Stafford Library
Columbia College
1001 Rogers Street
Columbia, Missouri 65216

WORLD LITERATURE CRITICISM

Supplement

WORLD LITERATURE CRITICISM
Advisory Board

William T. Balcom
Villa Park Public Library, Villa Park, Illinois

Candy Carter
Tahoe Truckee High School, Truckee, California

Carlota Cardenas De Dwyer
Tom C. Clark High School, San Antonio, Texas

Ken Holmes
E. St. Louis Lincoln Senior High School, E. St. Louis, Illinois

Barbara Hull
Library Media Specialist, Forest Hills High School, Forest Hills, New York

Larry R. Johannessen
Director of English Education, St. Xavier College, Chicago, Illinois

Lois Kaplan
Shaker Heights High School Library, Shaker Heights, Ohio

Sara Karow
Reference Librarian, Carnegie Branch, Houston Public Library, Houston, Texas

D'nis L. Lynch
Upper St. Clair School District, Pittsburgh, Pennsylvania

Kathy Lee Martin
Perry Meridian High School, Indianapolis, Indiana

Mike L. Printz
Librarian, Topeka West High School, Topeka, Kansas

Nancy L. Rosenberger
Phoenixville, Pennsylvania

Joyce Saricks
Coordinator, Literature and Audio-Visual Services, Downers Grove Public Library, Downers Grove, Illinois

Mary Southwell
Murray City Public Library, Murray City, Utah

Pam Spencer
Coordinator, Library Services, Fairfax County Public Schools, Virginia

Ute Stargardt
Alma College, Alma, Michigan

Patricia G. Stockner
Director, Warrenville Public Library District, Warrenville, Illinois

Gladys Veidemanis
Oshkosh, Wisconsin

Carolyn Calhoun Walter
St. Xavier College, Chicago, Illinois

Hilda K. Weisburg
Library Media Specialist, Sayreville War Memorial High School, Parkin, New Jersey

Brooke Workman
West High School, Iowa City, Iowa

WORLD LITERATURE CRITICISM

Supplement

A Selection of Major Authors from Gale's Literary Criticism Series

Kingston-Wilson

POLLY VEDDER, Editor

DETROIT · NEW YORK · TORONTO · LONDON

STAFF

Polly Vedder, *Editor*

John P. Daniel, Pamela S. Dear, Christopher Giroux, Josh Lauer, Patricia Onorato,
Deborah A. Stanley, Kathleen Wilson, and Janet Witalec, *Contributing Editors*

Jeffrey W. Hunter and Thomas Wiloch, *Associate Editors*

Tim Akers and Timothy White, *Assistant Editors*

Jennifer Daniels and Andrew Spongberg, *Editorial Assistants*

Susan M. Trosky, *Permissions Manager*
Margaret Chamberlain, Maria Franklin, and Kimberly F. Smilay, *Permissions Specialists*
Sarah Chesney, Edna Hedblad, Michele Lonoconus, and Shalice Shah, *Permissions Associates*
Stephen Cusack, Kelly Quin, Andrea Rigby, and Jessica Ulrich, *Permissions Assistants*

Victoria B. Cariappa, *Research Manager*
Barbara McNeil, *Research Specialist*
Laura C. Bissey, Julia C. Daniel, Tamara C. Nott,
Tracie A. Richardson, and Cheryl L. Warnock, *Research Associates*

Mary Beth Trimper, *Production Supervisor*
Shanna Heilveil, *Production Assistant*

Barbara J. Yarrow, *Graphic Services Manager*
Mikal Ansari, *Macintosh Artist*
Randy Bassett, *Imaging Database Supervisor*
Robert Duncan and Michael Logusz, *Imaging Specialists*
Pamela A. Reed, *Photography Coordinator*

Because this page cannot legibly accommodate all copyright notices, the acknowledgments constitute an extension of the copyright notice.

While every effort has been made to ensure the reliability of the information presented in this publication, Gale Research neither guarantees the accuracy of the data contained herein nor assumes any responsibility for errors, omissions, or discrepancies. Gale accepts no payment for listing; and inclusion in the publication of any organization, agency, institution, publication, service, or individual does not imply endorsement of the editors or publisher. Errors brought to the attention of the publisher and verified to the satisfaction of the publisher will be corrected in future editions.

This book is printed on acid-free paper that meets the minimum
requirements of American National Standard for Information Sciences—
Permanence Paper for Printed Library Materials, ANSI Z39.48-1984.

This publication is a creative work copyrighted by Gale Research and fully protected by all applicable copyright laws, as well as by misappropriation, trade secret, unfair competition, and other applicable laws. The authors and editors of this work have added value to the underlying factual material herein through one or more of the following: unique and original selection, coordination, expression, arrangement, and classification of the information.

Gale Research will vigorously defend all of its rights in this publication.

Copyright © 1997 by Gale Research
835 Penobscot Building
Detroit, MI 48226

All rights reserved including the right of reproduction in whole or in part in any form.

ISBN 0-7876-1696-6 (2-volume set)
Vol. 1: ISBN 0-7876-1912-4
Vol. 2: ISBN 0-7876-1913-2

Printed in the United States of America
10 9 8 7 6 5 4 3 2 1

Table of Contents

Introduction ix

Aeschylus 525 B.C.-456 B.C. 1:1
Considered the father of tragedy, Aeschylus has influenced the entire history of Western drama. He was recognized by his contemporaries as the leading figure in Attic drama, and his plays are still widely respected.

Dante Alighieri 1265-1321 .... 1:19
Dante is regarded as the finest Italian poet and a major influence in Western culture. His masterpiece, *La divina commedia* (*The Divine Comedy*), is known as one of the greatest poems of world literature.

Isabel Allende 1942- 1:39
Blending realism and fantasy into her fiction, Allende examines the social and political heritage of South America. Her most notable work, *The House of Spirits*, is typical of her writing, which draws upon her own experiences.

Maya Angelou 1928- 1:54
Angelou is one of the most admired contemporary African-American authors. She has received critical acclaim for her poetry as well as for autobiographical books such as *I Know Why the Caged Bird Sings*.

Aristophanes 450 B.C.-385 B.C. 1:71
Widely considered the greatest comic dramatist of ancient Greece, Aristophanes is admired for his imagination, earthy and irreverent style, and critical insight. His eleven complete plays represent the largest surviving body of work of any classical Greek writer.

Aristotle 384 B.C.-322 B.C. 1:88
One of the greatest intellectuals in Western history, Aristotle has influenced the development of philosophy, theology, and science. Additionally, his *Poetics* has set the standard for theoretical approaches to literature.

St. Augustine 354-430 .... 1:105
A Roman theologian and philosopher, St. Augustine became a champion of Christianity. His literary genius is most evident in his *Confessions,* the chronicle of his conversion.

Toni Cade Bambara 1939-1995 .... 1:122
Bambara, a writer and social activist, first gained critical acclaim for her short fiction, which has been praised for its insights into youth and the human condition, politics and music, and African-American culture.

Amiri Baraka 1934- 1:137
Having written in a wide variety of genres, Baraka is a prolific and influential African-American writer. His controversial work is designed to shock audiences into awareness of the political concerns of black Americans.

Beowulf **c. 8th century** 1:156
The oldest surviving English poem, *Beowulf* concerns the virtue and exploits of a Scandinavian hero. Linguists, historians, and literary critics have treasured it for its insight into early medieval life and thought as well as its poetic beauty.

Bible 1:175
The Bible is regarded as the most influential collection of writings in human history. It contains the sacred writings of Judaism and Christianity and has been translated into more than 1,800 languages.

Robert Browning 1812-1889 .... **1:197**
A prominent Victorian poet, Browning is regarded as the master of the dramatic monologue. His versatile approach and innovations in language helped bring the form to new levels of technical sophistication and are evident in much of his work, including "Fra Lippo Lippi" and his masterpiece, *The Ring and the Book*.

Geoffrey Chaucer 1340?-1400 .... **1:217**
Chaucer's *Canterbury Tales* is one of the most widely known pieces of Middle English literature. It is a unique blend of the poet's humor, satire, linguistic style, and knowledge of the human condition.

Kate Chopin 1851-1904 .... **1:235**
In the nineteenth century, Chopin received harsh criticism for her frank depictions of feminine independence, sexuality, and adultery in her short novel *The Awakening* and short stories such as "The Story of an Hour." Today she is praised for her realistic depiction of the plight of women in modern society.

Confucius 551? B.C.-479 B.C. **1:252**
Confucius influenced the development of both Eastern philosophy and Western thought with his short sayings collected in the *Lun-yu* (*The Analects*). The collection comments on subjects ranging from politics and war to personal conduct and family.

Countee Cullen 1903-1946 .... **1:271**
A leading poet of the Harlem Renaissance, Cullen strove to write literature that transcended race, blending traditional style and contemporary racial issues in his poetry.

Euripides 485 B.C.-406 B.C. **1:288**
Euripides modified the structure of classical Greek drama in innovative ways. The Peloponnesian War influenced Euripidean tragedy, filling it with uncertainty, injustice, and suffering.

Benjamin Franklin 1706-1790 .... **1:310**
Franklin is often remembered as a scientist, inventor, and colonial American statesman, yet he was also widely known for his *Poor Richard* almanacs, satires, and political essays. Perhaps his best work is his *Autobiography of Benjamin Franklin*, published after his death.

***Sir Gawain and the Green Knight* c. 14th century** **1:333**
Though little is known about its author, *Sir Gawain and the Green Knight* is considered the best and most intriguing of the English medieval romances. It receives steady critical review from a variety of perspectives.

Nikki Giovanni 1943- **1:350**
Giovanni became popular in the 1960s with her revolutionary poems. Her work is influenced by rhythm and blues and concentrates on the themes of family, race, womanhood, and sexuality.

Nadine Gordimer 1923- **1:367**
Writing mostly about the effects of apartheid, Gordimer captures the intricate human tensions in South Africa. She produces powerful fiction anchored by authentic portrayals of apartheid's effects on both whites and blacks.

Seamus Heaney 1939- **1:385**
Heaney has been lauded as the greatest Irish poet since William Butler Yeats. His Nobel Prize-winning poetry, which explores self-discovery, spiritual growth, and issues related to Irish history, is characterized by sensuous language, sexual metaphors, and nature imagery.

Homer c. 8th century B.C. **1:403**
The *Iliad* and the *Odyssey* created the framework for Western literary epics. With his relatively simple narrative technique, Homer wove together the themes of heroism, fate, honor, loyalty, and justice with ancient myths and folk motifs.

A. E. Housman 1859-1936 .... **1:424**
Housman was a popular success in the early 1900s. Written in the pastoral tradition, his poetry is marked by emotional force and classical beauty and often deals with religious disillusionment and the loss of youthful dreams.

Zora Neale Hurston 1903-1960 .... **1:439**
Hurston's place as an important writer of the Harlem Renaissance has been

only recently revived after decades of neglect. She wrote novels, short stories, and various works of nonfiction, and one of her most important contributions was the collection and publication of African-American folklore.

Martin Luther King, Jr. 1929-1968 .... **1:455**
King's "I Have a Dream" speech has become symbolic of the civil rights movement. An inspirational speaker who called for equality and social reform, King wrote essays with a sermon-like quality and often used biblical references.

Maxine Hong Kingston 1940- **2:473**
Kingston melds Asian legend with autobiographical elements and fictionalized history to show the cultural conflicts faced by Americans of Chinese descent.

Doris Lessing 1919- **2:485**
Widely considered one of the most important writers of the postwar era, Lessing focuses on major social issues such as racism, communism, and feminism in her works.

Henry Wadsworth Longfellow 1807-1882 .... **2:501**
Longfellow was the first American poet to gain favor with the international literary community. He is credited with introducing European culture to the American readers of his day.

Niccolò Machiavelli 1469-1527 .... **2:518**
Perhaps one of the most controversial political figures in history, Machiavelli is best remembered for his political treatise *The Prince*.

Malcolm X 1925-1965 .... **2:537**
As national minister of the Nation of Islam, Malcolm X was one of the most influential African-American leaders of the twentieth century. *The Autobiography of Malcolm X*, written with Alex Haley, chronicles his search for identity.

Sir Thomas Malory 1410?-1471? **2:553**
Malory's masterpiece, *Le Morte Darthur*, which was based on French prose romances, is regarded as the best-known treatment of Arthurian legend in English.

Edgar Lee Masters 1868-1950 .... **2:572**
Though he was a prolific writer in several genres, Masters is primarily remembered as a poet. He shattered the myth of traditional American values with his classic collection of poetry, *Spoon River Anthology*.

Edna St. Vincent Millay 1892-1950 .... **2:588**
Millay employed traditional poetic devices to convey nontraditional ideas about the role of women in society. Her early volumes of poetry boldly asserted an independent perspective rarely expressed by female authors of her time.

Czesław Miłosz 1911- **2:605**
Miłosz's writings are concerned with metaphysical issues such as good and evil, identity, and the nature of existence. He was the recipient of the Nobel Prize in Literature in 1980.

N. Scott Momaday 1934- **2:622**
Winner of the Pulitzer Prize for fiction in 1969 for his novel *House Made of Dawn*, Momaday focuses primarily on the plight of Native Americans in the modern world. His unique narrative style weaves native myth, history, and contemporary experience.

Marianne Moore 1887-1972 .... **2:638**
One of America's foremost literary figures, Moore is noted for her close attention to detail and observation of human character. Her poetry often displays a preoccupation with the relationships between the common and the uncommon.

Muhammad 570?-632 .... **2:655**
Muhammad, the founder of Islam, provided the divine revelations that were later transcribed to create the Koran, the sacred text of Islam. The Koran has dictated Islamic religious practices for over 1,300 years.

Alice Munro 1931- **2:673**
Munro is one of Canada's most critically acclaimed contemporary authors. Her works juxtapose the mundane with the fantastic in an effort to allow readers fresh insight into the familiar.

Gloria Naylor 1950- 2:689
Naylor's portrayal of the black woman's condition in America has won her critical acclaim. Her most popular novel, *The Women of Brewster Place*, has been adapted for television.

Sean O'Casey 1880-1964 .... 2:706
O'Casey is best remembered for dramas such as *The Shadow of a Gunman* and *The Plough and the Stars*, which deal with the tragedy of political violence in Ireland. His later plays are characterized by a formalistic style that highlights his poetic and ideologic sensibilities.

Plato 428? B.C.-348? B.C. 2:724
Many consider Plato the father of philosophical idealism and the preeminent writer of Greek prose. His words and ideas serve as the foundation for Western philosophy.

Salman Rushdie 1947- 2:742
Rushdie's style is characterized by a blend of history, myth, politics, and fantasy. His most famous work, *The Satanic Verses*, touched off an international furor for its controversial treatment of people, places, and objects sacred to Islam.

Leslie Marmon Silko 1948- 2:757
One of the foremost authors to emerge from the Native American literary renaissance of the 1970s, Silko blends contemporary narrative style with the oral traditions of her heritage.

Sophocles 496? B.C.-406? B.C. 2:772
Over 2,000 years after his death, Sophocles remains one of the greatest figures in world literature. His tragedies, which include his masterpiece, *Oedipus Rex*, initiated several theatrical conventions that have influenced drama throughout the Western world.

Jean Toomer 1894-1967 .... 2:789
Even though he was noted for his exploration of African-American culture, Toomer rejected the label of "black author"; instead, he considered himself part of a new "American" race made up of elements of all humanity. His major work, *Cane*, reflects this universalist philosophy.

Vergil 70 B.C.-19 B.C. 2:806
Drawing from Greek literary traditions, Vergil produced a body of work that has influenced virtually all subsequent Western literature. His writings, which include the *Aeneid*, provide the most insightful perspective on the anxieties of the Augustan Age.

Alice Walker 1944- 2:827
Walker's writing explores racial, sexual, and political issues, particularly as they relate to the lives of African-American women. Walker won the Pulitzer Prize for her novel *The Color Purple*.

Elie Wiesel 1928- 2:841
A survivor of the Nazi concentration camps, Wiesel attempts to comprehend the apparent indifference of God as suggested by the horror of the Holocaust. He won the Nobel Prize for Peace in 1986.

August Wilson 1945- 2:858
Wilson has been a major figure in the American theater since the 1980s. His plays—including an ambitious cycle devoted to twentieth-century African-American experience—have won enormous critical acclaim, including two Tony Awards and two Pulitzer Prizes.

Acknowledgments 2:877

WLC Cumulative Author Index 2:883

WLC Cumulative Nationality Index 2:889

WLC Cumulative Title Index 2:893

Introduction

A Comprehensive Information Source on World Literature

World Literature Criticism Supplement presents a broad selection of the best criticism of works by major writers from the pre-Christian era to the present. Among the authors included in *WLC Supplement* are ancient Greek poet Homer; Chinese philosopher Confucius; Greek philosophers and dramatists such as Plato, Aristotle, Aeschylus, Sophocles, Aristophanes, and Euripides; Roman poet Vergil; Christian apologist St. Augustine; Muslim prophet Muhammad; Italian poet Dante Alighieri; English poet Geoffrey Chaucer and prose writer Thomas Malory; Italian political philosopher Niccolò Machiavelli; American philosopher and autobiographer Benjamin Franklin; and major nineteenth- and twentieth-century authors including Robert Browning, Kate Chopin, Sean O'Casey, Nadine Gordimer, Seamus Heaney, Martin Luther King, Jr., Czesław Miłosz, N. Scott Momaday, Salman Rushdie, Leslie Marmon Silko, Elie Wiesel, and August Wilson.

Coverage

This two-volume set extends the coverage of *World Literature Criticism: 1500 to the Present* (1992), a six-volume collection designed for high school, college, and university students as well as for the general reader interested in learning more about literature. *WLC* was developed in response to strong demand by students, librarians, and other readers for a one-stop, authoritative guide to the whole spectrum of world literature from the sixteenth to the twentieth centuries. *WLC Supplement* broadens the coverage to important pre-Christian authors and influential first- through fifteenth-century writers and works, adds widely read authors who could not be included in the first volumes, and updates the set with additional twentieth-century writers whose works are increasingly studied in modern classrooms.

Inclusion Criteria

Authors were selected for inclusion in *WLC Supplement* based on the advice of leading experts on world literature as well as on the recommendations of a specially formed advisory panel made up of high school and undergraduate teachers and high school and public librarians from throughout the United States. Additionally, the most recent major curriculum studies were closely examined, notably Arthur N. Applebee, *A Study of Book-Length Works Taught in High School English Courses* (1989); Arthur N. Applebee, *A Study of High School Literature Anthologies* (1991); and Doug Estel, Michele L. Satchwell, and Patricia S. Wright, *Reading Lists for College-Bound Students* (1990). All of these resources were collated and compared to produce a reference product that is strongly curriculum driven. To ensure that *WLC Supplement* will continue to meet the needs of students and general readers alike, an effort was made to identify a group of important new writers in addition to the most studied authors.

Scope

Each author entry in *WLC Supplement* presents a historical survey of critical response to the author's works. Typically, early criticism is offered to indicate initial responses, later selections document any rise or decline in literary reputations, and retrospective analyses provide modern views. (In a handful of entries, early views were favored over more contemporary ones, since the early material was judged more likely to be useful to students.) Wherever possible, the editors strove to include seminal essays on each author's work along with commentary providing broad perspectives on major issues. Interviews and author statements are also included in many entries. Thus, *WLC Supplement* is both timely and comprehensive.

Organization of Author Entries

Information about authors and their works is presented through ten key access points:

- The **Descriptive Table of Contents** guides readers through the range of world literature, offering summary sketches of authors' careers and achievements.

- In each author entry, the **Author Heading** cites the name under which the author most commonly wrote, followed by birth and, where appropriate, death dates. Uncertain birth or death dates are indicated by question marks. Name variations, including full birth names when available, are given in parentheses in the caption below the **Author Portrait.**

- The **Biographical and Critical Introduction** contains background information about the life and works of the author, clearly divided into sections: 1) brief summary of the author's achievements and reputation; 2) **Biographical Information** that helps reveal the life, character, and personality of the author; 3) descriptions and summaries of the author's **Major Works**; and 4) commentary on the **Critical Reception** of the author's works. The concluding paragraph of the **Biographical and Critical Introduction** directs readers to other Gale series containing information about the author.

- Every *WLC Supplement* entry contains an **Author Portrait** or manuscript illustration.

- The **List of Principal Works** is chronological by date of first book publication and identifies the genre of each work. Ancient works are usually given in the more familiar English versions, but well-known foreign titles such as *Oedipus Rex* also appear in some listings. For non-English-language authors whose works have been translated into English, the title and date of the first English-language edition are given in brackets. Unless otherwise indicated, dramas are dated by first performance rather than first publication.

- Many entries contain an **Adaptations** section listing important treatments and adaptations of the author's works, including feature films, TV miniseries, and radio broadcasts. This feature was specially conceived for *WLC* to meet strong demand from students for this type of information.

- **Criticism** is arranged chronologically in each author entry to provide a useful perspective on changes in critical evaluation over the years. Most entries contain a detailed, comprehensive study of an author's career as well as book and performance reviews, studies of individual works, and comparative examinations. To ensure timeliness, current views are most often presented, but not to the exclusion of important early pieces. For the purpose of easy identification, the critic's name and source citation are given at the beginning of each piece of criticism. Unsigned criticism is preceded by the title of the source in which it appeared. Within the criticism, titles of works by the author are printed in boldface type. Publication information (such as publisher names and book prices) and certain numerical references (such as footnotes or page and line references to specific editions of works) have been deleted at the editor's discretion to provide smoother reading of the text.

- Critical essays are prefaced by **Explanatory Notes** as an additional aid to readers of *WLC Supplement*. These notes may provide several types of valuable information, including: 1) the reputation of the critic; 2) the importance of the work of criticism; 3) the commentator's approach to the author's work; 4) the purpose of the criticism; and 5) changes in critical trends regarding the author. In some cases, **Explanatory Notes** cross-reference the work of critics within an entry who agree or disagree with each other.

Other Features

WLC contains three distinct indexes to help readers find information quickly and easily:

- The **Cumulative Author Index** lists all the authors appearing in *WLC Supplement* as well as all those who appeared in the original six-volume set. Users need only consult the *Supplement* index to locate information on any author included in either set. To ensure easy access, name variations and changes are fully cross-indexed.

- The **Cumulative Nationality Index** lists all authors featured in *WLC Supplement* and the original *WLC* by nationality. For expatriate authors and authors identified with more than one nation, multiple listings are offered.

- The **Cumulative Title Index** lists in alphabetical order all individual works by the authors appearing in *WLC*. English-language translations of original foreign-language titles are cross-referenced so that all references to a work are combined in one listing.

Citing *World Literature Criticism Supplement*

When writing papers, students who quote directly from *WLC Supplement* may use the following general forms to footnote reprinted criticism:

For material drawn from periodicals:

Roger Dickinson-Brown, "The Art and Importance of N. Scott Momaday," *The Southern Review,* Vol. XIV, No. 1 (January 1978), 30-45; excerpted and reprinted in *World Literature Criticism Supplement,* ed. Polly Vedder (Detroit: Gale Research, 1997), pp. 625-31.

For material reprinted from books:

Mona Knapp, *Doris Lessing* (Frederick Ungar, 1984); excerpted and reprinted in *World Literature Criticism Supplement,* ed. Polly Vedder (Detroit: Gale Research, 1997), pp. 491-95.

Acknowledgments

The editor wishes to acknowledge the valuable contributions of the many librarians, authors, and scholars who assisted in the compilation of *WLC Supplement* with their responses to telephone and mail inquiries. Special thanks are offered to the members of *WLC*'s advisory board, whose names are listed opposite the title page.

Comments Are Welcome

The editor hopes that readers will find *WLC Supplement* a useful reference tool and welcomes comments about the work. Send comments and suggestions to: Editor, *World Literature Criticism Supplement,* Gale Research, Penobscot Building, Detroit, MI 48226-4094.

WORLD LITERATURE CRITICISM

Supplement

Maxine Hong Kingston

1940-

(Born Maxine Ting Ting Hong) American autobiographer, novelist, journalist, and short story writer.

INTRODUCTION

A highly acclaimed memoirist, Kingston integrates autobiographical elements with Asian legend and fictionalized history to show the cultural conflicts confronting Americans of Chinese descent. Her works bridge two civilizations in their examination of social and familial bonds from ancient China to contemporary California. Kingston relates the anxiety that often results from clashes between radically different cultural sensibilities. Her exotic, myth-laden narratives are informed by several sources: the ordeals of emigrant forebears who endured brutal exploitation as they labored on American railroads and cane plantations; the "talk-stories," or cautionary tales of ancient heroes and family secrets told by her mother; and her own experiences as a first-generation American with confused cultural allegiances. From these foundations, Kingston forms epic chronicles of the Chinese immigrant experience that are esteemed for their accurate and disturbing illumination of such social patterns as Asian cultural misogyny and American institutional racism.

Biographical Information

Born October 27, 1940, at Stockton, California, Kingston is the daughter of stern immigrant parents from China. She attended University of California, Berkeley, where she earned an A.B. in 1962 and a teaching certificate in 1965. For the next two years Kingston taught high school English in California until she moved to Hawaii in 1968. Kingston continued to teach at several high schools in Honolulu during the 1970s, while writing the autobiographical *The Woman Warrior* (1976), which won the National Book Critics Circle Award for general nonfiction. She was appointed visiting associate professor of English at the University of Hawaii in 1977. Shortly thereafter she published *China Men*

(1980), which won a National Book Critics Circle Award and an American Book Award. In 1986, Kingston was named the Thelma McCandless Professor at Eastern Michigan University. Since 1990, Kingston has been the Chancellor's Distinguished Professor at her alma mater in Berkeley.

Major Works

Primarily a memoir of Kingston's childhood, *The Woman Warrior* synthesizes ancient myth and imaginative biography to present a kaleidoscopic vision of female character. It also features the lives of other women in her family, as embellished or imagined by the author. The narrative begins with Kingston's mother, Brave Orchid, relating the story of No Name Woman, young Maxine's paternal aunt, whose disrepute has rendered her unmentionable. Left in their village by her emigre husband, No Name Woman became pregnant—perhaps by rape—and was forced by the villagers to drown herself and her baby. Brave Orchid affirms traditional attitudes, describing such practices as foot-binding and the sale of girls as slaves, and she threatens Maxine with servitude and an arranged marriage to a retarded neighborhood boy. Subsequent chapters, however, provide sharp contrast to these bleak visions, for Brave Orchid also recites the colorful legend of Fa Mu Lan, the woman who wielded a sword to defend her hamlet. The book concludes with a description of Brave Orchid's own incongruent character: independent enough to become one of rural China's few female doctors, she returns to her customary submissive role upon joining her husband in America. Kingston applies similar techniques to the plight of immigrant men in *China Men,* which is narrated by female storytellers. While Kingston's mother dominates *Woman Warrior,* her father dominates *China Men,* along with imaginative, epic biographies of other male ancestors—laborers who endured harsh anti-Chinese immigration laws and legalized abuse to establish family citizenship before returning to China. *China Men* opens with a calligrapher and poet in China, "the father from China," who emigrates to New York City, where he becomes part-owner of a laundry. He struggles with the temptations of his new-found bachelorhood until his wife joins him, and they move to California. A later section of the book relates the story of Kingston's father in Stockton, and the book concludes with the tale of her younger brother's tour of duty in Vietnam and his attempts to locate relatives in Hong Kong. An analysis of contemporary social and artistic values, *Tripmaster Monkey: His Fake Book* (1989), blends Chinese history and myth with wild humor through the character of Wittman Ah Sing, a young, fifth-generation Chinese-American Berkeley graduate. His creates turmoil during his picaresque adventures in San Francisco, while he explores his Chinese heritage and rages against white Americans who regularly ask if he speaks English.

Critical Reception

Commentators have admired Kingston's fanciful description and poetic diction, through which she imparts her fear and wonder of Chinese legacies. Jane Kramer remarked that *The Woman Warrior* "shocks us out of our facile rhetoric, past the clichés of our obtuseness, back to the mystery of a stubbornly, utterly foreign sensibility . . . Its sources are dream and memory, myth and desire. Its crises are crises of a heart in exile from roots that terrorize and bind it." Critics also have commented that Kingston's detailed technique elegantly blends the factual and the fantastic to create a magical, incisive depiction of Chinese-American identity. Mary Gordon observed that "*China Men* is a triumph of the highest order, of imagination, of language, of moral perception." While some reviewers complained that Wittman's invectives in *Tripmaster Monkey* were occasionally verbose and lacked the fevered eloquence of Kingston's earlier works, most praised the book's dynamic pace and psychological depth. Anne Tyler noted: "That Wittman is Chinese give his story depth and particularity. That he's American lends his narrative style a certain slangy insouciance. That he's Chinese-American, with the self-perceived outsider's edgy angle of vision, makes for a novel of satisfying complexity and bite and verve."

(For further information, see *Authors and Artists for Young Adults,* Vol. 8; *Contemporary Authors,* Vols. 69-72; *Contemporary Authors New Revision Series,* Vols. 13, 38; *Contemporary Literary Criticism,* Vols. 12, 19, 58; *Dictionary of Literary Biography Yearbook: 1980; Dictionary of Literary Biography,* Vol. 173; *DISCovering Authors Modules: Multicultural Authors Module, Novelists Module; Major Twentieth-Century Writers; Something about the Author,* Vol. 53.)

CRITICAL COMMENTARY

SARA BLACKBURN

SOURCE: Sara Blackburn, "Notes of a Chinese Daughter," in *Ms.,* January, 1977, pp. 39-40.

[*In the following excerpt, Blackburn favorably reviews* The Woman Warrior.]

Maxine Hong Kingston illuminates the experience of

> **Principal Works**
>
> *The Woman Warrior: Memoirs of a Girlhood among Ghosts* (autobiography) 1976
> *China Men* (autobiography) 1980
> *Tripmaster Monkey: His Fake Book* (novel) 1988
> Hawai'i One Summer 1997
>
> *Excerpts from these works were reprinted in *Through the Black Curtain*, 1988.

everyone who has ever felt the terror of being an emotional outsider. It seems to me that the best records of the immigrant experience and the bittersweet legacy it bestows upon the next generation fascinate us because of the insights they provide into the life of the family, that mystified arena where we first learn, truly or falsely, our own identities. It should therefore not be very startling—as it was to me—that this dazzling mixture of pre-revolutionary Chinese village life and myth, set against its almost unbearable contradictions in contemporary American life, could unfold as almost a psychic transcript of every woman I know—class, age, race, or ethnicity be damned. Here is the real meaning of America as melting pot.

Kingston alternates the experiences of her parents and their generation, in China and the Chinatowns of California, with her own. In a starving society where girl children were a despised and useless commodity, her mother had become a physician, then joined her long-ago immigrated husband in America, where she was hence to labor in the laundry which was their survival in the terrifying new land. Their children, raised in the aura of the old myths and their parents' fears for their children and themselves, alternated between revering and despising them....

In the book's finest scene, which somehow manages to be both hilarious and devastatingly painful, Kingston's elderly aunt is brought over from China and forced to try to reclaim the now-Americanized husband she had married years before at home. In the traditional style, he had been supporting her from California though he had long ago married another woman. The confrontation is a microcosm of the book's impact: he is a svelte, classy brain surgeon, surrounded by all the American trappings of wealth and prestige; she is a provincial old village woman, and falls back, dumbfounded, at his eerie power....

A tragic dynamic gets played out here. Taught that our own needs are illegitimate, too many of us repress them and spend our lives serving what we perceive to be the more legitimate needs of others. It is in this way that Kingston's ambivalent responses to growing up in this family and culture evoke the history of women around the world. The author's own early fantasies dwelt on how she is miraculously trained to be a fierce, proud warrior, who liberates the suffering people of the Chinese past from the terrible oppression of the landowners. Only her lover knows that she is, in reality, a woman!

In the book's climax, Kingston, now in high school, lashes out at her mother in an extraordinary, liberating tirade in which she claims at last her own shaky identity. And her mother, who once struggled so valiantly for her own, first denies her feelings and then tries to convey the dangers, real and imagined, which have molded her own attitude toward this beloved, maddening stranger. The gap is too wide, for the teenage Maxine has perceived more of her mother's fear than her love, more of her culture's confines than its richness and beauty. The possibilities of love and forgiveness will have to be postponed for the more immediate necessities: the struggles for autonomy, on the one hand, and assimilation on the other. The depiction of these twin struggles is this memoir's great strength.

The Woman Warrior is not without flaws: much of the exquisite fantasy material comes too early in the book, before we're properly grounded in the author's own "reality," and we can appreciate its full impact only in retrospect. There's often a staccato, jarring quality in transition from one scene to another, and we have to work hard placing ourselves in time and event. Prospective readers should not be discouraged by these minor problems. What is in store for those who read on is not only the essence of the immigrant experience—here Chinese, and uniquely fascinating for that—but a marvelous glimpse into the real life of women in the family, a perception-expanding report for the archives of human experience. Praise to Maxine Hong Kingston for distilling it and writing it all down for us....

LINDA CHING SLEDGE

SOURCE: Linda Ching Sledge, "Maxine Kingston's *China Men*: The Family Historian as Epic Poet," in *MELUS*, Vol. 7, No. 4, Winter, 1980, pp. 3-22.

[*In the following excerpt, Sledge discusses the role of family in Kingston's work.*]

Maxine Hong Kingston has been widely praised by

American critics for her two visionary biographical accounts of Asian-American life, **Woman Warrior** and **China Men.** Nevertheless, her reputation among some Chinese-American writers is still debated. The most serious allegation made by Kingston's detractors is that she does not paint an accurate portrait of ethnic culture and society. However, due to the currently undeveloped state of Asian-American literary criticism, this sweeping charge has yet to be fully supported by conventional historical methods of inquiry, by systematic literary theory, or by substantive analyses of Kingston's own writings. It already seems apparent that for sheer literary talent, originality of style, and comprehensiveness of vision, Kingston is a major American writer and the most formidable Asian-American writer in this nation's history. What is at issue is in part the question of genre. Are her works histories or novels? If they are histories, how realistic and verifiable is her evidence? If they are novels, why do they substitute separate, generally unconnected personal and family experiences for the contrivances of an "internal fiction" or "plot"? In some respects, **China Men** is so close to the "facts" of history that it can serve as a casebook for the evolution of Chinese-American family life over the last century; in other respects, it is wildly inventive and poetic.

Yet if it is an ethnic family history, **China Men** can only in the most limited sense be identified with the classic and definitive study in that discipline, Herbert Gutman's analytical and documentary *The Black Family in Slavery and Freedom*. Rather than accumulating and examining documentary evidence in a systematic fashion, Kingston in **China Men** attempts an imaginative reconstruction of one particular Cantonese family's emigration to America as the prototypical history of all immigrant American Chinese. That authentic, if idealized, family history is reified in the distinctive dialect of immigrant forebears; it is an extremely rich, consciously verbal style springing from a Cantonese village society that "talks" or "sings" its history, or what the distinguished linguistic scholar, Walter Ong, would call an "oral culture."

I would argue that **China Men** is neither novel nor history but represents the transmutation of "oral history" into cultural literary epic. It records a dramatization of real-life family stories in the form Asian-Americans recognize as "talk-story." As a chronicle of archetypal racial heroes, it is thus an "oral history" in the generic sense as well. Kingston is a sophisticated and contemporary artist, and her work is laden with eastern sources, but to my mind, **China Men** looks back to the traditional western epic, particularly the *Aeniad* in its cultural exegesis, its conscious formation of racial myths from earlier folk legends and its central theme of heroic wandering from "Troy" (China) to "New Troy" (America). It appears to imitate the epic's principal formal characteristics and functions. It is episodic in structure and told in a generally ceremonial, first-person voice. It continually intermingles supernatural beings with flesh and blood personalities, myth with history in a continuous present. It rehearses the exploits of wandering sojourner-heroes on whose actions depend the fate of a new nation or "race" and embodies in written discourse the oral poetic structures, customs, values, and psychology of a bardic community.

As a family history in epic form, **China Men** recounts the odyssey of a family of male sojourners across America and away from womenfolk and children in China. This dispersed arrangement of family members was the predominant form the traditional Chinese extended patrilineal family system took during the peak years of emigration, and although familiar to students of ethnic history and to Chinese themselves, it has not been the subject of any major scholarly study or literary work before **China Men.** Comparisons with pertinent findings of recent historians and sociologists of the family will show that Kingston remains faithful to the broad outlines of sojourner family history. Nevertheless, I hope to prove that her aim is not necessarily documentation but the celebration of the mystical continuity of the family, a triumphant vision that runs counter to the historical fact of family dispersion and dislocation. Thus without ignoring general historical trends and specific events, Kingston transmutes these into epic form with mythic content by idealizing selected values, problems, and personalities in her family's evolution. **China Men** also recalls the epic form in its stylistic recreation of "orality" or public verbal performance before a listening audience. The forefathers are poets, singers, tellers of tales. Song and story pervade the first-person voice of history, quicken the land and the sea, join past to present and homesick sojourners with loved ones far away.

The paradigmatic family in **China Men** functions as the principal arena in which universal human experiences such as birth, death, work, love, failure, and fear are tested, judged, and ultimately understood. So potent among ethnic women writers as a whole is this image of the family as touchstone of values and behavior that the ethnic literary critic, Edith Blicksilver, has designated it a chief literary theme of "female social protest" cutting across the boundaries of culture, race, and time. Kingston herself makes clear her lofty mission as "female social protester" (surely this, too, is the controlling notion of **Woman Warrior** as embodied in the narrator, Brave Orchid and Mu Lan): she intends to revise history from her race's point of view, to "claim America" for her male ancestors, a forgotten and misrepresented family of "American pioneers" and "Gold Mountain heroes." Their story unfolds as the retelling of exemplary tales composed by her forebears, preserved as accumulated family lore and handed down to the children. All concern family heroes driven by fate to seek an unknown destiny in barbarian lands. The ideal of family continuity gives these men strength to win at arduous "epic" tests of manhood. The traditional authority ascribed to male family members gives them a core of selfhood allowing them to withstand danger and defeat.

The preservation of these family values inevitably means the survival of heroes, their families, kin and clan, and the eventual proliferation of the larger community of sojourner families that constitutes their nation or "race." Just as the eccentric, feuding Dead family in Toni Morrison's brilliant novel, *Song of Solomon,* share a primal family bond that divides them from the black community yet grants them a generous vision of human possibility, Kingston's ancestors have a fierce family loyalty that isolates them culturally from mainstream America yet sustains them with a mystical belief in the oneness of all life. The fabled "Middle Kingdom" of T'ang heroes to which the family bears continued allegiance throughout its journey casts a long, protective shadow over lives lived in *Mei Kwok,* the "beautiful" but brutal new overseas home. Both places constitute the legendary frontiers which the author herself, in retracing the steps of her voyaging forefathers, hopes to explore.

> I want to talk to Cantonese, who have always been revolutionaries, nonconformists, people with fabulous imaginations, people who invented the Gold Mountain. I want to discern what it is that makes people go West and turn into Americans. I want to compare China, a country I made up, with what country is really out there.

In order to dramatize her ancestors' memories of a perfected homeland, a wandering race of family heroes and a legendary country of barbarian "demons" and spirits, Kingston recreates abstract versions of real-life family members and situations as I hope subsequently to show. Yet it is clear to me that the issue of authenticity that arose after the publication of ***Woman Warrior*** troubles the author. Kingston has thus included a lengthy central digression in ***China Men*** containing purely factual testimony of Chinese-American legal history ("The Laws") perhaps because some detractors have persisted in faulting her works for not being radical revisionist histories. Risking narrative discontinuity, the inclusion of this section balances the remaining chapters on "invented" or idealized history with substantial documentary material. But as a formal digression, it functions to provide the general American reading public, mostly ignorant of the history of Chinese in the U.S., with a brief chronicle of oppression against which the heroic deeds of the idealized fathers can be judged.... This brief chronology is a pertinent, persuasive reminder of America's long history of Sinophobia. It points to the harsh facts of peonage and discrimination under which Chinese were forced to labor for nearly a century....

Despite the carefully drawn central digression on Chinese-American legal history, however, the overall design of ***China Men*** demonstrates that the author's intention is not to write a factual account of Chinese servitude but a celebration of her ancestors as protagonists in a triumphant saga of survival and family continuity. Except for the factual summary, the work is shaped more by the lives of individual heroes than by the passage of key events in Chinese-American history. Main characters are treated in separate narrative chapters identified by legendary patronyms ("The Great Grandfather of the Sandalwood Mountains"). These forefather portraits provide ***China Men's*** scaffolding: they offer vivid exemplary exploits that westerners can identify as "epic-like." They also embody the Confucian practice of ancestor worship and as such offer an eastern equivalent of what Greek rhetoricians called *epidexis* ritual literary praise of renowned individuals. The legendary characteristics of these sojourner ancestors are enhanced by the proliferation of honorific titles and by the narrator's conscious obscuring of dates and locales of significant events. The circumstances surrounding the mental deterioration of "The Grandfather of the Sierra Nevada Mountains," for example, are purposely clouded so that his decline is not so much pitiful as noble and tragic....

In between these narrative episodes are small literary myths based on Chinese folk legends that provide fictional parallels to the historical chapters. These are not definitive, "pure" myths in the textual sense but are consciously contrived literary imitations that may be ironic analogues of western tales ("The Adventures of Lo Bun Sun") or variations of actual folk tales ("On Mortality Again"). Some are the author's own private ethnic "myths" in the Yeatsian sense ("The Hundred-Year-Old Man"). Authenticity of sources and materials are not of paramount concern here. What is important is the function these myths serve as epic conventions widening the dramatic scope of the narrative in order to encompass a coexistent supernatural plane of existence and in thus aggrandizing the themes and characters of the historical chapters.

The ancestors who people this saga of journey and return are also characters of epic proportions. The two founding fathers in ***China Men,*** Bak Goong of the Hawaiian Islands and Ah Goong of California, are prototypes of the family hero, fashioned in the image of the valiant, long-suffering Prometheus. Both are Cantonese "explorers and Americans" who pit themselves courageously against monumental natural obstacles to win at epic tests of manhood based not on lofty achievement so much as the endurance of great physical danger and psychological stress. Great Grandfather (Bak Goong) "hacks a farm out of the wilderness" in the impenetrable Hawaiian backland. Grandfather (Ah Goong) literally moves mountains and hews through time with his bare hands along the rugged Pacific coast. Yet each tale has a different shape. Great Grandfather is the paradigmatic Chinese-American epic hero whose journey finally ends at home.... Like the wily Odysseus or the Nordic trickster Loki, he makes fools of his enemies, the "police demons" or the "pesky missionary Jesus demons." Finally, he returns to China to die, having endured and thus affirmed his manhood, his life harmoniously complete and "of a piece." By contrast, Grandfather's story plays a variation on Great Grandfather's theme of epic wandering and homecoming. He is both tragic and heroic: although he sacrifices mind and health in order to defy immovable rock, "dust devils," earthquake, and fire, his homecoming is tinged with gall for his family treats the ill and exhausted sojourner as an idiot....

[Heroism] in **China Men** is not defined by the conventional Chinese standards of masculine authority nor by western standards of physical prowess. Kingston inverts the notion of masculinity and femininity in order to define "heroism" according to the standard of sheer survival of humiliating social and economic setbacks. The description of footbinding in the introductory myth of the captive "Tang Ao," a Chinese "Everyman," shows the hobbling of a male. Footbinding thus becomes a symbol for the immigrant male's "emasculation," his loss of power and position after his emigration to America.

> The women who sat on him turned to direct their attention to his feet. They bent his toes so far backward that his arched foot cracked. The old ladies squeezed each foot and broke many tiny bones along the sides. They gathered his toes, toes over and under one another like a knot of ginger root. Tang Ao wept with pain. As they wound the bandages tight and tighter around his feet, the women sang footbinding songs to distract him: "Use aloe for binding feet and not for scholars."

The womanization of Tang Ao is not to be interpreted as a diminution of stature or character. Like the crafty Odysseus biding his time in the land of the nymph Calypso, the Chinese hero's strength consists of an ability to find new methods by which to endure, in this case to acquiesce and hence to outlast his captivity. The myth also speaks of the growing equality of the sexes as a result of the male's adventuring into unknown territories.

If we compare the above myth with the chapters on "The Father from China" (BaBa), we see the father similarly "emasculated" or metamorphosed in a succession of unsuccessful male roles: talented scholar, village teacher, carefree American bachelor, ambitious entrepreneur.... He becomes the most fully realized "hero" in the work, for he is shown from many sides, as husband, son, "legal" and "illegal" father. He is heroic, too, in his ambitions for himself and for his family. It is he who defies the ancient edict that "a woman too well educated is apt to create trouble" by encouraging his wife to become a doctor, and by his heroic dream of achievement, he learns the realism of failure in American society. Even when he fails at his duty as father-provider, and retreats from his family in bitterness, he remains the family's *titular* authority by virtue of his wife's and children's love for him (**Woman Warrior** depicts the mother as the central figure and myth maker in the children's lives). They respect him even though they do not understand him. His belongings have for them a sacred aura despite their air of poverty and failure. His children regard his wingtip shoes, his expensive but threadbare suits, his private "father places" as touched with a special grace.

If Kingston's "Gold Mountain heroes" are heroic because they are survivors, despite having sometimes relinquished their responsibilities as male family authorities, her heroines too are special, for they redefine conventional notions of femininity within the sojourner family. There is strong historical testimony for this role-reversal. As historians have remarked, Cantonese women were forced to assume total family governance after the emigration of male villagers to foreign lands. Thus, there arose a strong tradition of womanly self-sufficiency and aggressiveness among Cantonese. Kingston shows the persistence of that tradition among those few Chinese women, like the mother, who were allowed to enter the U. S. during the lengthy period of exclusion.

In **China Men**, the Cantonese mother's independence and self-reliance is not simply a product of historical necessity and village tradition but a way of preserving sacred family bonds even when the conventional function of the male collapsed. The mother from China is forced by the father's increasing passivity to take on "masculine" traits of aggressiveness and authority.... She preserves family solidarity by her never ending stream of advice, philosophy, stories, and reproaches, her energy, and her iron will. When her husband is psychologically immobilized by failure, it is she, a former physician, who supports the family by joining the hordes of migrant fruit and vegetable pickers in the fields of Stockton.

The inversion of sexual roles not only creates another notion of "heroism" based on the necessity of adapting to the conditions of poverty and unemployment in the sojourner family, it also illuminates the internal tensions accumulating in such families as a result of the erosion of sex differentiation in the household. The strain on husband, wife, and children as a result of the father's "emasculation" or failure as provider is clear. His silence and impotent rage deepen as the wife takes on more active power in the family. He screams "wordless male screams in his sleep." He erupts in furious misogynistic curses that frighten his daughter. Yet it seems to me that despite these tensions, the behavioral accommodations within the family enable it to remain integral and strong. Moreover, the ancient family values are still viable, for the mother's aggression is apparently born out of love and necessity, not frustration and shame, and through it, the father eventually finds a way of regaining his former authority.... Like the father, the heroism of the prototypical Chinese-American mother consists of an ability to alter traditional roles in order to prevent the dissolution of the family as an economic and cultural unit....

Kingston's depiction of sojourner family life also takes into account the broad trends in western family which have undeniably influenced the course of ethnic family systems as well. *China Men*, to my mind, generally concurs with well known familists such as Philippe Aries, Peter Laslett, Edward Shorter, and Christopher Lasch who have presented persuasive if varied historical arguments on the "crisis" of western family life in the twentieth century. Like these professional historians of western family structures, Kingston defines the family as a flexible domestic arrangement varying in intensity and configuration over time and buffeted by external forces beyond its control. One particular issue addressed by *China Men* is what the historian John Demos has called the "overloading" of the modern family "with the most urgent of human needs and responsibilities" due to the breakup of the reciprocal social relationships between individual and community. Pertinent details in *China Men* reveal that the sojourner family is like the western family described by recent historians of family life: it, too, is a nexus of shifting human relationships and deteriorating cultural values....

Kingston also recounts occasional American accommodations of Chinese family traditions, such as the keeping of lunar holidays with special foods. These meals dramatize the family's shifting fortunes in the new world and the subsequent deliquescence of tradition....

However, the details and situations which attest to the historical fact of cultural erosion and family dislocation remain part of the background. Kingston, in the final analysis, gives an overwhelmingly heroic account of sojourner family life.... Throughout *China Men*, the continuing hold of certain fundamental aspects of the primordial Confucian ideal of family unity, economic interdependence, and mutual help is maintained....

A closer look at the details which purportedly show the deterioration of traditional family and cultural values also affirms this impression. The leaf-wrapped legumes passed around by laborers in California are not merely substitutes for ritual feasts. They conceal secret political codes: the message to strike against the railroads which were cruelly exploiting their labor. The laborers have pressed holiday tradition into the service of another Chinese tradition—grass-roots rebellion against a hated oppressor. Ah Goong ties the strike plan into the bundles of food and happily recalls a precedent for their actions: "The time and place for the revolution against Kublai Khan had been hidden inside autumn mooncakes." These men are not slaves helplessly adrift in a hostile environment: they are heroes carrying their traditions into a new frontier.

Kingston's depiction of sojourner attitudes toward traditional Chinese family life may prompt some critics to accuse her of romantic nostalgia for an outmoded and unjustly authoritarian system that was "intended to extend the relations of domination and subordination." Yet this criticism would misrepresent her obvious intention to recreate mythic, not documentary, history. Nor does she espouse what Raymond Dawson has called the erroneous "fiction of 'eternal standstill'" that led westerners for many centuries to extol the Chinese mind for its stability, "uniformity and unvariability" and the homogenous, family oriented Confucian state as "an example and model even for Christians." China men all too often drink deeply of loneliness, misunderstanding, and bitter despair as a result of their fidelity to ethnic and family unity. Such a loyalty has made assimilation into American society a long and painful struggle, as the father's saga of thwarted ambition and schizoid bicultural identities reveals. For China men, "home" is the absent and *real* family whose claims are continually reasserted in dreams, holiday feasts, mothers' and wives' scolding letters. Memories of home preserve their ethnic values and identities and teach them how to adjust to unexpected, even forbidden, social situations that may arise in the Gold Mountain....

It is important to note the effect of Kingston's heroic method upon the thorny issue of miscegenation. It is well known that intermarriage was strictly forbidden to Chinese by Confucian teachings, for it went against the classical notion established in the *Li Chi* that marriage was a religious duty between consenting families "to secure the services in the ancestral temple for the predecessors and to secure the continuance of the family line for posterity...."

Why does Kingston choose to exalt a controversial issue in Chinese-American history which Chinese commentators have generally avoided? To my mind, this pastoral treatment allows Kingston to explore typical and long ignored problems of sojourner history—loneliness, homesickness, sexual frustration—without cultural bias. We also come to understand and accept the emotional needs motivating these men to enter relationships which violated so profoundly cherished family and religious attitudes because we view such relationships from a sojourner's (Bak Sook Goong) own point of view. Literary myth is a way of dramatizing objectively the immigrants' general belief that their American experiences were illusory when compared with the more binding claims of the "real" family far away....

If Kingston's aim, then, in *China Men* is the celebration and not the analysis of racial and family history, how can the troubling question of her credibility even as "epic" historian be addressed? It occurs to me that through the forms and conventions of the epic, she comes closer than other commentators on the family to the actual truth about sojourner family history. Kingston proposes in *China Men* that the sojourner family is an indigenous American system whose evolution parallels but does not necessarily duplicate the major trends in family history in the west. The sojourner family is neither a "haven in a heartless world" nor an "encounter group" nor a simple domestic "construct designed for social purposes." Kingston, by contrast, shows that the special historical conditions and cultural traditions of sojourners have created unusually strong family ties that have intensified over the generations despite the reality of long-term separation of its members, the blurring of family and sex roles necessitated by economic hardship, even the gradual fragmentation of the ethnic American communities themselves. This development parallels in many ways that of the black family which survived despite slavery.

Nor does Kingston put forth the popular "mimetic" view that Chinese-American families are transplanted models of the traditional Confucian system. Rather, Kingston affirms that family traditions have always altered with the unique pressures of American society. The surprising result is that the sojourner family system has proven far more resilient than its counterpart in modern China where traditional family values have decayed markedly or have been wholly rejected.

The unusual persistence of sojourner family unity was noted over thirty years ago by Olga Lang in her groundbreaking study of Chinese families: Lang notes that Chinese in foreign countries, particularly in the U.S. and Hawaii, show no weakening but a strengthening of family ties, and attributes this to their need for mutual protection....

Finally, I would contend that Kingston's greatest achievement in *China Men* is her transmogrification of her forebears' language into a heroic tongue. To this end, she skillfully uses the myriad devices of the bard: mnemonic formulae; myths that parallel and enlarge the historical narration and are obviously stitched from the author's memories rather than taken from textual sources; a preoccupation with titles, recitations of names, name-calling; sensuous pictorial descriptions and descriptive catalogues; frequent authorial intrusions with translations of Sze-Yup terms (these are evocative conceptual translations, not literal translations); long summaries; and commentaries on previous action. These techniques are proof to me that Kingston's is above all a consciously verbal or oral literary performance of the sort described by Walter Ong in his seminal essay on ethnic language, "Oral Culture and the Literate Mind." Out of the indigenous Chinese-American tongue, Kingston recreates the spirit and beauty of the original myth-laden "oral culture" of her predecessors and fuses this with the rational "literate" craft of the western writer. It is not enough for her to embody in prose an authentic Asian-American diction by merely transcribing immigrant speech, slang, curses, cliches into English. She recognizes, perhaps, that the act of literal transcription is a mechanical exercise and results in lifeless, precious dialect. Her own characters do not speak in dialect or pidgin. Theirs is a simple, formal, generally grammatically correct diction that ranges from colloquial speech ("We need to go-out-on-the-road again," Kau Goong roared.), to flowery histrionics ("Old Uncles and Young Uncles, I have an appropriate story to tell. It cannot be left unsaid."), to monosyllabic chant ("I want my home," the men yelled together. "I want my home. Home. Home. Home. Home.") She depends not on dialect but on certain literary formulae, recognizable since Homer, to recreate the actual conceptual processes from which her ancestors' speech sprung, not reason and logic so much as memory and the psyche....

The verbal character of Kingston's language is also reflected in the protagonists' preoccupation with poetry or song, an important thematic motif in the work. Song pervades the men's primary activity, work. Its presence or absence is a measure of their happiness and success as workers. Yet even when the men's voices fail, they find song everywhere around them. It is present in memory, in the voices of wives and children talking-story, and especially in nature. The singing of the ground, the cane, the rocks, the sea, even the railroad affirms that the new world, though often hostile, is governed by the same benevolent natural process as the old.

> He sucked in deep breaths of the Sandalwood Mountain air, and let it fly out in a song, which reached up to the rims of volcanoes and down to the edge of the water. His song lifted and fell with the air, which seemed to breathe warmly through his body and through the rocks. The clouds and frigate birds made the currents visible, and the leaves were loud.... He sang like the heroes in stories about wanderers and exiles, poets and monks and monkeys, and princes and kings out for walks. His arias unfurled and rose in wide, wide arcs.

The critic John Leonard somewhat misleadingly describes Kingston's prose as "sensual." Perhaps a better term is "sentient," for her "singing" language is identified inevitably with a monistic and animistic view of humanity and nature and with an idealized image of the family as an organism encompassing disparate traditions into itself. It is this evolutionary understanding of family and ethnic history as derived from "song" or oral culture that gives **China Men** its encyclopedic scope and architectonic vision. Song transforms what could well be interpreted as a cruel, randomly violent America into an elemental force, an opponent worthy of "Gold Mountain heroes," the author's preferred title. Song touches the harsh world of work with grace and transforms the most formidable obstacles—towering cliffs of granite, impenetrable stands of cane—into part of the cosmic order.

Like that other American singer, Walt Whitman, Maxine Kingston raises private experience to the level of American myth. The structure of her song is epic—that most heroic and elastic of literary forms—by which she is able to encapsulate the data of history, the deep dreams of myth, and the archetypal drama of one American family....

ANNE TYLER

SOURCE: Anne Tyler, "Manic Monologue," in *The New Republic*, Vol. 200, No. 16, April 17, 1989, pp. 44-6.

[*In the following excerpt, Tyler favorably reviews* Tripmaster Monkey.]

[*Tripmaster Monkey* is] a great, huge sprawling beast of a novel, over 400 pages densely packed with the rantings and ravings and pranks and high jinks of one Wittman Ah Sing, a young Chinese-American (but how he would hate that term! Correction: American) rattling around San Francisco at some indeterminate point in the early 1960s. Just a year out of Berkeley, Wittman divides his time between writing poetry and clerking in a toy department, and when we first meet him he's considering suicide, but in such animated and slapdash terms that he doesn't have us worried for a moment.

A few of Wittman's mottoes are: "Better to be dead than boring," "Always do the more flamboyant thing," and "Do something, even if it's wrong." You see where all this could lead—and it does. Wittman's life is anything but dull. During the course of this novel, which encompasses just two months or so, Wittman gets fired for staging a pornographic scene between a Barbie doll and a battery-operated monkey, marries a virtual stranger in an impromptu ceremony performed by a mail-order minister, and produces a marathon play whose cast consists of nearly everyone he's ever met. And that's just the plot's stripped skeleton. There's much, much more, all of it related in his own highly exclamatory interior voice....

Many of Wittman's most impassioned monologues, private or public, have to do with his resentment of the way white Americans perceive him. Why, he wonders, do readers always assume a character is white unless they're told otherwise?... And why, he asks his theater audience, do white Americans always focus immediately upon his Chineseness?...

Tripmaster Monkey is a novel of excesses—both the hero's and the author's. Wittman careens through the story with that oversupply of manic energy often found in bright, idealistic, not-yet-mellowed young men; and Kingston describes his adventures in a style equally manic, equally energetic. If we didn't know better, we could imagine this book had been written by, say, a 23-year-old newly graduated college student.

Sometimes this is dazzling. How does she do it? we marvel. Where, for instance, does she find the vitality to embark upon a minutely detailed five-page description of what a roomful of high and contact-high party guests sees while staring at a blank TV screen? How has she managed to summon the youthful quirkiness, the youthful sense of limitless time and entirely idle curiosity, that allows Wittman to delight in the reflection of his own naked crotch as distorted by the handguard of a fencing sword? Or, for that matter, the youthful cruelty with which he surveys his fellow human beings?...

But at other times the effect is exhausting—much as if that 23-year-old had taken up residence in our living room, staying way too long, as 23-year-olds are wont to do, and wearing us out with his exuberance. The myths and sagas are particularly tiring. Wittman loves to tell lengthy stories that possess the grandiosity and the meandering formlessness common to folk legends. It's hard to believe that his friends, who tend to be as frenetic as Wittman himself, would sit still for what amounts to hours of this. Certainly the reader has trouble doing so. After a while, the merest mention of Liu Pei or Sun Wu Kong, the Monkey King, is enough to make our eyes glaze over.

No, what keeps us with *Tripmaster Monkey* (and we do stay with it, wholeheartedly) is not the larger-than-life sagas that Wittman finds so compelling but the tiny, meticulously catalogued details that fill his quieter moments. Just listen to the jumbled conversation of his mother and aunts as they play mah-jongg, or watch the hilarious lengths to which his father will go to save money, or observe Wittman's extended, gently humorous encounter with an elderly applicant in the Unemployment Office. When he lists the outward signs of a disintegrating marriage (the shrimp shells rotting on the dinner table, the off-the-hook telephone lost among the dirty clothes), or when he announces his resolutions for self-improvement ("decant the catsup . . . wash coffee cup between usings. . . . Peel an orange into the garbage bag, okay, but then walk a ways off, don't slurp over the bag"), the miracle is that we are riveted to his words no matter how long they go on. These passages refuel us; they remind us how infinitely entertaining everyday life can be when it's observed with a fresh eye.

Chinese, American, Chinese-American—Wittman is all three, whether he likes it or not, and the reader benefits. That Wittman is Chinese gives his story depth and particularity. That he's American lends his narrative style a certain slangy insouciance. That he's Chinese-American, with the self-perceived outsider's edgy angle of vision, makes for a novel of satisfying complexity and bite and verve. . . .

JOHN LEONARD

SOURCE: John Leonard, in a review of *Tripmaster Monkey*, in *The Nation*, New York, Vol. 248, No. 22, June 5, 1989, pp. 768-72.

[*In the following excerpt, Leonard favorably reviews* Tripmaster Monkey.]

We won't get much of anywhere with *Tripmaster Monkey* unless we understand that Maxine Hong Kingston is playing around like a Nabokov with the two cultures in her head. In *Ada,* by deciding that certain wars, which were lost, should have been won, Nabokov rearranged history to suit himself. There were Russians all over North America, making trilingual puns. This odd world was a parody of Russian novels.

In *Tripmaster Monkey,* America in the 1960s is looked at through the lens of a half-dozen Chinese novels, most of them sixteenth century. I will fall on this sword in a minute.

First, a disabusing. What everybody seems to have wanted from Kingston, after a decade of silence, is another dream-book, like *The Woman Warrior.* Or another history lesson, like *China Men.* Anyway: more magic, ghosts, dragonboats, flute music from the savage lands. Never mind that she's earned the right to write about whatever she chooses, and if she chooses to write about looking for Buddha in the wild, wild West, we'd better pay attention because she's smarter than we are. Nevertheless, the reviewers are demanding more memoir. Where's the female avenger?

Instead of the female avenger, we get Wittman Ah Sing, a 23-year-old fifth-generation Chinese-American male, Cal English major, playwright and draft dodger. . . . He wants to be an authentic American, but America won't let him. Racist jokes enrage him, but he also worries that a rapprochement of black and white might still exclude his very own yellow, which color determines his wardrobe, his slick performance. . . . He's done time at a dog pound, and among DNA biologists, and they all look alike: "A liberal-arts education is good for knowing how to look at anything from an inquisitive viewpoint, to shovel shit and have thoughts." He's into drugs, movies, comic books and modern masters. He wants to be, if not Lenny Bruce or Allen Ginsberg, at the very least "the first bad-jazz China Man bluesman of America." And what he'll do, like Judy Garland, is put on a show in his garage, a kind of Cantonese *Gotterdammerung*.

In other words: Huck Finn, Holden Caulfield, Augie March, maybe even Stephen Dedalus and probably Abbie Hoffman. Wittman is a "tripmaster," a friendly guide to the stoned in their travels through acid-time. But he's also, and this is where it gets tricky, an incarnation of the Monkey King in Wu Ch'eng-en's sixteenth-century *Journey to the West,* a kind of Chinese *Pilgrim's Progress.* He's the rebel/mischief-maker who helped bring back Buddha's Sutras from India; the shape-changer (falcon, koi fish, cormorant) who annoyed Laotse by eating the peaches of the Immortals, even though he hadn't been invited to their party. The weeklong play this Monkey stages to finish off Wittman's "fake book" is nothing less than a reenactment of *Romance of the Three Kingdoms,* a kind of Chinese *Terry and the Pirates.* And the actors he press-gangs into service for that play—everybody he knows in California, including his Flora Dora showgirl mother, his "aunties" and a kung fu gang—are nothing less than symbolic stand-ins for the 108 bandit-heroes of *Water Margin,* a kind of Chinese Robin Hood—enemies of a corrupt social order, hiding out in a wetlands Sherwood Forest, like Chairman Mao in misty Chingkangshan or the caves of Yenan.

This Wittman is stoned on books. Imagine one culture, ours, reimagined in the classic literature of another's—late imperial Ming—so much older, no less bloody. Sixties grandiosity!

A word here about language. What so excited readers of **The Woman Warrior** and **China Men** was that shiver of the exotic, the Other's static cling. It was as if we'd eavesdropped on a red dwarf and picked up these alien signals, this legend stuff, from an ancestor culture that despised its female children, that bound their feet and threw them down wishing wells and killed their names. Kingston achieved such a shiver by a sneaky art—disappearing into people who couldn't think in English, and translating for them. She had to invent an American language commensurate with their Chinese meanings. In the way that Toni Morrison arrived at all the transcendence of *Beloved* by stringing together little words *just so,* rubbing up their warmth into a combustion, Kingston dazzled us by pictographs, by engrams.

She made it look easy, but imagine the price. She denied and abolished herself. There wasn't room for a grown-up Maxine in her portraits of a mother who devoured her children and a father who buried wine bottles upside-down in the garden so that "their bottoms made a path of sea-color circles." This grown-up Maxine, after all, was a Cal English major just like Wittman; a reader of Rilke and Proust, Pound, Joyce and Eliot, the original Whitman and his grandchild Ginsberg, Charles Olson and Gary Snyder and Brother Antoninus. From these books dissolved in brain, from a slang of be-ins and love-ins and trippings-out in the psychedelic 1960s, from radical chitchat and the calisthenics of Left Coast Zen, an adult Kingston had fashioned a language of her own. But she'd no place to put it in her first two books. Like Bak Goong in **China Men,** forbidden to talk on the Hawaii sugarcane plantation, she shouted into a hole in the ground. To sing herself, she needed someone like the unbuttoned Wittman.

The result in **Tripmaster** is less charming but more exuberant. Instead of falling into pattern or turning on wheel—there's something inevitable about everything in **The Woman Warrior** and **China Men,** something fated—this language bounces, caroms and collides; abrades and inflames. instead of Mozart, Wittman's rock and roll. . . .

Wittman's too easily wowed. He's a one-man *I Ching*—"a book and also a person dressed in yellow," jumping from "reality to reality like quantum physics." He needs watching. And a female narrator—usually affectionate, always ironic, occasionally annoyed—looks down on him. Don't ask me how I know the narrator's female. I just do. She's as old as China, and remembers what happened in five dynasties and three religions. She's also foreseen the future: America will lose the war in Vietnam, which Wittman's dodging; the 1960s will be sadder than he hopes; feminism's in the works. She explains things Wittman has no way of knowing: . . . "Ho Chi Minh's favorite reading was *Romance of the Three Kingdoms* and it's a text at West Point too. Uncle Ho and Uncle Sam were both getting their strategy and philosophy from Grandfather Gwan, god of war." Though seldom a bully, she does at one point tell Wittman to shut up.

It's a nice tension. Wittman is the ultimate innocent himself, the last romantic, all virtue and passion and energy and funk. He will go up like a balloon in every weather: "They hung over the balcony and watched the skaters going around. If we run downstairs and rent skates, could we be Orlando and the Russian princes zipping on the frozen Thames above the apple woman in the deep ice? Wittman, the fool for books, ought to swear off reading for a while, and find his own life. . . ."

Now about that play. *Romance of the Three Kingdoms* is required reading for every literate Chinese child. (If you don't already know this stuff, you probably wonder if you need to. Only if you want to get a tenth as much out of Kingston's novel as she's put into it.) It glorifies a third-century revolt of Liu Pei and his mentor, Chu-ko Liang, against the military dictatorship of Ts'ao Ts'ao. . . .

This, of course, isn't good enough for Wittman. As well as the god of warriors, Gwan was the god of actors, writers, gamblers and travelers. Wittman will rewrite *Three Kingdoms.* His play is a "fake war." He'll substitute his theater for all the wars in the history of the world. From Monkey King and Havoc Monster, Pure Green Snake and White Bone Demoness, Dwarf Tiger and Dry Land Water Beast, American movies and Peking opera, vaudeville and puppets and brothel music, fireworks and kung fu, he will ordain a Peaceable Kingdom: "Night mirages filled the windows reflecting and magnifying—a city at war and carnival. All aflare and so bright that we understand: why we go to war is to make explosions and lights, which are more beautiful than anything...."

Well, the hippies wanted to be Indians. Why not Chinese, instead? And what, after all, was the trial of the Chicago Seven but Wittman's sort of theater? And wouldn't it have been something if the Quakers, Women's Strike for Peace, Martin Luther King Jr. and the vegetarians had prevailed? Instead, the garrison state, which had most of the violence, stopped this show, and the left regressed into little-league Leninism—a tantrum of cadres, Weatherpeople, Baader-Meinhof. And the rest is Heavy Metal. "It must be," says poor Wittman, "that people who read go on more macrocosmic and microcosmic trips—Biblical god trips. *The Tibetan Book of the Dead,* Ulysses, *Finnegans Wake* trips. Non-readers, what do they get? (They get the munchies.)"

You can stop looking for the Novel of the Sixties. It took 3,000 years on its journey to the West. But here are the peaches and the Sutras.

SOURCES FOR FURTHER STUDY

Chun, Gloria. "The High Note of the Barbarian Reed Pipe: Maxine Hong Kingston." *The Journal of Ethnic Studies* 19, No. 3 (Fall 1991): 85-94.

> Delineates the relations between *The Woman Warrior* and its publisher, reading audience, academia, and the author, showing how "the text reflects the goals of mainstream literary production."

Nishime, LeiLani. "Engendering Genre: Gender and Nationalism in *China Men* and *The Woman Warrior.*" *MELUS* 20 (Spring 1995): 67-82.

> Discusses Kingston's deconstruction of the opposition between fictional and nonfictional forms, use of mythology to explore issues of national identity, and manipulations of genre and mythology by introducing race and gender.

Rabinowitz, Paula. "Eccentric Memories: A Conversation with Maxine Hong Kingston." *Michigan Quarterly Review* 26 (Winter 1987): 177-87.

> Interviews Kingston about the significance and politics of memory in her works.

Slowik, Mary. "When the Ghosts Speak: Oral and Narrative Forms in Maxine Hong Kingston's *China Men.*" *MELUS* 19 (Spring 1994): 73-88.

> Describes the relation of Chinese immigrant history to oral and written narrative forms, concluding that Kingston's success in combining both elements makes *China Men* "a seminal study in multicultural literature."

Williams, A Noelle. "Parody and Pacifist Transformation in Maxine Hong Kingston's *Tripmaster Monkey: His Fake Book.*" *MELUS* 20 (Spring 1995): 83-100.

> Explores Kingston's use of parody to confront the conflicting desires of individuality and community in *Tripmaster Monkey.*

Yu, Ning. "A Strategy against Marginalization: The 'High' and 'Low' Cultures in Kingston's *China Men.*" *College Literature* 23 (October 1996): 73-87.

> Examines the particular way in which Kingston challenges the "low" status imposed on Chinese-Americans by resisting the constraints of binary thinking in *China Men.*

Doris Lessing

1919-

(Born Doris May Tayler; has also written under the pseudonym Jane Somers) Persian-born English novelist, short story writer, essayist, dramatist, poet, nonfiction writer, journalist, and travel writer.

INTRODUCTION

Considered among the most significant writers of the postwar generation, Lessing has explored many of the most important ideas, ideologies, and social issues of the twentieth century. Her works display a broad range of interests and concerns, including racism, communism, feminism, psychology, and mysticism. The major unifying theme of her work is the need for the individual to confront his or her most fundamental assumptions about life as a way of avoiding preconceived belief systems and achieving psychic and emotional wholeness.

Biographical Information

Lessing was born in Persia (now Iran) to English parents who moved their family to Rhodesia (now Zimbabwe) when she was still very young. She was educated in a convent school and then a government-run school for girls, which she left at the age of thirteen. Always a precocious reader, Lessing had excelled at school and continued her education on her own through the wealth of books her mother ordered from London. By age eighteen Lessing had written two drafts for novels and was selling stories to South African magazines, although her first novel, *The Grass Is Singing*, which confronts the effects of apartheid in rural Rhodesia from a woman's perspective, did not appear until 1950. Between 1924 and 1949 Lessing worked as a nursemaid, a lawyer's secretary, and a typist. In 1939 she married Frank Wisdom, with whom she had two children that she later abandoned to the care of relatives, but the marriage lasted only four years. Lessing joined the Communist Party in the early 1940s, but she left it during the early 1950s. Her second marriage, to Gottfried Lessing in 1945, also failed, and in 1949 she and their son Peter moved to London, where she has lived ever since.

Major Works

The Grass Is Singing established two of Lessing's early major concerns: racism and the way that historical and political circumstances can determine the course of a person's life. Early in her career Lessing explored similar issues in short story form. Among her most acclaimed collections—*Five: Short Novels* (1953), *The Habit of Loving* (1957), and *African Stories* (1964)— deal with racial concerns in African settings and the emancipation of modern women. The highly acclaimed "Children of Violence" series—comprising the novels *Martha Quest* (1952), *A Proper Marriage, A Ripple from the Storm* (1958), *Landlocked* (1966), and *The Four-Gated City* (1969)—traces the intellectual development of Martha Quest, a "child of violence" who progresses from personal, self-centered concerns to a larger awareness of others and the world around her, all the while pursuing various beliefs in order to achieve psychic wholeness. *The Golden Notebook* (1962), widely considered Lessing's masterpiece, centers on Anna Freeman Wulf. Parts of a novel that Anna is writing are juxtaposed with various aspects of her life which have been collected in one of four corresponding and color-coded notebooks. A fifth, "golden notebook," represents her desperate attempt to integrate through art her fragmented experiences and to become whole in the process. Lessing's so-called "inner space fiction," including *Briefing for a Descent into Hell* (1971) and *The Memoirs of a Survivor* (1974), reveals the influence of psychiatrists Carl Jung and R. D. Laing; the latter proposed that insanity is merely a convenient label imposed by society on those who do not conform to its standards of behavior. In the late 1970s Lessing began a five-volume "space fiction" series, "Canopus in Argos: Archives." The series involves three competing galactic empires—the benign Canopeans, self-centered Sirians, and evil Shammat—who manipulated earth history in order to retain a gene pool for their own immortality. These forces continue to influence events on earth through the intervention of immortal beings. Lessing also wrote two novels under the pseudonym Jane Somers, *The Diary of a Good Neighbour* (1983) and *If the Old Could . . .* (1984), to make a point about the problems faced by unknown writers, who usually are doomed to oblivion. Rejected by ten publishers, the major concerns of the Somers books reflect those of Lessing's feminist works: relations between women, the question of identity, and psychological conflict. Since her pseudonymous period, Lessing has written *The Good Terrorist* (1985), a satirical novel about romantic politics, and *The Fifth Child* (1988), about a violent, antisocial child who wreaks havoc on his family and society. The first volume of Lessing's autobiography, *Under My Skin* (1994), covers her life in Persia and Rhodesia until she departed for London.

Critical Reception

Lessing is generally regarded as one of the most important writers of the twentieth century. Using detailed, realistic descriptions, symbolism, and imagery to evoke a wide range of environments and moods, Lessing achieved what Edward J. Fitzgerald termed "tension and immediacy" in her work. Critics argue that her portrayal of marriage and motherhood, her anti-apartheid stance, and her experimentation with genre and form have made her an exciting and often controversial literary figure. Many critics have not thought highly of her science fiction and mystical works, contending that by abandoning realism Lessing neglected the social analysis that made her earlier works so valuable. However, Jeannette King found that "in her most experimental fantasies, Lessing has consistently explored the relationship between the individual psyche and the political, sexual, and religious ideologies that structure it." As Paul Schlueter remarked, "[Her] work has changed radically in format and genre over the years, . . . [but] the fact remains that she is among the most powerful and compelling novelists of our century."

(For further information, see *Concise Dictionary of British Literary Biography:* 1960 to Present; *Contemporary Authors,* Vols. 9-12R; *Contemporary Authors Autobiography Series,* Vol. 14; *Contemporary Authors New Revision Series,* Vols. 33, 54; *Contemporary Literary Criticism,* Vols. 1, 2, 3, 6, 10, 15, 22, 40, 94; *Dictionary of Literary Biography,* Vols. 15, 139; *Dictionary of Literary Biography Yearbook: 1985; DISCovering Authors; DISCovering Authors: British; DISCovering Authors: Canadian; DISCovering Authors Modules: Most-studied Authors Module, Novelists Module; Major Twentieth-Century Writers; Short Story Criticism,* Vol. 6.)

CRITICAL COMMENTARY

MARY ANN SINGLETON

SOURCE: Mary Ann Singleton, in her *The City and the Veld: The Fiction of Doris Lessing,* Bucknell University Press, 1977, 243 p.

[*In the following excerpt, Singleton examines the dual concepts of city and veld, or hope for an ideal*

Principal Works

The Grass Is Singing (novel) 1950
*Martha Quest (novel) 1952
This Was the Old Chief's Country (short stories) 1952
Before the Deluge (drama) 1953
Five: Short Novels (novellas) 1953
*A Proper Marriage (novel) 1954
Retreat to Innocence (novel) 1956
Going Home (essays) 1957
The Habit of Loving (short stories) 1957
*A Ripple from the Storm (novel) 1958
Fourteen Poems (poetry) 1959
In Pursuit of the English: A Documentary (documentary) 1960
The Golden Notebook (novel) 1962
A Man and Two Women (short stories) 1963
African Stories (short stories) 1964
*Landlocked (novel) 1966
Particularly Cats (autobiographical essay) 1967
Nine African Stories (short stories) 1968
*The Four-Gated City (novel) 1969
Briefing for a Descent into Hell (novel) 1971
The Story of a Non-Marrying Man and Other Stories (short stories) 1972; also published as The Temptation of Jack Orkney and Other Stories, 1972
The Summer before the Dark (novel) 1973
The Memoirs of a Survivor (novel) 1974
A Small Personal Voice: Essays, Reviews, and Interviews (essays, reviews, and interviews) 1974
†Shikasta (novel) 1979
†The Marriages between Zones Three, Four, and Five (novel) 1980
†The Sirian Experiments (novel) 1981
†The Making of the Representative for Planet 8 (novel) 1982
The Diary of a Good Neighbour [as Jane Somers] (novel) 1983
†Documents Relating to the Sentimental Agents in the Volyen Empire (novel) 1983
‡The Diaries of Jane Somers (novel) 1984
If the Old Could . . . [as Jane Somers] (novel) 1984
The Good Terrorist (novel) 1985
Prisons We Choose to Live Inside (essays) 1987
The Wind Blows Away Our Words (nonfiction) 1987
The Fifth Child (novella) 1988
African Laughter: Four Visits to Zimbabwe (nonfiction) 1992
The Real Thing (short stories) 1992
Playing the Game Graphic Novel (graphic novel) 1993
Under My Skin: Volume One of My Autobiography, to 1949 (autobiography) 1994
Love, Again (novel) 1996

*These novels are collectively called the "Children of Violence" series and the "Martha Quest" novels.
†These novels are collectively called the "Canopus in Argos: Archives" series.
‡This work comprises two earlier novels, The Diary of a Good Neighbour and If the Old Could . . . , which Lessing published under the pseudonym Jane Somers.

Adaptations

Adaptations of Lessing's works include the films Memoirs of a Survivor, directed by David Gladwell, 1981, and Killing Heat, an adaptation of The Grass Is Singing, directed by Michael Raeburn, 1982.

---

future as opposed to the unconscious, physical world of nature, as central to Lessing's fiction.]

[Doris Lessing] believes (with many others) that our civilization is slipping ever-faster toward the precipice. Almost from the beginning, her work has explored what in human nature is causing this catastrophe and what, if anything, can be done about it. . . .

Lessing's attention is always turned toward humanity's destructive weaknesses and potential strength, and it is essentially these that I have called the two *cities* and the *veld*. For Lessing, the African veld is the unconscious, physical world of nature that nourishes mankind with its unity but also inflicts its own mindless repetition and, in human terms, cruelty and indifference. The city is half-evolved consciousness, the destructive fragmentation of partial awareness. The ideal City is a hope for the future: the unified individual in a harmonious society. To impose such an intellectual scheme upon Lessing's work goes against its spirit; however, if it leads to increased understanding of her writing, perhaps to do so is forgivable. . . .

The ideal of the City stands behind everything Lessing has written, an expression of her firm sense of purpose, put most explicitly in an important essay, **"The Small Personal Voice,"** There she affirms a belief in "committed" literature, in which the writer considers himself/herself "an instrument of change." For if the ideal of the City stands in the background of Lessing's work, the Armageddon of technological disaster looms there as well. . . .

Lessing believes that mankind is at a crucial point in history and that artists must paint the possible evil as well as strengthen "a vision of good which may defeat the evil"; that is, art for society's sake. Lessing's criteria for art fit her own work. Not simply an artist, she is also critic and prophet, dissecting in minute detail the faults of a society "hypnotized by the idea of Armageddon" and prophesying the calamitous results of those faults. At the same time, she attempts to delineate possible solutions to the world's problems.

There are three main motifs in Lessing's work, which I have called the two *cities* and the *veld,* and they are apparent in her themes, imagery, and structures. The veld represents the unity of nature, whole and complete, but in which the individual counts for nothing. Before the birth of self-consciousness, as it is known today, mankind readily participated in this natural world and at times was scarcely differentiated from it; but the price of unity was to be caught in the ceaseless round of natural repetition, all instinct with no reason.

The city represents modern consciousness, expressed in a strife-torn society. Its origins are the loss of mythic consciousness that prevailed in early, simpler cultures; its power, the ability to use the tools of reason; its culmination, the achievements and excesses of the last two hundred years, when logic and reason have come to be valued by society as a whole almost to the exclusion of other modes of perception. Reason has the power to raise mankind above the brute, instinctual level, but in its present form it is partial, fragmented.... According to Lessing, such fragmented perception is presently leading mankind to certain disaster—much like fire in the hands of a child—causing unbalanced, private lives and conflict in society. As citizens of the contemporary city, mankind is a victim of a second type of repetition, not of natural cycles this time, but the constant replaying of destructive patterns of behavior. Both here and in the veld he has no hope of change except from natural evolution, in which he is simply acted upon: Jude rather than Prometheus.

The third motif is the ideal City, a new and more unified form of consciousness, ... expressed as a harmonious society of unified citizens. The human imagination holds the key: "[we must] force ourselves into the effort of imagination necessary to become what we are capable of being." Nature's harsh unity is no longer compatible with human self-consciousness and values. Partial truths have proved disastrous. The next step is to create new, whole forms that will somehow contain intuition along with reason, both myth and logic, with all the complexities the terms suggest. When—and if—this new unity is accomplished, the ideal City will be possible, the Golden Age finally at hand. The City in the veld is a man-made harmony—part of nature, yet at the same time separate from it, as consciousness is of and yet above nature.

Most of Lessing's fiction may be seen within this overall pattern. For the most part, Lessing depicts the psychically warped citizens of the city, all inexorably headed for disaster. The early *The Grass Is Singing* concerns Mary Turner's complete destruction by social and psychic forces of which she is not even aware, and many of the short stories dramatize the fragmented lives of people who have varying degrees of awareness. *Retreat to Innocence* shows Julia Barr's refusal to leave the superficial life of the city.

After *The Grass Is Singing,* Lessing's major protagonists and more visionary characters search for ways to integrate the city and the veld, even while they are inextricably caught in the tangles of the mass psyche and society. *The Golden Notebook* is an odyssey of the individual is search of wholeness, and while Anna Wulf's story is central, the reader sees beyond it to the society that conditions her and limits what she can be. **"Children of Violence"** is Lessing's most complete portrait of the fragmented city. Here, half a century passes before one's eyes, as Martha and her closest friends search in vain for inner and outer versions of the City, as society races with increasing speed toward its destruction. In **"Children of Violence"** Lessing comes closest to the first half of her criterion for the committed writer—to paint a vision of evil; her view of the good that may defeat it has evolved slowly and is therefore more clearly presented in the later works....

There is a substantial difference between Lessing's view of humanity's possibilities and the predominant attitude of most twentieth-century novels, in which the hero is perforce an anti-hero, stumbling gallantly through the world. Certainly Lessing's view of man in his present condition is bleak: in these lost generations, too, everyone is sick. Nevertheless, she extends a glimmer of hope that somewhere latent in man is, after all, the possibility of psychic health....

Lessing is a writer of great variety. Her short stories are usually economical and carefully crafted, while **"Children of Violence"** sprawls over five long novels, finally moving away almost entirely from customary narrative techniques.... But if her forms vary, her metaphysic, which I have summed up in the images of the two cities in the veld, remains essentially the same....

Most of Lessing's fiction deals with the need to join the mythic and discursive, the veld and the city—to be in touch with the mythic state, unified and close to experience, yet without losing the uniquely human values of ego-consciousness and logic. It is to be a hard-won wholeness based on a joining of reason and myth: something new. This is the unity suggested by the image of the City in the veld. The ideal City represents a man-made achievement, a triumph of consciousness and mental and physical harmony, standing apart from and yet integral to the cruel, unconscious, yet harmonious veld.

Lessing has said that people must force themselves, through effort of imagination, to become what they are capable of being; her image of the City, superimposed upon her picture of fragmented and violent society is such an attempt, as are all descriptions of Utopia....

If Lessing shares in this Utopian dream, she usually describes the world of here and now, trying to analyze what is going wrong. As a result, she seems to combine two extreme views of man. On the one hand, ... mankind seems always to be a victim of "grim fatality." From this point of view, if a finer consciousness should arise, willed human creativity will have no hand in it: at the end of *The Four-Gated City* Martha writes of the new children who are mutations, affected by the radiation of the catastrophe. Their consciousness is a product of natural evolution, comparable to the first sea creatures who crept up to land. On the other hand, Lessing's work never quite relinquishes the possibility that a "willed mutation" will be possible, that through new modes of perception men and women have the power to catapult themselves back to the top of the great chain of being; this time even higher than the angels and perhaps on a godly level themselves, as their own creators....

GORE VIDAL

SOURCE: Gore Vidal, "Paradise Regained," in *The New York Review of Books*, Vol. XXVI, No. 20, December 20, 1979, pp. 3-4.

[*Vidal is an American novelist, short story writer, dramatist, and essayist. He is particularly noted for his historical novels and his iconoclastic essays. In the following excerpt, he assesses Lessing's novel* Shikasta.]

Although Doris Lessing has more in common with George Eliot than she has with any contemporary serious-novelist, she is not always above solemnity, as opposed to mere seriousness. Somewhat solemnly, Lessing tells us in the preface to her new novel *Shikasta* that there may indeed be something wrong with the way that novels are currently being written. She appears not to be drawn to the autonomous word-structure. On the other hand, she is an old-fashioned moralist. This means that she is inclined to take very seriously the quotidian. The deep—as opposed to strip—mining of the truly moral relationship seems to me to be her territory. I say seems because I have come to Lessing's work late. I began to read her with *Memoirs of a Survivor,* and now, with *Shikasta*, I have followed her into the realms of science fiction where she is making a continuum all her own somewhere between John Milton and L. Ron Hubbard.

Lessing tells us that, originally, she thought that she might make a single volume out of certain themes from the Old Testament (source of so much of our dreaming and bad behavior) but that she is now launched on a series of fables about interplanetary dominations and powers. "I feel as if I have been set free both to be as experimental as I like, and as traditional." I'm not sure what she means by "experimental" and "traditional." At best, Lessing's prose is solid and slow and a bit flat-footed. She is an entirely "traditional" prose writer. I suspect that she did not want to use the word "imaginative," a taboo word nowadays, and so she wrote "experimental."

In any case, like the splendid *Memoirs of a Survivor, Shikasta* is the work of a formidable imagination. Lessing can make up things that appear to be real, which is what storytelling is all about. But she has been sufficiently influenced by serious-writing to feel a need to apologize. "It is by now commonplace to say that novelists everywhere are breaking the bonds of the realistic novel because what we all see around us becomes daily wilder, more fantastic, incredible.... The old 'realistic' novel is being changed, too, because of influences from that genre loosely described as space fiction." Actually, I have seen no very vivid sign of this influence and I don't suppose that she has either. But it is not unusual for a writer to regard his own new turning as a highway suddenly perceived by all, and soon to be crowded with other pilgrims en route to the City on the Hill.

If this book has any recent precursor, it is Kurt Vonnegut, Jr. Lessing has praised him elsewhere: "Vonnegut is moral in an old-fashioned way ... he has made nonsense of the little categories, the unnatural divisions into 'real' literature and the rest, because he is comic and sad at once, because his painful seriousness is never solemn. Vonnegut is unique among us; and these same qualities account for the way a few academics still try to patronize him...."

Lessing is even more influenced by the Old Testament. "It is our habit to dismiss the Old Testament altogether because Jehovah, or Jahve, does not think or behave like a social worker." So much for JC, doer of good and eventual scientist. But Lessing's point is well taken. Because the Old Testament's lurid tales of a furious god form a background to Jesus' "good news," to Mohammed's "recitations," to the Jewish ethical sense, those bloody tales still retain an extraordinary mythic power, last demonstrated in full force by Milton.

In a sense, Lessing's **Shikasta** is a return more to the spirit (not, alas, the language) of Milton than to that of Genesis. But Lessing goes Milton one better, or worse. Milton was a dualist. Lucifer blazes as the son of morning; and the Godhead blazes, too. Their agon is terrific. Although Lessing deals with opposites, she tends to unitarianism. She is filled with the spirit of the Sufis, and if there is one thing that makes me more nervous than a Jungian it is a Sufi. Lessing believes that it is possible "to 'plug in' to an overmind, or Ur-mind, or unconscious, or what you will, and that this accounts for a great many improbabilities and 'coincidences.'" She does indeed plug in; and **Shikasta** is certainly rich with improbabilities and "coincidences." Elsewhere (**"In the World, Not of It"**), Lessing has expressed her admiration for one Idries Shah, a busy contemporary purveyor of Sufism (from the Arab word *suf*, meaning wool . . . the costume for ascetics).

Idries Shah has been characterized in the pages of this journal as the author of works that are replete with "constant errors of fact, slovenly and inaccurate translations, even the misspelling of Oriental names and words. In place of scholarship we are asked to accept a muddle of platitudes, irrelevancies, and plain mumbo-jumbo." Lessing very much admires Idries Shah and the woolly ones, and she quotes with approval from Idries Shah's *The Dermis Probe* in which *he* quotes from M. Gauquelin's *The Cosmic Clocks*. "An astonishing parallel to the Sufi insistence on the relatively greater power of subtle communication to affect man, is found in scientific work which shows that all living things, including man, are 'incredibly sensitive to waves of extraordinarily weak energy — when more robust influences are excluded.'" This last quotation within a quotation is the theme of **Shikasta**.

It is Lessing's conceit that a benign and highly advanced galactic civilization, centered on Canopus, is sending out harmonious waves hither and yon, rather like Milton's god before Lucifer got bored. Canopus lives in harmony with another galactic empire named Sirius. Once upon a time warp, the two fought a Great War but now all is serene between the galaxies. I can't come up with the Old Testament parallel on that one. Is Canopus Heaven versus Sirius's Chaos? Anyway, the evil planet Shammat in the galactic empire of Puttiora turns out to be our old friend Lucifer or Satan or Lord of the Flies, and the planet Shikasta (that's us) is a battleground between the harmonious vibes of Canopus and the wicked vibes of Shammat which are constantly bombarding our planet. In the end, Lucifer is hurled howling into that place where he prefers to reign and all is harmony with God's chilluns. Lessing rather lacks negative capability. Where Milton's Lucifer is a joy to contemplate, Lessing's Shammat is a drag whose planetary agents sound like a cross between Tolkien's monster and Sir Lew Grade.

Lessing's narrative devices are nothing if not elaborate. Apparently, the Canopian harmonious future resembles nothing so much as an English Department that has somehow made an accommodation to share its "facilities" with the Bureau of Indian Affairs. The book's title page is daunting: "Canopus in Argos: Archives" at the top. Then "Re: Colonised Planet 5" (as I type this, I realize that I've been misreading "Re: Colonised" as recolonised); then "Shikasta"; then "Personal, Psychological, Historical Documents Relating to Visit by JOHOR (George Sherban) Emissary (Grade 9) 87th of the Period of the Last Days." At the bottom of the page, one's eye is suddenly delighted by the homely phrase "Alfred A. Knopf New York 1979." There is not much music in Lessing spheres.

Like the Archangel Raphael, Johor travels through Shikasta's time. The planet's first cities were so constructed that transmitters on Canopus could send out benign waves of force; as a result, the local population (trained by kindly giants) were happy and frolicsome. "Canopus was able to feed Shikasta with a rich and vigorous air, which kept everyone safe and healthy, and above all, made them love each other. . . . This supply of finer air had a name. It was called SOWF — the substance-of-we-feeling — I had of course spent time and effort in working out an easily memorable syllable." Of course. But the SOWF is cut off. The cities of the plain are blasted. The Degenerative Disease begins and the race suffers from "grandiosities and pomps," short life spans, bad temper. The Degenerative Disease is Lessing's equivalent for that original sin which befell man when Eve bit on the apple.

There is a certain amount of fun to be had in Johor's tour of human history. He is busy as a bee trying to contain the evil influence of Shammat, and Lessing not only brings us up to date but beyond: the Chinese will occupy Europe fairly soon. Lessing is a master of the eschatological style and **Memoirs of a Survivor** is a masterpiece of that genre. But where the earlier book dealt with a very real London in a most credible terminal state, **Shikasta** is never quite real enough. At times the plodding style does make things believable, but then reality slips away . . . too little SOWF, perhaps. Nevertheless, Lessing is plainly enjoying herself and the reader can share in that enjoyment a good deal of the time. But, finally, she lacks the peculiar ability to create alternative worlds. For instance, she invents for the human dead a limbo she calls Zone 6. This shadowy place is a cross between Homer's Hades and the Zoroastrian concept of the place where eternal souls hover about, waiting to be born. Lessing's descriptions of the undead dead are often very fine but when one compares her invention with Ursula Le Guin's somewhat similar land of the dead in the *Earthsea* trilogy, one is aware that Le Guin's darkness is darker, her coldness colder, her shadows more dense and stranger.

Lessing's affinity for the Old Testament combined with the woolliness of latter-day Sufism has got her into something of a philosophical muddle. Without the idea of free will, the human race is of no interest at all; certainly, without the idea of free will there can be no literature. To watch Milton's Lucifer serenely overthrow the controlling intelligence of his writerly creator is an awesome thing. But nothing like this happens in Lessing's work. From the moment of creation, Lessing's Shikastans are programmed by outside forces—sometimes benign, sometimes malign. They themselves are entirely passive. There is no Prometheus; there is not even an Eve. The fact that in the course of a very long book Lessing has not managed to create a character of the slightest interest is the result not so much of any failure in her considerable art as it is a sign that she has surrendered her mind to SOWF, or to the woollies, or to the Jealous God.

Obviously, there is a case to be made for predetermination or predestination or let-us-now-praise B. F. Skinner. Lessing herself might well argue that the seemingly inexorable DNA code is a form of genetic programming that could well be equated with Canopus's intervention and that, in either case, our puny lives are so many interchangeable tropisms, responding to outside stimuli. But I think that the human case is more interesting than that. The fact that no religion has been able to give a satisfactory reason for the existence of evil has certainly kept human beings on their toes during the brief respites that we are allowed between those ages of faith which can always be counted upon to create that we-state which seems so much to intrigue Lessing and her woollies, a condition best described by the most sinister of all Latin tags, *e pluribus unum*.

Ultimately, **Shikasta** is not so much a fable of the human will in opposition to a god who has wronged the fire-seeker as it is a fairy tale about good and bad extraterrestrial forces who take some obscure pleasure in manipulating a passive ant-like human race. Needless to say, Doris Lessing is not the first to incline to this "religion." In fact, she has considerable competition from a living prophet whose powerful mind has envisaged a race of god-like Thetans who once lived among us; they, too, overflowed with SOWF; then they went away. But all is not lost. The living prophet has told us their story. At first he wrote a science fiction novel, and bad people scoffed. But he was not dismayed. He knew that he could save us; bring back the wisdom of the Thetans; "clear" us of badness. He created a second holy book, *Dianetics*. Today he is the sole proprietor of the Church of Scientology. Doris Lessing would do well to abandon the woolly Idries Shah in favor of Mr. L. Ron Hubbard, who has already blazed that trail where now she trods—treads?—trods. . . .

MONA KNAPP

SOURCE: Mona Knapp, in her *Doris Lessing,* Frederick Ungar Publishing Co., 1984, 210 p.

[*In the following excerpt from her critical study* Doris Lessing, *Knapp offers an overview of Lessing's career and critical reception.*]

Doris Lessing has regretted only in passing her early decision to wash her hands of formal schooling. She has often expressed her contempt for the "horserace mentality" of educational institutions, which regard children as "commodities with a value in the success-stakes." She sees modern education—far from teaching individuals to think—as a tool to mass-produce compliant citizens who will run with the herd and fit society's needs by bowing mindlessly to authority.

The farmhouse in which Doris Tayler grew up is a prototype for the important motif of rooms and houses in Lessing's work. It symbolizes the limited possibilities of separating the individual from the environment. . . .

Houses are the single image which best illustrate Lessing's distrust of partitioning and compartmentalizing. They are always depicted as vulnerable and temporary, like our efforts to encapsulate experience. Lessing puts it categorically: "For me all houses will always be wrong." For they are impotent against existential homelessness, an illness of our century: "The fact is, I don't live anywhere; I never have since I left that first house on the kopje. I suspect more people are in this predicament than they know.". . .

At seventeen, Lessing had written and destroyed two

entire novels and fragments of others. She began writing at the age of nine, "poetic mush about sunsets mostly." With the modesty readers know as typical for her, she disclaims any literary worth of her writings prior to *The Grass Is Singing.* While still in Africa, she had submitted this novel without success to half a dozen English publishing houses. She signed a contract for it with a South African publisher, but when after her arrival in England it still had not been printed, she was advised to submit it to Michael Joseph Publishers in London. They accepted the manuscript at once. It was reprinted even before the official publication date and reached seven printings within five months. This enabled Lessing to give up a secretarial job. The successful first novel was quickly followed by *This Was the Old Chief's Country* (1951), *Martha Quest* (1952) and *Five* (1953). For the latter she earned the 1954 Somerset Maugham Award for the best work of a British author under thirty-five. Lessing lived thenceforth exclusively from her writing.

Despite the struggle to survive in economically ailing postwar Britain, the years after her arrival there were marked by breathtaking productivity in all literary genres. She was relieved to have escaped the oppressive Rhodesian society, where writers were constantly "in a torment of conscientiousness" over social injustice. England appeared to her in contrast as a calm haven for serious writing. There she further analyzed and increasingly rejected all forms of collective behavior. Though Marxist theory, which "looks at things as a whole and in relation to each other," provided the formative basis for Lessing's thought and works, her idealistic participation in the Rhodesian group was to remain her only wholehearted alliance with an ideologically defined collective. In England, her political activity was considerably less fervent and often concentrated on individual causes (such as circulating a petition for the Rosenbergs). Like many liberal intellectuals in the 1950s, she joined the British Communist Party, but attended meetings only sporadically; she had decided to leave it again well before she actually did so in 1956. She was also a member of a socialist writers' group, but has described herself as an "agitator manquee," whose main energy was poured onto paper rather than into active politics. Lessing disclaims any involvement with England's New Left of the 1960s, at which time she viewed all political formations with increasing distrust. Her viewpoint in 1980 is unequivocal: "Certainly I would never have anything to do with politics again unless I was forced at the point of a gun, having seen what happens." All this, of course, does not change the fact that Lessing's books frequently have a politically mobilizing effect on her readers, and that her prose is at its very finest when examining the political relationship between individuals and the historical process.

Political groups are only one aspect of the *collective*, which can be defined as one of three major poles in Lessing's work. Collectivism includes nationalist affiliations, clubs of all sorts, mass support of authority and Fuhrer-figures, and all caste or class systems. It further includes groupings determined by sex or social standing: in brief, all the structures with which individuals identify and conform in order to belong to something greater, more powerful than themselves. Collective identifications, which Lessing dissects with ever increasing acridity, are the source of lamentable human behavior: at best they produce docile and manipulable followers, at worst outbursts of mob spirit. Standing in a triad with the collective are the *individual* and the *whole:* the tension among the three runs through Lessing's work from beginning to end. Where in the early work the protagonists measure themselves against a collective standard, after *The Golden Notebook* they increasingly abandon collectives in favor of their own inner reality. Her newest, nonrealist books relegate both individuality and collectivism to second place, emphasizing instead the *whole* of nature: the organic configuration of atoms and planets which dwarfs human beings and their scrawny institutions. The holistic motif as presented in Lessing's work can lend itself to mystical, religious or back-to-nature interpretation. Of main importance is that it be distinguished from the pseudowholes presented by collectives. For where collectives level and demean individuals, Lessing sees in their linkage with the whole a possible redemption.

In the first ten years after leaving Africa, Lessing wrote four more novels, dozens of short stories, reviews, and articles, two book-length essays and three plays. In 1952 she accompanied the Authors' World Peace Appeal delegation to the Soviet Union. In the later 1950s she became involved with theater, both as an author and, as a leave replacement for Kenneth Tynan of *The Observer*, as a critic. So far she has written five plays, four of which were produced between 1958 and 1962. In addition to a translation of Alexander Ostrovsky's *The Storm* for the National Theatre, she has written four television plays (two of which are adaptations of prose works).

In 1956 Lessing traveled to South Africa and Rhodesia, where she had in the meantime been declared a "prohibited immigrant" because of her Communist affiliation and unconcealed criticism of the white-supremacist regime. She was never officially informed that she was "prohibited." In 1953 Southern Rhodesia, Northern Rhodesia, and Nyasaland had been linked by Britain into a Federation, which was dissolved in 1964. Lessing's trip thus came at a time of temporary and fragile political equilibrium: she was among the first to diagnose that the Federation was not working. Her account of this journey is found in *Going Home* (1957), her major journalistic work. Lessing was not to return to Africa again until over twenty-five years later, in the summer of 1982.

While the early books received consistent and emphatic acclaim, it was *The Golden Notebook* in 1962 that really brought Lessing international prominence. It is generally considered to be her finest achievement. New translations of this novel invariably touch off an explosion of interest in her works—as demonstrated in eight non-English-speaking countries to date. The novel was instrumental in establishing her reputation in Western Europe. Since its publication in Germany in 1978, she has held an active place in the West German literary forum, and received two literary prizes from German-speaking countries in 1982.

The Golden Notebook is a sweeping examination of an individual's final reckoning with many collectives, ranging from communism to feminism. Its viewpoint is that of disillusionment: with the socialist dream, with the hope for a better world, and with traditional femininity. Feminists in English-speaking countries (who are, ironically, one of the collectives whose *causa* is partially invalidated by the book), immediately adopted the novel as a spearhead for the movement. Lessing herself has adamantly refused to take sides in the war between the sexes, which, as she correctly diagnoses, often serves as a modish substitute for serious class conflict: "I say we should all go to bed, shut up about sexual liberation, and go on with the important matters." Nevertheless, the book set a milestone in British literature through its uninhibited depiction of female sexuality. It continued to be a favorite of feminist readers throughout the 1970s, since it formulates so potently many of the movement's arguments. (A good many of them, in fact, can already be found in *A Proper Marriage,* published in 1954.) Its undiminished popularity with an increasingly political feminist movement provides proof of the author's own premise: that there can be no women's cause independent of humanity's social and political causes on the whole front. *The Golden Notebook* must be seen as a first zenith of Lessing's work, which in 1962 was only at the beginning of its multifaceted and unpredictable development.

In 1964, Lessing reviewed *The Sufis* by Idries Shah, the chief proponent of modern Sufism. Using her usual autodidactic method, she immersed herself in reading about Sufism throughout the 1960s. Since that time, many critics have investigated Sufi mysticism as a key to understanding Lessing's work, especially the two last volumes of **"Children of Violence."** Though mysticism undoubtedly plays a role in the development of Lessing's thought, it is important to keep it in perspective. Doris Lessing is not an esoteric writer, and it is perfectly possible to appreciate and interpret her novels without deeper knowledge of Sufism—which is, after all, still an ism. The school of belief is over a thousand years old, and differs from similar religious and mystic groups in that there is no official hierarchy. Any person in any walk of life can be "a Sufi." This is a crucial point: Lessing would never subscribe to a doctrine dependent on gurus and authority figures. Sufism emphasizes the individual expansion of consciousness and, concurrently, repudiation of propaganda, ideology, and prejudice: "Sufism believes itself to be the substance of that current which can develop man to a higher stage in his evolution." Sufi mysticism transcends national, religious, material and racial boundaries and encourages individuals to recognize their importance to the greater scheme of the human race. Clearly, this canon did not revolutionize Lessing's thinking, but rather reinforced insights which were present from the beginning: "I became interested in the Sufi way of thought because I was already thinking like that, before I had heard of Sufis or Sufism. My most 'Sufi' book was the *Golden Notebook,* written before I had heard of mysticism."

The Four-Gated City, published in 1969, represents a major turning point in Lessing's production. It is the fifth and last volume of the sequence **"Children of Violence,"** which was begun in 1951 as an exhaustive exploration of our century's "whole pattern of discrimination and tyranny and violence" as it affects one heroine, Martha Quest. While the first four volumes depict her grappling with various collectives, the fifth book breaks up this polarity, which appears petty and confining once Martha envisions the "whole" spectrum of human experience. She discovers the subconscious, the extrasensory and the "mad" parts of her consciousness. The book transcends the previous realist boundaries of Lessing's narrative scope; by abandoning an empirical time framework it ends around the year 2000. This is a first in Lessing's oeuvre, and probably the most crucial step in the development of her vision away from individual-bound realism and toward holistic fantasies.

On the basis of both *The Four-Gated City* and *Briefing For a Descent Into Hell* (1971), many of Lessing's critics connected her works to those of the popular British psychiatrist R. D. Laing. Though she is familiar with his writings, she was already deeply involved with her own assessment of madness before reading Laing's *The Divided Self* (1959). Laing was only one of a host of psychologists and sociologists, among them Erich Fromm, who concluded in the late fifties that psychoanalysis is often used to stifle individuality, to force the patient to conform to the "normal" standards of a sick society. A more fruitful comparison would be that of Lessing's work to the documentation on schizophrenia by Bert Kaplan, which she read in the late 1960s. But the insight which links her to this school of thought—that insanity is in fact a rational reaction to a violent society—can be traced back to the first decade of her literary work....

While Lessing has always worked to enlighten, sensitize, and edify, her belief in the possible betterment of humanity's situation has consistently dwindled. Where she once insisted that black and white, East and West could coexist if only true human contact were established, she has long come to view the catastrophic self-annihilation of civilization, looming since the cold war, as inevitable. Even without the atom bomb, humanity's chances of feeding and clothing, much less educating itself, are slim. Of a world in which 42,000 children per day die of malnutrition and disease (United Nations/World Health Organization Statistics for 1982), Lessing says, "This is the apocalypse, here and now."

Another phase of prolific production in the early 1970s attests to the author's growing pessimism. She released three novels within four years: *Briefing For a Descent Into Hell* was followed by *The Summer Before the Dark* (1973) and *The Memoirs of a Survivor* (1974). The books explore "inner space": their protagonists retreat into the realm of the subconscious in search of meaning after their external, collective identifications break down. Though the heroes' "madness" is shown as a viable response to society's demands, the first two ultimately resume their "sane" roles, and the third novel suspends rather than solves the conflict through a mystical vision.

After *Memoirs*, Lessing shifts her focus from individual madness and collective doom toward that "whole" of humanity glimpsed in *The Four-Gated City*. Ending a lull of nearly five years, she embarked in 1979 on an unprecedented novel series, *Canopus in Argos: Archives*. Once again, the novels attest to furious productivity—at the time of this writing, five volumes have been published in less than four years. Lessing now abandons realism to invent a counteruniverse, in which individuals are not plagued by the illusion of free will, and collective action appears as a mere Band-Aid on civilization's festering wounds. Wholeness, on the other hand, can be envisioned and even put to paper, as Canopus's industrious archivists prove. With this series, it is necessary to draw an unavoidably simplistic line between the "old," realist Lessing, and the "new" Lessing. Most of her readers clearly identify with one or the other. Where older readers are often perplexed and disappointed by the new books, many under thirty are enthusiastic, and dismiss the 1960s realism of *The Golden Notebook* or the no-exit racial and social dilemmas of *The Grass Is Singing* as boring and depressing....

In explanation of her productivity, which has continued untiringly for over thirty years, she admits that she writes very fast, drawing from inspiration rather than calculation: "I share with D. H. Lawrence the belief that often it is the first writing that has the vitality. If you mess about and tinker with a thing, it loses freshness." She also emphasizes her reliance on the subconscious, which she allows to surface through slumber: "When I'm stuck in a book I deliberately dream.... I fill my brain with the material for a new book, go to sleep, and I usually come up with a dream which resolves the dilemma." No doubt her unconventional methods contribute to the superior momentum of her prose, but also to a reckless style which is frequently criticized as careless and gangling. Paradoxically, the reader is often confronted with ungrammatical sentences oblivious to words like "whom," full of badly placed commas and relative pronouns—but whose substance is singularly well-put and persuasive.

Lessing's influence and popularity have increased steadily since the publication of her first novel. Her works have always provoked vehement reactions: she has been scorned as a communist and as a traitor to communism; labeled a radical, a feminist, a liberal. She has the distinction of being banned from certain bookstore shelves as "not decent." In fact, most of her work up to 1974 is traditional in style and theme, designed to communicate with a large readership through its feet-on-the-ground diagnosis of the human situation. The "radicalism" of her realist works lies only in their insistence on calling things by their right names. The newer books, despite their intergalactic perspective, still have as their main subject the exploration of social and psychological processes, and are designed to deepen the reader's concept of self in relation to the universe....

A sweeping backward glance over Lessing's literary production...reveals an overwhelming and often contradictory medley of ideas, themes, fictional techniques, and perspectives. The very heterogeneity of this oeuvre makes it a fitting illustration of its own foremost premise: that truth and substance cannot be smoothly compartmentalized and labeled, but are rather in constant flux. Lessing began her work in 1950 as a proponent of socialist commitment and nineteenth-century realism. Today she envisions a fantastic universe which has long cast its sights beyond the abortive isms of the twentieth century. Staid tradition complements experimental fervor; penetrating close-up portraits of individuals stand in contrast to a sublime cosmic panorama.

Though it would be simplistic to divide Lessing's production into phases, three milestones provide distinct orientation points for any survey. These are, first, the publication of *The Golden Notebook* in 1962; second, the break with realism after *The Four-Gated City* in 1969; and third, the step into space fiction after 1979. Lessing's works up to 1962 reflect the formation of her thinking through Marxist theory and her idealistic hope, as she recently joked, "that something like ten years after World War II, the world would be communist and perfect." After 1962, she discarded the Kantian postulate that humanity as a whole will eventually accomplish its own enlightenment. Collective action (in the form of political groups, sex roles, institutions) increasingly became the target of her polemics, and her works concentrated on the possible expansion and evolution of the individual consciousness. After *The Four-Gated City*, the individual's quest for better, truer vision becomes progressively more detached from the problems of "reality," and Lessing's fiction concurrently turns its back on realism. Between 1971 and 1974 her novels delve in the mad, the subconscious, and the mystical spheres as wellsprings of perception. In 1979 then, the author completely trades off the real for the irreal, and invents a cosmos where virtually anything is possible in the battle between good and evil.

Scholarly research on Lessing's work is well established. Since the 1960s she has been a cause celebre in the literary forum. Whereas noticeable reticence characterizes the reception of her later works beginning with *Briefing*, critics return again and again to the realist novels and stories of the 1950s and 1960s....

To generalize or to draw subtotals regarding an author as unpredictable and prolific as Lessing is risky. If we search for a common denominator in her work to date, it must lie in her insistence that there *is* an alternative way of viewing life—politics, sexuality, culture, sanity—a new vista open to anyone willing to take off the blinders of collectivism and seek it. This idea is supported thematically by the child, the new generation on whom everything depends, and who epitomizes the possibility of a better future. The search for something finer unites protagonists as diverse as Martha Quest, who finds another geographic and psychic country, and Charles Watkins, who manages at least temporarily to drift through sea space. The Survivor is able to step through the wall, and Planet 8's Representative transcends the elements to achieve another form of being. Completely apart from the contextual plausibility of these figures' fates, they convey a common message responsible for the magnetic, regenerative effect of Lessing's books on her readers: that human beings are not trapped, boxed, and filed inside immutable boundaries. But this hopeful keynote also contains a challenge. Before individuals can find a new sphere and breed something better than themselves, they must wake from their daily drowse in front of the TV set, question the authority of the group mind and ultimately find the courage to swim against the collective stream. Lessing's chides those who resign themselves to their own limitations, for "this need to break out of our ordinary possibilities—the cage we live in that is made of our habits, upbringing, circumstances, and which shows itself so small and tight and tyrannical when we do try to break out—this need may well be the deepest one we have...."

PEARL K. BELL

SOURCE: Pearl K. Bell, "Bad Housekeeping," in *The New Republic*, Vol. 193, No. 18, October 28, 1985, pp. 47-50.

[*In the following excerpt, Bell reviews Lessing's novel* The Good Terrorist *and assesses Lessing as a novelist.*]

It is not easy to understand why Doris Lessing became such a formidable presence among contemporary novelists. She is often a clumsy writer. Her early novels and stories, despite their exotic setting in Southern Rhodesia, were conventional accounts of growing up in a racist society, and rebelling against the constrictions of family and class. Much of her later work, which she sought to make complex, is hard to read, capricious in form, and grimly didactic. She can be dismally humorless, and a sucker for specious answers to thorny questions. In the course of her prolific career, she has frequently spelled out her various and drastic changes of faith in novels that are laborious tracts rather than works of literary conviction or skill. In ... *The Good Terrorist,* a lifeless account of radical squatters in present-day London, she's grimly realistic, but what she means to convey by this squalid reality is obscure.

An early convert to communism while she was still living in colonial Africa, Lessing joined the British party after moving to England in the late 1940s. In 1956, the year of the Hungarian revolution and of Khrushchev's revelations about the horrors of Stalinism, she left the party and began searching for new ideological commitments in Jungian therapy and R. D. Laing's seductive metaphysics of madness. When Laing's ideas eventually proved insufficient, she plunged into Sufi mysticism. She is an avatar of the intellectual yearning for belief a la mode.

Yet the book that established Doris Lessing as an influential feminist mentor, *The Golden Notebook* (1962), was informed by aching honesty and a probing intelligence, as she described her disenchantment with communism, her troubles with men, with writer's block, with a world she found difficult to comprehend or accept. Why did this intricate novel become a sacred text of feminism? It is by no means the uplifting morality tale of an emancipated woman struggling toward the light of freedom that so many of its admirers have taken it to be. The heroine, Anna Wulf, is not much better off at the end than she was at the beginning. As Diana Trilling has shrewdly noted, "There is a certain anomaly in taking as a guide to female freedom a book whose ultimate conclusion . . . is that the special problem of what it means to be a woman is an insoluble one." Years after its publication, Lessing insisted—largely to deaf ears—that "this novel was not a trumpet for women's lib. . . . It described many female emotions of aggression, hostility, resentment. It put them into print."

What turned the novel into a book of revelation for feminists was its justification of self-absorption. In the notebooks of different colors kept by Anna Wulf, the self was examined with unblinking intensity from different angles—psychoanalytic, political, sexual, literary—and this extraordinarily detailed concentration on every aspect of the self was embraced as a stepping-stone to liberation. The influence of *The Golden Notebook* derives from its indulgences, its exercises in narcissism. It beatified the minutiae of self-regard, and its form could accommodate every political thought, however wrongheaded, and every failed love affair. It gave the confessional mode the sanctity of moral passion.

Lessing has always seen herself as a rebel. But after *The Golden Notebook*, she began to think on a more grandiose scale than rebellion, and to conceive of herself as a latter-day Cassandra, foreseeing cataclysm and disaster for a corrupt and evil world. She is a restless Seeker of Truth, though the later versions of this quest reveal an extravagance of temperament that must inflate the slightest sign of political and social disorder into apocalyptic premonitions of doom. In those years she became increasingly obsessed with the illuminations of madness and the imminence of holocaust and global catastrophe. As she remarked in 1971, "I am so sure that everything we now take for granted is going to be utterly swept away in the next decade." Toward the end of *The Golden Notebook* she had dramatized, through Anna's tortured involvement with a schizophrenic American, Saul Green, her growing conviction that "breakdown" and "crackup" (invariably enclosed in impatient, denying quotation marks) are "a way of self-healing, of the inner self's dismissing false dichotomies and divisions."

Her certainty that the world is on a course of disaster stemmed, paradoxically, from her new enthusiasm for the Sufist teachings of Idries Shah, a self-appointed heir to the crackpot mysticism of Gurdjieff and Ouspensky. Under Shah's tutelage, moving up what William James called the "ladder of faith," Lessing came to believe in a cosmic consciousness that all mankind shares, and a process of cosmic evolution that will raise humanity to higher and higher levels of being. Such mystical visions of a utopian ideal scarcely agreed with her prophecies of nuclear devastation. If mankind is moving inexorably toward a higher consciousness, how could she simultaneously feel sure that mankind is about to blow itself to pieces? It was a contradiction that Lessing never tried to resolve, but then she has never been a notably coherent thinker. Seekers of the Light never are, for the feverish wanderings of the apocalyptic imagination do not leave much energy for rational thought. Lessing in her Sufist devotions increasingly resembled a dotty English prophetess like Annie Besant, who began as a Fabian Socialist, became an exponent of Madame Blavatsky and her occult theosophy, and ended by anointing an Indian mystic, Krishnamurti, as the future Teacher of the World.

More fervently than most intellectuals of our time, Doris Lessing has hungered for a grand design, a panacea that promises release from the tyranny of reason and safe passage into the soothing purity of the unknown. She spelled out this longing in the novels that followed *The Golden Notebook*. In *The Four-Gated City*, which ends in the 1990s with a world in ruins after a nuclear war, Martha Quest looks after a deranged woman whose psychotic ramblings convince Martha that society's definition of sanity is a delusion and a trap for destroying "those people now considered to be in the main line of evolution." She immerses herself in books on telepathy, levitation, second sight, witches and mystics, and becomes a seer. In *Briefing for a Descent Into Hell*, a professor at Cambridge, yet another of Lessing's holy lunatics, is swept away from earth for a celestial briefing by the gods. In an interplanetary conference, they appoint him their emissary, who must warn the misguided residents of earth that they must change their ways or be destroyed. But it is not always possible to know where Lessing's fantasies end and belief, literal belief, takes over.

This adventure in space was the sketchiest of rehearsals, it is now clear, for *"Canopus in Argos: Archives,"* the stupefying and unreadable "space fiction" series, with five volumes to date and perhaps more to come, which Lessing churned out at breakneck speed between 1979 and 1983. The novels are a cosmological circus performance, in science fiction dress, of Lessing's frenetic obsessions and eschatological divagations. Among many other turns, we are given the Last Days of Earth, wars between galactic empires, the coming of a new Ice Age, and UFOs (of course she believes they exist). In the last volume, ***Documents Relating to the Sentimental Agents in the Volyen Empire,*** she attempts a satire, heavy-handed and platitudinous, of political rhetoric on earth, and finally tosses everything—politics, language, history, "words, words, words"—into the dustbin of meaninglessness. It is all part of cosmic mysteries beyond human control. Science fiction is supposed to be entertaining, but Lessing's glum didacticism is no fun at all. If her admonitory vision of a universe in perpetual conflict and lethal deterioration is an effort to reform the homicidal corruption of earthlings, surely klutzy prose, bizarre names, spurious moral abstractions, and elephantine symbols are not the way to go about it.

On and on she writes: Doris Lessing is not so much a novelist as a torrent. Crashing to earth after her speedy gallop through the galaxies, Lessing has now gone back to the kind of realistic fiction that, as she wrote many years ago,

> springs so vigorously and naturally from a strongly held, though not necessarily intellectually defined, view of life that it absorbs symbolism. . . . The realist novel is the highest form of prose writing.

Unfortunately, these recent books are not the highest form of Lessing. When she submitted the realistic ***Diary of a Good Neighbor*** and ***If the Old Could*** to her publisher under a pseudonym, in a stunt to prove that editors are swayed not by literary merit but by names, they were swiftly rejected—and deserved to be. The only parts worth a second glance deal with an impoverished old woman who lives in dreadful squalor. Lessing's description of the filthy, littered rooms would seem to be a domestic version of her hyped-up visions of global destruction, as though the rubble of a nuclear-devastated planet can be anticipated in the decay of an old woman's life. Bad housekeeping enforced by poverty and old age reflects, in small, Lessing's compulsive preoccupation with pollution, nuclear bombs, and the end of the universe—the consequences of bad political and spiritual housekeeping.

In ***The Good Terrorist,*** she again picks up the bad-housekeeping theme in a story about a group of young revolutionary drifters who take over an abandoned house in North London. With unremitting diligence she itemizes the rubbish choking the garden, the maggoty wreckage within the once elegant rooms, the toilets and kitchens vandalized at the order of local officials to keep squatters out. But the radicals' den mother, Alice Mellings, has a skewed genius for bringing order out of chaos, and the "squat" is shipshape in no time. On the other hand, this "all-purpose female drudge" is a pathetic fool and often out of her head. (All of Lessing's women, even in her first novel, ***The Grass Is Singing,*** are either born mad, go mad, or have madness thrust upon them.) She defiles her parents' generosity with vicious obscenities and rocks through the window, is slavishly devoted to a nasty homosexual who has exploited her for years, and bursts into hysterical tears on every other page. Her idea of a really good time is spray-painting defiant slogans on public walls, and being arrested at demos. Most of her squatting comrades, for whom she cooks, cleans, paints, lies, and steals, are a lazy bunch of ungrateful louts, ranting an endless litany about "bringing down the shitty fascist system." When two of the would-be terrorists go to Ireland to offer their services to the IRA, they are dismissed with a sneer as bumbling amateurs. When the group decides to set off a bomb at a grand London hotel, symbol of rotten capitalism, they botch the job, in the process killing one of their own along with innocent bystanders. In the end, Alice, "the poor baby," is about to bare her soul to a British intelligence officer whom she idiotically mistakes for a Russian agent.

Doris Lessing, as a presence, has been the Modern Woman. But her various explorations of that persona reveal that she cannot settle upon a stable identity, so she remains rootless, not earthbound, with no hobbling ties to community, family, or class. She yearns to be authentic, but ***The Good Terrorist*** shows how much she still lacks a center of gravity that would allow her to know which persona fits—realist, fabulist, doomsayer, mystic, or perhaps just a disenchanted old radical tired of the dangerous naivete of the young. Yet these squatters are her children. And all that they can do is squat, in every sense of the word, on the bourgeois world.

The question that finally remains is Lessing's ambiguity of purpose and judgment. When Alice screams at her long-suffering mother that "your world is finished, the day of the selfish bourgeoisie is over. You are doomed," what sounds like an old Lessing refrain cannot, at this point, arouse our sympathy. Does Lessing despise the feckless terrorists for their mindless rage and immaturity, their knee-jerk raving against "fascist-imperialistic" Britain? Or does she pity them for being so ill-equipped for the tasks of revolution, for being such unserious and unprofessional babies in the struggle for social justice? We don't know; and it is not clear that she does either. . . .

MAUREEN CORRIGAN

SOURCE: Maureen Corrigan, "Improbably Star-Crossed," in *The Nation*, Vol. 262, No. 18, May 6, 1996, pp. 62-63, 66.

[*Corrigan is an educator and broadcast journalist. In the review below, she provides a somewhat mixed assessment of* Love, Again.]

The other day, I showed my sophomore English class a videotaped interview that Bill Moyers did with Maxine Hong Kingston. My students thought they were watching an earnest conversation about art and responded accordingly — some took notes, others dozed. But what was really being enacted for them in that darkened classroom was a pornographic fantasy peculiar to reviewers, interviewers, editors, professors and other lowly laborers on the shop floor of the literature factory. Squinting intently at Kingston, Moyers would murmur questions and declarations about her books and she, in turn, would light up with pleasure and eagerly respond. The critical rapport between the two was intoxicating to behold. (If Kingston was faking it for the cameras, she was doing a brilliant job.) As their intimate conversation continued, a thought bubble all but materialized above Moyers's head: "I, alone, really understand your work."

Though I greatly admire her writing, I've never entertained that particular fantasy about Doris Lessing. Her high seriousness, her intellectual chilliness, her stern lack of sentimentality cause me to esteem rather than embrace her books, and make me suspect that Lessing and I would not hit it off. Rather than breathlessly affirm my readings of her books, Lessing would, I imagine, treat me like Marshall McLuhan did that gasbag of a Columbia professor who was discussing his theories in a movie lobby in *Annie Hall*. You remember how McLuhan suddenly popped up behind him and sneered, "You know nothing of my work."

I never discuss Doris Lessing in public spaces; I dread the thought of being forced to talk with her about her books face to face — and with good reason. Lessing is a notorious scold who routinely swats down the interpretations of her novels proffered by academic suppliants, literary journalists and naïve fans. Reading *Doris Lessing: Conversations* (1994), a collection of interviews with Lessing over the past four decades, one can almost hear the egos of Lessing's interlocutors shredding with every dismissive reply. She reprimands the misguided who refer to *Canopus in Argos: Archives* as "science fiction" rather than her preferred term "space fiction," and bristles when a radio interviewer asks her to describe the protagonist of *The Temptation of Jack Orkney*. "I use fifty thousand words describing him, don't I?" Lessing replies. But she reserves her most blatant contempt for those who reductively read her 1962 masterwork, *The Golden Notebook,* as some kind of feminist manifesto. In her 1971 preface to a new edition, Lessing insists that "the essence of the book, the organisation of it, everything in it, says implicitly and explicitly, that we must not divide things off, must not compartmentalise." Warned repeatedly that to affix any kind of label — "feminist," "political," "realistic," "mythic" — to her books is to misunderstand them, critics who nevertheless tackle Lessing's work must forsake the occupational fantasy of mind-melding and, instead, approach her as we would a Gorgon, carefully averting our anxious eyes from her stern orbs, which would gladly turn us to stone.

Love, Again is Lessing's first novel in eight years, and (I have my own eyes squeezed protectively shut) it is, by turns, an exhilarating and disquieting meditation on old age and romantic love. Lessing makes a self-conscious reference to *Death in Venice*, which seems entirely apt. But she also leavens *Love, Again* with the fairy dust of *A Midsummer Night's Dream*. Sixty-five-year-old Sarah Durham is a widow of long standing and a founding member of The Green Bird, a successful fringe theater in London. When the novel opens, Sarah is working on an avant-garde operatic play about a turn-of-the-century West Indian woman named Julie Vairon — a beautiful quadroon like Napoleon's Josephine. Vairon, who lived most of her life in an isolated French village where she wrote music and painted, was "discovered" in the 1970s and hailed as a great composer and feminist icon. Sarah, however, is drawn as much to Vairon's tortured love life, recorded in her diaries, as she is to her eerie music. During her youth, Vairon was romantically involved with two Frenchmen, both of whom eventually left her at the insistence of their scandalized families. As she approached middle age, Vairon received an unexpected marriage proposal from a master of a printing works. For a woman like Vairon, whose social and financial situation was precarious, such an offer was a godsend. Yet, a week before she was to marry the printer, Vairon drowned herself in the village pond.

As rehearsals for The Green Bird's production of *Julie Vairon* get under way, the company falls under Julie's erotic spell. Stephen Ellington-Smith, a wealthy backer of the production who's written his own play about Julie, confesses to Sarah that he's been romantically obsessed with the dead woman ever since he first heard her music. Sarah, who hasn't been in love for decades and who describes herself as having reached the "heights of common sense . . . the evenly lit unproblematical uplands where there are no surprises," allows herself to be seduced by a dashing young actor who's playing one of Julie's feckless lovers. When Sarah, at last, wills herself out of this *amour fou*, she falls even more deeply in love with Henry Bisley, the thirtyish American director of the play. (One of the great pleasures of reading Lessing is being privy to her female characters' dead-on assessments of their male counterparts. Upon first meeting Henry, Sarah comments: "There are men who carry with them, as some half-grown fishes are attached to yolk sacs, the shadow of their mothers, at once visible in an overdefensiveness and readiness for suspicion.") Yet another actor becomes smitten with Sarah while the actress playing Julie falls for Stephen. All around these principal players, character actors and producers are besotted with one another.

"This is the silliest stuff that ever I heard," remarks Hippolyta in *A Midsummer Night's Dream*, and readers of Lessing might be tempted to say the same upon hearing about the plot of **Love, Again**, whose frenzied couplings outnumber those of even its Shakespearean inspiration. But the novel is too anguished to be deemed silly. The various romances here are all the more wrenching because of their improbability—and because most of them are not consummated. Lessing makes us feel the terrible yearning and grief stirred up by these star-crossed loves, eliciting sympathy rather than sniggering. As she does in so many of her other novels and stories, Lessing leads readers of **Love, Again** deep into the irrational zones her characters inhabit and invites us to settle in and make ourselves uneasily at home.

Stylistically, **Love, Again** has little in common with its immediate predecessor, **The Fifth Child**—a sleek horror story about the moral responsibilities of maternity—or with her other more socially engaged novels. Intricate, internalized and allusive, this latest Lessing owes something to that more traditional genre of double-tiered storytelling represented by John Fowles's *The French Lieutenant's Woman*, A.S. Byatt's *Possession* and their many imitators. The melancholy tale of the fictitious Julie Vairon acts as a template for the contemporary romances that run aground: Her destructive ghost haunts the narrative just as it bewitches the unfortunate Stephen. The central subject here, however, is one that Lessing has probed before—that of an aging woman struggling with the changing importance her sexuality and her attractiveness have to her identity. Sarah Durham is an older incarnation of Kate Brown, the heroine of Lessing's 1973 novel **The Summer Before the Dark**. In that book, 45-year-old Kate breaks down when her husband and children scatter during the summer holidays. Kate tries to bolster her wobbly sense of self by initiating an affair with a young man, but when he, too, deserts her and an illness, surely partly psychosomatic, robs Kate of her glossy good looks, she is forced to come to terms with the newly invisible older woman she's become. "She knew now, she had to know at last, that all her life she had been held upright by an invisible fluid, the notice of other people. But the fluid had been drained away."

Sarah has already passed through the life stage that so panics Kate. Her children grown, all passion seemingly spent, she has crafted a self-sufficient, purposeful life. She has buried her sexual self, though she still mourns the loss. Surveying her naked body in a mirror, Sarah comments:

> Legs. Well, they weren't too bad now, never mind what they were. In fact her body had been a pretty good one, and it held its shape (more or less) till she moved, when a subtle disintegration set in, and areas shapely enough were surfaced with the fine velvety wrinkles of an elderly peach. But all this was irrelevant. What she could not face (had to keep bringing herself face to face with) was that any girl at all, no matter how ill-favoured, had one thing she had not. And would never have again. It was the irrevocableness of it. There was nothing to be done. She had lived her way into this.

At such a stage in life, it's better not to feel, not to crave. But when Sarah suddenly finds herself the object of fervent male gazes, the well-maintained crypt in which she has laid to rest her desire crumbles away. The resurrection is a painful one, because although Sarah once again burns with lust, she recognizes that to most of the outside world she is, in the self-loathing words of the sexagenarian W. B. Yeats, "a paltry thing, / A tattered coat upon a stick." Still, there are those three handsome young suitors circling around Sarah who simultaneously stroke and frustrate her passion. One toys with her; the other two truly, deeply—and most assuredly madly—fall in love with her.

To be frank, this is the part of Lessing's novel that's hardest to swallow. One young man with eclectic erotic tastes or an Oedipus complex is plausible; three is a preposterous embarrassment of riches. In the hands of almost any other author, this plot device would be seen as a cynical maneuver to capture the aging female baby-boomer readership. But Lessing's trademark gravity serves her well here. By describing Sarah's romantic predicaments in the language of carefully deliberated emotion, she keeps our titters, if not our skepticism, in check. And always looming on the horizon is the melancholy certainty that Sarah, by choice or circumstance, will eventually return to the sexual life-in-death state of solitary older woman. The *Midsummer Night's Dream* atmosphere aside, Lessing doesn't have the right temperament for fairy tales. In the riveting final scene of the novel, a somber Sarah watches a mother and two children on a park bench. The mother showers her infant son with love, all the while ignoring the daughter who cleaves longingly to her side. Silently addressing the little girl, Sarah says: "Quite soon a door will slam shut inside you because what you are feeling is unendurable.... And at that moment... you will be free." Like a scythe implacably cutting through a field, Lessing strips away Sarah's sense of possibility. In her "space fiction," Lessing may be forward-looking, but here she refuses to be seduced by the illusion of a future. It's almost as if she's telling us: Of course, the old must shield themselves from torrents of yearning; of course, things end badly and too soon. Of course. But I'm an anxious late-twentieth-century American who prefers a few therapeutic bromides to cushion the long free fall into the abyss. We may never bond, sister (can I call you that?), but you keep writing and I keep reading. As Woody Allan admits at the end of *Annie Hall*, I guess I need the eggs.

SOURCES FOR FURTHER STUDY

Brightman, Carol. "Doris Lessing: Notes of a Novelist." *Book World—The Washington Post* (16 October 1994): 1, 14.

Favorably reviews *Under My Skin*.

Burroway, Janet. "An Unfashionable Woman." *The New York Times Book Review* (6 November 1994): 1, 42.

Argues that the two major themes shaping *Under My Skin* are "the twin workings of memory and projection."

Innes, Charlotte. "A Life of Doing It Her Way." *Los Angeles Times* (8 December 1994): E1, E8.

Essay based on an interview in which Lessing discusses *Under My Skin*.

Leonard, John. "The African Queen." *The Nation* 259, No. 15 (7 November 1994): 528-36.

Reviews *Under My Skin*, noting relationships between Lessing's autobiographical account and her fiction.

Rubin, Merle. "Author Doris Lessing Turns a Writer's Spotlight on Herself." *The Christian Science Monitor* 86, No. 248 (17 November 1994): 14.

Argues that although "*Under My Skin* is sprinkled with provocative, often contradictory, sides on topics from abortion, sexual attraction, and parent-child bonding, to race relations, left-wing zealots, and the colonial legacy," few of these questions are resolved.

Schemo, Diana Jean. "A Portrait Unwinds, as in Life." *New York Times* (2 November 1994): C1, C10.

Discusses *Under My Skin*, modern art, and biography. The essay is based on an interview with Lessing.

Henry Wadsworth Longfellow

1807-1882

American poet, novelist, essayist, and translator.

INTRODUCTION

During the nineteenth century, Longfellow was the most popular American poet, whose nostalgic, inspirational verse was embraced by Americans and Europeans enduring rapid social change. After his death, however, his reputation suffered a serious decline. The very characteristics that made his poetry popular in his own day—gentle simplicity and a melancholy reminiscent of the German Romantics—are those that fueled the posthumous reaction against his work. Although the debate over Longfellow's literary stature continues, he is credited for introducing European culture to the American readers of his day. Moreover, he simultaneously popularized American folk themes abroad, where his works enjoyed an immense readership.

Biographical Information

Longfellow was born in Portland, Maine, the son of Stephen Longfellow, a lawyer and member of Congress, and Zilpah Wadsworth, whose ancestors arrived on the *Mayflower*. Despite his father's wish that he study law, Longfellow preferred a literary career and began publishing poems in numerous newspapers and periodicals while attending Bowdoin College. Before he graduated in 1825, the college trustees offered him a professorship of modern languages, provided he first prepare himself by touring Europe. Grateful for the opportunity to make literature his profession, he accepted and went abroad. The journey greatly influenced his future work, which evinces a blend of American and European elements. After his three-year tour, Longfellow returned to Bowdoin to teach and soon published *Outre-mer* (1833-34), a collection of travel sketches. In 1835 he accepted a modern languages professorship at Harvard University, where he remained for eighteen years. Meanwhile, he again traveled to Europe, discovering in Heidelberg the works of the German Romantic poets, whose artistic sensibilities he incorporated into his writing. After returning to Cambridge, he published the romantic novel *Hyperion* (1839) and the poetry collection *Voices of the Night* (1839), which met with popular acclaim. During the 1840s and 1850s Longfellow continued to write poetry, notably the narrative poems *Evangeline* (1847), and *The Song of Hiawatha* (1855), increasing his popular appeal with each successive volume. After leaving Harvard in 1854, Longfellow published *Tales of a Wayside Inn* (1863) and *The Divine Comedy of Dante Alighieri* (1865-67), which is regarded among the finest translations of Dante's work. Longfellow died in 1882, while working on two dramatic poems intended to supplement the dramatic trilogy *Christus: A Mystery* (1872).

Major Works

Outre-mer is modeled on Washington Irving's *Sketch Book*. *Voices of the Night* is distinguished by his "Psalm of Life" and "Light of the Stars," popular inspirational poems characterized by simple truths and maxims, while the ballads, lyrics, and sonnets from *Ballads and Other Poems* (1842) to *The Seaside and the Fireside* (1850) feature nostalgic, melancholic reflections on life's transience and generally conclude with didactic or romanticized expressions of the poet's religious faith. The longer narrative poems for which he is best remembered, *Evangeline, The Song of Hiawatha,* and *Tales of a Wayside Inn,* address American themes and subjects, often presenting vivid descriptions of the American landscape. *Evangeline,* written in classical dactylic hexameters, relates the sentimental tale of two lovers separated when the British claimed the French colony of Acadia (Nova Scotia today) during the French and Indian War. *The Song of Hiawatha* grafts source material from Ojibwa and Dakota tribal folklore onto the meter and plot structure of the Finnish folk epic *Kalevala. Tales of a Wayside Inn,* a series of narrative poems reminiscent of Geoffrey Chaucer's *Canterbury Tales,* reveals Longfellow's versatility and mastery of the narrative form and includes "Paul Revere's Ride," which introduced the legend of his "midnight ride" into American culture. *Christus: A Mystery,* a trilogy comprising dramatic poems that Longfellow intended to be his masterpiece, traces Christianity from its beginnings through the Middle Ages to the time of the American Puritans.

Critical Reception

Longfellow was the first American poet to gain a favorable international reputation. Praised by such eminent authors as Charles Dickens, Victor Hugo, and Alfred Tennyson, Longfellow was accorded a bust in the Poet's Corner of Westminster Abbey, making him the first American to be so honored. With the advent of Realism, Naturalism, and Modernism, Longfellow's verse fell out of favor with younger poets and critics alike, especially during the first half of the twentieth century, when his poetry was reviled as superficial and didactic. Since then, Longfellow has often been praised for his technical skill, particularly as shown in his lyrics and sonnets, and many continue to regard him a pioneer in adapting European literary traditions to American themes and subjects. Commenting on Longfellow's unique and important position in American letters, Odell Shepard stated: "To every educated American it should be a pride and pleasure to know Longfellow well, to defend him wisely, and to hold him dear."

(For further information, see *Concise Dictionary of American Literary Biography:* 1640-1865; *Dictionary of Literary Biography,* Vols. 1, 59; *DISCovering Authors; DISCovering Authors: British; DISCovering Authors: Canadian; DISCovering Authors Modules: Most-studied Authors Module, Poets Module; Nineteenth-Century Literature Criticism,* Vols. 2, 45; *Something about the Author,* Vol. 19.)

CRITICAL COMMENTARY

EDGAR ALLAN POE

SOURCE: Edgar Allan Poe, "Longfellow's Ballads," in his *The Complete Works of Edgar Allan Poe, Vol. VI,* Colonial Press Company, 1856, pp. 374-91.

[*One of the foremost American authors of the nineteenth century, Poe is widely regarded as the architect of the modern short story and the principal forerunner of aestheticism in modern literature. His self-declared intention, both as a critic and a literary theorist, was the articulation and promotion of strictly artistic ideals in a milieu he viewed as overly concerned with the utilitarian value of literature. In the following excerpt from an essay that first appeared in* Graham's Magazine *in 1842, he criticizes the didactic purposes of Longfellow's poetry.*]

Much as we admire the genius of Mr. Longfellow, we are fully sensible of his many errors of affectation and

> **Principal Works**
>
> *Outre-mer; a Pilgrimage Beyond the Sea.* 2 vols. (travel sketches) 1833-34
> *Hyperion* (novel) 1839
> *Voices of the Night* (poetry) 1839
> *Ballads and Other Poems* (poetry) 1842
> **The Spanish Student* (verse drama) 1843
> *The Poets and Poetry of Europe* [editor and translator] (poetry) 1845
> *The Belfry of Bruges and Other Poems* (poetry) 1846
> *Evangeline: A Tale of Acadie* (narrative poetry) 1847
> *Kavanagh* (novel) 1849
> *The Seaside and the Fireside* (poetry) 1850
> ***The Golden Legend* (dramatic poetry) 1851
> *The Song of Hiawatha* (narrative poetry) 1855
> *The Courtship of Miles Standish, and Other Poems* (poetry) 1858
> *Tales of a Wayside Inn* (narrative poetry) 1863
> *The Divine Comedy of Dante Alighieri.* 3 vols. [translator] (poetry) 1865-67
> ***The New England Tragedies* (dramatic poetry) 1868
> ***The Divine Tragedy* (dramatic poetry) 1871
> *Kéramos and Other Poems* (poetry) 1878
> *Ultima Thule* (poetry) 1880
> *In the Harbor: Ultima Thule, Part II* (poetry) 1882
> *Michael Angelo* (narrative poetry) 1883
> *The Works of Henry Wadsworth Longfellow.* 11 vols. (poetry, drama, novels, travel sketches, and translations) 1886
>
> *This is the date of first publication rather than first performance.
> **These were published together as *Christus: A Mystery* in 1872.
>
> **Adaptations**
>
> Adaptations of Longfellow's works include the films *Evangeline*, directed by E. P. Sullivan, 1913, *Hiawatha*, 1913, *Midnight Ride of Paul Revere*, 1914, *Evangeline*, directed by Raoul Walsh, 1919, *The Courtship of Miles Standish*, directed by Frederick Sullivan, 1923, *The Wreck of the Hesperus*, 1927, *Evangeline*, directed by Edwin Carewe, 1929, *Hiawatha*, 1952, and *The Word and the Echo*, 1971.

imitation. His artistic skill is great, and his ideality high. But his conception of the *aims* of poesy *is all wrong*.... His didactics are all *out of place*. He has written brilliant poems—by accident; that is to say, when permitting his genius to get the better of his conventional habit of thinking—a habit deduced from German study. We do not mean to say that a didactic moral may not be well made the *under-current* of a poetical thesis, but that it can never be well put so obtrusively forth as in the majority of his compositions.

We have said that Mr. Longfellow's conception of the *aims* of poesy is erroneous; and that thus, laboring at a disadvantage, he does violent wrong to his own high powers; and now the question is, what *are* his ideas of the aims of the Muse, as we gather these ideas from the *general* tendency of his poems? It will be at once evident that, imbued with the peculiar spirit of German song (in pure conventionality) he regards the inculcation of a *moral* as essential. Here we find it necessary to repeat that we have reference only to the *general* tendency of his compositions; for there are some magnificent exceptions, where, as if by accident, he has permitted his genius to get the better of his conventional prejudice. But didacticism is the prevalent *tone* of his song. His invention, his imagery, his all, is made subservient to the elucidation of some one or more points (but rarely of more than one) which he looks upon as *truth*. And that this mode of procedure will find stern defenders should never excite surprise, so long as the world is full to overflowing with cant and conventicles....

In common with all who claim the sacred title of poet, [Professor Longfellow] should limit his endeavors to the creation of novel moods of beauty, in form, in color, in sound, in sentiment; for over all this wide range has the poetry of words dominion. To what the world terms *prose* may be safely and properly left all else. The artist who doubts of his thesis, may always resolve his doubt by the single question—"might not this matter be as well or better handled in *prose?*" If it *may*, then is it no subject for the Muse....

Of the pieces which constitute [**Ballads and Other Poems**], there are not more than one or two thoroughly fulfilling the ideas we have proposed; although the volume, as a whole, is by no means so chargeable with didacticism as Mr. Longfellow's previous book [*Voices of the Night*]. We would mention as poems *nearly true*, **"The Village Blacksmith"; "The Wreck of the Hesperus,"** and especially **"The Skeleton in Armor."** In the first-mentioned we have the *beauty* of simplemindedness as a genuine thesis; and this thesis is inimitably handled until the concluding stanza, where the spirit of legitimate poesy is aggrieved in the pointed antithetical deduction of a *moral* from what has gone before. In **"The Wreck of the Hesperus"** we have the *beauty* of child-like confidence and innocence, with that of the father's stern courage and affection. But, with slight exception, those particulars of the storm here detailed are not poetic subjects. Their thrilling *horror* belongs to prose, in which it could be far more effectively discussed, as Professor Longfellow may assure himself at any moment by experiment.... In **"The Skeleton in Armor"** we find a pure and perfect thesis artistically treated. We find the beauty of bold courage and self-confidence, of love and maiden devotion, of reckless adventure, and finally of life-contemning grief. Combined with all this, we have numerous *points* of beauty apparently insulated, but all aiding the main effect or impression. The heart is stirred, and the mind does not lament its mal-instruction. The metre is simple, sonorous, well-balanced, and fully adapted to the subject. Upon the whole, there are fewer truer poems than this. It has but one defect—an important one. The prose remarks prefacing the narrative are really *necessary*. But every work of art should contain within itself all that is requisite for its own comprehension. And this remark is especially true of the ballad.... [Its] effect will depend, in great measure, upon the perfection of its finish, upon the nice adaptation of its constituent parts, and, especially, upon what is rightly termed by Schlegel *the unity or totality of interest*. But the practice of prefixing explanatory passages is utterly at variance with such unity.... [The] totality of effect is destroyed.

Of the other original poems in the volume before us, there is none in which the aim of instruction, or *truth*, has not been too obviously substituted for the legitimate aim, *beauty*. We have heretofore taken occasion to say that a didactic moral might be happily made the *under-current* of a poetical theme...; but the moral thus conveyed is invariably an ill effect when obtruding beyond the upper-current of the thesis itself. Perhaps the worst specimen of this obtrusion is given us by our poet in **"Blind Bartimeus"** and **"The Goblet of Life,"** where it will be observed that the *sole* interest of the upper-current of meaning depends upon its relation or reference to the under....

Of the translations we scarcely think it necessary to speak at all. We regret that our poet will persist in busying himself about such matters. *His* time might be better employed in original conception....

WALT WHITMAN

SOURCE: Walt Whitman, "Death of Longfellow," in *The Critic*, New York, Vol. II, No. 33, April 8, 1882, p. 101.

[Whitman is regarded as one of the most important and influential poets in American literature. His Leaves of Grass—in which he celebrated the "divine average," democracy, and sexuality—was a major influence on free verse. In the following excerpt, he praises Longfellow's achievement as a poet.]

Longfellow in his voluminous works seems to me not only to be eminent in the style and forms of poetical expression that mark the present age (an idiocrasy, almost a sickness, of verbal melody), but to bring what is always dearest as poetry to the general human heart and taste, and probably must be so in the nature of things. He is certainly the sort of bard and counteractant most needed for our materialistic, self-assertive, money-worshipping, Anglo-Saxon races, and especially for the present age in America—an age tyrannically regulated with reference to the manufacturer, the merchant, the financier, the politician and the day workman—for whom and among whom he comes as the poet of melody, courtesy, deference—poet of the mellow twilight of the past in Italy, Germany, Spain, and in Northern Europe—poet of all sympathetic gentleness—and universal poet of women and young people. I should have to think long if I were asked to name the man who has done more, and in more valuable directions, for America.

I doubt if there ever was before such a fine intuitive judge and selecter of poems. His translations of many German and Scandinavian pieces are said to be better than the vernaculars. He does not urge or lash. His influence is like good drink or air. He is not tepid either, but always vital, with flavor, motion, grace. He strikes a splendid average, and does not sing exceptional passions, or humanity's jagged escapades. He is not revolutionary, brings nothing offensive or new, does not deal hard blows. On the contrary his songs soothe and heal, or if they excite, it is a healthy and agreeable excitement. His very anger is gentle, is at second hand, (as in **'The Quadroon Girl'** and **'The Witnesses'**).

There is no undue element of pensiveness in Longfellow's strains. Even in the early translation, **'The Manrique,'** the movement is as of strong and steady wind or tide holding up and buoying. Death is not avoided through his many themes, but there is something almost winning in his original verses and renderings on that dread subject....

To the ungracious complaint-charge ... of his want of racy nativity and special originality, I shall only say that America and the world may well be reverently thankful—can never be thankful enough—for any such singing-bird vouchsafed out of the centuries, without asking that the notes be different from those of other songsters;—adding what I have heard Longfellow himself say, that ere the New World can be worthily original and announce herself and her own heroes, she must be well saturated with the originality of others, and respectfully consider the heroes that lived before Agamemnon.

Without jealousies, without mean passions, never did the personality, character, daily and yearly life of a poet, more steadily and truly assimilate his own loving, cultured, guileless, courteous ideal, and exemplify it. In the world's arena, he had some special sorrows—but he had prizes, triumphs, recognitions, the grandest.

Extensive and heartfelt as is to-day, and has been for a long while, the fame of Longfellow, it is probable, nay certain, that years hence it will be wider and deeper. . . .

ODELL SHEPARD

SOURCE: Odell Shepard, in an introduction to *Henry Wadsworth Longfellow: Representative Selections* by Henry Wadsworth Longfellow, edited by Odell Shepard, American Book Company, 1934, pp. xi-lv.

[*In the following excerpt, Shepard examines the strengths and weaknesses of Longfellow's poetry.*]

[Longfellow] has long been an American institution. His poems, whether good or bad, are woven in among our heartstrings, so that the effort to see them as they really are involves the strain of self-analysis and adverse criticism of them seems to tear at our very roots. . . .

Longfellow's work is of utmost value to America in her effort to see what she has been and what, therefore, she is and is to be. In studying him we study ourselves. It is true that he has little to say about the America of his time, and that his remarks about the America of any time are seldom acute; yet in the total temper of his mind he represents us, without fully intending it, more truly than other poets do who intend little else. Considering this, and also the range and depth of his influence upon us, it is clear that no view of American culture which leaves him out or treats him with contempt can be either sound or complete. Those who think him a great poet may be naive, but those who think him unworthy of careful consideration are something worse than that. . . .

From whatever angle we consider Longfellow's relation to his environment, . . . we find that his grasp of contemporary fact was weak and incomprehensive. Between him and the actual American scene there intervened an Indian-summer haze, dreamily dim, which blurred and softened every hue and line and angle, hiding the coarse and the familiar, substituting the colors of the heart's desire. This haze it is that we see in his writings, and not the crude reality behind it. Machinery, science, labor disputes, social unrest, the roar of industry and the din of war, all the strife and toil and anxious mental questing up and down which must be forever associated with his century, make little stir in his still pages. . . .

Whether a fault or not, this is a major trait of Longfellow's, that he does not bring the force of his mind to bear upon things near at hand. His thoughts and loves are otherwhere. Self-indulgently romantic, he uses imagination rather for escape from reality than for penetration of it. And even when concerned with things remote, his thought needs to dally with superficial hues and contours and seldom pierces to essences. This we feel in reading his several attempts at dramatic writing such as the inanimate *New England Tragedies,* and even more in his prose fiction. The stage is set for action, but no actors that draw the breath of life appear upon it. In an early story called **"The Baptism of Fire,"** published in *Outre-Mer,* he writes a cool description of an execution by fire and hanging which gives, at first, the effect of a callous brutality. One soon realizes, of course, that the writer is half asleep, that he has failed to bring the terrible experience home to himself as a thing that once actually happened—as a thing the like of which was happening in his own country in his time as in ours. Had he keenly realized this, either he would not have written the story at all or else he would have written it with an anguish of mind that would have made it live. But it remained for him, as it does for us, merely something in a book, distant in time and place, a faintly lurid spot in the light and shade of history.

The haze that dimmed and all but hid Longfellow's America from his eyes was composed, so to speak, of time. That is, he looked at the present through the past—through an illusory and highly romantic past, to be sure, of his own dreaming. What he saw in America was chiefly the enduring of the old rather than the emergence of the new. In fancy and imagination he was at least as antiquarian as Washington Irving, whose writings he admired as a boy, imitated as a young man, and never quite outgrew. Like Hawthorne, whose fancy clothed with mosses a house not seventy years old when he went to live in it, Longfellow had a deep delight in all things established and timeworn— a delight all the stronger because the America about him had so few of such things. . . .

Longfellow failed to establish living contact either with his own time or with the earlier ages into which he retreated. Even the world of nature was for the most part a blur to him, or a storehouse of metaphors and similes. His poems of the sea are indeed uniformly excellent, possibly because the images in them were stamped upon his mind before he began the rhetorician's quest of analogies, but elsewhere his observation was slight, superficial, and inaccurate. . . .

The harsh facts of life seldom touched him. He knew to the full the grief of personal bereavement, but the world's woe and misery never lay heavy upon his heart. He knew even less of sin, apparently, than Emerson did, and far less of moral and intellectual struggle. . . .

There is an important sense . . . in which we may say that this man, who spent his long life in reading and discussing and writing books, simply did not know enough, in the more vivid and poetic ways of knowing. One looks vainly through his pages for any sign of the amateur's acquaintance with science that gives bone and sinew to the writing of Emerson, providing it with a thousand flashing metaphors and profound analogies. He had none of Thoreau's knowledge of nature and skill in handicraft. He had nothing to correspond with Whittier's passionate concern about politics, with Melville's knowledge of the outer world of toil and danger, or with Hawthorne's grasp of the inner realities of the conscience. He lacked, moreover, a precious trait clearly seen in all these men—the sense of place and of utter devotion to it. Although he loved Portland and Cambridge, he could not have said, with Hawthorne, that New England was the largest lump of earth his heart could hold, nor did he draw strength of mind and spirit, as Whittier and Thoreau and Emerson learned to do, from the old familiar scene. In his *wanderjahre* he escaped provincialism in its good as well as in its bad aspects, to that—absurd though it is to regard him as a man without a country—even in his Americanism there is something diffuse, diluted, and faintly German. . . .

Though the stream of his thought may be shallow, it is clear, and it flows. Always chiefly concerned to convey his thought and feeling, he used verse not as an end in itself but as a vehicle of communication. He had the good craftsman's liking for the finished task, and he felt that the task of the creative artist is not finished so long as there remains in his work anything difficult or obscure which a greater care of his might clear away. Thus, for example, he used the normal prose order of words rather more consistently than other poets of his time, consulting not his own ease but that of his reader. . . . His art is of that good kind which conceals itself. What may seem at first to be mere triteness in his style often turns out to be exact rightness. That stultifying fear of the hackneyed expression by which the poets of our day are tormented was unknown to him, partly because he wished to say not new and clever and startling things but the things that had been tried by the ages and found true. Moreover, he wished to hold attention upon his thought or story and not upon himself. . . .

Longfellow's ability to sink himself and his own moods out of sight enabled him to excel as a translator and as a narrative poet. There are, to be sure, many dull passages in *Evangeline* and many shallows in the *Tales of a Wayside Inn*, which betray the hand of a professional writer doing his hundred lines a day. Longfellow's deficiency in first-hand experience and his shrinking from violence enfeebles not a few of his stories. Even the most decided success in his narrative writing, the account of the fight between Miles Standish and the Indians, falls far short of the terrible tale told in his source. On the other hand, most of his narrative work is straight-grained, objective, moving steadily onward with a strong sense of the goal.

In every poem he wrote Longfellow had a definite thing to say. This might be, and often it was, a platitude. For that he had little care, because he knew that we live in an old and iterative world and that the mere novelty of an idea is a supposition against it. Together with his thought, he had at the same moment a clear notion of the form in which it could be expressed most effectively. Form and substance seem to have occurred to him at the same instant, as two aspects of one thing, and it is for this reason that in all his better work the thought seems to fill the form without crowding or inflation.

Even the more acute readers of Longfellow have seldom recognized that his sense of form was at all uncommon, partly because the simple stanzas and meters of his familiar work—most of them derived from the popular ballad, Protestant hymnology, and the Romantic poets of Germany—are seldom associated with this Latin trait. Close reading of even his feebler early lyrics will show, however, that they usually contain little that could be dispensed with. For all their apparent laxity or ease, they are likely to be succinct, though seldom terse or laconic. Nearly everything irrelevant has been pruned away.

Only when this is realized are we prepared to understand Longfellow's remarkable success in the sonnet. It is here, more clearly than elsewhere, that we see him working as a conscious artist, making beauty for its own sake, shaping form unhastily with a slow-pulsed hand that never trembles. And it is perhaps from his sonnets that the sophisticated reader is most likely to gain that respect which may induce an intelligent re-reading of the poet's entire work. In the single sonnet **"Nature"** the best of his qualities are all implicit. Without a word too many or too few it phrases an ancient unchanging verity with quiet precision. The thought is obvious and the feeling familiar; the "as-so" design is hackneyed; the metaphor is by no means fresh; yet the poem is so beautifully constructed, its music is so delicate an echo of the mood, it is so perfectly one and indivisible, that it lives in memory as a piece of still perfection.

The beauty of this sonnet is not in the single lines and not in any of its aspects taken separately, but in the architectonic, the just proportion, the harmony and unity of the whole composition. And it is precisely in what may be called his sense of the whole that Longfellow is most remarkable as technician and creative artist. Herein, and not in the verbal virtuosity of a Swinburne or the finished texture of a Tennyson, lies his chief aesthetic excellence. In this important respect, moreover, his art improved and ripened with the years. . . .

Both the verse and the prose of Longfellow reveal a habit of mind, common in his time but not in ours, which impedes his direct communication with the reader. For our taste he is too heavily metaphorical. Moreover, his metaphors are often used rather for decorative purposes than for clarification. . . . This is due to that vice of professional and self-conscious phrase-making which the ancient rhetoricians foisted upon western literature, making it appear that the work of the literary artist is that of external adornment rather than that of imaginative penetration. Of this vice Longfellow was a late though not a flagrant example. He acquired it in his schooling, from public oratory, from sermons, and from the prevailing philosophy of his time. . . .

Longfellow's function in our literature was to release energy and not to restrict or guide it, certainly not to suggest that it might come to a tragic end. He was the poet of sentiment. The steeps of ecstasy and the pits of despair he never scaled or descended. He did what his times demanded and made possible, or, in a sense, necessary. . . . Different men, to be sure, were even then doing a different work. While Longfellow sat by the fire in his luxurious study, dreaming out the acquiescent lyrics that would soon lull a million readers to his mood, there was a young man sitting by a sheet-iron stove not fifteen miles away, in a shanty he had built with his own hands beside a lake in the woods, and this young man was writing a prose book intensely, even bitterly, critical of nearly all that was then going on in the land. But the poems of Longfellow were sold by the hundred thousand in some twenty languages, and the full fame of Thoreau has not even yet arrived. . . .

[Longfellow] considered the past our chief guide through the present and our best clue to the future; and also he thought it a main task of the poet to appraise the work of those who have gone before and so make it live anew in each generation. Such work he thought particularly urgent in America, where there had been so sharp a break with tradition. He thought America needed to be enriched in mind and spirit before she was corrected, and he set himself to the task of bringing her the wealth of other times and lands. Dominated by this motive, he did not wish to be unique, bizarre, eccentric. He wished to be faithful, sane, normal, and representative. . . .

What [this literary retrospection has] cost is obvious. It withdrew Longfellow's attention from events and ideas of the first magnitude, thus giving apparent sanction to the belief that the business of poetry and of the arts in general is to provide a temporary escape from actuality, rather than to pierce and illumine that actuality and so to transform it. . . . Thus he relegated art to a Sabbatical position, leaving the Philistine free for at least six days of unrestricted Philistinism. True though it may be that if he had claimed more he might have secured less, we cannot suppose that his actual claim was the result of any such calculation. He asked for poetry what he thought it deserved, and in asking so little he represented the attitude of his country. . . .

If Longfellow had been able to see precisely what sort of poetry America needed and had been endowed with the will and the power to make precisely that, it is not clear that his work would have been in many ways different. She needed a deeper sense of beauty, respect for the arts, wider mental horizons, veneration for the past, and tradition. He provided at least the means of getting these. There were other things equally necessary, such as restraint, humility, depth of thought, free play of ideas, but most of these are the gift of the critic. It was Longfellow's task to initiate the difficult transition from a moralistic to an aesthetic regime in literature. He did this the more effectively because he himself stood halfway between the extremes, and it is interesting to observe how, as the decades went by, the didactic element in his work was steadily subordinated. The pressure of necessity was lessening for many thousands in America. They were untrained in leisure or delight, which they regarded as dangerous if not reprehensible. Any such pure beauty as that in the Odes of Keats they would have ignored. They had enjoyed so little "schooling in the polite pleasures" that these had to come at first in the familiar guise of edification. In the poems of Longfellow they did so come. Moreover, he drew us gently back, after a long period of intellectual isolation, toward the main currents of the world's thought. As scholar and teacher, translator and editor, travel-writer and poet, he did much valuable work in what Barrett Wendell called the "transplanting of culture." He deepened our sense of the American past. His example taught us that a life devoted to thought and artistic creation may be dignified and useful. He probably did more than all our other poets together to enlarge in America the audience for poetry, and certainly he did more than all of them combined to apprise the rest of the world that we are not entirely songless. In his unquestioning idealism, in his moral simplicity and directness, in his natural honesty of mind and heart which could afford to go unadorned because it was beautiful in its essence, Americans have always recognized qualities to which they aspire....

In reading him we read ourselves. His poetry provides a bridge by means of which we may return at will into an America simpler and quieter than that of the present, yet indefeasibly our own. It lends depth and distance to our time, linking what we are with what we have been. Here is an assurance and a serenity not easy to find elsewhere. Here is beauty and charm and glamour that are part of our birthright. If this treasure is lost through our ignorance or impatient scorn of the past, we shall all be the poorer. To every educated American it should be a pride and a pleasure to know Longfellow well, to defend him wisely, and to hold him dear....

ALEXANDER COWIE

SOURCE: Alexander Cowie, "The Mixed Thirties," in his *The Rise of the American Novel*, American Book Company, 1948, pp. 276-326.

[*In the following excerpt, Cowie provides an overview of Longfellow's major prose works.*]

Longfellow began to write at an early age, but he matured his art slowly.... He blossomed lazily when conditions were propitious. Steady growth, not spurts, revealed the law of his nature. The ambition to succeed was no stronger in him than the instinct to perfect his work. His productions were quiet-toned; his colors were pastels. He uttered few piercing notes of sudden grief or shouts of exultant joy. All was measured, settled, and slow. The poet of the fireside was at his best when the fire had reached the stage of embers. The prose writer too was unhurried, pensive, dreamy. He waited for his thoughts to mature; he was content if growth continued. He may be said to have ripened his stories rather than constructed them. Accordingly they are stories to be enjoyed for their flavor and texture, rather than for the stimulation they afford. Longfellow was a good prose writer but not a very good narrative writer.

Most of his prose exhibits the same properties. *Outre-Mer* was a skilful blending of the same sort of sentiment and picturesqueness as Irving had purveyed in the *Sketch Book*. His two long stories [*Hyperion* and *Kavanagh*] ... were almost wholly lacking in the dynamic qualities that are popularly associated with novel and romance. They are both drowsy books—bred out of dream and mist, heavy with reminiscence, reluctant to deliver their burden of plot. Generations since their time have largely passed these books by with a vague phrase of recognition. Yet they deserve better than the fate that has befallen them. Their defects of plot are obvious to him who runs; their pallid characterizations are as easy to overlook as many of Hawthorne's. Nevertheless in most respects they are quite the equal of most of the poetical pieces of Longfellow that appear perennially in the "litercher books" of our school children. They are not so well proportioned as many of the poems, but they contain much extremely skilful writing, and they contain more that is of interest to the adult mind than do most of the poems. Their practical defect is that they are books of miscellany. Likewise, although they are "earnest" books, they lack profundity. Their general aspect is one of tameness and simplicity. Yet it is a mistake to reserve the laurel for those writers who undertake an enterprise of obvious magnitude, weight, and scope. A writer should not be condemned because it is not his gift to plumb the depths of the ocean in its farthest reaches; he may be reflecting life with as much truth and brilliance in cove or estuary. Not timidity but a true discernment of his real powers kept Longfellow from the truly sublime and terrible. He could translate, but not emulate, the author of *The Divine Comedy*.

[In *Hyperion*,] the novel is unrecognizable. Even the "romance" gets lost if by romance one means a knot of adventure cunningly tied and untied by a conscious craftsman. But the romantic quest of Paul Flemming exists in the warm emotion created by contemplation of an ancient atmosphere and old pageantry. This dreamy re-creation of old Germany and some of its modern exemplars serves as a matrix wherein is born a pattern of faith, a mode of life for a hero in the strife of life. The book is as unordered as a field of flowers; its atmosphere uncertainly alternates between mist and sunshine. The hero stumbles from time to time on his uneasy pilgrimage but finally reaches a resolution of his doubts. *Hyperion* is a sort of spiritual journal of Paul Flemming.

Kavanagh [is] Longfellow's only other extended piece of prose fiction.... By this time Longfellow had had the narrative experience of writing *Evangeline,* but he had not tasked himself in the stricter demands of the story-writer's art. He succeeded in narrative in spite of rather than because of his narrative habits. Only about half as long as *Hyperion, Kavanagh* is somewhat more unified than its predecessor, but it is just about as guileless in narrative technique. Compared with a narrative of Poe, it would seem to be the work of an amateur story-teller. Once this defect has been granted, the book can be enjoyed for its idyllic tone—its utterly simple and natural quality. Passing through summer into the first frosts of autumn, it is not without sadness for some of its characters, but it preserves an air of tranquility. *Kavanagh,* for all its technical defects is a charming book, and a valuable contribution to the literary history of New England—a kind of extended elegy of a village people....

NEWTON ARVIN

SOURCE: Newton Arvin, in his *Longfellow: His Life and Work,* Atlantic-Little, Brown, 1963, 338 p.

[*In the following excerpt, Arvin surveys Longfellow's major works.*]

A reader who was familiar with Longfellow's boyish poems, and who opened *Voices of the Night* when it first appeared, would surely have been struck very soon by the tones of a new manner.... [One is] aware at once of a firmness of tone, a boldness in attack, a freshness of image, that one would have found nowhere in Longfellow's juvenilia....

[*Voices of the Night*] is pervaded, as its title promises, by ... nocturnal symbolism.... The author of these poems was always to be, in one of his roles, a poet of the Night, or the Twilight; Night was to have for him an emotional significance that the day never quite had.... Almost always it brings thoughts, as it does in **"Hymn to the Night,"** of repose, assuagement, release from care. At moments one discerns a longing for unconsciousness, even oblivion, in this poet, that runs strangely counter to other reaches of his feeling....

There is no wildness of terror or fierceness of anger in this melancholy of Longfellow's, as there is in Poe's or Melville's, and no such dull and continuous pain as he himself saw in Hawthorne's; at its most acute, it never goes beyond a bearable despondency. It could be described as romantic nostalgia of the less passionate and rebellious sort, but it is as far as possible from being a mere literary convention; it was as inherent in Longfellow's temperament as a similar vein of feeling was in Heine's—without, as a rule, the recoil of irony....

There was never a time, however, when Longfellow was willing, as some greater and even some lesser writers have been, to yield himself wholly to the evidence of his sensibilities and make a coherent world-view out of his sufferings. His aversion to the tragic was as temperamental as his sensitiveness to pain, and as all mankind knows, or once knew, he insisted from the outset on correcting—one might say, on contradicting—the evidence of his sensibilities by opposing to it a doctrine of earnest struggle, of courageous resolution, of cheerful and productive action.... His resolute hopefulness is quite as genuine as his melancholy, only it is the product not of spontaneous emotion but of conscious effort and self-discipline. Perhaps it is expressed most acceptably in **"The Light of Stars,"** one of the two or three better poems in *Voices of the Night.* In this poem he confesses that in his breast, as in the night, there is no light but a cold and starry one, and especially the light of "the red planet Mars," to which he declares he is giving the first watch of the night. Mars, cold as he may be, is the planet of heroic action, and the poet is determined to accept that stern influence.... **"The Light of Stars"** was never one of Longfellow's extravagantly popular pieces, perhaps because there is too nice a balance in it between the confession of suffering and the voice of the resisting will. There was no such balance, and no such expressive metaphor, in **"A Psalm of Life"** or **"The Village Blacksmith"** or **"Excelsior";** and the slack commonplace of these inferior poems insured their universal currency for many decades....

Longfellow's moralizing poems fail, either wholly or relatively, because he was not a moralist. His gifts were quite different from that. Nothing, to repeat, could be more sincere than his moral convictions, but they are at second hand; they were not the fruit, as Emerson's (for example) were, of solitary and independent cogitation.... [Honorable] as they were, they have no intrinsic intellectual interest, and they usually do nothing for his poetry but enfeeble it. All this is only too evident.

Longfellow was obeying a truer instinct when he turned to the equally popular, but for him less treacherous, form of the ballad or short balladlike poem. He had a strain of the genuine folk poet in his make-up—in his unaffected naivete, his simplicity of mind and heart, his love of rapid and usually pathetic storytelling, and his power of improvisation—for some of these poems were written with as little effort as a folksinger puts into a new ballad on an old and familiar kind of subject. Hackneyed as it is, **"The Wreck of the Hesperus"** could hardly be surpassed as a literary imitation of the border ballad.... It is a poem for the young, of course, without any more underfeeling than the subject itself carries with it, but on its youthful level, it has in it the authentic terror of the sea. So, too, has the equally familiar **"The Skeleton in Armor,"** which is a little triumph of seaworthy narrative verse....

[Few poets] have had a stronger sense of the sea than Longfellow; and the best poems in *The Seaside and the Fireside,* for the most part, are the poems in the section, **"By the Seaside,"** to which both **"Sir Humphrey Gilbert"** and **"The Secret of the Sea"** belong. The longest of these is **"The Building of the Ship."** One regrets that this poem, like some others of Longfellow's, was staled and shopworn almost from the beginning by constant use in school readers and in youthful recitation, for, flawed as it is by some of Longfellow's habitual faults—the too facile family sentiment of one or two passages, for example—it has, to a robust taste that can overlook these flaws, a vivacity, a swiftness of movement, and a painterly concreteness of detail, as in an old-fashioned genre-painting or print, that save it from simple banality....

It goes without saying, now, that there is much that is facile and flaccid in [his collections of poetry]; like most minor poets who have been prolific as well as minor, Longfellow had no clear sense of the distinction between his weaknesses and his real strength. He seems to have taken as much pleasure in some of his inferior poems as in the better ones.... His nature was so genuinely sensitive and *gefuhlvoll* that, with the best conscience in the world, he could fall a victim to the bad sentimental taste of his age—there is of course a good sentimental taste—and there were subjects that normally betrayed him into the sort of false and misplaced feeling that one finds in Lydia Hunt Sigourney. One of these subjects was childhood **("To a Child")**; he is almost always at his feeblest on this theme. Another treacherous subject for him was that of innocence or simple unstained purity **("Maidenhood")**; one need not make light of this virtue in order to find Longfellow's celebration of it painfully wanting in moral complexity or edge. Death, too, sometimes inspired in him a soft and second-rate moral response, not a tragic one **("Footsteps of Angels")**; and the fact that he shared this weakness with greater writers of the age—Dickens, Tennyson, and others—does not conduce to greater patience with him.

Both morally and artistically speaking, when such subjects are in question, there is something suspect in emotions that well up so easily as these do, and that express themselves with so little stress or struggle. In general, it was a double-natured gift that the gods bestowed on Longfellow when, as it were in his cradle, they endowed him with the talents of an improvisator.... [When] thoughts or feelings sprang up in him that needed to be resisted, he gave them as free a rein as the thoughts or feelings that could safely be trusted....

His art, with some ups and downs, was to go on refining and enhancing itself perceptibly to the very end, but already the poems down to *The Seaside and the Fireside* furnish pretty much the measure of his capacities as a lyrical and narrative poet. There are states of feeling that remain this side of either ecstasy or despair—sadness, weariness, a half-pleasurable fear, elation, the simple apprehension of beauty—that Longfellow could express with a veracity that has nothing in it of falseness or the meretricious. Moods of the weather, seasons of the year, divisions of the day or night—to these external states he was delicately sensitive, and they often become the expressive equivalents of his emotions.... He had something like a genius for narrative poetry—not, to be sure, of the psychologically or philosophically interesting sort, but in the popular and romantic sense—and he could almost always draw, to happy effect, on legend or literary tradition. His sense of form was fallible, but at his best he is an accomplished, sometimes an exquisite, craftsman, like a master in some minor art, a potter or a silversmith; and his command of his materials, at such times—language, meter, rhyme, imagery—though it is not that of a great artist, is wholly adequate to his purposes....

Evangeline suggests a minor poetic form, not the epic, and it suggests a more archaic literary form than the novel. It is enough if the tenderness and the tenacity of the lovers' devotion to each other—for, after all, Gabriel does prove constant—are made credible, as they are; enough if the two of them move through the poem not as realistic lovers of the mid-eighteenth century in the colonies, but as figures of the frankest romanticism, dimly outlined, quietly moving, grave and gentle, and speaking hardly at all. Gabriel's father, the blacksmith Basil Lajeunesse, has enough choler and enough heartiness to give him a certain definition, but it is no more than that; and Evangeline's father, the prosperous farmer Benedict Bellefontaine, who dies of heartbreak on the sea beach during the night before the deportation, is a figure of pure pathos. The minor characters ... fill in the human scene pleasantly and rescue it from the bareness that might so easily have impoverished it....

[Plenty] of readers and critics at the time protested vigorously, as plenty have done since, against the metrical form in which Longfellow chose to cast his poem. This was of course the very controversial form of the allegedly classical hexameter. No really successful English poem had yet been written in this form, although experiments with it had been made ever since Elizabethan times....

[*Evangeline* stands or falls] not on the correctness of its hexameters, classically speaking, but on their intrinsic charm and their appropriateness to its inner character. When we read *Evangeline* in this spirit, we are likely to feel that, at its most successful, the verse has a kind of grave, slow-paced, mellifluous quality, like a slightly monotonous but not unmusical chant, which is genuinely expressive of its mournful and minor theme....

The real interest of *Hyperion*, only too obviously, lies not in the moral action, but in the divagations of one sort or another—they bulk too large to be called digressions—that make up the staple of the book. It was a great age of travel literature, not in the heroic Elizabethan sense, but in a more personal and impressionable one; and what doubtless most attracted Longfellow's readers at the time was *Hyperion*'s character as a pleasantly fictionalized guidebook....

Not that Longfellow proves himself, here any more than in *Outre-Mer*, a descriptive writer of great power; side by side with the great writers of this kind—with Ruskin, let us say—he is meager and hasty. He relies, for his effects of romantic wandering, not so much on sustained pieces of landscape painting or architectural evocation, as on his general genial movement from place to place by stagecoach or on foot; on his stops at inns with picturesque names, the White Horse or the Rheinischen Hof or the Golden Ship; and indeed, to a considerable extent, on the mere suggestive charm of the storied place-names themselves.... The whole narrative is bathed in so sunny and ingenuous an atmosphere of vagrant nostalgia that the mere name of a village or a lake, a river or a mountain, is enough to set the fancy vibrating pleasantly, if not with much sonority. And so of the glimpses one is furnished of "real" life in Germany and Austria; they never draw one's eye to the reactionary realities of the thirties—the censorship, the repression, the political imprisonments—any more than similar glimpses in *Outre-Mer* draw one's eye to the Italy of the early Risorgimento....

Much more than to [the] rather set pieces of social description, however, *Hyperion* owes its undeniable, and even now appreciable, flavor and color to its pervasive and almost obsessive literariness. Longfellow, when he wrote it, was still living in the first glow of his enthusiasm, his *Begeisterung*, for German literature, and *Hyperion* is the engaging memento, like a giftbook or album, of his love affair with the German mind. No one before him, in this country, had plunged so eagerly into those romantic waters, or come up with so rich a haul of literary impressions; and he poured them out, in *Hyperion*, with a youthful prodigality. No doubt he was rifling his own lectures at Harvard when he did this, but if so, his stylistic sense saved him from an obvious error; he does not merely thrust passages from his lectures, like inorganic lumps of commentary, into the structure of his narrative. The literary talk in which the book abounds is always, and with real naturalness, worked into the fabric of the whole....

[On the strength of such talk,] Longfellow is entitled to a small but secure niche in the history of our literary criticism. His critical writing, it is true, like his lecturing, is frankly subjective, appreciative, affirmative; his general literary *principles* are the commonplaces of romantic aesthetics, and his taste, fine as it often was, often too went sadly astray. At his best, however, he wrote sensitively, warmly, and imaginatively, like the poet he was, about the writers who delighted him....

It is characteristic of his criticism to express itself not only in metaphor but in metaphor that depends for its appreciative effect on allusions and references that are charming in themselves.... But it is not only in his criticism that Longfellow's mind habitually reveals its natural grain through metaphor and allusion: his prose in general sparkles with imagery and reference, fanciful, pretty, sometimes witty, sometimes inapt, but almost always delightful in itself. The prose of *Hyperion* owes its pleasantness, to a considerable extent, to this rococo ornament....

[*Kavanagh*,] is even slighter and more imponderous than *Hyperion;* one feels that the merest puff from the lips of criticism would shatter it, and indeed it seems to have proved to Longfellow himself that prose fiction was not, for him, a mode worth pursuing any further. Yet it was written, as he said, *con amore*, and an indulgent criticism will find, even now, elements of tenuous, but not merely imaginary, interest in it.... It *has* a certain veracity, just as it has a certain faint and flowerlike fragrance.

It is the fragrance of American pastoral. Like the stories of the local colorists which began to appear some time afterward, *Kavanagh* is an elegy on the old-fashioned village life of New England that was already, when he wrote, beginning to recede into oblivion, though Longfellow felt this before it had become a commonplace....

The main action of *Kavanagh* [however] is wholly without fictional solidity or serious truth. Longfellow had some but not most of the specific gifts of the novelist, and *Kavanagh,* despite the pleasure he took in writing it, seems to have taught him this. Very fortunately, on the whole, he was done with prose fiction for the rest of his literary life. . . .

[Whatever his success in the writing of the *Song of Hiawatha*], Longfellow was attempting an interesting experiment, and one that had not been made before. The Indian, of course, had already figured for decades in our literature; the subject, in a general way, may be said to have become hackneyed. Yet it had been viewed in only a few of its aspects. For the poets, the Indians of their time were appealing almost solely for the pathos of their fate, as members of a doomed and tragic race. . . .

What none of these writers, not even Cooper, had done, except in the most incidental way, was to interest themselves in the Indians' own mythology; in what had already begun to be called the "folklore" of this primitive race, the tales and legends inherited from a remote, ante-historic past, and preserved for generations in the form of oral tradition. This, and not the prowess of splendid savages or even the tragedy of their passing, was what now fascinated Longfellow. . . .

Longfellow's self-chosen task was to select among [the American Indian legends], translate them into his own imaginative terms, and make a coherent poem of them. This is what he did in *Hiawatha*. . . .

If "primitive" means only savage, bloodthirsty, and fierce, then Longfellow's Hiawatha is a romantic caricature of the real culture-hero of primitive peoples. . . . [He] is essentially human in his proportions, despite his magic resources; eternally young, slender, graceful, and kindly. . . . Hiawatha is not the Savage as Devil—the savage of the Puritans—or the Noble Savage of Cooper or the Heroic Savage of Melville; he has to be called something like the Gentle Savage. . . .

If we can regard Hiawatha indulgently in this milder light, he has a minor but genuine imaginative truth not merely to Indian but to human reality. He is a composite product—the image of an Indian prophet conjured up by a sensitive nineteenth-century imagination, with its own freshness and naivete, which had steeped itself in the somewhat expurgated legends that the early ethnologists had brought together. . . . [He] has a quasi-primitive veracity of his own—a childlike seriousness, an archaic ingenuousness, that ring perfectly true to one aspect of primordial human experience. . . .

There is no recondite symbolism in [the Indian] myths or legends as Longfellow retells them; if there is any symbolism, it is perfectly transparent, and Longfellow saw in them no such suggestiveness for romantic allegory as Melville, in *Mardi,* saw in his Polynesian myths and legends. They lack a certain resonance as a result, a certain penumbra of emotion or intellectual meaning. But Longfellow's mind was both more and less "primitive" than Melville's; he delighted in these traditions simple-mindedly for their own sake, and as a result they have, in his handling of them, a clarity of shape, an unambiguous freshness, which they would have lost in the handling of a greater poet. This points to a defect in the poem, but the defect is not without its compensations, and between them they signalize the weakness and strength of *Hiawatha* as a whole. There is another aspect, too, in which its qualities and its defects may be viewed. There was next to no *negative* strain in Longfellow's cult of the primitive; it was not—as it was with most writers in his time—the reverse of any deep loathing he may have felt for civilization or progress. . . . There is thus no painful complexity, no rich contradictoriness, in what Longfellow does with primitive life, and this keeps *Hiawatha* from having the intensity one finds in the work of more passionate men like Thoreau or Melville or even Cooper. The compensation is that it has a greater simplicity of truth to some aspects of primitive life. Was it a fatal mistake for Longfellow to pitch upon the meter that he thought the only right one for what he called his "Indian Edda"? . . . It is not only the meter, of course, but the trick of reiteration, especially at the beginning of lines . . . that has affected so many readers as laughable; but it is the meter that has been the real sticking-point. Is it not as hopelessly monotonous and even maddening as a primitive drumbeat, without the excuse that no better instruments are available to civilized composers? It is a painful question to any reader who cannot forswear the modest pleasure-giving quality of the poem as a whole. Does this quality simply survive in spite of the meter?—for a poem need not be utterly shipwrecked even by an infelicitous pattern. . . .

Both the meter and the language come to life, and the poem frees itself from mere monotony, when the action is playful, innocent, or *maerchenhaft,* or even when it is violent if the violence is half sportive. . . . [In] the description of Pau-Puk-Keewis's dancing there is a fine kinetic sense of choreographic movement, slow at first, then accelerated, and finally whirling. So with the hunting of Pau-Puk-Keewis; the verse keeps pace with the swift, unflagging movement of the flight and pursuit, and the mannerisms of style fall away almost completely.

This is even truer of the passages in which the moods of external nature—of languor or drowsiness, stillness or hush, even grimness—are in harmony with the emotions of the human figures. The most genuine feeling in the poem is the feeling that is reflected back from the landscape or the season or the time of day, and the verse is capable of expressing this without deflation....

Even now Longfellow had not done with the Indians; they reappear in *The Courtship of Miles Standish,* only now they are not legendary prophets and singers, boasters and tricksters, but historical Wampanoag Indians, such as the settlers of Plymouth had encountered in all their solid actuality on the shores and in the woods of Massachusetts. As a result, they are seen not through an Indian Summer haze of poetic primitiveness but with a certain harshness of "realism." They are seen, as a matter of fact, as if through the eyes of the Pilgrims themselves, and if that is a distorting medium, it is clearly the right one for this poem....

The hexameters of *The Courtship* are looser, more relaxed, more frequently trochaic, and less sonorous than those of *Evangeline;* sometimes, in their colloquial ease, ... they are merely jejune, and sometimes they are painfully prosaic.... [Yet] *The Courtship* has a sharp tonality of its own—to which the verse and the language of course contribute—somewhat reminiscent of the "primeval" opening and close of *Evangeline,* but quite unlike its luxuriant and subtropical middle passages....

The Puritan color of the poem is kept up not only by the austere landscape and seascape, but by the constant and always natural recurrence, as in a sacred cantata, of Scriptural language and imagery, usually in an Old Testament spirit. Alden and Priscilla, on their way home from the wedding, recall ... Rebecca and Isaac; and earlier, when John has been plunged in remorse for his "excessive" love of Priscilla, he accuses himself of "worshipping Astaroth blindly, and impious idols of Baal." ... [The] poem comes to an end in a burst of feeling that is both Israelitish and pastoral. It has that kind of truth to the life of the Plymouth Colony; and *The Courtship of Miles Standish,* modest as it is in the claims it makes, is a minor but honorable achievement in poetic narrative....

[Longfellow] had reached a kind of upland of his powers as a lyric poet with *The Seaside and the Fireside,* and after that he held his ground with no really startling ascents or descents until perhaps his late sixties, when there is an appreciable, but by no means a miserable, failure of energy. Almost everything he was later to say had been said, or implied, by the time of *The Seaside and the Fireside,* and what remained was, fortunately, not mere self-repetition, but a steady, slight, unsensational, but beautiful refinement and enhancement of what he had already done....

It remained for Longfellow in his middle fifties, and after the crushing blow of his wife's death, to hit upon the most fortunate plan—of an ambitious sort, that is—in his whole career as a poet, the plan of a series of tales in verse contained within a narrative frame [and titled *Tales of a Wayside Inn*]. No literary undertaking could have made a happier or more fruitful use of his powers and his equipment than this—of his storytelling genius, his sense of narrative form, his versatility, and the opulence of his literary erudition. He had considered projects of this sort long before, but nothing had come of them—in part, surely, because the right *kind* of frame had not suggested itself to him, as it did now....

As we read the *Tales of a Wayside Inn,* we feel ourselves in the presence of a poet who is at work in his most natural and spontaneous vein, a poet whose matter and form are at one with each other, and who has found his happiest means of expression. As we read Longfellow's dramatic poems, we feel ourselves, a good deal of the time, baffled and, sometimes, bored by writing that clearly expresses an aspiration, an ambition, but that is somehow not quite naturally directed; writing that is willed, even determined, but only intermittently borne up and carried along by a true afflatus....

Never did he undertake a task more mistakenly than when he set himself to compose a first panel for his sacred trilogy, *Christus: A Mystery,* and attempted, as he did in *The Divine Tragedy* to dramatize poetically the life of Christ. It is a subject beyond the powers of any poet, certainly of any poet since the Middle Ages, as even *Paradise Regained,* even Klopstock's *Messias,* should have demonstrated, and it was wholly beyond the powers of a poet whose Christian faith, sincere as it certainly was, was New England Unitarianism in its coolest, most reasonable, and most optimistic form.... Longfellow's awareness of human evil, of sin, was almost nonexistent, or so intermittent as to be largely ineffectual in his work, and the redemption of mankind from its burden of guilt by a transcendent Saviour was a theme of which he was utterly unable to make dramatic poetry of any but the most unconvincing sort....

The two *New England Tragedies,* **"John Endicott"** and **"Giles Corey of the Salem Farms,"** have a kind of vitality that is missing from *The Divine Tragedy:* in writing them, Longfellow was not oppressed by the constraint and self-consciousness that evidently weighed on him in writing the first part of the trilogy. The subjects themselves were fresher, closer at hand, and more purely human than the Gospel subject, and Longfellow could, and did, handle his historical authorities with much greater freedom. Neither play succeeds in arousing the emotions of tragedy in any profound way, but of the two **"John Endicott"** comes closer to doing so, no doubt because the heroism of the Quakers in resisting persecution had a reality for Longfellow that the suffering of the "witches" at Salem did not quite evoke....

"John Endicott" communicates something of the emotional tension of a community in the grip of heresy-hunters; **"Giles Corey"** fails, in the end, to communicate with any real power the emotional tension of a community pathologically attacked by a peculiarly virulent hysteria. There was a morbid horror in the subject of Salem witchcraft, unlike that of theological persecution, which Longfellow's kindly spirit shrank, perhaps half-consciously, from rendering with any real sternness or rigor; the poisons of panic terror, of malignant hostility, of superstitious cruelty were so alien to his own nature that, in this connection at least, he could not master them imaginatively, and though they are present in **"Giles Corey,"** they are never represented with full dramatic conviction. Correspondingly, Longfellow fails to evoke any deep tragic sense of the heroism, the moral grandeur, of those who held out against the hysteria and, in some cases, went to their deaths in unavailing innocence....

The subject of *Judas Maccabaeus* was almost as unsuitable a subject for Longfellow's gifts as *The Divine Tragedy* had been, and the poem has even fewer elements of interest than the other has. It is on an almost perversely small scale—five tiny acts divided into even tinier scenes and amounting to hardly a thousand lines in all. As a result, the poem produces somewhat the effect of an epic drama in a puppet theater or an oratorio reduced to a few brief and rather thin recitatives. Naturally, the theme that had struck Longfellow as so fruitful for a play—the collision of Judaism and Hellenism—could not be, and is not, developed in this space with any real richness or complexity: it is broached, but it is not worked out; grazed lightly, but not seriously *treated*.

The character and career of a great artist made less unnatural demands on Longfellow's power than the character and career of a great patriot-warrior, and the "Fragment" of *Michael Angelo,* which he never regarded as finished, has too much vitality, autumnal as that vitality mostly is, to be disposed of as a mere failure....

As a whole, *Michael Angelo,* whatever its shortcomings, is by no means unimpressive as a poetic and even as a "dramatic" treatment of its difficult and complex subject; fragmentary as it is, along with *The Golden Legend* it is the most interesting of all Longfellow's dramatic experiments....

Certainly Longfellow will never again "enjoy" the excessive popularity he enjoyed in his own time and for some years afterward, and this is as it should be....

Longfellow may continue to seem minor, but one rebels against describing him as small. There is a certain largeness not only in his conception of his role but in his actual performance, which is inconsistent with the label of littleness, even of perfection in littleness; his mind was simply, with all its limitations, too venturesome to allow him to remain content with the mastery of one or two forms or modes, and if this meant that he sometimes essayed to do a larger kind of thing than his gifts warranted, the result often has the value of interesting failure, and sometimes a greater value than that. The author of *Hiawatha,* of *Tales of a Wayside Inn,* of *Michael Angelo* was a lesser but not a little writer, a minor poet but not a poetaster....

In the great bulk of his work.... he is a demotic poet pure and simple, like Bryant, Whittier, and Holmes—only richer in resources, more various, more *genialisch* than any of them. And there are poems, early and late, which do not belong to the sphere of popular poetry at all; poems that are simply expressions of an authentic poetic gift, of course of a secondary order. These are the poems most worth holding on to, but much of the rest of his work deserves to be retained in the literary memory in much the same spirit in which Byron's narrative poems, or Tennyson's ballads, or the best of Whittier's demotic pieces deserve to be retained. It is still pleasure-giving to a catholic taste; it still speaks appealingly, for an American mind, to the sense of the American past; and now and then it disengages itself from historic circumstances and takes on the aspect, modestly and even obscurely, of timelessness. Our literature is not so rich in writing of this kind that we can afford to discard any of it....

EDWARD L. HIRSH

SOURCE: Edward L. Hirsh, "Henry Wadsworth Longfellow," in *Six Classic American Writers: An Introduction,* edited by Sherman Paul, University of Minnesota Press, 1970, pp. 122-59.

[*In the following excerpt from an essay that first appeared in 1964, Hirsh discusses themes and techniques in Longfellow's work.*]

The major ideas underlying Longfellow's poetry are characteristically expressed in a conventional nineteenth-century terminology that invites partial misreading, partly because of subsequent changes in meaning, especially in connotation, and partly because important terms are often so inclusive as to seem indeterminate. Longfellow's constant appeal to the heart is frequently understood as the consequence of a vague, sentimental notion that the gentler emotions could resolve problems and order life, to the near-exclusion of thought. His usage, however, like that of his contemporaries, reflects an older and wider meaning of *heart*. The word refers not only to the emotions, but also to will and intuitive reason. The heart is the source of insight as well as of joy or grief; it embraces the moral sensibility that accepts or rejects truth and that acts as conscience in its unstudied response to generally self-evident laws. . . . [In] his simple division of man into body and soul, Longfellow assigned all thoughts, all feelings, all desires to the soul, not the body, which is only the instrument. "It is the soul," he insisted, "that feels, enjoys, suffers . . . " Thus the affections themselves are spiritual, and, directed to good ends, can properly be called "holy."

Longfellow's frame of ultimate reference is formed by his religious convictions. . . . Like his father, Longfellow in general accepted the teaching of William Ellery Channing: that man is fundamentally good, endowed by God with reason, conscience, and an intuitive awareness of the divine; and that Christianity, the purest faith known to man, is progressing toward a full realization of its ideals in a universal church of the future. . . .

For so optimistic a belief, the chief problem is that of sin and evil, and the greatest imaginative failure of Longfellow's poetry is its inability to probe life's dark or sordid aspects. . . . Especially in his long poems, Longfellow represents or alludes to the malicious, fanatic, and selfish behavior men are capable of, but he suggests no deeper cause than a defect incidental to man's present condition, reformable although not yet reformed. . . .

The simply held ideas by which Longfellow attempted to order experience are frequently unable to contain the strong current of feeling that is a distinctive quality of his romantic sensibility. Although he was sharply critical of what he considered the excesses and absurdities of romanticism, his own poetry is saturated with a romantic sense of life's fragility. . . . However tempered in expression by his almost classical restraint and social poise, the dominant mood of Longfellow's poetry is a melancholy not unlike that of Washington Irving, compounded of nostalgia, the sadness of personal loss, and the painful awareness of transience and mortality. . . .

Like much nineteenth-century poetry, Longfellow's seems in retrospect leisurely, even too relaxed. The slow development of ideas, the elaboration of details, the multiplication of parallels, the explication of the already-evident are practices that destroy some of his poems and in varying combinations and degrees characterize most of them. The language, too, bears the stamp of its time in its tendency to expansive statement, its often predictable vocabulary and phraseology, and its fondness for literary diction. . . . Historically considered, the kind of poetry Longfellow wrote lay within a poetic tradition that with various adaptations served the larger part of a century, and was imaginatively satisfying to the romantic-Victorian sensibility. Within the age's literary conventions, Longfellow used language skillfully and sensitively. At its best, his language is simple and economical, natural in movement, emotionally exact in its use of words and phrases, and restrained in statement. Furthermore, Longfellow's handling of language is largely responsible for his achievement of an impressive tonal range from the formality of semi-epic narrative to the humor-seasoned easiness of the discourse of polite society. He makes the traditional poetic language, with often minimal alteration, express distinctively his own insights and feelings.

As a poet more evocative than creative of experience, Longfellow employs language with a notable awareness of the way in which it becomes charged with meaning from the inescapable situations of human life. Frequently he depends not upon connotations or overtones developed within the context of a poem, but upon a resonance provided immediately by general experience itself and renewed in the poem by allusions to the appropriate common events or situations, or by brief descriptions of them. . . .

Like other aspects of his poetry, Longfellow's prosody is remarkable for resourcefulness and variety within traditional limits. His uncommon talent in versification and his absorption in its technical problems led to no prosodic revolution; indeed, a dangerous facility, combined with a taste for euphony, brings his verse at moments close to that of the typical Victorian "sweet singer." Within accepted bounds, however, Longfellow's versatility in rhythmical, metrical, and rhyming patterns and his constant experimentation, directed toward the creation of a unique effect for each poem, reveal a technical mastery rarely approached in American poetry. Although his prosodic variety is most obvious in the surprisingly various patterns of his stanzaic verse, it is perhaps more subtly displayed in meeting the resistance of a set form like the sonnet, where, employing the Italian pattern and almost invariably observing a strict octet-sestet division, Longfellow achieves striking rhythmic differences by ingenious handling of metrical substitution, run-on and end-stopped lines, and caesuras. In freer forms, his skill is no less evident: the extremely uneven blank verse of *The Divine Tragedy* has reflective passages in which comparative rhythmic freedom works with approximately normal word order to produce lines that sometimes collapse into prose but that occasionally attain a thoroughly natural movement barely but unmistakably tightened into poetry....

The technical virtuosity of Longfellow's art is manifested in several accomplishments: the successful maintenance of falling rhythm in spite of English poetry's strong tendency to rising rhythm; the dexterous control of varied rhythm and free rhyming by an organization based on parallelism, balance, and alliteration; and the giving of widely varied movement to such uncomplicated verse forms as the quatrain....

The major irony of Longfellow's literary career was the commitment of his hopes for distinctive major achievement to the form in which he was most consistently unsuccessful, the poetic drama. From 1849 to 1872 he intermittently labored over what he regarded as "his loftier song" in "sublimer strain," as his greatest work, "the equivalent expression for the trouble and wrath of life, for its sorrow and mystery." The completed *Christus: A Mystery* consists of three parts comprising four poetic dramas, all so manifestly closet dramas that they could be properly described as dramatically organized poems. The first part is *The Divine Tragedy*, the last to be published; the second part is *The Golden Legend*, the first published; the third part, *The New England Tragedies*, consists of two dramas, *John Endicott* and *Giles Corey of the Salem Farms*. The three parts are linked by interludes and the whole *Christus* is provided with an "Introitus" and "Finale." No other works of Longfellow's had such intended scope or received such dedicated attention; and none were so disappointing in result....

Longfellow's general failure in dramatic form is understandable. His talent was narrative and lyrically meditative, and he could not refrain from reliance on narration and exposition, even to the destruction of dramatic effect.... It is his least pretentious dramatic work, the early *Spanish Student*, that is in many respects the most successfully realized; in spite of its lack of intellectual significance, it is a colorful, pleasant comedy of intrigue, technically more proficient than the later poetic dramas. Two minor dramatic works, *Judas Maccabeus* and *The Masque of Pandora*, have interesting themes but are extremely weak in execution. Only the partly completed *Michael Angelo*, closely related to Longfellow's own life and work, and containing in a few passages some of his strongest poetry, shows an apparently emerging mastery of dramatic form in the 1870's. The fundamental obstacle to the *Christus'* success, however, is not simply a flawed dramatic technique, but an internal conflict in the work between its ostensible intention and its meaning. Originally planned as a dramatizing of the progress of Christianity, the *Christus* loosely employs the theological virtues of faith, hope, and charity as the basis of organization, *The Divine Tragedy* expressing hope through its representation of Christ's life and mission, the *Golden Legend* depicting faith in its full medieval flowering, and the *New England Tragedies* pointing to the religious freedom of the age of charity or love. The optimism of the design is realized in some scenes and is recurrently asserted as a proposition, but it is not borne out in the *Christus'* development and accumulated feeling, which are finally somber and even pessimistic in their tendency. Longfellow's emotional recoil from several aspects of the contemporary religious scene apparently caused him to lose much of his professed hope for the future and left its mark especially on the first and third parts, the latest composed, of the *Christus.*

Perhaps the most successful part of *Christus* is the *Golden Legend*, which, in spite of an elementary plot, an unmedievally melancholy hero, and a sentimentalized heroine, effectively profits from Longfellow's knowledge of the Middle Ages. Although the deepest intellectual and spiritual life of the medieval world is not mirrored here, the varied contrasts and conflicts of the medieval surface, as well as the immediately underlying crosscurrents, are colorfully represented through skillfully shifted scenes presented in a freely handled answerable verse....

SOURCES FOR FURTHER STUDY

Allen, Gay Wilson. "Henry Wadsworth Longfellow." In *American Prosody*, pp. 154-92. New York: American Book Company, 1935.

    Provides detailed analysis of Longfellow's poetry.

Brenner, Rica. "Henry Wadsworth Longfellow." In *Twelve American Poets before 1900*, pp. 80-108. 1933. Reprint. Freeport, N.Y.: Books for Libraries Press, 1968.

    Presents an overview of Longfellow's life and works.

Fletcher, Angus. "Whitman and Longfellow: Two Types of the American Poet." *Raritan* 10, No. 4 (Spring 1991): 131-45.

Compares Longfellow with Whitman, concluding that "these two paths in the wilderness are in fact different ways of reaching the same goals."

Gohdes, Clarence. "Longfellow." In his *American Literature in Nineteenth-Century England,* pp. 99-126. New York: Columbia University Press, 1944.

Discusses the reception of Longfellow's poetry in England.

Long, Orie William. "Henry Wadsworth Longfellow." In his *Literary Pioneers: Early American Explorers of European Culture,* pp. 159-98. Cambridge, Mass.: Harvard University Press, 1935.

Discusses the influence of European writers, particularly Goethe, on Longfellow's art and thought.

Ward, Robert Stafford. "Longfellow's Roots in Yankee Soil." *The New England Quarterly* 41 (June 1968): 180-92.

Examines the New England heritage of Longfellow's poetry.

Niccolò Machiavelli

1469-1527

(Also Nicolo, Niccholo, and Nicolas; also Machiavegli, Machiavello, Machivel, and Machiavel) Italian essayist, dramatist, historian, sketch writer, biographer, writer of novellas, and poet.

INTRODUCTION

A Florentine statesman and political theorist, Machiavelli remains one of the most controversial figures of political history. He addressed a wide range of political and historical topics, while embracing strictly literary forms and has come to be identified almost exclusively with his highly controversial manual of state, *Il principe* (1532; *Nicholas Machiavel's Prince*). Over the centuries, this straightforward, pragmatic treatise on political conduct and the application of power, which is commonly known as *The Prince*, has been variously hailed, denounced, and distorted. Seldom has a single work generated such divergent and fierce commentary from such a wide assortment of writers. Commenting on Machiavelli's colorful critical heritage, T. S. Eliot has remarked that "no great man has been so completely misunderstood."

Biographical Information

Machiavelli was born in Florence to an established middle-class family whose members had traditionally held positions in local government. As a boy he learned Latin and quickly became an assiduous reader of the ancient classics. In 1498, Machiavelli helped the political faction that deposed Girolamo Savonarola. That same year Machiavelli was appointed to the second chancery of the republic, a position that allowed him to participate both in domestic politics and in diplomatic missions to foreign governments. For the next fourteen years Machiavelli closely examined the inner workings of government and met prominent individuals, among them Cesare Borgia, whom Machiavelli prominently profiled in *The Prince*. By 1502 he was a well-respected assistant to the republican head of state, Piero Soderini. In 1512, when Spanish forces invaded Italy, the Florentine political climate changed abruptly. The Medici—for centuries the rulers of Florence, but exiled since 1494—deposed Soderini, replacing the republican government with their own autocratic regime. Machiavelli was purged from office, jailed, and tortured for his republican sentiments, and finally banished in 1513 to his country residence in Percussina, where he composed *Discorsi di Nicolo Machiavelli* (1531; *Machivel's Discourses upon the First Decade of T. Livius*) and *The Prince*. Around 1518 he debuted the comedy *Comedia di Callimaco* (*Mandragola*), which proved popular with Italian audiences for several years. Machiavelli's only political work published during his lifetime was the military treatise *Libro della arte della guerra* (1521; *The Art of War*). Meanwhile, Machiavelli had made several attempts to gain favor with the Medici, including dedicating *The Prince* to Lorenzo. When he was appointed official historian of Florence in 1520, he began writing *Historie di Nicolo Machivegli* (1532; *The History of Florence*), which carefully dilutes his republican platform with the Medicean bias expected of him. In 1525 Pope Clement VII recognized his achievement with a monetary stipend. Two years later, the Medici were again ousted, and Machiavelli's hopes for advancement under the revived republic were frustrated, for the new government was suspicious of his ties to the Medici. He became disheartened and disillusioned by his country's internal strife, and soon thereafter fell gravely ill and died.

Major Works

The Prince delineates a typology of sovereignties and the deployment of available forces—military, political, or psychological—to acquire and retain them. As the first political treatise to divorce statecraft from ethics, *The Prince* posits two fundamentals necessary for effective political leadership: *virtu* and *fortuna*. *Virtu* refers to the prince's own abilities (ideally a combination of leonine force and vulpine cunning); *fortuna* to the unpredictable influence of luck. In a significant departure from previous political thought, the designs of Providence play no part in Machiavelli's scheme. *The Prince* presents Machiavelli's theses in direct, candid, and often passionate speech, using easily grasped metaphors and structuring the whole in an aphoristic vein that lends it a compelling authority. *Machivel's Discourses* is the acknowledged companion piece to *The Prince*. All of the author's subsequent studies treating history, political science, and military theory stem from this dissertation containing Machiavelli's most original thought. Less flamboyant than *The Prince* and narrower in its margin for interpretation, *Machivel's Discourses* reveals his undisguised admiration for ancient governmental forms, offering his most eloquent, thoroughly explicated republicanism. *Machivel's Discourses* also presents that methodical extrapolation of political theory from historical documentation that is intermittent in *The Prince*. *Mandragola* firmly predicates, as do all of Machiavelli's writings, an astute, unsentimental awareness of human nature as flawed and given to self-centeredness. The drama concerns Callimaco's desire to bed Lucrezia, the beautiful young wife of a doddering fool, Nicia, who is obsessed with begetting a son. Masquerading as a doctor, Callimaco advises Nicia to administer a potion of mandrake to Lucrezia to render her fertile, but also warns that the drug will have fatal implications for the first man to have intercourse with her. He slyly suggests to Nicia that a dupe be found for this purpose. Persuaded by her confessor, a knavish cleric, to comply with her husband's wishes, the virtuous Lucrezia at last allows Callimaco into her bed, where he has no difficulty convincing her to accept him as her lover on a more permanent basis.

Critical Reception

A decided influence on the philosophies of Thomas Hobbes and Sir Francis Bacon and on the thought of such modern political theorists as Vilfredo Pareto, Gaetano Mosca, Georges Sorel, and Robert Michels, Machiavelli has been called the founder of empirical political science, primarily on the strength of *Machivel's Discourses* and *The Prince*. Taken in historical perspective, *The Prince* understandably dwarfed Machiavelli's other works for with this slim treatise the author confronted the ramifications of power when its procurement and exercise were notably peremptory—not only in his own country but throughout Europe as well. Commentators have weighed the integrity of Machiavelli's controversial thought against the pressing political conditions that formed it. Some, like Roberto Ridolfi, have endeavored to dislodge the long-standing perception of Machiavelli as a ruthless character: "In judging Machiavelli one must . . . take account of his anguished despair of virtue and his tragic sense of evil. . . . [On] the basis of sentences taken out of context and of outward appearances he was judged a cold and cynical man, a sneerer at religion and virtue; but in fact there is hardly a page of his writing and certainly no action of life that does not show him to be passionate, generous, ardent and basically religious." "Far from banishing religion or ethics from politics," Peter Bondanella has stated, "Machiavelli created a new religion out of politics, with all its fateful implications for modern intellectual history."

(For further information, see *DISCovering Authors; DISCovering Authors: British; DISCovering Authors: Canadian; DISCovering Authors Modules: Most-studied Authors Module; Literature Criticism from 1400 to 1800,* Vols. 8, 36.)

CRITICAL COMMENTARY

JAMES BURNHAM

SOURCE: James Burnham, "Machiavelli: The Science of Power," in his *The Machiavellians: Defenders of Freedom*, The John Day Company, Inc., 1943, pp. 29-80.

[*In the following excerpt, Burnham discusses a number of Machiavelli's views and concepts.*]

There have been many critical discussions about Machiavelli's supposed views on "human nature." Some defend him, but he is usually charged with a libel upon mankind, with having a perverted, shocking, and detestable notion of what human beings are like. These discussion[s], however, are beside the point. Machiavelli has no views on human nature; or, at any rate, none is presented in his writings. Machiavelli is neither a psychologist nor a moral philosopher, but a political scientist.

It is clear from a study of Machiavelli that what he is trying to analyze is not "man" but "political man," in somewhat the same way that Adam Smith analyzed "economic man." Adam Smith did not suppose for a moment — though he, too, is often enough misunderstood — that he was exhaustively describing human nature when he said that economic man seeks a profit, that, when a man operates in the capitalist market, he seeks the greatest possible economic profit. Of course Adam Smith realized that men, in the course of their many and so various activities, are motivated by many other aims than the search for profit. But he was not interested in human nature as a whole. Man's nature was relevant to his studies only insofar as man functioned economically, in the market. Adam Smith was abstracting from human nature, and introducing the conception of an "economic agent," which he believed, with some justice, would aid him in formulating the laws of economics. . . .

Similarly with Machiavelli. He is interested in man in relation to political phenomena — that is, to the struggle for power; in man as he functions politically, not in man as he behaves toward his friends or family or god. It does not refute Machiavelli to point out that men do not always act as he says they act. He knows this. But many sides of man's nature he believes to be irrelevant to political behavior. If he is wrong, he is wrong because of a false theory of politics, not because of a false idea of man. . . .

From studying the facts of politics, then, Machiavelli reached certain conclusions, not about man but about "political man."

First, he implies everywhere a rather sharp distinction between two types of political man: a "ruler-type," we might call one, and a "ruled-type," the other. The first type would include not merely those who at any moment occupy leading positions in society, but those also who aspire to such positions or who might so aspire if opportunity offered; the second consists of those who neither lead nor are capable of becoming leaders. The second is the great majority. There is a certain arbitrariness in any such distinction as this, and obviously the exact line between the two groups is hazy. Nevertheless, it is clear that Machiavelli — and all those, moreover, who write in the tradition of Machiavelli — thinks that the distinction reflects a basic fact of political life, that active political struggle is confined for the most part to a small minority of men, that the majority is and remains, whatever else happens, the ruled.

The outstanding characteristic of the majority is, then, its political passivity. Unless driven by the most extreme provocation on the part of the rulers or by rare and exceptional circumstance, the ruled are not interested in power. They want a small minimum of security, and a chance to live their own lives and manage their own small affairs. . . .

When Machiavelli concludes that no man is perfectly good or bad, he is not making a primarily moral judgment. He means, more generally, that all men make mistakes at least sometimes, that there are no supermen, that no man is always intelligent and judicious, that even the stupid have occasional moments of brilliance, that men are not always consistent, that they are variable and variously motivated. Obvious as such reflections may seem, they are easily forgotten in the realm of political action, which is alone in question. The tendency, in political judgments, is toward black and white: the leader, or the proletariat, or the people, or the party, or the great captain is always right; the bosses or the crowd or the government, always wrong. From such reasoning flow not a few shocks and dismays at turns of events that might readily have been anticipated.

The ruled majority, changeable, weak, short-sighted, selfish, is not at all, for Machiavelli, the black to the

> **Principal Works**
>
> *Comedia di Callimaco: E di Lucretia [Mandragola] (drama) [first publication] 1518?
> Libro della arte della guerra [The Art of War] (treatise) 1521
> La Clizia [Clizia] (drama) 1525
> Discorsi di Nicolo Machiavelli... sopra la prima deca di Tito Livio, a Zanobi Buondelmonte, et a Cosimo Rucellai [Machivel's Discourses Upon the First Decade of T. Livius] (treatise) 1531
> Historie di Nicolo Machivegli [The History of Florence] (history) 1532
> **Il principe de Niccholo Machivello... La vita di Castruccio Castracani da Lucca... Il modo che tenne il Duca Valentino per ammazar Vitellozo, Oliverotto da Fermo il S. Paolo et il Duca di Gravini Orsini in Senigaglia [Nicholas Machiavel's Prince. Also, the Life of Castruccio Castracani of Lucca. Also the Meanes Duke Valentine Us'd to Put to Death Vitellozzo Vitelli, Oliverotto of Fermo, Paul, and the Duke of Gravina] (treatise, biography, and essay) 1532
> Favola: Belfagor arcidiavolo che prese moglie [A Fable: Belfagor, the Devil Who Took a Wife] (novella) 1559
> Tutte le opere storiche e litterarie di Niccolò Machiavelli (treatises, history, dramas, biography, prose, and poetry) 1929
> The Literary Works of Machiavelli (dramas, poetry, and novella) 1961
> Machiavelli: The Chief Works and Others. 3 vols. (treatises, history, dramas, biography, and prose) 1965
>
> *With the third edition of 1524 this work assumed the title of its prologue, La Mandragola.
> **La vita di Castruccio Castracani... and Il modo che tenne il Duca Valentino... were appended to and originally appeared in print with the first edition of Il principe.

rulers' white. Indeed, for him, the ruler-type is even less constant, less loyal, and on many occasions less intelligent....

In understanding Machiavelli, there are confusions that may result from his use of certain words.

In *The Prince*, Machiavelli divides all governments, with respect to their form, into "monarchies" (principalities) and "commonwealths" (republics). A monarchy means a government where sovereignty rests, formally, in a single man; a commonwealth means a government where sovereignty rests, formally, in more than one man. A commonwealth, therefore, need not be "democratic" in any usual sense; nor a monarchy, tyrannical.

At the beginning of the ***Discourses on Livy***, Machiavelli distinguishes three kinds of government: monarchy, aristocracy, and democracy. Through this distinction, which is taken from Aristotle, he is referring not only to differences in governmental form, but also to differing social relations in the state. In particular, by the terms "aristocracy" and "democracy" he is taking account of the relative power of "nobility" and "people."

When Machiavelli discusses the nobility and the people, he has in mind the distinction between "patricians" and "plebs" in Rome, and between the feudal nobility and the burghers in the Italian cities. Originally, in Rome, the patricians were the heads of the families belonging to the ancient tribes. Their class included, in a subordinate status, the rest of their families, their clients, servants, slaves, and so on. At first, the patricians alone were eligible to the senate and the consulship.

The class of the "plebs," or "people," was sub-divided primarily according to wealth. Its articulate and politically active members, who gradually won citizenship in Rome, the creation of the office of tribune, and eligibility to the senate and consulship, were for a long time only a small minority of the entire plebs—just as the patricians proper, who were the descendants of the early family heads in the eldest male line, were only a minority of the entire patrician class. In speaking of the "people," therefore, in connection with Rome, the reference is not to everyone, or even to "the masses" in an indiscriminate sense, but ordinarily to the upper stratum of the plebs.

Analogously in the case of the Italian cities, "people" meant in the first instance the burghers and the leading members of the guilds. These were opposed to the class of the nobility, dominated by the heads of the noble houses. In the course of time, the class of "people" expanded. It became necessary to distinguish between the richer burghers and chiefs of the major guilds (*popolo grasso*), and the lesser people (*popolo minuto*), whom Machiavelli sometimes calls "people of the meaner sort." But when Machiavelli wants to refer to the lower strata of "the masses," to the apprentices and workmen and those not regularly employed, he ordinarily calls them, not "people," but "rabble," or sometimes "multitude."

There are two important consequences of this terminology: The form of government—monarchy or commonwealth—is independent of the social ascendancy or subordination of the "people," since the people could set up a monarchy or tyranny as well as a commonwealth, and the nobility could rule through a republic or commonwealth, as it did during much of the history of Rome, in Venice, and typically in a long period of the history of the ancient cities. Second, the distinction between "ruler-type" and "ruled-type" is also independent: specifically, both types are to be found among the "people" as well as in other classes.

The ruler-type, then, is not distinguished by Machiavelli from the ruled by any moral standard, nor by intelligence or consistency, nor by any capacity to avoid mistakes. There are, however, certain common characteristics that mark the rulers and potential rulers, and divide them from the majority that is fated always to be ruled.

In the first place, the ruler-type has what Machiavelli calls *virtu*, what is so improperly translated as "virtue." *Virtu* is a word, in Machiavelli's language, that has no English equivalent. It includes in its meaning part of what we refer to as "ambition," "drive," "spirit" in the sense of Plato's *Oupos*, the "will to power." Those who are capable of rule are above all those who want to rule. They drive themselves as well as others; they have that quality which makes them keep going, endure amid difficulties, persist against dangers....

The ruler-type has, usually, strength, especially martial strength. War and fighting are the great training ground of rule, Machiavelli believes, and power is secure only on the basis of force.

Even more universal a quality of the ruler-type, however, is fraud. Machiavelli's writings contain numerous discussions of the indispensable role of fraud in political affairs, ranging from analyses of deceptions and stratagems in war to the breaking of treaties to the varied types of fraud met with daily in civil life. In the ***Discourses***, Book II, Chapter 13, he generalizes "that from mean to great fortune, people rise rather by fraud, than by force."...

The combination of force and fraud is picturesquely referred to in the famous passages of ***The Prince*** which describe the successful ruler as both Lion and Fox....

> Seeing, therefore, it is of such importance to a Prince to take upon him the nature and disposition of a beast, of all the whole flock, he ought to imitate the Lion and the Fox; for the Lion is in danger of toils and snares, and the Fox of the Wolf: so that he must be a Fox to find out the snares, and a Lion to fright away the Wolves, but they who keep wholly to the Lion, have no true notion of themselves....

Finally, political man of the ruler-type is skilled at adapting himself to the times. In passage after passage, Machiavelli returns to this essential ability: neither cruelty nor humaneness, neither rashness nor caution, neither liberality nor avarice avails in the struggle for power unless the times are suited....

Machiavelli does not have a systematically worked out theory of history. The many generalizations which he states are for the most part limited, dealing with some special phase of political action, and a list of them would be a summary of most of his writings. There are, however, in addition to those that I have already analyzed, a few wider principles of great influence in the later development of Machiavellism.

I. Political life, according to Machiavelli, is never static, but in continual change. There is no way of avoiding this change. Any idea of a perfect state, or even of a reasonably good state, much short of perfection, that could last indefinitely, is an illusion.

The process of change is repetitive, and roughly cyclical. That is to say, the pattern of change occurs again and again in history (so that, by studying the past, we learn also about the present and future); and this pattern comprises a more or less recognizable cycle. A good, flourishing, prosperous state becomes corrupt, evil, degenerate; from the corrupt, evil state again arises one that is strong and flourishing. The degeneration can, perhaps, be delayed; but Machiavelli has no confidence that it could be avoided. The very virtues of the good state contain the seeds of its own destruction. The strong and flourishing state is feared by all neighbors, and is therefore left in peace. War and the ways of force are neglected. The peace and prosperity breed idleness, luxury, and license; these, political corruption, tyranny, and weakness. The state is overcome by the force of uncorrupted neighbors, or itself enters a new cycle, where hard days and arms purge the corruption, and bring a new strength, a new virtue and prosperity. But once again, the degeneration sets in....

2. The recurring pattern of change expresses the more or less permanent core of human nature as it functions politically. The instability of all governments and political forms follows in part from the limitless human appetite for power....

3. Machiavelli assigns a major function in political affairs to what he calls "Fortune." Sometimes he seems

almost to personify Fortune, and, in the manner that lingered on through the Middle Ages from ancient times, to write about her as a goddess. He discusses Fortune not merely in occasional references, but in a number of lengthy passages scattered throughout his works.

From these passages it becomes clear what Machiavelli means by "Fortune." Fortune is all those causes of historical change that are beyond the deliberate, rational control of men. In the case both of individuals and of states, Machiavelli believes that those causes are many, often primary, and in the long run probably dominant. He does not altogether exclude from history the influence of deliberate human control, but he reduces it to a strictly limited range....

This conception of Fortune fits in closely with the idea, which we have already noted, that the ruler-type of political man is one who knows how to accommodate to the times. Fortune cannot be overcome, but advantage may be taken of her....

Beyond such accommodation ("opportunism," we might nowadays call it), men and states will make the most of fortune when they display *virtu*, when they are firm, bold, quick in decision, not irresolute, cowardly, and timid....

4. Machiavelli believes that religion is essential to the well-being of a state. In discussing religion, as in discussing human nature, Machiavelli confines himself to political function. He is not engaged in theological dispute, nor inquiring whether religion, or some particular religion, is true or false, but trying to estimate the role that religious belief and ritual perform in politics. He is analyzing, we might say in a general sense, "myth," and myth he finds to be politically indispensable....

5. We have already seen that Machiavelli's chief immediate practical goal was the national unification of Italy. In the review of his descriptive conclusions about the nature of political activity, no reference has been made to any more general goals or ideals to which Machiavelli adhered. I return now to this problem of goal, in order to answer the question: What kind of government did Machiavelli think best?

Machiavelli's writings, taken in their entirety, leave no doubt about the answer. Machiavelli thinks that the best kind of government is a republic, what he called a "commonwealth." Not only does he prefer a republican government; other things being equal, he considers a republic stronger, more enduring, wiser and more flexible than any form of monarchy. This opinion is above all clarified by Machiavelli's most important work, the *Discourses on Livy,* but it is at least implicit in everything that he wrote. When, in his Letter to Zenobius, he replies to the accusation that in all his writings he "insinuates" his "great affection to the Democratical Government," he accepts frankly the justice of the accusation....

Nor does this preference for a republic contradict his conclusion that the leadership of a prince was required for the national unification of Italy. If a republic is the best form of government, it does not follow that a republic is possible at every moment and for all things. Machiavelli's preferences are always disciplined by the truth. The truth here, as he correctly saw it, was that Italy could not then be unified except, in the initial stages at least, through a prince.

But in preferring a republican form of government, Machiavelli paints no utopia. He states the defects of his ideals as honestly as their virtues. It is true, moreover, that he does not attach quite the ultimate importance to the choice of form of government that would be attributed to that choice by utopians who believe that all human problems can be solved if only their own private ideal can be realized. There is no way, Machiavelli believes, to solve all or even most human problems.

Beyond and superior to his preference among the forms of government, Machiavelli projects his ideal of "liberty." For any given group of people, "liberty," as Machiavelli uses the word, means: independence—that is, no external subjection to another group; and, internally, a government by law, not by the arbitrary will of any individual men, princes or commoners....

As protectors of liberty, Machiavelli has no confidence in individual men as such; driven by unlimited ambition, deceiving even themselves, they are always corrupted by power. But individuals can, to some extent at least and for a while, be disciplined within the established framework of wise laws. A great deal of the *Discourses* is a commentary on this problem.

In chapter after chapter, Machiavelli insists that if liberty is to be preserved: no person and no magistrate may be permitted to be above the law; there must be legal means for any citizen to bring accusations against any other citizen or any official; terms of office must be short, and must never, no matter what the inconvenience, be lengthened; punishment must be firm and impartial; the ambitions of citizens must never be allowed to build up private power, but must be directed into public channels.

Machiavelli is not so naive as to imagine that the law can support itself. The law is founded upon force, but the force in turn will destroy the law unless it also is bridled; but force can be bridled only by opposing force. Sociologically, therefore, the foundation of liberty is a balancing of forces, what Machiavelli calls a "mixed" government. Since Machiavelli is neither a propagandist nor an apologist, since he is not the demagogue of any party or sect or group, he knows and says how hypocritical are the calls for a "unity" that is a mask for the suppression of all opposition, how fatally lying or wrong are all beliefs that liberty is the peculiar attribute of any single individual or group—prince or democrat, nobles or people or "multitude." Only out of the continuing clash of opposing groups can liberty flow....

Liberty, then—not the rhetorical liberty of an impossible and misconceived utopia, but such concrete liberty as is, when they are fortunate, within the grasp of real men, with their real limitations—is the dominant ideal of Machiavelli, and his final norm of judgment. Tyranny is liberty's opposite, and no man has been a clearer foe of tyranny. No man clearer, and few more eloquent....

Men are fond of believing that, even though they may for a while be mistaken, yet in the long run they do suitable honor, if not to the persons then at least to the memories, of those who have brought some measure of truth and enlightenment to the world. We may burn an occasional Bruno, imprison a Galileo, denounce a Darwin, exile an Einstein; but time, we imagine, restores judgment, and a new generation recognizes the brave captains of the mind who have dared to advance through the dark barriers of ignorance, superstition, and illusion. Machiavelli was so plainly one of these. His weapons, his methods—the methods of truth and science—he shared with Galileo and Darwin and Einstein; and he fought in a field of much greater concern to mankind. He tried to tell us not about stars or atoms, but about ourselves and our own common life. If his detailed conclusions were sometimes wrong, his own method, as the method of science always does, provides the way to correct them. He would be the first to insist on changing any of his views that were refuted by the evidence.

Though this is so, Machiavelli's name does not rank in this noble company. In the common opinion of men, his name itself has become a term of reproach and dishonor. He is thought of as Marlowe, not so long after his death, has him speak of himself in the prologue of *The Jew of Malta*:

> To some perhaps my name is odious,
> But such as love me guard me from their
>   tongues;
> And let them know that I am Machiavel,
> And weigh not men, and therefore not
>   men's words.
> Admired I am of those that hate me most.
> Though some speak openly against my
>   books,
> Yet they will read me, and thereby attain
> To Peter's chair: and when they cast me
>   off,
> Are poisoned by my climbing followers.
> I count religion but a childish toy,
> And hold there is no sin but ignorance.
> Birds of the air will tell of murders past!
> I am ashamed to hear such fooleries.
> Many will talk of title to a crown:
>   What right had Caesar to the empery?
>   Might first made kings, and laws were
>   then most sure
>   When like the Draco's they were writ in
>   blood.

Why should this be? If our reference is to the views that Machiavelli in fact held, that he stated plainly, openly and clearly in his writings, there is in the common opinion no truth at all. We face here what can hardly be, after all these centuries, a mere accident of misunderstanding. There must be some substantial reason why Machiavelli is so consistently distorted.

It might be argued that there have indeed been oppressors and tyrants who learned from Machiavelli how to act more effectively in the furtherance of their designs, and that this justifies the common judgment of his views. It is true that he has taught tyrants, from almost his own days—Thomas Cromwell, for example, the low-born Chancellor whom Henry VIII brought in to replace Thomas More when More refused to make his conscience a tool of his master's interests, was said to have a copy of Machiavelli always in his pocket; and in our own time Mussolini wrote a college thesis on Machiavelli. But knowledge has a disturbing neutrality in this respect. We do not blame the research analyst who has solved the chemical mysteries of a poison because a murderer made use of his treatise, nor a student of the nature of alloys because a safe is cracked with the help of his formulas, nor chemists and physical scientists because bombs explode when they drop on Warsaw or Chungking. Perhaps we should do so; perhaps, as the story in *Genesis* almost suggests, all knowledge is evil. But the mere fact that the knowledge made explicit by Machiavelli has been put to bad uses, which is a potential fate of all knowledge, cannot explain why he is singled out for infamy.

It may be remarked that the harsh opinion of Machiavelli has been more widespread in England and the United States than in the nations of Continental Europe. This is no doubt natural, because the distinguishing quality of Anglo-Saxon politics has always been hypocrisy, and hypocrisy must always be at pains to shy away from the truth. It is also the case that judgments of Machiavelli are usually based upon acquaintance with *The Prince* alone, an essay which, though plain enough, can be honestly misinterpreted when read out of the context of the rest of his writings. However, something more fundamental than these minor difficulties is at stake.

We are, I think, and not only from the fate of Machiavelli's reputation, forced to conclude that men do not really want to know about themselves. When we allow ourselves to be taken in by reasoning after the manner of Dante, we find it easy to believe such remarks as Aristotle made at the beginning of his *Metaphysics:* "All men naturally desire knowledge"; and to imagine that it is self-evident that knowledge will always be welcomed. But if we examine not what follows from some abstract metaphysical principle but how men behave, some doubts arise. Even in the case of the physical world, knowledge must often hammer long at the door. Where they are themselves the subject-matter, men still keep the door resolutely shut. It may even be that they are right in this resistance. Perhaps the full disclosure of what we really are and how we act is too violent a medicine.

In any case, whatever may be the desires of most men, it is most certainly against the interests of the powerful that the truth should be known about political behavior. If the political truths stated or approximated by Machiavelli were widely known by men, the success of tyranny and all the other forms of oppressive political rule would become much less likely. A deeper freedom would be possible in society than Machiavelli himself believed attainable. If men generally understood as much of the mechanism of rule and privilege as Machiavelli understood, they would no longer be deceived into accepting that rule and privilege, and they would know what steps to take to overcome them.

Therefore the powerful and their spokesmen—all the "official" thinkers, the lawyers and philosophers and preachers and demagogues and moralists and editors—must defame Machiavelli. Machiavelli says that rulers lie and break faith; this proves, they say, that he libels human nature. Machiavelli says that ambitious men struggle for power: he is apologizing for the opposition, the enemy, and trying to confuse you about us, who wish to lead you for your own good and welfare. Machiavelli says that you must keep strict watch over officials and subordinate them to the law: he is encouraging subversion and the loss of national unity. Machiavelli says that no man with power is to be trusted: you see that his aim is to smash all your faith and ideals.

Small wonder that the powerful—in public—denounce Machiavelli. The powerful have long practice and much skill in sizing up their opponents. They can recognize an enemy who will never compromise, even when that enemy is so abstract as a body of ideas....

BERTRAND RUSSELL

SOURCE: Bertrand Russell, "Modern Philosophy: Machiavelli," in his *A History of Western Philosophy, and Its Connection with Political and Social Circumstances from the Earliest Times to the Present Day,* Simon & Schuster, 1945, pp. 504-11.

[*A respected and prolific author, Russell was an English philosopher and mathematician known for his support of humanistic concerns. In the following excerpt, he summarizes Machiavelli's political platform.*]

The Renaissance, though it produced no important theoretical philosopher, produced one man of supreme eminence in *political* philosophy, Niccolo Machiavelli. It is the custom to be shocked by him, and he certainly is sometimes shocking. But many other men would be equally so if they were equally free from humbug. His political philosophy is scientific and empirical, based upon his own experience of affairs, concerned to set forth the means to assigned ends, regardless of the question whether the ends are to be considered good or bad. When, on occasion, he allows himself to mention the ends that he desires, they are such as we can all applaud. Much of the conventional obloquy that attaches to his name is due to the indignation of hypocrites who hate the frank avowal of evil-doing. There remains, it is true, a good deal that genuinely demands criticism, but in this he is an expression of his age....

The Prince is concerned to discover, from history and from contemporary events, how principalities are won, how they are held, and how they are lost. Fifteenth-century Italy afforded a multitude of examples, both great and small. Few rulers were legitimate; even the popes, in many cases, secured election by corrupt means. The rules for achieving success were not quite the same as they became when times grew more settled, for no one was shocked by cruelties and treacheries which would have disqualified a man in the eighteenth or the nineteenth century. Perhaps our age, again, can better appreciate Machiavelli, for some of the most notable successes of our time have been achieved by methods as base as any employed in Renaissance Italy. He would have applauded, as an artistic connoisseur in statecraft, Hitler's Reichstag fire, his purge of the party in 1934, and his breach of faith after Munich....

The Prince is very explicit in repudiating received morality where the conduct of rulers is concerned. A ruler will perish if he is always good; he must be as cunning as a fox and as fierce as a lion....

The tone of the *Discourses*, which are nominally a commentary on Livy, is very different. There are whole chapters which seem almost as if they had been written by Montesquieu; most of the book could have been read with approval by an eighteenth-century liberal. The doctrine of checks and balances is set forth explicitly. Princes, nobles, and people should all have a part in the Constitution; "then these three powers will keep each other reciprocally in check...."

The love of "liberty," and the theory of checks and balances, came to the Renaissance from antiquity, and to modern times largely from the Renaissance, though also directly from antiquity. This aspect of Machiavelli is at least as important as the more famous "immoral" doctrines of *The Prince*.

It is to be noted that Machiavelli never bases any political argument on Christian or biblical grounds. Medieval writers had a conception of "legitimate" power, which was that of the Pope and the Emperor, or derived from them. Northern writers, even so late as Locke, argue as to what happened in the Garden of Eden, and think that they can thence derive proofs that certain kinds of power are "legitimate." In Machiavelli there is no such conception. Power is for those who have the skill to seize it in a free competition. His preference for popular government is not derived from any idea of "rights," but from the observation that popular governments are less cruel, unscrupulous, and inconstant than tyrannies.

Let us try to make a synthesis (which Machiavelli himself did not make) of the "moral" and "immoral" parts of his doctrine. In what follows, I am expressing not my own opinions, but opinions which are explicitly or implicitly his.

There are certain political goods, of which three are specially important: national independence, security, and a well-ordered constitution. The best constitution is one which apportions legal rights among prince, nobles, and people in proportion to their real power, for under such a constitution successful revolutions are difficult and therefore stability is possible; but for considerations of stability, it would be wise to give more power to the people. So far as regards ends.

But there is also, in politics, the question of means. It is futile to pursue a political purpose by methods that are bound to fail; if the end is held good, we must choose means adequate to its achievement. The question of means can be treated in a purely scientific manner, without regard to the goodness or badness of the ends. "Success" means the achievement of your purpose, whatever it may be. If there is a science of success, it can be studied just as well in the successes of the wicked as in those of the good—indeed better, since the examples of successful sinners are more numerous than those of successful saints. But the science, once established, will be just as useful to the saint as to the sinner. For the saint, if he concerns himself with politics, must wish, just as the sinner does, to achieve success.

The question is ultimately one of power. To achieve a political end, power, of one kind or another, is necessary. This plain fact is concealed by slogans, such as "right will prevail" or "the triumph of evil is short-lived." If the side that you think right prevails, that is because it has superior power. It is true that power, often, depends upon opinion, and opinion upon propaganda; it is true, also, that it is an advantage in propaganda to seem more virtuous than your adversary, and that one way of seeming virtuous is to be virtuous. For this reason, it may sometimes happen that victory goes to the side which has the most of what the general public considers to be virtue. We must concede to Machiavelli that this was an important element in the growing power of the Church during the eleventh, twelfth, and thirteenth centuries, as well as in the success of the Reformation in the sixteenth century. But there are important limitations. In the first place, those who have seized power can, by controlling propaganda, cause their party to appear virtuous; no one, for example, could mention the sins of Alexander VI in a New York or Boston public school. In the second place, there are chaotic periods during which obvious knavery frequently succeeds; the period of Machiavelli was one of them. In such times, there tends to be a rapidly growing cynicism, which makes men forgive anything provided it pays. Even in such times, as Machiavelli himself says, it is desirable to present an appearance of virtue before the ignorant public.

This question can be carried a step further. Machiavelli is of opinion that civilized men are almost certain to be unscrupulous egoists. If a man wished nowadays to establish a republic, he says, he would find it easier with mountaineers than with the men of a large city, since the latter would be already corrupted. If a man is an unscrupulous egoist, his wisest line of conduct will depend upon the population with which he has to operate. The Renaissance Church shocked everybody, but it was only north of the Alps that it shocked people enough to produce the Reformation. At the time when Luther began his revolt, the revenue of the papacy was probably larger than it would have been if Alexander VI and Julius II had been more virtuous, and if this is true, it is so because of the cynicism of Reniassance Italy. It follows that politicians will behave better when they depend upon a virtuous population than when they depend upon one which is indifferent to moral considerations; they will also behave better in a community in which their crimes, if any, can be made widely known, than in one in which there is a strict censorship under their control. A certain amount can, of course, always be achieved by hypocrisy, but the amount can be much diminished by suitable institutions.

Machiavelli's political thinking, like that of most of the ancients, is in one respect somewhat shallow. He is occupied with great law givers, such as Lycurgus and Solon, who are supposed to create a community all in one piece, with little regard to what has gone before. The conception of a community as an organic growth, which the statesmen can only affect to a limited extent, is in the main modern, and has been greatly strengthened by the theory of evolution. This conception is not to be found in Machiavelli any more than in Plato.

It might, however, be maintained that the evolutionary view of society, though true in the past, is no longer applicable, but must, for the present and the future, be replaced by a much more mechanistic view. In Russia and Germany new societies have been created, in much the same way as the mythical Lycurgus was supposed to have created the Spartan polity. The ancient law giver was a benevolent myth; the modern law giver is a terrifying reality. The world has become more like that of Machiavelli than it was, and the modern man who hopes to refute his philosophy must think more deeply than seemed necessary in the nineteenth century....

GARRETT MATTINGLY

SOURCE: Garrett Mattingly, "Machiavelli's 'Prince': Political Science or Political Satire?" in *The American Scholar*, Vol. 27, No. 4, Autumn, 1958, pp. 482-91.

[*In the following excerpt, Mattingly proposes that* The Prince *be interpreted as a satire.*]

The notion that this little book [*The Prince*] was meant as a serious, scientific treatise on government contradicts everything we know about Machiavelli's life, about his writings, and about the history of his time.

In the first place, this proposition asks us to believe that Niccolo Machiavelli deliberately wrote a handbook meant to help a tyrant rule the once free people of Florence....

He has left proof of his devotion in the record of his activities and in the state papers in which he spun endless schemes for the defense and aggrandizement of the republic, and constantly preached the same to his superiors. One characteristic quotation is irresistible. The subject is an increase in the defense budget that Machiavelli's masters were reluctant to vote. He reminds them with mounting impatience that only strong states are respected by their neighbors and that their neglect of military strength in the recent past has cost them dear, and he ends with anything but detached calm: "Other people learn from the perils of their neighbors, you will not even learn from your own, nor trust yourselves, nor recognize the time you are losing and have lost. I tell you fortune will not alter the sentence it has pronounced unless you alter your behavior. Heaven will not and cannot preserve those bent on their own ruin. But I cannot believe it will come to this, seeing that you are free Florentines and have your liberty in your own hands. In the end I believe you will have the same regard for your freedom that men always have who are born free and desire to live free."

Only a man who cared deeply for the independence of his city would use language like this to his employers. But Machiavelli gave an even more impressive proof of his disinterested patriotism. After fourteen years in high office, in a place where the opportunities for dipping into the public purse and into the pockets of his compatriots and of those foreigners he did business with were practically unlimited (among other duties he acted as paymaster-general of the army), Machiavelli retired from public life as poor as when he had entered it. Later he was to refer to this record with pride, but also with a kind of rueful astonishment; and, indeed, if this was not a unique feat in his day, it was a very rare one....

Machiavelli emerged from prison in mid-March, 1513. Most people believe that *The Prince* was finished by December. I suppose it is possible to imagine that a man who has seen his country enslaved, his life's work wrecked and his own career with it, and has, for good measure, been tortured within an inch of his life should thereupon go home and write a book intended to teach his enemies the proper way to maintain themselves, writing all the time, remember, with the passionless objectivity of a scientist in a laboratory. It must be possible to imagine such behavior, because Machiavelli scholars do imagine it and accept it without a visible tremor. But it is a little difficult for the ordinary mind to compass.

The difficulty is increased by the fact that this acceptance of tyranny seems to have been a passing phase. Throughout the rest of his life Machiavelli wrote as a republican and moved mainly in republican circles....

The notion that *The Prince* is what it pretends to be, a scientific manual for tyrants, has to contend not only against Machiavelli's life but against his writings, as, of course, everyone who wants to use *The Prince* as a centerpiece in an exposition of Machiavelli's political thought has recognized. Ever since Herder, the standard explanation has been that in the corrupt conditions of sixteenth-century Italy only a prince could create a strong state capable of expansion. The trouble with this is that it was chiefly because they widened their boundaries that Machiavelli preferred republics. In the *Discorsi* he wrote,

> We know by experience that states have never signally increased either in territory or in riches except under a free government. The cause is not far to seek, since it is the well-being not of individuals but of the community which makes the state great, and without question this universal well-being is nowhere secured save in a republic.... Popular rule is always better than the rule of princes.

This is not just a casual remark. It is the main theme of the *Discorsi* and the basic assumption of all but one of Machiavelli's writings, as it was the basic assumption of his political career.

There is another way in which *The Prince* is a puzzling anomaly. In practically everything else Machiavelli wrote, he displayed the sensitivity and tact of the developed literary temperament. He was delicately aware of the tastes and probable reactions of his public. No one could have written that magnificent satiric soliloquy of Fra Timotheo in *Mandragola*, for instance, who had not an instinctive feeling for the response of an audience. But the effect of the publication of *The Prince* on the first several generations of its readers in Italy (outside of Florence) and in the rest of Europe was shock. It horrified, repelled and fascinated like a Medusa's head. A large part of the shock was caused, of course, by the cynical immorality of some of the proposals, but instead of appeasing revulsion and insinuating his new proposals as delicately as possible, Machiavelli seems to delight in intensifying the shock and deliberately employing devices to heighten it. Of these not the least effective is the way *The Prince* imitates, almost parodies, one of the best known and most respected literary forms of the three preceding centuries, the handbook of advice to princes. This literary type was enormously popular. Its exemplars ran into the hundreds of titles of which a few, like St. Thomas' *De Regno* and Erasmus' *Institutio principis christiani* are not quite unknown today. In some ways, Machiavelli's little treatise was just like all the other "Mirrors of Princes"; in other ways it was a diabolical burlesque of all of them, like a political Black Mass.

The shock was intensified again because Machiavelli deliberately addressed himself primarily to princes who have newly acquired their principalities and do not owe them either to inheritance or to the free choice of their countrymen. The short and ugly word for this kind of prince is "tyrant." Machiavelli never quite uses the word except in illustrations from classical antiquity, but he seems to delight in dancing all around it until even the dullest of his readers could not mistake his meaning. Opinions about the relative merits of republics and monarchies varied during the Renaissance, depending mainly upon where one lived, but about tyrants there was only one opinion. Cristoforo Landino, Lorenzo the Magnificent's teacher and client, stated the usual view in his commentary on Dante, written when Niccolo Machiavelli was a child. When he came to comment on Brutus and Cassius in the lowest circle of hell, Landino wrote: "Surely it was extraordinary cruelty to inflict such severe punishment on those who faced death to deliver their country from slavery, a deed for which, if they had been Christians, they would have merited the most honored seats in the highest heaven. If we consult the laws of any well-constituted republic, we shall find them to decree no greater reward to anyone than to the man who kills the tyrant." So said the Italian Renaissance with almost unanimous voice. If Machiavelli's friends were meant to read the manuscript of *The Prince* and if they took it at face value—an objective study of how to be a successful tyrant offered as advice to a member of the species— they can hardly have failed to be deeply shocked. And if the manuscript was meant for the eye of young Giuliano de Medici alone, he can hardly have been pleased to find it blandly assumed that he was one of a class of whom his father's tutor had written that the highest duty of a good citizen was to kill them.

The literary fame of *The Prince* is due, precisely, to its shocking quality, so if the book was seriously meant as a scientific manual, it owes its literary reputation to an artistic blunder....

Perhaps nobody should be rash enough today to call *The Prince* a satire, not in the teeth of all the learned opinion to the contrary. But when one comes to think of it, what excellent sense the idea makes! However you define "satire"—and I understand that critics are still without a thoroughly satisfactory definition—it must include the intention to denounce, expose or deride someone or something, and it is to be distinguished from mere didactic condemnation and invective (when it can be distinguished at all) by the employment of such devices as irony, sarcasm and ridicule. It need not be provocative of laughter; I doubt whether many people ever laughed or even smiled at the adventures of Gulliver among the Yahoos. And though satire admits of, and in fact always employs, exaggeration and overemphasis, the author, to be effective, must not appear to be, and in fact need not be, conscious that this is so. When Dryden wrote, "The rest to some faint meaning make pretense / But Shadwell never deviates into sense," he may have been conscious of some overstatement, but he was conveying his considered criticism of Shadwell's poetry. And when Pope called "Lord Fanny" "this painted child of dirt that stinks and strings," the language may be violent, but who can doubt that this is how Pope felt? Indeed the satirist seems to put forth his greatest powers chiefly when goaded by anger, hatred and savage indignation. If Machiavelli wrote *The Prince* out of the fullness of these emotions rather than out of the dispassionate curiosity of the scientist or out of a base willingness to toady to the destroyers of his country's liberty, then one can understand why the sentences crack like a whip, why the words bite and burn like acid, and why the whole style has a density and impact unique among his writings.

To read *The Prince* as satire not only clears up puzzles and resolves contradictions; it gives a new dimension and meaning to passages unremarkable before. Take the place in the dedication that runs "just as those who paint landscapes must seat themselves below in the plains to see the mountains, and high in the mountains to see the plains, so to understand the nature of the people one must be a prince, and to understand the nature a prince, one must be one of the people." In the usual view, this is a mere rhetorical flourish, but the irony, once sought, is easy to discover, for Machiavelli, in fact, takes both positions. The people can only see the prince as, by nature and necessity, false, cruel, mean and hypocritical. The prince, from his lofty but precarious perch, dare not see the people as other than they are described in Chapter Seventeen: "ungrateful, fickle, treacherous, cowardly and greedy. As long as you succeed they are yours entirely. They will offer you their blood, property, lives and children when you do not need them. When you do need them, they will turn against you." Probably Machiavelli really believed that this, or something like it, happened to the human nature of a tyrant and his subjects. But the view, like its expression, is something less than objective and dispassionate, and the only lesson it has for princes would seem to be: "Run for your life!"

Considering the brevity of the book, the number of times its princely reader is reminded, as in the passage just quoted, that his people will overthrow him at last is quite remarkable. Cities ruled in the past by princes easily accustom themselves to a change of masters, Machiavelli says in Chapter Five, but "in republics there is more vitality, greater hatred and more desire for vengeance. They cannot forget their lost liberty, so that the safest way is to destroy them—or to live there." He does not say what makes that safe. And most notably, with savage irony, "the duke [Borgia] was so able and laid such firm foundations ... that the Romagna [after Alexander VI's death] waited for him more than a month." This is as much as to put Leo X's brother on notice that without papal support he can expect short shrift. If the Romagna, accustomed to tyranny, waited only a month before it rose in revolt, how long will Florence wait? Tactlessness like this is unintelligible unless it is deliberate, unless these are not pedantic blunders but sarcastic ironies, taunts flung at the Medici, incitements to the Florentines.

Only in a satire can one understand the choice of Cesare Borgia as the model prince. The common people of Tuscany could not have had what they could expect of a prince's rule made clearer than by the example of this bloodstained buffoon whose vices, crimes and follies had been the scandal of Italy, and the conduct of whose brutal, undisciplined troops had so infuriated the Tuscans that when another band of them crossed their frontier, the peasants fell upon them and tore them to pieces. The Florentine aristocrats on whom Giovanni and cousin Giulio were relying to bridge the transition to despotism would have shared the people's revulsion to Cesare, and they may have been rendered somewhat more thoughtful by the logic of the assumption that nobles were more dangerous to a tyrant than commoners and should be dealt with as Cesare had dealt with the petty lords of the Romagna. Moreover, they could scarcely have avoided noticing the advice to use some faithful servant to terrorize the rest, and then to sacrifice him to escape the obloquy of his conduct, as Cesare had sacrificed Captain Ramiro. As for the gentle, mild-mannered, indolent Giuliano de Medici himself, he was the last man to be attracted by the notion of imitating the Borgia. He wanted no more than to occupy the same social position in Florence that his magnificent father had held, and not even that if it was too much trouble.

Besides, in the days of the family's misfortunes, Giuliano had found shelter and hospitality at the court of Guidobaldo de Montrefeltre. Guiliano lived at

Urbino for many years (there is a rather charming picture of him there in Castiglione's *Il Cortegiano*), and all his life he cherished deep gratitude and a strong affection for Duke Guidobaldo. He must have felt, then, a special loathing for the foreign ruffian who had betrayed and plundered his patron, and Machiavelli must have known that he did. Only a wish to draw the most odious comparison possible, only a compulsion to wound and insult, could have lead Machiavelli to select the Borgia as the prime exemplar in his "Mirror of Princes."

There is one last famous passage that reads differently if we accept *The Prince* as satire. On any other hypothesis, the final exhortation to free Italy from the barbarians sounds at best like empty rhetoric, at worst like calculating but stupid flattery. Who could really believe that the lazy, insipid Giuliano or his petty, vicious successor were the liberators Italy awaited? But if we have heard the mordant irony and sarcasm of the preceding chapters and detected the overtones of hatred and despair, then this last chapter will be charged with an irony turned inward, the bitter mockery of misdirected optimism. For before the Florentine republic had been gored to death by Spanish pikes, Machiavelli had believed, as he was to believe again, that a free Florentine republic could play the liberator's role. Perhaps, since he was all his life a passionate idealist, blind to reality when his desires were strong, Machiavelli may not have given up that wild hope even when he wrote *The Prince*.

HANNA FENICHEL PITKIN

SOURCE: Hanna Fenichel Pitkin, in her *Fortune Is a Woman: Gender and Politics in the Thought of Niccolo Machiavelli*, University of California Press, 1984, 354 p.

[*In the following excerpt, Pitkin examines several of Machiavelli's works, arguing that while Machiavelli's "themes are political and public, . . . the imagery in which they are expressed is often personal and sexual."*]

Though his explicit concerns are overwhelmingly political and public, Machiavelli's writings show a persistent preoccupation with manhood. What matters for both security and glory, for both individuals and states, is autonomy; and autonomy constantly refers back to psychic and personal concerns. Beginning with the obvious, Machiavelli's most characteristic, central, and frequently invoked concept is that of *virtu*, a term by no means regularly translatable by "virtue," and certainly not equivalent to virtue in the Christian sense. Though it can sometimes mean virtue, *virtu* tends mostly to connote energy, effectiveness, virtuosity. Burckhardt described it as "a union of force and ability, something that can be summed up by force alone, if by force one means human, not mechanical force: will, and therefore force of ability." The word derives from the Latin *virtus*, and thus from *vir*, which means "man." *Virtu* is thus manliness, those qualities found in a "real man." Furthermore, if *virtu* is Machiavelli's favorite quality, *effeminato* (effiminate) is one of his most frequent and scathing epithets. Nothing is more contemptible or more dangerous for a man than to be like a woman or, for that matter, a baby or an animal — that is, passive and dependent.

The themes are political and public, yet the imagery in which they are expressed is often personal and sexual. Political, military, and sexual achievement are somehow merged. Political power and military conquest are eroticized, and eros is treated as a matter of conquest and domination. In Machiavelli's plays, love is discussed in the military and political terms of attack and defense, the rousing of troops, and the mastery of states. The city is a woman and the citizens are her lovers. Commentators often see Italy, in the famous last chapter of *The Prince,* as a woman "beaten, despoiled, lacerated, devastated, subject to every sort of barbarous cruelty and arrogance," who will welcome a rescuing prince as "her redeemer," but also as her lover, "with what gratitude, with what tears!" And of course fortune is explicitly called "a woman," favoring the young, bold, and manly, to be confronted with whatever *virtu* a man can muster.

But what does being a man really mean, and how does one go about it? Machiavelli's writings are deeply divided on these questions, presenting conflicting images of manly autonomy. I shall begin by delineating two such images, one founded mainly in his own political experience, the other in his reading and fantasy about the ancient world: "the fox" and "the forefathers."

At the outset of both of his most important political works, Machiavelli ascribes his knowledge to two sources: "lengthy experience with recent matters" and "continual reading of ancient ones." To begin with the former and the vision of manliness to which it gives rise, what can be learned from experience depends of course on the nature of that experience (just as what can be learned from reading depends on the works read)....

Within this world, one can discern an ideal that becomes centrally (though not, as will emerge, exclusively) formative of Machiavelli's understanding of politics and autonomy. The ideal is of a manliness aiming not toward the actual, overt rewards of power, but rather toward indirect gratifications: the pleasures of identification with great men, the secret pride of being smarter than they and able to manipulate them.

One way to make that ideal of manliness accessible is through an examination of Machiavelli's greatest play (and the only one that is entirely original), **Mandragola.** It is a bawdy comedy, whose young hero, Callimaco, has lost his heart to the beautiful Lucretia. Unfortunately, she is already married to a foolish and aged lawyer, Nicia. But Callimaco's friend, Ligurio, invents a plot to help him win Lucretia. The marriage is childless, and Nicia desperately wants a son and heir. Ligurio convinces him that his wife will conceive if she drinks a potion of mandrake root, but that the first man to sleep with her after she drinks it will surely die. So Nicia is tricked into letting Callimaco sleep with Lucretia after she drinks the potion. The plot is successful, Lucretia falls in love with Callimaco, and the lovers agree to continue their illicit relationship, and to marry after old Nicia dies. It is a sordid story, without a single really admirable character; yet in the end everyone is, in a sense, better off. Nicia will have an heir, Callimaco and Lucretia have each other. As Ligurio says, contemplating his plan unfolding, "I believe that good is what does good to the largest number, and with which the highest number are pleased."

If one were to select one character in this play with whom Machiavelli might best be identified, the choice seems clear enough. It is not, despite the possible pun on his name, Nicia, nor, as one might conventionally suppose, the hero Callimaco. Instead, it is Ligurio, the author of the plot. Ligurio is an erstwhile "marriage broker" who has fallen on hard times and taken to "begging suppers and dinners"; he has become "a parasite, the darling of Malice." Not only are both Ligurio and Machiavelli authors of the play's plot, and both of them negotiators and go-betweens, but the play's prologue stresses the parallel by identifying the playwright as a man now constrained to "play the servant to such as can wear a better cloak than he," writing comedies only because he "has been cut off from showing other powers with other deeds." Like Ligurio, he is on intimate terms with malice, which was "his earliest art"; he is an expert at "how to find fault" and "does not stand in awe of anybody" in the Italian-speaking world.

The suggestion that **Mandragola,** in some ways parallels **The Prince**—with Machiavelli as counselor in the latter resembling Ligurio in the former—has been made repeatedly by Machiavelli scholars. Like Ligurio, Machiavelli seeks to manipulate the prince into seizing power—for both the prince's glory and the good of Italy. If we were to succeed, the prince would get the actual power just as Callimaco gets the girl: poor despoiled Lady Italy as she appears in the last chapter of **The Prince,** eager to receive him so that on her he may father a new state and perpetuate his name. Machiavelli himself is pimp to the union, rearranging present disorder and conflicting desires in a way that leaves all concerned better off; the real credit should be his.

The point, however, is not establishing the parallel between Ligurio and his creator, so much as exploring its meaning and what it can teach about their shared role or character. One might, for instance, pose this naive question: why would someone creating a fantasy imagine himself in a subordinate role rather than that of the hero who gets the girl? At the close of her night with the hero, Lucretia tells him that she loves him, having been tricked into doing what she would never otherwise have consented to do—tricked by "your cleverness, my husband's stupidity, my mother's folly, and my confessor's rascality." But it was not Callimaco's cleverness that won him access to his lady; actually he isn't very bright. Ligurio is the clever one who deserves the credit, and thus the lady's love. Why, then, does he not take her for himself? Why is he content to serve Callimaco?

Or, to put the question in a different way, instead of calling Callimaco the hero, should one not say the play is thoroughly problematic with respect to heroism? Callimaco gets the material reward, and gets the credit in the heroine's eyes, but Lingurio deserves the credit and receives it in the eyes of the audience. Yet Machiavelli also mocks and abuses Ligurio in the play, calling him a parasite and a glutton. It would not be difficult to read **Mandragola** as an Oedipal tale, like a hundred other bedroom farces in which a foolish old husband is cuckolded. The old man is bested by the young man, his wife becomes the young man's lover. In this vein, one might even suggest that the real point of the young man's victory is symbolic rather than physical—the conquest not of Lucretia but of her husband. Such a reading finds support in the fact that the old man is, like the playwright's own father, a lawyer. But is it not remarkable that in Machiavelli's Oedipal tale it takes *two* young men to do the job? It is as if the hero of this play were split into a matched pair, two halves of a hero, each incomplete without the other: the clever but somehow sexless adviser, agent of the victory, and the physically virile but rather dull advisee. Indeed, Ligurio tells Callimaco that they are (figuratively) of one blood, twins. Is such splitting the price paid for an Oedipal victory in Machiavelli's world?

Perhaps such speculations seem irrelevant and excessively psychological. The more precise question of why Ligurio might be content to serve Callimaco instead of furthering his own cause is addressed explicitly within the play. . . .

Despite the disparaging things said in **Mandragola** about Ligurio, he represents a character type, a pattern of skill and achievement that is familiar and much admired in Machiavelli's world. It is a pattern characteristic of Machiavelli himself in important ways, though never exhausting his aims and ideals as a man. To make this suggestion more plausible, we might tentatively revive the old cliche of national character, as it is treated, for instance, in John Clarke Adams and Paulo Barile's *The Government of Republican Italy*. Opening, as many such texts do, with sections on the Italian land and people, it then lists as one of the "main characteristics of the Mediterranean culture . . . an inordinate desire to be a '*furbo*' coupled with an obsessive fear of being '*fesso*.' " *Furbo* is described as "an untranslatable word," characterizing Renard the Fox in medieval French stories and Jeha in Arab tales, and meaning something like "skill in employing ruses that are usually, but not necessarily, dishonest." In such a culture, everybody wants to be outstandingly *furbo*, and a man may be scrupulously moral in his relations with family and friends, yet take pride in his ability to cheat someone outside his intimate circle or, better still, to defraud an organization or public agency. . . .

Even small trickery can be a source of pride if it is done with particular skill or against a worthy opponent. "A *furbo* often gets more satisfaction out of taking an unfair advantage in a single business deal than from making an honest profit in a series of deals with the same man."

The counterpart of the desire to be *furbo* is the fear—perfectly reasonable in a society where each is trying to outfox the others—of being a *fesso*: the person whom the *furbo* cheats, someone whose lack of character or ability condemns him to be a victim. The fear of being *fesso*, the textbook adds, "leads to an inordinate amount of mutual suspicion and naturally makes amicable or honest relations . . . exceptional" outside of the immediate family. . . .

Call him the fox, then, after Renard—this *furbo* who runs the show from behind the scenes through his cleverness; who never himself wins the girl or the glory but takes his pleasure in the secret knowledge of his own surpassing foxiness; and whose pride and skill lie in the ability to deceive without being deceived. Cynic and doubter, nobody's fool, inside dopester, master of maneuver, the fox struggles to survive and even to do good in a world where no one can be trusted. The metaphor of the fox is not central in Machiavelli's writing, though it does appear occasionally. . . . [In] **The Prince,** the fox appears in the famous passage asserting that a successful prince must know how to fight corrupt men with the weapons of corruption, to fight animals like an animal when necessary. Since a prince must sometimes

> play the animal well, he chooses among the beasts the fox and the lion, because the lion does not protect himself from traps; the fox does not protect himself from the wolves. The prince must be a fox, therefore, to recognize the traps and a lion to frighten the wolves.

Despite this unequivocal recommendation, much of the rest of the book suggests that Machiavelli intends not for the prince to be a fox himself but for him to employ a foxy counselor (Machiavelli himself is available). The fox is the clever one without overt power or glory. He remains inconspicuous. . . .

The fox prides himself on his ability to see the unsavory truth and on the courage to tell it. But he also prides himself on his ability to dissemble. Is there a conflict here? Perhaps not if he is employed as a diplomat for a government of his choice and in a city he loves, for then the world is divided between friends and (potential) enemies. The diplomat must convey *la verita effettuale* ["the actual truth"] to his superiors and deceive enemies abroad. In modern terms, one might say that diplomacy can provide a relatively stable level of gratification for a fox's conflicting psychological needs, which makes possible a "partially sublimated discharge" of drives and impulses and allows a "corresponding reduction in the warding-off activities of the ego." That is, when employed as a diplomat for a government he supports, a fox can both unmask and dissemble, know when to do each, and achieve both personal satisfaction and external rewards. And so it may have been for Machiavelli: through his diligence and skill, he supported his dependents and served both the Florentine Republic and his friend and leader. . . .

The fox is an underling, and it is characteristic of underlings both to despise and to glorify their masters. They are likely to resent their subordination to "such as can wear a better cloak," and to entertain fantasies of revenge or of displacing the master; but they may also derive gratification from their association with "so great a master," or at least from fantasies of serving some imaginary great master. To be an underling means to endure continual frustration and deprivation, and thus to have continual reason for envy and resentment. The resentment born of frustrated ambition is what makes Ligurio "the darling of Malice," and no doubt it is also what makes "the author" of *Mandragola* so skilled at "finding fault," his "earliest art." But underlings cannot afford too much of such angry feelings, or at least they must learn to contain and disguise them through self-control, and through the safe and indirect devices of humor and wit, paradox and ambiguity.

The device of humor and "playing the fool" can be particularly useful here, as a safe and even rewarding outlet for malice. For the fool, as everyone knows, is exempt from the usual rules of decorum and courtesy; he is not a serious competitor and therefore can say what is forbidden to others: the fool may insult the king and be praised for his wit to boot. Indeed, the court fool's special license is traditionally symbolized by the jester's cap, whose jagged points figure an inverted crown. Machiavelli himself was noted among his friends as a jokester and raconteur, and his writings frequently display a mordant, satirical wit. Commentators often have difficulty deciding when Machiavelli is being serious and when satirical. He himself comments in a letter to a friend by quoting Petrarch: "If sometimes I laugh or sing, I do it because I have just this one way for expressing my anxious sorrow."

Playing the fool, moreover, can lead to better things; it can be a prudent form of self-concealment while one awaits the right time for revenge or even for an open seizure of power. Thus the jester can not only express his anger indirectly in the present, but can also comfort himself with fantasies of later, more direct expressions. . . .

Themes and fantasies of inversion, or reversing convention or established authority, are pervasive in Machiavelli's work, both in its substantive content and in its style. Again and again he takes up an established form, a conventional assumption, a familiar doctrine, only to reverse it. *The Prince* inverts the moralistic outlook of the medieval "mirror of princes" literature it culminates, teaching the opposite of conventional moral precepts: that apparent kindness can turn out to be cruel, that apparent stinginess in a prince amounts to liberality, that the conventional keeping of faith can be a betrayal of public trust. The passage about the lion and the fox already cited appears to be a similar reversal of a passage in Cicero. More generally, Machiavelli often makes use of Christian themes for his own secular or anti-Christian purposes, speaking of "redemption," "rebirth," "sin," all in transmuted form. . . .

The inversion of conventional hierarchies or established rule is also a familiar theme in many of Machiavelli's literary works. In *Belfagor* one finds a kingdom of devils, in [*The Golden Ass*] a kingdom of women ruled by a woman, and in *Mandragola* Ligurio calls Lucretia "fit to rule a kingdom." The rules Machiavelli draws up for a hypothetical "pleasure company" are direct reversals of conventional fashion and manners: no member may tell the truth or speak well of another; the minority is to win in any vote; whoever reveals a secret must do so again within two days or incur "the penalty of always having to do everything backwards." . . . Even more significant, though less obvious, is the role of imitation and inversion in Machiavelli's literary style; he often prefers adapting or reversing in inherited form to following it or creating a new one. Besides *The Prince*, there is his play *Clizia*, essentially a translation of a play by Plautus, though its prologue explicitly reverses the announced theme of the ancient play. *The Art of War* derives its form from Ciceronian dialogue, its content from ancient writers on warfare like Vegetius, yet with a new twist. [*The Golden Ass*] owes its form to Apuleius and Plutarch, and many of its lines play off of Dante. *Mandragola* is probably an inversion of an incident central to Livy's history of Rome. And of course the *Discourses on Livy* themselves take the form of a commentary on an ancient authority, though Machiavelli often uses Livy to prove his own, somewhat different doctrines. It is a thoroughly foxy way of both disguising and presenting the self, promoting its goals from behind another ostensible authority: simultaneously serving and assaulting authority, identifying with the master's power and prestige while scheming to manipulate and use him for one's own purposes. The fox may wish to overthrow authority, but it may never come to that, for he adapts for survival in his situation. Whether or not Machiavelli sometimes imagined himself as Cesare Borgia or Brutus, in his life and in his writing he remained an underling, a go-between who transmitted the ideas and adopted the forms of others for his own purposes—an intellectual Ligurio, as it were.

And yet Machiavelli the playwright speaks of Ligurio with contempt. But of course he often speaks of himself with contempt as well, and of those associated with him, those concerning whom he might want to say "we": we Florentines, we Italians, we modern men. "The present age in every way is degenerate," he says, over and over; the Italians have become the "scorn of the world." ". . . I and my kind—we are poor, ambitious, cowardly." Perhaps it is only an objective assessment in a list that is, after all, flattering to hardly any European nation. But perhaps it is also a scornful self-assessment by a fox in a world of foxes; as Hale has suggested, Machiavelli's letters indicate "some core of reserve, some disappointment or self-disgust."

If a person, an action, or a pattern of character seems

contemptible, that implies the existence of some standard against which it has been measured and found wanting. By what standard might Machiavelli have judged his best skill, his pride and delight, as also a source of shame, a sign of degeneracy or a lack of manhood? That standard is found in Machiavelli's second great source of knowledge, his reading, and particularly his reading in ancient works....

Returning to *Mandragola* one can now see that Machiavelli has there created a circumscribed world — a world of foxes and their prey, of *furbi* and *fessi*, a world devoid of *virtu*. For that reason, it is a mistake simply to identify *Mandragola* with *The Prince* and both with the whole of Machiavelli's teachings, as some commentators do.... Social relations in the play are "in essence ... exploitative." But a world devoid of *virtu* cannot be the political world of Machiavelli's theorizing. He may well have been a fox, but he was not merely a fox. Indeed, the play's prologue says explicitly that the present age is "degenerate" by comparison with "ancient worth [*virtu*]." And it is surely not pure coincidence that the play's heroine, Lucretia, bears the same name as an ancient lady central to the establishment of the Roman Republic, as described by Livy.

The ancient Lucretia, a virtuous wife, kills herself after being raped by one of the sons of the Roman king. Brutus, who had been playing the fool, waiting for his opportunity, uses the occasion to arouse popular indignation against the monarchy, overthrow it, and establish a republic. In both Livy's account and Machiavelli's *Mandragola* a virtuous wife is sexually conquered. In both, the man who takes her has first heard of her while abroad, in a conversation in which men have boasted competively about the merits of their women. In both tales, old and formally legitimate authorities that are substantively inadequate are displaced by new, younger, and better ones. Yet nothing could be more different than the two sexual conquests, the two overthrowings of authority, the "virtues" of the ancient and modern world. In *Mandragola*, the violated wife does not kill herself but happily adapts to an adulterous life; is it for that sensible flexibility that Machiavelli (through Ligurio) calls her "wise" and "fit to rule a kingdom"? A fox would surely mock at a conception of virtue that brings a woman to suicide simply because she has been raped under the threat of death and because her husband's effort to absolve her of blame have failed. Yet the ancient rape of Lucretia led to the transformation of a social world, the birth of a republic of true *virtu*. The modern comic version leads only to the birth of a child, in a world that remains as corrupt as before. Though the cuckolded husband tells Lucretia after her adulterous night that "it's exactly as though you were born a second time," one knows that no regeneration — either Christian or classical — has taken place. *Mandragola* is not a recapitulation of the tale of Lucretia and Brutus in ancient Rome, but a satire on or an inversion of it.

Once again it is ancient Rome that supplies the standard by which modern times and modern people are measured and found wanting. Rome was the culture that invented the concept of *virtus* and best exemplified its pursuit. It was the very model of masculinity and autonomy. As a state, Rome kept itself strong, independent, and healthy; it grew and prospered among states and won its battles. And the Roman citizenry exemplified *virtu* as well, being courageous and public-spirited, and serving in a citizen militia that was sufficiently disciplined and effective to protect their collective autonomy. Here was an uncorrupted community of real men, competent to take care of themselves without being dependent on anyone else, sharing in a fraternal, participatory civic life that made them self-governing. Nor was their public-spiritedness a spineless, deferential uniformity; in their domestic politics, as in their relations abroad, they were strong and manly: fighters. Political conflict — that "fighting by laws" of which only true men are capable — was what made and kept Rome free, healthy, and honorable.

In this respect, Rome stands in marked contrast to modern Florence, where all is weakness and cowardice, privatization and corruption. There is plenty of domestic political conflict, but it is factional, divisive, destructive of power and manliness; it is fighting in the manner of beasts. A world of foxes and their victims is incapable of true manliness or virtuous citizenship, for its members cannot trust each other and cannot genuinely subscribe to any standards or ideals. They are essentially *privatized* — that is, absorbed in their immediate and direct relationship, unable to perceive the larger whole, incapable of sustaining a public, political life. For a public life depends on a living structure of relationships among citizens, relationships that extend beyond the personal and face-to-face to the impersonal, large-scale, and remote....

It will help to recall the special significance that ancient Rome had for Machiavelli's time, and the distinctive character of ancient Roman society, since both are intimately bound up with paternity. The Romans, after all, were not an ideal that Renaissance Italians picked arbitrarily from the catalogue of past greatness. For Machiavelli and his audience, the Romans were literally forefathers. Where Florence stood, the Roman state had once ruled; the ancestors of the men of Florence had been Roman citizens. Rome had founded Florence. To be sure, the questions of exactly who founded Florence, when it was founded, and what relationship the city had to Rome in ancient times are a central and revealing problem for Machiavelli. But the ambiguities and problems arise within an imagery of fathers and children, not as an alternative to this imagery....

All of the qualities of character central to the Roman table of virtues had to do with this original, sacred patriarchal founding and its transmission: *pietas,* which we call piety, but which to the Romans meant reverence for the past and proper submission to ancestors; *gravitas,* the ability to bear the sacred weight of the past, like armor, with courage and self-mastery; *dignitas,* a manner worthy of one's task and station; *constantia,* to guarantee that one never strays or wavers from the ancient path. All of these together make up Roman *virtus:* that quality of stern, serious, strong-minded, courageous manliness that despises pleasure and playfulness, cleaving to duty and strenuous effort. With their strongly patriarchal households and ancestor-oriented religion, this society of soldiers, builders, lawyers, and administrators proves the very model of significant (fore)fatherhood. Often on the verge of being pompous but never frivolous, perhaps stolid but never petty, they were always a little larger than life. Add to this Roman self-conception the Renaissance glorification of all things ancient, and one begins to see how Rome and the ancients might serve as an alternative model of manhood that puts the fox to shame. By comparison with a forefather, a fox is impotent and contemptible; a forefather need not stoop to the weapons of a fox, for he can put his imprint on the world openly and directly.

Yet the model of the forefather is not really a single, coherent image but is deeply divided into two visions of manhood, as much in conflict with each other as with the image of the fox. On the one hand, there is a singular forefather as founder, whose potent generativity transforms beasts into men; on the other hand, there are the forefathers of Roman republican citizenship, the members of a self-governing community who fight by laws. The images differ as much as paternity differs from fraternity, as uniqueness differs from mutuality, as unanimity differs from conflict....

The seemingly exclusively masculine world of Machiavelli's political writings, where men contend in the arena of history, is actually dominated or at least continually threatened from behind the scenes by dimly perceived, haunting feminine figures of overwhelming power. The contest among the men turns out to be, in crucial ways, their shared struggle against that power. The feminine constitutes "the other" for Machiavelli, opposed to manhood and autonomy in all their senses: to maleness, to adulthood, to humaneness, and to politics....

[At] the same time as they are contemptible, foolish, and weak, women also somehow possess mysterious and dangerous powers; they constitute a threat to men, both personally and politically. Looking particularly at Machiavelli's fiction, one might say that these mysterious and dangerous powers seem to be of two distinct kinds, the one corresponding to young or unmarried women or daughters, the other to older women, wives, mothers, matrons. Often the two types of women appear in linked pairs: daughter and mother, servant and queen, or beautiful virgin who is transformed into shrewish wife.

The young women or daughters are, almost without exception, depicted as sex objects, in the proper sense of that term: they are beautiful, desirable as possessions, potentially sources of the greatest pleasure for men. They are somehow simultaneously both virginal or chaste and passionate or potentially capable of sexual abandon. But they are passive, and themselves scarcely persons at all. They have no desires or plans of their own, initiate no deliberate action, are not significant agents in the world. They are objects of the men's desire, conquest, or possession. As desirable objects, however, they do have great "power" of a sort to move and hold men; without meaning to or actually doing anything, they are the central force that makes the plot move forward. Their power is like the power of gold; or, as the priest says in *Mandragola,* "he who deals with them gets profit and vexation together. But it's a fact that there's no honey without flies."

Lucretia, the "heroine" of *Mandragola,* is not totally devoid of personality or characterizations, yet what we learn about her is inconsistent and puzzling. On the one hand, she is the paragon of virtue and chastity and must be so for purposes of the plot, both to make her desirable and to make her inaccessible. Thus her "beauty and manners" are so exemplary that men who hear of her are "spellbound"; she is a "cautious and good" woman, "very chaste and a complete stranger to love dealings." She kneels praying for hours at night and has already successfully defended her virtue against the advances of lecherous friars. Her character is so pure and steadfast that no servant in her house would dare to plot against her or take bribes; her husband is certain she would never consent to any illicit scheme. Indeed, when she hears of Ligurio's plan she objects strenuously to the "sin" and "shame" of it, as well as to the idea of taking an innocent man's life. In short, she is, as Ligurio says, "virtuous, courteous, and fit to rule a kingdom." Yet this paragon of virtue not only turns out to be so malleable in the hands of her foolish husband, wicked mother, and a corrupt priest that she agrees to commit an obvious sin (which may still be within the bounds of credulity) but is transformed after one night with her lover into a resolute and competent adultress who, without any pang of conscience, knows just how to arrange things so that she and her lover may continue to cuckold her husband as long as he lives. As the characterization of a real person, a person in her own right, this is hard to accept. As an account of an object of desire and action whose contradictory characteristics make the plot move forward, however, it makes fairly obvious sense.

This somewhat inconsistent image of the romantic heroine is not, of course, unique to Machiavelli; it is, indeed, a stock image for many comedies. Yet Machiavelli's ambiguity about Lucretia runs deeper than the convention. There is the question, already raised, of her relationship to the ancient, historical Lucretia, suggesting that *Mandragola* plays out as farce, in relation to family life, what Livy relates as heroic tragedy in relation to ancient Roman political life. The modern Lucretia is a paragon of virtue, yet easily corrupted; the ancient one, though she knows that "only my body has been violated. My heart is innocent," nevertheless kills herself as a public example and insists on taking her "punishment...."

SOURCES FOR FURTHER STUDY

Adams, Robert M. "Machiavelli Now and Here: An Essay for the First World." *The American Scholar* 44, No. 3 (Summer 1975): 365-81.

   Briefly summarizes past reactions to Machiavelli's ideals and determines their validity and significance.

Adeney, Douglas. "Machiavelli and Political Morals." In *Political Thinkers,* edited by David Muschamp, pp. 51-65. London: Macmillan, 1986.

   Surveys Machiavelli's major political writings.

Anglo, Sydney. *Machiavelli: A Dissection.* London: Victor Gollancz, 1969, 300 p.

   Learned, insightful study of Machiavelli's works.

Fleisher, Martin, ed. *Machiavelli and the Nature of Political Thought.* New York: Atheneum, 1972, 307 p.

   Seven essays on various aspects of Machiavelli's thought by such essayists as J. G. A. Pocock, Brayton Polka, and Harvey C. Mansfield, Jr.

Pocock. J. G. A. "The Medicean Restoration: Machiavelli's 'Il Principe'" and "Rome and Venice: Machiavelli's 'Discorsi' and 'Arte della Guerra'." In his *The Machiavellian Moment: Florentine Political Thought and the Atlantic Republican Tradition,* pp. 158-62, pp. 183-218. Princeton: Princeton University Press, 1975.

   Analyzes three of Machiavelli's principal works in humanistic terms and in relation to medieval and Renaissance political thought.

Ridolfi, Roberto. *The Life of Niccolò Machiavelli.* Chicago: University of Chicago Press, 1963, 337 p.

   Noncritical biography detailing Machiavelli's life and career.

Malcolm X

1925-1965

(Born Malcolm Little; changed name to Malcolm X; also known by adopted religious name El-Hajj Malik El-Shabazz) American autobiographer and orator.

INTRODUCTION

A dynamic and influential twentieth-century African-American leader, Malcolm X rose to prominence in the mid-1950s as the outspoken national minister of the Nation of Islam (Black Muslims) under Elijah Muhammad, who characterized the black race as superior and the white race as inherently evil; he also opposed the mainstream civil rights movement, publicly called for black separatism, and rejected nonviolence and integration as effective means of combating racism. Malcolm repudiated Muhammad and the Nation of Islam in the mid-1960s, however, and embraced conventional Islam. He documented this change and his various identities and experiences throughout his life in *The Autobiography of Malcolm X* (1965), a work prepared with the help of American writer Alex Haley. Published after his assassination, Malcolm X's autobiography has been called "a compelling and irreplaceable book" about "a great American life."

Biographical Information

Born Malcolm Little on May 19, 1925, at Omaha, Nebraska, Malcolm was exposed to white supremacists and the black separatist movement at an early age. His father, a Baptist minister and a follower of Jamaican-born black nationalist Marcus Garvey, was murdered by a group of white supremacists shortly after he moved his family to Mason, Michigan. When the strain of raising her family alone became too much for his mother, she was placed in a mental institution and the children sent to separate foster homes. Despite the traumas of his early youth, Malcolm was perhaps the best student in his class, although he quit school in eighth grade and went to live with his half-sister in Boston. He held several menial jobs and acquired a reputation as a hustler, pimp, and drug dealer as well as the nickname "Detroit Red." In early 1946 Malcolm was arrested, charged with robbery, and sentenced to ten years in prison. There he acquired another nickname, "Satan," and read Elijah Muhammad's teachings at the prison library. Upon his release in 1952, Malcolm became a follower of Muhammad, rejecting the "slave name" of Little and assuming the name "Malcolm X" to signify the loss of his true African name. Appointed assistant minister of Detroit's Temple Number One of the Nation of Islam in 1953, Malcolm rose through the ranks, becoming a national minister in 1963 and overseeing a major mosque in Harlem. There he achieved an impressive status as an articulate, mercurial spokesman for the Black Muslims' radical agenda, denouncing integration, nonviolence, and Martin Luther King, Jr. Malcolm termed the assassination of John F. Kennedy a case of "chickens coming home to roost"—a statement that severely damaged Malcolm's career and cost him his position in the Nation of Islam. Following a pilgrimage to Mecca, where he took the religious name El-Hajj Malik El-Shabazz, Malcolm worked to unite blacks around the world, establishing the Organization of Afro-American Unity in 1964 in New York City. He soon discovered that members of the Nation of Islam were plotting to kill him. While addressing an audience of four hundred at Harlem's Audubon Ballroom on February 21, 1965, Malcolm X was assassinated by Talmadge Thayer, Norman 3X Butler, and Thomas 15X Johnson.

Major Works

The Autobiography of Malcolm X, published the same year as his death, is a moving account of Malcolm's own experiences with racism, his criminal past, and his years as an activist for both the Black Muslims and his own African-American organization. Together with his speeches and comments that have been collected in such volumes as *Malcolm X Speaks* (1965), *Malcolm X on Afro-American History* (1967), and *Malcolm X and the Negro Revolution* (1969), Malcolm's writings offer numerous insights into America's social climate from the mid-1950s to the mid-1960s, articulating the concerns of a significant segment of the black community in those years. In addition, these books serve as an imposing indication of Malcolm's beliefs, his achievements, and his potential, which was violently rendered unrealized.

Critical Reception

The Autobiography of Malcolm X has prompted diverse critical readings, including analyses of its properties as a political and rhetorical text, as a conversion of narrative reflecting Malcolm's search for identity, and as a work that both affirms and challenges the tradition of American autobiography. Of the work's significance, Charles H. Nichols asserted in 1985: "*The Autobiography of Malcolm X* is probably the most influential book read by this generation of Afro-Americans. For not only is the account of Malcolm Little an absorbing and heart-shattering encounter with the realities of poverty, crime and racism. It is a fantastic success story. Paradoxically, the book, designed to be an indictment of American and European bigotry and exploitation, is a triumphant affirmation of the possibilities of the human spirit." Although Malcolm's speeches also have been published, his autobiography remains by far his greatest contribution to literature. As Malcolm X has increasingly been recognized as a leading figure in the African-American struggle for recognition and equality, *The Autobiography of Malcolm X* has grown in stature. Truman Nelson concluded: "Viewed in its complete historical context, this is indeed a great book. Its dead-level honesty, its passion, its exalted purpose, even its manifold unsolved ambiguities will make it stand as a monument to the most painful of truths: that this country, this people, this Western world has practiced unspeakable cruelty against a race, an individual, who might have made its fraudulent humanism a reality."

(For further information, see *Black Literature Criticism; Black Writers,* Vol. 1; *Contemporary Authors,* Vols. 111, 125; *Contemporary Literary Criticism,* Vol. 82; *DISCovering Authors; DISCovering Authors: British; DISCovering Authors: Canadian; DISCovering Authors Modules: Most-studied Authors Module, Multicultural Authors Module; Major Twentieth-Century Writers.*)

CRITICAL COMMENTARY

WARNER BERTHOFF

SOURCE: Warner Berthoff, "Witness and Testament: Two Contemporary Classics," in *New Literary History,* Vol. II, No. 2, Winter, 1971, pp. 311-27.

[*In the following excerpt, Berthoff declares* The Autobiography of Malcolm X *"a contemporary classic."*]

No one can read very much of Malcolm's writing, more precisely listen to the voice transcribed in *The Autobiography of Malcolm X* (dictated to the journalist Alex Haley) or the printed versions of his public speeches,

Principal Works

The Autobiography of Malcolm X [with Alex Haley] (autobiography) 1965

Malcolm X Speaks: Selected Speeches and Statements (speeches) 1965

Malcolm X on Afro-American History (speeches) 1967

The Speeches of Malcolm X at Harvard (speeches) 1968

Malcolm X Talks to Young People (speeches) 1969

Malcolm X and the Negro Revolution: The Speeches of Malcolm X (speeches) 1969

Two Speeches by Malcolm X (speeches) 1969

By Any Means Necessary: Speeches, Interviews, and a Letter by Malcolm X (speeches, interviews, and letter) 1970

The End of White World Supremacy: Four Speeches (speeches) 1971

Malcolm X: The Last Speeches (speeches) 1989

Adaptations

James Baldwin adapted portions of *The Autobiography of Malcolm X* as *One Day, When I Was Lost: A Scenario*, Dial, 1973.

---

without forming the sense of an extraordinary human being: fiercely intelligent, shrewdly and humanely responsive to the life around him despite every reason in the world to have gone blind with suspicion and hate, a rarely gifted leader and inspirer of other men. The form of autobiographical narration adds something further; he comes through to us as the forceful agent of a life-history that was heroic in the event and has the shape of the heroic in the telling, a protagonist who (in Francis R. Hart's fine description) has himself created and now recreates "human value and vitality in each new world or underworld he has entered" [*New Literary History*, Spring 1970].

The power of Malcolm's book is that it speaks directly out of the totality of that life-history *and* the ingratiating openness of his own mind and recollection to it. It seems to me a book that ... does not require any softening or suspension of critical judgment. In the first place it is written, or spoken, in a quick, pungent, concrete style, again the plain style of popular idiom, improved and made efficient by the same sort of natural sharpness and concentration of attention that gives life and color to the best of Mark Twain's recollective writing, or Franklin's, or Bunyan's. In the run of the narrative the liveliness of observation and recollection, the "histrionic exuberance" (Professor Hart again), are continuously persuasive—and incidentally confirm as elements of a true style Alex Haley's assurance that the book is indeed Malcolm's own and not a clever piece of mimicry or pastiche. The casually vivid rendering of other persons is worth remarking, a test some quite competent novelists would have trouble passing. People who were especially important to Malcolm—his strong-minded half-sister Ella; the motherly white woman who ran the detention home he was sent to at 13, who was always kind to him and would call his people "niggers" to his face without a flicker of uneasiness; Shorty from Boston, who set him up in business; West Indian Archie, who "called him out"; or the tough convict Bimbi in Charlestown prison, strange little man of unexpected thoughts and arguments, who broke through the wall of rage and hate Malcolm was closing around himself—all these figures are precisely defined, according to their place in the story. The grasp of the narrative extends in fact to whole sociologies of behavior. The Harlem chapters in general, with their explanation of hustling in all its major forms—numbers, drugs, prostitution, protection, petty in-ghetto thievery—offer one of the best accounts in our literature of the cultural underside of the American business system, and of the bitter psychology that binds its victims to it; Malcolm came to see very clearly how the habituations bred by ghetto poverty operate to destroy individual efforts to break out of it, and he could use that insight with force and point in his preaching. Most generally it is just this blending of his own life-story with the full collective history of his milieu and the laws of behavior controlling it that gives Malcolm's testimony its strength and large authority—and sets it apart, I think, from the many more or less skillfully designed essays in autobiography we have had recently from writers like Frank Conroy, Claude Brown, Norman Podhoretz, Willie Morris, Paul Cowan, David McReynolds, to mention only a few; sets it apart also from the great run of novels about contemporary city life.

But it is Malcolm himself, and his own active consciousness of the myth of his life's progress, that most fills and quickens the book, making it something more than simply a valuable document. His past life is vividly present to him as he speaks; he gives it the form, in recollection, of a dramatic adventure in which he himself is felt as the precipitating agent and moving force. It is not unreasonable that he should see himself as someone who has a special power to make things happen, to work changes on the world around him (and to change within himself); and thus finally as one whose rise to authority is in some sense in the natural order of things, the working out of some deep structure of fortune. That is my way of putting it; Malcolm himself, as a Muslim, of course uses other words.

The force of this continuously active process of self-conception and self-projection is fundamental to the book's power of truth. It gives vitality and momentum to the early parts of the story, the picture of Malcolm's salad days as a Roxbury and Harlem sharpie, with conked hair and "knob-toed, orange-colored 'kick-up' shoes," the wildest Lindy-hopper and quickest hustler of all, delighting always in his impact on others—as in the interlude of his first trip back to Lansing, Michigan, to wow the yokels with his Harlem flashiness—finding satisfaction, too, in the names, the folk-identities, that attach to him at each new stage: "Homeboy," "Harlem Red" or "Detroit Red," "Satan" in the storming defiance of his first imprisonment. Most decisively, this force of self-conception is what brings alive the drama of his conversion, and his re-emergence within the Nation of Islam as a leader and teacher of his people. For Malcolm's autobiography is consciously shaped as the story of an "education," and in so describing it I am not merely making the appropriate allusion to Henry Adams or the *Bildungsroman* tradition; "education" is Malcolm's own word for what is taking place.

Above all, the book is the story of a conversion and its consequences. We can identify in it various classic features of conversion-narrative. A full detailing of the crimes and follies of his early life makes more astonishing the change of changes that follows ("The very enormity of my previous life's guilt prepared me to accept the truth"). In the central light of this new truth, particular events take on symbolic dimensions; they stand as the exemplary trials and challenges which the redeemed soul must pass through and by which it knows the meaning, feels the reality, of its experience. That meaning and reality, to repeat, are not merely personal. The outlines of grander historical patterns are invoked and give their backing to the story—the whole long history and tragedy of the black race in America; then, at the crisis, the radically clarifying mythology of the Black Muslim movement (a mythology which, to any one willing to consider it objectively, has the character of a full-blown poetic mythology; a source, once you place yourself inside it, of comprehensive and intrinsically rational explanations for the life-experience it refers to, that of the mass of black people in a historically racist society).

And always there is Malcolm's own fascination with what has happened to him, and what objectively it means. As if establishing a leitmotif, the climaxes of his story repeatedly focus on this extraordinary power to change and be changed that he has grown conscious of within himself and that presents itself to him as the distinctive rule of his life. Malcolm speaks with a just pride of his quickness to learn, to "pick up" how things are done in the world; of his readiness, even when it humiliates him, to accept schooling from those in possession of some special competence or wisdom; of a "personal chemistry" of openmindedness and quick realism that requires him to find out the full vital truth of his own experience and that keeps it available to consciousness from that time forward. His curiosity about life is unquenchable ("You can hardly mention anything I'm not curious about"). He has a driving need to understand everything that happens to him or around him and to gain a measure of intelligent control over it; it is a passion with him to get his own purchase on reality.

It thus makes *narrative* sense, of a kind only the best of novelists are in command of, that he should discover his calling in life as a teacher and converter. Malcolm has his own theories for nearly everything that interests him—theories of language and etymology (he has an autodidact's sense of word-magic, dating from the time in prison when studying a dictionary, page by page, in a folklorish fury of self-improvement, began quite literally to give him an extravagant new intuition of power and freedom, as of one suddenly finding a key to his enemy's most treasured secrets); theories about how Socrates' wisdom came from initiation into the mysteries of black Egypt and about the persecuted black philosopher Spinoza and the black poet Homer (cognate with Omar and Moor) and about who really wrote Shakespeare and translated the English Bible and why. Of course we can laugh at a lot of this from the pewboxes of a more orderly education, but I find myself impressed even in these odd instances with the unfailing rationality of the uses to which Malcolm put his thought, the intelligence even here of what really matters to him—which is the meaning of his life as a black man in the United States and the enormous responsibilities of a position of authority and leadership in which he can count on no help from the official, institutionalized culture but what he wrenches out for himself.

But it is, again, the prodigy of his own conversion that gives him the most direct confirmation of his beliefs; the awareness of himself as a man capable of these transforming changes that gives him confidence in his testimony's importance, that lets him say, "Anything I do today, I regard as urgent." The *Autobiography* was written to serve at once a religious and a political cause, the cause of the religion of Islam and the cause of black freedom, and it is filled with the letter of Malcolm's teaching. In the later chapters especially, more and more of the text is portioned out to explanations of essential doctrine and to social and political commentary and analysis. But here, too, it is a personal authority that comes through to us and makes the difference. I should like to try to characterize this authority a little further. I first read Malcolm's autobiography when I happened also to be reading through the Pauline epistles in the New Testament; the chance result was a sharp consciousness of fundamental resemblances. Resemblances, I mean, to the voice and manner of the Paul who not only is teaching his people the law of the new faith (to which he himself is a late comer, and by hard ways) but who suffuses his teaching with all the turbulence of his own history and masterful personality. Two recent students of Paul's letters, Charles Buck and Greer Taylor, have commented on the singularity of this element in Paul: "a presumption of personal authority on the part of the writer which is quite unlike that of any other New Testament author." Malcolm, too, writes as the leader of a new, precariously established faith, which he is concerned to stabilize against destructive inner dissensions yet without losing any of the priceless communal fervor and dedication that have been released by it. So at every point he brings to bear the full weight of his own reputation and active experience, including his earlier follies and excesses—precisely as Paul does in, for example, the astonishing final chapters of Second Corinthians, full as they are of the liveliest and most immediate self-reference. The tangible genius of both Paul and Malcolm as writers is to bring the authority of living personality, and of self-mastery, into the arena of what is understood to be an argument of the utmost consequence; a matter of life and death for those who commit themselves to it.

Malcolm's concerns are of course civil and political as well as sectarian. In his last years he had become, and knew it, a national leader as important as Dr. King; a leader moreover who, as the atmosphere of the Washington March of August 1963 gave way to the ghetto riots of the next summer, was trusted inside Harlem and its counterparts as the established black leadership no longer was. And the last academic point I want to make about the literary character of Malcolm's book is that in this regard, too, as a political statement, its form is recognizably "classic." The model it quite naturally conforms to is that of the Political Testament, the work in which some ruler or statesman sets down for the particular benefit of his people a summary of his own experience and wisdom and indicates the principles which are to guide those who succeed him. The historian Felix Gilbert has called attention to this rather special literary tradition in his study of the background of Washington's Farewell Address. It is necessarily, in the number of its members, a limited tradition; besides Washington's address Professor Gilbert mentions examples attributed to Richelieu, Colbert, the Dutch republican Jan de Witt, Robert Walpole, Peter the Great, and Frederick the Great, who wrote at least two of them. My argument is not that Malcolm was in any way guided by this grand precedent, merely that in serving all his book's purposes he substantially recreated it—which is of course what the work of literature we call "classic" does within the occasion it answers to....

PAUL JOHN EAKIN

SOURCE: Paul John Eakin, "Malcolm X and the Limits of Autobiography," in *Criticism*, Vol. XVIII, No. 3, Summer, 1976, pp. 230-42.

[*In the following essay, Eakin argues that Malcolm X's memoirs challenge traditional definitions of the genre of autobiography.*]

When a complex and controversial figure writes a book that has achieved the distinction and popularity of *The Autobiography of Malcolm X*, it is inevitable that efforts will be made to place him and his work in the perspective of a literary tradition. Barrett John Mandel, for example, has identified in Malcolm X's story the paradigm of the traditional conversion narrative. His reading of Malcolm X's autobiography, and it is a characteristic one, assumes that the narrative expresses a completed self. Further, Ross Miller has suggested that such an assumption is central to the expectations we bring to the reading of any autobiography: "The pose of the autobiographer as an experienced man is particularly effective because we expect to hear from someone who has a completed sense of his own life and is therefore in a position to tell what he has discovered." Even Warner Berthoff, who has admirably defined Malcolm X's "extraordinary power to change and be changed" as "the distinctive rule of his life," seems to have been drawn to this sense of the completed self when he attempts to locate the *Autobiography* in a special and limited literary tradition, that of the political testament in which "some ruler or statesman sets down for the particular benefit of his people a summary of his own experience and wisdom." The rhetorical posture of Malcolm X in the last chapter would seem to confirm Berthoff's reading and to fulfill Miller's autobiographical expectations, for it is indeed that of the elder statesman summing up a completed life, a life that has, as it were, already ended:

> Anyway, now, each day I live as if I am already dead, and I tell you what I would like for you to do. When I *am* dead—I say it that way because from the things I *know*, I do not expect to live long enough to read this book in its finished form—I want you to just watch and see if I'm not right in what I say: that

the white man, in his press, is going to identify me with "hate."

If Malcolm X's anticipation of his imminent death confers on this final phase of autobiographical retrospection a posthumous authority, it is nevertheless an authority that he exercises here to defend himself against the fiction of the completed self that his interpreters—both black and white, in the event—were to use against him. Each of his identities turned out to be provisional, and even this voice from the grave was the utterance not of an ultimate identity but merely of the last one in the series of roles that Malcolm X had variously assumed, lived out, and discarded.

Alex Haley's "Epilogue" to the *Autobiography* reveals the fictive nature of this final testamentary stance which Berthoff regards as definitive. Here Haley, Malcolm X's collaborator in the *Autobiography*, reports that the apparent uncertainty and confusion of Malcolm X's views were widely discussed in Harlem during the last months of Malcolm X's life, while Malcolm X himself, four days before his death, said in an interview, "I'm man enough to tell you that I can't put my finger on exactly what my philosophy is now, but I'm flexible." Moreover, the account of the composition of the *Autobiography* given by Haley in the "Epilogue" makes it clear that the fiction of the autobiographer as a man with "a completed sense of his own life" is especially misleading in the case of Malcolm X, for even Haley and the book that was taking shape in his hands were out of phase with the reality of Malcolm X's life and identity. Thus Haley acknowledges that he "never dreamed" of Malcolm X's break with Elijah Muhammad "until the actual rift became public," although the break overturned the design that had guided Malcolm X's dictations of his life story to Haley up to that point. The disparity between the traditional autobiographical fiction of the completed self and the biographical fact of Malcolm X's ceaselessly evolving identity may lead us, as it did Malcolm X himself, to enlarge our understanding of the limits and the possibilities of autobiography.

The original dedication of the *Autobiography*, which Malcolm X gave to Haley before the dictations had even begun, places the work squarely in one of the most ancient traditions of the genre, that of the exemplary life:

> This book I dedicate to the Honorable Elijah Muhammad, who found me here in America in the muck and mire of the filthiest civilization and society on this earth, and pulled me out, cleaned me up, and stood me on my feet, and made me the man that I am today.

This dedication (later cancelled) motivates more than half of the *Autobiography* in its final version. This book would be the story of a conversion, and Malcolm X's statement recapitulates in capsule form the essential pattern of such narratives: in the moment of conversion a new identity is discovered; further, this turning point sharply defines a two-part, before-after time scheme for the narrative; the movement of the self from "lost" to "found" constitutes the plot; and, finally, the very nature of the experience supplies an evangelical motive for autobiography.

What concerns us here, however, is not the much-studied features of conversion and the ease with which they may be translated into the formal elements of autobiographical narrative, but rather the natural and seemingly inevitable inference that the individual first discovers the shape of his life and then writes the life on the basis of this discovery. Some version of this temporal fiction, of course, lies behind most autobiography, and I would emphasize it as a corollary to Miller's definition of the completed self: the notion that living one's life precedes writing about it, that the life is in some sense complete and that the autobiographical process takes place afterward, somehow outside the realm of lapsing time in which the life proper necessarily unfolds. The evangelical bias of conversion narrative is especially interesting in this regard, for it supplies a predisposition for such an autobiographer to accept this supporting fiction as fact, since he believes that conversion works a definitive transition from shifting false beliefs to a fixed vision of the one truth. It is, accordingly, when a new discovery about the shape of one's life takes place during the writing of one's story that an autobiographer may be forced to recognize the presence and nature of the fictions on which his narrative is based. The experience of Malcolm X in his final period did foster such a recognition, and this knowledge and its consequences for autobiographical narrative may instruct us in the complex relation that necessarily obtains between living a life and writing about it. However, before we consider the *Autobiography* from the vantage point of the man who was becoming "El-Hajj Malik El-Shabazz" . . . let us look at the *Autobiography* as it was originally conceived by the man whose first conversion in prison had transformed him from "Satan" . . . to "Minister Malcolm X" . . . This is, of course, the way we do look at the *Autobiography* when we begin to read it for the first time, especially if we are relatively unfamiliar with the life of Malcolm X.

The Malcolm X of these years was firmly in command of the shape of his life, tracing his sense of this shape to the pivotal and structuring illumination of conversion itself. At this point his understanding of the design of his experience, especially his baffled fascination with the radical discontinuity between the old Adam and the new, closely parallels the state of St. Augustine, Jonathan Edwards, and many another sinner touched by gracious affections, so much so that the student of spiritual autobiography is likely to feel himself at home on familiar ground:

> For evil to bend its knees, admitting its guilt, to implore the forgiveness of God, is the hardest thing in the world.... When finally I was able to make myself stay down—I didn't know what to say to Allah.... I still marvel at how swiftly my previous life's thinking pattern slid away from me, like snow off a roof. It is as though someone else I knew of had lived by hustling and crime. I would be startled to catch myself thinking in a remote way of my earlier self as another person.

If we consider Malcolm X's account of his life up to the time of his break with Elijah Muhammad..., what we have in fact is a story that falls rather neatly into two sections roughly equal in length, devoted respectively to his former life as a sinner... and to his present life as one of Elijah Muhammad's ministers.... This two-part structure is punctuated by two decisive experiences: his repudiation of the white world of his youth in Mason, Michigan, and his conversion to Islam in prison at Norfolk, Massachusetts.

Malcolm X describes the "first major turning point of my life" at the end of the second chapter, his realization that in white society he was not free "to become whatever *I* wanted to be." The shock to the eighth-grade boy was profound, for despite his traumatic childhood memories of the destruction of his family by white society, Malcolm X had embraced the white success ethic by the time he was in junior high school: "I was trying so hard...to be white." What follows, in Chapters 3 through 9, is Malcolm X's account of his life as a ghetto hustler, his first "career," just as his role as a Black Muslim minister was to be his second. If Allah preserved him from the fate of an Alger hero or a Booker T. Washington, from a career as a "successful" shoeshine boy or a self-serving member of the "black bourgeoisie," he was nevertheless destined to enact a kind of inverse parody of the white man's rise to success as he sank deeper and deeper into a life of crime. This is the portion of the *Autobiography* that has been singled out for its vividness by the commentators, with the result that the conversion experience and its aftermath in Chapters 10 through 15 have been somewhat eclipsed. It would be possible, of course, to see in the popularity of this section nothing more than the universal appeal of any evocation of low life and evil ways. In addition, this preference may reflect an instinctive attraction to a more personal mode of autobiography with plenty of concrete self-revelation instead of the more formal testimony of an exemplary life. Certainly Alex Haley responded strongly to this narrative, and so did Malcolm X, though he tried to restrain himself:

> Then it was during recalling the early Harlem days that Malcolm X really got carried away. One night, suddenly, wildly, he jumped up from his chair and, incredibly, the fearsome black demagogue was scat-singing and popping his fingers, "re-bop-de-bop-blap-blam-" and then grabbing a vertical pipe with one hand (as the girl partner) he went jubilantly lindy-hopping around, his coattail and the long legs and the big feet flying as they had in those Harlem days. And then almost as suddenly, Malcolm X caught himself and sat back down, and for the rest of that session he was decidedly grumpy.

Haley captures here the characteristic drama of the autobiographical act that the juxtaposition of the self as it is and as it was inevitably generates. Malcolm X's commitment to his public role as "the fearsome black demagogue" conflicts with his evident pleasure in recapturing an earlier and distinctly personal identity, the historical conked and zooted lindy champ of the Roseland Ballroom in Roxbury, the hustling hipster of Small's Paradise in Harlem.

If the *Autobiography* had ended with the fourteenth or fifteenth chapter, what we would have, I suggest, is a narrative which could be defined as an extremely conventional example of autobiographical form distinguished chiefly by the immediacy and power of its imaginative recreation of the past. It is true that this much of the *Autobiography* would usefully illustrate the survival of the classic pattern of conversion narrative in the contemporary literature of spiritual autobiography, but this interest would necessarily be a limited one given Malcolm X's reticence about the drama of the experience of conversion itself. For Malcolm X the fact of conversion is decisive, life-shaping, identity-altering, but unlike the most celebrated spiritual autobiographers of the past he chooses not to dramatize the experience itself or to explore its psychological dynamics.

It seems probable that when Malcolm X began his dictations to Haley in 1963 he anticipated that his narrative would end with an account of his transformation into the national spokesman of Elijah Muhammad's Nation of Islam.... This was not destined to be the end of the story, however, for the pace of Malcolm X's history, always lively, became tumultuous in 1963 and steadily accelerated until his assassination in 1965. In this last period Malcolm X was to experience two events that destroyed the very premises of the autobiography he had set out to write. The most well-known convert to the Black Muslim religion was first to break with Elijah Muhammad . . . and then to make a pilgrimage to Mecca . . ., where he underwent a second conversion to what he now regarded as the true religion of Islam. The revelation that Elijah Muhammad was a false prophet shattered the world of Malcolm X and the shape of the life he had been living for twelve years:

> I was like someone who for twelve years had had an inseparable, beautiful marriage—and then suddenly one morning at breakfast the marriage partner had thrust across the table some divorce papers. I felt as though something in *nature* had failed, like the sun or the stars. It was that incredible a phenomenon to me—something too stupendous to conceive.

The autobiographical fiction of the completed self was exploded for good, although Malcolm X, with a remarkable fidelity to the truth of his past, was to preserve the fragments in the earlier chapters of the *Autobiography*, as we have seen.

The illumination at Mecca made Malcolm X feel "like a complete human being" for the first time "in my thirty-nine years on this earth," and he assumed a new name to symbolize this new sense of identity, El-Hajj Malik El-Shabazz. In the final chapters of the book (18 and 19) we see Malcolm X in the process of discarding the "old "'hate' and 'violence' image" of the militant preacher of Elijah Muhammad's Nation of Islam, but before he created a design for the life of this new self he was brutally gunned down on February 21, 1965. In fact, it is not at all certain that Malcolm X would have arrived at any single, definitive formulation for the shape of his life even if he had continued to live. In the final pages of the last chapter he observes:

> No man is given but so much time to accomplish whatever is his life's work. My life in particular never has stayed fixed in one position for very long. You have seen how throughout my life, I have often known unexpected drastic changes.

With these words Malcolm X articulates a truth already latent but ungrasped in the autobiographical narrative he originally set out to write in his evangelical zeal: his life was not now and never had been a life of the simpler pattern of the traditional conversion story. Because this complex vision of his existence is clearly not that of the early sections of the *Autobiography*, Alex Haley and Malcolm X were forced to confront the consequences of this discontinuity in perspective for the narrative, already a year old. It was Haley who raised the issue when he learned, belatedly, of the rift between Malcolm X and Elijah Muhammad, for he had become worried that an embittered Malcolm X might want to rewrite the book from his new perspective, and this at a time when Haley regarded their collaboration as virtually complete ("by now I had the bulk of the needed life story material in hand"). Malcolm X's initial response settled the matter temporarily: "I want the book to be the way it was." Haley's concern, however, was justified, for a few months later, following Malcolm X's journey to Mecca, Haley was "appalled" to find that Malcolm X had "red-inked" many of the places in the manuscript "where he had told of his almost father-and-son relationship with Elijah Muhammad." Haley describes this crisis of the autobiographical act as follows:

> Telephoning Malcolm X, I reminded him of his previous decision, and I stressed that if those chapters contained such telegraphing to readers of what would lie ahead, then the book would automatically be robbed of some of its building suspense and drama. Malcolm X said gruffly, "Whose book is this?" I told him "yours, of course," and that I only made the objection in my position as a writer. He said that he would have to think about it. I was heart-sick at the prospect that he might want to re-edit the entire book into a polemic against Elijah Muhammad. But late that night, Malcolm X telephoned. "I'm sorry. You're right. I was upset about something. Forget what I wanted changed, let what you already had stand." I never again gave him chapters to review unless I was with him. Several times I would covertly watch him frown and wince as he read, but he never again asked for any change in what he had originally said.

Malcolm X's refusal to change the narrative reflects, finally, his acceptance of change as the fundamental law of existence, and yet, curiously, by the very fidelity of this refusal he secures for the remembered past, and for the acts of memory devoted to it, such measure of permanence as the forms of art afford.

The exchange between the two men poses the perplexing issue of perspective in autobiography with an instructive clarity: to which of an autobiographer's selves should he or even can he be true? What are the strategies by which he may maintain a dual or plural allegiance without compromise to his present vision of the truth? In fact, the restraint of the "telegraphing" does leave the climax intact, and yet Malcolm X's decision not to revise the preceding narrative does not produce the kind of obvious discontinuity in authorial perspective that we might expect as a result. Haley's part in this is considerable, for his contribution to the ultimate shape of the *Autobiography* was more extensive and fundamental than his narrowly literary concerns here with foreshadowing and suspense might seem to suggest. Despite his tactful protest that he was only a "writer," Haley himself had been instrumental in the playing out of the autobiographical drama between one Malcolm X, whose faith in Elijah Muhammad had supplied him with his initial rationale for an autobiography, and another, whose repudiation of Elijah Muhammad made the *Autobiography* the extraordinary human document it eventually became. If the outcome of this drama was formalized in Malcolm X's expulsion from the Nation of Islam, it was already in the wind by the time the dictations began in earnest in 1963. Alex Haley was one to read between the lines.

Haley recalls in the "Epilogue" that at the very outset of the project he had been in fundamental disagreement with Malcolm X about the narrative he would help him write. He reports that Malcolm X wanted the focus to be on Elijah Muhammad and the Nation of Islam: "He would bristle when I tried to urge him that the proposed book was *his* life." At this early stage of the collaboration Haley portrays two Malcolms: a loyal public Malcolm X describing a religious movement in which he casts himself in a distinctly subordinate and self-effacing role, and a subversive private Malcolm X scribbling a trenchant counter-commentary in telegraphic red-ink ball point on any available scrap of paper. Determined to feature this second Malcolm X in the autobiography, Haley lured this suppressed identity out into the open by leaving white paper napkins next to Malcolm X's coffee cup to tap his closed communications with himself. Haley carefully retrieved this autobiographical fall-out, and taking his cue from one of these napkin revelations, interestingly about women, Haley "cast a bait" with a question about Malcolm X's mother. Haley reports that with this textbook display of Freudian savvy he was able to land the narrative he was seeking:

> From this stream-of-consciousness reminiscing I finally got out of him the foundation for this book's beginning chapters, "Nightmare" and "Mascot." After that night, he never again hesitated to tell me even the most intimate details of his personal life, over the next two years. His talking about his mother triggered something.

From the very earliest phase of the dictations, then, the autobiography began to take on a much more personal and private coloration than Malcolm X originally intended. What Elijah Muhammad accomplished, autobiographically speaking, when he "silenced" Malcolm X, was to legitimatize the private utterance of the napkins which had already found its way into the mainstream of a narrative initially conceived as an orthodox work of evangelical piety. After his separation from the Nation of Islam, Malcolm X comments that he began "to think for myself," "after twelve years of never thinking for as much as five minutes about myself." Haley reports two napkin messages of this period that signal the consequences of Malcolm X's new sense of himself and his power for the nearly-completed *Autobiography:*

> He scribbled one night, "You have not converted a man because you have silenced him. John Viscount Morley." And the same night, almost illegibly, "I was going downhill until he picked me up, but the more I think of it, we picked each other up."

Not only was Malcolm X rejecting the simple clarity of the original conversion narrative he had set out to tell, but he was no longer disposed to sacrifice to the greater glory of Elijah Muhammad his own agency in the working out of his life story.

In the final chapters of the *Autobiography* and in the "Epilogue," as Malcolm X moves toward a new view of his story as a life of changes, he expresses an impressive, highly self-conscious awareness of the problems of autobiographical narrative, and specifically of the complex relationship between living a life and writing an autobiography. All of his experience in the last packed months, weeks, and days of his life worked to destroy his earlier confident belief in the completed self, the completed life, and hence in the complete life story. Thus he writes to Haley in what is possibly his final statement about the *Autobiography:* "I just want to read it one more time because I don't expect to read it in finished form." As Malcolm X saw it at the last, all autobiographies are by nature incomplete and they can not, accordingly, have a definite shape. As a life changes, so any sense of the shape of a life must change; the autobiographical process evolves because it is part of the life, and the identity of the autobiographical "I" changes and shifts. Pursuing the logic of such speculations, Malcolm X even wonders whether any autobiography can keep abreast of the unfolding of personal history: "How is it possible to write one's autobiography in a world so fast-changing as this?" And so he observes to Haley, "I hope the book is proceeding rapidly, for events concerning my life happen so swiftly, much of what has already been written can easily be outdated from month to month. In life, nothing is permanent; not even life itself."

At the end, then, Malcolm X came to reject the traditional autobiographical fiction that the life comes first, and then the writing of the life; that the life is in some sense complete and that the autobiographical process simply records the final achieved shape. This fiction is based upon a suspension of time, as though the "life," the subject, could sit still long enough for the autobiographical "I," the photographer, to snap its picture. In fact, as Malcolm X was to learn, the "life" itself will not hold still; it changes, shifts position. And as for the autobiographical act, it requires much more than an instant of time to take the picture, to write the story. As the act of composition extends in time, so it enters the life-stream, and the fictive separation between life and life story, which is so convenient—even necessary—to the writing of autobiography, dissolves.

Malcolm X's final knowledge of the incompleteness of the self is what gives the last pages of the *Autobiography* together with the "Epilogue" their remarkable power: the vision of a man whose swiftly unfolding career has outstripped the possibilities of the traditional autobiography he had meant to write. It is not in the least surprising that Malcolm X's sobering insights into the limitations of autobiography are accompanied by an increasingly insistent desire to disengage himself from the ambitions of the autobiographical process. Thus he speaks of the *Autobiography* to Haley time and again as though, having disabused himself of any illusion that the narrative could keep pace with his life, he had consigned the book to its fate, casting it adrift as hopelessly obsolete. Paradoxically, nowhere does the book succeed, persuade, more than in its confession of failure as autobiography. This is the fascination of *The Education of Henry Adams*, and Malcolm X, like Adams, leaves behind him the husks of played-out autobiographical paradigms. The indomitable reality of the self transcends and exhausts the received shapes for a life that are transmitted by the culture, and yet the very process of discarding in itself works to structure an apparently shapeless experience. Despite—or because of—the intractability of life to form, the fiction of the completed self, which lies at the core of the autobiographical enterprise, cannot be readily dispatched. From its ashes, phoenix-like, it reconstitutes itself in a new guise. Malcolm X's work, and Adams' as well, generate a sense that the uncompromising commitment to the truth of one's own nature, which requires the elimination of false identities and careers one by one, will yield at the last the pure ore of a final and irreducible selfhood. This is the ultimate autobiographical dream.

GORDON O. TAYLOR

SOURCE: Gordon O. Taylor, "Voices from the Veil: Black American Autobiography," in *The Georgia Review*, Vol. XXXV, No. 2, Summer, 1981, pp. 341-61.

[*Taylor is an American educator and critic. In the following excerpt from a discussion of the autobiographies of Malcolm X, Richard Wright, and James Baldwin, Taylor places* The Autobiography of Malcolm X *within a black American autobiographical tradition, asserting that the works of these authors share "the urge to articulate, as if for the first time, a sensibility at once determined and precluded by history."*]

"The problem of the twentieth century is the problem of the color-line," says [W.E.B.] Du Bois, "1900" to him as critical a symbolic juncture as Henry Adams would soon claim, for different reasons, in his [*Education of Henry Adams*]. The problem shared with Du Bois by Wright, Baldwin, Malcolm X, and others is that of voicing black self-consciousness so as to create it, or to recreate it in the context of twentieth-century America. At the common core of *Black Boy, Notes of a Native Son*, and *The Autobiography of Malcolm X*, in addition to [Du Bois's] *The Souls of Black Folk*—granting crucial differences among them—is the urge to articulate, as if for the first time, a sensibility at once determined and precluded by history. The same urge is felt in, and is itself a subject of, such novels as James Weldon Johnson's *The Autobiography of an Ex-Coloured Man* and Ralph Ellison's *Invisible Man*. Never fully possessed of what Baldwin calls the "white centuries" of European culture, dispossessed as well of the African past, the Afro-American protagonists in these works, whether fictional or autobiographical personae, project themselves in terms of both being and nothingness. They imagine their lives as both shaped and negated by historical pressures rooted in race—lives in at least one respect over before begun. Yet they also envision their individualities as unformed, and therefore open to unbounded possibility residing in personal energies compressed and awaiting release. . . .

"How is it possible to write one's autobiography in a world so fast-changing as this?" asks Malcolm X, in a letter quoted by Alex Haley in his epilogue to *The Autobiography of Malcolm X* (1965). The question is one asked implicitly by Henry Adams from first page to last of [*The Education of Henry Adams*], the outer world as ostensible subject having long since given way to demands of the inner, the autobiographical act compelled by the changes within and without which seem to prevent it. Change is for Malcolm X a matter of escalating tension between the idea of black life in America, as fixed in the design imposed by slavery, and a contrary notion, inseparable from the first, of possibilities achievable through black resistance to that design. This is essentially the double-consciousness Du Bois projects in *The Souls of Black Folk*, which gave Malcolm his first "glimpse into the black people's history before they came to this country." Under pressure of double-consciousness reminiscent of Wright, between narrowing lines of historical force, Malcolm's voice accelerates toward the end he foresees, creating in the process a self who survives before in fact destroyed. Considered in relation to the literary patterns surveyed above—of interplay between the written and the unwritten record, of the urge to articulate black self out of silence—the fact that the book was spoken to Haley is of secondary importance. *The Autobiography of Malcolm X* is what it has been called (here in Peter Goldman's words) by many, "a great American life, a compelling and irreplaceable book." The life violently ended (but no more violently, Malcolm argued before the fact, than the inner lives of black Americans continue to be lived) is now begun on a pilgrimage of text, which Haley makes clear is in its essence Malcolm's. The issue is finally one of readership as much as authorship, as Du Bois suggested in his plea to God the Reader that his book be truly heard. As Ellison's narrator says in *Invisible Man* (the words welling in the silence after "There's Many a Thousand Gone" is sung), "A whole unrecorded history is spoken then, . . . listen to what is said."

The story is told as Baldwin said it must be, compulsively, in symbols and signs, in hieroglyphics such as the cryptic notations Malcolm made on paper napkins Haley learned to leave near him during interviews. Malcolm X speaks from beyond his conversion to "the Lost-Found Nation of Islam here in this wilderness of North America," beyond also his break with Elijah Muhammad, a change in a "life of changes" moving him toward a core of constant self. He speaks at times from a sense of being "already dead," premonitions of assassination blending with the "whispered" rather than the documented truth of his father's lynching, with the historical fatality of his race's enslavement. Violence, as he puts it, "runs in my family." Such "posthumousness" of voice, recalling moments of similar sensibility in Baldwin, Wright, and Du Bois, is no less emotionally convincing for being a rhetorical pose. The making of the book is on one level a political act, like Malcolm's reenactment of his father's involvement in Marcus Garvey's "back to Africa" movement in his own commitment to the Muslim doctrine of separation from white America. The personal progressively absorbs the political statement, however. He presents himself throughout as embodying the historical situation of "the black man in North America" (the equivalent but also the revision of "the Negro in America," the phrase in which Baldwin asserted his representative role), and the psychological tension collectively experienced by blacks.

Although the *Autobiography* contains no indication that he knew *Native Son*, in several passages Malcolm *is* Bigger, holding within him the same prophecy of our future. He accepts (without limiting himself to) the role of "America's most dangerous and threatening black man, . . . the one who has been kept sealed up by the Northerner in the black ghetto." This type, like the conditions which create it, "needs no fuse; . . . it spontaneously combusts from within." Malcolm makes of himself the archetypal "black prisoner," in whose ineradicable "memory of the bars" is also remembrance of the "first landing of the first slave ship." Such memory, from which historical identity has been erased, is itself the historical identity here reclaimed.

In prison, however, Malcolm also first felt free. "Transformed" by conversion, he also was liberated into the "new world" of books. The acts of reading and writing coalesced, as they had for Wright, into a means of self-verification against the cultural record from which he felt absent. He developed this more in terms of the spoken than the written word, his discovery of oratorical power simultaneous with the Muslims' discovery of its uses (as with narrator and Brotherhood in *Invisible Man*). But he emphasizes in the *Autobiography* his release through reading, and a consequent control of self in writing. After "lights out," the lamp's faint glow inversely suggesting the 1,369 bulbs blazing in Ellison's narrator's room, Malcolm feigns sleep as the guard passes, then re-enters the "area of that light-glow" to read on. As he listens to Elijah Muhammad "make a parable of me" while introducing him to the Muslims after he leaves prison, he is already launched on an effort to recompose himself in words.

Thus the fixity of each image of imprisonment is countered, though not negated, by a sense of fluid potentiality. Anger remains a creative force—"I *believe* in anger," Malcolm proclaims. He also comes to believe, however, in a different power of emergence from the past. The mental "wings" bestowed by conversion to Islam are those he rhetorically spreads as an angel of black vengeance against the white devil. They are also the wings on which the Muslims accuse him of flying too near the sun of Elijah's Muhammad's supremacy within the sect. But Malcolm X experiences the growth of other wings, within the chrysalis of personal history, to be spread in imaginative self-reincarnation.

His names, shed like snakeskin, convey the metamorphosis—Malcolm Little, "Homebody," "Detroit Red," "Satan," Malcolm X, El-Hajj Malik El-Shabazz. Whole phases of inner experience slide away "like snow off a roof," each previous phase "back there, without any remaining effect." During a pilgrimage to Mecca, carrying him past Black Muslim brotherhood to the true fulfillment of his Muslim life, he recalls a vision which takes him back in time as easily as the flow of time (with which he is obsessed) has taken him forward through his narrative. Lying awake among sleeping pilgrims,

> my mind took me back to personal memories I would have thought were gone forever . . . as far back, even, as when I was just a little boy, eight or nine years old. Out behind our house . . . there was an old, grassy "Hector's Hill," we called it—which may still be there. I remembered there in the Holy World how I used to lie on top of Hector's Hill, and look up at the sky, at the clouds moving over me, and daydreaming all kinds of things. And then . . . I remembered how years later, when I was in prison, I used to lie on my cell bunk—this would be especially when I was in solitary. . . .

His dreamings of the future are unencumbered by the past; in solitary reflection he can feel his immersion in—more than his racial removal from—the world. In Mecca, but in memory as well, he feels for the first time "like a complete human being." Prison at the time of his conversion was in Concord. He notes a link between Thoreau and himself forged in political resistance, suggesting in the process that one exists in the act of literary self-creation too. Hector's Hill, from which in the telling he reads again in moving clouds the symbols and signs of human possibility, is for a moment the imaginative place from which Thoreau would "fish in the sky, whose bottom is pebbly with stars."

In idiom also Malcolm slides easily through time and space, metamorphically slipping into the breaks of colloquial speech as Ellison's narrator [in *Invisible Man*] slips into the breaks in Louis Armstrong's music, descended ("What did I do/ To be so black/ And blue?") from the sorrow songs. He naturalizes the hustler's language into the narrative (after flaunting it at the outset, a verbal equivalent of the zoot suit he wears while inducting his Gentle Reader into the Harlem underworld). He then moves past it, as he moves beyond that phase of experience, but a fund of street intelligence remains, stenciled in his mind like the memory of the bars. As he says when he realizes that his discredit among the Muslims is being subtly arranged, "I hadn't hustled in the streets for years for nothing. I knew when I was being set up."

"What if history was a gambler," wonders the narrator in *Invisible Man*. "What if history was not a reasonable citizen, but a madman full of paranoid guile," life thus a matter of "running and dodging the forces of history instead of making a dominating stand." Malcolm presents hustling as a way of life rooted in a sense similar to Ellison's, paranoid guile the only sane response. "Internally restrained by nothing," the hustler is also in Malcolm's terms a "gambler," a Rinehartian being to whom anything is possible, inhabiting a world in which anything can happen. In the act of narration Malcolm's voice runs and dodges, talk from those days spilling into the present, from one form of the dangerous and reverberating silence of which Baldwin spoke. At the heart of the hustler's life is what Wright saw in his earliest stories, a "yawning void," an autobiographical vacuum with "no plot, . . . nothing save atmosphere, and longing and death." In the hustler's inability to "appraise" his own activity, lest in such distraction he fall prey to another, is the analogue to Baldwin's sense of being prohibited by external pressure from examining his own experience, a similar loss of experience the result.

Rescued from this death-in-life by the religion he encountered in prison, Malcolm found the Muslim precept "The white man is the devil" an echo, in his role as "the black prisoner," of the general experience of the black man in North America. Hence his susceptibility to conversion, and his insistence on the emotional truth (long after rejecting the historical absurdity) of the Muslim creation myth of "Mr. Yacub." Of a "tale" told in the ghetto, about a black woman's revenge against the whites who lynched her husband, Wright wrote in *Black Boy*:

> I did not know if the story was factually true or not, but it was emotionally true because I had already grown to feel that there existed men against whom I was powerless, men who could violate my life at will. . . . The story of the woman's deception gave form and meaning to confused defensive feelings that had long been sleeping in me.

Baldwin reports in *Notes of a Native Son* a "rumor" of a black soldier's being shot in the back by a white policeman in Harlem's Hotel Braddock, and dying while protecting a Negro woman from the officer. Baldwin's correction of the facts—the soldier was neither shot in the back nor dead, and the woman did not necessarily need protection—is secondary to the force with which the rumor swept the streets. An "instantaneous and revealing invention," it gave form and meaning to confused feelings in those who heard it: "They preferred the invention because [it] expressed and corroborated their hates and fears so perfectly." In this sense, for "that black convict" (as Malcolm calls himself) at the time of conversion, as for Malcolm having passed through self-narration beyond such faith, "The teachings ring true—to every Negro."

Malcolm also mentions the incident in the Hotel Braddock, but makes no interpretive comment, relating the "flash" of the rumor of the shooting without inquiring into its factuality. For him factuality is in that flash, out of which a riot spontaneously combusts. This is an instance of the *Autobiography*'s lack of "literary" development of its material. The sequence is perfectly aligned, however, with the sense of reality governing this phase of Malcolm's life. "A writer is what I want, not an interpreter," Haley says Malcolm told him when the publishing contract was signed. Or, as Ellison's narrator puts it, "This is not prophecy, but description." In such description, nonetheless, is a cumulative prophecy, igniting as inevitably in Malcolm's mind as the riot explodes in Harlem.

Whatever the mix of Malcolm X's motives—outrage at a leader's lapses from Muslim morality, perhaps the pride of a "Satan" who would rule—in breaking and in turn being cut off from the Muslims, he finds himself, in his final year, again on his own. "Thinking for myself," running and dodging through the psychological debris of the failure for him of Muslim historical design, he is exhilarated by freedom yet desperate for the new community he has set out in his mind to create in this wilderness of North America. He experiences the return—it had never really left him—of the old double-consciousness. THEM, hieroglyphically inscribed by Malcolm on one of Haley's napkins and meaning The Honorable Elijah Muhammad, becomes a Pynchonesque suggestion of the justifications in reality for resumption of paranoid guile, like WASTE in *The Crying of Lot 49*.

As Malcolm begins to see in former friends the faces of those who will end his life, he feels (like Ellison's narrator and in Ellison's words) that in the Brotherhood "was the only historically meaningful life that I could live. If I left it, I'd be nowhere," that place of internal emptiness so often arrived at in the works discussed above. Then he begins to feel (in his own words as we learn from Haley's epilogue, but also like Ellison's narrator for whom in the novel's epilogue invisibility has become a form of strategic flexibility) that while "I can't put my finger on exactly what my philosophy is now, . . . I'm flexible." The statement, made in an interview not printed until after his death, reflects his having gone (in Ellison's sense) underground. It also reflects his posthumous determination, reemergent in text, on lower narrative frequencies to keep on speaking for us all. This is where Malcolm X—his voice turning inward in a tightening gyre like the same tight circles he often walked while talking to Haley—makes his dominating stand.

When Malcolm lost faith in Elijah Muhammad, he felt "as though something in *nature* had failed, like the sun, or the stars." Elijah Muhammad, interpreting to the Muslim faithful Malcolm's fall from grace, said "He was a star, who went astray." Malcolm is yet another of Du Bois' falling stars, dying throughout history. But he is also in his book—in which he steps into self-fulfilling imagination rather than into Rinehart's mastery of chaos—the embodiment of Du Bois and of other black American autobiographers of this century. His parents' seventh child, he is also Du Bois' "seventh son, born with a veil, and gifted with second-sight in this American world," the gift of insight being the curse of double-consciousness. When Eldridge Cleaver says, "Black history began with Malcolm X," he ignores a history begun long before Du Bois yet testifies truly to the seminal as well as the culminating power of the record of Malcolm's personal journey up from slavery.

In the last lines of his *Narrative of the Life of Frederick Douglass, An American Slave, Written by Himself* (1845), Douglass states:

> The truth was, I felt myself a slave, and the idea of speaking to white people weighed me down. I spoke but a few moments, when I felt a degree of freedom, and said what I desired with considerable ease. From that time until now, I have been engaged in pleading the cause of my brethren—with what success, and with what devotion, I leave those acquainted with my labors to decide.

Malcolm's voice encompasses without overriding the voices of those who have spoken "from that time until now." In tones reminiscent of Douglass he says:

> I have given to this book so much of whatever time I have because I feel, and I hope, that if I honestly and fully tell my life's account, read objectively it might prove to be a testimony of some social value.

He dares humbly as well as in anger and pride "to dream to myself" back now on Hector's Hill as well as nearing death—"that one day, history may even say that my voice . . . helped to save America from a grave, possibly even a fatal catastrophe." With what success remains unknown, to be revealed in cities of words as yet unbuilt in the wilderness of North America, in signs yet to appear on the open pages beneath Wright's pencil at the end of *American Hunger*. With what devotion, however, is amply answered in *The Autobiography of Malcolm X*.

Malcolm's fallen star merges with the morning star of Thoreau, his "two-edged sword" of Islamic truth with the scimitar in *Walden*, "the sun glimmer[ing] on both its surfaces," its edge "dividing you through the heart," as in *Invisible Man* the narrator hears the shattering stroke of his heart in "There's Many a Thousand Gone." In his parable of unfinished self, Malcolm X moves time-haunted toward the perfect work into which time does not enter, an autobiographical act in which the tale Du Bois called "twice told but seldom written" becomes one in which (in a sense other than, yet comprehending that of the Islamic prophecy Malcolm invokes) "everything is written."

JOE WOOD

SOURCE: Joe Wood, "His Final Days," in *The Nation*, Vol. 249, No. 18, November 27, 1989, pp. 650-2.

[*In the following excerpt, Wood provides a mixed assessment of* Malcolm X: The Last Speeches.]

Do we measure activists' lives by the breadth of their hopes or their earnestness in trying to make them real? Or do we measure activists by where they actually end up, failures and disillusionments included? And how do we figure someone like Malcolm X?

In Malcolm's case, myth has long since taken the place of research in the imagination of Americans, black and white. Malcolm's myth, widely circulated in [*The Autobiography of Malcolm X*], makes him a very current African-American figure: the resistant seminationalist, a hero for the "lost and (now I'm) found" strain of gritty American individualism. In the popular view, Malcolm represents the real black thing; one's reaction to Malcolm's myth, then, becomes a measure of one's understanding of, or sympathy with, the "strong side" of black experience—the side that is ready to embrace other Americans without forfeiting any self-respect. Unfortunately, [*Malcolm X: The Last Speeches*] smoothes over significant details about Malcolm's life.

In March 1964, Malcolm X left the Nation of Islam, the organization that had both nurtured him into responsible adulthood and shaken America's political consciousness. The break was real. During the last eleven months of his life, Malcolm made an eye-opening pilgrimage to Africa and the Middle East, and he publicly renounced Elijah Muhammad's theology as unorthodox and racist. He also began pondering conceptual alternatives to the movement's black nationalism, eventually deciding to activate a human rights campaign in America, and to place new emphasis on brotherhood, internationalism, anti-imperialism and, most important, progressive action.

But never did he cease being, as is said in the vernacular, hard. After establishing the orthodox Muslim Mosque Inc., Malcolm formed the ecumenical Organization of Afro-American Unity (O.A.A.U.), and he gave it the slogan "By Any Means Necessary." He never failed to remind audiences that while he didn't advocate violence, he did believe in the right to self-protection, particularly in a country as racially inequitable as the United States. And while white liberals and black (dare I say it) integrationists like to stress his embrace of brotherhood, even a cursory examination of his speeches reveals that Malcolm never changed his mind about what the chief enemy was: white American racism.

In 1965 Pathfinder Press published *Malcolm X Speaks*, a collection of speeches, interviews and correspondence that, with one exception, are from the last year of his life. The editing of both that book and *Malcolm X: The Last Speeches* emphasizes Malcolm's political evolution; its obvious intent is to reinforce the notion that Malcolm was loosening up, becoming more intellectually honest and, most significant, more willing to embrace white revolutionaries and traditional leftisms.

Malcolm X: The Last Speeches actually offers readers glimpses of more than that. The book's first two examples are standard Black Muslim fare, delivered in 1963 to predominantly white audiences at Michigan State University and the University of California at Berkeley. In the book's pair of radio interviews (December 1964), Malcolm distances himself from speeches like these, contending that he was only "parroting" Elijah Muhammad's propaganda. But as parrot propagandists go, Malcolm performed brilliantly, making points he would later alter but never abandon:

> [The] new type [of black man] rejects the white man's Christian religion. He recognizes the real enemy. That Uncle Tom can't see his enemy. He thinks his friend is his enemy and his enemy is his friend. And he usually ends up loving his enemy, turning his other cheek to his enemy. But this new type, he doesn't turn the other cheek to anybody. He doesn't believe in any kind of

peaceful suffering. He believes in obeying the law. He believes in respecting people. He believes in doing unto others as he would have done to himself. But at the same time, if anybody attacks him, he believes in retaliating if it costs him his life. And it is good for white people to know this. Because if white people get the impression that Negroes all endorse this old turn-the-other-cheek cowardly philosophy of Dr. Martin Luther King, then whites are going to make the mistake of putting their hands on some black man, thinking that he's going to turn the other cheek, and he'll end up losing his hand and losing his life in the try. [*Commotion and laughter*]

Malcolm is giving voice to this "new" type of black man; he is tapping into a rather traditional African-American will to self-determination and proclaiming his strength in terms anybody can understand and respect. In such talk one can witness the genesis of Malcolm's slogan, By Any Means Necessary, and observe the reason for his appeal to black *and* white audiences.

Yet behind Malcolm X's incredible ability to pick metaphors from the air, and behind his clarity and brutal earnestness, lurked a basic deception: Malcolm didn't believe a lot of what he was saying. In 1960, for instance, Elijah directed Malcolm to conduct secret talks with the Ku Klux Klan about the possibility of carving a black nation out of South Carolina. These negotiations made Malcolm uncomfortable—cutting deals with the blue-eyed devils simply did not sit well. But like any disciplined revolutionary, Malcolm felt he couldn't break ranks and did so only after internal politics and personal disillusionment forced him out.

In the last year of his life, Malcolm offered piecemeal explanations for his abrupt departure. Among these were what he described as the movement's willful lethargy and its racist unorthodoxy; these concerns surface with passionate cogency in the book's only gem, a speech Malcolm made the night after his house was firebombed (allegedly by members of Elijah's movement). Delivered on February 15, 1965, at Harlem's Audubon Ballroom—the site of his assassination less than a week later—these remarks show the profundity of his disappointment with the movement:

> And there has been a conspiracy across the country on the part of many factions of the press to suppress news that would open the eyes of the Muslims who are following Elijah Muhammad. They continue to make him look like he's a prophet somewhere who is getting some messages direct from God and is untouchable and things of that sort. I'm telling you the truth. But they do know that if something were to happen and all these brothers, their eyes were to come open, they would be right out here in every one of these civil rights organizations making these Uncle Tom Negro leaders stand up and fight like men instead of running around here nonviolently acting like women.
>
> So they hope Elijah Muhammad remains as he is for a long time because they know that any organization that he heads, it will not do anything in the struggle that the black man is confronted with in this country. Proof of which, look how violent they can get. They were violent, they've been violent from coast to coast. Muslims, in the Muslim movement, have been involved in cold, calculated violence. And not at one time have they been involved in any violence against the Ku Klux Klan. They're capable. They're qualified. They're equipped. They know how to do it. But they'll never do it—only to another brother. [*Applause*]

What throbs at bottom here is a very painful distress: Malcolm is rejecting, and has been rejected by, his spiritual/political father. Elijah's movement made Malcolm, forming him even as he helped form the Nation. Like any good lieutenant, Malcolm served with his eyes open. He'd heard the rumors about Elijah's character, had sat across table from the Klan and had also concealed any doubts that had occurred to him. For his faith Malcolm was given the truth, which hurt.

By the time he made that speech, Malcolm had traveled through newly postcolonial Africa, and thereby broadened and sharpened his thinking. His essential "Black Muslim" outrage, however, remained, only with complications. The problems clearly did not come from his broader understanding of internationalism or anticapitalism or brotherhood. Malcolm never had much time to investigate these ideas thoroughly, nor did he ever abandon the sexism attendant on his notions of black manhood, nor did he fool himself about the privileges whites enjoy in this country. Rather, Malcolm's new perspective was made more complicated by his realization that he hadn't known his friends from his enemies, just like the Uncle Tom house Negroes he harped on in his Black Muslim speeches. Where in his old scheme, after all, does one place Elijah? The awful and unavoidable truth is that he must be classed alongside other useful revolutionaries turned sorry despots, men seduced by the jeweled trappings of institutional power.

What emerges, then, as Malcolm's most significant final year revelation is not his admission of the possibility of white good, but his encounter with the disillusioning reality of "new" Negro corruption. *The Last Speeches* records Malcolm's most significant postrevolutionary change: his realization that he could not be *sure*. Readers will be reminded that the gun Malcolm holds in that famous photograph was being readied not for enemies who were white, but former comrades who were black.

SOURCES FOR FURTHER STUDY

Clarke, John Henrik. *Malcolm X: The Man and His Times.* Toronto: The MacMillan Company, 1969, 360 p.

> Collects speeches by and interviews with Malcolm X, as well as analytical and commemorative essays and personal reminiscences.

Groppe, John D. "From Chaos to Cosmos: The Role of Trust in *The Autobiography of Malcolm X.*" *Soundings* LXVI, No. 4 (Winter 1983): 437-49.

> Argues that *The Autobiography* is "the story of loss, and then the regaining, of the capacity to trust," which ensures Malcolm's "pilgrimage from self to cosmos."

Hoyt, Charles Alva. "The Five Faces of Malcolm X." *Negro American Literature Forum* 4, No. 4 (Winter 1970): 107-12.

> Divides Malcolm X's life into five stages and five identities: Malcolm Little, Detroit Red, Satan, Malcolm X, and El-Hajj Malik El-Shabazz.

Nichols, Charles H. "The Slave Narrators and the Picaresque Mode: Archetypes for Modern Black Personae." In *The Slave's Narrative,* edited by Charles T. Davis and Henry Louis Gates, Jr., pp. 283-98. New York: Oxford University Press, 1985.

> Analyzes the influence of slave narratives on modern black autobiographies, including *The Autobiography of Malcolm X.*

Perry, Bruce. *Malcolm: The Life of a Man Who Changed Black America.* Barrytown, N.Y.: Station Hill Press, 1991, 568 p.

> Comprehensive biography of Malcolm X, focusing on the more personal aspects of the leader's life.

Rustin, Bayard. "Making His Mark: A Strong Diagnosis of America's Racial Sickness in One Negro's Odyssey." *Book World—New York Herald Tribune* (14 November 1965): 1, 8, 10, 12, 16-17.

> Review of *The Autobiography of Malcolm X* in which the critic surveys the life of Malcolm X and his role as a leader in the black community.

(Sir)Thomas Malory

1410?-1471?

(Also Maleore, Maleorre, Malleorr, and Malorye) English prose writer.

INTRODUCTION

Malory is recognized as a towering figure of medieval English literature. His masterwork, *The Noble and Joyous book entytled le morte Darthur* (1485)—which is commonly known as *Morte Darthur*—is the best-known treatment in English of the tales of the exploits and deeds of King Arthur and the knights of the Round Table. *Morte Darthur* is esteemed on several counts; it is a mirror of medieval culture and manners, a seminal work of English prose, and an enduring, entertaining narrative. *Morte Darthur,* however, remains an enigma— scholars, for example, frequently debate whether Malory wrote the book and historically have focused on the author's sources and intentions, as well as the book's structure and thematic content. Whatever puzzles it presents, the *Morte Darthur* is an acknowledged literary milestone. In the words of critic William Henry Schofield, it is "the fountainhead of [English] Arthurian fiction."

Biographical Information

Although the authorship of the *Morte Darthur* has long been hotly disputed, most scholars generally agree that the "syr Thomas Maleore knyght" named in the colophon of the 1485 printing of the text is Sir Thomas Malory of Newbold Revel, Warwickshire. His birth date is uncertain, but it is believed to be around 1410. He was probably the son of John Malory, esquire, also of Newbold Revel. As a young man, Thomas served with the earl of Warwick's forces in France and succeeded to his father's estate in 1433 or 1434. Far from being the sort of man likely to write what William Caxton called a "Noble and Joyous book," Sir Thomas is suspected to have been a ruffian of the most extreme kind. (Some critics, however, such as C. S. Lewis, assert that is is impossible to know the validity of the charges and emphasize that the possible mitigating circumstances remain unknown to modern audiences because of lack of evidence.) Malory, for instance, was indicted for theft in 1443 and served in parliament later in the decade. In 1450, he evidently embarked upon an appalling career of rape, robbery, and brutal violence. In spite of the seriousness of the charges brought at Nuneaton in 1451, Malory was never brought to trial for the crimes enumerated, though he was summoned in March 1452 to answer charges not sufficiently explained the year before. For a time he apparently continued his criminal enterprises, and he jumped bail in 1454 to avoid felony prosecution. He was called before the King's Bench on January 16, 1456. Two years later he was committed to Marshalsea prison. Nothing more is known of him until 1468, when he was specifically excluded from Edward IV's general pardon of August 25 of that year. Malory died in March 1471, probably having completed the *Morte Darthur* a year or two earlier. According to the seventeenth-century English antiquary William Dugdale, he was "buryed . . . in the Chappell of St Francis at the Grey Friars, near Newgate in the Suburbs of London."

Major Works

The central story of the *Morte Darthur* consists of two main elements: King Arthur's reign ending in disaster with the dissolution of the Round Table and the quest for the Holy Grail. The work begins with the adulterous conception of Arthur, who later establishes his kingship by pulling a sword from a stone. This infamous "sword in the stone" was better known as "Excalibur." Arthur and his legendary knights then form the Order of the Round Table and engage in battles in its and the realm's defense. After a series of stirring adventures and victories, Arthur conquers Rome, where he is welcomed by the pope. Tales of Arthur's knights follow: the prowess of Sir Palomides and Sir Lancelot, the pursuit of the mysterious Questing Beast, the rescue of prisoners held by rogue knights, the ventures of Sir Tristram and his paramour, and other accounts. After the quest for the Holy Grail is initiated, the vexing and ill-fated undertaking leads to the loss of some of Arthur's finest knights, among them Lancelot's son, the purehearted Sir Galahad. During the quest, the beginning of the end of the Round Table is foreshadowed in the shortcomings and spiritual imperfections of men once considered paradigms of knightly virtue. With the return of the knights from the failed attempt to recover the Grail, the dissolution of the Round Table proceeds in earnest. Lancelot proves his moral and spiritual failings by committing adultery with Arthur's consort, Queen Guinevere, while Arthur himself is increasingly thwarted by challenges to the throne. The conflict between knightly and Christian behavior remains unresolved, which precipitates the tragic and bloody collapse of Arthur's society at the treacherous instigation of the king's bastard son, Sir Mordred. In the end, Arthur is dead, Guinevere has entered a nunnery, and the kingdom is in ruins.

Critical Reception

The *Morte Darthur* has generated scores of textual and critical controversies among scholars who have yet to reach a consensus on questions about the book's sources and intent, structural unity, historical veracity, artistic viability, and moral authority. For example, much debate focuses on Sir Thomas's editing of his sources and the inclusion of French legends and how his choices shaped the final product. Before the nineteenth century, commentary focused more on the entertainment value of the *Morte Darthur* than on anything else. Since then, critics have explored many other aspects of the *Morte Darthur*. The "moral paradox" of a criminal author having written a work on "love, curtosye, and veray gentylnesse" has emerged as a major concern, while such issues as novelistic elements, characterization, allegorical imagery, "courtly love," the passage of time, formulaic language, neologisms, and dialogue in the work have been treated repeatedly. The width and variety of response to the *Morte Darthur* suggests the strong appeal of the work. As the single greatest repository of Arthurian Legend in English, its influence upon poets, novelists, and scholars has been tremendous. Equally, the *Morte Darthur* has stirred the imaginations of generations of readers whose love of the Round Table and all it represents is abiding. Eugène Vinaver commented on its longevity and popularity: "Many writers had worked on the French Arthurian prose romances between the thirteenth and the fifteenth centuries; there had been adaptations of it in Spain and in Germany. All this is now dead and buried, and Malory alone stands as a rock defying all changes of taste and style and morals; not as a grand paradox of nature, but as a lasting work of art."

(For further information, see *Concise Dictionary of British Literary Biography: Before 1660; Dictionary of Literary Biography,* Vol. 146; *DISCovering Authors; DISCovering Authors: British; DISCovering Authors: Canadian; DISCovering Authors Modules: Most-studied Authors Module; Literature Criticism from 1400 to 1800,* Vol. 11; *Something about the Author,* Vols. 33, 59.)

CRITICAL COMMENTARY

WILLIAM CAXTON

SOURCE: William Caxton, "Caxton's Preface," in *The Works of Sir Thomas Malory, Vol. I*, edited by Eugène Vinaver, Oxford at the Clarendon Press, 1947, pp. cxi-cxv.

[*Caxton is revered as the first English printer. In 1475, while living in Bruges, he set up and published* The Recuyell of the Historyes of Troye, *the first book printed in English. One year later, he established a press in Westminster, where, during the next decade and a half, he produced over eighty separate works. Caxton was a gifted editor, translator, and author in his own right. He often wrote prefaces to the works he published, supplying information (when available) about authorship, textual history, genre, intended audience, narrative structure, and other critical and aesthetic matters. His most famous publications include Geoffrey Chaucer's* Canterbury Tales *(1478 and 1484), John Gower's* Confessio amantis *(1483), a translation of* The Golden Legend *(1483), and Malory's* The Noble and Joyous book entytled le morte Darthur *(1485). In the following excerpt from the preface of the latter, Caxton argues that Arthur's reputation is chiefly literary and notices the didactic, historical, and entertainment value of the* Morte Darthur.]

After that I had accomplysshed and fynysshed dyvers hystoryes as wel of contemplacyon as of other hystoryal and worldly actes of grete conquerours and prynces, and also certeyn bookes of ensaumples and doctryne, many noble and dyvers gentylmen of thys royame of Englond camen and demaunded me many and oftymes wherfore that I have not do made and enprynte the noble hystorye of the Saynt Greal and of the moost renomed Crysten kyng, fyrst and chyef of the thre best Crysten, and worthy, kyng Arthur, whyche ought moost to be remembred emonge us Englysshemen tofore al other Crysten kynges.

For it is notoyrly knowen thorugh the unyversal world that there been nine worthy and the best that ever were, that is to wete, thre Paynyms, thre Jewes, and thre Crysten men. As for the Paynyms, they were tofore the Incarnacyon of Cryst whiche were named, the fyrst Hector of Troye, of whome th'ystorye is comen bothe in balade and in prose, the second Alysaunder the Grete, and the thyrd, Julyus Cezar, Emperour of Rome, the londe of byheste, the second Davyd, kyng of Jerusalem, and the thyrd Judas Machabeus, of these thre the Byble rehercethal theyr noble hystoryes and actes. And sythe the sayd Incarnacyon have ben thre noble Crysten men stalled and admytted thorugh the unyversal world into the nombre of the nine beste and worthy, of whome was fyrst the noble Arthur, whos noble actes I purpose to wryte thys present book here folowyng. The second was Charlemayn, or Charles the Grete, of whome th'ystorye is had in many places, bothe in Frensshe and Englysshe; and the thyrd and last was Godefray of Boloyn, of whos actes and lyf I made a book unto th'excellent prynce and kyng of noble memorye, kyng Edward the Fourth.

The sayd noble jentylmen instantly requyred me t'emprynte th'ystorye of the sayd noble kyng and conquerour kyng Arthur and of his knyghtes, wyth th'ystorye of the Saynt Greal and of the deth and endyng of the sayd Arthur, affermyng that I ought rather t'enprynte his actes and noble feates than of Godefroye of Boloyne or ony of the other eyght, consyderyng that he was a man borne wythin this royame and kyng and emperour of the same, and that there ben in Frensshe dyvers and many noble volumes of his actes, and also of his knyghtes.

To whome I answerd that dyvers men holde oppynyon that there was no suche Arthur and that alle suche bookes as been maad of hym ben but fayned and fables, bycause that somme cronycles make of hym no mencyon ne remembre hym noothynge, ne of his knyghtes.

Wherto they answerd, and one in specyal sayd, that in hym that shold say or thynke that there was never suche a kyng callyd Arthur myght wel be aretted grete folye and blyndenesse, for he sayd that there were many evydences of the contrarye. Fyrst, ye may see his sepulture in the monasterye of Glastyngburye; and also in Polycronycon, in the fifth book, the syxte chappytre, and in the seventh book, the twenty-thyrd chappytre, where his body was buryed, and after founden and translated into the sayd monasterye. Ye shal se also in th'ystorye of Bochas, in his book DE CASU PRINCIPUM, parte of his noble actes, and also of his falle. Also Galfrydus, in his Brutysshe book, recounteth his lyf. And in dyvers places of Englond many remembraunces ben yet of hym and shall remayne perpetuelly, and also of his knyghtes: fyrst,

> **Principal Works**
>
> *The Noble and Joyous book Entytled le Morte Darthur Notwythstondyng It Treateth of the Byrth, Lyf, and Actes of the Sayd Kyng Arthur, of His Knyghtes of the Rounde Table, Theyr Meruayllous Enquestes and Aduentures, Thachyeuyng of the Sangreal, & Thende the Dolorous Deth & Departyng out of Thys World of Them Al (prose) c. 1469
>
> *The Works of Sir Thomas Malory.* 3 vols. (prose) 1947; revised edition, 1967
>
> *There is no evidence that Malory gave this work a title. The present title was apparently supplied by William Caxton, the printer of the first edition. This work is also known as *The Booke of the Noble Kyng, Kyng Arthur, Sometyme Kynge of Englonde, of his Noble Actes and Feates of Armes and Chyvalrye, his Noble Knygtes and Table Rounde*; *The Whole Book of King Arthur and of His Noble Knights of the Round Table*; *Le Morte d'Arthur*; *Le Morte Darthur*; *Morte D'Arthur*; *Morte Arthur*; and, most commonly, *Morte Darthur*.
>
> **Adaptations**
>
> Adaptations of Malory's work include the films *Knights of the Round Table*, directed by Richard Thorpe, 1953, and *Excalibur*, directed by John Boorman, 1981.

in the abbey of Westmestre, at Saynt Edwardes shryne, remayneth the prynte of his seal in reed waxe, closed in beryll, in whych is wryton PATRICIUS ARTHURUS BRITANNIE GALLIE GERMANIE DACIE IMPERATOR; item, in the castel of Dover ye may see Gauwayns skulle and Cradoks mantel; at Wynchester, the Rounde Table; in other places Launcelottes swerde and many other thynges.

Thenne, al these thynges consydered, there can no man resonably gaynsaye but there was a kyng of thys lande named Arthur. For in al places, Crysten and hethen, he is reputed and taken for one of the nine worthy, and the fyrst of the thre Crysten men. And also he is more spoken of beyonde the see, moo bookes made of his noble actes, than there be in Englond; as wel in Duche, Ytalyen, Spaynysshe, and Grekysshe, as in Frensshe. And yet of record remayne in wytnesse of hym in Wales, in the toune of Camelot, the grete stones and mervayllous werkys of yron lyeng under the grounde, and ryal vautes, which dyvers now lyvyng hath seen. Wherfor it is a mervayl why he is no more renomed in his owne contreye, sauf onelye it accordeth to the word of God, whyche sayth that no man is accept for a prophete in his owne contreye.

Thenne, al these thynges forsayd aledged, I coude not wel denye but that there was suche a noble kyng named Arthur, and reputed one of the nine worthy, and fyrst and chyef of the Cristen men. And many noble volumes be made of hym and of his noble knyghtes in Frensshe, which I have seen and redde beyonde the see, which been not had in our maternal tongue. But in Walsshe ben many, and also in Frensshe, and somme in Englysshe, but nowher nygh alle. Wherfore, suche as have late ben drawen oute bryefly into Englysshe, I have, after the symple connynge that God hath sente to me, under the favour and correctyon of al noble lordes and gentylmen, enprysed to enprynte a book of the noble hystoryes of the sayd kynge Arthur and of certeyn of his knyghtes [***The Noble and Joyous Book Entytled Le Morte Darthur***], after a copye unto me delyverd, whyche copye syr Thomas Malorye dyd take oute of certeyn bookes of Frensshe and reduced it into Englysshe.

And I, accordyng to my copye, have doon sette it in enprynte to the entente that noble men may see and lerne the noble actes of chyvalrye, the jentyl and vertuous dedes that somme knyghtes used in tho dayes, by whyche they came to honour, and how they that were vycious were punysshed and ofte put to shame and rebuke; humbly bysechyng al noble lordes and ladyes wyth al other estates, of what estate or degree they been of, that shal see and rede in this sayd book and werke, that they take the good and honest actes in their remembraunce, and to folowe the same; wherin they shalle fynde many joyous and playsaunt hystoryes and noble and renomed actes of humanyte, gentylnesse, and chyvalryes. For herein may be seen noble chyvalrye, curtosye, humanyte, frendlynesse, hardynesse, love, frendshyp, cowardyse, murdre, hate, vertue, and synne. Doo after the good and leve the evyl, and it shal brynge you to good fame and renommee.

And for to passe the tyme thys book shal be plesaunte to rede in, but for to gyve fayth and byleve that al is trewe that is conteyned herin, ye be at your lyberte. But al is wryton for our doctryne, and for to beware that we falle not to vyce ne synne, but t'exersyse and folowe vertu, by whyche we may come and atteyne to good fame and renomme in thys lyf, and after thys shorte and transytorye lyf to come unto everlastyng blysse in heven; the whyche He graunte us that reygneth in heven, the Blessyd Trynyte. AMEN.

Thenne, to procede forth in thys sayd book, whyche I

dyrecte unto alle noble pryncis, lordes, and ladyes, gentylmen or gentylwymmen, that desyre to rede or here redde of the noble and joyous hystorye of the grete conquerour and excellent kyng, kyng Arthur, somtyme kyng of thys noble royalme thenne callyd Brytaygne, I, Wyllyam Caxton, symple persone, present thys book folowyng whyche I have enprysed t'enprynte: and treateth of the noble actes, feates of armes of chyvalrye, prowesse, hardynesse, humanyte, love, curtosye, and veray gentylnesse, wyth many wonderful hystoryes and adventures. . . .

SIR WALTER RALEIGH

SOURCE: Sir Walter Raleigh, "The Romance and the Novel," in his *The English Novel: A Short Sketch of Its History from the Earliest Times to the Appearance of "Waverly,"* John Murray, 1894, pp. 1-24.

[*A renowned lecturer and literary critic, Raleigh was the first professor of English literature at the University of Oxford. His critical approach to literature, evident in his lectures and in such works as* The English Novel *(1894) and* Shakespeare *(1907), was that of a highly perceptive, urbane commentator. In his literary exegeses he aimed to bring about the nonspecialist's understanding of English literature through concise textual commentary. In addition, Raleigh often illuminated his subject through insightful examination of the personality of the writer under discussion. In the following excerpt from* The English Novel, *he considers the prose style and structure of the* Morte Darthur.]

The scholars who are unwilling to admit that the Arthur legends grew up on Breton soil have also claimed Sir Thomas Malory, on the authority of Bale, for a Welshman. It is quite certain, at least, that he was, as Bale calls him, "heroici spiritus homo," a man of a heroic temper; the facts of his life are lacking. His book, **Le Morte Darthur,** a compilation mainly from French sources, was finished, as he himself states, in the ninth years of the reign of King Edward IV, that is to say, either in 1469 or 1470. It was secured for posterity by Caxton, who printed it in 1485.

In the preface which he contributed to his edition of the work, Caxton discusses at some length the existence of an historical Arthur. He had delayed printing the noble history of King Arthur because, like Milton later, he was troubled with the doubt whether such a king had ever existed. Divers gentlemen of this realm of England had attempted to conquer his scepticism, alleging, among other things, that in the castle of Do-

ver "ye may see Gawaine's skull." He concludes by remarking that, true or not, the book is exemplary and profitable. "And for to pass the time this book shall be pleasant to read in, but for to give faith and belief that all is true that is contained herein, ye be at your liberty; but all is written for our doctrine, and for to beware that we fall not to vice ne sin, but to exercise and follow virtue; by the which we may come and attain to good fame and renown in this life, and after this short and transitory life to come unto everlasting bliss in heaven."

The words are memorable as marking the beginning of prose fiction; history and fable, so long inextricably entangled, are here drawing apart from one another; literature is proclaiming itself as an art, and declaring a purpose beyond the scope of the humble chronicle.

To attain to a finely ordered artistic structure was beyond Malory's power; the very wealth of legend with which he had to deal put it beyond him, and he is too much absorbed in the interest of the parts to give more than a passing consideration to the whole. His simple forthright narrative is admirably lucid and effective, and makes amends for an inevitably rambling structure, while his flashes of chivalrous feeling illuminate the plains through which his story wanders. He is a master in the telling use of the Saxon speech, although he translates from the French. When Queen Guinevere escaped from the insolent overtures of Sir Mordred, she took the Tower of London and suddenly "stuffed it," says Malory, "with all manner of victual, and well garnished it with men, and so kept it." Sir Launcelot, after her death, "dried and dwined away . . . and ever he was lying groveling on the tomb of King Arthur and Queen Guenever." The Holy Grail descends amidst "cracking and crying of thunder." Sir Bedivere, when he was sent to throw away Excalibur, "saw nothing but the waters wap and the waves wan." And this fascinating simplicity of diction is matched by the clearness of outline that distinguishes Malory's pictures; the figures he employs, few in number, are of the natural and unsought kind dear to Saxon speech. A knight appears in the lists as "bright as an angel," two combatants rush together "like two rams," the children that King Arthur finds the giant roasting are broached on a spit, "like young birds." The allegorical habit has left traces here and there on Malory's work, but indeed it may be said for allegory that it fosters simplicity in prose narration. Where words are to bear a double meaning it is important that the first should be clearly defined, and perfectly distinguished from the second; the elaborated metaphorical style of a later and more sophisticated age mingles the fact and its figurative associations as early narrative prose never does. The Renaissance troubled the waters, and it was long ere prose ran clear again. There is no better prose style for the purposes of simple story-telling than that which many English writers have at command from Malory to Latimer.

The human emotions enshrined in this style have an irresistible appeal. Pity, anger, love, and pride, speak straight to the heart. The passionate and rebellious cry of Queen Guinevere, "I trust through God's grace after my death to have a sight of the blessed face of Christ, and at doomsday to sit at His right side, for as sinful as ever I was are saints in heaven," has parallels in modern literature. Burns expresses the same hope, but his surmise that after all he may—

> Snugly sit among the saunts
> At Davie's hip yet,

has lost more in pathos than it can make good by its gain in humour.

The work of Sir Thomas Malory became for the following age the embodiment of the ideas of chivalry and the well-head of romance. It was twice reprinted by Wynkyn de Worde, in 1498 and 1529, and again by William Copland in 1557. The demand continued, and there are later reprints, belonging to the reigns of Elizabeth and Charles I respectively, by Thomas East and William Stansby. But in the Elizabethan age, as in our own, it became the feeder of poetry rather than of prose; Spenser knew it well and Shakespeare read it; traces of its influence on the greater prose writers, even on Sir Philip Sidney, are scant enough.

C. S. LEWIS

SOURCE: C. S. Lewis, "The English Prose 'Morte'," in *Essays on Malory* by Walter Oakeshott and others, edited by J. A. W. Bennett, Oxford at the Clarendon Press, 1963, pp. 7-28.

[*Lewis is considered one of the foremost twentieth-century authors to write on Christian and mythopoeic themes. Indebted principally to George MacDonald, G. K. Chesterton, Charles Williams, and the writers of ancient Norse myths, he is regarded as a formidable logician and Christian polemicist, a perceptive literary critic, and—perhaps most highly—as a writer of fantasy literature. In the following excerpt, Lewis investigates what he considers five key "paradoxes" concerning Malory's intentions in the* Morte Darthur. *For a response to Lewis's essay, see the following excerpt by Eugene Vinaver.*]

I begin by considering certain paradoxes which have been thrown up by the remarkable discoveries made in the last fifty years about Malory and the book (or books) which he translated with modifications, from the French and which Caxton printed in 1485. They are five in number.

I. The work has long passed for a mirror of honour and virtue; the author appears to have been little better than a criminal.

II. The work strikes every reader as a rich feast of marvels, a tale 'of faerie damsels met in forest wide'; but a comparison of it with its sources seems to show Malory almost everywhere labouring to eliminate the marvellous and introduce the humdrum.

III. The work seems to many of us the typical specimen (because it is the first specimen we met) of Interwoven or Polyphonic narrative. But once again, comparison with the sources shows everything proceeding as if Malory detested this technique and did his best to pluck the threads apart.

IV. Its handling of the Grail story sounds deeply religious, and we have the sense that it is somehow profoundly connected with the final tragedy. But a case can be made out for the view that Malory evaded the religious significance and ignored or severed the connexion.

V. Malory seemed to Saintsbury (and doubtless to many) the man who alone "makes of this vast assemblage of stories one story and one book". The evidence of the Winchester MS. convinces Professor Vinaver that he really wrote several works which were never intended to form a whole.

If all these Paradoxes stand, they build up into a single grand Paradox. It is not of course paradoxical that a man's work should be other than he intended. What is paradoxical is that a man's work should succeed by its failure to realize every single intention he had when he made it. For it is as a mirror of honour, as a feast of marvels, as a Polyphonic narrative, as a romance of chivalry haunted by the higher mystery of the Grail, and as (in some sort) a unity, that the *Morte Darthur* has pleased. And not only pleased, but so far outstripped its rivals that it alone of all medieval prose romances has survived as a living book into our own century. In Malory's case, apparently, nothing succeeds like failure.

The reader should be warned at once that I am not attempting a *reductio ad absurdum*. I am not sure whether all the Paradoxes, in their sharpest form, will stand; but neither am I sure that all of them will completely fall. It therefore may be true that something like this paradoxical 'success by failure' has actually happened. If it has, then I want to draw a conclusion from it. But that will come later; in the meantime I will proceed to examine the five Paradoxes one by one.

I. The apparent discrepancy between the man and the work has seemed to some so formidable that they seek refuge in the possibility that the wicked Malory of the records is not our author but another man of the same name. But this is rather a desperate expedient. By all sound methodological principles a Malory whose Christian name was Thomas, who was a knight, who lived at the right time, and who was sometimes (like our Malory) in prison, must be assumed to be the author until any evidence to the contrary turns up. A far more respectable alternative is Professor Vinaver's view [presented in his edition of *The Works of Sir Thomas Malory* (1947)] that the discrepancy is an illusion because the book (or books) are not in fact noble; the common belief in their 'morality' is based mainly on Caxton's preface.

Yet I cannot quite accept this. It must of course be admitted that there are in the text untransmuted lumps of barbarism, like Arthur's massacre of the children. And even when we discount these, no one can claim (or should demand) that the general tone conforms to the standards either of the New Testament or of modern, peace-time respectability. But I find in it, sometimes implicit, sometimes explicit, an unforced reverence not only for courage (that of course) but for mercy, humility, graciousness, and good faith. The best way to see it is to compare Malory's heroes, the characters he obviously admired, with those of Homer, Virgil, Renaissance drama, or even our earlier novelists. I cannot conceive that even the best of them—even Hector, Pallas, Othello, or Tom Jones—could ever have been made to understand why Lancelot wept like a beaten child after he had healed Sir Urry. A character from Corneille might understand the scene when Gawain, unhorsed, bids Marhaus to dismount, 'or else I will slay thy horse', and Marhaus, instantly obeying, replies, 'Grammercy, of your gentleness ye teach me courtesy'; I doubt if he could equally have understood Lancelot's unresponsive endurance of Gawain's challenges. I cannot deny either 'morality' (it is not a word I love) or something better to the imagination that shows us Lancelot refusing to take Gareth's victory from him at the tournament, or Pelleas laying his sword across the throats of Gawain and Ettard, or all Lancelot's contrition in Book XV, or the last message of Galahad, now almost a blessed spirit, to his father, or the final lament of Ector. In such passages, and indeed almost everywhere, we meet something which I chiefly hesitate to call 'morality' because it is so little like a code of rules. It is rather the civilization of the heart (by no means of the head), a fineness and sensitivity, a voluntary rejection of all the uglier and more vulgar impulses. We can describe it only in words derived from its own age, words which will now perhaps be mocked, such as *courtesy, gentleness, chivalry*. It makes the *Morte* a 'noble' as well as a 'joyous' history. I at any rate will never blacken the book to make it match the man.

But was the man so black? At first sight it would seem hard to deny, for he was convicted of cattle-lifting, poaching, extortion, sacrilegious robbery, attempted murder, and rape. The record suggests to Professor Vinaver a man who at the age of forty 'from being a peaceable and presumably well-to-do citizen . . . became a law-breaker'. And if we apply certain habitual conceptions of our own to Malory's record, this result seems inevitable. But are these conceptions possibly too local and modern? 'Citizen', 'law-breaker', and (why has that come in?) 'well-to-do'. I suspect that a man of Malory's class and time would not much have relished the titles 'peaceable' or 'citizen'; and the real question about his actions probably was for him, and should be for us, not whether they broke the law but whether they were cowardly, discourteous, treacherous, and (in a word) unknightly. It is not clear that they need have been. Our record of them comes from lawyers. In that age evidence was not scientifically sifted and accusers laid it on thick. In every county civil war exploited, and was exploited by, local feuds. Legal proceedings, whether civil or criminal, were often primarily moves in family quarrels. We need not assume that he did all the things he was accused of. But even if he did, he need not have been, by all standards, a villain. Cattle-lifting was a gentlemanly crime. If he killed other men's deer, so did the Douglas at Otterburn. A knightly ambush and encounter could be attempted murder. Rape need mean no more than abduction; from the legal point of view Lancelot committed rape when he saved Guinevere from the fire. If Malory, loving Joan Smyth *par amours*, and knowing her cuckoldy knave of a husband to be little better than a King Mark, carried her off behind him at 'a great wallop' and perhaps thus saved her from a broken head and two black eyes at home, he may have done what a good knight and a true lover ('of a sinful man') should. That he often fell below the highest standards of chivalry, we may well believe; we need not believe that he fell flagrantly below them. He might, on the evidence, have been as good a knight as Tristram; for what should we think of Tristram himself if our knowledge of him were derived only from King Mark's solicitors?

Of course this picture is conjectural; but it is equally conjecture to represent him, on the strength of the records, as the sort of man who in our days becomes a 'criminal'. We don't know what he was really like, and I suppose we never shall.

II. This Paradox, like the next two, of course involves the assumption that differences between Malory's text and the extant MSS. of his originals are due to Malory. I think this is very probably so. I agree with Professor Vinaver that it is monstrous to set out by assuming that Malory had no spark of originality and therefore to trace everything in which he differs from those MSS. to a hypothetical, lost, intermediary. But probability is not certainty. We cannot be absolutely sure that any given passage, peculiar to Malory, or even any given omission, was his own. Everything I say about Paradoxes II, III, and IV must be understood with this *caveat*.

There are fewer marvels in Malory than in the corresponding French romances. There are, to be sure, at least two places where he introduces a marvel which they lack. But one of these seems to me to be almost certainly the (not unhappy) result of a graphic error. In C XVII. 19 the *sword* 'arose great and marvellous and was full of great heat that many men fell for dread'. In the French it was a wind (*ung vent*) that so arose. I suppose that either Malory or the scribe of the French MS. he was using, having the sword in his head from the preceding passage, wrote it here, intending to write *wind*. The other is in C IV. 6, where a sudden, presumably miraculous light of torches in Malory replaces the French text's ordinary arrival of torches carried by ladies. But this, or both these, amount to nothing against the opposite instances. No one disputes that Malory's text naturalizes, negatively, by the omission of wonders, and positively, by introducing practical, mundane details. When Arthur defeats Damas he makes proper legal arrangements for the righting of the wrongs Damas has done: 'I will that ye give unto your brother all the whole manor with the appurtenance, under this form, that Sir Ontzlake hold the manor of you, and yearly to give you a palfrey'. Similarly (in C VII. 35) the defeated knights swear homage and fealty to Gareth 'to hold of him for evermore'. King Anguysh sending Marhaus to Cornwall, assures him that his expenses will be amply covered. When Tristram bleeds over the lady's bed in C VIII. 14, we are told the extent of damage almost as if Malory had made up the laundry list—'both the over-sheet and the nether-sheet and the pillows and the head-sheet'. Mordred explains at length, and very sensibly, why young knights are at a disadvantage on horseback. Lancelot's habit of talking in his sleep is noted. Best of all, we are told exactly how much it had cost the Queen (£20,000) to send out knights in search of him.

The Paradox here is not very strong, for it turns on the contrast between Malory's supposed intentions and the known effect of his work. For, clearly, even if we know what he did, we can only guess what he intended. It is possible to imagine a burly, commonsensible man who was always trying to turn the faerie world of the romances into something much more earthy and realistic. Accepting that picture, we may smile at the 'success by failure', the happy frustration of his vain labour which has made his book for centuries the chief delight of all who love 'the fairy way of writing'. But a quite different picture is equally possible. If you write fairy-tales and receive letters from your child readers, you will find that children are always asking the sort of questions that Malory is always answering. A simple and serious delight in marvellous narrative most emphatically does not involve any indifference to mundane details. The more seriously you take the story the more you want to tie everything up and to know how people got from one place to another, and what they had to eat, and how all outstanding issues were settled. Neglect of these points, whether in writer or reader, means that the whole thing is merely conventional or playful. Multiplication of marvels goes with the same attitude. Those who love them, as alone they can be loved, for their suggestiveness, their quality, will not increase their number. Two enchanters, two ghosts, two ferlies are always half as impressive as one. Every supposedly naturalistic change that Malory made in the story might proceed from a far fuller belief and a more profound delight in it than the French authors had ever known. He would not be the less English for that.

Once more, I ask no one to choose between these two pictures. Either, as it seems to me, will fit the facts. We shall never know which is true.

III. The excellent remarks of Professor Vinaver on what I have called Interwoven or Polyphonic narrative will have made it clear to all readers that this is a real technique, not, as an earlier generation supposed, a mere muddle or an accidental by-product of conflation. It is a technique not peculiar to medieval prose romance. We find it fully developed over long stretches of Ovid's *Metamorphoses*. The rudiments of it are there in parts of *Beowulf*. The epic poets of Italy took it over from the romance, and Spenser took it over from them. Sidney re-wrote the *Arcadia* to make it more polyphonic. Milton seems to have toyed with the idea of using it for a great epic; he certainly acknowledged that to depart from Aristotelian unity in a narrative might be an enriching of art.

Quite clearly the method continued to be used for centuries, not in blind obedience to tradition but because it gave pleasure. Dante selected this feature of chivalrous romance for special praise: *Arturi regis ambages pulcerrime*. Tasso confesses that all knights and ladies prefer it; everyone reads Ariosto, and no one reads Trissino. He even records how his father discovered by sad experience that 'unity of action gave little pleasure'. The vogue of the Polyphonic in fact lasted longer than that of the modern novelistic technique has yet done. It would be interesting to analyse, and perhaps not difficult to account for, the pleasure it gave. But that would be too long a digression. What matters for the moment is that it did please and can please still. To the present day no one enjoys Malory's book who does not enjoy its *ambages*, its interweaving.

For it is certainly interwoven. Arthur has a war against five kings. To repair his losses he must make new knights. His selection sends Bagdemagus, malcontent, from the court, and the story of his wanderings crosses the latter end of Merlin's story. Arthur meanwhile has got involved in the affairs of Damas and Ontzlake, which in their turn involve both him and Accolon in the machinations of Morgan, which lead to the banishment of her son Uwain, which leads to his joint errantry with Gawain, which brings them both (now in company with Marhaus) to those three damsels at the river-head who fork the story into three . . . and so on. Those who dislike this sort of thing will not much like Malory.

Yet it may be, as Professor Vinaver concludes, that Malory 'strongly disliked' it himself. Certainly the evidence that he constantly simplified is irresistible. Whether he wanted to simplify still further and get rid of the Polyphonic altogether, or whether he wanted to go just as far as he has gone and liked the degree of Polyphony which survives under his treatment, we do not know. If he wanted to get rid of it altogether, he has undoubtedly failed. To anyone who comes to his work fresh from modern literature its Polyphonic character will be at first one of the most noticeable things about it. And the work will be liked, where it is liked, not despite of this peculiarity but (in part) because of it.

IV. This Paradox involves us in two subjects: Malory's treatment of the holy quest, and the connexion, if any, between it and other matters in his text.

Professor Vinaver's view on the first subject depends on the interpretation of a great many different passages. I shall refer to them both by the Book and Chapter of Caxton's edition and by the page and line of the Professor's (which I indicate by the letter *W*). They fall into four classes.

1. A passage held to indicate Malory's 'confidence in the unfailing merits of Arthurian chivalry' (*W* 1524). This is *C* XVI. 3 (*W* 946.18) where a Hermit in the French text condemns the Round Table for *luxure* and *orgueil*; but in Malory, for 'sin and wickedness'. I cannot myself see that the substitution of the general for the particular makes the condemnation less severe.

2. Passages where Malory substitutes the worldly for the religious. Thus in *C* XVI. 3 (*W* 945.10) the dying Uwain in the French asks that prayer be made for his soul; in Malory he asks to be remembered to Arthur and the court, 'and for old brotherhood, think on me'. (This phrase itself might imply a request for prayers, but I would not press that.) Again, in *C* XVI. 6 (*W* 955.9) Bors, surprisingly, and without authority from the French, says that he who achieves the Grail will win 'much earthly worship'. Both these, and especially the latter, are strong evidence for Professor Vinaver's view: if it is felt that they are sufficient to colour the whole narrative, then that view will be unassailable. Two other passages which might be quoted here seem to me, on the other hand, to rank as 'worldly' only if we adopt standards of worldliness which are almost intolerably severe. In *C* XIII. 19 (*W* 896.11) Malory allows the contrite Lancelot to be 'somewhat comforted' when day breaks and he hears the birds sing. In the French (which is finely imagined) the morning and the birds directly produce the conviction of God's anger, which in Malory comes home to Lancelot only when he realizes that he has lost his horse and his armour. This is certainly very practical, homely, English, and (in a word) Malorian; but it does not for me empty the scene of all religious significance. Again in *C* XVII. 13 (*W* 1011.31- 1012.1) Malory's Lancelot (not his French equivalent) after a month of fasting on board ship with no one but a dead lady for company, 'was somewhat weary of the ship' and went ashore 'to play him'. (Middle English *play* in such a context is of course a very mild world; we should have said 'to stretch his legs' or 'to relax'.) Now I think a man might have done that and yet be a very good sort of penitent on the whole. Both passages, indeed, are for me specimens of that Malorian realism which brings the story to life; they make Lancelot, not a stained-glass figure, but a real man, though a contrite one. It is proper, however, to point out that the difference between Professor Vinaver and myself may be simply the same difference there was between the French originals and Malory, the difference between the hard lines and rigid schematization of Latin thought, and the softening, compromising temper of us islanders. (For some say our best Christians are all Pelagians, and our best atheists all Puritans, at heart.)

3. The third class is, for me, the hardest to feel sure about. In *C* XIII. 14 (*W* 886.18) the qualification for success in the holy quest is, in the French, *chevaillierie celestiale*; in the English, 'virtuous living'. In *C* XIII. 16 (*W* 891.32) it is again, for Malory, 'knightly deeds and virtuous living'; for the French author it is service to the Creator, defence of Holy Church, and the offering to Christ of the treasure (one's soul) which has been entrusted to one. In *C* XVI. 6 (*W* 956.2) Bors is praised in the French for his 'religious', in Malory for his

'stable', life. In C XVI. 13 (W 968.11) Lionel is condemned by the French author because *n'a an soi nule vertu de Nostre Seignor qui en estant le tiegne;* by Malory, because 'he is a murderer and doth contrary to the order of knighthood'. These are I think the strongest specimens. That in C XV. 5 (W 931.25) seems to me weak. It is true that the motive which Malory gives Lancelot for joining in a certain fray is, as Professor Vinaver claims, incongruous with the Quest; but then Malory is fully aware of this and in the very next chapter (C XV. 6; W 933.32-934.4) makes his recluse tell Lancelot that such 'bobaunce and pride of the world' must be abandoned. The insertion of both these passages by Malory would seem to emphasize the very point which, it is claimed, he was ignoring. We might perhaps add C XVI. 17 (W 974.15-17) where the edifying mutual forgiveness of Bors and his brother is also peculiar to Malory.

But the earlier passages remain, and I will not for a moment dispute that they all indicate an important change made by Malory and affecting his version throughout. The question is how we are to define it. At first sight I am tempted to say that where the originals used specifically religious, Malory uses ethical, concepts: *virtuous* for *celestial, knightly* and *virtuous* for the offering of the heart to Christ, *stable* for *religious*. This certainly means that the choice before Malory's knights is not that between 'religion' in the technical sense and active life in the world. They are to go on being knights (C XIII. 20; W 899.1-5); just as the soldiers who came to the Baptist were told to go on being soldiers. Malory in fact holds the same view as Langland and Gower and many other English medieval moralists. No man need leave the Order to which he has been called, but every man must begin really to fulfil the functions for which that Order exists. The recall is not from knighthood to the cloister, but from knighthood as it has come to be (full of 'sin and wickedness') to knighthood as it was intended to be, grounded in 'patience and humility' (C XVI. 3; W 945-7). Admittedly, then, the story is ethical, as against mystical. But we must not say 'ethical, as against religious', for the ethical claim and the attempted ethical response, when prompted by a vision, purged by confession and penance, supported and corrected at every turn by voices, miracles, and spiritual counsels, is precisely the religious as it most commonly appears in secular vocations. And *stability* (perseverance to the end, or consistency) is of course essential.

4. Finally, we have those passages which exalt the supremacy of Lancelot over all other knights. There may be some difference of opinion as to which we should include in this class. I certainly would not include C XVII. 22 (W 1035.11-12) where Galahad, almost at the threshold of Heaven, sends to his father a message bidding him 'remember of this unstable world'. The words are full of knightly courtesy, filial duty, and Christian charity, but of course they are a warning and (by delicatest implication) a reproof. It is Galahad whom they exalt. Nor do I find much 'rehabilitation' of Lancelot in Malory's insertion at the end of C XVII. 23 (W 1036.19-1037.7). Lancelot does not relate the adventures of the Grail *simpliciter*, but those 'that he had seen'. Bors had seen, and Bors told, what Lancelot had not seen. One would expect the surviving knights each to contribute to the report which Arthur naturally demanded. And the passage repeats Galahad's message, with its grave implication. Another doubtful place is C XVI. 1 (W 941.20-22). Here Gawain says that 'if one thing were not' (surely beyond all doubt the 'one thing' is his adultery?) Lancelot would be matchless. But as things are, far from rising (for purposes of this Quest) to the level of Galahad, Perceval, and Bors, Lancelot 'is as we be', is just like the rest of us, *nous autres*, Ectors and Gawains —'but if he take the more pain on him'. I cannot imagine a better way of making us feel how Lancelot has sunk than thus to let us hear lesser men exclaiming that at last he's no better than they.

The passages on which the Vinaverian view must finally rest are those where Malory deliberately inserts the praise of Lancelot. A damsel in C XIII. 5 (W 863.30), a hermit in C XV. 4 (W 930.14), and a second hermit in C XV. 4 (W 930-14), and a third hermit in C XVI. 5 (W 948.27-8) all remind us that Lancelot was the best knight, for a sinful man, that ever lived. The reservation is of course important; but in spite of it, I am prepared to admit that all these passages may be meant to blunt for us the edge of the abasement which Lancelot undergoes in the French text. But it also seems to me equally possible that they were intended to have—and for me they have—a very different effect. It is a question of what may be called the logic of the imagination. If one wanted to exhibit in a novel the theme that intellectual achievements were no passport to heaven, one would not choose for one's protagonist some mediocrity who has 'got a good second'. Only a fool would labour to show the failure, on the highest level, of pretensions which were doubtfully adequate even on their own. Obviously one would build one's protagonist up to the stature of a Porson, a Sherrington, or a Mahaffy. If you want to show that one sort of achievement is inferior to, even incommensurable with, another, then of course the more splendid (in its own kind) your specimen is, the more impressive its failure (in another kind) will be. Every word said in praise of Lancelot as a good knight 'of a sinful man'— as the bravest, most courteous, most faithful in his love, but not seriously hitherto attempting that perfection of chastity and all other virtues which the Christian law demands of the knight, in his own fashion, no less than of the contemplative—serves all the more to drive home the moral of the whole story, makes it all the clearer that with the Quest we have entered a region where even what is best and greatest by the common standards of the world 'falls into abatement and low price'.

But, as before, I end in uncertainty. I am sure that Malory's handling has not on me the effect, and therefore need not have been meant to have the effect, which Professor Vinaver supposes. I know it has the opposite effect on me. I cannot rule out the possibility that it was intended to have this opposite effect. I do not claim to know that it was.

So much for his treatment of the Quest. As regards its relation to other parts of his work, I feel a little more confident. I appears to me to be unmistakably linked with the *Morte*. Before the Quest begins, before Galahad is begotten, when the Grail first appears before Lancelot in the house of Pelles, Malory inserts the prophecy that 'when this rich thing goeth about, the Round Table shall be broken for a season'. (*C* XI. 2; *W* 793.32-36). I do not know what to make of 'for a season', and how right (as often) Caxton was to omit it! But it is Malory who had introduced, even if Caxton perfected, the note of doom: the dreadful hint that the best is fatal to the good. Then in the Quest itself (*C* XIII. 20; *W* 897.27-28) Lancelot promises 'by the faith of his body' never to come in Guinevere's 'fellowship' again if he can avoid it. Then, when the Quest is over, almost immediately, Lancelot 'forgat the promise and the perfection that he made in the Quest'. This is in the French; but as if this were not enough Malory must add that this was the inadequately repented 'bosom-sin' which had led him to fail in that attempt (*C* XVIII. 1; *W* 1045.12-16). Notice too that in thus forgetting his promise Lancelot is verifying the diagnosis ('not stable, but . . . likely to turn again') made upon him by the hermit in *C* XVI 5.—a passage, so far as we know, of Malory's own making. The connexion here, if unintended, is singularly fortunate. But Malory still feels he has not done enough. Returning to *C* XVIII. I, we find a dialogue between Lancelot and Guinevere inserted (*W* 1045.30-1048.14) in which he almost begs the terrible woman to release him, pleading, 'I was but late in the quest,' confessing that 'privy thoughts to return to your love' were the lime-twigs he could not escape, trying to make her understand that such experiences 'may not be lightly forgotten'. Then later (*C* XIX. 10-12) we have what is perhaps the greatest of all passages peculiar to Malory, the healing of Sir Urry. Here Lancelot is proved by infallible signs to be in one sense (he knows too well in what and how limited a sense) the best knight of the world. Hence, while all praise him to the skies, he can only weep like a beaten child. As he failed on the Quest, so (for the same reason) he is failing now. In him, its highest specimen, the whole Round Table is failing; on it and him, as the result of his illicit love, the prophecies begin to be fulfilled. They are, no doubt, worked out through a tangle of human motives, the spite of Agravain and Mordred, the assumption of the blood-feud by Gawain. Of course, the fulfilment of the prophecies about Oedipus came about through seemingly free agents obeying human motives. That is how prophecies are fulfilled in good stories; no one ever suggested that the motivation somehow abolishes the connexion between the prediction and the event. And when all is nearly over and the doom worked out, Lancelot again recalls to us the source of the whole tragedy: 'For in the quest of the Sangreal I had forsaken the vanities of the world had not your love been' (*C* XXI. 9; *W* 1253.14-15).

And still, though I cannot see how any reader fails to see the connexion, I cannot be certain whether Malory himself saw it or not.

V. Finally, did Malory write one book or eight? Close study of the Winchester MS. has convinced Professor Vinaver that he wrote eight; instead of the *Morte Darthur* we have the 'Works' of Malory, and inconsistencies between them no longer matter—indeed, no longer exist, for independent worlds of invention cannot be inconsistent with one another. This view has been seriously criticized by Mr. D. S. Brewer [in his 1952 *Medium Aevum* article "Form in the Morte Darthur"]. He points out that the eight 'works' are full of backward and forward references, their order not alterable, and 'bridge' passages often supplied. I think I should be on Mr. Brewer's side in this question, if I were not bogged down in a preliminary doubt as to what precisely the question is.

I believe I know fairly well what we mean if we say, '*Pickwick* is one work, but *Pickwick* and *Great Expectations* are two works'. We mean that within *Pickwick*, as within *Great Expectations*, there are characters that continue or recur, and that there are causal connexions, and the later parts presuppose the earlier; whereas there are no common characters and no causal connexions shared by both. But ask me the same questions about *Barchester Towers* and *The Last Chroncicle*; already a shade of ambiguity has crept in. Now go to a step further. What of *Paradise Lost* and *Paradise Regained*? Here there are characters common to both, and the later poem presupposes and recalls events in the earlier. Satan's temptation of Christ presupposes his rebellion against God and his expulsion from Heaven. And if Satan, and the whole story, were as purely Milton's invention as Archdeacon Grantly is Trollope's, the two poems would stand in the same not very easily defined relation as the two novels. Actually, however, Satan's career with all its causal and chronological structure already exists in the Fathers and in popular belief, before Milton sets pen to paper, and continues to exist whether he wants us to treat *Regained* as a sequel or as a wholly separate poem. Presupposals of events in *Paradise Lost,* and backward references, are bound to occur. It may be impossible to say whether a given instance of them illustrates the unity of the two poems or whether it merely exhibits at one point the external, pre-existing, non-Miltonic unity of the matter he worked on. Hence we may generalize: wherever there is a matter (historical or legendary) previous and external to the author's activity, the question, 'One work or many?' loses a good deal of its meaning. And of course Malory's matter was of this kind.

On top of this a special difficulty arises from the fact that Malory was a medieval author. If it were possible to question him directly, in what form should we put our question? It would be no use asking him how many books he thought he had written; he would think we meant the material volumes or 'quairs'. If we asked him, 'How many tales?' he might enumerate more than eight. Such expressions as 'Thus endeth the tale of . . .' (C II. 19; W 92.22), or 'the adventure of' (C III. 8; W 108.28) or 'the quest of' (C III. 11; W 113.34) occur within the Vinaverian units. If we talked to him about 'artistic unity', he would not understand. We might finally, in desperation, try to find out whether he was at all worried at the appearance in one passage of some knight whose death had been recorded in an earlier passage. He would, I feel certain, simply refer us to 'the French book' as his authority. For the difficulty between Malory and us would not be merely linguistic. We should by the very form of our questions be presupposing concepts his mind was not furnished with. Did any Middle English author conceive clearly that he was writing fiction, a single work of fiction, which should obey the laws of its own inner unity but need not cohere with anything else in the world? I cannot believe it. They are all, even Chaucer, handing on, embellishing, expanding, or abridging a matter received from some source. They feel free to illuminate it at any number of points with their own vivid imagination, and even to correct what seems to them improbable, improper, or unedifying. But whatever their own degree of actual belief or of scepticism (were they clearly aware of either? did they for the most part even raise such questions?) they all proceed as if they were more or less historians; unscholarly, decorating, and emotional historians to be sure, like Livy or Plutarch, but (by and large) historians still. I do not for a moment believe that Malory had any intention either of writing a single 'work' or of writing many 'works' as we should understand the expressions. He was telling us about Arthur and the knights. Of course his matter was one—the same king, the same court. Of course his matter was many—they had had many adventures. .

The choice we try to force upon Malory is really a choice for us. It is our imagination, not his, that makes the work one or eight or fifty. We can read it either way. We can read it now one way, now another. We partly make what we read.

As will be seen, the examination of all five Paradoxes produces in me varying degrees of doubt (weakest as regards the Third, strongest as regards the Second and Fifth) about Professor Vinaver's idea of Malory's intentions; but it produces no confidence in any alternative theory. The net result is that Malory eludes me. Perhaps, then, I shall be able to find him in his style, for they say that a man's style is himself. Unfortunately, Malory turns out to have not a style, but styles. The inverted and alliterative language of the Roman War has little likeness to the limpid, unobtrusive prose in which we follow the adventures of knights errant. And we know why. The one is from the Alliterative *Morte,* the other renders, and copies as closely as English can, the style of the French prose romances. In both, Malory writes such a style as he has most lately read. And we cannot say that this subjection to the model is a prentice weakness which he outgrew in his maturity. At the very end, as soon as the Stanzaic *Morte* comes before him, the tell-tale features, the tags, inversions, and alliterations, creep into his prose: 'while we thus in holes us hide'—'that was wary and wise'—'droop and dare'—'shred them down as sheep in a fold' (C XX. 19; W 1211-12). And when he leaves his originals altogether to reflect upon the story (C XVIII. 25; W 1119-20), we have a style different from all these. There are more (ultimately) Latin derivatives close together (*constrain, divers, negligence, stability,* and *rasure*), and doublets like 'bring forth fruit and flourish', 'springeth and flourisheth', 'arase and deface', 'deface and lay apart'. This is quite unlike the prose used in his own (or what we take to be his own) additions to the narrative parts, especially those dialogues which he inserts more freely as he nears the end. These are no doubt admirable; but who, on purely internal evidence, could have picked them out (as almost anyone could pick out the alliterative passage about the dream in C V. 4)? They may be better than the surrounding prose which reproduces the French, but they are all of a piece with it. Malory's greatest original passages arise when he is most completely absorbed in the story and realizes the characters so fully that they begin to talk for him of their own accord; but they talk a language he has largely learned from his sources. The very ease with which he wanders away from this style into that of some inferior source or into a language of his own (which he may have thought 'higher') suggests that he hardly knows what he is doing. Thus, while in one sense it would be monstrous to say that he 'has no style' (he has written prose as musical, as forthright, as poignant, as was ever heard in England) it would be true in another. He has no style of his own, no characteristic manner. (If you were searching all literature for a man who might be described as 'the opposite of Pater', Malory would be a strong candidate.) In a style or styles so varied, everywhere so indebted to others, and perhaps most original precisely where it is most indebted, one cannot hopefully seek *l'homme meme*. Here also Malory vanishes into a mist.

And this result neither surprises nor disappoints me. I have called this essay 'The English prose *Morte*', because I think we may deceive ourselves by such expressions as 'Malory's **Morte Darthur**' or **'The Works of Sir Thomas Malory'**. They sound so dangerously like 'Browning's *Sordello*' or 'The Works of Jane Austen'. But there is no real parallel. Our familiar concept of 'author-and-his-book' is foiled by the composite works of the Middle Ages. Even in *Troilus and Criseyde*, where the whole is much shorter and the last worker's additions are much larger and known more certainly, we are foiled. We can sort out the Boccaccian and the Chaucerian passages. But not the Boccaccian and the Chaucerian element. For of course the surviving Boccaccio is modified by the interpolated Chaucer, and the Chaucer modified (this is less often stressed) by the Boccaccio. In the end we cannot really say that either author, nor even in what proportion each author, is responsible for the total effect. The prose **Morte** is very much more complicated. Whatever Malory's intentions—if he had any intentions—may have been, it is agreed on all hands that he has changed the tale very little. From the nature of the case he could not have changed it much. It is too vast, too filled with its own strong life, to be much affected by alterations so comparatively short and sporadic as his. This does not mean that his contribution is of negligible value. Like so many medieval authors (like, for example, the poet of *Cleanness* and *Patience*), at point after point he adds vividness, throws some figure into bolder relief, cuts away an excrescence, or sweetens some motive that he rightly found odious. The process may be described as 'touching up'. But there is no question of a great artist giving to a pupil's work those strokes of genius 'which make all the difference'. Rather, a deft pupil has added touches here and there to a work which, in its majestic entirety, he could never have conceived; and from which his own skill has been chiefly learned. Though he has in fact improved it, it was (by our standards, not by those of the Middle Ages) rather cheek of him to try. But even if he had done harm, he would not have done much harm.

If some people find it distressing to have a work which cannot be assigned to any single author, let me remind them that in another art we are familiar with this sort of thing. I am thinking of a great cathedral, where Saxon, Norman, Gothic, Renaissance, and Georgian elements all co-exist, and all grow together into something strange and admirable which none of its successive builders intended or foresaw. Under Malory's work lies that of the French prose romancers; under theirs, that of Chretien, Wace, and other poets; under that, Geoffrey, and perhaps the Breton *lais;* deepest of all, who knows what fragments of Celtic myth or actual British history? Malory is only the last of many restorers, improvers, demolitionists; if you will, of misunderstanders. Meanwhile, the great cathedral of words stands solidly before us and imposes on us a meaning which is largely independent of their varying and perhaps incompatible purposes. Who, if any, first saw or intended the tragic and ironic parallel between Mordred's begetting and Galahad's? Or the necessity that the Grail should bring not peace but a sword? Or the three-storied effect inevitably produced by the intermediate position of the good knights between the villains like Mark and the perfect knights like Percivale? Or the deep suggestiveness of Arthur's relation to that dark family (Morgan, Morgause, and the rest) from whom he emerges, who lie in wait for him, and who mysteriously return in his last hour to take him away?

I said just now that Malory was only the last of the makers of the **Morte.** I should have said, last but one (or even last but two). It follows from the view I am trying to put that Caxton's text is not most usefully regarded as a corruption. He touched up Malory as Malory touched up his predecessors and by the same right. The greatest service that he did the old fabric was one of demolition. Most unluckily (and probably, as Professor Vinaver thinks, early in his career) Malory had come across the Alliterative *Morte*. It is not a first-class poem, not comparable in epic quality to the battle scenes of Layamon, and it treats the dullest and most incredible part of the whole Arthurian legend. It is far easier to suspend one's disbelief in enchantments than in vast contradictions of known history scrawled across a whole continent; and a narrative of unbroken military successes, dull even when true, is insufferable when feigned. It is defeat, or (as in the *Iliad*) discords within one of the armies, that we need for epic. Malory swallowed this poem almost whole, except that by separating it from the **Morte** he deprived it of the tragic close and the moral judgement which had saved it from total paltriness. He also surrendered his style without resistance to the influence of the alliterative metre, which, degenerate even in the original, becomes in prose a noisy rumble. Caxton wisely abridged the whole dreary business, and removed (he might well have used the knife more boldly) some of the traces of the metre. Thus where Winchester's (and no doubt Malory's) text read

> Now fecche me, seyde sir Pryamus, my vyall that hangys by the
> gurdyll of my haynxman, for hit is full of the floure of the four
> good watyrs that passis from Paradyse, the mykill fruyte in fallys
> that at one day fede shall us all. . . .

Caxton gives

> And Priamus took from his page a vial full of the four waters that came out of Paradise.

Notice that Caxton has made it much more Malorian, more like the best and most typical parts of Malory, than Malory himself had done. This is 'forcing a man to be free', making him himself C V. 10; W 234.11-14). Again in C V. 8 (W 219.16-17) we owe to Caxton 'the ground trembled and dindled' instead of 'all the vale dyndled'. The division into chapters, if sometimes unskilfully done, has made the book everywhere more readable. The rubrics he prefixed to the chapters have become as much part of its beauty as the glosses of the *Ancient Mariner*'s. Sometimes, as in 'how Lancelot fell to his old love again', they direct us unerringly to the pith of what follows (C XVIII. 1); again and again they are evocative in the highest degree.

I am not of course suggesting that Caxton's share in the final effect is remotely comparable to Malory's; only that he too, in his degree, has helped a little, and that it is no misfortune if his text has counted for so much in the English imagination. That is why I have usually quoted not only from Caxton but even from Caxton edited by Pollard; the household book. I enjoy my cathedral as it has stood the test of time and demand no restoration. I have no more wish to discard Caxton for Malory than to discard Malory for the French romances.

It would distress me if anyone took this to imply the slightest depreciation of Professor Vinaver's great edition. It is an indispensable work of which English scholarship may well be proud, and my own debts to it will be obvious. Indeed the view I have taken allows me to give Professor Vinaver a place higher, in my opinion, than scholarship of itself could claim. I hesitated a while ago whether to call Malory last but one, or last but two, of the many who worked at the prose *Morte*. For has not Professor Vinaver some right to be numbered among them? He has not, naturally, allowed himself the liberties of a Malory or even of a Caxton. His chisel has touched no stone of the building. But he has made a new approach, and one which many modern pilgrims will find more congenial. His book smacks of our own century as Caxton's smacked of his. The division into eight romances, and above all the title, ***The Works of Malory,*** whether right or wrong (or neither), makes it far more digestible by contemporary critical conceptions than the old *Morte*. The ***Works,*** the Complete Works—that is what our libraries are used to. Already Malory fits more comfortably on the shelf beside the 'works' of everyone else. And the mere look of the pages—the paragraphing and the inverted commas—acclimatizes the book still further. Beyond question, Professor Vinaver has shown the cathedral from a new angle; placed the modern pilgrim where he will enjoy it best. And now that his edition is deservedly reaching the stage of cheap reprints, it may in its turn become the household book; until perhaps *alter Achilles,* some second Vinaver (a little cold to the first one as he is a little cold to Caxton) recalls his generation to the long forgotten book of 1485 or even to the French, and someone like myself puts in a plea for what will then be the old, the traditional, 'Works of Malory'. And all these preferences will be legitimate and none of them 'right' or 'wrong'. The cathedral of words is so large that everyone can find in it the work of his favourite period; and here, as you could not do in a real cathedral, you can always strip that favourite work of later accretions without pulling the whole thing down. What you must not do is to call those bits 'the' or 'the real' cathedral. They might have been. The whole might have been designed by one man and finished in one style. But that is not what happened. Though every part of it was made by a man, the whole has rather grown than been made. Such things have a kind of existence that is almost midway between the works of art and those of nature. . . .

EUGENE VINAVER

SOURCE: Eugene Vinaver, "On Art and Nature: A Letter to C. S. Lewis," in *Essays on Malory* by Walter Oakeshott and others, edited by J. A. W. Bennett, Oxford at the Clarendon Press, 1963, pp. 29-40.

[Vinaver is recognized as a pioneer in Malory studies. He wrote one of the first comprehensive studies of the author, Malory *(1929), and edited the three-volume* Works of Sir Thomas Malory *(1947) from the Winchester Manuscript of the text. He is best known for his controversial view that the* Morte Darthur *is a collection of related tales but not a continuous narrative. In the following excerpt, he responds to C. S. Lewis's investigation of "paradoxes" in the* Morte Darthur *(see preceding excerpt), focusing on whether Malory conceived the*

work as a single, unified narrative or as a series of related but discrete tales.]

My dear Lewis, of all the contributors to this volume I am the most fortunate. You have shown me your essay [see excerpt dated 1963] and asked me to write a reply to it or, to quote your own words, 'a development from it'. The privilege is a perilous one, and at first I hesitated to take up the friendly challenge; but the prospect of a dialogue with you on the vital issues you have raised is irresistible.

Everything you say is enlightening and much of it is revealing. I have lived with Malory for many years and I think I know how he impresses me; but I would rather leave the reader with *your* impressions firmly fixed in his mind, for I consider them an acquisition for us all and not a matter for discussion. What might usefully be discussed is not what you feel about Malory, but the way in which you account for your feelings—your interpretation of your reaction to the book.

I find this interpretation debatable, and there you probably agree. You sum it up by saying: 'the net result is that Malory eludes me.' I confess that up to that point, as I went on reading your essay, the familiar but invariably fresh magic of your language and thought lulled me into a delightful state of acquiescence. But when I came to these words I had to pause. Surely, I reflected, if there is one critic whom Malory does *not* elude it is C. S. Lewis; hence, if the 'net result' of his argument is to make him deny so obvious a fact there must be something wrong with his argument. I did not, and I could not, ask myself *why* Malory 'eluded' you, because he quite clearly had not done so. The only question in my mind was why you *thought* he had eluded you. What was it that gave you the feeling that you were faced with something strange and 'paradoxical': not even with one paradox, but with as many as five? There is no simple and uniform answer to this question. But as I was looking for a possible answer a passage from *A Winter's Tale* came to my mind—the lines spoken by Polixenes in Act IV:

> You see, sweet maid, we marry
> A gentle scion to the wildest stock,
> And make conceive a bark of baser kind
> By bud of nobler race. This is an art
> Which does mend Nature, change it rather,
>   but
> The art itself is Nature.

Art itself is nature. It plays, as Spenser said not long before these words were written, 'second Nature's part', and while it is totally different from Nature in the ordinary sense, which includes the artist's personality, his outlook and his intentions, it is part of a natural process which we can occasionally observe and which would be the greatest paradox of all, were it not 'itself Nature'.

The first of the five 'paradoxes' which you list at the outset is the cleavage between the man and the book. 'The work has long passed for a mirror of honour and virtue; the author appears to have been little better than a criminal.' Let us leave aside for the moment all questions of fact. The evidence on which the notion of Malory's 'immorality' rests is very slight indeed. Considering the state of justice in fifteenth-century England, even a conviction would not have been sufficient to prove that he was guilty of any of the charges brought against him; and there was in fact no conviction, or at least we have no record of one. Your own assessment of Malory's probable misdeeds is as fair a hypothesis as any that can reasonably be advanced in the present state of our knowledge. But even if he were as 'immoral' a character as some of his other biographers want him to be, what difference would this make to our understanding of his work? What except the romantic myth of the work being an expression of the 'whole man' makes you think that there would be anything abnormal about a cleavage between the man and the book? I should have thought that it would be more contrary to the natural course of things if there were no such cleavage, for in that case the two 'natures' would be identical, whereas in fact they hardly ever are: no reader of your *Personal Heresy in Criticism* will ever take their identity for granted. Proust in his *Methode de Sainte-Beuve* contrasts them as two distinct entities, totally unlike one another.... On this showing it seems singularly fortunate that our knowledge of Malory the man is not only limited but apparently inconsistent with the nature of his work: we are not even tempted to explain one through the other. It is, as you put it, 'a desperate expedient' to question Malory's identity simply because we cannot square the known facts of his life with the meaning and the message of his book; desperate to the extent of being perverse. Malory's biography has its uses: it is entertaining in itself, and it is an interesting sidelight on the social history of his time. But to feel 'disconcerted' about it as, for instance, E. K. Chambers did, is to misuse the results of biographical research, which are no more—and no less—puzzling in this case than such results normally are.

Your second and fourth 'paradoxes' are more difficult to dispose of, if indeed they can be disposed of at all. The problem they raise is a fundamental one. You find a curious contrast between Malory's efforts 'to eliminate the marvellous and introduce the humdrum' and the result of these efforts (Paradox II), and you suggest that there is an equally curious contrast between what seems to be a 'deeply religious' handling of the Grail story and a constant tendency to evade the religious issue (Paradox IV). What you say is not only true, but illuminating and very important. In Malory the feeling of the marvellous is not lessened, but intensified in spite of his 'practical realism'; and again, in his version of the Quest of the Holy Grail, much as he tries to cut down the religious exposition and even substitute the worldly for the divine, he produces a work which makes a more deeply religious impression on one's mind than the strictly orthodox original upon which it is based. How does this come about? I think you have supplied the answer. The work is not 'what any single individual either intended or foresaw'. 'Though every part of it was made by a man, the whole has rather grown than been made. Such things have a kind of existence that is almost midway between the works of art and those of nature.' I hope these words will long be remembered by all those who read Malory and induce others to read him. Perhaps you will allow me to illustrate them by a brief quotation:

> Lorde, I thanke The, for now I se that that
>   hath be my desire many
> a day. Now, my Blessed Lorde, I wold nat
>   lyve in this wrecched
> worlde no lenger, if hit myght please The,
>   Lorde.

This is Galahad's last prayer, and perhaps one of the most profoundly religious moments ever recorded in any version of the Grail story. If you look at the corresponding place in Pauphilet's edition of the *Queste del Saint Graal* you will find that every single word used by Malory is there, but that about three-quarters of the French text is missing in Malory. Among the omissions there are some important phrases and sentences which by the strict standards of the author of the French *Queste* the occasion required. And yet when you read the two passages together you realize that one has a power and a greatness totally absent from the other. Is this not, in miniature, the process you are thinking of? But why contrast in this instance 'art' and 'nature'? Why not say with Polixenes that this is 'an art that Nature makes'? The discrepancy between the intention and the result occurs daily in every branch of art, not because nature 'takes over' from the artist, but because the artist's genius takes control of the situation and modifies what we call his intention—his conscious self, his 'design'. It is again art 'playing second nature's part', acting much in the same way as nature is supposed to act, but *within* the artist's mind. Malory the man was certainly not a believer in the supernatural: the simple method of collation shows how consistently he cut it down in adapting his French books. And he was certainly not interested in the complexities of the Grail doctrine, as the same method amply demonstrates. But when we say this we describe the mind—or what happened in the mind—of Sir Thomas Malory when he was thinking about the supernatural and the Grail: we do *not* describe the process of his work, which is something very different and much more difficult to understand. The greater the author and the theme, the more room there is for this inner logic of the work, which alone, in the last analysis, determines the 'result'. It is the logic of the supernatural and the logic of the Grail theme that make the work into 'something which none of its successive builders intended or foresaw', but that logic only becomes active in the artist's hands; when it defeats his intentions and his beliefs the triumph is his: it is the triumph of his art over his conscious self, and each time it occurs he may well experience a 'more profound delight' in the result than the French authors had ever known.

Perhaps for the sake of clarity I ought to put it another way. If I understand your reasoning correctly, it is something like this: there was an excess of the supernatural in Malory's French originals; because he was out of sympathy with the supernatural he reduced the overall amount of it, and because 'two enchanters, two ghosts, two ferlies are always half as impressive as one' the reduction added to the impressiveness of the marvellous. But does this mean that anybody applying the same equation (2 = 1/2) to the same material might achieve the same result? Surely not. And if you agree, that is to say, if you think as I do that the equation taken by itself is inoperative, would you not say that it became operative in Malory because of something that happened *in* Malory and did not happen elsewhere—something that for want of a better word we call his art? The equation is, of course, a paradox, and a splendid one, but not the process which makes the equation work. The essence of it is the co-existence of two 'natures', the conscious and the creative, one 'mending' the other—clearly something rare, but no more paradoxical or accidental than any art 'which adds to Nature'. This is not a criticism, but a development of your argument. Alone among critics you have perceived the significance of Malory's treatment of the supernatural and the religious, and the interpretation I suggest is simply a means of describing this treatment in more explicit terms while 'walking stumblingly' after you.

The two remaining sections—III and V—are no less illuminating and thought-provoking. You formulate your 'paradox V' as follows:

> Malory seemed to Saintsbury (and doubtless to many) the man who alone 'makes of this vast assemblage of stories one story and one book.' The evidence of the Winchester MS.

convinces Professor Vinaver that he really wrote several works which were never intended to form a whole.

A thorny problem, and one which has engaged the attention of a considerable number of critics ever since I published my edition of the **Works.** But it seems to me that you have found the answer—if you can bear another paradox—by saying that you are 'bogged down in a preliminary doubt as to what precisely the question is'. Malory would have been 'bogged down' in very much the same doubt. It would be no use asking him, if he came back to life, 'how many books he thought he had written; he would think we meant the material volumes or "quairs". . . . If we talked to him about "artistic unity" he would not understand.' And you put the entire problem in a nutshell when you say: 'We should by the very form of our questions be presupposing concepts his mind was not furnished with.' But there are two issues we might consider: (*a*) how did Malory intend his romances to be presented to his readers? and (*b*) do these romances *in fact* make one romance? From the editor's point of view the first question is the only one that matters; the critic, on the other hand, is—or should be—interested primarily, if not exclusively, in the second, i.e. in the result, not in the intention. And either question can be answered without prejudice to the other.

What Malory *intended* could have been gathered long ago from his own words had they not been partly distorted in the process of transmission and partly misunderstood—or ignored. The Pierpont Morgan copy of Caxton's edition is the only existing record of what Malory wrote in his last colophon. In the other extant copy—the John Rylands— the last pages are missing. They have been replaced by Whittaker's facsimiles, which Sommer reproduced in his reprint, and everybody has since looked upon Sommer's text as a convenient and entirely reliable substitute for Caxton's. Unfortunately it is not at all reliable and the fault is not Sommer's, but Whittaker's. The Pierpont Morgan copy read as follows:

> Here is the ende of the hoole book of kyng
>   Arthur and of his noble
> knyghtes of the rounde table that whan they
>   were hole togyders
> there was euer an hondred and forty
> And here is the ende of the deth of Arthur

The word *hoole* is the last word on the last page but one of the text; it is perfectly legible, but if one is a little careless, and especially if one is thinking of the next word (the first on the following page)—*book*— one can easily misread *hoole* as *booke*. This is precisely what Whittaker did. In Sommer we find, as a result, *here is the ende of the booke book,* which all later editors took for a dittography and reduced to *here is the end of the book.* Next came the critics who, looking at the passage, decided, quite naturally, that from Malory's point of view the 'book of King Arthur', &c., was the same as the 'Death of Arthur': that the words after the first *the ende of* were a description of the work of which the words after the second *the ende of* supplied the title. Hence, they concluded, Malory did give his romances one general title, and Caxton did not betray the author's intentions by saying in his own colophon: 'Thus endeth thys noble and ioyous book entytled le morte Darthur.' There was clearly no harm in 'anglo-normanizing' *the death of.* Who can say, then, that Malory did not intend to write one book or that **Le Morte Darthur** is not its legitimate title?

I am not suggesting that without Whittaker's error critics would not have accepted Caxton's title and all that it involves, or even that the belief in Malory's 'unifying' design, shared by so many and denied by so few, rests to any appreciable extent on Malory's colophon; but I do think that now that we have at last got the correct reading of this colophon we ought to take some notice of it. Its implication seems to me crystal-clear. On the one hand there is 'the whole book', the entire collection, or series, of romances about King Arthur and his knights; and on the other, there is the *Death of Arthur,* the last work in the series, which presumably stands in the same relation to the whole as does each one of the romances—or 'works'—that occur earlier on. If we add to this the fact that, as the Winchester MS. shows, each romance has a separate title given to it in its colophon, that five out of the eight colophons end with the word *Amen*—the medieval equivalent of THE END—that four of these plus one other give the author's name (the equivalent of the signature with which not so long ago authors used to conclude their books), can there be much argument as to what Malory *intended* 'the whole book' to be? I am deliberately refraining for the moment from any discussion of its internal 'unity' or lack of 'unity': I am concerned purely and simply with what the text was meant to be; in other words I am arguing as an editor, not as a critic. And as an editor I feel that Malory has given us as clear an indication as any medieval author has ever done as to how his text should be presented to his readers. The only hesitation one might have concerns the words *the whole book of King Arthur and of his noble knights that when they were wholly together there was ever a hundred and forty.* Is this a title or a description of the series? My own feeling is—but I may be wrong—that both the qualifying adjective 'whole' and the subordinate clause after 'knights' tip the balance against the 'title' theory, and this is why I did not think I would be justified in replacing **Le Morte Darthur** (which, incidentally, *nobody* used as a title after Caxton until

Haslewood revived it in 1816) by another title. I called my edition ***The Works of Sir Thomas Malory***, which is clearly not a 'title'. You say, quite rightly, 'I do not for a moment believe that Malory had any intention either of writing a single "work" or of writing many "works" as we should understand the expression.' Of course not. But what author ever starts off with the idea of writing 'many works'? Can you honestly say that you ever did? And yet, if at some not distant date there appears a series of volumes entitled *The Works of C. S. Lewis* will you regard it as something contrary to your intentions as a writer?

I now come to the other and perhaps more important aspect of the problem: the 'critical' as distinct from the 'editorial'. I agree entirely with your concluding remarks: 'It is our imagination, not his (Malory's), that makes the work one or eight or fifty. We can read it either way. We can read it now one way, now another. We partly make what we read.' *We partly make what we read* describes a general phenomenon; what matters to us at the moment is the particular phenomenon: *We can read it now one way, now another*. We certainly can, but why? My explanation would be that the kind of 'unity' that people occasionally look for, and find, in Malory's romances is not the essential or the 'binding' kind. It is a kind without which any one of his romances could very well exist and be appreciated to the full. Remove from Malory's text all the occasional references to what is going to happen in a later work or to what has happened already in an earlier one, and nothing of importance will be lost. You are right in saying that some of these references are 'singularly fortunate', and it does not matter at this point in the argument whether they are of Malory's own making or whether they come straight from his sources: we are discussing the effect of the work, not its genesis. But by and large I can see only two 'areas' in which these references occur in a way that is at all significant: between the *Tale of King Arthur* and the *Quest of the Holy Grail* and between the *Quest* and the romance that comes immediately after it, *The Book of Sir Lancelot and Queen Guinevere*. The examples you quote are from the latter area; other critics have made a good deal of those which occur in the former. I cannot help feeling that too much has been read into some of these examples. Does the sentence 'and ever Sir Launcelote wepte, as he had bene a chylde that had bene beatyn' in *The Healing of Sir Urry* really mean that 'as he failed in the Quest, so (for the same reason) he is failing now'? Lancelot has healed Sir Urry after everyone else has failed in the attempt. He and all the 'kings and knights' kneel down and give 'thankynges and lovynge unto God and unto Hys Blyssed Modir'. And tears—not, I think, of sorrow or contrition, but of joy and gratitude, flow down Lancelot's face. What can be more natural? And why think of the Quest at this point, and of Lancelot's failure in it, when there is not the slightest indication in the text that any such thoughts crossed his mind? I mention this example simply because so much has been made of it by the champions of 'unity' (E. K. Chambers was, I think, the first to suggest the interpretation which you have adopted). But there are, of course, others which cannot be dismissed, and which I have no intention of querying. Lancelot certainly refers to the Quest in speaking to Guinevere (*W* 1046.3-14), and Malory in describing the effects of the Dolorous Stroke clearly refers to the Grail theme (*W* 85.27-9). There are other reminders and anticipations of the same kind. But how much do they really mean to Malory's readers? Not to compilers of concordances, nor to Ph.D. candidates who laboriously dig them out and exhibit them as precious finds, but to people who read Malory as he was meant to be read, that is to say for pleasure, as a 'noble and joyous book'? I am sure you have guessed already the thought behind this question, but let me make it clearer still. In a work such as the Arthurian Cycle of romances commonly known as the 'Vulgate'—the great cycle containing the *Estoire del Graal*, the *Merlin*, the *Lancelot* proper, the *Queste del Saint Graal*, and the *Mort Artu*—references and cross-links of this kind not only occur more frequently, but have an entirely different function: without them the work would not make sense; it could be neither understood nor enjoyed (this, incidentally, is the reason why critics who have not taken the trouble to follow them up find the Vulgate unreadable). Hence there is, I think, some justification for calling such a composition 'one work'; none of it could be appreciated by a reader who did not carry the whole of it in his head. I have often wondered whether the changes in the form of the European novel are not determined, in the last analysis, by the variations in the quantity of things that one *can* carry in one's head: our modern novel does seem to correspond to our present capacity, while the thirteenth-century cyclic novel leaves us far behind, just as it left Malory and his readers far behind. Of course, it is always pleasant to be reminded in passing of something one remembers; but it is also pleasant to know that it does not really matter whether one remembers it or not, and this is what to my mind makes Malory's echoes from one work to another 'singularly fortunate'. It would be disastrous if we made the entire edifice of his romances rest upon them: **Le Morte Darthur** would immediately collapse. If we don't want this to happen we must not let our imagination 'make the work one'; but on the other hand, it would be a pity if we lost altogether the feeling which you describe so well in your Preface to extracts from Spenser in *Major British Writers*, the feeling that 'adventures of this sort are going on all round us, that in this vast forest (we are nearly always in a forest) this is the sort of thing that goes on all the time, that it was going on before we arrived and will continue after we have left'.

Here, then, the achievement, the final result is not in any way contrary to the intention: we read Malory more or less as he thought one ought to read him, and enjoy the arrangement and the somewhat capricious sequence of romances as he intended it to be enjoyed. The difficulty upon which so much thought and effort have been expended in recent years does not arise (and this is indeed a paradox) until we 'presuppose concepts Malory's mind was not furnished with' either at the reflective or at the creative level.

There is much the same relationship between intention and achievement in his narrative technique (Paradox III). You agree that he made a valiant effort to 'straighten out' the unbelievably complex pattern of interwoven narratives which he found in his French books. If he had done this very few people in post-medieval England would have bothered to read him, just as in post-medieval France very few people have bothered to read in the original the great Arthurian Cycle of the thirteenth century. Of course, he did not carry the process of straightening-out to the end; and of course it is true that such 'interweavings' as he left in the text often add to our enjoyment of it. But it is entirely a question of degree: he carried his modifications far enough to make the work 'pleasant to read in' by modern standards. Here again the reader's reaction is conditioned partly by the author's efforts and partly by what he allowed to survive from the earlier state of his stories. With all its component elements and techniques the work has grown, as you say, 'into something strange and admirable', something which none of its successive builders can claim to have foreseen exactly as it is. This great cathedral 'stands solidly before us' and imposes upon us a structure of its own. Nothing else survives. Many writers had worked on the French Arthurian prose romances between the thirteenth and the fifteenth centuries; there had been adaptations of it in Spain and in Germany. All this is now dead and buried, and Malory alone stands as a rock defying all changes of taste and style and morals; not as a grand paradox of nature, but as a lasting work of art. Is it not, then, right that we should be thinking of the work in terms of what *he* did when he called it back to life? To create does not necessarily mean to invent or even to build; it may mean to leave out or to undo what others have done; it may even be something less tangible, which somehow transforms what had no existence into something that has. And our task as interpreters is really much more modest than people think. We can neither define nor explain. But we can point in the direction where were feel the path of genius lies and hope that in this way we may bring ourselves and others a little closer to its understanding. This is what you have done. Hence my gratitude....

SOURCES FOR FURTHER STUDY

Altick, Richard D. "The Quest of the Knight-Prisoner." In his *The Scholar Adventurers*, pp. 65-85. New York: Macmillan Co., 1950.

> A lively survey of scholarly efforts undertaken to establish the identity of the author of the *Morte Darthur*.

Benson, Larry D. "Sir Thomas Malory's *Le Morte Darthur*." In *Critical Approaches to Six Major English Works: "Beowulf" through "Paradise Lost,"* edited by R. M. Lumiansky and Herschel Baker, pp. 81-131. Philadelphia: University of Pennsylvania Press, 1968.

> A comprehensive overview of Malory criticism, providing commentary on textual matters, the structural unity, sources, and major themes, of the *Morte Darthur*.

Bradbrook, M. C. *Sir Thomas Malory*. Writers and Their Work, No. 95. London: Longmans, Green & Co. for the British Council and The National Book League, 1958, 40 p.

> A concise study of the *Morte Darthur*, with commentary on its authorship, focus on the Round Table, and the tragic themes in the work.

Erskine, John. "Malory's *Le Morte d'Arthur*." In his *The Delight of Great Books*, pp. 53-71. Cleveland: World Publishing Co., 1941.

> A general appreciation of the incidental and episodic merits of the *Morte Darthur*.

Moorman, Charles. *The Book of Kyng Arthur: The Unity of Malory's Morte Darthur*. Lexington: University of Kentucky Press, 1965, 106 p.

> Examines the treatment of courtly love, religion, and chivalry in the *Morte Darthur*.

Takamiya, Toshiyuki, and Derek Brewer, eds. *Aspects of Malory*. Arthurian Studies, No. 1. Cambridge: D. S. Brewer, 1981, 232 p.

> Contains eleven specially commissioned essays on Malory and the *Morte Darthur*, treating the sources of the work, its structure, and the identity of its work's author.

Edgar Lee Masters

1868-1950

(Also wrote under pseudonyms Lucius Atherton, Elmer Chubb, Webster Ford, Harley Prowler, Lute Puckett, and Dexter Wallace) American poet, novelist, dramatist, biographer, autobiographer, and essayist.

INTRODUCTION

A prolific writer in several genres, Masters is primarily remembered as the author of the highly acclaimed *Spoon River Anthology* (1915), a collection of free verse poems admired for their brevity in depicting the realities of small-town life. The poems, which take the form of epitaphs for the dead citizens of a Midwestern town, explicitly deal with both the admirable and ignoble aspects of life. Transforming American poetry, Masters exploded the myth of traditional American values, as did Sinclair Lewis and Sherwood Anderson in their fiction. Although many literary traditionalists deemed the volume's innovative format, free verse, and subject matter inappropriate for poetry, *Spoon River Anthology* became a widely discussed phenomenon in American poetry, and the collection made Masters famous. However, he never again approached fame during the rest of his literary career, which spanned more than a quarter of a century.

Biographical Information

Masters was born on August 23, 1868, in Garnett, Kansas, but soon moved with his family to Lewistown, Illinois, on the Spoon River. After one year of classes at Knox College, he studied law in his father's law office until he was admitted to the Illinois bar in 1891. Masters practiced law with his father for a year, then moved to Chicago, where he established a successful legal career that lasted until 1920 and was marked by a partnership from 1903 to 1911 with acclaimed criminal defense attorney Clarence Darrow. While setting up his legal practice, Masters continued to write poetry and associated with other writers of the Chicago Renaissance, most notably Theodore Dreiser and Carl Sandburg. His first book, *A Book of Verses,* appeared in 1898. In 1907 Masters met William Marion Reedy, editor of the St. Louis weekly *Reedy's Mirror,* who published some of his verse and introduced Masters to *Epigrams from the Greek Anthology,* a work that provided structural inspiration for *Spoon River Anthology.* Masters wrote several more volumes of poetry using pseudonyms and a number of plays, none of which were produced. Upon publication of *Spoon River,* Masters achieved status as a respected poet. He continued to write until 1942, when health problems prevented him from working. He died March 5, 1950, in a convalescent home.

Major Works

Masters originally intended to present a history of the Spoon River area by describing the interconnected lives of its inhabitants in a novel, but his friend Reedy inspired him to write otherwise. *Spoon River Anthology* contains over two hundred brief poetic monologues, which appear under the names of the dead buried in Spoon River's cemetery. Each person reveals the circumstances of his or her death and, usually, a concealed fact of his or her life. For instance, a crusading prohibitionist admits that he died of cirrhosis of the liver caused by drinking; the heir to a fortune, that he killed to inherit it; husbands and wives, that they despised their spouses. Into small-town America, wrote Robert Narveson, "came Masters's ghosts, avowing the presence of vice, corruption, greed, and pettiness," revelations which made *Spoon River* something of a *success de scandale.* Other poetry collections include *The Great Valley* (1916), which mourns the agrarian past and attacks the corruptions of cities and religions; *Domesday Book* (1920), a long narrative poem written in blank verse, about the life and death of free-spirited Elenor Murray, whose body washes onto a riverbank; and *The New Spoon River* (1924), which reiterates such themes as the invasion of urban and industrial values and the restructuring of small-town values. The novels *Mitch Miller* (1920), *Skeeters Kirby* (1923), *Kit O'Brien* (1927), and *Mirage* (1924) are set in the Spoon River area and present thinly disguised portraits of Masters and members of his family. Although the novels *Children of the Market Place* (1922), *The Nuptial Flight* (1923), and *The Tide of Time* (1937) contain some autobiographical elements, their focus is American sociological and historical themes. Masters's biographies of Abraham Lincoln, Walt Whitman, and Mark Twain reflect his intense interest in "representative" American figures, while *Vachel Lindsay: A Poet in America* (1935), considered his finest effort in biographical writing, offers insights into Lindsay's character and poetry.

Critical Reception

Extremely popular with the public, *Spoon River Anthology* generated renown, and even notoriety, almost unprecedented for a work of American poetry. "The portraits were strongly ironic, pathetic, heroic, comic," according to Narveson. "Along with the notoriety due to scandal, came a fame based on the book's solid virtues," and *Spoon River* became "an established American classic." Many critics commented on the particularly American quality of the epitaphs in *Spoon River.* Ezra Pound, for example, proclaimed Masters the first American poet since Walt Whitman to remain in his country and to treat themes unique to America in innovative poetry. Commentators often complained of the negative presentation of small-town American life, but some pointed out that many of the most famous poems from the collection—"Lucinda Matlock," "Sarah Brown," and "Rebecca Wasson"—are joyous celebrations of life rather than bitter or ironic comments. Critics found Masters's longer narrative poetry lacking sustained dramatic power and prolonged character development—flaws of Masters's fiction as well. John H. Wrenn and Margaret M. Wrenn pointed out that much of Masters's fiction, as his poetry, attempts "to portray America through a faithful depiction of her representative men and women, towns and cities, realities and illusions," a tendency also detected in biographies. The Wrenns concluded that Masters "never recovered from the success of *Spoon River Anthology.* And he never fully understood it."

(For further information, see *Concise Dictionary of American Literary Biography:* 1865-1917; *Contemporary Authors,* Vols. 104, 133; *Dictionary of Literary Biography,* Vol. 54; *DISCovering Authors; DISCovering Authors: Canadian; DISCovering Authors Modules: Most-studied Authors Module, Poets Module; Major Twentieth-Century Writers; Poetry Criticism,* Vol. 1; *Twentieth-Century Literary Criticism,* Vols. 2, 25.)

CRITICAL COMMENTARY

EZRA POUND

SOURCE: Ezra Pound, "Webster Ford," in *The Egoist,* Vol. II, No. 1, January 1, 1915, pp. 11-12.

[*An American poet and critic, Pound was "the principal inventor of modern poetry," according to Archibald MacLeish. He is chiefly renowned for his ambitious poetry cycle, the* Cantos, *which he re-*

Principal Works

A Book of Verses (poetry) 1898
The New Star Chamber and Other Essays (essays) 1904
The Blood of the Prophets [as Dexter Wallace] (poetry) 1905
Songs and Sonnets [as Webster Ford] (poetry) 1910
Songs and Sonnets: Second Series [as Webster Ford] (poetry) 1912
Spoon River Anthology (poetry) 1915
Songs and Satires (poetry) 1916
The Great Valley (poetry) 1916
Toward the Gulf (poetry) 1918
Starved Rock (poetry) 1919
Mitch Miller (novel) 1920
Domesday Book (poetry) 1920
The Open Sea (poetry) 1921
Children of the Market Place (novel) 1922
Skeeters Kirby (novel) 1923
The Nuptial Flight (novel) 1923
Mirage (novel) 1924
The New Spoon River (poetry) 1924
Selected Poems (poetry) 1925
Lee: A Dramatic Poem (poetry) 1926
Kit O'Brien (novel) 1927
Levy Mayer and the New Industrial Era (biography) 1927
Jack Kelso: A Dramatic Poem (poetry) 1928
The Fate of the Jury: An Epilogue to Domesday Book (poetry) 1929
Lichee Nuts (poetry) 1930
Lincoln: The Man (biography) 1931
Godbey: A Dramatic Poem (poetry) 1931
The Serpent in the Wilderness (poetry) 1933
The Tale of Chicago (history) 1933
Richmond: A Dramatic Poem (poetry) 1934
Invisible Landscapes (poetry) 1935
Vachel Lindsay: A Poet in America (biography) 1935
Poems of People (poetry) 1936
The Golden Fleece of California (poetry) 1936
Across Spoon River: An Autobiography (autobiography) 1936
Whitman (biography) 1937
The Tide of Time (novel) 1937
The New World (poetry) 1937
Mark Twain: A Portrait (biography) 1938
More People (poetry) 1939
Illinois Poems (poetry) 1941
The Sangamon (nonfiction) 1942
Along the Illinois (poetry) 1942
The Harmony of Deeper Music: Posthumous Poems of Edgar Lee Masters (poetry) 1976
The Enduring River: Edgar Lee Masters's Uncollected Spoon River Poems (poetry) 1991
Spoon River Anthology: An Annotated Edition (poetry) 1992

---

vised and enlarged throughout much of his life. These poems are noted for their lyrical intensity, metrical experimentation, literary allusions, varied subject matter and verse forms, and incorporation of phrases from foreign languages, including Chinese ideographs and Egyptian hieroglyphs. Pound considered the United States a cultural wasteland; his series of satirical poems Hugh Selwyn Mauberly *(1920), has often been ranked with T. S. Eliot's* The Waste Land *(1922) as a significant attack on the decadence of modern culture. In the following excerpt, Pound enthusiastically hails "Webster Ford" (the pseudonym under which Masters wrote* Spoon River Anthology*) as the first American poet since Walt Whitman to treat American themes in vigorous poetry.*]

At last! At last America has discovered a poet. Do not mistake me, America that great land of hypothetical futures has had various poets born within her borders, but since Whitman they have invariably had to come abroad for their recognition. "Walt" seems to have set the fashion. . . .

At last the American West has produced a poet strong enough to weather the climate, capable of dealing with life directly, without circumlocution, without resonant meaningless phrases. Ready to say what he has to say, and to shut up when he has said it. Able to treat Spoon River as Villon treated Paris of 1460. The essence of this treatment consists in looking at things unaffectedly. Villon did not pretend that fifteenth-century Paris was Rome of the first century B.C. Webster Ford does not pretend that Spoon River of 1914 is Paris of 1460.

The quality of this treatment is that it can treat actual details without being interested in them, without in the least depending upon them. The bore, the demnition bore of pseudo-modernity, is that the avowed modernist thinks he can make a poem out of a steam shovel more easily and more effectively than out of the traditional sow's ear. The accidents and detail are made to stand for the core.

Good poetry is always the same; the changes are superficial. We have the real poem in nature. The real poet thinking the real poem absorbs the *decor* almost unconsciously. . . .

I have before me an early book by Webster Ford, printed in 1912, and much more old fashioned than [the eighth-century Chinese poet] Rihoku. Nineteen-twelve was a bad year, we all ran about like puppies with ten tin cans tied to our tails. The tin cans of Swinburnian rhyming, of Browningisms, even, in Mr. Ford's case, of Kiplingisms, a resonant pendant, magniloquent, Miltonic, sonorous.

The fine thing about Mr. Ford's *Songs and Sonnets, Second Series,* is that in spite of the trappings one gets the conviction of a real author, determined to speak the truth despite the sectionised state of his medium. And despite cliches of phrase and of rhythm one receives emotions, of various strength, some tragic and violent. There is moral reflection, etc., but what is the use discussing faults which a man has already discarded.

In the *Spoon River Anthology* we find the straight writing, language unaffected. No longer the murmurous derivative, but:—

My wife hated me, my son went to the dogs.

That is to say the speech of a man in process of getting something said, not merely in quest of polysyllabic decoration.

It is a great and significant thing that America should contain an editor (of the St. Louis Mirror) with sense enough to print such straight writing, and a critic sane enough to find such work in a "common newspaper" and quote it in an American review (i.e. *Poetry*).

The silly will tell you that: "It isn't poetry." The decrepit will tell you it isn't poetry. There are even loathsome atavisms, creatures of my own generation who are so steeped in the abysmal ignorance of generations, now, thank heaven, fading from the world, who will tell you: "It isn't poetry." By which they mean: "It isn't ornament. It is an integral part of an emotion. It is a statement, a bare statement of something which is part of the mood, something which contributes to the mood, not merely a bit of chiffon attached. . . ."

I have read a reasonable amount of bad American magazine verse, pseudo-Masefieldian false pastoral and so on. Not one of the writers had had the sense, which Mr. Ford shows here, in calling up the reality of the Middle West by the very simple device of names.

CARL SANDBURG

SOURCE: Carl Sandburg, "Notes for a Review of 'The Spoon River Anthology'," in *The Little Review,* Vol. II, No. 3, May, 1915, pp. 42-3.

[*Sandburg was one of the central figures in the Chicago Renaissance, an early twentieth-century flowering of the arts, which vanquished the myth that the Eastern cities were the only centers of legitimate creativity in America and established the Midwest as the home of major writers, sculptors, and painters, as well as an important source of artistic subject matter. A lifelong believer in the worth of the common, unsung individual, Sandburg expressed his populist beliefs in poetry and songs, and in his Pulitzer Prize-winning biography of Abraham Lincoln. In the following excerpt, he praises the highly personal nature of the poems in the* Spoon River Anthology.]

I saw Masters write this book [the *Spoon River Anthology*]. He wrote it in snatched moments between fighting injunctions against a waitresses' union striving for the right to picket and gain one day's rest a week, battling from court to court for compensation to a railroad engineer rendered a loathsome cripple by the defective machinery of a locomotive, having his life amid affairs as intense as those he writes of.

At The Book and Play Club one night Masters tried to tell how he came to write the *Anthology.* Of course, he couldn't tell. There are no writers of great books able to tell the how and why of a dominating spirit that seizes them and wrenches the flashing pages from them. But there are a few forces known that play a part. And among these Masters said he wanted emphasis placed on *Poetry,* voices calling "Unhand me," verses and lines from all manner and schools of writers welcomed in Harriet Monroe's magazine.

Once in a while a man comes along who writes a book that has his own heart-beats in it. The people whose faces look out from the pages of the book are the people of life itself, each trait of them as plain or as mysterious as in the old home valley where the writer came from. Such a writer and book are realized here.

Masters' home town is Lewiston, Illinois, on the banks of the Spoon River. There actually is such a river where Masters waded bare-foot as a boy, and where the dead and the living folk of his book have fished or swam, or thrown pebbles and watched the widening circles. It is not far, less than a few hours' drive, from where Abraham Lincoln was raised. People who knew Lincoln are living there today.

Well, some two hundred and twenty portraits in free verse have been etched by Masters from this valley. They are Illinois people. Also they are the people of anywhere and everywhere in so-called civilization.

Aner Clute is the immortal girl of the streets. Chase Henry is the town drunkard of all time. The railroad lawyer, the corrupt judge, the prohibitionist, the various adulterers and adulteresses, the Sunday School superintendent, the mothers and fathers who lived for sacrifice in gratitude, joy,—all these people look out from this book with haunting eyes, and there are baffled mouths and brows calm in the facing of their destinies....

In the year 1914 Masters not only handled all of his regular law practice, heavy and grilling. Besides, he wrote the *Spoon River Anthology*. There were times when he was clean fagged with the day's work. But a spell was on him to throw into written form a picture gallery, a series of short movies of individuals he had seen back home. Each page in the anthology is a locked-up portrait now freed....

There is vitality, drops of heart blood, poured into Lee Masters' book. He has other books in him as vivid and poignant. Let us hope luck holds him by the hand and takes him along where he can write out these other ones.

HARRIET MONROE

SOURCE: Harriet Monroe, "Edgar Lee Masters," in her *Poets and Their Art*, revised edition, Macmillan Publishing Company, 1932, pp. 46-55.

[*As the founder and editor of* Poetry *magazine, Monroe was a key figure in the American "poetry renaissance" that took place in the early twentieth century.* Poetry *was the first periodical devoted primarily to the works of new poets and to poetry criticism, and from 1912 until her death Monroe maintained an editorial policy of printing "the best English verse which is being written today, regardless of where, by whom, or under what theory of art it is written." In the following excerpt, she calls Masters an epic poet on the strength of what she considers his best poems.*]

Edgar Lee Masters, whatever else one may say of him, has size. He bulks large, and it may be that in that "next age," to which we accord the ultimate accounting, he will make a number of other figures now conspicuous look small. He has, not unnaturally, the faults that go with size—careless technique, uncritical sanctionings, indelicacies of emotional excess, far-sightedness which misses obvious imperfections of detail. The world will sift out and throw away many poems in his numerous books of verse; and much of his prose—not all—will go into the discard. But when hurrying time has done its worst, enough will remain to prove a giant's stature and other attributes of power in this Illinois lawyer-poet of a changing age....

A Book of Verses, published under the author's own name in 1898, was almost as mild an affair as Byron's *Hours of Idleness*— indeed, these two poets offer many proofs of kinship. But Masters developed more slowly; already thirty years old when this first book appeared, he had reached thirty-four, with his sense of humor still in abeyance, when he put out a solemn blank-verse tragedy [*Maximilian*] on the subject of that bewhiskered busy-body of pitiable history, Maximilian, so-called emperor of Mexico.

Of course there was a drama in Mexico at that moment, but it did not follow academic lines. One would have expected a modern mind to find it, but Masters' theories of poetic art were intensely academic, and even eight years later, in 1912, when he issued *Songs and Sonnets* under the pseudonym of Webster Ford, we find him writing such things as an **"Ode to Fame"** in the most approved all-hail-to-thee style. This book also fell flat, of course; and its author, at forty-four a failure as a poet, was in danger of becoming embittered when even his friend Bill Reedy sent back his classic poems; for he could contrast the silence around him with the reclame which was beginning to salute the imagists and other free-versifiers during 1913.

One can almost see the satiric smile with which he said to himself, "If that's what they want, I'll give it to them!" But *Spoon River Anthology,* begun as a more or less satirical challenge to "the new movement," soon caught him up and carried him out to the depths. For the first time he found a theme which drew upon his humor as well as his knowledge and fervor and sympathy; and a form which made him forget old-fashioned prejudices, and thereby freed his art. By the time the world found him he had found himself. And it was a big discovery.

It is hardly necessary to repeat certain things that were said of this book in the first flush of its success. It fulfilled the old time-honored principle: present a local group completely, in its heights and depths and averages, and you present the race as it is in every time and clime. *Spoon River,* with its humors and tragedies and commonplaces, its strange interweavings of destiny, is precisely central Illinois, the very heart of Middle-west America; yet Lucretius or Omar or Li Po would recognize its types and incidents, and probably the poets of the twenty-fifth century will still pronounce it true. And not only true but beautiful, for the form of those terse little epitaphs is not only a perfect fit but that triumphant completion and fulfillment which marks the masterpieces of all the arts.

Spoon River classed its author as essentially an epic poet—that is, a poet whose chief urge is to tell the tale of the tribe. And although Mr. Masters has written fine lyrics, most of his best poems emphasize the epic quality of his vision. There be critics who aver that he has done nothing since *Spoon River,* but such a myopic verdict can come only from minds groping for details and blind to mass effects. Since *Spoon River* the very titles of his books have spread a large canvas; he has travelled down the Mississippi in *The Great Valley, Toward the Gulf, Starved Rock* and *The Open Sea,* with *Domesday Book* crossing the Atlantic and accepting the immensities of the World War; and finally he has given us *The New Spoon River,* with its philosophical development of the earlier subject. And although each of these volumes needs weeding out, each of them, except perhaps *The Open Sea,* contains a few essential and memorable poems which help to symmetrize and complete this poet's record of our time and place.

Throughout one is swept along by the man's impassioned quest of truth. In this quest he is absolutely sincere and uncompromising; yet, though he admits humanity's crimes, and lashes our smug and faulty civilization with laughter or even fury, one feels always the warmth of a big-hearted wistful sympathy with all God's sorely tried and tempted creatures as they move about among illusions and are ignorantly stirred by appearances and dreams. He is the attorney for the defense before the bar of ultimate justice, admitting the strong case against his client but pleading the sadness and bitter irony of man's endless struggle between good and evil, between beauty and sordidness.

If he plies the whip on Thomas Rhodes and Editor Whedon, and stings with laughter Bryan and Mrs. Purkapile and the Reverend Percy Ferguson, he has a sympathetic smile for Daisy Frazer and Roscoe Purkapile and "dear old Dick," a wrench of the heart for Doc Hill and the pair at Perko's, and a splendid burning candleflare of beauty for Anne Rutledge and Lucinda Matlock . . . , and a few other simple and loyal souls. And always one feels these more or less imperfect creatures cast into their true perspective by the poet's ever-present, clearsighted sense of humor. It is a humor enormous, like [Jonathan] Swift's, in its satirical sweep and power, but more genial than that of the Queen Anne cynic. It permeates all his work, of course, and helps to make his portraits so intensely and sympathetically alive. But his sense of pity is just as keen, and the two in perfect unison sometimes combine to produce a masterpiece of portraiture as incisive as [Diego Rodríguez de Silva] Velasquez, like **"Slip-shoe Lovey," "Archibald Higbie"** or **"Fiddler Jones."**

Indeed, the human tenderness of this often harsh poet, in his handling of such a battered bit of flesh and blood as Elinor Murray of the *Domesday Book,* cannot be too highly praised: in spite of her manifest and numerous slips and sins, he reveals her as nobody's slave—a free and generous spirit capable of heights as well as depths, and escaping vulgarity by a certain inner flare of something like a hidden and hunted love of truth. The poet turns more lights on her than Browning on Pompilia in *The Ring and the Book,* indulging too far his lawyer's love of presenting the complete and voluminous testimony of many witnesses. But, however over-laden, the book is a powerful modern epic of democratic human averages; an episode of the eternal struggle of the race to save its soul, like Browning's and every other epic that ever was written. To complain that much of it is prose masquerading as bad blank verse, and that even its best passages are guilty of excruciating banalities of style and technique, is as idle as criticism of a mountain. The mountain is there, imperfect in line, rough and craggy in detail; but massive and mighty as it rests broadly on the solid earth and lifts its brow into the clouds.

His capacity for fierce living and hard thinking is what gives size and depth to this poet's work. One pictures his imagination as a battle-ground of ecstasies and agonies—more completely than with most poets his puppets' feelings become his own. His philosophy therefore is built on human examples—abstract reasoning apart from life is impossible to him. It is an epicurean philosophy, no doubt, one which follows earthly paths and finds happiness a sufficient aim; but beyond this immediate goal lies the remote horizon of mystery. Mr. Masters may be a realist, but we are constantly reminded that his realism transcends mere fact, that the finite and the infinite are equally real to him and equally of the tenuous stuff of dreams. He makes **"Elza Ramsey"** say:

> Do you know what makes life a terror
> And a torture, Spoon River?
> It is due to the conflict between the little minds
> Who think life is real,

And who therefore work, save, make laws,
Prosecute and levy wars—
Between these and the big minds
Who know that life is a dream,
And that much of the world's activity
Is pure folly, and the chattering of idiots.

Again and again he chants the praise of life—this splendid garment of happiness which is offered so often in vain, and which most of us, at the best, wear so clumsily:

O life, O unutterable beauty!—
To leave you, knowing that you were
 never loved enough,
Wishing to live you all over,
With all the soul's wise will!

The desecration of life—that is the unpardonable sin which he lashes in countless poems. The magnificence of the opportunity and the insignificance of our response to it—that is the gods' food for laughter, and the poet's stuff of satire. Mr. Masters does not predict, though he does not deny, that some future life may give us another chance; in his mind that is irrelevant to the immediate and important issue—our unworthy and inadequate use of the life we have.

And of course our efforts at religion are the chief of our inadequacies. His **"Sarah Dewitt,"** receiving her husband as a gift of God and then finding he is "just a thief," says:

Friends, it is folly to prison God
In any house that is built with hands,
In man or woman, in passionate hopes,
In the love of Truth, or the Rock of Ages. . . .
For God is Proteus, and flies like magic
From earth to heaven, from hope to hope.
You never can catch Him, and this is the reason:
The game of the soul is never to find,
The game of the soul is to follow.

Indeed, it is the narrow and self-righteous patterns of respectability whom Masters whips with his sharpest satire, the static immovable human clods who obstruct the path of the adventurers, of the free and open-minded children of light. Perhaps **"Emmett Burns,"** in *The New Spoon River,* sums up most keenly his feeling about this blundering world:

Passer-by, do you know who are the slickest
 schemers
And the most excellent despots?
They are those who say this is right and this
 is wrong,
And who ascend the throne of what they call
 the right
And then hedge the right with a law.
Is there no way to beat these shallow souls?
Follow me, passer-by:
Be young, be wise,
Be indifferent to good and evil
And the laws they make—
Seek only the truth,
And die!. . .

Mr. Masters has little patience with the "Europe-blinded." Here at least is a poet who makes full use of our rich "epic material." If he satirizes the republic and its individual citizens, he also glorifies them. He makes no apologies to the past or the far-away, he deals with the stuff of his own time and place, and he is absolutely fearless and sincere. At the heart of his philosophy is love of the race and a fierce desire for its "pursuit of happiness" and reasonableness; but with humor putting all this in perspective and tempering his bitter wrath with a laugh.

If this poet is fundamentally epic in the sweep of his vision, his prolific art indulges also other moods. Certain fine poems of more or less cosmic motive are epic corollaries, no doubt—such things as **"The World's Desire," "The Loom," "The Star," "Silence," "Worlds."** And many poems about real or typical characters—**"Autochthon," "William Marion Reedy," "Cato Braden," "Widow La Rue," "Emily Brosseau," "Sir Galahad"** and others—as well as out-door poems like **"Grand River Marshes," "The Landscape,"** and the supremely joyous **"Lake Boats,"** may be classed as details of that story of his place and people which is his chief legacy to art.

Sometimes his prolific genius is tempted by the past, and we have monologues from Shakespeare, Byron, Voltaire, and others. These are always interesting, whether one agrees or not with the poet's analysis of motives. But such excursions are tangents from the main curve of his orbit, and when they are pursued too deliberately, as in certain dialogues in *The Open Sea,* which elaborate the Brutus theme through the centuries, they become the most ineffective chapter of Mr. Masters' artistic history. Occasionally, however, one finds an intensely vivid study of remote and alien character, as in that rather early lyrical ballad **"Saint Francis and Lady Clare,"** which has all the emotion of a personal song.

Now and then he utters a real lyric cry. One would like to quote such poems as **"I Shall Never See You Again," "Song of Women," "Poor Pierrot," "Recessional," "My Light With Yours," "Sounds Out of Sorrow," "The Sign"**—poems which make a strong bid for remembrance because their intense rhapsodic passion burns away all imperfections and sweeps the reader along in its flame of beauty unstudied and sincere. Even the poet's technique, so often slipshod, has nobilities of its own at ecstatic moments. Perhaps the great thing about him is that he is *capable* of ecstasy, that he lives hard and deep, and knows the extremes, the agonies. Thus his art is sincere, convincing; one never doubts the emotion behind it. And to a poet who believes, who feels to the utmost, much may be forgiven.

EDGAR LEE MASTERS

SOURCE: Edgar Lee Masters, "The Genesis of Spoon River," in *American Mercury*, Vol. XXVIII, No. 109, January, 1933, pp. 38-55.

[*In the following excerpt, Masters reminisces about writing* Spoon River Anthology.]

About 1904 I began to see copies of the St. Louis *Mirror*; and soon I met its editor, William Marion Reedy, and we became fast friends. He had had a classical training under the Jesuits, and was an acute judge of literature, a book-taster of the surest sense. He filled his weekly with his own remarkable comments, and with original verse, and verse copied from English journals, and translated from the French and the Russian. Before the tango started, when jazz was fumbling to an emergence, before American free verse was heard of, he was publishing the prose poems of Turgenev, and those of the French Symbolists. . . .

There was nothing new about free verse except in the minds of illiterate academicians and quiet formalists like William Dean Howells, who called **Spoon River** "shredded prose." Reedy understood all these things as well as I. He knew that Imagism was not a new thing, though he kept urging me to make the *Anthology* more imagistic, and I refused, except where imagism as vivid description in the Shakespearean practice was called for. I had had too much study in verse, too much practice too, to be interested in such worthless experiments as polyphonic prose, an innovation as absurd as Dadaism or Cubism or Futurism or Unanimism, all grotesqueries of the hour, and all worthless, since they were without thought, sincerity, substance.

Reedy was always referring to the classics, to rich old books like the *Greek Anthology*, and I used to buy these books as he brought them to my attention. He used to present me with books; he may have given me the *Greek Anthology*. I remember distinctly his references in the *Mirror* to it, from which I gathered that I could have Plato and Simonides and Theocritus in one book. At any rate, I read the *Greek Anthology* about 1909.

Along these years I was publishing poems in the *Mirror*, in rhyme, in standard measures. All the while there was implicit in Reedy's criticisms the idea that I should do something distinctively American, that my experience and background should not go unexpressed, and should not be smothered under verses of mere skill, which did not free what was really within me. I may have told him that I contemplated a novel with Lewistown as a microcosm; I don't remember now. But he did not suggest that I use this material for poetry, though he implied in all that he said that I should use life for poetry. I was trying to do that; I was doing it, but not in the way I did in the Anthology. He did not tell me to use epitaphy as a form. He merely acted like a friend who thought I could do something more distinctive than I was doing, somehow, some way, but without telling me how to do it.

But when I sent him the first pieces of the *Anthology*—**"The Hill,"** and two others, **"Fletcher McGee," "Hod Putt,"** I think,—back came a letter immediately saying that this was the stuff. I was astonished for reasons too numerous to be briefly covered, and his extravagant praise seemed like irony. When I wrote these first pieces, and scrawled at the top of the page *Spoon River Anthology*, I sat back and laughed at what seemed to me the most preposterous title known to the realm of books. Hence when I saw that he really liked the work I wanted to change the title to *Pleasant Plains Anthology*; but he dissented so earnestly that I yielded to his judgment. . . .

I could go into the matter of the prosody of the *Anthology* if I were writing a technical exposition. I could refer to the bald stark prose of the Bohn *Greek Anthology*, and then parallel it with rhythmical pieces like **"Thomas Trevelyn,"** and **"Isaiah Beethoven,"** and in this connection I could cite the fact that the **"Spooniad"** is in blank verse, quite conventional enough; and that the **"Epilogue"** is in rhymed lyrics. I could show that there are sixty-seven pieces which are both rhythmical and metrical; and that I invented a rhythmical pattern for such pieces as **"Henry Tripp,"** which are distinctive of the book and expressive of the mood which created it. I could appeal to Aristotle's *Poetics*, which laid down the dictum that the difference between poetry and prose is the difference between literature which imitates action and emotion, and literature which imitates nothing, like arguments and the like. I could as justification for the freedom I took, and the rebellion I asserted against technical groves and academicians, appeal to Goethe's instruction to use in poems alliteration, false rhymes and assonance, which in 1831 he said he would do if he were again young.

However, I did not know of Goethe's doctrines on that subject at the time. Nor did I know of Sainte-Beuve's words that "the greatest poet is not he who has done the best, but he who suggests the most," not he who writes the *Aeneid*, but he who gives to the world that which most stimulates the reader's imagination, and excites him the most to poetize himself, which remote things like the *Aeneid* cannot so much do. I could go into all this to repel the savage attacks that were made on the *Anthology* at the time and since to the effect that it was prose, and bald prose, that it was without harmony and beauty, that in a word it was not poetry at all. I shall do none of these things here; but I shall refer to some matters of substance before resuming the history of the *Anthology* and of myself during its composition.

There are two hundred and forty-four characters in the book, not counting those who figure in the **"Spooniad"** and the **"Epilogue."** There are nineteen stories developed by interrelated portraits. Practically every ordinary human occupation is covered, except those of the barber, the miller, the cobbler, the tailor and the garage man (who would have been an anachronism) and all these were depicted later in the *New Spoon River*. What critics overlook when they call the *Anthology* Zolaesque, and by doing so mean to degrade it, is the fact that when the book was put together in its definitive order, which was not the order of publication in the *Mirror*, the fools, the drunkards, and the failures came first, the people of one-birth minds got second place, and the heroes and the enlightened spirits came last, a sort of Divine Comedy, which some critics were acute enough to point out at once.

The names I drew from both the Spoon river and the Sangamon river neighborhoods, combining first names here with surnames there, and taking some also from the constitutions and State papers of Illinois. Only in a few instances, such as those of Chase Henry, William H. Herndon and Anne Rutledge and two or three others, did I use anyone's name as a whole....

As the Fall of 1914 came along, and as my memories of the Sangamon country and the Spoon river country became more translucent and imaginative under the influence of pale sunlight and falling leaves, I departed more and more from the wastrels and failures of life and turned more and more to gentle combinations of my imagination drawn from the lives of the faithful and tender-hearted souls whom I had known in my youth about Concord, and wherever in Spoon river they existed. As December came I was nearing exhaustion of body, what with my professional work and the great drains that the *Anthology* were making on my emotions. The flame had now become so intense that it could not be seen, by which I mean that the writing of the pieces did not seem to involve any effort whatever; and yet I should have known that I was being sapped rapidly. I had no auditory or visual experiences which were not the effect of actuality; but I did feel that somehow, by these months of exploring the souls of the dead, by this unlicensed revelation of their secrets, I had convoked about my head swarms of powers and beings who were watching me and protesting and yet inspiring me to go on.

I do not mean by this that I believed that I was so haunted; I only mean I had that sensation, as one in a lonely and eyrie room might suddenly feel that someone was in the next room spying upon him. Often, after writing, during which I became unconscious of the passing of time, and would suddenly realize that it was twilight, I would experience a sensation of lightness of body, as if I were about to float to the ceiling, or could drift out of the window without falling. Then I would go out of the room and catch up one of the children to get hold of reality again; or I would descend for a beer and a sandwich. These nights I was playing on the Victrola the Fifth Symphony of Beethoven, out of which came the poem **"Isaiah Beethoven,"** and such epitaphs as **"Aaron Hatfield," "Russell Kincaid,"** and **"Elijah Browning."**

I might have made the *Anthology* fuller and richer and longer at this time except for my professional distractions, and if I had not been begged to stop by some of my relatives, who said that the work was long enough. If I had not been at this time descending rapidly to a sick bed, I should have gone on despite every obstacle, and so long as the spirits swarmed....

For myself, now that I am writing about the book, I may say that if I had any conscious purpose in writing it and the *New Spoon River* it was to awaken that American vision, that love of liberty which the best men of the Republic strove to win for us, and to bequeath to time. If anyone is interested in my cosmology let him read **"Clifford Ridell"** in the *New Spoon River*, I think my poems, **"Mournin' For Religion,"** and **"The Mourner's Bench,"** are as much in the genre of America as anything in either anthology; that I have written many poems better than anything in either *Spoon River*, and that both *Domesday Book* and its epilogue, *The Fate of the Jury*, surpass them.

JAMES HURT

SOURCE: James Hurt, "The Sources of the Spoon: Edgar Lee Masters and the 'Spoon River Anthology'," in *The Centennial Review*, Vol. XXIV, No. 4, Fall, 1980, pp. 403-31.

[*In the following excerpt, Hurt analyzes how* Spoon River Anthology *reflects Masters's personal psychology.*]

To regard Spoon River merely as a sociological microcosm, the small town as world, is to leave out a great deal of the book—the highly personal mysticism of many of the epitaphs of the last section, for example, the systematic imagery that runs throughout the collection, and the almost obsessive recurrence through the epitaphs of certain subjective motifs.

To do justice to the complexity of the *Anthology*, the reader must recognize the highly personal nature of the epitaphs, the extent to which they present not just the small town as world but also the poet himself as small town. Masters' constant presence in the book behind the formally "objective," dramatic epitaphs is inescapable, but it is usually dismissed or deplored as distortion, a skewing of "the truth" about Spoon River in the direction of Masters' various prejudices and preconceptions. The book's subjectivity might instead be regarded as its strength, its very reason for being, not as an objective critique of village life but as a sustained piece of self-revelation, a portrait of the artist as a small town. . . .

Masters wrote himself into the *Spoon River Anthology* not only as **"Webster Ford,"** his pseudonym for the magazine publication of the *Anthology*, but in a number of other epitaphs as well. But in 1933, he declared that his "cosmology" was best represented not by any epitaph in the original *Anthology* of 1915 but by the epitaph of **"Clifford Ridell"** in the *New Spoon River* of 1924. This epitaph is significant enough in the interpretation of the *Spoon River Anthology* to merit quotation in full:

> Nothing outside of it,
> Boundless and filling all space.
> At one with itself, being all,
> And bent to no will but its own.
> Changing forever, but never diminishing.
> Every part of it true to the whole of it,
> However a part of it wars with a part of it.
> Disharmony comes from two, not one.
> Friendly with itself, for otherwise
> It would perish.
> Is it good or evil? But how evil,
> Since there is nothing with which to compare it,
> And make it a blunder, a mistake?
> Without disaster, having no fate, being fate itself.
> Unutterable unity,
> Eternal creation,
> Changing, but never destroying, not even me!

The Ridell epitaph is an extreme example of the cloudy abstraction and pseudo-philosophy which mar much of the *New Spoon River* as well as some of the last-written epitaphs in the original *Anthology*. What is the subject of the speaker's discourse, the referent of "it" in the first line? Is it Life? Reality? The Universe? Creation? There is no way of knowing, and the poem does not make us care very much; it seems as if almost any capitalized abstraction will serve to make the poem an equally meaningful or meaningless piece of vaguely mystical wisdom.

Read philosophically, the poem is insignificant; read psychologically, it is considerably more revealing. The last three words of the poem are a startling plunge from the heights of abstract impersonality into the personal and the dramatic: "not even me." With these words, we are forced to rethink the entire poem, not as a philosophical generalization, but as a dramatic utterance, an expression by a specific person of his perceptions of the world and of himself. The tone of those last three words is a complex combination of self-loathing and defiance. If "it" ever turned to destruction, the first to be destroyed would be "me," a self which is perhaps especially guilty or especially vulnerable. Mingled with this attitude is a suggestion of defiance, as well, a sense of daring "it" to do its worst and determining not to be destroyed.

If we read back from these final words, the entire poem expresses not so much a philosophy or a "cosmology" as a psychological position. The speaker is tormented by conflicts and divisions in which "a part of it wars with a part of it." But he attempts to transcend these divisions by looking beyond them to a vision of seamless unity, "every part of it true to the whole of it," beyond the categories of will, of good and evil, and of fate, endlessly changing but never destroying.

Such a vision seems to have more in it of a wish than of a firm belief. The self-hatred of the last three words gives a retrospective reality to the disharmony, evil, and disaster of the preceding lines, compared to which the perhaps overvehement assertion of an "unutterable unity," an "eternal creation," seems an expression of yearning rather than of faith. The epitaph has in it none of the pithy, anecdotal detail that makes many of the poems in the earlier *Anthology* so memorable. Nevertheless, it conveys a strong sense of the personality of **"Clifford Ridell"** as a man tormented to the point of obsession with disharmonies, perhaps both internal and external, and yearning, almost beyond hope, for integration and unity.

This psychological position is the one that underlies the *Spoon River Anthology*; this is the "cosmology" that governs the "microcosm" of Spoon River, however it may be rationalized into political views, theories of society, and various other doctrines.

Masters himself repeatedly made clear that the composition of the *Spoon River Anthology* coincided with the most important psychological crisis in his life and that the epitaphs were both an expression of that crisis and a means of working through it. He began to write the epitaphs without previous planning and in a style unlike his voluminous earlier work, and as the composition proceeded over a period of about eight months, it became the means and expression of a gradual loss of self, the collapse of strained psychological defenses, a rapid psychological regression, and ultimately a kind of symbolic death. The characters in the *Anthology* were not the products of ordinary memory or nostalgia, but Masters' own ghosts, internalized images of primal conflicts dredged up and confronted through the medium of his art.

Masters left two full and moving accounts of the psychological crisis that produced the *Anthology*. The earliest published account appeared in the *American Mercury* in 1933 in an article called **"The Genesis of Spoon River."** This account was the basis of the fuller account which appeared in Masters' autobiography *Across Spoon River* (1936).

The book and the crisis began on the weekend of May 20, 1914, when Masters' mother, Emma Masters, visited him in Chicago, and they spent the weekend reminiscing about people and events in Petersburg and Lewistown. Masters describes this as a "truly wonderful" experience, and uses the language of regression to describe his feelings: "Along the way I was reinvested with myself in those incarnations that had long since surrendered their sheaths to the changes of the years." On Sunday, he walked her to the train station and then walked back home, "full of a strange pensiveness." He particularly recalls the sound of a church bell and a feeling of spring in the air. He immediately went to his room and wrote **"The Hill,"** the opening piece in the *Anthology*, and wrote "two or three" of the epitaphs....

Once he had begun, Masters produced the epitaphs very rapidly, despite heavy court commitments which his law practice required. The only block seems to have been Masters' initial uncertainty about the merit of the new work. Actually, one epitaph had been written earlier as an experiment in using the *Greek Anthology* poems as models, that of **"Theodore the Poet,"** a whimsical tribute to Theodore Dreiser. The first submission to William Marion Reedy, the *Mirror*'s editor, was **"The Hill," "Fletcher McGee,"** and **"Hod Putt,"** and Masters reported that he had scrawled across the top of the manuscript the title *Spoon River Anthology*, regarding it as "the most preposterous title known to the realm of books," apparently as a friendly jibe at Reedy's tastes. When Reedy immediately accepted the poems, Masters wanted to change the title to the conventionally pretty *Pleasant Plains Anthology*, but Reedy insisted that it remain the *Spoon River Anthology*. Once this initial doubt had been overcome, Masters apparently surrendered to what seemed to him an almost miraculous flooding out of material. He wrote the epitaphs, he said, on Saturday afternoons and Sundays, "on the street car, or in court, or at luncheon, or at night after I had gone to bed...."

As the writing proceeded over an eight-month period, Masters began to experience feelings of possession and depersonalization.... He also describes himself [in *Across Spoon River*] as being in a "hypersensitive" state of "clairvoyance and clairaudience," and describes a recurring feeling of "lightness of body," in which he felt he could "float to the ceiling" or "drift out the window without falling."

Masters himself points out that the progress of his state of mind during this period can be retraced by examining the order of composition of the poems and their publication in Reedy's magazine. (The order in which they appear in the final book is unrelated to the order of composition). This progress seems to have been from comparatively recent memories, treated more or less whimsically or ironically, to earlier, more personal, and more deeply repressed ones....

In [the *Mirror's*] issue of January 15, Masters epitaphed himself as **"Webster Ford,"** the pseudonym under which the poems had appeared. "That was the last. And I was about ready to be laid away and given a stone with these verses." When Reedy revealed the identity of "Webster Ford," against Masters' better judgment, in the issue of November 20, 1915, Masters reported that he read the article announcing him as the author "with a kind of terror, a kind of sickness, such as one might feel who has died and for a moment is permitted to look down upon the body that he has abandoned." Almost immediately after the publication of the **"Webster Ford"** epitaph Masters developed a severe cold which confined him to his home, and ten days later, he contracted pneumonia. The illness was severe, the doctor warned Mrs. Masters that he might not recover, and his father came for a deathbed visit. He reached the crisis of the illness precisely one week after it had begun.... [Hallucinatory] sensations are of course not uncommon in cases of high fever, but in association with the recurring feelings of loss of self over the preceding several months, they take on a particular significance. It appears likely that the composition of the *Spoon River Anthology* was intimately linked with a severe ego-crisis on the part of Masters, which began with his mother's visit in May, which stretched through eight months of regressive activity accompanied by increasingly powerful feelings of loss of self and which culminated in this powerful experience, during a high fever and physical collapse, of ultimate regression and symbolic death....

The materials for understanding the background of Masters' collapse, its meaning, and the part the composition of the *Spoon River Anthology* had in it are to be found in *Across Spoon River* itself. The autobiography is a working out of the themes of the Ridell epitaph in terms of a life history. Masters' personal world he sees as locked in a web of desperate conflict, each part of it warring with another part. Every thesis—father, Petersburg, the South, the law—has its antithesis—mother, Lewistown, the North, poetry—and the two stand frozen in perpetual opposition. Nothing is ever forgotten or softened by the passing of time; childhood sibling rivalries are wounds as fresh at the age of sixty-seven as at the age of six. The rare images of fusion or unity, for example his grandparents' home, are presented as almost impossibly remote, more objects of helpless yearning than attainable goals. All these labyrinthine conflicts are, however, externalized, projected onto the outside world. Masters presents himself as assaulted by division, but seldom as divided himself. For the most part, his favorite image of himself suggests a powerful bull, set about by bulldogs (or more often, stinging insects), but doggedly pushing his way forward. "As always in my life," he writes in a characteristic passage, "my head was down, and I was thrusting my way forward."

As *Across Spoon River* recasts the vision of **"Clifford Ridell"** as an autobiographical narrative, so the *Spoon River Anthology* projects the same vision as an imaginary town. Or rather two towns, for the most fundamental conflict in the *Anthology* is between the worlds of Petersburg and Lewistown. It is part of the plan of the sequence that the towns be melded in a single composite, but the melding is not quite complete, and the careful reader of the *Anthology* can still see the joints. It is not quite accurate to write, as some have done, of Masters' "ambivalence" or his "love-hate relationship" with the small town. The ambivalence is, typically for Masters, translated into radical conflict, with all the love going to Petersburg and all the hate going to Lewistown. He makes the contrast explicit in his article... "The Genesis of Spoon River." Petersburg was a "genial neighborhood of fiddlers, dancers and feasters," and it "furnished the purest springs for the *Anthology,* and colored the noblest portraits of the book." Petersburg was heavily Southern in population and spirit; it had "no New England influences of any moment," including Calvinism and such Puritan constraints as Prohibitionism or taboos on dancing. While Petersburg was rural and Southern, Lewistown was urban and Northern; it was "inhabited by a people of tough and muscular minds, where political lines were bitterly drawn by the G.A.R., and competition at the bar was intense, and where New England and Calvinism waged a death struggle on the matter of Prohibition and the church with the Virginians and free livers." "It was this atmosphere of Northern light and cold winds," Masters wrote, "that clarified my mind at last to the beauty of the Petersburg material, and pointed with steel the pen with which I drew the microcosm of the Spoon river country."

Masters himself hints that the distinction between Petersburg and Lewistown survives in the final version of the *Anthology* when he writes that there were "fifty-three poems with names drawn from the Petersburg-New Salem-Concord-Sandridge country; and sixty-five from the Spoon river country." But one does not need to know the origins of the names; the distinction is clear on internal evidence alone. Characters in the *Anthology* tend to fall into two groups, the members of which refer to each other but not to members of the other group. Thus references to the Hatfields, the Sievers, Fiddler Jones, etc. identify epitaphs as "Petersburg" epitaphs, while references to Thomas Rhodes, Editor Whedon, Doctor Meyers, the Reverend Abner Peet, etc. mark the "Lewistown" epitaphs. Internal evidence of this kind allows us to place twenty-eight of Masters' fifty-three epitaphs in Petersburg, and sixty-five of Masters' sixty-six in Lewistown....

These figures are not significant in themselves—certainly the effect the *Anthology* leaves on a casual reader is that there is only one town—but they do demonstrate the way Masters built into his composite "Spoon River" not a vague ambivalence but a precise and well articulated polarity, the one he associated with Petersburg and Lewistown.

Fortunately, Masters did not extend this polarity to the individuals in the *Anthology.* Not all the villains come from Lewistown and not all the heroes come from Petersburg. Most of the people in the collection are of "mixed character," complex mixtures of good and bad, strength and weakness. One of the most striking sustained groups of epitaphs is the "Pantier" group, which includes seven epitaphs grouped together—**"Benjamin Pantier," "Mrs. Benjamin Pantier," "Reuben Pantier," "Emily Sparks,"** and **"Trainor the Druggist"**—and two later in the collection: **"Dora Williams"** and **"Mrs. Williams."** The models for the Pantier family are complex and instructive. The chief model would appear to be Masters' own family. The conflict between the earthy, "common" country lawyer Benjamin Pantier and his "delicate," "artistic" wife seems to duplicate fairly exactly the relationship between his parents described in *Across Spoon River*. This would make **"Reuben Pantier,"** their son, Masters himself, and again the identification seems accurate. Reuben, scarred by the conflict between his mother and father and the object of gossip about his sex life in Spoon River, goes out into the world and passes through "every peril known / Of wine and women and the joy of life." The model for his idealistic teacher, **"Emily Sparks,"** is also implicitly identified in *Across Spoon River* as Mary Fisher, who encouraged Masters' early literary ambitions and later became a writer herself.

Looked at from a slightly different angle, however, the Pantiers seem to be Masters himself and his wife. Some of the tensions in Masters' first marriage replicated, perhaps not coincidentally, those in his parents' marriage, and certainly we can hear behind Mrs. Pantier's distaste for whiskey, onions, and sex the voice of Helen Jenkins, who made Masters serve a year of churchgoing and abstinence from whiskey and cigars before she would marry him....

Whatever its models, the Pantier misalliance, and all the other relationships it sets in motion, is a complex tissue of opposing forces which are never reconciled though the multiple points of view temper the bitterness of individual voices. Trainor, the Druggist, has an important part of the truth when he says that Pantier and his wife were "good in themselves, but evil toward each other: / He oxygen, she hydrogen, / Their son, a devastating fire." Pantier himself is full of bitterness and self-pity: "she, who survives me, snared my soul / With a snare which bled me to death." But his wife, when she speaks for herself, is by no means an unsympathetic character, absurd perhaps in her pride at being a "lady" and having "delicate tastes," but as tragic a victim as Pantier in that "law and morality" have trapped her in a marriage with a man with whom having the "marital relation" "fills you with disgust / Everytime you think of it—while you think of it / Everytime you see him."

Dora Williams is the indirect victim of the Pantiers' conflicts. Seduced by Reuben Pantier, their troubled son, and rejected by him, she has, however, managed to turn the tables on men. A series of rich husbands who died quickly left her "versed in the world and rich" until her last husband, an Italian count, poisoned her. She finds in death release from the Pantiers' conflicts as they were transmitted to her: on her tomb in Rome is carved, "*Contessa Navigato / Implora eterna quiete....*"

The chief victim of the combination of oxygen and hydrogen that was the Pantiers' marriage, however, is their son Reuben, who has become a "devastating fire" of dissipation and self-destructiveness. It takes Emily Sparks, his former teacher with "the virgin heart," to see that Reuben is torn between "the clay" and "the fire" and that Reuben's fire could be not the fire of self-destruction but the purifying fire of the spirit. "My boy," she calls, "wherever you are, / Work for your soul's sake, / That all the clay of you, all of the dross of you, / May yield to the fire of you, / Till the fire is nothing but light ... / Nothing but light!"

The story of the Pantiers' marriage and its multiple reverberations may be taken as a paradigm of life in Spoon River. There is always the potentiality—perhaps a memory, perhaps a hope—of a seamless unity, but actual life is a clash of opposites; everywhere "a part of it wars with a part of it." The rift that runs through the Pantier marriage reappears in every aspect of life in Spoon River: religion, politics, art, work. The life-hating Puritanism of the Rev. Abner Peet wars against the tolerant compassion of a Doctor Meyers; Elliott Hawkins' political conservatism wars with John Cabanis' liberal idealism; Petit the Poet's fashionable but trivial verses triumph over the ridiculed but passionate poetry of Minerva Jones, and the self-destructive work ethic of a Cooney Potter clashes with the joyful playfulness of a Fiddler Jones.

This desperate vision of life as ceaseless, radical conflict is not unrelieved by rays of hope, however. Masters' Dantean division of the book into an Inferno of "fools, drunkards, and failures," a Purgatory of "people of one-birth minds," and a Paradise of "heroes and enlightened spirits" has perhaps obscured a more fundamental historical division among past, present, and future. A small group of epitaphs, most notably those of Lucinda and Davis Matlock, are voices out of a past culture that was unified and coherent. In their lives, work, play, marriage, religion, and social relationships were harmonious and fulfilling, welded together by a passionate joy in living. The photographer Rutherford McDowell senses this lost unity in the photographs of the old pioneers and studies their faces to try to understand their secret....

It is not so much that the "third generation," that of

the present, are "fools, drunkards, and failures" as that they live in a society at war with itself. There are many heroes even in the first, "Inferno" section of the *Anthology*: Kinsey Keene, Emily Sparks, Doctor Meyers, Doc Hill, Dorcas Gustine. If such people are failures, it is not through any deficiency of their own but because they are caught up and sometimes crushed in the forces clashing around them.... Many transformations of Masters' father and of one aspect of Masters himself move through this section in figures forced by their society into a perpetual stance of defiance, figures such as Dorcas Gustine, Jefferson Howard, and Kinsey Keene, who says, with Cambronne at Waterloo, "merde" to the whole Spoon River establishment. Such men are admirable but tragically reduced from the models of the past such as Davis Matlock or Aaron Hatfield. To be involved in such a society is to be involved in eternal warfare.

Many of the "heroes and enlightened spirits" of the last section of the *Anthology*, those who have risen above the conflicts of Spoon River to a vision of integration and unity, are therefore outside the mainstream of Spoon River life, eccentrics, recluses, and dropouts who have rejected the establishment or have been rejected by it and who live in the private world of the imagination where they find the hope of some future redemption of the fallen world of Spoon River. This final section opens with the **"Anne Rutledge"** epitaph and contains most of the idealized pioneer epitaphs as well as those of the visionaries of the future. This juxtaposition of the harmony of the past and the hope of the future enriches the implications of each. The epitaph of Davis Matlock, for example, is immediately followed by that of the contemporary hero Herman Altman, whose very name suggests that in his idealism he is an "old man" like Matlock. And the epitaph of the pioneer Aaron Hatfield is immediately preceded by that of Russell Kincaid, who finds the same unity in the identification with nature that Hatfield found in the communion at Concord Church.

Images of a unity to counter the fragmentation of Spoon River life appear throughout the *Anthology*, though they are concentrated in this last third. The most pervasive and important of these is announced by Emily Sparks (a significant name in itself) when she tells Reuben Pantier to work that his clay may yield to his fire, "Till the fire is nothing but light! . . . / Nothing but light!" The patron god of the *Spoon River Anthology*, as Masters makes clear in the Webster Ford epitaph, is Apollo, and imagery of fire, light, and the sun appear throughout in connection with the ecstatic achievement of unity. The image is treated comically in the epitaph of Jonathan Swift Somers, the voice along with Webster Ford of Masters as poet, perhaps his satirical, "cyclopean" eye as opposed to the "dreaming," "mystical" eyes of Webster Ford. Somers hopes that when, after he has risen to a total vision of the world, his soul takes fire, life will not "fiddle" as Nero did. . . .

But the earth and the clay are not always images of blindness and the flesh. As in much mystical thought, Masters' images of ecstatic integration tend to be double. Reuben Pantier's fire may be either a "devastating fire" of self-destruction or a purifying fire of self-transcendence. In the same way, the earth may be not the prison of the spirit but the gateway to it. The symbol of Siever's apple orchard moves through the *Anthology* as a means of mystic integration with natural process. Siever himself lies under the roots of a northern-spy apple tree, to "move in the chemic change and circle of life, / Into the soil and into the flesh of the tree, / And into the living epitaphs / Of redder apples!" And the village idiot Willie Metcalf attains to a kind of wisdom denied wiser heads when he has the feeling that he was not "a separate thing from the earth." "I never knew," he says, "whether I was a part of the earth / With flowers growing in me, or whether I walked— / Now I know."

The stars and music similarly stand as images of mystic unity. Alfonso Churchill has an astronomer's vision of the stars, while Elijah Browning has a mystic's apprehension of them. In his strange dream-vision which immediately precedes the final epitaph of Webster Ford, he ascends through levels of life and experience—childhood, commerce, love—to a mountain peak with a solitary star above it. . . .

These various images of harmony and unity are all highly private and mystical; there is not much sense in the concluding sections of the *Anthology* of a political solution to the conflicts in Spoon River, little more than Anne Rutledge's hope that the Republic may "bloom forever" from the dust of her bosom. A strong death wish moves behind these images of transcendent unity. To achieve peace and integration one must move beyond consciousness itself into the "final flame" or the cycles of nature or the high, cold star beyond life.

The movement toward the peace of death culminates in **"Webster Ford,"** the last epitaph in the book and Masters' own literary epitaph. In this extraordinary poem, addressed to the "Delphic Apollo," Masters associates himself with Mickey M'Grew, a minor figure from earlier in the *Anthology*. Mickey M'Grew is one of Masters' many doubles in the *Anthology*; he expresses the familiar Masters attitude that "It was just like everything else in life; / Something outside myself drew me down, / My own strength never failed me." Forced to give up the money to his father that he had saved for an education, he has became a man-of-all-work in Spoon River. Atop the town water-tower, which he is cleaning, he unhooks his safety rope and laughs as he flings his arms over the lip of the tower. But they slip on the "treacherous slime" and he plunges to his death, "down, down, down . . . Through bellowing darkness!"

Masters seems to feel a deep kinship with Mickey M'Grew and his one heroic, defiant gesture followed by a plunge into a "bellowing darkness." This affinity is further explored in **"Webster Ford."** Ford, M'Grew, and the banker's son have seen a vision of Apollo on the river bank at sunset. The banker's son has denied the vision: "It's light / By the flags at the water's edge, you half-witted fools." Ford and M'Grew, as spiritual brothers, acknowledge the vision; M'Grew, though he recognizes the vision only as "a ghost," carries the vision of Apollo with him to his death. Ford's own stewardship of the vision is a sad summary of Masters' own spiritual life. He has hidden the vision, "for fear / Of the son of the banker," and Apollo has avenged himself by turning Ford into a tree, "growing indurant, turning to stone." But as the metamorphosis progresses, from the gradually hardening trunk and branches there burst forth laurel leaves, the pages of the *Spoon River Anthology.* "'Tis vain, O youth," he cries, "to fly the call of Apollo. . . ."

The shadows are gathering fast in the last pages of the *Spoon River Anthology,* and "Webster Ford's" last words are a race against the spreading numbness of death, that goal toward which the entire collection has been increasingly directed, a death which is the only real release from the painful conflicts of life.

Within days after writing this epitaph, Masters actually felt the numbness moving into his limbs and approached the threshold of death. And after a prolonged recovery and the appearance of the *Anthology* in book form, he felt that the book was alien to him, as if it had been written by another person. It seemed, he wrote, to be a "creation which had come from me and now seemed to have no relation to me." And in a sense it had been written by another person. The man who, under the influence of his mother's reminiscences, had begun the *Anthology* in the spring of 1914 had been engaged for years in an exhausting psychological struggle, preserving his own self-image as an invulnerable stoic, head down and pushing his way forward, by denying his own inner conflicts and projecting them into competing figures in the external world. The writing of the *Anthology* functioned both as an attempt to preserve this strategy by dramatizing it and as the signal of its ultimate collapse. The "swarms of powers and beings" Masters sensed hovering over his head as he wrote, both protesting and inspiring him to go on, were the projections of his own conflicts, now assuming an independent existence and taking their leave. The act of writing was an act of undoing, of moving backward through his life, symbolically killing the images of his conflicts, returning to his origins, and attempting to begin again. This act culminated in the symbolic suicide of the Webster Ford epitaph and the final fantasy of his illness, the music, the flame, the "black disk" of annihilation, and the "vast warm tide" of oceanic peace. Perhaps unfortunately, "rebirth" in fantasy is seldom a permanent transformation in real life. After a period of recovery, Masters appears to have gradually reconstructed a similar defense system, and the Masters of 1916 was not markedly different from the Masters of 1914.

The origins of a work of art are not necessarily relevant to its meaning. But in the case of the *Spoon River Anthology,* consideration of the poet in the poems suggests levels of depth and complexity in the poems that have generally been ignored. The collection is on its most fundamental level a spiritual autobiography, an account of "the poet's mind." Only upon this substructure are the microcosm of small-town life and the macrocosm of social criticism of American life constructed. It is largely beside the point to try to determine whether Spoon River presents a true "cross-section" of a real village, whether marriage was really as dreadful in 1900 as it seems to be in the *Anthology,* or whether such war really existed in small-town political life. Spoon River is a highly personal, highly subjective vision of small-town life and the national life, not an objective or scientific account. To ignore the personal dimension in the *Anthology* is to ignore its underlying structure, the significance of its symbolism, the nature of its emotional power and much else that makes it continue to command our interest.

SOURCES FOR FURTHER STUDY

Burgess, Charles E. "Ancestral Lore in *Spoon River Anthology*: Fact and Fancy." Papers on Language and Literature 20, No. 2 (Spring 1984): 185-204.

    Examines ancestral lore that Masters drew on in writing the Spoon River poems by focusing on the Southern branches of Masters's family and his paternal grandmother Lucinda Masters.

Chandran, K. Narayana. "Revolt from the Grave: *Spoon River*

Anthology by Edgar Lee Masters." *The Midwest Quarterly* XXIX, No. 4 (Summer 1988): 438-47.

> Discusses the symbolic significance of the rural community Spoon River.

Childs, Herbert Ellsworth. "Agrarianism and Sex: Edgar Lee Masters and the Modern Spirit." *The Sewanee Review* XLI (1933): 331-43.

> An analysis of Masters's poetry and novels that identify his position among writers of the 1920s, placing Masters as a leader.

Flanagan, John T. *Edgar Lee Masters: The Spoon River Poet and His Critics*. Metuchen, N.J.: Scarecrow Press, 1974, 175 p.

> Collection of critical responses to Masters's poetry and prose, including references from William Rose Benét, Amy Lowell, and H. L. Mencken.

Narveson, Robert. "*Spoon River Anthology*: An Introduction." MidAmerica VII (1980): 52-72.

> Discusses principal themes and structure of *Spoon River Anthology*.

Wrenn, John H., and Wrenn, Margaret M. *Edgar Lee Masters*. Boston: Twayne, 1983, 144 p.

> Critical overview of Masters's life and writings.

Edna St. Vincent Millay

1892-1950

(Also wrote under the pseudonym Nancy Boyd) American poet, dramatist, essayist, librettist, and translator.

INTRODUCTION

Millay was an exceptionally popular poet whose verse captured the rebellious mood of post-World War I youth. She is primarily remembered for her early volumes of poetry, which boldly asserted an independent, nonconformist perspective toward contemporary life rarely expressed by women authors of her time. An advocate of individualism and romanticism in her verse, Millay commonly employed rhyme and traditional metrical patterns to convey her nontraditional ideas about the role of women in relationships and society. Millay was one of the most skillful writers of sonnets in the twentieth century, and her candid investigations of mental states are credited with prefiguring the confessional school of poetry.

Biographical Information

Born February 22, 1892, in Rockland, Maine, Millay was raised by her mother after her parents divorced when she was eight years old. Encouraged by her mother to be self-reliant and to pursue her interests in music and books, Millay proved to be a precocious poet, publishing several poems as a teenager in the children's magazine *St. Nicholas*. Her first major poem, "Renascence" (1912), garnered widespread acclaim for its refreshing exploration of the poet's spiritual and emotional progress. The poem helped Millay secure a scholarship to Vassar, where she received the education that helped her develop into a cultured and learned poet. In 1917, after graduation, she published her first collection of poetry, *Renascence, and Other Poems*. Millay moved to New York's Greenwich Village, where she worked with the Provincetown Players theater troupe and wrote poetry. At the center of the bohemian milieu in Greenwich Village during the 1920s, Millay became as famous for her hedonistic lifestyle as she did for her poetry. Millay's popularity peaked when she received the Pulitzer Prize in 1923 for *The Ballad of the Harp-Weaver* (1922). Millay also wrote several lyric dramas and an opera libretto, *The King's Henchman* (1927), which is considered an important contribution to American opera. By 1930, however, Millay reexamined her poetic priorities and became more interested in social and international political problems. During the last decade of her life, Millay was plagued by isolation, illness, and artistic stagnation. In 1944 she suffered a nervous breakdown that prevented her from writing for several years. Millay completed *Mine the Harvest* (1954) shortly before she died from a heart attack on October 19, 1950.

Major Works

The lyrics and sonnets collected in *Renascence* celebrate spiritual rebirth, nature, and beauty. Louis Untermeyer praised *Renascence* for its "lyrical mastery," adding that Millay "has made ecstasy articulate and almost tangible." Although *A Few Figs from Thistles* (1920) varies greatly in tone from *Renascence,* the collection displays a brazenly unconventional attitude toward modern life and extols the virtues of women's liberation and individuality. *Second April* (1921) contains many sonnets detailing Millay's passionate relationship with Arthur Davison Ficke, a sonneteer who influenced her style with the form. Despair and disillusionment appear in many poems throughout the volume, which exalts the rapture of beauty but laments its inevitable passing. *The Ballad of the Harp-Weaver* primarily concerns Millay's emotional life. *The Buck in the Snow, and Other Poems* (1928) and the sonnet sequence "Epitaph for the Race of Man," included in *Wine from These Grapes* (1934), address political and philosophical issues. "Justice Denied in Massachusetts," for instance, decries the executions of political radicals Nicola Sacco and Bartolomeo Vanzetti. Millay's later poetry signals an increasingly didactic and journalistic approach to her art; *Conversation at Midnight* (1937) and *Make Bright the Arrows* (1940) reflect her efforts at wartime propaganda.

Critical Reception

After an initial period of resounding praise, critical opinion of Millay's poetry diverged. Later critics most often categorized her as a minor lyric poet who failed to develop beyond her early successes. Detractors termed her writing verbose, pretentious, and artificial, citing Millay's use of archaic words, traditional structures, and a coy tone that weakened her feminist statements. However, some commentators, such as Edmund Wilson, considered Millay one of the few twentieth-century poets whose stature equals that of great literary figures from the past. Millay's champions supported this contention by pointing to her pervasive wit, lyric skill, and distinguished contribution to the sonnet form.

(For further information, see *Concise Dictionary of American Literary Biography:* 1917-1929; *Contemporary Authors,* Vols. 104, 130; *Dictionary of Literary Biography,* Vol. 45; *DISCovering Authors; DISCovering Authors: British; DISCovering Authors: Canadian; DISCovering Authors Modules: Most-studied Authors Module, Poets Module; Major Twentieth-Century Writers; Poetry Criticism,* Vol. 6; *Twentieth-Century Literary Criticism,* Vols. 4, 49.)

CRITICAL COMMENTARY

HARRIET MONROE

SOURCE: Harriet Monroe, "Edna St. Vincent Millay," in *Poetry,* Vol. XXIV, No. 5, August, 1924, pp. 260-67.

[*As the founder and editor of* Poetry, *Monroe was a key figure in the American "poetry renaissance" that took place in the early twentieth century.* Poetry *was the first periodical devoted primarily to the works of new poets and to poetry criticism. In the highly laudatory essay excerpted below, Monroe discusses why she believes Millay may be "the greatest woman poet since Sappho."*]

Long ago . . . I used to think how fine it would be to be the greatest woman poet since Sappho. . . .

I am reminded by that old dream to wonder whether we may not raise a point worthy of discussion in claiming that a certain living lady may perhaps be the greatest woman poet since Sappho. . . .

[The] woman-poets seem to have written almost exclusively in the English language. Emily Bronte, Elizabeth Barrett Browning, Christina Rossetti, Emily Dickinson—these four names bring us to 1900. . . .

Emily Bronte—austere, heroic, solitary—is of course the greatest woman in literature. Not even Sappho's *Hymn to Aphrodite* . . . can surpass *Wuthering Heights* for sheer depth and power of beauty, or match it for the compassing of human experience in a single mas-

Principal Works

Renascence, and Other Poems (poetry) 1917
*Aria da capo (drama) 1919
A Few Figs from Thistles: Poems and Four Sonnets (poetry) 1920
Second April (poetry) 1921
*The Lamp and the Bell (drama) 1921
*Two Slatterns and a King: A Moral Interlude (drama) 1921
The Ballad of the Harp-Weaver (poetry) 1922
The Harp-Weaver, and Other Poems (poetry) 1923
Distressing Dialogues [as Nancy Boyd] (essays) 1924
The King's Henchman (libretto) 1927
The Buck in the Snow, and Other Poems (poetry) 1928
Fatal Interview (sonnets) 1931
Wine from These Grapes (poetry) 1934
Conversation at Midnight (poetry) 1937
Huntsman, What Quarry? (poetry) 1939
Make Bright the Arrows: 1940 Notebook (poetry) 1940
Letters of Edna St. Vincent Millay (letters) 1952
Mine the Harvest (poetry) 1954
Collected Poems (poetry) 1956
Collected Lyrics of Edna St. Vincent Millay (poetry) 1967
Collected Sonnets of Edna St. Vincent Millay (poetry) 1988
Edna St. Vincent Millay: Selected Poems (poetry) 1991

*These works were published as *Three Plays* in 1926.

---

terpiece. But *Wuthering Heights,* though poetic in motive and essence, classes as a novel rather than a poem.... As a poet, she has not the scope, the variety, of Edna St. Vincent Millay, whose claim to pre-eminence we are considering....

"**Renascence**" remains the poem of largest sweep which Miss Millay has achieved as yet — the most comprehensive expression of her philosophy, so to speak, her sense of miracle in life and death — yet she has been lavish with details of experience, of emotion, and her agile and penetrating mind has leapt through spaces of thought rarely traversed by women, or by men either for that matter.

For in the lightest of her briefest lyrics there is always more than appears. In [*A Few Figs from Thistles*], for example, in "**Thursday**," "**The Penitent**," "**To the Not Impossible He**" and other witty ironies, and in more serious poems like "**The Betrothal**," how neatly she upsets the carefully built walls of convention which men have set up around their Ideal Woman, even while they fought, bled and died for all the Helens and Cleopatras they happened to encounter! And in *Aria da Capo,* a masterpiece of irony sharp as Toledo steel, she stabs the war-god to the heart with a stroke as clean, as deft, as ever the most skilfully murderous swordsman bestowed upon his enemy. Harangues have been made, volumes have been written, for the outlawry of war, but who else has put its preposterous unreasonableness into a nutshell like this girl who brings to bear upon the problem the luminous creative insight of genius?

Thus on the most serious subjects there is always the keen swift touch. Beauty blows upon them and is gone before one can catch one's breath; and lo and behold, we have a poem too lovely to perish, a song out of the blue which will ring in the ears of time. Such are the "little elegies" which will make the poet's Vassar friend, "**D. C.**" of the wonderful voice, a legend of imperishable beauty even though "her singing days are done." Thousands of stay-at-home women speak wistfully in "**Departure;**" and "**Lament**" — where can one find deep grief and its futility expressed with such agonizing grace? Indeed, though love and death and the swift passing of beauty have haunted this poet as much as others, she is rarely specific and descriptive. Her thought is transformed into imagery, into symbol, and it flashes back at us as from the facets of a jewel.

And the thing is so simply done. One weeps, not over D. C.'s death, but over her narrow shoes and blue gowns empty in the closet. In "**Renascence**" the sky, the earth, the infinite, no longer abstractions, come close, as tangible as a tree. "**The Harp-Weaver**," presenting the protective power of enveloping love — power which enwraps the beloved even after death has robbed him, is a kind of fairy-tale ballad, sweetly told as for a child. Even more in "**The Curse**" emotion becomes sheer magic of imagery and sound, as clear and keen as frost in sunlight. Always one feels the poet's complete and unabashed sincerity. She says neither the expected thing nor the "daring" thing, but she says the incisive true thing as she has discovered it and feels it.

Miss Millay's most confessional lyrics are in sonnet form, and among them are a number which can hardly be forgotten so long as English literature endures, and one or two which will rank among the best of a language extremely rich in beautiful sonnets....

Beyond these, outside the love-sequence, the **"Euclid"** sonnet stands in a place apart, of a beauty hardly to be matched for sculpturesque austerity, for detachment from the body and the physical universe. Other minds, searching the higher mathematics, have divined the central structural beauty on which all other beauty is founded, but if any other poet has expressed it I have yet to see the proof. That a young woman should have put this fundamental law into a sonnet is one of the inexplicable divinations of genius.... If Miss Millay had done nothing else, she could hardly be forgotten.

But she has done much else. Wilful, moody, whimsical, loving and forgetting, a creature of quick and keen emotions, she has followed her own way and sung her own songs. Taken as a whole, her poems present an utterly feminine personality of singular charm and power; and the best of them, a group of lyrics ineffably lovely, will probably be cherished as the richest, most precious gift of song which any woman since the immortal Lesbian has offered to the world.

EDD WINFIELD PARKS

SOURCE: Edd Winfield Parks, "Edna St. Vincent Millay," in *The Sewanee Review*, Vol. XXXVIII, No. 1, Winter, 1930, pp. 42-9.

[*Parks was an American critic, editor, and novelist. In the excerpt below, he asserts that* The Buck in the Snow *is technically and thematically Millay's most fully realized volume of poetry.*]

According to our convention, a woman feels rather than thinks, and is governed by emotion rather than intellect. Until she reached the age of thirty-five, Edna St. Vincent Millay seemed an almost perfect example of this belief: her poetry was intimate rather than conventional, emotional rather than intellectual, realistic rather than philosophical, and inconstant to an extreme. In brief, feminine. True, she occasionally exhibited remarkable insight into the problems of life, the miracle of death, but even these strengthened the conception: they seemed lightning-clarifying flashes of that intuition so freely granted to women, but behind them no philosophy of life, nor even a sustained intellectual curiosity.

Until the appearance of *The Buck in the Snow*, then, Miss Millay was in line for comparison with the gifted women poets of the world, Sappho, Mrs. Browning, Christina Rossetti, Emily Dickinson, and the feminine poets of the present day—a comparison that, in itself, would limit her work to a definitely narrow range.

There is a close unity, a cohesion of matter and manner in her work from *Renascence* through *The King's Henchman*....

Though her poems hint at embryonic intellectual processes and a growing interest in mortality, her best work and brief, lyrical moods clothed in gossamer silk, pointed *vers de societe*, such work as might be expected from one whose mother was a leprechaun and whose father was a friar. **"The Blue Flag in a Bog,"** the **"Ode to Silence"**—these and other poems that attempt the philosophical are her poorest work. They drag, repeat, wander: common faults when a poet has nothing to say....

[In the later poems] she has experimented with many techniques. Too often this experimentation with new forms is a first sign of sterility, the autumn of the mind. His vein of poetry almost exhausted, the craftsman attempts concealment by the dexterity of his rhyme and diction. One cannot believe this to be the case with Miss Millay. *The Buck in the Snow* is a richer, *fuller* book than any of its predecessors, the emotions, though changed, glow with the same intense flame. A tragic note replaces the old joyous one; mortality and the terrible uncontrollable machine that man has built, society, are her chief interests: society menacing all who may endanger its peace or its dollars....

[These] are transitional poems, the end of one poet and the birth of a new, perhaps a greater, poet. Something more than greater skill in craftsmanship, a more flexible technique, is present, though almost for the first time Miss Millay has tried new rhyme-schemes, assonance, slant-rhymes, a longer line, even free verse; in addition to this there begins to appear a philosophy of life, tragic, Hardy-esque, but immature....

Certain it is that her mind can no longer be called feminine, in the derogatory sense. For these poems, though they lack greatness in themselves, have the inherent qualities of which great poetry is made: not only emotion, but a philosophy of life appears; the intimacy remains, but surging underneath one feels universality.

JOHN CROWE RANSOM

SOURCE: John Crowe Ransom, "The Poet As Woman," in *The Southern Review*, Louisiana State University, Vol. 2, No. 4, Spring, 1937, pp. 783-806.

[*An American critic, poet, and editor, Ransom is considered one of the most influential literary theorists of the twentieth century. He is best known as a prominent spokesman for the Fugitive, Agrarian, and New Criticism movements in American literature. In* The New Criticism *(1941), which delineated a system of critical thought that dominated the American academic scene for nearly three decades, Ransom proposed a close reading of poetic texts and insisted that criticism should be based on a study of the structure and texture of a given poem, not its content. In the excerpt below, he outlines limitations and strengths in several of Millay's poems and dramas.*]

Miss Millay is an artist of considerable accomplishments. She is the best of the poets who are "popular" and loved by Circles, Leagues, Lyceums, and Round Tables; perhaps as good a combination as we can ever expect of the "literary" poet and the poet who is loyal to the "human interest" of the common reader. She can nearly always be cited for the virtues of clarity, firmness of outline, consistency of tone within the unit poem, and melodiousness. Her career has been one of dignity and poetic sincerity. She is an artist. . . .

[The limitation of Miss Millay] is her lack of intellectual interest. It is that which the male reader misses in her poetry, even though he may acknowledge the authenticity of the interest which is there. . . . It is true that some male poets are about as deficient; not necessarily that they are undeveloped intellectually, but they conceive poetry as a sentimental or feminine exercise. Not deficient in it are some female poets, I suppose, like Miss Marianne Moore; and doubtless many women are personally developed in intellect without having any idea that poetry can master and use what the intellect is prepared to furnish. . . .

Such are Miss Millay's limits. . . . We come finally to her quite positive talent or, if anybody quarrels with that term, genius. But I still have to identify by restriction the field in which I find it displayed.

The formal, reflective, or "literary" poems fall for the most part outside this field. She is not a good conventional or formalist poet, and I think I have already suggested why: because she allows the forms to bother her and to push her into absurdities. . . .

Then, the young-girl poems fall outside it; and I am afraid I refer to more poems than were composed in the years of her minority. This charming lady found it unusually difficult, poetically speaking, to come of age.

"**Renascence**" is genuine, in the sense that it is the right kind of religious poem for an actual young girl of New England, with much rapture, a naive order of images, and a dash of hell-fire vindictiveness. . . . But the volume *A Few Figs from Thistles* is well known as a series of antireligious and Bohemian shockers, and that stage should have been far behind her when she published the work at the age of twenty-eight. The college plays were exactly right for their occasions, but ***Aria da Capo*** comes long afterward and still suggests the prize-winning skit on the Senior Girls' Stunt Night of an unusually good year. And then come the poems of *Second April,* whose author at twenty-nine is not consistently grown up. . . . [Grandually] the affectations of girlhood in Miss Millay disappear.

When they are absent, she has a vein of poetry which is spontaneous, straightforward in diction, and excitingly womanlike; a distinguished objective record of a natural woman's mind. The structures are transparently simple and the effects are immediate. There are few poems, I think, that do not fumble the least bit, unless they are very short, but she has the right to be measured as a workman by her excellent best. Her best subjects are death, which she declines like an absolute antiphilosopher to accept or gloze, a case of indomitable feminine principle; personal moods, which she indulges without apology, in the kind of integrity that is granted to the kind of mind that has no direction nor modulation except by its natural health; and natural objects which call up her love or pity. I have to except from this list the love of a woman for a man, because, in her maturity at least, she has reserved that subject for the sonnets, and they are rather unconventional in sentiment, but literary, and corrupted by verbal insincerities. . . .

The most ambitious single work of Miss Millay's would be her operatic play, *The King's Henchman;* ambitious, but suited to her powers, and entirely successful. . . . Operatic drama lends itself to Miss Millay's scope. Its action is a little brief and simple, and it permits the maximum number of lyrical moments and really suits Poe's idea of the long poem as a series of short poems rather than a single consecutive whole. The work does not prove Miss Millay to be a dramatist, but it shows what an incessant fountain of poetry is a woman's sensibility in the midst of simple human and natural situations. It should be remarked that, being tenth century, the properties have the advantage of being a little picturesque, and the tone of the language slightly foreign, like a Scottish or Irish idiom perhaps. But these are the arrangements of the artist, of whom it cannot so fairly be said that she is in luck as that she is a competent designer.

HILDEGARDE FLANNER

SOURCE: Hildegarde Flanner, "Two Poets: Jeffers and Millay," in *After the Genteel Tradition: American Writers since 1910*, edited by Malcolm Cowley, Peter Smith, 1959, pp. 155-67.

[*Flanner was an American poet, essayist, and dramatist whose verse focused on religious and nature themes. In the excerpt below from an essay that first appeared in the* New Republic *in 1937, she praises Millay's fresh use of such traditional poetic forms as the sonnet and the elegy.*]

In reading Miss Millay's poetry one is always struck by the thought that she has been fortunate in her time of emergence—or that the time was fortunate in her. After the War and during the early twenties she expressed, particularly for women and for youth, a spirit that was symptomatic of the moment....

It is interesting to note that many of her more serious poems coming at a later period, especially the sonnet sequence *Fatal Interview*, are in celebration of the opposite practice, that of romantic love or what is more crudely (or exactly) called transference. It is this state to which literature is indebted for some of the most treasured examples of the poetic art.... Since the sonnets of *Fatal Interview*, however, she has come a noticeable distance from the private drama of the early and middle poems. One cannot prophesy, but it is unlikely that she will return to write of romantic passion and the crises of personal attachment. That something is thus lost from poetry is true. But any gain in objectivity is, after a few years, a gain for feeling and hence for the heart, when it again enjoys authority.

Miss Millay is not to be classed among the "makers" who have left language altered and disturbed by their experiments, and ready for new forms and sensibilities.... She is one of those who take the known forms that offer the readiest vehicle, technically and emotionally, and thus save themselves much loss of time, much doubt. Of her own day in modernism of intellect, she has yet been nearest another age technically. The sonnet was ideally suited to her wants and she surrendered herself to the iambic line and all the machinery of the form, certain to work and work so musically in her hands. Its good brevity, its psychological moments, its fine style of being a capsule of infinity, the effect of an idea ravished and made quotable, all this she was familiar with. That she was able with no hesitation to accept the continuity of a traditional form meant that she wrote in measures already possessing emotional associations for all readers. There was an exchange of gifts, for the sonnet received something from Miss Millay. She took the principle of surprise common to the final lines and developed it into a clever note of drama.... She gave to it, as to her other lyrics, homely and modern details and sometimes the grandeur of folk heroism.... She brought to the sonnet the interest and ferment of conversation. She made the form sophisticated, versatile and highly feminine.

It is not easy now to recapture in one's own words the sense of freshness and transparent revelation that her early lyrics conveyed. In these also it had been her fortune to take frequently a traditional form, the elegy, and make it immediate and tender. Her contribution to method has been chiefly in two directions: an infusion of personal energy and glow into the traditions of lyric poetry, and the deceptively artless ability to set down the naked fact unfortified. She has pleased the fastidious and did not scorn to please the simple, for even a limited poetic appreciation found in the identical performance something that gave pure pleasure....

It is true, however, that an extravagance of feeling, an indulgence of legendary anguish that belongs to the ultra places and not to the heart of poetry, have thrived beyond wisdom in her lines. One deplores the overdramatic ring in a brilliant measure. Yet it is equally true that an egotism never weak, and one of the best talents for lyrical anger in all literature, have saved her from a problem that other women poets have been torn by. Miss Millay has never been apologetic about the right to love or to suffer....

[Miss Millay] contemplates the end of civilization. Her mind, however, is on the elegy, not the revulsion. **"Epitaph for the Race of Man"** is eminent writing. But now that the content of her work is changing, these sonnets still run as smoothly as perfect engines. That is the fate of a traditional measure, no matter how strong may be our sense of continuity in using it. It begins to alarm with the bland ease of the mechanical. One does not ask Miss Millay to forgo the exceptional command of her medium. Yet there could be possible an eloquence neither disinherited nor upstart, an eloquence closer to its own necessity than these sonnets are, a kind of language less dependent on the perfection of the form.

WINFIELD TOWNLEY SCOTT

SOURCE: Winfield Townley Scott, "Millay Collected," in *Poetry*, Vol. LXIII, No. VI, March, 1944, pp. 334-42.

[*Scott was an American poet, editor, and critic. In the excerpt below, he offers a mixed assessment of Millay's verse upon the publication of her* Collected Lyrics.]

A new attitude toward Edna St. Vincent Millay has pretty thoroughly been adopted by the literati, and if her popular audience is still not only faithful but large, she has—so far as I can determine—failed to excite any recent collegiate intelligentsia. The greatest insult you can offer any young woman poet in this country is to warn her that she may be the Edna Millay of her generation; which, being interpreted, means that she is in danger of glibness and of popularity.

Now if under the praise and the dispraise there are reasons for both to be found in Miss Millay's poetry, the fact remains that the adulation and the abuse have little to do with the worth of that poetry, since both have been excessive. They do merit preliminary mention because they make so difficult an attempt to write of a body of poetry that is neither the most unworthy nor the greatest since Sappho's....

All her poems may be said to be variations on a theme announced by Housman: "Let us endure awhile and see injustice done." Occasionally this injustice is political and social in the sense uppermost in Housman's line; but generally with Miss Millay it is personal, and at her best it is always personal. Here are some of the things she has said so often in her verse:

This is a lovely world, almost unbearably beautiful as a work of nature; but the poet is usually, in this expression, writing from some particular point on earth which is markedly less desirable than another she is recalling, and therefore she writes in sorrow. Sorrow in general is a constant mood with her, and its most typical expression is through sorrow in love. Though her love poetry has ranged from the flip to the marmoreal, from the casual to the frenzied, it has elaborated at both extremes and all the way between that love is (1) fickle and (2) irresistible....

From her poem **"Mariposa"** the conviction that

> Whether I be false or true,
> Death comes in a day or two

was lightened and extenuated through the famous *A Few Figs from Thistles*, and this theme runs with its own small variations through her work, the impudence changing to bitterness and sometimes ... to wholly humorless arrogance.

As deliberately as anywhere in her work, I suppose, Miss Millay seeks to objectify her conclusions in the eighteen sonnets called *Epitaph for the Race of Man*. I like a couple of these as well as anything Edna Millay has ever written, but as a whole it is a sequence that suffers from repetitiousness and from the later grand manner of the poet. No one can sound so profound as Miss Millay at her falsest! However, as I understand them, these sonnets portray man's victories over his environment and conclude that his tragedy lies in his inevitable defeat by himself. It is a great theme, and sometimes Miss Millay handles it with great beauty and genuine (not bogus) dignity. Two of the sonnets are certainly among her best: the much admired **"See where Capella with her golden kids"** and the not enough admired **"Observe how Myanoshita cracked in two...."**

Her poems say a hundred times that life is sad. At least as often, her poems say that death is the bitterest pill of all; and they fight against it, wail upon it, and defy death. This, when you come to think of it, adds up to a lot of troubled emotion. Maybe if Miss Millay had ever made up her mind, we should have had less poetry from her, and that would be unfortunate; nonetheless, by these conflicting emotions she has remained in an intellectual jam. There is obvious sentimentality in this contradiction; it afflicts a great deal of her verse and explains, I think, why the verse leaves us dissatisfied. Here too I suspect we come closest to the reason for Miss Millay's attractiveness for the undergraduate, or adolescent, mind....

In other words, the mood of self-pity is exceptionally attractive to the young, and Miss Millay's verse has employed that mood (or vice versa) many, many times. The popularity of her poetry, of course, stems very largely from what we may call its familiarity: simple forms in rhyme and stanza, resemblances (whether or not fortunate) to poetry already well known, occasionally skillful reworkings of particular styles all the way from the Elizabethan to that of Robinson Jeffers. At her best, Miss Millay brings vigor and freshness to traditional forms and stamps them with a new personality more positively than any of her contemporaries has ever done....

Edna Millay has pursued her art according to lights that have varied in her career, but according to those lights with integrity. This is not a small matter.

Where her poetry has, so to speak, gone wrong is where she has mistaken attitudes for convictions, or mere moods for profound truths (as we all do). Thus, you get the absurd blather, "O world, I cannot hold thee close enough!", in **"God's World,"** and the astounding insistence on so desiring the seashore that she is crying aloud for death by drowning. This is the common error of requiring an emotion to bear ... a little more than it can bear. And along with such sentimentality in Miss Millay's work there has been a rapid loss of humor in its largest or smallest sense and a consequent gain in a grand manner that not only permits medieval impedimenta as aforesaid but even allows such solemn absurdities as celebrating the cleaning of a canary's cage....

These elements were always in Miss Millay's poetry. The humorless dullness of her early **"Ode to Silence"** is a pertinent example. The disproportionate overloading of an emotion was done full-length in **"The Blue Flag in the Bog."** But the simpler elements have persisted, too, and it is those we come back to....

There is in the poem **"Renascence"** a simplicity which is at times girlish; legitimately so, of course. It holds the seed of Edna Millay's best poetry. In her subsequent work this girlishness sometimes became unpleasantly coy and mawkish, as for instance in the poem called **"The Little Hill."** On the other hand, in **"Elaine"** and **"A Visit to the Asylum,"** bathos, however perilously, is really escaped; something pathetic and moving takes place.

JAMES GRAY

SOURCE: James Gray, in his *Edna St. Vincent Millay*, University of Minnesota Press, Minneapolis, 1967, 48 p.

[*In the following excerpt, Gray discusses major themes and stylistic traits of Millay's poetry.*]

Seen whole [Edna St. Vincent Millay] emerges out of myth not as a gay figure but as a tragic one; not as a precocious perennial schoolgirl but as an artist born mature and burdened with a scrupulous sense of responsibility toward her gift; not as a changeling child of mysticism but as a creature whose essential desire was to find identity with the balanced order of nature; not as a woman merely but as a creator who inevitably contained within her persona masculine as well as feminine attributes.

The theme of all her poetry is the search for the integrity of the individual spirit. The campaign to conquer and control this realm of experience is conducted always in terms of positive and rigorous conflict—the duel with death, the duel with love, the duel of mind pitted against heart, the duel with "The spiteful and the stingy and the rude" who would steal away possession of beauty.

It is not too fanciful to say that she was born old while she remained forever young....

[Quiet] reverence for vitality under discipline is the distinguishing quality of her poetry. At its best it is characterized by a kind of orderly surrender to ecstasy....

It is often said of the major figures of the arts that each seems to create a universe all his own and to measure its vast dimensions with untransferable techniques....

No such gigantic stature can be claimed for a poet like Edna Millay. Her theme was too personal, too intimate to herself to fill out the dimensions of a supernatural realm of imagination. Indeed it might be said that her unique effort was to perform the miracle of creation in reverse. A universe already made pressed its weight on the sensibility, the aptitude for awareness, of one individual....

The journey in search of wholeness for the individual, an adventure which has obsessed the minds of the philosophers of the past and the psychiatrists of the present, cannot be left safely to further exploration by the computers of the future. It continues, therefore, to be of no trivial interest as it is presented in the poems of Edna St. Vincent Millay.

It should not be taken as an indication of a failure to grow that Edna Millay produced when she was only nineteen years old one of the most characteristic, most memorable, and most moving of her poems. The intuitions of artists do not reach them on any schedule of merely logical development.... In **"Renascence"** Edna Millay announced the theme to which four more decades of her life were to be spent in the most intense kind of concentration. "The soul can split the sky in two, / And let the face of God shine through." This confrontation with the divine can be dared and endured because man is one with the divine.

Edna Millay presented the inner life of the spirit always as a conflict of powerful forces. The will to live and the will to die are elementally at war in **"Renascence."**... The impulse toward surrender *itself* has roused the counter impulse toward a participation more passionate than ever before in the values of human existence.... The meaning of this battle of the wills is clear. The anguish of existence must be endured as the tribute owed to its beauty....

An account of the running battle between life and death claimed first place among the poet's preoccupations through her writing career. The effectiveness of the report is heightened by an awareness, sometimes bitter and sometimes merely rueful, that now one side commands ascendancy over will and now the other....

[Variations] of tone in her report on the duel of life against death lend the best and most original of her personal qualities to the development of an old, familiar theme. The parallel may be suggested that, just as a mother must have faith in her child lacking any evidence to justify it, so the believer in life must show a similar courageous unreasonableness. Edna Millay is perhaps at her best when she casts her vote of No Confidence in death....

So many of Edna Millay's pages are devoted to critical moments of the love duel that it has been possible, even for reasonably well informed readers, to be aware only of her confidences about "what arms have lain / Under my head till morning." To their loss they have ignored her equal preoccupation with other themes. Still it is true that some of her most searching observations about the human condition are concerned with the approach to ecstasy through the identification of man with woman. It would, however, be to deceive oneself to approach these poems as if they were exercises in eroticism. Despite the many sidelong references to the physical relationship, the enclosing interest is that of human love as a total experience of the psyche involving, on the positive side, intellectual communication and sympathy of taste and, on the negative side, the endless warfare of two egos that cannot effect a complete surrender into oneness.

The limp endorsement of correct and appropriate sentiments which has made up so much of love poetry, particularly that written by women, is conspicuous for its total absence from these ardent but anxious confrontations of man and woman. It is significant of Edna Millay's approach to the psychological crisis of love versus hate—and to the even more destructive tragicomedy of love slackening away into indifference by the influences of time, change, and disillusion—that she does not speak of these matters simply as a woman. Often in her highly dramatic representations of the love duel she assumes the man's role and she plays it with no nervous air of indulging in a masquerade. She is concerned with the mind as the retort in which all the chemical reactions of love take place and, because her own intelligence partook of both masculine and feminine characteristics, the poems convey the impression that the exactitude of science, in control of the impulses of intuition, has been brought to bear to reveal much that those changes involve in a man's temperament as well as in a woman's.

Again, as in her account of the conflict of the will to live and the will to die, the love duel is presented with high drama as one that is destined to go on and on indecisively because the adversaries are only too well matched in aggressiveness and submissiveness, in strength and weakness, in sympathy and treachery....

[A reverential gaiety] which finds room for humor in the midst of the contemplation of bliss, characterizes much of Edna Millay's love poetry. Its popularity may be accounted for by the intoxicating quality that brings the immediacy of a highly personal emotion to the poetic statement. The merit that gives the work permanence is the fastidiousness of the style in which the spontaneity is captured.

In her younger days Edna Millay sometimes allowed her exuberant vitality to escape into verses the levity of which made her famous, perhaps to the injury of her reputation as a serious poet....

These flourishes of audacity do not touch at all closely on the center of her understanding of the love duel. There she held a formidable awareness of the power of change which is not in the least like the vague consciousness of impermanence in which so many poetic spirits have fluttered with languid futility.... Edna Millay used the sharpest tools of her intelligence to hew out for herself a unique place among poets by undertaking to discover *why* no love endures. What she says is that the loophole in commitment offers the necessary escape route by which the self saves its integrity. There can be no such thing as total surrender except with degradation or with, what is worse, dishonesty. In love the giving must be generous and free, but there must be withholding, too, if the self is to remain whole....

The immediacy of experience is communicated in images that are piercingly personal. Very often the suggestions of the figurative language are so unexpected that they seem to spring out of an immediate passion which catches deliberately and desperately at punishing words....

It is because she was bold enough to examine the problem of the psychological distance between man and woman—one that cannot be breached and should not be violated—that Edna Millay may be said to have made an original contribution to the literature of the love duel....

[It] is the ability to capture in colloquial language and in one brief thunderclap of drama the essence of a tragic psychological struggle that lends to Edna Millay's long discussion of the love duel its effects of variety and flexibility.

The tone of melancholy misgiving in the face of the emotional crisis is pervasive in these studies, but the warming, the nourishing, the half-maternal aspects of the experience of love are not neglected....

It is characteristic of Edna Millay's temper—not merely

its prevailing but its almost uninterrupted mood—that she enters upon the search for beauty as if this, too, were a struggle....

This is to say that the mind has its right to evaluate beauty. It should not yield in limp acceptance as if faced by something of divine origin and therefore, like a god of Greek mythology, not to be denied its will. What Edna Millay persuades a reader that she does indeed know is that beauty must be endured as well as enjoyed. To surrender to beauty without resistance would be to lose an exhilarating aspect of the experience. It must be participated in, but the terms of one's compact with beauty must be understood to be one-sided. "Beauty makes no pledges." In return for the awe that the observer feels in its presence nothing is promised other than awareness itself....

That she is not entirely consistent in developing her religion of beauty need not be found disturbing. She is no more given to shifts of interpretation than mystics must ever be. Beauty may be aloof and impersonal but it is also an element in the process of rebirth, the faith in which the poet takes her deepest comfort. It even becomes in certain poems the food on which she feeds. Her figures of speech suggest again and again that, as a woman, she felt an almost organic closeness to the working of gestation....

Part of the nourishment that she receives from awareness of beauty is provided by what is for her the immediate actuality of sensuous experience....

She was always an actor in the drama: a militant defender of herself against beauty, a militant defender of beauty against its defilers. And she was resolutely faithful to the integrity of her own perceptions. She never attempts to encompass more of a sense of the wonder of the natural world than her own eyes can see. What moves her is the recollection of a familiar scene, fixed in memory by some small detail of local color.... Armed with awareness, the one who is "waylaid" by beauty may find exultation in the simplest of experiences. Edna Millay did indeed seem to write all her poems to give permanence to a moment of ecstasy....

From first to last, through every phase of her development, Edna Millay continued to be intensely herself and no other. Whether her theme was death, love, beauty, or the refreshing impulse of the will to live she spoke always with an accent that was unique to her. Of language she made a homespun garment to clothe her passions and her faith.

That she was able to create effects of striking originality is discovered to be only the more remarkable when a characteristic poem is examined closely and its thought is found to wear "something old" and "something borrowed" from the left-over wardrobe of tradition. Edna Millay was a product as much of the nineteenth century as of the twentieth. The influence of tradition moved her a little backward in time. A too great reverence for her early instruction—not only at her mother's knee but also at Keats's—probably accounts for all the "O's" and "Ah's," the "would I were's," the "hast's," the "art's," the "wert's," the "Tis's." It must account also for the inversions of normal word order which sometimes impede the plunge of her hardihood in thought.

Even in more important matters of vocabulary, imagery, and symbolism her impulse toward expression was governed by convention. Despite her interest in science she felt its discipline to be alien to her always personal style of utterance. She did not find in its language a new source of imaginative power such as Auden has exploited. Despite her obsession in the late years with the crisis of war, such a reference as one to "Man and his engines" reveals an uninvolved attitude toward the special concerns of the machine age.... The familiar image, drawn from the treasury of metaphor upon which Shakespeare also depended for imaginative resource, seems never to have dismayed her. She was not inhibited by fear of intelligibility; she was not tempted to prod the imagination with tortured similes. For her, death still swung his scythe and the poems in which he does so with the old familiar ruthlessness betray no nervous apprehension that the instrument may have become rusty or blunted with the use of ages.

Because she absorbed tradition deeply into herself she seems able to revitalize its language with the warmth of her own temper. Her words become fertile from the nourishment which, as woman, she communicated to them as if by an umbilical link.

Simplicity, spontaneity, the seeming absence of calculation combine to produce her best effects....

More often than with either definitely declared voice she speaks as a detached observer of natural sights and sounds. These souvenirs of experience are shared with a reader in language that seems entirely casual; it has been borrowed for the moment from more studied performers in the realm of poetry simply to convey a passing impression.... More typical of the poet's method is the device of catching a symbolic significance, some warning of the threat against survival, in an image that seems to be, all at once, spontaneous, startling, and inescapably true....

Edna Millay's wit was never petty. She was generous

toward all her adversaries except mediocrity, war, and death. And in fashioning an epigram she revealed her most fastidious respect both for truth and for elegance. In the later poems her wit is so unobtrusive, so modest, that it might be missed entirely by a reader hoping to find a showy attribute identified by a capital letter. But it is always subtly present, embedded in a theme, as is the wit of Henry James. The tight-packed phrase, the unexpected revelation of how opposites of impulse may be found to blend, the sudden illumination of an ambiguity—these are the veins of wisdom through which wit runs in the sonnets....

A close examination of the work of any artist is certain to reveal flaws. The very urgency of the desire to communicate must tempt any poet sometimes to override obstacles recklessly. With Edna Millay the individual line seldom limps though it may now and again betray an obvious determination to be vigorous. There is little sense of strain in the use of rhyme and, even in the early poems when her effects threaten to become self-conscious, she avoids the temptation to indulge in the verbal acrobatics of clever versifiers as even Byron does. What troubles her appraisers most of all is the willingness to snatch up old trophies of metaphor and set them up among her own inspirations as if she were unaware of the difference of freshness between them.

But in the end vigor and spontaneity prevail in technique as they do in passion. The singing quality of the lyrics, of the free forms of verse and of the formal sonnets, too, is consistently clear and true....

She wrote prose, as she wrote poetry, with an at once witty and intensely sober regard for her own values. The personal letters glow— sometimes they seem feverishly to glitter—with the elan that sustained her, however precariously, through the crucial moments of her experience. Her preface to the volume of Baudelaire translations reveals a critical intelligence of distinction. Only the adroit satiric sketches written under the pseudonym Nancy Boyd depart from her preoccupation with poetry. These exercises, too, display a kind of coloratura virtuosity. They draw freely on her gift of wit and have importance as lucid indirect reflections of her attitudes: her unwavering honesty, her distaste for pretense, sentimentality, and concessiveness....

Conversation at Midnight remains pseudo-drama, lacking a concentrated drive toward effective vicarious experience....

The faults of the work are inherent in the original concept. This requires a group of men, met for a session of late-night drinking and ratiocination, to use the occasion for a kind of war game in which they fire rounds of ammunition over each other's heads, hitting only distant, theoretical targets. Each guest represents a point of view, aesthetic, social, or moral; each in turn has his say, in a piece of stylized elocution, about capitalism, Communism, commercialism, Nazism, and, of course, love in a world that is out of sorts with spontaneity. All is spoken in earnest; much of the talk is witty and stimulating; some of it inevitably seems trivial in its cloudy references to situations in the lives of the characters which there has been neither time nor occasion really to evoke. Nothing resembling dramatic tension can rise out of these arguments which never intermingle, never affect each other, never in the end manage to clarify idea....

There were crises of social life which gave gross affront to the most fundamental of her convictions and she could not withhold her protests. These took poetic form but—as she later knew to her chagrin—she was able at such times only to rear up the framework of a poem, gaunt and horrifying. To the lines with which she clothed the structure she could communicate her impotent rage but not the essence of compassion which she wished to memorialize.

There was, for example, her involvement in the Sacco and Vanzetti case....

When Sacco and Vanzetti were finally ordered to be executed, Edna Millay wrote the poem **"Justice Denied in Massachusetts,"** a desperate and bitter threnody.... The unwilling, half-stifled protest that a reader makes in his turn against these utterances springs from the impression that a just and honest sentiment is being overdramatized. Is the abject surrender to despair really congenial to the poet's spirit or does this lamentation have to be brought under the charge of being tainted by hysteria? The conviction is clearly genuine but the excess of passion with which it is expressed still seems dubious. The literary crisis is not ameliorated when the poet yields her mind to the most cliche of imaginings: "We shall die in darkness, and be buried in the rain."

It is right for a poet to be a participant in the affairs of everyday living. With her special talent for doing precisely this, Edna Millay could not withhold her world. Nor is it relevant that the guilt or innocence of the two men whose part she took is still a moot question. The respect must be paid her of considering anything she wrote as a work of art. Viewed in that light it becomes evident that poems written for occasions come forth misshapen at their birth by the influence of propaganda. In work that was truly her own even her bitterest protests against the will to destroy were informed by a still abiding faith; such poems reveal her militant spirit at its most staunch. The weakness of "**Justice Denied in Massachusetts**" must be attributed to the fact that it was not nourished by an inner will but fed on the inadequate substitute of propaganda....

Edna St. Vincent Millay has been praised extravagantly as the greatest woman poet since Sappho. She has also been dismissed with lofty forbearance as a renegade from the contemporary movement in poetry and sometimes been treated almost as a traitor because she never broke defiantly with the past. But both eulogy and denigration seem to hang upon her figure like whimsical investitures. Neither costume suits the occasion when her enduring presence rises up before us to bespeak a mind that has not lost its vigor....

She belongs to an impressive company of artists who came to maturity and found their voices during the second quarter of this century. Many of these have undertaken to explore the darkest caves of the secret mind of man and they have developed new poetic forms in which to record their experiences. Among them the figure of Edna St. Vincent Millay is conspicuous because she stands alone and in a blaze of light. It is impossible not to understand what she has to say, impossible not to be moved by the simple, direct, eloquent statements of her convictions. The world, which she had held no closer at the beginning of her life than she did at the end, gave her as much of pain as it did pleasure. Love, beauty, and life itself had all to be endured as well as enjoyed. But the human experience had meaning for her. The round of the seasons still kept to its pledge of rebirth and renewal. From that faith she drew the strength to impart dignity and beauty ... to even the most cruel phases of the adventure of our time.

JEANNINE DOBBS

SOURCE: Jeannine Dobbs, "Edna St. Vincent Millay and the Tradition of Domestic Poetry," in *Journal of Women's Studies in Literature*, Vol. 1, No. 2, Spring, 1979, pp. 89-106.

[*In the following excerpt, Dobbs asserts that although Millay's domestic poems have suffered critical neglect, they are among her best works.*]

Despite the quality and quantity of Millay's domestic poetry, her reputation was built on poems expressing disillusionment with people and on those celebrating sexual freedoms for women. Two of her sonnet sequences, "**Epitaph for the Race of Man**" and *Fatal Interview* typify these concerns. The former is abstract philosophizing on the folly of humankind; the latter a proficient but somewhat academic exercise in the tradition of the courtly love sonnet sequence.

Many of Millay's New Women type poems are successful and interesting; but the speakers usually are not portrayed as real, individualized women. They are witty and clever and sexually emancipated, but as women they are a stereotyped abstraction. The speaker of the following sonnet, for example, is a disembodied voice:

> I, being born a woman and distressed
> By all the needs and notions of my kind,
> Am urged by your propinquity to find
> Your person fair, and feel a certain zest
> To bear your body's weight upon my breast:
> So subtly is the fume of life designed,
> To clarify the pulse and cloud the mind,
> And leave me once again undone, possessed.
> Think not for this, however, the poor treason
> Of my stout blood against my staggering brain,
> I shall remember you with love, or season
> My scorn with pity,—let me make it plain:
> I find this frenzy insufficient reason
> For conversation when we meet again.
> *The Harp-Weaver,* 1923

The impersonal speaker works here because she represents all women: "I, being born women...." There is no personality here. There is no environment, no dramatic interplay. There is no real man involved, only a "person fair," a "body." There is not even any particularized emotion, just generalities: a "certain zest," a "frenzy." When the speaker is stereotyped and the situation generalized in this way, identification with the speaker must be made totally on an intellectual level. Many of Millay's burning-the-candle-at-both-ends type poems portray only a voice, and all portray the same voice.

In more successful poems, Millay places the speakers in a setting or in a situation with which women can identify. "**The Fitting**" (*Huntsman, What Quarry?*, 1939) is such a poem. Here the speaker's body is portrayed as being impersonally, even roughly handled by dressmakers, "doing what they were paid to do." As this activity proceeds, the woman thinks of her lover. The brief mention of the lover invites comparisons between the present touch of the dressmakers and the anticipated evening with the lover, when his touch, as [Norman A. Brittin in his *Edna St. Vincent Millay*] notes, will not have to be paid for.

It was these kinds of love poems—love poems declaring or illustrating women's independence in the face of social conventions—which most interested Millay's public. Many of these poems appear to be autobiographical, confessional. Therefore, as much attention was paid to guessing the identity of the lover(s) as to the poems themselves. With the appearance of this type of heroine and this kind of love poem (especially in *A Few Figs from Thistles*), Millay began to be encouraged to write for all the wrong reasons: shock, titillation, idle speculation. "Gossip and scandal . . . enhanced her sales," Dorothy Thompson reports [in "The Woman Poet" in *Ladies Home Journal*, January 1951]. The fact that *Fatal Interview* describes an illicit affair may help to explain the popularity of that sonnet sequence. Also, it was undomestic, academic, and abstract. It was, therefore, pronounced "intellectual" and "masculine," a superior work according to Millay's critics. Thus, Millay's public, her editors and critics have emphasized and praised some of her less successful and actually less important work and have neglected or ignored work that best reveals her talent, her domestic poetry.

Millay was one of the number of bright, young women who converged on New York and the capitals of Europe in the early 1920s to pursue the new liberated life women felt they had won along with suffrage. By this time, Millay was a published and recognized poet; and, for a while, she undertook a simultaneous career as an actress. During this time, she half-heartedly agreed to marry two or three of her numerous suitors; meanwhile she practiced her belief in free love. She feared marriage because she thought it might kill her creative voice. Floyd Dell, one of the rejected lovers, recalls "that she was probably afraid that by becoming a wife and mother, she might be less the poet. She wanted to devote herself exclusively to her poetry and did not want to 'belong' to any one except herself. She did not want to spend her energies on domestic affairs." In spite of her fears, Millay married Eugene Boissevain in 1923. She was thirty-one; he was forty-three. He gave up his career in order to take up the household duties and free Millay for her writing. When Allan Ross MacDougall interviewed Boissevain for an article in the *Delineator* some years after the marriage, Boissevain recalled: "When we got married I gave up my business. It seemed advisable to arrange our lives to suit Vincent. It is so obvious to anyone that Vincent is more important than I am. Anyone can buy and sell coffee—which is what I did . . . But anyone cannot write poetry."

In the same year as her marriage, Millay published a sonnet that warns a husband what may happen if he scorns his wife's intellect and insists instead on subjugating her to stereotyped wifely roles—to being submissive, non-intellectual and vain:

> Oh, oh, you will be sorry for that word!
> Give back my book and take my kiss
>   instead.
> Was it my enemy or my friend I heard,
> "What a big book for such a little head!"
> Come, I will show you now my newest
>   hat,
> And you may watch me purse my mouth
>   and prink!
> Oh, I shall love you still, and all of that.
> I never again shall tell you what I think.
> I shall be sweet and crafty, soft and sly;
> You will not catch me reading any more:
> I shall be called a wife to pattern by;
> And some day when you knock and push
>   the door,
> Some sane day, not too bright and not too
>   stormy
> I shall be gone, and you may whistle for
>   me.
>   *The Harp-Weaver*, 1923

Perhaps because Millay was so aware of the potential threat to her career posed by her marriage and certainly because of Boissevain's willingness to accept an untraditional domestic situation, the marriage endured until his death twenty-six years later.

Although some of Millay's domestic poems seem clearly autobiographical, it is difficult to discern any over-all correlation between the events of her life and the periods when she wrote on domestic subjects. She alternates between writing some domestic poems and writing none at all, but for no apparent reasons. She wrote about marriage before she became a wife, culminating with **"Sonnets from an Ungrafted Tree."** After her marriage, domesticity virtually disappeared from her work until the 1939 volume *Huntsman, What Quarry?*, a rather strange mixture of war and domestic concerns. During the war years, propaganda held her captive; but the poems collected posthumously in 1954 in *Mine the Harvest* reveal that she ultimately returned to her more basic subjects: nostalgia for childhood, nature, and domesticity. Hence, it is more useful and enlightening to see her domestic poetry not in terms of chronological progression, but in terms of certain recurrent themes.

The same domestic themes run through all three of the periods of Millay's career in which she wrote about her own or other women's experiences. The **"Sonnets from an Ungrafted Tree"** sequence deals with one of the most common: the relationship between husband and wife. This sequence appeared in the May 1923 issue of *Harpers* before it was collected in **The Harp-Weaver** volume. Millay did not marry until August 30th of that year. Thus, the poems were written before she herself could have had any actual experience as a wife. This fact makes the sequence all the more remarkable since it is one of the most striking portraits of a wife's situation in twentieth-century American poetry.

These sonnets tell the story of a wife who returns to the deathbed of her estranged husband. The wife Millay creates or describes here is a woman whose body has trapped her into marriage with a man she knows to be her intellectual and spiritual inferior. The woman was aware that her husband was "not over-kind nor over-quick in study / Nor skilled in sports nor beautiful" when she met him in school, but she married him anyway. Apparently even his physical passion did not prove to be a match for hers. In Sonnet IV, the woman's "desolate wish for comfort" and her intense efforts at starting a fire among "the sleeping ashes" seem a metaphorical experience suggesting the woman's frustrated efforts to kindle a physical passion in her past marital relationship. The woman is "mindful of like passion hurled in vain / Upon a similar task in other days." She brings her whole body to bear upon the "hilt" of the coals.

The woman's story is told primarily through such small domestic actions, rather than through explicit statements. We are told that the man does not measure up to the woman's dreams, that she married him because she was "so in need." But we are not told explicitly how their previous life together progressed or why they separated. What we are given are subtle insights into the woman's character and flashes of what her life in the house once was. Thus, we see her in Sonnet I in the past, presumably a new wife, "big-aproned, blithe, with stiff blue sleeves ... plant[ing] seeds, musing ahead to their far blossoming." There is something promising and maternal in this picture of the woman planning ahead to a distant crop. In contrast are the geraniums, the "rotted stalks" of the present. She has not provided the necessary care to ensure that her plants survive the winter season. She abandoned them when she left her husband.

Sonnet I provides a further contrast with the woman's actions later in the sequence. Her figure, "big-aproned" and "blithe" in a past spring is contrasted to her discovery in Sonnet XI of an apron which she had lost in a long ago snowstorm. Finding the apron, she is struck "that here was spring, and the whole year to be lived through once more." It is as if the resurrection of the apron represents not a new year at all, but only the same year to be lived again. In fact, none of the promise of the image of the woman from her past is fulfilled. She comes back only to mother her dying husband and to muse, in the end, upon his corpse.

These poems do not reveal what has motivated the woman to return to care for her dying husband. Perhaps it is a sense of guilt or perhaps a sense of duty — certainly it is not love that has brought her. Her behavior, her desire to remain invisible to the eyes of the neighbors, suggests guilt. Her instinct is always to flee. She leaves only the fanning of a rocker to the eyes of the grocer, just as the small bird she thinks she may have seen has left only its flash among the dwarf nasturtiums (shades of Emily Dickinson!). And the train's whistle at night brings her magic visions of cities that call to her as the whistle must have done when she first lived with the man as his wife.

The woman immerses herself in housekeeping as a distraction from her dying husband's "ever-clamorous care." She discovers that there is a "rapture of a decent kind, / In making mean and ugly objects fair." (It is to this kind of rapture that her desires have come.) She polishes the kitchen utensils, changes shelf paper, and replaces the table's oilcloth; but she is now only a visitor to the kitchen that once was hers. She has not been the one to position the soda and sugar; thus, they seem strange to her.

It is unclear whether or not the woman views domestic chores as a part of the trap of marriage. Perhaps it is only her disillusionment with the man and not her functions in the house which have caused the estrangement. The clean kitchen seems to give her pleasure; on the other hand, she finds saving the string and paper from the groceries a routine that is "treacherously dear" and "dull." And this is a woman who needs magic in her life, a woman for whom the common and everyday must be transformed.

As a girl she was blinded by a reflected light in a mirror held by the boyfriend, not by the vision of the boy himself. When it occurs to her that his dazzling her with a mirror is unmiraculous, she persists in viewing him by moonlight rather than by the clear and truthful light of day. The unsuccessful outcome of her marriage has not disillusioned the woman in general; she is still affected by the magic of the train's whistle. Only in matters concerning her husband has she given up hope of magic or surprise. She anticipates that in death he will be "only dead." But there is irony here. In Sonnet XVII, the last and perhaps the finest of the sequence, the woman is surprised by her dead husband. Considering him as "familiar as the bedroom door," she is surprised to discover in him a new dimension. In death he has a mystery about him that, in life, he had long since lost, or that she had only pretended was his.

These sonnets are serious, quiet, delicate pieces of work. Except for the epiphany in the final poem, the grand emotions of these characters are over. But the work is not slight or trivial. Much of Millay's work is uneven; however, except for the somewhat weak concluding couplet to Sonnet IX, this sequence is extremely well-written. Also, the sequence reveals a remarkable degree of imagination and insight into the female condition. Even though the essence of the story is said to be true [according to Jean Gould in her *The Poet and Her Book*], and even though Millay had done some housekeeping as the eldest daughter of a divorced and working mother, her understanding of the woman's emotional responses toward her husband—especially the epiphany in the concluding sonnet—is unaccounted for by what we know of her actual experience.

Whenever Millay writes about marriage, it is usually in the sad tone of **"Sonnets from an Ungrafted Tree,"** or in a disillusioned or cynical voice. A person is trapped, biologically, into marriage, or, like the husband in **"On the Wide Heath"** (*Wine from These Grapes*, 1934), trapped out of loneliness. This husband goes home "to a kitchen of a loud shrew" and

> Home to a worn reproach, the disagreeing,
>   The shelter, the stale air, content to be
> Pecked at, confined, encroached upon,—it being
> too lonely, to be free.

Also, the married person is one who resists being totally possessed. The speaker of **"Truck-Garden-Market Day"** (*Mine the Harvest*) for example, is happy to remain at home while her husband takes the produce to town because solitude gives her relief from his "noises." The time she is left alone represents to her the small part of herself she keeps from giving to him. She has already given him so much: "More than my heart to him I gave," she says, "who now am the timid, laughed-at slave." But she must not allow him to see how she feels, because:

> He would be troubled; he could not learn
> How small a part of myself I keep
> To smell the meadows, or sun the churn,
> When he's at market, or while he's asleep.

The woman is portrayed as preferring even a small housekeeping chore to the man's company. The woman's experience is different from her husband's, but by choice; and it is not necessarily inferior.

Perhaps Millay's most successful poem about marriage is one titled, **"An Ancient Gesture"** [from *Mine the Harvest*]:

> I thought, as I wiped my eyes on the
>   corner of my apron:
> Penelope did this too.
> And more than once; you can't keep
>   weaving all day
> And undoing it all through the night;
> Your arms get tired, and the back of your
>   neck gets tight;
> And along towards morning, when you
>   think it will never be light,
> And your husband has been gone, and
>   you don't know where, for years,
> Suddenly you burst into tears;
> There is simply nothing else to do
>
> And I thought, as I wiped my eyes on the
>   corner of my apron:
> This is an ancient gesture, authentic,
>   antique,
> In the very best tradition, classic, Greek;
> Ulysses did this too.
> But only as a gesture,—a gesture which
>   implied
> To the assembled throng that he was much
>   too moved to speak.
> He learned it from Penelope...
> Penelope, who really cried.

This combining of the classic and the homely is surprising but perfectly appropriate. The poem expresses the universality of domestic experience for women as well as the differences in the nature of experience between women and men: Penelope, the stay-at-home, the weaver, contrasted with Ulysses, the venturer, adventurer, orator. Penelope's weaving, which according to myth never gets done, is a perfect symbol for woman's condition. Ulysses learns something from his wife but then uses it superficially—to further his own ends. The sincerity and suffering of the woman are contrasted effectively with the political expediency of the man.

"Menses" (*Huntsman, What Quarry?*) is another poem that deals with marriage and with the differences between the sexes. The speaker is a man who humors the woman in a patronizing way. When the woman attacks him brutally, however, he forgives her, thinking to himself merely that she is "unwell." (She says at one point: "Lord, the shame, / The crying shame of seeing a man no wiser that the beasts he feeds—/ His skull as empty as a shell!") The poem ends with the woman's denunciation of her own weakness: "Just heaven consign and damn / To tedious Hell this body with its muddy feet in my mind!" Thus, it seems that the woman is as much or more concerned with the effect psychologically of her menstrual period on her intellect as with the effect on her relationship with the man.

The relationships between women and men and the differences between the sexes are thematically important to Millay's work. Maternity as subject or theme concerns her much less, although **"The Ballad of the Harp-Weaver,"** the poem for which she won the Pulitzer, tells the story of a mother's sacrifice for her child. In other poems, Millay oddly enough envisions herself (or her speakers) in strangely intense, maternal relationships with nature. Sometimes these visions are bizarre. In the apocalyptic poem **"The Blue-Flag in the Bog"** (*Second April*, 1921) she adopts a maternal posture toward the last flower left on earth. In **"The Little Hill"** (also *Second April*), she pictures herself as the mother of the hill where Christ died. But these conceits are mere oddities. Millay, although she had no children, could and did write successful poems about them. One example is an untitled poem [included in *Mine the Harvest*] in which she identifies with a child rather than with its mother. This poem deals with an adult's perception of birth as a betrayal. The second half reads:

> If you wish to witness a human counte-
> nance contorted
> And convulsed and crumpled by helpless
> grief and despair,
> Then stand beside the slatted crib and say
> There, there, and take the
> toy away.
>
> Pink and pale-blue look well
> In a nursery. And for the most part Baby is
> really good:
> He gurgles, he whimpers, he tries to get
> his toe in his mouth; he
> slobbers his food
> Dreamily—cereals and vegetable juices—
> onto his bib:
> He behaves as he should.
>
> But do not for a moment believe he has
> forgotten Blackness; not the
> deep
> Easy swell; nor his thwarted
> Design to remain for ever there;
> Nor the crimson betrayal of his birth into a
> yellow glare.
> The pictures painted on the inner eyelids
> of infants just before they
> sleep
> Are not pastel.

The sentiment almost inherent in this subject—baby in its pretty crib—is played off effectively against the strong ending of the poem. Removing the child's toy, which to the child is incomprehensible loss, signifies the incomprehensible losses and terrors life holds. The child still recalls the "betrayal" of its birth; and thus its dreams are not, as we might sentimentally like to believe, "pastel."

Another major theme, although not a familial one, is the preference for nature to housekeeping. One early (1920) and possibly autobiographical poem entitled **"Portrait by a Neighbor"** describes this preference. The poem begins:

> Before she has her floor swept
> Or her dishes done
> Any day you'll find her
> A-sunning in the sun!
>   *A Few Figs from Thistles*

And the same subject is more effectively treated in a late (1954), untitled poem in which the speaker recalls the discovery of nature's beauty and wonders how as mere child she could have withstood "the shock / Of beauty seen, noticed, for the first time." The speaker, now adult, still is staggered by the experience of encountering natural beauty—to the extent that she finds it impossible to turn from it to mundane, domestic chores:

> How did I bear it?—Now—grown up and
> encased
> In the armour of custom, after years
> Of looking at loveliness, forewarned
> And face to face, and no time
> And too prudent,
> At six in the morning to accept the unen-
> durable embrace,
>
> I come back from the garden into the
> kitchen,
> And take off my rubbers—the dew
> Is heavy and high, wetting the sock above
> The shoe—but I cannot do
> The housework yet.
>   *Mine the Harvest*

"Cave Canem" (*Mine the Harvest*), another seemingly autobiographical poem (probably written after Boissevain's death), also reveals her preference for nature as well as continued concern over the encroachment of domesticity on her writing. In this lyric, the speaker complains that she must "throw bright time to chickens in an untidy yard"; and that she is "forced to sit while the potted roses wilt in the case or the / sonnet cools."

In **"The Plaid Dress"** (*Huntsman, What Quarry?*), Millay uses something feminine in much the same way that Edward Taylor used the homely and commonplace as an emblem through which to treat larger concerns:

Strong sun, that bleach [sic]
The curtains of my room, can you not render
Colourless this dress I wear?—
This violent plaid
Of purple angers and red shames; the yellow stripe
Of thin but valid treacheries; the flashy green of kind deeds done
Through indolence, high judgments given in haste;
The recurring checker of the serious breach of taste?

No more uncoloured than unmade,
I fear, can be this garment that I may not doff;
Confession does not strip it off,
To send me homeward eased and bare;

All through the formal, unoffending evening, under the clean
Bright hair,
Lining the subtle gown . . . it is not seen,
But it is there.

The speaker's violently-coloured dress is used as a metaphor to represent her emotions—her "purple angers and red shames." She can suppress these, but she cannot purge them from her personality.

Millay's letters to her editors reveal her own opinions about some of her work. They indicate that she preferred poems such as **"The Plaid Dress"** to what she called her more "modern" poems, poems of "the revolutionary element" concerning "the world outside myself today." It is revealing that she felt it necessary to defend her more personal, feminine poems, almost to apologize for them. The reason for her attitude undoubtedly lies in the critical reception to her work: when she wrote in the male tradition—that is, "abstract" and "intellectual" poetry—or when she wrote "shocking" verse, she was praised; when she wrote outside that tradition—the domestic poems—she was usually ignored or downgraded.

Of course Millay's "feminist" verse is important. It was flippant, fresh, and fun. It was popular with the public and helped gain her fame, and it was widely imitated by Dorothy Parker and other women poets of the period. But a reassessment of Millay suggests that her greater contribution and achievement have been in the poems she wrote of a more personal, more immediate nature, poems out of her own experience as a woman and out of her understanding of that experience on the part of other women.

SOURCES FOR FURTHER STUDY

Benét, William Rose. Introduction to *Second April and The Buck in the Snow* by Edna St. Vincent Millay, pp. v-xii. New York: Harper & Brothers Publishers, 1950.

> Discusses Millay's writing style and her themes of nature and childhood.

Burch, Francis F. "Millay's 'Not in a Silver Casket Cool with Pearls'." *The Explicator* 48, No. 4 (Summer 1990): 277-79.

> Discusses Sonnet XI of *Fatal Interview*, concluding that "Millay introduces a feminine viewpoint to the English sonnet sequence, but her views are not new."

Gould, Jean. "Edna St. Vincent Millay—Saint of the Modern Sonnet." In *Faith of a (Woman) Writer*, edited by Alice Kessler-Harris and William McBrien, pp. 129-42. New York: Greenwood Press, 1988.

> Examines the origins of the sonnet sequences "Fatal Interview" and "Epitaph for the Race of Man" in relation to Millay's life.

Gregory, Horace, and Zaturenska, Marya. "Edna St. Vincent Millay and the Poetry of Feminine Revolt and Self-Expression." In their *A History of American Poetry, 1900-1940*, pp. 265-81. New York: Harcourt, Brace & Company, 1946.

> Discusses the development of Millay's literary personality and the structure and lyricism of her sonnets.

Hahn, Emily. "Mostly about Vincent." In her *Romantic Rebels: An Informal History of Bohemianism in America*, pp. 231-41. Boston: Houghton Mifflin Co., Riverside Press, 1966.

> Discussion of Millay's life in Greenwich Village during the 1920s.

Sheean, Vincent. *The Indigo Bunting: A Memoir of Edna St. Vincent Millay*. New York: Harper & Brothers, 1951, 131 p.

> Memoir of the critic's acquaintance with Millay during the 1940s. Sheean recounts significant events and relationships in Millay's life in those years and considers her verse in relation to her philosophical and spiritual perspectives.

Czesław Miłosz

1911-

(Has also written under the pseudonym J. Syruc) Polish poet, essayist, novelist, translator, nonfiction writer, diarist, autobiographer, and editor.

INTRODUCTION

The recipient of the 1980 Nobel Prize in Literature, Miłosz is widely considered Poland's greatest contemporary poet, although he has lived in exile since 1951. Miłosz's writings are concerned with humanistic and Christian themes, the problem of good and evil, political philosophy, history, metaphysical speculations, and personal and national identity. Jonathan Galassi noted: "[Miłosz's] entire effort is directed toward a confrontation with experience—and not with personal experience alone, but with history in all its paradoxical horror and wonder. . . . His own work provides dramatic evidence that in spite of the monumental inhumanities of our century, it is still possible for an artist to picture the world as a place where good and evil are significant ideas, and indeed active forces."

Biographical Information

Born in Szetegnie, Lithuania, in 1911, Miłosz spent much of his childhood in czarist Russia, where his father worked as a civil engineer. After World War I the family returned to their hometown, which had become part of the new Polish state, and Miłosz attended local Catholic schools. In 1933 he published his first collection of poems, *Poemat o czasie zastyglym*. While attending the University of Vilnius in Lithuania during the 1930s, Miłosz won respect for his poetry and associated with a literary group called the Catastrophists, who prophesied the subversion of cultural values and a cataclysmic global war. In the early 1940s, when these predictions were realized by the events of World War II, Miłosz began writing anti-Nazi poetry, which was published clandestinely. Living in Nazi-occupied Warsaw during the war, he worked as a writer, editor, and translator for Polish Resistance forces. After the war, he served as cultural attaché in Paris for the postwar Polish communist regime, whose hypocrisy and authoritarianism disgusted him. When Miłosz defected to the West in 1951, he was declared a nonperson by the Polish government, which also banned his writings for the next 30 years. He lived in Paris until 1960, then accepted a teaching position at the University of California, Berkeley, where he established permanent residence. After he was awarded the Nobel Prize, Miłosz received his first officially sanctioned publication in Poland since 1936. In 1981 he visited that country for the first time since his exile and was hailed as a symbol of the resurgence of freedom in Poland. Miłosz was named professor emeritus of Slavic languages and literature at Berkeley in 1978.

Major Works

Most of Miłosz's poetry avoids the experimentation with language that characterizes modern poetry, concentrating instead on the clear expression of his ideas; it also is strongly emotional and conveys a transcendent spirituality, deriving from his Roman Catholic background and his fascination with good and evil. His earliest poetry collections, *Poemat o czasie zastyglym, Trzy zimy* (1936), and *Wiersze* (1940), feature pastoral lyrics, meditations on the poetical process, and commentary on social problems. The restrained approach of Miłosz's anti-Nazi poetry communicates the horror and anguish of the times. *Ocalenie* (1940), a volume that reflects the poet's maturing skills, contains several of his most famous poems, including "The World" and "Voices of Poor People." Miłosz's next two volumes, *Swiatlo dzienne* (1953) and *Trak tat poetycki* (1957), blend lyrical, classical, and modernist forms to create poems that are alternately discursive, visionary, and somber. Miłosz's later poetry in such volumes as *The Separate Notebooks* (1984) and *Gdzie wschodzi slonce i kedy zapada* (1974; *The Rising of the Sun*) sometimes verges on rhythmical prose and contains many classical elements, including a respect for balance and form as well as an economical style. Miłosz's prose works delineate his personal experiences, his interest in history and politics, and his aesthetic theories. For example, the essay collection *Zniewolony umysl* (1953; *The Captive Mind*) studies the effects of totalitarianism on creativity, and *Rodzinna Europa* (1959; *Native Realm*) lyrically recreates the landscape and culture of Miłosz's youth. *Ziemia Ulro* (1977; *The Land of Ulro*) laments the modern emphasis on science and rationality, evoking a symbolic wasteland that has divorced human beings from spiritual and cultural pursuits, and *Beginning with My Streets* (1992)—an amalgam of literary criticism, philosophical meditations, and narrative essays—probes contemporary life, art, and politics, yielding astonishing insights. Miłosz's two novels combine explorations of twentieth-century world events with autobiographical elements. *Zdobycie wladzy* (1955; *The Seizure of Power*) examines the fortunes of intellectuals and artists within a communist state. Blending journalistic and poetic prose, the novel elucidates the relationship between art and ideology and offers vivid descriptions of the Russian occupation of Warsaw following World War II. In *Dolina Issy* (1955; *The Issa Valley*) Miłosz evokes the lush river valley where he was raised to explore a young man's evolving artistic sensibility. The mythical structure of this work explores such dualities as innocence and evil, regeneration and death, and idyllic visions and grim realities.

Critical Reception

Critics frequently emphasize Miłosz's important contributions to the development of contemporary Polish poetry, citing his application of modernist and classical verse forms, his lyricism, and his command of synecdoche and irony. In the United States Miłosz is known not only for his work written in Polish, but also for his English translations of his own poems and those of other prominent Polish poets. Many critics cite the profound awareness of history that informs his poetry, a quality sometimes considered lacking in American verse. Despite the broad range of historical and political themes in his poetry, Miłosz is regarded primarily as a metaphysical poet because of his pervasive concern with the nature of existence and identity. Affirming Miłosz's universal relevance, the prize-winning poet and former U.S. Poet Laureate Joseph Brodsky has written: "I have no hesitation whatsoever in stating that Czesław Miłosz is one of the greatest poets of our time, perhaps the greatest."

(For further information, see *Contemporary Authors*, Vols. 81-84; *Contemporary Authors New Revision Series*, Vols. 23, 51; *Contemporary Literary Criticism*, Vols. 5, 11, 22, 31, 56, 82; *DISCovering Authors Modules: Most-studied Authors Module, Poets Module; Major Twentieth-Century Writers; Poetry Criticism*, Vol. 8.)

CRITICAL COMMENTARY

TERRENCE DES PRES

SOURCE: Terrence Des Pres, "Czeslaw Milosz: The Poetry of Aftermath," in *The Nation*, New York, Vol. 227, No. 23, December 30, 1978, pp. 741-43.

[*In the following excerpt, Des Pres surveys autobiographical elements in Miłosz's work, especially*

Principal Works

Poemat o czasie zastyglym (poetry) 1933
Trzy zimy (poetry) 1936
Wiersze [as J. Syruc] (poetry) 1940
Ocalenie (poetry) 1945
Swiatlo dzienne (poetry) 1953
Zniewolony umysl (essays) 1953
 [*The Captive Mind*, 1953]
Dolina Issy (novel) 1955
 [*The Issa Valley*, 1981]
Zdobycie wladzy (novel) 1955
 [*The Seizure of Power*, 1955; also published as *The Usurpers*, 1955]
Trak tat poetycki (poetry) 1957
Kontynenty (poetry) 1958
Rodzinna Europa (essays) 1959
 [*Native Realm: A Search for Self-Definition*, 1968]
Czlowiek wsród skorpionów: Studium o Stanislawie Brzozowskim (history) 1962
Krol popiel i inne wiersze (poetry) 1962
Gucio zaczarowany (poetry) 1965
Lied vom Weltende (poetry) 1967
The History of Polish Literature (nonfiction) 1969; revised edition, 1983
Miasto bez imienia (poetry) 1969
Widzenia and Zatoka San Francisco (essays) 1969
 [*Visions from San Francisco Bay*, 1982]
Wiersze (poetry) 1969

Prywatne obowiazki (essays) 1972
Selected Poems (poetry) 1973
Gdzie wschodzi slonce i kedy zapada (poetry) 1974
 [*The Rising of the Sun*, 1985]
Utwory poetyckie (poetry) 1976
Emperor of the Earth: Modes of Eccentric Vision (nonfiction) 1977
Ziemia Ulro (nonfiction) 1977
 [*The Land of Ulro*, 1984]
The Bells in Winter (poetry) 1978
Dziela zbiorowe (poetry and prose) 1980
Ogrod nauk (nonfiction) 1980
Nobel Lecture (lecture) 1981
Hymn O Perle (poetry) 1982
The Witness of Poetry (lectures) 1983
Niobjeta ziemia (aphorisms, letters, poetry, and prose) 1984
 [*Unattainable Earth*, 1986]
The Separate Notebooks (poetry) 1984
Rok myśliwego (diary) 1990
Provinces (poetry) 1991
Beginning with My Streets: Essays and Recollections (essays) 1992
A Year of the Hunter (autobiography) 1994
Facing the River: New Poems (poetry) 1995
Striving towards Being: The Letters of Thomas Merton and Czesław Miłosz (letters) 1996

---

his focus on spiritual survival, moral survival, and renewal in modern times.]

Political catastrophe has defined the nature of our century, and the result—the collision of personal and public realms—has produced a new kind of writer. Czeslaw Milosz is the perfect example. In exile from a world which no longer exists, a witness to the Nazi devastation of Poland and the Soviet takeover of Eastern Europe, Milosz deals in his poetry with the central issues of our time: the impact of history upon moral being, the search for ways to survive spiritual ruin in a ruined world.

Translation of his early work, collected in **Selected Poems,** is foremost a poetry of loss and aftermath. A more recent collection, **Bells in Winter,** reaches toward a poetry of recovery. The basis of his art, however, remains constant. In **"Ars Poetica?,"** for example, the question mark in the title alerts us to the poem's theme: that although no aesthetic principle is absolute or safe from abuse, some notions of poetic practice are more responsible than others, especially in a world as violent as ours. Art should serve more than itself, and in an age of wreckage, with nations dispersed and loyalties divided, "The purpose of poetry is to remind us / how difficult it is to remain just one person." Milosz thus abjures modernism and pledges himself to values of "a time when only wise books were read / helping us to bear our pain and misery."

People, places, objects, everything for Milosz is densely historical. Destiny, for him, is shared, it is *human* destiny. The self cannot escape its larger, collective fate; and the norms of perception—in poetry as in life—are judged by the extremity of modern experience. An art which embodies these principles is essentially political, a way of seeing things which, in his brilliant book **The Captive Mind,** Milosz calls "the vision of the cobblestones":

> A man is lying under machine-gun fire on a street in an embattled city. He looks at the pavement and sees a very amusing sight: the

cobblestones are standing upright like the quills of a porcupine. The bullets hitting against their edges displace and tilt them. Such moments in the consciousness of a man *judge* all poets and philosophers.

In this way, at least, Milosz would measure his own art. Death in itself is not the issue but rather the manipulation of death for dehumanizing purposes and what this does to human beings, as when those bullets, those machine-guns spraying random streets, makes men and women crawl. At such moments, the innocence with which poetry would celebrate the world is lost. The poet is stopped by ugliness too fierce for song to bear:

> The first movement is singing, A free voice, filling mountains and valleys.
>
> The first movement is joy, But it is taken away.

And yet the poetic will does not die. I know of no poet more driven to celebration, to sing of the earth in its plainness and glory, and therefore no poet more tormented ("We, whose cunning is not unlike despair") by the terrible detour through history which must be taken if, in pursuit of joyous song, the authority of poetic affirmation is not to remain untested or open to the charge of ignorance. But after witnessing the liquidation of the Warsaw Ghetto, after the Soviet betrayal of the Polish uprising, after the protracted misery of the Baltic resettlement, the will to praise life meets hard objections. What is left to nourish and uphold? Where is joy to take root? Above all, as Milosz repeatedly says in the *Selected Poems*, how can we live with ourselves after the awful revelations of our own time?—

> We learned so much, this you know well: how, gradually, what could not be taken away is taken. People, countrysides.
>
> And the heart does not die when one thinks it should, we smile, there is tea and bread on the table.

The pain of memory is compounded by the anguish of self-revelation, as if one's failure to embrace "the poor ashes of Sachsenhausen / with absolute love" were a terminal diminishment, a deformation of spirit severe enough to cancel our right to praise, our right to find life good. The burden of aftermath, for those who must bear it, would seem to be final. And yet it is not. "You could scream / Because mankind is mad. / But you, of all people, should not." Thus the poet's responsibility is defined in *Bells in Winter*. The poet's aim is to behold "not out of sorrow, but in wonder." In a short poem called **"Proof,"** Milosz writes: "You remember, therefore you have no doubt: there is a Hell for certain." But in a companion poem called **"Amazement,"** Milosz finds that the wholeness of the world is greater than its horror; that everything, not excluding "hue of fir, white frost, dances of cranes," goes on simultaneously and, as he concludes, that the earth's plenitude is "probably eternal...."

In a deceptively simple poem entitled **"An Hour"** Milosz goes so far as to say that all of us, by the very fact of our own mortality, of our rootedness in time and events, experience moments of transcendent richness, moments which become, in turn, the basis of affirmation in times truly dark:

> So that they might praise, as I do, life, that is, happiness.

To equate life with happiness *and mean it* is an astonishing victory in our brute century—against terror, death camps, war's constant eruption and now too, the threat of nuclear holocaust. But this is precisely the labour of art in Milosz's eyes: to recover rapport with existence "earlier than any beginning," to regain that which was taken away, the first movement, joy. And that Milosz so often succeeds in his poems is no small victory. His poems argue the complexity of poetic endeavour in a world such as ours, and argue also a principle central to the kind of poetry Milosz writes: to grasp this particular art in its fullness, it cannot be separated from the world, it cannot be detached from the circumstances of its birth. In sharp contrast to prevailing notions of poetry in America—for which the self and nature are still the only important realities—literary fulfillment for a poet like Milosz depends on extraliterary consciousness; it depends on knowing the historical situation to which the poem implicitly responds, which is a kind of awareness the poem then incorporates back into itself.

Milosz's recent **"From the Rising of the Sun,"** which is his most ambitious and perhaps his greatest poem, is likewise the outstanding example of his kind of poetry. It fills nearly half the pages of *Bells in Winter*, and while it takes as its subject the development of Milosz's own unique and unlikely career, it is also a wonderful poem about its own becoming. Replete with historical detail, this is nevertheless the most personal poem Milosz has written—or rather, it stands as his successful integration of self and larger world, of destiny both private and collective. In it the poet pulls into vivid form the fragments of his abnormally scattered life, from his childhood in Lithuania, through his years as witness and exile, up to the present time in California. And simply as a journey, Milosz's lyrical recovery of his life is surely one of the archetypes of our age, beginning one acrid morning "where a black dog barks, and someone chops wood," arriving finally at this most lucky destination:

> In the morning we were cutting logs with a chain saw. And it is a strong, fierce dwarf, crackling and rushing in the smell of combustion.
>
> Below, the bay, the playful sun, And the towers of San Francisco seen through rusty fog.

Descriptions of cities, events, and persons central to his life are juxtaposed with meditations upon the historical significance of his experience, its representative character, its possible value within a realm time-bound *and* transcendent. More than a little this vast undertaking resembles T. S. Eliot's "Four Quartets," but with one crucial difference: where Eliot saw the world in terms of his own spiritual predicament, Milosz sees *his* life in terms of the world—a reversal which in his autobiographical book, **Native Realm,** he sums up this way: "Instead of thrusting the individual into the foreground, one can focus attention on the background, looking upon oneself as a sociological phenomenon. Inner experience, as it is preserved in the memory, will then be evaluated in the perspective of the changes one's milieu has undergone."

And yet the aim of both Milosz and Eliot is identical: to go back and work through the detritus of one's own time on earth, to gather up the worst along with the best, integrate past and present into a culminating moment which transcends both, which embraces pain and joy together, the whole of a life and a world redeemed through memory and art, a final restoration in spirit of that which in historical fact has been forever lost. And when Milosz says, in the poem's last line, "I was judged for my despair because I was unable to understand this," we see how very far he has come. . . .

Clearly, through his art Milosz has earned a solution to the most pressing spiritual dilemma today: how to bear the burden of historical consciousness without despair. Facing life's terror and injustice, Milosz began by using irony and remorse tinged with cynicism. Facing life's intrinsic goodness, he struggled toward praise. No matter if these two positions contradict each other; as a poet Milosz's great contribution has been to make them join to his, and our, benefit. From the perspective of political responsibility, morality and mysticism clash and tend to cancel each other. Or so I thought until I began to appreciate Milosz's particular genius, his double vision as honest as it is resilient. The air is thick with horror and no one remains untouched. The air is thick with horror and some part of the soul must stay inviolate or the core of human worth will perish. . . .

To celebrate life while at the same time rejecting its perversions is the basis of all thought and art which deserves—in the pure, ideal sense—to be called "political," and we should not be fooled by literary critics of a certain type (mainly American and academic) who tell us that poetry and politics cannot successfully meet. Milosz is proof to the contrary, and his work is exemplary for the way it stands so firmly in contrast to the kind of poetry (again, mainly American) which proceeds, after Auschwitz, after Hiroshima, as if between self and history there were no tie or common ground. On the contrary, Milosz's poetry is enhanced by its fund of historical sense. Rooted directly in political realities—in events in their impact and consequence—this kind of poetry yields a new aesthetic, which in Milosz's case I would call a *poetics of aftermath.*

Given, then, the increasing burden of history, the accelerating intrusion of political forces into private life, or simply the brutality of events as we witness them, what claim can poetry put forth to command our respect? What sort of art can stand as proof that the human spirit shall prevail? The sort Milosz gives us, for which we must surely be grateful. I do not suggest that our poets must take up arms and join the underground as Milosz did, or like him endure the plunder and dispersal of one's homeland, suffer exile and historical shame, before a poetry worth writing can emerge. The point—abundantly clear in Milosz's work—is not direct participation but the confrontation, assessment, and assimilation of events in their aftermath; and the hoped-for outcome of this process is artistic liberation sufficient to free us from time not by avoidance but through brave engagement.

For a poet like Milosz, who saw Warsaw levelled and was among the handful to survive his generation's murder, this could never be an easy task. His art is indeed difficult. But the difficulty is not, as with so many modern poets, chiefly a matter of assess[ment] and comprehension; more simply and deeply, it is a matter of courage. Do we, as responsible adults who care for beauty and mourn its loss, have the strength to acknowledge the world at its worst and still rejoice? In answer we have Milosz, we have a poetry which helps us, as he put it, to bear our pain and misery, but which also confirms that, yes, joy is possible. The virtue of Czeslaw Milosz, quite apart from his worldly intelligence, his will to stay sane amid madness, his modest steady voice—apart from these, his virtue resides in his example.

JOSEPH C. THACKERY

SOURCE: Joseph C. Thackery, "Czeslaw Milosz: The Uses of a Philosophy of Poetry," in *The Hollins Critic*, Vol. 19, No. 2, April, 1982, pp. 1-10.

[*In the following excerpt, Thackery examines Miłosz's view of history in* Bells in Winter.]

[In] the modern poetry of the West there has been an almost exclusive concentration on perception for perception's sake, ignoring both myth and history. For years one would not have known from the pages of American poetry magazines that there were dangers from fallout, war in Vietnam, starvation abroad, or nations striving for freedom while immersed in bondage....

However, to poets like Milosz, Tadeusz Rozewicz, and Zbigniew Herbert, all of whom saw the Warsaw ghetto gutted and later beheld Warsaw itself leveled and then throttled by a new authoritarianism, philosophy became an imperative of spiritual survival. As Milosz himself points out in his *History of Polish Literature*, 1969, the imperative centered on poetry for the very pragmatic reason that poetry took up less physical space in the Underground. Its adventures and its explorations thrived. Nevertheless, as Milosz has written: "Nazi rule did not spur clear thinking about the future. Literature registered emotional reflexes ranging from pain, hatred of the occupier, through horror, pity, sarcasm, and irony." The Occupation had revealed society not as an entity in itself, but as a dilating and fragile shell in which human relationships could be molded at will. The writer was well fed, but held to account for every word.

Between 1945 and 1949, the censors became more quiescent; there were few forbidden subjects and debate centered on what literature should "be" under socialism. But from 1949 to 1955, the new ruling class thoroughly suffocated free expression. Soviet models, forced upon writers in the interest of "modernization" of the state, drew a sterile pall over literature....

From 1956 to the present, however, a broad new realism has intervened.... Poets have dared the censors in order to produce unconventional and adventuresome work.... However, the earlier spiritual affliction suffered by the experimenters in reconstituting their philosophy is poignantly illustrated by Milosz in his *History:* "The act of writing a poem is an act of faith, yet if the screams of the tortured are audible in the poet's room, is not his activity an offense to human suffering?"

The work of the three Catastrophists, ... Rozewicz, Herbert and Milosz himself, exemplifies this dilemma. Each sought spiritual survival in a different way....

All three Catastrophists blend history and myth. But it is preeminently Milosz who fixes on history as backdrop, with man as an absurd social phenomenon, thrust into the *mise en scène* as if at the hands of some ironic and impersonal god. Although analogies to Eliot's "Four Quartets" are observable in Milosz's conceptions of time past, time future and time merging, he has refused to examine the world, as did Eliot and Lowell, in terms of his own anxiety. Instead, the authority of poetry is to be tested by a journey through history, the response to the pilgrimage being a rejuvenating sense of wonder....

Wonder and philosophical absolution ... inform Milosz's **"A Song on the End of the World,"** in which Armageddon is always *in esse*, but an old man, knowing that "the whole of the world is greater than its horror" (*Selected Poems* ...), goes on tying up his tomato plants. Appreciation of how this poet has been able to synthesize history and a sense of its horror with survival and absolution may be gained by a discussion of his syntactic intentions. These aims are powerfully illustrated by six poems in a section of his major *oeuvre*, **Bells in Winter.** They are **"The Unveiling," "Diary of a Naturalist," "Over Cities," "A Short Recess," "The Accuser,"** and the apotheosis poem, **"Bells in Winter."** Together they search for a poetry that will be at once harsh and mollifying, that will enable men to understand, if not to rationalize, the debasement of the human spirit by warfare and psychic dismemberment, while simultaneously establishing a personal *modus vivendi* and a psychology of aesthetic necessity.

Three concerns appear to influence the poet's approach: (1) his sense of the betrayal of speech, (2) his conception of Heraclitean change, and (3) his belief in *apokatastasis* or restitution and restoration, *versus katastasis* or establishment and fixity. A fourth phenomenon, which may arise only in subliminal consciousness of the reader, is what might be called "the third language," deriving from unexpected shifts of meaning in the transitions from one vocabulary to another. We consider these categories in order. Thus, in **"The Unveiling,"** the poet suggests the fallibility of the tools of literary creation—words.... **"Over Cities"** expands the scope of betrayal; it deals with the dangers of reason itself and the trivialization of art by "intelligence": "Yet while we hear everyone advising us to understand clearly causes and effects, let us beware of those perfectly logical though somewhat too eager arguments...."

"The Accuser" is in effect a trial at law in which a generalized Other, perhaps God (though certainly an impersonal God), acts as the poet's prosecutor, judge and jury. He charges that the optimism of creativity cannot gloss over horror and that there is never either time enough or a *locus poenitentiae* when all are guilty. Words fail in the end and leave only the life impulse: " — Yet I have learned how to live with my grief. / — As if putting words together has been of help."

The title poem, **"Bells in Winter,"** sets forth the poet's belief in restoration and recovery — the conviction that form is eternal — the cut oak, the sacrificed lamb are "annihilated" but their forms "exist forever." It is the vehicle of the form — the word — that is inadequate. . . .

Milosz's second major semantic trend is toward the full apprehension of Heraclitean change. In this mode, evidence of the influence of Eliot, the Bergsonian *élan vital* and the Symbolists echo through his conception of "reality." It is as though he had pulled together the remotest philosophical insights into a pragmatism that is both the rock in the river and the water that flows over the rock. . . .

The form of **"The Unveiling"** itself suggests a time past merging into time present and future, as in Eliot's "Burnt Norton." Thus, the poet repeatedly shifts back and forth from his early life to his San Francisco refuge. Interspersed are "choruses" like those in Greek drama, half-accusatory, half-grieving, as if the poet were keeping a sharp eye on himself that he might not betray his aesthetic responsibility. But, as **"Diary of a Naturalist"** implies, permanence is not to be achieved in mere survival: "That boy, does he already suspect / That beauty is always elsewhere and always delusive?" . . .

Though it is not the most powerful of the six poems (in this writer's opinion, **"Over Cities"** has that distinction), **"A Short Recess"** comes closest to the poet's insight that man is an absurd "occurrence" in the immensity of time and history and that evanescence overhangs every artistic effort. . . .

"A Short Recess" teems with an action imagery in the manner of Shakespeare's *Tempest*. The subjunctive mood suggests time lost, squandered, never to come again. . . . In this poem, and indeed, in the generality of Milosz's work, we are cast against a four-dimensional landscape of sky, mountain, plain, horizon and time — primordial and indeterminate. Man cowers in the foreground, indistinguishable in his own perspective. Let him begin to concentrate on detail, on the putatively definite, and meaning becomes progressively indefinite. The same displacement occurs at the other end of the reality scale: in the world of the quark, the neutrino, the particle, man is as absurd and inconsequential as when he is pasted like a wafer against the universe. . . .

Milosz's third preoccupation is with the tensions between *katastasis* (fixity) and *apokatastasis* (restoration). In these opposing conceptions, set forth in **"Bells in Winter,"** the poet struggles with his hatred and unwillingness to forgive. . . . He wonders if his sense of the immortality of form coupled with the promise of restitution in the Christian Bible is sufficient to stem the anxiety of never measuring up to self-image. Similar doubt occurs in **"The Unveiling"**: "When will that shore appear from which at last we see / How all this came to pass and for what reason?"

In **"Diary of a Naturalist"** a schoolroom lecture by a Doctor Catchfly suggests that because of his learning, man wrongly sees himself as the center of all importance; he must therefore account for his waste of nature and his insensitivity to the agony of non-human life. The drive of the intellect toward science fails as salvation, but religious awakening may be no adequate substitute because it contains its own denial and the hope for peaceful stasis is vain. . . .

The poet's impulse toward renewal wilts under the impact of savagery, but under the principle of *apokatastasis*, it cannot be killed. He submerges himself in the creative process so that the muse, the "other," may take over the task for which he feels inadequate. Though this release to subconscious powers creates anxiety, there is always a new vision, hard-won, but uplifting, as in **"The Unveiling"**. . . .

A kind of distorted salvation arises just because humanity is so vulnerable. In **"Bells in Winter"** the poet dreams that his double, a Greek youth, is relating the story of this condemnation by St. Paul in Corinth for having committed incest. . . .

This dream releases the poet from anxiety. He can once again picture the writing room of his youth. His imagination restores his one-time servant Lisabeth to her rightful human importance. The city is roofed with a canopy of bells as she, the personification of all persecuted womankind — tortured witch, outcast wench, mourning wife, mother of felon — attends mass and lines out her missal with her dirty fingernail. The memory saves the poet from hatred and confirms that form is eternal and therefore aesthetics, its vehicle, is timeless. . . .

Milosz adventures far beyond metaphor to plunge the reader into the sense of double existence, inside and outside time; indeed into the "cosmogonic moment of creation" in which there is in effect no time, only the creative *élan* and its reverberations in the soul. . . .

Analysis of Milosz's poetry leads one to the opinion that no other poet in the world could have written it in quite the way it exists. This statement is not a tautology; nor is it self-evident; it is the product of an empathy that moves the reader to elect this great man as spokesman of the millions of dead of the Holocaust, the Gulags, the Polish and Czech uprisings, and the added millions of those who will go on dying in an imperfect world. The former captive of authoritarianism is the living analogue of the double metaphor—the outsider released by virtue of his alienation from the obligation to follow the crowd. The Catastrophists, and especially Milosz, have expanded their reach precisely because they have achieved freedom from the self-absorption that inhibits the poetry of western democracies: the you-under-this-tree-sensing-me-under-that-treesyndrome. Their holistic sweep of expression is comparable to the shared necessity of micro- and macro-physics to hypothesize in metaphor: "neutrino," "helix," "black holes," "googol." It suggests that when mankind's bus stops extend to the stars, poetry may once again, as in primordial times, become a part of everyday life.

CHRISTOPHER CLAUSEN

SOURCE: Christopher Clausen, "Czeslaw Milosz: The Exile as Californian," in *The Moral Imagination: Essays on Literature and Ethics*, University of Iowa Press, 1986, pp. 139-53.

[*In the following excerpt, Clausen examines Miłosz's efforts to unify his experience as a Polish political exile and as an immigrant to California.*]

[Milosz's] poems since 1960 balance past and present, native and alien life and language. They are the work of a man who has led two lives in radically different times and places and is trying to unite them in thought and art. The result is a major and unique contribution to American literature, one that has gone virtually unnoticed by commentators who have been content to think of Milosz simply as an exile whose career since 1960 has been no more than a prolongation of his earlier life on native soil.

Milosz's first reaction to exile, he explains in **"To Raja Rao"** (significantly, the only poem in his *Selected Poems* that was written originally in English), was very much what one might expect:

> For years I could not accept
> the place I was in.
> I felt I should be somewhere else.
>
> . . . . .
>
> Somewhere else there was a city of real presence,
> of real trees and voices and friendship and love.

Exchanging Poland for France and then America was no help; like Solzhenitsyn, although less apocalyptically, he found East and West animated by opposite vices.

> Ill at ease in the tyranny, ill at ease in the republic,
> in the one I longed for freedom, in the other for the end of corruption. . . .

There is a subsequent stage in exile, however, at least if the one exiled is fortunate and brave enough. The poem continues:

> I learned at last to say: this is my home,
> here, before the glowing coal of ocean sunsets,
> on the shore which faces the shores of your Asia,
> in a great republic, moderately corrupt.

This stage marks not an end but a new beginning. It does not, needless to say, fully resolve the problems that have been left behind, the guilt and disorientation of the witness to history, the émigré, the survivor in lotus-land. Guilt of this kind is a major theme in the poetry that Milosz has written over the last forty years. He speaks again and again of scenes of horror half-recalled in dreams, of friends and strangers killed by the Gestapo, of various forms of desertion. In many of his poems, the landscape itself is deformed by history into nightmare. . . .

The brief section of *Selected Poems* that contains works written before the war is entitled, with a wistful irony, "How Once He Was." That section is followed by "What Did He Learn," which comprises poems written during and after the German occupation. The last section, including nearly half the poems in the book, is "Shore." As in the poem quoted above, the shore is that of California. It is in "Shore" that the ghosts of Europe are—not exactly exorcised, but made to cast a different shadow in a landscape whose paucity of rooted things bears some relation to the clarity and intensity of its sunlight. The lowering clouds of history may encourage richer vegetation; they also sometimes obscure things that are close at hand.

The English-bound reader whose interest in Milosz is as an American poet of European background, rather than a European poet accidentally resident in America, will be delighted to discover rumors of Walt Whitman in a poem entitled **"Hymn,"** written as early as 1934.... Milosz's admiration for Whitman and the visionary tradition has been an abiding influence, one which naturally reappears in the poems written after he came to this country. In **"Album of Dreams,"** Whitman's name is even mentioned ("With a broad white beard and dressed in velvet, / Walt Whitman was leading dances in a country manor / owned by Swedenborg, Emanuel."). More significantly, **"Throughout Our Lands,"** a long work in which present California and past Lithuania are contrasted in a series of concrete meditations, begins with an invocation of a valued predecessor....

It would be going too far to say that Milosz finds Whitman an altogether kindred spirit. No skeptical twentieth-century intellectual could possibly make such an affirmation, whatever his background. The following passage from [**"Throughout Our Lands"**] is both like and unlike Whitman's dream sequences:

> Between the moment and the moment I lived
>   through much in my sleep
> so distinctly that I felt time dissolve
> and knew that what was past still is, not was.
> And I hope this will be counted somehow in
>   my defense:
> my regret and great longing once to express
> one life, not for my glory, for a different
>   splendor.

The distinction in the last line would have been alien to Whitman, even after his own harrowing encounters with history. Nevertheless, in the tormented dreams, the merging of past and present, the aspiration (however thwarted) towards universal celebration, the similarities run deep.

A California poet whom Milosz has long admired in a more qualified way is Robinson Jeffers. Like Whitman and Milosz, Jeffers yearned for what critical prose can identify only as a mystical sense of the wholeness and saving beauty of reality, a lasting vision of the world's oneness in which all the accidents and terrors of actual life cease to be important. Milosz is drawn towards such a vision even while he remains skeptical of it; Jeffers found its fulfillment, rather precariously, in nature at its most inhuman. For both poets, history is a personal burden. But while Jeffers' solution was to apotheosize predatory hawks, cruel splendor, a rocky coast with few human inhabitants, Milosz finds nature in the raw just as repellant as the mindless atrocities of conquerors. The psychic problem of history has many possible solutions, with varying degrees of satisfactoriness. **"To Robinson Jeffers"** is Milosz's answer to one of the most seductive. The opening is suitably brusque:

> If you have not read the Slavic poets
> so much the better. There's nothing there
> for a Scotch-Irish wanderer to seek.

The "Slavic poets," as Milosz conceives them here, inhabited a peaceful, anthropocentric landscape where "the sun / was a farmer's ruddy face" and nature a place where humans found themselves (naturally) at home. Jeffers' landscapes, on the contrary, are filled with violence and solitude, the heritage of a northern warrior race that listened too long to the ocean....

Nevertheless, human values—however fragile—remain at the center of the poet's vision. The inhumanity of Jeffers' God is no more admirable than the inhumanity of historical processes. Perhaps direct experience of the latter is an inoculation against falling in love with the former.... Far from being Eden, the wilderness is simply a void. Civilization with its morality may be a frail creation, but there is no substitute for it. How could there be, for a poet whose mind is filled with such images of nightmare as the following (from **"Album of Dreams"**)?

> They ordered us to pack our things, as the
>   house was to be burned.
> There was time to write a letter, but that let-
>   ter was with me.
> We laid down our bundles and sat against
>   the wall.
> They looked when we placed a violin on the
>   bundles.
> My little sons did not cry. Gravity and curi-
>   osity.
> One of the soldiers brought a can of gaso-
>   line. Others were tearing down curtains.

The category of experience here is altogether outside Jeffers' awareness, despite his professions of complacency towards the destruction of civilization.

And yet the comparatively historyless California landscape does make a healing difference. Vanished Lithuania and burning Warsaw look different in its light.... There is a serenity about California that is profoundly appealing. The softer features of the landscape offer a vision of an order that is not human, but at the same time is by no means inimical to the values of civilization. Even basalt cliffs, even birds of prey, may have their place in easing the burdens of history. Here, one feels, is a good place for civilization to flower. If it has not altogether done so, Milosz seems at times to be thinking, neither has tyranny. (The works of humanity are always ambiguous; Berkeley and Hollywood are equally products of California.) There is the sweetness of air (though, alas, neither in Berkeley nor in Hollywood), the clarity of light, the mystery of fog, the grandeur of mountains in the distance—an inviting place even to the unwilling exile; a combination, perhaps, of a Van Gogh painting and a Japanese print, those pictorial legacies of great troubled civilizations. If it is not the fulfillment of history, it is more than lotus-land.... To be sure, painful memories come back immediately—of childhood, of war, of the remote historical past of Europe. But the context is different from what it was. It is too much to say that images of the Golden State overpower the sad past. But they certainly change it into something richer and more universal. Looked at this way, the tragedy of Eastern Europe ceases (for the reader) to be remote and becomes part of the American landscape of imagination, even as (for the writer) something of the opposite process occurs. For each party, a new relationship is established between two disparate and important experiences, one alien, the other relatively familiar, in which each element is enriched by the other.

California is not as devoid of history as all that, of course; it only seems so because of the fluidity of life there and because few of its inhabitants have lived there for more than a generation or two. One of the ways in which Milosz the poet assimilated himself to his new home was by meditating on its history. It would have been very surprising if such a writer had rested content with landscape. In fact he has had more to say about California's past than most native poets. In **"Throughout Our Lands"**... he casts his mind back to the first Europeans who lived in the Far West: among them Junipero Serra, the Franciscan friar who founded the California missions in the eighteenth century. Perhaps Milosz sees (at least playfully) a certain parallel between his own situation and that of the missionary who wandered earnestly west from Spain and north from Mexico.... The focus soon shifts, however, from the exile to his flock, and Junipero comes to seem a rather naive bearer of European civilization to barbarians who are probably better off without it. His message of salvation falls at first on deaf ears ("poor people, they had lost the gift of concentration"). In fact, it is to the soon-displaced Indians that Milosz feels a deeper sense of gratitude. The Indians lacked writing and had primitive tastes.

> Nonetheless it was they who in my place took possession
> of rocks on which only mute dragons
> were basking from the beginning, crawling out of the sea.
> They sewed a cloak from the plumage of flickers, hummingbirds, and tanagers,
> and a brown arm, throwing back the mantle, would point to: this.

An earlier explorer than Junipero Serra, Cabeza de Vaca, met an even less enviable fate among the pre-European inhabitants of the West. Not a missionary whose journey was deliberate, he was only an exile who landed from "a boat thrown up on the sand by surf, / crawling naked on all fours, under the eye of immobile Indians." Alternately worshipped as a long-expected god and punished when his miracles miscarried, he endured a life not altogether dissimilar to that of the European intellectual exile in the twentieth century. Whether such a parallel was in Milosz's mind it is impossible to say, but the episode comes at the end of the poem in which he goes furthest to set up reverberations between the settler of the past (Indian, missionary, castaway) and himself; between memories of Europe and images of the American West; between simple realities like a pear and the difficulty of naming it when one has had to live in too many languages. Perhaps the best writing about places is often done by exiles. It is nonetheless surprising, but true, that some of the best poems ever written about California and the West were composed in Polish.

In **"Ars Poetica?"** (from *Bells in Winter*), Milosz writes:

> The purpose of poetry is to remind us
> how difficult it is to remain just one person,
> for our house is open, there are no keys in the doors,
> and invisible guests come in and out at will.

For obvious reasons, that difficulty is one of which Milosz has been unusually aware. In *Native Realm* (1958; English translation, 1968), he wrote, "My own case is enough to verify how much of an effort it takes to absorb contradictory traditions, norms, and an overabundance of impressions, and to put them into some kind of order." The continuing effort to do so, in the second stage of his exile and at an age when most poets have long ceased to assimilate new experience into their art, is what gives Milosz a special claim on American readers. Its success is what most amply justifies, at least to the reader who has no Polish, his Nobel Prize.

> The first movement is singing,
> A free voice, filling mountains and valleys.
> The first movement is joy,
> But it is taken away.

So Milosz declared in **"The Poor Poet,"** in the burning Warsaw of 1944. His "first movement," of course, was life as a young writer before 1939, sometimes prophesying bad days to come but living nonetheless in a sort of prehistorical present. The "second movement" was the war, defeat, what has come to be known as the Holocaust (which, he reminds us in his Nobel address, was not restricted to Jews), and then the greater betrayal that followed the coming of peace. For the first half-decade of Soviet rule, Milosz chose not to become an exile, just as he had chosen to witness and resist the German occupation. But of the taking away of joy there was no end, and in 1951 his "second movement" ended in emigration.

It is with the American poems of his "third movement" that I have been mainly concerned, not only because they are the ones most accessible to American readers, but also because in them some of the harshness of history is mitigated, if not quite overcome. In them Milosz finds himself—sometimes—in a present that is no longer haunted, that has room for other things besides memory, even for joy. His passage through the horrors of history to a degree of posthistorical serenity testifies powerfully to the resources of both imagination and poetic art—resources which have been greatly in demand during his lifetime. . . .

One of the spiritual dangers of exile is that the one exiled may believe his own experiences, his own history, to be the only kind that lead to wisdom. This belief may manifest itself in an arrogant condescension towards those people among whom his exile is spent, a condition as unfavorable to art as the fanaticism of a Pearse. To judge by his poems of exile that have appeared in English, Milosz's art has avoided this fate by remaining open to the possibility of making a new home for itself, without of course forgetting the old one. Three concerns have preoccupied—one might almost say obsessed—Milosz's writings since the war: the value of European civilization, the persistence of history, and the artist's duty to tell the truth, both for his own sake and for the sake of his society. Dwelling on these preoccupations in the benign but alien setting where they seem at first to be drastically out of place; allowing the literal and symbolic extremes of past and present, old Europe and new California, to interpenetrate and illuminate each other; at his frequent best, doing all this with great power and inventiveness—it was these accomplishments that signalled his transformation from a promising young poet of early-twentieth-century Eastern Europe into a major poet of worldwide significance in the late twentieth century.

DONALD DAVIE

SOURCE: Donald Davie, "A Clamor of Tongues," in *The New Republic*, Vol. 206, No. 11, March 16, 1992, pp. 34-7.

[*An English poet, critic, educator, and translator, Davie is well respected for both his creative and his critical contributions to literature. During the 1950s Davie was associated with the Movement, a group of poets including Philip Larkin, Kingsley Amis, and Thom Gunn, whose verse emphasized formal structures, restrained language, traditional syntax, and the moral and social implications of poetic content. In the following excerpt from his review of Miłosz's poetry collection* Provinces, *his essay collection* Beginning with My Streets, *and Leonard Nathan and Arthur Quinn's critical study* The Poet's Work: An Introduction to Czesław Miłosz, *Davie focuses on Miłosz's rejection of American lyrical poetry and his concern with metaphysical themes.*]

In his latest gathering of essays, **Beginning with My Streets**—more a medley than a collection, with a deceptive air of being "thrown together"—Czeslaw Milosz includes an interview from 1988 in which he intimates, mildly enough, his dissatisfaction with the poetry of today, in many languages. His charge against contemporary poetry is that it has been impoverished from within by closing off too many doors in a search for "purity in lyricism." This accusation has been leveled before by Milosz, but never emphatically, because being emphatic is seldom his style. All the same, it is the clue to his achievement; he is one modern poet who has no interest in being a lyrical poet, who thinks indeed that exertions to that end are morally and politically often dubious.

Rather than the lyrical "I," emoting out of its own subjectivity (as Robert Lowell did, or Sylvia Plath), Milosz favors, and in his own poems puts into play, not one voice but several: voices that cross over, contradict one another, dissolve just when we think we have learned to trust them. This can be seen in poems short enough to look like lyrics. For instance, **"Should, Should Not"**:

> A man should not love the moon.
> An axe should not lose weight in his hand.
> His garden should smell of rotting apples
> And grow a fair amount of nettles.
> A man when he talks should not use words that are dear to him
>
> Or split open a seed to find out what is inside it.
> He should not drop a crumb of bread, or spit in the fire
> (So at least I was taught in Lithuania).
> When he steps on marble stairs,

He may, that boor, try to chip them with his
    boot
As a reminder that the stairs will not last for-
    ever.

Leonard Nathan and Arthur Quinn valuably place this in a series specifically addressed in the first place to Milosz's Berkeley students in the 1960s, when he saw the frivolity of the Parisian intelligentsia monstrously combined with the solemn habits of the Californian mentality: the worst of both worlds. Milosz himself has identified the marble stairs as those of "the Berkeley library." Accordingly, the poem is a series of admonitions. But each new admonition differs, grammatically and in versification, from the one before it. Thus any one admonition may be in isolation challenged. For instance, "a man . . . should not use words that are dear to him": what, *never*? That remonstration is allowed for. More crucial, the person whose boot tries to chip the marble stairs is called "a boor," but is not his endeavor underwritten by what his teachers of the 1960s or even today may rightly impress on him or her as a duty: the questioning of the marmorealized "canon"? A vast amount of work is done by the simple monosyllable "may," breaking into a sequence of "should" and "should not." Does "may" mean "is likely to," or "is permitted to"?

Recognizing these ambiguities, Nathan and Quinn advise us that this poem's "celebration of the acceptance of limitations" is "ironic." On the one hand, this opens up the possibility that the shifts of perspective are just rhetorically determined, on the assumption that no one would have attended to the poet-professor laying down the law over and over. On the other hand, it opens up the more dismaying perspective that the poet doesn't know where he stands on these issues, and is content to leave the matter suspended.

It is instructive, and I think conclusive, to see how Milosz responded when another interviewer offered to him the term "ironic" in relation to this poem. Milosz ducked the question, but conceded that the poem is spoken through a mask: "Yes, it's a mask. What can you do with a strange guy who doesn't understand himself?" And then he happily endorsed something said to him by an admirer of his translations from Scripture: "An instrument, not a human being but a device." The voice that speaks the poem is not that of a human being, whose lyrical "I" might declare itself in love with lunar purity (and sterility), but instead a device, perhaps divine, for which admonitions and prohibitions from Lithuanian folklore are no less binding than others arrived at on other grounds. It is not just the expatriate poet-professor who admonishes his misguided students, but a being more mysterious, drawing its authority from more occult sources. The poet in propria persona, the lyrical "I," is merely "a strange guy who doesn't understand himself," and so he must be discounted.

Normally one would not bear down in this way on a poem translated from a foreign tongue. There is always the possibility that substituting "may" for "should" is the result merely of a translator's inattention. But once Milosz's **Collected Poems** appeared in English in 1988, his poetry became a very abnormal phenomenon indeed, perhaps unprecedented. He has busied himself so constantly with the translation of his poems into English, assembling and training and collaborating with an exceptionally gifted team of translators, that we do not hear from him, or from his Polish-speaking admirers, the familiar wail of "how much is lost in translation." Undoubtedly much is lost; but Milosz's position seems to be that he will stand as stoutly by a poem of his in its American-English version as in its original Polish version.

He is even prepared to regard himself as an American poet. It is hard to see how a lyrical poet could take this position, however gifted and devoted his translators. On the contrary, it is the proudest boast made by or on behalf of the lyricist—Keats or Hart Crane, Lermontov or Mandelstam—that he is "untranslatable." Milosz makes no such boast. But this humility should not deceive us; Milosz is on his own admission a haughty man, not at all ingratiating toward the American public. What looks like humility derives not from the sort of person he is, but from the sort of poetry he writes—which is not a lyrical poetry.

Because most American readers have been led to believe that lyrical poetry is the only poetry there is, or the only poetry that can earn respect in modern times, there is a gulf that they have to bridge before they can encounter Milosz's poetry on its own terms. Nathan and Quinn's study is excellent and long overdue. (Nathan has for many years been Milosz's translator, collaborator, and, we may suppose, confidant.) Still, to my mind they concede too much to the assumption that a poet's poems, collected, bear witness to an agon: to an individual going his own way, against the socially or ideologically determined consensus.

This is one way of looking at Milosz's poetic achievement; but it is not the only way, nor is it the way that the poet invites. For instance, the long and forbidding and formally reckless poem in seven sections, **"From the Rising of the Sun"** (1973-74), can be addressed, as they address it, in terms of ecstasy and pessimism, as an expression of ecstatic pessimism. But if we cut the poem free from the moods of its creator, we can see that it is concerned with, and structured about, the historically verifiable facts of what the Roman Catholic Church has declared orthodox and heterodox. There is much drama, for Milosz is greatly drawn to some of the heresies, which he finds borne out by his own experience: for instance, Socinianism, which in the seventeenth century was the form that Protestantism took in Transylvania and northern Poland, produced martyrs whose nonconforming witness Milosz admires as heroic. More readers will think they understand ecstasy and pessimism than are at home with "Socinian" or "Manichaean." But it is these latter words that are exact and definable.

This is not at all to say that Milosz's poetry is "impersonal," as Eliot's aspired to be. Milosz continually draws or drives us back to circumstances peculiar to him, in particular to the Lithuanian/Polish crossroads where he was born and nurtured, which has given him, so he powerfully persuades us, an outlook on the intellectual and factual history of the present century such as we cannot get from any other source. In the same way, by repeatedly harking back, he plainly discerns in his own track through life a development, an Odyssey or a Pilgrim's Progress. If we can't discern that track as he wants us to, part of the reason is that we remain bewildered about the simple chronology, because of the waywardness with which his poetry has been bit by bit disclosed to us in English. It is a bewilderment that the *Collected Poems* alleviates but cannot altogether dispel. What does seem clear is that when Milosz looks back, he judges his actions and the actions of his contemporaries against a standard more ancient and more exacting than we are used to—against, for instance, the scale of the Seven Deadly Sins.

Milosz is very sensitive to the allegation that his constant harkings back convict him of nostalgia. Against this charge he can call on the rather powerful precedent of Proust. Milosz will not much relish this association; though two of his books are customarily described as novels, he is very sniffy about the novel as a genre, making a momentous exception for Dostoyevsky. However that may be, I find the Proustian presence helpful especially with *The Separate Notebooks*, which were separately published alone in English in 1984 and are also confusingly part of an erstwhile unheard-of collection called *Hymn of the Pearl* (1982). "Where is the truth of unremembered things?" is a question at the heart of *The Separate Notebooks;* and it is surely a question that Proust prompts if he doesn't explicitly pose it.

This explains, I think, why, in the latest pieces added to *Collected Poems,* there appears a seven-part quite straightforward and entertaining sequence, **"La Belle Epoque."** Milosz was born just early enough to experience Proust's world of "women in corsets and tournures, of whom one says either 'ladies' or 'cocottes,' the catechism, the list of sins before confession, music lessons, French verbs." The point is not to mourn the passing of that world, but to wonder at how substantial it seemed, as much in a coach of the Trans-Siberian Railway as on a Paris boulevard. The last thing that Milosz wants is to transcend historical time, to "soar above" it. Like an epic poet, he wants on the contrary to be mired in history in all its particularity—and in geography, too. The effect of such evocations is to locate the speaker of the poems in a segment of historical time as well as in a geographical space. And yet all these particulars are mustered to answer a question that must be called metaphysical.

Certain things he remembers or can reconstruct, others have gone out of mind. And "where is the truth of unremembered things?" Where else but in the mind of God? That is, no doubt, the right answer. But it is not an answer that satisfies Milosz, and we should think the worse of him if it did. For though he is a Christian poet—there's that scandalous cat out of the bag!—he can hardly give offense to unbelievers or to adherents of other faiths. Although he can usually persuade himself that the orthodox Christian answer to tormenting questions is the best on offer, he never deludes himself into thinking that having the answer removes the torment. Who remembers the unremembered dead? The question torments him as much when he's been given an answer as before.

And so, though it is true that in recent years Milosz has written Christian poems unprecedentedly serene and exhilarating, the nature of that serenity must be understood. It is not the serenity of a man who at last has all the answers, but of a man who acknowledges that some tormenting questions are unanswerable. The orthodox answers may be humbly acceded to, but the hurt remains nonetheless. Healing the hurt may be within the capacity of the priest, but the poet cannot and should not pretend to heal it. The priestly and the poetic vocations are distinct; and it is part of the case against the lyrical poets that too often they, or their admirers, blur the one office into the other. It is the business of the learned poet (and Milosz is certainly that) to know the answers on offer, now and in the past, and to discriminate among them; but it is not his duty or his privilege to administer comfort, beyond saying: "Yes, I've wondered about that myself."

There arises, for those few who perhaps pedantically care, the question of how far and in what way Milosz's poetry is related to "modernism" or "the modern movement," to what Amy Clampitt lately ... called "the fault line that opened in 1912, and has been no more than precariously spanned from that day to this." Though he was only 1 year old in 1912, Milosz recognizes that fault line, and locates himself in relation to it. He is certainly not of those who believe that modernism in poetry was an aberration that he may equably ignore. (His Christianity did not give him that cop-out: Eliot and Claudel, not to speak of Mandelstam and Pasternak, were modernist poets who professed themselves to be Christians.)

What is astringent and refreshing about Milosz's attitude to poetic modernism is that, as an Eastern European moving in and into a society that idolized Paris, he recognized how modernism, the Anglo-American version as much as the Polish version, took its bearings from France, and from a France culturally exhausted, in decline. Not for him the Francophilia that too often predetermined the judgments of Eliot and Pound. He is sure that Baudelaire is a very great poet, but not on the grounds to which Eliot appealed. Thus Milosz will endorse the modernist endeavor in poetry, will even enlist in the enterprise, but with a special sardonic awareness of how tainted its origins were. For him, it is modernism that has reintroduced into poetry the use of multiple voices, as against the single voice of the lyricist.

This explains why, when he looked at the American poetry that he had pitched himself into in 1960, he lit upon the unfashionable figure of Robinson Jeffers. Milosz was searching in American poetry not for a confirmation of truths that he had brought with him from Europe, but for a radical alternative—one that, as it turned out, he could not accept, but for which he was deeply grateful because it posed the alternatives in the starkest terms. Those alternatives were, at bottom, Nature or Culture. Milosz, inescapably European, opted in the end for culture; that is to say, for history. But he honored Jeffers's insistence that whereas Nature might seem at times to be comforting, in truth it was merciless—as Milosz already knew from his hunting in the Lithuanian forests. Whatever Warsaw or Paris or New York might hint, Milosz's attachment to Jeffers's poetry was not a matter of one provincialism calling to another. What was at issue between the Polish poet and the California poet was something on which programmatic "modernism" hardly impinged. Optimism and hope are diffident. Milosz can hope, where Jeffers can't. But he's at one with the Californian in scorning optimism, because nature plainly is pessimist. And of course Jeffers wasn't a lyrical poet, any more than Milosz.

To readers with short memories, it may seem that Milosz is now invulnerable, a consecrated icon carrying himself around—with unflagging energy, astonishing at 80—to artistic occasions here and abroad. But Milosz's international honors shouldn't obscure the true image of him as an intransigent loner. His latecome laurels aren't anything he can rest upon. For he is much resented. Some of the resentments—the Polish ones, for instance—I sense but cannot with confidence explain. He has made enemies; though his style is mostly suave, he does not suffer fools gladly, and his judgments are unsparing, even peremptory.

One Anglo-American class or coterie is particularly resentful. These are the literary warriors of the cold war, who made Milosz's *The Captive Mind* (1953) one of their founding texts. With the end of the cold war, these warriors find themselves out of a job, and it particularly irks them that Milosz isn't thrown on the scrap heap as they are, since *The Captive Mind* turns out to have been only an episode—heartfelt and never disowned—in a career that was focused on metaphysical, not political, issues; on the human condition at all times, not just in the second half of the twentieth century; on love and death, not chiefly or exclusively on political liberty.

This is what was at issue in Milosz's protest to *The New York Review of Books* about A. Alvarez's review of the *Collected Poems*—not that the review was grudging, it was laudatory, but in Milosz's view his poems were being applauded for the wrong reason:

> Perhaps some Western writers are longing for subjects provided by spasms of historical violent change, but I can assure Mr. Alvarez that we, i.e., natives of hazy Eastern regions, perceive History as a curse and prefer to restore to literature its autonomy, dignity, and independence from social pressures. . . . The voice of a poet should be purer and more distinct than the noise (or confused music) of History.

And so, considering art in its relation to the polis, we need to look, in his new collection of poems, at **"The Thistle, the Nettle,"** which has for an epigraph something from the poet's kinsman, the Lithuanian poet in French, Oscar de Milosz:

> The thistle, the nettle, the burdock, the belladonna
> Have a future. Theirs are wastelands
> And rusty railroad tracks, the sky, silence.
>
> Who shall I be for men many generations later?
> When, after the clamor of tongues, the award goes to silence?
>
> I was to be redeemed by the gift of arranging words
> But must be prepared for an earth without grammar,

> For the thistle, the nettle, the burdock, the belladonna,
> And a small wind above them, a sleepy cloud, silence.

I do not know whether to thank Milosz, or his collaborator Robert Hass, for the exquisite cadence of that last line. Is it too much to hope that after Auschwitz (which is certainly in Milosz's mind) the end may indeed be in pitiful and appalled silence, not in arguments for and against? Poetry can articulate that silence. Argument cannot, nor priestcraft either. . . .

SALLY LAIRD

SOURCE: Sally Laird, "Poetic Pathology of Our Century," in *Observer*, November 22, 1992, p. 64.

[*In the following appreciative review, Laird assesses* Beginning with My Streets.]

The essays contained in *Beginning With My Streets*, says Milosz in his Preface, 'may be considered a travel guide to a certain literary sensibility nourished by "another", less known Europe'. The description is characteristically impersonal, self-distancing. With a modesty that borders occasionally on pomposity, the Nobel prizewinner offers us not just his thoughts, but his mind itself as an object of scrutiny—a case-study for the pathologists of the twentieth century, of whom Milosz has been among the most searching.

If nowadays we can pretend to some familiarity with the mind of 'the other Europe' and its wounds, that is in large part due to Milosz and his endeavour, begun some 40 years ago in *The Captive Mind*, to acquaint the West with the reality of totalitarianism and to fight amnesia and indifference. Here, in essays dating mainly from the 1970s, Milosz shows undiminished contempt for the failure of Western *'belles-lettres'* to come to grips with reality, and his observations can leave us wincing. Are Tintin, Maigret and Frodo Baggins really the only heroes worth a name in modern Western literature?

But the prevailing tone is solemn, not spiteful. Totalitarianism, Milosz argues, left everyone speechless: what words could be found to name what had happened, especially when language itself had been usurped by ideology? 'How much reality is poetry able to bear?' Under such circumstances, the defencelessness of literature could not be condemned. What deserves punishment is the failure to recognise the threat or search for tactics to combat it.

These essays—a mixture of 'chatty narratives' in the Polish tradition, philosophical meditation, literary criticism and portraits of friends and writers—are an account of Milosz's own search for an art that could, without false innocence, maintain a 'cool and fastidious distance', yet preserve its vigour and will for truth. Such a feat, Milosz found, was possible only when distance was lent by time, not indifference, and poetic recollection—of every detail, 'beginning with my street'—became a sacred rite.

In his essay on 'Saligia' (the Russian acronym for the seven deadly sins), poet and engaged historian combine to reflect on the meaning of the sins, first in the mind of a Vilnius schoolboy, then in the context of a century that had given new meanings to envy, pride and anger.

The sins which occupied the highest terraces in Dante—covetousness, gluttony and lust—were those, Milosz argues, that derived from an excess of love: a 'centrifugal' will to possess, trained on the rich prodigal world outside, not on the self. That such a love is possible, even in our benighted century, is affirmed in Milosz's tributes to writers who never erred by 'mistaking their life for the world': the Polish émigré Stanislaw Vincenz, whose view of 'permanent, archetypal things' remained unobscured by the tribulations of his time; the seventeenth-century poet Thomas Traherne, able to find 'Paradise on Earth', despite the travails of his century; the poet Aleksander Wat, celebrating, from the prison of his physical sufferings, the 'young day, young times, young world'.

Included in the collection is Milosz's obituary of Zygmunt Hertz, the ebullient editor of the émigré Paris journal *Kultura*. Just as the image of the photographer may by chance be captured in the backdrop of his photograph—mirror, shadow or window—so we catch a suddenly human glimpse of Milosz, 'Czesiu', reproached and cherished friend of the dead man. The essay works as a two-way tribute. Somehow it is reassuring to find that in Milosz's severe world, where we're too often reminded of our failings, there's room in the pantheon for a fat, jolly man with a generous laugh, a liking for gossip, a permanent readiness to feast.

DAVID HERD

SOURCE: David Herd, "A Life in History," in *The Times*

Literary Supplement, No. 4832, November 10, 1995, p. 27.

[*In the following review, Herd discusses* Facing the River *in the context of Miłosz's life and previous writings.*]

Introducing his autobiographical work, *Native Realm: A search for self-definition,* Czeslaw Milosz sets out his approach to the genre: "Instead of thrusting the individual into the foreground, one can focus attention on the background, looking upon oneself as a sociological phenomenon. Inner experience, as it is preserved in the memory, will then be evaluated in the perspective of the changes one's milieu has undergone." Broadly speaking, it is this intention, to view himself as a "sociological phenomenon", that has shaped all of Milosz's writing. Stated in these borrowed terms, the intention can seem rather barren, as if the writer had a formula for personal identity. In practice, what it has meant in Milosz's best work, poetry and prose alike, is a deeply informed and ceaselessly nuanced investigation into the way history forms an individual life.

Milosz was born into the Lithuanian gentry in 1911. He escaped Soviet-occupied Lithuania in 1940, for Warsaw, where he served in the Polish Resistance, editing anti-Nazi books and pamphlets. He joined the Polish Diplomatic Service in 1945, defected to the West in 1951, and moved to California in 1960. In recounting these events in *Native Realm,* Milosz maintains throughout a quiet irony which enables him to get sufficiently outside his circumstances to comment upon them. And yet even as he does so, he is forever extending the backdrop, digging deep into his reading in religious and political history in an effort to understand the actions of modern Europe. What results is a learned and provocative study of nationhood, and as impressive an account of the growth of the mind of a poet as one is likely to find.

Supple as his prose is, however, it is clear that there have been times in Milosz's life when he has found it necessary to do his thinking in poetry. The group of poems collectively titled **"Voices of Poor People"**, which were written in Warsaw between 1942 and 1945, are evidence of this. Prior to these poems, Milosz had written in the Polish avant-garde style known as "catastrophist", a style constantly straining to make statements of global proportions, but actually always slipping back into what he himself calls a "lyricism of self-pity". These poems sound muffled in English, and one feels that the problem lies not with the translator, but with the young poet who was not yet thinking sufficiently clearly. The poems written in Warsaw have all the force of really clear dialectical thought. Choices and sensations are counterpoised; appalling human bargains are presented, their gains and costs given equal weight. Milosz felt that through these poems he had made an alloy of "individual and historical elements", the strength of which is perhaps most evident in **"Mid-Twentieth-Century Portrait"**, written in Cracow in 1945:

> Keeping one hand on Marx's writings, he reads the bible in private.
> His mocking eye on processions leaving burnt-out churches.
> His backdrop: a horseflesh-coloured city in ruins.
> In his hand: a memory of a boy "facist" killed in the Uprising.

Milosz's writing lost its edge for a while after his defection to the West, and it was not, again, until he began really to think his situation through poetically that he recovered his power for discriminating. In a number of poems written in America in the early and mid-1960's (**"Thesis and Counter-Thesis"**, **"To Robinson Jeffers"** and **"Three Talks on Civilisation"** are good examples), Milosz undertook to cross-examine the American poetic tradition. He begins to sound like himself again in these poems, and one suspects that it was only by arguing with the dominant celebratory note in American poetry that he could being his own antinomic cadences to bear on his new environment. This is not to say that Milosz has not sometimes tried to celebrate in the American manner. But such poems (**"Gift"** is one) feel only half formed in his hands. They lack that severe critical intelligence which makes his best writing truly urgent.

Facing The River is, at times, quite as critically intelligent as anything Milosz has written. Its strength lies in its willingness to face up to the question asked in **"Capri"**: "What did you do with your life, what did you do?" Thus a number of poems count the cost of devoting a life to poetry in the twentieth century. This, of course, is a late question, and *Facing The River* is, in every respect, a late collection. The question of self, for instance, is still prominent, but now the poet is trying to understand in what sense that "old Professor with an accent" can be said to be "identical with a boy" who walked from "Bouffalowa Hill" to "Tomasz Zan Library". The question induces a certain vertigo, in reader and poet alike, and Milosz steadies himself by revisiting scenes from a Lithuanian childhood. He is very careful in these poems, working hard not to succumb to nostalgia, but wanting to give an accurate picture of what was lost to Modernity.

Not everything is quite so careful. **"Realism"**, for instance, carries the aphoristic style typical of a number of the poems here to a problematic extreme. The poem presents the virtues of Dutch painting, from which it is happy to conclude that: "thus abstract art is brought to shame, / Even if we do not deserve any other". One has worries about what this easy dismissal of abstract art does not say; worries one would not presume to raise with Milosz, except that he previously raised them himself. As he says of his youthful resistance to abstraction in *Native Realm:* "I could have been very menacing, had I been given the power as an exterminator of 'degenerate art'—though I would have understood it in my own way, which had nothing to do with the primitive views of politicians." One feels that **"Realism"** is insufficiently argued without an acknowledgement of this sort.

The fact, though, that one can answer questions raised in *Facing The River* by looking back to Milosz's earlier writings indicates a most important truth. Which is that while many of the poems here can speak for themselves, the real value of the collection is the way it returns us to the immensely pressing arguments that Milosz has been having in and with poetry for the past sixty years.

SOURCES FOR FURTHER STUDY

Airaudi, Jesse T. "Eliot, Milosz, and the Enduring Modernist Protest." *Twentieth Century Literature* 34, No. 4 (Winter 1988): 453-67.

Argues that Miłosz belongs to the Modernist tradition because, like T. S. Eliot's, his work shares a "sense of catastrophe and the need to remember," and both poets "offer schemes for transforming society through imaginative synthesis."

Czarnecka, Ewa, and Aleksander Fiut. *Conversations with Czeslaw Milosz*. Translated by Richard Lourie. San Diego: Harcourt Brace Jovanovich, 1987, 332 p.

Contains interviews with Miłosz.

Gardels, Nathan. "The Withering Away of Society." *New Perspectives Quarterly* 5, No. 3 (Fall 1988): 55-8.

Interview in which Miłosz discusses his work and the implications of contemporary politics for artists.

Grosholz, Emily. "Milosz and the Moral Authority of Poetry." *The Hudson Review* XXXIX, No. 2 (Summer 1986): 251-70.

Examines the capacity of Milosz's poetry to influence individual morality.

Mozejko, Edward, ed. *Between Anxiety and Hope: The Poetry and Writings of Czeslaw Milosz*. Alberta: University of Alberta Press, 1988, 190 p.

Collection of critical essays about Miłosz and his work.

Nathan, Leonard, and Arthur Quinn. *The Poet's Work: An Introduction to Czelaw Milosz*. Cambridge, Mass.: Harvard University Press, 1991, 178 p.

Comprehensive discussion of Miłosz's themes.

N. Scott Momaday

1934-

American novelist, poet, and memoirist.

INTRODUCTION

Momaday's Kiowa Indian heritage enriches his writings, which often focus on the plight of Native Americans in the modern world and communicate a reverence for nature and traditional tribal customs. He has been praised for his imaginative interweaving of native myth, history, and contemporary experience, as well as for a unique narrative style that has led critics to compare him to William Faulkner. Although best known for his novel *House Made of Dawn* (1968), he considers himself primarily a poet. The novel received the Pulitzer Prize for fiction in 1969—the first written by a American Indian author recognized for the award—and initiated what has come to be known as a Native American renaissance in literature.

Biographical Information

Momaday was born in Lawton, Oklahoma, and spent his early years among the Kiowa Indians on his family's farm. When he was less than a year old, Momaday was named Tsoaitalee, or "Rock-Tree-Boy," after a 200-foot volcanic butte in Wyoming that is sacred to the Kiowas and known to Anglo-Americans as Devil's Tower. Edward Abbey notes that "to be named after that mysterious and mythic rock was, for the boy, a high honor and a compelling one. For among the Indians a name was never merely an identifying tag but something much more important, a kind of emblem and ideal, the determining source of a man or woman's character and course of life." Momaday grew up in New Mexico, where his parents worked as teachers among the Jemez Indians in the canyon and mountain country. He began writing seriously as an undergraduate at the University of New Mexico. Momaday was awarded a creative writing fellowship at Stanford University, where he earned a M.A. in 1958 and a Ph.D. in 1963. His first published book, *The Complete Poems of Frederick Goddard*

Tuckerman (1965), was originally his doctoral dissertation. A professor of English and comparative literature at various universities from the early 1970s through the mid-1980s, Momaday has served as a consultant to the National Endowment for the Arts since 1970.

Major Works

Momaday's poetry and prose reflect his Kiowa Indian background in structure, theme, and subject matter. Although he does not actually speak Kiowa, he treats language in his work as not only a reflection of the physical environment, but also as a means of shaping it. The Native American perception of man's relationship to the earth is a central concern in Momaday's writing. He believes that his poetry, in particular, grows from and sustains the Native American oral tradition. In *House Made of Dawn* Momaday used a sophisticated and fragmented narrative technique to explore the problem of mixing Native Americans and Anglos and the associated effort of living in two worlds. After serving in the U.S. Army during World War II, the protagonist, Abel, returns to his ancestral landscape and culture, where he kills an albino, serves a prison term, and is relocated to Los Angles upon release. Unable to cope with his factory job and city life, Abel returns to the reservation to carry on tradition for his dying grandfather. *The Way to Rainy Mountain* (1969) melds myth, history, and personal recollection into a narrative about the Kiowa tribe. In this work Momaday uses form to convey a reality that has largely been lost. Comprised of twenty-four numbered sections grouped into three parts, each part is subdivided further into three passages: the first contains Kiowa myths and legends, the second is based on historical accounts of the tribe, and the third is an autobiographical rendering of Momaday's rediscovery of his American Indian roots and homeland. *The Names: A Memoir* (1976) is another autobiographical exploration of Momaday's heritage, comprising tribal tales, boyhood memories, and genealogy. The title refers to the names given by the Kiowa Indians to the objects, forms, and features of their land. His second novel, *The Ancient Child* (1989) concerns a modern Native American searching for his identity.

Critical Reception

Baine Kerr has described *House Made of Dawn* as an attempt "to transliterate Indian culture, myth, and sensibility into an alien art form without loss." Although critics have praised the visionary prose of *House Made of Dawn,* some have maintained that Momaday met difficulty in his attempt to convey Indian sensibility in novelistic form. Roger Dickinson-Brown explained that the sequence of events is "without fixed order.... The result is a successful depiction but not an understanding of what is depicted: a reflection, not a novel in the comprehensive sense of the word." Others have viewed the novel as "a return to the sacred art of storytelling and myth-making that is part of Indian oral tradition," according to Vernon E. Lattin. *The Way to Rainy Mountain* is widely considered Momaday's best work, "a work of discovery as well as renunciation, of finding but also of letting go," as Kenneth Fields stated. *The Names* is admired for successfully bridging the gulf between native and white ways. Wallace Stegner has called *The Names* "an Indian book... a search and celebration, a book of identities and sources." Dickinson-Brown concluded that Momaday has "maintained a quiet reputation in American Indian affairs and among distinguished *literati*" for his works' brilliance and range, but especially for "his fusion of alien cultures, and his extraordinary experiments in different literary forms."

(For further information, see *Authors and Artists for Young Adults,* Vol. 11; *Contemporary Authors,* Vols. 25-28R; *Contemporary Authors New Revision Series,* Vols. 14, 34; *Contemporary Literary Criticism,* Vols. 2, 19, 85, 95; *Dictionary of Literary Biography,* Vols. 143, 175; *DISCovering Authors; DISCovering Authors: British; DISCovering Authors: Canadian; DISCovering Authors Modules: Most-studied Authors Module, Multicultural Authors Module, Novelists Module, Popular Fiction and Genre Authors Module; Major Twentieth-Century Writers; Native North American Literature; Something about the Author,* Vols. 30, 48.)

CRITICAL COMMENTARY

MARSHALL SPRAGUE

SOURCE: Marshall Sprague, "Anglos and Indians," in *The New York Times Book Review,* June 9, 1968, p. 5.

[*Sprague is an American journalist, critic, and nonfiction writer who has written about the history of the American West. In the following review, he offers praise for* House Made of Dawn.]

This first novel [*House Made of Dawn*], as subtly wrought as a piece of Navajo silverware, is the work of a young Kiowa Indian who teaches English and writes poetry at the University of California in Santa

> **Principal Works**
>
> *The Complete Poems of Frederick Goddard Tuckerman* [editor] (poetry) 1965
> *The Journey of Tai-me* (folktales) 1967
> *House Made of Dawn* (novel) 1968
> *The Way to Rainy Mountain* (autobiography) 1969
> *Colorado: Summer, Fall, Winter, Spring* (nonfiction) 1973
> *Angle of Geese and Other Poems* (poetry) 1974
> *The Gourd Dancer* (poetry) 1976
> *The Names: A Memoir* (autobiography) 1976
> *The Ancient Child* (novel) 1989
> *In the Presence of the Sun: Stories and Poems, 1961-1991* (stories and poems) 1993
> *Circle of Wonder: A Native American Christmas Story* (novella) 1994

Barbara. That creates a difficulty for a reviewer right away. American Indians do not write novels and poetry as a rule, or teach English in top-ranking universities either. But we cannot be patronizing. N. Scott Momaday's book is superb in its own right.

It is the old story of the problem of mixing Indians and Anglos. But there is a quality of revelation here as the author presents the heart-breaking effort of his hero to live in two worlds. Have you ever been to the Rio Grande country of New Mexico and wandered through the adobe Pueblo village there? It is a frustrating experience. The long-haired Indians with their blankets and headbands are not hostile—just indifferent. One returns to the comfort of Santa Fe feeling vaguely discontented and wondering why everything Anglo seems callow and obvious compared with this ancient culture that doesn't even bother to pave the streets.

Young Abel comes back to San Ysidro to resume the ancient ways of his beloved long-haired grandfather, Francisco. Abel is full of fears that he has relaxed his hold on these ways, after living like an Anglo in the Army. He is our tortured guide as we see his Indian world of pollen and rain, of houses made of dawn, of feasts and rituals to placate the gods, of orchards and patches of melons and grapes and squash, of beautiful colors and marvelous foods such as piki, posole, loaves of sotobalau, roasted mutton and fried bread. It is a wantless "world of wonder and exhilarating vastness."

The task of seeing it is made easier for us by the grandfather, who symbolizes the long and static continuity of Pueblo tradition. He shows us the richness of the Indian mixture through New Mexico's ages. The Jemez of San Ysidro have Navajo and Sia and Domingo and Isleta relatives—even a strain of Bahkyush, who fled from the East long ago, bringing to San Ysidro the finest of rain makers and eagle hunters. The Mexican priest, Father Olguin, is also a symbol of tradition. He is devoting his life to understanding these poetic people, just as other Catholic priests did in 17th-century New Mexico. He can smile as they smiled when he notes how they rank his shrine of Our Lady of the Angels second in spiritual importance to the adjoining kiva.

Abel's troubles begin at once. He has a brief and lyrical love affair with a white woman from California seeking some sort of truth at San Ysidro. Then he runs afoul of Anglo jurisprudence, which has no laws covering Pueblo ethics. He is paroled to a Los Angeles relocation center and copes for a time with that society, neither Anglo nor Indian. He attends peyote sessions; he tries to emulate his Navajo roommate, who almost accepts the glaring lights and treadmill jobs, the ugliness of the city and the Anglo yearning to own a Cadillac. Abel cannot "almost" cope. Because of his contempt, a sadistic cop beats him nearly to death. But he gets home in time to carry on tradition for his dying grandfather.

There is plenty of haze in the telling of this tale—but that is one reason why it rings so true. The mysteries of cultures different from our own cannot be explained in a short novel, even by an artist as talented as Mr. Momaday.

CHARLES A. NICHOLAS

SOURCE: Charles A. Nicholas, "N. Scott Momaday's Hard Journey Back," in *The South Dakota Review*, Vol. 13, No. 4, Winter, 1975-76, pp. 149-58.

[*In the following excerpt, Nicholas explains how* The Way to Rainy Mountain *demonstrates the similarity of inherited and created myths and "the convergence of personal and cultural experiences."*]

As a modern, historical consciousness and a member of a largely desacralized society, [Momaday] knows that he cannot return to the mythopoesis and archaic ontology of his Indian ancestors, that the Kiowa verbal tradition "has suffered a deterioration in time," ... and that the Kiowa culture can no longer establish identity and compel belief solely through the authority of its myths and rites. As a Kiowa who "feels Indian" in spite of all this, he is intent on reconciling his "primitive," tribal, "blood" consciousness with his modern, individual consciousness; but he is also bothered by a fear of presumption and sacrilege, a suspicion that he is evoking his dead relatives along with their myths, visions and rites without really being able to believe in them, or, to put it more precisely, to believe in what he has made them—in his imagination and through his art.

Put in yet another way, *The Way to Rainy Mountain* is one man's intensely personal discovery of what Joseph Campbell has called the collapse of traditional mythology and its displacement by creative mythology. But Momaday has gone one step farther, for he has sought to posit the essential continuity between these two kinds of mythology, insisting that both are acts of the imagination and both are capable of generating the same kind of belief. And he has done so in two ways: through the development of a complex structure in which to cast these many journeys he hopes to make . . . and through a series of memories or visions of his Kiowa ancestors through which he claims to have achieved a full sense of identification with them.

The numbered sections which make up the main body of his text—there are 24 grouped into three parts, The Setting Out, The Going On, and The Closing In—are divided into three passages. . . . Passage one contains fragments, told or retold, of Kiowa myths and legends; passage two contains bits and scraps from historical and ethnographic accounts of the Kiowas; and passage three contains autobiographical comments on his actual return to his Kiowa homeland and his personal past.

This division and fragmentation is offset however by less obvious but eventually more significant indications of continuity and convergence. Each of the sections, with a few exceptions, is devoted to the elaboration and development of a single theme. Section I establishes the pattern: it is concerned with "coming out" in each of the three modes— as mythic emergence, as historic migration, and as self discovery. Also, as the journey proceeds, Momaday explores the differences and similarities between these many journeys until, by the middle of Part III, he has interfused them in his mind, transformed his threefold division into mythic, historic, and autobiographical journeys into a single, all encompassing but nonetheless personal one. . . .

[The] attempt to reconcile Kiowa myth with the imaginative re-creation of his personal experience culminates in the closing sections of Part III. There the mythic passages are no longer mythic in the traditional sense, that is Momaday is creating myth out of his memories of his ancestors rather than passing on already established and socially sanctioned tales. Nor are the historical passages strictly historical, presumably objective, accounts of the Kiowas and their culture. Instead they are carefully selected and imaginatively rendered memories of his family. And, finally, the personal passages have become prose poems containing symbols which link them thematically to the other two, suggesting that all three journeys are products of the imagination, that all have become interfused in a single memory and reflect a single idea. . . .

[Momaday] is not only functioning as a creative mythologist, an indication of his modern, individualistic perspective; but he is also dramatizing the process whereby traditional mythology becomes creative — an indication that the two are continuous and reconcilable.

The last structural indication that Momaday has been moving toward the convergence of personal and cultural experience, poetry and myth, can be found in the poems which frame the entire work. Their positioning is itself an indication that creative art, that is the authority of the imagination, is most responsible for the integrity of the work, the journey it recalls, and the idea of the self which it reveals. . . .

ROGER DICKINSON-BROWN

SOURCE: Roger Dickinson-Brown, "The Art and Importance of N. Scott Momaday," in *The Southern Review*, Louisiana State University, Vol. XIV, No. 1, January, 1978, pp. 30-45.

[*In the excerpt below, Dickinson-Brown offers a stylistic examination of* House Made of Dawn, The Way to Rainy Mountain *and several of the poems in* Angle of Geese.]

The Kiowa Indian N. Scott Momaday came to public attention in 1969, surprising everyone, including himself and his editors, by winning the Pulitzer Prize for his novel *House Made of Dawn*. He has before and since maintained a quiet reputation in American Indian affairs and among distinguished *literati* for his genius, his extraordinary range, his fusion of alien cultures, and his extraordinary experiments in different literary forms.

House Made of Dawn is a memorable failure. Some of its passages attain a prose surface brilliance and also a depth, not at all like the historic depth of Macaulay or the ancient, almost etymological depth of Hardy, but a kind of depth of physical perception simultaneous with a post-Romantic understanding of man's relationship to nature—an understanding and a sensory perception which are both great and unique:

> He was a young man, and he rode out on the buckskin colt to the north and west, leading the hunting horse, across the river and beyond the white cliffs and the plain, beyond the hills and the mesas, the canyons and the caves. And once, where the horses could not go because the face of the rock was almost vertical and unbroken and the ancient handholds were worn away to shadows in the centuries of wind and rain, he climbed among the walls and pinnacles of rock, adhering like a vine to the face of the rock, pressing with no force at all his whole mind and weight upon the sheer ascent, running the roots of his weight into invisible hollows and cracks, and he heard the whistle and moan of the wind among the crags, like ancient voices, and saw the horses far below in the sunlit gorge. And there were the caves. He came suddenly upon a narrow ledge and stood before the mouth of a cave. It was sealed with silver webs, and he brushed them away. He bent to enter and knelt down on the floor. It was dark and cool and close inside, and smelled of damp earth and dead ancient fires, as if centuries ago the air had entered and stood still behind the web. The dead embers and ashes lay still in a mound upon the floor, and the floor was deep and packed with clay and glazed with the blood of animals. The chiseled dome was low and encrusted with smoke, and the one round wall was a perfect radius of rock and plaster. Here and there were earthen bowls, one very large, chipped and broken only at the mouth, deep and fired within. It was beautiful and thin-shelled and fragile-looking, but he struck the nails of his hand against it, and it rang like metal. There was a black metate by the door, the coarse, igneous grain of the shallow bowl forever bleached with meal, and in the ashes of the fire were several ears and cobs of corn, each no bigger than his thumb, charred and brittle, but whole and hard as wood. And there among the things of the dead he listened in the stillness all around and heard only the lowing of the wind . . . and then the plummet and rush of a great swooping bird—out of the corner of his eye he saw the awful shadow which hurtled across the light—and the clatter of wings on the cliff, and the small, thin cry of a rodent. And in the same instant the huge wings heaved with calm, gathering up the dead weight, and rose away.

The book glitters with similar passages, a shining tension between the cultural and the wild, between language and wind. But it is also filled with awkward dialogue and affected description ("There was no sound in the house, save the seldom crackling of the fire," etc.). And the novel falls apart rather than coming together: it remains a batch of often dazzling fragments, a kind of modern prose Sutton Hoo—perhaps because the young Momaday yielded to the deadly, fashionable temptation of imitative form in dealing with contemporary identity crisis, here specifically the fragmented personality of the misfit Abel. The book's own fragmentation is not quotable, since the problem is an incoherence of large parts, but any reader will readily grant that the sequence of items—say, the bear hunt and the murder that parallels it; the night scenes with Father Olguin; Abel's flashbacks; his encounter with the enemy tank; and his encounter with Angela—is without fixed order. The parts can be rearranged, no doubt with change of effect, but not always with recognizable difference. The fragments thus presented *are* the subject. The result is a successful depiction but not an understanding of what is depicted: a reflection, not a novel in the comprehensive sense of the word. (This is ironic, since Momaday's teacher Yvor Winters made such associational forms one of his major betes noires, but it is no more ironic than the pervasive associationism of that other great student of Winters, J. V. Cunningham, and of Winters himself.)

House Made of Dawn has other annoying peculiarities. In such an episodic narrative the reader tends to depend upon clues and keys, thematic links and the like. Momaday increases this tendency with historical parallels and contrasts which are essential to his meaning, such as those between Father Olguin and Fray Nicolas, and Abel and his grandfather. But the reader is misled by a false parallel between the albino Abel kills and the albino stillbirth recorded in the psychologically superb journal of Fray Nicolas. Albinism is not uncommon among Native American people, and the record of detail is a traditional and important function of narrative; but the details should not mislead. Momaday once indicated to me in conversation that he was unaware of the possibility of a connection between the albinos, and there is, after all, nothing in the novel to establish a connection. Yet most readers look for one. And there is at least one other important occurrence of the same problem: there seems to be, finally, no particular relationship between the old witch and the young one, in spite of misleading hereditary suggestions.

The book is therefore an intelligent miscellany of more and less well-written facets that together represent a historical and contemporary situation of great importance, but it is not a successful understanding of or coping with that situation, and so it fails as a novel—right through its evasive ending.

What remains is nonetheless sometimes rare photography with scraps of great prose. The prose is often rhythmically distinguished: long in its rhythms, with neither the complex clauses of James and Macaulay nor the streams of Joyce and Faulkner, yet very far indeed from the syntactical and artistic simplifications of Hemingway. And there are other successes. The long unified description of the bear hunt is remarkable for its psychological perception of the sexual relationship between hunter and hunted (the prose, the psychology, and the bear owe something to Faulkner). And the great description of the Eagle Watchers Society approaches the barren courage of Melville's *The Encantadas*.

But probably the most successful general feature of the novel is its landscape, which is both intensely sensory and symbolic in its implication of a human and historically specific relationship to that landscape:

> There is a kind of life that is peculiar to the land in summer—a wariness, a seasonal equation of well-being and alertness. Road runners take on the shape of motion itself, urgent and angular, or else they are like the gnarled, uncovered roots of ancient, stunted trees, some ordinary ruse of the land itself, immovable and forever there.

This is extraordinary physical detail; no one has achieved anything quite like it before. But it is even more abstract than it is physical, with neither quality detracting from the other. Nor is the abstraction figurative; it is implicit in the detail, and the detail is implicit in it. This kind of symbolism was called post-symbolic by Winters and has come to be associated with him, although he did not invent it but only observed, named, and practiced it. In any case Momaday's use of it is peculiar to him and to his Indian culture. It is a landscape and a way of living nowhere else available, and gives us reason to remember the book, if only in the way in which Hume's *History of England* and the poems of Edmund Waller are remembered.

In *The Way to Rainy Mountain* (starkly illustrated by Momaday's father Al), Momaday adopts a more apparently associational structure, adapts it to his purposes more distinctively, controls it better, and therefore writes better. The book makes an almost Jamesian symmetry: the whole, brief history of the Kiowa people is recounted, from "The Setting Out" from unknown beginnings in the Northwest mountains, through "The Going On" of a fiery nineteenth-century horse culture in the desert Southwest, to "The Closing In," the murder of their culture by the white European settlers of the same century. Each of these primary sections is composed of "triplets":

> Once there was a man who owned a fine hunting horse. It was black and fast and afraid of nothing. When it was turned upon an enemy it charged in a straight line and struck at full speed; the man need have no hand upon the rein. But, you know, that man knew fear. Once during a charge he turned that animal from its course. That was a bad thing. The hunting horse died of shame.

> . . . . .

> In 1861 a Sun Dance was held near the Arkansas River in Kansas. As an offering to Tai-me, a spotted horse was left tied to a pole in the medicine lodge, where it starved to death. Later in that year an epidemic of smallpox broke out in the tribe, and the old man Gaapiatan sacrificed one of his best horses, a fine black-eared animal, that he and his family might be spared.

> . . . . .

> I like to think of old man Gaapiatan and his horse. I think I know how much he loved that animal; I think I know what was going on in his mind: If you will give me my life and the lives of my family, I will give you the life of this black-eared horse.

The three primary sections are flanked on either side: at first by a Prologue and an Introduction, both vehicles for recounting the book's occasion, which was the author's personal journey retracing simultaneously both his ancestry and his tribe's migration; and at last by an Epilogue. These in turn are flanked by short beginning and closing poems.

These symmetries are simple and the story is simple, and dignified, and rich in coherent detail. Much critical comment upon it would be offensive and tedious. The prose resembles that of the better parts of ***House Made of Dawn***, but the associationism succeeds here because no larger structure than a chronological anthology of details is attempted; the parts accrue rather than compose. Here and elsewhere Momaday's diction, rhythm, or syntax can be inflated and sentimental, but the fault is not usually ruinous and is often entirely avoided:

> In the Kiowa calendars there is graphic proof that the lives of women were hard, whether they were "bad women" or not. Only the captives, who were slaves, held lower status. During the Sun Dance of 1843, a man stabbed his wife in the breast because she accepted Chief Dohasan's invitation to ride with him in the ceremonial procession. And in the winter of 1851-52, Big Bow stole the wife of a man who was away on a raiding expedition. He brought her to his father's camp and made her wait outside in the bitter cold while he went in to collect his things. But his father knew what was going on, and he held Big Bow and would not let him go. The woman was made to wait in the snow until her feet were frozen.

It is surprising that Momaday has published so few poems. *Angle of Geese* contains only eighteen—the considered work of a great poet around the age of forty. But the poems are there, astonishing in their depth and range. **"Simile," "Four Notions of Love and Marriage," "The Fear of Bo-talee," "The Story of a Well-Made Shield,"** and **"The Horse that Died of Shame"** are variously free verse (the first two, which are slight and sentimental) or prose poems. They partake of the same discrete intensity that characterizes the storytelling in *The Way to Rainy Mountain*, and which makes them some of the few real prose poems in English.

The poems written in grammatical parallels are much better: **"The Delight Song of Tsoai-talee"** and **"Plainview: 2."** In the latter, Momaday has used a form and created emotions without precedent in English:

> I saw an old Indian
> At Saddle Mountain.
> He drank and dreamed of drinking
> And a blue-black horse.
>
> Remember my horse running.
> Remember my horse.
> Remember my horse running.
> Remember my horse.
>
> Remember my horse wheeling.
> Remember my horse.
> Remember my horse wheeling.
> Remember my horse.
>
> Remember my horse blowing.
> Remember my horse.
> Remember my horse blowing.
> Remember my horse.
>
> Remember my horse standing.
> Remember my horse.
> Remember my horse standing.
> Remember my horse.
>
> Remember my horse hurting.
> Remember my horse.
> Remember my horse hurting.
> Remember my horse.
>
> Remember my horse falling.
> Remember my horse.
> Remember my horse falling.
> Remember my horse.
>
> Remember my horse dying.
> Remember my horse.
> Remember my horse dying.
> Remember my horse.
>
> A horse is one thing,
> An Indian another;
> An old horse is old;
> An old Indian is sad.
>
> I saw an old Indian
> At Saddle Mountain.
> He drank and dreamed of drinking
> And a blue-black horse.
>
> Remember my horse running.
> Remember my horse.
> Remember my horse wheeling.
> Remember my horse.
> Remember my horse blowing.
> Remember my horse.
> Remember my horse standing.
> Remember my horse.
> Remember my horse falling.
> Remember my horse.
> Remember my horse dying.
> Remember my horse.
> Remember my blue-black horse.
> Remember my blue-black horse.
> Remember my horse.
> Remember my horse.
> Remember.
> Remember.

A chant or a parallel poem is necessarily bulky and especially oral. I have often recited this poem to individuals and groups, in part to test its effect upon an English-language audience. My own voice is consciously based upon the oral readings of Pound, Winters, and Native American chant, with a dash of childhood Latin Mass. I read the lines without musical intonation but with emphatic regularity and little rhetorical variation. The results are extreme: about half the listeners are bored, the other half moved, sometimes to tears. The poem is obviously derived from Momaday's experience of Indian chant, in which, as in most other cultures, small distinction is made between music and poetry. In this respect **"Plainview: 2"** is a part of the abandoned traditions of Homer, *The Song of Roland,* oral formulas, the Christian, Muslim, and Jewish chant, and even certain Renaissance poems. The various forms of repetition in these works are still common in the Islamic and black African and certain other worlds, but they survive in the West (where individual originality has destroyed community), only through such traditional popular genres as commercial song (which, unlike "modern intellectual" poetry and "classical" music, preserves the fusion), nursery rhymes, and among the non-white minorities. These are our surviving traditions of form, which is by nature repetitive.

In addition to the obvious repetitions in **"Plainview: 2,"** the repetition of stanza 1 at stanza 10, and the two-line rehearsal of the four-line stanzas turn the poem. The whole poem is, in fact, simply a subtle variation, development, and restatement of the first stanza, with the extended, reiterated illustration of both the beauty of the horse's actions and its death. The ninth stanza occupies the poem like a kernel of gloss, but even its third and fourth lines are simply restatements of its first and second.

The form of this poem distinguishes with rare clarity what we call denotative and connotative. In a literate age of recorded language, where memory and repetition—sides of a coin—have each faded from our experience, we are inclined to regard such hammering as a waste of time—but it can, instead, be an intensification and a kind of experience we have lost. That is precisely the division of modern response to the poem.

The rest of Momaday's poetry is traditionally iambic or experimentally syllabic. Winters has called the iambic pentameter **"Before an Old Painting of the Crucifixion"** a great poem, and perhaps it is, in spite of a certain stiltedness and melodrama, reminiscent of the worst aspects of *House Made of Dawn.* Yet the iambic poems are certainly among the best of their kind in Momaday's generation, and it is only the exigency of space that limits me to a few lines from **"Rainy Mountain Cemetery"**:

> Most is your name the name of this dark
>   stone.
> Deranged in death, the mind to be inheres
> Forever in the nominal unknown....

Momaday's theme here is an inheritance from Winters, though it is as old as our civilization: the tension, the gorgeous hostility between the human and the wild—a tension always finally relaxed in death. Winters did a great deal to restore and articulate that consciousness, after and in the light of Romanticism. And it was Winters too who taught Momaday one of his greatest virtues, the power and humanity of abstraction—heresy in the cant of our time: *deranged* is a pure and perfect abstraction.

And there is more Winters:

> ... silence is the long approach of noon
> Upon the shadow that your name defines—
> And death this cold, black density of stone.

We have already seen this in *House Made of Dawn.* Winters called it post-symbolist method. The physical images carry the full force, often through double sense, of abstraction: the shadow *defines;* and death is the impenetrability, the incomprehensibility, of black *density.* Yet the images are not metaphors, for they are not subservient to the abstractions they communicate, nor are they synecdochical. They persist in the very mortal obstinacy which they mean. This style is everywhere in Momaday, but it is something which Winters could not have duplicated, for it is also profoundly Kiowa....

Momaday's syllabic poetry is his best and experimentally most exciting work. Even deprived of the rest of the poem, the middle stanza of **"The Bear"** seems to me among the perfect stanzas in English, rhythmically exquisite in its poise between iamb and an excess of syllabic looseness, utterly comprehensive in its presentation of the motionless wild bear and its relationship to time:

> Seen, he does not come,
> move, but seems forever there,
> dimensionless, dumb,
> in the windless noon's hot glare.

"Comparatives" is a tour-de-force of alternating unrhymed three-and four-syllable lines, again with Momaday's abstract and physical fusion. Momaday succeeds in presenting such unrhymed, short lines rhythmically, in spite of a necessarily high incidence of enjambment; the faint lines convey a melancholy appropriate to the antiquity and death which are the consequence of his juxtaposition of the dead and the fossil fish:

> ... cold, bright body
> of the fish
> upon the planks,
> the coil and

crescent of flesh
extending
just into death.

Even so,
in the distant,
inland sea,
a shadow runs,
radiant,
rude in the rock:
fossil fish,
fissure of bone
forever.
It is perhaps
the same thing,
an agony
twice perceived.

Momaday's greatest poem is certainly **"Angle of Geese,"** a masterpiece of syllabic rhythm, of modulated rhyme, of post-symbolic images, and of the meaning of language in human experience. Although perhaps none of its stanzas is equal to the best stanza of **"The Bear,"** each functions in a similar way, shifting from perfect to imperfect to no rhyme with the same supple responsiveness Dryden mastered, but with more range. Nevertheless the largest importance of this poem, even beyond its extraordinary form is its theme, which is probably the greatest of our century: the extended understanding of the significance of language and its relation to identity—an understanding increased not only by the important work done by the linguists of our century but also by the increased mixture of languages which has continued to accelerate over the last hundred years or so: French or English among Asians and Africans, often as first or only languages among nonetheless profoundly non-European people; Spanish established on an Indian continent; and, of course, English in America. These are non-native native speakers of English, as it were, further distinguishing literature in English from English literature. Their potential has much to do with their relative freedom from the disaster and degeneracy which Romantic ideas have created among their European-American counterparts: many of these new English writers still have deep connections with their communities, instead of the individualistic elitism which characterizes contemporary European-American art, music, and poetry. They are more like Shakespeare, Rembrandt, and Homer. And they often have fewer neuroses about the evils of form. Momaday, as a Kiowa, a university scholar, and a poet of major talent, is in an excellent position to take advantage of these multi-cultural possibilities. The result is **"Angle of Geese"**:

How shall we adorn
Recognition with our speech?—
Now the dead firstborn
Will lag in the wake of words.

Custom intervenes;
We are civil, something more:
More than language means,
The mute presence mulls and marks.

Almost of a mind,
We take measure of the loss;
I am slow to find
The mere margin of repose.

And one November
It was longer in the watch,
As if forever,
Of the huge ancestral goose.

So much symmetry!
Like the pale angle of time
And eternity.
The great shape labored and fell.

Quit of hope and hurt,
It held a motionless gaze,
Wide of time, alert,
On the dark distant flurry.

The poem is difficult and a little obscure, mostly because the subject is—but also because Momaday has indulged a little in the obscurantism that makes modern poetry what it is—and an explication of the poem is therefore necessary.

The first stanza presents the subject and observes that the Darwinian animal which we were, who is our ancestor, cannot be rediscovered in our language, which is what moved us away and distinguished us from the animal.

The second stanza explains the divorce: we have become civilized, but not wholly. "The mute presence" may, by syntax, seem to be the presence of language, but it is not. It is the presence of wilderness which is mute. We live in connotation, which is wild response. "Mulls" and "civil" are odd diction.

The third stanza contemplates this ambivalence, this incompleteness, and moves from the general to the particular. We are almost whole, or wholly civilized and conscious, and to precisely this extent we have lost our own wilderness. The speaker, introduced at this point, is slow to realize, outside language, what is wild in him. The language is typical of Momaday in its outright and exact abstraction: "mere" in the old sense of pure or unadulterated—here, by language and civilization; "margin" because this is where humans, with their names and mortality, overlap with wilderness, which has neither; "repose" because what is wild is forever and at every moment perfect and complete, without urgency, going nowhere, perpetuating itself beautifully for no sake at all. It is useful to remember wilderness here primarily in terms of immortal molecules and galaxies, without number or name—except those collective names imposed upon them by men who have to that extent simply perceived and thought about that which is unaltered by thought, which does not know the thinker, and which is, finally, a kind of god—not a god, as Stevens said, "but as a god might be." It is a kind of altered Romantic god, but one supported rather more by the pure sciences than by Deism and Benevolism: a nature pure and perfect, composed of sub-atomic particles and framed in an unimaginable universe with no edge. Language contradicts itself with this god, who is its enemy. It is the wilderness of our century, deprived of Romantic benevolence but retaining its old terrifying innocence and immense and nameless beauty, which ignores us and must destroy us, one by one. It is a god of mere repose. The goose, which the hunter waits for one November, is almost perfectly a part of the god (Momaday only implies the word), although a goose shares with men certain forms of individual consciousness of itself and others. Some animals have some language, and to this extent the goose knows the same clear and lonely condition we do, and is an imperfect symbol of the wilderness. The long watch, in any case, implies the eternity which is the whole of which the goose is an indiscriminate part: *as if forever*. The goose is huge because it is inseparable from the wild deity: what Emerson called the "not I," which neither names nor knows itself, which cannot die—whatever is, like the grasshopper of the ancient Greeks, immortal because the individuals have no name. That is our ancestor who does not know us, whom we hardly know.

So, in the fifth stanza, the symmetry of the angle or V of the flock of geese implies the perfection for which geometry and symmetry have always served as imaginary means. A goose is shot, and falls out of the angle, into the speaker's world.

The last stanza gives the goose a little of that hope and hurt which grants this sophisticated animal a part of what will kill the speaker: a conscious identity. But the goose is essentially wild, and it holds, like an immortal cockatrice, an inhuman gaze—motionless, outside the time in which we live and die, wildly, purely alert—fixed on the receding flurry of the flock out of which it fell, growing as dark and distant physically as it is in truth to the dying speaker who watches it too and for whom, alone, something has changed. The word "flurry" fuses with the flock all the huge vagueness which is our blind source.

seems to me the best example both of Momaday's greatness and his importance to contemporary literature: it profoundly realizes its subject, both denotatively and connotatively, with greater art in an important new prosodic form than anyone except Bridges and Daryush. It also presents, better than any other work I know—especially in the light of what has only recently been so developed and understood—perhaps the most important subject of our age: the tragic conflict between what we have felt in wilderness and what our language means.

HOWARD MEREDITH

SOURCE: Howard Meredith, "N. Scott Momaday: A Man of Words," in *World Literature Today*, Vol. 64, No. 3, Summer, 1990, pp. 405-07.

[*In the excerpt below, Meredith describes how Momaday reworks the traditional oral narratives of the Kiowa tribe to emphasize the symbolic unity possible within this disintegrating Native American culture.*]

N. Scott Momaday marks a decisive line of demarcation in the cultural tradition of the Kiowa people. In doing so, he has struck a responsive chord among the other diverse peoples of North America. He is a collector of the ancient traditions that circulated orally among the Kiowa people and others of the American Southwest. With him begins a literary tradition of those prose narratives which previously had circulated almost exclusively within specific tribal contexts. This process is one in which a great literary work, ***House Made of Dawn***, issued at a stroke.

Such a collecting and refashioning of old material cannot be ascribed to the initiative of Momaday alone. The time and place are ripe for it. Indeed, what is most important is that the presuppositions for this collecting and refashioning are present in the ancient tribal traditions themselves. The majority of these old narratives are etiologies. Their purpose is to explain some facts in tribal heritage, about a place or in the spiritual tradition. Previously the validity of these traditions and the interest in them have been regionally limited to the lands occupied by the Kiowa in Oklahoma and the Navajo-Pueblo country farther west. The ancient spiritual traditions in particular are previously unthinkable outside the sacred context. Only in the course of traditional acts could a person meet and experience them. These sacred narratives are not some kind of ornamental addition to the tribe. Rather, they are its inmost nerve. It is by this that the tribal community lives and from this that the content and form of the ceremonials and dances proceed.

What a profound change occurs as these materials from different Kiowa societies and diverse places along their line of migration became unified and even altered by a superimposed plan! In a word, they became available as literature in Momaday's *House Made of Dawn, The Way to Rainy Mountain, The Names,* and *The Ancient Child.* Above all an inner shift occurs in the meaning of these narratives. Momaday lives in a time of continuing crisis for the Kiowa tribe and all native peoples of the Americas. Connected with this crisis is the decline of the ancient Kiowa tribal unity. The translation of oral traditions into literary ones is fostered to a degree by this disintegration. Focus in the literary narrative is brought to bear on unifying elements. Some of these are explained in personal terms that have become intimately associated with traditions surrounding the Tai-me, a sacred figure of the Kiowa, and the tribal migration story ending at Rainy Mountain. In each of these Momaday uses words and formal variations to provide for emphasis in meaning and purpose which the material once possessed in its oral tribal context. He does not forget that the narrative has changed by virtue of the context in which he has placed it.

One conceptual problem about Momaday's work is that of making explicit the criteria by which a narrative is recognized as coherent or incoherent. He chooses Kiowa tradition in his fictional and personal narratives as a measured angle of vision. Consistent reference is made to the Tai-me and its central place in Kiowa understanding of the world in both narrative and conversational form. In *House Made of Dawn* we read of how the Tai-me came to the Kiowa.

> Long ago there were bad times. The Kiowas were hungry and there was no food. There was a man who heard his children cry from hunger, and he began to search for food. He walked four days and became very weak. On the fourth day he came to a great canyon. Suddenly there was thunder and lightning. A Voice spoke to him and said, "Why are you following me? What do you want?" The man was afraid. The thing standing before him had the feet of a deer, and its body was covered with feathers. The man answered that the Kiowas were hungry. "Take me with you," the Voice said, "and I will give you whatever you want." From that day Tai-me has belonged to the Kiowas.

In *The Way to Rainy Mountain* the Tai-me is described and brought within a personal memory.

> The great central figure of the *kedo*, or Sun Dance, ceremony is the *taime*. This is a small image, less than 2 feet in length, representing a human figure dressed in a robe of white feathers, with a headdress consisting of a single upright feather and pendants of ermine skin, with numerous strands of blue beads around its neck, and painted upon the face, breast, and back with designs symbolic of the sun and moon. The image itself is of dark-green stone, in form rudely resembling a human head and bust, probably shaped by art like the stone fetishes of the Pueblo tribes. It is preserved in a rawhide box in charge of the hereditary keeper, and is never under any circumstances exposed to view except at the annual Sun Dance, when it is fastened to a short upright stick planted within the medicine lodge, near the western side. It was last exposed in 1888. — Mooney

> Once I went with my father and grandmother to see the Tai-me bundle. It was suspended by means of a strip of ticking from the fork of a small ceremonial tree. I made an offering of bright red cloth, and my grandmother prayed aloud. It seemed a long time that we were there. I had never come into the presence of Tai-me before—nor have I since. There was a great holiness all about it in the room, as if an old person had died there or a child had been born.

Finally the Tai-me is referred to in terms of the imagination in *The Ancient Child.*

> And Tai-me was exposed there, Tai-me, the sacred Sun Dance doll and most powerful medicine in the tribe, more powerful even than the *tal-yi-da-i*, the ten bundles containing the "boy medicine," one of which was kept by her uncle T'ene-taide. She dared to look upon it, the stiff polished figure gleamed in a splinter of light, and the downy feathers of his headdress trembled on the warm, sluggish breeze. She placed a patch of blue wool among the other, richer offerings. The presence of Tai-me was palpable; it was as if she had walked into a warm, slow-moving stream; the presence lay against her like water.

Momaday places the Tai-me and its specific context in relation to the earth and sky. This place is in southwest Oklahoma on and around Rainy Mountain, which becomes "the center of the world, the sacred ground of sacred grounds."

In the same instance, structures and processes are determined in large part by what Momaday leaves out of his representations as much as by what he places in the literary versions. As with many American Indian traditions, family relationships are paramount. Although Momaday's Kiowa relations are discussed prominently, his Cherokee background is less well known. It is critical to remember that Momaday perceived how his mother's native heritage enabled her to assume an attitude of defiance. Natachee Scott Momaday's knowledge of her Cherokee ancestry allowed her to take an intellectual perspective that might have eluded her otherwise.

This decision by Momaday's mother, in turn, provided freedom of choice to her son. The defiance of the mother allowed added cultural perspectives through which to make critical choices. The tension between the requirements of the system in place and those of change, between order and adventure, were brought into bold relief through the native heritage. In his memoir Momaday wrote of his mother's choice of the cultural and intellectual forces that would provide her with life's perspective.

> It was about this time that she began to see herself as an Indian. That dim native heritage became her fascination and a cause for her, inasmuch, perhaps, as it enabled her to assume an attitude of defiance, an attitude which she assumed with particular style and satisfaction; it became her. She imagined who she was. This act of the imagination was, I believe, among the most important events of my mother's early life, as later the same essential act was to be among the most important of my own.

To both mother and son, the attitude existed in all kinds of narrative practice, including oral tradition, as well as literary fiction. This intellectual tension at certain moments became acute enough to become the principle of narrative works. In his graduate study Momaday examined the "literatures of resistance." He echoed this theme in his dissertation, an edition of the collected verse of the nineteenth-century poet Frederick Goddard Tuckman. In his study of Tuckman's poem "The Cricket" he wrote that this poem "must concern us with the matter of intellectual integrity in a context of intellectual dissolution." He returned to the theme of resistance in *The Ancient Child,* emphasizing the concept that all art was resistance.

Momaday challenges readers to accept the knowledge bound up in the themes of imagining the self and resisting the disintegrating intellectual climate. In a talk given in 1970, "Man Made of Words," he stated: "We Americans need now more than ever before—indeed more than we know—to imagine who and what we are with respect to the earth and sky." As the West European roots of Anglo-American culture become less relevant, the need is for each person and family of people to know themselves. New means of communication and mass media allow the oral traditions of America to emerge to influence segments of society as never before possible. Americans need to know themselves for what they are and not as a fading colonial image.

Momaday describes the world in which he lives as derived from mental schemata rather than from observation. He can discern the essential features of an order that happens to suit him. He highlights the essence of traditional narratives by emphasizing that the various traditions construct their objects. The terms are objects of language, not entities of which words are in some way copies. On the nature of the relationship between language and experience, Momaday states: "It seems to me that in a certain sense we are all made of words; that our most essential being consists in language." *The Way to Rainy Mountain* exhibits this ideal. As such it is an integration of old Kiowa tales, historical commentary, and autobiographical commentary. In large part, living memory and the oral tradition that transcends it outline the terms of Momaday's resistance. He is careful to define these integrating elements.

> The oral tradition is that process by which the myths, legends, tales, and lore of a people are formulated, communicated, and preserved in language by word of mouth, as opposed to writing. Or, it is a *collection* of such things....
>
> In the context of the remarks, the matter of oral tradition suggests certain particularities of art and reality. Art, for example, ... involves an oral dimension which is based markedly upon such considerations as memorization, intonation, inflection, precision of statement, brevity, rhythm, pace, and dramatic effect. Moreover, myth, legend, and lore, according to our definitions of these terms, imply a separate and distinct order of reality. We are concerned here not so much with an acute representation of actuality, but with the realization of the imaginative experience....
>
> Generally speaking, man has consummate being in language, and there only. The state of human *being* is an idea, an idea which man has of himself. Only when he is embodied in an idea, and the idea is realized in language, can man take possession of himself.

Momaday's sense of native literature is unified, intelligible, based on proper subordination of the part to the ends of the whole, whereas academic ethnology and history of the same subject matter know only the paratactic organization of contiguity or succession. This is a distinct sense of reality in comparison with that of oral tradition. Both oral tradition and written literature are realized in and through narrative. The shape of narrative and the angle of vision that particular narrative forms convey are thereby common to both at any given time.

Tradition has come to be associated with the singular, the unexpected, the uncontrollable, the unsystematic, whereas literature, especially fiction, on the other hand, is associated with the ordered, the coherent, the general. Momaday undercuts the narrative coherence of his novels through appeals to traditions other than the Anglo-American. The important thing for him in this context is not "objective" truth, as distinct from subjective belief, but the fact that the material is part of an accepted tradition. He finds an angle of vision from which readers can allow their gaze to embrace the entire sequence of facts—a pregnant principle for which each particular fact would be only a development. Isolated facts that cannot be related to the principal action are treated in digressions, as they are important in themselves.

Momaday's appeal to tradition—in fact, to a number of traditions, including Kiowa, Navajo-Pueblo, and Anglo-Saxon—raises questions and creates conditions in which the individual subject, the critical reason, could exercise and assert its freedom. It is not presented as an objectively true and therefore compelling discovery of reality itself. On the contrary, its verity and validity are always problematic, provoking the readers' reflections and thus renewing their own freedom. Discontinuity, rather than continuity, is placed at the heart of Momaday's use of the various traditions, as it has been placed at the heart of his fiction. He reaches through to past-present-future reality by a process of symbolic interpretation of the evidence. The older distinction between fiction and history or tradition, in which fiction is conceived as the representation of the imaginable and historical narrative as the representation of the actual, gives way to the recognition that this author knows the actual as the imaginable.

The cognitive function of Momaday's use of narrative form is not just to relate a succession of events but to bring forth an ensemble of interrelationships of many different elements as a single whole. In fictional narrative the coherence of such complex forms affords esthetic and emotional satisfaction. Momaday relates to the reader his figures' lives in language, "and of the awful risk involved." On one level he prepares his readers for the risk of experiencing another plane of existence, one that can be realized through acceptance of the oneness of past, present, and future in accord with spatial terms. Momaday provides for the defiance of renewal. He points the way to mental sanctuary. He brings American readers to a new sense of maturity through the use of the traditions of America. He asks readers to imagine themselves, but always in relationship to the American earth and sky. . . .

SCOTT EDWARD ANDERSON

SOURCE: Scott Edward Anderson, in a review of *In the Presence of the Sun: Stories and Poems, 1961-1991*, in *The Bloomsbury Review*, Vol. 13, No. 4, July-August, 1993, pp. 14, 22.

[Here, Anderson provides a thematic and stylistic review of In the Presence of the Sun.]

There have been a number of notable collected and selected volumes of poetry over the past few years, including award-winning books by Mary Oliver and Hayden Carruth, as well as important editions from Gary Snyder, Donald Hall, Derek Mahon, Cynthia Macdonald, Adrienne Rich, and others. The significance of this is not lost: As we approach the end of the millennium, many of our poets are at the top of their form. These collections allow us to assess their accomplishments as well as gauge the state of the art over the past several decades.

We are fortunate to add to the growing list of retrospective collections this new book from N. Scott Momaday. *In the Presence of the Sun* offers "stories," poems, and drawings from over 30 years. Many of us first became aware of Momaday through his Pulitzer Prize-winning novel, *House Made of Dawn*, but it was as a poet that he first appeared on the literary scene.

Momaday's early work, still some of his best, bears the influence of his teacher at Stanford, Yvor Winters. These are, nonetheless, poems of grace and resonance. Winters encouraged the young Momaday to work in a variety of traditional forms, including syllabic verse, in which the number of syllables in a line determines the rhythmic structure. Momaday used this method to great effect in such early poems as **"Buteo Regalis,"** and again in **"The Bear"**:

> What ruse of vision,
> escarping on the wall of leaves,

rending incision
into countless surfaces,

would cull and color
his somnolence, whose old age
has outworn valor,
all but the fact of courage?

In **"Angle of Geese,"** from the same period, the poet examines the differences between the human concept of death and death in wild nature:

> Almost of a mind,
> We take measure of the loss;
> I am slow to find
> The mere margin of repose.
>
> . . . . .
>
> So much symmetry!—
> Like the pale angle of time
> And eternity.
> The great shape labored and fell.

This is perhaps the first of Momaday's poems to reject, philosophically if not technically, Winters' influence. In the wake of this poem, Momaday turned increasingly to nature and to his Kiowa heritage, exploring native themes and the old ways and employing forms that more accurately present these concerns. This change is further exemplified by the incantatory style of his **"The Delight Song of Tsoai-talee"**:

> I am a flame of four colors
> I am a deer standing away in the dusk
> I am a field of sumac and the pomme blanche
> I am an angle of geese in the winter sky
> I am the hunger of a young wolf
> I am the whole dream of these things
> You see, I am alive, I am alive

Momaday participates annually in the Gourd Dance Society, where he is the successor to his grandfather, Mammedaty. His poem **"The Gourd Dancer"** is at once an homage to his grandfather and an expression of respect for the tradition:

> Someone spoke his name, Mammedaty, in which his essence was and is. It was a serious matter that his name should be spoken there in the circle, among the many people, and he was thoughtful, full of wonder, and aware of himself and of his name.

Here magic and tradition, reality and the dreamland come together for the poet and, through his storytelling, for the reader.

Myth, too, plays an important part in his work. Included in this volume is a long sequence of poems titled "The Strange and True Story of My Life with Billy the Kid." The mythic figure of Billy the Kid represents a significant influence on the imagination of Scott Momaday. While Momaday's choice of the legendary outlaw as a subject for a sustained sequence might at first seem odd, it illustrates the unique bicultural nature of both his outlook and his work. "The Kid" died in Momaday's home territory of New Mexico; we can imagine the young poet heard of his legend alongside the stories of his native culture, and the sequence has all the earmarks of the oral tradition in its form and function. Composed of songs, epigraphs, and prose poems as well as narrative poems, this sustained imaginative meditation captures the essence of the myth and its effect on the psyche of the author. For Momaday, Billy is not only an outlaw hero (and hence, like the poet's own people, both outcast and venerated presence), he is also a sensitive individual, a youth with a sense of valor if not a conscience:

> Billy fetched a plug of tobacco from his coat pocket, cut it in two with a jackknife, and gave the old man half. We said goodbye . . . Later, on the way to Santa Fe, I said to Billy: "Say, amigo, I have never seen you chew tobacco." "No, and it isn't likely that you ever will," he said. "I have no use for the weed. . . . I bought the tobacco at La Junta because I knew that we were coming this way . . . to see the old man . . . He has a taste for it. And I offered him half instead of the whole because he should prefer that I did not give him something outright; it pleased him that I should share something of my own with him. . . . I have thrown away my share . . . But that is an unimportant matter . . . this the old man understands and appreciates more even than the tobacco itself."

When Billy (ne Henry McCarty) witnesses the marriage of his mother, we see another side of the outlaw, one the tall tales never revealed:

> She is pale, lovely, and lithe.
> Her sons are stiff and homely,
> And they make hard witnesses.
> Joe is careless, distant, dumb;
> Henry imagines marriage,
> The remorse and agonies
> Of age. He looks upon her,
> His mother, and his mind turns
> Upon him; the beautiful
> His example of despair.

Yet Billy can also instill terror in an individual: He is

"the only man I have ever known in whose eyes there was no expression whatsoever."

In the **"Gathering of Shields,"** which gives *In the Presence of the Sun* its title, Momaday turns to a further exploration of myth and legend. Each shield, carefully executed in ink, is rendered on the facing page in a brief prose translation. "The Sun Dance Shield," "The Shield That Died," "The Floating Feathers Shield," and "The Shield That Was Touched by Pretty Mouth" are all brought to life by the poetry. Take, for example, the tragic story of "The Shield of Which the Less Said the Better":

> A man—his name is of no importance—owned a shield. The shield came down in the man's family. The man's grandson carried the shield into a fight at Stinking Creek, and he was killed. Soldiers took away the shield. Some years ago old man Red Horn bought the shield in a white man's store at Clinton, Oklahoma, for seventeen dollars. The shield was worth seventeen dollars, more or less.

The shield drawings are powerful, in part because the form is such an intriguing one: circles, objects of protection, ornament, and deep spiritual value. Each shield tells a story, but its decoration only provides the skeleton of a narrative—the trick, Momaday implies, is to *listen* to the shield.

In "The Shield of Two Dreams," a woman named Dark Water inherits her father's shield through the simple act of dreaming. This, we imagine, is a fairly radical event, for nothing else like it appears in this gathering of shields; no other woman receives this power. Momaday has, rather appropriately, placed this shield at the end of the section, as if to underscore its adaptation of the old ways to new times.

Of the "New Poems" in this collection, only a few seem to live up to the promise of Momaday's earlier work: **"The Great Fillmore Street Buffalo Drive," "Carnegie, Oklahoma, 1919," "Mogollon Morning,"** and **"Wreckage"**:

> Had my bones, like the sun,
> been splintered on this canyon wall
> and burned among these buckled plates,
> this bright debris; had it been so,
> I should not have lingered so long
> among my losses. I should have come
> loudly, like a warrior, to my time.

The other poems in this section seem vague and affected, and their weakness stands out in the face of the strong earlier work of the collection.

The drawings throughout the volume are evocative, especially the various bears, which in many ways resemble the author. (Momaday's biography proclaims: "He is a bear.") They are robust creatures, well rounded yet full of energy. It is a contradiction that serves well this bear of an artist—poet, painter, and storyteller, and in all these things a "man made of words." *In the Presence of the Sun* gives us the unique opportunity to witness this bear as he articulates "the appropriate expression of his spirit."

SOURCES FOR FURTHER STUDY

Antell, Judith A. "Momaday, Welch, and Silko: Expressing the Feminine Principle through Male Alienation." *The American Indian Quarterly* XII, No. 3 (Summer 1988): 213-20.

> Examines Momaday's *House Made of Dawn*, James Welch's *The Death of Jim Loney*, and Leslie Marmon Silko's *Ceremony*, arguing that their treatment of the alienated Native American male underscores the role and power of Native American women in tribal communities.

Brumble, H. David, III. "N. Scott Momaday: Oral to Written Tradition." In his *American Indian Autobiography*, pp. 165-80. Berkeley: University of California Press, 1988.

> Argues that Momaday's autobiographical writings are informed by Native oral traditions, tribal history, and a desire to return to the "old ways."

Lincoln, Kenneth. "Comic Accommodations: Momaday and Norman." In his *Indi'n Humor: Bicultural Play in Native America*, pp. 280-308. New York: Oxford University Press, 1993.

> Discusses Momaday's use of humor, irony, caricature, and the Trickster figure in *House Made of Dawn*. This chapter also includes an examination of these and similar elements in Howard Norman's novel *The Northern Lights*.

Reynolds, Susan Salter. Review of *In the Presence of the Sun: Stories and Poems, 1961-1991*, by N. Scott Momaday. *Los Angeles Times Book Review* (27 December 1992): 6.

> Praises Momaday's focus on identity, nature, and Native chants, artifacts, and traditions in *In the Presence of the Sun*.

Scarberry-García, Susan. *Landmarks of Healing: A Study of "House Made of Dawn."* Albuquerque: University of New Mexico Press, 1990, 208 p.

> Provides essays on the motif of the twin, animal imagery, Native myths, and the theme of healing as presented in *House Made of Dawn*. The critic notes: "This study attempts to interpret the dialectical relationship between the text and the cultural worlds that engendered the text by examining the ethnographic record as it pertains to Navajo, Pueblo, and Kiowa events in the novel."

Trimble, Martha Scott. "N. Scott Momaday (1934-)." In *Fifty Western Writers: A Bio-Bibliographical Sourcebook,* edited by Fred Erisman and Richard W. Etulain, pp. 313-24. Westport, Conn.: Greenwood Press, 1982.

> Provides an overview of Momaday's life, a discussion of the major themes of his works, critical reception of his writings, and a listing of primary and secondary sources.

Marianne Moore

1887-1972

(Full name Marianne Craig Moore) American poet, essayist, translator, short story writer, editor, playwright, and author of children's books.

INTRODUCTION

One of the foremost American literary figures, Moore created poetry characterized by loose rhythms, carefully chosen words, close attention to detail, and acute observation of human character. Her poems often reflect her preoccupation with the relationships between the common and the uncommon, advocate discipline in both art and life, and espouse virtues of restraint, modesty, and humor. She frequently used animals as a central image to emphasize themes of independence, honesty, and the integration of art and nature. Although some critics consider much of her poetry overly precious and her subject matter inconsequential, Moore has been praised as an important poetic voice by such literary figures as T. S. Eliot, William Carlos Williams, Hilda Doolittle, and Ezra Pound.

Biographical Information

Moore was born November 15, 1887, in Kirkwood, Missouri. She attended Bryn Mawr College, where she published her early poetry in the campus literary magazine, and received a degree in biology and histology in 1909. At Bryn Mawr Moore established an enduring friendship with Doolittle as well as with Williams, Pound, and Eliot, to whom her work would later be compared. In 1915 her poems began to appear in respected literary periodicals; her first volume, *Poems* (1921), gathers many of these pieces. While Doolittle and others had arranged the content of *Poems,* Moore chose the poems in her second volume, *Observations* (1924), to represent the variety of her themes and forms. In 1925, Moore became editor of the *Dial,* a position she retained until the magazine ceased publication in 1929. Her experiences at the *Dial* brought her into contact with many notable literati, who helped advance her international reputation. At the urging of friends, Moore published *Selected Poems* in 1935; other volumes of this time include *The Pangolin and Other Verse* (1936), *What Are Years* (1941), and *Nevertheless* (1944), perhaps her most impassioned work. Many of the poems in these books later were included in *Collected Poems* (1951), which was awarded both the Pulitzer Prize in poetry and a National Book Award in 1951. In the latter part of her life Moore received a host of awards and honors for her literary contributions, including the Poetry Society of America Gold Medal, the National Medal for Literature, and an honorary doctorate from Harvard University. Moore died February 5, 1972.

Major Works

Much of Moore's early verse is marked by stylistic originality, unique subject matter, and unconventional humor. Such poems as "Critics and Connoisseurs" and "Poetry" indicate her concerns with literature and art. One of the more striking pieces in *Observations*, "Marriage," a long experimental work written in free verse, features collage-like assemblages of quotations and fragments, using wit and satire to comment on the tensions of marital coexistence. Another poem from the same volume, "An Octopus," scrupulously describes the flora and fauna of Washington state's Mount Rainier, deriving its name from the shape of the glacier that surrounds the mountain peak; it is often regarded as one of the twentieth century's great odes to nature. *Selected Poems* features an introduction by Eliot and includes poems from *Observations* as well as pieces that had been published between 1932 and 1934. *The Pangolin and Other Verse* attests to Moore's interest in animals as subjects for art; *What Are Years* combines poems from *The Pangolin* with several previously uncollected works; and *Nevertheless* contains the highly regarded and much discussed "In Distrust of Merits," Moore's condemnation of the atrocities of war, which W. H. Auden singled out as the best of all the poems to emerge in reaction to World War II. Moore's later works include *Like a Bulwark* (1956), *O to Be a Dragon* (1959), *Tell Me, Tell Me: Granite, Steel, and Other Topics* (1966), and *The Complete Poems of Marianne Moore* (1967), which presents all of *Selected Poems*, several uncollected works, and selections from her translations, *Selected Fables of La Fontaine* (1955). However, many poems in the collection reveal extensive revisions, particularly "Poetry," which Moore reduced from its original thirty-one lines to only three. The dismay many critics expressed over this change was exacerbated by Moore's note in *Complete Poems*: "Omissions are not accidents—M. M."

Critical Reception

Although initial reviews of Moore's work were highly favorable, later criticism has varied. Critics have noted a distant, often sexless, perspective in all Moore's work. For instance, Gilbert Sorrentino dismissed her later work as contrived and detached from reality. Moore's poetry has been the subject of feminist criticism, too. Some feminists found her work exemplary of a strong female voice, highlighting specific elements of her poetry as well as her gender and prominence in literary society. Suzanne Juhasz, however, contended that Moore emerged as an important poet because she denied femininity and sexuality in her poetry. Others fault Moore for this denial, claiming that her disregard of gender and sexuality simply reinforce the limitations society places on women. Nonetheless, Moore is esteemed as one of the most important poets in modern literature. John Ashbery predicted that Moore's work "will continue to be read as poetry when much of the major poetry of our time has become part of the history of literature."

(For further information, see *Concise Dictionary of American Literary Biography:* 1929-1941; *Contemporary Authors,* Vols. 1-4R, 33-36R; *Contemporary Authors New Revision Series,* Vol. 3; *Contemporary Literary Criticism,* Vols. 1, 2, 4, 8, 10, 13, 19, 47; *Dictionary of Literary Biography Documentary Series,* Vol. 7; *Dictionary of Literary Biography,* Vol. 45; *DISCovering Authors; DISCovering Authors: British; DISCovering Authors: Canadian; DISCovering Authors Modules: Most-studied Authors Module, Poets Module; Major Twentieth-Century Writers; Poetry Criticism,* Vol. 4; *Something about the Author,* Vol. 20.)

CRITICAL COMMENTARY

T. S. ELIOT

SOURCE: T. S. Eliot, in an introduction to *Selected Poems* by Marianne Moore, The Macmillan Company, 1935, pp. vii-xiv.

[*Perhaps the most influential poet and critic to write in the English language during the first half of the twentieth century, Eliot is closely identified with many of the qualities denoted by the term Modernism: experimentation, formal complexity, artistic and intellectual eclecticism, and a classicist's view of the artist working at an emotional distance from his or her creation. He introduced a number*

Principal Works

Poems (poetry) 1921
Observations (poetry) 1924
Selected Poems (poetry) 1935
The Pangolin and Other Verse (poetry) 1936
What Are Years and Other Poems (poetry) 1941
Nevertheless (poetry) 1944
Collected Poems (poetry) 1951
Predilections (essays and reviews) 1955
Selected Fables of La Fontaine [translator] (fables) 1955; revised edition published as *The Fables of La Fontaine*, 1964
Like a Bulwark (poetry) 1956
Idiosyncrasy and Technique: Two Lectures (lectures) 1958
O to Be a Dragon (poetry) 1959
A Marianne Moore Reader (poetry) 1961
The Absentee: A Comedy in Four Acts (drama) 1962
The Arctic Ox (poetry) 1964
A Talisman (poetry) 1965
Tell Me, Tell Me: Granite, Steel, and Other Topics (poetry and prose) 1966
The Complete Poems of Marianne Moore (poetry) 1967; revised edition, 1981
Selected Poems (poetry) 1969
Unfinished Poems (poetry) 1972
The Complete Prose of Marianne Moore (prose) 1986

---

of terms and concepts that strongly affected critical thought in his lifetime, among them the idea that poets must be conscious of the living tradition of literature in order for their work to have artistic and spiritual validity. In general, Eliot upheld values of traditionalism and discipline, and in 1928 he annexed Christian theology to his overall conservative worldview. His best-known poems include "The Love Song of J. Alfred Prufrock" and The Waste Land (1922). In the excerpt below, Eliot discusses what he believed to be Moore's significant contributions not only to poetry but to the English language.]

I am aware that prejudice makes me underrate certain authors: I see them rather as public enemies than as subjects for criticism; and I dare say that a different prejudice makes me uncritically favourable to others. I may even admire the right authors for the wrong reasons. But I am much more confident of my appreciation of the authors whom I admire, than of my depreciation of the authors who leave me cold or who exasperate me. And in asserting that what I call *genuineness* is a more important thing to recognise in a contemporary than *greatness*, I am distinguishing between his function while living and his function when dead. Living, the poet is carrying on that struggle for the maintenance of a living language, for the maintenance of its strength, its subtlety, for the preservation of quality of feeling, which must be kept up in every generation; dead, he provides standards for those who take up the struggle after him. Miss Moore is, I believe, one of those few who have done the language some service in my lifetime.

So far back as my memory extends, which is to the pages of *The Egoist* during the War, and of *The Little Review* and *The Dial* in the years immediately following, Miss Moore has no immediate poetic derivations. I cannot, therefore, fill up my pages with the usual account of influences and development. There is one early poem, **"A Talisman,"** which I will quote in full here, because it suggests a slight influence of H. D. [Hilda Doolittle], certainly of H. D. rather than of any other 'Imagist':

>Under a splintered mast
>Torn from the ship and cast
>   Near her hull,
>
>A stumbling shepherd found
>Embedded in the ground,
>   A sea-gull
>
>Of lapis-lazuli,
>A scarab of the sea,
>   With wings spread—
>
>Curling its coral feet,
>Parting its beak to greet
>   Men long dead.

The sentiment is commonplace, and I cannot see what a bird carved of *lapis-lazuli* should be doing with *coral* feet; but even here the cadence, the use of rhyme, and a certain authoritativeness of manner distinguish the poem. Looking at Miss Moore's poems of a slightly later period, I should say that she had taken to heart the repeated reminder of Mr. Pound: that poetry should be as well written as prose. She seems to have saturated her mind in the perfections of prose, in its precision rather than its purple; and to have found her rhythm, her poetry, her appreciation of the individual word, for herself.

The first aspect in which Miss Moore's poetry is likely to strike the reader is that of minute detail rather than that of emotional unity. The gift for detailed observation, for finding the exact words for some experience of the eye, is liable to disperse the attention of the relaxed reader. The minutiae may even irritate the unwary, or arouse in them only the pleasurable astonishment evoked by the carved ivory ball with eleven other balls inside it, the full-rigged ship in a bottle, the skeleton of the crucifix-fish. The bewilderment consequent upon trying to follow so alert an eye, so quick a process of association, may produce the effect of some 'metaphysical' poetry. To the moderately intellectual the poems may appear to be intellectual exercises; only to those whose intellection moves more easily will they immediately appear to have emotional value. But the detail has always its service to perform to the whole. The similes are there for use; as the mussel-shell 'opening and shutting itself like an injured fan', . . . the waves 'as formal as the scales on a fish'. They make us see the object more clearly, though we may not understand immediately why our attention has been called to this object, and though we may not immediately grasp its association with a number of other objects. So, in her amused and affectionate attention to animals—from the domestic cat, or 'to popularize the mule', to the most exotic strangers from the tropics, she succeeds at once in startling us into an unusual awareness of visual patterns, with something like the fascination of a high-powered microscope.

Miss Moore's poetry, or most of it, might be classified as 'descriptive' rather than 'lyrical' or 'dramatic'. Descriptive poetry is supposed to be dated to a period, and to be condemned thereby; but it is really one of the permanent modes of expression. In the eighteenth century—or say a period which includes *Cooper's Hill*, *Windsor Forest*, and Gray's *Elegy*—the scene described is a point of departure for meditations on one thing or another. The poetry of the Romantic Age, from Byron at his worst to Wordsworth at his best, wavers between the reflective and the evocative; but the description, the picture set before you, is always there for the same purpose. The aim of 'imagism', so far as I understand it, or so far as it had any, was to induce a peculiar concentration upon something visual, and to set in motion an expanding succession of concentric feelings. Some of Miss Moore's poems—for instance with animal or bird subjects—have a very wide spread of association. It would be difficult to say what is the 'subject-matter' of **"The Jerboa."** For a mind of such agility, and for a sensibility so reticent, the minor subject, such as a pleasant little sand-coloured skipping animal, may be the best release for the major emotions. Only the pedantic literalist could consider the subject-matter to be trivial; the triviality is in himself. We all have to choose whatever subject-matter allows us the most powerful and most secret release; and that is a personal affair.

The result is often something that the majority will call frigid; for to feel things in one's own way, however intensely, is likely to look like frigidity to those who can only feel in accepted ways.

> The deepest feeling always shows itself in
>   silence;
> not in silence, but restraint.

It shows itself in a control which makes possible the fusion of the ironic-conversational and the high-rhetorical, as

> I recall their magnificence, now not more
>   magnificent
> than it is dim. It is difficult to recall the ornament,
> speech, and precise manner of what one
>   might
>   call the minor acquaintances twenty
>   years back. . . .
>
> strict with tension, malignant
> in its power over us and deeper
>   than the sea when it proffers flattery in exchange
>   for hemp,
> rye, flax, horses, platinum, timber and fur.

As one would expect from the kind of activity which I have been trying to indicate, Miss Moore's versification is anything but 'free'. Many of the poems are in exact, and sometimes complicated formal patterns, and move with the elegance of a minuet. ('Elegance', indeed, is one of her certain attributes.) Some of the poems (e.g. **"Marriage"**, **"An Octopus"**) are unrhymed; in others (e.g. **"Sea Unicorns and Land Unicorns"**) rhyme or assonance is introduced irregularly; in a number of the poems rhyme is part of a regular pattern interwoven with unrhymed endings. Miss Moore's use of rhyme is in itself a definite innovation in metric.

In the conventional forms of rhyme the stress given by the rhyme tends to fall in the same place as the stress given by the sense. The extreme case, at its best, is the pentameter couplet of Pope. Poets before and after Pope have given variety, sometimes at the expense of smoothness, by deliberately separating the stresses, from time to time; but this separation—often effected simply by longer periods or more involved syntax—can hardly be considered as more than a deviation from the norm for the purpose of avoiding monotony. The tendency of some of the best contemporary poetry is of course to dispense with rhyme altogether; but some of those who do use it have used it here and there to make a pattern directly in contrast with the sense and rhythm pattern, to give a greater intricacy. Some of the internal rhyming of Hopkins is to the point. (Genuine or auditory internal rhyme must not be confused with false or visual internal rhyme. If a poem reads just as well when cut up so that all the rhymes fall at the end of lines, then the internal rhyme is false and only a typographical caprice, as in Oscar Wilde's *Sphynx*.) This rhyme, which forms a pattern *against* the metric and sense pattern of the poem, may be either heavy or light—that is to say, either *heavier* or *lighter* than the other pattern. The two kinds, heavy and light, have doubtless different uses which remain to be explored. Of the *light* rhyme Miss Moore is the greatest living master; and indeed she is the first, so far as I know, who has investigated its possibilities. It will be observed that the effect sometimes requires giving a word a slightly more analytical pronunciation, or stressing a syllable more than ordinarily:

>   al-
>   ways has been—at the antipodes from the init-
>   ial great truths. 'Part of it was crawling, part
>   of it
>   was about to crawl, the rest
>   was torpid in its lair.' In the short-legged, fit-
>   ful advance. . . .

It is sometimes obtained by the use of articles as rhyme words:

>   an
>   injured fan.
>   The barnacles which encrust the side
>   of the wave, cannot hide . . .
>   the
>   turquoise sea
>   of bodies. The water drives a wedge . . .

In a good deal of what is sometimes (with an unconscious theological innuendo) called 'modernist' verse one finds either an excess or a defect of technical attention. The former appears in an emphasis upon words rather than things, and the latter in an emphasis upon things and an indifference to words. In either case, the poem is formless, just as the most accomplished sonnet, if it is an attempt to express matter unsuitable for sonnet form, is formless. But a precise fitness of form and matter mean also a balance between them: thus the form, the pattern movement, has a solemnity of its own (e.g. Shakespeare's songs), however light and gay the human emotion concerned; and a gaiety of its own, however serious or tragic the emotion. The choruses of Sophocles, as well as the songs of Shakespeare, have another concern besides the human action of which they are spectators, and without this other concern there is not poetry. And on the other hand, if you aim only at the poetry in poetry, there is no poetry either.

My conviction, for what it is worth, has remained unchanged for the last fourteen years: that Miss Moore's poems form part of the small body of durable poetry written in our time; of that small body of writings, among what passes for poetry, in which an original sensibility and alert intelligence and deep feeling have been engaged in maintaining the life of the English language.

WALLACE FOWLIE

SOURCE: Wallace Fowlie, "Marianne Moore," in *The Sewanee Review*, Vol. LX, No. 3, Summer, 1952, pp. 537-47.

[*Fowlie is among the most respected scholars of French literature. His work includes translations of major poets and dramatists of France and critical studies of the major figures and movements of modern French letters. Broad intellectual and artistic sympathies, along with an acute sensitivity for French writing and a firsthand understanding of literary creativity, are hallmarks of his career. In the excerpt below, he extols Moore's poetic form, subject matter, and linguistic style.*]

The world was made to end in a poem, as Mallarme taught, and as Marianne Moore illustrates in each of the seventy-one **Collected Poems,** composed during the past thirty years and published in England and America just after the turn of the mid-century, in 1951. She owes nothing, specifically, to other poets, and yet she was preceded by a host of eminent poets. Her will, as courageously as that of any other modern poet's will, has been focused on the naming of all the objects in the world which are not to be forgotten. Her poetry is an extraordinary manifestation, a song of that reality by means of which man attaches himself firmly to the entire universe. . . .

The first impression in reading a Marianne Moore poem is that of following a movement which must adhere to a concerted, and often, complex design. It is the experiencing of a construction. The lines support one another and explain one another and all move upward toward the reconstruction of the whole. But one learns, in reading her, that the immediate lines do not exhaust what they say, that they announce a secret end, a higher degree of accomplishment. This is as true of the early poems, such as **"The Fish"** . . . as it is of the later poems where in some instances the poet speaks directly of the world's "sick scene."

>   These, laid like animals for sacrifice,
>   like Isaac on the mount, were their own substitute.
>
>   **("Keeping their world large")**

The exceptional gravity of these poems comes, perhaps, from their secret end, never explicitly defined, but which remains with them, in some restless unsatisfied form, a complement of the full verbal expression. The poems are the words, so competently, so exquisitely arranged on the page itself, but they are consigned to the reader by the poet in some secret kind of treaty signed with a future belief in common understanding. Doctrine could be extricated from this poetry only with the greatest labor, and yet it is poetry manifesting the progress of a soul, announcing in its own particular resonance the story of a life.

The acceptance of the physical world, when it is as vibrant and accurate as in these poems, may be quite as "mystical" as any rejection of the world. Mystics of all beliefs have vacillated between embracing the fullness of the world, or renouncing it. The vision of the poet is likewise double, likewise seemingly contradictory. Everything may be represented outside the soul or consumed within it. Such deliberate coolness of rhythm and rhyme, such precise weight and density of syllables, combine knowledge with prudence in degrees that seem almost equal. The atmosphere of each poem ends by becoming a desert. The humility of this spirit is religious, not only when she writes of the "Sahara field-mouse" **("The Jerboa")**, but when she writes of such an experience as war:

>   There is hate's crown beneath which all is death.
>   **("In distrust of merits")**

Each poem is self-contained in much the same way as this poet is the prisoner of her own substance. Miss Moore's poetry testifies at every step to this very principle, whereby song becomes more total, more unified, as the spiritual concentration deepens. The work is patient and even cruel at times in its constant measuring of the poet's relationship with the world. Claudel's celebration of the world is sung with greater magnificence, by means of his more overtly expressed religious faith, but Miss Moore's is perhaps more vigilant and pathetic. She is a strong defender of the world of beings and objects, no detail of which is useless.

There are few writers who have a clearer and more penetrating awareness of the means, the purpose, the significance of their art than Marianne Moore. Yet her attitude is not "aesthetic" in any narrow sense of the word. It is not the result of some historical or dialectical theory which joins her with any particular group or literary school. She has something to say and she is unable not to say it. I rather imagine that only when she is saying it, does she discover that her cause is one with the cause of many of her contemporaries. She hardly believes in the ancient theory of Inspiration which makes of the poet the blind instrument of the gods or of the muses. The intellect presides over the creation of this poetry, seeking to overcome or circumvent all the obstacles that may exist between the idea and the achievement. And yet under the appearance of the poem's problem, under the intellectual demonstration of the poem's surface, there is a frenzy and a living source, which in Marianne Moore's case are almost invisible. She has not created her poetic universe with the sole resource of her intelligence.

The critics and the poets who have written about Miss Moore's poetry . . . have all been struck by the strict economy of her images. The next step in the critical analysis of her work should be the study of how far she has extended, and in some degree of violence, the field of our memory, of the vast effort of memory she forces on her readers. The forms of her favorite animals help to create an illusion almost of centuries. In verse this work has its parallels with the paintings of Hieronymous Bosch and the Breughels. The elements she describes are not always familiar to our immediate memory, and the arabesques of the spaces surrounding these favorite forms are organized into a composition of endless little scenes. Flowers, insects, fish, all help to describe the freedom of nature, and their poems help to describe a living contemplation, a permanent love. But the fantasy of the mind has its laws as surely as biological evolution. . . .

Miss Moore's experimentation with English prosody is quite in keeping with this possible theory of her "poetic inspiration." Its basis is surely in the center of life, in the concrete world, in spoken language, in experience. Her research leads her much farther than the mere use of sounds in their rhythmical function. It is more elemental, in the utilization of their substance, of their verbal hardness. The mouth itself, rather than the ears, is the judge of the pleasure of articulation. It only is able to weight and feel the words as they are chosen by the poet. I imagine that a phonetician could measure the points of articulation which dictated a given verse. The origin of such a "poetic act" lies surely in vital depths where flesh becomes speech.

Most contemporary poets are also theorists of poetry. The practice of their art seems to be at the same time the exercise of a will to consider poetry not merely as an end in itself but as a means of knowledge which may even extend beyond thought itself. In this respect Marianne Moore demonstrates none of the metaphysical anguish we associate with Rimbaud or Mallarmé.

But she is the kind of poet who experiences what others discern. Every poet yearns for more participation than his individual existence will allow. His cry is often that of someone dismembered. The poet begins always with his solitude of which each poem in some way is a transformation....

The poet's solitude is no moral place. The shades invading it grow more and more real, and the poet's faith speaks of them finally without reticence. Marianne Moore in our day has become one of the most skilled mediators between the objects of a poet's solitude and objects in the outer world. What a miraculous absence of antagonism between the exterior world and the world of this poet's imagination! Her poetry defines poetic activity by being it. So many of our contemporary debates on the means of poetry, on the degree of reality, on the conditions for its appearance, are here resolved by their very manifestation. She reconciles without effort the two great antagonistic views of poetry: the hard specific labor advocated by the classical poets, and the exaltation of "dictated" verse believed in by the romantics. Reconciled to the advantage, it is true, of the classical labor. One sees in Marianne Moore's poetry objects resembling a carriage made in Sweden more often than a dark sky pierced with lightning.

"Classical," then, and endowed with a highly critical spirit, Miss Moore gives the impression of maintaining a continual surveillance over self, on the alert at all times, and refusing to accept as real whatever exceeds her conscience and her consciousness, in a fear, perhaps, of losing hold of the object for its shadow, and of giving consent to an extreme or an unwarranted rashness. The poet must be, for her and for every classically-minded poet, the master of his instrument.

If her poetry, according to this definition, does illustrate the classical mode, it is warmly human in its descent toward the reader, in its appeasement and reassurance. Between readers and what they might consider modern poetry, these poems establish a dyke. What might appear in other poets as capricious and confused, is here lucid and organized. The animals are in a cage and the fish in an aquarium....

I do not believe Miss Moore the kind of poet who is innocent or optimistic or unarmed. If she senses the advent of an enemy, she is quite capable of poisoning her arrows and mining her territory. She is able to give to the meekest of words an unusual pressure and explosive power. The act of writing is always for her, I would say, a sign that she is present in front of the enemy who, although he is nameless, will not surprise her.

The poet's language remains a permanent defiance to the laws of human communication. It is a violation of language in the sense that it tries always to speak the ineffable and ends by creating some kind of form around the ineffable. Miss Moore, in a justly celebrated line, writes

> Ecstasy affords
> the occasion and expediency determines the
> form.
> **("The past is the present")**

The solidity of the poem's form and its precisely impeccable appearance on the page, are compensations for what cannot be said, for the indecipherable part of every poem's genesis. In this effort to give language a meaning, the spontaneity of pure verbalism is far surpassed. The equivocal nature of poetry lies precisely in this tendency to subjugate by language what exists outside of language. No poet is more respectful of this equivocation than Miss Moore, or more knowing of the principle of poetry whereby the explicable is married with the inexplicable.

The "genuineness" of Miss Moore's poetry, referred to by Eliot, Burke and Blackmur as having to do with the literalness of her vision, may be explained in a slightly different way. It seems to me to concern the poetic act itself, namely to converting into formal language what is by essence unfamiliar to language....

Over and over again, Miss Moore chooses for the subject matter of her poetry the ordinary, the factual, the trite, and reveals about them something incomprehensible which had been heretofore missed. This is her personal way of explaining miracles.... The pleasures she provides are those of a world perpetually new. In the flash of a line she can often help us to see something new about our human condition. She provides us therefore with what must be called the poetic form of knowledge. She refuses resolutely to substitute for the real world a world of fantasy or dream. The daily world cannot exhaust our need for surprise. The real poet is a greater mathematician than a dreamer, she keeps telling us. The dignity of the poetic act is in its rigor, its high responsibility, its will to move beyond the commonplace. It is demiurgic in the sense that it endows language with something more than its usual power. The naming of each object in this verse has almost a baptismal seriousness. Whereas we can look at these same objects in the world with considerable indifference, we contemplate them in the poems with unexpected fervor. They are the same, but they have been transformed.

The lessons on poetry which this poetic work provides are not facile, but they are central and well worth the trouble of exploring. I don't believe that Marianne Moore is telling us that the poet necessarily prefers the difficult. (In some way or other the problem of "obscurity" returns each century.) The poet certainly doesn't write in order not to be understood. But he does address his poems to those who have a knowledge somewhat comparable to his, and a turn of mind like his. The poet's land stretches out between language and meaning, between the simple power of speech and the universal mystery it conceals. This concealed light when it suddenly flashes before the astonished reader or listener is the poem's miracle. A poem of Marianne Moore's has its periods of waiting, for its final surprise, as any common melodrama. As poetic language moves from comparatively simple speech toward the inexhaustible regions behind speech, the poem is engendered in a dazzling effulgence. . . .

The *Collected Poems* of Marianne Moore seem to be inhabited by an ever-present need of purification and reduction. If the scrupulosity of this poet has been defined by some as being Protestant-American by nature, it can be defined also as belonging to a more universal and modern view of poetics which is a process of deleting the uselessly poetical without ever impoverishing the fundamental vigor. . . .

Miss Moore brings to American poetry, after the theories of Poe and the efforts of the imagists, her own passion for poetic purity, expressed in a desire to rid her poetry of whatever is not really hers, to circumscribe her art to such an extent that only what has been tested and verified is allowed to appear on the printed page. This will to deliver poetry from some of the romantic exaggerations comes from a poetic conscience which may also be puritanical. The good it has done American poetry cannot be overestimated. More traditionally, poetic purity has been sought in extreme forms of simplicity (or clarity) and hermeticism. Miss Moore's art is never one or the other extreme. It is poetry more concerned with creation than effusion, with construction rather than freedom. The tradition of Poe was to make of poetry a pure kind of music. With Marianne Moore we learn all over again that poetry is not music, but language. . . .

This is "new" poetry, but not created through any simple need for innovation. Its character of newness has unquestionably something to do with its particular search for poetic purity. Marianne Moore combines a need for continuity and a will for discontinuity, a recognizable scientific definition and a new unprecedented relationship. What Miss Moore eradicates from traditional poetics and established modes had already entered a phase of sterility. A literary revolution, like a political one, never takes place in a period of fullness. Like most innovators, Miss Moore has only a very imperfect awareness of what she has done and of the extent of her goal. Her poems will have to be surrounded by more time for any explicit measurement of their relationship with the past and the present, but that measurement will have something to do with the explicit need for renovation which American poetry felt during the second quarter of the Twentieth Century.

A certain transparent dignity was reestablished in American poetry in such a poem, for example, as **"In distrust of merits."** Miss Moore's poems stood quite alone for some years, different in their formal rigor from other poetry, until now they have relegated into an historical past the poetry with which they first contrasted, and have grown into some of the fixed patterns of our contemporary poetic conscience. But far more than answering the need of releasing poetry from the outmoded, Marianne Moore's writing answers the need for creation, which in poetry is always the discovering for a work what is suitable and right for its expression. What is most personal to Marianne Moore as a poet coincides miraculously with the purest and most durable forms of the English language. The magic she has performed has to do with the coexistence of an inner elaboration and an exterior form lucidly communicable.

TAFFY WYNNE MARTIN

SOURCE: Taffy Wynne Martin, "Marianne Moore's 'Foiled Explosiveness,'" in *Virginia Quarterly Review*, Volume 58, Number 4, Autumn, 1982, pp. 733-45.

[*In the following excerpt, Martin analyzes the 1981 edition of* Complete Poems, *hailing Moore for challenging traditional notions of poetry.*]

[Marianne Moore's] work is as difficult as it is distinctive. A puzzle to her friends and a challenge to her critics, Moore was either savagely attacked or nearly enshrined by her contemporaries. Her quaint facade and extraordinarily conventional life, which baffled and occasionally infuriated those who envied her discipline and admired her productivity, eventually gained as much attention as her convoluted poetry. In subsequent years, Moore's tame public image seems even to have affected her critical reputation. . . . [The] recent publication of her *Complete Poems* is a welcome event. Like its predecessor [*Collected Poems*], this volume remains quite deliberately incomplete and offers a corrective but not yet a full solution to the predicament. . . .

Although these late poems, along with those collected after 1951, are a welcome addition to the available Moore canon, the new *Complete Poems* is not an entirely satisfactory edition of her work. Moore's working habits were such—she revised her poems incessantly, usually shortening them, often ruthlessly—that by the time some work appeared in *Complete Poems*, it had been revised almost beyond recognition. Some pieces disappeared entirely. Certainly Moore's own cryptic introduction to the volume, "Omissions are not accidents. M.M.," failed, even in 1969 to satisfy the many readers who objected to her rigorous editing. Their dissatisfaction was well-founded. Moore revised **"Poetry"** almost beyond recognition, including in her "Notes" what the new *Complete Poems* calls the "longer version" but omitting several other significant drafts which are essential to a study of her poetry.

Although this poem is unusual since Moore's changes in it are so drastic and so numerous, the baroque history of her poems and the byzantine workings of her mind cannot be appreciated until more of her work is available, regardless of what her "final intentions" may have been. When a truly *Complete Poems*, which includes all of the important versions of those pieces Moore changed most drastically finally appears, we shall see a more complex, less easily stereotyped Marianne Moore than is possible at present.

For instance, in **"Melancthon,"** which does not appear in either edition of *Complete Poems*, Moore armors some remarkable statements in the words of an animal-speaker, a practice common to many of her poems. Her speaker, an elephant, is Black Earth (the title of the poem at one point), "black glass through which no light / can filter," and impenetrable "soul which shall never / be cut into / by wooden spear." But the speaker is also Melancthon (Philip), Martin Luther's colleague who longed to be liberated from the "wrath of the theologians" and who tempered the Reformation with humanism. This double perspective, so much a part of Moore's subject is, in part, the difficulty of communicating, particularly through language. At one point the poem presents both the necessity and the difficulty of acknowledging and of incorporating another's perspective while remaining oneself....

[Even] without the powerful statements of **"Melancthon,"** the new *Complete Poems* presents a Marianne Moore much enamored of complexities of any sort. She repeatedly denies the possibility of simplification and offers instead arguments for multiple perspective, unresolvable contradiction, and—that "savage's romance"—"accessibility to experience." Her perspective was so inclusive, her point of view so likely to shift and detour at a moment's notice, that in some poems it is almost impossible not to become lost in the confusion which she presents with absolute precision. Such is the case, although in different ways, with two early poems—her two longest—**"Marriage"** and **"An Octopus."** In **"Marriage"** Moore examines with unremitting equanimity and precision

> This institution,
> perhaps one should say enterprise
> out of respect for which
> one says one need not change one's mind
> about a thing one has believed in,
> requiring public promises
> of one's intention
> to fulfil a private obligation:

One devastating anecdote follows another as Moore exposes the undertaking as preposterous and painful. Again, as in **"Melancthon,"** there exists the dilemma of both attempting and withdrawing from communication.... In the attempt at "this amalgamation which can never be more / than an interesting impossibility," neither party escapes her scorn. Failure seems predetermined....

The relentless and impartial dispassion with which Moore presents the "institution" offers as the best possible hope the half success of "cycloid inclusiveness," a "striking grasp of opposites / opposed each to the other, not to unity...." Her refusal to offer even the slightest hope of resolution intensifies throughout the poem. Having already established that there can be no answer, Moore asks:

> What can one do for them
> these savages
> condemned to disaffect
> all those who are not visionaries
> alert to undertake the silly task
> of making people noble?

Since nothing can be done to aid the self-deluded, Moore ruthlessly concludes that this naive but mistaken belief in the efficacy of "public promises ... to fulfil a private obligation," dictates that "the statesmanship / of an archaic Daniel Webster / persists to their simplicity of temper / as the essence of the matter." Meaningless contradiction, a passive symbol of church or state, and the withdrawal of personal contact close the poem as her enigmatic representation of "the essence of the matter...."

This is Moore presenting confusion and deluded vision at its most devastating, but it is also a rare exception. More commonly she focuses on contradiction and complexity as positive qualities. As if to counter the effect of the dismal mood of **"Marriage,"** Moore follows the shock of her conclusion with another long, dense poem, **"An Octopus,"** which begins somewhat ominously but turns quickly into a delighted appreciation of the indecipherable density of Mt. Tacoma's glacier. Every specimen of disarray offers a form of delight, precisely because of its inherent contradiction....

[Delusion is not so devastating] in **"An Octopus,"** where the density of growth makes vision difficult, even misleading, but pleasurable.... Thus it is pleasant to discover that "Completing a circle, / you have been deceived into thinking that you have progressed." In fact, the confusion "prejudices you in favor of itself." Throughout this poem, Moore holds in suspension and demonstrates the simultaneity of two opposing qualities of the glacier. "Damned for its sacrosanct remoteness," it presents a challenge to those who would "'conquer the main peak of Mount Tacoma.'" Nevertheless, combined with that remoteness, "Relentless accuracy is the nature of this octopus / with its capacity for fact." Offering partial shelter, the mountain "receives one under winds that 'tear the snow to bits / and hurl it like a sandblast / shearing off twigs and loose bark from the trees." It also challenges its visitors' perceptions.... The poem ends with an explosion of motion which emphasizes the mysterious calm and self-possession of the mountain even in the midst of unpredictable violence. She persuades us to "believe it / despite reason to think not."

Moore's later poems make it increasingly clear that she presents contradiction in a deliberate attempt to undermine not only our expectations but every attempt at and every supposition of reason....

Concealed power, particularly as it turns toward implosion, so dominates her late poems that they become almost impenetrable. When those poems turn to epigram, as they often do, the foil works so effectively and the clipped endings so dominate that many poems have been dismissed as embarrassing, lamely occasional works, devoid of power. Another look is now in order. It will reveal that in her late works, while continuing with her early subjects such as armoring, complexity, and the difficulty of accurate perception, Moore also persisted in her attempt to undermine every expectation of what poetry is and can do. That is her subject in **"Baseball and Writing / Suggested by post-game broadcasts,"** which takes her use of quotations beyond what she described as "lines in which the chief interest is borrowed."

That poem captures in a riotous but absolutely controlled volley of observations and partial quotations from innumerable viewpoints the rapidly shifting perceptions and moods of a baseball game and the fragmentary nature of broadcast coverage of games. In what might serve as an apologia for her difficult style, Moore opens the poem by anticipating and answering a question.

> Fanaticism? No. Writing is exciting
> and baseball is like writing.
>   You can never tell with either
>   how it will go
>   or what you will do:

What Moore did was unlike the work of any other poet of the past decade. Her verse, at times intricately patterned and at others expansive and sprawling, contained precise, half-hidden, internal, and off rhymes. Her subjects ranged from contemporary politics to scientific discovery, and the "Notes" she provided to document her "hybrid method of composition" sometimes raise more questions than the poems themselves. She has consistently been recognized as a craftsman, but she was far more than that. Marianne Moore used the relentless accuracy of her craft to challenge and to subvert every preconception of poetic discourse....

GILBERT SORRENTINO

SOURCE: Gilbert Sorrentino, "An Octopus / of Ice," in *Something Said*, North Point Press, 1984, pp. 157-66.

[*A respected American novelist, poet, and editor, Sorrentino has also gained notice as a critic of considerable insight. In the following excerpt, he examines what he believes to be Moore's literary decline with the publication of* Complete Poems.]

From an elegant, restrained, restricted verse of enormous glitter and craft to the greeting-card doggerel of a dear old lady—such is the progress of Marianne Moore's ***Complete Poems***. It is a volume that paralyzes the reader with sadness. A poet, presented as "major," who has worked for half a century, has avoided confronting, even once, in her entire body of work, the fact that the nation is brutalized, corrupted, and perhaps hopelessly psychopathic. But the clearly inept verse of the later books is strikingly prefigured in her early work. What happened to Miss Moore is that the costuming gave out; the language failed her. And the language failed her because it lost any touch with the reality that language bears. Miss Moore retreated from life; and her language retreated with her, until it finally died, it finally became good copy, bright and slick and incapable of carrying emotion to the page, to the reader. But since the poet had no emotion save that of the most bitterly conformist, no response but that which is the expected one in this time of the planned tear, the carefully bizarre, the language fits the poem to perfection.

What it is, really, is that the verse was always rooted in itself, i.e., was verse as artifact, as protection for the "refined" sensibilities of the poet. So the poem wore itself out upon itself as the poet grew older and further removed from the world. It is hideous to listen to the claptrap concerning Miss Moore's baseball fanaticism being an instance of her interest in the "regular things." It has nothing to do with what is true. It is a luxury for silly people. If Miss Moore could not, and would not, and most certainly did not engage the real when her juices were flowing, how much less could she do so in her old age: the poem, which sustained itself, sucked its own substance for nourishment, wore itself out over the years, grinding on itself, grinding itself to death. Miss Moore cast about for subject matter outside her own human terrors and desire and meanness—outside, that is, her own humanity, much like a classy Ogden Nash. The formal structuring of the poem, set in motion to poeticize the Brooklyn Dodgers, or Yul Brynner, or some footnoted speaker of some dull cliche, fell into cuteness, the scribbling of a harmless old eccentric. But this is the final product of what began as a harmless young eccentric. (Who knows how harmless?)

The formal composition of the early poems had a value to it: it made sense, that is, aesthetically. The prosy slabs with the careful internal rhyme, the subtle end rhymes, the enjambement used with such precision that the rhymes were muted and rang in the head alone, while devoid of the nervous energy of Williams' early work and the nobility of Pound's, had their verve, their poetic rationale. In the late poems, with the language drained of charge, the "look" of the poems is the same in many instances; but the sound, the formality of the made work is lacking. To compensate for her failed language, Miss Moore used the old suits in the closet. You can check, for example, **"The Steeple-Jack"** against **"Rescue with Yul Brynner"** for an exhibit of decadence.

But there are many other such exhibits. The wretched doggerel of **"Baseball and Writing"**; **"I May, I Might, I Must"** which hardly displaces the white of the page; . . . **"Hometown Piece for Messers Alston and Reese."** These are not simply the flagging energies of a tired poet displayed. The reason for the dreary failure of this work is that it is the perfect culmination of the Moore "machine" slowly coming to a halt—and it is indeed a machine that Miss Moore has been at work on all these years, one of glass. And although it still glitters with the look of beauty, and delicacy, and careful attention to detail, the machine is, after all, a toy. As it was from the start.

What is specifically salient about Miss Moore's poems? First, there is no sexuality. Which is incredible—i.e., that she should avoid such a basic human situation. So there are few men and women, those that exist are resplendent in their flat dimensions, clothed in the finery of the slow profundity. (Which takes the place of sex?) They are statues, or they are safely dead; they are ghostly words of wisdom, "Superior people never make long visits . . ." and "The deepest feeling always shows itself in silence; / not in silence, but restraint." Which, apart from the fact that both of these statements are patently untrue, except in Miss Moore's subworld, that is, the world where such dilettantish eccentricity passes for engagement and "trouble," are interesting in the use of "superior"—who are *they*? We know, though, who they are. They're the people who stand outside the world, annoyed at trifles, life a congeries of good manners. And "restraint" is, of course, like "continence." Thus, the whole crushing microcosm of Marianne Moore's universe, made clear in a very early poem.

What else? The animals are always pointed out as Miss Moore's private domain. Yet a look at the animal poems is enlightening because they come through, finally, as creatures out of Walt Disney. A bitterly ironic poem is the one, **"Peter,"** with the last lines

> To tell the hen: fly over the fence, go in the
>   wrong way in your perturbation—this is life;
> to do less would be nothing but dishonesty.

—which agrees with the need for the cat to maim and destroy the hen, since that is his nature. Yet the "nature" of Miss Moore's poems is such use of it as to defend her very life, her heart, against all the incursions of a *human* nature as terribly compelling. She uses the exotic animal and the exotic habits of commonplace animals (with all their animalism removed) to draw pretty conclusions about a world which the animals, and myself, do not recognize—because it does not exist except within the shining machine of words.

In **"Critics and Connoisseurs,"** she sweetly scolds against "conscious fastidiousness" using a metaphorical swan who was guilty of this. Miss Moore deprecates the swan's actions, drawing the moral to extend to the human world. She brings an ant in, to the same effect. She does not like this kind of *person* and springs upon that attitude by using these picture postcard animals, these Walt Disney creations. (Who really did the same sort of dishonest thing in his anthropomorphic obsessions.) It is not, at this point, that one is complaining about anthropomorphism: it is that the animals are so *used*, lacking much of their juices. Miss Moore's cat, springing after the hen, will rend, slaughter, and tear the hen to bits when caught. This is also his nature, though this is the part of it that she will not see. The **"Critics and Connoisseurs"** works the same way. How can a poet *ask* of the humanized ant, what good the "experience of carrying a stick" is? She asks because the ant does not please her; he is metaphorically at fault in his "nature." The cat is not, so long as he doesn't engage in the ultimate rending.

A final note on this poem: She says, "Disbelief and conscious fastidiousness were / ingredients in its / disinclination to move." If Miss Moore's poems are not examples of "conscious fastidiousness," then what are they? Perhaps, at this time, she was struggling with herself, for it is in this book, published in 1935, that she includes **"The Fish,"** her best poem, with its absolutely awed, non-cute sense of the terror and evil inherent in the creation. There was never to be another poem like it.

The poems, as suggested, refuse to admit that living people live. One recalls William Carlos Williams defending his *Paterson IV* against Miss Moore's attack: "To me the world is something which to you must seem foreign. I won't defend my world. I live in it. Those I find there have all the qualities which inform those about them who are luckier," thinking, here, I'd guess, of himself as one of "those who are luckier." But Miss Moore does not, nor did she ever, want to be informed—to her, Lesbianism is evil and foul, so it does not exist. It is not for the poet to treat. I will be careful to state here that I do not take issue with Miss Moore's right as a poet to select her materials—but when the selection *grazes* that which lives, when it selects, then, from these living things, those qualities which render them nonliving, a mere projection of Miss Moore's hazy fantasy about what the world is, this selection is pernicious and ultimately destructive of the poem.

The fear of life, it seems obvious, is not really the same as being distrustful of life, or bitter about it. Nor is it the same as *being afraid*. One can be afraid, and *in life*—Miss Moore fears the entire slate, she withdraws herself and her poem, she scolds. **"In the Days of Prismatic Color,"** which I take to be her aesthetic, says:

> Principally throat, sophistication is as it always
> has been—at the antipodes from the initial great
> truths.

Which leads the reader to two points: What are these poems if not "sophistication"?—and, what does Miss Moore think the "initial great truths" are? The cat who stops short of killing? The "superior people" who don't stay too long? The ant with his stick, baldly anthropomorphized to use in a metaphorical or allegorical battering? Or is "the quadrille of Old Russia" as against "a documentary / of Cossacks" the truer image of reality? It is, of course, not an obeisance to "truths" at all that she cares for; it is an instance of Miss Moore's despair at the world which does not care about her Walt Disney creatures and her fantastic politics: people do not die; ideas die. (And a lot of them are such *nice* ideas.) Or people die so that ideas (Miss Moore's) may live and find their way into poems which are ideational set-pieces about people who are unconnected to reality....

The poems truly take on, beginning with *Like A Bulwark* (1956), the cadence and shine of ad copy. They engage "subject" since there has been, for years, nothing left to engage, and the "subject" is the "Real Thing." Here is the beginning of Miss Moore's status as "beloved poet." Poetry, loved by everyone, loved by those who never read poetry, is produced. If one accepts the facade of America, as in 1956 Miss Moore had been doing for some thirty-five or forty years, one accepts the absolute language of that facade, and that language is the copywriter's. America, it must be obvious to even the most benighted by now, would literally cease to exist as the familiar entity it is without advertising copy: I would say that a great majority of the population would feel cheated, robbed, strangely empty and vague, without the advertisement. It is an integral part of the America Miss Moore loves and cherishes, i.e., the fake America. It is indeed an official language, violently opposed to the language of the poem, since its intent is to conceal. The concretists of today embrace the ad, and rightly so, since they have lost all pretension of caring about the use of clear language. It *is* the poem—the poem *is* the copy....

"Spenser's Ireland" is remarkable in that it works clearly on the two levels of decadence I have spoken of: The quick stab and glossiness of good ad copy and the blithe dismissal of certain facts that ad copy is better off ignoring, e.g., Swift, Parnell, the IRA, the Sinn Fein, Black and Tan butchery, Yeats, Joyce, Wolfe Tone, Robert Emmett, and so on. I am amazed that the Irish Tourist Board has not asked Miss Moore for permission to quote the first three or four lines of this poem, since it functions with great clarity on that plane they function on—dear old Ireland, ah, the peat, ah, the old priests, etc., etc. But how could Miss Moore write clearly of Ireland when she cannot write clearly of her own American experience? Of her own human experience?

It is impossible to lose all touch with the world without losing touch with the language; the language will betray you at every turn if you try to break and humble it to display an abstraction which you insist on believing is true. I am not sure if the converse is true, but I think it must be. So, as Miss Moore continually faced a world which frightened her, except in its more eccentric delights, mostly bookish, so she falsified her language. Emily Dickinson most certainly did not tell us of the "world" in her poems, probably knowing less about it than Miss Moore. Then why do we still, to our profit, read her?—it is, of course, because she went down into her own tortured heart and wrote of that specific. In Miss Moore's poems, we have neither the world nor herself; her anger is clearly removed from all emotion, save that which is safely to be vented. Who Miss Moore is, these poems will not tell, unless it is by default: what they do *not* say. Or, what they say charmingly, and offhandedly, as in the tensely hysterical assault on sex and sexuality in **"Marriage,"** surely one of the greatest attempts at sterilization in the language—all of it understanding, spinsterish language, skipping about "hearth and home"—never the bed. The language failed her as it lost its engagement with the real; and as time passed, Miss Moore added more and more supplementary material to her poems, in the form of scattered quotes from "public" sources mostly—newspapers, magazines, the writings of naturalists, etc. What is the effect of this cluttered poem, the strings of quote marks, the sounding of flat journalese in the body of the poem which builds itself around the quotes—not the opposite—the quotes used to heighten the effect of a particular line or stanza? The poem takes on the whole linguistic sense of the quotes; it creaks under the barrage of them; and, most importantly, the quotes elaborate on the idea of the poem, or elucidate it. We have the really juiceless phenomenon of the poem, rooted in sand, bolstered by secondhand quotes out of context, from sources whose sense of style is decidedly apoetic. The blind lead the blind.

I have mentioned the poem **"In the Days of Prismatic Color"** as striking me as Miss Moore's aesthetic, and her phrase therein, "great truths." Earlier on in the poem she says:

> complexity is not a crime, but carry
> it to the point of murkiness
> and nothing is plain.

These "great truths," however, are strangely missing in Miss Moore's work. They are not found in the formal structuring of the poems and their engagement with the world; they are, indeed, these "great truths," a series of pegs upon which the poet hangs "ideas." She *says* it, but they are not to be found anywhere in the poems. We all know what she means by "great truths," don't we? Why, the "great truths" are ... are ... the, well, the "GREAT TRUTHS"! But the poem retreats at bewildering speed, and with a display of the most fantastic sleight-of-hand, from any sense of the real, at all. This, the shoring up of the poem with grand statements about Life, and Art, and Love, and Death, and so on, while the poem in its bones refuses to confront any of these things, is another instance of irony in Miss Moore's work. For what is this dazzling footwork but her proscribed "complexity"?—"carried to the point of murkiness" where "nothing is plain"?

"Style" reveals the poem destroyed as clearly as anything in this volume: The casting about for "subject" (there is nothing left, at this date, 1956), the "look" of the early poems, the bathos of the rhyme drawn out in great pain and carelessness, the great lack of sincerity, and the ever-present quotes. The rhyme is most instructive here, the fantastic wrenching of good straight syntax to get the rhyme to fall: "have an Iberian-American champion yet" to rhyme with "alphabet"—and that latter word used gratuitously, since it is followed by the phrase, "S soundholes in a 'cello"—this is bad enough, but the rhythmic sense of the poem falls from the merely incompetent and weary to the ludicrous with "fast fast fast and faster" to rhyme with "Etchebaster."

"In the Public Garden" is notable in that it mistakes Eisenhower for a "hardest-working citizen." This was in 1958, when he was President, and in a poem read at the Boston Arts Festival. It is on a level with Frost's inaugural poem in 1960—the public poem to delight the poetry-hating audience....

For the poem **"Combat Cultural"** I refer the reader to Robert Duncan's remarks in his essay "Ideas on the Meaning of Form." Also, his general comments on the decline of Marianne Moore's work in the same essay.

James Dickey calls *Tell Me, Tell Me* Miss Moore's best book. In it we are presented with such poems as **"Baseball and Writing,"** which continues the bathetic note struck in **"Hometown Piece"; "In Lieu of the Lyre,"** which must be read to be believed; **"Granite and Steel,"** a poem about the Brooklyn Bridge, which, curiously, neglects to quote from the finest poem on that bridge, Hart Crane's "To Brooklyn Bridge"; and **"To Victor Hugo of My Crow Pluto,"** which must stand as the classic attempt at a conscious doggerel that doesn't succeed in its own intent.

"W. S. Landor" is a curious poem in its praise of Landor as someone Miss Moore would like. He throws a man through the window and worries about the plants beneath. It is not Landor's act which I hit at here, nor Miss Moore's approval of this gruff, "no-nonsense" English virility, all roast beef and Yorkshire pudding and baying hounds. It is the failure shown here to distinguish this kind of anecdote as being the propaganda of masculinity. There was a guard at Auschwitz who left his chores of murdering to return to his university and take his examinations in philosophy. A brilliant student, soft-spoken, well-educated, immaculately dressed. Perhaps he loved flowers. The man thrown through the window is a literary abstraction, like the swan, the ant, etc. The language in a vacuum.

"Rescue with Yul Brynner" carries on the spirit of **"Style."** It is Miss Moore crying in the movies.

In **"Hitherto Uncollected"** no further aberrations are revealed.

So, in reading through this body of work, these poems of an entire lifetime, one sees the clearest graph of decline imaginable in the work of a "major" contemporary poet. What I have tried to show in these notes, however, is that this decline did not come about through a sudden failure of power on the poet's part; but that the later, really bad verse, was absolutely prefigured in the earliest poems. The poet failed as her language failed, and her language failed because she shut out the real.

ALAN NADEL

SOURCE: Alan Nadel, "Marianne Moore and the Art of Delineation," in *Sagetrieb*, Vol. 6, No. 3, Winter, 1987, pp. 169-80.

[*Nadel is an American educator and critic. In the following excerpt, he presents reasons for classifying Moore as a modernist and outlines the differences between her work and that of such contemporaries as T. S. Eliot and William Carlos Williams.*]

What makes Marianne Moore a "modernist"?

This question, which has focussed much Moore criticism, is usually addressed by associating her with Pound and/or Eliot and/or Stevens and/or Williams. Although Grace Schulman omits Williams completely from her discussion, he seems to be the modernist most consistently connected with Moore. In her recent study of American modernism, Lisa Steinman, for example, notes the ways both poets engage twentieth-century science and technology: "like Williams, [Moore] admires not only the creativity of scientists but also the achievements of American technology and even of American business. Also like Williams, Moore sometimes draws parallels between poetry and other more accepted fields to grant authority to poetry." Discussing modernist "long poems," Laurence Stapleton similarly connects Moore with Williams, noting that although Moore does not produce anything like *The Waste Land, The Cantos,* or "Notes toward a Supreme Fiction," **"An Octopus"** "is more like Paterson at its best . . . than it is like anything written by [Eliot, Pound, or Stevens]."

Moore is particularly connected with Williams in her treatment of objects and images. This connection forms the basis of A. Kingsley Weatherhead's *The Edge of the Image*. Whatever the merit of these connections, however, I want to suggest that Moore diverges not only from Williams's but also from Pound's and Eliot's treatment of objects in some crucial ways, ways that both differentiate her from other modernists and help delineate her role as a modernist. It is important to note, for example, that she does not follow Williams's dictum: "No ideas but in things."

There are, nevertheless, a lot of *things* in her poetry. . . .

Her poetry is a virtual compendium of things, aligning Moore with the great catalogers in American poetry, Whitman before her and Elizabeth Bishop after. Even her titles could be read as items on the inventory list of an eclectic curio shop. . . .

Her abundance of "ideas" sets her apart. Her poetry abounds with ideas, presented in the form of direct statement. . . .

The residence for her abundance of ideas is not in things but in "poems," poems that do not privilege the image, even though Moore, as Weatherhead pointed out, shared with Williams a love of the sharply delineated, of images with edges. No matter how sharp their edges, however, Moore's images do not quite fit Pound's definition either: that which presents an "emotional and intellectual complex in an instant of time." In Moore's poetry, the impact of her intellect, or of the intellect in general, remains discrete from the emotional response of recognition through the senses. Her exegetical stance seems almost to force the separation, so that an object or image, sharply delineated, often serves to exemplify a point.

In **"The Hero,"** for example, sites which contain "snakes' hypodermic teeth" illustrate ground "where love won't grow." "The startling El Greco / brimming with inner light" exemplifies a "rock crystal thing to see . . . that covets nothing that it has let go." And preference for seeing such a "rock crystal thing" identifies the "hero." The poem presents the image, then, only to illustrate an abstract concept which in turn is useful only to explain how to recognize an intangible quality. In other poems the separation results from making the object a focus of discussion, a source of contemplative wisdom. Considering the elaborately described bowls, in **"Bowls,"** Moore learns "that we are precisionists, / not citizens of Pompeii arrested in action / as a cross-section of one's correspondence would seem to imply."

These examples suggest that Moore does not rely on "objective correlatives," if we infer that Eliot meant objects which focus emotion by representing it, by becoming its manifestation, instead of complementing a direct assertion. If for Eliot emotion recollected in tranquility is an inexact formula, it is not nearly so inexact for Moore nor so formulaic. Perhaps this is so because the tranquility of Moore's poetry provides the site not so much of recollection as of delineation. . . .

Traditional English language poetics — according to the line of Pound's argument — dominated by iambics (usually by pentameters) and often by regular rhyme schemes was inadequate to delineate the connection between poetry and its subject matter. Only by breaking with tradition and employing the full array of poetic devices available could poetry achieve the necessary precision and exactitude.

This concern, shared by Moore also, as Bonnie Costello notes, set her apart from other modernists: "While [they] made the major claim of achieving the genuine in form, closing the gap between human constructions and the order of nature, Moore admits the allusiveness of truth, connecting the genuine with the acknowledgment of limits." "For Moore," Costello explains, "accuracy is always an ideal." From this perspective, we can see Moore as articulating the problems with Pound's suggestion of the adequacy of poetry — a suggestion of adequation that marks the story of its own failure, a story that follows this line: Once upon a time we could presume that a direct line connected art to what it signified in nature — an emotion, vision, or idea, that could be re-collected and retold. The *mode* of representation was believed to function independently of the *object* of representation, but now the nature of nature has been shown to be more complex than we thought, and simple signification no longer delineates it adequately. Now we must marshall more to the endeavor, employ all the devices once used merely as decor. What we once took as the surplus, the supplement, now we recognize as crucial, necessary, that without which poetry is merely a bunch of inadequate lines.

Along the same line, we can construct the story of many modernist arts. In painting too the adequacy of the line to render reality had come under scrutiny. The sense of a subject not stable and timeless but fragmented and timebound shook the foundation upon which pictorial representation relied. The line itself — that basic unit of the pictorial — was recontextualized in a fourth dimension, in a time-frame that was, after Einstein, relative and spatial, not constant and linear. The same storyline, as well, could be adapted to narrate the fate of prose narrative, in which the privileged position of the chronological, the model of historical linearity, was flooded by a stream of consciousness on whose currents rode the model of the psychological present. In that model, time lines dissolved and the lines which connected perceptions with one another or with external experiences became muddled, crossed, hard to identify and/or to disentangle.

To put it most simply, the idea of linear reality — *that old story* — had lost its authority. Hence followed strategies of containment which tried to salvage thought and emotion by locating them within the image, object, thing. But this move toward self-containment simultaneously required contextualization, required the extra-textual explanations necessary, paradoxically, to assert the self-sufficiency of the artistic work. The footnotes to *The Waste Land,* Pound's literary essays, *The Necessary Angel,* etc., can be viewed — alongside their critical codifications in the name of "New Criticism" — as ways of defending the mimetic quality of modernist art.

This modernist line of defense delineates the point, as I have suggested, at which Moore departs from the picture, but in the way that she reconstitutes that point of departure, that place where the line itself is in question, she marks her quintessential modernism. In any case, that is the line I am — more or less — arguing.

And it begins appropriately with the line of argumentation, for that is the line Moore's compositions make new. Whereas Pound, Williams, Eliot, H.D., even Frost, and often Stevens, relied on juxtaposition — just as Picasso and Duchamp did — to substitute for commentary, Moore foregrounded commentary itself. The resulting observations — as she called her works — find their structure best described not in the vocabulary of poetics but in the vocabulary of rhetoric. **"When I Buy Pictures,"** for example, is a verse essay delineating the qualities in visual art that Moore values. It fits clearly into the genre of the personal essay, purporting not to identify universal principles but principles of personal taste, those things, she tells us, that "would give me pleasure in my average moments." Like the ideal student of, let's say, *The Harbrace Handbook,* she has begun the perfect "topic/restriction" paragraph. Fixing on the topic of acquiring art, she has used the word "when" to delineate the scope of her composition; it will tell us *under what conditions* Moore finds paintings desirable. Not when they soar to the sublime, her argument indicates, but when they replicate what gives her pleasure in her "average moments." This means works of two sorts: "the satire upon curiosity in which no more is discernible / than the intensity of the mood; / or quite the opposite. . . . " A list of examples follows, and then the next point, which is that these effects cannot be achieved through disproportion, overemphasis. She concludes by appealing to an authority (A. R. Gordon, her endnotes indicate) and then heightening the appeal by reiterating in her own words the common quality her two sorts of pleasure-giving paintings have:

> it comes to this: of whatever sort it is,
> it must be "lit with piercing glances into the life
>   of things";
> it must acknowledge the spiritual forces which
>   have made it.

The rhetorical structure of this work is clear—a classification achieved by topic/restriction/example, developed by further modification and resolved by moving from the differences to the similarities; similarly the argument moves from the personal ("when I") to the universal ("it must") and from the subjective qualities of the poet ("what would give me pleasure") to the objective (in the sense of being authoritative and shared) of A. R. Gordon. If these rhetorical qualities are somewhat obvious, that is all the more reason to say that this is a fairly good "composition" (i.e., short piece of expository prose).

But it is also a composition in the sense that the pictures it discusses are compositions, works of art arranged by an intelligence in such a way that the whole effect is greater than the sum of its parts. The pictures are assemblies of lines that do not allow their being viewed simply as lines nor even as lines of reference, but rather as references that effect commentary. If these lines, then, are no longer transparent—no longer merely referential—they act as a method of classification, a way of delineating. When the voice in *The Waste Land* can connect nothing with nothing, it voices another aspect of the dilemma Moore investigates here and elsewhere when she shows the line of connection between something and something.

Eliot's line and Moore's share a recognition of limitation, a willingness to forego the other possibility—that of connecting something (or nothing) with *everything*. Both recognize—as all modernists did—the ways in which the modern sensibility had rent the connection between the temporal and the eternal. Moore responds, I am arguing, by drawing smaller lines, making connections not authorized by a cosmology but by the rules of argumentation, the science of rhetoric. It is worth noting in this light that virtually all the critics who discuss Moore's poems on some or many occasions refer to them as arguments. . . . In that regard, then, my argument is not particularly new; it merely foregrounds what many critics have taken for granted—that one must talk about Moore's poetry in the same way that one talks about Williams's essays, but not his poems. More than delineating this implicit line which runs through Moore criticism, I am arguing that Moore in her poems is drawing out the lines which connect not only her critics to one another, but also connect her contemporaries—the modernists—to their own work. Each of their works can be viewed as part of an argument about the nature of connections, about the kinds of lines that can be drawn between life and art, art and art, tradition and the individual talent. . . .

In foregrounding the unarticulated process of argumentation upon which modernist art depends, Moore also exposes the problematic nature of arguments. . . .

"Complexity," "fragility," "soundness," "defensiveness"—these words not only qualify her arguments but also name themes which run through them. Others have discussed aspects of these themes in her work, and space does not permit even an adequate outline of their arguments. But it is worth noting that these themes again help identify some margins of modernism. The "soundness" of poetic argument, for example, suggests not only Pound's and Eliot's insistence on a poetics based on the paradigm of musical composition but also connects their arguments with those of the French symbolists. If for Pope the sound must seem a sequel to the sense, for Moore (like her contemporaries) sound helps create sense. She shows as well that poetry makes sense sound—a double pun or perhaps a triple suggested by the phrase "sound sense" in the last line of **"To a Strategist."** Poetry gives us the sensation of sound and as well replicates sensate sounds, the sounds of the senses. It also contextualizes sounds so as to make them sensible. Sensibility, in turn, renders the sensate experience of poetry stable, firm, sound. Poetry thus sounds an argument made sound through that argument.

Or through nothing. The pun "sound sense" thus delineates as well the margins of the modernist/symbolist argument that makes sound and sense a self-contained unit.

Beyond the soundness of that argument resides only silence, which is equally sensible and sensate in its restraint, Moore's poetry argues, as sound is in its indulgence. Against the anonymity of the author, Moore outlines the idea of privacy which is a form of silence created by self-possession and presence, not anonymity and absence. As silence supplements sound, presence supplements anonymity, a connection delineated most clearly in the second stanza of **"Injudicious Gardening"**:

> However, your particular possession;
>   the sense of privacy,
>   indeed might deprecate
>   offended ears, and need not tolerate
>   effrontery.

The sense (of privacy), which is a form of silence, deprecates access to sound, the offended (and off ended) ear channels through which sounds pass on their way to becoming sensible. Or sense might do that, indeed. The kind of deed that might indeed allow such deprecation remains unsaid, as does the nature of the offense. The first stanza suggests that the offense is liking yellow flowers—a "symbol" of infidelity—but indeed this is more a visual than an aural offense. In the poem's contentious reversibilities, Moore takes us inside the sounds of words that make them (in)sensible. In this imaginary garden, in judiciousness, in fidelity, she finds again possibly, in action (in deed), in possession (in deed), a place for the genuine (indeed).

Indeed the pun is the line of aural association that takes us into that garden as it does into the words of which the garden is composed. In such judicious gardening one finds the best arguments for modernism, just as Moore found in the Armory Show its best defense. I am suggesting, in other words, that **"Armor's Undermining Modesty"** glosses the Armory Show that Moore found so inspirational. The poem—which is about words and etymologies, surfaces and self-possession, gloss and tarnish—connects visual with linguistic by highlighting the power of understatement as well as its vulnerability. This is what the Armory Show delineated for Moore, and the pun on armor creates another outline of modernism in her work.

The observance of that outline takes us to a final observation on Moore's observations: they merge not only the seen with the scene, the sense with the said, the argument with the example; they also merge in some ways the temporal with the eternal. For the making of her poetry outlines the argument that contextualizes observed phenomena and thus turns the observation into a form of observance. By constructing the argument in judiciousness and in fidelity that connects thought and phenomena, one must not only observe the phenomena in the sense of seeing it but also observe it in the sense of paying homage to it. The act of temporal observance thus becomes a form of religious observance, and the poem itself becomes a rite of passage and a passage of rites. In this way Moore aligns with Eliot by completing the line of his argument that leads us out of the Waste Land and back to the Garden.

SOURCES FOR FURTHER STUDY

Engel, Bernard F. *Marianne Moore*. Rev. ed. Boston: Twayne Publishers, 1989, 160 p.

> Biographical and critical study of Moore and her works.

Koch, Vivienne. "The Peaceable Kingdom of Marianne Moore." *Quarterly Review of Literature* IV, No. 2 (1948): 153-69.

> Looks at Moore as a fabulist, examines her poetic influences, and reviews her work through 1948.

Molesworth, Charles. *Marianne Moore: A Literary Life*. New York: Atheneum, 1990, 472 p.

> Extensive biography and survey of Moore's literary career.

Rosenthal, M. L. "'Nerved by What Chills / The Blood': Passion and Power in Marianne Moore." *The American Poetry Review* 17, No. 4 (July-August 1988): 45-7.

> Analyzes several of Moore's poems, including "The Mind Is an Enchanting Thing," "Marriage," and "The Steeple-Jack."

Schulman, Grace. *Marianne Moore: The Poetry of Engagement*. Urbana: University of Illinois Press, 1986, 137 p.

> Assesses Moore's imagery, observations, and rhythmic methods.

Tomlinson, Charles, ed. *Marianne Moore: A Collection of Critical Essays*. Englewood Cliffs, N.J.: Prentice-Hall, 1970, 185 p.

> Contains essays by many of Moore's most highly regarded critics, including Pound, Eliot, Williams, Stevens, Hugh Kenner, and Randall Jarrell.

Muhammad

570?-632

(Original name Abu al-Qasim Muhammad 'Abd Allah ibn 'Abd al-Muttalib ibn Hashim) Arabian religious leader and statesman.

INTRODUCTION

Muhammad, or The Prophet, exerted a profound, enduring influence on global religion and politics when he established the Islamic faith during the seventh century. The principal vehicle of Muhammad's influence—and one of the seminal works of Arabic literature—is the Koran (also transliterated as Qur'an), the sacred text of Islam. Comprising transcriptions of divine revelations Muhammad received concerning the nature of the universe, the role of Allah (God), and the responsibilities of humanity, the Koran has propounded Islamic creeds and dictated Islamic religious practice for over 1,300 years. "Islam," an Arabic term denoting the religion's central tenet, complete submission to God, delineates a comprehensive set of personal devotions and social injunctions. Stylistically, the Koran epitomizes the northern Arabic dialect used for most literary works of the period. Alternately lyrical and harsh, mystical and precise, the work's rhythmic language is the standard by which all subsequent Arabic literature has been measured. Like the Bible for Christians, the Torah for Jews, or the Vedas for Hindus, the Koran is for Muslims both a superlative literary artifact and the definitive source of information about the will of Allah and humankind's relationship to Him.

Biographical Information

According to Ibn Ishaq (died c.768), Muhammad's first biographer, Muhammad was born in Mecca after the death of his father, a prominent member of the Quraysh tribe that controlled Mecca. At age six his mother died, and a grandfather and an uncle cared for him. Traveling with his uncle in merchant caravans, he eventually began working as the trading agent for the wealthy widow Khadijah, who eventually proposed marriage to Muhammad. Their union produced four daughters and provided Muhammad with the capital to become a successful independent trader. Because his background made him sensitive to the corruption prevalent in Mecca at that time, Muhammad often contemplated the city's social problems. One night in 610 he claimed to have been visited by the angel Gabriel, who informed him that he had been chosen as the messenger of God and imparted the first of the some 650 revelations he received periodically over the next twenty years. The Prophet fulfilled his charge almost immediately, converting friends and family members of the Quraysh tribe. As Muhammad's following increased, so did opposition to his growing influence, and the head of Muhammad's clan withdrew familial protection for the Muslims about 619, the year his wife and uncle died. Deprived of religious advantages and relieved of family obligations in Mecca, Muhammad sought converts in other Arab towns. Eventually he contracted with a group from Medina to lead a Muslim emigration to that city in 622, which marks the beginning of the Islamic calendar. He formed alliances throughout Arabia, undertook a series of increasingly successful raids on Meccan caravans, and became less tolerant of detractors and nonbelievers. Recurrent skirmishes with Mecca culminated in that city's surrender and conversion to Islam in 630. That same year Muhammad conquered the tribes that inhabited the Syrian border, consolidating Muslim hegemony in the Arabian Peninsula. He died at Mecca in 632.

Major Works

The Prophet never transcribed any of God's revelations himself. After his death one of his companions, Zayd ibn Thabit, collected all oral and written versions of the divine messages in the first Koran, which is composed in rhyming prose and concludes with two brief exhortations to avoid evil. Each of the resulting 114 surahs, or chapters, records at least one revelation. The surahs are arranged according to diminishing length, and the shorter chapters, which scholars consider the earliest, appear near the end of the Koran. Each surah is preceded by a heading consisting of a title (usually a word or phrase prominent in the chapter), a formulaic prayer, an explanation of whether the revelation occurred at Mecca or Medina, and the number of verses in the surah. Earlier surahs are characterized by shorter verses, vivid description, rhythmic rhyme, and dramatic impact. The later surahs contain longer verses of greater complexity and detail. Their rhyme scheme is less regular and, many maintain, less natural; the overall effect of these longer passages is more prosaic. The Koran also employs refrains that recur at the ends of sections within surahs: while they reinforce the content of earlier surahs, the refrains of later surahs often have little or no connection to the import of the verse. The perspective, structure, and syntax of the Koran serve didactic purposes. The surahs usually feature a nonlinear sentence structure: non sequiturs abound; comparisons are but faintly implied; conditional clauses are incomplete or wholly absent; allusions to unexplained events are frequent. These syntactical tendencies are said to foster Muslim acceptance of human limits relative to divine omniscience. Much of the Koran comprises ambiguous parables attributed to God, while some narrative passages recount several biblical stories.

Critical Reception

The Islamic community approaches the Koran as the literal word of God. Among Westerners, however, critical response to the Koran has depended largely on prevailing attitudes toward Islam. Since the late nineteenth-century, Koranic studies in the West have benefited from an improved understanding of Arabic language and culture, although the tendency to disparage the Koran for failing to embody such Western literary conventions as concreteness, linear narrative, and closure has persisted. Much twentieth-century Koran scholarship examines how Muslims have reworked Jewish and Christian materials to serve Islamic purposes. The Koran's literary influence has been extensive in part because the northern Arabic literary language has survived. This "high" dialect evolved into the medium of classical Arabic literature during the twelfth century and continues today as the idiom of Arabic education, literature, and journalism. The Koran exemplifies literary Arabic as it had developed up to the seventh century; however, it is the spread of Islam that accounts for the work's broader social, political, and religious significance.

CRITICAL COMMENTARY

W. MONTGOMERY WATT

SOURCE: W. Montgomery Watt, "Novelty in the Content of the Qur'an," in his *Islamic Revelation in the Modern World,* Edinburgh at the University Press, 1969, pp. 44-56.

[*In the excerpt below, Watt contends that the Koran interprets contemporary events and reworks Christian, Judaic, and Arabian polytheistic precepts to serve Muslim purposes.*]

It was fashionable at the beginning of the twentieth

> **Principal English Translations**
>
> *The Alcoran of Mahomet* (translated by Alexander Ross) 1649
> *The Koran, commonly called the Alcoran of Mohammed* (translated by George Sale) 1734
> *The Koran* (translated by J. M. Rodwell) 1861
> *The Qur'an* (translated by Edward Henry Palmer) 1880
> *The Qur'an* (translated by Richard Bell) 1937
> *The Koran* (translated by N. J. Dawood) 1956
> *The Meaning of the Glorious Qur'an* (translated by Marmaduke Pickthall) 1930
> *The Koran Interpreted* (translated by Arthur J. Arberry) 1955
> *The Qur'an and Its Exegesis: Selected Texts with Classical and Modern Muslim Interpretations* (translated and edited by Alford T. Welch) 1977

century to present the **Qur'an** as a selection of ideas from Judaism and Christianity with little distinctive merit and no novelty or originality. Such a view is a belated survival from the war-propaganda of the crusading period when Western Europe, in great fear of Muslim armies, had to embody its defensive attitudes in a falsified picture of Islam. When one considers the view out of context, merely by comparing the **Qur'an** with the Bible, there seems to be much to be said for it. This, however, is to assume that Muhammad made his proclamations in a vacuum. When one looks at both scriptures in their historical context, the matter takes on a different complexion. The Old Testament prophet did not speak in an intellectual vacuum any more than did Muhammad, but spoke to people familiar with the messages of previous prophets and with something of the past religious history of their people. This religious situation was presupposed. The novel and original message of each prophet assumed familiarity with many ideas, was expressed in terms of these ideas, and dealt with contemporary problems....

The message of the earliest passages of the **Qur'an** was adapted to the situation in Mecca when Muhammad began his mission there. Among the passages generally agreed to be early [were those] in which opposition to Muhammad was neither expressly stated nor implied. In these passages five main points appeared to be insisted on: (1) God is all-powerful and good; (2) men will appear before God on the Last Day to be judged and assigned to heaven or hell according to their deeds; (3) man ought to be grateful to God and worship him; (4) man should be generous with his wealth and upright; (5) Muhammad has been sent as a warner to bring this message from God to his fellows. Now the first four of these points might be said to be derived from Judaism or Christianity, though there are some differences of emphasis; for example, the older religions usually lay far less emphasis on generosity with wealth. The pivot of the new religious movement, however, was the fifth point; and, though the idea of conveying a divine message may be derived, the assertion that in particular Muhammad is such a messenger cannot be derived. Here at least is one element of originality.

Even the other ideas, however, when looked at in their historical context, are seen to be specially relevant to Mecca at that period. Mecca was a prosperous commercial centre whose caravans went as far as Damascus in the north and the Yemen in the south. Some of its trading enterprises had even wider ramifications. The great merchants were very wealthy men, and had come to believe that almost anything could be achieved by finance and careful planning. Besides this they were so engrossed in making money that they neglected the traditional duties falling upon them as clan leaders of looking after the poorer members of the clan. There had been a breakdown of the traditional desert morality with its insistence on most of the virtues essential to life in society. Only those aspects of morality connected with the *lex talionis* were still in force.

Now the five points listed are all relevant to this situation. To counteract the exaggerated views of human power and the failure to recognize its limitations men are called upon to acknowledge God's power, to be grateful to him and to worship him. To counteract the breakdown of traditional morality and the failure of the traditional sanctions to deal with this, it is insisted that a man's ultimate fate depends on the Last Judgement, and the basis of this is the man's conduct as an individual. Thus a sanction for morality is provided which is suited to the individualistic outlook of the great merchants. To counter the close-fistedness of the merchants with their wealth and their neglect of the needy of their kin, it is insisted that in the Judgement an important question will be whether the man was niggardly or generous with his wealth. Thus, in respect of the first four points, even if the **Qur'an** is presenting old ideas, it is selecting and emphasizing aspects which were specially relevant to the Mecca of the early seventh century.

The fifth point—that Muhammad has been sent as a messenger and warner to his people—is in part an assertion of the special application of the message to Muhammad's environment. The **Qur'an** itself acknowledges that its message is in essentials a repetition of that to which the earlier monotheistic religions are a response; but this message has been freshly revealed to Muhammad. Yet as the conception of revelation and the first recipient of revelation is developed in the **Qur'an** it comes to have several elements of originality. Because a large part of the message is the proclamation that wrongdoers and unbelievers will be punished, both eschatologically and temporally, Muhammad is told in early passages to say that his function is that of a 'warner' and that he has no political ambitions. After the Hijra to Medina, however, the concept of 'messenger'—the commonest title for Muhammad as recipient of the revelation—is enlarged; besides communicating the divine messages it is his task to administer the community of Muslims in accordance with these messages. In this way a political role is, as it were, thrust upon him. The Old Testament prophet also had a political role, but 'the Messenger of God' came to have vastly greater responsibilities.

When one turns from the earliest passages of the **Qur'an** to later ones, it is clear that many of the regulations for the Muslim community of Medina are original at least in their details. The Muslim community grew and developed gradually, chiefly by adapting existing Arabian usages. Even the ideals which may be said to have guided the process of adaptation, though in a sense shared by other peoples, had a special Arabian flavour. It is hardly necessary, however, to examine these matters at length. It will be more instructive to look at the development of the Qur'anic attitude to pre-Islamic Arabian religion.

It is noteworthy that in the earliest passages of the **Qur'an** there is no attack on the existing religion. The five points are positive, except that punishment is threatened for niggardliness and for unbelief in God and the Last Judgement. The verse calling on the Meccans to worship the Lord of the Ka'ba seems to hope that existing believers in a supreme deity (with other lesser ones) will see in the Qur'anic proclamations a purified version of what they already believe. In other words the **Qur'an** may be said to envisage a smooth transition from the higher forms of the existing religion to the new religion; that is to say, the emphasis is on amplifying and adding to existing beliefs, not on discarding old ones, though it may have been hoped that old beliefs incompatible with the new beliefs would in due course fade away. The change of direction (if this metaphor be allowed to pass for the moment) came about with bitter Qur'anic attacks on the polytheistic aspects of the existing religion. This presumably followed on the appearance of vigorous opposition to Muhammad's movement, and this opposition—no doubt for complex reasons—was linked with some resurgence of idol-worship. Thus Islam has come to be noted for its insistence that God is one and that there are no other beings to whom worship may properly be offered.

In describing this development it is impossible to avoid anthropomorphic metaphors, and to say, according to the form of words adopted in this study, that the **Qur'an** 'hoped' and 'changed its direction or policy'. It must be insisted that this is not a mere verbal trick to avoid saying that Muhammad hoped or changed his policy. It might be suggested to the European reader that he think of the **Qur'an** as proceeding from some kind of social force operative in the community as a whole. This would be something beyond Muhammad's consciousness, though working through him. The observer sees that this force, as it directs the society towards a more satisfactory condition, will naturally first explore the direct road forwards, that is, to build a new order of society on a modified form of existing beliefs. In course of time it becomes clear that other social forces resistant to change are linked with aspects of the old beliefs. In order to weaken these forces and allow the social reform to proceed it was necessary to have a criterion to distinguish between the supporters of reform and those who wanted to retain the *status quo*. The social force behind the reform produced this criterion by its new 'policy' of attacking the polytheistic aspects of the old beliefs.

Despite the bitterness of the attack on idols much of the old religion was absorbed into Islam. Conceptions which are shared with Judaism and Christianity come in the **Qur'an** to have a distinctive Arabian form. There is less emphasis on God's creation of the world and of man in the distant past and more on his all-embracing activity in the world at the present time. Although he is the merciful and compassionate, he comes to have some of the inscrutability ascribed by the pre-Islamic Arabs to Time. There are many passages about God's control of the whole process of human birth; and one wonders whether in this he has taken over some of the attributes of the old Arabian and Semitic deities who were identified with male and female creative powers. Thus both in the **Qur'an**'s rejection of Arabian polytheism and in its implicit acceptance of features of the old Arabian religion, there is something not derived from Judaism or Christianity and to be reckoned original.

This relationship of Islam to the old Arabian religion is paralleled by the relationship of Old Testament religion to the old Canaanite religion. There is the same fierce denunciation of aspects of polytheism. At the same time animal sacrifice, which really belonged to Canaanite religion, and was closely linked with the ideas of that religion, came to have an important place in the worship of the Israelites. Indeed, in so far as Christianity is the consummation of the Old Testament, sacrifice may be said to have become central, since the crucifixion of Jesus was interpreted both by himself and by his followers in terms of sacrifice. The parallelism in this matter between Islam and the Old Testament religion is no accident, but is rather something which is implicit in a true monotheism.

This examination, then, of the relation of the **Qur'an** to the Meccan and Arabian environment has made it clear that the message is specially suited to the needs of the people among whom Muhammad lived, and is not a mere repetition of older ideas. If the **Qur'an** contains truths that are in some sense eternal, yet they have been adapted to the particular milieu. Or perhaps, in the light of the later spread of Islam it would be better to say that the particular message conveyed to the people of Mecca and Medina had from the first implicit in it aspects of universality.

One of the functions of the religious leader of the prophetic type is to show his people how their faith is confirmed by events which happen to them, and how certain other events, which might seem to destroy that faith, need not be interpreted in such a way. Before looking at some of the Qur'anic interpretations it will be useful to look at an Old Testament instance. The incidents in the story of the 'sin of Achan' (*Joshua*, 7) are selected for this purpose, partly because the story is nowadays unfamiliar, partly because the matter is relatively unimportant (and unlikely to raise theological passions), and partly because the element of the supernatural is at a minimum. There are also some parallels to the situation of the Muslims after the battle of Uhud.

The incidents took place shortly after the entry of the Israelites into Palestine across the Jordan and their capture of the city of Jericho. They were filled with elation at their success. When it came to attacking a small place called Ai, which lay in their line of advance, they were so confident that they thought it unnecessary for the whole army to attack Ai, and sent a relatively small force of three thousand men. To their consternation this force was put to flight. Joshua in deep despair spent the whole day in prayer prostrate on his face before the ark of God, and eventually was told by God that the discomfiture was due to the fact that the people had sinned. Next day lots were drawn and the lot fell upon Achan. He confessed that he had taken a rich robe, some silver and a wedge of gold from the spoils of Jericho, although this had been forbidden by Joshua. Thereupon he, his family, his domestic animals and all his material possessions were taken apart, and killed and destroyed by stoning and burning. The attack on Ai was renewed and was successful; but it may be noted that thirty thousand men were placed in an ambush while the rest of the army made a frontal attack.

The important point in this story is that, once the rout before Ai had taken place, it was necessary to restore confidence by showing that it was not due to military inferiority but to something else, namely, sin or disobedience. According to the ideas of primitive religion this sin was felt to be a pollution or infection of the whole body; but the steps taken led to the effective cleansing of the whole body. The modern historian may be inclined to ask some questions. He will want to know whether the lot was manipulated, or whether nearly everybody had in fact taken something. The latter may well have been the case, for it is nowhere stated that no other spoils had been taken privately. The phrase in verse 26 that 'the Lord turned from the fierceness of his anger' could mean that there were no further polluting articles in the camp; but it could also mean that Achan and his goods were taken as representing all sinful men and wrongfully-taken spoils, so that their removal entailed the complete removal of the pollution. The modern historian might rather say that the defeat was due to the fact that most of the army was thinking chiefly of the spoil, while the punishment of Achan helped to curb any undue desire for self-enrichment.

Though there can be no question of imitation, there is a parallel between the inspired interpretation of the rout at Ai in the Old Testament and that of the reverse at Uhud in the **Qur'an**. The Muslims were greatly elated after their victory at Badr, and were therefore correspondingly depressed after Uhud. From a military point of view Uhud was not a serious reverse; the Meccans had still failed to take even one life for each life lost, although they had sworn they would take several. The difficulty was that the Muslims had taken Badr as a sign that God was fighting for them, and this had become the basis of their confidence. After Uhud they began to doubt if God was really fighting for them, and their confidence ebbed away. The **Qur'an** dealt with this loss of confidence by showing that the reverse was due, not to any change on God's part, but to the disobedience of the archers who left their posts because they were eager for plunder. This interpretation and Muhammad's own steadiness in the crisis led in due course to the Muslims regaining confidence.

The **Qur'an** is constantly interpreting contemporary events and situations. Early in the Meccan period it asserts or implies that Meccan commercial prosperity is due to God. The theistic interpretation of earlier events like the expedition of the elephant and the destruction of various peoples was probably first made in the **Qur'an**, but it is conceivable that interpretations along similar lines were already current among the Arabs. For most of the Meccan period the Muslims could not but be aware of the opposition to their religious movement, and this no doubt made them wonder why, if Muhammad was really sent by God, he should yet have to meet such opposition. The **Qur'an** asserts again and again that it was common and indeed normal for a 'messenger' to meet such opposition, and cited many Biblical and Arabian instances. Eventually the messenger was saved, despite the opposition, even when the whole community was destroyed. Against this background it was to be expected that the **Qur'an** would interpret the victory at Badr as a punishment of the Meccans for disbelieving the message, and a vindication of Muhammad's claim to be a messenger.

Another aspect of the contemporary situation where the Qur'anic interpretation was important was the relationship of the Muslims to the established communities of Jews and Christians with which they were in contact. One of the factors in this situation was the recognition by Islam of the essential identity of its message with that of Judaism and Christianity. Another factor was the criticism of Muhammad and the **Qur'an** by the Jews of Medina. In so far as a Muslim was able to appreciate the criticisms, they were likely to make him doubt the genuineness of the **Qur'an** and of Muhammad's claim to be a messenger. The behaviour of the Jews was thus a serious threat to the growing community of Muslims. Difficulties with Christians came chiefly towards the end of Muhammad's life when Christian tribes opposed the Islamic advance northwards in the direction of Syria.

One of the points in the Qur'anic interpretation of this situation was that the Jews opposed Muhammad and criticized him because they themselves had deviated from the original pure form of their own religion; and the same came to be said also of the Christians. It was not surprising, then, that they rejected the **Qur'an,** since it basically repeated the pure religion and not the corruptions of the Jews and Christians. This pure religion was further identified with the religion of Abraham, and it was insisted that he was neither a Jew nor a Christian. This last point, of course, is quite correct, since a Jew may be defined either as a descendant of Jacob (also called Israel) or as an adherent of the religious community based on the revelation to Moses; and both Jacob and Moses are descendants of Abraham. The **Qur'an** connects Abraham and Ishmael with Mecca, but does not speak of any Arabs as descended from Ishmael, though later Muslims accepted the Old Testament genealogies on this matter. There was a certain fitness in the claim that Islam was a restoration of the religion of Abraham in its purity; in this way Muslims were protected from the intellectual attacks of Jews and Christians, and yet the relationship to the two older religions was maintained. In its original form the claim approved itself to people who had no knowledge of the Jewish and Christian scriptures; later when Muslim scholars had gained some knowledge of the Bible and were meeting people familiar with it they had to elaborate further the theory of 'the corruption of the scriptures'.

From all this it will be clear that the Qur'anic interpretation of contemporary events and situations was no academic exercise, but was practical guidance for the community in the handling of actual problems. The guidance was no mere mechanical application of some rule, but was a creative response to the particular challenge. There can be no question but that in these matters the **Qur'an** shows originality....

MICHAEL COOK

SOURCE: Michael Cook, in his *Muhammad*, Oxford University Press, Oxford, 1983, 94 p.

[*In the excerpt below, Cook identifies basic Muslim tenets concerning the nature of the universe, human history, Muhammad's role, the future, law, and politics.*]

There are two components of Muhammad's universe: God and the world. Of these, God is the more remarkable. He is eternal—He has always existed, and always will. He is omniscient: not a leaf falls without His knowledge. He is omnipotent: when He decides something, He has only to say 'Be!' and it is. Above all, He is unique: He is one, and there is no other god but Him; He has no partners in His divinity. Furthermore, He is merciful and beneficent—but for reasons we shall come to, He is frequently angry.

The rest of the universe—the seven heavens, the earths, and their contents—was created by Him and belongs to Him. This feat of creation was achieved in six days (though the days in question would seem to have been divine days, each equivalent to a thousand human years). The basic structure of the world is fairly simple, although the scanty Koranic data have to be completed from tradition. The lower part, which was created first, consisted originally of a single earth which God then split into seven. The seven earths are arranged one above another like a stack of plates; we inhabit the top one, and the devil the bottom one, which is hell. Above the earths God placed an analogous stack of heavens; the lowest heaven is our own sky, the topmost is Paradise. The scale is generous by terrestrial standards: the standard distance, that between any two neighbouring plates, takes five hundred years to traverse, and larger dimensions are encountered at the top and bottom. The whole structure is said to have posed serious underpinning problems, to which colourful solutions were found; but these and other details need not detain us. God, in so far as He may be said to be in any particular place, is at the top of the world. Having created it, He did not leave it to run itself, or delegate the responsibility to others. Rather He continues to attend to it in every detail. He holds back the sky to prevent it falling on the earth; and He it is who makes rain to fall and trees to grow.

The world contains more than one form of intelligent life; but it is mankind which receives the lion's share of divine attention. The human race is monogenetic: we all descend from Adam, who was made from dust, and his consort, who was fashioned from him. We too belong to God. Tradition, slightly adapting a Koranic passage, relates that after creating Adam God rubbed his back, and there issued from him the souls of all future humanity. God then called them to bear witness, asking: 'Am I not your Lord?', to which they replied 'Yes, we bear witness'.

Despite this admission, the record of human conduct has to a large extent been one of disobedience to God. In the varied repertoire of human disobedience, one sin is particularly prominent: the failure to accord to Him the exclusive worship which is His due. This sin of polytheism is one into which men keep falling, and which then acquires for them the spurious authority of ancestral tradition. Hence the repeated dispatch of divine messengers to prise men loose from the ways of their fathers and revive their primordial allegiance to God alone. The story of these reminders, and the mixed reception they met with, makes up the core of human history....

Sooner rather than later, this history will end in a cataclysmic destruction of the world as we know it. The sky will be split, the stars scattered, the earth pounded to dust. The entire human race will be brought back to life—an easy matter for God to bring about, as the **Koran** insists. He will then proceed to judge men according to their deeds with the aid of balances; the saved will spend the rest of eternity amid the colourful delights of Paradise, while those found wanting are consigned to the pains of hell.

In these basic outlines, Muhammad's universe does not differ radically from those of other monotheist faiths. What comment it requires will accordingly depend on whether the reader is himself from a monotheist background. If he is, it will be enough to identify the more significant points of comparison. If he is not, he may legitimately find the entire conception puzzling; and this is perhaps where we should begin.

Historically, monotheism is descended from the polytheism of the ancient Near East. Near Eastern gods were often human beings writ large: they had bodies of human shape, quarrelled, behaved irresponsibly when drunk, and so forth. The God of the Old Testament was not given to such undignified behaviour, but He retained considerable traces from this past. The Bible speaks of Him as creating man in His own image, and as taking a day's rest after the labour of creation; and it treats in detail of the manner in which the Deity is to be housed and supplied with food. The tendency in monotheism has, however, been away from such a human conception of God, and towards a more transcendent one. Muhammad's God in some respects illustrates this trend. Admittedly the **Koran** still speaks freely of God's 'hand', and refers to Him settling into His throne; but it strongly denies that He found the work of creation tiring, and Islam does not accept the notion that God created man in His own image.

This dehumanisation of God had one rather serious implication, and we can best identify it by going back to the Mesopotamian myth which explains the creation of man. Even after the basic work of creation had been done, it must be understood, the running of the universe made heavy demands on the gods; and as might be expected, it was the junior gods who were saddled with the drudgery. Under these conditions, serious labour unrest developed among the junior gods, and a critical situation was defused only when discussions among their seniors issued in the creation of a substitute race, namely mankind. Since then men have done the hard work, and by and large the gods have lived a life of leisure. The whole story turns on the assumption that the gods have needs close enough to our own to be immediately intelligible to us, and that their powers to satisfy these needs, though considerable, are not unlimited.

The monotheist God, by contrast, needs nothing and nobody: 'God has no need of the worlds' and 'no need of you'; and if He were to need anything, He has only to say 'Be!' and it is. What then can be the point of His having human servants, or indeed a created world at all? Yet the **Koran** often refers to such servants of God, and explicitly assures us that God did not create heaven and earth for fun; had He wished to amuse Himself, He could have done so without resorting to the creation of an external world. But by the same token, the world cannot be considered to meet any other divine need. The strong and often immediate sense of God's purposes that characterises monotheism thus fits badly with the sublimer notions it has developed about His nature.

The reader who is himself from a monotheist background will of course be inured to this tension. He should also find the basic conception of Muhammad's universe a familiar one; it is not so distant from that found in the first chapter of the Book of Genesis, and ultimately derives from it. Other features have parallels in monotheist cosmology as it existed closer to the time of Muhammad. Thus the seven heavens, the five-hundred-year module, and the underpinning arrangements can all be matched from Jewish tradition. Similarly homespun ideas were also current among the Christians of the Middle East; here, however, they were under strong pressure from the very different style of cosmological thought represented by Greek philosophy. A sixth-century Nestorian Christian found it necessary to write at length to defend his traditional monotheist image of God's world against this pernicious influence. The same influence was later at work in the Islamic world, but not in the period which concerns us.

The feature of Muhammad's universe which is most likely to strike a non-Muslim monotheist as alien is a certain bleakness in the relationship between God's power and human action. This point is intimately related to the general tension within monotheism that we have already explored: on the one hand God frequently engages in behaviour that can be understood in much the same way as our own (e.g. He keeps sending messengers to disobedient communities with warnings they mostly disregard); and on the other hand, He is an omnipotent God who can realise His wishes immediately (e.g. He could if He wished have all men believe in Him). The first conception suggests that men act of their own free will, and sooner or later get their deserts for it. The second suggests that human acts, like other events, take place because God in His omnipotence has decreed that they will. The two conceptions do not go well together, if indeed they are compatible at all.

In the circumstances, there are two obvious ways to respond to the dilemma. One is to cut back the operation of God's omnipotence to allow at least a minimal domain for the freedom of human choice; for if men are not given enough moral rope to hang themselves, we are confronted with the unwelcome implication that their sin and damnation are the fault of God. This, essentially, was the option chosen by the other monotheist faiths of the day. The second course is to stand unflinchingly by God's omnipotence, and to allow human free will to be swamped by it; this, essentially, is the direction in which Islam inclines. God 'leads astray whom He will and guides whom He will'. He has created many men for hell, and pledged His word to fill it. The unbelievers will not believe, whether Muhammad warns them or not, for 'God has set a seal on their hearts'. This idiom was not new in monotheism; the God of Exodus repeatedly hardened the heart of Pharaoh the better to display His signs (see for example Exod. 7.3, and compare Rom. 9.17-18). Nor is it one consistently used in the **Koran.** Thus Muhammad is told to say: 'The truth is from your Lord; so let whosoever will, believe, and let whosoever will, disbelieve'. Such verses were duly cited by the proponents of the doctrine of human free will in Islam. But for better or worse, they fought a losing battle. . . .

Early Muslim scholars assigned to this world a duration of some six or seven thousand years. By the standards of ancient Indian or modern Western cosmology such a figure is breathtakingly small, but it agreed well enough with the views of other monotheists. Of this span, it was clear that the greater part had already elapsed—perhaps 5,500 out of 6,000 years. Muhammad's mission thus fell decidedly late in the day. He himself is said to have told his followers, with reference to the prospective duration of their community: 'Your appointed time compared with that of those who were before you is as from the afternoon prayer to the setting of the sun.' The formulation is problematic, but there is learned authority for the view that it represents about one-fourteenth of the total.

An early scholar who reckoned the age of the world at 5,600 years avowed that he knew about every period of its history, and what kings and prophets had lived in it. We can disregard the kings; it is the prophets who constitute the backbone of monotheist history. The list given below shows the most important of them. (The dates, which may be taken to represent years elapsed since the expulsion of Adam from Paradise, have the authority of Ibn Ishaq; but conflicting opinions abound on such details.)

Adam	-
Noah	1200
Abraham	2342
Moses	2907
Jesus	4832
Muhammad	5432

A chronology of this kind is not to be found in the **Koran;** but all the prophets listed here appear there, and their order in time is clearly envisaged as shown.

Every name in the list bar the last is familiar from the Bible. The first four names are major figures of the Pentateuch, and as such the common property of Judaism and Christianity. The parts they play in the Koranic view of monotheist history are more or less in accordance with their Biblical roles—though a good deal of material is altered, added or lost. Adam remains the common ancestor of humanity, and is expelled from Paradise with his consort for eating forbidden fruit. Noah is the builder of the ark whose occupants alone survive the flood in which God destroys the human race. Abraham is still the father who nearly sacrifices his son to God. Moses confronts Pharaoh, leads the Israelite exodus from Egypt, and meets God on Mount Sinai; to him is revealed a scripture, the Pentateuch. Other Old Testament figures also appear, notably Joseph, David and Solomon.

All this is familiar. Yet there are differences, and of these the most significant is a subtle shift of emphasis. The original Biblical figures play roles of considerable diversity; the **Koran,** by contrast, has a tendency to impose on them a stereotyped conception of the monotheist messenger. Thus in the **Koran,** Noah's mission is to warn his polytheist contemporaries to worship God alone; whereas in the Bible their sin is moral corruption rather than polytheism, and Noah has in any case no message to deliver to them.

With the next name on the list we come to a specifically Christian figure. As might be expected, the Jesus of the **Koran** is still recognisable as the Jesus of the New Testament: he is styled the Messiah, is born of a virgin, works miracles, has disciples, is rejected by the Jews, and eventually ascends to heaven. There are, however, divergences. For no obvious reason the **Koran** insists that Jesus was not really crucified; and there is no sense of his mission being addressed to an audience wider than the Children of Israel. But the crucial point of divergence is the insistence that Jesus, though a messenger of God, was not His son, still less God Himself. He is accordingly quoted in the **Koran** as denying his own (and his mother's) divinity. Closely related to this emphasis on the humanity of Jesus is the rejection of the Christian doctrine of the Trinity: it is unbelief to say that God is 'the third of three', for there is but one God. The Koranic doctrine of Jesus thus establishes a position quite distinct from that of either the Jews, who reject him, or the Christians, who deify him. Here, then, we have a parting of the ways.

It will be evident from this that the Koranic respect for Moses and Jesus does not extend to the bulk of their followers. The **Koran** does have some friendly things to say of the Christians, despite its strong sense of their fundamental error with regard to the status of their founder. But it also advances a good deal of miscellaneous polemic against them—they consider Mary, the mother of Jesus, to be divine; they hold themselves to be sons of God; they are riven by sectarianism; and so forth.

The Jews receive considerably more attention than the Christians. There is a long appeal to the Children of Israel to fulfil their covenant with God, and to accept Muhammad's message confirming the revelation that had already come to them; some of them would seem to have responded positively. There is a large amount of polemic. Misdeeds of the Biblical Israelites are raked over, such as their worship of the golden calf; the Jews are accused of speaking slanderously of Mary, the mother of Jesus, and are said to be among the most hostile of men towards the true believers. Many of the charges are petty or obscure (e.g. the curious allegation that the Jews consider Ezra to be the son of God), and in general there is more bad feeling towards the Jews than there is towards the Christians. But by contrast, the polemic is not focused on any central issue of doctrine—other than the Jewish refusal to accept Muhammad's own credentials.

Before leaving this stretch of monotheist history, a negative point implicit in all this should be brought out. The **Koran** is much concerned with the missions of the various monotheist messengers; but it displays little interest in whatever structure of religious authority may have existed in the intervals between these prophetic episodes. Aaron appears in the **Koran** as the brother of Moses and a participant in the events of his career, but never for his role in the establishment of the Israelite priesthood. The case of the twelve disciples of Jesus is similar: they never figure as the nucleus of the Christian church. Admittedly the **Koran** has a few things to say about the rabbis and monks of contemporary Judaism and Christianity, and it once mentions Christian priests. It is clear that these figures are thought to have legitimate roles to play in their respective communities; but they tend to be a bad lot, and to be worshipped by their followers in the place of God. One verse refers to monasticism as an institution; it describes it as an innovation of the Christians, not a divinely imposed duty, but does not reject it out of hand. Yet the attention given to these matters is slight.

From this survey, it might appear that Arabia played no role in monotheist history until the coming of Muhammad himself. In fact there are two Koranic conceptions which serve to endow Arabia with a monotheist past in its own right; one is rather modest, the other extremely bold.

The first conception is that of the ethnic warner. The idea is that God sends to every people a messenger, usually of their own number, who warns them in their own language to worship God alone; they regularly disregard the warning, and God destroys them in some spectacular fashion. We have already seen the shift of emphasis whereby the **Koran** presents Noah's career in this light. There is in fact a whole cycle of such stories which appear and reappear in the **Koran;** what concerns us here is that this stereotype is also extended to Arabia. To take a single example, a certain Salih (a good Arabic name) was sent to Thamud (an attested people of ancient Arabia) with such a message; they ignored it, and were destroyed by a thunderbolt, or some equivalent expression of divine irritation. These Arabian warners are unknown to Jewish or Christian tradition, and their presence in the **Koran** does something to place Arabia on the monotheist map. But by their very nature, they make no mark on the grand scheme of monotheist history. The episodes are parochial side-shows, and establish no continuing monotheist communities; all that is left is some archaeological remains and a cautionary tale.

The other conception, the 'religion of Abraham', is of a quite different calibre. Its starting-point is the Biblical account of Abraham and his sons. According to the Book of Genesis, Abraham was married to Sarah; but she only bore him a son, Isaac, in their extreme old age. At that time Abraham already had a son, Ishmael, by an Egyptian concubine named Hagar. This had led to considerable ill-feeling between the two women, and already while Hagar was pregnant she had run away into the wilderness. On this occasion an angel had found her by a spring, and sent her home with somewhat qualified promises for the future of her unborn son. When eventually Isaac was born to Sarah, Hagar was sent packing together with her son. This time her water supply ran out, and the child was about to die of thirst when again an angel intervened. Hagar was promised that a great nation would arise from her son, and was miraculously shown a well. Thereafter, we are told, God was with the lad; he grew up in the wilderness and had twelve sons, from whom were descended the twelve Ishmaelite tribes. But for all that, Abraham's heir was Isaac, the ancestor of the Israelites; it was with Isaac, not Ishmael, that God made His everlasting covenant.

The message of this colourful narrative of patriarchal family life is a simple one. Abraham was the common ancestor of the Israelites and the Ishmaelites—or as posterity would put it, of the Jews and the Arabs. Thereafter sacred history was concerned only with the Israelites; the Ishmaelites might be a great nation, but in religious terms they were a dead end.

Much of this picture was accepted by Islam. Muslim scholars thought in the same genealogical idiom, and considered the Arabs (or more precisely, the northern Arabs) to descend from the sons of Ishmael. Equally, as we have seen, Islam accepts the Israelite line of sacred history running from Isaac to Moses and on (in the Christian view) to Jesus. Where Islam departed radically from the Biblical conception was in opening up the Ishmaelite dead end, thereby creating a second line of sacred history that was specifically Arabian.

One Muslim tradition describes the aftermath of the quarrel between Sarah and Hagar. Abraham took Hagar and Ishmael to an uninhabited spot in the wilderness, and left them there. Hagar's water-skin was soon empty, and her child was about to die when Gabriel appeared; he struck the ground with his foot, and a spring gushed forth. The uninhabited spot was Mecca, and the spring was Zamzam, the water-supply of the Meccan sanctuary which we met in connection with Muhammad's grandfather. Other traditions depart more strongly from the Biblical narrative. God ordered Abraham to build Him a sanctuary where He would be worshipped. Abraham was at first in some perplexity as to how to proceed, but was supernaturally guided to Mecca, accompanied by Hagar and Ishmael. There Abraham and Ishmael built the sanctuary and established the rites of pilgrimage to it. Abraham seems in due course to have departed to resume his Biblical career; but Hagar and Ishmael remained, and at their deaths were buried in the sanctuary. Some say that Ishmael was the first to speak in pure Arabic. He was also a prophet in his own right—and the ancestor of a prophet, Muhammad.

The Arabs thus inherited from their ancestor a monotheist faith and sanctuary. In the course of time, however, this heritage was greatly corrupted. As Mecca became overcrowded with Ishmael's rapidly multiplying descendants, groups of them would move away and subsequently fall into local idolatry. Idols even appeared in the sanctuary itself (Hubal, the most noteworthy, being acquired by a leading Meccan while travelling on business in Moab). In the meantime, the descendants of Ishmael had lost possession of their sanctuary to others, not to regain it till Quraysh settled in Mecca five generations before Muhammad. Yet for all that the Arabs had lapsed into pagan superstition, monotheism remained their birthright.

The elaborate narrative traditions drawn on here are not to be found in the **Koran**, but the basic conception is present in force. The **Koran** emphasises that Abraham was a monotheist long before there was such a thing as Judaism or Christianity. 'Abraham was neither a Jew nor a Christian; but he was one of the true religion (*hanif*) who submitted to God (*muslim*)'. That Abraham is here described as, in effect, a Muslim is no surprise; the **Koran** uses similar language of other monotheists (e.g. Noah, Joseph, the Queen of Sheba, the disciples of Jesus). Its tendency to link the term *muslim* with Abraham in particular is nevertheless a pronounced one. The term *hanif* is also significant. Although its exact sense is obscure, the **Koran** uses it in contexts suggestive of a pristine monotheism, which it tends to contrast with (latter-day) Judaism and Christianity. It associates the idea strongly with Abraham, but never with Moses or Jesus.

Abraham in turn bequeaths his faith to his sons, warning them to be sure that when they die, they do so in a state of submission to God (*muslim*). He prays that they may not succumb to the worship of idols, and asks God to raise up from his and Ishmael's posterity a people (*umma*) who submit to God (*muslim*). Abraham's religion accordingly remains valid for his descendants. The **Koran** frequently recommends it, and tells the believers that their religion is that of 'your father Abraham'. (The phrase is to be taken literally; this is not the Christian image of 'our father Abraham' as the *spiritual* ancestor of all believers, whatever their actual descent.) At the same time the story of the building of the sanctuary by Abraham and Ishmael has a prominent place in the **Koran;** and Abraham speaks of the settlement of some of his posterity in a barren valley beside it (i.e. Mecca).

The effect of these ideas is simple but crucial: they endow Arabia and the Arabs with an honoured place in monotheist history, and one genealogically independent of the Jews and Christians.

The view of sacred history just analysed is in some ways a very consistent one—relentlessly monotheist, and by Biblical standards rather stereotyped. It nevertheless puts side by side two notions between which there is a certain tension. On the one hand there is the conception of a linear succession of monotheist messengers, among whom the founders of Judaism and Christianity find their places. Yet on the other hand we have the idea of an alternative, Arabian monotheism in a line branching off from Abraham. These two conceptions are closely linked to the role, or roles, which the **Koran** ascribes to Muhammad.

The least adventurous role is that of an ethnic warner. Muhammad's mission is to 'warn the mother of cities (i.e. Mecca) and those round about her'; those to whom he is sent have received no previous warning. The parallel with the earlier ethnic warners is explicit: 'This is a warner, of the warners of old'. This simple conception is a prominent one in the **Koran,** and each retelling of the cautionary tales about earlier warners helps to underline it. Yet it does not quite fit. For one thing, we find in these passages references to Muhammad as the recipient of a revealed book. Aptly, this scripture is an 'Arabic **Koran**'—a common Koranic phrase, and a characteristic example of the Koranic emphasis on Arabic as the language of Muhammad's mission. Yet the revelation of a scripture is not a motif that appears in the cautionary tales of earlier warners. And for another thing, Muhammad's people did in the end listen to him, an outcome for which the model of the ethnic warner hardly provided.

A more ambitious conception of Muhammad's role arises out of the religion of Abraham. This pristine monotheism having fallen on evil days, Muhammad could be seen as a messenger sent to restore it. Such a need had been anticipated by Abraham himself. In the course of the major Koranic account of the foundation of the sanctuary, we read that Abraham prayed in these terms on behalf of his descendants: 'Lord, send among them a messenger of their own number who may recite your signs to them, teach them the Book and wisdom, and purify them'. A little later, it is stated that such a messenger has now been sent—a clear reference to Muhammad.

This gives Muhammad a definite position in the structure of monotheist history, and one that goes well with the Arabian setting. But it does not really define his position with regard to the main line of succession, and in particular to Moses and Jesus. It is here that a third conception of Muhammad's role appears. This conception is nicely illustrated in a Koranic sketch of the history of scriptural law: first the Pentateuch was revealed, i.e. to Moses; then Jesus was sent, and to him was revealed the Gospel, confirming the Pentateuch; then the Book (i.e. the **Koran**) was revealed to Muhammad, confirming what had already been revealed. Conversely, the **Koran** describes the earlier scriptures as foretelling the coming of Muhammad: he is inscribed in the Pentateuch and the Gospel, and his future mission was part of the good news announced by Jesus. Muhammad is thus authenticated as a new prophet with a new scripture in the direct line of succession to Moses and Jesus.

He is accordingly much more than just a local Arabian prophet. The **Koran,** after speaking of the endorsement of Muhammad in the Pentateuch and Gospel, goes on to refer to him as 'the messenger of God to you all'; and from this it is but a short step to conceiving him as God's messenger to mankind at large. In practice, as the **Koran** makes clear, it is not the will of God that mankind should again become the 'one community' they originally were; He guides whom He wills, and by the same token He leads astray whom He wills. But for all the persistence of error, there is now but one true religion for all mankind.

This assertion gains poignancy from the fact that Muhammad is not just the most recent of the prophets, but also the last—the 'seal of the prophets', in a Koranic phrase which has come to be understood in this sense. Tradition has it that Muhammad comparing his role to those of the earlier prophets, likened himself to the final brick to be laid in the corner of an edifice otherwise completed. His career is accordingly the last major even in monotheist history before the end of the world.

We may end this account with a brief relation of the

future course of history as it appeared to early Muslims. This is not a topic treated in the **Koran;** but it is abundantly (and by no means consistently) treated in early tradition, from which what follows is selected.

The future is nasty, brutish and short. The Muslim community will break up into a mass of conflicting sects, just as the Children of Israel had done before them. Sedition will follow sedition like strips of the darkest night, and the living will envy the dead. Eventually God will send a redeemer, a descendant of Muhammad. This redeemer, the Mahdi, will receive allegiance at the sanctuary in Mecca, whence his emigration (*hijra*) will be to Jerusalem; there he will reign in justice. Yet this interlude will last less than a decade. Thereafter Antichrist (the Dajjal) will appear from Iraq, reducing the Muslims to a remnant making their last stand on the peak of a mountain in Syria. In the hour of their need, Jesus will descend to earth in armour and lead them against Antichrist, slaying him at the gate of Lydda in Palestine; then Jesus will reign in justice and plenty, exterminating the pig and breaking the crosses of the Christians. Yet this too will pass, giving way to the final horrors of human history. At the last a wind takes up the souls of the believers, the sun rises in the west, and history gives way to the cataclysmic eschatology of the **Koran.**

The Koranic view of history is in some ways rather repetitive. Successive messengers arrive with the same doctrinal message. There is, however, a certain ringing of changes with regard to the outward form and precise content of the messages. Sometimes they are in writing; sometimes, apparently, they are not. What is more, the various revealed books, while of course confirming each other in general terms, may differ significantly in points of detail. God tells Muhammad that 'to every term there is a book', that is, each age has its scripture; in it God erases or confirms what He pleases, the 'mother of the Book' (presumably a kind of archetype) being with Him. In other words, the content of revelation is liable to change from one prophetic epoch to another.

The field in which this instability is most marked is divine law—law which God Himself makes and unmakes. To each community God assigned its particular way; thus each has its own way of slaughtering (or sacrificing) animals, and yet 'their God is one god'. Whereas the truth of monotheist doctrine is timeless, the validity of monotheist law is a more relative matter. Even within the **Koran** itself, the Muslim scholars found scriptural support for the view that earlier verses could be abrogated by later ones.

The pivotal event in the Koranic view of the history of law is the revelation of the Pentateuch to Moses. There is little indication that law played much part in God's dealings with mankind before this event. We learn incidentally that God had revealed the duties of prayer and almsgiving to Abraham, Isaac and Jacob, and that Ishmael imposed them on his family; but for the most part Abrahamic law remains as shadowy as the scripture with which the **Koran** occasionally endows him. With Moses, we are on firmer ground. The Pentateuch contains the 'judgement of God', and by it the Prophets judged the Jews. Some of its concrete legal stipulations are cited—a couple of dietary laws, for example, and the principle of 'a life for a life'. The Pentateuch (or the set of tablets which God gave to Moses) deals fully with all questions; in it are guidance and light.

There is nevertheless a strong sense in the **Koran** that the yoke of the Pentateuchal code was an unduly heavy one, and that this, though God's responsibility, is the fault of the Jews. This idea finds clear expression with regard to dietary law. The **Koran** insists that dietary prohibitions of divine origin were first introduced in the Pentateuch: 'Every food was lawful to the Children of Israel, except what Israel (i.e. Jacob) forbade to himself, before the revelation of the Pentateuch'. That God then forbade to the Israelites foods previously permitted to them was a punishment for their own misdeeds.

The tendency since the revelation of the Pentateuch has accordingly been for God to ease the yoke of the law. The mission of Jesus is conceived in a manner rather similar to that of Moses, in the sense that the scripture revealed to him, the Gospel, is a law-book according to which his followers are to be judged. Yet at the same time it is part of his mission 'to declare lawful to you some of what was forbidden to you'. Muhammad's role is similarly conceived, and is perhaps thought of as going further in the direction of liberalisation. Much, of course, is carried over from earlier dispensations; thus the obligation to fast is laid upon the believers 'as it was laid upon those who were before you'. Dietary law, however, is drastically pruned: the prohibitions are reduced to a few key points, and these provisions are expressly contrasted with the more elaborate restrictions which God had imposed on the Jews. The case of the Sabbath is similar. Without question it had been imposed on the Jews, and one verse which was to cause a considerable theological flurry tells how God metamorphosed Sabbath-breakers into apes. Yet this did not mean that the Sabbath was binding on Muhammad's own community. It had been imposed only on 'those who differed concerning it' (presumably the Jews), and—so the context seems to imply—forms no part of the religion of Abraham.

Historically, this Koranic perspective on the history of

law is in some ways an apt one. Law was a late starter in religious history. The gods of the ancient Near East did not usually concern themselves with legislation, and law was not a central feature of the culture of their priests. The salience of law in ancient Israelite religion was thus unusual—and still more so the later elaboration of the Biblical heritage into the law-centred culture of the Jewish rabbis. It is also legitimate to think of a trend towards liberalisation, and to place both Jesus and Muhammad within it. Yet there is a fundamental difference here which the **Koran,** in bringing Jesus firmly into line between Moses and Muhammad, has glossed over. The Gospel is not a law-book. Its message is rather that the Law is not enough; and the followers of Jesus soon went on to infer that most of it was not necessary at all. The dietary code of the Pentateuch still stands in the Christian Bible as 'appointed to be read in churches', but it would be bizarre, indeed sinful, for Christians to observe it. Christianity, in short, is not a law-centred religion. Islam, for all its liberalisation, unmistakably remains one. . . .

R. PARET

SOURCE: R. Paret, "The Qur'an-I," in *Arabic Literature to the End of the Umayyad Period*, edited by A. F. L. Beeston and others, Cambridge University Press, 1983, pp. 186-227.

[*In the following excerpt, Paret discusses stylistic aspects of the* Koran.]

The language of the **Qur'an** is essentially identical with the standard Arabic high language which in Muhammad's day had already been developed by the ancient Arabic poets and was subsequently to live on through the centuries as the language of classical Arabic literature. . . .

The **Qur'an** is written throughout in rhyming prose (*saj'*), and appears therefore, to a greater or lesser extent, artistically constructed and strongly rhetorical in comparison with ordinary prose. The individual parts of a sentence, the sentence or combination of sentences which end with a rhyme and are called verses (*ayah*, plural *ayat*) follow the rhyme scheme a-a, b-b, c-c. The same rhyme is repeated not only once but as often as the author pleases, e.g. a-a-a, b-b, c-c-c-c (*surah* [chapter] ci). Short *surahs* sometimes have only one rhyme. Ideally, as in the earliest *surahs*, the rhymes follow in rapid succession at fairly equal intervals; this also seems to have been the case with the rhymes of the ancient Arabic soothsayers. (Presumably the Prophet in fact adopted the alternation of short rhyme sequences from the practice of these soothsayers.) In the *surahs* from the latter years of Muhammad's career the verses lengthen increasingly, and the rhymes no longer have the effect of rhetorically enlivening elements, but sound monotonous and often forced, as though they have been added later.

As far as the rhymes themselves are concerned, they are handled with great freedom. . . .

Frequently the demands of the rhyme scheme determine the choice of word or construction. . . .

In a few *surahs* the same verse occurs again and again at the end of individual sections, retaining the same rhyme and thus forming a kind of refrain. The sections identified in this way as being similar are not, however, proper stanzas. In *surahs* liv and xxvi it is above all sections referring to earlier prophets and their incredulous contemporaries which close with this sort of verse. In *surah* lxxvii, in another context, the refrain *waylun yawma-'idhin li-'l- mukadhdhibina* ("Woe on that day to those who declare [our message] to be a lie!") occurs ten times. *Surah* lv reveals the same refrain repeated as many as thirty-one times. It runs thus: *fa-bi-ayyi ala'i rabbi-kuma tukadhdhibani* ("which of the good deeds of your Lord do you want to deny?"), and through the use of the dual it fits in at least superficially with the rhyme scheme of this *surah*. At the beginning the refrain also suits the context, which praises the creative power of God. But by the end it is being repeated mechanically without any real connection, even after verses depicting the torment of sinners in Hell. The whole thing is an ill-judged attempt to endow an already spirited text with even more rhetorical artistry through the constant repetition of a refrain.

A large number of early pronouncements in the **Qur'an** are introduced by strange oaths, or rather asseverations, a stylistic device which Muhammad in all probability copied from the old Arab soothsayers. These declarations, some of which are difficult to comprehend, are designed to prepare the way for the subsequent statement with rhetorical, if not magical, pathos. As an example let us take the opening of *surah* lxxxix. "By the dawn, by [a certain period of] ten nights, by the even and uneven [of number] and by the night when it runs its course! Is this not for the man of understanding a [powerful] oath?" The Prophet made extensive use of this device, but related it more and more closely to the content of his message, and eventually abandoned it altogether. The process whereby the incantations were gradually assimilated to Islamic doctrine cannot be demonstrated in detail here. But let us look at three more quotations to illustrate the development in question. Surah lxxvii.1ff.: "By those who are sent one after the other [in bands?] surge onwards, breach [?] and scatter [?] [everything] and exhort [men] to forgiveness or as a warning! Whatever threats are made against you will certainly come to pass." Surah lxxv.1-2: "No, in truth! I swear by the day of resurrection and by [each] one who [will then?] reproach himself bitterly." Surah xxxvi.2-4: "By the wise **Qur'an!** Your are truly one of [God's] messengers and [your foot is] upon a straight path."

The formulation of the early pronouncements makes a forceful, even inspiring impression without any preceding asseveration, especially in the texts dealing with the impending apocalypse and the threat of judgement, one of the main themes of Muhammad's message. Since the event as such is unimaginable, it is symbolized by its omens and attendant phenomena, and thus impressed upon the heat of the listener through an accumulation of terrifying occurrences. Often this happens through temporal clauses introduced by the particles *idha*, "[one day] when" or *yawma* "on the day when". Sometimes the balancing clause is missing. To complete the sense we then have to add something like "then the fateful moment will have arrived" or "then you must be prepared for the worst". Surah lxxiv.1-5: "When the heavens are rent, hearken to the Lord and it is meet for them [to obey His will?], when the earth is spread out [and brought low], casts forth all [the dead] concealed within it, empties itself [completely], hearkens to the Lord and it is meet for it [to obey His will?]!" Surah ci. 1-4: "The castrophe! What does it signify? How can you know what it should signify? On the day when men will be as [singed] moths, scattered about [on the ground], and the mountains like tangled wool!"

Abbreviated temporal clauses with *idh* ("in those days past when") occur even more frequently. They are found in texts which point back in time and recall episodes from the story of salvation, or events which happened not long before. We can best understand them in their truncated form as exclamations, and should supply the missing clause in our own minds with something like "that was indeed a noteworthy event". Two examples refer ... to the battle of Badr. We can add to these another example from a section about the story of Abraham. Surah ii.127: "And [in those days] when Abraham erected the foundations—those of the house [the Ka'bah]—[he] and Ishmael [and prayed to God]: 'Lord! Accept this our gift! You are He who hears and knows [all].'" (The preceding verses 124, 125 and 126 are similarly introduced by *wa-idh*.) In so far as the abbreviated temporal clauses like the last example refer back to episodes from the history of religion, rather than to familiar events in living memory, they have become a purely stylistic device. They inform about episodes from the dim and distant past by adopting a formulation which purports to remind the listeners of something that, as a rule, they did not know before. Only Muhammad enjoys such knowledge. For his part he believes that through revelation he has access to knowledge denied to ordinary mortals. Surah ii.133: "Or were you [perhaps] witnesses, when Jacob reached the point of death [so that you could give an authentic account of it]? When he spoke to his sons 'Whom will you serve when I am no longer with you?'?" Surah iii.2-4 (preceded by a section about Zacharias and Mary): "And when the angels said: 'Mary! God has chosen you and made you pure! ... Be a humble servant of the Lord ... !' This [i.e. the story of Mary] is one of the stories which remain concealed [from ordinary mortals]. We impart it to you [as revelation]. You were not of their number [i.e. among Mary's companions] when they drew lots [to decide] which one should attend Mary. And you were not of their number when they quarrelled among themselves [over this]."

When reading the **Qur'an** one must always bear in mind that the text was originally meant to be spoken out loud and presupposes an audience. As the mouthpiece of God Muhammad is often bidden by the word *qul* ("speak") to proclaim something orally. The vocatives "O you believers!" or "O you people!" sometimes allude to the listeners. Sometimes the audience or the Prophet himself is directed by an introductory *a-ra'aytum, a-ra'ayta* ("What do you think about this?") to adopt a critical attitude to a particular subject. Everything is couched in a living, spoken language. Only later was the **Qur'an** turned into a book that silently bears its message within itself and only when read aloud—and even then only to a limited extent—makes a lively and spirited impression. In the narrative passages direct speech is used freely and we sometimes even find statements and replies. There are positively dramatic eschatological scenes with regular dialogues, some between the damned in Hell and the blessed in Paradise, others between the damned and their previous seducers. God, too, appears in person at the Last Judgement and speaks, as does even Hell itself: "On the Day [of Judgement], when we shall say to Hell: 'Are you [now] full?', whereupon it will reply: 'Are there still more [for me to swallow up]?'" (surah l.30). When we read these passages (lxxiv.38-48; l.19-30; xxxvii.19-33, 50-60; xxxviii.59-64) it is not always clear who exactly is speaking or being addressed. We also find impersonal phrases before direct speech ("Then it is said, 'And they are told, the Angels of the Judgement are told'"). In the original oral delivery the identity of the speaker could easily be indicated by a change of voice or gesture.

The language of the **Qur'an** is rich in images, though not as extensively so as the *logia* of Jesus in the Gospels. Now and then the image has already become a metaphor. It then denotes directly the object or event which it originally served to paraphrase and elucidate. Thus, for instance, the performing of moral actions is indicated by *kasaba*, a word taken from commercial life and meaning in fact "acquire". Words from the sphere of nomadic life such as *dalla*, "lose one's way" and *hada*, "lead along the right path" become expressions of religious conduct. Terms denoting the behaviour of birds such as *khafada 'l-janaha* ("[the bird] folded up the wing [signifying compliance, gentleness]") are applied without demur to human beings (xv.88; xvii.24; xx.22; xxviii.32). But as a rule the image is used only for purposes of comparison and not identified with the object or event in question. In this context we must distinguish carefully between a mere simile and the aesthetically more ambitious parable, which has a didactic function. The distinction, it is true, is not always easy to preserve.

Similes are to be found, for example, in *surah* ci.4-5, where we read during a description of the apocalypse that men "will be as [singed] moths, scattered about [on the ground], and the mountains like tangled wool", or in *surah* lxxiv.50-1, where it is said of the infidels who shut their ears to the tidings of salvation that they turn away "like startled [wild] asses fleeing from a lion" (incidentally, the word for lion – "powerful" – is itself a metaphor). The following two examples can also be regarded as ordinary similes. *Surah* lxii.5: "Those who are laden with the Torah are like an ass carrying books." *Surah* vii.176, where we read of one who could not be won over to Islam: "He is like a dog. His tongue hangs out, you may beat him or leave him alone."

The parables proper are impressed upon men by God, so that they may perhaps take heed (xiv.25; xxxix.27; lix.21). The peculiar "light-verse", "God is the Light of the Heavens and the Earth; the likeness of His light is as a niche wherein is a lamp . . . ", (xxiv.35), which undoubtedly belongs to this category, has been the object of much speculation and debate. But impressive too are the parables of the mirage and of the darkness in the depths of the ocean (xxiv.39-40) that follow shortly afterwards. The material of the other twenty or more Quranic parables is drawn from various spheres: natural phenomena such as thunderstorms, gales, cold, rain, flood, growth and drought; from agriculture and horticulture, from the institution of slavery. Even a spider's web provides the starting point for an edifying reflection (xxix.41): "God is not ashamed to coin any parable, even one involving a gnat. Those who believe know that it is the truth [and comes] from their Lord. Those, however, who do not believe say 'What does God intend with such a parable?' He leads many astray thereby. But He [also] thereby leads many along the right path. And only the evil-doers are thus led astray" (ii.26). It is very often the case that the short life of plants gives rise to edifying reflections. Sometimes, as in *surah* xxxix.21, the emphasis is then placed on the natural phenomenon itself, so that one cannot, strictly speaking, call it a parable any longer. In other cases strange hybrids are formed. Thus, for instance, in *surah* iii.117: "That which they [i.e. the infidels] expend in this life is like an ice-cold wind which blew over the corn-fields of men who [with their sinful ways] had transgressed against themselves, and destroyed it [i.e. the seed or corn]. God did not transgress against them, but they transgressed against themselves." Here the parable merges into a reference to an earlier event (somewhat like the story of the gardens of the Sabaeans in *surah* xxxiv.15-17). A theme such as that of the transitoriness of earthly life can be seen from many different points of view. It is, after all, inexhaustible.

The **Qur'an** was not written all at once. Certain of Muhammad's opponents reproached him for this (xxv.32). But no book has ever materialized out of the blue. And even if it did, what purpose would this serve? "If we had sent down to you a scripture [written] on parchment [or papyrus? *qirtas*] and they [i.e. your people] were able to lay their hands upon it, those who do not believe would [still] say: 'That is clearly witchcraft'" (vi.7). In reality the individual revelations were proclaimed over a period of twenty years or more and in separate sections (xvii.106), which were presumably fairly short but were later for the most part combined into longer chapters. Later still the chapters, called *surahs*, were collected into a book, the **Qur'an.** Thereby they were arranged on the purely mechanical basis of diminishing length, though exceptions were made for the short prayer-like prefatory *surah* and the two apotropaic concluding *surahs*. This is not the place to discuss in detail the composition of individual *surahs*. What we can justifiably discuss here, however, is the problem of changes in the style of individual chapters and at the same time the question of how far it is possible to date the chapters concerned on the basis of stylistic features.

When one tries to put a date to particular *surahs*, either in part or as a whole, one naturally pays due attention to references to historical events such as the battle of Badr, the Trench war or the expedition to al-Hudaybiyah. This has already been done by Muslim historians and commentators. But such allusions are in fact relatively rare. A more significant basis for the dating of the texts is provided by stylistic traits. Changes of style in the **Qur'an** are accounted for by the mere fact that Muhammad grew considerably older in the course of his activity as a prophet and accordingly moved away from a more dynamic to a calmer mode of expression. At the same time we must not fall into the trap of denying the Prophet all rhetorical sweep in his later years. The more measured tone of the later *surahs* is also determined by their purpose and content. Rules governing matters of family law, and especially the laws of inheritance, could scarcely be formulated in as spirited a fashion as the prophecies of impending doom with which Muhammad had first addressed the citizens of Mecca. However that may be, Muslim scholars tried many centuries ago to divide up the *surahs* according to their subject matter into those dating from the Meccan period and those from the Medinan period, and to establish their chronological sequence. They also considered the possibility that small sections of a *surah* might date from a later period than the bulk of its verses. Utilizing these preliminary studies and taking into account stylistic features, the European orientalists Gustav Weil, Richard Bell and (in particular) Theodor Noldeke worked out a more precise chronological arrangement of the *surahs*, whereby they subdivided the Meccan *surahs* into three groups. The results of their research into modifications of style may be summed up as follows.

Of the three groups belonging to the Meccan period, the first and oldest group amounts, according to Noldeke's reckoning, to forty-eight mostly short *surahs*, and is distinguished by its passionate and forceful style. "The diction is grand, noble and full of bold images, the rhetorical sweep is still tinged with poetry. The impassioned verve, which is not infrequently interrupted by simple but powerful, measured maxims and colourful descriptions, is reflected in the short verses, the whole manner of speaking is rhythmical and often of considerable, though completely artless euphony.

The emotions and intuitions of the Prophet are sometimes expressed with a certain obscurity of meaning; the meaning indeed is intimated rather than fully articulated." (Thus Noldeke's classic formulation of 1860.)

In the twenty-one *surahs* comprising each of the other two Meccan periods we witness a gradual transition to a more serene reflection. Examples from nature and history that are meant to serve the unbelievers as a warning and the faithful as edification and comfort are depicted in detail and arranged in sequence. The descriptions grow more expansive, the verses longer. The *surahs*, too, increase in length. The similarity between the accounts of various men of God from earlier times makes for a somewhat monotonous effect. The angry tone of the polemic against the incorrigible representatives of polytheism and their worldly philosophy makes itself clearly felt. All these characteristics develop slowly in the *surahs* of the second Meccan period, to emerge fully fledged, as it were, in those of the third period.

The twenty-four *surahs* originating in Medina are for the most part lengthy because they comprise many different individual sections. Here the new set of tasks confronting the Prophet after his migration makes relatively little impact on the style. The polemic rumbles on, though it acquires rather more specific forms vis-a-vis the Jews of Medina and the "hypocrites". References to past historical events are enlivened in the same way as the references to earlier religious situations, through the occasional use of abbreviated temporal clauses. As is to be expected, the requisite legal rulings and other instructions sound truly prosaic. The rhymes still customary at the end of the long verses are here redundant and give an impression of having been stuck on arbitrarily....

JOHN L. ESPOSITO

SOURCE: John L. Esposito, "The Quran: The Word of God," in his *Islam: The Straight Path*, expanded edition, Oxford University Press, 1991, pp. 19-21.

[*Esposito is an educator and writer whose works include* Voices of Resurgent Islam *(1983),* Islam and Politics *(1984), and* Islam: The Straight Path *(1988). In this excerpt from the expanded edition of the latter book, published in 1991, he discusses Muslim beliefs about the Quran.*]

For Muslims, the **Quran** is the Book of God. It is the eternal, uncreated, literal word of God sent down from heaven, revealed one final time to the Prophet Muhammad as a guide for humankind ([**Quran**] 2:185). The **Quran** consists of 114 chapters of 6,000 verses, originally revealed to Muhammad over a period of twenty-two years. It is approximately four-fifths the size of the New Testament, and its chapters are arranged according to length, not chronology. The longer chapters, representing the later Medinan revelations, precede the shorter, earlier Meccan revelations to Muhammad.

Islam teaches that God's revelation has occurred in several forms: in nature, history, and Scripture. God's existence can be known through creation; nature contains pointers or "signs" of God, its creator and sustainer (3:26-27). The history of the rise and fall of nations, victory and defeat, provides clear signs and lessons of God's sovereignty and intervention in history (30:2-9). In addition, God in His mercy determined to reveal His will for humankind through a series of messengers: "Indeed, We sent forth among every nation a Messenger, saying: 'Serve your God, and shun false gods'" (16:36) (see also 13:7, 15:10, 35:24). The verses of revelation are also called signs of God. Thus, throughout history, human beings could not only know that there is a God but also know what God desires and commands for His creatures.

If Scripture is a sign from God sent to previous generations, what can be said about these Scriptures and prophets? Why was the **Quran** subsequently revealed, and what is the relationship of the **Quran** and Muhammad to previous revelations?

Although God had revealed His will to Moses and the Hebrew prophets and later to Jesus, Muslims believe that the Scriptures of the Jewish community (Torah) and that of the Christian church (the Evangel or Gospel) were corrupted. The current texts of the Torah and the New Testament are regarded as a composite of human fabrications mixed with divine revelation. Of God's revelation to the Jews, the **Quran** declares:

> Surely We sent down the Torah, wherein is guidance and light; thereby the Prophets who had surrendered themselves gave judgment for those of Jewry, as did the masters and rabbis, following that portion of God's book as they were given to keep and were witness to. (5:47)

Muslims believe that after the deaths of the prophets, extraneous, nonbiblical beliefs infiltrated the texts and thus altered and distorted the original, pure revelation. The Jews, and later the Christians, are portrayed as having distorted their mission to witness into a doctrine of their divine election as a chosen people:

> And the Jews and Christians say, "We are the sons of God, and His beloved ones." Say: "Why then does He chastise you for your sins? No you are mortals, of His creating; He forgives whom He will, and He chastises whom He will." (5:20)

The **Quran** teaches that a similar degeneration or perversion of Scripture occurred in Christianity. God sent Jesus as a prophet: "He [God] will teach him [Jesus] the Book, the Wisdom, the Torah, the Gospel, to be a messenger to the Children of Israel" (3:48-49). Yet, the **Quran** declares that after his death, Jesus' meaning and message were soon altered by those who made him into a god:

> The Christians say, "The Messiah is the Son of God." . . . God assail them! How they are perverted!. . . They were commanded to serve but One God; There is no God but He. (9:30-31)

After the falsification of the revelation given to the Jews and the Christians, Muslims believe that God in His mercy sent down His word one final time. The **Quran** does not abrogate or nullify, but rather corrects, the versions of Scripture preserved by the Jewish and Christian communities: "People of the Book, now there has come to you Our messenger making clear to you many things you have been concealing of the Book, and effacing many things" (5:16).

Thus, Islam is not a new religion with a new Scripture. Instead of being the youngest of the major monotheistic world religions, from a Muslim viewpoint it is the oldest. Islam represents the "original" as well as the final revelation of the God of Abraham, Moses, Jesus, and Muhammad. The **Quran,** like the Torah and the Evangel, is based on a preexisting heavenly tablet, the source or mother of Scripture. It is a book written in Arabic that exists in heaven with God; from it, the discourses or teachings of the three Scriptures are revealed at different stages in history: "Every term has a book . . . and with Him is the essence of the Book" (13:38-39).

Since Muslims believe that the **Quran**'s Arabic language and character are revealed (26:195; 41:44), all Muslims, regardless of their national language, memorize and recite the **Quran** in Arabic whether they fully understand it or not. Arabic is the sacred language of Islam because, in a very real sense, it is the language of God. In contrast to Judaism and Christianity, whose Scriptures were not only translated into Greek and Latin at an early date but also disseminated in vernacular languages, in Islam Arabic has remained the language of the **Quran** and of religious learning. Until modern times, the **Quran** was printed only in Arabic; it could not be translated in Muslim countries. Even now, translations are often accompanied by the Arabic text.

Since the **Quran** is God's book, the text of the **Quran,** like its author, is regarded as perfect, eternal, and unchangeable. This belief is the basis for the doctrine of the miracle of inimitability of the **Quran,** which asserts that the ideas, language, and style of the **Quran** cannot be reproduced. The **Quran** proclaims that even the combined efforts of human beings and jinns could not produce a comparable text (17:88). The **Quran** is regarded as the only miracle brought by the Prophet. Muslim tradition is replete with stories of those who converted to Islam on hearing its inimitable message and of those pagan poets who failed the Quranic challenge (10:37-38) to create verses comparable with those contained in the **Quran**. Indeed, throughout history, many Arab Christians as well have regarded it as the perfection of Arabic language and literature.

In addition to its place as a religious text, the **Quran** was central to the development of Arabic linguistics and provided the basis for the development of Arabic grammar, vocabulary, and syntax. As Philip K. Hitti observed [in his *Islam: A Way of Life*, Henry Regnery, 1971, p. 27]:

> In length the **Koran** is no more than four-fifths that of the New Testament, but in use it far exceeds it. Not only is it the basis of the religion, the canon of ethical and moral life, but also the textbook in which the Moslem begins his study of language, science, theology, and jurisprudence. Its literary influence has been incalculable and enduring. The first prose book in Arabic, it set the style for future products. It kept the language uniform. So that whereas today a Moroccan uses a dialect different from that used by an Arabian or an Iraqi, all write in the same style.

Today, crowds fill stadiums and auditoriums throughout the Islamic world for public **Quran** recitation contests. Chanting of the **Quran** is an art form. Reciters or chanters are held in an esteem comparable with that of opera stars in the West. Memorization of the entire **Quran** brings great prestige as well as merit. Recordings of the **Quran** are enjoyed for their aesthetic as well as their religious value.

SOURCES FOR FURTHER STUDY

Arberry, A. J. *Aspects of Islamic Civilization: As depicted in the original texts.* London: George Allen and Unwin, 1964, 408 p.

> Presents a panorama of Muslim life and thought, illustrating the development of Islamic civilization and illuminating its literary, intellectual, and religious movements, politics, and sociology.

Cleary, Thomas. An introduction to *The Essential Koran: The Heart of Islam,* pp. vii-xviii. San Francisco: HarperCollins, 1993.

> Brief summary of the literary origins and the contents of the Koran.

Gibb, H. A. R. "The Age of Expansion." In his *Arabic Literature: An Introduction,* pp. 32-45. Oxford: Clarendon Press, 1963.

> Traces the influence of the Koran on subsequent Arabic literature.

Pellat, Charles. "Jewellers with Words." In *Islam and the Arab World: Faith, People, Culture,* edited by Bernard Lewis, pp. 141-60. New York: Knopf, 1976.

> Examines the significance of literature in Arabic culture, demonstrating the Koran's influence.

Rodinson, Maxime. *Muhammad.* New York: Pantheon Books, 1980, 363 p.

> Interpretive biography, focusing on how Muhammad's "psychological make-up. . . combined with the sociological conditions of his time and place to produce a lasting historic impact on a world scale."

Rubin, Uri. *The Eye of the Beholder: The Life of Muhammad As Viewed by the Early Muslims.* Princeton, N.J.: The Darwin Press, 1995, 289 p.

> Concentrates on the story of Muhammad's prophetic emergence in Mecca through textual analysis, demonstrating how medieval Islamic society sought to establish itself as a worthy monotheistic community.

Alice Munro

1931-

(Born Alice Laidlaw) Canadian short story writer and essayist.

INTRODUCTION

Munro is one of Canada's most critically acclaimed contemporary authors. Often referred to as a regional writer because her fiction frequently centers on the culture of rural southwestern Ontario, Munro credits the short story writers of the American South, particularly Eudora Welty and Flannery O'Connor, with shaping her fictional perspective. Her works juxtapose the mundane with the fantastic, often using paradox and irony to expose superficial appearances, and feature autobiographical elements by chronicling the emotional development of adolescent and adult female characters. Munro's first collection, *Dance of the Happy Shades* (1968)— as well as two subsequent collections, *Who Do You Think You Are?* (1978) and *The Progress of Love* (1986)— won the Governor General's Literary Award, and with *Lives of Girls and Women* (1971), her second book, she established a reputation as a gifted short story writer. "Few people writing today can bring a character, a mood or a scene to life with such economy," observed Beverley Slopen, adding that Munro "has an exhilarating ability to make the readers see the familiar with fresh insight and compassion."

Biographical Information

Munro grew up on the outskirts of Wingham, Ontario, where her family struggled to maintain a decent living from her father's silver fox farm. She has characterized this locale as belonging neither to the town nor the country, an ambiguous area in which many of her stories are set. A diligent student, she earned a scholarship to the University of Western Ontario in 1949. Married two years later, she moved with her husband to British Columbia, where she concentrated on raising a family. There, she compiled over a twelve-year period the stories that comprise *Dance of the Happy*

Shades. In the early 1970s, after her marriage had dissolved, Munro accepted a position as writer-in-residence at the University of Western Ontario and later moved with her second husband to Clinton, Ontario, a few miles from her childhood home. In 1974 some of her stories were accepted by *The New Yorker*, to which she has been a longtime regular contributor. Between 1979 and 1982 Munro extensively toured Australia, China, and Scandinavia. In 1986 she received the first Marian Engel Award, given to a woman writer for an outstanding body of work, and in 1990 she won the Canada Council Molson prize for her "outstanding lifetime contribution to the cultural and intellectual life of Canada."

Major Works

The fifteen stories in Munro's first book, *Dance of the Happy Shades,* explore the personal isolation that fear, ridicule, and the inability to communicate often impose. Consistently focusing on social and personal divisions throughout the collection, Munro examines the segregation of a town's misfits in several stories. Characters who initially seem certain of their identities gradually begin to question the basic assumptions under which they live. Other stories in the collection include "coming-of-age" tales. The stories in *Lives of Girls and Women* and *Who Do You Think You Are?* offer no resolution, which leaves readers to draw their own conclusions about the protagonists' actions. *Lives of Girls and Women* concerns specific experiences that affect protagonist Del Jordan's perceptions of her changing environment. Critics have likened this collection to James Joyce's *Portrait of the Artist as a Young Man* (1916), for Munro's portrayal of Del as an alienated and misunderstood artist is akin to Joyce's portrait of Stephen Dedalus. A volume of related stories, *Who Do You Think You Are?* introduces Rose, a wealthy, middle-aged divorcee who grew up in poverty, as she fits together the pieces of her life. A depressive quality permeates these stories which feature harsh depictions of Rose's relationships with men. Abrupt time shifts and overlapping experiences in this work develop a multifaceted characterization of Rose. Munro's other collections, *Something I've Been Meaning to Tell You* (1974), *The Moons of Jupiter* (1982), *The Progress of Love,* and *Friend of My Youth* (1990), focus on the lives of mature characters and deal primarily with adult themes. The eleven stories in *The Progress of Love* examine the ways love endures and changes in the midst of divorce, separation, and death. *Friend of My Youth* explores the movements of relationships and characters with respect to the passage of time, while *Open Secrets* (1994) largely concerns the politics of sex.

Critical Reception

Catherine Sheldrick stated that Munro's stories present "ordinary experiences so that they appear extraordinary, invested with a kind of magic." Munro's emphasis on the seemingly mundane progression of female lives prompted Ted Solataroff to call Munro a "great stylist of 1920's realism, a Katherine Anne Porter brought up to date." Similarly, Joyce Carol Oates found that "the evocation of emotions, ranging from bitter hatred to love, from bewilderment and resentment to awe . . . [in] an effortless, almost conversational tone [indicate] we are in the presence of an art that works to conceal itself, in order to celebrate its subject." Occasionally faulted for limiting herself to a narrow thematic range, Munro is widely regarded as a talented short story writer whose strength lies in her ability to present the texture of everyday life with both compassion and unyielding precision.

(For further information, see *Authors in the News,* Vol. 2; *Contemporary Authors,* Vols. 33-36R; *Contemporary Authors New Revision Series,* Vols. 33, 53; *Contemporary Literary Criticism,* Vols. 6, 10, 19, 50, 95; *Dictionary of Literary Biography,* Vol. 53; *DISCovering Authors: Canadian; DISCovering Authors Modules: Most-studied Authors Module, Novelists Module; Major Twentieth-Century Writers; Short Story Criticism,* Vol. 3; *Something about the Author,* Vol. 29.)

CRITICAL COMMENTARY

BRANDON CONRON

SOURCE: Brandon Conron, "Munro's Wonderland," in *Canadian Literature,* No. 78, Autumn, 1978, pp. 109-23.

[*In the following excerpt, Conron discusses Munro's style and technique in her early short story collections.*]

[Alice Munro's writing] captures the flavour and mood of rural Ontario. . . . During an interview in 1971, after acknowledging Eudora Welty as probably her favourite author, Munro remarked, "If I'm a regional writer, the region I'm writing about has many things in common with the American South. . . . "

Although there are obviously vast differences between Munro's own country and the American South, some

> **Principal Works**
>
> *Dance of the Happy Shades* (short stories) 1968
> *Lives of Girls and Women* (short stories) 1971
> *Something I've Been Meaning to Tell You: Thirteen Stories* (short stories) 1974
> *Who Do You Think You Are?* (short stories) 1978; also published as *The Beggar Maid: Stories of Flo and Rose*, 1979
> *The Moons of Jupiter* (short stories) 1982
> *The Progress of Love* (short stories) 1986
> *Friend of My Youth* (short stories) 1991
> *Open Secrets* (short stories) 1994
> *Selected Stories* (short stories) 1996
>
> **Adaptations**
>
> "Baptising," in *Lives of Girls and Women*, was adapted and filmed for the CBC *Performance* series, 1975.

attitudes are common to both societies: an almost religious belief in the land and the old rural cultural values; a sense of the past and respect for family history, however unremarkable or bizarre it may seem to outsiders: a profound awareness of the Bible which is reflected in the very language and images of speech; and a Calvinistic sense of sin.

Also influential in Munro's artistic development was journalist James Agee's experiment of integrating photography and text. . . .

[Her] intense feeling for the exact texture of surfaces and the tone of responses makes far greater demands than any cinemagraphic technique can adequately meet. It requires a style more akin to what in contemporary painting is often called "magic realism." Among those loosely categorized in this group, Alice Munro has noted a particular appreciation for the American Edward Hopper's paintings of ordinary places—a barber shop, seaside cottages, a small town street, roadside snack bar or gasoline station. Canadian painters like Alex Colville, Tom Forrestal and Jack Chambers have also influenced her. While all of these artists express themselves in individually different styles, the overall impression which they convey is one of acute perception of their environment. They exercise the selectivity of the expert photographer; yet by some personal, humanizing stroke each object or nuance in their painting somehow appears to have a special significance in its relationship to the rest of the picture. There is a kind of illusionary three dimensional aspect, a super realism or magical and mysterious suggestion of a soul beyond the objects depicted, which leaves the viewer participant with greater insights and an increased sensitivity towards the world around.

Such an impression Alice Munro can create in her extended images, which often evoke in the reader an intuitive awareness of a story's entire impact. In *Dance of the Happy Shades* this technique can be observed in a number of descriptive passages. Frequently the author arrests or suspends motion before returning to action, as in the still painting description from **"Thanks for the Ride"** of a typical small town near Lake Huron, after the summer vacationers have gone home. . . .

[While such Southern writers as Truman Capote, Carson McCullers, Flannery O'Connor, Reynolds Price, and Eudora Welty] undoubtedly influenced Munro's descriptive style, it was their expression of the profound dignity of even the most trivial events of every day life to which she especially responded. Later, when she first discovered Patrick White through his *Tree of Man* . . . , this feeling for the inherent beauty of every earthly thing was reinforced: for her, too, a lowly ant or a gob of spittle could be worthy of appreciative contemplation. There is a remarkable similarity between the imagery of White and Munro—probably because of their similar apprehension of the "holiness" of all aspects of life, in which "beautiful or ugly had ceased to matter because there was in everything something to be discovered. . . ."

[The stories of *Dance of the Happy Shades*] treat the maturing process of the young as recalled later, and depend partly for their effect on a bifocal point of view that sees a situation from both an adolescent and an adult perspective. . . .

A central story in this collection . . . is **"Images,"** a young woman's recollections of an outing with her father. An intricate series of contrasts is presented: outdoor activity and the pervasive aura of an unexplained malady; apparent jollity and genuine misery; death and life; images and actuality. . . . This is a strange story, replete with concrete imagery and suggestive overtones, that demonstrates the author's acute perception of smells and tastes as well as of sights and sounds and their associations. . . .

This first volume reveals that Alice Munro can treat a wide range of themes with a technical framework that is, in her own words, "very traditional, very conventional." In all but three of these fifteen stories the point of view is that of a child or adolescent, modified or controlled to some extent by the lapse of time, new insights and perspectives between an incident and its recording. In only one is the narrator or reader's sensorium a male. In each, the characters are seen in a strongly presented physical setting, in which the surfaces of life, its texture, sounds and smells are described with exactness of observation and delicacy of language. The focus is fairly narrow and highly personal, in the sense that "the emotional reality," though not the events, is "solidly autobiographical."

Although the stories have no formal sequence, they effectively trace the development of a sensitive young girl into womanhood. They capture in dialogue, characterization and description the practicality and hardships, seasonal rhythms and vitality of rural and small town life, the barriers between the young and the old, the poor and the affluent, the sick and the well. Secrets and a lack of genuine communication between family members or friends often lead to guilty estrangements; unawareness of a situation, perhaps because of a selfish distaste for unpleasant things or a fear of ridicule, is common; the pressure to conform is relentless, and failure of will to make one's own life is too frequent. The treatment of these various themes is everywhere touched with humour, compassionate irony, and a comprehension of the absurd and grotesque. Common experiences become unique, yet universal, expressions of what it means to be alive during this period.

In . . . *Something I've Been Meaning to Tell You* (1974), Alice Munro moves into a larger, more cosmopolitan world. Only six of the thirteen stories are rooted in what was formerly considered Munro country. The other seven have contemporary urban settings. . . . There is a wider variety of characters also, fewer girls and young women and more middle-aged or elderly people. Most of the stories are longer. There is a mature awareness of the complexity and fragility of human relationships, the confusing standards of modern city life, and the conflict of generations. Satire is more common. These new aspects are ordered with the same characteristic perception, subtle interplay of emotions, droll sense of humour, and ironic compassion.

Although arbitrarily chosen thematic headings cannot adequately reflect the overlapping and variety of minor motifs in individual tales, four kinds of stories seem to emerge: first, those in which are blended a number of related themes—the essential individualism of each person, the impossibility of complete comprehension of one's own self let alone another's, the self-deception, buried resentments, and often unwitting vindictiveness of human personality; second, stories reminiscent of *Dance* in their focus on relatively simple emotional situations; third, stories which offer especially revealing insights into the author's technique; and finally, narratives in which a sense of personal guilt is pervasive.

The title piece, **"Something I've Been Meaning to Tell You,"** a good example of the first group, is a finely orchestrated dramatization of the underlying tensions and ironies of close relationships. . . . Through the recurring images and allusions time flows easily backwards and forwards as on the little stage of Mock Hill a range of human emotions is portrayed with a gently comic undertone that is conveyed overtly in the names of the setting and characters.

Et's fantasy, plausible and ambiguous enough for a reader to speculate about its validity, is presented with splendid irony. She also sees a mythical parallel when Arthur in a foursome game of "Who am I?" chooses to be Sir Galahad. . . .

Among the stories [appearing in *Something I've Been Meaning to Tell You* which are] most arresting for their critical insights into the author's technique are **"Material"** . . . [and] **"Tell Me Yes or No."** . . . **"Material"** tells how a writer, Hugo, transforms a personal incident into fiction. His former wife muses about his publication with devastating satire. . . . Mocking the book jacket blurb, tearing apart its half lies of Hugo's experiences as "lumberjack, beer-slinger, counterman," she ridicules his image as "not only fake but out of date." . . . This is a very complex, ironic and comical story that touches on such themes and tensions as the amorality of artists, creating from "scraps and oddments, useless baggage," a "hard and shining, rare intimidating quality"; the tenuous tie that holds men and women together in love, "as flimsy as a Roumanian accent or the calm curve of an eyelid, some half-fraudulent mystery"; the way that men, whatever their temperaments, know "how to ignore or use things. . . . They are not *at the mercy*." Dialogue, description, and reflection all unite in a realistic and ironic interplay of character and events to evoke in the reader a rich and varied response. . . .

In **"Tell Me Yes or No"** a narrator has an imaginary conversation with a dead lover as she recalls their affair and tells of a later trip to his home city. . . .

Moving with the temporal fluidity of internal monologue, the story is rich in imagery, descriptive detail, and inner revelation as the narrator attempts to understand the deceased as well as their relationship for the previous two years. . . .

In many of the stories already commented upon there can be noted an expression of a sense of guilt for uncharitable thoughts, acts of deceit or omission. In the last group to be discussed, regret and remorse are pervasive motifs. **"Walking on Water,"** set in Victoria and suggested by a publicity stunt there of television comic Paul Paulsen, describes the tragic failure of a young

Zen adherent's experiment in psychic control over matter, as seen through the perspective of a retired druggist. The difficulty of bridging the generation gap is vividly portrayed in realistic dialogue and sharp imagery, as he attempts to understand the sense of values of the flower people. His touching concern for their welfare and poignant foreboding reach a climactic note with his eventual feeling of disorientation in their brutally existential dismissal of the victim's fate. . . .

"The Ottawa Valley," final story of this volume, is another reminiscence of a childhood experience by a mature woman. . . . In recalling [childhood incidents], the cousins' versions often vary and their different responses are comically revealing of their different temperaments and sensibilities. . . .

The spectre of a gifted, eccentric and ailing mother haunts much of Munro's fiction, and appears either briefly or as a dominating figure in several of the collected stories. She is a central character in *Lives of Girls and Women*. Frequently associated with her is a daughter whose growing maturity brings a sense of guilt for her own lack of understanding or compassion. Another less individualized but equally recurring figure in various aspects is the man, whether single or married, who uses or ignores women and events at his own whim. There is also a whole range of other characters that have been imaginatively created out of vividly recalled memories. For the most part they are unsophisticated people who only vaguely comprehend the meaning of their own lives. The reader is taken with them through a series of rather subtle, low-keyed circumstances in which the continuum is often disrupted and then reestablished in a way that alters both the reader's as well as the characters' emotional awareness, and leads them both to a significant or fresh conception of the world. Most of the tales are presented from the first person point of view. Even in those few which happen to be written in the third person the narrative voice is that of the central figure. This technique allows an intimate rapport between reader and narrator. The blending of past and present often generates the energy of the story as the perspective continually shifts. In some tales the first paragraph is a microcosm of the whole; in others the ending contains the vital clues required to reveal the full deployment of fictional forces. Some move forward more by dialogue than description. In virtually all, the rhythm is achieved by a balance of the parts which defies rational analysis. . . .

Alice Munro's special distillation of personality is revealed in the quiet humour, gentle irony, and compassionate understanding with which she treats her themes. Her uniqueness lies not only in the special angle of vision from which her characters are seen, but also in the lasting impact which they have on the reader. They are memorable for themselves as well as for their symbolic significance. Many are representative of particular life patterns, revealed often in a single picture, in the fashion of Sherwood Anderson, of "lives flowing past each other." But they still remain individuals who become permanent personal possessions of the reader. Her writing is original, not for its technical innovation or interpretations of the atomic age, but rather for its fragile insights into the complexity of personal relationships. Her narratives spring from an imaginative, intelligent and unpretentious individuality to which fiction is a natural recourse. They are independent, absorbing, and realistic expressions of the profound disturbances and magic of ultimate human reckonings. . . .

HELEN HOY

SOURCE: Helen Hoy, "'Dull, Simple, Amazing and Unfathomable': Paradox and Double Vision" in *Studies in Canadian Literature*, Vol. 5, 1980, pp. 100-15.

[*In the following excerpt, Hoy examines how Munro uses language and imagery to reveal paradox in her characters, their behavior, and reality itself.*]

Royal Beating. That was Flo's promise. You are going to get one Royal Beating.

The word Royal lolled on Flo's tongue, took on trappings. Rose had a need to picture things, to pursue absurdities, that was stronger than the need to stay out of trouble, and instead of taking this threat to heart she pondered: how is a beating royal?

In this delight in language and exuberant pursuit of absurdities despite ensuing complications, Rose reveals herself, in Alice Munro's . . . work *Who Do You Think You Are?*, to be very much a child of the author herself. Munro's own sensitivity to individual words and images, her spare lucid style, and command of detail have given her fiction a precision which is one of her most distinctive accomplishments. What an examination of the texture of her prose reveals, in particular, is the centrality of paradox and the ironic juxtaposition of apparently incompatible terms or judgements: "ironic and serious at the same time," "mottoes of godliness and honor and flaming bigotry," "special, useless knowledge," "tones of shrill and happy outrage," "the bad taste, the heartlessness, the joy of it." This stylistic characteristic is closely related to the juxtaposition, in the action, of the fantastic and the ordinary, her use of each to undercut the other.... The linking of incongruities in language or action, however, is more than a stylistic technique or fictional quirk. It reflects Munro's larger vision, one which underlies all her fiction and which emerges as a central theme in *Lives of Girls and Women* and in several of the short stories in *Dance of the Happy Shades* and *Something I've Been Meaning To Tell You.* Paradox helps sustain Munro's thematic insistence on the doubleness of reality, the illusoriness of either the prosaic or the marvellous in isolation.

The freshness of language and image, which is Munro's great strength, she herself explains in an interview with Graeme Gibson: "I'm not an intellectual writer. I'm very, very excited by what you might call the surface of life, and it must be that this seems to me very meaningful in a way I can't analyze or describe.... It seems to me very important to be able to get at the exact tone or texture of how things are." This impulse she, of course, embodies in *Lives of Girls and Women* in Del Jordan who, as a maturing writer, attempts to pin her town to paper and realizes, "no list could hold what I wanted, for what I wanted was every last thing, every layer of speech and thought, stroke of light on bark or walls, every smell, pothole, pain, crack, delusion, held still and held together—radiant, everlasting." The last words hold the clue to Del's, and Munro's obsession with external realities: it is an obsession which Munro, in her interview with Gibson, says can best be compared to a religious feeling about the world. So too when another interviewer John Metcalf asks perceptively whether she glories in surfaces because she feels them not to be surfaces, she agrees, adding, "It's just a feeling about the intensity of what is *there.*" In the struggle to capture this intensity about very ordinary things, paradox not surprisingly becomes one of Munro's most important tools.

Sometimes this persistent "balance or reconcilement of opposites or discordant qualities" (to echo Coleridge's celebrated definition of the imagination) occurs almost in passing as an unobtrusive feature of Munro's style, in her description, for instance, of the way children whimper monotonously "to *celebrate* a hurt." Often, though, the inherent contradictions in people and situations are more explicitly confronted. Paradox becomes Munro's means of capturing complex human characteristics whether wittily as in the description of successful academics as "such brilliant, such talented incapable men" or more seriously, gropingly as in Del's discussion of an egotism women feel in men, something "tender, swollen, tyrannical, absurd." In an attempt, in **"Dance of the Happy Shades,"** to convey the reality of the Marsalles sisters, "sexless, wild and gentle creatures, bizarre yet domestic," Munro extends paradox into physical description itself, characterizing both as having kindly, grotesque faces, and eyes which are at the same time tiny, red, short-sighted, and sweet-tempered. The same incongruities multiply in the world encompassing Munro's characters. A housewife and writer finds herself sheltered and encumbered, warmed and bound by her home; a growing girl is both absolved and dismissed by her father's casual acceptance of her moment of rebellion; the struggle of wills between an amateur hypnotist and a stubborn old woman ends with her "dead, and what was more, victorious"; a teenage girl feels that her mother's concern creates for her an oppressive obligation to be happy, as another feels that her mother loves her but is also her enemy; a maiden aunt, stumbling on her niece and a lover naked and passionate, perceives them as strange and familiar, both more and less than themselves. A character's feelings for her relatives are described as "irritable ... bonds of sympathy," a writer's techniques as "Lovely tricks, honest tricks." In these examples as in many, Munro employs not an elaborated paradoxical statement but a more concentrated phrase, an oxymoron, most often in the form of two parallel but incompatible verbs or adjectives. The startling fusion of warring terms gives to her style at its best a denseness and precision characteristic of poetry.

Paradox is most prominent in the fiction's portrayal of human character and emotional reaction. At times this is simply a means of suggesting inconsistencies, variations over time, as in Del's discovery (in contrast with her youthful belief in the absolute finality of some quarrels) that people can feel murderous disillusionment and hate, then go on to love again. More often, Munro explores the emotional contradictions persisting side by side in time. A character in **"Tell Me Yes or No"** not only expects her lover, like a knight, to be capable alternately of "acts of outmoded self-sacrifice and also of marvellous brutality," she also goes on to describe him as *simultaneously* mild and inflexible. Paradox, therefore, is frequently an admirable means of conveying the intense emotional ambivalence of adolescence: in response to an example of purely decorative femininity, for example, Del reveals, "I thought she was an idiot, and yet I frantically admired her." She finds the idea of sex totally funny and totally revolting, hopes and fears she will be overheard shouting the forbidden word "bugger," and later is both relieved and desolate at the loss of her lover Garnet. In the same way, of other adolescent girls, we are told that "any title with the word popularity in it could both chill and compel me," that "she was quivering ... with pride, shame, boldness, and exhilaration" (note how "shame" here is even flanked by two differing contraries), and that the pregnancy and marriage of a friend "made me both envious and appalled." (In the last example, the friend herself is concomitantly characterized as "abashed and proud.") Lest we conclude, however, that Munro is mainly recording the confusions of youth, we might note that almost the same formula is applied to an adult woman, in her response to some men's invulnerability: "I envy and despise." Rose's friend Clifford argues that his marital dissatisfaction is not simply a change of heart over time, informing his wife, "I wanted to be married to you and I want to be married to you and I couldn't stand being married to you and I can't stand being married to you. It's a static contradiction."

In fact, the matter-of-fact union of incompatible tendencies is Munro's means of bringing life, precision, and complexity to her depiction of emotions generally. Occasionally, as in the example just given, she actually acknowledges and spells out the paradoxical nature of such feelings: "They [Del's aunts] respected men's work beyond anything; they also laughed at it. This was strange; they could believe absolutely in its importance and at the same time convey their judgement that it was, from one point of view, frivolous, non-essential." Compare this incidentally with a later character's mingling of "flattery and a delicate sort of contempt" in her conversation with a man. Similarly the reader is deliberately drawn into a contemplation of the paradoxical quality of Milton Homer's unsocialized behaviour in *Who Do You Think You Are?* as the narrator, describing his goggling, leering expressions as both boldly calculating and helpless, involuntary, asks if such a thing is possible. More often, we simply have subtle touches in the portrayal of characters, even minor characters—a landlord with an "affable, predatory expression," an aunt "flashing malice and kindness," a grandmother whose renunciation of love is a "self- glorifying dangerous self-denying passion," the same grandmother predicting problems with "annoyance and satisfaction," an unhappy lover bound by rules "meaningless and absolute." The same duality is found on a larger scale with more central characters too, like the pathetic heroine of **"Thanks for the Ride,"** whose combination of defiance and need, scorn and acquiescence is summed up in the final sound of her voice, "abusive and forlorn."

At one point in *Lives of Girls and Women,* Del somewhat ironically characterizes the Anglican liturgy as presenting "lively emotion *safely* contained in the most *elegant* channels of language." In contrast to this, Munro's own technique, rather than using language to defuse emotion, creates a resonance or current, releases an intensity through the juxtaposition of oppositely charged words or ideas. The effect is not a wild splattering of emotion—in the careful precision of Munro's language, and a certain intellectual detachment as well, there is some of the control attributed here to the liturgical ritual—but it is controlled *energy,* a galvanic interaction between the poles of the paradox rather than a safe elegance. Through the originality not of craziness but of unexpected revelation, Munro's oxymorons have something of the same vitality as the bizarre childhood rhyme about fried Vancouvers and pickled arseholes, which so pleases Rose for what she calls "The tumble of reason; the spark and spit of craziness."

So positive emotions are unexpectedly qualified—"heartless applause," "smiling angrily," "hungry laughter," "accusing vulnerability," "aggressive bright spirits"; negative ones are similarly—"tender pain," "semitolerant contempt," "happy outrage," "terrible tender revenge"; and even an epithet like absurd, which might seem sweeping and inarguably dismissive, must coexist with its opposite: Del's mother in her youthful enthusiasm is "absurd and unassailable," Del, naked, feels "absurd and dazzling," and a boy reassures a drunken girl, with "a very stupid, half-sick, absurd and alarming expression." While such pairings can sometimes become automatic or mechanical in Munro's writing, most often the originality of the details produces a slight, revelatory wrenching of assumptions and perspective.

We should note that the effect of paradox in Munro is never to invalidate, rarely even to diminish either of the contradictory impulses. Characteristically, in fact, she employs the unifying conjunction "and," disregarding for her purposes conjunctions of limitation or concession. As Cleanth Brooks says of the technique in poetry, the ironic or paradoxical union of opposites "is not that of a prudent splitting of the difference between antithetical overemphases." So, Del in ignoring her aunts' dreams feels "that kind of tender remorse which has as its other side a brutal, *unblemished* satisfaction," quotes sentimental poetry "with absolute sincerity, absolute irony," and comments explicitly about her youthful curiosity over sex, "Disgust did not rule out enjoyment, in my thoughts; indeed they were inseparable." The contradictory emotions retain their individual intensity.

In her examination of human inconsistency, Munro presents the contradictions not only within emotions but also between emotion and behaviour. Again there is often little attempt to reduce the inconsistency or explain why actions defy their motivations; the two conflicting realities are simply juxtaposed—"The thought of intimacies with Jerry Storey was offensive in itself. Which did not mean that they did not, occasionally, take place," "The ritual of walking up and down the street to show ourselves off we thought crude and ridiculous, though we could not resist it," "not bothering to shake off our enmity, nor thinking how the one thing could give way to the other, we kissed." At times, in fact, Munro actually uses human perverseness itself as the explanation for behaviour, in identifying the "aphrodisiac prickles of disgust" in the appeal of the idiotic saintly whore or the perversely appealing lack of handsomeness of the lecherous minister Rose encounters. Faced with an invitation to sneak away to a dance, Del feels paradoxically, "I had no choice but to do this ... because I truly hated and feared the Gay-la Dance Hall."

The unexpected challenge to common assumptions which is the source of such paradoxes' power need not always be spelled out. The same shock of recognition, Coleridge's union of "the sense of novelty and freshness, with old and familiar objects," is achieved when, for instance, Del's mother's radical defence of women's independence is described unexpectedly as innocent in its assumption of women's damageability, when Del comments on the concealed jubilation and eagerness to cause pain in parents' revelations of unpleasant realities, when the narrator of **"Shining Houses"** makes a matter-of-fact, parenthetical reference to the way people admire each other for being drunk, or when Rose reveals that outspoken hostility does not pose the threat to one of her friendships which genteel tact would. The freshness of perception which Alice Munro brings to very familiar situations lends itself to the creation of observations such as these which remain startling, although the underlying paradox is never articulated.

Indeed Munro sometimes even seems to go through an initial process of making the strange familiar so that she can then go on paradoxically to justify the originally familiar (but now strange) as also possible. An interesting example of this occurs in *Who Do You Think You Are?* in Rose's analysis of her reconciliation with Patrick, her fiance. Disregarding any immediate, popular explanations like romantic love (and through silence apparently dismissing them as naive), Munro accustoms the reader to more sophisticated, sceptical analysis by consideration of such similarly complex motivations as comradely compassion, emotional greed, economic cowardice, and vanity (with only subtle hints of glibness). Only then, ironically, does she reveal Rose's secret explanation, which Rose has never confided and which she cannot justify, namely that she may have been motivated, oddly enough, by a vision of happiness. The paradoxical revelation of unacknowledged, even denied, but recognizable aspects of human behaviour has, in the context of worldly characters and readers, been taken a step further here and turned on itself. Having directed attention towards less obvious explanations of behaviour, Munro then revitalizes from a new perspective a vision of innocence and good will which has paradoxically become unexpected.

Verbal paradox, however, particularly cryptic oxymoron, remains a more distinctive feature of Munro's style, and, as many of the examples already cited suggest, functions particularly as a means of definition, of zeroing in on the individual qualities of an emotion or moment. More than evocativeness, it is precision which she seeks in the description of "a great unemotional happiness," "sophisticated prudery," or a character "kind but not compassionate." In light of Munro's love for clear images and her insistence on her inability to put characters in a room without describing all the furniture, it is interesting that many of these paradoxes involve abstract not concrete language (an aspect of her style easily overlooked). It is the exactness and poetic explosiveness of the internal contradiction which give them their vividness. Admiring the discontinuities of modern experimental prose, Munro has complained that her writing tends "to fill everything in, to be pretty wordy." As this discussion suggests, however, while within a traditional narrative form and concerned with articulating rather than simply suggesting, her use of language generally is not discursive or rambling, but tight, economical, exact.

HALLVARD DAHLIE

SOURCE: Hallvard Dahlie, "Alice Munro," in *Canadian Writers and Their Works, Vol. 7*, Robert Lecker, Jack David, Ellen Quigley, eds., ECW Press, 1985, pp. 215-56.

[*A Norwegian-born Canadian critic and educator, Dahlie is the author of such works as* Brian Moore *(1981) and* Varieties of Exile: The Canadian Experience *(1986). In the following excerpt, he discusses critical reaction to Munro's works.*]

Though Alice Munro has been writing for some three decades, critical attention of any extended sort did not appear until the beginning of the 1970s, when serious response to her 1968 collection of stories began to formulate. She had received, it is true, some attention during the 1950s and 1960s, particularly from *Tamarack Review* editor Robert Weaver, who was consistent and perceptive in his praise of her work, but she earned only a line or two of objective mention in the 1965 edition of the *Literary History of Canada: Canadian Literature in English* (compared to more than a page of strong praise in the revised 1976 edition). It was, however, the awarding of the Governor General's Award for *Dance of the Happy Shades* that signalled to the country as a whole the arrival of a new force in Canadian literature, even though the initial response to that event focused more on who Alice Munro was than on the substance of her fiction.

To date, serious critical attention has been limited to interviews, articles, and reviews published in scholarly and academic journals; no monograph or full-length study as yet exists, though I know of one that is under way as I write this. The first graduate thesis on Munro's work came out of Queen's University in 1972, and in the ensuing decade her fiction has received increasing attention from graduate students across the country as well as abroad. A half dozen or so interviews with Munro have been conducted since Mari Stainsby published the first one in 1971 [in *British Columbia Library Quarterly* (July 1971)] and though some of these are livelier than others, all elicit much the same information about her life and career, about the various influences on her work, and about her opinions on being simultaneously a writer and a woman in Canada.

Scholarly articles on Munro show a steady but not spectacular growth, with the majority of them thematic in nature, though a few also address structural and stylistic matters. The titles of the articles are revealing, suggesting not only the richness of Munro's fiction but also the versatility of her critics. Where one speaks of isolation and rejection, another counters with confinement and escape, a third with resolution and independence, and yet another with transience; one discusses her vision, and not to be outdone, another her double vision; we have private landscapes and wonderlands, both with and without the looking glass; child-women and primitives vie with the masculine image and the growth of a young artist in her fiction; two critics link her with James Joyce, one with the American South, and a third with myth and fairy tale. In short, scholarly criticism of Munro to date seems to be following the standard exegetical route that all writers routinely undergo, perhaps particularly those whose fiction is relatively uncomplicated and accessible to a wide range of readers.

The articles which examine *Dance of the Happy Shades*—and only one is concerned exclusively with this book—have in common a tendency to set up either opposing or complementary tensions within the stories and thus to formulate keys to specific interpretations. In some cases, it is Munro's own phrases that provide the opening the critic requires, particularly when the situation evoked by that phrase seems to constitute a repeating pattern in her fiction. Thus, for example, in my 1972 article on *Dance* [in *World Literature Written in English* (April 1972)], I picked up on Helen's parenthetical observation in **"The Peace of Utrecht"** about the depressive effect of "unconsummated relationships" and saw this as a recurring dilemma for those many Munro characters caught up in situations of isolation and rejection. Similarly, Rae McCarthy Macdonald in her 1976 article [in *Modern Fiction Studies* (Autumn 1976)] takes the observation that the scissors-man in **"The Time of Death"** is in some respects like "a madman loose in the world" to buttress her convincing argument that a central pattern in Munro is the tension between the normal world and the irrational "other" world which so many characters appear to be partially occupying. In an earlier article that same year, Beverly Rasporich saw much the same pattern operating throughout Munro's three books, but with a persuasive narrowing of focus: what she sees as Munro's central concern, the exploration of the feminine psyche, receives a vivid reflection through what she calls "the grotesque and hysterical reality of Munro's 'other' world."

Extended criticism of *Lives of Girls and Women* began appearing about the mid-1970s, and to date it is this book that has attracted the greatest amount of attention. In a 1975 article [*Essays on Canadian Writing* (Fall 1975)], Tim Struthers analyses this novel within the perspective of its being a *Kunstlerroman*, drawing a number of parallels between it and Joyce's *Portrait* [*of the Artist as a Young Man*] as well as making an interesting observation on the closing words of *Lives* and *Ulysses*. Del's final word, "Yes," Struthers suggests, moves this novel, as did Molly Bloom's in *Ulysses,* from irony to affirmation, a position, I think, that the "Epilogue" itself supports. W. R. Martin in a 1979 article [in *Journal of Canadian Fiction* (1979)] pursues the Joycean parallels in Munro, observing, as Struthers does, the "artist" similarities that link *Lives* and the *Portrait*. But he concentrates his analysis on the tonal and structural similarities between *Dance* and *Dubliners*, particularly the correspondences between two of Munro's stories, **"Dance of the Happy Shades"** and **"The Time of Death,"** and Joyce's "The Dead." Struthers' other article on Munro (1974, rev. 1978) [in *The Canadian Novel*, ed. John Moss, vol. 1: *Here and Now*] constitutes an interesting analysis of her frequently asserted debt to writers of the American South, arguing that it is manifested both thematically and formally. His demonstration of Munro's debt to Eudora Welty is more convincing, I think, than the case he makes for her formal affinities with the journalism/photography combination of James Agee and Walker Evans in their *Let Us Now Praise Famous Men*, though one can certainly find in many of Munro's stories tonal echoes of Agee's novel *A Death in the Family*.

The three articles on Munro published in 1977 reflect the eclectic nature of current criticism of her work: David Monoghan concentrates on the twin relationships of vision and form that the opening **"Flats Road"** section of *Lives* has with the rest of the novel; Marcia Allentuck argues that *Lives*, along with the stories **"The Office"** and **"Material,"** provide evidence that the emotional dependence women experience with men is difficult, if not impossible, to overcome; and John Moss shapes his analysis of *Lives* to the overall theme of his *Sex and Violence in the Canadian Novel*. Del's progress from childhood to maturity, he argues, that is, her evolution as an artist, is reflected among other ways by her progression from the vicarious sexuality adumbrated in Uncle Benny's world to her total sexual fulfilment in the **"Baptizing"** section, where in effect the artist merges with the person she has created.

In the last four years or so, criticism of Munro has begun moving away from its thematic slant towards a concern with structure and style, though there is as yet no study exclusively devoted to these formal aspects. In a detailed study of *Lives* [in *Studies in Canadian Literature* (Summer 1978)], Rae McCarthy Macdonald picks up on her earlier article and demonstrates how Del is compelled to make continuous commitments to one world or the other—to the ordinary world or to the "other country," as it were. The process, she suggests, is rendered credible and dramatic through the episodic structure of the novel, a structure which paradoxically reveals by the time of Del's maturity that the two worlds were not that separate after all, that, indeed, this dual vision of the world was in fact an illusion. This notion, the doubleness of reality, is central to a fine study by Helen Hoy [in *Studies in Canadian Literature* (Spring 1980)], who argues convincingly that Munro consistently employs the stylistic devices of paradox, juxtaposition, and oxymoron to reflect the coalescing of the seemingly prosaic and the seemingly marvellous in life. Hoy's is the only article to date to deal to any extent with *Who Do You Think You Are?*, and with respect to that book she tentatively explores the idea that it introduces a new layer of ambiguity to this concept of reality, wherein the commonplace achieves its own intrinsic mystery.

If there is the beginning of a consistent ideological stance in Munro criticism, it lies, not surprisingly, in the feminist approach. Both Rasporich and Allentuck, in the articles referred to above, edge into this area, but the strongest position taken to date is that by Bronwen Wallace in an article published in 1978 [in *The Human Elements: Critical Essays*, ed. David Helwig]. Wallace pursues, with reference mainly to the collections of stories, Munro's own implication made in an interview that women, as members of a subject race, have visions and perceptions that are qualitatively different from those of men; indeed, she concludes her perceptive study by arguing that the presence of so many selves in a woman constitutes her unique strength rather than a weakness. In an article published the following year [in *Canadian Literature* (Spring 1979)], Nancy Bailey combines a feminist approach with a Jungian analysis of the androgynous nature of the female-artist figure. It is an intriguing study, though for me it was more instructive at times about Jung than about Munro, as, for example, when she interprets Bobby Sherriff as "the Wise Man or the fourth stage of animus development." Nevertheless, Bailey's article may well mark the advent of the kind of sophisticated and intellectual approach that will be required if Munro's subsequent fiction assumes more complexity.

In general, however, there is as yet no sustained body of Munro criticism which adopts any consistent dialectic or ideological stance, even though some of the titles of the articles discussed here bear family resemblances to one another. What we have at the moment is a growing collection of discrete articles, eclectic in nature, all of which shed interesting and useful light on the meanings and structures of Munro's fiction.

JOYCE CAROL OATES

SOURCE: Joyce Carol Oates, "Characters Dangerously Like Us," in *The New York Times Book Review*, September 14, 1986, pp. 7, 9.

[In the following excerpt, Oates commends the rich texture of Munro's style.]

Like her similarly gifted contemporaries Peter Taylor, William Trevor, Edna O'Brien and some few others, the Canadian short-story writer Alice Munro writes stories that have the density—moral, emotional, sometimes historical—of other writers' novels. As remote from the techniques and ambitions of what is currently known as "minimalist" fiction as it is possible to get and still inhabit the same genre, these writers give us fictitious worlds that are mimetic paradigms of utterly real worlds yet are fictions, composed with so assured an art that it might be mistaken for artlessness. They give voice to the voices of their regions, filtering the natural rhythms of speech through a more refined (but not obtrusively refined) writerly speech. They are faithful to the contours of local legend, tall tales, anecdotes, family reminiscences; their material is nearly always realistic—"Realism" being that convention among competing others that swept all before it in the mid and late 19th century—and their characters behave, generally, like real people. That is, they surprise us at every turn, without violating probability. They so resemble ourselves that reading about them, at times, is emotionally risky. Esthetically experimental literature, while evoking our admiration, rarely moves us the way this sort of literature moves us.

From the start of her career in 1968 with the Canadian publication of the short-story collection *Dance of the Happy Shades* (published in the United States in 1973) through *Lives of Girls and Women, Something I've Been Meaning to Tell You, The Beggar Maid, The Moons of Jupiter* and this new collection, *The Progress of Love*, Alice Munro has concentrated on short fiction that explores the lives of fairly undistinguished men and women—but particularly women—who live in southwestern rural Ontario. When her characters move elsewhere to live, to British Columbia, for instance, like the couple whose precarious marriage is explored in **"Miles City, Montana,"** it is still Ontario that is home. (But: "When we said 'home' and meant Ontario, we had very different places in mind.") Though Ms. Munro's tonal palette has darkened considerably over the last 20 years, her fictional technique has not changed greatly, nor has the range of her characters. By degrees, of course, they have grown older. Their living fulfills the prophetic conclusion of a beautiful early story, **"Walker Brothers Cowboy"** (from *Dance of the Happy Shades*):

> I feel my father's life flowing back from our car in the last of the afternoon, darkening and turning strange, like a landscape that has an enchantment on it, making it kindly, ordinary and familiar while you are looking at it, but changing it, once your back is turned, into something you will never know, with all kinds of weathers, and distances you cannot imagine.

The most powerful of the 11 stories collected in *The Progress of Love* take on bluntly and without sentiment the themes of mortality, self-delusion, puzzlement over the inexplicable ways of fate. In **"Fits"** it is observed that "people can take a fit like the earth takes a fit" after an unaccountable murder-suicide has been discovered in a small rural town. (Indeed, **"Fits"** would have made an excellent title for this collection.) The story yields its secrets slowly, with admirable craft and suspense: the surprise for the reader is that the "fit" at its core is less the sensational act of violence than a woman's mysteriously untroubled response to it.

"A Queer Streak" is a tragically comic (or comically tragic) tale of an ambitious young woman named Violet, a "holy terror" in her youth, whose life is permanently altered by the bizarre behavior of an emotionally unbalanced younger sister. It is a familiar temptation to which Violet succumbs: she decides, against the very grain of her personality, that the loss of her fiance is a "golden opportunity" and not a disaster. Henceforth she will give up her own life, live for others:

> That was the way Violet saw to leave her pain behind. A weight gone off her. If she would bow down and leave her old self behind as well, and all her ideas of what her life should be, the weight, the pain, the humiliation would all go magically. And she could still be chosen. . . . If she prayed enough and tried enough, that would be possible.

But this moment of revelation is the high point of Violet's life, as we see it.

Violet, who takes on, by degrees, the "queer streak" of her family, is one of Ms. Munro's unromantic, independent heroines—country bred, proud, resilient, courageous even in her old age. Her story might have been even more moving if it did not unaccountably accelerate in its second half (where the point of view shifts to Violet's cousin Dan about whom we know virtually nothing and who is merely used as an instrument to observe Violet). Also, Ms. Munro is curiously perfunctory in summarizing Violet's love affair with a married man—the most intense emotional experience of Violet's life, presumably. Like the adulterous love affair at the heart of **"White Dump,"** it is alluded to rather than dramatized: the reader knows very little about it, and consequently feels very little.

Recurring in Alice Munro's fiction is a certain female protagonist, clearly kin to Violet, but generally more capable of establishing a life for herself. She is intelligent, though not intellectual; "superior," though often self-doubting. She has the capacity to extract from frequently sordid experiences moral insights of a very nearly Jamesian subtlety and precision. She tells us what she thinks; tells us, often, what we would think. Not conventionally beautiful, she is nonetheless attractive to men: which leads her sometimes, as an adolescent, into dangerous situations—as in the new story **"Jesse and Meribeth"** in which the adolescent Jesse is scolded by a near-seducer, an older man, for what he correctly perceives as her overwrought romantic imagination: "You shouldn't go inside places like this with men just because they ask you. . . . You're hot-blooded. You've got some lessons to learn." In the more complex, multigenerational **"White Dump"** a kindred girl is drawn into marriage with a man who "depended on her to make him a man," and who will prove inadequate to her passionate nature. In **"Lichen,"** one of the bleakest of the new stories, the heroine, middle-aged, cheerful, at last adjusted to a solitary life, achieves a moral triumph over her fatuous ex-husband simply by maturing beyond him. She is fully accepting of the terms of her freedom:

> This white-haired woman walking beside him ... dragged so much weight with her— a weight not just of his sexual secrets but of his middle-of-the-night speculations about God, his psychosomatic chest pains, his digestive sensitivity, his escape plans, which once included her.... All his ordinary and extraordinary life—even some things it was unlikely she knew about—seemed stored up in her. He could never feel any lightness, any secret and victorious expansion, with a woman who knew so much. She was bloated with all she knew.

She has become, ironically, a kind of mother to him; but she looks so much older than he that he is shamed and frightened at the very sight of her.

In one of the collection's finest stories, **"The Progress of Love,"** the daughter of a woman who sacrificed both herself and her children to presumably Christian ideals of integrity chooses deliberately not to believe in those ideals, or to marry conventionally as her mother had done; she becomes, in fact, a real estate agent, selling off the old houses and farms that made up the world of her youth. Long divorced, alone but not really lonely, Euphemia—who calls herself Fame—seeks moments of "kindness and reconciliation" rather than serious love; she wonders "if those moments aren't more valued, and deliberately gone after, in the set-ups some people like myself have now, than they were in those old marriages, where love and grudges could be growing underground, so confused and stubborn, it must have seemed they had forever." But without the old marriages and all that they yielded of sorrow, repression, loss, romance—what remains? Fame's love affairs are affairs merely, matters of convenience. To celebrate birthdays "or other big events" she goes with friends from work to a place called the Hideaway where male strippers perform.

(While Ms. Munro's Ontario countryside has come to bear a disconcerting resemblance to Andrew Wyeth's stark, bleached-out, clinically detailed landscapes, her small towns have been tawdrily transformed—dignified old country inns recycled as strip joints, convenience stores stocked with video games: "jittery electronic noise and flashing light and menacing, modern-day, oddly shaved and painted children.")

More than *The Beggar Maid* and *The Moons of Jupiter*, the two story collections preceding this one, *The Progress of Love* does contain less fully realized stories. So thinly executed is **"Eskimo"** that it reads like an early draft of a typically rich, layered, provocative Munro story: its male protagonist is off-stage, its female protagonist senses, or imagines, a psychic kinship with a young Eskimo girl she tries to befriend on an airplane flight, but their encounter comes to nothing and the story dissolves in a self-consciously symbolic dream. **"Miles City, Montana"** recounts a child's near-drowning but fails to integrate the episode with what precedes and follows it, and ends with a rather forced epiphany: "So we went on, with the two in the back seat trusting us, because of no choice, and we ourselves trusting to be forgiven, in time, for everything that had first to be seen and condemned by those children: whatever was flippant, arbitrary, careless, callous—all our natural, and particular, mistakes." **"Monsieur les Deux Chapeaux"** and **"Circle of Prayer"** are each rather sketchily imagined, though brimming with life; and **"White Dump,"** potentially one of the strongest stories in the collection, suffers from a self-conscious structure in which time is fashionably broken and point of view shifts with disconcerting casualness from character to character. We catch only a glimpse of Isabel and her lover and must take Isabel's word for it, that she feels "rescued, lifted, beheld, and safe"; we are not even certain whether the author means her conviction to be serious, or self-deluded. And the image of the "white dump"—the biscuit factory sugar dump—is rather arbitrarily spliced onto the story, poetically vivid as it is.

Even the weaker stories, however, contain passages of genuinely inspired prose and yield the solid pleasures of a three-dimensional world that has been respectfully, if not always lovingly, recorded. And Ms. Munro's minor characters, though fleetingly glimpsed, are frequently the vehicles for others' gestures of compassion and pity. (As in **"The Moon in the Orange Street Skating Rink,"** where decades are compressed within the space of a few pages, and Edgar, whom we have seen as a bright, attractive boy of 17, emerges as an elderly stroke victim, seated in front of a television screen, indifferent to the visit of his cousin and to his cousin's offer to take him for a walk. His wife says of him, simply: "No. He's happy.")

The Progress of Love is a volume of unflinching audacious honesty, uncompromisingly downright in its dissection of the ways in which we deceive ourselves in the name of love; the bleakness of its vision is enriched by the author's exquisite eye and ear for detail. Life is heartbreak, but it is also uncharted moments of kindness and reconciliation.

ALICE MUNRO WITH PLEUKE BOYCE AND RON SMITH

SOURCE: Alice Munro with Pleuke Boyce and Ron Smith, "A National Treasure," in *Meanjin*, Vol. 54, No. 2, 1995, pp. 222-32.

[*In the following interview, Munro discusses the purpose of her fiction, which is to relate the perplexing experiences and open-ended nature of human behavior, and not to present neatly packaged, specifically themed stories with lessons.*]

It would not be exaggerating to suggest that for many Canadians Alice Munro is a national treasure. Her eight books have been greeted with reviews that range from stating 'She is our Chekhov' to 'One of the best short story writers alive' (*The Times*, London). She has won Canada's prestigious Governor General's Award three times, for ***Dance of the Happy Shades*** (1968), ***Who Do You Think You Are?*** (1978) and ***The Progress Of Love*** (1986), which was also selected as one of the best books of that year by the *New York Times*. Her other books include ***Lives of Girls and Women*** (1971), ***Something I've Been Meaning To Tell You*** (1976), ***The Moons Of Jupiter*** (1982), ***Friend Of My Youth*** (1990) and, most recently, ***Open Secrets*** (1994). She is a frequent contributor to the *New Yorker*, the *Paris Review*, and *Atlantic Monthly*.

Her work has been translated into several languages and she has been a guest speaker in countries as diverse as China, Norway, England and Australia. Her success as a writer stems not only from her obvious love and care for craft, but from her gift, as one reviewer has suggested, to make 'the unremarkable seem remarkable'. She touches our lives in a way that is at once subtle and disturbing.

Born and raised in Wingham, Ontario, she and her second husband now divide their time between Clinton, Ontario, and Comox on Vancouver Island. Alice Munro was interviewed for *Meanjin* by Pleuke Boyce (her Dutch translator) and Ron Smith in Errington, B.C., on 30 January 1995.

[Meanjin:] *How does a story get started?*

[Munro:] Story telling is continuous. Story doesn't stop, at least not the sort of stories I'm interested in writing. There are certain types of stories which do, in fact, end. Which do come to a conclusion. Political stories conclude. Because they have some purpose to fulfil which is separate from telling a story. Such stories want to engage and challenge us with the issues they present, usually in the hope of satisfying some political or social agenda. The problem with issue-driven fiction is that it doesn't arouse feelings or disturb us in the way I think good fiction should. The message becomes more important than the questions or puzzles nurtured by human experience or behaviour.

Are you suggesting then that your stories do not make a political or social comment?

No. I'm certain my stories do have social and political content, at least in the broadest sense of those terms. Obviously every human action has some political impulse and social consequence. But I'd rather leave any interpretation of these motives in my work to the reader or the critic. Why invent characters if they simply embody some polemical goal? I don't like messages attached to my reading. This is why I'm not too fond of [Leo] Tolstoy or D. H. Lawrence. While some of the writing in both writers is beautiful, I'm not at all interested in the sermons attached to their stories. On the other hand, Eudora Welty makes a southern American town feel absolutely magical, but she may be in fact, often is politically incorrect. The experience she relates, though, is both accurate and authentic. And emotionally and intellectually disturbing. Her book, *The Golden Apples*, is one of my favourite books. But I guess if I were black and had grown up in the South, I would have felt excluded from that book.

By contrast, I was annoyed with the dialogue in a novel I read recently because the exchange between the characters appeared to be little more than a political debate. I think my response here has something to do with the fact that I proceed from induction rather than deduction. I also think that writing about 'current issues' dates very quickly. Still, in certain contexts I can see where writing that's overtly political can be 'useful' fiction.

How have your views of writing changed from the publication of ***Dance of the Happy Shades*** *(1968) to the recent publication of* ***Open Secrets*** *(1994)?*

When I started to write I wrote about things that puzzled me — death, love, all the obvious concerns that tend to confuse us throughout our lives. Describing life made life bearable for me. While I'm still puzzled, I realize the questions we ask are far more intriguing than the answers we give or sometimes think we've discovered. This is why ***Open Secrets*** is not a good introduction to my work. These stories don't close in the way people expect or want them to.

You're suggesting that some readers are challenged when their expectations are unfulfilled? They feel cheated, perhaps, because part of their sense of anticipation as a reader is that you will bring the story to a satisfactory resolution?

Yes. The stories in **Open Secrets** aren't about what they seem to be about. Clearly some people find this quite disconcerting. My sister, who is a conservative reader—she reads good books, but nothing too experimental—phoned me after she'd read the first story in **Open Secrets** and said 'I can't stand it.' She had wanted a normal ending, where everything was resolved. One woman, who I consider to be a fairly sophisticated reader, wrote to me recently about the new book and accused me of having betrayed a trust, a trust presumably that had been built up through her reading of the earlier books. She signed her letter 'Still a fan', but she was obviously upset. Certainly I'm grateful for readers, but my response to her was that we never had a contract. When I write there is a reader there for me, an imagined ideal reader, someone I'm definitely talking to, but no writer can be handcuffed by reader expectations. I don't mind negative reactions because they make me reflect on what I'm doing. Criticism is more helpful then unadulterated praise. I realize that when people object to certain things they bring their own biases. This forces me to re-examine my ideas and usually confirms what I'm doing. On the other hand, I'm bothered when people say how grim or depressing my stories are. This has been particularly true with **Open Secrets**. I disagree with this response to my work. **'Spaceships Have Landed'** has a lightness about it of which I'm quite fond.

I would agree, although I don't think your stories are ever 'light', at least not in the sense that most people would use that word. Your stories are beautifully balanced, and humour and irony are a part of that balance.

Obviously I don't mean to suggest that violence of any sort, mental or physical, done to any human being is 'light' subject matter.

But you are concerned that the full range of emotional experience be recognized in your work?

Yes.

Does it bother you, then, when certain critics use the terms 'provincial' or 'regional' to describe your writing? Do you think these words, which are used by Brian Fawcett and others in a way that is accusatory, accurately reflect what you are doing?

Outside of Canada readers are much more receptive to what is regional. Americans see this quality in [William] Faulkner or Welty as a virtue.

Or, more recently, in Raymond Carver.

Yes. Fawcett compared my work to Carver's. In Canada these are pejorative terms. Patronizing. I'm not certain what either word means to these people. They appear to be limiting their use of the terms to geography. They're usually talking about a place they think is unimportant. I write about what I know well. My people go back one hundred and fifty years in that place. I know what's going on in a bar, a house, a church, a store; I have a feeling for what's going on. This is essential! Those who criticize my work as being too provincial seem to be suggesting that people live very different lives in different places. To a certain extent this is true, but the implication is that the rural experience is limited. Hence, less valid. I think we should celebrate those differences. At the same time those differences are not so great that we cannot share in the emotional experiences that are common to us all. I think this criticism is a desperate attempt to legitimize Canadian literature. Urban equals legitimacy. How can Canadian literature be world class if written about rural Ontario? This is such a parochial complaint to begin with. By extension, I guess they would dismiss all the southern American women writers I like so much. Or many of the Latin American writers who have become so popular. After all, [Gabriel] García Márquez is regional, at least as I understand their use of the term. I think Fawcett is probably equally concerned that I'm not pushing a particular ideology.

In **Open Secrets** *you've extended the short story form. It's easy for an established writer to settle back and repeat successes, but you've refused to do this. You take risks which, with all due respect to your detractors, doesn't surprise me.*

It's pointless to go on if you don't take risks. While the stories in **Open Secrets** have elements of mystery and romance, for example, themes which have always attracted readers, the stories don't satisfy in the same way as a traditional mystery or romance would. As I stated earlier, I wanted these stories to be open. I wanted to challenge what people want to know. Or expect to know. Or anticipate knowing. And as profoundly, what I think I know.

Also, I wanted to record how women adapt to protect men. The emotional and intellectual pull in **'The Albanian Virgin'** is the legitimacy given to the female who denies her sexuality. This is similar to the school marm in the old west who gave up her female identity to become the teacher. The different woman. The emotional pull is the strength of denial. Women have been pulled in half this way for a long time. Well into this century, marriage and having children have not been attractive options for a lot of women. And, frankly, nor have the alternatives.

Equally important in this new collection, I've been concerned with time. How do we relate to time and space. In **'Carried Away'** I began with a conventional romantic plot, but from the start I knew Louisa would lose the man. The reality is you don't always get the man you want. And what if there are alternate realities? I felt it was important that the man age in the story, but that Louisa encounter the several potential realities available to her in her future. Our own lives are made up of this sort of mix. We are the ones who impose the notion of succession on our lives. Perhaps this is how we avoid confronting what is fantasy and what is reality. That is, if it is ever possible to make a meaningful distinction between the two. We rarely live beyond the one reality we define or choose for ourselves. Yet things happen simultaneously in the universe. Something completely unimportant really does matter, at least in one version of the future. And rarely is it what we expect. I suspect these are the concerns which caused some of my readers to feel uneasy about the new book. Form is never stationary or static. Much of the material might appear to be familiar but the security that familiarity offers the reader is illusory. For some first-time readers of my work, these stories must appear quite strange or fragmented indeed. Quite disjointed.

The word displacement comes to mind. Events in time are not necessarily sequential, especially when we factor memory into the equation. Your work has been evolving in this direction for some time. Figurative gaps, what we usually define as metaphor, have been supplanted by spatial and temporal gaps. Does this explain why the stories in the new collection are all quite long? All have the scope, the range, the vision of novels. As the inspiration for your work becomes more complex, have you considered writing novels? I should admit here that I really don't think **Lives of Girls and Women** *is a novel.*

I don't know if **Lives** is a novel or not. That's for you to decide. Certainly each section in the book is quite separate. Quite distinct. Yet the book is unified.

The answer is yes. I'm always trying to write a novel. In fact, I'm working on one right now, but I have trouble making them long enough because I'm incapable of doing the in-between stuff. You know, the things that keep it moving along, but that aren't important in themselves. If I finish this novel I'm working on, it will probably be too short. But I feel somewhat encouraged by a Dutch writer I'm reading, Cees Nooteboom. His novels are very short, often less than a hundred pages. I could write a novel of that length, but I don't think my publisher would go for it.

I've tried to write several novels and they've all failed. When I try to write a novel it flies in too many directions. From a little clot it moves out and I can't rein it in. Most, if not all, of these efforts have eventually become stories. For example, three stories in *Open Secrets*, which started as a novel, come from a single source: **'The Albanian Virgin'**, **'Carried Away'**, and **'A Real Life'**. A book by Edith Durham, *High Albania*, provided the initial information and inspiration for **'The Albanian Virgin'**. She travelled the country extensively around 1908, a bit earlier than the time I set my story in. And the concept of the Albanian virgin, about which she had written, fascinated me. There was this possibility for women that if they opted out of marriage and sex they could become independent. They could be some kind of honorary man. They would be all alone and had to do everything for themselves. But there was this possibility they could reject the traditional role and be just themselves. As I said earlier, we've had something similar in our culture, a modern counterpart. The spinster. The woman who didn't marry but carved out a life for herself and became a music teacher or librarian. She, too, had to renounce sex and everything that went with it. You couldn't have it both ways.

Then in writing the first drafts of that story, I attempted to use **'A Real Life'** as a framing device. Needless to say, that didn't work. Dorrie's character grew into something unexpected. And quite special. Her liberation is exhilarating. Her potential, while unrecognized by others in her community, is as huge as the world she is prepared to explore. She is capable of change in a way that threatens Millicent. **'A Real Life'** became its own story. Next, the protagonist in the first version of **'The Albanian Virgin'** was a librarian, but I soon found myself doing research on librarians and popular titles of the day. The next thing I knew I had kidnapped my librarian from **'The Albanian Virgin'** and brought her to **'Carried Away'**.

But I still wanted to write about the Albanian Virgin. The two people who supply the tale are based on a couple who used to come into the bookstore my first husband and I started in Victoria. They were English and had very strong accents. They were always trying to sell us books for cash. Anything for cash, in fact. Once, when I admired a bracelet the woman was wearing, mostly to make conversation, she immediately offered to sell it to me. But I didn't want it, of course. With the money they managed to make, they played the horses. The man went around with a wheelbarrow and wore a long cloak. They were quite a sight. At that time, this was around 1963, you did not see many eccentrics in Victoria.

This is the way in which my potential novels tend to fly to pieces. Ideas for stories need an emotional pull and once I sense that pull I go with it. I lose control over my original intention.

Does this matter? I would have thought that if the work is complete on its own terms, then it has fulfilled whatever obligation it has to the reader. [Jorge Luis] Borges suggests that you should provide no more than what the reader needs to complete the work in his or her own imagination.

Yes, I can accept that. I'm certainly not intentionally withholding anything from the reader. I feel the stories are complete. They're simply not novels.

The label is really unimportant. Your stories are as long as many of Marguerite Duras's novels. And, while different, I would suggest they have comparable depth and complexity. Maybe it's these qualities that define a novel?

I don't know. However, I do know that I must pursue the emotional life my stories demand of me. I guess I've learned to accept what is given. As long as the stories disturb people or point to the ways in which they should be dissatisfied with the status quo, then I assume I've done my job.

Then writing is more than merely 'a way of getting on top of experience', as you said in an earlier interview?

When did I say that? It must have been a long time ago. Certainly I never managed to achieve that goal.

Your stories often deal with sexual experience and often that experience is very sensual. Is this important in your writing?

Yes. Sex and sexuality are central to our being.

In this respect, you seem equally comfortable in your creation of female or male protagonists. For example, in 'Thanks For The Ride' *from* Dance Of The Happy Shades *you write from the male point of view with amazing accuracy and insight. And in the new book both* 'Spaceships Have Landed' *and* 'Carried Away' *capture the male psyche as well as any male writer. How do you feel about voice appropriation?*

I love it! I intend to do more! Is this really still an issue? Are there people who actually believe that a woman can't write from the point of view of a man? I would have thought it was the intensity and colour of perception and the quality of writing that mattered.

SOURCES FOR FURTHER STUDY

Carrington, Ildikó de Papp. "What's in a Title: Alice Munro's 'Carried Away'." *Studies in Short Fiction* 30, No. 4 (Fall 1993): 555-64.

    Explores how the title "Carried Away" reflects the story's structure and action.

Fowler, Rowena. "The Art of Alice Munro: *The Beggar Maid* and *Lives of Girls and Women*." *Critique* 25, No. 4 (Summer 1984): 189-98.

    Compares the heroines of *The Beggar Maid* and *Lives of Women and Children* and discusses Munro's writing process.

Smythe, Karen. "Sad Stories: The Ethics of Epiphany in Munrovian Elegy." *The University of Toronto Quarterly* 60, No. 4 (Summer 1991): 493-506.

    Essay explores the meanings of melancholy and realism in Munro's fiction.

Thomas, Sue. "Reading Female Sexual Desire in Alice Munro's *Lives of Girls and Women*." *Critique* XXXVI, No. 2 (Winter 1995): 106-20.

    Feminist discussion of Del's sexuality in *Lives of Girls and Women*.

Warkwick, Susan J. "Growing Up: The Novels of Alice Munro." *Essays on Canadian Writing*, No. 29 (Summer 1984): 204-25.

    Discusses issues of communication and maturation in respect to Del in *Lives of Girls and Women* and Rose in *Who Do You Think You Are?*

Weinhouse, Linda. "Alice Munro: Hard-Luck Stories or There Is No Sexual Relation." *Critique* XXXVI, No. 2 (Winter 1995): 121-29.

    Analyzes "Hard Luck Stories" in terms of the theories of Jacques Lacan.

Gloria Naylor

1950-

American novelist, critic, and short story writer.

INTRODUCTION

Naylor is best known as the author of *The Women of Brewster Place* (1982), which won the American Book Award for best first novel in 1983 and was adapted as a television production starring Oprah Winfrey, Lynn Whitfield, and Cicely Tyson in 1989. "While *The Women of Brewster Place* is about the black woman's condition in America," Naylor explained, "I had to deal with the fact that one composite picture couldn't do justice to the complexity of the black female experience. So I tried to solve this problem by creating a microcosm on a dead-end street and devoting each chapter to a different woman's life. These women vary in age, personal background, political consciousness, and sexual preference. What they do share is a common oppression and, more importantly, a spiritual strength and sense of female communion that I believe all women have employed historically for their psychic health and survival."

Biographical Information

Naylor was born and raised in New York City. After high school graduation, she served as a missionary for Jehovah's Witnesses in New York, North Carolina, and Florida until 1975, when she returned to New York City. Discouraged about the dearth of books on black women by black women, Naylor endeavored to write one. *The Women of Brewster Place* was conceived as a short story, but Naylor expanded it into a novel. She completed most of the manuscript while working as a hotel switchboard operator and studying at Brooklyn College of the City University of New York, where she earned a B.A. in 1981. By the time she obtained her master's degree in African-American studies from Yale University in 1983, she was already recognized as an impressive new writer. During the 1980s Naylor was named visiting lecturer or writer-in-residence at several American universities. Later she published the novels *Linden Hills* (1985) and *Mama Day* (1988). Since 1990 Naylor has presided over her own production company, One Way Productions, and has continued to lecture on campuses.

Major Works

The Women of Brewster Place focuses on seven black female residents of Brewster Place—a dilapidated ghetto housing project in an unidentified northern city—and their relationships with one another. As they cope with living in a racist and sexist society, they encounter further abuse from their own husbands, lovers, and children. *Linden Hills* abandons the gritty realism of Naylor's first novel, creating instead an allegorical commentary on the fallacies of black mobility and material success. The novel revolves around Willie and Lester, two young handymen who do odd jobs over the Christmas holidays for the residents of Linden Hills, an exclusive suburb located near Brewster Place and controlled by Luther Nedeed, a real estate tycoon and mortician. As Willie and Lester offer their services throughout the neighborhood, they witness Nedeed's malevolence and expose the idleness, hypocrisy, and bigotry of the townspeople. Set in the all-black island community of Willow Springs off the coasts of South Carolina and Georgia, *Mama Day* centers on Mama Day, an elderly mystical healer, and Cocoa, Mama Day's strong-willed grandniece who lives in New York but spends the summer on the island. Both women are descendants of Sapphira Wade, an African slave and sorceress who married and later murdered her master after forcing him to bequeath to his slaves and their offspring his land, which included the island. When Cocoa brings her rational husband, George, to visit Mama Day, their lives collide after Cocoa becomes deathly ill, and George is forced to put aside reason to save her. *Bailey's Cafe* (1992) combines first and third person narration to depict the desperate patrons of a Brooklyn diner in the years following World War II. Their stories of loss and survival capture black life in New York City during the late 1940s.

Critical Reception

Despite the critical acclaim of Naylor's other works, *The Women of Brewster Place* remains her most popular book. Assessing Naylor's appeal, Deirdre Donahue observed that "Naylor is not afraid to grapple with life's big subjects: sex, birth, love, death, grief. Her women feel deeply, and she unflinchingly transcribes their emotions." Donahue also found that "Naylor's potency wells up from her language. With prose as rich as poetry, a passage will suddenly take off and sing like a spiritual." Critics have cited similarities between *Linden Hills* and Dante's *Inferno,* while others have compared *Mama Day* to William Shakespeare's *Tempest.* Michiko Kakutani affirmed that "although the notion of using Dante's *Inferno* to illuminate the co-opting of black aspirations in contemporary America may strike the prospective reader as pretentious, one is quickly beguiled by the actual novel—so gracefully does Naylor fuse together the epic and the naturalistic, the magical and the real." Naylor's novels "sing of sorrows proudly borne by black women in America," concluded Donahue.

(For further information, see *Authors and Artists for Young Adults,* Vol. 6; *Black Literature Criticism; Black Writers,* Vol. 2; *Contemporary Authors,* Vol. 107; *Contemporary Authors New Revision Series,* Vols. 27, 51; *Contemporary Literary Criticism,* Vols. 28, 52; *Dictionary of Literary Biography,* Vol. 173; *DISCovering Authors; DISCovering Authors: Canadian; DISCovering Authors Modules: Most-studied Authors Module, Multicultural Authors Module, Novelists Module, Popular Fiction and Genre Authors Module; Major Twentieth-Century Writers.*)

CRITICAL COMMENTARY

ANNIE GOTTLIEB

SOURCE: Annie Gottlieb, "Women Together," in *The New York Times Book Review,* August 22, 1982, pp. 11, 25.

[*In the following excerpt, Gottlieb reviews* The Women of Brewster Place, *concluding: "Miss Naylor bravely risks sentimentality and melodrama to write her compassion and outrage large, and she pulls it off triumphantly."*]

Ten or 12 years ago, the vanguard of the women's movement began exhorting the rest of us to pay attention to our relationships with other women: mothers, daughters, sisters, friends. How important those neglected bonds were, said representatives, how much of the actual substance of daily life they were. But it was hard, at first, for most women to *see* clearly the significance of those bonds; all our lives those relationships had been the backdrop, while the sexy, angry fireworks with men were the show.

Now, it seems, that particular lesson of feminism has been not only taken to heart, but deeply absorbed. Here are two first novels in which it feels perfectly natural

> **Principal Works**
>
> *The Women of Brewster Place* (novel) 1982
> *Linden Hills* (novel) 1985
> *Centennial* (nonfiction) 1986
> *Mama Day* (novel) 1988
> *Bailey's Cafe* (novel) 1992
>
> **Adaptations**
>
> *The Women of Brewster Place* was adapted as a television miniseries, produced by Oprah Winfrey and Carole Isenberg, ABC, 1989.

that women are the foreground figures, primary both to the reader and to each other, regardless of whether they're involved with men. In Gloria Naylor's fierce, loving group portrait of seven black women in one housing development . . . , the bonds between women are the abiding ones. Most men are incalculable hunters who come and go. They are attractive—but weak and / or dangerous—representatives of nature and of violence who both fertilize and threaten the female core.

Gloria Naylor's *The Women of Brewster Place* is set in one of those vintage urban-housing developments that black people (who are, in truth, "nutmeg," "ebony," "saffron," "cinnamon-red" or "gold") have inherited from a succession of other ethnic groups. The difference is that while the Irish and Italians used it as a jumping-off place for the suburbs, for most of its "colored daughters" Brewster Place is "the end of the line": "They came because they had no choice and would remain for the same reason." But the end of the line is not the end of life. With their backs literally to the wall—a brick barrier that has turned Brewster Place into a dead end—the women make their stand together, fighting a hostile world with love and humor.

There's Mattie Michael, dark as "rich, double cocoa," who defied her overprotective father to take a man who was pure temptation, almost a force of nature—a Pan. Pregnant and disowned, she made the instinctive matriarchal decision (I mean that word in the mythic, not the sociological, sense) to live without a man and invest all her love back into her child. Left in the lurch by the grown, spoiled son who results, she becomes the anchor for the other women of Brewster Place.

There's Etta Mae Johnson, survivor and good-time woman, who comes home to Mattie when her dream of redemption by marrying a "respectable" preacher is sordidly ended. There's Ciel Turner, whose husband, Eugene, ominously resents her fertility: "With two kids and you on my back, I ain't never gonna have nothin' . . . nothin'!" There's Kiswana (formerly Melanie) Browne, idealistic daughter of middle-class parents, who has moved to Brewster Place to be near "my people." Cora Lee, a welfare mother, likes men only because they provide babies, but she can't cope with children once they are older. She is *almost* lifted out of the inertia of her life by the power of art when Kiswana takes her to see a black production of Shakespeare in the park. And, finally, there are Theresa and Lorraine, lovers who embody the ultimate commitment of woman to woman and yet arouse uprise or loathing in most of the other women of Brewster Place.

Despite Gloria Naylor's shrewd and lyrical portrayal of many of the realities of black life (her scene of services in the Canaan Baptist Church is brilliant), *The Women of Brewster Place* isn't realistic fiction—it is mythic. Nothing supernatural happens in it, yet its vivid, earthy characters (especially Mattie) seem constantly on the verge of breaking out into magical powers. The book has two climaxes, one of healing and rebirth, one of destruction. In the first, Mattie magnificently wrestles Ciel, dying of grief, back to life. In the second, Lorraine, rejected by the others, is gang raped, a blood sacrifice brutally proving the sisterhood of all women. Miss Naylor bravely risks sentimentality and melodrama to write her compassion and outrage large, and she pulls it off triumphantly.

LOYLE HAIRSTON

SOURCE: Loyle Hairston, in a review of "The Women of Brewster Place," in *Freedomways*, Vol. 23, No. 4, 1983, pp. 282-85.

[*In the following essay, Hairston favorably reviews* The Women of Brewster Place, *praising the book's rich and "well-drawn" characters.*]

The personal stories of several women whose lives intertwine by virtue of their residence on the same block comprise the subject matter of this award-winning first novel [*The Women of Brewster Place*]. Brewster Place, like so many urban areas, had more prosperous times as a lily-white community. Now, it has become what the media during the '60s christened a "ghetto"—that is, a black slum. But inhabiting this piece of urban real estate is a colorful cast of characters, who throb with vitality amid the shattering of their hopes and dreams.

We meet Mattie Michael first. Seduced and made pregnant in late adolescence by the local dandy in her native Tennessee town, Mattie is later beaten by her father for refusing to divulge the man's name and must leave home. With her son, Basil, she eventually finds her way to Brewster Place, where she develops quickly into a hard-working, resourceful woman bent on giving her son a good start in life. Indulged and doted upon, Basil grows into a trouble-prone teenager whose reckless ways lead to a manslaughter charge. Mattie mortgages her home to pay his bail only to be betrayed by her beloved son, who jumps bail and skips town, leaving his mother heartbroken and destitute.

In the course of her travails, Mattie has met Etta Mae Johnson, a confirmed hedonist whose dreams have been dissipated in her pursuit of "good times." For Etta, happiness is a man. Thus, attending church services with Mattie Michael one Sunday, she finds herself listening, not to the reverend's sermon, but to her old instincts telling her to lasso someone who can support her in the style "that complemented the type of woman she had fought all these years to become." The good reverend, however, proves to be as much a man of the world as of the cloth, experienced in exploiting the wiles of his congregation's female members.

We also meet Kiswana Browne, a naive, middle-class apostate given to revolutionary idealism. When Kiswana's mother visits her estranged daughter in her third-floor walkup on Brewster Place, readers are afforded an insightful look at the generation gap. Kiswana is a bright-eyed product of the '60s who received the dictum "black is beautiful" as political ideology. Mom, though upbraided for her "backwardness," proves to be more than a match for her militant daughter, who finally succumbs to a force more potent than her revolutionary zeal—a mother's love.

The saddest story in this collection is also the most amusing. It features young, overweight Cora Lee—a stereotypical "welfare mother." Cora has not given much thought to why she had her brood of children, nor has she considered what kind of future awaits them. Her more troubling concerns are the tragic lives of her favorite TV soap opera characters. Persuaded by Kiswana to take the children to an Afro-American cultural affair, she finds the event so stimulating that she goes home and jumps into bed with her current lover. Several stories later, we find her pregnant again.

For me the most penetrating of the stories is **"The Two,"** with its well-drawn lesbian characters, Theresa and Lorraine. Sharp contrasts between the young lovers' personalities surface when Lorraine befriends Ben, the building superintendent and handy man. Although she doesn't see a rival in Ben, Theresa opposes the friendship for more complex reasons. The women's domestic conflict is exacerbated by their different reactions to the hostility directed at them by their neighbors, who are portrayed as harboring the bigoted social attitudes common to many Americans. The story ends in a spate of violence, with Ben being brutally murdered when he is mistaken for Lorraine's attacker.

Other characters are, for the most part, equally well-drawn each with a strong individuality shaped out of the pathetic circumstances of their lives and all sharing a common fate—life has turned on them with a vengeance. Naylor's prose embraces them warmly, revealing in a vivid, fast-paced narrative their various levels of consciousness. While her subjects are Afro-American, these are not racial stories except in the context of U.S. life. They are primarily stories about the human will to survive for as long as possible.

The world of Brewster Place is a familiar one in that it mirrors a real world of poverty and all of its attendant ills—humiliation, pain, powerlessness, loneliness, despair. As slice of life tales, however, Naylor's offerings leave unanswered the questions of social causality and how folk like those depicted are to overcome their degrading condition. Is individual initiative a la Horatio Alger the way out? Or is radical change in society required? In the flyleaf of her book, Naylor quotes the Langston Hughes poem which asks, regarding "a dream deferred," "Does it dry up / like a raisin in the sun," or, as Hughes posed in the last line, "Does it explode!" Naylor's characters are unlikely to explode in the sense that Hughes meant. For even though most of them are shown as being vital, scrappy and endowed with the varieties of inner strength that spawns wisdom—the sagacity to attack their circumstances with a determination to alter the course of their lives—none, except for the young militant, envisions any hope of better times.

Understanding the dialectics of change would seem to be the moral task of the writer who quests for illuminating truths about people whose lives are under assault from an oppressive society. But perhaps Naylor, like most U.S. writers, is a kind of closet social Darwinist who does not see the U.S. as oppressive; who sees, rather, a nation with surmountable social problems that test the mettle of individual citizens. In any case, the narrative gives no hint that its author is in serious conflict with fundamental U.S. values. Consequently, questions arise about the moral and philosophical premises underlying her fiction. Whereas works like *Huckleberry Finn* and *Native Son* endure partly because they are critical of society, Naylor's first effort seems to fall in with most of the fiction being published today, which bypasses provocative social themes to play, instead, in the shallower waters of isolated personal relationships.

Indeed, in some recently published Afro-American fiction, the black man has eclipsed a hostile society as the archest villain in our midst, his image as brute and rapist having graduated from white supremacist myth to gospel truth. While *Brewster Place* does not suffer from this dreary perspective, it does confine its concerns to the warts and cankers of individual personality, neglecting to delineate the origins of those social conditions which so strongly affect personality and behavior.

I'm not suggesting that Naylor should have written a different book. I'm merely noting that what I look for in a story is absent—namely, some new insight into, some purposeful probing of, mundane reality. For a writer to achieve this requires, first and foremost, the courage to write from strong conviction, in addition to talent and knowledge—a stance that, to me, is especially incumbent upon Afro-Americans. Even though this may work against one's striving for recognition and success in the literary world, one might well ask whether recognition by an establishment committed to maintaining a status quo that subjugates third world people at home and abroad is truly meritorious. In any case, the works of writers who lack conviction seldom survive as solid literature.

Notwithstanding the many questions it provokes about what is happening in contemporary Afro-American literature, *The Women of Brewster Place* is an enjoyable read. Naylor displays a fine talent as both story teller and prose stylist, armed as she is with a poetic feeling for the English language, folk speech and the contradictory nuances of personality. Here is a good beginning, rich in marvelous detail about characters with whom we can easily identify. Hopefully, her next offering will plumb further the depths of human experience.

MICHIKO KAKUTANI

SOURCE: Michiko Kakutani, "Dante in Suburbia," in *The New York Times*, February 9, 1985, p. 14.

[*In the following review, Kakutani praises Naylor's fusing of "the epic and the naturalistic, the magical and the baroque" in* Linden Hills.]

In *The Women of Brewster Place,* her award-winning first novel, Gloria Naylor conjured up an entire fictional world by sifting through the lives of eight black women, trapped in an urban housing development, at "the end of the line." . . . [In *Linden Hills*], she is again concerned with the foundering of black dreams within a particular community, but she has moved up the social ladder, to an upper-middle class neighborhood of mock-Tudor homes and Georgian mansions known as Linden Hills.

By letting her mythic imagination spring free from the constraints of old-fashioned realism, Miss Naylor has produced an ambitious novel that aspires to be nothing less than a contemporary reading of Dante's *Inferno*. Not only are the residents of Linden Hills lost souls, condemned to a "city of woe" for their embracing of material pleasures, but they also live on a series of circular drives that correspond, geographically, to Dante's nine circles of hell. At the bottom of the hill, there's a frozen lake—just like the one in which Lucifer was immersed—and on the lake lives Miss Naylor's own version of Satan, a short, frog-eyed real estate tycoon, named Luther Nedeed, who maintains his hold over Linden Hills by appealing to its citizens' baser ambitions. . . .

Although the notion of using Dante's *Inferno* to illuminate the co-opting of black aspirations in contemporary America may strike the prospective reader as pretentious, one is quickly beguiled by the actual novel—so gracefully does Miss Naylor fuse together the epic and the naturalistic, the magical and the real. If the narrative relies rather too much on baroque symbols and withheld secrets—What terrible rites take place in the mortuary at the bottom of the hill? Whatever happened to Luther Nedeed's wife and baby son?—it is redeemed by the author's confident way with a story; her sassy, street-wise humor; her ability to empathize with her characters' dilemmas.

As written by Miss Naylor, those characters represent a spectrum black opinions. One member of Linden Hills denounces his ancestors for their passivity and their faith: "These people, his people, were always out of step, a step behind or a step ahead, still griping and crying about slavery, hanging up portraits of Abraham Lincoln in those lousy shacks. They couldn't do nothing because they were slaves or because they *will* be in heaven."

Another mocks his wealthy family and their neighbors as yuppified Uncle Toms: They're the "saddest niggers you'll ever wanna meet."

And a third sympathizes with these same people for wanting a better life: "My mom got beat up every night after payday by a man who couldn't bear the thought of bringing home a paycheck only large enough for three people and making it stretch over eight people, so he drank up half of it." . . .

There is a certain sociological impulse at work here, as though Miss Naylor wanted to play Studs Terkel—wanted to make sure to include every representative viewpoint. And yet for all their symbolic value, her characters never become caricatures, outlined by a condescending observer. Roxanne, the bright, spoiled princess who wants to grow up to be a combination of Eleanor Roosevelt and Diana Ross; Xavier, her ambitious boyfriend who's afraid to declare his love; Michael, the Harvard track star who becomes a minister, only to lose his faith—these people emerge, bit by bit, as conflicted individuals whose dilemmas are as much products of personal chemistry, as abstract, environmental forces.

We get to know these residents of Linden Hills through the eyes of Lester and Willie, two characters out of an Eddie Murphy movie and two of the most charming heroes to talk their way through a recent novel. These two hip dudes are doing odd jobs in Linden Hills to earn some extra Christmas money, and in narrating their adventures there, Miss Naylor captures, perfectly, the flavor of youthful male friendship—that peculiar combination of boasting and joke-telling that belies deeper bonds of shared insecurities and fears.

Both young men happen to be poets, blessed with sensitivity and a way with words, but as our guides through the inferno of Linden Hills they remind us less of Virgil and Dante, than of another pair of friends—Tom Sawyer and Huckleberry Finn.

JEWELLE GOMEZ

SOURCE: Jewelle Gomez, "Naylor's Inferno," in *The Women's Review of Books*, Vol. II, No. 11, August, 1985, pp. 7-8.

[*In the following excerpt, Gomez offers a negative review of* Linden Hills, *stating that the work leaves her "unsatisfied, somewhat like I've felt after my grandmother's* Reader's Digest *condensations."*]

It's hard for me to be overly critical of a young, black woman writer who has achieved national success, something so rarely offered to women of color in this country. It is doubly difficult when the work of that writer, Gloria Naylor, shows seriousness and intelligence, and, next to Toni Morrison, creates the most complex black women characters in modern literature. Still, Gloria Naylor's first novel, *The Women of Brewster Place* and now her second, *Linden Hills*, leave me unsatisfied, somewhat like I've felt after my grandmother's *Reader's Digest* condensations. I sense something important was happening but the abridgement left a bare skeleton, not a full experience. . . .

Perhaps it is the sweeping scope of her story which makes Naylor believe she must wave characters and situations before us quickly rather than let us interact with them in an intimate way. But given her flair for lyrical narrative and pungent dialog there is no reason not to expect more from her. Too often, [*Linden Hills*] reads like a screenplay. Naylor gives us a visual effect or the rhythm of an event but we get no clear sense of either the impact on the characters or the emotional subtext. If there is no subtext, if this is merely the unfolding of a tapestry of diverse characters whose paths cross at random, then it is even more crucial for Naylor to attach her characters more firmly to the framework.

The Inferno motif shapes the narrative—which is fine, as the lives of black people are more than suitable for epic legends—but it often feels like a literary exercise rather than a groundbreaking adaptation. But having chosen a classical European tale to emulate, Naylor then does nothing to utilize the endless and rich African mythology to embellish the story and give it a more timeless significance. The first disappointment comes early and is woven throughout the book. Skin color has been a source of contention for Afro-Americans since we were forced onto these shores. Our color marked us as slaves and as inferior. We, as well as Europeans, have been taught that the fairer our skin the closer we are to human. Naylor uses that symbology liberally: the endless Nedeed men are coal black, squat, ugly and evil but Ruth, Willie's dream girl, has a face like "smokey caramel." All of the Nedeed wives have been fair-skinned and nearly invisible presences in the household. The current Mrs. Nedeed, somewhat darker, ironically delivers the first fair-skinned son; both are doomed from the beginning of the book. Given the complex and oppressive part that skin color has played in the economic, social and psychological lives of Afro-Americans I expected a more meaningful treatment of it. If "black" only symbolizes evil here, just as it does in most western literature, then why does neither the author nor her characters comment on that, either directly or obliquely? Perhaps Naylor feels she has done so by giving Willie the nickname "White," awarded to him because of his dark skin. But the reiteration of the symbolism here feels like simple acceptance of it.

Another weakness in the novel is the preponderance

of mad people. This is, perhaps, where clinging to Dante has been most disadvantageous. On their descent Willie and Lester encounter their old friend Norman, a man who appears healthy most of the time until he is attacked by "the pinks." Then he claws madly at his skin, gouging and scraping to rid himself of imagined pink ooze which threatens to envelope him. His wife has reduced their household to the most harmless furnishings (paper plates, plastic flatware, only two chairs) in order to protect him when he is possessed. Laurel, the beautiful, "coffee-colored" heir to a house in Linden Hills, retreats into silence, classical music and endless swims in her backyard pool. She leaves her devoted grandmother bewildered and her "sketch" of a husband impatient. Laurel finally does a high dive into her empty pool on a snowy Christmas eve to escape the demons that haunt her—demons which, like "the pinks," are rather fantastic and ill-defined.

The Nedeed patriarchs pursue riches and power through their mortuary business and the conversion of Linden Hills into a desirable property. They shape the competition which drives others to scheme and connive to win a place in Linden Hills. The last Luther Nedeed loses control when his dark-skinned wife gives birth to a light-skinned son: he locks them both in the basement of their home. (And as if that were not enough, he has already been seen doing unsettling things with the corpses at the mortuary.) Then there are the Nedeed wives, most of whom have been chosen for their obsequiousness and malleability. The current Mrs. Nedeed (whose name, Willa, we learn only at the end of the book) seems to be in atypically good control of her faculties until her son dies in the basement and Luther refuses to let her out. Leafing through journals and photograph albums during her imprisonment, Willa sees a pattern of overbearance and abuse that has left the Nedeed women less than whole. And in one particularly chilling section she flips through a picture album that begins with the wedding of a vibrant girl named Priscilla to an antecedent Luther. As the pictures progress the shadow of Priscilla's son, yet another Luther, grows ominously until it covers her completely. Soon all traces of her once lively face appear to have been deliberately burned away from the photos. In another journal Willa watches the normal check list of groceries and recipes metamorphose into a grotesque catalogue of binging and purging.

Willa's explorations of the past prove to be the most engaging parts of the book, although so many people (good and evil) are crippled with neuroses it is hard to find one to hold on to. Perhaps that is part of the relentless descent into hell; but after a while I longed for one ordinary somebody who just goes home and watches television. Naylor sets a tone of relentless gothic horror but her bedlam is out of hand.... There are no innocents here except for Willie and Lester, and they are her weakest characters. Perhaps in light of the insanity around them their mundane concerns (where to find a job, what to do about being in love with a friend's wife) can only seem insignificant. Naylor does not give these concerns nearly as much attention as the more histrionic ones. A paragraph here and there touches on one boy's unease at the real intimacy he feels with his pal, or the other's bitterness toward his mother, but these are only passing moments on the way to the snake pit. Willie and Lester should be our link but they have neither wisdom or naivete. They are young boys who have opted out of the system for no particular reason; they are not significantly oppressed by poverty nor inspired by genius; they have no driving vision of their own and so cannot compete dramatically with the really extraordinary characters.

I would have loved to see this trip through the eyes of Ruth, who does battle against her husband's "pinks" with a fierceness and love unmatched by any other character in the novel (a battle dropped half way through the book!). Or through the testimony of the alcoholic Reverend Hollis who is the only active adversary of Luther Nedeed. The telescope of Dr. Braithwaite, the town historian, would certainly have been revealing: he has killed the roots of the willow trees surrounding his home to provide an unobscured perspective from which to observe the life of most residents, including Luther, while he writes the definitive history of Linden Hills.

Time is another problem. As in *The Women of Brewster Place*, I am never secure in my sense of time. The history of Linden Hills is laid out from before the Civil War to the recent present but all events are set curiously adrift on the social and political sea that buffets Afro-Americans in this country. I don't need to know exactly where Willie and Lester are in relation to Brown vs. Board of Education, but even Dante worked within a specific sociopolitical milieu which shaped his vision. In Linden Hills some people behave like it is still the turn of the century while others talk about "disk cameras." For many of the issues Naylor touches upon, a clear sense of historical time is pivotal. For example, one character disavows a liaison with his male lover in order to marry the appropriate woman and inherit the coveted Linden Hills home, all at the direction of Luther Nedeed. This feudal machination is certainly not completely outdated (and never will be as long as there is greed), but who is the young man beset by this trauma? We receive so little personal information about him that his motivations are obscure. For a middle-class, educated gay man to be blind to alternative lifestyles in 1985 is not inconceivable but it's still hard to accept the melodrama of his arranged marriage without screaming "dump the girl and buy a ticket to Grand Rapids!" Naylor's earlier novel presented a similar limitation. While she admirably attempts to portray black gays as integral to the fabric of black life she seems incapable of imagining black gays functioning as healthy, average people. In her fiction, although they are not at fault, gays must still be made to pay. This makes her books sound like a return to the forties, not a chronicle of the eighties....

All of that said, the reason I have such high expectations is that Naylor is talented. Her writing can be lyrical and powerful, so I demand more than emulation....

I want Gloria Naylor to engage me, to intrigue, horrify and move me. She is eminently capable of that and more. But her writing jumps around from character to event as if it's not important how we feel about them. Naylor's work is important and intelligent. She takes black people and black women in particular more seriously than most writers do today. I want her craft to be equal to her vision. We know that we can master European forms. That's easy. I'm still looking for the evenly shaped work that I know will be crafted from Naylor's raw talent. A work that stands on its own in world literature.

MICHIKO KAKUTANI

SOURCE: Michiko Kakutani, in a review of "Mama Day," in *The New York Times*, February 10, 1988, p. C25.

[*In the following excerpt, Kakutani negatively appraises* Mama Day *and criticizes the novel's "pasteboard figures."*]

In her previous novel, *Linden Hills*, Gloria Naylor created an intimate portrait of a "perverted Eden," in which upper-middle-class blacks discover that they've achieved wealth and success at the expense of their own history and identity, that they've sold their souls and are now living in a kind of spiritual hell. *Mama Day*, her latest novel, similarly describes a hermetic black community, but this time, it's a pastoral world named Willow Springs—a small, paradisal island, situated off the southeast coast of the United States, somewhere off South Carolina and Georgia, but utterly sovereign in its history and traditions.

Legend has it that the island initially belonged to a Norwegian landowner named Bascombe Wade, and that one of his slaves—"a true conjure woman" by the name of Sapphira, who "could walk through a lightning storm without being touched"—married him, persuaded him to leave all his holdings to his slaves, then "poisoned him for his trouble." Before killing him, she bore him seven sons. The youngest of that generation also had seven sons, and the last of them fathered Miranda, or Mama Day. The great-nieces of Mama Day are Willa Prescott Nedeed, who readers of *Linden Hills* will recall came to an ugly and untimely end; and Ophelia, the heroine of this novel, who is likewise threatened with early and disfiguring death....

To set up the fast-paced events that conclude *Mama Day*, Ms. Naylor spends much of the first portion of the book giving us menacing hints and planting time bombs set to detonate later. We're told that Ophelia's the namesake of another Day, an unhappy woman who never recovered from one of the misfortunes that befell the family, and that her own hot temper is liable to get her into trouble. We're told that George [Ophelia's husband] suffers from a bad heart and that he shouldn't over-exert himself. We're told that Miss Ruby, a neighbor in Willow Springs, plans to use her magical powers against any woman who comes near her husband, and that her husband happens to be attracted to Ophelia. We're also told that Mama Day herself possesses potent conjuring powers, which she will use to defend her family.

One of the problems with this information is that it's force-fed into the story line, at the expense of character development and narrative flow. The plot is made to pivot around melodramatically withheld secrets (concerning the history of Willow Springs, the nature of Mama Day's second sight, the mysterious "hoodoo" rites practiced on the island); and we are constantly being reminded of the novel's themes by trite observations that are meant to pass as folk wisdom: "Home. You can move away from it, but you never leave it"; "they say every blessing hides a curse, and every curse a blessing" or "nothing would be real until the end."

To make matters worse, the island's residents, who are given to uttering such lines, come across as pasteboard figures, devoid of the carefully observed individuality that distinguished their counterparts in *Linden Hills*. Mama Day is just the sort of matriarchal figure that her name indicates—strong, wise and resolute; her neighbor, a "hoodoo" man known as Dr. Buzzard, is a folksy con man, who plays a crooked game of poker and makes moonshine on the side, and Ruby is the manipulative devil woman, absurdly possessive of her man. As for the visitors to Willow Springs, they're initially just as two-dimensional: Ophelia is a bigoted, demanding woman, who seems lucky to have found a husband at all, given her large mouth and even larger ego, while George appears to be a conscientious yuppie, neatly dividing his time between work, his wife and his passion for football.

Fortunately, as *Mama Day* progresses, Ms. Naylor's considerable storytelling powers begin to take over, and her central characters slowly take on the heat of felt emotion. The bantering exchanges between George and Ophelia demonstrate their affection, as well as their knowledge of each other's weaknesses, and George's gradual immersion in the world of Willow Springs serves to reveal much about both him and his wife.

Still, for all the narrative energy of the novel's second half, there's something contrived and forced about the story. Whereas Toni Morrison's recent novel *Beloved*, which dealt with many of the same themes of familial love and guilt, had a beautiful organic quality to it, weaving together the ordinary and the mythic in a frightening tapestry of fate, *Mama Day* remains a readable, but lumpy, amalgam of styles and allusions. The reader eventually becomes absorbed in George and Ophelia's story, but is never persuaded that the events, which overtake them, are plausible, much less inevitable or real.

BHARATI MUKHERJEE

SOURCE: Bharati Mukherjee, "There Are Four Sides to Everything," in *The New York Times Book Review*, February 21, 1988, p. C25.

[*Mukherjee is an Indian-born American novelist, short story writer, and journalist. Her fiction often focuses on sensitive protagonists who lack a stable sense of personal and cultural identity and are victimized by racism, sexism, and other forms of social oppression. In her review of* Mama Day *excerpted below, she lauds Naylor's ability to render "the wondrous familiar."*]

On a note card above my writing desk hang the words of the late American original, Liberace: "Too much of a good thing is simply wonderful."

Excess—of plots and subplots, of major characters and walk-ons, of political issues and literary allusions—is what Gloria Naylor's *Mama Day*, her third and most ambitious book, is blessed with. "There are just too many sides to the whole story," Cocoa, Mama Day's grandniece, explains at the end of this longish novel, and the story obviously feels urgent enough to both Cocoa and to Ms. Naylor that they present it to us whole.

If novels are viewed as having the power to save, then novelists are obliged, first, to relive the history of the errors of earlier chroniclers and filling in the missing parts. Recent novels like *Mama Day*, Toni Morrison's *Beloved* and Louise Erdrich's *Love Medicine* resonate with the genuine excitement of authors discovering ways, for the first time it seems, to write down what had only been intuited or heard. These are novelists with an old-fashioned "calling" (to bear witness, to affirm public virtues) in a post-modernist world; their books are scaled down for today's microwavable taste, but still linked to the great public voice of 19th-century storytelling.

Mama Day has its roots in *The Tempest*. The theme is reconciliation, the title character is Miranda (also the name of Prospero's daughter), and Willow Springs is an isolated island where, as on Prospero's isle, magical and mysterious events come to pass. As in *The Tempest*, one story line concerns the magician Miranda Day, nicknamed Mama Day, and her acquisition, exercise and relinquishment of magical powers. The other story line concerns a pair of "star-crossed" (Ms. Naylor's phrase, too) lovers: Ophelia Day, nicknamed Cocoa, and George Andrews.

Willow Springs is a wondrous island, wonderfully rendered. We learn its secrets only if we let ourselves listen to inaudible voices in boarded-up houses and hard-to-reach graveyards. We find out the way the locals do, "sitting on our porches and shelling June peas, quieting the midnight cough of a baby, taking apart the engine of a car—you done heard it without a single living soul really saying a word."

On this wondrous island, slavery and race relations, lovers' quarrels, family scandals, professional jealousies all become the "stuff as dreams are made on." The island itself sits just out of the legal reaches of Georgia and South Carolina. "And the way we saw it," ghosts whisper, "America ain't entered the question at all when it come to our land.... We wasn't even Americans when we got it—[we] was slaves. And the laws about slaves not owning nothing in Georgia and South Carolina don't apply, 'cause the land wasn't then—and isn't now—in either of them places."

America, with all its greed and chicanery, exists beyond a bridge. The island was "settled" (if that word is ever appropriate in American history) in the first quarter of the 19th century by an Africa-born slave, a spirited woman named Sapphira who, according to legend, bore her master, a Norwegian immigrant named Bascombe Wade, and maybe person or persons unknown, a total of seven sons. She then persuaded Bascombe to deed the children every square inch of Willow Springs, after which she either poisoned or stabbed the poor man in bed and vanished ahead of a posse. We find out the conditions of Sapphira's bondage only at the end of the novel: love, and not a bill of sale, had kept Bascombe and Sapphira together. Bascombe had given up his land to her sons willingly. This disclosure may make for "incorrect" politics, but it is in keeping with the *Tempest*-like atmosphere of benevolence, light and harmony that Ms. Naylor wishes to have prevail on Willow Springs.

Mama Day, who made a brief appearance in Ms. Naylor's earlier novel, **Linden Hills,** as the toothless, illiterate aunt, the wearer of ugly, comfortable shoes, the hauler of cheap cardboard suitcases and leaky jars of homemade preserves, the caster of hoodoo spells, comes into her own in this novel. . . .

Mama Day—over 100 years old if we are to believe what folks in Willow Springs say, unmarried, stern, wise, crotchety, comforting—is the true heir of Sapphira Wade. Sapphira and Bascombe's love nest, a yellow house set deep in the woods, yields secrets about the future as well as the past to the witch-prophet-matriarch Mama Day. She is the ur-Daughter to Sapphira's ur-Mother and, in turn, through a Leda-and-the-Swan kind of mysterious dead-of-night visitations, she peoples the land herself. . . .

As long as the narrative confines itself to Mama Day and daily life on the bizarre island full of rogues, frauds, crazies, martyrs and clairvoyants, the novel moves quickly. Curiously, the slow sections are about the love story of 27-year-old Cocoa, who has relocated from Willow Springs to New York, and George Andrews, who is meant to be emblematic of the good-hearted, hard-driving but culturally orphaned Northern black man. The courtship occurs all over Manhattan—in greasy diners, in three-star restaurants, in midtown offices, on subways—giving Ms. Naylor a chance to accommodate several set pieces. But she is less proficient in making the familiar wondrous than she is in making the wondrous familiar. Discussions of black bigotry (Cocoa uses kumquats, tacos and bagels as race-related shorthand and has to be scolded into greater tolerance) or of the alienating effects of Barnard College on black women ("those too bright, too jaded colored girls" is George's put-down) seem like arbitrary asides.

The love story suffers from a more serious flaw. Ms. Naylor, through strident parallels, wants us to compare Cocoa and George to Romeo and Juliet, and their courtship process to the taming of Katharina, the "shrew." The literary plan calls for George to sacrifice his life so that Cocoa might be saved, but the lovers never quite fill out their assigned mythic proportions. Cocoa just seems shallow and self-centered; and George is a priggish young man who wears dry-cleaned blue jeans for roughing it on weekends. For their love story to overwhelm us, with "all passion spent," the lovers' intensity should make whole paragraphs resonate. This, unfortunately, Ms. Naylor does not do. It seems the unchallenged domain of the 19th-century novel to link personal passion with the broader politics of an age. Cocoa is not Madame Bovary, Anna Karenina, Jane Eyre, Dorothea Brooke.

But I'd rather dwell on **Mama Day**'s strengths. Gloria Naylor has written a big, strong, dense, admirable novel; spacious, sometimes a little drafty like all public monuments, designed to last and intended for many levels of use.

ANGELS CARABI

SOURCE: Angels Carabi, "Belles Lettres Interview," in *Belles Lettres*, Vol. 7, No. 3, Spring, 1992, pp. 36-42.

[*In the following interview, Naylor speaks about her novels as well as the roles and responsibilities of a black woman writer.*]

Toni Morrison told me that, despite growing up in the North, she was surrounded by grandmothers and aunts who told stories from the South. Did you have a similar experience?

Exactly. I listened to stories about fishing and going to the woods and picking berries. I heard about working in the cotton fields and about the different characters who were in Robinsonville: the women who worked with roots and herbs, the guy who ran the church, and the man who was always drunk. A whole microcosm lived in that little hamlet. I heard all the stories because I was a quiet, shy child. I was the kid in the corner listening when they were talking about themselves. And I loved books with a passion. So my mother was rewarded by her oldest daughter in that way.

I understand that your parents migrated from Robinson, Mississippi.

That's right. My mother was eight months pregnant when she moved with my father from Robinson, Mississippi, to New York City. She decided to travel before I was born because she was adamant that none of her children would be born in the South. My mother loved to read, but she was a share cropper and could not afford to buy books. The only access to reading material was through the public libraries, the entrance to which was forbidden to black people. To buy books, my mother had to work extra hours. On Saturdays, she would go to somebody else's field and do day labor. At the end of the month, she would have about two dollars that she would send to book clubs. She was not formally educated, because schools went up to the ninth grade and children were supposed to start working afterwards. Yet she was a visionary in that she wanted her children to grow up in a place where they could read, if nothing else. She was so determined to accomplish her goal that she would say to anybody who wanted to date her: "If you marry me and if we have children, I want to leave the South." So when she married my father, she reminded him of the promise he had made to her. My grandparents had left the South a few months before, so it was easier for her to make that move; she was going where her mother had already gone. They came to New York in 1949, and I was born in 1950.

How did that move affect the family?

Often people ask me why I write about the South when I was born in New York. The reason is that although we lived in the North, I grew up in a Southern home in terms of things like food and language. The grownups no longer worked in the fields but did other kinds of manual labor. My father started working in the garment district and ended as a frame finisher. My mother did not work full-time until the 1960s, when my sisters and I were older. We lived first in Harlem, then in a housing project in the Bronx, then in Harlem again. My parents wanted a nicer place for the children to grow up in and good schools to go to, but they discovered that, because of our race, we encountered the same racism that existed in the South, although it was subtler. Job discrimination was not openly stated in the newspapers, but the truth was, even educated black people could not find jobs or live in certain high-rent neighborhoods. Middle-class black people fought against this policy because they were educated and they had money, but even in the North they were not able to obtain what they wanted. My folks' priority was to work extremely hard so their children would not have to go through what they had experienced in the South.

You received your Master's degree at Yale. Was it common among women of your generation to pursue higher education?

I went to college later than most of the young women who were with me in high school. They entered professions; many soon married. But it was different for me because I was a bit of a rebel and chose to try my wings in the world. At that time I did not believe in higher education. But the women growing up in the 1960s had opportunities open up because of the Civil Rights and Women's Movements. The black woman profited from both, to a certain degree. Those who were talented and determined could push their way through; the assumption was no longer that your only goal in life was to find a "good man" and take care of the home and the kids. Women were being shown that they had a choice. Before the 1960s, it was very different. Whether or not you were talented, you encountered a stone wall in front of you.

How did the 1960s affect you?

I learned how deep the problems were, not only in my country but in the world. The problems were so widespread and serious that they could not be solved just by marching and demonstrating. I believed that I had to rebuild our whole social system. I could see no reason for the war in Southeast Asia, a war against children and women. . . . I could not understand the assassination of Martin Luther King. He was a man who had been preaching peace and love and brotherhood. I thought that there was not much hope. So I went around with a religious group for seven years that preached about a coming theocracy. I became a sort of radical, praying for the earth to be cleansed. In 1975 this new theocracy still had not taken place and I was twenty-five with no remarkable skills. I decided to go back to school.

In the last two decades, there has been a explosion of Afro-American writers, especially of women writers. Can you talk about this phenomenon?

The phenomenon lies in the exposure of what has been taking place for quite a while in this country. A writer will write, a singer will sing, a dancer will dance. You do that because you have no choice: Either you create or you explode. Black women have been writing in this country for over a hundred years. They began to proliferate in the 1930s during the Harlem Renaissance, and they continued to grow and build on each other. In the mid 1960s and the 1970s, we began to question definitions of "American literature." Is it just simply the literature produced by the white-upper-middle-class male? Or are there other realities that constitute this country? Look at those "invisible" black females making all that noise. Do they have a history? Do they have a reality? Yes, definitely, they do. Slowly, they began to enter the institutions. I had read Faulkner, Hemingway, the Brontes, Dickens, Thackeray, Emerson, Melville, Poe, and Hawthorne, and it had been wonderful and fine. I loved that kind of literature and it taught me about language, but it did not teach me about my reality. When black Americans and women found their way into the institutions, we realized that there was another history, other meanings. We started to change our vision of American literature. Then this trend infiltrated the publishing industry. So attention is now being paid to an effort that has always been made. I don't think that more black women are writing now, but I know there's a difference in perspective.

Can you talk about some of the aspects of black women's vision that you consider uniquely rich?

Oh my God! What the black woman is bringing is a whole hidden part of American history, of the female experience. What is so rich about it, I think, is that the black woman brings both her history as a black person and her living reality as a female. Black women writers make drama out of the so-called "small matters" of life. Their portrayal of the irony of what it has been like to have a dual existence in this country becomes a celebration of the self, of transcendence. The black woman brings to literature the merging of two hidden realities.

From the beginning of your work, you create a sense of place, a sense of community where people interact.

For various reasons, I am drawn to this sense of community. What makes a writer do what he or she does derives from so many rivulets of influences. I come from a very large, close-knit, and extended family. My parents were both from families of nine children each and I grew up with about twenty cousins on my mother's side. I also come from the black working class, and in my generation, they tended to converge class in communities. Besides, family and class community is my communal history as a black American. Our survival today has depended on our nurturing each other, finding resources within ourselves. The women in Robinson, Mississippi, who dealt with herbs, for instance, played a crucial role in our community. They weren't just magical women. They had a definite medical purpose, because you could not depend on the outside hospitals to take care of your needs. So people grew up within a community that birthed you and laid you away when you died. Community is what I know and what I feel most comfortable with.

Brewster Place, in your novel **The Women of Brewster Place,** *is an urban island where only black people live. It seems to me that, by isolating the place from white people, you are more able to concentrate your attention on the black community, instead of analyzing the effects of racism on black people.*

That is a trend you can find when you look at black women's literature in general. Men have a need to confront the world, to flex their muscles, if you will. The female confronts what is immediately around her.

I knew that there was richness to be found within the black community. I'm not concerned with the reaction of white Americans to me. That goes back to how I was raised. At home, we were told that no one can tell you who or what you are, whether or not you have value. You must tell that to yourself. I learned to look inward, to explore the problems "we" have and discover what the realities are.

To talk about "the black experience" is to engage yourself in a vast field of inquiry. It seems that you provide a variety of characters who come from different backgrounds, with different problems that illustrate individual aspects of that experience.

Exactly. By exploring the lives of different women in Brewster Place, I'm attempting to create a microcosm of the black female experience in America. This is why the book is structured the way it is, with the women on different levels in those apartment buildings. Where I placed them and how they lived meant something in relationship to the wall in Brewster Place.

People tend to talk about "the black experience," lumping it all as one mass searching but there is no one thing that can stand for that experience because it is indeed so rich and so varied. This agglomeration is done for the sake of expediency and also because race is something that people don't want to think about much, so they pick one or two examples and figure that they have thought about the whole problem. It's intellectual and moral laziness.

Let's look at some of the distinct characters that you create in **The Women of Brewster Place.** *For instance, when Mattie Michael arrives in Brewster Place, the smell of the herbs brings her memories of the South. Maybe it is the sense of the South that encourages her to live the ideal of community. It is Mattie who holds the place together.*

Yes, she does do that, which is why she is the first to arrive. The South has taught her that. Her personal experience is with her son. Mattie, for me, overcame one of the most painful things a woman can overcome, the loss of child. By coming to Brewster Place she creates a new home and a new family.

I have never been a mother and I was worried about how my story would develop. I always worry when my characters come to an experience that I have never had because I want to do them justice. I know I have the power of language and I know this can be abused, so I worried about whether I could write about a mother. So I talked to several friends, one of them being Amanda, a single parent who has two children. I could tell that the boy was her heart. It's not that she loved one child more than the other, but she had that attraction for her son. I never forgot what she told me: "I think the boy is so special to you because you know that's the one man that could never leave you." This is how Mattie's story got structured. She lost her father, and Butch, her lover, but she could keep this boy. I think there's a line in the story when she realizes that her son is empty and selfish and she says something like "she got what she prayed for, a little boy who would always need her, except that now he was a grown man."

What is extraordinary about Mattie is that, in spite of having all these problems, she's generous and calm-almost magic yet very human. She allows people to feel free in her presence.

Like an earth mother, I guess.

Your characters are dreamers.

Yes, every single one. And **Brewster Place** opens with Langston Hughes's poem "A Dream Deferred." I have always been a daydreamer. I come from a family of dreamers, and I'm from a nation of people who are dreamers, the black nation. I always dreamed that I would be a writer and now I know what it takes to have dreams come true. Now I'm dreaming to be a producer, and I will become one. But I know the work that goes into it. In **Brewster Place,** each of the women has a dream of her own.

However, some of their dreams are unattainable. Etta, for instance, dreams of achieving respectability by marrying the Reverend; Ciel dreams that her husband will change; Kiswana is dreaming about becoming a revolutionary and changing the social situation of the black community.

I guess they all have a dream they never quite realize. The idea was just to see them trying.

Let's talk about Kiswana. She's from a bourgeois family, she's a poet activist, she's a social worker, and she dreams that she will be able to help poor people. However, at the beginning of the book, you associate with Kiswana the image of a bird that is sent to fly to the center of the universe. The bird, of course, cannot fly that high.

That was intentional. And later, I think that there are bird droppings on the fire escape! You know, Kiswana was doing all the bad dreaming that wasn't going to be reality. But she's brought back to base, I think, in a softer way and, ultimately, she begins to work with what she has. And the people show that to her. They tell her that it's not for her to tell them what to do, but that she should work with them.

Kiswana changes her name from Melanie to Kiswana, an African name.

Often in the 1960s people turned away from what they thought was oppression. Our names were associated with a past of slavery and people began looking at Africa for a sense of worth and pride. But actually, in the cotton fields and within the slavery system, many people found strategies that kept them mentally and physically strong. The dignity of the recent past has been restored, and I believe that you take from what is really yours. We are not Africans, we are Americans of African descent. Therefore, we have to root ourselves in this country and find pride in what happened here. There can be some pride in what happened in Africa, but there's so much glorious black history here.

Kiswana had every right to change her name, but Melanie was not a bad name. Considering the type of Melanie she was named after—a women that stood her ground—she should actually be very proud of having such a name. This is what her mother is trying to tell her.

How about her mother's opinions, like telling Kiswana that the best way she can help the people in Brewster Place is by going to school and occupying a position of power?

I think a woman from her background could say little else. I believe, though, that there are two ways of empowering people. You can be in a position where you can influence national policy or you can work at the grassroots level. You can open a social center, or teach people how to register and vote . . . both ways are equally meaningful.

Even though your characters don't always fulfill their dreams, they are able to go on living with dignity. I'm thinking of Etta finding her way through Mattie's friendship, of Kiswana going to night school and helping the people, of Ciel cleansing herself with Mattie's help, of Cora Lee taking children to a summer school. I think that the message that these women are not lost and that they take responsibility over their lives is very important.

Yes, you are indeed able each day to decide how you will live that day. You can decide whether or not your dreams die. You can see these women doing something that I saw women do all my life. The poor women that I grew up with knew it was Monday morning because they had to get up, get the kids bathed, get themselves dressed, and go out to the laundry and work for eight hours. And then they had to pick up a chicken on their way home and stretch it for six people. Then they had to sweep up, get homework done, go to bed that night, get up in the morning, and do it all again. And each day when they would bathe their kids they would be dreaming of the day that the children would go to college and they would not have to work so hard. And there was laughter in all that. They had good times. I saw more people depressed in graduate school than in Harlem! Only the privileged people have the luxury of feeling depressed. My mother did not know such a word. She started using it when we children grew up and spoke of being depressed.

I think this attitude is reflected in your work, in the sense that your characters do not play the role of victims.

You cripple yourself when you think of yourself as a victim. You can be victimized yet still go on with your life. When I walk the streets of Harlem, I think about the people with whom I grew up and about the people who are there now. They are very different. There were more men in the homes then; there were two parents who care for the future of their children. There was more community. I think that what is lacking is hope. Younger and younger women are having children, and those children are having other children and they stay in a vicious circle. They see no way out.

How can the writer help to improve this situation?

To be honest, I think that writing, like all of the arts, is an elite occupation. When **Brewster Place** came out I said to myself, how ironic for the women who I am celebrating and writing about, because the majority of them would not read the book. However, I think that the writer as creator provides people with resources to help with literacy. So the value in writing books lies in telling people, "Learning to read will open your imagination. You will see a way out of no way." The writer can also show the discipline it takes to do something.

In Brewster Place you solve problems through female friendship.

Women only had each other in our history. Around the kitchen table or at the laundromat, they would go to other women with their problems about children, about the men in their lives, about their jobs. And they would share that in places that were unimportant to the outside world, gaining strength from each other in quiet ways. Yes, I was celebrating this in my novel.

Most of the men in Brewster Place are portrayed as immature, and they try to solve their problems through violence against women.

When I decided who was going to be the focus of this work, I had to introduce conflicts into the heroines' lives so they could demonstrate what we have been talking about: How their dreams had been interfered with and how they achieved transcendence in spite of that. Well, with women of this social group, nine times out of ten, the conflict bearers will be male. However, I had hoped the reader would see that there are two sides in most of my male characters; for instance, even though Mattie's father rejects her, he loves her. But for a man like that—an old man, a hard man who is demanding obedience—it is not possible to accept disobedience. To him love equals obedience. So, when he beats Mattie, he's beating out the disobedience. Most of my male characters are three dimensional. Eugene, Ciel's husband, is immature and can't take pressure, but I think he is the only one.

Your chapter on the two lesbian women is impressive and very moving. The fact that the community does not help them hurts the reader. Were they being rejected because the community was not ready to accept the presence of two lesbians?

That was exactly what it was about. They could not reach over that difference. Just like the world had put a wall in Brewster Place, they had put a wall between themselves and Lorraine and Theresa.

So when Lorraine dies, the community's reaction is to have dreams.

I must correct that. People often think that she has died. She doesn't. She just remains insane. At the end she utters the word "please," which she will be repeating for the rest of her life.

Mattie's dream at the end of the book is a dream of bonding between women. Is it a deferred dream?

This is going to depend on the reader. When she wakes up, the party is going to take place, but the clouds are coming and you know it's going to rain. Is this going to be a deferred dream? Well, I decided to let each reader decide. Will they tear down the wall? Or won't they? They are not quite ready yet. It's an open ending.

Let's move to your second novel, **Linden Hills.** *You begin, as you did in Brewster Place, by creating a sense of place; this time, however, the neighborhood is middle class and the novel revolves around a central metaphor associated with Dante's Inferno.*

In **Linden Hills** I wanted to look at what happens to black Americans when they move up in America's society. They first lose family ties, because if you work for a big corporation, you may have grown up in Detroit but may end up living in Houston. Then there are the community ties. You can create a whole different type of community around you—mostly of a mixture of other professional, middle-class people—but you lose the ties with your spiritual or religious values. And ultimately, the strongest and most difficult ties to let go of are your ties with your ethnocentric sense of self. You forget what it means to be an African American. Black Americans with a higher social status, often have to confront issues of racism without the things that have historically supported the working class, like the family, the community, the church, or just their own sense of self.

So that's what *Linden Hills* was about on one level. I thought Dante's *Inferno* was the perfect work for symbolizing when up is down. Dante presents an image of Florentine society and then slowly moves from the lesser sins to the greater sins. So that's what I did in *Linden Hills*. When you move down the hill, you encounter a greater alienation, the repercussions of upward mobility.

Let's move now to your latest book **Mama Day.** *Again, from the beginning there's a sense of place very carefully described.*

Yes, I think this is going to be my *modus operandi* until I die!

Willow Springs is nonurban island, away from civilization. In **Mama Day** *you fuse the world of the supernatural and the realistic world of New York City. What inspired you to write it?*

It goes back to the stories I listened to when I sat in the corner of the kitchen, and to the different ideas that my parents had regarding the old women who not only worked as quasitraditional doctors, but who used roots and herbs and had supernatural kinds of powers. My mother believed that there were things that happened in life that you could not question but my father was very reluctant to accept "superstition." The structure of *Mama Day* emerged from this dual interpretation. I wanted as well to look at women in history, especially at women connected to the earth who could affect behavior. Until the Middle Ages, when the so-called "witches" were persecuted, women were the primary healers who knew how to abort or how to stop conception. They showed women how to have control of their process of creation. So these wise women were chastised and burnt for stepping over those bounds.

A writer, I think, begins to exorcise demons with her work when she writes about what she fears as well as about what she dreams. I had to get rid of some demons with *Brewster Place.* I had first to confront what it meant to be to be a black woman and to celebrate it. In *Linden Hills* I had to come to terms with what it meant to change class, which is actually what I did and what my parents had been working so hard for. But when a child from a poor class enters another class, there is tension. When I got to *Mama Day,* I wanted to rest and write about what I believed. And I believe in the power of love and the power of magic—sometimes I think that they are one and the same. *Mama* is about the fact that the real basic magic is the unfolding of the human potential and if we reach inside ourselves we can create miracles.

Beautiful. You're working on another book, [**Bailey's Cafe**]. *What is it about and where do you locate it?*

[*Bailey's Cafe*] is going to deal with the various ways women respond to sex. It exists within the jazz and blues milieu of the 1940s, among the Duke Ellingtons, the Ella Fitzgeralds. Bally has a juke box in his cafe. As you walk down 125th Street towards the Hudson River you head west, and if you don't happen to pick up a few spare notes coming out that juke box, you would simply walk into the river. So you pick up those notes and you enter Bally's Cafe. My characters are the music and each has some sort of song.

In what direction is black American literature moving?

I think it's moving towards reflecting a middle-class experience. The people that are now writing don't share my experience or that of Alice Walker or Toni Morrison. They may be second or third-generation urban blacks and they speak about other aspects of life. Surreal novels and novels of the absurd are coming out that deal with how to confront America, and what it means to be young, black, professional women.

When you write, do you address your writing primarily to black people?

I address it to myself. I talk to myself and to my characters—and I let speak to me. I feel that they have chosen me, for whatever reason, to convey their stories to the world. I try really hard to listen internally. I often do things with my own life to make myself a more fitting vessel to communicate their stories. I always worry if I am saying the right thing, because I have the words and they have the story, which I am recording. The best writing comes out when you just are quiet and you let happen what must happen.

RICHARD EDER

SOURCE: Richard Eder, "Grounds for the City," in *Los Angeles Times Book Review*, August 30, 1992, pp. 3, 7.

[*Eder reviews Naylor's novel* Bailey's Cafe *and focuses on the characters developed therein.*]

Call him Bailey though that, he says, is not his name. But it is the name of his mission, in both senses of the word. Bailey's Cafe is located in a broken-down premises that bore the name when he took it over at the end of the Second World War. "Located" is a manner of speaking; the entrance is on a ghetto street in any or all of our cities; the back looks out on a timeless cosmic void.

Gloria Naylor's new novel [*Bailey's Cafe*] is devotional at heart, though it is told in contrasting shades of harsh, comic and magic realism. Its stories of ravaged urban blacks, most of them women, are savage and sardonic, but they float in a mystical lyricism. They are the stories of the regulars who frequent Bailey's, and they are told by the proprietor, doorkeeper and gritty good shepherd who both runs it and expounds it, along with his laconically nurturing wife, Nadine. It stands "on the margin between the edge of the world and infinite possibility," he tells us.

Naylor writes consummately well of the real world's edge. Her infinite possibility is shakier. It is cloudy or downright sentimental at times, though it can also be moving. Magic is a tricky proposition; when it doesn't transport you, it strands you. The seedy watering-place as a place of dreams—Saroyan's saloon in "The Time of Your Life," the End of the Line Cafe in "The Iceman Cometh," Lanford Wilson's Hot L Baltimore and Bailey's place need a vigilant bouncer to keep bathos out. Bailey, like some of his predecessors, can grow distracted.

At the start, when he is telling of his own life, Bailey's voice crackles with passion and wit. He grows up in a mix of comfort and humiliation as the son of the butler and cook in a rich black household. Baseball is his passion—he speaks with infectious pride of the history of the Negro Leagues—and so are women.

His courtship of Nadine is a gem. He meets her at a game; he is so uncharacteristically silenced by her beauty that he jams an ice-cream cone down her dress. Somehow it works, though; she lets him take her out, though his ebullience is flattened by her steadfast refusal to smile. She is enjoying herself, she says, but why—"I'm more than my body"—should she have to smile? And we get Bailey's hapless reasonableness as the baffled male:

"Go to Upper Borneo and smile, they'll say He's happy. Go there and slit your throat, they'll say He's dead," he expostulates, and subsides into complaint: "While most of what happens in life is below the surface, other people come up for air and translate their feelings for the general population now and then. Nadine doesn't bother."

Bailey fights in the stinking hell of World War II's Pacific campaign. It will take away his bounce, it will make him old. What makes him infinitely old is Hiroshima. He had prayed for his ordeal to end; the prayer was "answered by the only God who would hear, a God of punishment and reprisal, a salvation that is a curse."

The horrors of our time—at war, and for blacks in the cities—defy practical remedy. And so, Bailey and Nadine—her silence takes on a magical aspect—move into the partly grounded, partly floating Cafe. It is a place of kindness but it is more than a refuge. It is a place for stories and for healing—not healing as a cure but as a power to endure—by primal power. Much of this power, which suggests female shamanic traditions from Africa and the Caribbean, is lodged in Eve. She runs a boarding house—as real and supernatural as the Cafe—that is a brothel too, and a convent. Many of the brutalized women, whose story Bailey tells, live there. Their "gentleman callers" cannot buy them. They must, however, buy flowers from Eve to present to them; and each woman has her own totemic flower.

The Eve figure, her flowers and ancient female mysteries, impart a certain forced wonder, an over-dosed and over-sweet exhortation; though Naylor gives her fierceness and resourcefulness as well. Some of the women's stories, such as that of the Ethiopian child, Mariam, who gives birth at the Cafe although she is a virgin; and disappears in a wall of water that her parched longings have summoned up, show similar indulgence.

In others, the sheer strength and color of the story more than make up for a spot of undigested uplift here and there. "Josie" tells of a righteous woman who is both undone and transfigured by abuse. As a child, she kept an immaculate house for her dissolute, whoring mother, as if scrubbing could redeem them both. She marries an older man, kind but beaten down by injustice, and defiantly tries to keep flowers and order in their sooty shack by the railroad track. When he dies, she loses the house, takes to living in the street, and sells herself to other vagrants; but only for the 20 or 25 cents she needs to survive.

When she sits in the cafe, her dream of a just and gracious life shines so strongly that she imparts grace to her shaking coffee mug. And when a kind and comic iceman recognizes her light and wants to marry her, she imagines making a perfect home with him. And in an impressive twist, Naylor suddenly suggests imagination as a kingdom more powerful than reality.

In counterpoint is the wonderfully sardonic story of Miss Maple. He is a man, in fact; a formidably powerful and intelligent black man. His forebears were visionary and wealthy pioneers in the Imperial Valley; he himself got a first rate education and developed a powerful talent for marketing.

Yet he spends years sending brilliant resumes and project proposals, being enthusiastically invited for job interviews, and seeing ardor extinguished like a candle when he shows up. Statistics were one of his specialties; eventually he calculates that his chances would be no worse if he wore dresses to his interviews. After all, for job rounds in the summer, they are much cooler than the regulation business suit.

The ending is upbeat, perhaps too glibly so; but the parable is brilliantly conceived and fleshed out. It is an unforgettable succesor to Ellison's metaphor of the invisible man, and as incandescent.

SOURCES FOR FURTHER STUDY

Brown, Rosellen. Review of *Mama Day*, by Gloria Naylor. *Ms.* XVI, No. 8 (February 1988): 74.

> Reviews *Mama Day*, finding that the novel is about "the healing power of women."

Denison, David C. "Interview with Gloria Naylor." *The Writer* 107 (21 December 1994): 21.

> Discusses Naylor's writing style and how she identifies with her characters as she writes.

Eko, Ebele. "Beyond the Myth of Confrontation: A Comparative Study of African and African-American Female Protagonists." *Ariel* 17, No. 4 (October 1986): 139-52.

> Compares Kiswana Browne of *The Women of Brewster Place* with Anowa of Ama Ata Aidoo's *Anowa*, Margaret Cadmore of Bessie Head's *Maru*, and Selina Boyce of Paule Marshall's *Brown Girl, Brownstones*. The critic traces the "many bonds and parallels" between all four characters.

Puhr, Kathleen M. "Healers in Gloria Naylor's Fiction." *Twentieth Century Literature* 40 (Winter 1994): 518-27.

> Discusses how black love, manifesting itself in caring for others, is presented in Naylor's novels.

Ward, Catherine C. "Gloria Naylor's *Linden Hills*: A Modern Inferno." *Contemporary Literature* 28, No. 1 (Spring 1987): 67-81.

> Overview of *Linden Hills*, likening the novel to "a modern version of Dante's *Inferno*."

Wood, Rebecca S. "'Two Warring Ideals in One Body': Universalism and Nationalism in Gloria Naylor's *Bailey's Cafe*." *African American Review* 30 (Fall 1996): 381-95.

> Presents overview of *Bailey's Cafe* in terms of other Western and African-American literary texts that Naylor often alludes to in her writing.

Sean O'Casey

1880-1964

(Born John Casey; also wrote under pseudonym Sean O'Cathasaigh) Irish dramatist, autobiographer, poet, short story writer, and critic.

INTRODUCTION

Considered by many critics as one of the most original and accomplished dramatists of the twentieth century, O'Casey is noted for formally innovative and aggressively iconoclastic plays in which he condemns war, satirizes the follies of the Irish people, and celebrates the perseverance of the working class. In addition, O'Casey is esteemed for his impassioned, combative criticism and an acclaimed series of autobiographies. O'Casey was a highly controversial figure, who openly expressed his Irish nationalist sympathies and advocated communism throughout his life.

Biographical Information

O'Casey was born John Casey to working-class Protestant parents in predominantly Catholic Dublin. His father died when he was only six years old, which exacerbated the family's already precarious financial position. Due to his family's economic standing, O'Casey, who suffered from a disease which seriously affected his eyes throughout his life, consequently received little formal education. In spite of these disadvantages, O'Casey read Shakespeare and the English classics extensively during his teens, simultaneously supporting himself with a series of clerical and manual labor jobs. Sometime around 1906, he left the Protestant church, became an agnostic, and began to cultivate ardent nationalist feelings. O'Casey joined The Gaelic League, which inspired him to learn the Gaelic language and its literature, and later joined the Irish Brotherhood, the radical organization responsible for planning the 1916 Easter Rebellion. After publishing several collections of lyrical ballads and poems under the Gaelic pseudonym Sean O'Cathasaigh in 1918, he turned to playwriting. Dismissing O'Casey's early submissions, the Abbey Theatre of Dublin eventually accepted *The Shadow of a Gunman,* staging it in 1923. Despite the success of *The Shadow of a Gunman, Juno and the Paycock* (1924), and *The Plough and the Stars* (1926), the Abbey's directors, including famed Irish poet W. B. Yeats, rejected *The Silver Tassie* (1929), which is noted for its deeply nihilistic depiction of war and disconcerting use of expressionistic technique. In subsequent plays O'Casey abandoned the conventions of dramatic realism and adopted a highly rhetorical and formalistic style that affirmed his poetic and ideological sensibilities. During the 1930s O'Casey published only one play, concentrating instead on his autobiography. Ostracized by most theater critics as much for his political affiliations as for his highly formalized style of playwriting, O'Casey had relatively few plays staged during the remainder of his career. In spite of a revived interest in O'Casey's work beginning in the 1960s, he remained aloof from the public and declined several honorary doctorates. He died in 1964.

Major Works

The Shadow of a Gunman, O'Casey's first staged play, is a lyrical tragicomedy about the political violence in Dublin's tenements told from the perspective of its working-class victims. Transcending propaganda, the play articulates one of O'Casey's central themes: the impersonal brutality and absurdity of war. His next two plays, *Juno and the Paycock* and *The Plough and the Stars,* focus on the civil war in Ireland—the former from the perspective of a troubled family whose dissension and strife mirror the national situation and the latter from the standpoint of an entire tenement house. Both plays dramatize the horrors of slum life in relation to the destruction of war, but they also suggest that life in the tenements is redeemed by the humanity of its women. Though similar in theme to his earlier plays, *The Silver Tassie,* which examines the impact of World War I on Irish and British soldiers, represents a significant departure from his previous style, particularly the second act, which features an expressionistic blend of colloquial speech, plainsong chants, and an apocalyptic setting representing the front lines in Flanders. O'Casey's penchant for expressionistic devices and stylized dialogue is even more evident in subsequent plays, including *Within the Gates* (1934), which dramatizes diverse interactions among people filtering through a crowded urban park, and *Cock-a-Doodle Dandy* (1949), which satirizes rural Irish customs and folklore. O'Casey's multi-volume autobiography begins with *I Knock at the Door* (1939) and concludes with *Sunset and Evening Star* (1954).

Critical Reception

While critical praise is fairly unanimous for O'Casey's first three major plays, which are naturalistic in style and presentation, some critics have condemned the works following *The Silver Tassie* as overly didactic, ideological propaganda pieces rather than exemplars of expressionist theater. Richard Gilman, for example, suggests that O'Casey's work cannot bear the weight of his reputation as a major dramatist: "There are too many bad and even deeply embarrassing plays in his *oeuvre* . . . and too many esthetic sins of naiveté, rhetorical excess, sentimentality and tendentiousness in all but his very best work." At the opposite extreme, O'Casey's most sympathetic advocates assert that his achievements in playwriting and autobiography have been insufficiently recognized, and that mainstream commentators have failed to appreciate the poetic richness of O'Casey's language and his virtuosic handling of expressionist technique. Carol Kleiman has viewed O'Casey as a visionary who pioneered some of the major trends in contemporary theater: "[The] 'humanly absurd' aspect of O'Casey's theatre, embodied in . . . all those elements which O'Casey uses to create his own kind of stage poetry . . . allows us to view his plays as an unacknowledged seedbed from which grew many of the dramatic motifs and techniques of the Theatre of the Absurd."

(For further information, see *Concise Dictionary of British Literary Biography:* 1914-1945; *Contemporary Authors,* Vols. 89-92; *Contemporary Literary Criticism,* Vols. 1, 5, 9, 11, 15, 88; *Dictionary of Literary Biography,* Vol. 10; *DISCovering Authors: British; DISCovering Authors: Canadian; DISCovering Authors Modules: Dramatists Module, Most-studied Authors Module; Major Twentieth-Century Writers.*)

CRITICAL COMMENTARY

THE NEW YORK TIMES BOOK REVIEW

SOURCE: A review of *Two Plays: Juno and the Paycock [and] The Shadow of a Gunman,* in *The New York Times Book Review,* March 8, 1925, p. 5.

[*In the following review of* Juno and the Paycock *and* The Shadow of a Gunman, *the critic hails O'Casey as an impressive talent whose early work "deserves serious consideration."*]

The chaotic Dublin of 1920 and 1922 furnishes Sean O'Casey the material for his two vivid dramas, ***Juno and the Paycock*** and ***The Shadow of a Gunman,*** in

Principal Works

Lament for Thomas Ashe [as Sean O'Cathasaigh] (prose) 1917
The Story of Thomas Ashe [as Sean O'Cathasaigh] (prose) 1917
Songs of the Wren No. 1 [as Sean O'Cathasaigh] (verse) 1918
Songs of the Wren No. 2 [as Sean O'Cathasaigh] (verse) 1918
More Wren Songs [as Sean O'Cathasaigh] (verse) 1918
The Story of the Irish Citizen Army [as Sean O'Cathasaigh] (essay) 1919
*The Shadow of a Gunman (drama) 1923
*Juno and the Paycock (drama) 1924
The Plough and the Stars (drama) 1926
The Silver Tassie (drama) 1929
Windfalls: Stories, Poems, and Plays (short stories, poetry, and drama) 1934
Within the Gates (drama) 1934
The Flying Wasp (criticism) 1937
I Knock at the Door: Swift Glances Back at Things That Made Me (autobiography) 1939
The Star Turns Red (drama) 1940
Pictures in the Hallway (autobiography) 1942
Purple Dust (drama) 1943
Red Roses for Me (drama) 1943
Drums Under the Windows (autobiography) 1945
Oak Leaves and Lavender; or A World on Wallpaper (drama) 1946
Cock-a-Doodle Dandy (drama) 1949
Inishfallen, Fare Thee Well (autobiography) 1949
Collected Plays. 4 vols. (drama) 1949-1952
Rose and Crown (autobiography) 1952
Sunset and Evening Star (autobiography) 1954
The Bishop's Bonfire: A Sad Play within the Tune of a Polka (drama) 1955
The Green Crow (criticism) 1956
Mirror in My House: The Autobiographies of Sean O'Casey. 2 vols. (autobiography) 1956
The Drums of Father Ned (drama) 1960
Behind the Green Curtains (drama) 1962
Feathers from the Green Crow [edited by Robert Hogan] (criticism) 1962
Figuro in the Night (drama) 1962
The Moon Shines on Kylenamoe (drama) 1962
Under a Colored Cap: Articles Merry and Mournful With Comments and a Song (criticism) 1963
The Letters of Sean O'Casey. 4 vols. [edited by David Krause] (letters) 1975–1992
The Complete Plays of Sean O'Casey (drama) 1984

*These works were collectively published as *Two Plays*.

Adaptations

Adaptations of O'Casey's works include the plays *Pictures in the Hallway*, 1956, *I Knock at the Door*, 1958, and *Drums under the Windows*, 1960, all by Paul Shyre.

Two Plays. These efforts, ruthless enough in their depiction of a reality that was a matter of blood and murder, move with surprising speed and comprehension of dramatic value, and yet, at the same time, they are lighted by a broad humor that is laughable enough on the surface but which, taken with the subject involved, reveals sardonic undercurrents. Mr. O'Casey is frankly melodramatic when its suits his purpose to be so, and his humor is often enough a stage matter, "fat stuff," as an actor would say, and calculated to arouse the laughter of a popular audience. And yet the reader will never lose the impression of a depth in these plays that is not always visible on the surface. There are tragic connotations that lose themselves in a befuddled sense of the obligations toward life that are part of a man's heritage.

Mr. O'Casey is no philosopher; he is a somewhat stark expositor, who is building plays that are meant to act well and which, from a reading, seem to fulfill all the requirements of suspense, thrill, humor and vivid characterization. But he is also an artist and it is within his province as a playwright to find form and sincerity in his material. Gifted with the power of creating a rich and colorful dialogue that is artful in its dramatic possibilities, he sets to work to show through two groups of people in two of the poorer tenements the chaotic whirlpool of that Dublin that passed through the guerrilla warfare of the Irregulars and the Black and Tans. The result is both thrilling and depressing. There are gunfire, ambushes, raids, seductions, cowardice, poverty, drunkenness, all the concomitants that follow hard on any liberating movement that depends on force. Through all this is threaded a spiritual revelation that is both pathetic and disturbing. It wounds the heart of man to think that life is so constituted, and yet it so smacks of the verisimilitude of life that the reader automatically accepts it as it is revealed.

Juno and the Paycock is the better of these two plays, for here Mr. O'Casey develops an essentially serious action in an almost constant comedy medium. Curiously enough, the reader will realize no disparity between the medium and the subject. This play presents as its central character a drunken loafer and braggart with an engaging tongue, who watches regardlessly as his little world, poverty-stricken enough in the first place, falls to pieces about him. "Captain" Jack Boyle is a character rich in acting possibilities, and as the reader follows him through his imbroglio, noting how the wastrel counts on the legacy that never comes to recoup his fallen fortunes, and leaves him careless and drunken in his wretched house, from which his wife has hurried to look upon the face of her dead son killed by the Irregulars for alleged treachery a violent desire must spring up to see some clever actor in this role. It is crammed with possibilities. The spiritual flavor of the play may be acrid but it rings true. Boyle is the engaging loafer altogether too fond of his poteen, singing his Irish patriotic songs with a high air, and letting his world fall into ruins about him. His daughter is seduced and deserted by a young Englishman. The very furniture is removed from the house for debt. Misfortune piles upon misfortune, and still Boyle exists in his boastful imaginative world of big words and no deeds. All this is deplorable enough, but the reader does not pity Boyle so much as the women as Boyle's wife Juno and his daughter Mary. It is upon their puny shoulders that the eventual degradations come.

In *The Shadow of a Gunman,* the second play in this impressive book, it is again the women who suffer. Donal Davoren is the typical poet, who is paralysed in the face of action. This hardly seems to ring true of those fierce Dublin days, for it was the poets, the writers, the thinkers, who crumpled up first of all before the withering gunfire. But for the sake of Mr. O'Casey's theme he is quite justified in making his leading male character a writer who constantly quotes Shelley. The pretty city girl is charmed by the poet who takes the suitcase of bombs to her room when the Black and Tans raid the tenement and is shot down when she tries to escape from the lorry. Davoren is under suspicion of being a gunman because he lives so quietly, and there is a subtle mockery in this characterization of a man who is incapable of action, who can hear an innocent girl being hurried from the house and to her death, and who yet receives the plaudits and admiration of the Republican-minded folk about him. Fate places him in this milieu and he is lacking in the strength of will to surmount the situation that leaves him a confessed coward. *The Shadow of a Gunman* is a more subdued play than *Juno and the Paycock,* in that it hardly depends upon comedy elements to carry it forward. But there is reason for this, because the characterization is of a different order. The theme does not permit such personages as the Jack Boyle, Joxer Daly and Mrs. Madigan of the first drama. Juno Boyle in *Juno and the Paycock* cries out, "Ah, what can God do agen the stupidity o' men!" and both of these plays seem to be more or less directly based upon this text.

It is through the stupidity, the fear, the avarice, the drunkenness of men, that all the woes of the women in these two plays come into being. Mr. O'Casey is an impressive realist here.

The playwright's name will be new to readers of Irish plays, but his two dramas should prove sufficient to show that that dramatic urge that began so many years ago with Yeats, Martyn, Colum and Synge has not died. It may have flickered down during the past decade, but the dramatic instincts of the Irish writers continue to exist, and every now and then something impressive like the work of Mr. O'Casey happens and those who know breathe a sigh of relief. It would be a rather foolish procedure to attempt any comparison of Mr. O'Casey with the older Irish dramatists on the strength of these two plays, for, fine as they are, they are no more than a beginning. If he is to be another Synge he will have to do better than this. He will have to reach the authentic plane of tragedy or of high comedy, and in neither *Juno and the Paycock* nor *The Shadow of a Gunman* has he reached those proud eminences as yet. But what he has done deserves serious consideration, for his plays are among the first things to come out of that new Ireland that was baptized with machine gunfire only a few years ago.

JACQUELINE DOYLE

SOURCE: Jacqueline Doyle, "Liturgical Imagery in Sean O'Casey's 'The Silver Tassie'," in *Modern Drama,* Vol. XXI, No. 1, March, 1978, pp. 29-38.

[*In the following excerpt, Doyle analyzes how* The Silver Tassie *relies on religious symbolism for its power and meaning.*]

The Silver Tassie represents a radical departure from Sean O'Casey's early work, and its most significant aspects have been almost consistently misunderstood by his critics. The play is a conscious blend of naturalism and symbolic expressionism, and as such is unified through language, imagery, and theme, rather than through character. O'Casey himself wrote to W. B. Yeats, in their famous controversy over the play [documented in O'Casey's *Blasts and Benedictions*]: "I'm afraid I can't make my mind mix with the sense of importance you give to 'a dominating character.' God forgive me, but it does sound as if you peeked and pined for a hero in the play. Now, is a dominating character more important than a play, or is a play more important than a dominating character?" Characterization in *The Silver Tassie* is clearly subordinate to the play's ritualistic structure and to its complex symbolic framework. Symbol and imagery throughout the four acts revolve around the trinity of war, religion, and sexuality—"the decorations of security." This imagery is placed within the dual context of a strong antiwar theme and the Sacrifice of the Mass. The thematic and structural function of the imagery is well expressed by the Croucher's lines in Act II: "Then the decorations of security/Become the symbols of self sacrifice...."

The ritual structure is manifested first and most obviously in the religious chanting. Despite the observations of the critics, the chant is not confined to the second, expressionistic act, but operates as a unifying element throughout the play, appearing in both naturalistic and expressionistic passages.... The intertwining of war, religion, and sexuality in the imagery of [the first] act is subtly manipulated. Susie chants Biblical platitudes as she polishes Harry's rifle, an activity that is prolonged almost to the end of the scene, and is unavoidably phallic. It is revealed that the roots of her religious belief lie in sexual frustration.... It becomes clear as the act progresses that hers is the chanting of the "faithful" and not of the "Faith." ... The tragedy of the "faithful" is in Susie's line at the conclusion of the scene, "the men that go with the guns are going with God...."

If Act I is the chant of the "faithful," Act II is the chant of the "Faith." The curtain rises on a starkly expressionistic set dominated by a broken crucifix. The beginnings of the Mass are heard faintly from the ruins of the monastery, while the Croucher, a ragged and blood-stained soldier, intones ironic reversals of the Book of Ezekiel over the traditional Latin chants. In Ezekiel God's question in the valley of bones was, "Son of man, can these bones live?" ... The Croucher's premonition is far darker: "And I looked and saw a great multitude that stood upon their feet, an exceeding great army. / And he said unto me, Son of man, can this exceeding great army become a valley of dry bones?" ... The Croucher concludes with a horrifying image of the ravages of war: "And I prophesied, and the breath came out of them, and behold a shaking, and their bones fell asunder, bone from his bone, and they died, and the exceeding great army became a valley of dry bones." The contrast is between God's vision of resurrection and man's vision of sacrifice; this is painfully in keeping with the thematic impulse of the play. The soldiers, the sacrificial victims, respond to the Mass rather than to the Croucher's ominous forebodings....

Act II could be interpreted as corresponding to the Offertory of the Mass—offering the soldiers as the sacrificial victims of the "faithful. The entire play participates loosely in the structure of the Mass. Ironically, it is a death Mass rather than a life Mass, and the Consecration results in desecration rather than in Resurrection. Both the play and the Mass are divided into four parts.... The first act of the play is the "Mass of the Catechumens," the portion of the Mass open to the uninitiated—O'Casey's "faithful." In ancient Christian ritual, the remainder of the Mass was for those initiated into the mysteries of the "Faith"; in the second act the stage is cleared of all but the soldiers. After the second act, the Offertory, the third act traces the Consecration. The reluctant bathing of Simon and Sylvester represents a sort of mock-purification, and certainly the breaking of the Host (Christ's Body) is tragically present in Harry Heegan's crippled body.... Surgeon Maxwell's "While there's life there's hope (*with a grin and a wink at Susie*)" ... is an ironic mockery of the "Faith" and hope of Act II and of Harry's timid hope for resurrection. In some senses it prepares the audience for the failed Communion of Act IV.

The soldier as Christ figure is implicit in O'Casey's manipulation of the Mass structure....

The soldier as Christ figure functions as both martyr and priest. *The Baltimore Catechism* describes the Christ-martyr-priest relation most simply: "In every Mass, *through the priest* at the altar, Jesus again offers himself as a sacrifice to God in an unbloody (not bloody) way, under the appearance of bread and wine." Most specifically, this Christ-priest figure is Harry Heegan. The play opens with a mythic chronicling of his strength by Simon and Sylvester ("Simon" and "Sylvester" perhaps functioning in their religious roles as disciple and saint; clearly the two act as commentators on the life of "Christ"). Harry briefly appears, associated with the Silver Tassie as chalice....

There exist overtones of the Last Supper throughout the conclusion of Act I, most explicitly in Harry's lines, "Jesus, a last drink, then!" ... The four acts (which I have identified as Public Mass, Offertory, Consecration, Eucharist) could also be seen as the last four days of Christ's life. Thus Act I includes the Last Supper and Holy Thursday (Gethsemane and the vision of the chalice); Act II is Holy Friday and the Crucifixion (and certainly the crucifix plays a prominent part in the act); Act III is Holy Saturday (with the body interred in the hospital rather than the tomb); and Act IV is Easter Sunday. Both Acts III and IV contain denials of miracle; the women came to Christ's tomb but Jessie refuses, and, of course, the Resurrection in Act IV is a failed one.

These overpowering religious overtones pervade the secular imagery, particularly the two major strands of imagery—color and dance. The images relate to the two martyrs: Teddy Foran, who is blinded, and Harry Heegan, whose legs are paralyzed. Color and dance are literal and symbolic losses which are not restored.

The colors red, green, white, and black recur constantly throughout the play, but critics seem to have done little or no work in interpreting them.... The color symbolism becomes even more striking when interpreted in the context of Catholic liturgical symbolism. *The Catholic Encyclopedia* reports:

> The variety of liturgical colours in the Church arose from the mystical meaning attached to them. Thus white, the symbol of light, typifies innocence and purity, joy and glory; red, the language of fire and blood, indicates burning charity and the martyrs' generous sacrifice; green, the hue of plants and trees, bespeaks the hope of life eternal; violet, the gloomy cast of the mortified, denotes affliction and melancholy; while black, the universal emblem of mourning, signifies the sorrow of death and the sombreness of the tomb.

The symbolism is most obvious in the sets, which appear to be restricted to these colors alone. In the set of Act I, the prominent colors are the purple velvet shield, the bedspread striped with black and vivid green, the picture of Harry in his red and yellow football uniform. In Act II he describes explicitly the red glare, the green star, the white star, and the expressionistic stained glass window with its green background and white-faced Virgin in black robes. Act III in the hospital contains the colors of martyrdom, of purity, and of death—the red quilt, the white quilt, the black quilt, white walls, green lampshade. The dance-hall of Act IV is hung with red and black striped curtains, green curtains, red and black ribbon, and its most startling image is that of the lanterns: "*the lanterns are black, with a broad red stripe running down the centre of the largest and across those hanging at each side, so that, when they are lighted, they suggest an illuminated black cross with an inner one of gleaming red.*" ... Harry is consistently associated with the papal colors, red and yellow (red for martyrdom and sacrifice), supporting his Christ-priest function. Colors are expressive of life throughout the play and become a poignant symbol of life lost (most literally for the martyr Teddy Foran)....

While the dance is not as integral a symbol as color, it is clearly a life symbol and central to the imagery of the last act.... The dance becomes part of the religious ritual of the Eucharist, the self-sacrifice of war, and sexual ritual. For the impotent and crippled Harry is deprived both of partner and dance. Sergeant Maxwell replaces Harry of the first act as the symbol of virility. The resumption of the dance by Susie and Sergeant Maxwell symbolizes life in both its indifference and survival....

Color and dance fuse in the major symbol of the play—the Silver Tassie. The tassie is a secular and a religious life symbol which is subject to a Joycean symbolist desecration at the end of the play. (Joyce, however, in taking the symbols of God, pits symbolist art against religion in *Portrait of the Artist,* whereas O'Casey pits art and the symbols of religion against war and the "faithful" in *The Silver Tassie.*) Reference to the first scene and Jessie's raising of the tassie as a chalice is helpful. Harry articulates the (trinity of) meaning in the tassie with an ironic pun on the trinity and the "One": "Won, won, won, be-God; by the odd goal in five. Lift it up, lift it up, Jessie, sign of youth, sign of strength, sign of victory." ... The values of the tassie are those of war and sexuality. The scene ends with a song, possibly a hymn, to the tassie. The cup reappears in Act IV, again associated with the trinity: "The Silver Tassie—that I won three times, three times for them.... " ... Miracle for the "faithful" is denied; Christ is not resurrected, and Barney hysterically calls Harry a "half baked Lazarus." In one of the most important passages of the play, Harry stages a mock-Eucharist.... The sacrilege demonstrates the tragedy of man's self-sacrifice—"The Lord hath given and man hath taken away!"

The importance of the tassie is best and most conclusively understood through the parallel structures of Acts I and IV. The hope, the faith, and the desecration implicit within the theme are a part of both acts. In Act I marriage (sexuality) is desecrated by war, and in Act IV religion (the chalice) is desecrated by war. In the first act, Teddy Foran, the later blinded martyr, throws down and breaks his wife's treasured wedding-bowl, as Harry, the Christ-martyr figure, later flings the treasured tassie to the floor.... [Aesthetic] affirmation and hope lies at the core of the play, despite the blasphemy of the "faithful." In the last act, Harry raises the cup three times and then smashes it, committing the final sacrilege. Susie's reply this time is intentionally blasphemous: "We can't give sight to the blind or make the lame walk. We would if we could. It is the misfortune of war." ... Her complacent reversal of the Bible tragically emphasizes Harry's insight: "The Lord hath given and man hath taken away!" For the despairing yet hopeful conclusion of the play is not that God does not exist, but that man through sacrilege, through *self*-sacrifice, through war, has driven God away....

COLBERT KEARNEY

SOURCE: Colbert Kearney, "Sean O'Casey and the Glamour of Grammar," in *Anglo-Irish and Irish Litera-*

ture *Aspects of Language and Culture, Vol. II*, edited by Birgit Bramsback and Martin Croghan, Almqvist & Wiksell International, 1988, pp. 63-70.

[*In the following essay, originally submitted at a major literary conference in 1986, Kearney describes how the "glamour" of language is used—both literally and metaphorically—to seduce and betray the uneducated slum-dwellers in O'Casey's Dublin Trilogy.*]

O'Casey's early trilogy—*The Shadow of a Gunman, Juno and the Paycock* and *The Plough and the Stars*—is set in Irish history and specifically in O'Casey's personal perspective on the recent political revolution—the 1916 Rising, the guerilla warfare for Independence (1919-1921) and the Civil War (1922-1923). The central theme is *delusion*. As a socialist, O'Casey believed that the common people and their trade union leaders had been duped by bourgeois nationalists who had little knowledge of or interest in the lot of the working-class. Each play is associated with a particular phase of the revolution and the political stress is on a Dublin working-class community as the victim rather than the beneficiary of the struggle. Each of the plays examines the ways in which a group of characters is deluded into taking part in an action which results in death and desolation.

In this brief submission, which can only be a crude summary of a broader and more detailed analysis of the trilogy, I want to focus on one of the dramatic means through which the plays present the process of delusion.

The working-class Dublin into which Sean O'Casey was born was a secondary oral culture in the sense that although literacy was well established it had not yet eradicated the oral tradition of the community. The working-class poor attributed an extraordinary value and prestige to 'high' literacy, associating its manifestations—'educated' speech and 'proper' behaviour—with the power of those who ruled over the working-class as naturally as gods or magicians controlled the fate of humans. (Much as we, perhaps, attribute almost infinite power and prestige to those who have mastered the new literacy, that of the computer.)

Almost all the characters in *The Shadow of a Gunman* (1923) are defined by their attitude to language and, more specifically, to the central character, Davoren, whom they believe to be a gunman. It is interesting that this popular fantasy identifies Davoren rather than Shields—never mind Maguire—as the gunman: after all, Shields once held violent views and was the companion of the substantial gunman in the play. What made Davoren the popular choice? Within the economy of the play, the answer must lie in Davoren's projection of himself as a poet, as one who could not only read but who could create the texts that others would read.

The play is set in a community which is in the process of change from an oral to a literate culture and which is in awe of the powers of 'high' literacy. Tommy Owens is the least advanced in this context. He is, for the most part, a repository of traditional lore. His character is a fabric of cliche, formula, historical reference (frequently mistaken) and verse—and yet even this degenerate child of an oral culture is ludicrously well prepared for the arrival of literacy. As Mr Gallogher produces his letter, "Tommy *takes out a well-worn notebook and a pencil stump, and assumes a very important attitude.*" Tommy is only one of the many characters who are fascinated by literacy. Minnie's view of the world has been formed by romantic fiction. Mr Gallogher seeks to make himself important by imitating—as best he can—the superior language of the legal profession. Mr Grigson does the same thing by drawing on his study of the Bible and, perhaps, of even more hard-boiled fiction. Mrs Henderson is a version of Mrs Malaprop—but so are all those characters who fail to master a language which is 'higher' than that which they have inherited. (One must remember that, as regards the reaction of an audience, only in a social context where *Prometheus Unbound* is considered more prestigious than *God Save Ireland* is Davoren considered less ludicrous than Tommy Owens.)

In *The Shadow of a Gunman* a society in awe of the powers of 'high' literacy pays a would-be poet the peculiar compliment of believing him to be a gunman; the poet amuses himself by allowing the cult to continue and the result is death. There is no avoiding the connection between literacy and death: the final emblem is the bloody piece of paper on which the name of the writer has been blotted out by Minnie's blood. The agent of delusion in this play is a poet whose reputed mastery of the 'highest' linguistic form (and, probably, of the new technology of typewriting) earns him a super-human status in a community where the only equivalent power is that of the gunman. Both the poet and the gunman offer a new and better life but in *The Shadow of a Gunman* they bring only death.

Juno and the Paycock is set in a similar community during the Civil War but political element is for the most part a backdrop for the domestic action which concerns the social fortunes of the Boyle family and especially their relations with Mr Charles Bentham. Again the central theme is delusion and again the theme is most vividly realised in the fate of a young woman. Mary Boyle is typical of a community caught between orality and literacy, where the elders are strikingly oral and the young are obsessed with the power of education in literacy.

> The opposing forces are apparent in her speech and her manners, both of which are degraded by her environment and improved by her acquaintance – slight though it be – with literature.

'Literature' has involved Mary in trade union politics and won her the attention of the upwardly mobile and linguistically erratic Jerry Devine. 'Literature' – in the form of the will – has also won Mary the attention of Mr Charles Bentham, the *outsider* of the play, a gentleman among tenement-dwellers, a speaker of 'proper' English among talkers of dialect, a theosophist among primitive Catholics, a 'high' literate in a secondary oral culture. It is interesting to notice that Bentham is the actual writer of the will, 'the thick [who] made out the Will wrong', the character responsible for most of the Boyles' troubles in the course of the play. In the context of this trilogy the old device of the will acquires a new lease of what might be termed, for want of a better word, life. The will is not merely a convenient device of *anagnoresis* and *peripeteia*: it is also, like the bloody paper in *The Shadow of a Gunman,* an emblem of the literacy which enters, transforms and ultimately destroys the oral community of the Boyle household.

The Captain and Joxer, casualties of capitalism, have had to fall back on their only resources, the devices of an earlier, oral culture. The Captain has created an alternative life for himself, as rich in romantic adventure and philosophical speculation as his actual circumstances are poor in everything. Given an ideal audience – and this is where Joxer earns his *sassige* – he can recite his greatness, believing it while the words are in the air. Within an oral culture, speech *is* action, performance is truth and, sound being evanescent and leaving no trace, there is little possibility of being convicted of what literates would understand as 'telling a lie'. But literacy changes all this: letters record and leave a trace which may be consulted by any *chiselur* who has learned to read and hence the Captain's venom on the point of Mary's reading:

> What did th' likes of her, born in a tenement house, want with readin'? Her readin's afther bringin' her to a nice pass – oh, it's madnin', madnin', madnin'!

Of course, the agent of the change in Mary's condition is Bentham, not books, and the immediate agent of the destruction of the house of Boyle is Bentham, not books, but in a way Boyle is right to see that it was literacy which gave Bentham the power to bring such *madnin'* confusion into the world of the Captain.

Just as the characters of *The Shadow of a Gunman* are fascinated by the idea of Davoren the poet, so too most of the characters of *Juno and the Paycock* are fascinated by the idea of Bentham the lawyer. Bentham has given up teaching – the promulgation of basic literacy – in order to master the 'higher' language of the law. Jerry Devine tries to mock this aura by calling Bentham a 'Micky Dazzler' but Bentham's social graces cause the other characters to treat him as a social superior in whose presence one wears one's good clothes and speaks as *properly* as one can. Of course, this is an aspect of a common phenomenon – the inferiority complex of one social class in the presence of a higher class – but it should be noted that Bentham's social superiority is established by his reputation for 'high' literacy and it should also be noted that when Captain Boyle aspires to the world of Bentham he immediately acquires an *attackey case* and *dockyments* and shortly afterwards begins to write poetry.

The house that is built on the will collapses quickly and only the strength of Juno remains. She is the only one who is granted any compensatory understanding, the only one capable of a genuinely revolutionary act. She sees through such false signifiers as *Diehard* and *Stater* when applied to the actual sons of actual mothers. This is not surprising, for, though she was in many ways an ordinary, selfish woman who wanted to better her life, Juno has always had the ability to subvert the cliche. In fact this is her characteristic virtue within the play, to point the weaknesses of the slogans which her children repeat with a fervour typical of an oral culture. When Mary protests that trade unionists could not allow a victimised member to 'walk the streets', Juno replies:

> No, of course yous couldn't – yous wanted to keep her company.

She has equally limited faith in the other struggle, represented by her son who also maintains that 'a principle's a principle':

> Ah, you lost your best principle, me boy, when you lost your arm. . .

And when he persists and sloganises that Ireland

> only half free'll never be at peace while she has a son left to pull a trigger –

Juno reduces the argument to absurdity:

> To be sure, to be sure – no bread's a lot better than half a loaf.

What makes Juno such a powerful character is that,

while staying within the ethos of her community she is able to break through the cultural determinism which limits the other characters. A Catholic, she can look at the disaster area which is her life, listen to the traditional responses around her and speak:

> These things have nothin' to do with the Will o' God. Ah, what can God do agen the stupidity o' men!

The *will* of God did not cause their misfortunes, not nearly as much as the *will,* in both the sexual sense and the legal sense, as represented by a stupid selfish man.

In *The Shadow of a Gunman* a society fascinated by 'high' literacy pays a writer the peculiar compliment of believing him to be a gunman; the writer allows the cult to flourish and to explode in fatal violence and death. *The Plough and the Stars* marks both an advance in general technique and also a considerable refinement of the motif under discussion. Almost the first action of the play is the act of writing—Mrs Gogan signs a receipt for Nora's new hat from Arnott's—and very shortly afterwards Fluther reads the handbill which advertises the 'Great Demonstration an' torchlight procession around places in the city sacred to the memory of Irish Patriots'. The handbill introduces the political theme and also begins the identification of nationalist politics with a cult of the dead. Reading—or incompetent reading—is satirised as the Covey attempts to enlighten the household with his selections from the classics of scientific materialism. But, of course, the most important documents in Act One are the invisible letter of promotion which Nora has concealed from Jack for the past two weeks and the dispatch from General Connolly which Captain Brennan delivers to Commandant Clitheroe. Jack must choose between a Sam Browne belt and the girdle of Venus: in this play it is a choice, as we shall see, between politics and erotics, between death and life.

As in the other plays there is, at the heart of the domestic action, the desertion of a female; but Jack is neither a thoughtless admirer nor a scheming manipulator but Nora's own newly-wed husband. Nor is Jack associated with writing, as Davoren and Bentham were. Jack is an insider, who speaks the same dialect as the other inhabitants. The dramatic problem at the end of Act One is to make credible the mental processes by which Jack rejects the love of his new wife in order to join his colleagues in the Citizen Army; this problem is bravely and brilliantly solved in the course of Act Two by the use of what O'Casey describes in the list of characters as *The Figure in the Window* and in the text as *The Voice of the Man.*

This device is a shadow seen and a voice heard through the medium of a public-house window. Although I think it would be bad for the production to identify the figure or the voice as those of Patrick Pearse, there is no doubt that early Irish audiences were—and to a lesser extent a modern Irish audience is—aware of the historical basis of the words in the speeches of the most venerated of the men who inspired and led the 1916 Rising. What all audiences see is a shadow as distinct from a physical body; what all audiences hear is a style of speech which is distinct from the speech of the other characters. The principal structural device of the Act is the Ironic counterpoint of the solemn rhetoric outside and the farcical language inside the pub. The asserted claim of the Voice is that

> bloodshed is a cleansing and sanctifying thing, and the nation that regards it as the final horror has lost its manhood... And we must be ready to pour out the same red wine in the same glorious sacrifice, for without shedding of blood there is no redemption... When war comes to Ireland she must welcome it as she would welcome the Angel of God!

The enacted 'counter-claim' of the latter part of the play is that blood is blood, that manhood is not best tested by the shedding of blood, that blood is not the wine of fertility and redemption, that war is not the annunciation of the Angel of God but the apocalypse of the Angel of Death. It is the Voice which wins out in Act Two. When the local men enter with flags and in uniform they have identified themselves totally with the Voice:

> *They are in a state of emotional excitement. Their faces are flushed and their eyes sparkle; they speak rapidly, as if unaware of the meaning of what they said. They have been mesmerized by the fervency of the speeches.*

They have been won over by the *speech*—the rhetoric—which they now imitate, speaking in pattern and devoting themselves to death and destruction for a female Ireland who has become for them greater than wife or mother.

When we analyse that *speech* we see that it is characterised by 'literary' qualities: it is strikingly different from the vernacular of the community. It is 'high', shaped by the literary tradition of Europe rather than by the experience of the Dublin tenements. Within the context of a public declamation it transforms suffering and death into redemption and resurrection: it claims to transmute an impoverished actuality into a glorious ideal. It is based on the imagery of death and miraculous resurrection and thus for a Catholic community constitutes a call to a holy war in which death is the ultimate victory. It operates only at a spiritual or symbolic level; physically speaking, great loss of blood results in pain and death and the end of the person.

The speech succeeds because of the enormous prestige of this kind of rhetoric among those who have never learned it. Western civilisation began when skillful public speaking was established as the art of rhetoric (*he rhetorike*) and this in turn developed into the study of language (*ars grammatica*) which was the basis of higher education and which distinguished the educated elite from the illiterate masses, i. e. those whose oral culture had not been eradicated by literacy. Those in primary oral cultures tend to view literacy with what strikes us as a superstitious awe. Those in secondary oral cultures — such as the tenement-dwellers of O'Casey's trilogy — are also in awe of this 'higher' education: they are either passionately dedicated to acquiring it themselves or they are, literally, lost in admiration of those who have already acquired it.

There are at least two noteworthy aspects of the men's acceptance of the speech. The first is that it is primarily and specifically male, perhaps anti-female — Ireland is greater than wife or mother — and this may have something to do with the history of literacy which was until a mere hundred years ago almost exclusively the preserve of male celibate colleges. The other is that it embraces a dedication to suffering and death. The primary validation of this comes, of course, from the Christian tradition of martyrdom but there is also in the play a strong sense of an Irish tradition — however closely related to the Christian — which is an older cult of the dead.

Within the play, in a fictional 1916, the Voice of the Man derives authority for the national struggle from the graves of earlier political martyrs; for the audience at the play there is the sense of hearing a ghost from the past — if the ghost is identified as that of Pearse, the *frisson* is greater but in the political atmosphere of our time even the vague idea of such a connection makes for a great moment in the theatre — speaking from one of those magical graves and urging the continuation of the struggle. Within the play, there is in Acts Three and Four the refutation of the claims of the Voice: there is no redemption, the belief of the once-mesmerized men is unable to withstand the actuality of battle, and whatever virtue there is in the play derives not from manliness (*virtus*) but from the generosity of women. Within the audience there is and always has been the awareness that the consequences of the Rising — no matter how acceptable overall — could hardly sustain the analogy with divine resurrection and eternal life. What made the first productions of the play so daringly shocking was the clear implication that the working people of Ireland had not been led to glory but had been deluded by the leaders of the 1916 Rising, by the spirit of the Christo-heroic nationalist tradition as expressed so brilliantly by the Voice of the Man.

There is one other character in the play who sometimes speaks in the same 'high spiritual' style as the Voice of the Man and this is, of course, Bessie who, being a working-class Protestant, derives her 'high' style from popular reading of the Bible rather than from scholastic education. She is quite comfortable with symbolic arrows and alters of heroic sacrifice and the speech which I wish to draw your attention to is when she draws on her Biblical armaments to attack Mrs Gogan. She imagines Mrs Gogan deluding the man from the Saint Vincent de Paul Society.

> mockin' th' man with an angel face, shinin' with th' glamour of deceit and lies!

Mrs Gogan is seen here in a way which reminds us of the traditional transfiguration, her face bright with divine enlightenment. But of course Bessie goes on to assert that the source of the transformation is not divine but diabolical: Mrs Gogan's intention is to delude the man from the charitable organisation. The phraseology is interesting, recalling the references of the Voice to the Angel of God and anticipating the entrance of the uniformed men at the end of Act Two when, under the influence of the Voice, "*their faces are flushed and their eyes sparkle*". But even more interesting, at least in the context of this paper, is the use of the term *glamour* to describe delusion: was it Bessie's — that is, O'Casey's — familiarity with the early modern English of the King James Bible or had it something to do with the conflict between oral and literate cultures in Dublin at the turn of the century that generated this phrase in which deceit and delusion are identified with a word with an etymology which recalls the time when literates were believed to have the power to use magic words, the power of glamour/grammar, to charm (*carmen*) helpless people with spells.

Pointing out that when the art of writing arrived in oral societies it was often regarded 'as an instrument of secret and magic powers,' Walter J. Ong reminds us [in his *Orality and Literacy*] that traces of this early attitude toward writing can still show etymologically: the Middle English 'grammarye' or grammar, referring to book-learning, came to mean occult or magical lore, and through one Scottish dialectical form has emerged in our present English vocabulary as 'glamor' (spell-casting power).

O'Casey's early trilogy shows how the poor uneducated people of Dublin were—in the opinion of some—deluded by the glamour/grammar, the deceitful language of Micky Dazzlers who promised eternal life but whose only gift was desolation.

CHRISTOPHER INNES

SOURCE: Christopher Innes, "The Essential Continuity of Sean O'Casey," in *Modern Drama*, Vol. XXXIII, No. 3, September, 1990, pp. 419-31.

[*In the following essay, Innes argues that the predominantly naturalist reading given to O'Casey's early plays ignores elements of expressionism which not only exist in his early work, but are a mark of continuity throughout his oeuvre.*]

There is a general assumption behind almost all critical approaches to Sean O'Casey's work, which deserves examination, if only because it is so common. Despite Denis Johnston's assertion in 1926, the year of *The Plough and the Stars*, that O'Casey's first three plays are increasingly poetic in dialogue and expressionistic in form, the Dublin trilogy is almost invariably held up as an example of naturalism. Equally, all his theatrical output from the 1934 production of *Within the Gates*, whether labelled expressionist or fantasy, is seen as the stylistic antithesis of the early plays. Biographic reference is used to support this: O'Casey's move from Ireland to England after the *Plough* riots is taken as the sign of a radical departure in subject matter. To some critics his 1928 break with the Abbey theatre gave him the liberty to explore new dramatic forms. To others it shows limitations that come from writing without the practical discipline of stage production, resulting in flawed language and abstract characterization. In both cases, *The Silver Tassie*, as the immediate cause of O'Casey's break with the Abbey, is considered an amalgam of opposing styles, signalling the transition from one to another.

One recent critic [Carol Kleiman] at least has tried to redress the balance by emphasizing the realistic basis of the symbolism in his two most expressionistic works. But this argument [in her *Sean O'Casey's Bridge of Vision*] for the unity of O'Casey's vision still accepts the unquestioned naturalism of his Dublin plays, and its premise is that throughout his career O'Casey employed a "basically realistic technique." By contrast, the continuity of O'Casey's work should be seen as far more radical, since his early trilogy can be shown to be no less non-naturalistic beneath its apparent surface than his later recognizably symbolic plays. Even the shift in characterization, from seemingly individualized and rounded figures towards the typical and two-dimensional, is demonstrably part of a consistent development, instead of being evidence of a break between two different styles. Indeed, the critical views that posit such division in O'Casey's career lead to inherently contradictory conclusions.

That O'Casey's post-war plays have had remarkably few performances is conventionally seen as being directly due to their poetic expressionism and overt political bias (the latter indeed being the reason for their adoption by the Berliner Ensemble). Conversely, the popularity of the early plays becomes evidence for the absence of specifically these qualities, leading to the type of judgement put most directly by Joseph Wood Krutch: "[O'Casey] offers no solution; he proposes no remedy; he suggests no hope." "His plays lack form, lack movement, and in the final analysis lack any informing purpose." More recently and more subtly this analysis has been used [by Desmond E. S. Maxwell in his *A Critical History of Modern Irish Drama*] to align O'Casey with the existentialist vision of "life as farce with which tragic experience must come to terms" in depicting "a world whose structures will never live up to their promise." Yet this line is highly problematic in the light of O'Casey's firmly held socialist principles, practically expressed in his association with the labour leader, Jim Larkin, and his involvement in founding the Irish Citizens' Army. Acknowledging that these form the background for the Dublin plays logically leads to the argument that they represent a repudiation of Marxism—a conclusion which can only be sustained by assuming there is no continuity with later works such as *The Star Turns Red* (1940) and *Red Roses for Me* (1943).

Another case in point is the influence of Bernard Shaw. Shaw, of course, intervened in defence of *The Silver Tassie*, and critics have generally followed Denis Johnston (who deplored the "damage done by the honeyed poison of G.B.S.") in seeing his influence as mainly limited to O'Casey's subsequent didactic work. Certainly the model of Shaw is most noticeable in *Purple Dust* (1940, first produced 1945), where the situation of a rich Englishman's attempt to impose his ethos on an Irish village, the major characters and the satiric contrast between neo-colonialism and the supposedly backward natives directly echo *John Bull's Other Island*. In particular the major thematic motif of O'Casey's last trilogy of symbolic fantasies is a clear reworking of Shaw's Life Force—though simplified to liberating sexuality—the vital principle embodied in the emblematic title figure of *Cock-a-doodle Dandy* (1949, first professional performance 1958), "a gay bird.... A bit unruly at times" who both tricks the police into shooting holes in the top hat of bourgeois respectability and conjures up a storm that whirls the puritanical priest away through the air, "rousing up commotion among the young and the souls zealous for life" as well as affirming though his dancing "the right of the joy of life to live courageously in the hearts of men." Following Shaw, the carriers of this Life Force are female: Loreleen, explicitly associated with the "Red Cock" by her dress and in the dialogue, who is victimized and banished by the life-denying representatives of the repressive society; the Every-woman figure of Jannice in *Within the Gates,* who obeys the call of the Dreamer-poet to "Sing them silent, dance them still, and laugh them into an open shame!" — thus overcoming Bishop, Atheist, dispossessed masses, all who "carry furl'd the fainting flag of a dead hope and a dead faith," and affirming the joyfulness of existence even as she dies.

However, key lines from *The Doctor's Dilemma* are also quoted in the opening stage directions to O'Casey's first play, *The Shadow of a Gunman* 1923), and again in the dialogue of *Within the Gates,* while the subtitles of plays throughout his career echo Shaw's use of subtitles: *A Political Phantasy* (*Kathleen Listens In,* 1923), *A Wayward Comedy* (*Purple Dust*), *A Sincerious Comedy* (*Hall of Healing,* 1951, unperformed). Indeed, O'Casey, who was still quoting Shaw in support of his own views up to the year of his death in 1964, stressed it was Shaw's example that weaned him from the Gaelic League and first inspired him to write for the stage: "I abandoned the romantic cult of Nationalism sixty years ago, and saw the real Ireland when I read the cheap edition of Shaw's *John Bull's Other Island*; hating only poverty, hunger, and disease." The type of objectivity, particularly in the satiric perspective on his own revolutionary ideals, on which the definition of O'Casey's early drama as naturalistic is based, can be seen as deriving from Shaw. So too can his characteristic use of irony, as for instance in the juxtaposition of the red glare of the burning city under bombardment with the British soldier's chorus of "Keep the 'owme fires burning" that closes *The Plough and the Stars,* which exactly repeats the ending of *Heartbreak House* in a different context.

This ironic objectivity gives his Dublin trilogy much of its dramatic power, and its qualities can be most clearly seen in relation to autobiographical material. In *The Shadow of a Gunman,* for instance, several characters are identifiable real life portraits and the poet-protagonist is in many ways a self-projection. Yet Davoren is explicitly an anti-hero, "on the run" (O'Casey's first title for the play) from the overcrowded poverty of the slums, political violence, and the "common people" for whom "beauty is for sale in a butcher's shop." A satiric representation of O'Casey's previous, pre-Shaw values, he stands for the sentimental idealism of the Gaelic League. His reference points are mythic heroes of Irish legend or the symbol of Kathleen ni Houlihan (which Yeats had made synonymous with the romantic image of Irish liberation, and which O'Casey tried to expropriate for his socialist vision in *Kathleen Listens In*—produced the same year). His poetry is used as an excuse for avoiding life; and a rhetorical line from Shelley substitutes for emotional involvement: "Ah me, alas! Pain, pain ever, for ever. Like thee, Prometheus, no change, no pause, no hope. Ah, life, life, life!"

All the characters are equally subject to this kind of posturing, with the action turning on the gap between their illusions and reality. Just like the timid Grigson, recasting his encounter with the brutal Auxiliaries into the heroic mode after his wife has just given a graphic description of his humiliating self-abasement, so Davoren fosters the admiration of the tenement's inhabitants in mistaking his subjective escapism for the bravery of a gunman "on the run," only to finally recognize his guilt and cowardice. Even then, the inflated language of his self-condemnation as "poet and poltroon, poltroon and poet," together with his repeat of the Shelley theme-note from the beginning, imply that this is nothing more than an alternative form of escapism—the sorrowing outcast instead of the dangerous shadow of the man of action—and that this pasteboard Prometheus will never break his chains of illusion.

The only possible exception is the real gunman. But Maguire is no more than a *deus ex machina,* the actual shadow of the ironic title that Davoren applies to himself, and the disregard for the safety of the innocent whose freedom he is so ready to kill—and die—for, in leaving the bag of bombs behind, implies an equivalent romanticism in his Cause. As Davoren's peddler-companion, who frequently seems to voice O'Casey's views, describes it, "their Mass is a burnin' buildin'; their De Profundis is 'The Soldiers' Song . . . —, an' it's all for 'the glory o' God an' the honour o' Ireland'." Even Minnie, whose openness and self-sacrifice give her the status of a tragic heroine, is governed by illusion. When the Auxiliaries beat down the door to search the house, it is sentimental attraction to an imaginary gunman-poet that motivates her to take responsibility for the bombs. The bravado of her cry, "Up the Republic!," is an attempt to live up to the expectations of this non-existent figure as she is dragged down the stairs outside his room. And she is not shot for her action in concealing weapons, nor for her revolutionary sentiments, but by mistake—and possibly by the gunmen she believes she is supporting—when the Auxiliaries' truck is ambushed.

The tragedy of her death is that it is not only pointless, but unnecessary. It underlines the real cost of the escapism illustrated in different degrees by other characters in rather over-literal terms, since she is killed while trying to escape from the violence that is not only the defining fact of their environment, but the touchstone for their illusions. The fighting off-stage not only undercuts pretensions to bravery:

> GRIGSON. If a man keeps a stiff upper front—Merciful God, there's an ambush! [*Explosions of two bursting bombs are heard on the street outside the house . . .*]

It dismisses philosophic detachment, poetic fervour, nationalist ideals, religious faith:

> SEAMUS. . . . No man need be afraid with a crowd of angels round him; thanks to God for His Holy religion!
>
> DAVOREN. You're welcome to your angels; philosophy is mine; philosophy that makes the coward brave; the sufferer defiant; the weak strong; the . . .
>
> [*A volley of shots is heard in a lane that runs parallel with the wall of the backyard. Religion and philosophy are forgotten in the violent fear of a nervous equality.*]

The boldness of the juxtapositions, the repetitions, and the presentation of all the characters as variations on the same theme, make O'Casey's use of irony crudely obvious in this early play. It is most effective when limited to the foreground situation, rather than based on contrasts between personal action and the historical background, as with the braces Seamus peddles:

> They're great value; I only hope I'll be able to get enough o' them. I'm wearing a pair of them meself—they'd do Cuchullian, they're so strong. (*Counting the spoons*) . . . And still we're looking for freedom—ye gods, it's a glorious country! (*He lets one fall, which he stoops to pick up.*) Oh, my God, there's the braces after breakin'.
>
> DAVOREN. That doesn't look as if they were strong enough for Cuchullian.
>
> SEAMUS. I put a heavy strain on them too sudden.

This broad farce is taken directly from the Music Hall—it is not coincidental that exactly the same comic turn provides the anti-climax of *Waiting for Godot*, since there is a clear kinship between Beckett's clown-like tramps and O'Casey's shabby self-deceivers—and carries over into the other parts of the Dublin trilogy, as does the same use of irony to control the audience's critical perception. However, both Music Hall elements and the opposition of character against context become progressively subtler, as well as better integrated with the action in the two following plays. Boyle and Joxer, as classic drunkards convinced the earth is reeling because they can't stand straight, illustrate the actual situation at the end of *Juno and the Paycock*: both their domestic circle and the society outside have indeed broken down "in a terr . . . ible state o' . . . chassis," but it is the failure of moral perception, not the existential nature of the world, that is responsible for the chaos. In the central scene of *The Plough and the Stars* the stock skit is more naturalistic, two disreputable women tearing each other's hair out over insults to their respectability, and barely indicated (the barman breaks up the fight before Mrs. Grogan and Bessie get their hands on one another), while the thematic reverberations are even wider. Set against the Republican rally outside the pub, it undercuts the orator's death-bound mysticism with its rhetoric of patriotic sacrifice and redemptive bloodshedding, reducing the coming battle for independence to a farcical squabble. Beyond that it points to the First World War—also a heroic analogue for the orator—undermining idealistic justifications for the slaughter in the trenches through the association of "poor little Catholic Belgium" with "poor little Catholic Ireland," which ironically puts the protestant loyalist in the position of her German enemies.

It was this scene, of course, that sparked the riots at the Abbey's 1926 production of the play. Focussing on the Flag of the title (degraded by its presence in a pub), the depiction of the men who fought in the Uprising as less than heroic (held back by their wives, fearful under fire, motivated by self preservation once the battle is lost), and the presence of a prostitute among the characters ("an abominable play. . . . There are no streetwalkers in Dublin!"), the public demonstration illustrated O'Casey's point exactly. As he pointed out in **"A Reply to the Critics,"** which emphasized the realistic basis of his portrayal, the romantic idealism "about 'the Ireland that remembers with tear-dimmed eyes all that Easter Week stands for' makes me sick. Some of the men cannot even get a job."

The Plough and the Stars is always cited as O'Casey's most developed naturalistic play. The multiple focus and interweaving strands of action replace the simplification of a dominant protagonist by a social panorama, without losing the human scale, and this form itself incorporates the thematic statement. It embodies an image of community, which is mirrored in the way the inhabitants of the slum tenement develop a sense of group responsibility under the pressure of external events that threaten the group's existence and destroy the narrower social unit of the family. Tenuous and contingent, in plot terms the actual community is always on the point of disruption through the deaths of its individual members; whether all too literally inflamed by delusive ideals (Jack Clitheroe, trapped in a burning building), a victim of circumstance (Bessie Burgess, shot in error by the British soldiers she supports), or a statistic of poverty (the young girl, Mollser, dying of consumption). On the stylistic level, however, comic dissension—the sword-waving chase around a kitchen table in Act I, the baby thrust into the arms of an unwilling man, and dumped on the pub floor, when the women square off in Act II—gives way to tragic unity. The positive social vision suggested in the structure, but not affirmed by the dramatic action, thus implicitly endorses the young socialist's response to the Republican ideal of independence: "Dope, dope. There's only one war worth havin': th' war for th' economic emancipation of th' proletariat."

Typically for this stage in O'Casey's development, while his views may be presented, their spokesman is treated satirically. Derogatorally named "the Covey," and incongruously trying to attract a prostitute's attentions or impress a British Corporal with the pretentious catchphrase of "Did y'ever read, comrade, Jenersky's *Thesis on the Origin, Development, an' Consolidation of th' Evolutionary Idea of the Proletariat?*," his political theorizing is contemptuously dismissed by all the other characters. Similarly, the first sign of solidarity among the tenement inhabitants is the anti-social activity of looting, which may create an unlikely team out of the former female antagonists, but discredits the socialist's ideological understanding—though not, as is often assumed, the political principles themselves—and shows materialistic greed banishing an appeal to common humanity in the other non-combatant men.

O'Casey's approach is exemplified in the treatment of Bessie Burgess; not only, as a pro-British Protestant and vocal anti-Republican, the outsider in the tenement group, but the least sympathetic character for the predominantly Catholic and Nationalist Dublin audience of the time. The sentimentally attractive Nora Clitheroe, retreating into an Ophelia-like madness when her husband rejects her for Republican ideals, offers a conventional (and deliberately illusory) tragic image. But the real heroine of the tragedy is Bessie, who becomes the human centre of the community, nursing the woman she had despised at the beginning of the play and sacrificing her own life for her safety. Bringing the Dublin spectators to identify with her forms a practical demonstration of the socialist's contention that "there's no such thing as an Irishman, or an Englishman, or a German or a Turk; we're all only human bein's." At the same time sympathy is not made easy. It is Bessie's insults that provoke Jack into returning to his death in the already hopeless battle, and her reaction when shot is to curse the helplessly terrified Nora as "you bitch."

Once the riots had subsided, the play was praised for "the astonishing accuracy of . . . photographic detail," and indeed the basis for several scenes is documentary. For instance the orator's rhetoric is taken verbatim from Pearse's speeches, while O'Casey emphasized that "of these very words Jim Connolly himself said almost the same thing as the Covey." Yet this factual background is set against a highly patterned thematic structure, which approaches melodrama at points such as the oath to the flags:

> CAPT. BRENNAN [*catching up The Plough and the Stars*]. Imprisonment for th' Independence of Ireland!
>
> LIEUT. LANGON [*catching up the Tri-colour*]. Wounds for th' Independence of Ireland!
>
> CLITHEROE. Death for th' Independence of Ireland!
>
> THE THREE [*together*]. So help us God!

The melodramatic tone of the speeches might be simply a naturalistic response to the passion of the moment, if the fate of each character did not exactly correspond to his vow. As this indicates, even the characterization is less naturalistic than it appears. With their emblematic names and identifying catchphrases—the Covey's grandiose book-title, Fluther Good's reiterated "derogatory" and "vice versa"—these are the equivalent of the stock figures that Strindberg rejected in the classic definition of naturalism that prefaces *Miss Julie*, while one has a clearly literary genesis. Nora, like the Ibsen heroine from whom she takes her name, deceives her equally patronizing husband in order to save him, and has her doll's house destroyed by her inability to intercept a letter.

Thus even O'Casey's most naturalistic work contains the seeds of his later development, and the connections are clearest in *Juno and the Paycock*. The original centre of the play, "the tragedy of a crippled IRA man, one Johnny Boyle," is typically melodramatic in concept and treatment. The guilty betrayer is hounded by conscience to the brink of self-betrayal, with his life linked to a flickering crimson votive light, which goes out as his executioners approach (even if the classic formula of Boucicault—or Irving's *The Bells*—is reversed by transforming villain into victim). At the same time, the surrounding action, which not only parallels and extends this core, but dominates it through the vivid vitality of the characters, is openly allegorical.

The reference to Mrs. Boyle and her husband in the title may be ironic, Juno only a nickname—but as the schoolmaster points out, it is still intended to remind "one of Homer's glorious story of ancient gods and heroes." On the symbolic level of the play she can be seen as a counter-type to the Yeatsian Kathleen Ni Houlihan, Ireland as the archetypal mother mourning the loss of her sons in place of the virginal siren welcoming the death of her lovers, a contrast parodistically encapsulated in her husband's linguistic confusion:

> BOYLE (solemnly).... Requiescat in pace... or, usin' our oul' tongue like St. Patrick or St. Bridget, Guh sayeree jeea ayera!
>
> MARY. Oh, father, that's not Rest in Peace; that's God save Ireland.
>
> BOYLE. U-u-ugh, it's all the same—isn't it a prayer?

Even the most naturalistic aspects of Juno's characterization have representative significance. O'Casey's description—"*twenty years ago* [ie. at the first performance of Yeats's *Kathleen Ni Houlihan*, 1902] *she must have been a pretty woman; but her face has now assumed ... a look of listless monotony and harassed anxiety, blending with an expression of mechanical resistance*"—measures the deterioration of Nationalist idealism in terms of its human cost and lack of material or political benefits for the working-classes.

This is the major motif of the play as a whole. Even more explicitly than in *The Plough and the Stars*, since here all the action takes place inside a single house, the tenement stands for the nation beneath its local specificity. Each of the women has a husband or son maimed or killed—with Johnny as a human calendar of revolutionary conflict: crippled by a bullet in the hip during Easter Week 1916 (a relatively minor wound analogous perhaps to the 15 rebels hanged by the British), losing an arm in the civil war period of *Shadow of a Gunman*, and finally his life (a progressive dismemberment mirroring the increasing bitterness of the fighting; in 1922 the Free State government executed 77 Republican leaders)—and the Boyle family fortunes are the vicissitudes of the Irish people in microcosm.

The legacy that provides an illusory windfall stands for the newly won national sovereignty. This is underlined for the audience by Boyle's assertion, significantly placed just after an unanswered knock of doom (in the shape of a trench-coated gunman) and immediately before the entry of Bentham to announce their unexpected good fortune, that "Today ... there's goin' to be issued a proclamation be me, establishin' an independent Republic, an' Juno'll have to take an oath of allegiance." The Captain's characteristic confusion of constitutional terms and ironic misinterpretation of liberty as the evasion of social responsibility is a clear criticism of the false expectations engendered by nationhood, tangibly illustrated in the cheap and garishly vulgar furnishing the family buys on credit, the pretentious gramophone and the bourgeois suit that replaces Boyle's labouring trousers. The pompous schoolmaster's incompetence in drawing up the will, which deprives them of the promised riches, can be seen as O'Casey's comment on the politicians' drafting of the constitution, while the resulting material destitution offers a graphic image of moral bankruptcy in the state. The stage set itself is dismantled by the two removal men who repossess almost all the family's possessions to pay their debts, paralleled by the forcible removal of Johnny by his two executioners. Juno has learnt from the loss of her own son the compassion she so signally lacked with her neighbour's exactly comparable bereavement. But she leaves to work elsewhere for the future in the form of Mary's unborn child, abandoned by the Bentham/politicians who seduced her and rejected by the other contender for her favour, the socialist/Labour Movement, whose narrow morality makes him incapable of living up to his humanitarian ideals. Juno's heavily-weighted prayer to "take away our hearts o' stone, and give us hearts o' flesh" counter-balances the pair of comic drunkards, who incongruously point the moral that "The counthry'll have to steady itself ... it's goin' ... to hell. ... No matther ... what any one may ... say ... Irelan' sober ... is Irelan' ... free." But the darkened and stripped stage is left to the inebriated forces of anarchy, O'Casey's most satiric version of the escape artists and "shadows" of sentimental patriotism, who form his major target from the title figure of the first play in the Dublin trilogy to the intoxicating silhouette of Pearse in *The Plough and the Stars*.

The discomforting irony of sharp juxtapositions at the end of *Juno*, may give an overwhelming impression of objectivity. However, as Samuel Beckett observed, reviewing *Windfalls* [in *The Bookman* 86, 1934]:

> Mr. O'Casey is a master of knockabout in this very serious and honourable sense—that he discerns the principle of disintegration in even the most complacent solidities, and activates it to their explosion. This is the energy of his theatre, the triumph of the principle of knockabout in situation, in all its elements and on all its planes, from the furniture to the higher centres.

This could be applied equally to *Juno*: practically none of the elements that combine in the final image are naturalistic. Despite O'Casey's vehement assertion that "I have nothing to do with Beckett. . . . his philosophy isn't my philosophy, for within him there is no hazard of hope," Beckett's approval of a specific play has sometimes been used to support a view of O'Casey in general as a proto-Absurdist, whose early plays express an existential nihilism. Yet, leaving aside the completely unBeckettian social reference, the sequence of impressions that define the ending is clearly intended as a protest and a warning, while the solution is suggested by the structure of the following play in the series. Rather than resigning an audience to the pointlessness of human effort in the face of a recalcitrant universe, the bleakness of the comic closing moment calls for a value judgement, conditioned by the preceding balance between the continuing cycle of violence and the call for a wider humanity.

The positive message becomes increasingly open and direct in O'Casey's subsequent plays; and as explicit statement replaces oblique suggestion, the realistic surface disappears. Settings symbolize philosophical oppositions or emotional states, while ideological manipulation replaces personal motive in the characters. At its extreme this results in the Morality play psychomachia of *Within the Gates,* where good and evil "angels" (The Dreamer/The Atheist) struggle for the protagonist's soul against a backdrop of war memorial and maypole. Similarly the conflict in *The Star Turns Red* is defined dialectically by the church spire and the foundry chimney seen through windows either side of the stage, the portraits of a Bishop and Lenin on the walls. The resolution is symbolized by the addition of *"a white cross on which a red hammer and sickle are imposed,"* and a single speech from Red Jim (an idealized projection of Jim Larkin) is sufficient to transform the grief of a weeping girl into triumphant affirmation:

> Up, young woman, and join in the glowing hour your lover died to fashion. He fought for life, for life is all; and death is nothing!
>
> [*Julia stands up with her right fist clenched. The playing and singing of "The Internationale" grow louder. Soldiers and sailors appear at the windows, and all join in the singing.*]

At the same time the language becomes poetic to reflect universal thematic intentions—all too often, as J.B. Priestley was the first to point out [reviewing *Oak Leaves and Lavender* (in *Our Time* 5, 1945-6)] resulting in "windy rhetoric that obscures the characters and blunts the situations. . . . O'Casey in Dublin created literature, whereas O'Casey in Devon is merely being literary."

Another factor frequently pointed to in critical discussions of *The Silver Tassie*, apart from O'Casey's isolation from both the society that provided the material for his early plays and the requirements of a specific theatre that shaped them, is the influence of German expressionism: in particular Toller's *Masse-Mensch,* performed by the Dublin Drama League under the title of *Masses and Man* in 1925, and *Transfiguration*. Given O'Casey's personal links to Denis Johnston, and Johnston's interest in Toller (which led him to direct *Hoppla!* for the League in 1929), it is certainly reasonable to suggest that O'Casey became exposed to the expressionist approach then. But at this point in O'Casey's career, the effect of Toller's example, even on the war sequence of Act II, seems rather general. It is only with *The Star Turns Red*—written for Unity Theatre, which was largely responsible for introducing Toller and Kaiser to the English stage, and to which O'Casey may have turned for precisely that reason as well as their shared Marxism—that the model of *Masses and Man* can be specifically traced. The expressionist combination of religious humanitarianism and leftwing politics, which made their radical dramatic form seem the proclamation of a new social order, corresponded with the views already implicit in the Dublin trilogy. But now, what before had remained on a thematic level, became embodied in the style. The decisive new element is the utopianism inherent in the expressionist approach. This is reflected in O'Casey's generic switch from the "Tragedy" of his early plays to "Comedy" for his subsequent work; and the nature of the change can be seen in the intermediate "Tragi-Comedy" of *The Silver Tassie.*

On the surface the opening has the characteristics of the previous plays: set in a Dublin tenement, with a pair of cowardly boasters, and focussing on group interaction. By itself the wedding bowl smashed by the physically dominating Teddy Foran is on the same level of significance as the red votive light in *Juno.* However, the parallel between the bowl and the *"silver cup joyously, rather than reverentially, elevated, as a priest would elevate a chalice"* transforms both into obvious symbols, with the thematic connection being emphasized by the crushing of the silver cup that ends the play. In addition, the naturalistically depicted characters have a single line of thought that in conventional terms would seem obsessive. "Tambourine theology" is an accurate description of all the speeches of one, while both Mrs. Foran and Harry Heegan's mother have no other concern in sending their men off to the First World War trenches but the maintenance money from the government for dependents of soldiers of Active Service. In fact the characters have hardly more developed personalities than the openly expressionistic figures of Act II, being designed to serve a didactic pattern. The dominant males of the opening are defined purely in terms of physical vitality to provide the maximum contrast to the war-cripples they become, the soccer hero Harry being paralysed from the waist down, the blinded Teddy being subservient to the wife he had terrorized, while in place of being a hero-worshipper spurned by the girls, Barney throttles the helpless Harry and wins his former fiancee.

At first glance the war sequence seems a complete contrast, with its class-conscious caricatures, anonymous soldiers and chanted verse. The only named character, Barney, is pinioned to a gun-wheel in direct comparison and contrast to a life-size Christ-figure with one arm released from the crucifix, either side of a howitzer to which the soldiers pray when the enemy attack. The tone is set by antiphonal chanting: "Kyrie eleison" from within the ruined monastery and an inverted version of Ezekiel's prophecy of resurrection from a blood-covered death figure. Stage directions stress the distinction between these symbolic objects and reality, *"Every feature of the scene seems a little distorted from its original appearance,"* and when the guns fire *"Only flashes are seen, no noise is heard."* Yet in the first production Harry doubled as 1st Soldier without any noticeable incongruity. Indeed, in the following hospital scene this surreal treatment coexists with the naturalistic surface—with the figures both interacting as individuals and reduced to numbers by the system, the same counterpoint between off-stage latin liturgy and human pain closing the episode—and the double image of reality is projected onto the final return to a Dublin setting. The bitter presence of the maimed makes the Football Club dance grotesque; conversational dialogue continually modulates into antiphonal patterns:

> SYLVESTER. . . . give him breath to sing his song an' play the ukelele.
>
> MRS. HEEGAN. Just as he used to do.
>
> SYLVESTER. Behind the trenches.
>
> SIMON. In the Rest Camps.
>
> MRS. FORAN. Out in France.
>
> HARRY. I can see, but I cannot dance.
>
> TEDDY. I can dance but I cannot see. . . .
>
> HARRY. There's something wrong with life when men can walk.
>
> TEDDY. There's something wrong with life when men can see.

We are challenged to look behind naturalistic surfaces. In retrospect the apparent normality of the tenement is as illusory as the balloons and coloured streamers of the dance hall. As Shaw commented in his defence of **The Silver Tassie,** "The first act is not a bit realistic; it is deliberately fantastic . . . poetry."

In much the same way, the "dramatic dehiscence" noted by Beckett undermines the apparent naturalism of the Dublin trilogy. The combination of Music Hall turn with melodrama, as well as stock characterization and, above all, the strongly allegorical action, are precisely the qualities that form the dramaturgical basis for O'Casey's later works. The change of style is more a shift in emphasis than a new approach. The mythic dimension is already present in **Juno,** and even in **Shadow of a Gunman,** where Minnie is "A Helen of Troy come to live in a tenement!" Exactly the same allegory, on which the action of Juno is based, reappears in more didactic and openly symbolic plays. The O'Houlihan house of **Kathleen Listens In,** bought in exchange for the family cow of living standards and its door painted green, stands for national independence, with the subsequent political conflict represented by the demands of the Worker that the house be painted red versus the Republican extremist's "Yous'll grow shamrocks or yous'll grow nothin'!." The decaying mansion of **Purple Dust** is Ireland again, with independence again embodied by the destruction of its interior. But there the terms are cultural rather than political, with the flood that drives out Stokes and Poges—the wealthy English neo-colonists, named after the village that inspired Gray's "Elegy," whose intention of reviving the feudal past is sabotaged by the down-to-earth vitality of the locals—symbolizing the sweeping away of cultural imperialism and capitalism by the river of time. Conversely, the celebration of the Life Force that finds its fullest expression in O'Casey's last fantasies is also present in **The Plough and the Stars,** with Rosie Redmond's song of sexual pleasure and procreation (censored in the original Abbey production) in counterpoint to the men marching off to their deaths in the Easter Uprising.

O'Casey's work, then, has a consistent unity. His early plays signal a move beyond the limits of dramatic naturalism as much as the later, more obviously experimental works. Though in different ways, both correspond to his concept of "The new form in drama [which] will take qualities found in classical, romantic and expressionistic plays, will blend them together, breathe the breath of life into the new form and create a new drama [O'Casey, *New York Times,* 21 October 1994]." As such his search is a prototype for the various attempts to develop new forms of social realism which can be found in the contemporary generation of politically oriented dramatists from Osborne to Hare or Edgar. Yet, with the exception of Denis Johnston's counter-play to *The Plough and the Stars, The Scythe and the Sunset* (1958) and a general influence on the later, marginalized Irish work of John Arden, O'Casey's work has had no specific effect on subsequent British or Irish theatre.

The critical misreading of O'Casey, interpreting his development in terms of a radical change in style, is arguably the major reason for O'Casey's lack of influence. Yeats's attack on *The Silver Tassie* for its apparent abandonment of the earlier plays' dramatic principles, based on a purely naturalistic reading of the Dublin trilogy, is typical. O'Casey's withdrawal to England and his increasingly overt political bias may have been contributing factors in banishing his later plays from the stage. But Yeats's criticism not only initiated the break with the Abbey. It established the terms for discussion of O'Casey's work by exaggerating the realism of his early plays as much as by singling out the expressionistic elements of *The Silver Tassie.* As a result, whether seeking to promote O'Casey's post-1930 stylistic experimentation, commenting on its problematic language and characterization, or choosing to focus exclusively on the Abbey plays, subsequent criticism has emphasized a division that is more apparent than actual.

SOURCES FOR FURTHER STUDY

daRin, Doris. *Sean O'Casey.* New York: Frederick Ungar Publishing, 1976, 216 p.

> Analyzes twelve of O'Casey's plays. daRin also provides an introductory profile of the author, an evaluation of his artistic stature, an epilogue on Irish politics, and a bibliography.

Jones, Nesta, ed. *File on O'Casey.* London: Methuen, 1986, 96 p.

> Collection of reviews of O'Casey's plays.

Kenneally, Michael. *Portraying the Self: Sean O'Casey and the Art of Autobiography.* Buckinghamshire, England: Colin Smythe, 1988, 268 p.

> Argues that O'Casey was a master in the autobiography genre. In the introduction Kenneally cites a number of eminent critics who contend "that O'Casey's reputation will rest, ultimately, not on his stature as a dramatist—however great it may be—but on his achievements as autobiographer."

Kilroy, Thomas, ed. *Sean O'Casey: A Collection of Critical Essays.* Englewood Cliffs, N.J.: Prentice-Hall, 1975, 174 p.

> Includes commentary by leading O'Casey scholars and such eminent literary figures as W. B. Yeats, George Bernard Shaw, and Samuel Beckett.

O'Connor, Garry. *Sean O'Casey: A Life.* London: Hodder & Stoughton, 1988, 448 p.

> Detailed biography in which O'Connor focuses on showing "how Sean O'Casey . . . painstakingly created himself out of the real-life John Casey."

Rollins, Ronald Gene. *Sean O'Casey's Drama: Verisimilitude and Vision.* Tuscaloosa: University of Alabama Press, 1979, 139 p.

> Analyzes selected O'Casey plays, focusing on his visual techniques, ritualistic patterns, and use of myths.

Plato

428? B.C.-348? B.C.

Greek philosopher and prose writer.

INTRODUCTION

A seminal thinker and a principal figure in the development of Western philosophy, Plato is the progenitor of philosophical idealism and, as many scholars contend, the preeminent Greek writer of prose. Ralph Waldo Emerson more forcefully stated that "Plato is philosophy, and philosophy, Plato." Plato's theory of Ideas, the doctrine that permeated his thought and all his writings, specifies a class of immutable entities, termed alternatively Ideas or Forms, existing in an unseen, eternal realm. These Ideas are the foundation of reality and render the material world simply the reflection of the eternal realm. His philosophy, which stresses ethics and reason, is not a distinctly formulated system but rather a general representation of his thought, expressed in the form of dialogues that are praised for their artistic craftsmanship and poetic character.

Biographical Information

A citizen of Athens and descendant of a distinguished family of statesmen, Plato was born about 428 B.C. and lived during a period of political tumult marked by the death of the great Athenian statesman Pericles in 429 B.C. and the strife of the Peloponnesian War, which lasted from 431 to 404 B.C. The era also exhibited remarkable cultural vitality, including the accomplishments of the great dramatists Sophocles, Euripides, and Aristophanes, of whom Plato was a younger contemporary. Plato abandoned his early political ambitions upon the death of Socrates (who had been condemned and imprisoned for impiety and for corrupting youth) in 399 B.C., which proved to him that politics was not a suitable arena for philosophers. Afterwards Plato traveled in Greece, Egypt, Italy, and Sicily. Around 387 B.C. Plato established the Academy, a school dedicated to philosophical and scientific research as well as the study of mathematics and jurisprudence. Considered the predecessor of the modern university, the Academy, located outside Athens, developed into one of the great philosophical schools of antiquity, lasting more than 900 years until it was suppressed with other pagan schools by the Byzantine emperor Justinian in 529 A.D. In 367 B.C. Plato was invited at the request of his friend Dion to Syracuse to tutor Dionysius II in the ways of the philosopher-king described in the Republic, but the plan failed, and Plato spent the rest of his life presiding over his Academy.

Major Works

All of Plato's known works, including the *Apology*, thirty-four dialogues of varying length, and thirteen epistles, are extant. However, a number of the dialogues, such as the *Alcibiades II, Hipparchus, Rivals, Theages, Clitophon,* and *Minos,* and most of the epistles, are presumed spurious for reasons of style and content. Although all of Plato's dialogues feature a Socratic style of thought called the dialectic method—a cooperative philosophical investigation in which participants search and learn by positing and critically examining conclusions—they generally are arranged according to early, middle, and late periods. The early period comprises the *Apology, Crito, Charmides, Laches, Euthyphro, Hippias Minor, Hippias Major, Ion,* and *Lysis.* These dialogues discuss such general moral terms as courage, justice, or virtue. Discussions are brief and free of dogmatism and the use of myth. In these works Socrates is the central interlocutor who criticizes others' opinions without providing constructive solutions. Works of the middle period include the *Gorgias, Protagoras, Euthydemus, Cratylus, Phaedo, Republic, Meno, Alcibiades I, Menexenus, Phaedrus, Symposium, Theaetetus,* and *Parmenides.* These dialogues discuss more complex concepts but use a more positive method of teaching that provides answers and employs myths. Socrates remains the chief speaker, but other interlocutors are present. The *Symposium* and the *Protagoras* are generally recognized as Plato's finest dramatic pieces, whereas the *Republic* is regarded as Plato's greatest work because it crystallizes Platonic thought. The latter dialogue illustrates Plato's theory of Ideas by using the so-called "allegory of the cave," which correlates the relation between particulars and Ideas to the relation between shadows and the material objects that cast them, noting that an inability to comprehend reality is the result in either case. Although its declared subject is justice as administered by the individual and the state, the *Republic* also contains Plato's theory of art, which calls for the banishment of poets from his utopian state since he considers art—including music, literature, and visual arts—a dangerous medium. His *Symposium* suggests that love, or Eros, attracts the soul to the Ideas, particularly to the supreme Idea of the Good that reigns over all Ideas, as the means to sharing in immortality. The later dialogues comprise the *Sophist, Politicus, Timaeus, Critias, Philebus, Laws,* and *Epinomis.* Socrates is less prominent or entirely absent in these dialogues, and the focus is on topics that scholars believe either originated entirely from Plato or arose from discussions at the Academy. These rather technical works, in which myths are fewer and less important, are also nearly continuous monologues.

Critical Reception

Although his philosophy is sometimes considered unsystematic and flawed, Plato remains an integral source of philosophic inspiration. He has most closely been associated with the development of philosophic idealism, but his words have been interpreted at one time or another as the source for all philosophies. "Nearly all the themes of philosophizing converge in Plato and spring from Plato," Karl Jaspers has written, "as though philosophy began and ended with him. Everything that preceded Platonic thinking seems to serve it, and everything that came after seems to interpret it." Critics agree that his dialogues are literary masterpieces and note that his dialogues exemplify the best of Greek prose. His early style is light and graceful, rhythmically imitative of natural conversation, whereas his later style is elaborate, highly mannered and copious, and often marked by archaic, poetical, or technical diction. With a rich vocabulary and command of rhetorical and colloquial language, Plato created masterful character sketches and individuated voices for his interlocutors, most of whom were historical persons. Despite this view, the artistic aspect of Plato's work is far overshadowed by the scholastic regard for the intellectual power and the pervasive influence of his thought, as evinced in Alfred North Whitehead's famous statement: "The safest general characterization of the European philosophical tradition is that it consists of a series of footnotes to Plato."

(For further information, see *Classical and Medieval Literature Criticism,* Vol. 8; *Dictionary of Literary Biography,* Vol. 176; *DISCovering Authors; DISCovering Authors: British; DISCovering Authors: Canadian; DISCovering Authors Modules: Most-studied Authors Module.*)

CRITICAL COMMENTARY

JOHN OF SALISBURY

SOURCE: John of Salisbury, in his *The Metalogicon of John of Salisbury: A Twelfth-Century Defense of the Verbal and Logical Arts of the Trivium*, translated by Daniel D. McGarry, 1955. Reprint by University of California Press, 1962, 305 p.

[*An English philosopher and prelate, John of Salisbury is regarded as one of the key figures in medieval intellectual history. His writings include* The Polycraticus, *which addresses political and philosophical issues, and* The Metalogicon *(1159), regarded as an eloquent defense of Aristotelian logic against dogmatism. In the following excerpt from the latter work, he discusses Plato's ideas on logic, intuitive understanding, and types of existence.*]

According to Apuleius, Augustine, and Isidore, the credit for completing philosophy belongs to Plato. For to physics and ethics, which Pythagoras and Socrates respectively had already fully taught, Plato added logic. By the latter, when the causes of things and the bases of the *mores* are being discussed, the real [proving] force of arguments may be determined. Plato, however, did not organize logic into a scientific art. Use came first, for here, as elsewhere, precept followed practice....

Just as reason transcends sense perception, so it, in turn, is surpassed by [intuitive] understanding, as Plato observes in his *Republic*. For [intuitive] understanding actually attains what reason investigates. [Intuitive understanding] enters into the very labors of reason, and treasures up the preparatory gains of reason unto wisdom. It is, in fact, the highest power of a spiritual nature. Besides comprehending what is human, it also contemplates the divine causes behind all reasons within the natural powers of its perception. For there are some divine reasons which utterly exceed, not merely human, but even angelic comprehension. And there are some divine truths, in like manner, which become either more fully or less fully known to us, according to the decree of the divine dispensation. [Intuitive understanding], according to Plato, "is possessed only by God and a few select individuals."...

In explaining the difference between things which really exist and those which only seem to exist, Plato states that intelligibles are impervious both to external incursion and to internal passion. They cannot be injured by any force, nor can they be wasted away by the wear and tear of time. Rather, they persevere continually in the unimpaired vigor of their [impregnable] state. Hence they truly exist [in a strict sense], and are second only to the first essence in their right to existence. This is the sure, secure state that is denoted by a substantive word, when the latter is correctly used. Temporal things seem to exist, since they are representative images of such intelligibles. But temporal things are not fully worthy of being called by substantive names, for they pass away with time. They are forever changing, and vanish like smoke. As Plato observes in his *Timaeus,* "They take flight without even waiting to receive names." Plato divides true existence into three categories, which he posits as the principles of [all] things: namely, "God, matter, and idea." For these are, by their nature, unchangeable. God is absolutely immutable, whereas the other two are in a way unchangeable, even though they mutually differ in their effects. Coming into matter, forms dispose it, and render it in a way subject to change. On the other hand, forms themselves are also to some extent modified by contact with matter, and, as Boethius observes in his *Arithmetic*, are [thereby] transformed into a state of mutable instability....

WILHELM WINDELBAND

SOURCE: Wilhelm Windelband, "The Systematic Period," in his *History of Philosophy*, translated by James H. Tufts, revised edition, The Macmillan Company, 1901. pp. 99-154.

[*Windelband was an eminent German Neo-Kantian philosopher whose writings include the influential* Geschichte der Philosophie *(1892; A History of Philosophy). In the following excerpt from the revised 1901 edition of that work, he presents a general overview of Plato's philosophy.*]

The origin and development of the Platonic *doctrine of Ideas* is one of the most difficult and involved, as well as one of the most effective and fruitful, processes in the entire history of European thought, and the task of apprehending it properly is made still more difficult

> **Principal English Translations**
>
> *The Works of Plato Abridg'd: With an Account of His Life, Philosophy, Morals, and Politicks* [translated by various individuals; from the 1699 French edition of M. Dacier] 1701
> *The Works of Plato* [translated by Thomas Taylor and Floyer Sydenham] 1804
> *The Theaetetus of Plato* [translated by Lewis Campbell] 1861
> *The Sophistes of Plato* [translated by R. W. Mackay] 1868
> *The Dialogues of Plato* [translated by B. Jowett] 1871
> *Gorgias* [translated by E. M. Cope] 1883
> *Plato, with an English Translation.* 12 vols. [translated by various individuals] 1914-35.
> *Thirteen Epistles of Plato* [translated by L. A. Post] 1925
> *Plato: Timaeus and Critias* [translated by A. E. Taylor] 1929
> *The Laws* [translated by A. E. Taylor] 1934
> *Parmenides* [translated by A. E. Taylor] 1934
> *Cratylus* [translated by H. N. Fowler] 1937
> *The Republic of Plato* [translated by F. M. Cornford] 1945
> *Phaedrus* [translated by R. Hackforth] 1952
> *Plato's Statesman* [translated by J. B. Skemp] 1952
> *Symposium* [translated by W. Hamilton] 1952
> *The Last Days of Socrates: Euthyphro, The Apology, Crito, Phaedo* [translated by Hugh Tredennick] 1954
> *Protogoras and Meno* [translated by W. K. C. Guthrie] 1956
> *Plato: The Collected Dialogues, Including the Letters* [edited by Edith Hamilton and Huntington Cairns; translated by various individuals] 1961
> *The Republic* [translated by G. M. A. Grube] 1974
> *Five Dialogues* [translated by G. M. A. Grube; includes *Euthyphro, Apology, Crito, Meno,* and *Phaedo*] 1981
> *Phaedrus* [translated by C. J. Rowe] 1986
> *Early Socratic Dialogues* [edited by Trevor J. Saunders; translated by various individuals; includes *Ion, Laches, Lysis, Charmides, Hippias Major, Hippias Minor,* and *Euthydemus*] 1987
> *Theaetetus* [translated by Robin A. H. Waterfield] 1987
> *Symposium* [translated by Alexander Nehamas and Paul Woodruff] 1989

by the literary form in which it has been transmitted. The Platonic dialogues show the philosophy of their author in process of constant re-shaping: their composition extended through half a century. Since, however, the order in which the individual dialogues arose has not been transmitted to us and cannot be established absolutely from external characteristics, pragmatic hypotheses based on the logical connections of thought must be called to our aid.

1. In the first place there is no question that the opposition between Socrates and the Sophists formed the starting-point for Platonic thought. Plato's first writings were dedicated to an affectionate and in the main, certainly, a faithful presentation of the Socratic doctrine of virtue. To this he attached a polemic against the Sophistic doctrines of society and knowledge marked by increasing keenness, but also by an increasing tendency toward establishing his own view upon an independent basis. The Platonic criticism of the Sophistic theories, however, proceeded essentially from the Socratic postulate. It admitted fully, in the spirit of Protagoras, the relativity of all knowledge gained through perception, but it found just in this the inadequacy of the Sophistic theory for a true science of ethics. The knowledge which is necessary for virtue cannot consist in opinions as they arise from the changing states of motion in subject and object, nor can it consist of a rational consideration and legitimation of such opinions gained by perception; it must have a wholly different source and wholly different objects. Of the corporeal world and its changing states—Plato held to this view of Protagoras in its entirety—there is no science, but only perceptions and opinions; it is accordingly an *incorporeal world* that forms the object of science, and this world must exist side by side with the corporeal world as independently as does knowledge side by side with opinion.

Here we have for the first time the claim of an *immaterial reality*, brought forward expressly and with full consciousness, and it is clear that this springs from the ethical need for a knowledge that is raised above all ideas gained by sense-perception. The assumption of immateriality did not at first have as its aim, for Plato, the explanation of phenomena: its end was rather to assure an object for ethical knowledge. The idealistic metaphysics, therefore, in its first draft builds entirely upon a new foundation of its own, without any reference to the work of earlier science that had been directed toward investigating and understanding phenomena; it is an *immaterial Eleatism*, which seeks true Being in the Ideas, without troubling itself about the world of generation and occurrence, which it leaves to perception and opinion.

To avoid numerous misunderstandings we must, nevertheless, expressly point out that the Platonic conception of immateriality (*asvmatou*) is in nowise coincident with that of the spiritual or psychical, as might be easily assumed from the modern mode of thinking. For the Platonic conception the particular psychical functions belong to the world of Becoming, precisely as do those of the body and of other corporeal things; and on the other hand, in the true reality the "forms" or "shapes" of corporeality, the Ideas of sensuous qualities and relations, find a place precisely as do those of the spiritual relations. The identification of spirit or mind and incorporeality, the division of the world into mind and matter, is un-Platonic. The incorporeal world which Plato teaches is not yet the spiritual.

Rather, the Ideas are, for Plato, *that incorporeal Being which is known through conceptions*. Since, that is, the conceptions in which Socrates found the essence of science are not given as such in the reality that can be perceived, they must form a "second," "other" reality, different from the former, existing by itself, and this immaterial reality is related to the material, as Being to Becoming, as the abiding to the changing, as the simple to the manifold—in short, as the world of Parmenides to that of Heraclitus. The object of ethical knowledge, cognised through general conceptions, is that which "is" in the true sense: the ethical, the logical, and the physical arch (ground or first principle) are the same. This is the point in which all lines of earlier philosophy converge.

2. If the Ideas are to be "something other" than the perceptible world, knowledge of them through conceptions cannot be found in the content of perception, for they cannot be contained in it. With this turn of thought, which corresponds to the sharper separation of the two worlds, the Platonic doctrine of knowledge becomes much more rationalistic than that of Democritus, and goes also decidedly beyond that of Socrates; for while the latter had developed the universal out of the opinions and perceptions of individuals inductively, and had found it as the common content in these opinions and perceptions, Plato does not conceive of the process of induction in this analytical manner, but sees in perceptions only the suggestions or promptings with the help of which the soul *bethinks itself* of the conceptions, of the knowledge of the Ideas.

Plato expressed this rationalistic principle in the form that *philosophical knowledge is recollection* . . . . He showed in the example of the Pythagorean proposition that mathematical knowledge is not extracted from sense-perception, but that sense-perception offers only the opportunity on occasion of which the soul recollects the knowledge already present within her, that is, knowledge that has purely rational validity. He points out that the pure mathematical relations are not present in corporeal reality; on the contrary, the notion of these relations arises in us when similar figures of perception offer but the occasion therefor, and he extended this observation, which is completely applicable to mathematical knowledge, to the sum total of scientific knowledge.

That this reflection upon what is rationally necessary should be conceived of as recollection is connected with the fact that Plato, as little as any of his predecessors, recognises a creative activity of the consciousness, which produces its content. This is a general limit for all Greek psychology; the content for ideas must somehow be given to the "soul"; hence, if the Ideas are not given in perception, and the soul nevertheless finds them in herself on occasion of perception, she must have already *received* these Ideas in some way or other. For this act of reception, however, Plato finds only the mythical representation, that before the earthly life the souls have *beheld* the pure forms of reality in the incorporeal world itself, that the perception of similar corporeal things calls the remembrance back to those forms forgotten in the corporeal earthly life, and that from this awakes the *philosophical impulse*, the *love of the Ideas* . . . , by which the soul becomes raised again to the knowledge of that true reality. Here, too, as in the case of Democritus, it is shown that the entire ancient rationalism could form no idea of the process of thought except after the analogy of sensuous perception, particularly that of the sense of sight.

What Socrates in his doctrine of the formation of conceptions had designated as induction, became transformed, therefore, for Plato, into an intuition that proceeds by recollecting . . . , into reflection upon a higher and purer perception (*Anschauung*). This pure perception, however, yields a plurality of ideas corresponding to the multiplicity of objects which occasion such perceptions, and from this grows the further task for science to know also the *relations of the Ideas to each other*. This is a second step of Plato's beyond Socrates, and is especially important for the reason that it led shortly to the apprehension of the *logical relations between conceptions*. It was principally the relations of the subordination and coordination of concepts to which Plato became attentive. The division of the class-concepts or logical genera into their species played a great part in his teaching. The possibility or impossibility of the union of particular conceptions is brought more exactly into consideration, and as a methodical aid he recommended the hypothetical method of discussion, which aims to examine a tentatively proposed conception by developing all the possible consequences that would follow from the possibility of its union with conceptions already known.

These logical operations taken as a whole, by means

of which the Ideas and their relations to one another . . . were to be found, Plato denoted by the name *dialectic*. What is found in his writings concerning it has throughout a methodological character, but is not properly logical.

3. The doctrine of knowledge as recollection stood, however, in closest connection with Plato's conception of the *relation of Ideas to the world of phenomena*. Between the higher world . . . and the lower world . . . , between what *is* and what is in process of Becoming, he found that relation of similarity which exists between archetypes . . . and their copies or images. . . . In this, too, a strong influence of mathematics upon the Platonic philosophy is disclosed: as the Pythagoreans had already designated things as imitations of numbers, so Plato found that individual things always correspond to their class-concepts only to a certain degree, and that the class-concept is a logical ideal which none of its empirical examples comes up to. He expressed this by the conception of *imitation*. . . . It was thus at the same time established that that second world, that of the incorporeal Ideas, was to be regarded as the higher, the more valuable, the more primitive world.

Yet this mode of representing the matter gave rather a determination of their respective values than a view that was usable for metaphysical consideration: hence Plato sought for still other designations of the relation. The logical side of the matter, according to which the Idea as class-concept or species represents the total unitary extent or compass, of which the individual things denote but a part, appears in the expression *participation* . . . , which means that the individual thing but partakes in the universal essence of the Idea; and the changing process of this partaking is emphasized by the conception of *presence*. . . . The class-concept or species is present in the thing so long as the latter possesses the qualities which dwell in the Idea. The Ideas come and go, and as these now communicate themselves to things and now again withdraw, the qualities in these things which are like the Ideas are successively changed to the eye of perception.

The precise designation of this relation was, for Plato, an object of only secondary interest, provided only the difference between the world of Ideas and the corporeal world, and the dependence of the latter upon the former, were recognised. Most important and sufficient for him was the conviction that by means of conceptions that knowledge which virtue needs of what truly and really *is*, could be won.

4. But the logico-metaphysical interest which Plato grafted upon the Socratic doctrine of knowledge carried him far beyond the master as regards the contents of this doctrine. The general characteristics which he developed for the essence of the Ideas applied to *all class-concepts,* and the immaterial world was therefore peopled with the archetypes of the entire world of experience. So many class-concepts, so many Ideas; for Plato, too, there are countless "forms." In so far criticism [particularly Aristotle in his *Metaphysics*] was right in saying that Plato's world of Ideas was the world of perception thought over again in conception.

In fact, according to the first draft of the Platonic philosophy, there are Ideas of everything possible, of things, qualities, and relations; of the good and the beautiful as well as of the bad and the ugly. Since the Idea is defined methodologically, in a purely formal way, as class-concept, every class-concept whatever belongs to the higher world of pure forms; and in the dialogue **Parmenides,** not only was Plato's attention called by a man schooled in the Eleatic Sophistic doctrine to all kinds of dialectical difficulties which inhere in the logical relation of the one Idea to its many copies, but he was also rallied, spitefully enough, with the thought of all the foul companions that would be met in his world of pure conceptual forms.

Plato's philosophy had no principle that could serve as a weapon against such an objection, nor is there in the dialogues any intimation that he had attempted to announce a definite criterion for the *selection* of those class-concepts that were to be regarded as Ideas, as constituents of the higher incorporeal world. Nor do the examples which he adduces permit such a principle to be recognised; we can only say that it seems as if in course of time he continually emphasised more strongly the attributes expressing worth (as the good and the beautiful), the mathematical relations (greatness and smallness, numerical determinations, etc.), and the types of species in the organic world, while, on the contrary, he no longer reckoned among the Ideas mere concepts of relation, especially negative notions and things made by human art.

5. Our knowledge of the *systematic connection and order* which Plato intended to affirm in the realm of Ideas remains ultimately as obscure as that in regard to the preceding point. Urgent as he was to establish co-ordination and subordination among the conceptions, the thought of a logically arranged pyramid of conceptions which must culminate in the conception that was most general and poorest in content seems not to have been carried out. A very problematical attempt to set up a limited number (five) of most general conceptions is presented in the **Sophist.** But these attempts, which tend toward the Aristotelian doctrine of the categories, are not to be traced back with certainty to Plato himself.

With him we find, rather, only the doctrine presented

in the *Philebus,* as well as in the *Republic,* that the *Idea of the Good* is the highest, embracing, ruling, and realising all others. Plato defines this Idea as regards its content as little as did Socrates; he determined it only by means of the relation, that it should represent in its content the highest *absolute end of all reality,* of the incorporeal as of the corporeal. The subordination of the other Ideas to this highest Idea is accordingly not the *logical* subordination of a particular under the general, but the *teleological* of the means to the end.

In the latest period of his philosophising, concerning which we have only intimations in the *Laws* and in critical notices of Aristotle, and in the teachings of his nearest successors, the imperfection of this solution of the logical problem seems to have led Plato to the unfortunate thought of developing the *system of Ideas* according to the method of the *Pythagorean number-theory.* The Pythagoreans also, to be sure, had the purpose of attaching the abiding arrangements of things symbolically to the development of the number series. But that was only a makeshift, because they had as yet no idea of the logical arrangement of conceptions: hence, when Plato, in connection with his other thoughts, fell back upon this makeshift, designated the Idea of the Good as the ... One, and attempted to derive from it the duality ... of the Infinite or Indefinite, and the Measure, and from this, further, the other Ideas in such a way as to present a series of the conditioning and the conditioned, neither this deplorable construction nor the fact that men like Speusippus, Xenocrates, Philippus, and Archytas undertook to carry it out in detail, would be worth more particular mention, were not this just the point to which the speculation of the Neo-Pythagoreans and the Neo-Platonists became attached. For by this gradation ... the world of true reality, the *division in the conception of reality,* which had developed out of the opposition between perception and thought, became *multiplied,* and thus dualism was again abolished. For when to the One, or the Idea of the Good, was ascribed the highest absolute reality, and to the various strata of the world of Ideas, a reality of constantly decreasing worth in proportion as they were removed from the One in the system in numbers, there arose from this a *scale of realities* which extended from the One down to the lowest reality,—that of the corporeal world. Fantastic as this thought may be, it yet evinced its force and influence in the development of thought, even to the threshold of modern philosophy. Its power, however, lies doubtless in all cases in its amalgamation of attributes of worth with these various grades of reality.

6. While as metaphysics, the doctrine of Ideas fell into such serious difficulties, it was carried out in an extremely happy, simple, and transparent manner in that domain which formed its proper home,—that of ethics. For the systematic elaboration of this, however, Plato needed a *psychology,* and that, too, of another sort than the psychology which had arisen in previous science, out of the presuppositions of natural philosophy, and with the aid of individual perceptions or opinions. When, in contrast with this, he developed his psychology from the postulates of the doctrine of Ideas, the result was of course a purely metaphysical theory which stood and fell with its postulate, yet it was at the same time, by reason of the import of the doctrine of Ideas, a first attempt to understand the psychical life from within, and in accordance with its internal character and articulation.

The conception of the *soul* or mind was in itself a difficulty in the dualism of the doctrine of Ideas. For Plato, also, "soul" was on the one hand the living element, that which is moved of itself and moves other things, and on the other hand, that which perceives, knows, and wills. As principle of life and of motion, the soul belongs, therefore, to the lower world of Becoming, and in this it remains when it perceives and directs its desires toward objects of the senses. But this same soul, nevertheless, by its true knowledge of the Ideas, becomes partaker in the higher reality of abiding Being. Hence it must be assigned a *position between the two worlds*—not the timeless, unchanged essence of the Ideas, but a vitality which survives change; *i.e. immortality.* Here, for the first time, personal immortality is brought forward by Plato as a part of philosophic teaching. Of the proofs which the *Phoedo* adduces for this, those are most in accord with the spirit of the system which reason from the soul's knowledge of Ideas to its relationship with eternity; in correspondence with the form of the system is the dialectic false conclusion that the soul cannot be or become dead, because its essential characteristic is life; the most tenable of the arguments is the reference to the unity and substantiality which the soul evinces in ruling the body.

In consequence of this intermediate position the soul must bear in itself the traits of both worlds; there must be in its essence something which corresponds to the world of Ideas, and something which corresponds to the world of perception. The former is the *rational nature...,* the seat of knowledge and of the virtue which corresponds to it; in the latter, the irrational nature, Plato made a further distinction of two elements,—the nobler, which inclines towards the Reason, and the lower, which resists it. The nobler he found in the ardent, spirited Will (*Spirit...*), the lower in the sensuous desire (*Appetite...*). Thus Reason, Spirit, and Appetite are the three forms of activity of the soul, the classes or species ... of its states.

These fundamental psychological conceptions which had thus grown out of considerations of ethical worth are employed by Plato to set forth the moral destiny of the individual. The fettering of the soul to the body is at once a consequence and a punishment of the sensuous appetite. Plato extends the immortal existence of the soul equally beyond the two boundaries of the earthly life. The sin for the sake of which the soul is ensnared in the world of sense is to be sought in a preexistent state; its destiny in the hereafter will depend upon how far it has freed itself in the earthly life from the sensuous appetite, and turned to its higher vocation—knowledge of the Ideas. But inasmuch as the ultimate goal of the soul appears to be to strip off the sensuous nature, the three forms of activity are designated also as *parts of the soul*. In the **Timoeus** Plato even portrays the process of the formation of the soul out of these parts, and retains immortality for the rational part only.

It is already clear from these changing determinations that the relation of these three fundamental forms of the psychical life to the none too strongly emphasised unity of the soul's nature was not clearly thought out; nor is it possible to give to these conceptions formed from the ethical need the significance of purely psychological distinctions, such as have since been made.

7. But at all events there followed in this way, from the doctrine of the two worlds, a negative *morals* that would fly from the world, and in which the withdrawal from the world of sense and the spiritualisation of life were praised as ideals of wisdom. It is not only the **Phoedo** that breathes this earnest disposition in its portrayal of the death of Socrates; the same ethical theory prevails in such dialogues as the **Gorgias**, the **Theoetetus**, and, in part, the **Republic**. But in Plato's own nature the heavy blood of the thinker was associated with the light heart-beat of the artist, and thus while his philosophy lured him into the realm of bodiless forms, the whole charm of Hellenic beauty was living and active within him. Strongly as he therefore combated root and branch the theory of Aristippus, which would fain regard man's strivings as satisfied with sensuous pleasure, it was nevertheless his opinion that the Idea of the Good becomes realised even in the world of sense. Joy in the beautiful, pleasure in the sensuous imitation of the Idea, painless because free from the element of wishing, the development of knowledge and practical artistic skill, the intelligent understanding of the mathematical relations which measure empirical reality, and the appropriate ordering of the individual life,—all these were valued by him as at least preparatory stages and participations in that highest good which consists in knowledge of the Ideas, and of the highest among them, the Idea of the Good. In the **Symposium** and in the **Philebus** he has given expression to this his estimate of the goods of life.

This same thought, that ethical values and standards must illumine the whole circuit of human life, was used in another form by Plato in that presentation of the system of the virtues which he developed in the **Republic.** Here he showed that each part of the soul has a definite task to fulfil, and so a perfection of its own to reach: the rational part, in *wisdom* . . . , the spirited . . . in *energy of will* (courage . . .), the appetitive . . . in *self-control* (moderation . . .); that, however, in addition to all these, as the virtue of the soul as a whole, there must be the right relation of these parts, complete *uprightness* (justice . . .).

The true significance, however, of these *four cardinal virtues,* is first unfolded upon a higher domain, that of politics.

8. The tendency of the doctrine of Ideas, directed as it was toward the general and the universal, exhibited its most perfect operation in the aspect now to be noticed, viz. that the ethical ideal of the Platonic philosophy lay not in the ability and happiness of the individual, but in the ethical perfection of the *species*. True to the logical principle of the doctrine of Ideas, that which truly *is* in the ethical sense, is not the individual man, but mankind, and the form in which this truly existent humanity appears is the organic union of individuals in the *state*. The ethical ideal becomes for Plato the *political*, and in the midst of the time which saw the dissolution of Greek political life, and in opposition to those doctrines which proclaimed only the principle of individual happiness, he raised the conception of the state to an all-controlling height.

He considered the state, however, not from the side of its empirical origin, but in reference to its task, viz. that of presenting in large the ideal of humanity, and of educating the citizen to that particular virtue which makes him truly happy. Convinced that his project could be realised, with force if necessary, he wove into its fabric not only features which he approved of the then-existing Greek political life, in particular those of the aristocratic Doric constitutions, but also all the ideals for whose fulfilment he hoped from the right formation of public life.

If the *ideal state* is to present man in large, it must consist of the three parts which correspond to the three parts of the soul,—the *teaching class*, the *warrior class*, and the *working class*. It belongs to the first class alone, that of the cultured . . ., to guide the state and to rule . . . to give laws and to watch over their observance. The virtue proper to this class is wisdom, insight into that which is for the advantage of the whole, and which is demanded by the ethical aim of the whole. To support this class there is the second class, that of the public officials . . . , which has to evince the virtue of the fearless performance of duty . . . as it maintains the order of the state within and without. It is, however, obedience which holds the desires in check, self-control . . . , that becomes the great mass of the people, the artisans and farmers . . . , who have to care for providing for the external means of the states by their labour and industry. Only when each class thus does its duty and maintains its appropriate virtue does the nature of the state correspond to the ideal of justice. . . .

The principle of *aristocracy in education,* which is of decisive importance in the Platonic ideal of the state, appears most clearly in the provision that for the great mass of the third class only the ordinary ability of practical life is claimed, and in that this is regarded as sufficient for their purpose, while the education, which the state has the right and duty to take in hand itself in order to train its citizens for its own ends, is given only to the two other classes. By means of a constantly repeated process of selection continued from birth to the late years, the government causes the two upper classes to be continually renewed, strata by strata; and in order that no individual interest may remain to hold back these classes, who are properly the organs of the whole body, in the fulfilment of their task, they are to renounce family life and private property. Their lot is that of education by the state, absence of family relations, community of life and of goods. He who is to live for the ends of the whole, for the ethical education of the people, must not be bound to the individual by any personal interest. To this thought, which found its historic realisation in the sacerdotal state of the mediaeval hierarchy, is limited whatever of communism, community of wives, etc., men have professed to discover in the Platonic teaching. The great Idealist carries out to its extreme consequences the thought that the end of human life consists in moral education, and that the entire organisation of a community must be arranged for this sole end.

9. With this a new relation between the world of ideas and the world of phenomena was discovered, and one which corresponded most perfectly to the spirit of the Platonic system: the Idea of the Good disclosed itself as the task, as the *end* . . . , which the phenomenon of human life in society has to fulfil. This discovery became of decisive importance for the final form taken by Plato's metaphysical system.

For, as first projected, the doctrine of Ideas had been precisely as incompetent as the Eleatic doctrine of Being to explain empirical reality. The class-concepts were held to give knowledge of the absolute reality, which, purely for itself, simple and changeless, without origin and imperishable, forms a world by itself, and, as incorporeal, is separated from the world where things arise. Hence, as was demonstrated in the dialogue the *Sophist,* in a keen polemic against the doctrine of Ideas, this doctrine formed no principle of motion, and therefore no explanation of facts, because it excluded from itself all motion and change.

But however little Plato's interests may have been directed toward this end, the conception of the Idea as true Being ultimately demanded, nevertheless, that the phenomenon should be regarded, not only as something other, something imitative, something that participated, but also as something dependent. It demanded that the *Idea be regarded as cause of occurrence and change.* . . . But that which is itself absolutely unchangeable and immovable, and excludes every particular function from itself, cannot be a cause in the mechanical sense, but only in the sense that it presents the *end* for the sake of which the occurrence takes place. Here for the first time the relation between the two worlds of Being and Becoming . . . is fully defined; all change and occurrence exists for the sake of the Idea; the Idea is the *final cause* of phenomena.

This foundation of *teleological metaphysics* Plato gives in the **Philebus** and in the middle books of the **Republic,** and adds at once a further culminating thought by introducing as the final cause of all occurrence, the world of Ideas as a whole, but in particular the highest Idea, to which all the rest are subordinate in the sense of means to end, — the *Idea of the Good.* This, referring to Anaxagoras, he designates as the *World-reason* . . . , or as the *deity.*

Side by side with this *motif* taken from Anaxagoras, another of a Pythagorean nature appears with increasing force in a later form of the doctrine of Ideas, a *motif* in accordance with which the imperfection of the phenomenon is pointed out as in contrast with the true Being. This inadequacy, however, could not be derived from Being itself, and just as Leucippus, in order to understand plurality and motion, had declared that in addition to the Being of Parmenides the Not-being was also "real," or "actual," and existent, so Plato saw himself forced, with like logical consistency, for the purpose of explaining phenomena and the inadequacy which they show with reference to the Ideas, to assume beside the world of Being or of cause, *i.e.* the world of Ideas and the Idea of the Good, a *secondary or accessory cause* . . . in that which has not the attribute of Being. Indeed, the parallelism in the two thinkers goes so far that this secondary cause, which is not Being . . . , is for Plato precisely the same as for Leucippus and Philolaus, viz. *empty space.*

Space was then for Plato the "nothing" out of which the world of phenomena is formed for the sake of the Idea of the Good, or of the deity. This process of formation, however, consists in *taking on mathematical form;* hence Plato taught in the *Philebus* that the world of perception was a "mixture" of the "unlimited" (*apeirou*), *i.e.* space, and of "limitation" . . . , *i.e.* the mathematical forms; and that the cause of this mixture, the highest, divine world-principle, was the Idea of the Good. Space assumes mathematical formation in order to become like the world of Ideas.

The importance which mathematics had possessed from the outset in the development of Plato's thought finds thus at last its metaphysical expression. The mathematical structures are the intermediate link, by means of which empty space, which *is* not, is able to imitate in phenomena the pure "forms" of the world of Ideas. Hence mathematical knowledge . . . , as well as purely philosophical knowledge . . . , has to do with an abiding essence . . . , and is therefore comprised together with this, as rational knowledge . . . , and set over against knowledge of phenomena. . . . But occupying thus an intermediate place, it takes only the position of a last stage in the preparation for the wisdom of the "rulers," as set forth in the system of education in the *Republic.*

10. The metaphysical preliminaries were now given for what Plato ultimately projected in the *Timoeus;* viz. *a sketch or rough draught of the philosophy of Nature,* for which, of course, true to his epistemological principle, he could not claim the worth of certainty, but only that of probability. Since, that is, he was not in a position to carry through dialectically, and establish in conceptions this project of explaining occurrence from the world's end or purpose, Plato gave an exposition of his *teleological view of Nature* in mythical form only,—a view intended only as an opinion, and not as science.

This view, nevertheless, takes a position sharply *opposed to the mechanical explanation of Nature,* and, as this latter is set forth, we can scarcely suppose that Plato had any other doctrine in mind than that of Democritus. In opposition to the theory which makes all kinds of worlds arise here and there from the "accidental" (meaning "purposeless" or "undersigned") meeting of "that which is in unordered, lawless motion," and perish again, he sets forth his own theory that there is only this one, most perfect and most beautiful cosmos, unitary in nature and unique as regards its kind, and that its origin can be traced only to a reason acting according to ends.

If, then, it is desired to form a theory concerning this origin, the ground of the world of phenomena must be sought in the telic relation of this world to the Ideas. This relation Plato expressed by the idea of a *"world-forming God"* (. . . demiurge) who formed or shaped out that which is not Being, *i.e.* space, "with regard to the Ideas." In this connection the Not-being is characterised as the indefinite plasticity which takes up all corporeal forms into itself . . . , and yet at the same time forms the ground for the fact that the Ideas find no pure representation in it. This counter-working of the accessory cause, or of the individual accessory causes, Plato designates as *mechanical necessity.* . . . he takes up then the conception of Democritus as a particular *moment* into his physics, in order to explain by it what cannot be understood teleologically. Divine activity according to ends and natural necessity are set over against each other as explaining principles, on the one hand for the perfect, and on the other hand for the imperfect in the world of phenomena. Ethical dualism passes over from metaphysics into physical theory.

The characteristic fundamental thought of the Platonic as contrasted with the Atomistic physics is, that while Democritus conceived of the movements of the whole as mechanical resultants of the original states of motion of the individual atoms, Plato, on the contrary, regarded the *ordered motion of the universe as a whole,* as the primitive unit, and derived every individual change or occurrence from this purposively determined whole. From this thought sprang the strange construction of the conception of the *world-soul,* which Plato characterised as the single principle of all motions, and thus also of all determinations of form, and likewise of all activities of perception and ideation in the world. In fantastic, obscure exposition he brought forward as the mathematical "division" of this world-soul, his astronomical theory, which was in the main closely connected with that of the younger Pythagoreans, but which was less advanced than theirs in its assumption that the earth stood still. The main criterion in this process of division was the distinction between that which remains like itself . . . and that which changes . . . ,—a contrast in which we easily recognise the Pythagorean contrast between the perfect stellar world and the imperfect terrestrial world.

A similar continuation of Pythagorean doctrine is contained in the Platonic *Timus,* with reference also to the purely mathematical construction of the corporeal world. Here, too, the four elements are characterised according to the simple, regular, geometrical solids. But it is expressly taught that these *consist of triangular surfaces,* and those, too, of a right-angled sort, which are in part equilateral, in part so formed that the shorter side is half the length of the hypotenuse. The *limiting surfaces* of these solids,—tetrahedron, cube, etc.,—may be thought of as composed of such right-angled triangles, and Plato would have the essence of space-filling, *i.e.* density or solidity of bodies, regarded as consisting in this composition of these limiting surfaces. By thus conceiving of physical bodies as purely mathematical structures, the metaphysical thought of the *Philebus* found expression also in physics,—the thought, namely, that the phenomenal world is a limitation of space formed in imitation of the Ideas. These triangular surfaces, which were, moreover, conceived of as being indivisible, have a suspicious similarity with the atomic forms . . . of Democritus. . . .

WILLIAM GEORGE DE BURGH

SOURCE: William George de Burgh, "The Greatness of Athens," in his *The Legacy of the Ancient World*, revised edition, Penguin Books, 1961, pp. 134-88.

[*De Burgh was an English historian and philosopher whose writings include* Towards a Religious Philosophy *(1937),* From Morality to Religion *(1938), and* The Life of Reason *(1949). In the excerpt below from the 1947 revised edition of his* The Legacy of the Ancient World, *he provides a concise introduction to Plato's thought.*]

[The Platonic dialogues] are consummate masterpieces both of scientific reasoning and of dramatic art; we can well appreciate how Plato in youth had been drawn to write poetry. The dialogue form not only gave free play to the imagination of the artist, but reflected naturally the living movement of the Socratic conversations, and Plato's own conception of philosophic method as the upward endeavour of kindred spirits, by challenge of mind to mind, in the search for absolute truth. Of these writings the **Republic,** composed . . . in the full maturity of his genius, affords the best approach to the study of Plato's philosophy. It is the most comprehensive in range of all the dialogues. Opening with the question 'What is justice?' it portrays the ideal society and the progress of the soul to philosophic wisdom, and closes with a picture of the life beyond the grave. The problems of ethics and politics, psychology and education, literature and art, religion and science, are handled in a living unity, as factors in the single problem of the universe, by a thinker whose proud boast it was to be 'the spectator of all time and all existence'. But Plato was inspired, not only by the impulse of philosophy to know the truth, but also by an ardent passion for practical reform. From his youth, when he looked to enter the public life of his native Athens, up to his last vain journey in old age to Sicily, he was possessed with a burning desire to save the souls of men, and to build, as far as earthly conditions allowed, the city of God on Hellenic soil. For him, as for his master Socrates, philosophy was always a 'way of life'. From Socrates too he had learnt that goodness was knowledge, and that the only sure basis of practical conduct was a reasoned apprehension of the principle of good. Thus both problems, the speculative and the practical, found for Plato their common solution in philosophy, in a knowledge that should reveal the inner truth of the world as ideal goodness, and form the goal of individual and social action. What is this knowledge? And how can man attain to it? These are the cardinal questions of Plato's philosophy.

That knowledge must be knowledge of what *is*, that its object must have true being, was never questioned by Plato; for him not merely must reality be knowable, but knowledge can be only of the real. Where, then, is true being to be found? Heraclitus had held that all in the sense-world was in ceaseless change, ever coming to be and ceasing to be, never abiding in being. The followers of Protagoras had applied this doctrine to show how, at least in the field of sense, each passing appearance was true to the individual percipient in the instant of his perception. Such views robbed truth of all its meaning, and Plato could not rest content with them. He was driven, therefore, like Socrates before him, to seek for being elsewhere than in the world of sense. Reflection on our actual thinking shows it to involve objects of a very different order from sense-data; for these can be known only by aid of general concepts, apprehended not by the senses but by thought. This is especially evident in mathematical judgements, and in those that express moral and aesthetic values. No sensible lines or circles are perfectly equal, and to call an action good or a picture beautiful implies a single standard of goodness or of beauty, to which the particular instances are imperfect approximations. Thus Plato was led to the belief in an intelligible world, wherein there existed in unchanging being, as substantial realities, the Forms or Ideas, the perfect archetypes, 'shared in' or 'imitated by' their manifold and changing copies in the world of sense. These Forms alone were the proper objects of scientific 'knowledge'; the particular instances of them in the sense-world, on the other hand, were objects of fallible and fluctuating 'opinion', the source alike of speculative error and of moral delusion. He who thinks and lives in bondage to the body and to things of sense, for all his keen insight into the particular circumstances around him, is as one walking amid dream-phantoms in his sleep; the philosopher, with his mind's eye fixed on the intelligible realities, alone has waking vision. Plato proclaimed the doctrine of two worlds and, perhaps for the first time in the history of western thought, ascribed true being to immaterial substances. Moreover, the Forms are not isolated spiritual atoms but constitute an intelligible economy or order, which it is the philosopher's main task to trace. Supreme in this super-sensible hierarchy is the Form of Good, the source both of knowability and of being in all the other

Forms, itself 'transcending knowledge and being'. In the *Republic* Plato evinces reluctance to expound directly this 'highest object of knowledge', nor does he supply the deficiency anywhere in his writings; indeed, in [his *Seventh Letter*] he states explicitly that 'There is no writing of mine on the subject nor ever shall be. It is not capable of expression like other branches of study; but, as the result of long intercourse and a common life spent upon the thing, a light is suddenly kindled as from a leaping spark, and when it has reached the soul, it thenceforward finds nutriment for itself.' We know, however, that the Good formed the goal of all Plato's intellectual endeavour, and that he lectured on the subject in the Academy to the close of his life. It gave unity and system to the intelligible world, harmonizing the Forms in one sovereign and universal purpose. As in the sense-world the sun is the source of light and life to all created things, so in the thought-world the Forms derive their rationality and being from the Form of Good. Such in outline was Plato's answer to the two questions, What is knowledge? and What is being? which form the burden of metaphysics in all ages. His solution is liable to misinterpretation, and in three directions. (i) The Forms, though apprehended by the mind through general concepts, are no thought-abstractions, but substances, existing independently of the mind of any thinker in an objective spiritual world. (ii) The Form of Good is not identified by Plato with God. God is not a Form, but a living and active soul, the self-moving source of the motion of the heavens and, as Plato relates in semi-mythical language in the *Timaeus*, the creator of the sensible universe, after the pattern of the Forms and in accordance with mathematical law. The doctrines that God is himself the supreme good, and that the Forms are his eternal thoughts, having their being in the divine intellect, were not Plato's, but modifications of Plato's theory which naturally suggested themselves to Neo-Platonic and medieval thinkers. Finally (iii) it must not be supposed that in denying scientific knowledge of things of sense, Plato rejected them as illusory or worthless. It is not because the sense-world has no truth, but because its partial truth is visible only to the mind that grasps its dependence on the Forms, that Plato insists that the latter are the true objects of scientific study. Plato, in fact, conceived the sense-world as fashioned by God in space out of geometrical figures, a theory not so far removed from Descartes' reduction of physical body to terms of figured extension. Plato was a deep student of the mathematical sciences, which he held to be the proper approach to philosophy; and there is a tradition that over the portals of the Academy were inscribed the words, 'Let no one who is not a geometrician enter here.' In his view, mathematics furnished the key to physical nature; his later theory of Forms was in all likelihood a doctrine of mathematical relations, akin to that of modern physics, save only that, for Plato, the mathematical interpretation, far from precluding explanation in terms of purpose, required for its foundation the essential Form of Good.

In the nature of man, the distinction between the intelligible order and the sensible appears as that between the soul and the body. For Plato, as for Aristotle after him, soul (*psyche*) is the principle of life and motion, so that, wherever these are present, there is soul; and the human soul, far from being the only or the chief expression of soul, is but one form of its manifestation. Greek philosophy stands in sharp contrast to the modern tendency to regard the human mind as the pivotal fact of experience. Beside human and infra-human souls, there is in Plato's universe the soul of God, the world-soul, and the divine souls that move the stars. With a passionate intensity of conviction, Plato believed all souls to be inherently immortal; his final proof, stated in the *Phaedrus* and again in his latest dialogue, the *Laws*, argues from the fact of motion to the necessity of a cause of motion which is self-moved, and therefore can never begin or cease to move. Consequently, human, like all other, souls existed before incarnation in the body, and will survive the body's death. Thus Plato explains how the imperfect copies of the Forms in the world of sense 'remind' the soul of the perfect archetypes which it had known before its embodiment, and solves the difficulty how man comes by a knowledge that transcends the limits of sense-experience. It enables him also to account for present suffering as expiation for evil done in a previous incarnation and to develop the genuinely ethical doctrines of rewards and punishments after death, and of progressive purification in a series of lives. Here Plato is building on the soil of Orphic teaching, which came to him through the Pythagoreans and Socrates. The body is the prison-house and tomb of the soul; its death is the soul's liberation; the life of philosophy, which fixes the mind's thought on the super-sensible Forms, is the prelude to this liberation and, in literal truth, the study of death. In temporal union with the body, the human soul appears, not in its native purity, but like the sea-god Glaucus in the tale, 'encrusted with shells and seaweed', so that its essential nature, reason, is concealed from outward view. In our actual experience, the soul forms a composite unity of three powers: reason, the philosophic faculty, the rightful authority in the soul's economy, whose rule ensures harmony within, and also with the kindred reason in other souls and in the universe; the 'spirited' or passionate faculty, impulsive and pugnacious, a willing servant of reason but liable, if undirected, to lead the soul astray on the path of self-assertion; and the appetites, associated with bodily pleasures, some lawful, others unlawful, but all alike insatiable in their thirst for satisfaction, and, unless sternly disciplined by reason, ever plunging the soul into a riot of anarchy and disunion. Under the outward semblance of a man, we can picture a creature compounded of three natures, those of a man (reason), a lion (passion), and a many-headed hydra (appetites). The ethical and educational scheme of the *Republic* is largely based on this three-fold psychological distinction; for example, the picture of three types of life, inspired respectively by love of pleasure, love of honour, and love of wisdom; the analysis of moral virtue into the specific forms of wisdom, courage, and temperance, which have their common root in justice, the principle enabling each part of the soul to do its proper work in the economy of the whole, and ensuring a harmony or 'music' through the entire soul; the division of education into music and gymnastic, the disciplines of the appetites and of 'spirit', forming the requisite moral basis for the use of reason in maturer years; and, finally, the conception of philosophy as a conversion of the soul from the darkness of the sense-world to the light of the world of Forms, and as a lifelong preparation for the unfettered exercise of reason in the world beyond the grave.

Against those who maintained that morality was mere convention and that the individual finds his true happiness in a life of self-assertion, Plato showed how many in the very core of his being was marked out for social co-operation. He formulated two positions in intimate conjunction, namely, that each individual has by nature a unique capacity which determines his particular function in society, and that this function can only be efficiently discharged, so as to bring happiness to the agent, when it is regulated by the general good. The economy of the state is dependent on the psychology of the citizens, and this analogy between the *Polis* and the individual governs the picture of their good and evil types throughout the whole of the *Republic*. Social functions will be apportioned on the basis of the individual characters of the citizens; those in whose souls appetite is dominant will perform physical labour, supplying the material needs of the community as artisans or farmers; the 'spirited' souls will constitute the military class; the philosophic souls, which have proved in repeated trials their capacity for the life of reason, will be entrusted with the highest task of government. Thus Plato is brought by logical steps to his famous paradox, that 'until philosophers are kings and kings philosophers there will be no salvation for states or for the souls of men'. There will be none for the state, since reason is the power in the soul that makes for unity, and the realization of reason in the philosophic life is the only safeguard against social anarchy. Nor will there be for the individual soul; for, unless reason be sovereign in the community, no private person can resist the corrupting influence of public opinion and the allurements of the world. Believing that it was possible for the philosopher to attain in the course of his earthly life to the culmination of speculative knowledge in the vision of absolute Good, he drew the natural corollary that failure to conform in conduct to that vision was inconceivable. Knowledge on this exalted plane entailed conformity of conduct. It was impossible to sin against the light. Christianity at once endorsed and modified the Platonic doctrine. On the one hand, it held for the redeemed in Paradise, who enjoyed the direct vision of God, the absolute Good (*non posse peccare*); on the other, that direct vision was unattainable by men in this life, even on the highest level of mystic contemplation. The saint, for all his saintliness, remains a sinner; he sees God only 'through a glass darkly' (*per speciem in aenigmate*), never 'face to face'. Plato's Form of Good was not identified by him with God (who was a 'soul', not a 'form'), but it was knowable by the philosopher 'face to face'. Thus, inspired partly by the conviction that in a perfect society all things must be in common, and each member feel joy and sorrow in the joy and sorrow of every other, partly by a sense of the danger even to the chosen few of the curse of private interests, Plato denied to the ruling classes the possession of private property and replaced the private household by a single state-family, regulated with uncompromising rigour by the philosopher-kings. In these provisions we see at once Plato's passionate longing for unity, and his clear grasp of the forces of evil that are ever ready to assert their claims in the life of the individual and of the community. His austere idealism and unrelenting logic combined to lead him, in the temper of a monastic founder, to banish all temptations, such as private possessions and the dramatic art, that might possibly provoke to moral licence. The world of his day, and especially the political and ethical tone of fourth-century Athens, is, in the *Republic*, unreservedly condemned. The individual Athenian seemed to him to have been swept off his bearings on a tide of emotional debauchery, the Athenian state to have been rent asunder by party faction and the self-aggrandisement of its leaders. If the souls of men or human societies were to win salvation, it must be through a radical change of heart, carrying with it the institution of severe self-discipline and a revolution in the principles of life and government. Plato's keen insight into the evil of human nature and his bitter sense of the hopelessness of actual society reminds us frequently of Tolstoy. But he differed from Tolstoy in that he was always also a philosopher. His remedy for the evils of the world was to place power in the hands of those who know. They alone, who, as the fruit of long moral and intellectual training, have attained to knowledge and love of the sovereign good, are qualified to mould the citizen's character and direct the policy of the state. In contrast to the ideal of Periclean democracy, Plato preaches professional socialism. In a famous simile in the sixth book of the *Republic* he likens the Athenian people to the captain of a ship, good-natured but sluggish, and easily influenced by the flattery of artful mariners who vie with one another in cajoling him to entrust the helm to one of themselves. None of them has ever learnt the pilot's art or has the true knowledge that alone avails to guide the ship aright. All the while, the true pilot who is master of his craft remains neglected and alone. Thus in Plato's view the Athenian *demos* had fallen into the hands of unscrupulous and incompetent adventurers, while the philosopher, by right of nature the true-born ruler, was condemned to the inactivity of private life.

Needless to say, Plato failed to convince his fellow-citizens, and Athens pursued her course until the advent of the Macedonian conqueror. Unwearying in his efforts after practical reform, he thrice visited Sicilian Syracuse, in the hope that as a despot's counsellor he might succeed in instituting the philosophic state. But already in the *Republic* he had come to see that the ideal city was 'a pattern set up in heaven', incapable of perfect realization upon earth. In two of the later dialogues, the *Statesman* and the *Laws,* he evinced a more tolerant temper towards existing forms of government and, in the last-named writing, sketched a second-best policy as an accommodation of the ideal to the facts of life. But his true vocation, during the last forty years of life, lay in the Academy, the college for scientific and philosophical research which he founded and endowed. The Academy can justly claim to be regarded as the earliest university in history. Students flocked thither from all quarters of the Hellenic world, notably Eudoxus, a mathematician and astronomer from Cyzicus, and the young Aristotle from Stagira on the Macedonian coast. The members of the school shared a common life, residing in the Academy, and engaging not only in strictly philosophical studies but in inquiries into mathematics, biology, and problems of morals and jurisprudence. Amongst its achievements was the development of solid geometry, and Plato, in sketching his programme of higher studies in the *Republic,* advocated state support for this new science. The subsequent course of educational thought and practice, alike in Graeco-Roman and in medieval times, is grounded on Plato's institution of the Academy. It became a custom to seek for legislative reformers in the ranks of the school. Plato's latest writing, the *Laws,* is an example of this branch of its inquiries. The Academy had a long and memorable history; it served as the model for subsequent foundations, such as Aristotle's college in the Lyceum, and those of the Stoics and the Epicureans, and continued in being as the central home of Platonic teaching for a thousand years, until the pagan schools were finally disendowed and disestablished by the Christian emperor Justinian (A.D. 529).

The philosophy of Plato, because of its other-worldliness and uncompromising idealism, has seemed to many minds more akin to the spirit of Christianity than to that of Greece, which looked to this life and its opportunities for the satisfaction of man's intellectual and moral aspirations. There is truth in this assertion, though the differences are more vital than the likeness. Plato's doctrines of the soul's salvation through laborious intellectual discipline, and of the spiritual direction of society by a scientific aristocracy, carry us a long way from the ideal of a spiritual kingdom to be entered, not by the wise and prudent, but in the spirit of a little child. Moreover, the root-conceptions of Plato's thought proved fruitful beyond expectation in moulding the Hellenic ideal of life. The conviction, expressed in the *Republic,* that the highest life is that not of pleasure or power, but of philosophical contemplation, remained the governing ideal of ancient thought. When the city-state lost its independence and the career of free public activity was closed to the Greek citizen, the best minds busied themselves more and more with the pursuit of knowledge. Aristotle, who, though often contrasted with Plato, yet builds at every point on his master's foundations and is rather to be regarded as the first great Platonist, shared his belief that the life of philosophy is that in which the soul finds fullest satisfaction and approaches most nearly to the divine. In the centuries that followed, the same conviction was held alike by Platonists and Aristotelians, by Stoics and Epicureans. Nor was it confined to the Pagan world. Stripped of its peculiarly intellectual interpretation as the life of philosophy, the ideal of contemplative activity dominated medieval Christianity. The Mary and Martha of the Gospels became the types of the theoretic and active life; and the former had chosen the better part. The institution of monasticism, the writings of Dante, and the sculptures that adorn the cathedrals of the Middle Ages, are evidence of the hold which this thought, the product conjointly of the Christian and the Hellenic genius, had won over the spiritual aspirations of mankind. Plato, like all the greatest of the Greeks, whether in literature or philosophy, stands for something of universal value. Whenever the spirit of man turns from the world of sense and change towards that which is eternal, unchanging, and one, whether it be in intellectual or religious contemplation, it has claimed kinship with the spirit of Plato....

R. M. HARE

SOURCE: R. M. Hare, "Plato's Achievement," in his *Plato,* Oxford University Press, 1982, pp. 69-75.

[*Hare is an English educator who has written a*

number of philosophical books. In the following excerpt, he discusses key points of Plato's thought and assesses his contributions to the development of philosophy.]

If the first of Europe's philosophers whose works survive does not have the same towering dominance as its first poet, Homer, that is not any reflection on Plato's genius. His actual achievement in his own field was as great. It is merely that we know a little more about what went before. Despite this, he, like Homer, presents to us the appearance (albeit a misleading one) of arising out of nothing, and also of a certain primitiveness which his marvellously polished style does not altogether conceal. He has a greater claim than anybody else to be called the founder of philosophy as we know it. But what, exactly, did he found? The answer will depend on who 'we' are; it will be different for Patonists [those who focus on the aspect of Plato that Hare calls "Pato," an ascetic moralist who advocated "the perennial philosophy" and drew a sharp line between eternal ideas and the material world] and Latonists [those who focus on the aspect of Plato that Hare calls "Lato," an intellectual and logician], and even that crude division does not do justice to the complexity of Plato's make-up, and of his influence on the subsequent history of philosophy.

Of the two Platos that we distinguished, it is difficult to think that the achievement of Pato was as great as that of Lato. The 'perennial philosophy' is perennial just because it is a very natural expression of human thinking about the mind and about values; it has appeared in many places at many times in different forms, and Plato's mind-body dualism, with its associated belief in the immortality of the soul, and his particular treatment of the objectivity of values, are not markedly different from anybody else's. What is unique in him is the progress from these quasi-religious speculations, which could have remained, as they have in others, vapid and evanescent, towards a much tougher, more precise logical and metaphysical theory, a moral philosophy and a philosophy of language; these were not entirely new, but, through discussion and criticism of them, they engendered the lasting achievements of Aristotle in those fields, and thus shaped the entire future of philosophy.

Let us start with Plato's development of the topic of 'The One and the Many'. We have seen how the early cosmologists sought an explanation of the bewildering variety of things in the world by seeking for them some common ground or reason. The search started with the question, 'What were their origins?'; went on to the question 'What are they all made of?'; but then divided. Natural scientists went on asking this second question in ever subtler forms and have been answering it ever since. But by this time problems had arisen which could not be answered by this method, and which demanded an entirely different sort of inquiry, whether we style it metaphysics or logic. For the puzzles generated by Parmenides could not be solved without asking 'What are they all?' in a quite different sense. This new inquiry, whether we call it conceptual or logical or even linguistic, consists in asking about the meanings of the words we use, or, to put it in a way more congenial to Plato, about the natures (in a quite different sense from the physical) of the things we are talking about. The Many are to be understood, not by seeking their physical constituents, nor even the efficient causes of their motions and changes, but by isolating and understanding the Idea to which we are referring when we use a certain word. This is to know in the deepest sense what it is to be a thing of a certain kind.

Plato had grasped the truth that conceptual understanding is different from natural science, and just as important. He had succeeded in distinguishing from each other the four different types of explanation (the four different kinds of 'Why?'-questions and their answers) which were duly classified by Aristotle in his doctrine of the 'four causes'. Of these we have just mentioned three:

1 The *material* cause, or explanation of the material constitution of a thing;

2 The *efficient* cause, or cause in the narrower modern sense, which made a thing do what it did;

3 The *formal* cause, or explanation of its form—of what it is to be that kind of thing;

and he also, as we shall see in a moment, distinguished

4 The *final* cause, or explanation of the purpose for which something comes to be as it is.

Plato was more interested in formal and final causes than in the other two kinds, and thought that they would both be understood by getting to know the Idea of the kind of thing in question. This association of the formal and final causes (having its origin in Plato's doctrine about the Good, already discussed) may have been a mistake; but, if so, it was a very momentous one which was taken over by Aristotle and by many philosophers to this day. The notion that what it *is to be* a thing of a certain kind (its essence) is logically tied to what a thing of that kind *ought to be* (its purpose) still has its adherents.

To have distinguished the four kinds of explanation would have been achievement enough, but Plato went further. He saw that there was a question about how we could claim to *know* the answers to the formal and final 'Why?'-questions. We may concede that in his theory of knowledge knowing is treated too much like mental seeing, and the objects of knowledge too much like objects of ordinary vision, being different from them only in being seen by the mind and not the eyes, and in having a perfection and abidingness which the objects of ordinary vision do not have. But nevertheless the Theory of Ideas does represent Plato's way of stating some very important discoveries.

The first of these is that the sort of knowledge we are after both in science and in mathematics and logic is something universal. A causal law or a mathematical or logical theorem, if it holds at all, holds for all similar cases. That moral principles too have to be universal is a feature of them whose importance has to be acknowledged even by those who do not follow Plato in his cognitivism—do not, that is, allow themselves to speak of moral *knowledge*.

The second is that all these disciplines including morality are capable of being structured into systems in which more general concepts or statements form the grounds of more specific ones. For both Plato and Aristotle this truth was expressed in their doctrine that in order to say what a thing is, we have to say to what genus it belongs, and then to say how it is differentiated from the other kinds of things in that genus. This is summed up in the Platonic method of dialectic, employing 'collection' and 'division'. . . . We must never forget that the word Plato used for his Ideas, '*eidos*', is the same word, and with very much the same meaning, as we translate 'species' when we meet it in Aristotle's logic. Plato's description in the **Republic** . . . of the way in which the Ideas are subordinated to one another in a hierarchy may sound too crudely physical to us (it is almost as if he were looking with his mind's eye at a lot of quasi-visible onions strung together in a rope); but this was his way of putting the thought that a discipline has to be logically ordered if its propositions are to be *connected* (the metaphor survives) with each other.

In this and other ways Plato's investigations of the Socratic 'What is. . .?' questions led him a very long way into the disciplines of logic and metaphysics. Aristotle's systematisation of logic—above all his theory of the syllogism which dominated logic for many centuries—could never have been achieved without Plato's insights.

Plato also, as we have seen, avoided a trap into which he might easily have fallen, given his assimilation of knowing to mental seeing: that of thinking, as [René] Descartes seems to have thought, that the clarity and distinctness of the vision was a certificate of its correctness. Instead, by recognising the difference between knowledge and right opinion, he was led to demand, as a qualification for knowledge, the ability to give and defend a reason or explanation for the thing known. This explanation normally took the form of a definition (ideally of the type just described). However, the importance of this distinction transcends Plato's particular theory of definition. Whenever anybody, whether in science or mathematics or moral philosophy, makes some statement on the basis of mere intuition, hoping that we will share the intuition and therefore agree with it, he should be disciplined by means of the Socratic-Platonic demand that he 'give an account' of what he has said. Even now too many philosophical frauds are unwilling to face the auditors in this way.

So far we have not, in this [essay], made much of any distinction between on the one hand science and mathematics, and on the other morals and politics. This is in accordance with Plato's practice; he thinks that all are subject to the same disciplines and methods, although in the application of them to this imperfect world rigour may be lost. But those who now wish to make a sharp distinction between evaluative and factual propositions, and thus between the methods appropriate to morality and science, do not have to part company with Plato completely even here. For one of the most remarkable things about him is how, even though he never wavered in his objectivism, and constantly assimilated moral to other kinds of knowledge, he also recognised quite early, following Socrates, the special feature of value judgements which distinguishes them from factual ones, their prescriptivity. This comes out above all in his equation of thinking something good with desiring and therefore being disposed to choose it, and thus in his acceptance, albeit in a modified form, of the links between knowledge and goodness which had led Socrates into paradox.

Nor did the prescriptivity of value judgements die with Plato. It is implicit in Aristotle's statement that the Good is what everything is after; and also in his doctrine known as the 'practical syllogism'. The conclusion of a piece of practical reasoning, he saw, can be an action just because its premises contain a value judgement which is prescriptive. He insists that practical wisdom, our guide in matters of evaluation and action, is 'epitactic' (meaning 'prescriptive')—a word he takes over, with the distinction it implies between active prescription and mere passive judgement, from Plato's **Politicus**. . . . The same intimate connection between value judgements and action became important again in the eighteenth century with the work of [David] Hume, who found in it an obstacle to the founding of morality on reason, and of [Immanuel]

Kant, who thought he had surmounted the obstacle; and it is still important today.

Plato was also the first person in history to attempt a systematic account of the structure of the mind. His account is no doubt crude compared with Aristotle's, let alone with what a satisfactory explanation of 'mental' phenomena would require. And he did not see the necessity for saying precisely what, in more literal terms, the metaphor of 'parts of the mind' really means. All the same, he started a very important and fruitful line of inquiry, and had much more excuse for his crude partition of the mind than some recent thinkers like [Sigmund] Freud. Although it is hard to take seriously, as constituents of 'the mind', entities like 'the intellect' and 'the will' (to use modern descendants of Plato's terms), the distinctions which have been made in this kind of way do nevertheless need making.

They need making, above all, in order to emphasise the importance of disciplined thought, if we are to have a satisfactory way of answering any of the more difficult questions that face us. Although we have to allow credit to Plato's predecessors, and especially to the Sophists, for bringing into emphasis the intellectual side of man's nature, we owe to Plato and Socrates more than to anybody else the idea, which has been current ever since, that man will have more success in almost everything he undertakes if he learns to *think* better.

This brings us to what, I am sure, Plato himself thought of as his most important practical contribution: his educational theory. He believed firmly that there could be a body of knowledge or understanding whose attainment and handing down would make possible the orderly solution of political problems such as had brought Athens and all Greece into chaos. In this he taught the world a valuable lesson. If we could fully understand the problems, which involves understanding first of all the words in terms of which they are posed, and then (even harder) understanding the situations and the people that generate them, we should be on a way to their solution. This, at any rate, is a more hopeful line than attributing them to human wickedness which can never be eradicated. Even the wicked can be coped with if we understand what makes them do what they do. Socrates did not think he had attained this understanding, and even Plato was not all that optimistic; but he saw it as the only way out of the troubles of Greece, and founded an institution, the Academy, which he thought would help towards attaining it.

His bolder plans for political reform are more questionable, and more tentative. If the education of the intellect, preceded by a thorough schooling of the will, is necessary in order to put human society to rights, how can this come about? Plato here took a short cut. If absolute power could come into the hands of good and wise men, would not that do the trick? We have seen how much of good sense can be extracted from this bold suggestion. It is not wholly devoid of merit, but simply ignores the difficulty (indeed the practical impossibility) of finding suitable incumbents, and the further difficulty of reconciling absolute power, however wise its possessor, with the attainment of ends which nearly everybody (and who shall say they are wrong?) will include in their requirements for the good life, above all liberty. When Plato, impressed with the practical difficulties, goes on in the *Laws* to subject human and fallible rulers to a rigid code, he only makes matters worse. In its final form the Platonic proposal shares many features with the Holy Inquisition.

Nevertheless, Plato's political theory presents the liberal with a challenge which he has to face, and in facing which he will find himself having to answer questions which too many liberals ignore. If some ways of organising society are better than others, in the sense that they do better for the people who live in the society, even on their own reckoning; and if some politicians and others are doing their very best to prevent it being organised, or kept organised, in these better ways, what am I to do about them, if not seek the power to frustrate their malign endeavours? If I think I know how a wise dictator would arrange things, ought I not to try to become a wise dictator? Plato has his answer to this question; what is the answer of the liberals?

Plato did not see his political proposals realised, nor perhaps did he expect to. His only excursion into politics, in Sicily, was a disaster. But a change did come over men's minds as a result of his thought. Greek political morality did not improve, it is true; nor was the Roman much better. But though the practice of politics remained as dirty as before, it is fair to claim that, gradually, through the work of Plato and his successors, the Stoics, Christians and others, ideals of a new and better sort came in the end to be current.

The rhetoric of present-day politics is still mostly nothing but rhetoric; but rhetoric does influence people (even its authors), and cause things to happen which otherwise would not. Our political rhetoric is permeated now by ideals which were simply non-existent in the rhetoric of Plato's day. This can be seen by comparing almost any political speech nowadays with almost any speech reported from the fifth and fourth centuries BC. Politicians do not always do what they commend in their speeches; but sometimes they do, and that has made a difference to the world. Part of this difference we owe to Plato. In the end he made many people see that personal or even national ambition and success are not the most important things in life, and that the good of other people is a worthier aim. For this we can forgive him for being also the father of political paternalism and absolutism.

SOURCES FOR FURTHER STUDY

Anton, John, and Anthony Preus, eds. *Essays in Ancient Greek Philosophy III: Plato.* Albany: State University of New York Press, 1989, 366 p.

> Collection of seventeen essays that explore "the richness and suggestive power of Plato's ontology, cosmology, philosophy of mind, political theory, ethics, and aesthetics," but "do not, on the whole, challenge or reject Platonic theses."

Brumbaugh, Robert S. *Platonic Studies of Greek Philosophy: Form, Arts, Gadgets, and Hemlock.* Albany: State University of New York Press, 1989, 296 p.

> Essays arranged in five groups of increasing generality as follows: the form of the Good as discussed in the *Republic,* Platonic dialogues other than the *Republic,* Aristotle's modification of Platonism, the importance of technology for Plato's thinking, and contemporary issues and relevant commentary in Plato's dialogues.

Cross, R. C., and A. D. Woozley. *Plato's "Republic": A Philosophical Commentary.* London: Macmillan & Co., 1964, 295 p.

> Serves "as something of an introduction to philosophy via the *Republic,* rather than a specialised Platonic study." The authors concentrate on main themes of the work, including "the problem of justice," "evolution of the ideal city," "justice in the soul," "art," and "the sun, line and cave."

Durant, Will. "Plato." In his *The Lives and Opinions of the Greater Philosophers,* pp. 1-48. New York: Pocket Books, 1953.

> Describes Plato's life and times and discusses ethical, political, and psychological aspects of his philosophy.

Gauss, H. *Plato's Conception of Philosophy.* New York: Haskell House Publishers, 1974, 272 p.

> Examines Plato's logic, ethics, and social philosophy.

Romilly, Jacqueline de. "Philosophers of the Fourth Century: Plato and Aristotle." In her *A Short History of Greek Literature,* translated by Lillian Doherty, pp. 142-55.

> Presents Plato's writings within "the historical circumstances and the internal development of Greek literature."

Salman Rushdie

1947-

(Full name Ahmed Salman Rushdie) Indian-born English novelist, critic, and nonfiction writer.

INTRODUCTION

Rushdie is perhaps best known as the author of *The Satanic Verses* (1988), an irreverent, iconoclastic novel that freely incorporates events depicted in the Koran and other aspects of Islamic culture. Although written in the self-reflexive and fragmented style that characterizes all of Rushdie's work, *The Satanic Verses* outraged devout Muslims and touched off an international furor, which included public demonstrations against the book, bans on its importation, and a *fatwa,* or decree, issued by Iranian leader Ayatollah Ruhollah Khomeini and renewed again in 1993, calling for the author's execution. Consequently, Rushdie was forced into hiding, where he remained until September 1995, making only infrequent and unannounced public appearances.

Biographical Information

Rushdie was born June 19, 1947, in Bombay, India. A member of a middle-class Muslim family, he attended the Cathedral Boys' High School. In 1964 the family moved to Pakistan, but by then Rushdie had been sent to Rugby School in England, returning home only for vacations. Rushdie entered King's College, Cambridge, where he received a M.A. with honors in 1968. After graduation, he acted for one year at an experimental theater, then supported himself as a freelance advertising copywriter during the 1970s. In 1975 Rushdie published his first novel, *Grimus,* which tells the story of a Native American who receives the gift of immortality and begins an odyssey to find life's meaning. With the publication of *Midnight's Children* (1981), which received the Booker McConnell Prize, Rushdie was able to commit all of his time to writing. Following *Shame* (1983) and *The Jaguar Smile* (1987), a nonfiction account of the political and social conditions he observed during a 1986 trip to Nicaragua, Rushdie wrote his most controversial work, *The Satanic Verses,* which forced him into hiding. Since then, Rushdie has written a fairy tale for children, several collections of essays and short stories, and the novel *The Moor's Last Sigh* (1995).

Major Works

Rich in allusions to Indian history, literature, and mythology, *Midnight's Children* concerns Saleem Sinai, one of a thousand and one babies who had been born during the first hour of the nation's independence, who is presented as a prematurely aged and impotent man in his early thirties. Read as allegory, Saleem and the thousand other babies, many of whom died at birth, represent the hopes as well as the frustrating realities of independent India. *Shame* presents fabulistic accounts of events in an unnamed country that strongly resembles Pakistan, examining related themes of shame versus honor and shame versus shamelessness as cultural influences that affect the personalities and actions of individuals. *The Satanic Verses* explores themes relating to good and evil, religious faith and fanaticism, illusion versus reality, and the plight of Indians who have relocated to Great Britain. Creating several levels of meaning by frequent use of puns, metaphors, similes, and allusions to popular culture and the sacred beliefs of Islam, the novel begins with the miraculous survival of two expatriate Indian men, Gibreel Farishta and Saladin Chamcha, who fall to Earth following an airplane explosion over England. These alter egos represent good and evil. Gibreel, a movie star in Indian religious films, experiences vivid dreams in which historical events of the founding of Islam are depicted in epic detail. Saladin, who metamorphoses into a satanic figure, journeys to London and encounters police brutality, prejudice, and other seamy elements that reflect deep-rooted social problems. The narrative follows these characters through the intertwining of past and present, various locations, reality, dream, and films until their final confrontation on a movie set. *Haroun and the Sea of Stories* (1990) is a fable that offers a clear message against literary censorship by despots. When Rashid the storyteller, who receives his talents from the Sea of Stories located on a moon called Kahina, loses his ability to tell stories, Rashid's son, Haroun, investigates and discovers that Walrus, who controls the sea, is at war with the evil ruler, Khattam-Shud, who poisons the sea in an effort to destroy all stories. After many adventures, Haroun destroys Khattam-Shud, thus saving the sea and restoring his father's powers of storytelling. *East, West* (1994), comprising nine short stories, is divided into three sections: "East," set in India; "West," set in Europe; and "East-West," set in England. Each story contains characters embodying diverse cultures who interact on a variety of social and emotional levels. *The Moor's Last Sigh* presents a satirical view of the politics of India. Framed by a dilemma reminiscent of Scheherazade's, Moraes "the Moor" Zogoiby must tell his famous mother's family history to regain his freedom.

Critical Reception

While most of Rushdie's works are generally admired for their blend of history, myth, politics, and fantasy, critical reaction to *The Satanic Verses* has been mixed. While some Muslims claimed that Rushdie violated taboos by making irreverent references to people, places, and objects sacred to Islam, most Western commentators defended Rushdie's freedom of expression. A. J. Mojtabai has stated: "As a display of narrative energy and wealth of invention, *The Satanic Verses* is impressive. As a sustained exploration of the human condition, it flies apart into delirium." Others have praised Rushdie's exuberant narrative and his far-ranging development of themes. Robert Irwin has noted: "Once an image, pun, or reference has been brought into play, Rushdie gallops off with it in all directions." Although many tend to read everything Rushdie has written since the imposition of the *fatwa* as a cloaked reference to the author's unfortunate personal dilemma, Rushdie has bravely continued to pursue his art, "living a nightmare, looking for words that will restore the rest of his days to him without compromising him as a writer," according to the editors of the *New Republic*.

(For further information, see *Bestsellers:* 89:3; *Contemporary Authors,* Vols. 108, 111; *Contemporary Authors New Revision Series,* Vols. 33, 56; *Contemporary Literary Criticism,* Vols. 23, 31, 55, 100; *DISCovering Authors: British; DISCovering Authors: Canadian; DISCovering Authors Modules: Most-studied Authors Module, Novelists Module, Popular Fiction and Genre Authors Module; Major Twentieth-Century Writers.*)

CRITICAL COMMENTARY

PATRICK PARRINDER

SOURCE: Patrick Parrinder, "Let's Get the Hell Out of Here," in *London Review of Books,* Vol. 10, No. 17, September 29, 1988, pp. 11-13.

[*In the following excerpt, Parrinder examines the "loosely Biblical structure" of several of Rushdie's works.*]

[In *The Satanic Verses*] Rushdie's prose, by design and

> **Principal Works**
>
> *Grimus* (novel) 1975
> *Midnight's Children* (novel) 1981
> *Shame* (novel) 1983
> *The Painter and the Pest* (screenplay) 1985
> *The Jaguar Smile: A Nicaraguan Journey* (nonfiction) 1987
> *The Riddle of Midnight* (screenplay) 1988
> *The Satanic Verses* (novel) 1988
> *Haroun and the Sea of Stories* (juvenile) 1990
> *Imaginary Homelands: The Collected Essays* (essays and criticism) 1991
> *The Rushdie Letters: Freedom to Speak, Freedom to Write* (letters) 1993
> *East, West* (short stories) 1994
> *The Moor's Last Sigh* (novel) 1995

also (I suspect) by accident, tends to impede realistic recognition. His favourite mode is caricature. Here, a new character, Rosa Diamond, is introduced:

> I know what a ghost is, the old woman affirmed silently. Her name was Rosa Diamond; she was 88 years old; and she was squinting beakily through her salt-caked bedroom windows, watching the full moon's sea. And I know what it isn't, too, she nodded further, it isn't a scarification or a flapping sheet, so pooh and pish to all *that* bunkum. What's a ghost? Unfinished business, is what.

Without pausing over 'beakily' or the Masefieldian 'salt-caked', we can say that 'scarification' is a malapropism, and it is Rushdie's and not Rosa's, as we learn from other passages in the novel. Poor Rosa's idiom is idiosyncratic indeed if she gets 'pooh', 'pish' and 'bunkum' all into one sentence. Her notion that a ghost is unfinished business will be repeated almost verbatim by one of Rushdie's twin protagonists some hundreds of pages later: he, however, cannot have been privy to Rosa's thoughts. The other protagonist, the Indian filmstar Gibreel Farishta, finds on a visit to London that 'fictions were walking around wherever he went . . . fictions masquerading as real human beings.' In Rushdie's novels they aren't difficult to spot.

This hardly matters, I agree, since his novels have a Dickensian expansiveness and a driving narrative energy. Rushdie may produce baggy monsters, but he is one of the very few current writers whose works are attempts at the greater Bible, the 'bright book of life'. He tends to use a loosely Biblical structure, beginning with a Creation and a Fall and a miraculous birth—in *Midnight's Children* (1981) the build-up is so tremendous that the hero's birth does not happen until page 116—and leading towards some kind of apocalypse: the last section of *Shame* (1983) is entitled 'Judgment Day'. Rushdie's fictive repertoire has mostly been based on the archetypal male figures of the wanderer and the storyteller, and the women who surround them. The storyteller, obviously enough, is a surrogate for the author himself: in *Midnight's Children,* for example, he appears as a bumbling, mock-heroic first-person narrator. The wanderer is a more grandiose but equally self-projective figure.

In Rushdie's first novel, the ungainly *Grimus* (1975), the themes were there but they had not yet found an adequate vehicle. The hero, Flapping Eagle (get it?), is an Axona Indian exiled from the language and the ways of his ancestors. He falls through a 'gate' in space, landing on Thera, a satellite of the Star Nus in the Gorf Nirveesu. Here he is found washed up on the shore and is escorted on his subsequent journey by one Virgil Jones. Much else in this tedious fantasy seems to have been composed by the anagrammatic method or with the help of a mythological dictionary: the title *Grimus,* for example, alludes to the Sufi legend of the Simurg. Rushdie's reputation was made with *Midnight's Children* and *Shame,* which combined fantasy and fairytale with social satire and political allegory. Saleem Sinai in *Midnight's Children* is, like Flapping Eagle, gifted with miraculous powers; Flapping Eagle is an orphan, Saleem is a changeling, and Omar Khayyam Shakil in *Shame* has not one but three mothers. These protagonists all become exiles and wanderers, and *The Satanic Verses* reminds us that the archetypal wanderer is the Devil. But the wanderer is also the storyteller, or so the narrator of *Shame* insists: 'I too, like all migrants, am a fantasist. I build imaginary countries and try to impose them on the ones that exist.'

The wanderer-storyteller has invariably suffered a Fall. Like the Fall into the Quotidian which caused Saul Bellow's Herzog so much merriment, we may, if we wish, think of this as an event in the spiritual and political history of our century. Thus in *Midnight's Children* and *Shame* the Fall is the shock of independence, the birth of the new nations of India and Pakistan. In *The Satanic Verses* it is a more general disrup-tion. 'Information got abolished sometime in the 20th-century . . . Since then we've been living in a fairy-story'—or so one of Rushdie's characters tells us. This hits off the carnivalesque note of these novels, but it does not mean that their author has failed to honour the poet's obligation, as stated in *The Satanic Verses* by the satirist Baal, to 'name the unnamable, to point out frauds, to take sides, to start arguments, shape the world and stop it from going to sleep'. The method of *Midnight's*

Children and *Shame* may be fabulous rather than informative, but where it matters these novels are unflinchingly political. In *The Satanic Verses* Rushdie turns from the political development of India and Pakistan to the immigrant Asian communities in Britain, and, above all, to the global resurgence of Islamic fundamentalism.

The title refers to a much-disputed incident in the life of the Prophet. Mohammed used to meet and converse with the angel Gabriel on a mountain near Mecca, and the verses of the Koran were dictated to him on these occasions. But one day, as a ninth-century historian tells us, while Mohammed was negotiating with the rulers of Mecca, the Devil 'threw upon his tongue' verses conceding semi-divine status to three local pagan deities. Later Gabriel showed the Prophet his mistake, and the verses were changed to those that now appear in the scriptures. To Western scholars this account shows Mohammed making, and hurriedly correcting, a political blunder. But it also raises puzzling questions about the status of creative and prophetic inspiration, and of those near-neighbours to inspiration—improvisation and what we call forgery. From the standpoint of the faithful the Satanic verses are apocryphal and hence forged, but of course the majority of Western translations of the Islamic scriptures argue that the Koran as a whole is a forgery.

Gibreel Farishta in *The Satanic Verses* is a film-actor specialising in the popular Indian genre movies known as 'theologicals'. In the beginning he and another actor, Saladin Chamcha, fall together from a hijacked airliner which has been blown up over the English Channel at 29,000 feet. The Air India plane was named the *Bostan*, after one of the two gardens of paradise. Gibreel, by flapping his arms (compare Flapping Eagle), is able to slow down their descent so that they fall safely to earth, where they are miraculously 'born again', an angel and a devil respectively. The angel Gibreel spends much of his time dreaming, though in his waking life he begins to suffer from paranoid schizophrenia. His dreams are the source of several of Rushdie's multiply-embedded narratives, and in one of these, set in the Arabian city of Jahilia, the prophet Mahound comes to Gibreel for advice and then, in his next public appearance, speaks the Satanic verses. It is Gibreel this time who admits to a mistake, and who later corrects the prophet.

If Farishta now sports an undeserved halo, Saladin Chamcha sprouts cloven hoofs and a pair of horns. Once they have landed on the Sussex coast Gibreel treacherously disowns his companion, leaving him in the hands of the police, who promptly beat him up. Formerly a well-known London character-actor—he was the source of the outlandish voices on the TV *Aliens Show*, and in advertisements featuring talking crisp-packets and baked-bean cans—Saladin is now a suspected illegal immigrant and a virtual outlaw. Thrown out by his wife, he goes to ground in Brickhall, an Asian district of Inner London. Here racial tension mounts, as Saladin becomes a cult-hero while awaiting his opportunity for revenge on Gibreel. The two meet at last at a wild party in Shepperton Studios, on the set of *Our Mutual Friend;* soon after this Gibreel, further maddened by a spate of anonymous phone calls reflecting Saladin's gifts of tongues and voices, brings rioting and melodrama to the streets of Brickhall. Gibreel is now transformed into Azraeel, the fire-breathing Islamic angel of death. The multiple film-within-a-film effect is typical of Rushdie, whose whole novel could be regarded as a species of 'theological'. And there is more, much more, as (once again) he digs deep into the mythographical bran-tub. The story of Othello, Aladdin and his lamp, the Battle of Hastings, Beauty and the Beast, and the legends of Everest (29,000 feet and all that), all play a part. Fortunately, the limpidity of Rushdie's interpolated tales provides a crucial relief from the pandemonium of his main narrative.

In *Shame,* his most tightly-controlled and perhaps his best novel to date, the burgeoning multiple folk-tale plot was harnessed to a transparently allegorical account of Pakistan's political history. It was as if the *Decameron* or *Arabian Nights* had been yoked with the Sub-Continental equivalent of *Animal Farm*. *Shame* tells of the overthrow and execution of the former playboy and democratically-elected prime minister, Iskander Harappa, leaving his tough and beautiful daughter, the 'Virgin Ironpants', to become his political heir. Harappa is succeeded by his former army commander General 'Razor Guts' Hyder, a tyrant who undergoes a richly Dickensian process of moral disintegration through guilt before succumbing in his turn to a bloodthirsty, fairy-tale vengeance. How ironic that the real-life General Zia, like Gibreel and Saladin but not like his counterpart in *Shame*, was to come to grief in a mid-air explosion.

In *Shame* Rushdie uses the novelist's privilege to exaggerate the dynastic nature of Pakistani politics. Almost everyone is related by birth or marriage to everyone else, and the novel begins with a genealogical table. Equally, the author is able to disclose the 'real' manner of Isky Harappa's death (the judicial hanging was solely for public consumption), and to predict his rival's downfall. *The Satanic Verses* looks, rather, at 'Mrs Torture's' England, endowing London with police violence, race-riots and (stretching credulity) with a tropical summer. The narrator's disclosures include the inside story of some brutal murders and the last fatal moments of a hijacking, but his most daring revelations are the theological ones.

Gibreel's dreams, in particular, 'name the unnamable' by portraying a bloodthirsty Imam's seizure of power, the tale of a pilgrimage of Indian villagers who end up drowning in the Arabian Sea, and some ungodly goings-on in Jahilia, the fictive equivalent of Mecca. As Mahound and his followers return from their flight to Yathrib to take over the city, we see two writers — the satirist Baal and his own Persian scribe Salman — becoming the prophet's mortal enemies. (Meanwhile, the inmates of the local brothel cheekily impersonate the prophet's 12 wives.) Salman finally admits to having changed the wording of some of Mahound's revelations, but saves his own skin by betraying Baal. Is there any way of escaping this fundamentalist universe — the universe as dreamed by Gibreel — or is a little verbal tinkering the best that can be done? Saladin Chamcha finally leaves behind his demonic powers, going off with a woman whose last words are 'Let's get the hell out of here.' Another woman, Gibreel's ex-lover Alleluia Cone, has turned herself into an intrepid mountaineer and Everest-explorer in order, as she hopes, to rise above good and evil: but she fails, so far as we can tell, since Gibreel in the end sends her prematurely to paradise. In a reversal of the story of *Paradise Lost*, it is Gibreel who gradually degenerates into a bringer of death, while Saladin finds some sort of redemption: but this, after all, is the Devil's version. It is all damnably entertaining, and fiendishly ingenious.

Rushdie wrote in *Shame* that 'every story one chooses to tell is a kind of censorship, it prevents the telling of other tales.' His own profuse and multiply-branching fictions do not give the impression that anything has been prevented from being told.

S. NOMANUL HAQ

SOURCE: S. Nomanul Haq, "Salmon Rushdie, Blame Yourself," in *The New York Times*, February 23, 1989, p. A23.

[*The following open letter to Rushdie was originally published in* The New York Times *in early 1989. Haq charges that Rushdie could have foreseen the outrage* The Satanic Verses *caused and that his decision to publish the book demonstrated his insensitivity to Muslim sensibilities.*]

Dear Salman Rushdie,

A few years ago, when I read your *Midnight's Children*, I was overwhelmed. It was not the exuberance of your narrative and stylistic craft, nor the threads of your rich imagination, woven with such effortless intellectual control that engulfed me. Rather, it was your formidable grasp of history and through that of the psyche of a complex culture in all its variations that formed the substratum of your tale.

And yet it is this question of your knowledge of history that I shall raise in connection with your seriously and alarmingly controversial *The Satanic Verses.*

Let me say at once that I do hold you as an artist, not as a historian or a psychologist — nor, indeed, as a theologian. But, at the same time you do make use of what are facts of history and psychology, giving them your own distinct treatment.

No writer, you will agree, writes in a historical vacuum. But then, a responsible artist does not, without powerful grounds, mutilate history. Nor, unless there exists a mammoth mystification, does he disregard the sensibilities and sensitivities of his own milieu, especially when it forms both the subject matter and the bulk of his or her audience.

Strangely, what I am saying is something that I learned from none other than yourself. You might recall your telling criticism of Sir Richard Attenborough's celebrated film *Gandhi*. You enraged Sir Richard, but in the controversy I remained your passionate supporter.

You censured the film for disregarding or minimizing certain important historical facts. And you said that in a work of an artistic nature, one cannot say everything, that there has to be a choice — but that there has to be a rationale of choice. One selects not to mislead but to make the story more meaningful. Ironically, this has precisely been your lapse in the *The Satanic Verses.*

Most of your Western audience are unable to gauge the acuteness of your blow to the very core of the Indian subcontinental culture. They cannot estimate the seriousness of the injury because they do not know the history of the aggrieved.

You do know it and therefore one feels that you foresaw, at least to some extent, the consequences.

There is in your book, for example, the phantasmagoria of your own namesake Salman's corruption of the revealed word by his erroneous rendering of the words of Mahound.

Here the veil is too thin to cover the identity of Mahound: he can be understood in no other way than as a caricature of the Muslim Prophet. You do know that Islam is consistently, acutely and uniquely sensitive to its scripture. Ordinarily, Arabic is written without short vowels, but no copy of the Koran today is vowelless. Muslims insist that it should and can be read only in one way. The Muslim view is that even incorrectly reading the Koran is a cardinal sin. The Koran is neither read nor recited in translation for the very reason that translation might introduce alteration.

This matter is deadly serious and to make it a subject of insensitive fantasy is equally serious.

There is a further issue that your Western reader does not sense: that your corrupt Salman is the namesake not only of you in your book but of a historical personage who was a Persian companion of the Prophet, a companion who has been accorded a particularly elevated status by the Shiites. Given the militancy of the Shiites, when you made Salman the polluter of the revelation, you knew that you were planting your hand in the cluster of bees!

Your response to the uproar has been wavering and inconsistent, and your defense has the odor of self-righteousness. You say that people who have not read your book have no right to criticize it. But do you really think that reading the book will drastically alter their opinions?

Then you talk about freedom of expression. Free speech is a tricky issue and cannot be taken too literally. What do you think the response of black Americans would be if you were to mock the Rev. Dr. Martin Luther King Jr.? Or the reaction of the Jewish community if you were to eulogize Hitler? Or the anger of a pious Hindu if you were to present a graphic description of the slaughtering of a cow?

And to say that the Muslim world has demonstrated a total lack of dignity and tolerance is to utter a historical irrelevance. The Muslim nations have not gone through the turmoils of the Enlightenment and they have seen no scientific revolution; their sensibilities are different. Often, a peaceful demonstration is not their way and we cannot change them overnight. The best thing is to avoid hitting their most sensitive chords. And, Mr. Rushdie, you knew that.

As for your waverings, you started out by expressing regret over the fact that you did not write even a more controversial book. You accused the leaders of the angry demonstration in Islamabad of exploiting a religious slogan for secular and political ends. They may have done so, but what about the innocent and ignorant people who died in the violence? You expressed no sympathy for them.

And now you issue a three-sentence statement that, at best, has the semblance of regret. Quite honestly, Mr. Rushdie, your heart does not beat in this statement, your expression is glaringly perfunctory.

I am saddened that a bounty has been placed on your head and that a great writer like you, rather than presenting himself to the public, is in hiding. You have elicited the rage of entire nations. This is a pity. But, Mr. Rushdie, you have cut them and they are bleeding. Do something quickly to heal the wound.

JOHN BANVILLE

SOURCE: John Banville, "An Interview with Salman Rushdie," in *The New York Review of Books*, Vol. XL, No. 5, March 4, 1993, pp. 34-6.

[*The following essay is based on an interview with Rushdie four years after he went into hiding. The author discusses the controversy surrounding* The Satanic Verses, *his seemingly inconsistent statements regarding the furor, and other literary, religious, and political topics.*]

Under an unknown picture somewhere in India there is hidden a portrait of Salman Rushdie's mother. The story goes like this. An artist, hired by Rushdie's father to paint Disney animals on the walls of the child Salman's nursery, went on to do a portrait of Mrs. Rushdie. When the painting was finished, Rushdie *pere* did not like it. The artist stored the picture in the studio of a friend of his, another artist, who, running out of canvases one day, painted a picture of his own over it. Afterward, when both had become famous artists, the friend could not remember which picture he had painted over the other's canvas, or to whom he had sold it.

When Rushdie told me the story recently when I was interviewing him for the *Irish Times* it struck me as peculiarly apt, given both the kind of artist Salman Rushdie is (the painted mother, the harsh father, the Disney creatures poking their anthropomorphic noses through the backdrop) and his present circumstances. He too has disappeared behind a work of art.

We met in the stillness of a post-Christmas bank holiday afternoon. I had not seen him for ten years. He had changed. How would he not? Yet the differences in him were a surprise. I had expected that he would be angry, tense, volubly outraged. However, what I sensed most strongly in him was an immense and somehow sustaining sadness. The confident, exuberant, funny thirty-five-year-old I met ten years ago had taken on a *gravitas* that was at once moving and impressive.

On February 14 Rushdie will have been in hiding for four years. The *fatwa*, or death sentence, imposed on him by Ayatollah Khomeini in retribution for his "blasphemous" novel *The Satanic Verses*, is still in force, backed up by the offer of $2 million in blood money to anyone who should be successful in murdering him. Over the years the world has accommodated itself to this extraordinary situation, but nevertheless it is, as Rushdie himself insists, a scandal.

I began by asking if he could discern any shift in the political situation in Iran that would give him hope that the *fatwa* might be lifted.

"I used to spend a lot of my time trying to keep up with the internal struggles there, but then I thought, to hell with that. It's not my business to understand the internal politics of Iran. The banning of my book and the imposition of the *fatwa* is a terrorist act by the state of Iran, and my business is simply to make sure that the Iranian state is dealt with on that basis, and is obliged to alter its position."

Does he have any contact with people in Iran—people in power? "There have been occasions when so-called intermediaries have popped up out of the woodwork, claiming to have great contacts in Iran. What tends to happen is that I talk to them for a couple of weeks and then they disappear and I never hear from them again.

"The question all these people ask is, What reparations would I be prepared to make? But my view is, who is injuring whom here? It's not for me to say I will withdraw *The Satanic Verses*. The whole issue is that a crime has been committed against the book."

How did the book come to the attention of the mullahs in the first place?

"Well, I think. . . " A hesitation, and a low chuckle; his delight in the rich absurdity of human affairs is one thing that has not changed over the years. ". . . I think it started in Leicester."

So I have my headline: *It Started in Leicester*.

"It does seem the first rumblings against the book started in a mosque or council of mosques there. They circulated selected lines and passages from the book to show how terrible it was. From there, it spread around Britain and out to India and Pakistan and Bangladesh, where there were riots and people were killed." There are a number of legends about how the book came to Khomeini's attention. There is a passage in the novel about an Imam in exile who is not unlike Khomeini, and there is a view that he took exception to it. "I don't find that very convincing because the book did not exist in a Farsi edition, and there were no copies of the book available in Iran at that time anyway. It's since been admitted by quite high-ranking Iranian officials that Khomeini never saw a copy of the book; whatever he did he did on the basis of hearsay."

I ask the only question I have come prepared with: Does he feel the affair has made him into a purely political phenomenon?

"One of the oddest things for me about the business is that while *Midnight's Children* and *Shame* were in some ways quite directly political, or at least they used history as part of their architecture, I thought *The Satanic Verses* was the least political novel I had ever written, a novel whose engine was not public affairs but other kinds of more personal and cultural crises. It was a book written really to make sense of what had happened to me, which was the move from one part of the world to another and what that does to the various aspects of one's being-in-the-world. But there I am thinking I'm writing my most personal novel and I end up writing this political bombshell!

"Certainly it is a big problem that people by and large don't talk to me about my *writing*. Even the novel I wrote after *The Satanic Verses* [*Haroun and the Sea of Stories*], which was a great pleasure for me, and which individual readers responded to warmly, was received on the public level as if it were something to be decoded, an allegory of my predicament. But it's not an allegory; it's a novel.

"All the same I can't avoid the situation; while I don't see myself as this entity that has been constructed with my name on it, at the same time I can't deny my life: this is what has happened to me. It will of course to some extent affect my writing, not directly perhaps but yet in profound ways. I have always to some extent felt unhoused. I feel very much more so now."

Is this not a good, a *necessary* way for an artist to feel?

"We are all in some manner alone on the planet, beyond the community or the language or whatever; we are poor, bare creatures; it's no bad thing to be forced to recognize these things."

An irony of the affair not much remarked on is that *The Satanic Verses* is very sympathetic and tender toward the unhoused, the dispossessed, the deracinated—the very people, in fact, who rioted in the streets and publicly burned what they had been told was a blasphemous book. He nods, smiling, in a kind of hopeless misery. It is deeply painful for him that the people whom he has made his subject, and for whom he has a deep fondness, are the ones who hate him most, or hate at least that image of him fostered by fanatics in the Muslim world.

He is adamant that what is most important here is the integrity of the text. "When at the start of the affair I was able to contact friends and allies and they asked me what I wanted them to do, I said, Defend the text. Simply to make a general defense of free speech doesn't answer the attack; the attack is particularized. If you answer a particularized attack with only a general defense then to some extent you are conceding a point, you're saying, Oh yes, we recognize that it may be an evil book, but even an evil book must be allowed to exist. But it is not an evil book. So I have always been most grateful when people have tried to defend the text, for that's at least as important to me as the defense of my life."

What interests me in Rushdie's fiction—in anyone's fiction—is not its public, political aspect, but the way in which in it the objective world is reordered under the pressure of a subjective sensibility. It struck me, rereading *The Satanic Verses* in preparation for this meeting, that the final section, a (relatively) realistic account of a father's death, is perhaps the most significant—and certainly the most moving—passage in the book, the moment toward which the whole work moves, no matter how fantastical what went before. Was this section grounded in personal experience?

"Very much. My father died of the same cancer that killed the character in the book. I was there when he died. He and I had always had a somewhat difficult relationship, and it was important for us to have some time together before the end. I felt a great moral ambiguity about using my father's death in that way, especially as it was so recent, but in the end I thought I would do it because it would be an act of respect. I was afraid that it might appear a stuck-on ending, but as it turned out it seemed to be just what the book needed, had been demanding."

He believes that one of the most important themes in the novel is loss: of parents, country, self, things which to a greater or lesser degree Rushdie himself has lost. Does he feel abandoned by those in the Muslim world who he might have thought would support him?

"Intellectuals in the Muslim community know the size of the crime that has been committed against the book. A few months ago a declaration of unequivocal support for me was signed by seventy or so leading Iranian intellectuals in exile [printed in the *New York Review of Books,* 14 May 1992], which was wonderfully courageous; after all, they are not receiving government protection, and in some cases, as a result of their support for me, their lives have been threatened by the Iranians.

"An important part of their statement was that blasphemy cannot be used as a limiting point on thought. If we go back to a world in which religious authorities can set the limits of what it is permissible to say and think, then we shall have reinvented the Inquisition and de-invented the whole modern idea of freedom of speech, which was invented as a struggle against the Church."

We turn to the subject of the book he is working on. "It's about someone who is thrown out of his family because of an unfortunate love affair. It begins with this expulsion from the family, and goes on to recount how he is forced to remake his life from scratch." We are back to the feeling of homelessness that weighs so heavily upon him.

He tells me the story of the lost portrait of his mother. "In my book, about a very different mother and a very different son, there is a similarly lost portrait, and one of the strands of the story is his finding this picture, and in this way the struggle there had been in life between mother and son continues beyond death."

The novel will be called *The Moor's Last Sigh,* which is a translation of the Spanish name of the place from which in 1492 the last Sultan of Granada, driven out of the city by the Catholic armies of Ferdinand and Isabella, looked back for a final time at the Alhambra palace.

"The idea of the fall of Granada is used throughout the book as a metaphor for various kinds of rupture. One can see Moorish Spain as a fusion of cultures—Spanish, Moorish, Jewish, the 'Peoples of the Book'—which came apart at the fall of Granada.

"This was the only time in history when there was a fusion of those three cultures. Of course, one should not sentimentalize that entity, for the basis on which it existed was Islamic imperialism; Islam was clearly the boss, and the other religions had to abide by the laws. All the same, there was a fusion of cultures which since then have been to some extent each other's other. In that fusion are ideas which have always appealed to me, particularly now; for instance, the idea of the fundamentalist, totalized explanation of the world as opposed to the complex, relativist, hybrid vision of things."

The last sultan, Boabdil (Muhammad XI, d. 1527), was "weak," that is, he was a "poetic type"—which means, I suppose, he was someone in whom all the cultures flowed and therefore was unable to take absolutist views; against him there was the absolutist Catholic Queen Isabella, and his own formidable mother, Aisha. As Boabdil paused on that last ridge, Aisha is reputed to have told him, "Yes, you may well weep like a woman for what you could not defend like a man."

"The story is a metaphor for the conflict between the one and the many, between the pure and the impure, the sacred and the profane, and as such is a continuation by other means of the concerns of my previous books. Boabdil's story is merely background—there is no direct 'historical' narrative—and is done rather like Sidney Nolan's series of Ned Kelly paintings.

"The book is grounded in my experiences of these past years, and what makes it particularly interesting for me is that this is true, not fiction; that this obscene thing could happen to me and my book, and could go on and cease to seem scandalous."

Rushdie feels that the reaction to the book was in part a result of the force of the political language of Iran. The Iranians saw the United States as the Great Satan, and Britain, a satellite of the US, as a Little Satan, whereas the Jews were seen as being responsible for everything that is wrong in the world. "So when, in the mullahs' view, a Jewish American publisher hired a self-hating race-traitor and (British) wog to write a book to attack Islam, the 'conspiracy' was complete.

"The thing I didn't understand—or underestimated the force of—was that whereas in the Judeo-Christian tradition it is accepted that one may at least dispute whether good and evil are external or internal to us— to ask, for instance, Do we need such beings as God and the Devil in order to understand good and evil?— the parts of my book that raised this question represented something that it is still very hard to say publicly in the Islamic world; and to hear it said with all the paraphernalia of contemporary fiction was very upsetting for many people, to which I'm afraid my only answer is, That's tough—because this kind of thing needs to be said."

He was looking forward to going to Ireland, believing that in such a country, with its recent memories of colonialism, and which is still to some extent engaged in nation-building, it would be easier for him to be understood than in many other, more "progressive," countries. "Also, the knowledge that people have who live in countries where God is not dead is very different to that of people who live in countries where religion has died.

"I have always insisted that what happened to me is only the best-known case among fairly widespread, coherent attempts to repress all progressive voices, not just in Iran but throughout the Muslim world. Always the arguments used against these people are the same: always it's insult, offense, blasphemy, heresy—the language of the Inquisition. And you can widen your view and look for the same process beyond the Muslim world, where the same battle is continuing, the battle between the sacred and the profane. And in that war I'm on the side of the profane."

I ask, with some hesitation, if he would like to say something about his public declaration, two years ago, of his espousal of Islam, which he subsequently recanted. He flinched, as at the resurgence of an old pain.

"I feel I've had to undo that; I'll probably be saying that for the rest of my life.

"What happened was this. First of all, I was probably more despairing in that moment than I've ever been. I felt that there was no energy or enthusiasm in the world to do anything about my plight. Secondly, a thing which people sometimes don't understand is how painful it was for me to realize that the people I had always written about were the very people who were now burning the book. The need in me to heal that rift was very profound—still is.

"Those two things came together—the despair, and the need to heal the rift—and what I felt was, look, I'd better do something very large in order to show these people whom I write about that I'm not their enemy; that, yes, I do have a very profound dispute with the way in which the people who are in power in Islam attempt to regulate their societies, but that maybe in the end I could carry on that dispute more effectively from inside the room than from outside it. I wanted to say, I am not outside the house of Islam throwing stones at the windows, I'm inside it trying to build it and redecorate it. That was the way I thought about it to myself at the time, but also I can see that in that process there was a large effort to rationalize the doing of something I thought might help.

"All I can say is that, having said what I said I felt sick with myself, for a very long time, not because so many people who had been supporting me found it bizarre or whatever—because my response to that was then, and remains today, that anyone who thinks he can do better is welcome to come and try.

"The problem for me was not other people's attitudes; the problem for me was my own sense of having betrayed myself.

"The issue was that the thing that has enabled me to survive in this affair has been that I have always been able to defend my words and writings and statements; always I said what I said and wrote what I wrote because it was what I felt, because it was what came out of me truthfully, and as a result I could stand by it; but at *that* moment I felt I had done something that I couldn't defend in that way, that did not represent my real feeling.

"There were good reasons for it—the attempt at peacemaking and so on—but it was not a statement I could put my hand on my heart and say I believed in.

"I found it agonizing that my public statements were at complete odds with my private feelings. That situation became untenable for me, and so I had to unsay it; and now I've been unsaying it for two years. I'll probably have to unsay it to the press in every country in the world.

"After what religion has done to me in the last four years, I feel much angrier about what it does to people and their lives than I ever did before; that's the truth. The writer who wrote *The Satanic Verses* was sympathetic to Islam, was trying very hard to imagine himself into that frame of mind, albeit from a nonbelieving point of view; I couldn't write that sympathetically now, because of the very intimate demonstration I have had of the power of religion for evil; that is now my experience, and for me to try to write from some other experience would be false.

"I can still accept at a theoretical level the power of religion for good, the way in which it gives people consolation and the way in which it strengthens people, and the fact that these are very beautiful stories and that they are codifications of human belief and human philosophy, I wouldn't deny any of that—but in my life religion has acted in a very malign way, and in consequence my reactions to it are what you would expect."

I suggest that in the matter of his "conversion" he is likely to be harder on himself than anyone else would be. A great many people do things which they come to be ashamed of, but these actions will never get into the headlines.

"Of course, that's true, Martin Amis very soon after the *fatwa* was imposed said I had 'vanished into the front page,' and I think that it was a very accurate phrase. I have been trying to escape from the front page. What I find now is that the ideas that present themselves as things I want to write about are much less public, much less politically generated than they used to be. I have now had enough politics to last a lifetime. I now want to write about other things."

Have circumstances got easier for him, or has he got used, insofar as one can get used, to the kind of life he has been forced to lead?

"They've got easier and more difficult. At the beginning, the first eighteen months, it was very hard for me to emerge from the safe place; it was a very sequestered time." In those early days did he have a garden, somewhere outside, where he could walk?

"Depends where I was; often, no. We had to be very careful because we had no knowledge of what was coming against us. It was a personally difficult time because of my marriage ending. That was the worst time, in terms of physical constraints. It's got a little easier now, even though it does still involve incredible paraphernalia, all this cloak and dagger stuff, but I'm not quite as confined as I was.

"On the other hand, psychologically I find it harder to tolerate now than I did then. When this began, nobody expected it to last very long. I remember the first day when the police came to offer me protection, they said, Let's just go away and lie low for a few days while the governments sort it out. People thought because what had happened was so outrageous it would have to be fixed and would be fixed very soon. This was why I agreed to dive underground, because everyone thought it would be just a matter or days. And here we are almost four years later.

"When it began I could say to myself, It's an emergency, and in such a case you do what is necessary to handle it, so I could accept the need for hiding, etc. Now, four years later, I realize it's not an emergency, it's a scandal. And what's worst about it is that people are behaving as if it were not a scandal."

Does he feel the British government is not doing enough?

"Well, let's face it, they saved my life. They are affording me in, I must say, a very ungrudging way, a level of protection that is equivalent to what the Prime Minister would get, and I'm just some novelist. To that extent they've done a great thing for me. But if we are to get to a position where none of this is needed, it's going to require not just a defensive act, but a positive act.

"As a result of the trips abroad I've been able to make there is a lot of interest in Europe and North America in doing something about the case. And I'm trying to make the government here see that this would be a wonderful moment for it to put itself at the head of that international effort."

Has he met John Major?

"No. I hope that might be rectified. It's a problem. This campaign requires practical acts and symbolic gestures. At that level, the fact the British Prime Minister has never allowed himself to be seen in public shaking my hand is an indication that the affair is being in some way downgraded. It's getting to the point where it's easier for me to meet the heads of other governments than the leaders of my own.

"Things are moving, however. The British government have now formally told the Iranians they will not normalize relations until the *fatwa* is canceled. Also, at the recent Edinburgh Summit the British delegation introduced into the conclusions of the summit a statement that all European nations should continue to pressurize Iran on the *fatwa*."

Was he very frightened at the start? Is he less frightened now?

"It's less now because the situation is less frightening. At first it wasn't a matter really of being frightened. When I first heard the news I thought I was dead. I thought I probably had two or three days at the most to live. That's beyond fear, it was the strangest thing I've ever felt.

"After that it was very shocking and unnerving to see the extent of the hatred that was being hurled at me; that was very disorienting, very bewildering. Then I came to the conclusion that I must not allow myself to be terrified; the only answer to a terrorist is to say, I'm not scared of you. That was an extraordinary moment. I felt free."

Has the experience of the past four years changed him?

"Yes, it's changed me very much. It has hurt me a great deal. If you are on the receiving end of a great injury you are never the same again; you may not be worse, you may not be better, but you're never the same again. It made me feel everything I thought I knew was false. I was always very impatient—with the exception of writing, where I'm very patient—but now I'm able to take a longer view of things."

The experience must have affected the quality of his life, must have thinned it out. His reply is simple.

"My life has been wrecked."

MICHAEL WOOD

SOURCE: Michael Wood, "Shenanigans," in *London Review of Books*, Vol. 17, No. 17, September 7, 1995, pp. 3, 5.

[*In the following review, Wood presents an in-depth analysis of Rushdie's career, culminating with* The Moor's Last Sigh.]

The Moor's last sigh is several things, both inside and outside Salman Rushdie's sprawling new novel [*The Moor's Last Sigh*]. It is the defeated farewell of the last Moorish ruler in Spain, the Sultan Boabdil leaving his beloved Granada in 1492, a year also known for other travels. It is Othello's last gasp of jealousy and violence. It is, in the novel, the name of two paintings depicting Boabdil's departure; and it is what the novel itself becomes, the long, breathless, terminal narration of the asthmatic Moraes Zogoiby, alias 'Moor'. *Old Moore's Almanac* flickers somewhere here ('Old Moor will sigh no more'), as does Luis Buñuel's *dernier soupir* (which appears as the Ultimo Suspiro petrol station). Ingrid Bergman and Humphrey Bogart were wrong, we learn, to think that a sigh is just a sigh: a sigh could be almost anything, and the name Zogoiby is a version of the Arabic *elzogoybi*, 'the unlucky one', the sobriquet traditionally attached to Boabdil.

Boabdil is elegiac shorthand for a delicate, plural civilisation unable to defend itself against single-minded religion; or rather against the single-minded political use of religion: the spirit of the Catholic Spanish kings of the Counter-Reformation, or the mosque and temple-destroying Hindus and Muslims of a later day. Boabdil, remote as he seems in time and space, is an aspect of India as it might have been in this century, and the novel gives him a legendary descendency of Indian Jews, one of whom finally marries an Indian Catholic of (probably also legendary) Portuguese descent. A Zogoiby weds a Da Gama; the dispossessed Moor meets up with an originator of empire. In South India; in Cochin, to be precise, one of the formerly (notionally) independent states which are now part of the state of Kerala. The date of the meeting is 1939, although most of the rest of the novel takes place in post-Independence India, and in Bombay.

The meeting is several centuries late and occurs only in the family imagination, and in what looks like the wrong place, but how else, Rushdie is suggesting, are we to understand, or even picture, the failed dream of a many-cultured peace, what the wreckage of empire might look like if it were not only a wreck. There are Chinese tiles in the synagogue in Cochin, 'pushy ladies, skirts-not-saris, Spanish shenanigans, Moorish crowns . . . can this really be India?' 'Shenanigans' is good, an entirely gratuitous dash of yet another culture. Rushdie's narrator continues his questions: 'Is this not the most eccentric of slices to extract from all that life—a freak blond hair plucked from a jet-black (and horribly unravelling) plait?' He knows we know the answer.

These characters and stories are not less Indian than for whom the claim is made. And the same goes for the stories. The supposed centre that makes them seem marginal, or (later) seeks to expel them, is the invention of a murderous ideology. A sigh is not just a sigh. But it's not a shout; even less a last battle. Scarcely a memory. It's appropriate—too appropriate, I think, too literary in the genteel old fashion—that the book should end in a clatter of names, phrases and scenery borrowed from *Don Quixote,* that great work of comic mourning written by a Spaniard pretending to be an Arab. On the last pages, the narrator gazes, for good measure, across a valley at the Alhambra, 'the glory of the Moors, their triumphant masterpiece and their last redoubt'. Is this Rushdie or the Granada tourist office?

Rushdie takes risks as a writer, apart from the obvious ones. Well, the obvious ones aren't risks, they are grave dangers, and to call them risks would be to suggest that Rushdie courted them. His life is in danger not because he wrote a clever, irreverent book, but because of the thuggish way his book was received. The question of a more diffuse hurt and offence caused by *The Satanic Verses*—well, caused by the idea or the description of *The Satanic Verses*—is different, and very complicated, not helped by knee-jerking in any direction. It seems to me monstrous to 'think of taking offence as a fundamental right', as someone says in *East, West.* But then it is heartless not to see that unintended offences can cause pain. The risks I have in mind are far less grave. The worst that can happen here is a little critical disagreement.

The risks are more or less lost in the sheer spilling high spirits of *Midnight's Children;* muted by a disciplined sense of outrage in *Shame;* converted into charm in the fantasy world of *Haroun and the Sea of Stories;* carefully rationed in the stories of *East, West.* But they are there all the time. In *The Satanic Verses* they become broadly visible, boldly taken *as* risks, so that great imaginative coups alternate with peeling patches of whimsy. *The Moor's Last Sigh* is steadier than that, more old-fashioned, a sort of hysterical family saga, and its risks play off each other more harmoniously; but they are still very visible, a sort of signature, and it may be worth trying to say what they are.

Garrulousness first of all. Rushdie's narrators not only talk a lot, they are their talk. They are not so much characters as voices—sometimes they are unconvincing as characters—and the less they understand about themselves, the more they talk. They represent brilliant, voluble evasions of the world, which is nevertheless evoked by these evasions—which leaks through their words and their scarce silences. When the young hero of *Haroun and the Sea of Stories* discovers that silence, too, has 'its own grace and beauty', the effect is one of major shock. He had thought that silence was evil, and the rest of the story he is in points that way. The arch-enemy is the Prince of Silence, destroyer of stories. He has imposed 'Silence Laws', and his more fanatical devotees sew their lips together with twine. Speech is the freedom of speech, of course, and such freedom dies if it is not exercised. Since *Haroun* is a form of fairy tale, liberal democracy not only gets a little plug, but wins the day, because the chattering good guys also form a fine army: 'All those arguments and debates, all that openness, had created powerful bonds of fellowship between them.' We wish. But words are also the foes of reality, as Conrad suggested, and it's not always good to like them so much. The narrator of *The Moor's Last Sigh* finds what he calls gabbiness erotic: 'When I chatter on, or am assailed by the garrulity of others, I find it—how-to-say?—arousing.' *Midnight's Children* is a triumph of such arousal; but we can all think of occasions, in and out of fiction, when chatter is either irrelevant or helpless or worse. Even *Midnight's Children* is a shallow masterpiece (Pauline Kael's phrase for *Citizen Kane*); it's no use looking for the depths it doesn't have.

Melodrama. Rushdie's narrative method is full of extravagant nods and winks: spoofed nods and winks, mostly, but maybe nods and winks, unlike sighs, are just what they are, spoofed or not. 'When I needed to move a mountain for love, I thought my mother would help. Alas for us all; I was wrong.' 'O mother, mother, I know why you banished me now. O my great dead mother, my duped progenitrix, my fool.' 'I brutally put an end to his accursed life. And in so doing called a curse down upon my own.' This is not the tourist office, it's some sort of fire-breathing, little-did-we-know romance. Rushdie is aware of what he is doing. He sets up Disney cartoons as a context, accuses his characters of 'old-style Indian melodrama', and when the narrator learns that his father is 'the most evil man that ever lived', the reference is made in contrast to the father of Superman. The trouble is that Rushdie really needs some of the emotions, and some of the power, that are being burlesqued here. At times he gets them, but it's a close thing; often the sheer lumpishness of the spoofed mode gets in his way.

Hyperbole. Rushdie specialises in a mode of fantasy which doesn't depart from the real but only exaggerates it; this exaggeration then becomes a brilliant or lurid metaphor for a different but related reality. A good example would be the elaborately twinned cracking-up of Saleem Sinai and India in *Midnight's Children.* In *The Moor's Last Sigh,* the narrator was born four and a half months after his conception, and has lived his whole life at twice the ordinary pace, double-quick, as people say in old-fashioned public schools and Rushdie's India. The idioms and the images begin to sprout, the narrator telling us, rather too helpfully, that he is living out 'the literal truth of the metaphors so often applied to my mother and her circle': 'In the fast lane, on the fast track, ahead of my time, a jetsetter right down to my genes, I burned—having no option—the candle at both ends.' The city connection is almost irresistible, in any case not resisted: 'I have always been, if only in my uncontrollable increases, prodigious. Like the city itself, Bombay of my joys and sorrows, I mushroomed into a huge urbane sprawl of a fellow, I expanded without time for proper planning.' Should that really be 'urbane'? I wouldn't ask if elsewhere a man's 'niece Sara' didn't turn into his 'daughter Sara' within half a page. There's magic realism and there's magic realism. But then if the narrator is Bombay, Bombay is India: the bastard child of a Portuguese-English wedding, and yet the most Indian of Indian cities ... Those who hated India, those who sought to ruin it, would need to ruin Bombay.'

Rushdie's hyperboles are often memorable, but sometimes work too hard, and they and the garrulousness are closely connected to another risk: the explanation. Rushdie is an extraordinarily intelligent and fluent writer, but he doesn't always trust the reader to get what he means. Sometimes the explanations are cogent enough, too explicit for some tastes, but loaded with the energy of anxiety: 'Children make fictions of their fathers, re-inventing them according to their childish needs. The reality of a father is a weight few sons can bear.' At other times perhaps Rushdie is just allowing his narrator a little sententiousness: 'That's not a star worth following; it's just an unlucky rock. Our fates are here on earth. There are no guiding stars.' But at other times we seem to be sinking into genuine soppiness: 'his willingness to permit the co-existence within himself of conflicting impulses is the source of his full, gentle humaneness ... that hate-the-sin-and-love-the-sinner sweetness, that historical generosity of spirit, which is one of the true wonders of India'; 'There is in us, in all of us, some measure of brightness, of possibility. We start with that, but also with its dark counter-force.' Or just wordiness: 'the tragedy of multiplicity destroyed by singularity, the defeat of Many by One'. At other times the explainer and the novelist in Rushdie seem to be telling different stories, and curious tensions arise.

The whole of *The Moor's Last Sigh* is predicated on an argument about the One and the Many, about the vulnerability and desirability of the world of the Many. All the stories run that way except one: that of a woman with a multiple personality disorder who ruins a whole series of lives by pretending to a number of people she was what each of them wanted. Singularity in this case would have been better than multiplicity, and the story thus becomes 'a bitter parable' in which 'the polarity between good and evil was reversed.' The narrator says that 'it did not fail to occur' to him that the woman's story—she is among other things his mistress and his nemesis—was 'a defeat for the pluralistic philosophy on which we had all been raised'. He doesn't do anything with this counter-example, though, and fifty pages later he is still lyrically allegorising his affair:

> I wanted to cling to the image of love as the blending of spirits, as mélange, as the triumph of the impure, mongrel, conjoining best of us over what there is in us of the solitary, the isolated, the austere, the dogmatic, the pure; of love as democracy, as the victory of the no-man-is-an-island, two's company Many over the clean, mean, apartheiding Ones.

Plainly Rushdie sees this attempt as doomed to failure, but he doesn't seem to disavow it, and the mention of apartheid dumps all the virtue on one side. There is no real tussle or dialogue here, and even the contradiction of a philosophy only reverses it, leaving us with the same polarity upside down. What if the polarity is the problem? What if the Many need to talk to the One as well as to each other? What if the whole proposition is just too general or too abstract to apply to any recognisable human situation, if even the impure and the mongrels can't quite rise to the Platonic dignity of their own idea, *the* impure, mongrel best of us? These are the questions that I think Rushdie the novelist is asking, that his novel is asking, in its intricate profusion. But the explainer doesn't seem to be listening; and the explainer takes over the whole last section of the book: an epilogue which limps along into a shoot-out sponsored by the Lone Ranger and other heroes of moral complexity.

Rushdie's last risk, that of writing in pictures, so rarely fails to deliver brilliant results that it doesn't look like a risk at all. But it is one; and only a writer of great gifts could make it look so safe. For all his talkiness, Rushdie also understands that less can be more, and there is a very moving moment in this novel when he tells us, through his narrator, 'another secret' about fear: 'the revolution against fear, the engendering of that tawdry despot's fall, has more or less nothing to do with "courage". It is driven by something much more straightforward: the simple need to get on with your life.' What Rushdie doesn't say is that that *is* courage, of the most exemplary sort.

And so his images, which rightly raise far more questions than we can answer, speak for themselves, and often quite laconically. A bridegroom on his wedding night takes off his clothes, his wife already undressed and waiting; puts on her wedding-dress, and takes off across the water for a homosexual rendezvous: 'the bridegroom's face beneath the bridal veil', as Rushdie's narrator puts it. A character in Cochin is given permission to train a group of actors as Lenin impersonators, eager to spread the great man's word to these far southern regions. They say his speeches in Malayalam, Kannada, Tulu, Konkani, Tamil, Telugu and English, but they don't look much like Lenin, and are exposed and dismissed by a Russian Lenin impersonator, who calls them a mockery: 'this is not adaptation but satirical caricature.' 'O, I was lost in fiction,' a character says, 'and murder was all around.' Fiction really feels like a place here, rather than a metaphor, and when another character is said to die, 'quickly, in great pain, railing against the enemy in her body, savagely angry with death for arriving too soon and behaving so badly', we are so caught up in the picture that the very idea of the figurative seems to fade.

I haven't said much about the plot of *The Moor's Last Sigh.* It details the lives of wealthy spice merchants and their eccentric children and in-laws; their colleagues and fellow conspirators, protégés and enemies; their loves and deaths. There is a great deal of violence and corruption ('one man one bribe' is a cynic's definition of democracy), and some good story twists. At the heart of the novel, though, is the work of the narrator's mother, the painter Aurora Zogoiby. She herself is a dazzling character, prematurely white-haired, beautiful, fearless, limitlessly talented — 'Listen: she was the light of our lives, the excitement of our imaginations, the beloved of our dreams. We loved her even as she destroyed us' — but she is not as memorable or as complicated as her paintings. Her *Moor's Last Sigh,* for instance, 170 x 247 cms, oil on canvas, 1987, the year of her death, is 'a picture which, for all its great size, had been stripped to the harsh essentials, all its elements converging on the face at its heart, the Sultan's face, from which horror, weakness, loss and pain poured like darkness itself'. Aurora has done all kinds of paintings since she covered the walls of her room with a vision of India when she was 13; and she has done a sequence of paintings about the defeated, departing Moor. 'She was using Arab Spain to re-imagine India,' and so 'Jews, Christians, Muslims, Parsis, Sikhs, Buddhists, Jains crowded into her paint — Boabdil's fancydress balls.' A pluralist's golden age.

'So there was,' her son thinks, 'a didacticism here, but what with the vivid surrealism of her images and the kingfisher brilliance of her colouring and the dynamic acceleration of her brush, it was easy not to feel preached at, to revel in the carnival without listening to the barker, to dance to the music without caring for the message in the song.'

It's easy to do the same with Rushdie, although he could make it easier, and it's worth remembering, as he always does, that the fantastic sometimes just is the historical. Here is another piece of picture-writing, showing the working poor of Bombay, who are not only poor and horribly exploited, but officially regarded as non-existent:

> They continued to be classified as phantoms, to move through the city like wraiths, except that these were the wraiths that kept the city going, building its houses, hauling its goods, cleaning up its droppings, and then simply and terribly dying, each in their turn, unseen, as their spectral blood poured out of their ghostly mouths in the middle of the bitch-city's all-too-real, uncaring streets.

SOURCES FOR FURTHER STUDY

Amanuddin, Syed. "The Novels of Salman Rushdie: Mediated Reality as Fantasy." *World Literature Today* 63 (Winter 1989): 42-5.

> Discusses *Grimus, Midnight's Children,* and *Shame* in terms of Rushdie's views of mediated and unmediated reality.

Cook, Rufus. "Place and Displacement in Salman Rushdie's Work." *World Literature Today* 68 (Winter 1994): 23-8.

> Examines Rushdie's novels in terms of his preoccupation with the relationship between imaginary constructs and real-life counterparts, noting Rushdie's acknowledgment that reality takes precedence over art.

"Salman Rushdie Talks to the London Consortium about *The Satanic Verses.*" *Critical Quarterly* 38 (Summer 1996): 51-70.

> Discusses the form of the text, his version of Indian cinema and the early history of Islam, and his use of Roman poet Ovid's *Metamorphosis.*

Harrison, James. "Reconstructing *Midnight's Children* and

Shame." University of Toronto Quarterly 59 (Spring 1990): 399-412.

> Demonstrates how Rushdie creates structure, cohesion, and unity in *Midnight's Children* and *Shame,* despite the novels's postmodernist presentation.

Rombes, Nicholas D., Jr. "*The Satanic Verses* as a Cinematic Narrative." *Literature/Film Quarterly* 21, No. 1 (1993): 47-53.

> Analyzes how Rushdie presents the opposition between an omniscient narrator and the camera's eye, discussing his use of film language in *The Satanic Verses* and the ways he incorporates cinematic techniques into the narrative structure.

Srivastava, Aruna. "'The Empire Writes Back': Language and History in *Shame* and *Midnight's Children*." *Ariel* 20 (October 1989): 62-78.

> Argues that Rushdie uses colonial history in his narratives to displace "more politically acceptable ones."

Leslie Marmon Silko

1948-

American novelist, poet, and short story writer.

INTRODUCTION

Silko is one of the foremost authors to emerge from the Native American literary renaissance of the 1970s. Her works blend Western literary genres with the oral traditions of her Laguna Pueblo heritage to communicate Native American concepts concerning time, nature, and spirituality and their relevance in the contemporary world. Her protagonists, often of mixed Laguna and European heritage, draw upon the moral strength of their native community and its traditions in order to overcome the repressive, alienating effects of white society.

Biographical Information

Born March 5, 1948, in Albuquerque, New Mexico, Silko descends from a mixed heritage of Laguna Pueblo, Plains Indian, Mexican, and Anglo-American ancestry. Raised on the Laguna Pueblo Reservation in northern New Mexico, she attended federal schools administered by the Bureau of Indian Affairs, but at home she also learned Laguna legends and traditions from her great-grandmother and other members of her extended family. She graduated magna cum laude from the University of New Mexico in 1969 and briefly attended law school before she decided to pursue a writing career. During the early 1970s, Silko published short stories, most notably "Lullaby," "Yellow Woman," and "Tony's Story," in several literary journals, but she first received critical attention from the novel *Ceremony* (1977), which depicts life on an Indian reservation and explores philosophical issues. While working on her fiction, Silko has taught English literature at universities and colleges throughout the Southwest.

Major Works

Ceremony weaves free verse poetry with narrative

prose and skillfully incorporates Native American storytelling techniques. Set primarily in the years following World War II, the novel concerns Tayo, a war veteran of mixed European and Laguna heritage, who returns to the reservation shattered by his war experiences. He ultimately finds healing, however, with the help of both Betonie, a wise old half-breed, and T'seh Montano, a medicine woman who embodies the feminine, life-giving aspects of the earth. Tayo learns from them that ancient ceremonies are not merely rituals, but a means of achieving one's proper place in the universe. *Storyteller* (1981) features some of Silko's earlier short stories and includes poetry from her earlier collection *Laguna Woman* (1974) as well. Among these stories, "Yellow Woman" derives from traditional abduction tales in which a kachina, or mountain spirit, kidnaps and seduces a young woman on her way to draw water. In Silko's tale, a contemporary Pueblo woman suspects that her liaison with a cattle rustler is a reenactment of the "yellow woman" legend. The boundary between her experience and the myth slowly dissolves as she becomes aware of her active role in the traditions of her community. "Lullaby" presents an old woman recalling the time when her children were taken away for education but later returned to a culture that no longer seemed familiar or comfortable to them. "Tony's Story" concerns an Indian who kills a vicious policeman. *With the Delicacy and Strength of Lace* (1985) is a collection of correspondence between Silko and the poet James Wright, who died of cancer in 1980. *Almanac of the Dead* (1991) offers an apocalyptic vision of North America when Native Americans reclaim their ancestral lands after whites succumb to crime, perversion, drug addiction, and environmental degradation.

Critical Reception

Ceremony established Silko as an important voice of the Native American community. Charles L. Larson called the novel "powerfully conceived" and "strongly rooted in the author's own tribal background [which is] especially valuable here." Frank MacShane hailed Silko as "without question... the most accomplished Indian writer of her generation." *Storyteller* revived interest in Silko's early short stories and poetry. N. Scott Momaday found the volume "a rich, many-faceted book," adding that Silko's "perceptions are accurate, and her style reflects the breadth, the texture, the mortality of her subjects." While some critics have objected to what they perceived as Silko's exaggeration of corruption in Anglo-American society in *Almanac of the Dead*—Malcolm Jones, Jr. observed that "in her cosmology, there are good people and there are white people"—most have praised her vivid characterizations and inventive plotting as a compelling portrait of a society founded upon the eradication of Native Americans and their cultures.

(For further information, see *Authors and Artists for Young Adults*, Vol. 14; *Contemporary Authors*, Vols. 115, 122; *Contemporary Authors New Revision Series*, Vol. 45; *Contemporary Literary Criticism*, Vols. 23, 74; *Dictionary of Literary Biography*, Vols. 143, 175; *DISCovering Authors*; *DISCovering Authors: Canadian*; *DISCovering Authors Modules: Most-studied Authors Module, Multicultural Authors Module, Popular Fiction and Genre Authors Module*; *Native North American Literature*.)

CRITICAL COMMENTARY

EDITH BLICKSILVER

SOURCE: Edith Blicksilver, "Traditionalism vs. Modernity: Leslie Silko on American Indian Women," in *Southwest Review*, Vol. 64, No. 2, Spring, 1979, pp. 149-60.

[*In the following excerpt, Blicksilver examines Silko's portrayal of Native American women in her short stories.*]

[Leslie Silko] attempts in some of her short stories and poems to explore the conflict between traditionalism and modernity. Fortunately, she has been able to transcend the limits of her minority experience.... Her intelligence, sensitivity, and remarkably controlled narrative techniques have produced fictional characterizations that do not typify the simplistic vision of the racial conflict. Even her extremely personal, semiautobiographical poetic renditions avoid the sentimental stereotype, revealing instead a vibrant human being, comfortable in her natural environment while exploring the dimensional limits of her multifaceted role as a child, lover, wife, and mother....

[Her short story] **"Lullaby"** describes the Anglo's exploitation of the Indian and the tragic consequences of forcing young children to choose between the old tribal reservation traditions and a materialistic, urban, sterile society so alien to their close-knit extended family culture. Unable to adjust, many Indians succumbed to disease, drunkenness, and despair.

Principal Works

Laguna Woman: Poems (poems) 1974
Ceremony (novel) 1977
Storyteller (poems and short stories) 1981
With the Delicacy and Strength of Lace: Letters Between Leslie Marmon Silko and James Wright [with James A. Wright] (letters) 1985
Almanac of the Dead (novel) 1991
Yellow Woman and a Beauty of the Spirit: Essays on Native American Life Today (essays) 1996

Told from the point of view of Ayah, a proud and sensitive old Navaho woman, Silko's story gives us a sense of layers unexposed, mysteries unsolved, and we are reminded that the creative pen of a skilled craftsman can make movingly poignant even the most prosaic situation. She has avoided the literary dangers inherent in writing from an ethnic woman's point of view, never presenting a mechanical and collectivist view of a human being or subordinating the individual in his complexity and unpredictability to the service of some sociopolitical cause. Silko is able to extricate her powerful feelings for this individual from her sympathetic involvement with her as a victim of racial oppression.... Ayah recalls the loss of her beloved son Jimmie in the war, the sickness, the poverty, and the snatching of her remaining two small children by Anglo educators. After their time in the white man's school they return only briefly and feel uncomfortable in what now seems to them her alien and culturally backward world....

The flashbacks and flash-forwards are artistically challenging, but fortunately Silko has a gift for quick, distinct characterizations, so that they are not lost in the fast-paced fragmentally sketched events of the old woman's life.

The Navaho woman emerges as a victim of ignorance, exploitation, and superstition....

Silko has used the impassive image of this Indian woman and the injustices she witnesses in her life to point an accusing finger at the white man who relegated her family to a reservation where diseases and alcoholism engulfed them, where they were refused the basic rights accorded other American citizens, and where they were relieved of their responsibilities as parents by being denied the control of their children's education....

Ayah's stony silence masks a deep hurt, and because she copes she is admired, not pitied, by the reader. Like Hemingway's heroic characters, she has learned to endure with dignity.... Silko skillfully juxtaposes the spiritual and the material needs in life....

This old Navaho woman represents the transitional link between old and new. To see the future, one must look back to understand these people, who they were and what they are becoming. Native Americans possess a rich culture strongly suffused with love of nature and an understanding of their place as part of the harmony of the natural environment. They respected the power of nature because in their arid Southwest the tribe's well-being was largely dependent upon the whims of the winds and the rains.

The Indian woman had her place; shielded by her man she was secure within her circumscribed world, never questioning her identity....

The Indian woman may not have been liberated according to modern definitions, but she knew her worth. Then life changed. A reservation environment and the white man's paternalism robbed the Native Americans of their self-esteem. The woman's role as wife and mother changed when her man no longer had freedom of movement, challenge, or self-determination in his life....

Perhaps one can criticize Silko because the story emphasizes the Indians' sorrows; the joys described are in the past. But this is her version of the Native American's present-day reality, and the old woman's heroic fortitude is the most sensitively delineated aspect of the characterizations depicted....

But what about the younger Indian woman? How has she adjusted to the liberation movement? Does she have a conflict between traditionalism and modernity? Leslie Silko describes such a woman, her link with tribal culture, and the demands of freedom in a short story called **"Yellow Woman."**

"Yellow Woman" relies upon religious symbolism, for it is the tale of a young Laguna Pueblo woman's casual love affair with a cattle rustler, who, she tries to convince herself and almost succeeds in believing, may be one of the *ka'tsina* mountain spirits that haunted the imaginative instincts of her tribal women since the beginning of time. Her hero is a mysterious stranger who may be a Navaho, but she never learns his origins or anything about his past, and this adds suspense to the relationship.

At first glance, the story can be interpreted as that of a contemporary, liberated Erica Jong heroine who leaves a devoted husband to satisfy her sexual desires with a handsome man whose name she has not even bothered to learn....

Upon closer scrutiny, the reader is soon made aware that the story was written by an Indian author steeped in tribal folklore traditions. The heroine remembers her beloved grandfather's fascinating tales about the *ka'tsina* spirit who lured the "Yellow Woman" to submit to his will, and she feels that this grandfather would understand why she had not returned to fulfill her duties as wife and mother.

Silko has performed an invaluable service for future generations of her people, who have only orally transmitted their folk mythology, by having her heroine tell a tale that her grandfather related to her. In this she is like those who wrote down the Homeric tales. . . .

Silko's poetry also reflects this attempt to retain ancient beliefs, and she uses the mythology of her Laguna Pueblo people, especially the symbol of the coyote as creator-trickster, to explore the imaginative richness and beauty of tribal folk tales. The relationships between human beings and natural forces, the animal and the vegetable kingdoms, are subjects of a series of poems describing different types of love relationships. . . .

Silko's close emotional union with nature and her respect for its power and vitality are evident in her imaginative dependence upon colors such as green and yellow, reminding one of Dylan Thomas's "Fern Hill." . . .

In her poetry she expresses the Native American convictions that the earth is vital, that there is a spiritual dimension in which she rightly belongs. Therefore, she affirms herself in the spirit of the earth; in turn, the earth nourishes and inspires the creative talent within her.

And so Silko, who is both a sensitive poet and a fine fiction writer, uses nature and folklore to tell about the Indian woman's role as child, lover, wife, and mother. She writes with a deep intensity that sets her work apart; hers is an emerging talent from which we can continue to expect new and impressive work.

Her stories sometimes reveal a deeply felt sadness, an awareness that her once great culture is being lost or replaced by an Anglo culture that does not have the same respect for nature that hers had, and in some ways is morally inferior to it. She gives her reader a sense of what it is like to live in a cultural sunset, in a society to which she does not completely belong, to which she frequently cannot relate.

Of course, for the Indian of mixed ancestry the search for acceptance is especially poignant. . . .

Aware that her Indian culture is threatened with extinction, and even more because of its oral tradition, Silko is determined to preserve literary treasures for future generations. In the past, books by white writers either romanticized red men or pictured them as bestial warriors and ravishers of women. Historically, Anglo readers have had access to pitifully few authentic Indian authors, especially women. In recent years, creative Native American writers have finally emerged as eloquent voices for their people; and Leslie Silko is one of the strongest and brightest. . . .

N. SCOTT MOMADAY

SOURCE: N. Scott Momaday, "The Spirit in Words," in *The New York Times Book Review,* May 24, 1981, pp. 8, 17.

[*Momaday is an American poet and critic whose works reflect the oral traditions of his Kiowa Indian heritage. In his review of* Storyteller *excerpted below, he contends that while several pieces from the collection "have the look and sound of ethnography," Silko generally succeeds in conveying the lyrical intensity of oral storytelling.*]

Storyteller is a rich, many-faceted book. It consists of short stories, anecdotes, folktales, poems, historical and autobiographical notes, and photographs. It begins with the description of an old Hopi basket in which there are hundreds of photographs, all taken, presumably, at Laguna Pueblo, N.M., near the turn of the century. "The photographs are here," we are told, "because they are part of many of the stories and because many of the stories can be traced in the photographs." Implicit in this statement, of course, is the very notion of an anthology or even a random sampling, rather than a "story" as such or a sustained narrative. The book is a melange. Here and there are moments of considerable beauty and intensity, moments in which, according to the central tenet of storytelling, the language is celebrated.

Leslie Silko . . . lived for a time in Alaska, and it evidently left a deep impression on her: the very best writing in [*Storyteller*] comes out of that experience. The title story, for example, is about a girl who lives with an old Eskimo man, a storyteller *par excellence.* When he dies, she is compelled to tell his story, just as he told it, slowly, entirely, for its own sake. Nothing must stand in the way of that commitment, that trust, that moral necessity. It is a lovely and haunting piece, not to be forgotten. . . .

[In] its poetic imagery, it conveys a nearly intuitive recognition of infinite distance and absolute cold. And the book also includes a poem entitled **"How to Write a Poem About the Sky"** on the same subject.

When Leslie Silko draws on her own Hopi Indian tradition, where it would seem she ought to be most at home, she writes to rather less effect, I think. The Laguna stories are there, to be sure, but they are, collectively, not quite so vital as one might wish. Some of them seem to disintegrate in the telling. **"Toe'Osh: A Laguna Coyote Story"** is a case in point. I'm not sure what the difficulty is here; the piece seems to proceed haltingly as the fragments of two or three unrelated (or, at best, loosely related) stories. Other stories have the look and sound of ethnography, rather than the lyrical intensity of oral tradition. The exceptions are notable. **"Uncle Tony's Goat"** is a fine bit of work. **"Yellow Woman"** is a remarkable mixture of folklore and sexual fantasy. Both seem familiar in the best sense; both are narrated in the first person.

At her best, Leslie Silko is very good indeed. She has a sharp sense of the way in which the profound and the mundane often run together in our daily lives. And her sense of humor is acute. . . .

We must take such words as "storyteller" very seriously. And we must make distinctions. A camera is not a storyteller. Neither is a novelist or a poet, necessarily. In view of the title of this book, let us make a distinction here. Leslie Silko is a writer, one of high and recorded accomplishment. If she is not yet a storyteller, she promises to become one. . . .

KENNETH LINCOLN

SOURCE: Kenneth Lincoln, "Grandmother Storyteller: Leslie Silko," in his *Native American Renaissance,* University of California Press, 1983, pp. 222-50.

[*In the following excerpt, Lincoln discusses the characteristics of Native American storytelling present in Silko's short story "Storyteller."*]

Indian storytelling, old and new, is drawn from living history. Its angle of truth derives from a belief in families telling their lives directly. Its sense of art turns on tribal integrity.

To tell a story the Indian way, no less than to write, means not so much to fictionalize, as to inflect the truth of the old ways still with us ("novel" may suggest making up new, even unreal events, considering the second definition for storyteller is "liar" in the Oxford English Dictionary). The Indian storyteller weaves a narrative less as a point-of-view, detached on the crosshairs of art, more as a human presence, attended by an audience taking part in the story. It is not a question of the "rhetoric of fiction," in Western terms for the novel, but of historical witness to human events.

Why do cultures tell stories? Storytelling personally brings people together; it engages them collectively in giving and receiving the events of their lives. In such storytelling times, people occupy space with focused attention; they enter their common world more fully. In the tribe, people share and pass on information, values, and beliefs through stories. They are entertained while learning their culture's crafts, skills, and means of survival. They historically mark and recount events worth remembering, so that culture extends history as a collective experience, across the spaces between peoples, over time that separates living and dead.

Religious stories or "myths" put people in touch with powers beyond themselves; they may plumb a deeper, or more interior, sense of reality through what Black Elk calls "the wonder and strangeness of the greening earth." The artistry of storytelling draws people as well into a world playfully heightened and crafted through language. An Indian "word sender" or "carrier of the dream wheel" *characterizes* reality: peoples, landscapes, seasons, tonalizes, lightens, spiritualizes, brightens, and darkens human experience, all the while working with the reality that is. . . .

The concept of a true, living story, the personal inflection embodied and embraced in communal history, bedrocks Leslie Marmon Silko's fiction. She describes her people: "My family are the Marmons at Old Laguna on the Laguna Pueblo Reservation where I grew up. We are mixed blood—Laguna, Mexican, white—but the way we live is like Marmons, and if you are from Laguna Pueblo you will understand what I mean. All those languages, all those ways of living are combined, and we live somewhere on the fringes of all three. But I don't apologize for this any more—not to whites, not to full bloods—our origin is unlike any other. My poetry, my storytelling rise out of this source."

ICE WOMAN

I have slept with the river and
he is warmer than any man.

At sunrise
I heard ice on the cattails,
      ["Indian Song: Survival"]

Silko's **"Storyteller"** cuts an ice-clear channel. The short story unfolds with an economy so lucid that nothing is lost. "It had come down suddenly, and she stood with her back to the wind looking at the river, its smoky water clotted with ice. The wind had blown the snow over the frozen river, hiding thin blue streaks where fast water ran under ice translucent and fragile as memory." Detail, tone, character, dramatic pacing, message: all are firmly placed and finely drawn, with the precision and certainty of crystals freezing on a dead man's face. Silko's "favorite" among her works, including the award-winning **"Lullaby"** the story carries no names, but works through "the interior landscapes of the characters." Presences, sounds, and shapes are shagged with ice and snow; people huddle around the warmth of an oil stove, a woman's body, or an old man's story, as the sun freezes white in the sky. This northern cold is the analogue to southwestern desert heat, the climate where Silko grew up and then left to write some of her finest prose in Ketchikan, Alaska.

"Storyteller" opens with an Eskimo woman in jail, listening. The lowering, pale yellow sun, "worn thin by winter," stands still, trapped in the frozen river. She knows it is time. The story begins and closes with this prophetic sense of end: inevitable cycles of temporality enclose human action, inexorable fates trap man in a vast and intricate scheme of things.

The Inuit or Eskimo tell an old myth of a hunter's daughter who fell into the sea. When she reached for the gunwale of her father's boat, he cut off her fingers and let her drown. Takanakapsaluk now sits in a cave at the bottom of the sea, guarded by a dog "gnawing on a bone and snarling." She is keeper of the game, key to Eskimo survival. When times come hard, the people dying of starvation, a shaman or "one-who-drops-down-to-the-bottom-of-the-sea" must go to propitiate this tragic goddess known as Mother of the Sea. Negotiating the watch dog and the girl's father, who waits to seize dead souls, the shaman faces Takanakapsaluk. She is turned away in anger from the light and animals in her pool. Knud Rasmussen recounts the scene:

> Her hair hangs down loose all over one side of her face, a tangled, untidy mass hiding her eyes, so that she cannot see. It is the misdeeds and offenses committed by men which gather in dirt and impurity over her body. All the foul emanations from the sins of mankind nearly suffocate her . . . he must grasp Takanakapsaluk by one shoulder and turn her face towards the lamp and towards the animals, and stroke her hair, the hair she has been unable to comb out herself, because she has no fingers; and he must smooth it and comb it, and as soon as she is calmer, he must say:

> "Those up above can no longer help the seals up by grasping their foreflippers."

> Then Takanakapsaluk answers in the spirit language: "The secret miscarriages of the women and breaches of taboo in eating boiled meat bar the way for the animals."

The shaman shoots back up a tube, held precariously open by his tribal namesakes, and addresses the assembled people:

> "I have something to say."

> "Let us hear, let us hear."

> "Words will rise."

The women, quiet until now, recite the names of their household and confess their miscarriages. They fear that all the "soft things"—skins, clothing, animal hide coverings—must be thrown away because they have been poisoned by the women's blood secrets.

"I seek, and I strike where nothing is to be found!" the shaman chants. "I seek, and I strike where nothing is to be found! If there is anything, you must say so!"

This myth, still ritualized, shadows Silko's **"Storyteller,"** Swithout necessarily structuring the narrative. Years back the Gussuck boats fired "big guns at the walrus and seals," and with nothing left to hunt, the girl's parents traded their rifle for a storekeeper's red can of "alcohol" that poisoned them. The memory of their death returns in the girl's menstrual nightmare of "something red in the tall river grass." A scabrous yellow dog now sleeps before the returned storeman's display case of knives and ammunition, where the reticent young woman, many times sexually defiled, unzips her parka and shakes "her long hair loose" by the stove. The lecherous white storekeeper, like a false shaman, will be sucked down into the river's current, never to rise.

The nameless girl's life shapes the narrative by way of her grandmother's prophecy: "It will take a long time, but the story must be told. There must not be any lies." It is a story of time's stern and just law—blood will out—told without contrition or forgiveness, no names, no slack, no dates, no sentiment. The figures are elemental: a girl, her grandmother, an old man, a sodomist, a drowned rapist. The story cuts to death's quick, sharp as a hunter crossing marshy tundra in early winter.

PATRICIA CLARK SMITH AND PAULA GUNN ALLEN

SOURCE: Patricia Clark Smith and Paula Gunn Allen, "Earthy Relations, Carnal Knowledge: Southwestern American Indian Women Writers and Landscape," in *The Desert Is No Lady: Southwestern Landscapes in Women's Writing and Art,* edited by Vera Norwood and Janice Monk, Yale University Press, 1987, pp. 174-96.

[*Allen is a Laguna Pueblo novelist, poet, nonfiction writer, educator, and critic. In the following excerpt, she and Smith provide a thematic analysis of the short story "Yellow Woman," suggesting that Silko's "flexible narrative point of view" has its roots in her experience of growing up without fully belonging to any of her ancestral cultures.*]

Leslie Marmon Silko is of mixed Laguna, Hispanic, and Anglo ancestry. Many members of her family were educated in Indian schools like Carlisle and Sherman Institute, and as a child she attended a private dayschool in Albuquerque. Her work reflects the mixedblood's sense of dwelling at the edges of communities: "We are . . . Laguna, Mexican, White—but the way we live is like Marmons, and if you are from Laguna Pueblo, you will understand what I mean. All those languages, all those ways of living are combined, and we live somewhere on the fringes of all three." That experience of growing up around Laguna life without being fully immersed in it gives Silko's work a certain doubleness, a flexible narrative point of view. At times there's a distance, an ironic edge, a sense that she is writing *about* a tradition as much as *out* of it.... In **"Yellow Woman,"** a modern heroine thinks about one of the old-time Yellow Woman stories, even as Silva, the man she has met by the river, makes love to her:

> He touched my neck, and I moved close to him to feel his breathing and hear his heart. I was wondering if Yellow Woman had known who she was—if she knew that they would become part of the stories. Maybe she'd had another name that her husband and relatives called her so that only the ka'tsina from the north and the storytellers would know her as Yellow Woman. But I didn't go on; I felt him all around me, pushing me down into the river sand....
>
> "Do you know the story?"
>
> "What story?" He smiled and pulled me close to him as he said this.... This is the way it happens in the stories, I was thinking, with no thought beyond the moment she meets the ka'tsina spirit and they go.

This flexible viewpoint enables Silko to take old tales like the ones of woman-abducted-by-wilderness-spirit and treat them simultaneously, or in successive retellings, with high humor, irony, and reverence. This does not always sit well with her critics, white and Indian alike, some of whom seem to expect all American Indian literature to be as pompously solemn as *Billy Jack* or *Hanta Yo.* But Silko knows that the real stories are large and true enough to contain many stories, to bear many interpretations. In her collection *Storyteller,* Silko juxtaposes a number of pieces that treat very differently the theme of a woman leaving home for the wilderness. **"Cottonwood"** is a fairly straight retelling of two Yellow Woman stories. In the first, Yellow Woman goes out around the fall equinox to meet the Sun himself:

> She left precise stone rooms
> That hold the heart silently
> She walked past white corn
> hung in long rows from roof beams
> The dry husks rattled in a thin autumn wind.
>
> She left her home
> her clan
> and the people
> (Three small children
> the youngest just weaned
> her husband away cutting firewood)

Her rendezvous with the sun, her willingness to join him, ensures that he will come out of his Sun House; he will not leave the earth locked forever in winter. The second part of the poem deals with her abduction by Buffalo Man; both the Buffalo People and she herself are finally slain by her jealous husband, Arrow Boy, once he discovers that she does not especially want to be rescued, but the end result is the gift of buffalo meat as food in time of drought,

> all because
> one time long ago
> our daughter, our sister Kochininako
> went away with them.

Storyteller also contains **"Yellow Woman,"** a masterfully ambiguous story, whose heroine, like Yellow Woman, meets a man by the river, a man named Silva (forest, in Spanish), who may be a Navajo cattle thief or the ka'tsina he laughingly tells her he is—or both. Many details in the story parallel the old Keres tales of Yellow Woman and Whirlwind Man or Buffalo Man. But what is most important in the story is the heroine's awakened consciousness of her own sexuality and her acute sensual awareness of the man, the river, and the mountain terrain they travel: "And again he was all around me with his skin slippery against mine, and I was afraid because I understood that his strength could hurt me. I lay underneath him and I knew that he could destroy me. But later, while he slept beside me, I touched his face and I had a feeling—the kind of feeling that overcame me that morning along the river. I kissed him on the forehead and he reached out for me." In letting herself open to Silva, she lets herself open to wilderness in all its wonder, its threat and vulnerability. The description fits her experience of both the man and the mountain.

"Yellow Woman" ends ambiguously. Silva may or may not get shot by a rancher, and he may or may not be a ka'tsina who will one day return for the heroine. Though she decides finally to tell her family only that she's been kidnapped by "some Navajo," what stays with her—and with the reader—is the lyrical evocation of Silva and his terrain: ants swarming over pine needles, the "mountain smell of pitch and buck brush," the danger and beauty she has experienced on those heights.

The heroine of **"Yellow Woman"** at times admits that hers is an unlikely story, but on the whole both she and the reader are inclined toward the belief in Silva as mountain spirit. Still, we understand there might be ways, in current parlance, to deconstruct that interpretation. Indeed, Silko does not need a critic to perform that task for her, just as the obscene and irreverent antics of Pueblo sacred clowns in a sense "deconstruct" ceremonies without the help of anthropologists. Her poem **"Storytelling"** begins with a straight-faced recap of the Yellow Woman and Buffalo Man tale, then proceeds in a rapid verbal montage:

> "You better have a damn good story,"
> her husband said,
> "about where you have been for the past
> ten months and how you explain these
> twin baby boys."

> . . . .

> It was
> in the summer
> of 1967.
> T.V. news reported
> a kidnapping.
> Four Laguna woman
> and three Navajo men
> headed north along
> the Rio Puerco River
> in a red '56 Ford
> and the FBI and
> state police were
> hot on their trail
> of wine bottles and
> size 42 panties
> hanging in bushes and trees
> all along the road.

> "We couldn't escape them," he told po
>   lice later.
> "We tried, but there were four of them
>   and only three of us."

> . . . .

> It was
> that Navajo
> from Alamo,
> you know,
> the tall
> good-looking one.

> He told me
> he'd kill me
> if I didn't
> go with him
> And then it
> rained so much
> and the roads
> got muddy.
> That's why
> it took me
> so long
> to get back home.

> My husband
> left
> after he heard the story
> and moved back with his mother.
> It was my fault and
> I don't blame him either.
> I could have told
> the story
> better than I did.

Whether deeply moving and ceremonial or slapstick, whether a woman abandons her water jar or her size 42 panties, whether she goes off with Whirlwind Man or the good-looking Navajo from Alamo, Silko conveys the sense that all these stories somehow concern an inevitable human need to go forth and experience wilderness—and the sexual wildness that it encompasses.

JAMES RUPPERT

SOURCE: James Ruppert, "The Reader's Lessons in 'Ceremony'," in *Arizona Quarterly*, Vol. 44, No. 1, Spring, 1988, pp. 78-85.

[*In the essay below, Ruppert discusses how* Ceremony *"fuses story and reality to define an identity for its protagonist and the reader."*]

When Leslie Marmon Silko published **Ceremony** in 1977, the critical reaction was good. The book was praised in the *New York Review of Books* and in other established critical publications. But, something of even greater significance happened for those interested in Southwestern literature and American Indian literature. A novel came into existence that challenged readers, Indian and White, to expand and merge their cultural frameworks. The novel was, at once, grounded in Indian tradition and informed by contemporary American fiction. While remaining a popular novel taught in many classes, it continues to open up fresh insights into fiction and culture, for it is not only a novel that presents a philosophical and cultural viewpoint, but a novel that teaches us how to read it and how to understand its special narrative structures. Through its formal and stylistic elements, it fuses story and reality to define an identity for its protagonist and the reader.

Perhaps the most immediate way the reader sees its uniqueness is in its form. **Ceremony** merges what we would call poetry and prose. Silko says that ideally these sections should be heard, not read, so that they approximate the position of a listener before the storyteller. The stories or myths told in the poems are broken up and placed periodically throughout the text, so that the completion of the poem stories and the prose narrative converge at the end. It would seem that Silko wants us to hear a different voice in the poetry, while still forcing the reader to acknowledge a unity of purpose underneath this apparent formal diversity. This discourse strategy is mirrored variously throughout the novel and is ultimately a reflection of the epistemological unity of Laguna narrative esthetic and world view.

When Thought-Woman thinks, whatever she is thinking about appears. "I'm telling you the story she is thinking," says Silko at the start. The story—the myth—is reality (a complete ontological system), and the novel leads the reader to an insight into that unity between myth and reality. Reality is a story, Silko explains. The mythic material presented in poetic form paces the reality of the prose, leading us to the climax of the novel, but it also comments on the action of the story and gives order. Only when we see the reality of the novel in terms of the mythic poem, do we see the order of the story. The loss of power and vision, or, as Tayo says, "how the world had come undone," the struggle to return the world to its proper order, the ultimate successful conclusion of the crisis, and the identity and harmony created by this successful conclusion of the story are all predicted, ordered, and directed by the myth/poem. The myth/poem expresses the reality of the prose meaning. It creates that meaning. It is not just an allegory or a quaint piece of local color. The drought, the Whites, the breakdown of tribal identity and integrity, World War II, and even nuclear power are given meaning through the interaction of the poetry and the prose; or, on another level, through the interface of story and reality.

When the speaker begins by saying that the stories are the only way to fight off illness, evil, and death, she is being quite literal, for it is the stories that grant order and form to the flow of events, and these stories codify meaning in such a way that the listener or reader can understand events in the world around him. Only when the reader understands the meaning of events can he act in an effective manner. But to do so, it is essential that the reader understands that the stories and reality in the novel are one.

Stylistically, the form of the prose aids this realization in a number of ways. First, Silko uses no chapter breaks. As the prose flows continuously from beginning to end, the reader is encouraged to perceive the novel as one unified experience. Any breaks in the flow are short, temporary, and tend to lead the reader to the poetic or mythic plane. The artificial structures of numerical separation or of dramatic scenes are eliminated in favor of structures inherent in the rhythm of the narrative and the movements of the mythic story. Events and interactions are not isolated into chapters but are superimposed until they build a structure that continues throughout the novel. They grow out of a developing narrative context and are to be understood on multiple levels of significance in the same way that events in Laguna culture can be understood on mythic, religious, cultural, sociological, and individual levels simultaneously.

This lack of expected breaking of the flow of the prose also discourages the reader from imposing a strict chronological order on the narrative, thus reinforcing the perception that the novel is a simultaneous, unified moment that circles out like the waves around a rock dropped in a quiet pond, rather than a linear progression of moments. The thematic center point of the novel is when Tayo and the reader realize this, and Silko writes, "He took a deep breath of cold mountain air: there were no boundaries; the world below and the sand paintings inside became the same that night." As the false boundaries of time, distance, truth, and individuality fall away, Tayo and the reader are left with the fused story / reality unifying all experience, defining time, event, and identity. Western distinctions which slice reality are put aside by the structure of the novel.

When the pattern of the narrative is analyzed, this concern with the unity of experience and the fusion of story and reality is seen reflected in the way that Silko uses a fragmented story structure which does not make clear distinction between past and present. Events seem to be happening on various planes of existence at the same time. One obvious explanation is that the form of the narrative mirrors the psychological state of the protagonist, Tayo. At the beginning of the novel, he is a shattered war veteran. As he goes through Betonie's ceremony, he reintegrated himself into psychic health and Laguna culture. The swirl of memory and reality which paralyzes his broken mental state is healed and the narrative proceeds in a more standard, linear fashion because Tayo's mental state is improving, becoming more normal, more standard, more Western.

Perhaps the story becomes clearer and more patterned for the reader later in the novel for another more reader-centered reason. At the beginning of the novel, the reader is unsure of the relationship between the prose and poetry, agitated with the fragmented vision of the narrative, and uncertain who is speaking and why, but those confusions seem to be clarified by the end of the novel so that the reader tends not to ask such questions when approaching the resolution at the end. Not only has the novel taught us to disregard those artificial Western distinctions such as time and space, it has approximated a holistic vision close to the Laguna experience of the world and oral tradition. Silko assures us that in the story, time and distance are overcome and anything is possible if one knows the right story. But even more deeply, the reader has learned to trust the fusion of the story and reality; he has enriched his epistemological conditioning so that the story makes better sense. The reader has grown; he perceives the events in the story with greater insight, perhaps even a cross-cultural insight. It could be said that the reader's story perception has improved, somewhat like the way one's depth perception or pattern-recognition skills can be enhanced.

The formal structure is, of course, an expression of the thematic content. Tayo's return to individual and cultural identity and health (or harmony) through ceremonial integration with a unified story/reality is central to the novel. Tayo's act of cursing the rain parallels the loss of rain in the mythic story. His personal breakdown reflects the breakdown of Laguna cultural integrity. His personal dryness of emotion, spirit, and communal identity find physical manifestation in the drought suffered by the people of Laguna. Betonie's ceremony is Tayo's path to reintegration back to identity on the personal, cultural, and mythic level. But it is also the Laguna path back to reintegration, and ultimately, the world's.

Tayo's recovery is contingent upon his realization that mythic and real worlds are one, just as the success of the novel is contingent upon the reader realizing the same thing. As Tayo finally understands, "His sickness was only part of something larger, and his cure would be found only in something great and inclusive of everything." He realizes that the world is in danger and that his cure and the world's cure require his action. He cannot remain passive. When Tayo enters the story, or as Night Swan, says, "you are now part of it," he is given an identity; he might be called the-one-who-brings-back-the-rain.He felt after the war that he had become white smoke, that he had no identity, but in the unified story that the reader comes to understand as containing the underlying pattern of significance, he did have an identity. He was the blasphemer, the-one-who-drove-the-rain-away.

The trip that Tayo makes to the mountain helps convince him of the fusion of story and reality. He realizes in the mountain that "Betonie's vision was a story that he could feel happening." As Tayo moves deeper into that fusion, he meets Mountain Lion and falls in love with Elk Woman. His understanding of story/reality increases and emotion comes back into his life. He realizes that he and the world around him have come under the influence of the destroyers, the witches. Ts'eh tells him, "Their highest ambition is to gut human beings while they are still breathing, to hold the heart still beating so the victim will never feel anything again. When they finish, you watch yourself from a distance and you can't even cry—not even for yourself." Tayo's emerging understanding of epistemological unity and the destruction of time and space boundaries are complete on the mountain when he realizes: The silence was inside, in his belly; there was no longer any hurry. The ride into the mountains had branched into all directions of time. He knew then why the oldtimers could only speak of yesterday and tomorrow in terms of the present moment: the only certainty; and this present sense of being was qualified with bare hints of yesterday or tomorrow, by saying, "I go up to the mountains tomorrow." The ck'o'yo Kaup'a'ta somewhere is stacking his gambling sticks and waiting for a visitor; Rocky and I are walking across the ridge in moonlight; Josiah and Robert are waiting for us. This night is a single night; and there has never been any other.

When Tayo returns to the pueblo, the old men of the tribe take him into the Kiva. As he tells them of his experiences, they realize that he has seen A'moo'ooh, the Elk Woman. The pueblo's shattered connection with the spirit world is now reestablished and they know the drought will end. The old men give Tayo the social identity he had always lacked as they take him in to become one of them, but they also acknowledge his mythic identity as the bringer of blessings, the gatherer of seeds, the lover of the Elk Woman.

Tayo's final realizations come only when he is able to end the story correctly. He understands enough about the witchery now to act on his own. He must not let the witchery encircle "slowly to choke the life away." He must draw strength from his vision, and then end the story in a way that completes the personal, social, and mythic story of the human beings and the destroyers. He gathers strength at this point from a unified vision of the interweaving of all life. Yet at that moment in the sunrise, it was all so beautiful, everything, from all directions, evenly, perfectly, balancing day with night, summer months with winter. The valley was enclosing this totality, like the mind holding all thoughts together in a single moment. The strength came from here, from this feeling. It had always been there.

Tayo is at that moment beginning to realize that the source of strength for him, Laguna, and those who would fight the destroyers is in a unified vision of experience, and he begins to act on it. Tayo looks out and sees the world as a giant sand painting and all humans as one clan — narrative and experience become one. "He cried the relief he felt at finally seeing the pattern, the way all the stories fit together — the old stories, the war stories, their stories — to become the story that was still being told. He was not crazy; he had never been crazy. He had only seen and heard the world as it always was: no boundaries, only transitions through all distances and time." This realization gives Tayo what he calls the "ear for the story, the eye for the pattern." His understanding of the story / reality creates meaning and identity.

As mentioned earlier, this fusion of story / reality is exactly the effect that the form and style of the novel encourage the reader to experience. As Tayo's confusion and lack of identity clear, the reader's confusion about the form and content of the narrative clears too. If the reader follows and understands the fusion of the story and reality, he too sees how all the stories merge into the story that is being told. He has effectively been educated into the unity that strengthens Tayo and brings back the rain and its blessings. Also, he has been introduced into the experience of the oral tradition. The perceptive reader, too, has the ear for the story, the eye for the pattern, and is encouraged to see the world as one large swirling sand painting.

But this realization brings obligations with it. He must understand the story and see the work of the destroyers in the world around him. Night Swan, Betonie, Ts'eh, or Tayo could also say to each of us, "you are part of it now." So the reader too must act. Great responsibility is placed on the shoulders of those who understand. They must see to it that the story ends properly. Consequently, the readers are also given an identity in the mythic story. They are members of a group of people who must tell the story correctly, who must defeat the destroyers. They are part of the story now. Others will speak of them when they learn the story.

Out of this new identity and these new understandings will come a new harmony with all that is. The reader knows that his presence is needed at the new ceremonies designed to defeat the destroyers. The new ceremonies are being made every day, for Silko explains the ceremonies and the stories must grow to meet the new conditions of evil and disharmony. The novel begins and ends with the word "Sunrise" because the Dawn people's ceremonial prayers do so. The novel itself is a prayer or a ceremony which continues in the world after the book is closed. The title *Ceremony* refers not only to the ceremony that Tayo experiences, but also to the harmony, healing, and increased awareness that the reader acquires through the reading and understanding of the novel itself. It has produced meaning, identity, and understanding in the reader. It has brought the reader into the story, brought him in touch with the unity of all that is, placed him at the center of the swirling sand painting of the world. It has brought him into harmony.

Silko's novel has amazingly fused contemporary American fiction with Native American story telling. Her novel uses narrative in a way unique to the Western literary tradition. But as she does so, she structures the reader's experience so that he will be forced to understand and participate in the cultural and epistemological framework of the people of Laguna. In a similar manner, a Native American reader is encouraged to utilize his understandings as a base for viewing White society, but he is also forced to use something of the Western psychological and social way of seeing. The cross-cultural racial tensions that surround the novel are ultimately dismantled and re-formed as the distinction between the destroyers and those who would stop the destroyers. Whites and Indians can unite through participation in the story / reality.

Silko's story brings all humanity together in a struggle to defeat the destroyers who "are working for the end of this world." The last page of the novel is not the finish of the fused story / reality. The ceremony continues and it is now the responsibility of the reader to act....

C. W. TRUESDALE

SOURCE: C. W. Truesdale, "Tradition and *Ceremony*: Leslie Marmon Silko as an American Novelist," in *North Dakota Quarterly*, Vol. 59, No. 4, Fall, 1991, pp. 200-228.

[*In the following excerpt, Truesdale highlights Silko's treatment of such subjects as the environment, identity, and tradition in* Ceremony.]

Leslie Marmon Silko is one of those writers who have become more and more of an anomaly in recent American literature, especially in fiction: she believes in writing as a craft, a discipline, and an act of discovery, and she takes it very seriously. Writing seems to be as much a necessity for her as eating, drinking, and trying to make ends meet:

> I think that in these times especially, but probably for all times, in the stories we tell or share we can only be guided by the heart—we cannot dictate or predict which stories will be "the ones." All we can do is remember and to tell with all our hearts, not hold anything back, because anything held back or not told cannot continue on with others.

That Silko has attained some popular success has made those mundane ends possible. But I have the feeling she would write whether that were true or not. Everything I have read by her emanates from inner compulsions she doesn't entirely understand and which are often in deep conflict with one another. Her motivation seems to be to resolve those conflicts in dramatic, meaningful, and truthful ways, which I regard as one of the few true motivations for the serious writer, whose proper business is to make some kind of unique order out of the chaos of conflicting impulses that beset most of us, especially in a society such as ours where no one body of traditions and conventions is anything like universal.

Not surprisingly, Silko's real subject involves her Pueblo heritage, but it is not limited to that. What really seems to interest and concern her is the survival of that heritage in the twentieth-century American world that surrounds and contains that heritage in usually destructive and often mindless—if not malicious—ways. (Like the recent resettlement of Navajos displaced from lands awarded to the Hopis. The Navajos, who had been shepherds and farmers, were given brand-new $70,000 houses in Flagstaff—and nothing to do. The bureaucrats responsible for this "transaction" cannot seem to comprehend why the Navajos are not grateful. Colin Turnbull, the brilliant English anthropologist, describes in harrowing detail in *The Mountain People* the devastating results of trying to force a group of nomadic, hunting tribesmen in Uganda to become settled agriculturists.)

Silko's novel, **Ceremony**, is in no sense a nostalgic celebration of the "old ways," though some of its characters are governed by such feelings. Like many first-rate novels, it questions not only the modern world but the old ways themselves in such a manner that her Pueblo heritage becomes a highly dramatic aspect of the book as a whole, partly because she doesn't really know (until she has finished writing this book) what the answers to the questions are: "Do the old ways have any meaning for today's Pueblo Indian? Are the traditions that have somehow managed to survive flexible and resilient enough not only to help us adapt to and live in the modern world but also to illuminate that same world in meaningful ways? In short, can the Lagunas survive as a community, as a people, in an alien and often hostile world?"

As a writer, there is another question or series of questions that are of perhaps equal importance to her: "Whom am I writing for? Does my audience consist wholly of my own people? Am I trying to summon them like an old-time prophetess back to the old ways? Or am I writing for a more general audience consisting of literate, compassionate, and intelligent individuals who are part of mainstream American culture? If the latter, do I want to invoke their guilt as perhaps unwitting participants in the powerful exploitation and humiliation of my people the way so many Indian writers have done or non-Indian liberals like Dee Brown? Or do I want to portray in my principal characters a terrible struggle towards identity that *anyone* in the modern world can relate to? Injustice is easy to portray—it's all around us and it's terribly important as a factor in political and judicial determinations that affect my people adversely. I *could* be that kind of writer," she seems to be saying (and one can certainly find many examples of injustice in **Ceremony**), "but what really concerns me is living itself and whether it is possible for people like me to find a way towards an identity that includes not only my Indian past but is also viable for me as a person in my own right for the future."

Silko's *Ceremony* is not by any standard a modernist novel at first glance, nor is it the traditional storytelling that goes on in so much of her next book, *Storyteller*. She does make use of techniques developed in the twentieth-century novel—near stream-of-consciousness writing at times, for instance, where appropriate. And she does not use ordinary chapter breaks, largely because the narrative being developed is not straight-line conventionalized plotting. The significant action of *Ceremony* happens in the mind of the protagonist and consists of his affirming himself and establishing his identity. Breaks in the story line and transitions are effected by using mostly English versions of traditional Laguna poems, which themselves take on ever greater importance as the novel develops. In many ways, especially thematic, it resembles the near-contemporary novel, *One Flew over the Cuckoo's Nest,* the protagonist of which, like Tayo in *Ceremony*, is victimized by the machinery of a society he neither accepts nor understands—on one level, but only too well on a deeper experiential level. . . .

Ceremony is a very rich novel. Although it has much to teach the willing and perceptive reader, Silko never preaches at us nor does she ever once patronize Tayo. She knows that Tayo's story is hers in some way—and ours too.

I'd like to . . . [call] the reader's attention to some of the important subjects dealt with—very graciously—in this novel:

—*On the Environment:* The novel celebrates the importance of oral wisdom about roots, seeds plants, the cycles of nature, and the configuration of the stars, which are figured here as bird-like navigational aids. Silko's thrust is positive, not satirical, though she does have plenty to say about man's rape of the land, about his "witchery" (as she repeatedly calls it) in the name of progress and weapons development. It is no accident that the murder of Harley takes place at the mouth of an abandoned uranium mine, since the development of the atomic bomb, which took place very near Laguna Pueblo in the Jemez Mountains, is the ultimate rape of nature.

—*On the Nature of Identity:* Tayo is a unique individual from the beginning, but he cannot see himself uniquely until he accepts the help of others, surrenders himself (but not without great resistance and skepticism) to their guidance (particularly old Betonie's and Ts'eh's), and eschews violence in the name of love, the sacred, and the good spirits. In other words he must identify himself in terms of his real heritage and its living, if beleaguered, vitality.

—*On the Woman Spirit:* Old Betonie's grandmother (apparently the "She" of his lore-stories) is Mexican and gives birth to his grandfather Descheeny's last daughter, Betonie's mother. When she is born and the villagers see the hazel color of her eyes, immediate evidence of mixed blood status, she is driven from the village and "Root Woman" (a Laguna version of the Greek goddess Ceres) is blamed for this, but all of the really powerful women in this novel are guided by her— Night Swan, Ts'eh, and even (to a certain extent) old Grandma, but decidedly *not* Tayo's Auntie. The Mexican girl who comes to Descheeny for his chants and ceremonies drops a blue lace shawl from a tree (an act which leads to her capture) and Ts'eh herself wears a blue silk shawl when Tayo finds her again. She uses this for gathering roots and herbs. It is clear that Silko regards them as the carriers of the sacred and akin to the good spirit of nature ("Root Woman"). Their gift is to nurture and to love, and without them the ceremonies could not be passed along to future generations. Many of them have—like Ts'eh herself and Night Swan and Betonie's mother—ambiguous origins, but there is nothing ambiguous about their power, their knowledge, and their wisdom. They do not belong to any specific tribe, as often as not, and some are not even Indian. The true Indian ceremonials are in their keeping, but Silko is implying a greater universality than that and something that might well be attended to by individuals from just about anywhere (including, of course, mainstream America). This brings Silko very close to the ideas and practices of many feminists.

—*On Healing: Ceremony* has little to do with the religious practices of the Western World. If anything, it is closer to some Oriental practices. But it does make some important, mostly negative connections with that modern "religious" practice called psychotherapy, particularly of the pragmatic/gestalt sort with its typical emphasis on self-improvement, self-assertion, the will, and the irrelevance of the past. ("You can be whatever you resolve to be," said Stonewall Jackson as a young professor of physics—what used to be called "natural philosophy"—at the Virginia Military Institute.) During the course of the novel Tayo is exposed to more or less traditional Indian healing practices (like the Scalp Ceremony), but he is also exposed to the therapeutic attention in the psycho ward of the veterans' hospital in Los Angeles, and a return there remains a constant, stomach-tightening threat to him throughout the novel. . . .

—*On Tradition:* . . . One thought of Tayo's . . . needs to be pondered carefully:

> He cried the relief he felt at finally seeing the pattern, the way all the stories fit together—the old stories, the war stories, their stories—to become the story that was still

being told. *He was not crazy; he had never been crazy.* He had only seen and heard the world as it always was: no boundaries, only transitions through all distances and time. (my emphasis)

What Tayo comes to realize here is that all societies—traditional or not—try to contain and control the extraordinary individual by working away at the weaknesses that inevitably occur even when someone, like Tayo, is doing nothing more than trying to find out who he is. Tayo's major strengths—his inquisitiveness, his refusal to accept a stereotyped role for himself, and his essentially loving nature (albeit unrequited for a long time)—are turned mindlessly against himself by his family, his so-called friends and fellow vets, his hospital experiences and most of all by his own nightmares, his self-doubt, and his total lack of conviction in his ability to accomplish anything at all....

Ceremony is a documentation of the futility of such destructive forces and is an affirmation of those positive, creative, and nourishing powers in the natural world and in society which are drawn from traditional wisdom and are certainly still viable for the Indian—and anyone else who is in tune with them. Silko rejects out of hand the sterile trappings of tradition (of the sort that emanate all the time these days from the White House) and goes right for its essence. Living tradition in her view must constantly be renewed and undergo changes. If it is really working, it takes individuals like Tayo into itself and allows them to grow freely and beautifully into themselves. If it isn't, it is as useless as anything else.

In Silko's view, as I see it, working tradition becomes a wonderfully adaptive vehicle for at once confirming the past and preparing us for the uncertain future.

And she has done this so convincingly in *Ceremony* that she just might make traditionalists of us all.

ELIZABETH TALLENT

SOURCE: Elizabeth Tallent, "Storytelling with a Vengeance," in *The New York Times Book Review*, December 22, 1991, p. 6.

[*In the following review, Tallent favorably comments on* Almanac of the Dead.]

One great possibility for the novel form is meditation upon the crucial death of a single character—think of Mrs. Ramsay in *To the Lighthouse,* the father in *A Death in the Family,* the mother in *Sons and Lovers.* But what if an entire culture reeks of cruelty and death, if the individual imagination confronts not a specific loss but fathomless brutality, if despair is no longer a matter of private experience but pervades an epoch?

Almanac of the Dead brilliantly grapples with just such questions, spinning tale after sanguinary tale with a vengeance. This wild, jarring, graphic, mordant, prodigious book embodies the bold wish to encompass in a novel the cruelty of contemporary America, a nation founded on the murder and deracination of the continent's native peoples.

Leslie Marmon Silko, who is of Laguna Pueblo, Mexican and Anglo descent, is the author of the novel *Ceremony* and the collection *Storyteller,* both works that honored the moral force of Native American tradition in conflict with intrusive, impoverishing Western European culture. Her new novel again treats the Native American ethos, reverence for the earth and especially one's ancestral land, as touchstone. It is not only scathing in its portrait of an ecologically catastrophic United States but sweeping in its chronology. The plot follows a far-flung conspiracy of displaced tribal people to retake North America toward the millennium's end.

There are sometimes ferocious, sometimes clinical accounts of savagery ranging from clitorectomy to serial murders. A Mexican revolutionary reflects that "the white man didn't seem to understand he had no future here because he had no past, no spirits of ancestors here." "No future" is literal: most whites must vanish, through massacre or migration, for the continent to be redeemed. The indigenous dead troubled even Cortez's soldiers, who talismanically dressed their wounds "in the fat of slain Indians." Now Native American ghosts direct "mothers from country club neighborhoods to pack the children in the car and drive off hundred-foot cliffs.... The spirits whisper in the brains of loners, the crazed young white men with automatic rifles who slaughter crowds in shopping malls or school yards." Still another character muses that "within 'history' reside relentless forces, powerful spirits, vengeful, relentlessly seeking justice." That ghosts urging slaughter in schoolyards could be as brutal as conquistadors is not an issue *Almanac of the Dead* illumines, and the novel's occasional blurred equation of "justice" with random violence is its shakiest imaginative leap.

As in Ms. Silko's previous work, one aspect of human experience is unequivocally celebrated: storytelling. Yoeme, a Yaqui woman who escaped a death sentence for sedition in 1918, "believed power resides within certain stories ... and with each retelling a slight but permanent shift took place." Yoeme's gift to her twin granddaughters, Zeta and Lecha, is the ancient, fragmentary almanac of tribal narratives: "Yoeme and others believed the almanac had living power within it, a power that would bring all the tribal people of the Americas together to retake the land."

There is genius in the sheer, tireless variousness of the novel's interconnecting tales. Settings include an Alaskan village with one communal television and a stark post-modern mansion set within a numinous rain forest. In addition to outlining the economy of the black market in human organs, the book includes a kidnapping, a hanging, a cocaine bust and an assassination franchise. There are scenes of politics in Tucson, Ariz., the country-club lunching of powerful men's wives and the organization of a ragged troop of homeless Vietnam veterans.

How does a subversive Mexican Indian group persuade foreign governments to send aid? They request uniforms and dynamite "for clearing land for new baseball diamonds." How does a computer whiz "safecrack" vast computer networks from his desert trailer? "His prospective clients were asked to supply entry codes. Ninety-nine percent of his clients had been former employees motivated by revenge."

Ms. Silko seems scarcely able to *name* a character without that character's beginning instantly to brood, to remember, to plot vengeance. The most minor figure in *Almanac of the Dead* possesses formidable id, and in a cast of more than 70 (my count), their individual obsessions are as unique as fingerprints.

Some repetitions could have used deft editorial excision, but for the most part the pace is fast. In Pueblo cosmology, duality, particularly twinship, is very powerful. The plot is set off as much by the 60th birthday shared by Zeta, matriarch of an isolated Arizona ranch and a paranoid connoisseur of security systems, and Lecha, a "TV talk show psychic," as by their decoding of the almanac. Lecha's eyes "know many things never meant to be seen. The contents of shallow graves. The thrust of a knife."

Earlier, in California, blond, cocaine-addicted Seese—her very name a cry—had discovered her baby missing from his crib and sought out the psychic Lecha in Tucson. In Mexico, torture, riots and carnage proliferate; twin brothers are told by sacred macaws to lead their barefoot tribal army north across the border into North America.

Lecha and Zeta, who have seen so much violence, now prepare, along with the other native prophets and revolutionaries, for a great deal more. While the novel stops short of the ultimate crisis, the signs point one way, implacably. Appearing on the eve of the quincentennial of Columbus's arrival in the Americas, *Almanac of the Dead* burns at an apocalyptic pitch—passionate indictment, defiant augury, bravura storytelling.

SOURCES FOR FURTHER STUDY

Blumenthal, Susan. "Spotted Cattle and Deer: Spirit Guides and Symbols of Endurance and Healing in *Ceremony*." *The American Indian Quarterly* XIV, No. 4 (Fall 1990): 367-77.

    Regards the spotted cattle and deer in *Ceremony* as "messengers of ancient wisdom vital to Tayo's quest for healing and identity."

Herzog, Kristin. "Thinking Woman and Feeling Man: Gender in Silko's *Ceremony*." *Melus* 12, No. 1 (Spring 1985): 25-36.

    Discusses Silko's unstereotypical portrayals of men and women in *Ceremony*.

Manley, Kathleen. "Leslie Marmon Silko's Use of Color in *Ceremony*." *Southern Folklore* 46, No. 2 (1989): 133-46.

    Examines Silko's use of certain ceremonial colors and their contribution to the novel's theme and structure.

Nelson, Robert M. "Place and Vision: The Function of Landscape in *Ceremony*." *Journal of the Southwest* 30, No. 3 (Autumn 1988): 281-316.

    Explores the significance of the natural world in *Ceremony*.

St. Andrews, B. A. "Healing the Witchery: Medicine in Silko's *Ceremony*." *Arizona Quarterly* 44, No. 1 (Spring 1988): 86-94.

    Applies Native American principles of spiritual healing to *Ceremony*.

Swan, Edith. "Healing Via the Sunwise Cycle in Silko's *Ceremony*." *American Indian Quarterly* XII, No. 4 (Fall 1988): 313-28.

    Follows Tayo's journey through the Laguna symbolic universe in *Ceremony*.

Sophocles

496? B.C.-406? B.C.

Greek dramatist.

INTRODUCTION

Sophocles is one of classical Greece's three great tragic dramatists whose works shaped the genre of the tragedy in Western literature. Along with Aeschylus and Euripides, Sophocles initiated several theatrical conventions that have influenced the development of dramatic art in the Western world. His surviving tragedies attest to his consummate craftsmanship in plot construction, characterization, and versification. Since the earliest evaluations of his work, commentators have been especially fascinated with Sophocles' use of irony in his masterpiece *Oedipous Tyrannos* (c. 425 B.C.; *Oedipus Rex*), affirming the observation of Aristotle, who declared that the play epitomizes effective dramatic technique and characterization. J. W. Mackail asserted that for all these reasons Sophocles "is the single poet who embodies centrally and completely the spirit of Athens."

Biographical Information

As a poet and a public figure, Sophocles is said to have represented "the spirit of Athens." His birth and death dates approximate the beginning and end of the Golden Age of Athens (480 B.C.-404 B.C.), a period when the city enjoyed unprecedented cultural and political supremacy in the Greek world. Born into a wealthy and respected family, Sophocles held important political positions because he belonged to the Athenian elite, and he showed his devotion to traditional religion by serving as a priest of the healing deity Amynos. Sophocles' victories at the Great Dionysia festival in Athens marked the beginning of his long career as an acclaimed dramatist. Held every spring since the sixth century B.C., the Dionysia festival honored the god Dionysus with plays performed by groups of traveling actors and included a renowned tragic competition, in which four plays (three tragedies and a comic satyr play) by rival dramatists were performed and judged. At the festival of 468 B.C., Sophocles defeated Aeschylus, winning first prize with *Triptolemos,* one of his many lost plays. According to biographical sources, he won first prize more than twenty times and never received a prize below second place, a unique feat among Greek dramatists.

Major Works

In his dramas, Sophocles focused on a strong-willed, highly principled, and passionate individual who encounters a seemingly insurmountable ethical or moral difficulty. His gift for portraying exceptional characters under stress is the hallmark of his dramatic style. In measured, simple, and piercingly direct language, his dramas move swiftly, logically, and inexorably toward their seemingly inevitable conclusions. Sophocles is believed to have written one hundred and twenty-three tragedies; titles and fragments of ninety exist, but only seven tragedies survive in their entirety. The earliest of these, *Aias* (c. 450 B.C.; *Ajax*), follows the sufferings of its title hero from his public humiliation by the Greek commanders Agamemnon and Menelaus to his suicide. *Antigone* (c. 442 B.C.) concerns the conflict between the title heroine and her uncle, King Creon, that stemmed from his refusal to allow the burial of Antigone's brother, Polyneices, who was condemned as a traitor to his city. *Antigone,* along with *Oedipus Rex* and *Oedipous epi Kolonoi* (c. 405 B.C.; *Oedipus at Colonus*), forms the Theban trilogy, which derives from an ancient story of King Oedipus of Thebes. *Oedipus Rex,* perhaps the most famous play ever written, describes the tragic events that lead unwitting Oedipus to murder his father and marry his mother; when their true identities are revealed, Oedipus blinds himself. *Oedipus at Colonus* reveals the mysterious death of King Oedipus, closing with his deification at Colonus, where he found lasting refuge. Other Sophoclean dramas include *Ichneutai* (c. 440 B.C.; *The Trackers*), a brief comic fragment dealing with the theft of Apollo's cattle by Hermes; *Trakhiniai* (c. 440-430 B.C.; *The Trachiniae*), which recounts the efforts of Deianeira to win back her unfaithful husband with a supposedly magic robe that is actually poisonous and consequently kills him; *Elektra* (c. 425-10 B.C.; *Electra*), which concerns the actions of Electra, who convinces her brother Orestes to avenge their father's murder by killing their mother Clytemnestra; and *Philoktetes* (409 B.C.; *Philoctetes*), which tells of Odysseus and Neoptolemus's search for Philoctetes, whose bow and arrows are vital to the successful capture of Troy, according to a prophecy. All the recurring themes in Sophoclean drama—the mysterious workings of divine justice, the nature and purpose of human suffering, and the role of knowledge—are rooted in Sophocles' fascination with human potential. Among the technical innovations Sophocles introduced to dramatic art, the most significant are the presence of a third actor, which permitted complex dialogue structure, and the development of more expressive masks, which brought greater realism to each scene.

Critical Reception

Sophocles' reputation as a dramatist has been secure ever since his own time, when he was held in such high regard that the Athenian government appointed officials to safeguard the purity of his texts. Aristotle argued in his *Poetics* that *Oedipus Rex* was a model tragedy, naming certain elements of Sophoclean tragedy, such as reversal and discovery, as the key concepts of his general theory of drama. Sophocles' subsequent impact on European literature has been tremendous. Although debate persists over certain aspects of Sophocles' oeuvre, there is complete consensus that his contribution to drama is inestimable. Scholars observe that classical Greek tragedy, founded by Aeschylus, attained perfection in the works of Sophocles. For his consummate technical skill as a dramatist, for his unforgettable characters, and for his haunting, perfectly plotted plays, he remains one of the greatest figures of world literature.

(For further information, see *Classical and Medieval Literature Criticism,* Vol. 2; *Dictionary of Literary Biography,* Vol. 176; *DISCovering Authors; DISCovering Authors: British; DISCovering Authors: Canadian; DISCovering Authors Modules: Dramatists Module, Most-studied Authors Module; Drama Criticism,* Vol. 1.)

CRITICAL COMMENTARY

ARISTOTLE

SOURCE: Aristotle, "Aristotle, The Poetics," translated by W. Hamilton Fyfe, in *Aristotle: The Poetics, "Longinus" on the Sublime, Demetrius on Style,* Vol. XXIII, William Heinemann Ltd., 1927, pp. 3-117.

[*In the following excerpt, written in the fourth century B.C., Aristotle discusses the principles of dramatic composition—focusing on the elements of reversal, discovery, and character—using* Oedipus tyrannus *by Sophocles as a model of effective theatrical style.*]

Principal Works

Triptolemos (drama) c. 486 B.C.
Aias [*Ajax*] (drama) c. 450 B.C.
Antigone (drama) c. 442 B.C.
Ichneutai [*The Trackers*] (drama) c. 440 B.C.
*Trakhiniai [*Trachiniae*] (drama) c. 440-430 B.C.
**Oedipous tyrannos [*Oedipus Rex*] (drama) c. 425 B.C.
Elektra [*Electra*] (drama) c. 425-410 B.C.
Philoktetes [*Philoctetes*] (drama) 409 B.C.
Oedipous epi Kolonoi [*Oedipus at Colonus*] (drama) c. 405 B.C.

*This work is also known as *The Women of Trachis*.
**This work is also known as *Oedipus the King*.

Principal English Translations

The Theban Plays (dramas) 1947
The Oedipus Cycle (dramas) 1949
The Complete Greek Tragedies: Sophocles (dramas) 1954-57
Plays (dramas) 1956
Complete Plays of Sophocles (dramas) 1982
The Three Theban Plays: Antigone, Oedipus the King, Oedipus at Colonus (dramas) 1984
Antigone (drama) 1989

Adaptations

Adaptations of Sophocles's works include the film *Oedipus Rex*, directed by Pier Paolo Pasolini, 1967.

Some plots [of tragedies] are "simple" and some "complex," as indeed the actions represented by the plots are obviously such. By a simple action I mean one that is single and continuous. . ., wherein the change of fortune occurs without "reversal" or "discovery"; by a complex action I mean one wherein the change coincides with a "discovery" or "reversal" or both. These should result from the actual structure of the plot in such a way that what has already happened makes the result inevitable or probable; for there is indeed a vast difference between what happens *propter hoc* and *post hoc*.

A "reversal" is a change of the situation into the opposite. . ., this change being, moreover, as we are saying, probable or inevitable—like the man in the *Oedipus* who came to cheer Oedipus and rid him of his anxiety about his mother by revealing his parentage and changed the whole situation. . . .

A "discovery," as the term itself implies, is a change from ignorance to knowledge, producing either friendship or hatred in those who are destined for good fortune or ill. A discovery is most effective when it coincides with reversals, such as that involved by the discovery in the *Oedipus*. There are also other forms of discovery, for what we have described may in a sense occur in relation to inanimate and trivial objects, or one may discover whether some one has done something or not. But the discovery which is most essentially part of the plot and part of the action is of the kind described above, for such a discovery and reversal of fortune will involve either pity or fear, and it is actions such as these which, according to our hypothesis, tragedy represents; and, moreover, misfortune and good fortune are likely to turn upon such incidents. . . .

Following upon what has been said above we should next state what ought to be aimed at and what avoided in the construction of a plot, and the means by which the object of tragedy may be achieved. Since then the structure of the best tragedy should be not simple but complex and one that represents incidents arousing fear and pity—for that is peculiar to this form of art—it is obvious to begin with that one should not show worthy men passing from good fortune to bad. That does not arouse fear or pity but shocks our feelings. Nor again wicked people passing from bad fortune to good. That is the most tragic of all, having none of the requisite qualities, since it does not satisfy our feelings or arouse pity or fear. Nor again the passing of a thoroughly bad man from good fortune to bad fortune. Such a structure might satisfy our feelings but it arouses neither pity nor fear, the one being for the man who does not deserve his misfortune and the other for the man who is like ourselves—pity for the undeserved misfortune, fear for the man like ourselves—so that the result will arouse neither pity nor fear.

There remains then the mean between these. This is the sort of man who is not pre-eminently virtuous and just, and yet it is through no badness or villainy of his own that he falls into the misfortune, but rather through some flaw in him, he being one of those who are in high station and good fortune, like Oedipus and Thyestes and the famous men of such families as those. The successful plot must then have a single and not, as some say, a double issue; and the change must be not to good fortune from bad but, on the contrary, from good to bad fortune, and it must not be due to villainy but to some great flaw in such a man as we have described, or of one who is better rather than worse. This can be seen also in actual practice. For at first poets accepted any plots, but to-day the best tragedies are written about a few families—Alcmaeon for instance and Oedipus and Orestes and Meleager and Thyestes and Telephus and all the others whom it befell to suffer or inflict terrible disasters.

Judged then by the theory of the art, the best tragedy is of this construction. . . .

Fear and pity sometimes result from the spectacle and are sometimes aroused by the actual arrangement of the incidents, which is preferable and the mark of a better poet. The plot should be so constructed that even without seeing the play anyone hearing of the incidents happening thrills with fear and pity as a result of what occurs. So would anyone feel who heard the story of Oedipus. To produce this effect by means of an appeal to the eye is inartistic and needs adventitious aid, while those who by such means produce an effect which is not fearful but merely monstrous have nothing in common with tragedy. For one should not seek from tragedy all kinds of pleasure but that which is peculiar to tragedy, and since the poet must by "representation" produce the pleasure which comes from feeling pity and fear, obviously this quality must be embodied in the incidents. . . .

Concerning "character" there are four points to aim at. The first and most important is that the character should be good. The play will show character if . . . either the dialogue or the actions reveal some choice; and the character will be good, if the choice is good. But this is relative to each class of people. Even a woman is "good" and so is a slave, although it may be said that a woman is an inferior thing and a slave beneath consideration.

The second point is that the characters should be appropriate. A character may be manly, but it is not appropriate for a woman to be manly or clever.

Thirdly, it should be "like." This is different from making the character good and from making it appropriate in the sense of the word as used above.

Fourthly, it should be consistent. Even if the original be inconsistent and offers such a character to the poet for representation, still he must be consistently inconsistent. . . .

In character-drawing just as much as in the arrangement of the incidents one should always seek what is inevitable or probable, so as to make it inevitable or probable that such and such a person should say or do such and such; and inevitable or probable that one thing should follow another.

Clearly therefore the "denouement" of each play should also be the result of the plot itself and not produced mechanically as in the *Medea* and the incident of the embarkation in the *Iliad*. The "god in the car" should only be used to explain what lies outside the play, either what happened earlier and is therefore beyond human knowledge, or what happens later and needs to be foretold in a proclamation. For we ascribe to the gods the power of seeing everything. There must, however, be nothing inexplicable in the incidents, or, if there is, it must lie outside the tragedy. There is an example in Sophocles' *Oedipus*. . . .

As for kinds of Discovery, first comes the least artistic kind, which is largely used owing to incompetence—discovery by tokens. These may be congenital, like "the spear the Earthborn bear" or stars, like those which Carcinus uses in his *Thyestes*; or they may be acquired and these may be on the body, for instance, wounds, or external things like necklaces, and in the *Tyro* the discovery by means of the boat. . . . In the second place come those which are manufactured by the poet and are therefore inartistic. . . .

The third kind is due to memory, to showing distress on seeing something. . . .

Best of all is the discovery which is brought about directly by the incidents, the surprise being produced by means of what is likely—take the scene in Sophocles' *Oedipus* or in the *Iphigeneia*—for it is likely enough that she should want to send a letter. These are the only discovery scenes which dispense with artificial tokens, like necklaces.

JOHANN WOLFGANG VON GOETHE AND JOHANN PETER ECKERMANN

SOURCE: Johann Wolfgang von Goethe, in a conversation with Johann Peter Eckermann on March 28, 1827, in *Conversations with Eckermann (1823-1832)*, translated by John Oxenford, 1850. Reprint by North Point Press, 1984, pp. 141-47.

[*Goethe has been called Germany's greatest writer, excelling in a variety of genres and literary styles. In the following excerpt, Goethe and Eckermann remark on several themes in the plays of Sophocles.*]

"An action should never be placed in the category of political virtue which is opposed to virtue in general. When Creon forbids the burial of Polyneices, and not only taints the air with the decaying corpse, but also affords opportunity for dogs and birds of prey to drag about pieces torn from the dead body and thus to defile the altars—an action so offensive to both gods and men is not politically virtuous, but a political crime. Besides, he has everybody in the play against him. He has the elders of the state, who form the chorus, against him; he has the people at large against him; he has Teiresias against him; he has his own family against him; but he hears not, and obstinately persists in his impiety until he has brought to ruin all who belong to him, and is himself at last nothing but a shadow."

"And still," said I, "when we hear him speak, we cannot help believing he is somewhat in the right."

"That is the very thing," said Goethe, "in which Sophocles is a master; and in which consists the very life of the dramatic in general. His characters all possess this gift of eloquence, and know how to explain the motives for their action so convincingly that the hearer is almost always on the side of the last speaker.

"Evidently, in his youth, he enjoyed an excellent rhetorical education, by which he became trained to look for all the reasons and seeming reasons of things. Still, his great talent in this respect betrayed him into faults: he sometimes went too far. There is a passage in *Antigone* which I always look upon as a blemish, and I would give a great deal for an apt philologist to prove that it is interpolated and spurious. After the heroine has explained the noble motives for her action, and displayed the elevated purity of her soul, she at last, when she is led to death, brings forward a motive that is quite unworthy and almost borders upon the comic. She says that, if she had been a mother, she would not have done, either for her dead children or for her dead husband, what she has done for her brother. 'For,' says she, 'if my husband died I could have had another, and if my children died I could have had others by my new husband. But with my brother, the case is different. I cannot have another brother; for, since my mother and father are dead, there is nobody to beget one.'

"This is, at least, the bare sense of this passage, which in my opinion, when placed in the mouth of a heroine going to her death, disturbs the tragic tone and appears to me very far-fetched—to savour too much of dialectical calculation."

We conversed further upon Sophocles, remarking that in his pieces he always less considered a moral tendency than an apt treatment of the subject, particularly with regard to theatrical effect.

"I do not object," said Goethe, "to a dramatic poet having a moral influence in view; but, when the point is to bring his subject clearly and effectively before his audience, his moral purpose proves of little use, and he needs much more a faculty for delineation and a familiarity with the stage to know what to do and what to leave undone. If there be a moral in the subject, it will appear, and the poet has nothing to consider but the effective and artistic treatment of his subject. If a poet has as high a soul as Sophocles, his influence will always be moral, let him do what he will. Besides, he knew the stage, and understood his craft thoroughly."

"How well he knew the theatre," answered I, "and how much he had in view a theatrical effect, we see in his *Philoctetes*, and the great resemblance this piece bears to *Oedipus in Colonos*, in both arrangement and course of action.

"In each piece we see a hero in a helpless condition; both are old and suffering from bodily infirmities. Oedipus has at his side his daughter as a guide and a prop; Philoctetes has his bow. The resemblance is carried still further. Both have been thrust aside in their afflictions; but, when the oracle declares that victory can be obtained with their aid alone, endeavour is made to get them back; Ulysses comes to Philoctetes, Creon to Oedipus. Both begin their discourse with cunning and honeyed words; but when these are of no avail they use violence, and we see Philoctetes deprived of his bow, and Oedipus of his daughter."

"Such acts of violence," said Goethe, "give an opportunity for excellent altercations, and such situations of helplessness excited the emotions of the audience; on which account the poet, whose object it was to produce an effect upon the public, liked to introduce them. In order to strengthen this effect in the [*Oedipus in Colonos*], Sophocles brings him in as a weak old man—whereas, according to all circumstances, he must have been a man still in the prime of life. But, at this vigorous age, the poet could not have used him for his play; he would have produced no effect, and he therefore made him a weak, helpless old man."

"The resemblance to *Philoctetes*," continued I, "goes still further. The hero, in both pieces, does not act, but suffers. On the other hand, each of these passive heroes has two active characters against him. Oedipus has Creon and Polyneices, Philoctetes has Neoptolemus and Ulysses; two such opposing characters were necessary to discuss the subject on all sides, and to gain the necessary body and fulness for the piece."

"You might add," interposed Goethe, "that both pieces bear this further resemblance: we see in both the extremely effective situation of a happy change; since one hero, in his disconsolate situation, has his beloved daughter restored to him, and the other his no less beloved bow."

The happy conclusions of these two pieces are also similar; for both heroes are delivered from their sorrows: Oedipus is blissfully snatched away; and as for Philoctetes, we are forewarned by the oracle of his cure, before Tory, by Oesculapius.

FRIEDRICH NIETZSCHE

SOURCE: Friedrich Nietzsche, "The Birth of Tragedy," in *Basic Writings of Nietzsche*, translated by Walter Kaufmann, The Modern Library, 1967, pp. 3-146.

[*A German philosopher and poet, Nietzsche exerted a profound yet volatile influence on contemporary thought. Central ideas in his writings included the will to power, the "overman" (or superman), and the death of God. In the following excerpt from a work written in 1872, Nietzsche emphasizes the ability of Sophocles to create powerful characters and briefly discusses* Oedipus tyrannus *in the context of the myth "that a wise magus can be born only from incest."*]

Everything that comes to the surface in the Apollinian part of Greek tragedy, in the dialogue, looks simple, transparent, and beautiful. In this sense, the dialogue is an image of the Hellene whose nature is revealed in the dance because in the dance the greatest strength remains only potential but betrays itself in the suppleness and wealth of movement. Thus the language of Sophocles' heroes amazes us by its Apollinian precision and lucidity, so we immediately have the feeling that we are looking into the innermost ground of their being, with some astonishment that the way to this ground should be so short. But suppose we disregard the character of the hero as it comes to the surface, visibly—after all, it is in the last analysis nothing but a bright image projected on a dark wall, which means appearance through and through; suppose we penetrate into the myth that projects itself in these lucid reflections: then we suddenly experience a phenomenon that is just the opposite of a familiar optical phenomenon. When after a forceful attempt to gaze on the sun we turn away blinded, we see dark-colored spots before our eyes, as a cure, as it were. Conversely, the bright image projections of the Sophoclean hero—in short, the Apollinian aspect of the mask—are necessary effects of a glance into the inside and terrors of nature; as it were, luminous spots to cure eyes damaged by gruesome night. Only in this sense may we believe that we properly comprehend the serious and important concept of "Greek cheerfulness." The mis-understanding of this concept as cheerfulness in a state of unendangered comfort is, of course, encountered everywhere today.

Sophocles understood the most sorrowful figure of the Greek stage, the unfortunate Oedipus, as the noble human being who, in spite of his wisdom, is destined to error and misery but who eventually, through his tremendous suffering, spreads a magical power of blessing that remains effective even beyond his decease. The noble human being does not sin, the profound poet wants to tell us: though every law, every natural order, even the moral world may perish through his actions, his actions also produce a higher magical circle of effects which found a new world on the ruins of the old one that has been overthrown. That is what the poet wants to say to us insofar as he is at the same time a religious thinker. As a poet he first shows us a marvelously tied knot of a trial, slowly unraveled by the judge, bit by bit, for his own undoing. The genuinely Hellenic delight at this dialectical solution is so great that it introduces a trait of superior cheerfulness into the whole work, everywhere softening the sharp points of the gruesome presuppositions of this process.

In *Oedipus at Colonus* we encounter the same cheerfulness, but elevated into an infinite transfiguration. The old man, struck by an excess of misery, abandoned solely to *suffer* whatever befalls him, is confronted by the supraterrestrial cheerfulness that descends from the divine sphere and suggests to us that the hero attains his highest activity, extending far beyond his life, through his purely passive posture, while his conscious deeds and desires, earlier in his life, merely led him into passivity. Thus the intricate legal knot of the Oedipus fable that no mortal eye could unravel is gradually disentangled—and the most profound human joy overcomes us at this divine counterpart of the dialectic.

If this explanation does justice to the poet one may yet ask whether it exhausts the contents of the myth—and then it becomes evident that the poet's whole conception is nothing but precisely that bright image which healing nature projects before us after a glance into the abyss. Oedipus, the murderer of his father, the husband of his mother, the solver of the riddle of the Sphinx! What does the mysterious triad of these fateful deeds tell us?

There is a tremendously old popular belief, especially in Persia, that a wise magus can be born only from incest. With the riddle-solving and mother-marrying Oedipus in mind, we must immediately interpret this to mean that where prophetic and magical powers have broken the spell of present and future, the rigid law of individuation, and the real magic of nature, some enormously unnatural event—such as incest—must have occurred earlier, as a cause. How else could one compel nature to surrender her secrets if not by triumphantly resisting her, that is, by means of something unnatural? It is this insight that I find expressed in that horrible triad of Oedipus' destinies: the same man who solves the riddle of nature—that Sphinx of two species—also must break the most sacred natural orders by murdering his father and marrying his mother. Indeed, the myth seems to wish to whisper to us that wisdom, and particularly Dionysian wisdom, is an unnatural abomination; that he who by means of his knowledge plunges nature into the abyss of destruction must also suffer the dissolution of nature in his own person. "The edge of wisdom turns against the wise: wisdom is a crime against nature": such horrible sentences are proclaimed to us by the myth; but the Hellenic poet touches the sublime and terrible Memnon's Column of myth like a sunbeam, so that it suddenly begins to sound—in Sophoclean melodies.

SIGMUND FREUD

SOURCE: Sigmund Freud, "The Material and Sources of Dreams," in his *The Interpretation of Dreams*, edited and translated by James Strachey, Basic Books, Inc., Publishers, 1955, pp. 163-276.

[An Austrian neurologist and author, Freud is known as the father of psychoanalysis, a method of seeking to understand the power of the unconscious over the conscious mind. His writings have exerted an enormous influence on literary criticism and on other fields of intellectual endeavor. In the following excerpt from a work written in 1900, he demonstrates how Sophocles' Oedipus Rex *supports his assumptions regarding the Oedipus complex, noting that Oedipus' "destiny moves us only because it might have been ours."]*

In my experience, which is already extensive, the chief part in the mental lives of all children who later become psychoneurotics is played by their parents. Being in love with the one parent and hating the other are among the essential constituents of the stock of physical impulses which is formed at that time and which is of such importance in determining the symptoms of the later neurosis. It is not my belief, however, that psychoneurotics differ sharply in this respect from other human beings who remain normal—that they are able, that is, to create something absolutely new and peculiar to themselves. It is far more probable—and this is confirmed by occasional observations on normal children—that they are only distinguished by exhibiting on a magnified scale feelings of love and hatred to their parents which occur less obviously and less intensely in the minds of most children.

This discovery is confirmed by a legend that has come down to us from classical antiquity: a legend whose profound and universal power to move can only be understood if the hypothesis I have put forward in regard to the psychology of children has an equally universal validity. What I have in mind is the legend of King Oedipus and Sophocles' drama which bears his name.

Oedipus, son of Laius, King of Thebes, and of Jocasta, was exposed as an infant because an oracle had warned Laius that the still unborn child would be his father's murderer. The child was rescued, and grew up as a prince in an alien court, until, in doubts as to his origin, he too questioned the oracle and was warned to avoid his home since he was destined to murder his father and take his mother in marriage. On the road leading away from what he believed was his home, he met King Laius and slew him in a sudden quarrel. He came next to Thebes and solved the riddle set him by the Sphinx who barred his way. Out of gratitude the Thebans made him their king and gave him Jocasta's hand in marriage. He reigned long in peace and honour, and she who, unknown to him, was his mother bore him two sons and two daughters. Then at last a plague broke out and the Thebans made enquiry once more of the oracle. It is at this point that Sophocles' tragedy opens. The messengers bring back the reply that the plague will cease when the murderer of Laius has been driven from the land.

> But he, where is he? Where shall now be read
> The fading record of this ancient guilt?

The action of the play consists in nothing other than the process of revealing, with cunning delays and evermounting excitement—a process that can be likened to the work of a psychoanalysis—that Oedipus himself is the murderer of Laius, but further that he is the son of the murdered man and of Jocasta. Appalled at the abomination which he has unwittingly perpetrated, Oedipus blinds himself and forsakes his home. The oracle has been fulfilled.

Oedipus Rex is what is known as a tragedy of destiny. Its tragic effect is said to lie in the contrast between the supreme will of the gods and the vain attempts of mankind to escape the evil that threatens them. The lesson which, it is said, the deeply moved spectator should learn from the tragedy is submission to the divine will and realization of his own impotence. Modern dramatists have accordingly tried to achieve a similar tragic effect by weaving the same contrast into a plot invented by themselves. But the spectators have looked on unmoved while a curse or an oracle was fulfilled in spite of all the efforts of some innocent man: later tragedies of destiny have failed in their effect.

If *Oedipus Rex* moves a modern audience no less than it did the contemporary Greek one, the explanation can only be that its effect does not lie in the contrast between destiny and human will, but is to be looked for in the particular nature of the material on which that contrast is exemplified. There must be something which makes a voice within us ready to recognize the compelling force of destiny in the *Oedipus*, while we can dismiss as merely arbitrary such dispositions as are laid down in [Grillparzer's] *Die Ahnfrau* or other modern tragedies of destiny. And a factor of this kind is in fact involved in the story of King Oedipus. His destiny moves us only because it might have been ours—because the oracle laid the same curse upon us before our birth as upon him. It is the fate of all of us, perhaps, to direct our first sexual impulse towards our mother and our first hatred and our first murderous wish against our father. Our dreams convince us that that is so. King Oedipus, who slew his father Laius and married his mother Jocasta, merely shows us the fulfilment of our own childhood wishes. But, more fortunate than he, we have meanwhile succeeded, in so far as we have not become psychoneurotics, in detaching our sexual impulses from our mothers and in forgetting our jealousy of our fathers. Here is one in whom these primaeval wishes of our childhood have been fulfilled, and we shrink back from him with the whole force of the repression by which those wishes have since that time been held down within us. While the poet, as he unravels the past, brings to light the guilt of Oedipus, he is at the same time compelling us to recognize our own inner minds, in which those same impulses, though suppressed, are still to be found. The contrast with which the closing Chorus leaves us confronted—

> ... Fix on Oedipus your eyes,
> Who resolved the dark enigma, noblest
>   champion and most wise.
> Like a star his envied fortune mounted
>   beaming far and wide:
> Now he sinks in seas of anguish, whelmed
>   beneath a raging tide...

—strikes as a warning at ourselves and our pride, at us who since our childhood have grown so wise and so mighty in our own eyes. Like Oedipus, we live in ignorance of these wishes, repugnant to morality, which have been forced upon us by Nature, and after their revelation we may all of us well seek to close our eyes to the scenes of our childhood.

There is an unmistakable indication in the text of Sophocles' tragedy itself that the legend of Oedipus sprang from some primaeval dream-material which had as its content the distressing disturbance of a child's relation to his parents owing to the first stirrings of sexuality. At a point when Oedipus, though he is not yet enlightened, has begun to feel troubled by his recollection of the oracle, Jocasta consoles him by referring to a dream which many people dream, though, as she thinks, it has no meaning:

> Many a man ere now in dreams hath lain
> With her who bare him. He hath least annoy
> Who with such omens troubleth not his
>   mind.

To-day, just as then, many men dream of having sexual relations with their mothers, and speak of the fact with indignation and astonishment. It is clearly the key to the tragedy and the complement to the dream of the dreamer's father being dead. The story of Oedipus is the reaction of the imagination to these two typical dreams. And just as these dreams, when dreamt by adults, are accompanied by feelings of repulsion, so too the legend must include horror and self-punishment.

JACQUELINE DE ROMILLY

SOURCE: Jacqueline de Romilly, "Drama in the Second Half of the Fifth Century: Sophocles, Euripides, and Aristophanes," in her *A Short History of Greek Literature*, translated by Lillian Doherty, The University of Chicago Press, 1985, pp. 66-89.

[*In the following excerpt from a work written in 1980, de Romilly explores Sophocles' views on the relation between gods and men, comments on aspects of the Sophoclean hero, and discusses the overall tenor of the dramatist's works.*]

[Two sets of themes can be identified in the tragedies of Aeschylus], those related to the city and those concerning the gods. The first group are of minor importance in the surviving plays of Sophocles. The second half of the *Ajax*, and more especially the *Antigone*, do include discussions of the problem of absolute authority. The *Antigone* also contains reflections on the subject of law, which have encouraged some scholars

(Victor Ehrenberg, among others) to compare Sophocles' position with that of Pericles. But it must be acknowledged that what Sophocles emphasizes are religious obligations or very broad moral ones. The political life of the city-state remains in the background except as it impinges on religious duties.

The relation between men and gods is ... a major theme in Sophocles. But it is nothing like the relation between men and gods as described by Aeschylus. In the first place, the gods are more distant. In the surviving plays, they almost never appear onstage (the sole exception is Athene, in the prologue to the *Ajax*). Likewise, their influence on human emotions is less immediate; and the principles by which they act are harder to discern.

Yet the gods make their presence known, most frequently by means of oracles. The plays of Sophocles often find their points of departure in prophecies; as the action unfolds, the characters look for the fulfilment of the various prophecies, weigh them against each other, and seek reassurance in them. Sometimes as many as three or four are cited in a single tragedy (e.g., in *The Women of Trachis*, in *Oedipus the King*, and in *Philoctetes*). Yet these oracles are not understood. Often they are enigmatic, as in Herodotus. Thus Heracles was told that he would be killed by a dead man (in fact, the drug which killed him was given to Deianira by the dying Centaur): how could he be expected to interpret this? Even when the oracles themselves are clear, their application may be deceptive; thus Oedipus mistook the identity of his father and mother. To put it another way, the mystery surrounding the gods' designs does not involve a principle; it is as if a veil were lifted only halfway, and mortals were expected to guess what lay behind it. The partial disclosures of oracles add pathos to human weakness without in any way illuminating it.

Indeed, the contrast between human fate and human ignorance is a source of profound irony. It is no accident that disaster strikes at the very moment when the protagonists are taking heart. Nor is it by accident that Sophocles so often puts words of double meaning into his characters' mouths—words whose full import the speakers themselves are unaware of. Oedipus curses the murderer of Laius without knowing that he is himself the murderer, and swears to act "as if the dead man were his own father"—which is in fact the case. To the ironies of fate Sophocles adds ironies in the structuring of scenes and in the choice of words. The gods almost seem to be laughing at mankind, just as Athene in the *Ajax* makes cruel sport of the pitiful, crazed hero.

Yet in Sophocles' world view there are no signs of revolt against this divine regime. He respects the gods; and in his plays only the arrogant who are about to be struck down dare to doubt the veracity of oracles. Instead of revolt or doubt we find an overwhelming sense of the distance between gods and men. Among men, everything passes, everything changes. Sophocles says so repeatedly, in choral odes of rare nobility and power. One such marks the opening of *The Women of Trachis:* "Never has the son of Cronus, the king who ordains all things, given to mortals portions without pain. Joys and pains come to all by turns, circling, even as the stars of the Great Bear resolve. For men, nothing endures—not the starry night, not misfortunes, not riches" [lines 126-33]. The sphere of the gods, by contrast, is the sphere of the absolute, which nothing disturbs; in this respect Sophocles mirrors the beliefs of Pindar. As the chorus in the *Antigone* declares, nothing can diminish Zeus's power; "neither sleep, which charms all creatures, nor the divine and weariless months can ever conquer him." The chorus then addresses Zeus directly: "Untouched by age and time, you remain absolute master of Olympus and its dazzling light" [605-10].

The awareness of this gulf between two worlds accounts for two aspects of Sophocles' thought that at first glance might appear contradictory. First, it explains what may be called his pessimism. How can man hope, in such circumstances, to understand divine acts or escape their effects? Such acts are equally mysterious whether they are generous (*Oedipus at Colonus*) or cruel (*Oedipus the King*): a man's efforts to act rightly may be his own undoing. Or, like Oedipus, he may do wrong in spite of himself, without knowing or wishing it.

At the same time, whatever comes from the gods derives from them a sacred quality that outweighs every other consideration. A man cannot be too pious; he must put nothing before the divine ordinances. For Sophocles, the "unwritten laws" (respect for the gods, for parents, for suppliants, for the dead) are not the projections of a human consciousness or, indeed, of a Greek consciousness; they are divine laws. It is they that Antigone puts before the edict against burying her brother; and she is exhilarated at the thought that these laws partake of the permanence of the distant gods: "They are not of today or yesterday; no one knows the day they first appeared" [456-57]. In the same vein, the chorus of *Oedipus the King* prays that it may never neglect the "laws begotten in the clear air of heaven, / whose only father is Olympus;" "No mortal nature brought them to birth, / no forgetfulness shall lull them to sleep; / for God is great in them and grows not old" [867-72]. In Sophocles, the eminence of the gods makes man's fate seem more tragic by contrast; but at the same time it increases the brilliance of the human ideal.

This brings us to another all-important aspect of Sophocles' thought that sets him apart from Aeschylus. In the absence of any clear understanding of the divine will, attention is focused on man: will he find an honorable response to the fate that threatens him? Sophocles shows us Ajax, Oedipus, Heracles, Philoctetes, even Electra at the moment when each is destroyed and brought low, though none of them can be said really to deserve such a fall; but it is at that very moment that their heroism is revealed—in the way they face the trial.

A primary feature of Sophocles' characters is the variety of positions they take, positions that are often in direct conflict with one another. This implies clear and effective characterization. After Aeschylus, literary expression had grown less rigid, and dialogue had gained in importance relative to the lyrical portion of tragedy. At the same time, the individual had gained a greater independence in society. As a result, we see more nuanced characterization, and frequent confrontations of two contrasting personalities. [We have] the pairs of sisters (Antigone/Ismene, Electra/Chrysothemis) and the contrasts between husband and wife or master and captive woman (Heracles/Deianira, Ajax/Tecmessa). Elsewhere Neoptolemus's candor is contrasted with Odysseus's guile, Odysseus's prudence with Ajax's reckless passion, Odysseus's moderation with Agamemnon's harshness. All these characters are vividly portrayed, the individuality of each brought out by such contrasts.

Yet a qualification is in order: Sophocles' characterization does not always presuppose a psychological study that can satisfy our modern expectations. In a famous but unjust critique, Tycho von Wilamowitz (son of the well-known classical scholar) went so far as to claim that Sophocles neglected psychology to the point of implausibility when it suited his dramatic purpose. Some passages are certainly problematic. When Ajax, just before killing himself, claims to be reconciled to life, is he partly sincere and partly dishonest? Sophocles never makes it clear. Nor does he say or even imply to what extent Deianira is sincere when she claims to forgive her husband's infidelity. Equally inexplicable is Antigone's sudden shift from a bold acceptance of death to plaintive laments over her fate.

These gray areas imply no contradictions; they merely indicate that Sophocles did not care to make every link explicit in a character's motivation. For psychological investigation was not his major concern in creating characters. His characters have different mentalities because each embodies a different moral ideal, to which he or she adheres. Each knows the basis for his actions and defends his principles, making them his cause; each stands in contrast to those among whom he lives as one philosophy of life stands in contrast to others.

As a result, we come to feel that the debate on stage transcends the characters and concerns us as well. In the opposition between Ajax and Tecmessa we can see the contrast between an aristocratic ethic based on honor and a more humane ethic based on obligations to individuals. In the same play there is the debate between the Atreidae, who represent the claims of discipline, and Teucer and Odysseus, who urge respect for a dead man's former stature. The conflict between Antigone and Ismene, like that between Electra and Chrysothemis, is based on the opposite reactions of revolt and submission. The scenes in which these characters confront one another are clearly designed to weigh conflicting duties. Thus we have long speeches balancing one another, or debates in lines of crackling riposte in which antitheses—sometimes on the level of individual words or syllables—follow one another in rapid succession. Finally, each play as a whole is built from a sequence of such contrasting scenes. Antigone debates her act first with her sister and then with Creon; one is a timid ally, the other an antagonist. Later, Creon must debate *his* position with his own allies—his son and the prophet Teiresias—who find him at fault. In this series of confrontations, positions are affirmed, vindicated, and clarified; at the same time, tension builds.

Such close identification between a character and the ideal in whose name he acts implies a rare lucidity on the part of the character; yet complexity is by no means excluded. As we have seen, the sudden reversals in some characters' positions can be surprising. Neoptolemus's change of heart—his decision to embrace the right cause—is the whole subject of the play. Seldom, however, can we label a character's moral position without misrepresenting it; bad and good are usually intertwined. Creon, in the *Antigone,* defends the rights of the city-state, and his arguments are impressive; but they are also inflexible, and he tends to confuse the state with himself. Haemon and Teiresias try, each in his own way, to convince Creon of this. The truth is complex and emerges only gradually, as scene follows scene. It can honestly be said that after twenty-five centuries we are still debating the precise meaning of the conflict between Antigone and Creon. When the philosopher Hegel claims that Antigone represents the family in conflict with the state, he is oversimplifying. At different periods it has been said that Antigone stands for humane feeling as opposed to intransigence, or for the right to rebel as opposed to any abuse of power; these too are oversimplifications. In Sophocles, as in Thucydides, we find a tendency to identify the particular with the general—without, however, distorting the particular. Sophocles does not simply choose an ideal to embody in Antigone; he puts a living Antigone before us. Yet at every juncture of the plot he manages to reveal in her a set of principles and an ideal of proper conduct that together make up her unique personality. An individual and a philosophy of life can be identified with one another in Sophocles because all his characters are passionately concerned to define and to defend their reasons for living.

Among these reasons, honor takes first place. It seems to a reader of the plays that the notion of honor evolves and increasingly asserts itself. Thus we move from the altogether external honor of Ajax, made up of acknowledged exploits and finding expression in public esteem, to the internalized honor of Neoptolemus, which requires only moral courage and finds expression only in a clear conscience (to the neglect, in Neoptolemus's case, of the glory he might win, and at the risk of being misjudged by the entire Greek army). Sophocles takes us, in other words, all the way from the world of Homer to that of Socrates. The plays in all their diversity retrace this movement toward ever purer and higher values. Transcending such contrasts and such progress, however, is a fundamental trait common to all of Sophocles' protagonists; each is prepared to sacrifice everything to his honor and to his values as he understands them. These are *heroic* characters. From a fierce warrior like Ajax to young women like Antigone or Electra, all share the same resolve, the same acceptance of death, the same refusal to be swayed.

The result is that the heroes are isolated from their intimates, who misunderstand them, try to restrain them, call them reckless and unrealistic. Their acts draw down the taunts of the powerful. Ajax dies alone, killing himself on enemy soil with a sword that was the gift of an enemy. Deianira dies misunderstood and cursed by her husband. She too withdraws to die alone, as do Eurydice in *Antigone* and Jocasta in *Oedipus the King.* Antigone is condemned to die in a subterranean vault, utterly alone; she is led away amid the sarcasms of the chorus ("They are laughing at me!"). Electra can count on no one but herself to act ("I am alone"). Philoctetes has spent years alone on his island, where the Greeks want to abandon him a second time. Finally, Oedipus, at the very height of his exaltation, is left alone to face a death only he may witness.

This solitude in fact corresponds to the greatness of the hero; he is condemned to it by his insistence on an absolute. At the same time, he finds in it a sort of obligation to rise above himself with renewed strength.

Even on this point, Sophocles leaves us with an antithesis. On the one hand are the heroes, in all their greatness; on the other, their more human intimates. Naturally the spotlight is on the heroes; the brilliance, the glory are theirs. But are those who try in vain to sway them necessarily wrong? Is Ajax right to kill himself, to abandon Tecmessa, his son, and the sailors of his fleet? Is the pliancy of the more tolerant Odysseus, who can forget injuries, less praiseworthy? And is Philoctetes right to refuse so obstinately to go to Troy? The heroes, in truth, are limiting cases, proof of the nobility that can coexist with the cruelest of trials. They are not models for our emulation, any more than Sophocles' plays are disembodied sermons. They are expressions of his faith in man.

For a pessimist, Sophocles radiates a rare confidence in everything beautiful. This side of him is often revealed in his choral odes. What I have said thus far about his arrangement of scenes, his lucid dialogue, and his forceful antitheses gives an idea of his dramatic art as expressed in the spoken parts of the plays. But I have given no hint of the beauty of his great odes, which are less directly related to the action than those of Aeschylus, yet for that very reason reveal more of the poet himself. Sophocles' odes are hardly divorced from the action; but in most cases they translate the themes of the preceding episode into more universal terms, reflecting Sophocles' propensity for combining the particular and the general. In *Antigone,* for example, after the announcement that Polyneices has been buried in spite of the royal edict, the chorus sings of the greatness of human accomplishments but recalls that men are bound to obey laws; when Antigone's guilt has been discovered, it sings of the ease with which disaster strikes; after the scene with Haemon, it describes the universal power of love; and when Antigone has gone to her death, it recalls the deaths of figures from mythology. In each case there is the same broadening of focus—the same echo, in a more serene key, of the preceding action.

In this way Sophocles' odes, though far shorter than those of Aeschylus, open up broad perspectives in which we can glimpse the poet's tastes and convictions. An example is the ode in the *Antigone* that begins, "Many are the wonders in this world, but none is greater than man" [332ff.]. There is no finer statement in Greek of man's preeminence, no greater praise for his discoveries and creative intelligence. In the spirit of his age, with its faith in progress, Sophocles evokes the whole series of human inventions, closing (in a vein more characteristic of his own thought) with the warning that if man uses his intelligence for ill, or against the law, it becomes ruinous.

Even expressions of grief and pain testify indirectly to Sophocles' love of life. When he wrote the poignant ode in *Oedipus at Colonus* deploring old age, the poet was in his nineties (the play was produced posthumously); it is a bitter piece, claiming that early death is best, and is often cited as evidence of Sophocles' pessimism. But behind the bitterness we can glimpse a sorrow at the loss of what made life worth living. In describing old age as "loathsome, impotent, unsociable, friendless" [1235-37], the poet may be suggesting nostalgia for the company, friendships, and happy life he had enjoyed as a younger man.

In this last tragedy, Sophocles even finds room for praise of his native Athens or, more precisely, his Attica. Oedipus comes there to die, and Sophocles takes advantage of the opportunity to describe the beauties of the Attic countryside—birds, growing things, and streams—which, together with the beneficent presence of the gods, inspire a great sense of peace. "In this land of good horses, stranger, you have found the best retreat on earth. This is white Colonus, favorite haunt of the sweet nightingale; she loves to sing in our green vales, amid the dark ivy, inviolable bower of the gods, sheltered by its thick growth of leaves from the sun and from every storm wind" [668ff.]. If Sophocles is elsewhere the tragedian who most insistently recalls the fragility of human happiness and portrays heroism at its highest pitch, the Colonus ode gives us a glimpse of the happier man suggested by his biography. In the contrast he so consistently draws between man's vulnerability and his greatness, the abiding impression is that vulnerability is not paramount. The mood of Sophocles' plays is not one of despair, and he is no more "pessimistic" about man's worth than he is about the beauty of life.

R. P. WINNINGTON-INGRAM

SOURCE: R. P. Winnington-Ingram, in his *Sophocles: An Interpretation*, Cambridge University Press, 1980, 346 p.

[*Below, Winnington-Ingram comments on several characters from Sophocles' plays, concluding that they generally exhibit "a dimension of greatness beyond the measure of normal humanity."*]

Each play of Sophocles exists in its own right, with its own situation, its own pattern, its own subtle variations upon common themes. The critic's primary task is no doubt to try and understand the individual play. Yet every play reveals a view of the world—and a view of heroes in that world; and a poet who saw the world in a certain way. The term "Sophoclean" is not an empty one, though its definition, because of the variety of the plays—and because they are so few and were selected for survival by a process largely irrelevant to the issues we are discussing, is a matter of extreme difficulty. Perhaps the surprising thing is that this small selection of plays does in fact contain so many common themes. The themes are social and religious.

The hero suffers a wrong, or what he regards as a wrong, done to himself or to those who are bound to him by kinship. This wrong he resents, in many cases to such a degree that it totally dominates his mind; moreover, it divides his world into friends and enemies who for him constitute, or should (he feels) constitute, irreconcilable camps. In one way or another he seeks to retrieve his position, to restore his honour or the honour of his kin; and in the process he is, or is like to be, destroyed. This pattern is clearest in *Ajax*, *Antigone*, *Electra*, and *Philoctetes*; it is an important aspect of *Oedipus Coloneus*, a minor feature in *Trachiniae*, and in *Oedipus Tyrannus* virtually absent. It will be convenient now to take the plays out of their (hypothetical) chronological order and, briefly, examine their themes, beginning with two plays which, separated by decades, unfold in a context of war.

Ajax might seem a simple matter of honour. "The man of good birth must either live nobly or be noble in his death." Ajax has no way of retrieving his honour in life, and so he kills himself. Honour is conferred by society. Ajax thinks it has been unjustly withheld from him by the Judgement of the Arms, which he resents to such a degree that he goes out to murder the Greek leaders as they sleep. He is frustrated by Athena; and this is the second and ultimate blow to his honour which necessitates his suicide. Sophocles has been at pains to show that the pride of Ajax is so hypertrophied as to be irreconcilable even with heroic society, a mental sickness, grown pathological in the course of time. Attempts have been made to extract a milder, wiser Ajax from the famous Deception Speech, even to represent his suicide as an act of *sophrosune*: on the contrary, it is the final assertion of his pride and his difference, the final rejection of a society whose values he has carried to an intolerable extreme. He dies calling upon the Erinyes to avenge him not only upon the Atridae but upon the whole Greek army—upon those who should have been his friends but have proved enemies. With Ajax is contrasted Odysseus, the "enemy" who ends by acting as a friend, refusing to accept that rigid polarity of friendship and enmity which was part of the creed of Ajax; a man of different temper who perhaps foreshadowed a different age; a man who, knowing the fragility of human fortunes, was capable of purity.

Philoctetes, like Ajax, had come to hate the Atridae and Odysseus. If Ajax had fought for ten years only to be cheated (as he thought) of his just reward, Philoctetes had spent those same ten years upon a desert island in company with a foul disease. As the action of the play unfolds, he is confronted with a dilemma. Not to mention the cure of his wound, this once mighty hero is offered the prospect of sharing the supreme honour of taking Troy, a thing which Achilles and Ajax and Diomede and the rest had failed to do; and, hero though he is, he rejects it. Some critics have argued that he rejects it because of the moral inferiority of the remaining Greek leaders, being unwilling to associate his heroism with their baseness, but the seductions of this hypothesis must be resisted. He rejects it, because it conflicts with another part of the heroic code, which is to resent an injury and pursue a grievance to the extreme point. And the reason why this prevails over the prospect of glory is to be found in the circumstances of the ten years' solitude during which he has brooded over his wrongs. Hatred of his enemies has become something he cannot abandon; he cannot benefit himself, if this means benefiting them. With him is contrasted Odysseus, who, as in *Ajax*, belongs to another world, but in its most repugnant aspect: a man of adaptable standards, who will be just and pious when he can, but will sacrifice everything to success. More important is Neoptolemus, who shares the main interest of the play. He has inherited a heroic—or if you will an aristocratic—code which does not reject violence but rejects deceit. For a time he is seduced by Odysseus, but repents, not simply because the deceit revolts him, but because he turns out to be one of those who are capable of pity—and of acting on it, even to his own detriment.

Antigone and *Electra,* also separated in time, fall to be considered together: both "family" plays, each with a formidable heroine who owes a duty derived from kinship. Antigone's duty is to bury, with humanity and decency on her side; Electra's to avenge by matricide. For Electra it is a point of honour first to lament and then to avenge her father, and no consideration of caution or moderation weighs with her; when she believes her brother dead, she urges Chrysothemis to join with her in killing Aegisthus (and by implication Clytemnestra) and so win honour in life and in death. "For those who are nobly born it is shameful to live shamefully"; and the Chorus sings that "none of the good, by living a base life, is willing to shame his fair repute, leaving no name," and that Electra is winning the noblest renown for observing the greatest natural laws, for her piety towards Zeus—the laws being those which demand filial piety. But piety towards one parent demands the sacrifice of the other, about which Electra has no qualms: indeed she is consumed with hatred for her. What is certain, in a play of vexed interpretation, is that her obsessive grief and obsessive hatred are the product of a long process of time which precedes and prepares the matricide. They are the work of Furies, of whom she is both the victim and the agent.

Antigone is rendered complex by the contrasted tragedies of Creon and Antigone—tragedies of different type of which Antigone's is typically Sophoclean. There is also a contrast of principles and of character. She acts out of an emotion which is at once narrow and generous: she is no reasoner, and the other side of the case simply does not exist for her. That other side is put by Creon, but the poet deliberately undercuts his position and shows his rationality as more apparent than real. He is crude and insensitive, and the sympathies of poet and audience are with Antigone, who, however, could not have done what she did, if she had not been hard, with a hardness inherited from her father. She too is made by her past, but the intensity of her emotion is the product, not (as with Electra) of long eroding time, but of a brief experience of unimaginable horror which has given her an obsession with the world of the dead. It is to this world that her "friends" belong; and it is in and through that world that, by a heroic resolve, she would cancel the hatreds which have dogged the house, retrieve its honour, declare peace and the restoration of love. Seeing things always in terms of "friends" and "enemies," she claims that it is her nature to join in friendship rather than in enmity, but, when her sister, who had failed to share her heroism, seeks out of mere affection to share her death, she cast her out into the ranks of the enemy. The heroic polarity prevails, as it will prevail in *Oedipus Coloneus.*

The work of time; heredity; friends and enemies; resentment and retaliation; the return of good for good and evil for evil; pity and the absence of pity. In the *Coloneus* all these familiar Sophoclean themes are present, woven into an intricate fabric: what marks it out is the ultimate destiny of an Oedipus who had seemed to be the paradigm of human fragility, of the breach between gods and men. Oedipus becomes a *heros.* Unlike the man of the *Tyrannus,* whose past is essentially personal to him, whose future is left in uncertainty, and in the treatment of whose destiny there is no word of the Erinyes, this Oedipus comes to a sanctuary of the Eumenides, which he recognizes as his final resting-place, and goes on, at a divine command, to assume himself the status of a chthonian power—powerful to benefit his friends and harm his enemies. What is the principle to which, inflexibly, he adheres? It is the principle of wrathful retaliation: so far from waning with time, his *thumos* grows into the gigantic curse upon his sons which foreshadows his role in the nether world. Pity belongs to Antigone.

A different Antigone; and a different Oedipus, if one

which the masterful king of the *Tyrannus* might—in time—have become. What, then, was the principle to which the latter adhered to the point of destruction? The contrast between appearance and reality, the fallibility of human knowledge, the late learning of truth, are common themes in Sophocles. One of the functions of time is to conceal and then to reveal; and one of the functions of those oracles whose terms are known but whose significance waits to be disclosed is to emphasize the breach between divine and human knowledge. Such oracles are prominent in *Trachiniae,* a highly ironical play, but, if there is one play in which irony runs riot, it is the *Tyrannus;* and, if there is one characteristic which marks out this Oedipus, it is his intellectual assurance and, one must add, his intellectual integrity, his determination to know the truth which blasts him by its discovery. It is this, not his character as a man of action, not his duty as a king, that marks him out as a Sophoclean hero.

We are left with *Trachiniae,* which moves in a different context from the other plays, being a tragedy of sex. Deianira, a wife of conventional virtue, a human-being who recognizes human status and is, like Odysseus in *Ajax* and like Neoptolemus, capable of pity, and who has therefore, it might seem, the qualities to safeguard her against tragedy, is led by the power of sex to perform an unscrupulous act with a consequence to be expected of a wicked woman. Which is ironical; it is no less ironical that the hero who has vanquished monsters—and has taken women as a requirement of his strong body—should be destroyed by his lusts and by the conjunction of two women. The only victor is Aphrodite, to whose power it is the fate of both Heracles and Deianira to fall victim. She is the force working within them that has inspired the actions for which they must pay. Yet they were deliberate actions, and in both cases they were the product of a past way of life, though in Deianira's case a paradoxical product. There is paradox and irony too in the case of Heracles. His career had consisted in a series of ordeals by which he had benefited humanity, freeing the Greek world of noxious monsters. If we look for a guiding principle of his life, he gives it to us, when he says: "Both living and dead, I have retaliated upon the evil"; and it seems that this theme—of retaliation and the perpetuation of evil through *talio*—is given some prominence in the later stages of the play. The irony is that his final ordeal, which Lichas invited us to see in terms of revenge, turns out to have been performed in pursuit of a lust; it is the monster that has his revenge.

This summary should have brought out two things: the frequent recurrence of certain themes and issues closely bound up with the heroism of the heroes, but also the variety of circumstance and tone and implication with which the themes are treated. The recurrences are important if we would form some general notion of the heroes and what they stand for; the variety, which involves the whole richness of the individual plays, should be cautionary when we come to generalize. One generalization at least is valid. The heroes have a dimension of greatness beyond the measure of normal humanity: they go on where ordinary men would stop. It is a kind of excess, and excess is dangerous. About their greatness there are two things to be said. It is just because they have this almost superhuman capacity of holding to their principles that the poet, through extreme cases, is able to unfold the tragic implications of those principles. Secondly, this kind of greatness does not comport with the conditions of mortal existence and tends towards disaster. If this is no world for them, as it is not, we are bound to ask how Sophocles saw the world in which they suffer their tormented destinies; and if it is governed by divine powers, as for Sophocles it was, to ask how he saw the gods at work in it.

Sophocles was a religious man. He held the priesthood of a minor deity. When a cult of Asclepius was being introduced into Athens during the Peloponnesian War, he took the god—or at least the sacred snake—into his house while a shrine was being prepared. The cult of the Eumenides at Colonus, where he was born, is described in loving detail, and all the sanctities of the place are celebrated in an ode. That he believed in the gods is certain, but how, precisely, he envisaged the anthropomorphic pantheon we are in no position to say. Nor is the question very important. Crude anthropomorphism was only one expression of Greek religious experience; and polytheism was the more acceptable that the gods were a part of nature and, being gods of power, reflected, as the Greek gods did, those aspects of life—physical, social, and emotional—where power resided and some impulse outside man was felt, feared or desired.

The personal religion of Sophocles is a matter of pure speculation: how religion and the gods enter into his tragedy we can attempt to discern, but must bear in mind that conventional piety need not imply untroubled acceptance of everything and anything attributable to the divine world. Greek polytheism represents the world as it impinges upon men. And as it is it must be accepted? A good pagan position, but even pagans are strangely reluctant to accept paganism. Are the gods just? Are men free? Greeks, like others, wrestled with these questions. The anxious wrestlings of Aeschylus, in particular, are reflected in the work of Sophocles at every point.

In the extant plays gods are seldom seen upon the stage. We have Heracles in *Philoctetes,* but it is essential to his role that he was recently a man and much of what he says is at the human level: indeed *qua* spokesman of heaven he says very little. We have Athena in *Ajax*.... Her role in the Prologos may be thought ambiguous, but is clarified by the words of Calchas, so that we see why she makes that pronouncement of the grounds of divine favour and disfavour: we see that her "wrath," which Ajax rightly recognizes without understanding its cause, was the appropriate penalty for his pride. Constantly, however, there are gods in the background, generally and specifically.

There is Aphrodite (with Eros). Athena punishes, but does not cause, the nature and action of Ajax: Aphrodite has worked powerfully within both Heracles and Deianira. It may be a misleading accident that this power is prominent in two of the extant plays and hymned in both. We must, however, take what we are given and recognize an aspect of the divine world of Sophocles which is seldom stressed, but should not be ignored. The power of sexual passion operating on, and in, the human mind is generative of tragedy because men may break under the strain and perform disastrous acts. There is some reason to suppose that Sophocles, like Aeschylus before him and like Euripides, saw another god of overwhelming emotion, Dionysus, as a potentially disastrous power. Both these powers are divine and part of the given world in which men have to play out their destinies. They are given, like the individual fates, and men have not asked for them.

There is Apollo, who enters particularly into the story of Oedipus, prominent in the *Tyrannus*, less so in the *Coloneus*. In the *Tyrannus* one gets the impression that Apollo is working against Oedipus, which is how the latter sees it. What, then, is Apollo's interest? Like Athena in *Ajax*, to punish a deliberate offence against divine law? The Chorus uses language of the unknown offender which might suggest such a thing, in an ode which immediately follows the all but explicit revelations of Teiresias. But Oedipus was not a deliberate offender. He was, however, deeply polluted; and Apollo was a god much concerned with pollution and purification. Or do we say that, as the god who knows what is to be and has foretold it, he has an interest in the fulfilment of his oracle? So stated, this sounds rather jejune. Better, perhaps, to remember that in Greek thought he was associated with the notion of self-knowledge.... This Oedipus is to acquire and becomes a symbol of human ignorance as Apollo and his oracle are symbols of divine knowledge.

Above and beyond Apollo, in point of knowledge and in point of power, stands Zeus. As in Homer, as in Aeschylus, he is the supreme authority, the divine king. The Chorus of the *Tyrannus*, when they think (how wrongly!) that oracles are not being fulfilled, pray to Zeus as ruler and king of all things. "There is none of these things that is not Zeus," says that Coryphaeus at the end of *Trachiniae*. If the prominence of Zeus in a play about Heracles owes something to his fatherhood, he looms in all the extant plays, and in some he looms larger as the play draws towards its close. The ways in which he enters into a play can be problematic. The prayer in the *Tyrannus* comes at the end of an ode whose tendency is to show that the fate of Oedipus was *not* the consequence of traditional wickedness. The choral comment in *Trachiniae* follows—and cannot fail to recall—the bitter complaint of Hyllus about the heartlessness of the gods. In *Antigone* Zeus is at once responsible for the troubles that have beset the house and also the authority to which the heroine appeals in defence of her action. There is no reason to suppose that for Sophocles he was a simpler and less troubling concept than he was for Aeschylus. As in Aeschylus so in Sophocles, he stands in an enigmatic relationship to the nether powers, to fate and the Erinyes.

Divine power bears upon the heroes in more than one way. Each of them comes into the world of human action and passion with a *moira*: he is of such-and-such a kind and will find himself in such-and-such a situation; and there is not a great deal that he can do about it. This is true of them, and it is true of us. To the question Why? there may be no ultimate answer or, if an answer is sought, it recedes into a vanishing distance. Sophocles wrote one play—and it is his most famous—which provides the parradigm of this aspect of human existence. It was the *moira* of Oedipus to kill his father and lie with his mother; and it is no good asking what the gods had to gain by this horror. That was what was going to happen to him and it did: everything stems from that. The story is given the greatest possible dramatic impact, because it did not happen, as it might have happened, to you or to me, but to a man of high station who fell into the depth of misery and so illustrated the precarious condition of humanity; it happened to a man of high intelligence, against his expectation, and so revealed the limitations of human knowledge. The world is such a world in which such a thing can happen. We cannot call the gods to account.

It was the *moira* of Philoctetes to be bitten by a sacred snake, receive a noisome wound and be in consequence abandoned by the Greeks. Here indeed there is some kind of divine purpose in the background, but it is neither very specific nor much stressed; it is an arbitrary datum, but it needs Philoctetes as a victim, it even needs him to forego his heroic resentment. This is of course a very different kind of play, in which the factor of destiny is hardly in the forefront and the consequences of the destined situation are worked out largely in terms of human psychology and social relationships. But the surd factor of an unaccountable destiny enters into all the plays in one way or another. Ajax has his *moira* no less than Oedipus; Antigone and Electra have theirs. It seems cruel to the sufferer who may cry out against it: so Oedipus speaks of a *daimon* which is *omos* and of himself as *echthrodaimon*.

We cannot say with what emotion, other than pity, Sophocles saw the dice loaded against his heroes in a pitiless world or contemplated, for that matter, the forces to which they were exposed. For if they have their individual fates assigned to them, they share—and exemplify—the general vulnerability of man, and this in many ways. Among those ways, they are subject to the forces of passion which assault the human mind, and which Sophocles, as a Greek, attributed to a divine origin, to an Aphrodite or a Dionysus, who, if they represent the irrational in man, are yet themselves gods. Nothing in the Greek conception of the divine is more characteristic or more revealing than these gods who work within the human *psyche* for delight or for tragedy. We may count it as a stroke of luck that mere chance has preserved two plays of Sophocles which exhibit Aphrodite in her tragic guise, in one of which she is protagonist. When she emerges sole victor from the destruction of Heracles and Deianira, she is not, as in *Hippolytus*, avenging a slighted divinity: she is merely being herself, nor is she responsible for the ironical fact that the physical strength which made Heracles a hero made him also her victim.

In the exposure to such forces, as in the individual *moira*, there is an arbitrariness which defies explanation, but this does not mean that Sophocles saw the divine dispensations as arbitrary—or wholly arbitrary. [He] had inherited from his predecessors—and indeed from early strata of Greek thought—two notions of *moira*; that, along with that of personal destiny, to all appearance arbitrary, there was a notion of *moira* as order, divinely sanctioned and entailing, by inexorable law, the punishment of offences against that order. It is a kind of justice and thus naturally associated with that clamant demand for justice in the gods which had led to the moralization of Zeus and so to all the problems of theodicy. It is in this connection that the relationship between the heroes and the gods becomes most difficult to determine and, thus, most interesting.

The gods represent—are responsible for—the world as it is and as it is governed. The heroes are obviously, in some sense, up against the world, hence their intransigence, hence their loneliness: they feel not only isolated from their fellow-men but (often) abandoned, even victimized, by the gods. Are they right to feel so, or are they wrong? If we apply to our old acquaintances, the pietists and the "hero-worshippers," we receive different answers. The gods of the pietists order all for the best; their harsh justice is in the interests of men, for whose welfare they care; learning comes by suffering, and those who lack the saving grace of *sophrosune* are taught a lesson; the intellectual pride of an Oedipus is humbled no less than the traditional heroic pride of an Ajax (the only matter in dispute being whether he learns his lesson or not). It follows that those who behave differently are right and favoured by the gods, Creon in the *Tyrannus* and Odysseus in *Ajax*. Of Odysseus this seems, broadly, to be true, but *Ajax* is a relatively early play, and there is nothing in later Sophocles quite so explicit as the motto-couplet of Athena which relates the love and hatred of the gods to the presence or absence of *sophrosune* in men. We turn to Antigone. What has she to learn, except that by being pious she has earned the reward of impiety? In that play Creon acts badly and, amid echoes of Aeschylus, is punished, learns—or half-learns—a lesson, but he does not share the typical attributes of a Sophoclean hero; Antigone, who does, claims to be acting in accord with divine law and is destroyed. Do we, then, go into reverse and say, with the hero-worshippers, that this is a bad world; that what the heroes do is great and right and exposes the badness of a world unworthy of them? We then take another look at Ajax; we bring Heracles and Electra into the picture; we begin to wonder, and we wait for the Colonean Oedipus.

The generalizations founder upon the variety of the heroes and of the situations in which they are placed, and extreme views can only be defended by interpretations which defy the text of Sophocles. Do we say the heroes are *per se* admirable? Or do we, rather, lay stress on their lack of *sophrosune*, that spirit of moderation and control which keeps men safe (as indeed it does), for which they suffer (as indeed they do), adding perhaps that they show their greatness above all in the moment of defeat? Are they approved or disapproved? But tragedy is not about approval and disapproval, which is why Ajax and Antigone can both be tragic figures, though no one could approve of the action of Ajax in seeking to kill his generals or (one might have hoped) disapprove of the action of Antigone in burying her brother; nor, for all they have in common, do we respond in the same way to those formidable heroines, Antigone and Electra. Indeed the engagement of our sympathies with these different figures varies notably in degree and in kind. These great and often terrible personages are neither models of how human-beings should behave nor models of how they should not behave. They are tragic figures who find themselves in tragic situations. Plato and Aristotle are bad guides. Aristotle encourages us to look for a *hamartia*, by which he presumably meant something different from the divine distraction, *ate*-produced and *ate*-producing, of early Greek thought (the kind of thing he was not interested in), but he does not make it clear how wide his conception of *hamartia* was (factual? moral?) nor, wisely perhaps, does he give examples. Of course tragic heroes make their tragic mistakes, but, if we seek in each case to identify a specific *hamartia*, we may end up discovering one of the least interesting things about them. For Plato it was a primary purpose to acquit the gods of responsibility for evil, in which he departed from the main stream of Greek thought, and by which he was led to banish tragedy. Can the gods of Sophocles, responsible for the conditions of human life, be so acquitted? May it not be that the gods whom the Chorus of *Oedipus Tyrannus*, appropriately, wished to worship were tragic gods, with whom the tragic heroes have an awful kinship?

There is a point of junction between the heroes—many or most of them—and the gods. (i) ... [Frequently] these plays turn on the sequence of injury, resentment and (as a matter of honour) retaliation. This is not a mere accident of mythology, or random selection. The emotions and motives involved belong to traditional Greek morals; ... the Greeks were taught to write tragedy (beginning of course, as Aristotle saw, with Homer, in part, by observing the consequences which followed when the code was carried inexorably into effect. (ii) ... [There] is a justice of the gods, whether it is viewed in terms of *moira* or of Zeus. It is a penal justice, a matter of retribution, of the past offence exacting payment in the present and laying up further retribution in the future. And this, too, for those who believed in divine justice, led in the direction of tragedy. Indeed, (i) and (ii) are meshed together. For it is the way of the gods to punish, not with thunderbolt or plague (though these may be used), but through human agency. Human retaliation is matched, in the proliferation of evil, by a divine law under which actions carry their inevitable penal consequences; divine *talio* is the sanction behind human *talio*; wrathful men are the agents of wrathful gods.

SOURCES FOR FURTHER STUDY

Bowra, C. M. *Sophoclean Tragedy.* Oxford: Clarendon Press, 1944, 334 p.

>Discusses the themes, characterizations, and structure of plays by Sophocles.

Gassner, John. "Sophocles the Serene." In his *Masters of the Drama,* pp. 40-55. Rev. ed. New York: Dover Publications, 1954.

>An overview of the life and works of Sophocles.

Hadas, Moses. "Sophocles." In his *A History of Greek Literature,* pp. 84-91. New York: Columbia University Press, 1950.

>A concise discussion of Sophocles' dramatic art.

Jones, John. "Sophocles." In his *On Aristotle and Greek Tragedy,* pp. 141-238. New York: Oxford University Press, 1962.

>Delineates Sophocles' use of myth in *Electra, Ajax, Antigone, Oedipus Rex,* and *Oedipus at Colonus.*

Letters, F. H. J. *The Life and Work of Sophocles.* London: Sheed and Ward, 1953, 310 p.

>Reviews the life, times, and style of Sophocles, with a chapter on each of the plays.

Seale, David. *Vision and Stagecraft in Sophocles.* Chicago: University of Chicago Press, 1982, 269 p.

>Traces various visual conventions and motifs used in Sophocles' dramas.

Jean Toomer

1894-1967

(Born Nathan Eugene Toomer) American poet, short story writer, and essayist.

INTRODUCTION

Toomer's greatest contribution to literature is *Cane* (1923), an innovative volume of avant-garde poetry, short stories, drama, and prose vignettes that explores African-American culture and spirituality in the rural South and the urban North. Toomer conceived *Cane* as an elegiac work commemorating a folk culture rooted in nature and myth that he believed would soon be superseded in a waxing industrial age. The child of a racially mixed ancestry, Toomer rejected racial chauvinism and the label "black author"; instead, he considered himself the representative of a new "American" race made up of elements of all humanity, and many of his writings reflect this universalist philosophy. *Cane* has been hailed since its release as one of the greatest works of the Harlem Renaissance period, and critics have praised Toomer for his rich use of language and symbolism. Although his later work, which reflects his increasing interest in mysticism and metaphysics, never attained the critical stature of *Cane*, Toomer is now regarded as a seminal figure of both African-American and Modernist literature.

Biographical Information

Born in 1894 in Washington, D.C., Toomer described his ancestry as "Scotch, Welsh, German, English, French, Dutch, Spanish, with some dark blood"; his grandfather was black, his mother of mixed race, and his father a white Georgia farmer. Toomer spent much of his childhood in an affluent white section of Washington, relatively free from racial prejudice, in the home of his maternal grandfather, P. B. S. Pinchback, a prominent Louisiana politician of the Reconstruction era. After the death of Toomer's mother in 1909, the Pinchbacks experienced extreme financial losses, requiring the family to move to a modest African-American neighborhood. As a young man, Toomer lived a transient existence, studying various subjects at several universities and working a number of jobs. He enjoyed a literary apprenticeship for several months in 1919 and 1920 in Greenwich Village, where he met such prominent New York intellectuals as Edwin Arlington Robinson and Waldo Frank. In the fall of 1921, Toomer accepted a temporary teaching position in Sparta, Georgia, a rural Southern town that gave him the opportunity to discover his African-American roots. In 1922 he toured the South with Frank; the trip inspired much of *Cane*. In 1923, Toomer became a follower of George Gurdjieff, an Armenian mystic whose philosophy aspired toward self-awareness of one's status as part of a larger, universal being. Toomer embraced this philosophy, spending the next summer at the Gurdjieff Institute in Fontainebleau, France, and devoting the next several years to proselytizing Gurdjieff's teachings in the United States. When he began writing again in the late 1920s, his work was dominated by Gurdjieffian metaphysics, which alienated publishers. Toomer spent the rest of his career in obscurity, although he continued to write prolifically. He renounced Gurdjieff when he converted to Quakerism in 1940 and wrote on Christian themes until his death in 1967.

Major Works

Divided into three sections, *Cane* contrasts the passionate, nature-bound life of rural black Southerners with the numbness and ineffectuality of urban black Northerners, demonstrating Toomer's belief that materialism and restrictive social values leave individuals spiritually crippled. Using a structure often compared to musical composition, *Cane* features recurring themes and motifs blended with poetic elements borrowed from gospel and blues music. The first section of *Cane* weaves six stories with twelve poems, using imagery drawn from nature to create lyrical, impressionistic, and often mystical portraits of six Southern women. Images of sunset, dusk, ripening fruit, and canefields in the stories "Karintha," "Becky," "Carma," and "Fern" suggest the richness of a passing way of life, while ghosts, full moons, and fire in "Esther" and "Blood-Burning Moon" announce its dissolution. The second section of *Cane* comprises seven prose sketches and five poems, shifting the setting to the urban North of Chicago and Washington, D.C. "Seventh Street," the opening piece, establishes the frenetic tone and urban landscape that characterize this section. Ragged, jazzy rhythms punctuate this section, while houses, alleys, asphalt streets, machines, theaters, and nightclubs function as symbols of confinement that limit growth and thwart self-understanding. Examinations of sexual and emotional relationships between men and women in such stories as "Avey," "Theater," "Box Seat," and "Bona and Paul" challenge the conventions of modern industrialized society. Variously described by critics as a play, novella, and short story, "Kabnis," the third section, is a thinly veiled autobiographical portrait of an educated but spiritually confused Northern black who travels to the South to teach school in a small rural town. This piece focuses on various men, each of whom embodies some part of the black experience: Kabnis, an idealist inflated by white values and disillusioned with his race; Lewis, an intelligent man who accepts his history; Hanby, a school principal who plays the aristocrat among his people; and Father John, a wise old African-American who experienced slavery and knows his heritage. "Kabnis," then, reflects the dilemma of black Americans caught between conflicting, alienating lifestyles and values. Only a few of Toomer's post-*Cane* works garnered critical attention, notably "The Blue Meridian," a long poem that heralds the coming of a united human race, spiritually enlightened and free of artificial barriers. Although most of these works went unpublished, some are collected in *The Wayward and the Seeking* (1978).

Critical Reception

Cane drew early critical interest because of its engaging approach to its subject and experimental form. Critics recognized that *Cane* is neither a diatribe on racial relations nor a strident reformist doctrine, but is instead a lyrical, passionate, and artistic creation. Literary scholars have also debated to which genre *Cane* belongs. However, many critics dismiss Toomer's work after *Cane* as sermonizing and lacking in the lyrical quality of his younger work; they suggest that Toomer allowed his intellectual agenda to overwhelm his aesthetics. Many were also disappointed with his refusal to expand upon the African-American themes of *Cane*. Darwin T. Turner concluded that "*Cane* still sings to readers, not the swan song of an era that was dying, but the morning hymn of a Renaissance that was beginning."

(For further information, see *Black Literature Criticism; Black Writers*, Vol. 1; *Concise Dictionary of American Literary Biography:* 1917-1929; *Contemporary Authors,* Vols. 85-88; *Contemporary Literary Criticism,* Vols. 1, 4, 13, 22; *Dictionary of Literary Biography,* Vols. 45, 51; *DISCovering Authors Modules: Multicultural Authors Module; Major Twentieth-Century Writers; Poetry Criticism,* Vol. 7; *Short Story Criticism,* Vol. 1.)

CRITICAL COMMENTARY

WALDO FRANK

SOURCE: Waldo Frank, in a foreword to *Cane* by Jean Toomer, 1923. Reprint by University Place Press, 1967, pp. vii-xi.

[*An American novelist, critic, and editor, Frank was a founder of* Seven Arts, *a distinguished magazine of leftist politics and avant-garde literature. After meeting Toomer in 1920, he became the young author's mentor and was instrumental in launching his career. In the following excerpt, taken from his foreword to the first edition of* Cane, *Frank acclaims Toomer's evocation of the South and praises him for choosing an aesthetic, rather than racially provincial, approach to the work.*]

Reading [*Cane*], I had the vision of a land, heretofore sunk in the mists of muteness, suddenly rising up into the eminence of song. Innumerable books have been written about the South; some good books have been written in the South. This book *is* the South. I do not mean that *Cane* covers the South or is the South's full voice. Merely this: a poet has arisen among our American youth who has known how to turn the essences and materials of his Southland into the essences and materials of literature. A poet has arisen in that land who writes, not as a Southerner, not as a rebel against Southerners, not as a Negro, not as apologist or priest or critic: who writes as a *poet*. The fashioning of beauty is ever foremost in his inspiration: not forcedly but simply, and because these ultimate aspects of his world are to him more real than all its specific problems. He has made songs and lovely stories of his land . . . not of its yesterday, but of its immediate life. And that has been enough.

How rare this is will be clear to those who have followed with concern the struggle of the South toward literary expression, and the particular trial of that portion of its folk whose skin is dark. The gifted Negro has been too often thwarted from becoming a poet because his world was forever forcing him to recollect that he was a Negro. The artist must lose such lesser identities in the great well of life. . . . The French novelist is not forever noting: "This is French." It is so atmospheric for him to be French, that he can devote himself to saying: "This is human." This is an imperative condition for the creating of deep art. The whole will and mind of the creator must go below the surfaces of race. And this has been an almost impossible condition for the American Negro to achieve, forced every moment of his life into a specific and superficial plane of consciousness.

The first negative significance of *Cane* is that this so natural and restrictive state of mind is completely lacking. For Toomer, the Southland is not a problem to be solved; it is a field of loveliness to be sung: the Georgia Negro is not a downtrodden soul to be uplifted; he is material for gorgeous painting: the segregated self-conscious brown belt of Washington is not a topic to be discussed and exposed; it is a subject of beauty and of drama, worthy of creation in literary form.

It seems to me, therefore, that this is a first book in more ways than one. It is a harbinger of the South's literary maturity: of its emergence from the obsession put upon its minds by the unending racial crisis — an obsession from which writers have made their indirect escape through sentimentalism, exoticism, polemic, "problem" fiction, and moral melodrama. It marks the dawn of direct and unafraid creation. And, as the initial work of a man of twenty-seven, it is the harbinger of a literary force of whose incalculable future I believe no reader of this book will be in doubt.

How typical is *Cane* of the South's still virgin soil and of its pressing seeds! and the book's chaos of verse, tale, drama, its rhythmic rolling shift from lyrism to narrative, from mystery to intimate pathos! But read the book through and you will see a complex and significant form take substance from its chaos. Part One is the primitive and evanescent black world of Georgia. Part Two is the threshing and suffering brown world of Washington, lifted by opportunity and contact into the anguish of self-conscious struggle. Part Three is Georgia again . . . the invasion into this black womb of the ferment seed: the neurotic, educated, spiritually stirring Negro. As a broad form this is superb, and the very looseness and unexpected waves of the book's parts make *Cane* still more *South*, still more of an aesthetic equivalent of the land.

What a land it is! What an Aeschylean beauty to its fateful problem! Those of you who love our South will find here some of your love. Those of you who know it not will perhaps begin to understand what a warm splendor is at last at dawn.

> A feast of moon and men and barking hounds,

> **Principal Works**
>
> *Cane* (poetry and short stories) 1923
> *Essentials* (aphorisms and apothegms) 1931
> *The Flavor of Man* (lecture) 1949
> *The Wayward and the Seeking: A Miscellany of Writings* (poetry and short stories) 1978
> *The Collected Poems of Jean Toomer* (poetry) 1988
> *Jean Toomer: Selected Essays And Literary Criticism* (essays and criticism) 1996

> An orgy for some genius of the South
> With bloodshot eyes and cane-lipped scented mouth
> Surprised in making folk-songs. . . .

So, in his still sometimes clumsy stride (for Toomer is finally a poet in prose) the author gives you an inkling of his revelation. An individual force, wise enough to drink humbly at this great spring of his land . . . such is the first impression of Jean Toomer. But beyond this wisdom and this power (which shows itself perhaps most splendidly in his complete freedom from the sense of persecution), there rises a figure more significant: the artist, hard, self-immolating, the artist who is not interested in races, whose domain is Life. The book's final Part is no longer "promise"; it is achievement. It is no mere dawn: it is a bit of the full morning. These materials . . . the ancient black man, mute, inaccessible, and yet so mystically close to the new tumultuous members of his race, the simple slave Past, the shredding Negro Present, the iridescent passionate dream of the To-morrow . . . are made and measured by a craftsman into an unforgettable music. The notes of his counterpoint are particular, themes are of intimate connection with us Americans. But the result is that abstract and absolute thing called Art.

ARNA BONTEMPS

SOURCE: Arna Bontemps, "Introduction," in *Cane*, by Jean Toomer, Harper, 1969.

[*The foremost scholar and historian of the Harlem Renaissance, Bontemps is best known for* Black Thunder, *a fictionalized account of a slave uprising that occurred in 1800 in Virginia. In the following excerpt, he assesses the influence of* Cane *and notes some of its literary features.*]

[The publication of *Cane* had an important effect on] practically an entire generation of young Negro writers then just beginning to emerge; their reaction to Toomer's *Cane* marked an awakening that soon thereafter began to be called a Negro Renaissance.

Cane's influence was by no means limited to the joyous band that included Langston Hughes, Countee Cullen, Eric Walrond, Zora Neale Hurston, Wallace Thurman, Rudolph Fisher and their contemporaries of the 'Twenties. Subsequent writing by Negroes in the United States, as well as in the West Indies and Africa, has continued to reflect its mood and often its method and, one feels, it has also influenced the writing about Negroes by others. Certainly no earlier volume of poetry or fiction or both had come close to expressing the ethos of the Negro in the Southern setting as *Cane* did. Even in today's ghettos astute readers are finding that its insights have anticipated and often exceeded their own.

There are many odd and provocative things about *Cane,* and not the least is its form. Reviewers who read it in 1923 were generally stumped. Poetry and prose were whipped together in a kind of frappé. Realism was mixed with what they called mysticism, and the result seemed to many of them confusing. . . .

The book by which we remember this writer is as hard to classify as its author. At first glance it appears to consist of assorted sketches, stories, and a novelette, all interspersed with poems. Some of the prose is poetic, and often Toomer slips from one form into the other almost imperceptibly. The novelette is constructed like a play.

His characters, always evoked with effortless strength, are as recognizable as they are unexpected in the fiction of that period. . . .

It does not take long to discover that *Cane* is not without design, however. A world of black peasantry in Georgia appears in the first section. The scene shifts, with almost prophetic insight, to the black ghetto of Washington, D.C. in the second. Rural Georgia comes up again in the third. Changes in the concerns of Toomer's folk are noted as the setting changes.

A young poet-observer moves through the book. . . . A native richness is here . . . and the poet embraced it with the passion of love.

ROBERT BONE

SOURCE: Robert Bone, "Jean Toomer," in *Down Home:*

A History of Afro-American Short Fiction from Its Beginnings to the End of the Harlem Renaissance, Columbia University Press, 1975, pp. 204-38.

[*In the following excerpt, Bone provides information about Toomer related to his literary career and examines three representative stories from* Cane.]

When Toomer writes of "a song-lit race of slaves," whose plaintive soul is "leaving, soon gone," he employs the language and the form of pastoral elegy. For *Cane* is in essence a pastoral interlude, like Thoreau's trip to the woods, through which the author seeks to achieve a consolidation of the self, in order to move forward to the fundamental task of prophecy.

Cane was Jean Toomer's hail-and-farewell to his blackness. Springing from a sojourn of several months in Sparta, Georgia, the impulse that gave birth to *Cane* was soon exhausted. Toomer was never to touch on these materials again. "The folk-spirit," as he explains in the *Outline of an Autobiography*, "was walking in to die on the modern desert. That spirit was so beautiful. Its death was so tragic. Just this seemed to sum up life for me. And this was the feeling I put into *Cane*, *Cane* was a swan song. It was a song of an end. And why no one has seen and felt that, why people have expected me to write a second and a third and a fourth book like *Cane* is one of the queer misunderstandings of my life." . . .

Toomer's intellectual gropings began in 1916, during his first sojourn in Chicago. Under the influence of Clarence Darrow and Carl Sandburg, he became an agnostic and a socialist. On moving to New York in 1917, he read intensively in Shaw and Ibsen, Santayana and Goethe. Brief employment in a Jersey shipyard cured him of his socialism, while a reading of Goethe's *Wilhelm Meister* made him an esthete. His esthetic tendencies were reinforced by a meeting with Waldo Frank in 1919. Back in Washington in the summer of 1920, he read "all of Waldo Frank, most of Dostoievsky, much of Tolstoi, Flaubert, Baudelaire, Sinclair Lewis, Dreiser, most all of the American poets, Coleridge, Blake, Pater—in fine, a good portion of the modern writers of all western countries."

From 1920 to 1923 Toomer lived in Washington, caring for his aging grandparents and serving his literary apprenticeship. Setting the most exacting standards, he accumulated a trunkful of manuscripts before he was satisfied with their quality: "I wrote and wrote and put each thing aside, regarding it as simply one of the exercises of my apprenticeship." For three months in the fall of 1921 he served as Acting Principal of a Negro school in Sparta, Georgia. This pilgrimage to his sources inspired Toomer's first book. *Cane* was written in approximately thirteen months, from November 1921 to December 1922. . . .

Of the twenty-nine units of which *Cane* is composed, fifteen are plainly poems, written for the most part in free verse. **"Kabnis"** is a free-form play, complete with stage directions. Six of the less substantial pieces are sketches, or vignettes, or prose poems, too slender to afford much narrative development. The seven that remain may reasonably be regarded as short stories. Of these seven stories, we have chosen to discuss three: **"Fern," "Theater,"** and **"Bona and Paul."** They will serve to illustrate the tendency of Toomer's art to move beyond mere surfaces to a realm of transcendent reality.

"Fern," which first appeared in the *Little Review* of Autumn 1922, has been as widely anthologized as it has been misconstrued. Restricting their vision to the psychological plane, critics have variously regarded Fern as a victim of sexual repression, a promiscuous, castrating female, and an emblem of the mystery of Negro womanhood. The bafflement of the young narrator, in short, has been shared by most commentators, who have failed to perceive that the story functions primarily on a philosophical or religious plane. The heroine's sexual passivity is evoked merely to accentuate her otherworldly qualities. The story's theme, which may be traced to Vachel Lindsay's poem, "The Congo," is the spirituality of the Negro race.

Fern spiritualizes everything and everyone with whom she comes in contact. The story opens with the sentence: "Face flowed into her eyes." The eyes, in Toomer, are windows to the soul, and in Fern's countenance they dominate, and even obliterate, the surrounding flesh. They seem to focus on some vague spot above the horizon, seeking always to transcend, or rise above, the Georgia landscape. The movement of the imagery is upward, and it defines Fern's relation to the world. Her domain is the unseen and intangible: the noumenal world that exists beyond the senses. The men that she encounters, including the narrator, are uplifted and ennobled by the contact, and struggle subsequently to transcend their selfishness.

Fern's spiritual force is redoubled by virtue of her mixed ancestry. The daughter of a Jewish father and a Negro mother, she is the inheritor of two sets of sorrow songs. At his first sight of her, the narrator recalls, "I felt as if I heard a Jewish cantor sing. As if his singing rose above the unheard chorus of a folk-song." Fernie May Rosen possesses the Jewish genius for suffering. She takes upon herself the agony of others, including the sexual torment of her lovers. She is the eternal scapegoat who must suffer in order that others (specifically the narrator) may be born. That is why, in the minds of the townspeople, she remains a virgin, and why she is associated, in Toomer's iconography, with the Virgin Mary.

Fern embodies not only the Negro of the folksongs, but also of the revival meeting and the emotional church. That is the point of the climactic episode in which the narrator—half curious concerning Fern, and half in love with her—escorts her through a canebrake. Vaguely conscious of her spiritual power, but acting from force of habit, he takes her in his arms. She responds by running off, sinking to her knees, swaying back and forth, and uttering convulsive sounds, "mingled with calls to Christ Jesus." She thus performs a priestly, if not a sexual office. Her body, although he doesn't recognize the gift, has been offered as the instrument of his salvation.

Fern is a symbol, in short, of the Negro folk-spirit. As such, she is the repository of a doomed spirituality. The quality of soul that she embodies, and whose cultural expression is folksong and revivalist religion, is about to disappear. It will not survive the Great Migration: "Besides, picture if you can, this cream-colored solitary girl sitting at a tenement window and looking down on the indifferent throngs of Harlem." Fern could not exist apart from her pastoral milieu, and yet this rural folk-culture is fading into memory. The elegiac note is unmistakable. It is in the Georgia dusk that Fern weaves her most potent spell. Images of evening suffuse the story, producing that peculiar blend of sadness and tranquillity which is the hallmark of pastoral elegy.

"Theater" was inspired by a two-week stint that Toomer served as assistant manager of the Howard Theater in Washington, D.C. It was long enough to absorb the atmosphere of a Negro vaudeville house and to fashion out of this milieu a complex symbol. In the opening paragraph, the walls of the theater are described as a kind of semipermeable membrane through which a complicated process of osmosis takes place. The "nigger life" of alleys, poolrooms, restaurants, and cabarets nourishes the shows that are presented within these walls, and conversely, the shows exert a shaping influence on the life-style that gave them birth. The theater thus emerges as an emblem of the two-way, reciprocal relationship of life and art.

The walls of the theater press in upon the human world until they become symbolic of the prison of the flesh, from which imagination alone can offer an escape. In the translucent glow of the lighted theater, human flesh seems to dissolve: "Stage lights, soft, as if they shine through clear pink fingers." The theater is a place of shadowy forms, of artificial contrivances, of elaborate mirrorings of life. Throughout the story, Toomer never lets us forget the paraphernalia of illusion: the scenery and costumes and lighting effects that function to transform reality. His theme is precisely the relationship between the image and the life it represents, or, in Ralph Ellison's illuminating phrase, between the shadow and the act.

Toomer's theater is a place where magical transformations occur. The throbbing life of Washington's black belt is translated by the black musicians into jazz forms. The raw sexuality of brown and beige chorus girls is converted before our very eyes into dance forms. Dorris, the most talented among them, is transfigured into a woman of surpassing loveliness by the writer-hero's dream. The instrument of all these metamorphoses is the human imagination, symbolized by the shaft of light that streaks down from a window to illuminate the afternoon rehearsal.

On this symbolic stage the plot unfolds. John, the manager's brother, and a writer, watches Dorris dance. He entertains erotic fantasies, but finally dismisses them, not because of the obvious barrier of background and education, but rather on complicated philosophic grounds. While he is dedicated, in a priestly vein, to contemplation of the noumenal, she represents precisely the attractions of the phenomenal world. Putting it another way, John is torn between the higher and lower functions of his being. Dorris, on her part, does her best to win him through the only art at her command: the dance. Failing to ignite his passion, she mistakenly concludes that he has rejected her on the grounds of social class.

Momentarily the philosophic gulf between them is bridged in the imagery of John's dream. This climactic episode, where daydream shades off into fiction, is emblematic of the transforming power of imagination. In it the raw materials of John's experience are transfigured by the writer's art. Dorris becomes a woman of surpassing beauty; their imagined union, disembodied and ideal: "But his feet feel as though they step on autumn leaves whose rustle has been pressed out of them by the passing of a million satin slippers." In this image of nature *dematerialized* by art, Toomer reveals the heart of his esthetic. John's dream is a vision of the union of flesh and spirit, of the phenomenal and noumenal worlds.

Art-as-transfiguration is Toomer's theme. He is concerned in **"Theater"** with the death of experience and its rebirth as art. Thus John's renunciation of a love affair with Dorris, and his distillation of their encounter into poetry. John is to Dorris as an artist to his material: she represents *untransformed* experience. But the artist, by definition, is a man who cannot tolerate the untransformed world. Through his imagination, he must remove the rustle from the autumn leaves. Paradoxically, the artist must renounce the phenomenal world, even as he celebrates it. The result is a tragic alienation, whose subjective mood is melancholy.

"Bona and Paul" derives from Toomer's undergraduate experience at the American College of Physical Training in Chicago. . . .

The kernel of the story is contained in the opening tableau. On the floor of a gymnasium, students are engaged in precision drilling. Paul, out of step with the rest, is dressed in nonregulation blue trousers. It is precisely this nonconformity that Bona finds appealing. The precision drilling is symbolic of a regimented society that not only marches, but thinks in rigid line formation. Paul's white companions, as the story unfolds, are alternately fascinated and repelled by his ambiguous exoticism. Tormented by uncertainty, and desirous of reassuring absolutes, they press him to declare his race. They remain, in short, *unawakened* to the possibilities of life, to the individual reality that lies beyond the social category.

The theme of the story is epistemological. Verbs of cognition predominate, as Paul and Bona grope across the color line for a deeper knowledge of each other. Toomer's central metaphor, which compares the lovers to opaque windows, is drawn from St. Paul's first epistle to the Corinthians: "For now we see through a glass darkly; but then face to face: now I know in part; but then shall I know even as I am known." The color line, symbolized by the South-Side L track that divides the city, constitutes an artificial barrier to human understanding. Based on *a priori* rather than *a posteriori* knowledge, it serves to blind rather than illuminate.

The story moves to a climax in the episode of the Crimson Gardens. As he enters the nightclub with Bona, Paul feels inclined to cheer, for the Crimson Gardens represents a yea-saying, an affirmation of life. With its white patrons and Negro music, the club is a symbol of cultural amalgamation. It is also the Garden of Eden, where Paul loses Bona by eating of the Tree of Knowledge. As the young couple whirl around the floor, "The dance takes blood from their minds and packs it, tingling, in the torsos of their swaying bodies." Intoxicated with passion, they head for the exit, but their progress is interrupted by a leering Negro doorman. Paul steps back to assure the man that something beautiful is about to happen, but when he returns for his companion, Bona has disappeared.

The resolution of the story is conveyed entirely through the imagery. The style becomes intensely lyrical, as it attempts to shape the moment of epiphany: "I came back to tell you, brother, that white faces are petals of roses. That dark faces are petals of dusk. That I am going out and gather petals. That I am going out and know her whom I brought here with me to these Gardens which are purple like a bed of roses would be at dusk." Reality, in other words, is not categorical, but contingent. A flower that is red in daylight is purple in the dusk. And dusk is the point in time when day and night mingle and become one.

What Paul has mastered, in short, is a new epistemology, a new way of knowing. He has discovered the imagination as a mode of knowledge. He has learned that while thought divides (categorizes), imagination synthesizes. Through metaphor, the language of poetry, the imagination transcends categories and frees the human mind for a genuine encounter with reality. At the same time, Toomer's hero pays an awesome price for his new knowledge. Intent on philosophic clarity, he loses the girl. It is Toomer's characteristic gesture of renunciation: the eternal paradox of earthly values lost, even as transcendent aims are realized.

"Bona and Paul" is a model of artistic economy and symbolic compression. In its density of texture and profundity of theme, it is one of Toomer's richest stories. On the face of it, the story seems to undermine the central thrust of *Cane*. Once we take account of its strategic position at the end of Part II, however, this difficulty is resolved. The urbanization of the Negro, Toomer feels, will lead inexorably to his assimilation. In the process, America will be transformed. Like Toomer's hero, we will one day discover within ourselves the courage to transcend our racial categories. Then we will see not through a glass darkly, but face to face at last.

BERNARD W. BELL

SOURCE: Bernard W. Bell, "Jean Toomer's 'Blue Meridian': The Poet as Prophet of a New Order of Man," in *Black American Literature Forum*, Vol. 14, No. 2, Summer, 1980, pp. 77-80.

[*In the essay below, Bell examines Toomer's "The Blue Meridian," which he describes as the poetic zenith of Toomer's quest for identity and a new world order.*]

It may come as a surprise to many of his new admirers, but Jean Toomer viewed himself as a cultural aristocrat, not a cultural nationalist. Recalling how the discovery of [Johann Wolfgang von] Goethe's *Wilhelm*

Meister helped him to pull together the scattered pieces of his life, he wrote in 1918:

> I was lifted into and shown my real world. It was the world of the aristocrat—but not the social aristocrat; the aristocrat of culture, of spirit and character, of ideas, of true nobility. And for the first time in years and years I breathed the air of my land.... I resolved to devote myself to the making of myself such a person as I caught glimpses of in the pages of *Wilhelm Meister*. For my specialized work, I would write.

More like the avant-garde of the Lost Generation than the vanguard of the Harlem Renaissance, Toomer was deeply involved in creating a synthesis of new forms and themes. In the wake of World War I he completely devoted himself to the task of learning the craft of writing. During this period he confessed to being strongly influenced by two approaches to literature. First, he was attracted to those American writers and works that used regional materials in a poetic manner, especially Walt Whitman, Robert Frost, and Sherwood Anderson. Secondly, he was impressed by the Imagists. "Their insistence on fresh vision and on the perfect clean economical line," he wrote, "was just what I had been looking for. I began feeling that I had in my hands the tools for my creation." The artistic fusion in *Cane* (1923) of symbols of the Black American's African and Southern experience and the Afro-American tradition of music bears witness to this influence and establishes the book as a landmark in modern American literature.

Following the publication of *Cane*, Toomer, convinced by personal experience and extensive reading that "the parts of man—his mind, emotions, and body—were radically out of harmony with each other," discovered the method for unifying these three centers of being in the teachings of George Ivanovitch Gurdjieff, the "rascal sage." A synthesis of Western science and Eastern mysticism, Gurdjieff's system was a rigorous discipline that taught self-development and cosmic consciousness through self-awareness, sacred exercises, temple dances, and various psychic feats. In 1934 Toomer began making annual retreats to the Institute for the Harmonious Development of Man, Gurdjieff's headquarters in Fontainbleau-Avon, France. He returned as a Gurdjieffian prophet to spread the gospel in Harlem—where his sessions included such talented artists as Aaron Douglass, Wallace Thurman, Harold Jackman, Nella Larsen, and Dorothy Peterson—and in Chicago. He also continued writing voluminously, but most of these writings, which repudiate racial classifications and celebrate a Gurdjieffian vision of life, were rejected by publishers.

The most significant exception is **"Blue Meridian,"** a long Whitmanesque poem. **"Blue Meridian"** is the poetic zenith of Toomer's quest for identity. It represents the resolution of a long process of agonizing emotional and intellectual turmoil over the problems of race and aesthetics as viewed through the prism of his own personal crisis. Toomer began grappling with the question of race in high school and began the first draft of the poem, then entitled "The First American," in the early 1920s. Completed in 1930, a section of the poem appeared as **"Brown River, Smile"** the following year in *The Adelphi*. But the entire poem was not published until 1936, when it appeared in Kreymborg, Mumford, and Rosenfeld's *The New Caravan*.

Toomer the poet/prophet sings exultantly of a new world order in **"Blue Meridian."** Neither Black nor white, Eastern nor Western, the new order of man is "The blue man, the purple man"; the new people are the "race called the Americans," and the new society is America, "spiritualized by each new American." Through evolution the regenerated American is also the harmoniously developed, universal man, free of definitions and classifications that restrict or confine the vitality of his being. For Toomer, as for Whitman, America was, in Whitman's exuberant words, "the greatest poem," "a teeming nation of nations," and "the race of races."

"Art," writes Toomer (in *Essentials*), "is a means of communicating high-rate vibrations," and the artist is he "who can combine opposing forms and forces in significant unity." Toomer splendidly fulfills both the letter and spirit of these definitions in **"Blue Meridian."** As with *Cane*, the chief symbol of **"Blue Meridian"** is implicit in its title. In the context of the poem, the meridian, which generally denotes the highest point of prosperity, splendor, and power, symbolizes the Spirit of mankind. On the geographical and astronomical planes it also represents the imaginary circles which connect both geophysical poles and the circle passing through the celestial poles. Other important symbols relating to the spiritual power of the new American include the Mississippi River, a pod, a grain of wheat, a waterwheel, crocks (i.e., earthenware receptacles), and the cross. The title of the poem thus generates a series of symbols which reinforce the themes of potential wholeness, evolution, and cosmic consciousness. So intricate is the symbolic pattern that the color progression of the meridian from black to white to blue corresponds to the movement of the poem through different stages of man's historical and organic development to a higher form.

Retracing the stages of man's development and the process by which the new American was born, Toomer invokes the primeval forces of life waiting to energize select men to a higher form of being. In the first section of the poem primal darkness is upon the face of the deep:

> Black Meridian, black light,
> Dynamic atom-aggregate,
> Lay sleeping in an inland lake.

In order to elevate himself man must let the "Big Light" in to awaken his dormant potential. Neither Christian nor mystical in the traditional sense, the genesis is an eclectic yet harmonious blend of Darwinian evolution and Gurdjieffian mysticism. The poet invokes the "Radiant Incorporal, / The I of earth of mankind" to crash through confining barriers, across the continent and spiral on into the cosmos:

> Beyond plants are animals,
> Beyond animals is man,
> Beyond man is the universe.

At this stage the Mississippi River, sister of the Ganges and main artery of the Western world, has the potential for becoming a sacred river, a potential which is realized in the White Meridian section of the poem. Similarly, each form that appears in the first section, the Black Meridian stage, contains the seed for its future growth. For, since Adam, man has been in a state of becoming, ready to unite parts and reconcile opposites into a moving whole of total body and soul:

> Men of the East, men of the West
> Men in life, men in death,
> Americans and all countrymen—
> Growth is by admixture from less to more,
> Preserving the great granary intact,
> Through cycles of death and life,
> Each stage a pod,
> Perpetuating and perfecting
> An essence identical in all,
> Obeying the same laws, unto the same goal,
> The far distant objective,
> By ways both down and up,
> Down years ago, now struggling up.

The poet is firm in the conviction that the capacity for growth is common to all men and has always been present in America. Past generations, however, have not fully realized their human potential and, by extension, the promise of the nation and the universe.

Toomer's purpose, then, is not the glorification of the common man but the celebration of "A million men, or twelve men," the result of a long process of natural selection and self-realization. Elitist in nature, Toomer's view of modern man in **"Blue Meridian"** is essentially Gurdjieffian. Comparing man to an acorn, Gurdjieff says (in Fritz Peters's *Boyhood with Gurdjieff;* 1964):

> Nature make many acorns, but possibility to become tree exist for only few acorns. Same with man—many men born, but only few grow. People think this waste, think Nature waste. Not so. Rest become fertilizer, go back into earth and create possibility for more acorns, more men, once in while more tree more real man. Nature always give— but only give possibility. To become real oak, or real man, must make effort.

For both Gurdjieff and Toomer, the real man, the new man, must manifest Understanding, Conscience, and Ability. Defective men—those who lack or fail to acquire these three attributes—become the fertilizer for perpetuating the promise of eternally awake souls.

Included among the defectives in **"Blue Meridian"** are old gods and old races. The old gods, "led by an inverted Christ, / A shaved Moses, a blanched Lemur, / And a moulting Thunderbird," have failed to transform the soul of man. All that remains of their existence is "Their dust and seed falling down / To fertilize the seven regions of America." The waves of old peoples have similarly failed. The European races, "displaced by machines" and "Baptized by finance," could not rise above materialism; the African races— moaning "O Lord, Lord, / This bale will break me— / But we must keep the watermelon"—were weighted down by racism and a negative self-image; and the red race, whose organic relationship with Nature was ruptured when its members were "serpentined" into reservations and towns, was annihilated by an alien culture. These were the early inhabitants of the New World, great races of nondescript persons waiting to be fused into the first Americans:

> Drawing, in waves of inhabitation,
> All the peoples of the earth,
> Later to weed out, organize, assimilate,
> Gathered by the snatch of accident,
> Selected with the speed of fate,
> The alien and the belonging,
> All belonging now,
> Not yet made one and aged.

The creation of the new man is a long evolutionary process engineered by Nature. This is the myth of America as told by a twentieth-century Gurdjieffian poet/priest.

In the past America did not fulfill its promise because each American did not lift himself "To matter uniquely man." Out of a past blind to the transcendent value of

Understanding, Conscience, and Ability—words the poet would give his life "to see inscribed / Upon the arch of our consciousness"—comes the hell of the Depression. The vital material and spiritual forces of mankind have gone wrong:

> An airplane, with broken wing,
> In a tail spin,
> Descends with terrifying speed—
> "Don't put me on the spot!"—
> From beings to no-things,
> From human beings to grotesques,
> From men and women to manikins,
> From forms and chaoses—
> *Crash!*

The eagle, majestic symbol of American extremes of production and destruction, has degenerated into a one-wing plane of death. And the heroic daring of a [Charles] Lindberg—"Flight symbol of the alone to the Alone"—is displaced in newspaper headlines by the unheroic exploits of Al Capone. Because man is responsible for his own downfall and spiritual blight, he must follow the poet's example and assume the responsibility for his own regeneration.

In the second section of the poem Toomer lustily calls forth the new American and shows him the highway to love and "unstreaked dignity." This stage opens with a heavenly white light, as the symbol of hope and emerging consciousness:

> White Meridian, white light,
> Dynamic atom-aggregate,
> Lay waking on an inland lake.

The poet exhorts modern man to break from a moneyed and machined death, urging him to move on to a new level of consciousness:

> Walk from it,
> Wake from it,
> From the terrible mistake
> That we who have power are less than we should
>   be.
> Join that staff whose left hand is
> Demolishing defectives,
> Whose right is setting up a mill
> And a wheel therein, its rim of power
> Its spokes of knowledge, its hub of conscience—
> And in that same heart we will hold all life.

Breaking free from his islandized condition and fixing his sight on universal man, Toomer, like Whitman, becomes the Creator calling into being a new world order:

> Uncase the races,
> Open this pod,
> Free man from this shrinkage,
> Not from the reality itself,
> But from the unbecoming and enslaving behavior
> Associated with our prejudices and preferences.
> Eliminate these.
> I am, we are, simply of the human race.
>
> Uncase the nations,
> Open this pod,
> Keep the real but destroy the false;
> We are of the human nation.
>
> Uncase the regions—
> Occidental, Oriental, North, South—
> We are of Earth.
>
> Free the sexes,
> I am neither male nor female nor in-between;
> I am of sex, with male differentiations.
>
> Open the classes;
> I am, we are, simply of the human class.
>
> Expand the fields—
> Those definitions which fix fractions and lose wholes—
> I am of the field of being,
> We are beings.
>
> Uncase the religions;
> I am religious.
>
> Uncase, unpod whatever impedes, until,
> Having realized pure consciousness of being,
> Sensing, feeling and understanding
> That we are beings
> Co-existing with others in an inhabited universe,
> We will be free to use rightly with reason
> Our own and other human functions.

Unlike Whitman's bombast and the unqualified democratic strain of his America, Toomer's social imperatives and expansive mood affirm a Gurdjieffian world of beings who have realized the value of intelligence, conscience, and ability.

But were it not for his imaginative use of concrete symbols, we would surely be lost in a sea of abstractions. In this section of the poem a waterwheel becomes the agent for invigorating the soul. But first the poet acknowledges the regenerative influence of a special woman in his life, probably Margaret Naumberg:

> Much that I am I owe to her
> For she was going where I was going,
> Except that on the way we parted.
> She, individualized and beautiful,
> Remarkable beyond most
> Followed, at one turn, her picture of herself—

The poet does not follow for fear he might lose himself and betray "the task of man." Instead he responds to the music of "sacred and profane extremes" and the song of himself:

> And some rare times
> I hear myself, the unrecorded,
> Sing the flow of I,
> The notes and language not of this experience,
> Sing I am,
> As the flow of I pauses,
> Then passes through my water-wheel—
> And these radiant realities, the living others,
> The people identical in being.

After invoking the waterwheel, "its rim of power, / Its spokes of knowledge, its hub of conscience," to transform their lives, the poet and his nameless female companion experience the White Meridian:

> Sun upon clean water is the radiance of creation—
> And once, far out in the vast spread,
> Our eyes beheld a sacrament;
> Her face was marvelously bright,
> My brain was fiery with internal stars,
> I felt certain I had brought
> The gods to earth and men to heaven;
> I blessed her, drawing with the fingers
> Of my spirit the figure of the cross;
> I said to her—
> "All my senses will remember you as sweet,
> Your essence is my wonder."

This mystical experience marks the spiritual rebirth of the poet.

The poem now approaches its final stage, the Blue Meridian, with the poet heralding the dawn of a new people, the synthesis of contrasting and conflicting forces:

> A strong yes, a strong no,
> With these we move and make drama,
> Yet say nothing of the goal.
> Black is black, white is white,
> East is east, west is west,
> Is truth for the brain of contrasts;
> Yet here the high way of the third,
> The blue man, the purple man
> Foretold by ancient minds who knew,
> Not the place, not the name,
> But the resultant of yes and no
> Struggling for birth through ages.

Earlier lines and images of the poem reappear in transfiguration, spiritualized by the regeneration of the poet, "America among Americans, / Man at large among men." While the Mississippi River fulfills its sacred potential, a fusion of Christian and Gurdjieffian symbols reflect the crowning achievement of an unbroken chain of millions of ancestors:

> Mankind is a cross,
> Joined as a cross irrevocably—
> The solid stream sourcing in the remote past,
> Ending in far off distant years,
> Is the perpendicular,
> The planetary wash of those now living
> Forms the transverse bar . . .

For Toomer, America was the majestic base "Of cathedral people," a people who were genuinely interracial and capable of cosmic consciousness. Thus, as the streams of humanity merge, as the forces of Nature are reconciled and all divisions harmoniously resolved, the poem reaches its final stage:

> Blue Meridian, banded light,
> Dynamic atom-aggregate,
> Awakes upon the earth;
> In his left hand he holds elevated rock
> In his right hand he holds lifted branches,
> He dances the dance of the Blue Meridian
> And dervishes with the seven regions of America.

At the end of *Cane*, the apparent analog for the Black Meridian section of the poem, Toomer left us with only the promise of self-realization. In **"Blue Meridian"** he moved beyond race to become the prophet of a new order of man known as the American. But rather than a betrayal of race for a cheap chauvinism, Toomer's poetic resolution of his private and public quest for identity represents a genuine effort to cast off all classifications that enslave human beings and inhibit the free play of intelligence and goodwill in the world.

DARRYL PINCKNEY

SOURCE: Darryl Pinckney, "Phantom," in *The New*

York Review of Books, Vol. 28, No. 3, March 5, 1981, pp. 34-36.

[*In the following excerpt, Pinckney explores the influence of Georges Gurdjieff and his philosophy on Toomer's post-*Cane *works.*]

Opaque and lyrical, *Cane* was much influenced by the imagists.... [The women of the first section are] isolated, suffering from impossible longings, doomed to live out their disappointments in men, or sustained by withdrawal, by sullen defiance—these characters, and their circumstances, are made vivid in a few, sudden strokes.... The characters are not full in the usual sense. Toomer is more interested in the drift of feelings, in elevated portraits of common events....

There is nostalgia for a natural and instinctive way of life in *Cane.* The second section contains six stories taking in the black life of Washington and Chicago, cities filled with repressed, frustrated souls. The contrast between the rural and the urban seems somewhat sentimental, but Toomer's language is sufficiently distant....

Here, too, irresolute, indolent women slip from man to man; irritated young men come to see the impossibility of getting what they want by conforming to conventional white values; a black man, self-conscious and apologetic to the outside world when he is attracted to a white woman, loses her; men and women are fearful of expressing love and lose it. A recurring theme of this section is how respectability, for middle-class blacks, is a kind of paralysis, an inhibition that results in self-denial....

When writing of the South, Toomer was a detached observer. In the city sketches he draws more on his own experience, and many of the male protagonists are reflections of an inflated image of himself. The long final section of *Cane,* **"Kabnis"** is an allegorical attempt to fuse the two themes of the Southland's naturalness and the repressed nature of an educated, northern black, Ralph Kabnis.... Hope is apparently represented by the strong-willed Lewis, also a northern black in search of his identity. Unlike Kabnis, he is able to leave the South rather than sink into it, able to learn from what he has seen and depart, as Toomer did in real life....

[Toomer] does not conceive of sex as exotic, demonic, or decadent. *Cane* does not have the appeal of the illicit; the characters are not having fun that will be paid for later. The pessimism here is so strong that even the seductions are solemn. There is a peculiar innocence in *Cane* which supports the yearning, elaborate language, the saturation in a wistful sensuality....

Cane, unlike most books of the period, is a psychological novel rather than a sociological one. Intimacy is seen as a path toward spiritual completion, and everyone in *Cane* is haunted by the wish to achieve some harmonious, perfected state. Life is seen and understood from the inside. The conflicts are internal, the rules of society merely assumed.... [It] reads like an *hommage* to the lost ways that were so attuned to "the orthodoxies of the body," as Kenneth Burke once called a fundamental aspect of black folk life.

Toomer was something of a mysterious figure to his friends, and perhaps this obscurity accounts for his legend.... **The Wayward and the Seeking** does much toward increasing our understanding of him. Included in this volume are excerpts from previously unpublished autobiographies...; three short stories...; two experimental dramas in an Expressionistic style; twelve poems; and selections from Toomer's privately printed book of aphorisms and maxims, *Essentials* (1931). It must be said, however, that the quality of the work is disappointing. The untutored genius of *Cane* seems here more like a chagrined auto-didact.

Toomer attempted several autobiographies, each with a different thematic emphasis. [Editor Darwin T. Turner] has drawn from these documents and arranged them in such a way as to form a coherent story of Toomer's life up to the publication of *Cane.*...

Toomer became an ardent disciple of Georges Gurdjieff.... It is Gurdjieff who has most influenced the tone of the autobiographical pieces. Toomer aspires to be, like Gurdjieff, the teacher, the guide, the sage, and this ends in much posturing, in a romantic imagining of himself and his family.

Moreover, the autobiographical passages make strange demands on the reader's patience and willingness to believe....

There is something very sad too in Toomer's idealized portrait of himself. He was never able to make an agreeable or interesting protagonist of himself.... Toomer apparently was certain that there were important lessons for everyone in his experience, but it is not clear what these were, especially as the pall of Gurdjieff hung more and more over the page. The autobiographies sag with tedious descriptions of Toomer's young life, his obsession with his transformation from an alert, clever, inquisitive, mischievous, popular boy to the morbid, sensitive iconoclast, thrilled and sickened by the discoveries of sex, anxious for an ennobling mission. There are intriguing references to domestic troubles..., but Toomer is self-servingly reticent. He concentrates on himself, on his path toward enlightenment and Gurdjieff, his "mission."

Still, one can piece together some clues, particularly to the emotional strain he must have suffered as a boy....

The experiences that Toomer recounts of his life after high school strike a thoroughly contemporary note in what they reveal of his restlessness. [He relocated often and returned to Washington several times, only to leave again.] . . . Finally, Toomer decided to remain in Washington until his writing "lifted him out."

It did so with *Cane.* But the three stories included in *The Wayward and the Seeking* reveal the difficulties Toomer had with his writing after *Cane.* **"Withered Skin of Berries,"** composed early in his career, is in the style of *Cane,* a lyrical exploration of a woman's inner life, her search for love, her confusion over the attentions of both a white and a black man. **"Winter on Earth"** is a sort of prose poem about wintry austerity and desolation. **"Mr. Costyve Duditch"** is the least successful story, a clumsily rendered narrative about a lonely and foolish man. Toomer attempts to bring ideas from Gurdjieff into his work, though it is not clear how Toomer interpreted his ideas beyond vague allegorical representations....

Toomer's work after *Cane* concentrates on themes of spiritual liberation, free development of mind, body, and soul, and the need for psychological reform. He also turned away explicitly from racial subjects. Yet the subtlety of his prose was lost—not so much because Toomer no longer wrote about blacks as because he was didactically urging his readers to strive toward a higher consciousness.... The plays [*Natalie Mann* and *The Sacred Factory*] show the same unfortunate tendency as the short prose works: an urge to preach. Toomer tries to create messianic young men who will educate the feelings of trusting females. But his dramatic gifts were not equal to his desire to portray the struggle for self-knowledge and freedom....

Though Toomer became disillusioned with Gurdjieff after various scandals, he never abandoned the philosophy and even headed several Gurdjieff groups across the country. In his fiction after *Cane* Toomer tried to convey his vision as a missionary. Much of the fiction was autobiographical, or had characters modeled on himself, and none of it worked. Even his most direct expressions in philosophical tracts and poems were failures....

The problem Toomer's work presents is not so much his attitude toward race—his ideas came from improvisation, the accommodation a passionately private person tried to make with the world. The problem, the sadness of Toomer, was that his lyrical gift could not hold his free-fall into philosophy. Toomer did not accept the limits of choice imposed by the tragedies of history and became a propagandist. He could not name the thing he longed to escape and retreated into a vestal masochism not unlike that of the little black boy in the lines of Blake. Once, however, during his quest for grace, Toomer suffered the sea change and had his transfiguring moment, which produced *Cane.*

ANN MARIE BUSH AND LOUIS D. MITCHELL

SOURCE: Ann Marie Bush and Louis D. Mitchell, "Jean Toomer: A Cubist Poet," in *Black American Literature Forum*, Vol. 17, No. 3, Fall, 1983, pp. 106-8.

[*In the following excerpt, Bush and Mitchell analyze Toomer's poems "Nullo" and "Storm Ending," claiming that these works establish him as a cubist poet.*]

Cubists perceive reality through intuitive vision of the mind rather than through reasoned logic of the senses. And cubists understand the reality of an object as the conceptual totality and essence of that object. They portray conceptual reality with techniques of form that manifest cubist concepts of time, space, and motion intertwined with four aesthetic concerns: dissociation of the elements of the object, simultaneity, relationship of the parts to the whole and the whole to its parts, and integrity of the object. What distinguishes cubist writers from cubist painters, sculptors, or composers is simply the particular medium of the art. While the cubist painter and sculptor are limited respectively by texture and color of paint and types of wood, metal, or stone, the cubist composer is limited by melody, rhythm, and harmony, and the cubist writer is limited by words, punctuation, and spacing on the page.

Having failed to recognize that Jean Toomer's works are essentially cubist in nature, critics have traditionally interpreted his work from sociological, psychological, archetypal, impressionist, or imagist points of view. Hopefully the following discussion of **"Nullo"** and **"Storm Ending,"** poems which offer particularly striking examples of the literary cubism so prominent throughout *Cane,* will permit scholars to begin viewing Toomer's work more clearly.

By compressing many images into one moment in **"Nullo"** and **"Storm Ending,"** Toomer abandons the conventional beginning-and-end or cause-and-effect scheme in chronological time and adopts the cubist non-sequential movement in synchronic time. Further,

Toomer dissociates, or fragments, his subject into many images, each of which is no more or less important than the whole and all of which advance and recede and blend instantaneously and simultaneously. As a consequence, the reader must respond with an intuitive perception of one conceptual compound image, the totality and essence of the subject.

For example, in **"Nullo"** Toomer flashes the texture of nature across the mind, and we react instantaneously with intuitive perception:

> A spray of pine-needles,
> Dipped in western horizon gold,
> Fell onto a path.
> Dry moulds of cow-hoofs.
> In the forest.
> Rabbits knew not of their falling,
> Nor did the forest catch aflame.

All at once within our imaginations we finger the sharpness of a smooth pine needle, the hardness of a caked hoof-print in the grainy earth, and the softness of a rabbit's fur. Simultaneously, we dive into five levels of space in nature: the sun above the earth, the pine needles in mid-air between the tree and the ground, the needles upon the ground, the prints of the cow's hooves that indent the earth, and the rabbits' homes, burrows under ground.

As we experience these varied textures and levels of space, we concurrently taste both chronological and cyclical time through samples of motion. The always-moving earth, gyrating on its axis and whirling about the sun, creates an instant of dusk in our cycle of day and night. But we know that dawn will also come, in time. The downward fall of pine needles marks a seeming moment of finality in nature's cycle of birth and death. But we know that, in time, the fallen needles will decompose, become the soil, and then again the tree. Contrarily, the remnants of hoof-prints focus on the linear movement of a cow's passage from place to place without recurrence. We know the animal has wandered the path and, with its horizontal motion, has recorded the past in the chronology of time.

Through it all, we synchronically experience the essence and the totality of nature at an unconscious level. Unlike the rabbit, we are not blind to the dynamism of light from flaming needles that spark no fire:

> A spray of pine-needles,
> Dipped in western horizon gold,
>
> . . . . .
>
> Rabbits knew not of their falling,
> Nor did the forest catch aflame.

Rather, we are cognizant of the intense light of all time compressed into the brilliant flare of the moment.

As a philosopher, Toomer appropriately entitles the poem **"Nullo,"** because nothing happens, yet everything *is*. As a cubist, he fittingly expresses the heart of **Cane** in **"Nullo,"** for the part is the whole, yet the whole is the part. As a master craftsman, Toomer aesthetically portrays nature by sketching the rabbit, a part of nature, unaware of the dynamism within its environment, and he symbolically portrays the Black American, a son of the soil, unaware of the dynamism within himself.

"Storm Ending" offers additional evidence of a cubist at work. Toomer, like every cubist, strives to imprint the essence and the totality of his subject on the mind of the audience. He endeavors to go beyond the illusion of his subject's mere visual appearance to the reality of its conceptual representation. Recognizing that only deftness of form can accomplish this intent, Toomer displays great finesse as he harnesses the power of form and generates true cubist art in his short lyric **"Storm Ending."**

Close scrutiny of the structure of **"Storm Ending"** produces two unique conceptual responses: one in which sound, sun, and rain fall to the earth simultaneously, and another in which only sound and sun concurrently fall. Each is a variation of the other; each helps to create the other; yet both reveal the same lasting symbolic effect: Black Americans reject their slave heritage rooted in the soil of the South, and white Americans reject Black Americans.

Taking note of all punctuation marks, we discover that three fragments comprise the poem. In the first fragment Toomer paints:

> Thunder blossoms gorgeously above our
>   heads,
> Great, hollow, bell-like flowers,
> Rumbling in the wind,
> Stretching clappers to strike our ears.

Here, Toomer hammers the fragment into two visual planes: the horizontal plane of clouds, "thunder blossoms," reverberating in the wind, and the vertical sheet of sound pouring from the clouds and resonating in our minds. Dynamic in its fusion of sound and motion, this fragment ironically concludes with two dots that indicate the need for a gentle pause.

In the second fragment Toomer sketches:

> Full-lipped flowers
> Bitten by the sun

Bleeding rain
Dropping rain like golden honey —

Again Toomer flattens the fragment into two definite planes: the horizontal plane of the sun, layers of space above the clouds, and the vertical (or even diagonal) plane of rays "like golden honey" radiating from the sun, rupturing the clouds, and dripping to the earth. The absence of punctuation within the fragment evokes a third plane, that of a vertical slice of rain bleeding from the clouds as does the sheet of sound in the first fragment.

With the falling of rain from the clouds and warm rays from the sun, we intuitively conceive the importance of both the sun and the clouds in the rich fertilization of the earth, and Toomer generates sensual imagery to support our conception. The lines "Full-lipped flowers / Bitten by the sun" suggest the culmination of the elements' mating as we visualize both the clouds and the sun bleeding and dripping their potent, life-giving seeds to the earth.

Dynamic in its fusion of color, warmth, motion, and sensuality, this second fragment concludes with a dash that indicates a lengthy pause. This pause is necessary, for here, as in all cubist art, the point of view changes. Through the first and second fragments, we stand on earth peering upward into the sun surrounded by clouds. Now, from space, we peer downward at the earth through an opening in those clouds. From no other position could we perceive the third fragment:

> And the sweet earth flying from the thunder.

Only from such a remote distance can we be objective enough to see the flattened plane of earth, in its cyclical motion about the sun, pass across our opening and appear to fly from the thunder of the clouds. . . .

Toomer cubistically smatters the mind with three fragments, yet there emerges a complexity of superimposed planar images that portray abundant activity in one moment's time, the ending of a storm. Absence of sequential narrative gives proof that we are not to perceive the abundant activity chronologically, but synchronically. In fact, as any cubist might do, we can rearrange the lines or the fragments without effectively changing our intuitive perception. For example:

> Full-lipped flowers
> Bleeding rain
> Bitten by the sun
> Dripping rain like golden honey —
> Thunder blossoms gorgeously above our heads,
> Rumbling in the wind,
> Great, hollow, bell-like flowers,
> Stretching clappers to strike our ears.
> And the sweet earth flying from the thunder.

No matter what the order of the images on the page, we still experience, on the literal level, the aesthetic effect described above. And, on the symbolic level, we witness Black slaves, dark clouds pierced by the sun on their backs, as they spill their lifeblood and tears to fertilize the soil of the South. We witness, also, as the sweet earth flies from the thunder, that Black Americans reject their slave heritage and that white Americans reject their Black brothers.

Although one sees and hears and feels clear images in both **"Nullo"** and **"Storm Ending,"** there is no indication of metaphor. Thus, critics such as Bernard W. Bell and Amritjit Singh, who claim that Toomer embraces imagism, are mistaken, for in an imagist poem the image is metaphor. Witness the image as metaphor in these two imagist poems, "In a Station of the Metro" and "Alba," by Ezra Pound:

> The apparition of these faces in the crowd;
> Petals on a wet, black bough.
>
> . . . . .
>
> As cool as the pale wet leaves of lily-of-the-valley
> She lay beside me in the dawn.

The metaphor in each poem by Pound is obvious. But no such metaphors exist in Toomer's **"Nullo"** or **"Storm Ending,"** because Toomer's works are cubistic rather than imagistic. Toomer as a cubist goes beyond the imagist. In his work the crystal-clear image is not metaphor; the image is object or subject.

Toomer's use of the image as object rather than metaphor shows that Toomer upholds the integrity of the subject. Beyond that, Toomer adheres to all of the basic cubist aesthetic concerns. He dissociates the elements of his subject and creates images for each fragment of that subject. He abandons sequential movement in chronological time and adopts non-sequential movement in synchronic time by smattering the mind with numerous images — equal in value to each other and to the whole — that must be perceived instantaneously. By compressing so many images into one moment, he forces the reader to perceive the images simultaneously. This forces the reader to respond with intuitive perception of the conceptual compound image of the subject in its totality and in its essence. And while Toomer follows this process, he plays with categories of time, types of motion, and levels of space. Toomer is a master of literary cubism.

ALVIN AUBERT

SOURCE: Alvin Aubert, "Archetypal Victim," in *The American Book Review*, Vol. 10, No. 6, January-February, 1989, pp. 12, 21.

[*In the following excerpt, Aubert offers a mixed assessment of* The Collected Poems of Jean Toomer *and argues that Toomer's early poems are his best.*]

An aura of melancholy surrounds Jean Toomer, an aura traceable to the writer's failure to reconcile a debilitating inner conflict involving his intellectual prowess, his artistic sensibility, his racially mixed African-European-American ancestry, and his familial circumstances. A mulatto who could pass for white, and the grandson of the Honorable P. B. S. Pinchback, the first and only Afro-American to serve as governor of a state (initially lieutenant governor, then acting governor of Louisiana during the Reconstruction era), Toomer nevertheless suffered intellectual and artistic frustration as a result of his ethnic marginality.

Had Toomer dealt more directly with these circumstances, rather than escaping into philosophical idealism in quest of a universal man—whose prototype he ultimately proclaimed himself to be—we might have been spared the tediously ingenuous "spiritualizing of experience" he undertook in his writings, to the detriment of his poetry in particular. Had he followed the course he set in the poems he wrote between 1919 and 1923, some written specifically for inclusion in his highly successful experimental novel *Cane*, Toomer would have left not only a more aesthetically viable poetic legacy but a more voluminous body of poetry and fiction as well. Instead, he ended up as the essentially one-book author he is likely to remain even if everything he left behind were to be published, judging from the qualitative description we have so far of his papers in the Yale Library.

Cane, indisputably an American classic, is a striking melange of prose sketches, poems, etc. in which Toomer both celebrates and bids farewell to his African-American heritage. It was in the creative atmosphere of *Cane* that Toomer produced the poems coeditors Robert B. Jones and Margery Toomer Latimer, Toomer's daughter, assign to what they call Toomer's "Ancestral Consciousness Period (1921-1923)." Relatively early in his long life (1894-1967), Toomer began to repudiate his African-American identity. Partly for this reason, and despite Cynthia Earl Kerman and Richard Eldridge's excellent biographical study of him in *The Lives of Jean Toomer: A Hunger for Wholeness* (1987), Toomer remains pretty much a figure of myth. And it is essentially his mythopoeic attraction that invests Toomer's collected poems with an extra-aesthetic appeal, perhaps to the point of inviting excuses for their aesthetic flaws.

It is Toomer's early poems that we find most aesthetically viable, most acceptable to our contemporary sensibility in their concreteness and existentiality—an experiential existentiality, rather than the philosophical one coeditor Robert B. Jones attributes to the later "Christian Existential" poems written out of Toomer's Quaker experience. Regrettably, in his twenty-one-page introduction Jones barely touches upon the aesthetics of the poems, although, as he himself remarks, there is no "comprehensive study" of them despite the considerable amount of critical writing done on Toomer since the 1970s.

Toomer's best poems, it would be easy enough to claim, are among those written between 1919 and 1923, before he came under the influence of Gurdjieffian idealism and, later, Quakerism. Among these are the apprentice poems he wrote, as Jones notes, under the influence of Orientalism, French and American symbolism, and Imagism (1919-1921), and those written under the same aesthetic impetus but with an African-American consciousness (1921-1923), the poems that appear in *Cane*. After these early periods, a deleterious abstractionism begins to creep into Toomer's poems, although in many of those written later (1924-1955) there remain traces of Toomer's recognition of the value of concrete representation.

Toomer's metaphysical, abstractionist tendency first appears in the poem **"As Eagles Soar"** and intensifies in the lengthy, rhetorically derivative Whitmanesque **"The Blue Meridian,"** which Jones calls "minor classic of American literature." That it may well be, but for reasons other than aesthetic. A much shorter poem of the same period, **"It Is Everywhere,"** better accomplishes a similar philosophical purpose, in less detail but with such felicitous lines as: "And what comes down goes up again / Within the view of purple hills." At any rate, **"It Is Everywhere"** is certainly more than the "local colorist . . . kaleidoscopic panorama of the American landscape" Jones calls it.

The short poem **"The Chase"** exemplifies Toomer's increasing tendency in his later poems to yoke poetry and rhetoric to the detriment of the former. The two-stanza poem opens in concrete description but virtually self-destructs in a sudden rhetorical shift in the second half of the second stanza, a pattern that marks subsequent poems in the book and Toomer's poetry generally. The first half of the second stanza, extending though markedly diluting the concrete descriptiveness of the first, works fine: "As the white bird leaves the dirty nest, / Flashes in the dazzling sky, / And merges in the blue." But then an aesthetically numbing metaphysical application rushes the poem toward its meaning: "May my spirit quit me, / And fly the beam straight / Into thy power and thy glory."

As an archetypal victim of the American color caste system, Jean Toomer stands with the likes of Beat poet Bob Kaufman. Toomer's poems, poetic prose, and critical commentary invite the speculation that under more equitable conditions he would have become a truly outstanding American Modernist, ranking with the likes of T. S. Eliot, Ezra Pound, and William Carlos Williams as a shaper of our modern and contemporary poetic sensibilities.

SOURCES FOR FURTHER STUDY

Benson, Brian Joseph, and Mable Mayle Dillard. *Jean Toomer*. Boston: Twayne Publishers, 1980, 152 p.

> Critical and biographical survey of Toomer's life and career.

Durham, Frank, ed. *The Merrill Studies in "Cane."* Columbus, Ohio: Charles E. Merrill Publishing, 1971, 113 p.

> Reprints, in whole or part, significant essays about Toomer and reviews of *Cane* by such critics as Robert Bone, Arna Bontemps, Alain Locke, and Gorham Munson.

Jackson, Blyden. "Jean Toomer's *Cane*: An Issue of Genre." In his *The Waiting Years*, pp. 189-202. Baton Rouge: Louisiana State University Press, 1976.

> Discusses the genre of *Cane*, examining how it has been classified by reviewers and scholars.

Kerman, Cynthia Earl, and Richard Eldridge. *The Lives of Jean Toomer: A Hunger for Wholeness*. Baton Rouge: Louisiana State University Press, 1987, 411 p.

> Detailed biography emphasizing Toomer's quest for spiritual enlightenment.

Rice, H. William. "Two Work Songs in *Cane*." *Black American Literature Forum* 23, No. 3 (Fall 1989): 593-99.

> Discusses the importance of song and lyric to the prose sections of *Cane*.

Thompson, Larry E. "Jean Toomer: As Modern Man." In *The Harlem Renaissance Remembered,* edited by Arna Bontemps, pp. 51-62. New York: Dodd, Mead, 1972.

> Examines Toomer's search for identity in his life and work.

Vergil

70 B.C.-19 B.C.

(Full name Publius Vergilius Maro; also Virgil) Roman poet.

INTRODUCTION

Considered the greatest poet of ancient Rome, Vergil is acclaimed for brilliantly transforming the Greek literary traditions that provided Roman writers with material, themes, and writing styles and conventions. His three major works—the *Eclogues,* the *Georgics,* and the *Aeneid*—have influenced virtually all subsequent Western literature, and Dante Alighieri, Geoffrey Chaucer, Edmund Spenser, John Milton, Percy Bysshe Shelley, and Matthew Arnold are numbered among his prominent literary heirs. As literary exemplars, revealing artifacts, and continuously pertinent, provocative portrayals of the human condition, Vergil's works endure among the great creations of world literature

Biographical Information

Vergil was born on October 15, 70 B.C., at Andes, near Mantua, in Cisalpine Gaul. His mother, Magia Polla, was the daughter of the landlord who employed Vergil's father, Maro, a day laborer. The couple's marriage elevated Maro's social status, which possibly enhanced the quality of his son's education. The boy received elementary schooling in Mantua, then studied rhetoric in Rome and philosophy in Naples. Vergil planned to practice law but proved too shy to speak comfortably in public. Returning to his family's small farm, he studied and wrote poetry until the land was confiscated in 41 B.C. to compensate retiring soldiers. Friends urged Vergil to appeal to Octavian (known as Augustus after he became emperor in 27 B.C.), Julius Caesar's adopted son and eventual successor. Octavian restored the farm—perhaps, scholars speculate, because he was impressed by Vergil's writings—but the poet soon moved to Naples, where he composed the *Eclogues* between 42 and 37 B.C. They attracted widespread praise and the sponsorship of Octavian's friend, the art patron Maecenas. Maecenas allegedly prevailed upon Vergil to compose his next work, the *Georgics*, which were written between 37 and 30 B.C. The work further enhanced Vergil's reputation upon its publication in 29 B.C. Octavian, to whom Vergil read the completed poem, honored him with two villas and a generous stipend, and Octavian's friends asked Vergil to compose an epic honoring the emperor. This project, which became the *Aeneid*, occupied the last ten years of Vergil's life. According to several of his friends, he first drafted the epic in prose, then laboriously reworked it in verse. Composition was slow and revision constant. When he left Naples in 19 B.C. to gather new material in Greece and Asia Minor, he planned to devote another three years to revisions, but he caught fever at Megara and died soon after returning to Italy.

Major Works

The ten poems comprising the *Eclogues* vary in length from 63 to 111 lines, and each depicts shepherds of poetic temperament who sing of unhappy loves in an idealized rural landscape. Although much of the *Ecologues* derive from the *Idylls* of Theocritus, Vergil substantially modified the Theocritan features that he borrowed, and he introduced much new material through numerous allusions to the figures, events, and concerns of Augustan Rome. Vergil's innovations are evident in the structure and style of the *Eclogues* as well: the ten poems are ordered very deliberately, creating an effect of balanced variety, and his sentences are simply connected and slowly paced, evoking a limpid, lyrical atmosphere. The *Georgics*, widely considered the most polished of Vergil's works, consists of four books, each between 500 and 600 lines long, that offer instruction in grain production, the cultivation of trees and vineyards, animal husbandry, and beekeeping. Lyrical and evocative in his description of the Roman countryside, Vergil interwove a myriad of mythical and literary allusions seamlessly, enriching his poem without encumbering it. Books One and Three are somber, depicting gruelling labor and emphasizing catastrophe; books Two and Four are livelier in tone, describing easier labor and offering some alternatives to despair. The *Aeneid*, commonly considered Vergil's best work as well as a masterpiece of Roman culture, consists of twelve books, each between 700 and 1,000 lines long. As scholars have maintained, Vergil forged a characteristically Roman epic from such disparate sources as archiac myths and mysteries, Homeric epic poetry, ancient beliefs (such as that of reincarnation), and Stoic precepts, while emphasizing the spirit of Augustan patriotism and imperialism throughout the epic. Conceived as a tribute to Augustus, the *Aeneid* concerns the founding of Rome and focuses on the adventures and exploits of Aeneas, who figures as a venerable ancestor of the emperor. But the epic also reflects the human cost of Roman power, particularly in the final books in which Vergil compassionately depicted characters who were ultimately sacrificed to the entwined destinies of Aeneas and Rome.

Critical Reception

Immensely popular in Augustan Rome, Vergil's works became part of the standard curriculum in Roman schools within fifty years of his death, ensuring the production of numerous copies and thus continuous availability of his writings to readers throughout the centuries. Critics in that time closely analyzed the narrative and stylistic aspects of Vergil's great poems and scrutinized his sources and models—particularly the adaptations of the Theocritan patterns in the *Eclogues* and the pervasive allusions to the works of Homer, Lucretius, and others in the *Georgics*. A consummate master of form, Vergil has been credited with significantly refining narrative technique and with contributing to psychologically credible characterization as illustrated in the *Aeneid*. He has also been praised for developing the typically Greek meter, the dactylic hexameter (a line consisting of six feet, with a predominance of dactyls—a long syllable and two short syllables—over spondees—two long syllables), into an outstanding instrument of Latin poetry. Scholars have also increasingly appreciated the encyclopedic description of Greco-Roman culture that Vergil's poetry provides. In particular, his work emphasizes the anxieties of the Augustan Age—Does progress necessarily entail and justify human suffering? Can art minister to that suffering?—Questions that remain relevant today.

(For further information, see *Classical and Medieval Literature Criticism,* Vol. 9; *DISCovering Authors; DISCovering Authors: British; DISCovering Authors: Canadian; DISCovering Authors Modules: Most-studied Authors Module, Poets Module; Poetry Criticism,* Vol. 12.)

CRITICAL COMMENTARY

QUINTILIAN

SOURCE: Quintilian, "Book X," in his *The Institutio Oratoria of Quintilian, Vol. IV*, translated by H. E. Butler, William Heinemann Ltd., 1922, pp. 1-151.

[*The Roman rhetorician Quintilian gained such esteem as a teacher of oratory that Emperor Vespasian named him Rome's first paid professor of rhetoric. He is best known for his treatise* Institutio oratoria *(ca. 96 A.D.; Education of an Orator), a veritable encyclopedia of rhetorical knowledge. In the following excerpt from that work, Quintilian briefly compares Vergil with Homer.*]

I now come to Roman authors.... As among Greek authors Homer provided us with the most auspicious opening, so will Virgil among our own. For of all epic poets, Greek or Roman, he, without doubt, most nearly approaches to Homer. I will repeat the words which I heard Domitius Afer use in my young days. I asked what poet in his opinion came nearest to Homer, and he replied, "Virgil comes second, but is nearer first than third." And in truth, although we must needs bow before the immortal and superhuman genius of Homer, there is greater diligence and exactness in the work of Virgil just because his task was harder. And perhaps the superior uniformity of the Roman's excellence balances Homer's pre-eminence in his outstanding passages. All our other poets follow a long way in the rear.

J. W. MACKAIL

SOURCE: J. W. Mackail, "The Augustan Age: Virgil," in his *Latin Literature*, 1895. Reprint by Charles Scribner's Sons, 1900, pp. 91-105.

[*In the excerpt below, Mackail traces the increasing sophistication of Vergil's artistry from the* Eclogues *through the* Georgics *and into the full maturity displayed in the* Aeneid.]

Publius Vergilius Maro was born at the village of Andes, near Mantua, on the 15th of October, 70 B.C. The province of Cisalpine Gaul, though not formally incorporated with Italy till twenty years later, had before this become thoroughly Romanised, and was one of the principal recruiting grounds for the legions. But the population was still, by blood and sympathy, very largely Celtic; and modern theorists are fond of tracing the new element of romance, which Virgil introduced with such momentous results into Latin poetry, to the same Celtic spirit which in later ages flowered out in the Arthurian legend, and inspired the whole creative literature of mediaeval Europe. To the countrymen of Shakespeare and Keats it will not seem necessary to assume a Celtic origin, on abstract grounds, for any new birth of this romantic element. The name Maro may or may not be Celtic; any argument founded on it is of little more relevance than the fancy which once interpreted the name of Virgil's mother, Magia Polla, into a supernatural significance, and, connecting the name Virgilius itself with the word *Virgo*, metamorphosed the poet into an enchanter born of a maiden mother, the Merlin of the Roman Empire.

Virgil's father was a small freeholder in Andes, who farmed his own land, practised forestry and bee-keeping, and gradually accumulated a sufficient competence to enable him to give his son—an only child, so far as can be ascertained—the best education that the times could provide. He was sent to school at the neighbouring town of Cremona, and afterwards to Milan, the capital city of the province. At the age of seventeen he proceeded to Rome, where he studied oratory and philosophy under the best masters of the time. A tradition, which the dates make improbable, was that Gaius Octavius, afterwards the Emperor Augustus, was for a time his fellow-scholar under the rhetorician Epidius. In the class-room of the Epicurean Siro he may have made his first acquaintance with the poetry of Lucretius.

For the next ten years we know nothing of Virgil's life, which no doubt was that of a profound student. His father had died, and his mother married again, and his patrimony was sufficient to support him until a turn of the wheel of public affairs for a moment lost, and then permanently secured his fortune. After the battle of Philippi, the first task of the victorious triumvirs was to provide for the disbanding and settlement of the immense armies which had been raised for the Civil war. The lands of cities which had taken the Republican side were confiscated right and left for this purpose; among the rest, Virgil's farm, which was included in the territory of Cremona. But Virgil found in the administrator of the district, Gaius Asinius Pollio, himself a distinguished critic and man of let-

Principal Works

Eclogae [*Eclogues* or *Bucolics*; title means "Selections"] (poetry) 42-37 B.C.
Georgica [*Georgics*; title means "Points of Farming"] (poetry) 37-30 B.C.
Aeneis [*The Aeneid*] (epic poetry) 31-19 B.C.

Principal English Translations

Eneydos (translated by William Caxton) 1490
Eneados (translated by Gawin Douglas) 1553
The Aeneid, Books II and IV (partial translation by Henry Howard) 1557
Aeneidos (translated by Thomas Phaer and Thomas Twyne) 1573
The Aeneis of P. Virgilius Maro, Books I-IV (partial translation by Richard Stanyhurst) 1582
The Bucoliks of Publius Virgilius Maro, Prince of all Latine poets, otherwise called his Pastoralls, or shepeherds meetings. Together with his Georgiks or Rurall, otherwise called his husbandrie, conteyning foure books (translated by Abraham Fleming) 1589
Virgil's Georgicks (translated by Thomas May) 1628
The Works of P. Vergilius Maro (translated by John Ogilby) 1649
The Works of Virgil: containing his Pastorals, Georgics, and Aeneis (translated by John Dryden) 1697
The Works of Virgil (translated by Christopher Pitt and Joseph Warton) 1753
The Georgicks of Virgil (translated by John Martyn) 1741
The Bucolicks of Virgil (translated by John Martyn) 1749
The Aeneid (verse translation by John Conington) 1866
The Aeneid (prose translation by John Conington) 1872
The Aeneid (translated by William Morris) 1876
The Aeneid (translated by John William Mackail) 1908
The Georgicks of Virgil in English Verse (translated by Arthur S. Way) 1912
The Aeneid of Virgil in English Verse (translated by Arthur S. Way) 1916
The Poems of Virgil (translated by James Rhoads) 1921
The Aeneid (translated by Henry Rushton Fairclough) 1932
The Eclogues of Virgil in English Verse (translated by Arthur S. Way) 1932
Virgil's Works: The Aeneid, Eclogues, Georgics (translated by John William Mackail) 1934
The Eclogues and the Georgics (translated by R. C. Trevelyan) 1944
The Pastoral Poems (translated by E. V. Rieu) 1949
The Aeneid of Virgil (translated by Rolphe Humphries) 1951
The Aeneid of Virgil (translated by C. Day Lewis) 1952
The Aeneid by Virgil (translated by W. F. Jackson Knight) 1958
The Aeneid: An Epic Poem of Rome (translated by L. R. Lind) 1962
The Aeneid (translated by Frank O. Copley) 1965
The Eclogues, Georgics, and Aeneid of Virgil (translated by C. Day Lewis) 1966
The Aeneid of Vergil (translated by Kevin Guinagh) 1970
The Aeneid of Virgil (translated by Allen Mandelbaum) 1971
The Aeneid of Virgil (translated by R. D. Williams) 1972-73
The Aeneid (translated by Robert Fitzgerald) 1981

---

ters, a powerful and active patron. By his influence and that of his friends, Cornelius Gallus and Alfenus Varus—the former a soldier and poet, the latter an eminent jurist, who both had been fellow-students of Virgil at Rome—Virgil was compensated by an estate in Campania, and introduced to the intimate circle of Octavianus, who, under the terms of the triumvirate, was already absolute ruler of Italy.

It was about this time that the *Eclogues* were published, whether separately or collectively is uncertain, though the final collection and arrangement, which is Virgil's own, can hardly be later than 38 B.C. The impression they made on the world of letters was immediate and universal. To some degree no doubt a reception was secured to them by the influence of Maecenas, the Home Minister of Octavianus, who had already taken up the line which he so largely developed in later years, of a public patron of art and letters in the interest of the new government. But had Virgil made his first public appearance merely as a Court poet, it is probable that the *Eclogues* would have roused little enthusiasm and little serious criticism. Their true significance seems to have been at once realised as marking the beginning of a new era; and amid the storm of criticism, laudatory and adverse, which has raged round them for so many ages since, this cardinal fact has always remained prominent. Alike to the humanists or the earlier Renaissance, who found in them the sunrise of a golden age of poetry and the achievement of the Latin conquest over Greece, and to the more recent critics of this century, for whom they represented the echo of an already exhausted convention and the beginning of the decadence of Roman poetry, the *Eclogues* have been the real turning-point, not only between two periods of Latin literature, but between two worlds.

The poems destined to so remarkable a significance are, in their external form, close and careful imitations of Theocritus, and have all the vices and weaknesses of imitative poetry to a degree that could not well be exceeded. Nor are these failings redeemed (as is to a certain extent true of the purely imitative work of Catullus and other poets) by any brilliant jewel-finish of workmanship. The execution is uncertain, hesitating, sometimes extraordinarily feeble. One well-known line it is impossible to explain otherwise than as a mistranslation of a phrase in Theocritus such as one would hardly expect from an average schoolboy. When Virgil follows the convention of the Greek pastoral his copy is doubly removed from nature; where he ventures on fresh impersonation or allegory of his own, it is generally weak in itself and always hopelessly out of tone with the rest. Even the versification is curiously unequal and imperfect. There are lines in more than one Eclogue which remind one in everything but their languor of the flattest parts of Lucretius. Contemporary critics even went so far as to say that the language here and there was simply not Latin.

Yet granted that all this and more than all this is true, it does not touch that specific Virgilian charm of which these poems first disclosed the secret. Already through their immature and tremulous cadences there pierces, from time to time, that note of brooding pity which is unique in the poetry of the world. The fourth and tenth Eclogues may be singled out especially as showing the new method, which almost amounted to a new human language, as they are also those where Virgil breaks away most decidedly from imitation of the Greek idyllists. The fourth Eclogue unfortunately has been so long and so deeply associated with purely adventitious ideas that it requires a considerable effort to read it as it ought to be read. The curious misconception which turned it into a prophecy of the birth of Christ outlasted in its effects any serious belief in its historical truth: even modern critics cite Isaiah for parallels, and are apt to decry it as a childish attempt to draw a picture of some actual golden age. But the Sibylline verses which suggested its contents and imagery were really but the accidental grain of dust round which the crystallisation of the poem began; and the enchanted light which lingers over it is hardly distinguishable from that which saturates the *Georgics. Cedet et ipse mari vector, nec nautica pinus mutabit merces*—the feeling here is the same as in his mere descriptions of daily weather, like the *Omnia plenis rura natant fossis atque omnis navita ponte umida vela legit*; not so much a vision of a golden age as Nature herself seen through a medium of strange gold. Or again, in the tenth Eclogue, where the masque of shepherds and gods passes before the sick lover, it is through the same strange and golden air that they seem to move, and the heavy lilies of Silvanus droop in the stillness of the same unearthly day.

Seven years following on the publication of the *Eclogues* were spent by Virgil on the composition of the *Georgics*. They were published two years after the battle of Actium, being thus the first, as they are the most splendid, literary production of the Empire. They represent the art of Virgil in its matured perfection. The subject was one in which he was thoroughly at home and completely happy. His own early years had been spent in the pastures of the Mincio, among his father's cornfields and coppices and hives; and his newer residence, by the seashore near Naples in winter, and in summer at his villa in the lovely hill-country of Campania, surrounded him with all that was most beautiful in the most beautiful of lands. His delicate health made it easier for him to give his work the slow and arduous elaboration that makes the *Georgics* in mere technical finish the most perfect work of Latin, or perhaps of any literature. There is no trace of impatience in the work. It was in some sense a commission; but Augustus and Maecenas, if it be true that they suggested the subject, had, at all events, the sense not to hurry it. The result more than fulfilled the brilliant promise of the *Eclogues*. Virgil was now, without doubt or dispute, the first of contemporary poets.

But his responsibilities grew with his greatness. The scheme of a great Roman epic, which had always floated before his own mind, was now definitely and indeed urgently pressed upon him by authority which it was difficult to resist. And many elements in his own mind drew him in the same direction. Too much stress need not be laid on the passage in the sixth Eclogue—one of the rare autobiographic touches is his work—in which he alludes to his early experiments in "singing of kings and battles." Such early exercises are the common field of young poets. But the maturing of his mind, which can be traced in the *Georgics*, was urging him towards certain methods of art for which the epic was the only literary form that gave sufficient scope. More and more he was turning from nature to man and human life, and to the contemplation of human destiny. The growth of the psychological instinct in the *Georgics* is curiously visible in the episode of Aristaeus, with which the poem now ends. According to a well-authenticated tradition, the last two hundred and fifty lines of the fourth Georgic were written several years after the rest of the poem, to replace the original conclusion, which had contained the praises of his early friend, Cornelius Gallus, now dead in disgrace and proscribed from court poetry. In the story of Orpheus and Eurydice, in the later version, Virgil shows a new method and a new power. It stands between the idyl and the epic, but it is the epic method towards which it tends. No return upon the earlier manner was thenceforth possible; with many searchings of heart, with much occasional despondency and dissatisfaction, he addressed himself to the composition of the *Aeneid*.

The earlier national epics of Naevius and Ennius had framed certain lines for Roman epic poetry, which it was almost bound to follow. They had established the mythical connection of Rome with Troy and with the great cycle of Greek legend, and had originated the idea of making Rome itself—that *Fortuna Urbis* which later stood in the form of a golden statue in the imperial bedchamber—the central interest, one might almost say the central figure, of the story. To adapt the Homeric methods to this new purpose, and at the same time to make his epic the vehicle for all his own inward broodings over life and fate, for his subtle and delicate psychology, and for that philosophic passion in which all the other motives and springs of life were becoming included, was a task incapable of perfect solution. On his death-bed Virgil made it his last desire that the *Aeneid* should be destroyed, nominally on the ground that it still wanted three years' work to bring it to perfection, but one can hardly doubt from a deeper and less articulate feeling. The command of the Emperor alone prevented his wish from taking effect. With the unfinished *Aeneid*, as with the unfinished poem of Lucretius, it is easy to see within what limits any changes or improvements would have been made in it had the author lived longer: the work is, in both cases, substantially done.

The *Aeneid* was begun the year after the publication of the *Georgics*, when Virgil was forty years of age. During its progress he continued to live for the most part in his Campanian retirement. He had a house at Rome in the fashionable quarter of the Esquiline, but used it little. He was also much in Sicily, and the later books of the *Aeneid* seem to show personal observation of many parts of Central Italy. It is a debated question whether he visited Greece more than once. His last visit there was in 19 B.C. He had resolved to spend three years more on the completion of his poem, and then give himself up to philosophy for what might remain of his life. But the three years were not given him. A fever, caught while visiting Megara on a day of excessive heat, induced him to return hastily to Italy. He died a few days after landing at Brundusium, on the 26th of September. His ashes were, by his own request, buried near Naples, where his tomb was a century afterwards worshipped as a holy place.

The *Aeneid*, carefully edited from the poet's manuscript by two of his friends, was forthwith published, and had such a reception as perhaps no poem before or since has ever found. Already, while it was in progress, it had been rumoured as "something greater than the *Iliad*," and now that it appeared, it at once became the canon of Roman poetry, and immediately began to exercise an unparalleled influence over Latin literature, prose as well as verse. Critics were not indeed wanting to point out its defects, and there was still a school (which attained greater importance a century later) that went back to Lucretius and the older poets, and refused to allow Virgil's preeminence. But for the Roman world at large, as since for the world of the Latin races, Virgil became what Homer had been to Greece, "the poet." The decay of art and letters in the third century only added a mystical and hieratic element to his fame. Even to the Christian Church he remained a poet sacred and apart: in his profound tenderness and his mystical "yearning after the further shore" as much as in the supposed prophecy of the fourth Eclogue, they found and revered what seemed to them like an unconscious inspiration. The famous passage of St. Augustine, where he speaks of his own early love for Virgil, shows in its half-hysterical renunciation how great the charm of the Virgilian art had been, and still was, to him: *Quid miserius misero*, he cries, *non miserante se ipsum, et flente Didonis mortem quae fiebat amando Aeneam, non flente autem mortem meam quae fiebat non amando tel Deus lumen cordis mei, non te amabam, et haec non flebam, sed flebam Didonem exstinctam, ferroque extrema secutam, sequens ipse extrema condita tua relicto te!* To the graver and more matured mind of Dante, Virgil was the lord and master who, even though shut out from Paradise, was the chosen and honoured minister of God. Up to the beginning of the present century the supremacy of Virgil was hardly doubted. Since then the development of scientific criticism has passed him through all its searching processes, and in a fair judgment his greatness has rather gained than lost. The doubtful honour of indiscriminate praise was for a brief period succeeded by the attacks of an almost equally undiscriminating censure. An ill-judged partiality had once spoken of the *Aeneid* as something greater than a Roman *Iliad*: it was easy to show that in the most remarkable Homeric qualities the *Aeneid* fell far short, and that, so far as it was an imitation of Homer, it could no more stand beside Homer than the imitations of Theocritus in the *Eclogues* could stand beside Theocritus. The romantic movement, with its impatience of established fames, damned the *Aeneid* in one word as artificial; forgetting, or not seeing, that the *Aeneid* was itself the fountain-head of romanticism. Long after the theory of the noble savage had passed out of political and social philosophy it lingered in literary criticism; and the distinction between "natural" and "artificial" poetry was held to be like that between light and darkness. It was not till a comparatively recent time that the leisurely progress of criticism stumbled on the fact that all poetry is artificial, and that the *Iliad* itself is artificial in a very eminent and unusual degree.

No great work of art can be usefully judged by comparison with any other great work of art. It may, indeed, be interesting and fertile to compare one with another, in order to seize more sharply and appreciate more vividly the special beauty of each. But to press comparison further, and to depreciate one because it has not what is the special quality of the other, is to lose sight of the function of criticism. We shall not find in Virgil the bright speed, the unexhausted joyfulness, which, in spite of a view of life as grave as Virgil's own, make the *Iliad* and *Odyssey* unique in poetry; nor, which is more to the point as regards the *Aeneid*, the narrative power, the genius for story-telling, which is one of the rarest of literary gifts, and which Ovid alone among the Latin poets possessed in any high perfection. We shall not find in him that high and concentrated passion which in Pindar (as afterwards in Dante) fuses the elements of thought and language into a single white heat. We shall not find in him the luminous and untroubled calm, as of a spirit in which all passion has been fused away, which makes the poetry of Sophocles so crystalline and irreproachable. Nor shall we find in him the great qualities of his own Latin predecessors, Lucretius or Catullus. All this is merely saying in amplified words that Virgil was not Lucretius or Catullus, and that still less was he Homer, or Pindar, or Sophocles; and to this may be added, that he lived in the world which the great Greek and Latin poets had created, though he looked forward out of it into another.

Yet the positive excellences of the *Aeneid* are so numerous and so splendid that the claim of its author to be the Roman Homer is not unreasonable, if it be made clear that the two poems are fundamentally disparate, and that no more is meant than that the one poet is as eminent in his own form and method as the other in his. In our haste to rest Virgil's claim to supremacy as a poet on the single quality in which he is unique and unapproachable we may seem tacitly to assent to the judgment of his detractors on other points. Yet the more one studies the *Aeneid*, the more profoundly is one impressed by its quality as a masterpiece of construction. The most adverse critic would not deny that portions of the poem are, both in dramatic and narrative quality, all but unsurpassed, and in a certain union of imaginative sympathy with their fine dramatic power and their stateliness of narration perhaps unequalled. The story of the last agony of Troy could not be told with more breadth, more richness, more brilliance than it is told in the second book: here, at least, the story neither flags nor hurries; from the moment when the Greek squadron sets sail from Tenedos and the signal-flame flashes from their flagship, the scenes of the fatal night pass before us in a smooth swift stream that gathers weight and volume as it goes, till it culminates in the vision of awful faces which rises before Aeneas when Venus lifts the cloud of mortality from his startled eyes. The episode of Nisus and Euryalus in the ninth book, and that of Camilla in the eleventh, are in their degree as admirably vivid and stately. The portraiture of Dido, again, in the fourth book, is in combined breadth and subtlety one of the dramatic masterpieces of human literature. It is idle to urge that this touch is borrowed from Euripides or that suggested by Sophocles, or to quote the Medea of Apollonius as the original of which Dido is an elaborate imitation. What Virgil borrowed he knew how to make his own; and the world which, while not denying the tenderness, the grace, the charm of the heroine of the *Argonautica*, leaves the *Argonautica* unread, has thrilled and grown pale from generation to generation over the passionate tragedy of the Carthaginian queen.

But before a deeper and more appreciative study of the *Aeneid* these great episodes cease to present themselves as detached eminences. That the *Aeneid* is unequal is true; that passages in it here and there are mannered, and even flat, is true also; but to one who has had the patience to know it thoroughly, it is in its total effect, and not in the great passages, or even the great books, that it seems the most consummate achievement. Virgil may seem to us to miss some of his opportunities, to labour others beyond their due proportion, to force himself (especially in the later books) into material not well adapted to the distinctive Virgilian treatment. The slight and vague portrait of the maiden princess of Latium, in which the one vivid touch of her "flower-like hair" is the only clear memory we carry away with us, might, in different hands—in those of Apollonius, for instance,—have given a new grace and charm to the scenes where she appears. The funeral games at the tomb of Anchises, no longer described, as they had been in early Greek poetry, from the mere pleasure in dwelling upon their details, begin to become tedious before they are over. In the battle-pieces of the last three books we sometimes cannot help being reminded that Virgil is rather wearily following an obsolescent literary tradition. But when we have set such passages against others which, without being as widely celebrated as the episode of the sack of Troy or the death of Dido, are equally miraculous in their workmanship—the end of the fifth book, for instance, or the muster-roll of the armies of Italy in the seventh, or, above all, the last hundred and fifty lines of the twelfth, where Virgil rises perhaps to his very greatest manner—we shall not find that the splendour of the poem depends on detached passages, but far more on the great manner and movement which, interfused with the unique Virgilian tenderness, sustains the whole structure through and through.

The merely technical quality of Virgil's art has never been disputed. The Latin hexameter, "the stateliest measure ever moulded by the lips of man," was brought by him to a perfection which made any further development impossible. Up to the last it kept taking in his hands new refinements of rhythm and movement which make the later books of the *Aeneid* (the least successful part of the poem in general estimation) an even more fascinating study to the lovers of language than the more formally perfect work of the *Georgics*, or the earlier books of the *Aeneid* itself. A brilliant modern critic has noted this in words which deserve careful study.

> The innovations are individually hardly preceptible, but taken together they alter the character of the hexameter line in a way more easily felt than described. Among the more definite changes we may note that there are more full stops in the middle of lines, there are more elisions, there is a larger proportion of short words, there are more words repeated, more assonances, and a freer use of the emphasis gained by the recurrence of verbs in the same or cognate tenses. Where passages thus characterised have come down to us still in the making, the effect is forced and fragmentary; where they succeed, they combine in a novel manner the rushing freedom of the old trochaics with the majesty which is the distinguishing feature of Virgil's style. Art has concealed its art, and the poet's last words suggest to us possibilities in the Latin tongue which no successor has been able to realise.

Again, the psychological interest and insight which keep perpetually growing throughout Virgil's work result in an almost unequalled power of expressing in exquisite language the half-tones and delicate shades of mental processes. The famous simile in the twelfth *Aeneid*—

> *Ac velut in somnis oculos ubi languida pressit*
> *Nocte quies, nequiquam avidos extendere cursus*
> *Velle videmur, et in mediis conatibus aegri*
> *Succidimus, nec lingua valet, nec corpore notae*
> *Sufficient vires aut vox et verba sequuntur*—

is an instance of the amazing mastery with which he makes language have the effect of music, in expressing the subtlest processes of feeling.

But the specific and central charm of Virgil lies deeper than in any merely technical quality. The word which expresses it most nearly is that of pity. In the most famous of his single lines he speaks of the "tears of things;" just this sense of tears, this voice that always, in its most sustained splendour and in its most ordinary cadences, vibrates with a strange pathos, is what finally places him along among artists. This thrill in the voice, *come colui che piange e dice,* is never absent from his poetry. In the "lonely words," in the "pathetic half-lines" spoken of by the two great modern masters of English prose and verse, he perpetually touches the deepest springs of feeling; in these it is that he sounds, as no other poet has done, the depths of beauty and sorrow, of patience and magnanimity, of honour in life and hope beyond death.

W. F. JACKSON KNIGHT

SOURCE: W. F. Jackson Knight, in an introduction to *The Aeneid* by Virgil, translated by W. F. Jackson Knight, revised edition, 1958. Reprint by Penguin Books, 1968, pp. 11-24.

[*In the following excerpt, Knight provides a comprehensive overview of Vergil's sources, themes, and style in the* Aeneid.]

The *Aeneid* of Virgil is a gateway between the pagan and the Christian centuries. Virgil, who was born in 70 B.C. and died in 19 B.C., left the poem unfinished at his death. That was eight years after the republican government of old Rome gave place to the rule of emperors, and only a few years before the Christian Era started. Virgil is the Poet of the Gate.

In the beginning, Rome had been a tiny settlement surrounded by enemies, and it had needed a strong will, proud, disciplined, and sustained, to survive at all. Rome did survive and was led on by successive hard-won victories to world dominion.

The early history is obscure, but the process seems to have taken at least five centuries of almost continuous warfare, and during that period the Romans achieved unparalleled success, apparently through unique merits of their own combined with a special share of divine favour and good fortune. The spectacular rise of Rome was a matter for wonder and a certain reverence to the Romans themselves, especially when, in the later years of the republican period, new chances of peace and prosperity, and a new access of scepticism threatened the old habits of loyalty, integrity, and self-sacrifice. People then looked back on their rich moral inheritance and became increasingly interested in the origins of Rome and in the Roman 'myth', which was both life-giving and poetically true. The valour of old Rome did not pass away before it could give to the Christian allegiance the devout and heroic fidelity which had made and saved the little Republic of long ago. Virgil was the supreme poet of this majestic phase of human experience. He distilled and epitomized it. And by the magic of creation he made it glow with a new light which was to brighten all the centuries to come.

Of Virgil's life something is known, but not very much. His full name was Publius Vergilius Maro. He was born near Mantua, in Cisalpine Gaul, as the north of Italy was then called. His parents had a farm there. The young Virgil was given a very good education and went to Rome to perfect it. He seems to have been interested in all subjects, including science. Though he early made friends with many important Romans, among them probably the young Octavius who was afterwards to become Augustus, the first emperor, Virgil preferred a quiet life, away from Rome. He was very shy and his health was always bad. He soon went to live at Naples, and there he spent most of his life, reading and writing. In 19 B.C. he started on a journey to Greece with Augustus. But he became very ill and had to return. He died at Brindisi. Before he died he asked his friends to burn the *Aeneid*. Apparently he was persuaded to change his mind, and agreed to let Varius and Tucca edit and publish it.

The Emperor Augustus had captured Virgil's imagination when they were both young. Virgil could apparently foresee that he would give the Roman World peace and order, as indeed he did. Virgil passionately believed in the restoration of Roman greatness and Italy's prosperity, and such too was the policy of Augustus and his chief minister Maecenas. They were Virgil's patrons, and in some sense and to some extent he wrote his poetry in conformity with their wishes. But Augustus sometimes used cruel methods, which Virgil could not condone, and indeed subtly criticized here and there in his late poetry. It is even possible that the influence of Virgil and his friend, the great lyric poet Horace, actually helped to reform Augustus, who became milder as he grew older.

Virgil left three literary works, all in verse. Some shorter poems were also attributed to him, but he is not now generally believed to be the author of any of them, at least in their present form, except two, both very short, but delightful.

Of the three certainly authentic works, the first is a collection of 'Pastoral Poems', otherwise known as the **Bucolics** or the **Eclogues.** They are ten short pieces, professedly fiction about imaginary goatherds and other country people, but sometimes mentioning real people, some of them contemporary, or hinting at realities in a highly elusive kind of allegory. The poetry is full of charming thoughts and pictures, and the music of the Latin is lovely beyond description; and underlying it is a deep wisdom.

The next poem is 'Poetry of the Farm', the *Georgics*, in four books, containing advice to farmers about crops, trees, and animals, especially bees, but clothing it in poetic feeling and colour, usually fascinating and sometimes sublime.

The *Aeneid* is the third, last, and longest, of Virgil's poems. It is a legendary narrative, a story about the imagined origin of the Roman nation in times long before the foundation of Rome itself. It is an epic poem. Epic poems form a large class, beginning for us with the Babylonian Epic of Gilgamesh over four thousand years ago and Homer's *Iliad* and *Odyssey* more than a thousand years after it, and appearing at many other times and places, principally in Asia and Europe. An epic poem is hard to define. But perhaps it can be fairly described as a long narrative poem, full of action, which tells us about human life and makes us think about the relation between man and the superhuman powers, having as the chief characters 'heroes', that is, people who are in some way stronger than ordinary mankind but below the divine level. Epics are either oral poems, poems composed among people who are not yet fully used to writing, or, in later phases of culture, written poems which have been developed, directly or indirectly, out of the old tradition of oral poetry.

The *Aeneid,* as any epic should be, is an exciting story extremely well told and full of incident: it can be read as a story and nothing more. However, besides being a story, it is a kind of moving picture carrying allusive, and in a sense symbolic, meanings.

According to legend some of the Romans could trace their descent back to the Trojans of the city of Troy which had been made famous by Homer. The Trojan prince Aeneas was said to have escaped after the capture of the city and sailed with other Trojans to the west coast of Italy, where he and they settled, and where their descendants afterwards founded, or helped to found, the earliest Rome. Virgil rewrote this legend elaborately and made it serve the purpose of his own vision.

When in the *Aeneid* we read of the Greeks sacking Troy,

it seems as if no Trojan can escape the final annihilation. The new destiny of the Trojan remnant starts from utter despair, and afterwards too, as they go on their adventurous way, they are sometimes inclined to hopeless despondency. Yet after immense efforts and much endurance they prevailed, and so made possible the future supremacy and grandeur of Rome. The Trojans succeeded not so much through their own strength as through divine help and divine encouragement. The whole story is threaded along a series of divine appearances and admonitions, with their commands, advice, and explanations, and sometimes with their practical assistance.

Aeneas, the leader of the Trojan band, was supposed to be the son of Venus, the Goddess of Love, and of a mortal father, Anchises. Venus protected Aeneas. But Juno, the Queen of the Gods and wife of the supreme god Jupiter, had been the enemy of Troy and she opposed Aeneas fiercely. Jupiter of course had to see both sides of the question, but he and Destiny, working together, helped the Trojans and endorsed their success. Other gods and goddesses were also involved, favouring or opposing one character or another or one side or the other. In the poem they communicate with mortal men either directly or through dreams, visions, omens, and the words of prophets and clairvoyants. Virgil had no doubt that the affairs of the earthly world are subject to the powers of another world, a world which is normally, but by no means always, invisible, but no less real for that; and near the middle of the poem he introduces an explanation of a part of his belief.

The belief is vital to the poem. For Virgil was presenting a true poetic picture of the world, showing how human affairs are controlled by human and superhuman qualities and deeds, and in particular how it had happened that Rome grew to greatness after a process which began in weakness and despair. Aeneas himself is more than once ready to abandon hope. But every time he is given some reassurance. And, whatever his faults, for he had many, he would never disregard the voice of Heaven.

The *Aeneid* shows the way things happen in the world. Some of it is strange to us at first sight, but after a little reflection we are likely to agree that everything in it is true to life. We are left to draw our own conclusions, and, if we do, we find important moral facts, not of course preached to us or pressed on us, but emerging from the situations and the results of the action. For example, the *Aeneid* strongly and frequently confirms two important rules of conduct: one principally Greek, 'Avoid excess', and the other principally Roman, 'Be true', that is, loyal to the gods, to the homeland, and to family, friends, and dependants. Virgil regularly calls Aeneas 'Aeneas the True'; and he introduces many examples of thoughtless excess leading to disaster, especially excesses of inordinate affection when someone is carried too far by an exclusive love for some person or thing. When the Trojans, after a storm at sea, came to shore at Carthage in north Africa, Aeneas and Dido the Queen of Carthage fell in love and settled down to live together, forgetting the destiny which required him to go on to Italy. During this part of the story Virgil even stops calling Aeneas 'The True'. Duly, after some months, the divine reproof came and Aeneas obediently sailed away. In fury at this betrayal, Dido cursed him and killed herself. The result of her curse was to be the terrible antagonism between Rome and Carthage which lasted, with intermissions, for a hundred years. Again, at the end of the *Aeneid,* Aeneas, to avenge his friend Pallas, vindictively killed his defeated enemy, Turnus. He let the memory of the friend whom he himself had failed to protect expel every other thought. We are led to wonder whether, if he had not spoilt his victory by this wanton cruelty, the subsequent history of Italy might have been less bloodstained and bitter.

Most great poems are concerned with wickedness, violence, and horror. But often, at least among civilized people, the whole tendency of the same poems is really towards peaceful goodness, humanity, and reconciliation. Virgil's poem pre-eminently has this tendency. Few if any poets have been so tender and sympathetic as Virgil; and for him the ideas of reconciliation and harmony amount almost to an obsession. And for Virgil it is not only by heroic champions in battle that valour is shown, and it is not only on their courage and resolution that a great future may depend.

Aeneas is to win a kingdom in Italy as a Prince of Destiny, and Divine Powers guide and aid him. He is even given by his mother Venus a set of arms and armour made specially for him by Vulcan, the god of fire and metal-working, who had giants, and all the volcanic might of Etna, to serve him. Now Virgil expresses much of his eloquent wisdom in his similes. These are short comparisons of divine and human characters and actions usually with animals or natural forces, but not always. It is worthwhile to give careful notice to all Virgil's similes, and to compare them with each other. When Vulcan leaps up from his bed to make the arms for Aeneas, Virgil provides a simile for him; and he compares his alacrity to the devoted will-power of some poor mother in a cottage who works all night at her weaving in order to keep her home together and bring up her children. It is as if Virgil had said that nothing is greater than the courageous fidelity and resolute will of a humble housewife, not even the determination of elemental powers commanding volcanic might and dominating empires.

That is how Virgil's poetry works. All the time there are hints in it which can easily be overlooked without spoiling the exciting story, but richly repay attention. To see, perhaps suddenly and unexpectedly, one of Virgil's deeper meanings softly emerging is to benefit from an artistic pleasure as keen and intense as any aesthetic experience can be. And a great many of these experiences may be enjoyed simply by reading the story and not overlooking the obvious.

Perhaps one should be content with that. Or perhaps it is not only fairer to Virgil but also advantageous to us, his readers, if we give some attention to his method of composition, and see how he went to work. The *Aeneid* was created with both mighty inspiration and immense labour.

There is a good and clear example of Virgil's way of working in an early scene where Venus prevents Aeneas from killing the beautiful but sinful Helen. When Aeneas is at the very lowest point of his fortunes, with his city, Troy, captured and burning and apparently nothing whatever left to him except such satisfaction as he might find in punishing the woman who had been the cause of it all, Venus suddenly appears and tells him not to be angry, but to think of good things, not bad things, and to be practical.

According to a rather second-rate, Greek, version of the sack of Troy, which Virgil knew, it was not Aeneas who found Helen and wanted to kill her, but Menelaus. Menelaus was a Greek king and Helen's former husband, from whom she had run away. The Greeks had fought the war in order to recapture her for him. But when at last he found her he was so angry that he wanted to kill her. Just in time, Venus appeared to Menelaus and reminded him that Helen would still make him a good wife and that to kill her would only be a foolish waste. So Menelaus spared Helen. The occurrence, as it is in this older version, is interesting in its way and perhaps amusing; it could be called a satisfactory part of a very plain tale. But it has no depth and no exaltation. Menelaus is naturally annoyed, but he has no high tragic passion. It would certainly have been foolish to fight for Helen throughout a ten-year war, and then not take her back after all. Venus appealed to Menelaus' selfish interest. It was her business to do this, as she was the Goddess of Love and had always favoured the beautiful Helen. But there are no high motives anywhere, no suggestive force, and nothing to make us think.

Genius works differently. This time Virgil had little to do, one or two touches perhaps; but enough. He simply substituted Aeneas for Menelaus. The consequences are startling. The whole scene is raised to the level of the sublime. Aeneas has a strong and not wholly selfish reason for killing Helen. The drama is intense. Venus is his own mother, not merely an irresponsible love-goddess. Her advice to him has a moral depth and a certain universality which are almost Christian. She tells Aeneas not to blame any human culprit, since Troy has fallen through the gods' inclemency; and here Virgil found in old poetry the phrase 'not Helen but Paris is to blame' and simply changed 'but' to 'or', saying 'not Paris or Helen . . .', thus delicately registering his protest against all hate and all revenge. By such subtle means Virgil contrived to charge his story and especially the critical moments in it with a depth of meaning new to poetry and nearer to ultimate truth than any poet had contrived before.

Virgil always worked like this. The whole *Aeneid* shows a coherent system interlaced with such mutually dependent brilliancies of insight. The great poets have a way of making what is seen reveal the unseen; and they seem to do this better if they collect an enormous quantity of observations on life, their own and other people's, and then condense it under strong pressure so that even a few words have a great power of suggestion and persuasion. No doubt they are all the time choosing with precise accuracy what is most important. The result is an allusive and partly symbolic kind of language able to communicate not merely single happenings but the universal truth behind them.

These greater poets also reach back across past time, and represent a view of the world which belongs not to one man or one generation of men but to the men of many succeeding generations or even a whole civilization. The experience which is distilled may be the experience of many centuries; and it may be condensed and focused by a single genius in a single poetic statement. That is what Virgil did to the experience of the Greeks and Romans in the *Aeneid.*

To do this, he needed to read and remember a very great number of books, and let his own phrases, and therefore the form of his own thought, grow out of them. That is how he worked. And it enabled him to keep in touch with many people, present and past, and especially the past poets, and to be friends with them all the time as he wrote. So well did Virgil succeed that he could almost be said to have written about many different things at once. It would be truer to say that he lived in an ideal world of poetry and found his way through it to new heights without ever losing contact with the poetry which had been there before. This poetic thought-world, compiled from countless previous poetic thoughts, Virgil reorganized and co-ordinated anew. That is how he created an allusive, partly symbolic language which could fitly communicate what he had to say about the real world behind appearances.

Virgil was sensitive and sympathetic to all points of view and all kinds of people, even wicked ones. He was not content to give only one side of a question. Indeed, he often needed to express the truth about people or things when the truth itself looked paradoxical or even illogical, and when probably no one but he could have shown the underlying sense. His allusive method, based on very wide reading, helped him to tell the whole truth, that is, 'the truth of art', not 'the trivial truth of fact'. He certainly had a rare gift for hitting off something vividly in a few words, and giving a rich and true impression. But in general he did not mean to be photographic. He was like a portrait painter who can make his picture a far more lifelike resemblance by a few inspired brush-strokes, not closely corresponding to anything which ordinary people see in the face to be painted, than ever he could by copying each individual wrinkle. The comparison can be continued. Virgil was like a portrait-painter who, in order to understand his sitter perfectly, looks at him as he is now, and also tries to see him as he was at all the earlier stages of his life with the help of portraits of him already painted by other artists at different times.

Virgil used his books as the painter might use the earlier portraits. He collected as much material as possible but never copied anything exactly and always tried to have more than one influence working at the same time. Homer was one of his main guides; and in the opening lines of the *Aeneid* he used suggestions from the beginnings of both Homer's poems. Reminiscences of Homer can be noticed all through the *Aeneid*; and Homer's works are only two among an immense number which helped to make it. Situations, and even characters, are composed in this way. For example, in Aeneas himself there are echoes not only of the rather different Aeneas who plays a small part in Homer, but also of Homer's Achilles, his Ulysses (or Odysseus), and his Hector, and, in addition to all these, of Hercules, no doubt drawn from various other books, and probably many more characters, besides the real and living Emperor Augustus, who, like other historical characters, 'shimmers through' the story. 'It was ever Virgil's way to merge the actual in the ideal and so to make its reality shine more brightly.' Even Virgil's philosophical ideas are drawn in part from different earlier writers. Lucretius was a very strong influence. Virgil knew his work well and made free use of many hundreds of his phrases in the *Aeneid*, and let them suggest ideas. But since he violently disagreed with the materialistic philosophy of Lucretius, he could not adopt his thought. Indeed, he apparently delighted in turning it upside down, and expressing something far more like the idealistic philosophy of Plato even when the phrases of Lucretius were influencing him.

When in the middle of the *Aeneid* Aeneas is allowed, like Dante in the *Divine Comedy*, to visit the Spiritual World beyond death, he has to find, pick, and take with him as his passport a 'golden bough'. Certainly, a great number of facts contributed to suggest the idea of this 'bough' to Virgil, but there is little doubt which was the most important. It was a passage in a Greek poem about the different Greek writers, composed not long before Virgil's time, in which the work of Plato is called a 'golden bough, sparkling all round with every virtue'. Virgil characteristically chose this way of saying that moral goodness is necessary for the spiritual discernment which is in its turn necessary for wise and progressive statesmanship.

Virgil worked with care and deliberation. Sometimes he produced an average of only one line a day. He spent about eleven years writing the *Aeneid*, and that was a very short time for so difficult a task, so elaborately conceived, and subject to so many conflicting requirements. He intended, if he had lived, to spend three years revising it. So the poem is imperfect; but what exactly he meant to do to it is not known. There are little misfits and incongruities in the *Aeneid* as we have it, but so there probably are in all long literary works, especially the greatest. The same remark or action may be attributed in one passage to one character and in another to someone else; and sometimes it is hard to see how a period of time, or a distance, squares with what Virgil has said in some other part of the poem. None of these little oversights matter. Possibly Virgil would have corrected at least some of them if he had lived.

There are also things in the poem which, though they may seem odd to us, are nevertheless a necessary part of Virgil's art, and will not even seem strange to us if we remember what sort of art Virgil's was. They may be there simply because Virgil was not content to be photographic, but preferred to tell more of the truth than he could tell by confining himself to plain fact. For example, the Trojans travel in a few quite small ships, but they seem to have with them everything that they need, including elaborate clothing and jewellery for presents to their various hosts, and even sometimes bulls and sheep for sacrifices to their various gods. The reason, put shortly, is that the imagery and symbolic suggestion are on these occasions more important than the ordinary restrictions of possibility; it matters that we should be impressed with the former wealth and power of the Trojans and the nobility and piety which they still had, but it does not matter whether we are convinced that the whole story really happened, which anyhow no one is likely to believe.

Then there is the warfare. Some of the battles seem to belong to no single place or time, but to involve different and incompatible fighting methods and weapons. This is quite in accordance with Virgil's principles of art, and his habitual way of writing of several things, or different stages in the evolution of one thing, at the same time. He could have made all his battles old-fashioned like Homer's battles, or contemporary, like Julius Caesar's. But he preferred to do more than that. It was his way of showing what all war is like, not only one particular battle, which may not be a good example of what usually happens in war.

There are also exaggerations. They are characteristic of epic poems but may surprise readers new to the epic manner. Exaggerations are quite in place in the fairyland of epic. Nor are they childish, but a serious and important symbolic means, used by gifted poets of many places and times, for expressing deep and true meanings. On the whole, Virgil, and Homer still more, were very moderate with their exaggerations. Even Virgil's Turnus, who has a helmet which discharges flames of fire, automatically hotter as the battle grows fiercer, and whose face actually emits sparks when he is in a hurry to fight, is not too fantastic. The flames and sparks are part of the recurring imagery used to express the nature of Turnus. He was a very attractive hero, young, noble, handsome, generous, valiant, and unfortunate, and certainly more attractive than his conqueror, Aeneas. But he had one fault: he was too fiery. And the fire of Turnus was not creative. This Virgil indicates in two similes, one for Turnus and one for Aeneas, and each about water in a bowl or cauldron. For Turnus, the water boils over and sends up steam and smoke. For Aeneas, rays of light are reflected from the surface, and presently, as the water ceases to sway, they become steady. Aeneas, with all his faults, can see the light in the end, but for Turnus the end is darkness. If Virgil had written his psychological analysis of Aeneas and Turnus in a scientific book, the length of it would have been frightening. As it is, a wealth of truth emerges from a few deft images here and there.

Virgil's art was not confined to images, symbolic allusion, and good story-telling. It included many kinds of symmetry and pattern, all subject to the great law of variety. The sun very frequently rises and sets in the *Aeneid*. The various descriptions, though similar, are never exactly the same; and apparently the expression chosen has to symbolize the events and situations which are to follow in the coming day or night. The words themselves throughout the poem are chosen and fitted according to many subtle principles. Their vowels, consonants, and rhythms had to be right in relation not only to the other words in the same line but to the words in other lines in the same passage. Words are chosen because they begin with the right letter, end with the right sound, and otherwise fit the designed patterns of both music and meaning. Lines near together are in elaborate relations of echo and contrast with one another, and a line in one place may significantly echo a line far away in the poem. There are several kinds of rhythm, some governed by long and short syllables, some by stress-accents, and some by vowel sounds; and the rhythms not only form their own and other patterns through interaction together, but also help the meanings. People who know not a word of Latin can enjoy the music of Virgil.

DOUGLAS J. STEWART

SOURCE: Douglas J. Stewart, "Morality, Mortality, and the Public Life: Aeneas the Politician," in *The Antioch Review*, Vol. 32, No. 4, Fall/Winter, 1973, pp. 649-64.

[*In the following essay, Stewart emphasizes the political didacticism of the* Aeneid, *claiming the "essential subject" of the poem "is the 'education' of a political leader."*]

In his 1961 lectures from the Oxford Chair of Poetry Robert Graves labeled Virgil the "anti-poet"—in *Gravespeak*, roughly, the Anti-Christ—and denounced him for "pliability ... subservience ... narrowness; his denial of the stubborn imaginative freedom that the true poets who preceded him had valued; his lack of originality, courage, humour, or even animal spirits...." Graves' performance, long awaited as the most spectacular clash of humors in a generation, was really rather tame, if not conventional. Most students of Virgil had heard that litany before, based as it is on the almost cliché image of the poet in the modern era, a shaggy rebel touchy to the point of oaths or tears at society's supposed attempts either to curb or ignore his personal feelings. How very different Virgil's role as a court poet, living on state funds and writing, on commission from Caesar Augustus, an epic poem that was not about the feelings of anybody in particular, but the destiny of a supra-national empire. The case against Virgil is just too simple: a toady, a propagandist, a man afraid of conflict and direct statement.

That of course is the trouble: the case is *too* easy, simply because a 15-year-old could make it. After reading Graves once, I found myself wondering what Virgil might have to say, if *he* were elected Oxford Professor of Poetry, about our modern poets (and critics). One thing I am sure he would stress is the deplorable political naivete of poets who seldom seem to know the first thing about politics, and rarely have exercised their "stubborn imaginative freedom" to explore the inner nature of *institutions* and the complex fate of men who are called upon to manage them.

There is nothing wrong with the literature of personal experience and the feelings; that indeed is what most literature has always concerned itself with. And it is difficult for a writer to come to grips imaginatively with the political element in life. Finally, institutions may well be both corrupt and corrupting. But none of these considerations proves *a priori* that literature cannot tackle a political subject, or that it cannot be successful, which is to say convincing to the reader, in doing so. And the task Virgil set for himself in the *Aeneid* was to write literature about institutions and the political vocation. He did not try to write imitation Homeric epic, or second-rate Apollonian romance, or philosophical cryptograms based on Stoic matter in Lucretian forms. Whatever Augustus was expecting from Virgil, one thing he certainly did *not* get was a patriotic hymn of praise for Rome, nor indeed is Rome the specific subject of the poem. Much less did he get simple propaganda favoring his own regime. The essential subject of the *Aeneid* is the "education" of a political leader.

As we shall see presently in greater detail, the most persuasive boast Roman culture could make was that it had objectified and codified the conditions of creating political leadership, which gave it title to rule the world. That being the claim, Virgil determined to produce in full detail a dry-eyed study of how that process occurs, using the persona of Rome's legendary founder, the Trojan hero Aeneas. Virgil's first insight was relatively simple, if hard for emotional people to absorb: that a politician, normally, is neither a gangstar nor a hero, but a frequently puzzled player of a fiendishly complicated game most of the rules of which change by the hour. A typical politician may find this fascinating or heartening, but to others a politician at work must seem a dull fellow, because most of his "adventures" are infinitesimal mental acts of deduction, appraisal and equivocation, seldom even verbalized, or not candidly so. The knowing or threatening look, the muffled conversation, the equivocal speech are perhaps the politician's most typical outward expressions of his feelings and functions, hardly comparable to the sweeping gestures of lofty oratory of an epic hero. In Homer, especially in the *Iliad*, heroism is for the human characters; politics is for the gods. Though the heroes have technical political roles as chiefs and kings, they seldom remember to fulfill them—except perhaps Agamemnon, who fills his incompetently, as Thersites reminds everyone. Making a politician out of Aeneas, who began his "career" as a Homeric hero, required the displacement, if not the disappearance, of Aeneas' epic personality, because a politician has very little time for a private set of feelings. To state this perspective would not of course make Robert Graves any happier with Virgil, because Graves like so many others limits the focus of real poetry ("true poets") to the personal realm; but all one can say in reply is that Virgil understood much better than his detractors what kind of poetry he had chosen *not* to write and how and where the *Aeneid* had to differ from the poetry of personal life.

The *Aeneid* is a study of the preternatural strains and anxieties a political vocation brings to mere natural man, and the ultimate surd presented to us when we consider the problem of political leadership: is such a thing possible at all; can one be both a human being and a leader; and will it not turn out that the claims of nature and politics will be mutually contradictory? Poetry of the more usual pattern, with its involvement in the fate and aspirations of the individual, stands at a great distance from politics, whose concern is the fate of groups—and indirectly the fate of individuals who act as their agents—and Virgil understood this better than anyone else. Eventually, it may be, poetry with its "higher" morality must come to judge even politics. But the right word is *eventually*. Not too quickly or too rashly, as is usually the case. And Virgil understood this too.

One source of the impatience even subtle readers experience with Virgil and all Latin literature is a curious system of retreat and apology that threads its way through the works of most Roman writers. They all seem so terribly conscious of having come, collectively, upon Greek literary themes and forms late in the day, *arrivistes* blundering in upon a cultural dialogue that had been going on a long time without them, as though the subjects of discussion, though old in fact, are new to them. They also seem embarrassed and distinctly modest about any contribution they could possibly make to the discussion already well under way. The poet Horace in one poem stakes his claim to immortality on his ability to make the rude Latin language dance in Greek meters, a very modest claim indeed, and probably not even an honest one, but that is all he *dares* to say, because no one would believe anything more. Lucretius grumbles about the *egestas*, the poverty of Latin for discussions of philosophy, and *claims* to be doing no more than versifying the ideas of Epicurus (though that too is probably false). Sallust apologizes for the absence of respectable Roman historiography by arguing that in Rome men competent in public affairs took part in them rather than wrote about them, unlike Greece where, if anything, the political genius of a writer like Thucydides exceeded the magnitude of the events he had to write about. Even Ovid, though evidently troubled and annoyed by the cautious, imitative tone of his fellow writers, found no better means of asserting his own originality than by farcical imitation of the imitators. The most famous of these apologetic texts—or so it is usually interpreted—is the great prophecy of Anchises in *Aeneid*

VI. In lines 847-853 Anchises (actually his ghost) foretells to Aeneas just which of the civilized arts it will be granted to Rome itself to practice, once Rome takes its ordained place on the world stage, and which must be conceded to subject peoples like the Greeks. The lines appear to acquiesce in a straight trade-off between Greek and Roman skills: let the Greeks (called simply, "the others") seek fame and excellence in the fine arts and the like, provided only that the Romans understand that their own fame will be secured through the exercise of the arts of legislation, politics and at least a modified form of imperial warfare:

> *excudent alii spirantia mollius aera*
> *(credo equidem), vivos ducent de marmore vultus*
> *orabunt causas melius, caelique meatus*
> *describent radio et surgentia sidera dicent:*
> *tu regere imperio populos, Romane, memento*
> *(hae tibi erunt artes), pacique imponere morem*
> *parcere subiectis et debellare superbos.*
> [847-853]

(Others, I dare say, will hammer out breathing bronzes more subtly, and draw living faces out of the marble; they will speak more eloquently, map the course of the heavens with instruments and predict the comings and goings of the stars. But you, a Roman, remember how to rule nations. These will be *your* arts: to enforce the habit of peace, to spare the conquered, but war down the proud.)

It is remarkable how much Virgil gives away here. I call attention to the phrases "breathing bronzes" (*spirantia aera*) and "living faces out of marble" (*vivos . . . de marmore vultus*). With more than a touch of the true artist's sadness he is admitting that by the turn of the fates the Greeks have been selectively and abundantly blessed with the ability to create an approximation of life from that which is naturally non-living (*spirantia* and *vivos* are key words here and much stronger than Virgil's usual metaphors), and that is the program and aspiration of all art, one may say.

This passage, as noted, is part of a pattern that frequently earns all of Latin literature the scorn of critics and scholars as a second-rate and "derivative" historical phenomenon. But this passage in particular has had a more specific, unbalancing effect on Virgil's individual reputation, because it has been used to call into question his respect for his own art, or even his attentiveness to what he was doing. Supposing it agreed that a Horace or a Sallust were but second-raters—at least they worked earnestly and believingly to the best of their ability. These lines have sometimes been taken to mean that Virgil had no stomach for his project, and it has even been thought that they amount to a moody, half-conscious resignation of the spirit from the whole enterprise. This interpretation is especially tempting to over-eager critics who read more than is there into the first half of the "bargain" conceding pre-eminence in the arts to the Greeks, and have seen much less than is there in the second half claiming political pre-eminence for the Romans. This in turn is intimately linked with the essential issue of what kind of poetry Virgil thought he was trying to write.

First of all, one may note that in the catalogue of Greek superiorities Virgil omits mention of poetry, his own medium. Yet poetry was obviously the supreme accomplishment of the Greeks. This omission can be given several explanations, all of them correct in their way. First, Virgil did not need to praise Greek poetry, since he was in the very act of imitating it, the highest form of praise. Second, and more important, no matter how humble one may feel, it would not do in the middle of a *Latin* poem to say too explicitly that the Greeks win all the prizes for poetry, too. It would simply jar the poetic frame too crudely, and the poem one was writing would perish in the saying of it. And third, though Virgil was in some ways a shy and self-critical man, I doubt he really failed to understand his own gifts. And surely he hoped by means of his own poem to render the case between Greek and Latin poetry not so entirely one-sided as it was before his coming.

But there is yet another way to explain this omission, and it brings us back to the opening question: what sort of poetry can one write about material that is, in the judgment of most people, so unpoetic so as to seem positively anti-poetic? And how is it to be made credible, given this very suspicion? Virgil's complex answer to this puzzle grows out of this passage. The first step is to admit that *by and large*, poetry and politics *are* antithetical and then to write poetry that portrays just why this is generally true.

Virgil says in the prophecy of Anchises that the Roman genius best expresses itself in the arts of politics. He also states, in effect, that politics is essentially alien to the whole realm of the arts. He omits any mention of poetry here because he realizes that he has undertaken an almost impossible task in the ***Aeneid***, to celebrate and justify a political quest and a political event, and to do it within the rules of art itself, not those of politics. Having accepted responsibility for this hybrid enterprise, Virgil—if not the world's greatest poet then surely its most *tactful* poet—immediately understood that to intrude the quarrel between poetry and politics just here would be to spoil the effect and reduce the results to a conundrum about his own personal position on politics and the Augustan settlement. As we have seen, Virgil did not escape posterity's inquisition on this subject, though the questions have normally been posed with un-Virgilian crudity: Was Virgil sincere? Was he hostile to his political assignment? And so on. So put, they are simply beneath intellectual consideration because Virgil himself obviously understood them, found the means to escape the false dilemma they posed, and passed on to his real work. The real question for us is: How did Virgil so manage his efforts that he could speak truth about his theme, politics, without foisting on it the often irrelevant petulancies of the artist, and without at the same time letting the expediencies of the politician (Augustus, or the whole herd collectively) make him descend indecently to propaganda. It was at once a terrifying exercise in restraint and an extravagantly ambitious program.

In practical terms this program meant that Aeneas, who begins as just one more epic "hero," must be conducted by the poet through a series of brain washings until he has developed into something totally different, a political leader, who is no hero at all. This, however, will entail a progressive estrangement of the poet from the hero, a loss of contact between the increasingly political figure of Aeneas and the mechanisms easily available to a poet for assessing character and penetrating the psyche.

Politics is very difficult for literature to portray, for except at extreme moments of either heroism or tyranny it displays very little of the sharp features of individual personality, which are what literature wants to find in life. Politics usually takes a little from the personalities of many people, and not much from the personality of any one man. On the other hand, it gives very little scope *to* the personality of any one man, or offers little room for the development of the individual personality. I think Virgil grasped this frustating state of affairs very early on, yet determined grimly to follow its implications to the end. The *Aeneid*, as a result, is perhaps the one really successful, though unappreciated, literary portrait of a politician's life and education.

Politics, sadly, is quite mute at its real center, the heart of the politician, the structure of his loves and cares. Literature, the carrier of fame and thus of historical approbation—at least as all poets believe—has rarely if ever solved the problem of handling quotidian politics with insight and conviction. If we look to Shakespeare we find that to make politics artistically tolerable he was forced to reduce it to mere crime (*Macbeth, Julius Caesar, Richard III*) or to gross quarrels over succession (*Richard II, Hamlet, Lear*)—the *coup d'état* in its various manifestations. These models are negative and suggest that politics can provide literature only with pathological material . . . which is largely true. Literature normally can only deal effectively with the boundary moments *between* regimes, the assassination, the *coup*—or with certain types of tyranny, because tyranny, as Tacitus made clear, treats *all* events as real or potential boundary moments. It is only when politics disguises itself as the individual concern of life-or-death that literature can normally get it in clear focus. Yet Virgil is probably the one clear exception to this rule: he really taught himself to understand politics in its standard operations, and created the epic of a political man—an agent, not a hero.

The typical politician does not spend his time thinking about assassination, *coup d'état* or tyranny. He enjoys most what we call "administration," *i.e.*, the marshalling of usually reluctant forces and factors— men, materials and money—into concerted action to produce a permanent and visible result, a "fixture" of some sort, that will survive on the landscape, both as a permanent addition to society's collection of amenities (or vanities) *and* as a witness to the fact that the politician responsible did not live entirely in vain. (Power comes in as a *means* to this end.) In other words, most politicians do not consciously think of power *per se* but of serviceable memorials to their skill at creation. Here is where the politician gains *his* immortality. Any Roman reading the prophecy of Anchises would instantly have understood that the background assumption of the passage was one of vicarious immortality gained through political achievement.

But fame requires a repository, a reliquary, an *object* in which it resides. Works of art are their own reliquaries and works of thought repose in written documents, books and treatises, verbal continuities speaking for themselves. The most obvious object a politician leaves behind him is the public building, the great monument in stone and steel. This is why politicians have engaged in an ages-long love affair with the construction industry. True, some politicians have believed that constitutional reform in the broad sense, a re-integration of a people's needs with their public law, is as good as, or better than, a building program. But they have not been in the majority, and even they have never entirely scorned the importance of buildings. For example, in the year 1800 one would have to say that the two shrewdest politicians living were Jefferson and Napoleon. Both effected massive changes in the political thought and basic law of their nations—both were thought of as law-givers—yet both men also with their left hands, as it were, were avid builders and possessed an almost professional eye for architectural style and proportion. It is probably only with Bentham that the idea began to grow that institutional re-design is *more important* than buildings, both *pro bono publico* and for the political leader's reputation. (Although, as I shall note shortly, even here Virgil may have anticipated history.)

Virgil, I suggest, having agreed to write an "epic" about a political leader, did the responsible thing: he studied political leaders to see how they really operated. He learned, if he had not known before, much of what I have been discussing: the typical politician is not really on easy terms with the poet; his ideals and aims are elsewhere. Despite the claims of ancient poets that politicians desire their attention because poetry alone confers immortality, in their actions politicians prove that they think otherwise. Politicians may be happy to hire the services of poets—in modern terms, journalists—to celebrate the regime for short-term public-relations purposes, but when the question is true immortality, politicians instinctively vote with the other side: a building or a program beats the poet's faint praise (or the historian's awe) every time. Thus Virgil set himself the chore of writing about a "hero" who would himself have very little use for, or interest in, the services of a poet like Virgil. The *Aeneid* then begins to sound very much like a series of long-distance telephone calls between a distracted central character and an intelligent poet whose fidelity to truth makes him understand why it is increasingly difficult to keep Aeneas on the line.

At the 31st line of the first book of the *Aeneid* Virgil, in his own voice, utters a remarkably quotable and intuitive line, *Tantae molis erat Romanam condere gentem.* "Such struggle would be needed to found the Roman nation." *Tantae molis*, to be sure, does mean "such struggle," and the line is a Stoicized expression of the extreme demands that duty will impose upon Aeneas as, like Hercules, he goes about his largely unpleasant labors. But *molis*, before it acquired the ethical sense of "struggle" had the primary physical meaning of "building stone" or another very large and heavy object solid and immovable enough to serve as the foundation of an enduring public building. And, appearing with the verb *condere*, "to lay down" or "fix" (in the ground), it makes a pretty clear case that the dominant image in Virgil's mind was that of building on a monumental scale.

I dwelt above on the fact that Roman culture contained a large admixture of defensive maneuvers whereby the supremacy of Greek culture was admitted, while spokesmen for Roman culture agree to compete only for secondary honors, those of re-doing Greek achievement in Latin phrases. Virgil, obviously, subscribed to this view, but only to a degree. Quite apart from his own self-respect, he realized that he had a different problem here—in fact one diametrically opposed to that accepted by most Roman writers: he was not trying to domesticate Greek ideas in Roman terms, but to discover the essence of Roman ideas and feelings and naturalize them in the Greek style, *i.e.*, in a verse form, the epic, that was foreign to Roman culture. (The older Roman "epics" of Naevius and Ennius were fabulized "annals" or history, not especially mythic.) I think he understood his own capacity to do just this, while also realizing, perhaps, just what the cost would be in critical incomprehension. Virgil, in contrast to other poets who never seemed to question the fact that they were educated in Greek terms to think like Greeks, deliberately reversed the pattern and successfully internalized true-to-character Roman enthusiasms and then sought to create freely with them in a Greek medium. This he largely succeeded in doing. The dominant ideal in the minds of upper-class Romans was the desire to appear in history as important and creative politically, and the surest token of political creativity is long-lasting public construction, as the careers of the great Roman magnates, from Appius Claudius Pulcher to Augustus himself make clear. As recorded in Suetonius (*Vita Divi Augusti*, 28) Augustus boasted that he found Rome brick and left it marble, and in his own record of his reign (*Res Gestae*, 19-21) Augustus gloats over the long list of buildings begun, finished and repaired in his reign, though he makes no mention of having sponsored the greatest of all Latin poems—as I have noted, when it comes down to cases politicians vote with the contractor and the architect, not with the poet. It just happened that this particular poet, Virgil, shrewdly noted this very fact and proceeded to elaborate his epic upon this basic understanding of the ways of politics.

The poem opens and wastes no time in lodging in the reader's mind the dominant image of construction, the heavier the better, the romance of public buildings, the most essential Roman image that could be set forth. The point is obviously to suggest to the perceptive reader that nearly all of the epic, and hence Greek-style, "adventures" of the story are a throwaway: they are never crucial. And in fact the most important passages in the *Aeneid* are those times when the poem reneges on pursuing an "epic" story to an epic conclusion, such as Aeneas' headlong flight from Dido (with nothing like Odysseus' doubts or complaints about Calypso) or his dropping out of action just when there is the chance to make the great epic speech. Even though the *Aeneid* is modeled, superficially, on both *Iliad* and *Odyssey*, and at a deeper level, follows the *Odyssey* in being the story of a man forced to introspection in order to find out who he is through the agency of his experience, in the last analysis it is not much like any "epic" before or since.

I have said that Aeneas began his heroic "career" in Homer's *Iliad*. I used that odd word "career" for a purpose, to imply that for him heroism was not to be a way of *being*, but simply a profession for a time. And that profession is aborted in *Aeneid* II (606 ff.): in a desultory skirmish with a band of Greek looters on the night Troy is taken, Aeneas is suddenly commanded by his mother Venus to break off the engagement and flee, because he has other *work* to do: "do not fear the commands of your mother, nor refuse to obey my orders" (*tu ne qua parentis / iussa time, neu praeceptis parere recusa*..., words which will never read quite the same to me after *Portnoy's Complaint*). Aeneas obeys instantly. He is no Achilles proclaiming to *his* mother his resolve to follow the heroic code until it kills him. Nor is Venus a Thetis: she simply will not stand by wringing her hands to see her boy killed for no purpose: he is destined to a political career as the founder of a new state, and she is determined that he will have it. The tone suddenly drops in this passage to the practical, if not the bourgeois. Epic assumptions are destroyed and Aeneas is propelled by his mother — playing a Roman matron on the model of the great political matriarchs like Cornelia — into the new world of policy, calculation, and caution. From here on he is searching for a new role to assume, and by the time he reaches Carthage he is already half a politician. At the sight of the rising walls of Carthage he bursts out to Achates: *O fortunati quorum iam moenia surgunt* (I, 437). Walls, structures, are now of primary concern to him because they are the surest tokens of social reality and continuity. Real epic heroes are not interested in buildings but in deeds of the moment. In her speech to Aeneas prevailing on him to abandon Troy, Venus had dwelt on the horror of seeing mightly buildings destroyed (II, 608-612) and implied that this was even worse than the destruction of people. She was teaching him a lesson about the permanence of society as represented by its buildings — buildings as a prerequisite for all civilized life, and even for life itself. And through his subsequent experience Aeneas will be forced to learn at first hand the malaise of an unhoused, non-political existence, to the extent that he quickly becomes an almost fantatical apostle of the civic life and the concrete artifacts upon which it depends.

Aeneas' ejaculation *O fortunati* came as he was gazing on the temple of Juno, his arch-enemy, and on the frescoes adorning its walls which told the story *of the destruction of Troy! Sunt lacrimae rerum* and all that. But none of this matters to him at this moment. Here is the most positive civic achievement known to him, the erection of great public buildings which somehow protect a people while encouraging them to believe in their own survival despite any challenge time may hurl upon them.

But a politician is more than a builder. He is a leader of people (not, as the phrase usually has it, a leader of *men* — readers often forget that Aeneas led a band of men *and women* from Troy). And a leader, except in the simplified terms of *warfare* — another boundary situation — is no hero. He is simply one who organizes other people's energies. He leads (often) by pretending that a given common aim is both realizable and beneficial, though he personally may doubt the first and not even understand the second. Those who have searched the *Aeneid* for a second Achilles and found only the "priest" of Yeats' story, have simply misunderstood the arena in which this "hero" is operating. All those flat, dull speeches of encouragement, all that weariness, that general hangover quality Aeneas both experiences and communicates when he looks out upon the world, are the politician's special burden. He must pretend to enthusiasms he does not feel, repress emotions he does feel, and generally behave not as a free individual but as the incorporation of a society's needs, a trust-officer for other people's future. The heraldic badge of the *Aeneid* is the vignette of Aeneas carrying his lame father and leading his small son away from the ruins of Troy. It sums up precisely the fate and role of Aeneas: go-between, maker or agent of continuity, link between past and future, doubly burdened by both. And finally of course the politician has the misfortune — and the wretchedness — of accepting responsibility for the actions of his subordinates. Aeneas must face the grim results of his son's ill-timed hunting expedition, and of the foolish bravado of Nisus and Euryalus. This is a world totally different from that of Achilles, whose sense of role is so personal as to be infantile: he quarrels with a superior, retires from action, delegates command to an inferior, and then reacts to the inferior's defeat only in terms that reflect his personal feeling of outrage and loss. A real leader, a politician, has no time for the ego-cultivation of an Achilles (Virgil might say); he is just a center around which effective historical action *may* take place. That is, if he's lucky, if he can hang on, hope for the best, and keep his power intact for as long as possible.

For such reasons as these Aeneas the politician is always on the point of escaping from the status of a literary character under his creator's control, into another world where the poet cannot easily follow. Again and again he turns his back on the kinds of action and self-expression that literature can normally take into its forms. His abandonment of Dido is the prime case in point. Virgil, and Aeneas, have been attacked a thousand times because Virgil has Aeneas, after one warning from Mercury, drop Dido with no complaints and no arguments, and certainly with no dramatic expressions of his passion or the loss he is incurring. Thus Aeneas is cold and calculating, a cad, a jellyfish, without backbone or balls — so the indictments run. But they are not to the point. Any politician with a capacity for introspection would instantly understand even this as simply an extreme case of what politics *always* demands from its practitioners, a readiness to deny and ignore the promptings of mere nature when policy, the duty of role-playing, the communal purpose demand it. True, the average politician suffers little more than the loss of regular dinners with his family, but the possibility of greater sacrifice is always there, as the fateful careers of two Kennedys have instructed us. The Dido story is a metaphor for what any politician must be prepared to do: to sacrifice every last personal tie, if necessary, to help keep the political enterprise going, to maintain the quest. Literature has never found this sort of thing very palatable, either because it is devoted to exploring the *private* passions of man, or because it holds an implicit ethics denying the validity, if not the reality, of the abstruse and probably corrupt doings of politics. Literature may be right, and politics wrong, in the final judgment. But insofar as politics exists and there are politicians to observe, Virgil is saying, it is proper to present what politics really is like and how a politician lives, since that is what Aeneas was.

I suggested above that Virgil anticipated the modern conviction that social programs, intangible institutional reforms (*e.g.*, Social Security), are even more significant monuments to a political career than memorials in stone. As evidence, consider the prophecy of Anchises in Book VI, already cited to make a narrower point. What Anchises declares, in effect, is not just how Greek and Roman cultures should compose their differences in a viable scheme that carries on the best of both; he also enunciates a new constitutional principle: *parcere victis et debellare superbos*, "spare the conquered and war down the proud." This, if finally understood, would accomplish the total conversion of Aeneas from a bloodletting epic hero to a wise philosopher-king. For it says that warfare, that plaything of epic heroes, is to be conducted *solely* under the guidance of cold-eyed impersonal policy. To a large extent Aeneas' own character manages to conform itself to this principle even though the following of principle so intently tends to obliterate and bury that character, which is only "rescued" by a horrid paradox at the end. It is noticeable that Aeneas begins to curtail all instinctive, natural reactions and replace them with political calculation, in the better sense. And for this the poet rewards him by switching from the epithet *pius*—which implied, in the first six books, his subjection to paternal and ancestral control, that of both Anchises and Venus—to the epithet *pater*, father, indicating his acceptance of, and title to, full responsibility and political authority in the last six books. Likewise, Aeneas ages significantly in the last six books: we can no longer imagine him appearing as a lover. In the words of Professor Clausen: "We see him, middle-aged and a widower, bound to pursue his reluctant way from Troy to Italy, from a past he has lost to a future he will never possess." The last phrase sums up a politician's vocation about as well as anything can. Aeneas becomes cautious and stiff; he develops a resistance to emotional appeals, whether to fear or vanity. And he becomes caught in the categorical imperative of politics: preservation of the leader's *person* is inextricably involved with the accomplishment of his *purposes*, to an extent that even he can grasp only in rare moments.

The *Aeneid* ends with the murder of Turnus. It *is* a murder precisely because it would have been a piece of behavior perfectly normal for an epic hero on the Homeric model. But it comes long after Aeneas has been taught, and has accepted, the new constitutional principle which subjects war, and all other behavior, to the demands of a rational, and humanitarian politics: *parcere victis*, "spare the conquered." Critics hostile to Virgil seem to blame this atrocity on the poet himself. Yet Aeneas does no more than what Achilles does to Hector, and Hector is admirable while Turnus most certainly is not. Yet a charge must be made: Aeneas is wrong. His act is one of excess. And worse, it is a *personal* act.

Political leaders cannot afford to act on personal grounds. Aeneas is no Achilles; he does not occupy that primitive sphere in the shame culture which countenances a permanent adolescence forever clamoring for attention and given to smashing the furniture if it does not get it. Aeneas is simply subject to different and higher standards, standards to which he with at least partial understanding, has lent himself. It is not even an excuse that he has considerable human grounds for his act. Turnus is a narrow, violent, and rather stupid egomaniac (*he* is an Achilles), and he had savagely killed the most unoffending and ideal human type who appears in the *Aeneid*, Pallas, the saintly son of Evander. The disparity between their characters can hardly be measured. Moreover Virgil supplies an extrairony. Pallas is clearly portrayed as a cadet-leader from the younger generation, possessing all the qualities of incipient leadership that would make him Aeneas' ideal successor. And any half-competent politician spends at least half his time worrying about the problem of capable and acceptable successors. In politics continuity is always *the* problem. It may be that Aeneas saw Pallas, rather than his own son Ascanius, at least for a few hopeful moments, as his own successor, *via* the procedure of adoption. This procedure was common among the great political families of Rome. Augustus was the adopted son of Julius Caesar. The saintly Marcellus was, likewise, the adoptive heir of Augustus, and the untimely and horrid death of Pallas at the hands of Turnus is perhaps a literary parallel with the ultimately and regrettable death of Marcellus. Yet even this does not excuse a political failure, which is what the murder of Turnus is. Aeneas has multiple motives, but a multiplicity of motives does not constitute a reason for political action, not for a politician.

The new constitutional order demands that he restrain himself—even as he had been restrained by Venus from killing Helen in Book II—and that he substitute policy for spontaneous, natural human action.

Aeneas fails the final political test, yet, paradoxically, he reasserts his humanity at the same time. Why? The answer is not that Virgil is an obtuse and disoriented writer. Rather he is a poet who is also a shrewd and reliable witness of the real world. Aeneas is shown in the last six books growing in political consequence and command. Meanwhile his personality deteriorates and fades. His motives are less and less subject to scrutiny as those of a simple human being. Yet in the end he fails as a politician because human nature finally breaks through. But it is too late, and the wrong moment. His world and his vocation have changed, but at the last moment he himself betrays the new system he has instituted. Virgil shows us that the tension between natural man and civic man will probably never be fully resolved. This point is given excruciating prominence in Book VI, near the end of Anchises' prophetic vision of the panorama of Rome's history. Of Brutus, the first consul after the overthrow of the Etruscan kings, Virgil writes:

> *consulis imperium hic primus saevasque securis*
> *accipiet, natosque pater nova bella moventis*
> *ad poenam pulchra pro libertate vocabit,*
> *infelix, utcumque ferent ea facta minores.*
> [819-822]

(He first will receive the power of the consulate and the dread axes, and he, as father, will call his sons, plotting revolution, to due punishment, for the sake of dear liberty—a wretched man—or so lesser men will think who retell these things.)

The phrase "wretched man, or so lesser men will think..." is the exact description of the terrible paradox of the political leader, the sensitivities of natural man meeting the leader's self-imposed duties to his society rather than to his blood and feelings. It is a tragedy, and tragedy quite beyond the matter of individual griefs, that political leadership, though indispensable, so often seems to end up in a situation in which a leader, having systematically educated himself to reject the promptings of mere nature, will either go a step too far and use policy in such an unnatural way that he disgusts other men, even if they appear to benefit from his acts, or else he will suffer a momentary lapse and abandon policy for a natural act at precisely the wrong point. The former was the fate of the first Brutus, who horrified the ancient Romans quite as much as the second Brutus horrified Plutarch and Shakespeare by killing Caesar; the latter is the fate of Aeneas. Virgil has planned the moment carefully: he has brought back personal motivation at the point where it is at one and the same time politically unacceptable, *but artistically necessary and conclusive.*

The politician is yet always a human being, even if the unique pressures of his profession tend to persuade him that this is not true. He cannot always see every problem presented to him as though it were a simple theorem in the geometry of power and of responsibility for the community. Usually his own humanity and weaknesses will at some point invade his behavior and this, though acceptable to art, will be disastrous for politics. It is not always the general dehumanization of politics that makes our collective social life especially dangerous, but sometimes its sudden *re*-humanization at the worst possible moment on an unpredictable schedule. The politician's existential risk is twofold, and probably intolerable for complete mental health: either he will lose his humanity entirely and become a robot or a fanatic, or he will reassert it at precisely the wrong moment, as Aeneas does, only to put everything wrong.

The ambiguity of critics and criticism when facing the *Aeneid* is simply a copy of the ambiguity an observer like Virgil must have felt in studying the careers of successful Roman politicians like Scipio, Sulla, Julius Caesar or Augustus. How can one do justice to a man who is both an individual and the embodiment of the *res publica*? It really can't be done. Virtually no one can stand the strain, ultimately, of both roles. Virgil's alleged and much-discussed demurrer against the Augustan system, if it exists, is not to be found at some superficial level like distrust of imperialism or autocracy. He is hardly interested in such abstractions. His entry into the political problem of Aeneas is effected at a much deeper point: he sees the acceptance of political leadership as a crucial denial of natural human feelings, which in the long run will probably rebel, and the eventuating crisis will destroy the characters of all but the strongest. Leadership is a necessary good—or evil, perhaps—but hardly ever can it provide ethical or personal satisfaction for the chosen vehicle. *Fata dederunt:* Aeneas often silences grumblers with such a phrase, but it only quiets lesser folk. For him all it means is that he personally has no escape and no prospect of contentment. What the fates have really granted is his own unwilled yoking to an enterprise that systematically overrules the feelings, or else guarantees that expression of natural life and feeling will bring him only gigantic troubles and endanger his civic aims. This honest and sympathetic account of the politician's dilemma in no sense makes the *Aeneid* an artistic failure. Far from it: it makes the poem a perfect portrayal of one of mankind's most serious and besetting problems, which no other literary work I know has expressed so convincingly.

SOURCES FOR FURTHER STUDY

Bloom, Harold, ed. *Modern Critical Views: Virgil*. New York: Chelsea House Publishers, 1986, 223 p.

> Collection of essays by such noted classical scholars as J. William Hunt, K. W. Gransden, Michael C. J. Putnam and others.

Camps, W. A. *An Introduction to Virgil's "Aeneid"*. London: Oxford University Press, 1969, 164 p.

> General study of the *Aeneid* containing discussion of the epic's characters, structure, style, and sources.

Commager, Steele, ed. *Virgil: A Collection of Critical Essays*. Englewood Cliffs, N.J.: Prentice-Hall, 1966, 186 p.

> Contains essays on the *Aeneid* by C. M. Bowra, C. S. Lewis, Brooks Otis, Adam Parry, Bernard Knox, and Viktor Pöschl.

Dudley, D. R., ed. *Virgil*. New York: Basic Books, 1969, 219 p.

> Contains essays on Vergil that address his originality, his influence on subsequent poets and artists, the fluctuations in his critical reception, and his depiction of the afterlife. Selection includes pieces by Brooks Otis, W. F. Jackson Knight, and R. D. Williams.

Gransden, K. W. *Virgil's "Iliad": An Essay on Epic Narrative*. Cambridge, England: Cambridge University Press, 1984, 219 p.

> Analyzes the structural significance of the last six books of the *Aeneid*, examining Vergil's adaptation of the *Iliad*. Gransden's approach is influenced by his study of narrative theory.

Williams, R. D. "The *Aeneid*." In his *Virgil*, pp. 23-44. Oxford at the Clarendon Press, 1967.

> Studies the conflicts between national destiny and individual tragedy, Stoicism and Epicureanism, Homeric and Roman values, and supernatural and mortal realms in the *Aeneid*, reviewing the history of critical responses to these tensions.

Alice Walker

1944-

American novelist, short story writer, essayist, poet, critic, editor, and author of children's books.

INTRODUCTION

The author of the Pulitzer Prize-winning novel *The Color Purple* (1982), Walker writes about the black woman's struggle for spiritual wholeness and sexual, political, and racial equality. Although most critics categorize her writings as feminist, Walker rebuffs the label, describing her work and herself as "womanist." She defines this term as "a woman who loves other women. . . . Appreciates and prefers woman's culture, woman's emotional flexibility . . . and woman's strength. . . . *Loves* the spirit. . . . Loves herself. *Regardless*." For this reason, some critics have faulted Walker's fiction for its unflattering portraits of black men. However, most applaud her lyrical prose, her sensitive characterizations, and her gift for rendering beauty, grace, and dignity in ordinary people and places.

Biographical Information

Walker was born in Eatonton, Georgia, a rural town where most blacks worked as tenant farmers. At age eight, when an older brother accidentally shot her with a BB gun, she was blinded in her right eye because her parents lacked transportation to seek immediate medical attention. Consequently, Walker spent most of her childhood withdrawn from others, writing poetry to ease her loneliness. In 1961 Walker won a scholarship to Spelman College, where she became involved in the civil rights movement and participated in sit-ins at local business establishments. In 1963, she transferred to Sarah Lawrence College, graduating in 1965. After her marriage in 1967 to Melvyn Leventhal, a Jewish civil rights attorney, Walker's published *Once* (1968), which includes poetry written while she attended college. The newlyweds spent the summer conducting activist work in Jackson, Mississippi, becoming the first legally married interracial couple to reside there. In

1970 Walker published her first novel, *The Third Life of Grange Copeland*. By the time the couple divorced in 1976, Walker had published two poetry collections, a short story collection, and the novel *Meridian* (1976), generally regarded as one of the best novels about the civil rights movement. In 1982, *The Color Purple* made Walker an overnight literary celebrity. Since then, Walker focused on her writing, while teaching at various colleges and universities.

Major Works

The Third Life of Grange Copeland introduces many of Walker's themes, particularly the domination of powerless women by equally powerless men. The novel chronicles three generations of a black sharecropping family, exploring the effects of racism and poverty in their lives. Because of his sense of failure, Grange Copeland drives his wife to suicide and abandons his children to seek a better life in the North. His legacy of hate and violence passes on to his son, who eventually murders his wife. When Grange returns to his family, the broken yet compassionate man attempts to atone for his past with the help of his granddaughter. In *Meridian* the title character, a college-educated woman committed to helping Southern blacks gain political and social equality, joins a black militant organization. Unable to reconcile her values to the group's violent actions, she leaves it but remains devoted to her legendary activist work. *The Color Purple*, written as a series of letters, traces the physical and emotional abuse endured by Celie, a poor Southern black woman, at the hands of both her stepfather, who repeatedly raped her as a teen and sold the two children she bore him, and her husband, who beat and psychologically tormented her. The letters Celie writes describe her ordeal to God and to her sister Nettie, who escaped a similar fate by serving as a missionary in Africa. Celie eventually finds solace through an intimate friendship with Shug Avery, a charismatic blues singer who gives her the courage to leave her marriage so that she can reunite with her children and sister. *The Temple of My Familiar* (1989) records 500,000 years of human history as witnessed by Miss Lissie, a goddess from primeval Africa who has been incarnated innumerable times throughout history. Through a series of conversations Miss Lissie relates her experiences—from the prehistoric world where humans and animals lived harmoniously in a matriarchal society to slavery in the United States. *Possessing the Secret of Joy* (1992) concerns Toshi, an African woman who struggles to overcome the physical and psychological consequences of her ritual genital mutilation as an adolescent, a common practice in African and Eastern cultures. Other notable works include the poetry collection *Good Night, Willie Lee, I'll See You in the Morning* (1979), which celebrates familial bonds and friendships; the short story collection *You Can't Keep a Good Woman Down* (1981), which highlights Walker's womanist philosophy; and the essay collection *In Search of Our Mothers' Gardens* (1984), which addresses such themes as the environment, animal rights, and nuclear war.

Critical Reception

One of the most prolific black women writers in America, Walker consistently has explored racial, sexual, and political issues, particularly as they relate to the lives of African-American women. Though her works have been faulted for reviving stereotypes of the dysfunctional black family, the negative portrayal of black men, and an "unabashedly feminist viewpoint," they also are admired for accurately rendered black folk idiom, intensely descriptive language, and believable characters. Walker explained: "The black woman is one of America's greatest heroes. . . . Not enough credit has been given to the black woman who has been oppressed beyond recognition." Walker's insistence on giving black women their due resulted in *The Color Purple*, "an American novel of permanent importance, [a] rare sort of book," according to Peter S. Prescott. "Perhaps even more than Walker's other works," announced Barbara T. Christian, "[*The Color Purple*] especially affirms that the most abused of the abused can transform herself. It completes the cycle Walker announced a decade ago: the survival and liberation of black women through the strength and wisdom of others."

(For further information, see *Authors and Artists for Young Adults*, Vol. 3; *Bestsellers*: 89:4; *Black Literature Criticism*; *Black Writers*, Vol. 2; *Concise Dictionary of American Literary Biography*: 1968-1988; *Contemporary Authors*, Vols. 37-40R; *Contemporary Authors New Revision Series*, Vols. 9, 27, 49; *Contemporary Literary Criticism*, Vols. 5, 6, 9, 19, 27, 46, 58; *Dictionary of Literary Biography*, Vols. 6, 33, 143; *DISCovering Authors*; *DISCovering Authors: British*; *DISCovering Authors: Canadian*; *DISCovering Authors Modules: Most-studied Authors Module, Multicultural Authors Module, Novelists Module, Poets Module, Popular Fiction and Genre Authors Module*; *Major Twentieth-Century Writers*; *Short Story Criticism*, Vol. 5; *Something about the Author*, Vol. 31.)

CRITICAL COMMENTARY

MARY HELEN WASHINGTON

SOURCE: Mary Helen Washington, "An Essay on Alice Walker," in *Sturdy Black Bridges: Visions of Black Women in Literature,* Roseann P. Bell, Bettye J. Parker, and Beverly Guy-Sheftall, eds., Anchor Press, 1979, pp. 133-49.

[*In the following excerpt, Washington examines the depiction of women in Walker's work.*]

From whatever vantage point one investigates the work of Alice Walker—poet, novelist, short story writer, critic, essayist, and apologist for black women—it is clear that the special identifying mark of her writing is her concern for the lives of black women.... [There] are more than twenty-five characters from the slave woman to a revolutionary woman of the sixties [about whom she has written]. Within each of these roles Walker has examined the external realities facing these women as well as the internal world of each woman.

We might begin to understand Alice Walker, the apologist and spokeswoman for black women, by understanding the motivation for Walker's preoccupation with her subject. Obviously there is simply a personal identification.... Moreover her sense of personal identification with black women includes a sense of sharing in their peculiar oppression....

Walker understands that what W. E. B. Du Bois called double consciousness ... creates its own particular kind of disfigurement in the lives of black women, and that, far more than the external facts and figures of oppression, the true terror is within; the mutilation of the spirit *and* the body. Though Walker does not neglect to deal with the external *realities* of poverty, exploitation, and discrimination, her stories, novels, and poems most often focus on the intimate reaches of the inner lives of her characters; the landscape of her stories is the spiritual realm where the soul yearns for what it does not have....

The true empathy Alice Walker has for the oppressed woman comes through in all her writings.... Raising an ax, crying out in childbirth or abortion, surrendering to a man who is oblivious to her real name—these are the kinds of images which most often appear in Ms. Walker's own writing....

What particularly distinguishes Alice Walker in her role as apologist and chronicler for black women is her evolutionary treatment of black women; that is, she sees the experiences of black women as a series of movements from women totally victimized by society and by the men in their lives to the growing developing women whose consciousness allows them to have control over their lives....

Walker's personal construct of the black woman's history [is] the woman suspended, artist thwarted and hindered in her desires to create, living through two centuries when her main role was to be a cheap source of cheap labor in the American society....

Most of Walker's women characters belong to the first part of the cycle—the suspended woman.... [These] are women who are cruelly exploited, spirits and bodies mutilated, relegated to the most narrow and confining lives, sometimes driven to madness....

In **"The Child Who Favored Daughter,"** the father presides over the destruction of three women in his family: his own wife, whom he drives to suicide after beating and crippling her; his sister, named Daughter, whose suicide is the result of the punishment her family exacts after she has an affair with a white man; and his own daughter, whom he mutilates because she will not renounce her white lover. To understand the violence of this man toward these three women in his family, author Walker makes us know that it is the result of an immense chaos within—the components of which are his impotent rage against the white world which abuses him, his vulnerable love for his child and his sister, both of whom chose white lovers. He is so threatened by that inner chaos that the very act of violence is a form of control, a way of imposing order on his own world. By killing his daughter, he has at once shut out the image of Daughter which haunts him, he has murdered his own incest, and he has eliminated the last woman who has the power to hurt him....

Walker [has] explored the tragedies in the lives of Black women—the tragedy of poverty, abuse from men who are themselves abused, the physical deterioration—but there is greater depth in Walker's exploration because not only does she comprehend the past lives of these women but she has also questioned their fates and dared to see through to a time when black women would no longer live in suspension, when there would be a place for them to move into.

Principal Works

Once: Poems (poetry) 1968
The Third Life of Grange Copeland (novel) 1970
Revolutionary Petunias and Other Poems (poetry) 1971
Five Poems (poetry) 1972
In Love and Trouble: Stories of Black Women (short stories) 1973
Langston Hughes: American Poet (juvenile nonfiction) 1974
Meridian (novel) 1976
Good Night, Willie Lee, I'll See You in the Morning (poetry) 1979
"Porn at Home" (essay) 1980; published in periodical *Ms.*
You Can't Keep a Good Woman Down (short stories) 1981
The Color Purple (novel) 1982
Horses Make a Landscape Look More Beautiful: Poems (poetry) 1984
In Search of Our Mothers' Gardens: Womanist Prose (essays) 1984
Alice Walker Boxed Set—Fiction: The Third Life of Grange Copeland, You Can't Keep a Good Woman Down, and In Love and Trouble (novel and short stories) 1985
Alice Walker Boxed Set—Poetry: Good Night, Willie Lee, I'll See You in the Morning; Revolutionary Petunias and Other Poems; Once: Poems (poetry) 1985
"Cuddling" (short story) 1985; published in periodical *Essence*
"Kindred Spirits" (short story) 1985; published in periodical *Esquire*
"Olive Oil" (short story) 1985; published in periodical *Ms.*
"Not Only Will Your Teachers Appear, They Will Cook New Foods for You" (essay) 1986; published in periodical *Mendocino Country*
Living by the Word: Selected Writings, 1973-1987 (essays) 1988
The Temple of My Familiar (novel) 1989
Her Blue Body Everything We Know (poetry) 1991
Possessing the Secret of Joy (novel) 1992

Adaptations

The Color Purple was adapted as a film starring Whoopi Goldberg, Oprah Winfrey, and Danny Glover, directed by Steven Spielberg, 1985.

In the second cycle of Walker's personal construct of the history of black women are the women who belong to the decades of the forties and fifties, those decades when black people (then "Negroes") wanted most to be part of the mainstream of American life even though assimilation required total denial of one's ethnicity....

The women in this cycle are also victims, not of physical violence, but of a kind of psychic violence that alienates them from their roots, cutting them off from real contact.

The woman named Molly from Walker's poem **"For My Sister Molly Who in the Fifties"** is the eldest sister in a poor rural family in Eatonton; she is, in fact, Alice Walker's sister and Walker is the child narrator of the poem mourning the loss of her talented and devoted "Molly." When Molly first comes home on vacation from college, she is very close to her brothers and sisters, teaching them what she has learned, reading to them about faraway places like Africa. The young narrator is enraptured by Molly, spellbound by the bright colorful sister who changes her drab life into beauty.... But being a child, the narrator does not realize or suspect the growing signs of Molly's remoteness. Molly goes off to the university, travels abroad, becoming distant and cold and frowning upon the lives of the simple folks she comes from.... From her superior position [Molly] can only see the negatives—the silent, fearful, barefoot, tongue-tied, ignorant brothers and sisters. She finds the past, her backward family, unbearable, and though she may have sensed their groping after life, she finally leaves the family for good....

The women of the second cycle are destroyed spiritually rather than physically, and yet there is still some movement forward, some hope that did not exist for the earlier generation of American black women. The women in this cycle are more aware of their condition and they have greater potential for shaping their lives, although they are still thwarted because they feel themselves coming to life before the necessary changes have been made in the political environment—before there is space for them to move into. The sense of "twoness" that Du Bois spoke of in *The Souls of Black Folk* is perhaps most evident in the lives of these women; they are the most aware of and burdened by the "double consciousness" that makes one measure one's soul by the tape of the other world....

The women of the third cycle are, for the most part, women of the late sixties, although there are some older women in Walker's fiction who exhibit the qualities of the developing, emergent model. Greatly influenced by the political events of the sixties and the changes resulting from the freedom movement, they are women coming just to the edge of a new awareness and making the first tentative steps into an uncharted region. And although they are more fully conscious of their political and psychological oppression and more capable of creating new options for themselves, they must undergo a harsh initiation before they are ready to occupy and claim any new territory....

Besides political activism, a fundamental activity the women in the third cycle engage in is the search for meaning in their roots and traditions. As they struggle to reclaim their past and to re-examine their relationship to the black community, there is a consequent reconciliation between themselves and black men.

In Sarah Davis, the main character of Walker's short story, **"A Sudden Trip Home in the Spring,"** we have another witness to the end of the old cycles of confusion and despair. Her search begins when she returns home to the South from a northern white college to bury her father. She is an artist, but because of her alienation from her father, whom she blames for her mother's death, she is unable to paint the faces of black men, seeing in them only defeat.... Through a series of events surrounding her father's funeral, Sarah rediscovers the courage and grace of her grandfather and reestablishes the vital link between her and her brother. Her resolve at the end of the story to do a sculpture of her grandfather... signifies the return to her roots and her own personal sense of liberation. This story, more than any other, indicates the contrast between the women of the second cycle who were determined to escape their roots in order to make it in a white world and the emergent women of the third cycle who demonstrate a sense of freedom by the drive to reestablish those vital links to their past....

ROBERT TOWERS

SOURCE: Robert Towers, "Good Men Are Hard to Find," in *The New York Review of Books*, Vol. XXIX, No. 13, August 12, 1982, pp. 35-6.

[*In the following excerpt, Towers praises Walker's use of black dialect in* The Color Purple, *but points out certain "inadequacies" in the work.*]

There is nothing cool or throwaway in Alice Walker's attitude toward the materials of her fiction. The first book by this exceptionally productive novelist, poet, and short-story writer to come to my notice was *Meridian* (1976), an impassioned account of the spiritual progress of a young black woman, Meridian Hill, during the civil-rights struggle of the 1960s and its aftermath.... Though beset by serious structural problems and other lapses of craft, **Meridian** remains the most impressive fictional treatment of the "Movement" that I have yet read.

In *The Color Purple* Alice Walker moves backward in time, setting her story roughly (the chronology is kept vague) between 1916 and 1942—a period during which the post-Reconstruction settlement of black status remained almost unaltered in the Deep South. Drawing upon what must be maternal and grandmaternal accounts as well as upon her own memory and observation, Miss Walker, who is herself under forty, exposes us to a way of life that for the most part existed beyond or below the reach of fiction and that has hitherto been made available to us chiefly through tape-recorded reminiscences: the life of poor, rural Southern blacks as it was experienced by their womenfolk....

I cannot gauge the general accuracy of Miss Walker's account [of Celie's life] or the degree to which it may be colored by current male-female antagonisms within the black community.... I did note certain improbabilities: it seems unlikely that a woman of Celie's education would have applied the word "amazons" to a group of feisty sisters or that Celie, in the 1930s, would have found fulfillment in designing and making pants for women. In any case, *The Color Purple* has more serious faults than its possible feminist bias. Alice Walker still has a lot to learn about plotting and structuring what is clearly intended to be a realistic novel. The revelations involving the fate of Celie's lost babies and the identity of her real father seem crudely contrived—the stuff of melodrama or fairy tales.

The extended account of Nettie's experience in Africa, to which she has gone with a black missionary couple and their two adopted children, is meant to be a counterweight to Celie's story but it lacks authenticity—not because Miss Walker is ignorant of Africa... but because she has failed to endow Nettie with her own distinctive voice; the fact that Nettie is better educated than Celie—and a great reader—should not have drained her epistolary style of all personal flavor, leaving her essentially uncharacterized, a mere reporter of events. The failure to find an interesting idiom for a major figure like Nettie is especially damaging in an epistolary novel, which is at best a difficult genre for a twentieth-century writer, posing its own special problems of momentum and credibility.

Fortunately, inadequacies which might tell heavily against another novel seem relatively insignificant in view of the one great challenge which Alice Walker has triumphantly met: the conversion, in Celie's letters, of a subliterate dialect into a medium of remarkable expressiveness, color, and poignancy. I find it impossible to imagine Celie apart from her language; through it, not only a memorable and infinitely touching character but a whole submerged world is vividly called into being. Miss Walker knows how to avoid the excesses of literal transcription while remaining faithful to the spirit and rhythms of Black English. I can think of no other novelist who has so successfully tapped the poetic resources of the idiom....

TRUDIER HARRIS

SOURCE: Trudier Harris, "On 'The Color Purple', Stereotypes, and Silence," in *Black American Literature Forum*, Vol. 18, No. 4, Winter, 1984, pp. 155-61.

[*In the following excerpt, Harris evaluates* The Color Purple, *stating of the work: "To complain about the novel is to commit treason against black women writers, yet there is much in it that deserves complaint...."*]

The Color Purple has been canonized. I don't think it should have been. The tale of the novel's popularity is the tale of the media's ability, once again, to dictate the tastes of the reading public, and to attempt to shape what is acceptable creation by black American writers. Sadly, a book that might have been ignored if it had been published ten years earlier or later has now become *the* classic novel by a black woman. That happened in great part because the pendulum determining focus on black writers had swung in their favor again, and Alice Walker had been waiting in the wings of the feminist movement and the power it had generated long enough for her curtain call to come.... While it is not certain how long Alice Walker will be in the limelight for ***The Color Purple***, it is certain that the damaging effects reaped by the excessive media attention given to the novel will plague us as scholars and teachers for many years to come.

The novel has become so popular that Alice Walker is almost universally recognized as a spokeswoman for black people, especially for black women, and the novel is more and more touted as a work representative of black communities in this country. The effect of the novel's popularity has been detrimental in two significant and related ways. Response to its unequaled popularity, first of all, has created a cadre of spectator readers. These readers, who do not identify with the characters and who do not feel the intensity of their pain, stand back and view the events of the novel as a circus of black human interactions that rivals anything Daniel Patrick Moynihan concocted. The spectator readers show what damage the novel can have: for them, the book reinforces racist stereotypes they may have been heir to and others of which they may have only dreamed.

The other, equally significant, detrimental effect is that the novel has been so much praised that critics, especially black women critics, have seemingly been reluctant to offer detailed, carefully considered criticisms of it. While that may be explained in part by the recent publication of the novel and by the limited access black women critics traditionally have had to publishing outlets, these possible explanations are partly outweighed by the fact that the novel has been so consistently in the public eye that it takes great effort not to write about it. *The Color Purple* silences by its dominance, a dominance perpetuated by the popular media. Those who initially found or still find themselves unable to speak out perhaps reflect in some way my own path to writing about the novel. From the time the novel appeared in 1982, I have been waging a battle with myself to record my reaction to it. For me, the process of reading, re-reading, and re-reading the novel, discussing it, then writing about it has reflected some of the major dilemmas of the black woman critic. To complain about the novel is to commit treason against black women writers, yet there is much in it that deserves complaint.... After all, a large number of readers, usually vocal and white, have decided that *The Color Purple* is the quintessential statement on Afro-American women and a certain kind of black lifestyle in these United States....

When I started asking black women how they felt about the book, there was a quiet strain of discomfort with it, a quiet tendency to criticize, but none of them would do so very aggressively. We were all faced with the idea that to criticize a novel that had been so universally complimented was somehow a desertion of the race and the black woman writer. Yet, there was a feeling of uneasiness with the novel. Instead of focusing upon the specifics of that uneasiness, however, most of the black women with whom I talked preferred instead to praise that which they thought was safe: the beautiful voice in the book and Walker's ability to capture an authentic black folk speech without all the caricature that usually typifies such efforts. They could be lukewarm toward the relationship between Celie and Shug and generally criticize Albert. However, they almost never said anything about the book's African sections until I brought them up. Do they work for you? Do you see how they're integrated into the rest of the novel? Does the voice of Nettie ring authentic and true to you? Only when assured that their ideas would not be looked upon as a desertion of black femininity would the women then proceed to offer valuable insights.

For others, though, silence about the novel was something not to be broken. One Afro-American woman critic who has written on contemporary black women writers told me that she would never write anything on the novel or make a public statement about it. Quite clearly, that was a statement in itself. Her avowed silence became a political confirmation of everything that I found problematic about the novel.

But shouldn't black women allow for diversity of interpretation of our experiences, you may ask? And shouldn't we be reluctant to prescribe a direction for our black women writers? Of course, but what we have with this novel is a situation in which many black women object to the portrayals of the characters, yet we may never hear the reasons for their objections precisely *because they are black women*. . . .

In Gloria Steinem's article on Alice Walker and her works, especially *The Color Purple,* which appeared in *Ms. Magazine* in June of 1982, Steinem reflects her own surprise at Walker's achievement; her response is condescending at times to a degree even beyond that latitude that might be expected in such works. She praises Walker for generally being alive, black, and able to write well. . . .

Steinem focuses on the language and the morality in Walker's novel. The language I have no problem with, but then I am not one of the individuals who assumes that black women have difficulty with folk idiom. Celie's voice in the novel is powerful, engaging, subtly humorous, and incisively analytic at the basic level of human interactions. The voice is perfectly suited to the character, and Walker has breathed into it a vitality that frequently overshadows the problematic areas of concern in the novel. . . . The form of the book, as it relates to the folk speech, the pattern and nuances of Celie's voice, is absolutely wonderful. The clash between Celie's conception and her writing ability, however, is another issue. I can imagine a black woman of Celie's background and education talking with God, as Mariah Uphur does in Sarah E. Wright's *This Child's Gonna Live,* but writing letters to God is altogether another matter. Even if we can suspend our disbelief long enough to get beyond that hurdle, we are still confronted with the substance of the book. *What* Celie records—the degradation, abuse, dehumanization—is not only morally repulsive, but it invites spectator readers to generalize about black people in the same negative ways that have gone on for centuries. Further, how Celie grows and how she presents other characters as growing is frequently incredible and inconsistent to anyone accustomed to novels at least adhering to the worlds, logical or otherwise, that they have created.

When I read lines such as " . . . I'm so beside myself," "She look like she ain't long for this world but dressed well for the next," "Look like a little mouse been nibbling the biscuit, a rat run off with the ham," and "Scare me so bad I near bout drop my grip," I felt a sense of deja vu for all the black women who made art out of conversation in the part of Alabama where I grew up. . . . That part of Celie I could imagine. And one might even understand, at least initially, her fear of her stepfather and the underdeveloped moral sense that leads to inactivity in response to abuse. Her lack of understanding about her pregnancy is also probable within the environment in which she grew up; as many black girls/women during those years were taught that babies were found in cabbage heads or in hollow logs.

But those years and years and years of Celie's acquiescence, extreme in their individuality, have been used too readily to affirm what the uninformed or the ill-informed believe is a general pattern of violence and abuse for black women. That is one of the dangerous consequences of the conceptualization of that powerful voice Celie has.

One of the saddest effects and the greatest irony of that voice is that, while it makes Celie articulate, it has simultaneously encouraged silence from black women, who need to be vocal in voicing their objections to, as well as their praises for, the novel. As Celie's voice has resounded publicly, it has, through its very forcefulness, cowed the voices of black women into private commentary or into silence about issues raised in the novel.

The voice led to Steinem's celebration of the wonderful morality in the novel, yet what she finds so attractive provides another source of my contention with the book. Steinem asserts that morality for Walker "is not an external dictate. It doesn't matter if you love the wrong people, or have children with more than one of them, or whether you have money, go to church, or obey the laws. What matters is cruelty, violence, keeping the truth from others who need it, suppressing someone's will or talent, taking more than you need from people or nature, and failing to choose for yourself. It's the internal morality of dignity, autonomy, and balance." What kind of morality is it that espouses that all human degradation is justified if the individual somehow survives all the tortures and uglinesses heaped upon her? Where is the dignity, autonomy, or balance in that? I am not opposed to triumph, but I do have objections to the unrealistic presentation of the path, the *process* that leads to such a triumph, especially when it is used to create a new archetype or to resurrect old myths about black women.

By no means am I suggesting that Celie should be blamed for what happens to her. My problem is with her reaction to the situation. Even slave women who found themselves abused frequently found ways of responding to that—by running away, fighting back, poisoning their masters, or through more subtly defiant acts such as spitting into the food they cooked for their masters. They did something, and Celie shares a kinship in conception if not in chronology with them....

I found so many white women who joined Steinem in praising the novel that I read it again just to recheck my own evaluations. Then, since I was on leave at The Bunting Institute at Radcliffe and had access to a community of women, the majority of whom were white, I thought it would be fitting to test some of my ideas on them. Accordingly, I wrote a thirty-three-page article on the novel and invited women in residence at the Institute to come to a working paper session and respond to what I had written. My basic contentions were that the portrayal of Celie was unrealistic for the time in which the novel was set, that Nettie and the letters from Africa were really extraneous to the central concerns of the novel, that the lesbian relationship in the book represents the height of silly romanticism, and that the epistolary form of the novel ultimately makes Celie a much more sophisticated character than we are initially led to believe....

During that session, I discovered that some white women did not like the novel, but they were not the ones controlling publications like *Ms*. One white woman commented that, if she had not been told the novel had been written by a black woman, she would have thought it had been written by a Southern white male who wanted to reinforce the traditional sexual and violent stereotypes about black people. That comment affirmed one of my major objections to the thematic development of the novel: The book simply added a freshness to many of the ideas circulating in the popular culture and captured in racist literature that suggested that black people have no morality when it comes to sexuality, that black family structure is weak if existent at all, that black men abuse black women, and that black women who may appear to be churchgoers are really lewd and lascivious.

The novel gives validity to all the white racist's notions of pathology in black communities. For these spectator readers, black fathers and father-figures are viewed as being immoral, sexually unrestrained. Black males and females form units without the benefit of marriage, or they easily dissolve marriages in order to form less structured, more promiscuous relationships. Black men beat their wives—or attempt to—and neglect, ignore, or abuse their children. When they cannot control their wives through beatings, they violently dispatch them. The only stereotype that is undercut in the book is that of the matriarch. Sofia, who comes closest in size and personality to the likes of Lorraine Hansberry's Mama Lena Younger and comparable characters, is beaten, imprisoned, and nearly driven insane precisely because of her strength.

The women had fewer comments on the section on Africa, but generally agreed that it was less engaging than other parts of the novel. I maintained that the letters from Africa were like the whaling chapters in *Moby Dick*—there more for the exhibition of a certain kind of knowledge than for the good of the work....

Other women from that session also commented on Walker's excessively negative portrayal of black men—not a new criticism leveled against her—and some thought the lesbian relationship was problematic. There were others, though, who couldn't see what all the fuss was about, who said that they had simply enjoyed reading the novel. I had not trouble with their enjoyment of the novel as a response to reading it; my problems centered on the reasons for their finding it so enjoyable. Those who did generally mentioned the book's affirmation: that Celie is able to find happiness after so many horrible things have happened to her. That is a response that would probably please Walker, who has indicated that the character Celie is based on her great-grandmother, who was raped at twelve by her slaveholding master. In reparation to a woman who had suffered such pain, Walker has explained: "I liberated her from her own history.... I wanted her to be happy." It is this clash between history and fiction, in part, that causes the problems with the novel.

On the way to making Celie happy, Walker portrays her as a victim of many imaginable abuses and a few unimaginable ones. Celie is a woman who *believes* she is ugly, and she centers that belief on her blackness. While this is not a new problem with some black women, a black woman character conceived in 1982 who is still heir to the same kinds of problems that characters had who were conceived decades earlier is problematic for me—especially since Celie makes a big deal of how ugly she believes she is. But, you may say, how can a woman affirm any standard of beauty in an environment in which men are so abusive? Allowance for the fact that Celie is "living" in the 1940s really does not gainsay the criticism about this aspect of her conception. I would say in response that Nettie was there during Celie's early years, and Nettie apparently has a rather positive conception of herself. If Celie believes her about some things, why not about others? Instead, Celie gives in to her environment with a kind of passivity that comes near to provoking screams in readers not of the spectator variety who may be guilty of caring too much about the characters. Before she can be made to be happy, Celie is forced to relive the history of many Afro-American women who found themselves in unpleasant circumstances, but few of them seem to have undergone such an intuitive devaluation of themselves.... I can imagine Celie existing forever in her situation if someone else did not come along to "stir her root life," as Jean Toomer would say, "and teach her to dream." It is that burying away of the instinctive desire to save one's self that makes me in part so angry about Celie—in addition to all those ugly things that happen to her. Plowing a man's fields for twenty years and letting him use her body as a sperm depository leaves Celie so buried away from herself that it is hard to imagine anything stirring her to life—just as it is equally hard to imagine her being so deadened. Ah—the dilemma.

Celie does have an awareness of right and wrong that comes from outside herself—as well as the one she will develop from her own experiences. She knows that Albert's abuse of her is wrong just as she knew her stepfather's sexual exploitation of her was wrong. And she does go to church; whether or not she believes what she hears, certainly something of the Christian philosophy seeps into her consciousness over the years. There are guidelines for action, therefore, to which she can compare her own situation and respond. Also, considering the fact that she cannot have children with Albert, the traditional reason for enduring abuse—one's children—is absent in her case. So why does she stay?...

From the beginning of the novel, even as Walker presents Celie's sexual abuse by her stepfather, there is an element of fantasy in the book. Celie becomes the ugly duckling who will eventually be redeemed through suffering. This trait links her to all the heroines of fairy tales from Cinderella to Snow White. Instead of the abusive stepmother as the villain, the stepfather plays that role. He devalues Celie in direct proportion to Nettie's valuing of her; unfortunately, as an inexperienced rather than an adult godmother, Nettie lacks the ability to protect Celie. The clash between youth and age, between power and powerlessness begins the mixed-media approach of the novel. Celie's predicament may be real, but she is forced to deal with it in terms that are antithetical to the reality of her condition....

The fabulist/fairy-tale mold of the novel is ultimately incongruous with and does not serve well to frame its message. When things turn out happily in those traditional tales, we are asked to affirm the basic pattern and message: Good triumphs over evil. But what does *The Color Purple* affirm? What were all those women who applauded approving of? It affirms, first of all, patience and long-suffering—perhaps to a greater degree than that exhibited by Cinderella or by the likes of Elizabeth Grimes in James Baldwin's *Go Tell It on the Mountain*. In true fairy-tale fashion, it affirms passivity; heroines in those tales do little to help themselves. It affirms silence in the face of, if not actual allegiance to, cruelty. It affirms secrecy concerning violence and violation. It affirms, saddest of all, the myth of the American Dream becoming a reality for black Americans, even those who are "dirt poor," as one of my colleagues phrased it, and those who are the "downest" and "outest." The fable structure thereby perpetuates a lie in holding out to blacks a non-existent or minimally existent hope for a piece of that great American pie. The clash of characters who presumably contend with and in the real world with the idealistic, suprarealistic quality and expectations of fairy-tale worlds places a burden on the novel that diffuses its message and guarantees possibilities for unintended interpretations.

With its mixture of message, form, and character, *The Color Purple* reads like a political shopping list of all the IOUs Walker felt that it was time to repay. She pays homage to the feminists by portraying a woman who struggles through adversity to assert herself against almost impossible odds. She pays homage to the lesbians by portraying a relationship between two women that reads like a schoolgirl fairy tale in its ultimate adherence to the convention of the happy resolution. She pays homage to black nationalists by opposing colonialism, and to Pan Africanism by suggesting that yes, indeed, a black American does understand and sympathize with the plight of her black brothers and sisters thousands of miles across the ocean. And she adds in a few other obeisances—to career-minded women in the characters of Mary Agnes and Shug, to born-again male feminists in the character of Albert, and to black culture generally in the use of the blues and the folk idiom....

I *will* teach *The Color Purple* again—precisely because of the teachability engendered by its controversiality. I will be angry again because I am not a spectator to what happens to Celie; for me, the novel *demands* participation. I will continue to react to all praise of the novel by asserting that mere praise ignores the responsibility that goes along with it—we must clarify as much as we can the reasons that things are being praised and enumerate as best we can the consequences of that praise. I will continue to read and re-

read the novel, almost in self-defense against the continuing demands for discussions and oral evaluations of it. Perhaps—and other black women may share this response—I am caught in a love/hate relationship with *The Color Purple;* though my crying out against it might be comparable to spitting into a whirlwind in an effort to change its course, I shall nevertheless purse my lips....

J. CHARLES WASHINGTON

SOURCE: J. Charles Washington, "Positive Black Male Images in Alice Walker's Fiction," in *Obsidian*, Vol. III, No. 1, Spring, 1988, pp. 23-48.

[*In the following excerpt, Washington disputes critics who claim that the portraits of men in Walker's fiction are excessively negative.*]

Now that the controversy over Alice Walker's Pulitzer Prize-winning novel *The Color Purple* has subsided, it might be worthwhile to re-examine her fiction, specifically, the short stories, in an attempt to resolve the issue of her purported attack on Black males. In particular, her critics charged her with presenting a grossly negative image of Black men, who were portrayed as mean, cruel, or violent, entirely without redeeming qualities. In a review of the film of the novel, the *Washington Post* of February 5, 1986 stated: "But what is being heatedly discussed is the characterization of Black males as cruel, unaffectionate, domineering slap-happy oafs." Gloria Steinem, a major source of these discussions, writes in the June 1982, issue of *Ms.* magazine, that "a disproportionate number of her (Walker's) hurtful, negative reviews have been by Black men."

This "disproportionate number" is significant, but only because, according to Trudier Harris, "black women critics have . . . been reluctant to offer . . . criticisms of it." The reason for this reluctance, Harris explains, is that "To complain about the novel is to commit treason against Black women writers, yet there is much in it that deserves complaint." With a tone that reveals the high degree of distress and frustration she feels, Harris complains not only about the negative, unrealistic and stereotypical portraits of Black men and women the novel presents, but also about its overall thematic development. . . .

The charge against Walker cannot be supported, for it is based on far too simplistic a view of an artist. Though her work is woman-centered, its wider focus is on the struggle of Black people—men and women—to reclaim their own lives. . . . Her exclusive concentration on what used to be called the weaker sex who, if no longer as weak as they once were, are still the most oppressed in society does not mean that she is anti-male, but that she has less time and energy to devote to exploring more fully the problems of men or the common causes of the oppression of both. . . .

Walker's works tell us a great deal about the lives of Black people, and it is ironic that her reward has often been controversy and harsh criticism. Her persistence in the face of it springs from her commitment to truth and honesty. Like most Black artists concerned about freeing Black people from their past mistakes, she too believes that "the truth shall set you free." In *Black Women Writers*, Barbara Christian writes that "there is a sense in which the 'forbidden' in the society is consistently approached by Walker as a possible route to truth." In contrast to many Black writers who are reluctant to criticize Black males because they fear it will exacerbate an already precarious situation between Black men and women, the "forbidden" Walker exposes is the role Black men, both the positive and negative types, have played in the oppression of Black women.

Examples of the purely negative type of Black male abound in Walker's work, among them the men in *The Color Purple;* however, as mentioned, one of the most glaring examples is the younger Grange Copeland, hero of *The Third Life*, of whom Barbara Christian writes in *Black Women Writers:* "Grange Copeland hates himself because he is powerless, as opposed to powerful, the definition of maleness for him. His reaction is to prove his power by inflicting violence on the women around him." The cyclical nature of this phenomenon is seen in the life of Grange's son Brownfield, perhaps the most monstrous character in all of Walker's fiction, who brutalizes his children and his wife and then murders her.

The role played by the positive type of Black male found in *In Love and Trouble* is no less destructive on the lives of Black women, for it often means only a change in the kind of violence inflicted; that is, emotional violence predominates over the physical kind. But there is a major difference in the men who cause the oppression, and it is this distinction which allows us to label them positive rather than negative and which supplies the hope that change is possible. While the men in *Purple* and *Third Life* shock us with their unspeakable cruelty and violence not only because they are fully aware of their immoral behavior but also because they often revel in and enjoy inflicting pain, the men in *In Love and Trouble* are never monsters of this type. On the contrary, they are at all times human beings who reveal a variety of human strengths and weaknesses.

The positive classification also depends on the perspective from which one views them. For instance, Ruel, the antagonist/husband in **"Really, Doesn't Crime Pay,"** who fails to recognize his wife's ambition to write or her need for her own identity because he only sees her as a housewife is, in my view, not a negative character. A product of the social mores of his time stemming from the morally sanctioned patriarchal tradition which fostered them, he is as much a victim as his wife of a seemingly permanent mind-set in society which neither of them created and which will bind them until they realize that they must set themselves free. Similarly, while it may be considered immoral by some, a man who marries for money, in this case at the invitation of the female, as Jerome Washington does in **"Her Sweet Jerome,"** is no more negative than a woman who does the same. To label him such would require applying to him the same pernicious double standard of which women have always been victim.

A second significant cause of the oppression of the Black women in these stories, as it relates to their interaction with Black men, is their mistaken definition of themselves as women. Their own blindness about themselves and about what they can and must do for themselves is given strong emphasis, which is another important sign that Walker is searching for the truth, and that her interest is in finding causes, not assessing blame. The female protagonist of **"Really, Doesn't Crime Pay,"** for example, is spiritually and emotionally imprisoned by her husband's limited definition of her humanity and sits waiting deliverance from her life of useless dissipation, completely unaware that what she desires most lies within her own power—that, in other words, she must be the agent of her own deliverance. Such behavior on the women's part does not correlate with positive male characters. It does mean, however, that the men's behavior is no worse than that of the women, their alleged victims. They are in fact equally responsible for their problems and for the suffering they inflict on each other. . . .

[Many] of the women in *In Love and Trouble* share culpability in their own downfall, and this fact plays an important part in softening the negative image of their Black men. For though it is not always the case, and a man or woman must bear responsibility for his/her immoral behavior no matter what the circumstances, the men's role in the oppression of these women is often aided by the women's contribution to or willful participation in—sometimes, even, a masochistic invitation of—their own victimization.

The variety of problems and character types found in these stories is perhaps the most convincing evidence of Walker's preoccupation with presenting the full range of Black humanity—"the survival whole" of her people—as seen in the individual lives of her characters. To reiterate, what we are seeing, then, is not a common theme of oppression, but a multiplicity of themes based on the individuals' responses to it. Like her female characters, the Black male characters are shown to be individual human beings. Regarding them as such, one will find among them several positive Black male images or characters, which is the thesis of this essay. Because most of the stories have female protagonists and male antagonists, in such a case the selection of stories has to be based on those in which the male antagonists are sufficiently developed to give a substantial view of their characters. From this group, two have been selected for examination: **"Really, Doesn't Crime Pay"** and **"To Hell with Dying. . . . "**

"Really, Doesn't Crime Pay" takes place within the pages of Myrna's writing notebook. "Myrna" is never used within the story itself. To identify her, the name appears in parentheses only as an undertitle.

On the surface, the notebook entries tell about Myrna's desire to be a writer and her dissatisfaction with her life as a housewife. Spending her days in idleness and useless dissipation—she does not have to work—she falls prey to a young Black charlatan or amateur writer, Mordecai Rich, who seduces and then abandons her, leading to an emotional breakdown. One day while sitting in the doctor's office, she discovers that he has published under his own name one of her stories that she had given him. Later that night while in bed, she attempts to murder her husband Ruel, who had ridiculed her desire to be a writer, insisting instead that she have a child and become a housewife.

On a deeper level, the story is a tragedy about a young Black woman who has talent but who lacks the understanding, courage and know-how to break the restrictions placed on her and to create the meaningful identity she craves and needs. Her insecurity about her talent and her own self-worth resulting in extreme self-hatred, leads to her victimization by Mordecai and to her attempted murder of her husband, whom she blames for her plight and to whom she transfers her frustration and hatred.

Myrna's entries in her notebook are significant in revealing her character and exposing the tragic nature of her situation. Walker skillfully establishes the interrelatedness of the literary elements of theme, character and plot. Allowing us to see inside Myrna's head and heart, we observe more than twenty years of rage and anger bottled up there, which is more than enough to drive anyone mad. Since the entries in her notebook are both the plot as well as samples of her writing, what they also allow us to see is not only the quality of her writing and the sensitivity and talent required to produce it, but also the tragic waste of them and her life due to her failure to act or to attempt to solve the dilemma she faced....

Walker never lets the reader forget that Myrna is conscious or fully aware of her acts. In fact, it is this awareness on her part that makes her appear less sympathetic, and the man with whom she commits adultery less villainous, in the readers' eyes.... What increases the antipathy toward her even more, however, is her use of her week-long sexual encounter with Mordecai, unknown to her husband, of course, as a way of striking back at him for his failure to recognize her need: "I gloat over this knowledge. Now Ruel will find out that I am not a womb without a brain that can be bought with Japanese bathtubs and shopping sprees."

Putting all her hope for a change in her life in Mordecai, she declares, "The moment of my deliverance is at hand." He abandons her, however, and soon thereafter she begins to reveal signs of an emotional breakdown. As her condition worsens, Ruel tells her she acts as if her mind is asleep, to which she makes the mental notes: "Nothing will wake it but a letter from Mordecai telling me to pack my bags and fly to New York." Clearly, this indicates the confusion in her mind about what change is needed to bring about the happiness she craves. This change is not an external one, although new scenes, sights and surroundings would no doubt help alleviate her mental depression. What she actually requires is a fundamental modification in the way she thinks about herself. Thus, it is not Ruel alone who needs to know that she is not "a womb without a mind," but she too must realize that she has the capability of being both "womb" and "brain"—both a housewife and artist; in separating the two or failing to see the alternative available to her, she commits the same kind of error that Ruel makes. Complementing this confusion in her mind is another serious mistake on her part: her lack of self-involvement in changing her condition. And so she sits waiting for deliverance, expecting Mordecai to do for her what only she can do for herself.

That Walker sees the solution to Myrna's problems as one of her own making is found in *Mothers' Garden*, in the author's analysis of the escape route by which Black women have traditionally sought and succeeded in securing their spiritual survival. This route, based on an intuitive sense which enabled them to know how to get what they needed, was their flexibility combined with an enormous capacity for work: this enabled them to be both worker and creator, both wife and artist. Using her mother, who bore and raised eight children, as an example, Walker first explains that many of the stories she writes are her mother's stories; then she adds:

> But the telling of these stories ... was not the only way my mother showed herself as an artist.... My mother adorned with flowers whatever shabby house we were forced to live in. And not just your typical straggly country stand of zinnias, either. She planted ambitious gardens ... with over fifty different varieties of plants that bloom(ed) profusely from early March until late November.

The conclusion of this anecdote illustrates the enormous will and energy required to maintain the garden:

> Before she left home for the fields, she watered her flowers, chopped up the grass, and laid out new beds. When she returned from the fields she might divide clumps of beds, dig a cold pit, uproot and replant roses, or prune branches from her taller bushes or trees—until night came and it was too dark to see.

With this as the norm, one can see how far from it Myrna is. Not compelled to work to support herself, her life of ease, which would have given her ample time for self-development, cannot be compared to the lives of drudgery of the generation of Black women to which Walker's mother belongs. Myrna's easy life is of little consequence, however, for in addition to her fragile emotional nature and her blindness about the deeper cause of her problem, she lacks the pragmatism which would have enabled her to find a solution to her problem. Without it, acting instead in response to her feelings of self-hatred, she continues to destroy the life she has by contemplating suicide and by commiting cruelty against her husband. Interestingly, no critic, male or female, has commented on the cruelty and violence this female character inflicts on her husband, actions which make her no less negative than some of the males in Walker's works. After release from the hospital, where she has recovered from her breakdown, she resumes her life of uselessness and idleness. She also continues to deceive her husband, who still hopes for the birth of a child, by religiously taking birth control pills. Illustrating her enjoyment of the pain she inflicts on him, it is, she says, "the only spot of humor in my entire day when I am gulping that little yellow tablet...." Her spiritual death, then, is seen not only in these acts of cruelty, but also in her refusal to give birth to life. As for her sterility and failure to come to grips with her life, she says:

I go to the new shopping mall *twice a day now* [emphasis added]; once in the morning and once in the afternoon, or at night. I buy hats I would not dream of wearing, or even owning.

Ruel, Myrna's husband, is cast in the traditional mold. A solid, lower middle-class type, he is a 40-year old Korean war veteran who works in a store and raises a hundred acres of peanuts. Steady, immovable and unchanging like the earth he cultivates, he clings to life in the same small southern town in which he was born and reared. In fact, he has traveled beyond its confines only once when he went off to war. Though he claims the experience broadened him, especially his two months of European leave, it did not change him or affect his thinking in any fundamental way. Because his character had already been shaped by the values of a Southern tradition hundreds of years old, the brief, passing moment in Europe did not—indeed, could not—penetrate the deeper core of his being.... Ruel's ideas of what married life entails, that is, the fixed roles that marriage partners must play, ... are the same ones he learned in childhood, passed down to him from his father. It must be noted, however, that these values are not limited to the South, for they are the foundation of the patriarchal tradition known and practiced throughout the world.

Men of this type do not permit their wives to work, as he does not, even though in his case, it may mean that he has to work two jobs to supply his wife with the things he thinks she needs or wants. Not just a reflection of the male ego, this social pattern is in keeping with the men's expectation that the freedom and time it gives their women will enable them to more easily perform their "duty" as wives and mothers. Seeing this duty as the only appropriate one for a female, Ruel naturally thinks that his wife's writing is "a lot of foolish vulgar stuff" and that she is "peculiar" for wanting to do it. This "unnatural" desire of hers is a threat to him, for its exposure to the public will cause him embarrassment. Conversely, the traditional role he urges on her will confirm his normalcy and masculinity. And so, whenever she mentions the subject of writing, "he brings up having a baby or going shopping...."

When Mordecai Rich appears, Ruel is slightly jealous but does not feel threatened. How could he be disturbed by such "a skinny black tramp," when he, Ruel, is all an ideal husband should be, which is how he sees himself. However, it is his preoccupation with himself, with his own needs and self-image, that blinds him to the needs of his wife. Failing to see his own shortcomings, he readily dismisses the signs of her distress because he cannot see that she has a problem.

Failing to do so, he would never believe that he might possibly be implicated in its cause. For this reason too, he only begins to notice her and to feel that something is wrong with his life after Mordecai abandons her and the signs of her oncoming nervous breakdown are too obvious to be ignored.

What we see in this couple, then, is an identically matched pair of individuals with an interesting kind of incompatibility that renders them incapable of helping each other. Both, therefore, share the blame for the deterioration or destruction of their relationship. In both individuals, the root of the problem is not immorality, but fundamental character flaws. In Ruel's case, it is his selfishness or egocentrism based on his belief that what is good or right for him is also good enough for his wife. It must be re-emphasized, however, that his behavior, which is typical of many men everywhere and therefore universal, has its basis in the mores of the patriarchal tradition, a tradition which regrettably makes little allowance for the spiritual needs of women.

Because he is a plain, common, everyday type who is unaware of any other tradition or set of values and therefore blameless, Ruel is not a negative character. In contrast to his wife, even his faults are virtues. For though he is preoccupied with his own image and his own life, it is devoted to and expressive of his love for her. Therefore, he is never cruel, brutal or violent. Rather, his life is characterized by hard work, as he struggles to provide her with a decent home to live in and other material possessions she needs or wants. Mindful of his role and image as provider, he feels ashamed of the wooden house he purchased for his wife, with its toilet in the yard. Constantly trying to improve their life, he dreams of a better home for her, telling her, "One day we'll have a new house of brick, with a Japanese bath." Finally, it is ironic that what Myrna considers his greatest fault, his insistence that she have a child, is in fact the greatest expression of his love for her, since he believes, as most men and women do, that a child will cure her illness and provide her with the self-fulfillment she needs.

It is not only his moral fiber and love that establishes Ruel as a positive male image, but also his innocence. All of these qualities produce the sympathy we feel for him. Such a solid, respectable person could not be the monster his wife makes him out to be. Such a decent person does not deserve to be the cuckold she makes of him or the victim of the cruel tricks she plays on him. Even after Myrna's attempt to murder him, it is clear that he never understands her, or the real source of their problem. Rather, Ruel blames Mordecai.... After Myrna's recovery, Ruel makes repeated attempts to impregnate her, never once suspecting that she is deliberately thwarting conception of the child he desperately wants. When she fails to become pregnant, he sends her to a gynecologist. When this step also fails to produce the desired result, he finally learns one irrelevant fact: irrelevant because it will not change him either: As Myrna says, "He knows now that I intend to say yes until he is completely exhausted."

Lacking knowledge of himself and therefore incapable of changing, Ruel faces a hopeless situation. But what he represents is an important part of what Walker wishes to show us. Even such basically good men as Ruel are often unwitting contributors to the destruction of relationships between Black men and women....

As David Bradley notes in his *New York Times Magazine* article, Walker's stories with older men protagonists (in their sixties onward) contain overwhelmingly positive Black male images. This change results from a major shift in theme. Sexual or marital relations between Black men and women, with all the attendant stress and pain they entail, are not the central focus. Rather, the author's interest is in presenting the experiences of the old as a legacy for the young....

PUBLISHERS WEEKLY

SOURCE: A review of *The Same River Twice: Honoring the Difficult*, in *Publishers Weekly*, Vol. 242, No. 51, December 18, 1995, p. 38.

[*Below, the reviewer gives a mixed assessment of* The Same River Twice.]

Walker's latest book finds the Pulitzer Prize-winning author still grappling with criticism of the film version of her novel *The Color Purple.* She continues to defend her depiction of an abusive black man as well as her decision to use Steven Spielberg as director. But now she also recognizes the project as a creative watershed. Walker's memoir pieces together assorted journal entries, magazine clippings, occasional photographs and even her original screenplay to form an intimate scrapbook of the period. We witness one of the seminal gatherings in Hollywood history: the original meeting of Walker, Spielberg, and producer/musician Quincy Jones, and we watch their collaboration unfold. Walker discusses the fortuitous casting of Whoopi Goldberg and Oprah Winfrey, who have evolved into two of the few female Hollywood powers. Yet Walker's recollections include few other voices. This makes for a perspective uncomfortably lopsided in parts. Also Walker's preoccupation with her old critics seems unnecessary and somewhat dated. However, the book wonderfully illuminates Walker's "born-again pagan" spirit and her boundless passion for the characters she creates and the audience she serves.

SOURCES FOR FURTHER STUDY

Bobo, Jacqueline. "Sifting through the Controversy: Reading *The Color Purple*." Callaloo 12, No. 2 (Spring 1989): 332-42.

> Discusses the controversy surrounding *The Color Purple* and public reaction to the film.

Bradley, David. "Novelist Alice Walker Telling the Black Woman's Story." *The New York Times Magazine* (8 January 1984): 25-37.

> Extensive biographical profile of Walker, interspersed with critical analysis of her work.

Callaloo 12, No. 2 (Spring 1989).

> Special issue devoted to Walker, with essays and reviews by Theodore O. Mason, Jr., Joseph A. Brown, and Keith Byerman.

Iannone, Carol. "A Turning of the Critical Tide?" *Commentary* 88, No. 5 (November 1989):57-9.

> Examines critical response to *The Color Purple* and *The Temple of My Familiar*, ascribing positive reactions to political reasons.

Ingoldby, Grace. "Fall Out." *New Statesman* 108, No. 2791 (14 September 1984): 32.

> Explores characterization in *You Can't Keep a Good Woman Down*.

Petry, Alice Hall. "Alice Walker: The Achievement of the Short Fiction." *Modern Language Studies* 19, No. 1 (Winter 1989): 12-27.

> Evaluates Walker's short stories, concluding that Walker is an uneven writer.

Elie Wiesel

1928-

(Full name Eliezer Wiesel) Romanian-born American novelist, memoirist, journalist, short story writer, essayist, and dramatist.

INTRODUCTION

A survivor of Nazi concentration camps and winner of the 1986 Nobel Peace Prize, Wiesel is one of the most important authors of Holocaust literature and an eloquent spokesman for contemporary Judaism. His works attempt to comprehend the horror of the concentration camps and the apparent indifference of God, thereby reaffirming his life and faith. His lyrical, impressionistic novels, mainly written in French, often juxtapose the past and present to examine the effect of the Holocaust on Jews as individuals and as a people. Although Wiesel focused on seemingly exclusive Judaic concerns, the relevance of his work lies in his ability to speak for all persecuted people, and, by extension, humanity.

Biographical Information

Wiesel was born September 30, 1928, in Sighet, Romania, the historical center of Jewish culture in Transylvania. In early 1944 Nazi officials deported fifteen-year-old Wiesel and his family to Birkenau; his mother and sisters were separated from him and his father, who were sent on to Auschwitz. When Soviet troops neared the concentration camp in 1945, the captives were marched to Buchenwald, where his father soon died of dysentery and starvation. When the camps were liberated, Wiesel learned that his mother and younger sister had perished in the gas chambers, but his older sisters had survived; years later they and Wiesel were reunited. Wiesel had hoped to emigrate to Palestine, but immigration restrictions proved insurmountable. He was placed on a Belgium-bound train with other Jewish orphans, but it was rerouted to France. Wiesel eventually moved to Paris, where he studied literature at the Sorbonne from 1948 to 1951. Since 1949 he has worked as a foreign correspondent and journalist at various times for the French-Jewish periodical *L'Arche,* which sent him to cover the formation of the Israeli state, the Tel Aviv newspaper *Yediot Ahronot,* and the *Jewish Daily Forward* in New York City. In 1954, Wiesel interviewed Francois Mauriac, the Roman Catholic novelist and Nobel Laureate, who persuaded Wiesel to break his vow of silence about his concentration camp experience and to bear witness for those who had died. Wiesel wrote an eight-hundred page memoir, *Un di Velt Hot Geshvign* (1956), which he later edited into a shorter version, *La nuit* (1958; *Night*), one of the most powerful works of Holocaust literature. Struck by a New York taxicab in 1956 while on assignment for *Yediot Ahronot,* Wiesel applied for and received U.S. citizenship during his long convalescence. In the mid-1960s Wiesel extended his commitment to speak for the persecuted by focusing on contemporary Jewish victims of oppression, publishing *Le Juifs du silence* (1966; *The Jews of Silence*), which reports on Jewish persecution in the former Soviet Union and pleads for global Jewish solidarity. With the success of his writings, Wiesel emerged as an important moral voice on religious issues, human rights, and the Middle East. He chaired the U.S. President's Commission on the Holocaust in 1979 and the U.S. Holocaust Memorial Council from 1980 to 1986. Since 1988, Wiesel has served Boston University as a professor of philosophy.

Major Works

Night is Wiesel's best known work and, in his words, what "all my subsequent books are built around." A powerful, moving account of his experiences at Auschwitz and Buchenwald, *Night* expresses his guilt as a survivor and anger at God for allowing people to be destroyed despite their faithfulness to God's law. In *L'aube* (1961; *Dawn*) a young survivor becomes a terrorist in the war to free Palestine from British rule, discovering that he has forsaken his religious ideals as a result. *Le jour* (1961; *The Accident*) tells of an Israeli foreign correspondent, who is struck by a taxicab and gradually realizes that the guilt he harbors as a survivor caused him to seek his own death. Wiesel's later novels elaborate his themes of self-discovery, moral choice, indifference and responsibility, and notions of an absurd and unjust God. In *La ville de la chance* (1962; *The Town Beyond the Wall*), a Holocaust survivor confronts his former Nazi guard only to learn that revenge and madness are denials of moral responsibility. The Jewish survivor of *Les portes de la foret* (1964; *The Gates of the Forest*) changes his perception of his relationship to the world when he realizes that "it's inhuman to wall yourself up in pain and memories as if in a prison. Suffering must open us to others. It must not cause us to reject them." *Le cinquieme fils* (1983; *The Fifth Son*) examines the impact of the Holocaust on the children of survivors. A young Jewish American travels to Europe with plans to kill his father's persecutor, but he relents when he is faced with the man's incomprehension of his deeds. The stories and autobiographical fragments collected in *Le chant des morts* (1966; *Legends of Our Time*) and *Entre deux soleils* (1970; *One Generation After*) examine the political and moral effects of world apathy toward any oppressed people. *Un Juif aujourd'hui* (1977; *A Jew Today*), a collection of autobiographical sketches, essays, and dialogues, expresses shame for the past and a cautious hope for the future. *Celebration hassidique* (1972; *Souls on Fire*), *Four Hasidic Masters and Their Struggle Against Melancholy* (1978), *Five Biblical Figures* (1981), and *Somewhere a Master* (1982)—Wiesel's collections of humanistic portraits of biblical figures and legends—address affirmative aspects of Judaism by their examples of how to live joyfully in an incomprehensible and absurd universe.

Critical Reception

Wiesel's work often generates disagreement among critics. Whereas some reviewers consider his plots and characters mere vehicles for rhetorical concerns and question whether his fiction is art or polemic, most praise his sensitive insight into human behavior, his moral candor, and his ability to objectively examine the Holocaust and its effect upon modern Jewish thought. Despite the range of critical opinion, Wiesel's fiction is widely regarded as among the most passionate and powerful of all Holocaust writing. Daniel Stern stated: "Not since Albert Camus has there been such an eloquent spokesman for man."

(For further information, see *Authors and Artists for Young Adults,* Vol. 7; *Authors in the News,* Vol. 1; *Contemporary Authors,* Vols. 5-8R; *Contemporary Authors Autobiography Series,* Vol. 4; *Contemporary Authors New Revision Series,* Vols. 8, 40; *Contemporary Literary Criticism,* Vols. 3, 5, 11, 37; *Dictionary of Literary Biography Yearbook: 1987; Dictionary of Literary Biography,* Vol. 83; *DISCovering Authors; DISCovering Authors: British; DISCovering Authors: Canadian; DISCovering Authors Modules: Most-studied Authors Module, Novelists Module; Major Twentieth-Century Writers; Something about the Author,* Vol. 56.)

CRITICAL COMMENTARY

ROBERT ALTER

SOURCE: Robert Alter, "Elie Wiesel: Between Hangman and Victim," in his *After the Tradition: Essays on Modern Jewish Writing,* E. P. Dutton & Co., Inc., 1969, pp. 151-60.

[*An American scholar, Alter has published highly respected studies of American Jewish writers. In the excerpt below from a 1966 essay, he characterizes Wiesel's novels as theological parables drawn from Hasidic teachings.*]

The novels of Elie Wiesel strike me as a singularly impressive instance of how the creative imagination can surprise our expectations of what its limits should be. It is natural enough to wonder whether it is really possible to write about the Holocaust, to use the written word, which by its very nature is committed to order, as a means of representing and assessing absolute moral chaos. . . .

The achievement, however, of Elie Wiesel's five published books reminds us of the danger in issuing prescriptions about things of the spirit. He has managed to realize the terrible past imaginatively with growing artistic strength in a narrative form that is consecutive, coherent, and, at least on the surface, realistic, in a taut prose that is a model of lucidity and precision. Yet by the very nature of his subject, what we might want to describe as the "realism" of his technique constantly transcends itself, as we are made to feel the pitiful inadequacy of all our commonsense categories of reality. . . . Before the fact of the Holocaust, perhaps only a great visionary poet like Dante could thoroughly imagine such a gruesome reality; after the fact, it still requires a peculiar imaginative courage to abandon all the defenses of common sense in order to remember and reconstitute in language such a reality. It is ultimately this imaginative courage that endows Wiesel's factually precise writing with a hallucinated more-than-realism: he is able to confront the horror with a nakedly self-exposed honesty rare even among writers who went through the same ordeal.

Wiesel's relation both to his subject and to his craft required that, before he could invent fiction, he should starkly record fact, and so his first book, ***Night,*** is a terse and terrifying account of the concentration-camp experiences that made him an agonized witness to the death of his innocence, his human self-respect, his father, his God. . . .

The closest literary analogy I can think of for Wiesel's imaginative landscapes is the kind of lyric love poetry where all existence is focused in the presence of the lover and the beloved (as in Donne's famous lines, "She's all states, and all princes, I, / Nothing else is."). In Wiesel's case, the world seems to contain only three classes of people, each with its own kind of guilt of complicity: executioners, victims, and spectators at the execution.

If this drastic selectivity in some ways foreshortens the view of reality in his novels, it also generates an extraordinary degree of intensity, at once dramatic and moral. The imponderable keys of life and death are placed in the hands of each of Wiesel's protagonists with the imperative to decide how they should be used. . . .

Wiesel's novels, for all the vividness with which they render certain contemporary situations, are more theological parable than realistic fiction: they are written for and about Abrahams on the mountain, Isaacs under the slaughtering knife, and a God who watches but no longer sends His messenger to stay the descending blade. In this kind of parabolic novel our expectations of what people will say, do, or even think are very different from what they would normally be. . . . It is a strange truth we are made to feel almost everywhere in Wiesel's fiction of ultimate confrontations.

Since most of the action and thought in Wiesel's novels take place on the broadest level of philosophical or theological generalization, it is entirely appropriate that the argument of the books should repeatedly crystallize in wisdom-statements, whether by one of the characters or by the narrator himself. . . .

The wisdom taught by the Teacher in his books is, of course, always "existential," never academic, because the figure for Wiesel always derives from the Hasidic spiritual guide—more particularly, from a kabbalistic master of his own childhood whose message was one of redemption, involving the secret knowledge through which man could learn to loose the chains in which the Messiah is bound. . . .

What the Teachers attempt to do is to exorcise these

Principal Works

La Nuit (novel) 1958
[Night, 1960]
L'Aube (novel) 1961
[Dawn, 1961]
Le Jour (novel) 1961
[The Accident, 1962]
La Ville de la chance, (novel) 1962
[The Town beyond the Wall, 1964]
Les Portes de la foret (novel) 1964
[The Gates of the Forest, 1966]
Le Chant des morts (short stories) 1966
[Legends of Our Time, 1968]
The Jews of Silence: A Personal Report on Soviet Jewry (nonfiction) 1966
Zalmen; ou, la Folie de Dieu (drama) 1966
[Zalmen; or, The Madness of God, 1968]
La Nuit, L'Aube, Le Jour (novels) 1969
[Night, Dawn, The Accident: Three Tales, 1972]
Entre deux soleils (short stories) 1970
[One Generation After, 1970]
Celebration Hassidique: Portraits et legendes (sketches) 1972
[Soulson Fire: Portraits and Legends of Hasidic Masters, 1972]
Celebration Biblique: Portraits et legendes (sketches) 1975
[Messengers of God: Biblical Portraits and Legends, 1976]
Un Juif aujourd'hui: Recits, essais, dialogues (essays) 1977

[A Jew Today, 1978]
Dimensions of the Holocaust (nonfiction) 1977
Four Hasidic Masters and Their Struggle against Melancholy (sketches) 1978
Le Proces de Shamgorod tel qu'il se deroula le 25 fevrier 1649: Piece en trois actes (drama) 1979
[The Trial of God (as It Was Held on February 25, 1649, in Shamgorod): A Play in Three Acts, 1979]
Le Testament d'un poete Juif assassine (novel) 1980
[The Testament, 1981]
Five Biblical Portraits (sketches) 1981
Somewhere a Master (sketches) 1982
Le Cinquieme Fils (novel) 1983
[The Fifth Son, 1985]
The Golem: The Story of a Legend as Told by Elie Wiesel (fiction) 1983
Le Crepuscule au loin (novel) 1987
[Twilight, 1988]
The Nobel Speech (lecture) 1987
From the Kingdom of Memory (essays) 1990
The Forgotten (novel) 1992
Tous les Fleuves Vont a la Mer: Memoires (memoirs) 1994
[All Rivers Run to the Sea: Memoirs, 1995]
Memoire a Deux Voix [with Francois Mitterrand] (memoirs) 1995
[Memoir in Two Voices, 1996]

*This volume was first published in a longer version as Un Di Velt Hot Geshvign (1956).

---

paralyzing visions without committing the spiritual folly of suggesting that they be forgotten, and this act has general, not merely personal, significance because all of us, to the extent that we have courage to think about the recent past, must be haunted in some way, however intermittently, by these same specters....

This striking summary of ultimate contradictions, which expresses so much of Wiesel's spiritual world, is reminiscent of a teaching of the Hasidic master, Simha Bunam of Pzhysha, who used to say that every man should have two pockets, one in which to put a slip of paper with the rabbinic dictum, "For my sake the world was created," and the other to carry Abraham's confession of humility before God, "I am dust and ashes." The transmutation that occurs in Wiesel's restatement of the paradox is instructive. In the Hasidic teaching, both man's awesome importance and his nothingness are conceived in terms of his stance before the Creator. In Wiesel, on the other hand, the theological center has shifted to the human spirit: it is pathetically finite man who is the source of miraculous aspiration, of regeneration, in a world where all life is inevitably transient. We may tend to be suspicious of affirmations, for it is often in their affirmative moments that even writers of considerable integrity yield to the temptation of offering a facile and superficial counterfeit of wisdom. In Wiesel, however, one senses that the affirmations are hard-earned, and, indeed, by incorporating as they do their own threatened negations, they may even be hard to assimilate. What is true of the affirmations is true of Wiesel's books in general, which are easy to read but difficult to assimilate. For they are the stages of his own way both from and toward faith, and, at this point in history, that way could not be easy, either to walk or to imagine.

HAMIDA BOSMAJIAN

SOURCE: Hamida Bosmajian, "The Rage for Order: Autobiographical Accounts of the Self in the Nightmare of History," in her *Metaphors of Evil: Contemporary German Literature and the Shadow of Nazism*, University of Iowa Press, 1979, pp. 27-54.

[In the excerpt below, Bosmajian focuses on Wiesel's focus on the self and the individual's relationship to God in Night.]

In *Night*, time ends for young Eliezer in the spring of 1944 when he and his family are torn from their idyllic world in Sighet and transported to Auschwitz. His mother and sister die immediately, and Eliezer begins work in the Buna factories. During the evacuation of Auschwitz, Eliezer, his father, and a multitude of prisoners are driven on the run through a raging blizzard, eventually herded into open cattle wagons which transport them to Buchenwald. It is there that his father, the mainstay of Eliezer's existence, dies. On the even of 28 January 1945 (the first date since he left Sighet), time begins again for Eliezer as he looks at his dying father for the last time and climbs into the bunk above him. The next morning his father is gone: "They must have taken him away before dawn and carried him to the crematory. He may still have been breathing. There were no prayers at his grave." If time before the concentrationary universe was one of Edenic innocence and ignorance, time after the experience defines knowledge of a world so totally fallen that, for Eliezer, at least there is no hope for redemption after liberation. He is locked in his memory of the antiworld: "From the depths of the mirror a corpse gazed at me. The look in his eyes, as they stared into mine, has never left me." Wiesel's autobiography is about the origin of that look.

The language of *Night* is deceptively simple, language that gives the reader the illusion of understanding the unspeakable situation. The familiar linguistic signals, however, reverberate and urge the discovery of a revelation of experience and truth behind the image as sign. It is the language of a religious imagination, demonstrated in the first chapter by the passion with which Eliezer studied not only the law of the Talmud but also the mysticism of the Kabbalah. In the final analysis, *Night* is not an attempt to realistically detail the experience of Auschwitz but rather to show how that experience transformed the religious personality's relation to God. The relation to God is brought about through the language of prayer, as Moche, the mystic Beadle of Sighet, tells Eliezer: "Man raises himself towards God by the questions he asks of Him . . . that is the true dialogue. Man questions God and God answers. But we don't understand His answers. We can't understand them. Because they come from the depths of the soul, and they stay there until death. You will find the true answers, Eliezer, only within yourself."

This is the most important thematic statement in *Night*. It defines the complex inner-outer relationship of the ego to the larger self; it defines the narrator and his language, in which the familiar phrase "depth of the soul" becomes a leitmotif. Charged with affirmation or negation, the phrase is used in all crucial moments of Eliezer's experience. Moche is unaware of the problems his definition can and will cause the boy; he is unaware that the "true dialogue" will be a monologue, a failure of communication. In Wiesel's autobiography, the creature finds himself in a catastrophic creation and concludes that the creator must have withdrawn defensively from that chaos. The creature, too, after viewing and absorbing the chaos, withdraws with defensive aggressiveness into a rigid posture. As Harold Bloom points out in *Kabbalah and Criticism*, "Such a concentration sets up defensive reactions in the self, making the subsequent creation a catastrophe, and rendering . . . representation a hopeless quest." The narrator's defensive reaction is that he, unlike the Creator, does not want his linguistic creation to be catastrophic but wants to shape it with a rage for order by means of a language that is obviously defective in its "imagery of limitation." Yet the familiar order of the narrator's linguistic cosmos reverberates, and the reader, receptive to these reverberations, will break the familiar vessels of the images in *Night* and approximate the catastrophe that underlies them. Such approximation necessarily involves a misreading; for the reader's defenses against the catastrophe in *Night* are likewise provoked, and the true dialogue becomes impossible.

Eliezer's experience at Auschwitz-Buna is shaped by the gradual stripping from him of everything he loves. There is the blind struggle for existence at all cost, but along with it the meaning for life is lost. As the boy deteriorates physically, as he is stripped of his flesh, he loses his potential for love as a force in a meaningful life. To be sure, this takes a long time, for love is strong. But in the end, however, only emptiness remains. During the first selection upon his arrival at Birkenau, he is as yet unaware that the stripping process has begun—"men to the left, women to the right." His mother and sister disappear forever. His father, who was somewhat on the periphery of Eliezer's world in Sighet, now becomes for him the fulcrum, the one stable point with which Eliezer can align himself even after his commitment to his father becomes hardly more than a conditioned reflex.

The reader of *Night* has to remain conscious of the fact that the events Eliezer witnesses in the inferno are experienced by him as a child. Although he is not innocent in the sense of being unreflective (for he had studied and interpreted the scriptures too much), he is still innocent in that the world into which he is cast is at first totally alien and incomprehensible to him. The child is father of the man and as such holds the promise for the future. In the concentration camps, that future was demolished and the innocence of the child perverted. The child in the camp did not only hear stories about evil such as the destruction of the Temple, over which he could weep with the empathy that distance permits, but the child lived in what has become for the twentieth century a myth of evil. The camp was never a metaphor for the child. His first consciousness of evil is aroused by the sight of infant damnation that pales all images of the slaughter of the innocent: a lorry filled with babies is emptied into a burning pit. "In the depths of my heart, I bade farewell to my father, to the whole universe; and in spite of myself, the words formed themselves and issued from my lips: '. . . May His name be blessed and magnified . . .'." Eliezer can still pray, prayer that has already become a reflex action.

Eliezer's rebellion against God is initiated by witnessing two hangings. The first, the execution of a heroic Polish youth, affects him hardly at all; the second, the hanging of an angelic-looking child, affects him deeply. On the eve of Rosh Hashanah, however, when hundreds of men prostrate themselves with love before their invisible and powerful God, "like trees before the tempest," Eliezer accuses God of breaking His covenant with men. He does not deny the existence of God; he contracts away from God, as God has withdrawn from him: "My eyes were open and I was alone—terribly alone in a world without God and without man. Without love or mercy. I had ceased to be anything but ashes, yet I felt myself stronger than the Almighty to whom my life had been tied for so long." Until now, his ego had identified with the archetypal symbols of his religion which he had projected, not only as an energy within "the depths of his soul," but also as existing externally. As a religious but powerless human being, he felt empathy at the sight of suffering, an onrush of powerful emotion that ought to be felt by the all-powerful god he had projected. Since the god remains silent, no matter how much the believer demonstrates love, Eliezer rejects the god through his ego's expression of will. With hope gone, his will makes him strong and allows him to say no to a cosmic system that is contradicted by the reality of Auschwitz. He turns to his weak, earthly father instead and achieves with him a wordless moment of perfect communion of love, a primal communication of touch assuring that the other is really there.

Even the bond with the earthly father is threatened, however, by the temptation that he might be better off without him. This temptation develops during the evacuation of Auschwitz as the inmates are forced to run through the snow and are eventually transported, snow and ice encrusted, on open cattle wagons. Torn between the need to protect and reject his parent, Eliezer projects images of how other sons treat their fathers. The most horrible of these images occurs in the cattle wagon when a nameless son, crazed with starvation, creeps towards his father who is chewing a crust of bread. He beats his father down only to be himself killed by his starving fellow prisoners. Eliezer, however, saves his father from being thrown out as dead from the cattle wagon, but increasingly these rescues become the prolonging of a death of which the son does not want to be guilty. He can never give enough love to keep his father alive; love is no longer enough, just as hate will not suffice to avenge the camp experience. He will be left with guilt because he survives, but at the time of his father's death he only feels drained: "And, in the depths of my being, in the recesses of my weakened conscience could I have searched it, I might perhaps have found something like—free at last!"

Having struggled between life and death for so long, he looks into a mirror at the end of his ordeal: "From the depths of the mirror, a corpse gazed back at me. The look in his eyes, as they stared into mine, has never left me." The image communicates the demonic epiphany of a Narcissus locked into the closed circuit of experiences that have robbed him of all interest in and love for life. He cannot love the world, and, since the world is reflected in his eyes, he cannot love himself. But Wiesel writes "a corpse" and "his eyes," and this implies that the reflection is experienced as *the other*, a life-saving disjunction which turns the camp experience at that moment into memory and all which the process of memory entails. The look in the mirror holds a memory of a loveless world, but it is in memory of a loved family who died in the camp that the book is created. In the re-creation of the struggle to maintain love and in the eventual defeat of love, the catastrophe is once more enacted: the mother once more carries the sister to the gas chamber, God is once more rejected, the father dies once more. But this time it happens in a verbal structure, in a record that preserves and stalls forgetfulness. *Night* is an homage to such love and its struggle; it is also, however, a denial of forgiveness and expiation, for the look of the corpse never leaves the autobiographer who incorporated the world of Auschwitz into his very being.

JOSEPHINE KNOPP AND ARNOST LUSTIG

SOURCE: Josephine Knopp and Arnost Lustig, "Holocaust Literature II: Novels and Short Stories," in *Encountering the Holocaust: An Interdisciplinary Survey*, edited by Byron L. Sherwin and Susan G. Ament, Impact Press, 1979, pp. 267-315.

[*Knopp is the director of research for the National Institute on the Holocaust and is the author of* The Trial of Judaism *(1971), a study of contemporary Jewish literature. In the excerpt below, she and Lustig discuss Wiesel's portrayal of the Holocaust and the effect of the concentration camps on Jewish perceptions of God and God's covenant with Israel.*]

As witness to the Holocaust Wiesel remains firmly within the Judaic tradition—established by Abraham, Moses, Jeremiah, and Job—of condemnation of God for failure to intercede on behalf of His creatures. Indeed, Wiesel's first five works can be read as a sustained developing revolt against God from within a Jewish context. Jewish tradition provides not only adequate precedents for such revolt, but legal and moral sanction as well, in the covenant with God into which the Jewish people entered: "We are to protect His Torah, and He, in turn, assumes responsibility for Israel's presence in the world.... when our physical existence was threatened we simply reminded God of His duties and promises deriving from the covenant." Against this background the reality of Auschwitz confronts the Jew with a dilemma, an "absurdity" which cannot be easily dismissed and which stubbornly refuses to dissipate of its own accord. Since the Jewish God is "Lord of actual history," the Jew must conclude that God was somehow part of Auschwitz, thus calling into question the continued validity of the covenant itself. Clearly, any recognition that the covenant might no longer be operative would strike a devastating blow at the very foundations of Judaism and leave the theologically serious Jew isolated, to struggle in an unaccustomed loneliness with an indifferent, or worse, hostile universe. After Auschwitz, he is joined to the French existentialists in confronting the absurdity of the universe, an absurdity engendered and given substance by the Holocaust and signaling the breakdown of the covenant. The only possible response that remains within the framework of Judaism is rebellion against God, a denunciation of God that at the same time demands that He fulfill His contractual obligation. This is the religious/moral context within which Wiesel attempts to apprehend and assimilate the events of the Holocaust.

In his early works Wiesel's role as witness to the Holocaust predominates, perhaps in response to the survivor's fear that the tale would not be told or, if told, not believed.

Hence, the autobiography *Night* exposes to view the inner life of the young Jewish inmate of a German concentration camp, while *Dawn* and *The Accident* are largely autobiographical works describing the torment that this survivor endures after liberation. As with other Holocaust writers, for Wiesel survival itself carries with it a stigma, engendering guilt and a sense that the survivor is no longer of the living, that he is—in Wiesel's phrase—"a messenger of death." If the enormities of the concentration camp experience lead Eliezer/Elisha, Wiesel's protagonist, to reject God in *Night*, the torment of survival brings him to question seriously and reject the Jewish moral commitment in *Dawn* and *The Accident*, not, however, without the sense that in violating the traditional Jewish code of morality he has violated his own being: "I've killed. I've killed Elisha." The rebellion against Jewish tradition, begun in the Nazi concentration camp of *Night* and continued in *Dawn* through Elisha's killing of a fellow human creature, reaches a climax in *The Accident* in the protagonist's act of attempted suicide. For the sacredness of life, God's gift to mankind, is basic to Judaism and, in fact, arguably the most basic tenet of the Jewish faith. Thus the Jew is not free to argue, as does Camus, that "there is but one truly serious philosophical problem, and that is suicide." It is not for the Jew to judge "whether"—in the words of Camus—"life is or is not worth living"; only the God of Israel, as Creator and Giver of Life, is to determine when life is to end. In Wiesel's Jewish context, therefore, the suicide attempt takes on significance as a kind of ultimate defiance of God, explainable only on the basis of a recognition, in reaction to Auschwitz, that God encompasses evil as well as good, that in violating His covenant with Man, God has not only withdrawn His protection, but has left man free of the restraints of His Laws and Commandments.

Wiesel's hero has thus come to share the attitude which characterizes Camus's protagonist, Meursault, at the beginning of *The Stranger*—a sense of the absurdity of the world and the pointlessness of human existence. In contrast to Meursault, however, Wiesel's character is obsessed by the relationship of man to God, never losing his belief in God's presence in the world, even while bitterly denouncing God's injustice toward man. While Meursault appears to have no past, living in a kind of timeless present devoid of history and human attachments, the narrator of *The Accident* cannot forget his past despite the horror of the memory, because

"I am my past. If it is buried, I'm buried with it." He is at great pains to explain his desire to die, to make understood the tragedy of those "living-dead," who came back after merely lasting through the Holocaust, devoid of joy, hope, or delusions about the future.

The Town Beyond the Wall represents a new point of view in Wiesel's writing, emphasizing the culpability of man for the crimes of the Holocaust and indicting the indifferent observers equally with the executioners. Here the problem is couched primarily in terms of man's cruelty and indifference to his fellows, and the solution is sought within man as well. Indeed, in this work Wiesel clearly seeks response to the Holocaust in the secular existential philosophy of Camus. Following Albert Camus, Wiesel suggests that man's proper stance in the face of suffering entails a rejection of suicide and madness; it involves struggling against indifference, assuming responsibility for one's fellow man, retaining an essential core of humanity at all costs.

In contrast to the Jewish victims of his childhood, who were unable or unwilling either to surrender faith or to acknowledge the possibility of evil within God, the protagonist of *The Town Beyond the Wall*—now named Michael—frees himself to take positive action by refusing to shrink from these alternatives. Michael's ultimate victory over the tortures and loneliness of imprisonment comes about, not through prayer, which he rejects in spite of the danger of heading to perdition, but by extending his help to another human being, the demented young prisoner whose life he saves, whose mind he struggles with all his being to bring out of its catatonic state. The struggle to cure the boy saves Michael because it is a meaningful protest against the world's indifference, and thus, as for Adam Stein, an effective antidote to clinical madness. As Byron Sherwin has pointed out, Michael does in fact display a kind of madness in *Town Beyond the Wall*, the "moral madness" (in the sense of A. J. Heschel) of the ancient Hebrew prophets, which entails remaining human and retaining a concern for others in a world in which the social norm is hate and indifference. It is in this sense that Sherwin interprets the novel's epitaph from Dostoevsky: "I have a plan: to go mad." The moral madman is closely linked in spirit to the "absurd man," in the sense of Camus; both are able to face the world's absurdity unflinchingly, with aversion perhaps, but without denial. Where the absurd man may succeed in doing this on the basis of a rational decision, executed by force of will, the moral madman, like the Hebrew prophets, often acts upon inner compulsion, unable to do otherwise. The end result is the same in either case—that genuine confrontation with the absurd advocated in *The Myth of Sisyphus*.

Moral madness reappears as a theme of some importance in Wiesel's succeeding novel *The Gates of the Forest*. At the beginning of the work it is not the young protagonist Gregor, but Gabriel, his philosopher-teacher, who displays moral madness by reacting with laughter to the horrors of the War. Gabriel clings to this position even in the face of death; exposing himself to capture in order to save Gregor, he bursts into overwhelming laughter at the very moment he falls into the hands of the German soldiers. A similar response to enormity is urged upon Gabriel—in New York after the War—by the Hasidic Rebbe, who renews the emphasis, so prominent in *Night*, upon the implication of God in evil, but with a difference. Here there is a new awareness that the recognition of God's guilt is, in itself, not a viable solution to the problem of evil in the world, that there must be a constructive response from man as well. That response, Wiesel suggests, can be expressed in the Hasidic way of prayer and joy, through clinging to God until he is forced to recognize once again his covenantal responsibility for the preservation of the Jewish people. Thus, Wiesel's protest against God is such that it allows him to remain a Jew, "within God"—in Wiesel's phrase. The object of this protest is not nihilism, not denial of God, but the very opposite—the reestablishment of God's order in a world which has witnessed the destruction of order. The boy of *Night*, who vows never to "forget those flames which consumed my faith forever," gives way to the man of *The Gates of the Forest*, who understands that "God's final victory . . . lies in man's inability to reject Him."

The Gates of the Forest provides the first instance within Wiesel's canon in which traditional Christian dogma concerning the historical role of the Jewish people assumes more than minor importance; this novel, indeed, marks only the beginning of an increasing preoccupation with that theme in the author's more recent writings. Wiesel's attention to the function of Christian attitudes in Jewish tragedy—especially in *The Oath*—where it serves as a framework supporting the entire plot—suggests that in the teachings of the Church, he has found (as have a number of Christian theologians in recent years) a clue toward understanding man's participation, whether active or passive, in Auschwitz. His recent work develops and builds upon the notion that men were freed to commit and accept the enormities of the Holocaust in part by the accumulation of centuries of Christian retribution against those among Jesus' people who did not accept him as Messiah.

Two episodes in *The Gates of the Forest* have particular interest in this connection. The first of these describes a school play performed in a Hungarian village upon the subject—"hatred of the Jews and its justification." During the performance the figure of Judas Iscariot—played, ironically, by Gregor, a Jew hiding from the Germans by posing as a mute Gentile—comes under verbal and physical attack as the other actors and the audience are carried away by hatred. As it happens, in his role of deaf-mute, Gregor has heard confessions of many guilty secrets by the villagers, who saw in him a completely safe confessor, one who could carry no tales. In danger of his life, Gregor briefly considers a public exposure of the villagers, who would then, he reasons, turn their hatred from him and toward each other. That Gregor rejects this plan in favor of a far more difficult and dangerous course of action indicates that this Jew-as-Judas, at least, is no betrayer. The impression seems unavoidable that Wiesel is attempting to reach a new understanding of the relationship between Judas and his master here, one that raises questions concerning the traditional Christian view of the betrayal, not only about the motivation of Judas, but about that of Jesus as well.

The second episode involves the village priest, who is harboring a Jewish fugitive. Having saved the Jew from capture by the Germans, he decides it is time to apply himself to the man's soul as well. The priest urges the Jew to accept Jesus, insisting that the trials of the Jewish people would end with their collective repentance. The Jew rejects the priest and his theology: "Stop thinking about our salvation and perhaps the cemeteries won't be so full of Jews." Unable to bear the Jew's dismissal of Jesus as Messiah, and indeed of the Hebraic God Himself, the priest loses control of his anger, ordering the man out of the house—and to certain death.

Consonant with Wiesel's reexamination of the figure of Judas is his reconsideration of the fundamental problem of the Crucifixion, from a Jewish perspective, in a brief episode in *A Beggar in Jerusalem*. The scene relates a conversation between the dying Jesus and one called Shlomo, who makes it clear to Jesus that he is not to be accepted as the Messiah by future generations of Jews: "You think you are suffering for my sake and for my brothers, yet we are the ones who will be made to suffer for you, because of you." Through Shlomo, Wiesel expresses his sympathy for Jesus and a grasp of the moral dilemma posed for him by the "actions his followers would undertake in his name to spread his word . . . the innumerable victims persecuted and crushed under the sign of his law." Wiesel perceives with Emil Fackenheim that "the returning Christ would have gone to Auschwitz . . . involuntarily if not voluntarily." His artistic perception as expressed here foreshadows a significant theological insight: it is not in Jesus as man and prophet, but rather in the Church's conception of Jesus as Messiah that the genesis of Christian anti-Semitism is to be found.

In *The Oath*, Wiesel makes his most extensive attempt to date to gauge the role of Christian doctrine in the formulation of the "Final Solution of the Jewish question," removing the major plot action to the Eastern European village of Kolvillag in the 1920's—well before Hitler's rise to power—in order to add a new dimension to his understanding of the Holocaust by viewing the future from the perspective of the tragic Jewish past. The plot is set into motion by the confrontation in the present between two victims of past Jewish persecutions: Azriel, sole survivor of the pogrom in Kolvillag some fifty years earlier, and a young man who shares in the agony of survival by virtue of his being the child of survivors of the Holocaust. The encounter between the two reveals that they are linked not only by the Jewish history of suffering but in their personal fates as well. It becomes apparent that only Azriel can prevent the young man's "abdication" from a life of despair, and only by revealing the secrets which he and the dead victims of the pogrom had sworn under oath not to reveal. After fifty years of silence Azriel, as the sole survivor and link between the victims of Kolvillag and the living present, speaks out in order to avoid "not suffering but . . . indifference to suffering." Azriel relates the circumstances leading to the final destruction of the Jewish community of Kolvillag, and with his tale as vehicle, *The Oath* emerges as a quasi-theological inquest into the Christian roots of anti-Semitism. Through the novel's dramatic action, Wiesel examines the consequences of confrontation between the teachings of Judaism and traditional Christian dogma relating to the Jews, and in so doing he raises a number of serious and difficult problems that challenge both Jewish and Christian theology in the post-Holocaust era.

Azriel's story incorporates into the present the medieval accusation of ritual murder—the Jews of Kolvillag are held responsible for the disappearance of a Christian youth—thus linking the circumstances leading to the destruction of Kolvillag and, by implication, those surrounding the Holocaust itself with the pogroms of the Middle Ages. While the tale of "ritual murder" is central to the implication of Christianity in the Holocaust, the consequences for Judaic thought issue from the theological debate between the Rebbe and Moshe. Arguing within the framework of traditional *halacha* (Jewish law), the Rebbe opposes Moshe's offer of martyrdom, which can be justified only when the Torah itself is in danger. Moshe's counter-argument cuts deeper, reaching for another level of understanding of the covenant and describing the dilemma of the theologically serious Jew threatened with pogrom: "We must save the divine Law even if it places us in contradiction to the Law . . . Without Jews there would be no Torah. . . . They are inextricably bound." Moshe understands the paradox inherent in affirming God's presence during the Kolvillag pogrom, that such affirmation would imply concomitant damnation of God for his complicity in the evil of the pogrom. Yet in characteristically mystical fashion, Moshe demands that the Jews of Kolvillag remain Jews, continuing to praise God, but in "silence" rather than as witnesses. He concludes that despite the importance in Jewish history of the witness to disaster, of the "survivor-story-teller," they must now "adopt a new way: silence ... we shall testify no more." Moshe's exhortation of his fellow Jews to remain with God does not in itself break new theological ground, reflecting rather the theological insight achieved in Wiesel's earlier work: man's need to define himself in relationship to God continues undiminished, even after Auschwitz. However—and we shall enlarge upon this presently—*The Oath* does offer fresh possibilities for assimilating the knowledge of God's implication in evil, despite Wiesel's assertion elsewhere of the impossibility of understanding Auschwitz on the level of God.

At the same time, the recognition with which *The Oath* is informed—clearer than elsewhere in Wiesel's writings—of the implication in Jewish suffering of Christian doctrine and Christian institutions, of the "love of God turned into hate of man," as Wiesel puts it, contributes to the possibility of comprehending Auschwitz on the level of man. This recognition is expressed in part through the concern with the history of Christian atrocity against the Jews displayed by Shmuel, who immerses himself in martyrology in an attempt to gain a better understanding of what is to come. In continuing to act as chronicler and witness, Shmuel rejects Moshe's oath, which has as its purpose the rupture of continuity in Jewish history, the abolition of suffering through an attack upon the history of suffering. This opposition of responses in Moshe and Shmuel serves as a focal point in the novel for the tension between the survivor's desire to remain silent and his need to record the event. This theme is a familiar one in the works of Wiesel, reflecting the author's personal dilemma as survivor, his feeling, often expressed, that the Holocaust demands response yet imposes silence. However, in *The Oath,* for the first time in Wiesel's fiction, this theme emerges as a central problem of the novel. Like Wiesel himself, Shmuel chooses to continue to serve as witness to history. Initiating Azriel into the tradition of the Book, he fulfills his chosen role, discharges his obligation to link Jewish past and future, denies the validity of Moshe's position.

With the killing already begun, the priest and the Bishop "decided this was the time to debate orthodoxy and heresy," giving credence to the Rebbe's position that "Help cannot come from the other side. A Jew must not expect anything from Christians, man must not expect anything from man. Consolation can and must come only from God." Consolation perhaps, but not rescue, and this is the heart of the difficulty Wiesel experiences in understanding the Holocaust on the level of God. Christian churchmen have not intervened on behalf of the Jews, but neither has the God of Israel, who, according to Jewish tradition, is bound to do so by virtue of the covenant. While Wiesel's earlier novels respond to this inherent paradox by declaring God guilty of complicity in evil, *The Oath* reaches toward a resolution within the Talmudic tradition of *Hester Panim*, the Hiding of the Divine Face, a point of view foreshadowed, however, in a legend appended to *The Town Beyond the Wall*, relating how God and man exchanged places, "so neither ... was ever again what he seemed to be." Thus God may forfeit omnipotence and become, like man, not indifferent to history, but unable to control it, powerless to combat man's destructive impulse. The legend suggests that in observing helplessly the suffering of man, God suffers with him as well, since "the liberation of the one was bound to the liberation of the other."

In contrast to Wiesel, who has consistently admitted his inability to reconcile the Holocaust with the traditional Jewish view of the God of history and the covenant, Nelly Sachs in the verse drama *Eli* has employed the notion of *Hester Panim* in an attempt to achieve precisely such a reconciliation. *Eli* presents a plea for the survivors of the Holocaust to "re-establish their relationship to God and to regain his attention—in effect to bring him out of hiding" and an examination of the thesis that through prayer this can, in fact, be accomplished. While Wiesel does not go nearly this far in establishing upon *Hester Panim* a theological vantage point from which to view God's silence during the Holocaust, in *The Oath* he seems to weigh seriously the possibilities for understanding inherent in the concept. Illustrative are the Rebbe's questioning in the face of a pogrom, whether God "could be turning His Face away from His people," and Moshe's understanding—on his own terms, in terms of silence—of God's role in the affairs of men: "rather than speak, God listens; rather than intervene and decide, He waits and judges only later."

Though Wiesel implies, through Moshe, that God may have no choice in the Hiding of the Face, the suggestion remains as well that God is implicated in evil by virtue of his ambivalence: "Satan is more than evil," Moshe declares, "he is evil disguised as good, the link between the two... his place is at God's right. An awesome concept, leading to horror. How is one to distinguish God in evil, Satan in good?" Moshe's perception of the ambiguous and elusive nature of God's role in good and evil finds its counterpart in "the perplexing duality of the knowledge of God"—as theologian

Eliezer Berkovits puts it—that confronts the Jew of faith after the Holocaust:

> He [the Jew of faith] knows of the numerous revelations of the divine presence as he knows of the overlong phrases of God's absence.... But he also knows that God's absence, even at Auschwitz, is not absolute.... There were many who found him even in his hiding.

Between Berkovits and Wiesel there is an essential convergence of overall outlook, a unanimity in stressing the interconnectedness of all of Jewish history, the unbroken continuity of Jewish tradition. Shmuel's immersion in the study of the atrocities punctuating Jewish history, Moshe's teaching that "nothing in Jewish tradition was unconnected," find their counterpart in the observation of Berkovits that "a straight line leads from the first act of Christian oppression against the Jews and Judaism in the fourth century to the Holocaust in the twentieth."

Kolvillag is a Jewish Everytown, whose destruction links past pogroms with future Holocaust. As he watched the town burn—destroying both Jew and Christian, both victim and executioner in a powerful evocation of the indivisibility of violence—Azriel, the sole survivor, the indispensable link needed to maintain the continuity of Jewish history, understood that he had just glimpsed the future. Kolvillag provides a backdrop against which Azriel can view the Holocaust to come in terms of the accumulation of past events, but his view of the future is only one side of a dual truth. A description of the other is provided by Berkovits:

> The rabbis of the Talmud could speak of the silence of God at the time of the destruction of the Temple ... and yet remain true to His word, because ... Israel survived, remained historically viable, full of future expectation.

Azriel not only survives, but he survives to rescue the young Jew from self-destruction, to maintain Jewish continuity in *that* man's future by passing on to him, through the tale of Kolvillag and its victims, the role of witness inherited from Shmuel. Like Azriel, who was saved from the flames of Kolvillag in order to testify as witness, this young Jew no longer has the right to die. In spite of his initial reluctance, Azriel ultimately has rejected silence in favor of history, understanding the nature of man's encounter with God not as Moshe understood it, but as did his father Shmuel. As witness to future generations, Azriel becomes the fictive counterpart of his creator, carrying out the role that Wiesel, as writer and survivor, has taken upon himself.

ELLEN S. FINE

SOURCE: Ellen S. Fine, in her *Legacy of Night: The Literary Universe of Elie Wiesel*, State University of New York Press, 1982, pp. 1-9.

[*In the excerpt below, Fine offers an overview of Wiesel's life and works.*]

The imperative to testify characterizes the life and literature of Holocaust survivor Elie Wiesel. Obsessed with the need to remember and to transmit the story and history of the six million Jews annihilated by the Nazis, Wiesel has committed himself to the role of witness (or what is called in French *temoin*) as the justification for his existence. He considers writing "not a profession, but an occupation, a duty," and his primary function as a writer is to give testimony. His *temoignages*, novels, plays, legends, essays, dialogues, and speeches form concentric circles around the dark event of the Holocaust and the identity of the Jew in its aftermath.

Essentially a messenger deeply concerned with informing and warning the world of the horrors of genocide, Wiesel tells his own tale—that of a young Orthodox Jewish boy growing up in a small Eastern European town destined to be destroyed by the Nazi invaders. He describes the odyssey that led from his native town of Sighet, nestled in the Carpathian mountains of Transylvania, to the macabre *univers concentrationnaire* of Auschwitz and Buchenwald, and finally to postwar France, Israel, and the United States. His works retrace this journey, recollecting and chronicling the personal and historical circumstances that have structured his life before, during, and after the Holocaust.

Wiesel writes from the perspective of a witness-storyteller who knows that the essence of his story—filled with unanswered political, philosophical, and theological questions—is impossible to communicate. Nevertheless he has chosen the vocation of writer, with the objective of using written language as a vehicle of communion. In his literary universe, he seeks to assimilate the multiple levels of his encounter with history, to form legends and myth out of memory. His response to the voyage into Night takes the form of artistic creation, which, as Albert Camus has noted, does not remove us from the drama of our time, but instead brings us closer. Elie Wiesel's books represent a mode of survival, an attempt to come to terms with existence in a post-Holocaust epoch. At the same time, they demonstrate a survivor's ability to fictionalize the raw material and transmute it into works of art....

In Wiesel's novels there is a general progression from witnessing to bearing witness. The survivor-protagonist, whose voice has been silenced by nocturnal flames, struggles to express himself and to recover the faculty of speech. He slowly learns to reach out to others and to reaffirm his identity as a member of the human community. The assertion of the voice is linked to the vocation of witness and is at the core of the thematic development. In their quest for a voice, the Wieselean characters pass through various stages, reflecting the author's own spiritual-intellectual itinerary. Their story is basically his, for he is very much a part of many of his protagonists. Yet, transposed into a fictional mode, Wiesel's story exposes the reader to the intensely problematic nature of the witness. The contradictions inherent in the act of testifying are revealed in both conscious and unconscious forms. A close study of the texts discloses an underlying tension between the compulsion to tell the tale and the fear of betraying the sanctity of the subject. The author has created characters who allow him to confront himself, and a new kind of protagonist—emblem of our times—issues forth from the literary mind after Auschwitz: *the protagonist as witness.*

Wiesel's novels lend themselves to a chronological investigation. They follow a logical sequence, each exploring a particular option open to the survivor after the journey to the end of night: killing, suicide, madness, faith and friendship, return from exile, silence, and involvement in revolutionary movements, in history itself. "The books came one after the other to answer the questions I was asking myself," Wiesel tells us. "Each time a gate closed, the possibilities diminished, and one hope after another was stripped away." But if each text shuts a door, it also points the way to the volume that follows. The continuity and cumulative force of his oeuvre are sustained by the repetition of themes and the reappearance of characters who resemble one other. The author even joins one work to the next by a deliberately chosen phrase. "I always smuggle into every book one sentence which is the substance of the next books—a Jewish tradition," he declares.

[The novels should be discussed] . . . in chronological order, not for the purpose of interpreting the manifest theme around which each book revolves, but rather to trace the course of the protagonist as witness: his sharpened consciousness as bearer of memory, the mythification and demythification of his role, as the act of speaking—and of writing—becomes more difficult. . . .

In order to understand the struggles of the fictional witnesses, let us first consider what personally motivated Wiesel to become an author. Two major factors influenced his dedication to the written word: his religious background as an Orthodox Jew and the event of the Holocaust.

Elie Wiesel was born on September 30, 1928 in Sighet, a border town with a long and complicated political history. Once a part of the Austrian Empire, the town was given up to Hungary, handed over to Rumania and then taken back by Hungary at the beginning of World War II. During the war, Germany incorporated Sighet into the Third Reich. The Soviet Union took over at the end of the war, finally rendering the town to Rumania. Presently located about a kilometer from the Soviet frontier, Sighet has approximately 120,000 inhabitants.

Wiesel grew up in the town's *shtetl,* or Jewish section. His father, Shlomo, was a middle-class shopkeeper who spent much of his time working for the community. In the early years of the war he helped save Polish Jews who had escaped to Hungary. Because of his efforts he spent a few months in jail. Shlomo instilled humanist values in his only son (Wiesel had three sisters) and encouraged him to learn modern Hebrew and to read its literature. His father, Wiesel tells us, represented "reason" and his mother "faith." The daughter of Dodye Feig, a fervent Hasid and a farmer who lived in a village near Sighet, Sarah Feig was a highly cultured woman who insisted that her son study the Torah, Talmud, mystical doctrines of the Kabbala, and the teachings of Hasidic masters. She wanted him to be both a rabbi and a Ph.D.

Immersed in religious texts, the young Wiesel learned to venerate the Book and to regard everything connected to the word as sacred. "Jewish theology made a writer of me," he states. At the age of twelve he wrote a long commentary on the Bible, which he found some twenty years later under a pile of discarded volumes in the only synagogue left in Sighet. Had it not been for the war, he probably would have continued to write commentaries on the Bible and Talmud. If anyone had told the pious youth pouring over the same page of the same book of the Torah for days on end that some day he would become a novelist—and a French novelist at that—he would have turned his back, convinced that he was being mistaken for someone else.

To an Orthodox Jew in the *shtetl,* novels were puerile, a waste of time. How could the fictional universe invented by man compare to the transcendent mystery of holy scripture? In the Orthodox tradition the scribe or *sofer* is highly respected in contrast to the writer of fiction, who is considered a *batlan,* someone who has nothing better to do. Several years after the war Wiesel returned to his grandfather's town to see the old Hasidic rabbi, who at once recognized him as "the grandson of Dodye Feig." Asked how he earned his living, Wiesel replied that he wrote. "You write?" the rabbi responded in disbelief. "That's your work? Are you serious? You do nothing else? No other profession? You spend your life writing, that's all?"

The Holocaust was to radically change Wiesel's destiny and take him far from the kingdom of Dodye Feig. In March 1944 the Germans came to Hungary; one month later they began the mass deportations from Transylvania, including fifteen thousand Jews from Sighet and approximately eighteen thousand from neighboring villages. At the age of fifteen, Wiesel was plunged from the stability of small-town life into the grotesque universe of *Night.* Along with his parents and three sisters, he was deported to Auschwitz, where his mother and younger sister were immediately sent to the gas chambers; his two older sisters managed to survive. Wiesel and his father stayed together as they were shunted from Auschwitz to Buchenwald where the youth watched his father slowly die. This was to mark him for the rest of his life, and his vow to bear witness to his father's murder is reflected throughout his writing. Indeed, Wiesel's entire literary structure appears to be founded on the need to transmit his father's legacy and to reaffirm the paternal authority by telling the story.

After his liberation from Buchenwald, Wiesel wanted to go to Palestine but was prevented by British immigration restrictions. Refusing to be repatriated to Sighet, he was put on a train with four hundred other child refugees who had been in Buchenwald. Originally destined to go to Belgium, the train was rerouted to France by De Gaulle. At the border the young passengers were asked if they wanted to become French citizens, and Wiesel, unable to understand, failed to respond. Consequently, he remained stateless until 1963, when he was granted American citizenship.

At first, Wiesel spent time in Normandy, France, under the auspices of the children's aid organization, Oeuvres du Secours aux Enfants, and then went to Paris where he studied the Talmud and earned a living as a tutor in Yiddish, Hebrew, and the Bible. A young French philosopher, Francois Wahl, helped him to learn French by introducing him to the great classical authors, beginning with Racine. Wiesel learned the language by listening in silence. He took courses at the Sorbonne in philosophy and literature and, although he never officially completed his studies, he wrote a long dissertation on comparative ascetism. In postwar France he was exposed to intellectual movements such as existentialism and to the thinking of such men of letters as Albert Camus, Jean-Paul Sartre, and Andre Malraux, whose philosophical and moral explorations of the human condition and whose notion of the writer as witness to his times were to influence his own work. Wiesel also seems to have incorporated into his writing the later stylistic techniques of the French *Nouveau Roman* which interrogate reality and question systems of time and causality found in established narrative forms.

Learning French for Wiesel was like entering a house that welcomed him; it offered him a haven, a refuge, a home, and meant a "new beginning, a new possibility, a new world." The adoption of French as his written language marked a significant change in consciousness—the death of one era and the initiation into another. It was the expression of a certain faith in the ability to start again, a distancing from the brutal experience of the Holocaust, a rejection of the past. Yiddish, his mother tongue, and Hebrew, the language of his early educational training, evoked painful emotions, while the Hungarian and German languages were those of the oppressors. Wiesel therefore chose French as the foundation for rebuilding his new house and for reconstructing his intellectual life. Although he eventually published newspaper articles in Hebrew, Yiddish, and even in English (which he learned on a trip to India in 1952), his books have always been written in French, a language that he says "lends itself to narrative."

Adapting to an unfamiliar linguistic framework demands discipline and a shift in orientation. For the young survivor of the Holocaust, French represented a Cartesian language, dominated by reason, logic, and clarity. To introduce Midrashic tales and mystical notions of the Kabbala into a nonmystical language was a challenge and form of defiance. "It is a question of plunging into a language that is foreign to me and expressing ideas not made for it," Wiesel observes. Piotr Rawicz, a survivor from the Ukraine who also writes in French, confirms this notion: "Elie Wiesel enriches the French domain with philosophical matters and emotional states that would have made their entrance into the letters of Descartes' land with difficulty if it had not been for him." Indeed, Wiesel's style is unique because of the way it fuses aspects of the French novel with Jewish lore. His narrative structure is often fragmented: characterized by shifts in points of view, disjointed images, contradictory statements, and a blending of fact and fiction, of history and imagination. The effect produced is similar to the mode of the *Nouveau Roman* and, at the same time, is in keeping with the tradition of the Jewish storyteller who weaves folktales, anecdotes, and parables into the fabric of his texts, transmitting messages that are highly ambiguous. This peculiar combination of French stylistics and Jewish legends has caused some critics to view Wiesel's works as collections of short sketches rather than completely developed novels, although in his most recent novel, *The Testament*, the main character and plot are more fully elaborated than in any of the previous books. Many commentators in France have called Wiesel a poet and a visionary rather than a novelist in the conventional sense....

The thrust of his writing does not lie in his literary techniques and he has openly rejected the notion of art for art's sake. He is basically a storyteller with something to say. If the French language has provided the edifice for Wiesel's creative endeavors, his motivation to become a writer and the subject matter of his publications are clearly not to be found in the French heritage. He first realized that he was going to write when he looked at his face after the liberation of Buchenwald and knew that he had to speak about "*that* face and *that* mirror and *that* change"; "I knew that anyone who remained alive had to become a storyteller, a messenger, had to speak up." The Holocaust thus imposed the vocation of writer upon Wiesel as it did upon other survivors living in France, such as Anna Langfus and Piotr Rawicz, who might never have written novels if it had not been for their concentration camp experience.

Although Wiesel made a vow to keep silent for ten years after the war, during that time he read widely and thought constantly about the Holocaust in his travels around the world as a correspondent for Israeli and French newspapers. Conscious of the need to bear witness, he did not know how to approach a subject so overwhelming in its magnitude that words could only distort it. Nonetheless, the ten years of silent reflection prepared him for his meeting in 1954 with the French Catholic writer Francois Mauriac, who encouraged the young journalist to write about his journey into darkness. Mauriac became a kind of patron to him, a protector, a friend.

Two years after his interview with Mauriac (described in detail in *A Jew Today*), Wiesel published his first work, written in Yiddish, *Un di Velt hot Geshvign* (*And the World Remained Silent*), an eight-hundred-page *temoignage* of his life in the death camp universe. In 1958 he condensed it and translated it into French as *La Nuit*. Deeply moved by the book, Mauriac wrote the foreword. The text became a personal Bible for Wiesel, forming the nucleus of his subsequent volumes, the center around which all of his tales revolve. The publication also marked the beginning of his literary career and affirmed his task as *temoin*: never to forget the voices of those who perished in the Nazi concentration camps.

In effect, the desire to commemorate the dead and to give expression to their presence through his voice is one of the primary sources of Wiesel's will to bear witness. His words mourn and elegize his family, friends and the little *shtetl* of his youth peopled with rabbis, teachers, beggars, and madmen—figures who frequently reappear in his works. By building a monument to them in the form of tales and myths, he creates a memorial to a community deprived of its graves. The dead hover over him as he engraves his testimony onto the printed page: "When one writes, thinking of those invisible victims who should be his readers and are actually his writers (because he's writing their story), then one is very humble and very daring at the same time—in writing a sentence or when translating an image." For Wiesel, the act of recording becomes analogous to inscriptions on a gravestone, a lasting message sculpted into the resistant matter: "For me writing is a *matzeva*, an invisible tombstone, erected to the memory of the dead unburied. Each word corresponds to a face, a prayer, the one needing the other so as not to sink into oblivion" [*Legends of Our Time*].

The author's resolution to establish a permanent testament to those who have disappeared signifies a commitment to his faith. The Jews have been traditionally considered witnesses in the historical and religious sense, upholding a legacy that commands them to record, transmit, and remember in order to assure the continuity of history. To be a Jew for Wiesel means to testify: "To bear witness to what is, and to what is no longer.... For the contemporary Jewish writer, there can be no theme more human, no project more universal" [*One Generation After*]. As a writer and a Jew (and Wiesel does not separate the two), he takes upon himself the entire destiny of his people from beginning to now and assumes the function of *le moi-somme*, or collective spokesman: "When I say 'I', I express a certain totality." He believes that all events in Jewish history are linked: every Jew must see himself as having received the Torah at Sinai, having witnessed the destruction of the Temple, and having participated in the Holocaust. According to Wiesel, "Any Jew born before, during or after the Holocaust must enter it again in order to take it upon himself." His strong sense of solidarity with his community has thus provided the framework for his position as a witness whose undying pledge is to work for the survival of his people.

The threat to the survival of the Jews is also a threat to mankind in general, and it is from his particular experience that Wiesel probes the more universal human condition, speaking out for nations oppressed and in danger of being destroyed: Cambodia, Biafra, Paraguay, and Bangladesh. "The Jewish and human conditions become one—a concentric circle, one within the other, not one against the other or one replacing the other," he declares. The isolation, dehumanization, and devastation of one-third of the Jewish population during the Nazi regime reflect the violence and victimization of twentieth-century man *in extremis*. Wiesel continues to protest the injustice of a civilization that permitted the massacre of six million Jews and still tolerates torture and genocide. He believes that the task of the writer-as-witness is "not to appease or flatter, but to disturb, to warn, to question by questioning oneself" [*A Jew Today*]. His moral obligation is to awaken the conscience of an indifferent society.

Yet he has felt frustrated in his attempts to communicate and has gravitated toward silence as an alternative form of testimony. Throughout his texts there is an unresolved conflict between the urge to cry out and the need to remain silent, resulting in a complex thematic interplay. Silence is both destructive and beneficial: it is death, absence, betrayal, and exile, as well as purification and affirmation of being. Words, too, are double-edged: they can misrepresent what they aim to describe but have the power to create, reconstruct, and render immortal. The dialectic of silence and language—of transmitting silence through language—is at the core of the theme of the witness.

Wiesel finds himself in a paradoxical situation. He insists that it is impossible to write about the Holocaust, that Auschwitz negates the foundations of art, defies the imagination, and lies beyond the grasp of literature. He has sought to change his focus and widen his concentric circles by turning to historical and contemporary Jewish themes outside the realm of the Holocaust. Yet, he persists in remembering and in transmitting the legacy of *Night* through the enduring power of his words and silence.

"True despair," says Albert Camus, "is the agony of death, the grave or the abyss. If he speaks, if he reasons, above all if he writes, immediately the brother reaches out his hand, the tree is justified, love is born." Elie Wiesel has chosen to reach out: he has given birth to a literary universe in which his protagonists testify for him. They tell his story, the story of how a young survivor, mute and passive, transforms himself into an articulate messenger. It is these characters—*the witnesses of the witness*—who provide insights for both the reader and the author. "Novelists ought not to speak," he observes. "Their mission consists in listening to other voices, including those of their own creations, of their own characters." We, too, as readers, will listen to the voices from Elie Wiesel's inner landscape so that we may behold the other face of history and may preserve its memory: for to listen to a witness is to become one.

DAPHNE MERKIN

SOURCE: Daphne Merkin, "Witness to the Holocaust," in *The New York Times Book Review*, December 17, 1995, p. 7.

[*Merkin, an American novelist and editor, judges* All Rivers Run to the Sea *"illuminating" but expresses perplexity at how little it reveals about how Wiesel developed from a studious, shy boy to a Nobel Prize-winning author and public figure.*]

It is 1936 and in Sighet—a small Hungarian village of which it was once said that "everyone had his own synagogue, even atheists"—an 8-year-old boy is taken by his mother to see a renowned rabbi who is passing through. The boy is a solitary, rather clinging child, in love with his mother as boys who grow up to be writers or artists often are. The rabbi spends a few minutes alone with the child and then confers with the mother, who emerges from their talk sobbing and refusing to answer any of her son's questions. Twenty-five years later the son visits the bedside of a dying cousin and discovers that the rabbi had predicted that the 8-year-old would grow up to be "a great man in Israel" but that neither he nor the boy's mother would "live to see the day."

We are told this story early on in Elie Wiesel's memoir, *All Rivers Run to the Sea,* but it is quickly passed over, leaving the reader somewhat puzzled as to its intended significance. Is this incident set forth as a touching throwaway anecdote about a rare moment of disharmony between mother and son? Or is it meant to be a revealing allusion to the ultimate value of the life that is about to unfold? Since this particular 8-year-old did in fact grow up to become a cultural icon, a Nobel Peace Prize-winning writer who, in his role as one of the first Holocaust witnesses, would eventually take on the mantle of spokesman for the oppressed, the rabbi who came to Sighet more than half a century ago would appear prescient indeed. But most people who write literary autobiographies are at pains to let their character speak for itself.

I bring up this ambiguity because it permeates to the very core of this memoir. We are allowed glimpses of the private man behind the public figure—the timid boy who bribed his way into his classmates' affection with gifts of food, the high-minded student in a beret whose idea of chatting up an attractive woman was to announce that he is in love with God, the penurious young journalist "imprisoned by . . . inhibitions" who pounded the typewriter keys in a small Upper West Side studio without ever really getting a clear sense of how that boy propelled himself into becoming the man who became Elie Wiesel.

None of which is to say that *All Rivers Run to the Sea* doesn't have illuminating—at times fascinating—moments. Mr. Wiesel remains unequaled at bringing home the experience of horrific, nullifying disorientation that was the first step in the program of genocide known as the Final Solution. "It was a beautiful, unusually hot, sunny day. The streets teemed with distraught men and women. They were thirsty, but the gendarmes prevented them from going back into what had been their last shelter, even for an instant. My sisters and I moved among them with pots and bottles filled with water.... The chief rabbi, his beard cut off, walked wearily, his bag slung over his shoulder."

Mr. Wiesel's literary voice—stately yet lyrical, poetic without being dreamy—fits itself to the cadences of suffering, to the way a feeling of anguish can attach itself to concrete events: "I freeze every time I hear a train whistle," he writes. It must also be said that the immediacy of his images often gets lost in the din of a second, more clamorous voice, imbued with a too-reflective sense of its own importance. You can hear Elie Wiesel, official Keeper of Burdens, in sentences that begin, with an orotund sweep, like this one: "And if I bear within me a nameless grief and disillusionment, a bottomless despair...." Or in de rigueur observations about racism: "In the South I was struck by ... the unforgivable humiliation of its blacks. Looking at the 'White Only' signs, I felt ashamed of being white."

The impulse on the part of writers like Primo Levi, Paul Celan, Ida Fink and Mr. Wiesel is to redress the enormous evil of Nazism by forcing the world to attend to the testimony of countless unmourned dead. But at times, Mr. Wiesel's original exhortation to remember—"I wrote to testify, to stop the dead from dying, to justify my own survival"—gets buried under something less authentic. Within the course of this book, the author himself alludes to disquieting charges in recent years that he has in some way appropriated a historic catastrophe and made it into an egotistic mission. He quotes a reporter who asked him upon the French publication of *The Town Beyond the Wall* in the mid-1960's, "How much longer are you going to wallow in suffering?" and the Prix Goncourt juror who commented in the 80's that "we'll give him the prize when he brings us a novel on some other theme."

The accusation of "collecting the dividends of Auschwitz" is a serious one, and can be fueled by petty as well as legitimate concerns. But the larger issue is that even the direst of tragedies, if publicized enough, begins to fall on resistant ears. Just 10 years after the liberation of the concentration camps—well before what has been called the Holocaust Industry had come into being, prompting the mordant observation "There's no business like Shoah business"—there were those who thought the messenger had outlived the message. Already in 1955 Francois Mauriac, who shepherded the manuscript of Mr. Wiesel's first book, *Night*, was blithely told by his own publisher: "No one's interested in the death camps anymore. It won't sell." The truth, of course, is that at that point few writers had taken on the Holocaust as a literary subject, and *Night* went on to win a worldwide audience.

Along the way to finding out very little about Elie Wiesel, we also find out a lot: that he wasn't particularly close to his father and that he was one of four children, three of whom survived the war (his parents did not). He lost his religious footing in Buchenwald, but as an adolescent refugee in Paris he fell in love once again with Jewish learning and traditions. He would eventually work as a translator for the Irgun, write a romantic spy novel under the pen name Elisha Carmeli and travel to India where he was briefly intrigued by the Hindu tradition. He is thin-skinned: "I am stung by the slightest offense, moved by the slightest act of generosity." One can infer too, that he holds grudges and that there is something remote in his affections.

And still after 400-odd pages, the mystery remains. How did this cautious man plagued by migraines—someone who, by his own account, "broke into a cold sweat whenever he had to open his mouth in public"—become an activist compelled to play out the dictates of his conscience on a world stage? "Success required daring," he writes, "which I lacked." Throughout this memoir the author presents himself—rather curiously, given the arc of his life—as a passive agent of circumstance: "When was it," he asks, "that I realized I was not in control of my destiny?"

One can hear in this question the same plaintive music that has made Mr. Wiesel such a successful speaker, a seductive modesty that goes in the face of the audience's expectations of a Great Man. "I promised myself," he writes with charming diffidence of his decision in 1949 to abandon Paris for the newly declared but still imperiled Jewish state, "I would be more daring in Israel, where everyone is daring." In this same spirit, *All Rivers Run to the Sea* makes references to Mr. Wiesel's growing access to power without sketching in the integral changes that presumably accompanied it; we hear of his close relationships with Mauriac and Golda Meir, his effective intervention on behalf of Soviet Jewry, his meetings with Marguerite Yourcenar, Samuel Beckett and the Lubavitcher Rebbe, without understanding what fed the intense drive of this man who as a student had so feared rejection that he thought it "better to die of hunger than of shame."

There is a beguiling, if not entirely convincing, lack of individual will throughout this recounting, as though the author has intuited that ambition yoked to moral purpose is so problematic that it is best to act as though he simply wandered into the Nobel Prize. Some, although not all, of this may be attributable to the fact that *All Rivers Run to the Sea* is the first of a projected two volumes (although this is never made explicit by the publisher or within the text) and leaves off in the late 60's before Mr. Wiesel had fully met up with fame and honor.

If the reader finishes this book with an impression that the public and private Elie Wiesel seem to dance around each other without ever really connecting, the author has foreseen this: "Some see their work as a commentary on their life; for others it is the other way around. I count myself among the latter. Consider this account, then, as a kind of commentary." In other words, the definitive text of Mr. Wiesel's life is not to be found between hard covers. The 19th-century Jewish sage the Chofetz Chaim said that the sign of a great man is that the closer you get, the greater he seems. It is undoubtedly a sign of Mr. Wiesel's canny elusiveness that he has chosen to protect himself from too close a personal scrutiny, either his own or others'. But perhaps the problem lies with those of us who demand authenticity from people who write accounts of their lives—and even more from people who shine brightly in the firmament—rather than with the book. At any rate, *All Rivers Run to the Sea* suggests that its author prefers to leave an informed assessment of his accomplishments and character not to human judgement but to the God whose existence he has never ceased believing in.

SOURCES FOR FURTHER STUDY

"Elie Wiesel." *America* 159 (19 November 1988): 397-404.

Examines the presence and absence of God in Wiesel's works, the importance of silence in his writings, and the theme of madness in his plays.

Brown, Robert McAfee. "The Need to Remember." *The Christian Century* 109 (20-27 May 1992): 548-50.

Favorable review of *The Forgotten* emphasizing Wiesel's theme that vengeance leads to a rise in evil.

Cargas, Harry J. "Messenger for the Ten Thousandth." *Commonweal* 113 (24 October 1986): 555-57.

Interview in which Wiesel talks about the art of writing and his literary motivation.

Freedman, Samuel G. "Bearing Witness: The Life and Work of Elie Wiesel." *The New York Times Magazine* (October 23 1983): 32-6.

Presents an overview of Wiesel's career and works.

Friedman, John S. "The Art of Fiction LXXIX: Elie Wiesel." *Paris Review* 26 (Spring 1984): 130-78.

Interview, originally conducted in 1978, in which Wiesel discusses his works and subjects, influences, characters, and writing habits.

Plank, Karl A. "Broken Continuities: Night and White Crucifixion." *The Christian Century* 104 (November 4 1987): 963-66.

Discusses crucifixion imagery in *Night*.

August Wilson

1945-

American dramatist.

INTRODUCTION

Wilson emerged in the 1980s as a major figure in American theater. His later dramas, which have received two Tony Awards out of five nominations, three New York Drama Critics' Circle Awards, and two Pulitzer Prizes for drama, are part of a play-cycle in progress devoted to the African-American experience throughout the twentieth century. "I'm taking each decade and looking at one of the most important questions that blacks confronted in that decade and writing a play about it," Wilson explained. "Put them all together and you have a history." *Ma Rainey's Black Bottom* (1984), *Fences* (1985), *Joe Turner's Come and Gone* (1986), *The Piano Lesson* (1987), *Two Trains Running* (1990), and *Seven Guitars* (1995) comprise this project so far. The leisurely pace and familial settings of his plays often evoked comparisons to the dramas of Eugene O'Neill. Praised for their vivid characterizations and richly poetic dialogue, Wilson's dramas often center upon conflicts between African Americans who embrace the harsh reality of their past and those who deny it. Wilson's perceptive, somber explorations of African-American history prompted Samuel G. Freedman to describe the dramatist as "one part Dylan Thomas and one part Malcolm X, a lyric poet fired in the kiln of black nationalism."

Biographical Information

Born Frederick August Kittel in 1945, Wilson grew up in a Pittsburgh, Pennsylvania, ghetto called "The Hill." Disgusted by the racist treatment he endured in many of the schools he had attended, Wilson dropped out in the ninth grade and educated himself at the local library. He discovered the works of such African-American writers as Ralph Ellison, Langston Hughes, and Arna Bontemps, whose powerful, skilled use of elements drawn from their heritage, inspired Wilson to write poetry and short stories, some of which he successfully submitted to black publications at the University of Pittsburgh. In 1968 Wilson co-founded with Rob Penny the Black Horizons on the Hill, a community theater whose goal was to raise consciousness among residents of the area; it also served as a forum for his early dramas. In 1978, when he was invited to write plays for a black theater in St. Paul, Minnesota, Wilson found his artistic voice in the language of his native city. Although *Black Bart and the Sacred Hills* (1981) and *Jitney* (1982) garnered little notice, *Ma Rainey's Black Bottom* attracted the attention of Lloyd Richards, artistic director at the Yale Repertory Theater, who worked with Wilson to refine the play. Richards produced *Ma Rainey* at Yale in 1984, then took it to Broadway, where Wilson was hailed as an important new playwright. Since then, with the exception of *Seven Guitars*, every play by Wilson has debuted at Yale Repertory under the direction of Richards. In addition, *Joe Turner's Come and Gone* debuted on Broadway while *Fences* was still running there, an unprecedented accomplishment in the New York theater for an African-American playwright.

Major Works

Ma Rainey's Black Bottom is about a black blues singer who exploits her fellow musicians. The title refers to the legendary blues singer Gertrude "Ma" Rainey, whom many consider the mother of the blues. Set in a recording studio in 1927, four musicians who are waiting for Ma's arrival discuss their abusive employer and the hardships of life in racist America. When Ma Rainey arrives, accompanied by the group's white manager and the owner of the studio, tensions mount until the bitter, cynical trumpeter, who has endured too much, vents his frustration in the violent climax of the play. *Fences*, set in the late 1950s, examines the destructive and far-reaching consequences of racial injustice and concerns an embittered former athlete, rejected by major league baseball because of the color of his skin, who forbids his son to accept an athletic scholarship. Set in 1911 in a Pittsburgh boardinghouse, *Joe Turner's Come and Gone* relates the struggles of blacks who migrated north after Reconstruction ended. The play focuses on Herald Loomis's search for his wife after seven years of forced labor at the hands of Joe Turner, an infamous Southerner who abducted blacks and held them as indentured servants. *The Piano Lesson*, set in 1936, pits a brother against a sister in a contest to decide the fate of a revered heirloom—a piano whose legs feature carved African totems of their ancestors who had been traded in exchange for the piano by the man who owned them as slaves. *Two Trains Running*, set on a single day in 1969 in a run-down diner on the verge of being sold, presents the reactions by regular patrons to the pending sale. *Seven Guitars*, set in the 1940s, recounts the tragic story of blues guitarist Floyd Barton. The play opens with his funeral, then continues as a series of flashbacks that recreate the events of the last week of his life.

Critical Reception

Nearly unanimous critical acclaim and immense popular appeal has greeted the premieres of each of Wilson's plays. Critics often have cited the vitality of the characters, authentic, lively dialogue, and use of African myths and legends as the basis of their praise. Many critics have detected the influence of such playwrights as Arthur Miller, Tennessee Williams, and Eugene O'Neill in Wilson's treatment of family divisions, although Wilson has stated that his main influences are collagist painter Romare Bearden, writers Amiri Baraka and Jorge Luis Borges, and blues music. Some reviewers, however, felt that *The Piano Lesson* did not met the high dramatic standards set by Wilson's earlier works, viewing the play as static and judging the playwright's use of a ghost onstage as glaringly ineffective. Despite such criticism, Wilson's subsequent plays have continued to command widespread respect. Discussing Wilson's body of work, Lawrence Bommer stated that "Wilson has created the most complete cultural chronicle since Balzac wrote his vast *Human Comedy*, an artistic whole that has grown even greater than its prize-winning parts."

(For further information, see *Authors and Artists for Young Adults*, Vol. 16; *Black Literature Criticism*; *Black Writers*, Vol. 2; *Contemporary Authors*, Vols. 115, 122; *Contemporary Authors New Revision Series*, Vols. 42, 54; *Contemporary Literary Criticism*, Vols. 39, 50, 63; *DISCovering Authors*; *DISCovering Authors: British*; *DISCovering Authors: Canadian*; *DISCovering Authors Modules: Dramatists Module, Most-studied Authors Module, Multicultural Authors Module*; *Drama Criticism*, Vol. 2; *Major Twentieth-Century Writers*.)

CRITICAL COMMENTARY

FRANK RICH

SOURCE: Frank Rich, "Wilson's *Ma Rainey's* Opens," in *The New York Times*, October 12, 1984, pp. C1, C3.

[*Rich provided drama reviews for* Time *and the* New York Post *prior to becoming the* New York Times *drama critic in 1980. In the following favorable review, he describes* Ma Rainey's Black Bottom *as "a searing inside account of what white racism does to its victims."*]

Late in Act I of *Ma Rainey's Black Bottom,* a somber, aging band trombonist (Joe Seneca) tilts his head heavenward to sing the blues. The setting is a dilapidated Chicago recording studio of 1927, and the song sounds as old as time. "If I had my way," goes the lyric, "I would tear this old building down."

Once the play has ended, that lyric has almost become a prophecy. In *Ma Rainey's Black Bottom,* the writer August Wilson sends the entire history of black America crashing down upon our heads. This play is a searing inside account of what white racism does to its victims—and it floats on the same authentic artistry as the blues music it celebrates. Harrowing as *Ma Rainey's* can be, it is also funny, salty, carnal and lyrical. Like his real-life heroine, the legendary singer Gertrude (Ma) Rainey, Mr. Wilson articulates a legacy of unspeakable agony and rage in a spellbinding voice.

The play is Mr. Wilson's first to arrive in New York, and it reached here, via the Yale Repertory Theater, under the sensitive hand of the man who was born to direct it, Lloyd Richards. On Broadway, Mr. Richards has honed *Ma Rainey's* to its finest form. What's more, the director brings us an exciting young actor—Charles S. Dutton—along with his extraordinary dramatist. One wonders if the electricity at the Cort is the same that audiences felt when Mr. Richards, Lorraine Hansberry and Sidney Poitier stormed into Broadway with *A Raisin in the Sun* a quarter-century ago.

As *Ma Rainey's* shares its director and Chicago setting with *Raisin,* so it builds on Hansberry's themes: Mr. Wilson's characters want to make it in white America. And, to a degree, they have. Ma Rainey (1886-1939) was among the first black singers to get a recording contract—albeit with a white company's "race" division. Mr. Wilson gives us Ma (Theresa Merritt) at the height of her fame. A mountain of glitter and feathers, she has become a despotic, temperamental star, complete with a retinue of flunkies, a fancy car and a kept young lesbian lover.

The evening's framework is a Paramount-label recording session that actually happened, but whose details and supporting players have been invented by the author. As the action swings between the studio and the band's warm-up room—designed by Charles Henry McClennahan as if they might be the festering last-chance saloon of *The Iceman Cometh*—Ma and her four accompanying musicians overcome various mishaps to record "Ma Rainey's Black Bottom" and other songs. During the delays, the band members smoke reefers, joke around and reminisce about past gigs on a well-traveled road stretching through whorehouses and church socials from New Orleans to Fat Back, Ark.

The musicians' speeches are like improvised band solos—variously fizzy, haunting and mournful. We hear how the bassist Slow Drag (Leonard Jackson) got his nickname at a dance contest, but also about how a black preacher was tortured by being forced to "dance" by a white vigilante's gun. Gradually, we come to know these men, from their elusive pipe dreams to their hidden scars, but so deftly are the verbal riffs orchestrated that we don't immediately notice the incendiary drama boiling underneath.

That drama is ignited by a conflict between Ma and her young trumpeter Levee, played by Mr. Dutton. An ambitious sport eager to form his own jazz band, Levee mocks his employer's old "jugband music" and champions the new dance music that has just begun to usurp the blues among black audiences in the urban North. Already Levee has challenged Ma by writing a swinging version of "Ma Rainey's Black Bottom" that he expects the record company to use in place of the singer's traditional arrangement.

Yet even as the battle is joined between emblematic representatives of two generations of black music, we're thrust into a more profound war about identity. The African nationalist among the musicians, the pianist Toledo (Robert Judd), argues that, "We done sold ourselves to the white man in order to be like him." We soon realize that, while Ma's music is from the heart, her life has become a sad, ludicrous "imitation" of white stardom. Levee's music is soulful, too, but

Principal Works

The Coldest Day of the Year (drama) 1979
The Homecoming (drama) 1979
Fullerton Street (drama) 1980
Black Bart and the Sacred Hills (drama) 1981
Jitney (drama) 1982
The Mill Hand's Lunch Bucket (drama) 1983
Ma Rainey's Black Bottom (drama) 1984
Fences (drama) 1985
Joe Turner's Come and Gone (drama) 1986
The Piano Lesson (drama) 1987
**August Wilson: Three Plays* (drama) 1991
Two Trains Running (drama) 1990
The Piano Lesson (teleplay) 1995
Seven Guitars (drama) 1995

*This volume contains *Ma Rainey's Black Bottom*, *Fences*, and *Joe Turner's Come and Gone*.

---

his ideal of success is having his "name in lights"; his pride is invested in the new shoes on which he's blown a week's pay.

Ma, at least, senses the limits of her success. Though she acts as if she owns the studio, she can't hail a cab in the white city beyond. She knows that her clout with the record company begins and ends with her viability as a commercial product: "When I've finished recording," she says, "it's just like I'd been some whore, and they roll over and put their pants on." Levee, by contrast, has yet to learn that a black man can't name his own terms if he's going to sell his music to a white world. As he plots his future career, he deceives himself into believing that a shoeshine and Uncle Tom smile will win white backers for his schemes.

Inevitably, the promised door of opportunity slams, quite literally, in Levee's face, and the sound has a violent ring that reverberates through the decades. Levee must confront not just the collapse of his hopes but the destruction of his dignity. Having played the white man's game and lost to its rigged rules, he is left with less than nothing: Even as he fails to sell himself to whites, Levee has sold out his own sense of self-worth.

Mr. Dutton's delineation of this tragic downfall is red-hot. A burly actor a year out of Yale, he is at first as jazzy as his music. With his boisterous wisecracks and jumpy sprinter's stance, he seems ready to leap into the stratosphere envisioned in his fantasies of glory. But once he crash lands, the poison of self-hatred ravages his massive body and distorts his thundering voice. No longer able to channel his anger into his music, he directs it to God, crying out that a black man's prayers are doomed to be tossed "into the garbage." As Mr. Dutton careens about with unchecked, ever escalating turbulence he transforms an anonymous Chicago bandroom into a burial ground for a race's aspirations.

Mr. Dutton's fellow band members are a miraculous double-threat ensemble: They play their instruments nearly as convincingly as they spin their juicy monologues. Aleta Mitchell and Lou Criscuolo, as Ma's gum-chewing lover and harried white manager, are just right, and so is Scott Davenport-Richards, as Ma's erstwhile Little Lord Fauntleroy of a young nephew. It's one of the evening's more grotesquely amusing gags that Ma imperiously insists on having the boy, a chronic stutterer, recite a spoken introduction on her record.

Miss Merritt is Ma Rainey incarnate. A singing actress of both wit and power, she finds bitter humor in the character's distorted sense of self: When she barks her outrageous demands to her lackeys, we see a show business monster who's come a long way from her roots. Yet the roots can still be unearthed. In a rare reflective moment, she explains why she sings the blues. "You don't sing to feel better," Miss Merritt says tenderly. "You sing because that's a way of understanding life."

The lines might also apply to the play's author. Mr. Wilson can't mend the broken lives he unravels in ***Ma Rainey's Black Bottom***. But, like his heroine, he makes their suffering into art that forces us to understand and won't allow us to forget.

HILARY DEVRIES

SOURCE: Hilary DeVries, "A Song in Search of Itself," in *American Theatre*, Vol. 3, No. 10, January, 1987, pp. 22-5.

[*In the following essay, DeVries examines the recurring themes in Wilson's cycle of plays regarding the black experience. She identifies the most pervasive theme as "the need for black Americans to forge anew their identity, an identity that is at once African and American."*]

In August Wilson's most recent play, ***The Piano Lesson***, the young protagonist Boy Willie declares: "That's all I wanted. To sit down and be at ease with everything. But I wasn't born to that. When I go by on the road and something ain't right, then I got to try and fix it." The speaker is the son of a slave determined to transform his family's racial legacy into a self-determining future; but the words also bear witness to their author's aspirations as one of this country's leading black playwrights.

In the black American theatrical tradition, often distinguished as much by political circumstance as individual accomplishment, August Wilson has emerged as a compelling new voice. Chronicling the history of black Americans through the 20th century, Wilson draws on his background as a poet to enrich his more recently honed talents as a dramatist. His three best-known plays, *Ma Rainey's Black Bottom*, *Fences* and *Joe Turner's Come and Gone*, evince both their author's fecund use of language and a storyteller's narrative touch.

The plays' cumulative intent, however, is as pedagogic as it is expository. Wilson describes his artistic agenda as an attempt to "concretize" the black American tradition, to demonstrate how that tradition "can sustain a man once he has left his father's house." Indeed, the theme that surges through Wilson's work is the need for black Americans to forge anew their identity, an identity that is at once African and American.

In the seven years he has been writing plays—his first efforts resulted in a handful of seldom if ever produced one-acts—Wilson has undertaken an ambitious, systematic project: each work is to be set in a different decade from 1900 to the present. "I'm taking each decade and looking back at one of the most important questions that blacks confronted in that decade and writing a play about it," says Wilson. "Put them all together and you have a history."

The dramatic chronicle that has resulted thusfar is peopled by striking protagonists earmarked by the eras in which they lived: Levee, the impetuous young trumpeter of *Ma Rainey*, struggles to survive in a white entertainment world during the '20s; Loomis, the forbiddingly Dickensian protagonist of *Joe Turner*, fights to regain his identity after seven years of forced labor in the early 1900s; Troy, the tyrannical patriarch of *Fences*, rages at social injustice prefiguring that of the explosive '60s. Collectively they constitute Wilson's overt literary intent: "You should be able to see a progression through the decades from Loomis to Levee to Boy Willie [in *The Piano Lesson*] to Troy." Says drama critic Ernie Schier, "August is a better chronicler of the black experience in this country than Alex Haley. In 40 years, he will be the playwright we will still be hearing about."

Ironically, Wilson is emerging at a time when few black American playwrights are finding and keeping a national audience, when politically and artistically the country is more attuned to the racial injustices of South Africa than to the dilemmas of its own black population. Nonetheless, after nearly two decades of writing both poetry and drama and four years of almost exclusive collaboration with director Lloyd Richards at the O'Neill Theater Center and Yale Repertory Theatre, Wilson is entering a new and broader arena.

The Piano Lesson received its first staged reading at the O'Neill this past summer. A trio of Wilson's other plays are currently crisscrossing the country. *Fences*, starring James Earl Jones, is set to open in New York in March after runs last season at the Goodman Theatre in Chicago and (with a different cast) at Seattle Repertory Theatre. The Yale production of *Joe Turner* has just completed the first of its regional theatre stopovers at Boston's Huntington Theatre Company. And—although *Ma Rainey* never recouped its investment during its commercial New York run two years ago, despite its critical heralding and a 1984 Tony nomination—Wilson is tilting anew at Broadway. In addition to the upcoming New York run of *Fences*, Wilson has just completed the book for a new musical about black jazz musician Jelly Roll Morton, which is to star Gregory Hines and open on Broadway in the spring under Jerry Zaks's direction. "I consider this a jazz-blues folk opera," says Wilson, "an encapsulation of the history of black music until 1928."

The undertaking is further evidence of Wilson's commitment to his delineated literary turf—history, that individual and collective process of discovery that, as the author says, "becomes doubly important if someone else has been writing yours for you." His plays maintain a contemporary involvement with the past, and punctuate each era with its own particular totems. By mining black American music, which Wilson sees as one of the few traditionally acceptable venues for black American culture, Wilson is able to reveal the cumulative history informing his protagonists: nearly all his characters are in search of their individual songs of identity. Wilson describes Loomis's metaphysical journey in *Joe Turner*, for example, as a "song in search of itself."

Its musical allusions aside, Wilson's writing is a poetic melding of African and Western imagery. His use of ethnographically specific folklore borders on the mystical and reinforces the distinctively non-linear narrative style which the playwright ascribes to an "African storytelling mode." While some have been slow to warm to this nontraditional dramatic structure, others have praised it as indigenous to the black oral tradition, a heritage that embraces African as well as Bible Belt oral patterns and serves as Wilson's own palimpsest. "It is writing based on centuries of 'hearing'," says director Claude Purdy, who staged Wilson's *Fences* at GeVa Theatre in Rochester, N.Y.

Wilson describes his work as an attempt to confront "the glancing manner in which white America looks at blacks and the way blacks look at themselves." By probing the sociological archetype with sufficient metaphor but without conspicuous didacticism, Wilson has set himself apart from many of the so-called angry young black playwrights, including Ed Bullins and Amiri Baraka, whose work proliferated during the late '60s. "I can only do what I do because the '60s existed," Wilson reasons. "I am building off that original conflict."

Although he maintains that "the one thing that has best served me as a playwright is my background in poetry," Wilson first came to the theatre out of a search for a broader forum in which to voice his social concerns; initially he thought about a legal career. But after a boyhood spent on the streets of Pittsburgh—Wilson dropped out of school at age 15—the playwright says "my sense of justice [became] very different from what the law says. It just happened that my talent lies with words." Claude Purdy, now director-in-residence at St. Paul's Penumbra Theatre, confirms Wilson's motives: "August came out of the '60s with a responsible attitude, eager to explore his community's culture and do something for his people."

As a co-founder of Pittsburgh's Black Horizons Theatre, Wilson wrote his early one-acts during the height of the black power movement as a way, he says, "to politicize the community and raise consciousness." Today Wilson prefers the label of "cultural nationalist."

"An interviewer once asked me if having written these plays I hadn't exhausted the black experience. I said, 'Wait a minute. You've got 40,000 movies and plays about the white experience, and we don't ask if you've exhausted your experience.' I'll never run out of material. If I finish this cycle, I'll just start over again. You can write forever about the clash between the urban North and the rural South, what happened when [blacks] came to the cities, how their lives changed and how it affected generations to come."

It is an outspoken assertion from this usually reserved 41-year-old Pittsburgh native now residing in St. Paul. Wilson's conversational style only hints at his transplanted Midwest roots. With his soft-spoken affability and almost old-fashioned politeness, he hardly appears the source for the chorus of vibrant voices—by turns soft and genial, angry and defiant—one hears in his plays.

"After I turned 20, I spent the next 10 to 15 years hanging out on streetcorners, following old men around, working odd jobs. There was this place called Pat's Cigar Store in Pittsburgh. It was the same place that Claude McKay mentioned in his book *Home to Harlem*. When I found out about that, I said, 'This is a part of history,' and I ran down there to where all the old men in the community would congregate."

Although Wilson originally channeled his literary efforts into poetry, his move to Minnesota in the early 1970s served as a catalyst, permitting those colloquial voices and his own skills as a dramatist to come into their own. Initially working as a script writer for the local science museum's children's theatre while firing off "five plays in three years" to the O'Neill, Wilson did not conceive of himself as a playwright until he received the first of several writing grants. After submitting *Jitney* to Minneapolis's Playwrights' Center, Wilson was awarded a Jerome Foundation fellowship in the late 1970s. (He has subsequently received Bush, Rockefeller, McKnight and Guggenheim fellowships.) "I walked in and there were 16 playwrights," Wilson remembers about that encounter with the Playwrights' Center. "It was the first time I had dinner with other playwrights. It was the first time I began to think of myself as one."

It was this "two hundred bucks a month for a year" that afforded Wilson the opportunity to rework a one-act about a blues recording session into what became the full-length *Ma Rainey*, his first play accepted by the O'Neill and the most naturalistic of his dramas. Set in a Chicago recording studio in 1927, the play is a garrulous and colloquially accurate look at the exploitation of black musicians. Through Wilson's carefully orchestrated verbal riffs, the characters' struggle for identity slowly escalates to a violent conclusion.

In *Ma Rainey*, the struggle is predicated not only upon friction between the white recording executives and the black musicians but also upon subtle conflicts within the black community itself. Ma, the recording star, knows the limits of her commercial success, admitting, "It's just like I been a whore"; the elderly pianist, Toledo, is an African nationalist who argues, "We done sold ourselves to the white man in order to be like him"; Levee, the headstrong trumpeter, is intent on making it in the white world, on seeing his name in lights. Unable to confront his white oppressors, Levee fatally lashes out at his own. Wilson describes Levee's condition in a rhetorical question: "How can I live this life in society that refuses to recognize my worth, that refuses to allow me to contribute to its welfare?"

It is a question that Wilson probes again in *Fences*, written partly as a response to criticism of *Ma Rainey's* bifurcated focus. "*Fences* was me sitting down saying, 'Okay, here is a play with a large central character.'" It was also the writer's attempt to create a protagonist who, unlike the impatient and intransigent Levee, had achieved a grudging parity with his times, albeit a smoldering suppression of desire suitable to the political realities of the 1950s. "Unlike Levee, Troy didn't sell his soul to the devil," says Wilson.

A former Negro League ballplayer past his prime by the time Jackie Robinson broke the color barrier, Troy Maxson can be considered Wilson's most overtly didactic character. "I had to write a character who is responsible and likes the idea of family," says the playwright. This sense of responsibility—for one's own destiny as well as one's own family—is pivotal for Wilson, not only in its metaphysical ramifications but in its more pragmatic applications as well. "We have been told so many times how irresponsible we are as black males that I try and present positive images of responsibility," says the writer. "I started *Fences* with the image of a man standing in his yard with a baby in his arms."

It is this sense of individual accountability that Wilson's other protagonists—Loomis in *Joe Turner* and Boy Willie in the yet-to-be-produced *Piano Lesson*—confront in more mystical terms. "In *Ma Rainey* and *Fences*," Wilson explains, "the two roads into white American society traditionally open to blacks, entertainment and sports, fail the characters." As a result, the leading figures in the subsequent plays do not establish their identities relative to the white world; they rediscover themselves as Africans. "If black folks would recognize themselves as Africans and not be afraid to respond to the world as Africans, then they could make their contribution to the world as Africans," says Wilson.

Set in 1911 in order to get closer to this "African retentiveness," *Joe Turner* is infused with so much non-Western mysticism and folklore—ghosts, myths, chants and spells—that the narrative can be seen as a spiritual allegory. Based partly on a painting by black artist Romare Bearden, "Mill Hand's Lunch Bucket," as well as the legend of the actual slave hunter Joe Turner, the play is rife with historical detail as well as religious feeling. Loomis's search for his own past after seven years of bondage symbolizes the quest of an entire race. "As a whole, our generation knows very little about our past," explains Wilson. "My generation of parents tried to shield their children from the indignities they'd suffered."

For Loomis, the journey towards self-knowledge includes two apocalyptic moments—baptismal exorcisms that bracket the play's two acts and reverberate with violence. In the first of these cathartic steps, Loomis confronts his vision of "bones walking on top of water," a mythic image of ancestral suffering. In the final scene, Loomis faces both Christianity and African myth, and with a single symbolic act, finds himself purged from his past and a free man. As Loomis states, "I don't need anyone to bleed for me, I can bleed for myself."

It is a moment of individual transmogrification that Wilson examines again, and to even stronger effect, in *The Piano Lesson*. Although Wilson intends to rewrite this latest entry in his historical cycle next summer, the play's inherent dramatic conflict—a brother and sister argue over their shared legacy, the family piano—and its crisp scenic construction bode well for its arrival on stage. The piano itself is Wilson's clearest, most fully realized symbol, one that resounds with African and Western significance while forming the fulcrum of the play's metaphysical debate: "The real issue is the piano, the legacy. How are you going to use it?" says Wilson.

There are two choices, one taken up by Berneice, who wants to preserve the blood-stained piano as a totem to the family's violence-wracked past. Her brother, Boy Willie, however, is intent on literally capitalizing on the family's history to create a new future; he wants to sell the piano and buy the land which their father originally farmed as a slave. "I ain't gonna be no fool about no sentimental value," Boy Willie says. "With that piano I get the land and I can go down and cash in the crop." As Wilson describes his character's position, "I often wonder what the fabric of American society would be like if blacks had stayed in the South and somehow found a way to [economically] develop and lock into that particular area. That's what Boy Willie is articulating. He wants to put his hands to better use."

Willie's desire encapsulates the playwright's overall intent. "I think it's largely a question of identity. Without knowing your past, you don't know your present—and you certainly can't plot your future," Wilson says. "You go out and discover it for yourself. It's being responsible for your own presence in the world and for your own salvation.". . .

SAMUEL G. FREEDMAN

SOURCE: Samuel G. Freedman, "A Voice from the Streets," in *The New York Times Magazine*, March 15, 1987, pp. 36, 40, 49, 70.

[In the excerpt below, Freedman traces Wilson's

life from early childhood to the present, illuminating aspects that helped determine the form and content of his plays.]

During the early 1960's, as August Wilson was reaching manhood, the church of St. Benedict the Moor took up a collection for a statue atop its steeple. The church straddled the border between the Hill, the black Pittsburgh slum where Wilson grew up, and the city's downtown district. And when the statue was unveiled, Wilson remembers, Saint Benedict was opening his arms to the skyscrapers and department stores, and turning his back on the Hill.

A generation later, as August Wilson walks its streets on a visit home, the Hill looks godforsaken indeed. Gone are Lutz's Meat Market, the Hilltop Club and Pope's Restaurant. The New Granada Theater is closed. An abandoned truck rusts in a weeded lot and a junkie lurches up the street, hawking a stolen television set. Beyond the decay, past the plywood and charred bricks, rise the new glass towers of Pittsburgh, glistening like shafts of crystal.

"Hey, professor," a man in a worn overcoat says to Wilson, extending a calloused hand for a soul shake.

"Hey, man," Wilson says, meeting his grip.

This passing moment is the ultimate compliment, for if August Wilson has wanted anything in his career as a playwright it is to be recognized by the people of the ghetto as their voice, their bard. Wilson gives words to trumpeters and trash men, cabbies and conjurers, boarders and landladies, all joined by a heritage of slavery. Their patois is his poetry, their dreams are his dramas. And while Wilson's inspiration is contained—a few sloping blocks in Pittsburgh—his aspiration seems boundless. He intends to write a play about black Americans in every decade of this century, and he has already completed six of the projected 10.

Fences, a drama set in the 1950's, is the second of the cycle to reach Broadway. It was preceded by *Ma Rainey's Black Bottom,* which won the New York Drama Critics Circle Award as the best play of the 1984-85 season and, as Frank Rich, chief drama critic for *The New York Times,* wrote, it established Wilson as "a major find for the American theater," a writer of "compassion, raucous humor and penetrating wisdom."...

Fences may prove the most accessible of Wilson's plays, faster-moving than *Ma Rainey* and less mystical than *Joe Turner's Come and Gone.* Several critics have likened this family drama to Arthur Miller's *Death of a Salesman,* centering as it does on a proud, embittered patriarch, Troy Maxson, and his teen-age son, Cory.

Their immediate conflict is kindled when Cory is recruited to play college football and Troy, once a baseball star barred from the segregated big leagues, demands he turn down the scholarship because he cannot believe times have truly changed. Behind the narrative looms Wilson's concern with legacy. As Cory Maxson almost grudgingly discovers the value in his father's flawed life, he accepts his part in a continuum that runs from Pittsburgh to the antebellum South and finally to Mother Africa.

For Wilson, at the age of 42, that journey is not only historical, but personal. His father was a white man who all but abandoned him. The playwright dismisses the subject of his parentage in a temperate tone more unsettling than any anger, and one can only speculate how Wilson's origins fueled the pursuit of blackness, his own and his people's. Troy Maxson of *Fences,* then, embodies not only the black stepfather Wilson found in his teens, but something rather more metaphysical.

"I think it was Amiri Baraka who said that when you look in the mirror you should see your God," Wilson says.

> All over the world, nobody has a God who doesn't resemble them. Except black Americans. They can't even see they're worshipping someone else's God, because they want so badly to assimilate, to get the fruits of society. The message of America is 'Leave your Africanness outside the door.' My message is 'Claim what is yours.'

Last April, when *Joe Turner's Come and Gone* was in rehearsal at the Yale Repertory Theater, a Jewish friend invited Wilson to a seder, the ritual Passover meal. *Joe Turner* is the story of Herald Loomis, a black freedman pressed into illegal bondage—decades after the Emancipation Proclamation—by the Tennessee bounty hunter of the play's title. Freed after seven years, he makes his way to Pittsburgh, looking for the wife who had fled north during his enslavement. He is in many ways a crippled man, driven to his knees by visions of slavery, of "bones walking on top of the water," and it takes the powers of an African healer named Bynum to raise him upright again. Set against *Joe Turner,* the seder was a powerful coincidence.

"The first words of the ceremony were, 'We were slaves in Egypt,'" Wilson recalls.

> And these were Yale students, Yale professors, in 1986, in New Haven, talking about something that happened thousands of years ago. Then it struck me that Passover is not just happening in this house in New Haven,

it's happening in Jewish homes all over the world. And the concluing line—'Next year in Jerusalem'—they've been saying that for thousands of years. And that is the source of Jewish power and Jewish pride.

I thought this is something we should do. Blacks in America want to forget about slavery—the stigma, the shame. That's the wrong move. If you can't be who you are, who can you be? How can you know what to do? He have our history. We have our book, which is the blues. And we forget it all.

If Wilson's mission is memory, his method is more artistic than archival. He is one part Dylan Thomas and one part Malcolm X, a lyric poet fired in the kiln of black nationalism. The highly polemical black theater of the 1960's made the play the vehicle for the message, but Wilson encountered literature before ideology, and he still abides by that order. He is a storyteller, and his story is the African diaspora— not because it suits a political agenda but because everything in his life conspired to make it so.

Most of Wilson's plays concern the conflict between those who embrace their African past and those who deny it. "You don't see me running around in no jungle with no bone between my nose," boasts one character in *Ma Rainey*. Wilson's answer is that Africa remains a pervasive force, a kind of psychic balm available to 20th-century blacks through blues songs, communal dances, tall tales. Wilson the mythologist coexists with Wilson the social realist. There is a broad historical truth to his characters—to Levee, the jazz musician who naively sells off his compositions to a white record-company executive; to Troy Maxson, whose job prospects go no further than becoming the first black truck driver in the Pittsburgh Sanitation Department.

Wilson makes these lives ring with dignity. "I do the best I can do," Troy tells his wife, Rose, in *Fences*.

> I come in here every Friday. I carry a sack of potatoes and a bucket of lard. You all line up at the door with your hands out. I give you the lint from my pockets. I give you my sweat and blood. I ain't got no tears. I done spent them. We go upstairs in that room at night and I fall down on you and try to blast a hole into forever. I get up Monday morning, find my lunch on the table. I go out. Make my way. Find my strength to carry me through to the next Friday.

There is an extraordinary acuity to Wilson's ear, a quality that has a black audience murmuring "That's right" or "Tell it" during his plays, as they might during a Jesse Jackson speech or a B. B. King concert. Wilson's virtuosity with the vernacular can lull an audience into laughter, too. Early in *Fences*, Troy Maxson's best friend needles him about flirting outside his marriage. "It's all right to buy her one drink," he says. "That's what you call being polite. But when you wanna be buying two or three—that's what you call eyeing her."

By evening's end, it is apparent that Troy has done more than eye her, and the kidding has assumed a prophetic power—a prime characteristic of Wilson's work. With one set and a half-dozen major roles, a Wilson play can seem talky and static, but if wordiness is a weakness at times, it is also a masterly way of deceiving the audience into amused complacency. By the end of his first acts, Wilson characteristically begins to detonate his dramatic bombshells, and at the final explosion—a murder, a madman's howl or a self-inflicted stabbing—a shudder ripples through the audience.

Wilson writes of the particulars of black life, elevating his anger to a more universal plane. As a thinker, if not a stylist, Wilson descends less from the Richard Wright tradition of social protest than from the ontological one of Ralph Ellison. Ellison's *The Invisible Man*, like Wilson's characters, confronts blackness not as a function of pigment but as a condition of the soul. The white man in Wilson's plays can be finessed, ignored, intimidated; it is the Almighty against whom his characters rail. After a musician in *Ma Rainey* hears of a white mob forcing a black reverend to dance, he shouts to the rafters, "Where the hell was God when all of this was going on? . . ."

Wilson received a positive racial identity from his mother, who died in 1983. Living on welfare and, later, on the wages of a janitorial job, Daisy Wilson kept her children healthy, fed, and educated. She would stretch eggs with flour to make breakfast go seven ways. She would wait until Christmas Eve for the $1 tree she could afford. She would get second-hand Nancy Drew mysteries and other books for the daily reading she required of her children. Wilson's favorite story about her, and her gifts, involves a radio contest:

> Morton Salt in the 1950's had come out with their slogan, 'When it rains, it pours.' When the announcer said the words, the first caller to identify it as the Morton slogan won a Speed Queen washer. My mother was still doing the wash with a rub board. One night, we're listening to the station and the contest comes on. We didn't have a telephone, so Mommy sends my sister right out with a dime to call in and say, 'Morton Salt.' When

they found out she was black, they wanted to give her a certificate to go to the Salvation Army for a used washing machine. And she told them where they could put their certificate. I remember her girlfriends' telling her, 'Daisy, get the used washer.' But she'd rather go on scrubbing.

As a writer, Wilson has honored his mother and imagined the father he might have had. "I know there are not strong black images in literature and film," he says, "so I thought, why not create them? Herald Loomis is responsible. Troy Maxson is responsible. Those images are important. Every black man did not just make a baby and run off."

But unlike the more politicized black writers of the 1960's—or, at the other end of the spectrum, the mass-market creators of television's *Julia* and *The Cosby Show*—Wilson has created fallible humans, not simplistic paragons. Troy Maxson can turn gales of rage on the son who adores him, but he also feeds him, clothes him, teaches him. Troy can sneak around on the wife who loves him, fathering a baby out of wedlock. But when the child is born, Troy brings it home and Rose, however hurt, agrees to raise it as her own.

It is not surprising that Wilson's fictive families form bulwarks against a hostile world, for his own encounters with white Pittsburgh offered the racist commonplaces of America—bricks through the window when the family tried moving into mostly white Hazelwood; "Nigger, go home" notes on his desk at an overwhelmingly white parochial high school; accusations of cheating when a term paper on Napoleon seems a bit too good to have been done by a black boy. Hounded out of one school, frustrated by another, Wilson dropped out in the ninth grade. At the age of 15, his formal education had come to an end.

He split his days between the street and the library, where he chanced upon a section marked "Negro." There were about 30 books, and he read them all—Arna Bontemps, Ralph Ellison, Richard Wright and Langston Hughes. He remembers especially a sociology text that spoke of "the Negro's power of hard work" because it was the first time anything ever suggested to him that a Negro could have any power in America. "I was just beginning to discover racism, and I think I was looking for something," Wilson recalls. "Those books were a comfort. Just the idea black people would write books. I wanted my book up there, too. I used to dream about being part of the Harlem Renaissance."

Supporting himself as a short-order cook and stock clerk, Wilson began to write: stories, poetry—even a college term paper on Carl Sandburg and Robert Frost for [his sister] Freda. She got an A, he made $20, and it bought a used Royal typewriter, the first he had owned. "The first thing I typed was my name," he would recall years later. "I wanted to see how it looked in print. Then I began to type my poems."

Around the neighborhood, Wilson kept his eyes and ears open: How Miss Sarah sprinkled salt and lined up pennies across her threshold. He listened to the men talk at Pat's Place, a cigar store and pool room, and if someone said, "Joe Foy's funeral's today," he would find out who Joe Foy was. Most of all, Wilson saw in the Hill a pageant of violence. One night, he watched a black man walk into a bar with a white woman. Another black man, passing the first, said to him, "Say, Phil, I see you got your white whore." Phil drew his knife and began slashing the man across the chest, slashing to the cadence of his cry, "That's my wife! That's my wife! That's my wife!" His rage spent, he got into his car with his wife and drove off.

One part of Wilson understood the futility of the violence, the self-destruction, and he summons it in his plays as the ultimate, diabolical triumph of white bigotry: turning blacks against themselves. **Ma Rainey's Black Bottom,** for instance, ends with Levee stabbing not the white man who has appropriated his music but the bandmate who accidentally steps on his shoe. *Fences* brings Cory to the brink of attacking Troy with a baseball bat, symbol of the father's manhood.

Yet another part of Wilson admired the Hill's criminals. His own family lived near the bottom of the Hill's social scale, which roughly conformed to its topography, and he grew up with a hot hate for the affluent blacks up in Sugar Top, the doctors and lawyers who would send their children to a Saturday movie downtown with the admonition "Don't show your color." In Wilson's plays, the black middle-class exists only as an object of contempt; if he had written *A Raisin in the Sun*, the Younger family would not have moved to the suburbs, it would have joined either the Blackstone Rangers street gang or the Nation of Islam. Wilson's characters are almost all the kind of street blacks for whom his longtime friend Rob Penny invented the term "stomp-down bloods."

"For a long time, I thought the most valuable blacks were those in the penitentiary," Wilson says, recalling his teens and 20's.

> They were the people with the warrior spirit. How they chose to battle may have been wrong, but you need people who will battle. You need someone who says, 'I won't shine shoes for $40 a week. I have a woman and

two kids, and I will put a gun in my hand and *take*, and my kids will have Christmas presents.' Just like there were people who didn't accept slavery. There were Nat Turners. And that's the spirit that Levee has, and Troy has, and Herald Loomis has.

In 1969, when Wilson was 24, his stepfather, David Bedford, died. The two had not been close for almost a decade, since Wilson quit his high school football team against Bedford's wishes, and the late 1960's was a time when young black men like Wilson often disparaged their fathers as a generation of compromisers. Then Wilson heard a story about Bedford that changed his life.

Bedford, it turned out, had been a high school football star in the 1930's, and had hoped a sports scholarship would lead to a career in medicine. But no Pittsburgh college would give a black player a grant and Bedford was too poor to pay his own way. To get the money, he decided to rob a store, and during the theft he killed a man. For the 23 years before he met Wilson's mother, Bedford had been in prison. By the time he was free, only a job in the city Sewer Department beckoned.

"I found myself trying to figure out the intent of these lives around me," Wilson says. "Trying to uncover the nobility and the dignity that I might not have seen. I was ignorant of their contributions. Part of the reason I wrote **Fences** was to illuminate that generation, which shielded its children from all of the indignities they went through."

Wilson's personal discoveries coincided with the rise of the black nationalist movement, which was based in large part on venerating the Afro-American past. Wilson and Rob Penny, a playwright and professor, founded a theater called the Black Horizon on the Hill, and it produced Wilson's earliest plays. Poetry readings, jazz concerts and art galleries all flourished. Wilson and Penny also belonged to a group of Pittsburgh's black artists and intellectuals who studied and discussed the writings of Ed Bullins, Richard Wesley, Ron Milner, Ishmael Reed, Maulana Karenga and, most importantly, Amiri Baraka and Malcolm X.

In some ways, though, Wilson didn't quite fit in. His sympathies resided with black nationalism, but as a writer he could not produce convincing agitprop. Nor had he yet found the true dramatic voice of the Hill. His development as a writer shared less with black American authors than with black Africans like novelist Chinua Achebe, who fell under the sway of white writers while studying abroad and only later returned home to adapt those influences to their indigenous oral tradition and tribal lore.

The self-educated Wilson counts among his strongest early influences Dylan Thomas, for the theatricality of his verse, and John Berryman, for the process of condensing language that the poet called "psychic shorthand." Wilson also admired the jazzy rhythms and street sensibility of Baraka's poetry and plays....

Between performance and publication royalties and grants—including Guggenheim and Rockfeller fellowships—Wilson has been able since 1982 to devote himself wholly to writing. Now, the posters, awards, programs and reviews from Wilson's first six shows line the long hallway of his St. Paul apartment. But, the playwright adds, there is plenty of wall space left to cover.

"You have to be willing to open yourself up," Wilson says of his approach to writing. "It's like walking down the road. It's the landscape of the self, and you have to be willing to confront whatever you find there."

ROBERT BRUSTEIN

SOURCE: Robert Brustein, "The Lesson of 'The Piano Lesson'," in *The New Republic*, Vol. 202, No. 21, May 21, 1990, pp. 28-30.

[*In the following excerpt, Brustein claims that Wilson's artistic vision is limited to the black experience and that he should "develop the radical poetic strain that now lies dormant in his art."*]

There are reasons why I didn't review the three previous August Wilson productions that moved from the Yale Repertory to Broadway. Lloyd Richards, who directed them all and guided their passage through a variety of resident theaters to New York, succeeded me as Yale's dean and artistic director eleven years ago, and protocol required that I hold my tongue about the progress of my successor. I broke my resolve in an article for *The New York Times* about the role of Yale and other resident theaters in what I viewed as the homogenization of the non-profit stage. I called this process "McTheater"—the use of sequential non-profit institutions as launching pads and tryout franchises for the development of Broadway products and the enrichment of artistic personnel. Since the universally acclaimed Broadway production of **The Piano Lesson** brings this process to some kind of crazy culmination—and raises so many troubling cultural questions—I'm going to break my silence once again.

First, let's take a look at the Wilson phenomenon. *The*

Piano Lesson is an overwritten exercise in a conventional style—to my mind, the most poorly composed of Wilson's four produced works. None of the previous plays was major, but they each had occasional firepower, even some poetry lying dormant under the surface of their kitchen-sink productions. I don't find much power or poetry at all in *The Piano Lesson*, though the play has earned Wilson his second Pulitzer Prize and inspired comparisons with O'Neill. (One critic likened him to Shakespeare!) In one sense, the comparison is apt. Like O'Neill, Wilson has epic ambitions, handicapped by repetitiousness, crude plotting, and clumsy structure. But where O'Neill wrote about the human experience in forms that were daring and exploratory, Wilson has thus far limited himself to the black experience in a relatively literalistic style.

Before his death, O'Neill determined to compose a nine-play cycle about the progressive degeneration of the American spirit. (Only *A Touch of the Poet* was completed to his satisfaction.) Wilson's four plays also have a historical plan: each attempts to demonstrate how the acid of racism has eaten away at black aspirations in the various decades of the twentieth century. *Ma Rainey's Black Bottom*, set in the 1920s, shows how black musicians were prevented from entering the mainstream of the American recording industry. *Fences*, set in the 1950s, shows how black athletes were prevented from participating in major league baseball. *Joe Turner's Come and Gone*, set in 1911, shows how blacks were reduced to poverty and desperation by the chain-gang system. And *The Piano Lesson*, set in the 1930s, shows how black ideals were corroded by slavery. Presumably Wilson is preparing to cover at least five more theatrical decades of white culpability and black martyrdom. This single-minded documentation of American racism is a worthy if familiar social agenda, and no enlightened person would deny its premise, but as an ongoing artistic program it is monotonous, limited, locked in a perception of victimization.

In comparison with the raging polemics of Ed Bullins or Amiri Baraka, Wilson's indictments are relatively mild. His characters usually sit on the edge of the middle class, wearing good suits, inhabiting clean homes. Securely shuttered behind realism's fourth wall, they never come on like menacing street people screaming obscenities or bombarding the audience with such phrases as "black power's gonna get your mama"—which may further explain Wilson's astounding reception. It is comforting to find a black playwright working the mainstream American realist tradition of Clifford Odets, Lillian Hellman, and the early Arthur Miller, a dignified protest writer capable of discussing the black experience without intimidating the readers of the Home section. Still, enough radical vapor floats over the bourgeois bolsters and upholstered couches to stimulate the guilt glands of liberal white audiences. Unable to reform the past, we sometimes pay for the sins of history and our society through artistic reparations in a cultural equivalent of affirmative action.

On its three-year road to Broadway, *The Piano Lesson* could have benefited from some more honest criticism; in its present form, it represents a step backward. A family drama, like *Fences*, it lacks the interior tension of that work . . . , and at three hours it's about an hour and a half too long for its subject matter. Buried inside much tedious exposition is a single conflict between Boy Willie and his sister, Berniece, over a carved piano. Boy Willie wants to sell the piano and buy some farmland down South. Berniece wants to keep it as a token of the family heritage (their mother polished it every day for seventeen years). A repetitive series of confrontations between the two adds little about the conflict but a lot more about the symbolic history of the piano. It belonged to Sutter, a slave owner, who sold members of their family in order to buy the piano for his wife as an anniversary present. Eventually, their father stole it back from Sutter and was later killed in a boxcar fire, while Sutter fell, or was pushed, down a well.

Wilson pounds this symbolic piano a little heavyhandedly. Like Chekhov's cherry orchard, it is intended to reflect the contrasting values of its characters—Berniece finds it a symbol of the past while Boy Willie sees only its material value. But Chekhov's people are a lot more complicated than their attitudes; and because Wilson's images fail to resonate, the play seems like much ado about a piano, extended by superfluous filler from peripheral characters. Frying real food on a real stove, turning on real faucets with real hot-and-cold running water, ironing real shirts on real ironing boards, and flushing real toilets . . . , these amiable supernumeraries natter incessantly on a variety of irrelevant subjects, occasionally breaking into song and dance. These superfluous riffs are partly intended as comic relief, and *The Piano Lesson* has been praised for its humor. But the domesticated jokes, most of them about watermelons, are about at the level of *The Jeffersons*—even the audience's laughter seemed canned. As for Wilson's highly lauded dialogue, his language here lacks music (except for one potentially strong speech by Boy Willie about his Daddy's hands), usually alternating between the prosaic and the proverbial: "God don' ask what you done. God asks what you gonna do."

What ultimately makes this piano unplayable, however, is the ending, which tacks a supernatural resolution onto an essentially naturalistic anecdote. Sutter's ghost is (inexplicably) a resident in this house, his presence signified from time to time by a lighting special on the stairs. In the final scene, Boy Willie, after numerous efforts to remove the piano (after three hours I was prepared to run on stage and give him a hand), is blown off his feet by a tumultuous blast. He rushes upstairs to do battle with the ghost, now represented through a scrim by flowing, glowing window curtains. Returning, Boy Willie renounces his desire to take the piano from the house, while the supernumeraries laugh and cry, and Berniece praises the Lord. Willie adds: "If you and Maretha don't keep playin' on that piano, me and Sutter both likely to be back." Curtain.

This ending is considerably more forced, though arguably less ludicrous, than the version I saw three years ago at one of the play's numerous station stops. There Willie rushed upstairs as the curtain fell on the illuminated portraits of his slave ancestors in the attic. Either way, the supernatural element is a contrived intrusion. When ghosts begin resolving realistic plots, you can be sure the playwright has failed to master his material. . . .

August Wilson is still a relatively young man with a genuine, if not yet fully developed, talent. O'Neill's early plays were just as highly praised, though he wrote nothing truly great until the end of his life. Premature acclaim was actually one of the obstacles to his development; only by facing the demons in his heart at the end of his days, a sick, lonely man in a shuttered room, was he able to write with total honesty about his true subject. To judge from *The Piano Lesson*, Wilson is reaching a dead end in his examination of American racism, though another play on the subject (appropriately titled *Two Trains Running*) is now gathering steam at Yale on its way through the regional railroad depots to its final Broadway destination. It will probably be greeted with the same hallelujah chorus as all his other work. But if Wilson wishes to be a truly major playwright, he would be wise to move on from safe, popular sociology and develop the radical poetic strain that now lies dormant in his art. It is not easy to forsake the rewards of society for the rewards of posterity, but the genuine artist accepts no standards lower than the exacting ones he applies to himself.

AUGUST WILSON

SOURCE: August Wilson, "How to Write a Play Like August Wilson," in *The New York Times*, Section 2, March 10, 1991, pp. 5, 17.

[*The following essay was adapted from a talk given by Wilson in 1991 at Manhattan's Poetry Center. Here, he discusses his personal writing techniques.*]

When I discovered the word breakfast, and I discovered that it was two words, I think then I decided I wanted to be a writer. I've been writing since April 1, 1965, the day I bought my first typewriter, for $20. That's, I don't know, 26 years now. And so, behind each one of the plays are all those thousands of poems and stories and things I wrote many, many years ago. I had begun writing then as a 20-year-old poet. And I don't care what anybody says, as a 20-year-old poet you cannot sit at home and write poetry, because you don't know anything about life. So you have to go out and engage the world.

My friends at the time were painters. I was not envious of them, because they were always trying to get money for paint and get money for canvas. I felt that my tools were very simple. I could borrow a pencil and write on a napkin or get a piece of paper from anyone. So I began to write out in bars and restaurants little snatches of things.

I still do it that way. I start—generally I have an idea of something I want to say—but I start with a line of dialogue. I have no idea half the time who's speaking or what they're saying. I'll start with the line, and the more dialogue I write, the better I get to know the characters. For instance, in writing the play *The Piano Lesson*, one of the characters, Berniece, says something to Boy Willie, her brother, and he talks about how "Sutter fell in the well." Well, this is a surprise to *me*. I didn't know that.

Then I say, "Well, who is Sutter?" You see, if you have a character in a play, the character who knows everything, then you won't have any problem. Whenever you get stuck you ask them a question. I have learned that if you trust them and simply do not even think about what they're saying, it doesn't matter. They say things like, "Sutter fell in the well." You just write it down and make it all make sense later. So I use those characters a lot. Anything you want to know you ask the characters.

0Part of my process is that I assemble all these things and later try to make sense out of them and sort of plug them in to what is my larger artistic agenda. That agenda is answering James Baldwin when he called for "a profound articulation of the black tradition," which he defined as "that field of manners and ritual of intercourse that will sustain a man once he's left his father's house."

So I say, O.K., that field of manners and ritual of intercourse is what I'm trying to put on stage. And I best learn about that through the blues. I discovered everything there. So I have an agenda. Someone asked the painter Romare Bearden about his work and he said, "I try to explore, in terms of the life I know best, those things which are common to all cultures."

So I say, O.K., culture and the commonalities of culture.

Using those two things and having the larger agenda, I take all this material, no matter what it is, and later, I sit down and assemble it. And I discovered—and I admire Romare Bearden a lot; he's a collagist, he pieces things together—I discovered that that's part of my process, what I do. I piece it all together, and, hopefully, have it make sense, the way a collage would.

As for the characters, they are all invented. At the same time they are all made up out of myself. So they're all me, different aspects of my personality, I guess. But I don't say, "Oh, I know a guy like this. I'm going to write Joe." Some people do that. I can't do that. So I write different parts of myself and I try to invent or discover some other parts.

I approach poetry and plays differently. For me, if there is such a thing as public art and private art, then the poems are private. They are a record, a private journey, if you will. I count them as moments of privilege. I count them as gifts.

In terms of influence on my work, I have what I call my four B's: Romare Bearden; Imamu Amiri Baraka, the writer; Jorge Luis Borges, the Argentine short-story writer; and the biggest B of all: the blues. I don't play an instrument. I don't know any musical terms. And I don't know anything about music. But I have a very good ear and I'm a good listener. And I listen mostly to the blues. I have been variously influenced by them and also by the 2,000 or some poets I have read. I have not been, per se, influenced by playwrights or any writers other than that. Some of the black writers I read. For instance, I read Ralph Ellison's *Invisible Man* when I was 14. I guess I've been influenced by him. I've certainly been inspired by examples like that.

In my own work, what I hope to do is to "place" the tradition of black American culture, to demonstrate its ability to sustain us. We have a ground that is specific, that is peculiarly ours, that we can stand on, which gives us a world view, to look at the world and to comment on it. I'm just trying to place the world of that culture on stage and to demonstrate its existence and maybe also indicate some directions toward which we as people might possibly move.

For instance, in the play **Two Trains Running**, there are so many references to death. The undertaker in the black community is the richest man. It's still true today. In the midst of all that, though, in the midst of all this death, you have that which doesn't die—the character of Aunt Esther, which is the tradition. And when the people, the characters in the play, go to see Aunt Esther, the main thing she tells them, each in a different way, is that if you drop the ball you have to go back and pick it up. If you continue running, if you reach the end zone, it's not going to be a touchdown. You have to have the ball.

And I think that we as black Americans need to go back and make the connection that we allowed to be severed when we moved from the South to the North, the great migration starting in 1915. For the most part, the culture that was growing and developing in the Southern part of the United States for 200 and some years, we more or less abandoned. And we have a situation where in 1991 kids do not know who they are because they cannot make the connection with their grandparents—and therefore the connection with their political history in America.

In *The Piano Lesson*, where you have a brother and sister arguing over a piano that is a family heirloom, and each with different ideas of ways to use it, the ending was a very difficult thing because I didn't want to choose sides.

We had about five different endings to the play. But it was always the same ending: I wanted Boy Willie to demonstrate a willingness to battle with Sutter's ghost, the ghost of the white man—that lingering idea of him as the master of slaves—which is still in black Americans' lives and needs to be exorcised. I wasn't so much concerned with who ended up with the piano, as with Boy Willie's willingness to do battle.

In staging it, there were also the ghosts of the guys in the play who had burned up in the boxcar. Ideally, I had wanted Boy Willie to fight it out himself. But then we thought, well, maybe we'll have those ghosts come in and they'll help him with this battle with Sutter. At the same time, Berniece must break her taboo about playing the piano and call up the ghost of her mother and her grandmother and all of her ancestors, whom she has been rejecting. And she does that, and it's a very powerful force. And Sutter's ghost leaves the house. And that's as clear as I can put it.

JOHN LAHR

SOURCE: John Lahr, "Black and Blues: 'Seven Guitars,' a New Chapter in August Wilson's Ten-Play Cycle," in *The New Yorker*, Vol. 72, No. 8, April 15, 1996, pp. 99-101.

[*Lahr is an American biographer and theater critic who has written a number of well regarded books. In the following review, he praises* Seven Guitars *as part of a "profound and persuasive" history of twentieth-century African-American experience.*]

Somewhere in the middle of August Wilson's exciting *Seven Guitars*, which sends us stirring news of black life in the late forties, I found my mind wandering from the tribulations of his seven memorable characters to the blues. The show flashes back to the final days of a Pittsburgh blues singer named Floyd (Schoolboy) Barton. Before the play begins, Willie Dixon's "Little Red Rooster" and Arthur (Big Boy) Crudup's "That's All Right" rock the Walter Kerr, and when the lights come up, on Floyd's wake, a landlady named Louise (Michele Shay)—dwarfed by the production designer Scott Bradley's mammoth ghetto warrens of creosoted wood and brick and stone wedged between telephone poles and laundry lines—keeps the blues mojo working with a bawdy offer to the mournful assembly. "Anybody here wanna try my cabbage," she sings, "just step this way." What a pinched, desiccated, joyless century this would be without the blues' swaggering refusal to surrender. The seven guitars of the title are the seven characters whose straightforward story lines Wilson turns into beautiful, complex music—a funky, wailing, irresistible Chicago blues.

"I take the same approach as a bluesman, the same ideas and attitudes," Wilson recently told me. "For instance, lines that say, 'I'm leavin' in the mornin', I'm gonna start out walkin', And take a chance I may ride.' I simply go back and look through that. Contained in the expression is your whole world view." He added, "When the old folks sang, 'Everything's gonna be all right,' it was all right, simply because they sang. They made it all right by their singing. They just changed their attitudes. The blues emboldened their spirits and enabled them to survive whatever the circumstance was." Here, in a Pittsburgh backyard in 1948, Wilson is bearing witness to a pivotal, ironic moment in black American history, when African-Americans were poised between their greatest hope and their greatest heartbreak. "We had just gone off and demonstrated our allegiance and willingness to fight and die for the country," Wilson said. "We actually believed that things would be different, and that we would be accorded first-class citizenship. We came back after the war, and that was not true." In the high times and dashed dreams of *Seven Guitars*, the seventh work in a ten-play cycle that will chronicle black experience in each decade of the twentieth century (his plays for the first decade of the century, the eighties, and the nineties still remain to be written), Wilson eloquently dramatizes this punishing contradiction.

Opportunity is what Floyd carries in his pocket when he is conjured up before us in all his high-stepping, smooth-talking glory. Floyd has discovered that there's a record deal waiting for him in Chicago if he can just find the money to get his guitar out of hock and a ticket to ride. Keith David, as Floyd, gives the character a bravura air of confidence and cunning. Fresh from the workhouse, where he's done ninety days for vagrancy (the judge called his crime "worthlessness"), Floyd flaunts his prowess and his hope, trying to win back his shy, saturnine ex-girlfriend, Vera (Viola Davis), so he can take her to Chicago with him. He shows her a letter from Savoy Records. "Look at that. 'Mr. Floyd Barton,'" he says. "You get you a hit record and the white folks call you Mister." In one throwaway laugh line, Wilson catches a lifetime of second-class citizenship. But Floyd is ever hopeful. "It's different now," he tells Vera. "You get a hit record and you be surprised how everything change." What doesn't change for any of the black folk onstage, though, is their access to money. "You got to take the opportunity while it's there," Floyd says. Yet in order to seize his moment Floyd needs not only his own guitar but all his band's instruments, which are also at the pawnshop. The band has a hit record but nothing to play music with.

To finance his move, Floyd has to rely on his erstwhile manager, a white man called T. L. Hall. The plot point neatly incorporates Wilson's views on the failure of African-Americans to progress in American society. The playwright told me, "The thrust for integration and the lack of a relationship to banking capital meant that we could not continue to develop the economic base that we'd begun."

The waste of talent is implied here by the inventive energy the characters bring to the ordinary activities of their stalled days. Wilson is writing an oral, not an economic, history of his time, and it is all the more profound and persuasive because it teaches through joy, not through reason. In a catalogue of song, superstitions, stories, homilies, and food, the folkways of a lost time and place are gorgeously reimagined. For instance, Floyd's harmonica player and good friend, Canewell (the superb Ruben Santiago-Hudson, whose every syllable of tall talk is etched with tenderness), explains how to test the sweetness of watermelons. "You don't thump them," Canewell, who has eyes for Vera, says. "You treat a watermelon just like you do a woman—you squeeze them." The drummer, Red Carter (the droll Tommy Hollis), is a portly repository of black legend, especially his own. He tells how he juggled affairs with seven women at one time: "I tried to move my Friday woman over to Sunday, but she got mad. My Sunday woman quit me and my Monday woman wanted to see me on Saturday. I got so confused I say the best thing for me to do was quit my job."

For these characters, work is hardscrabble, but fun isn't. Wilson makes a point of showing off their high spirits and their talent when, after some artfully engineered badinage, the band members find themselves making wonderful music out of nothing. Canewell produces a spare harmonica and makes it "talk"; Floyd bangs his beat-up wooden guitar; Red produces drumsticks and beats out time on a card table and the backs of chairs. It's one of several showstopping moments that Wilson uses to make larger, powerful points about the personalities onstage. During another such scene, everyone sits outside on a sweltering night listening intently to a radio broadcast of the Joe Louis-Billy Conn championship fight. Boxing is the crudest of Darwinian metaphors; but, if the black man can't always survive in the real world, here, at least, he's victorious. (To underline the dramatic point, Wilson has moved the date of the Louis-Conn bout from 1946 to 1948.) The group erupts in a frenzied dance to celebrate the Brown Bomber's knockout—a victory that must stand for the characters' own frustrated battles against the white man. Red tries to teach Vera "the Joe Louis Victory Walk," telling her, "Now just let it roll. You ain't got to worry about rocking it—it'll rock by itself." Vera, who is slow to kindle, finally burns. It's a fabulous, ecstatic moment, and Vera's heat prompts Floyd to pull a gun on Red. (All the men are armed for the tough world they hustle in.) Later, in the second act, the dance is reprised by Vera and the others to celebrate the band's own victory at a local club called the Blue Goose. Life, briefly, looks as if it might come good.

Floyd's obsession is to get to Chicago and his record contract. "More people means more opportunity," he says. A lot of the play's talk focusses on whether or not to go to the Windy City. Pittsburgh is a kind of way station in the migration from the rural South to the urban North, and the implications of this migration are what Wilson is trying to trap in all the banter. A barnyard rooster that belongs to a next-door neighbor and announces itself in the play's second scene becomes the subject of much comic abuse, and a symbol of the spiritual dilemma of this shifting population. "You ain't gonna find no rooster living next to you making all that noise in Chicago," Floyd says. To Canewell, who has told us earlier that he owes his name to his grandfather's cutting cane in Louisiana ("Otherwise my name would be Cottonwell," he jokes), the rooster is a totem of the painful past. "The rooster didn't crow during slavery," he says. "If you think I'm lying go and find you somebody from back in slavery time and ask them if they ever heard the rooster crow." One character refuses to participate in the rooster jive: the demented wise man Hedley (Roger Robinson), who makes his living selling chicken sandwiches, and honors his black heritage with the sure knowledge that "the white man walk the earth on the black man's back." Hedley speaks in riddles, and he dreams that one day his dead father's inheritance will come to him from the cornet player Buddy Bolden, whom his father idolized. Sometimes Hedley's actions seem as capricious as his pronouncements. After all the grousing about the rooster, Hedley bolts from the back yard and returns with the offending piece of poultry in his hand. "God ain't making no more roosters," he declares. "It is a thing past. Soon you mark my words when God ain't making no more niggers. They, too, be a done thing." He continues, "You hear this rooster you know you alive." Then Hedley wrings its neck and slits its throat. The chilling moment works as both a curse and a prophecy. Wilson told me, "Hedley's whole warning is 'If the rooster has become useless, then what about you? Maybe you'll become useless, too.' If you don't connect to the past, then you don't know who you are in the present. You may prove to be unworthy of the past."

When Floyd's manager is jailed for an insurance scam, Floyd finds himself between a rock and a hard place. "Everything can't go wrong all the time," he says quietly. "I don't want to live my life without. Everybody I know live without. I don't want to do that. I want to live with.... Floyd Barton is gonna make his record. Floyd Barton is going to Chicago." He seizes his opportunity in the only way left to him: he robs for it. One of his friends is killed. Wilson allows Floyd a moment of glory at the Blue Goose before making him pay for his actions. Hedley discovers Floyd counting his stolen cash in the moonlight. In his dementia, Hedley mistakes Floyd, in his white city suit, for Buddy Bolden, and claims the cash as his. They quarrel, and Hedley kills Floyd.

"The odyssey of the African-American throughout the twentieth century has been one of loss and reclamation," Wilson told me. "It's about reclaiming those things which were lost during slavery." At Floyd's wake, Vera maintains that she saw him being taken up to Heaven, but his death is a necessary part of what Wilson sees as the African-American reclamation of "moral personality"—of taking responsibility for one's actions. "I always say that if the African who arrived drained and malnourished in the hold of a three-hundred-and-fifty-foot slave ship is still, after four hundred years, chained and malnourished, then it can't be anybody's fault but his," Wilson told me.

When Wilson was growing up, in the Hill district of

Pittsburgh in the late forties and fifties, his parents used to admonish him, "Don't go out there and show your color," but Wilson has dedicated his life and his art to doing just that: making a spectacle of blackness. No other theatrical testament to African-American life has been so popular or so poetic or so penetrating. In Wilson's long and successful partnership with the director Lloyd Richards, whose hand has guided this play through a protracted and difficult birth, he has won two Pulitzer Prizes, for *Fences* (1987) and *The Piano Lesson* (1990). If there were any justice in these things (there isn't), *Seven Guitars* would make it a hat trick. No one else—not even Eugene O'Neill, who set out in the mid-thirties to write a nine-play cycle and managed only two plays—has aimed so high and achieved so much. On Broadway, where shows are filled with bogus recipes for happiness, it's thrilling finally to hear a useful one. "You get you about three pounds of turnips and about three pounds of mustard," Canewell says, describing his method of making turnip greens. "I like to mix them together.... Put you in a little piece, about a quarter pound of salt pork in there with them. Turn the fire way down real low and let them cook up about six hours. Throw you some red pepper seeds in there first. Cook that up and call me when it get done." Me, too.

SOURCES FOR FURTHER STUDY

Brown, Chip. "The Light in August." *Esquire* III, No. 4 (April 1989): 116, 118, 120, 122-27.

>Detailed article tracing Wilson's literary career through events in his personal life.

DeVries, Hilary. "A Street-Corner Scribe of Life in Black America." *Christian Science Monitor* (27 March 1987):1, 8.

>Discusses the themes, imagery and language of Wilson's play-cycle on the black American experience.

Harrison, Paul Carter. "August Wilson's Blues Poetics." In *Three Plays*, by August Wilson, pp. 291-317. Pittsburgh: University of Pittsburgh Press, 1991.

>Examines the influence of the oral and blues music traditions in Wilson's plays, linking his dramas to the Harlem Renaissance and the Black Arts Movement.

Poinsett, Alex. "August Wilson: Hottest New Playwright." *Ebony* XLIII, No. 1 (November 1987): 68, 70, 72, 74.

>Biographical article focusing on Wilson's career and the impact of cultural heritage on his writing.

Smith, Philip E. II. "*Ma Rainey's Black Bottom:* Playing the Blues as Equipment for Living." In *Within the Dramatic Spectrum,* edited by Karelisa V. Hartigan, pp. 177-86. Lanham, Md.: University Press of America, 1986.

>Explores Wilson's portrayal of the black American instinct for survival.

Staples, Brent. "August Wilson." *Essence* 18, No. 4 (August 1987): 51, 111, 113.

>Examines blues music and oral tradition as used by Wilson in his dramas.

WORLD LITERATURE CRITICISM

Supplement

ACKNOWLEDGMENTS

ACKNOWLEDGMENTS

The editors wish to thank the copyright holders of the excerpted criticism included in this volume and the permissions managers of many book and magazine publishing companies for assisting us in securing reproduction rights. We are also grateful to the staffs of the Detroit Public Library, the Library of Congress, the University of Detroit Mercy Library, Wayne State University Purdy/Kresge Library Complex, and the University of Michigan Libraries for making their resources available to us. Following is a list of the copyright holders who have granted us permission to reproduce material in *WLCS*. Every effort has been made to trace copyright, but if omissions have been made, please let us know.

COPYRIGHTED EXCERPTS IN *WLCS* WERE REPRODUCED FROM THE FOLLOWING PERIODICALS:

A Current Bibliography on African Affairs, v. 17, 1984-85. Reproduced by permission.—*America,* v. 126, February 19, 1972. Reproduced by permission.—*The American Book Review,* v. 10, January-February, 1989. Reproduced by permission.—*American Mercury,* v. XXVIII, January, 1933, renewed 1960. Reproduced by permission.—*The American Scholar,* v. 27, Autumn, 1958. Reproduced by permission.—*American Theatre,* v. 3, January, 1987. Reproduced by permission.—*The Antioch Review,* v. 32, Fall-Winter, 1973. Copyright © 1973 by the Antioch Review Inc. Reproduced by permission of the Editors.—*Arion,* v. 8, Autumn, 1969. Reproduced by permission of the publisher and the translator.—*Arizona Quarterly,* v. 44, Spring, 1988. Reproduced by permission of the publisher and the author.—*Belles Lettres: A Review of Books by Women,* v. 7, Spring, 1992. Reproduced by permission.—*Black American Literature Forum,* v. 14, Summer, 1980; v. 17, Fall, 1983; v. 18, Winter, 1984. All reproduced by permission of the publisher and the authors.—*The Bloomsbury Review,* v. 13, July-August, 1993. Reproduced by permission.—*Book World—The Washington Post,* February 14, 1988; July 26, 1992. © 1988, 1992, Washington Post Book World Service/Washington Post Writers Group. Reprinted with permission.—*Boston Review,* v. XVI, April, 1991. Reproduced by permission.—*Canadian Literature,* Autumn, 1978. Reproduced by permission.—*The Centennial Review,* v. XXIV, Fall, 1980. Reproduced by permission.—*CLA Journal,* v. XXXVI, December, 1992. Reproduced by permission.—*The Commonweal,* v. LIX, October 23, 1953; v. LXXXVIII, June 28, 1968. Copyright (c) 1953, 1968 Commonweal Publishing Co., Inc. Both reproduced by permission of Commonweal Foundation.—*Critical Inquiry,* v. 5, Winter, 1978. Reproduced by permission.—*Criticism,* v. XVIII, Summer, 1976. Reproduced by permission.—*Early American Literature,* v. 14, Winter, 1979-80. Reproduced by permission.—*The Economist,* v. 319, June 22, 1991. © 1991 The Economist Newspaper Group, Inc. Reprinted with permission.—*Freedomways,* v. 23, 1983; v. 24, 1984. Both reproduced by permission.—*The Georgia Review,* v. XXXV, Summer, 1981. Reproduced by permission.—*The Hollins Critic,* v. 19, April, 1982; v. 25, October, 1988. Both reproduced by permission.—*Journal of Biblical Literature,* v. 103, 1984. Reproduced by permission.—*Journal of Women's Studies in Literature,* v. 1, Spring, 1979. Reproduced by permission.—*Latin American Literary Review,* v. XVI, July-December, 1988. Reproduced by permission.—*London Review of Books,* v. 10, September 29, 1988; v. 17, September 7, 1995, for "Shenanigans" by Michael Wood. Appears here by permission of the London Review of Books and the author.—*Los Angeles Times Book Review,* August 30, 1992. Reproduced by permission.—*The Massachusetts Review,* v. XXVIII, Summer, 1987; v. XXVIII, Autumn, 1987. Both reproduced by permission.—*Meanjin,* v. 54, 1995. Reproduced by permission of the authors.—*MELUS,* v. 7, Spring, 1980. Copyright, MELUS, The Society for the Study of Multi-Ethnic Literature of the United States, 1980. Reproduced by permission.—*Modern Drama,* v. XXI, March, 1978; v. XXXIII, September, 1990. Reproduced by permission.—*Modern Fiction Studies,* v. 28, Autumn, 1982. Reproduced by permission.—*Ms.,* January, 1977. Reproduced by permission.—*The Nation,* v. 227, December 30, 1978. ;v. 248, June 5, 1989; v. 249, November 27, 1989; v. 262, May 6, 1996. All reproduced by permission.—*National Review,* v. 47, April 3, 1995. Reproduced by permission.—*New Literary History,* v. II, Winter, 1971. Reproduced by permission.—*New Statesman & Society,* v. 8, September 22, 1995. Reproduced by permission.—*The New Republic,* v. 193, October 28, 1985; v. 200, April 17, 1989; v. 202, May 21, 1990; v. 206, March 16, 1992. All reproduced by permission.—*The New York Review of Books,* v. IX, August 24, 1967; v. XXVI, December 20, 1979; v. 28, March 5, 1981; v. XVIII, October 8, 1981; v. XXIX, August 12, 1982; v. XXXI, June 14, 1984; v. XXXII, March 14, 1985; v. XXXIX, March 5, 1992; v. XL, March 4, 1993; v. XLI, December 1, 1994. Copyright © 1967, 1979, 1981, 1982, 1984, 1985, 1992, 1993, 1994, Nyrev, Inc. All reproduced by permission.—*The New York Times Book Review,* March 8, 1925; June 9, 1968; February 13, 1972; December 16, 1979; June 1, 1980; May 24, 1981; February 21, 1988; December 22, 1991; December 17, 1995. Copyright © The New York Times Co. All reprinted by permission.—*The New York Times Company,* August 22, 1982; September 14, 1986. Copyright © The New York Times Co. Reprinted by permission. Both reprinted by permission.—*The New York Times,* October 12, 1984; February 9, 1985; May 9, 1985; March 15, 1987; February 10, 1988; February 23, 1989; March 10, 1991. Copyright © The New York Times Co. All reprinted by permission.—*The New Yorker,* v. 72, April 15, 1996. Reproduced by permission.—*North Dakota Quarterly,* v. 59, Fall, 1991. Reproduced by permission.—*The Observer,* November 22, 1992. Reproduced by permission.—*Obsidian,* v. III, Spring, 1988. Reproduced by permission.—*The Ontario Review,* Spring-Summer, 1987. Reproduced by permission.—*PHYLON: The Atlanta University Review of Race and Culture,* v. XXXVI, December, 1975 for "The Rhetoric of Martin Luther King, Jr.: `Letter from Birmingham Jail'" by Wesley T. Mott. Reproduced by permission of the author.—*PMLA: Publications of the Modern*

Language Association of America, v. 91, May, 1976. Reprinted by permission of the Modern Language Association of America.—*Poetry,* v. LXIII, March, 1944. Reproduced by permission of the publisher and the author.—*Publishers Weekly,* v. 242, December 18, 1995; v. 243, December 30, 1996. Both reproduced by permission.—*Rhetoric Society Quarterly,* v. 19, Winter, 1989. Reproduced by permission.—*Sagetrieb,* v. 6, Winter, 1987. Reproduced by permission.—*Salmagundi,* Winter, 1994. Reproduced by permission.—*The Sewanee Review,* v. 60, Summer, 1952. Copyright 1952, 1980 by the University of the South; v. 94, Fall, 1986. Copyright 1986 by John W. Stevenson. Both reprinted with the permission of the editor and the authors.—*The South Dakota Review,* v. 13, Winter, 1975-76. Reproduced by permission.—*The Southern Humanities Review,* Fall, 1973. Reproduced by permission.—*The Southern Review,* v. 2, Spring, 1937; v. XIV, January, 1978. Both reproduced by permission. *Southwest Review,* v. 64, Spring, 1979. Reproduced by permission.—*Studies in Canadian Literature,* v. 5, 1980. Reproduced by permission.—*The Times Literary Supplement,* November 10, 1995. Reproduced by permission.—*The University of Michigan Papers in Women's Studies,* v. II, 1977. Reproduced by permission.—*Victorian Poetry,* v. 7, Summer, 1969; v. 14, Winter, 1976. Both reproduced by permission.—*Virginia Quarterly Review,* v. 58, Autumn, 1982. Reproduced by permission.—*Women's Studies,* v. 13, 1986. Reproduced by permission.—*The Women's Review of Books,* v. II, August, 1985; v. IV, October, 1986. Both reproduced by permission.—*World Literature Today,* v. 64, Summer, 1990. Reproduced by permission.

COPYRIGHTED EXCERPTS IN *WLCS* WERE REPRODUCED FROM THE FOLLOWING BOOKS:

Alter, Robert. From *After the Tradition: Essays on Modern Jewish Writing.* E. P. Dutton & Co. Inc., 1969. Reproduced by permission.—Arrowsmith, William. From *Four Plays by Aristophanes,* translated by William Arrowsmith, Richmond Lattimore and Douglass Parker. New American Library, 1984. Reproduced by permission.—Baker, Jr., Houston A. From *A Many-Colored Coat of Dreams: The Poetry of Countee Cullen.* Broadside Press, 1974. Reproduced by permission.—Bambara, Toni Cade and Claudia Tate. From an interview in *Black Women Writers at Work.* Edited by Claudia Tate. Continuum, 1983. Copyright © 1983 by Claudia Tate. All rights reserved. Reprinted by permission of the publisher.—Blake, William. From *Blake: Complete Writings.* Edited by Geoffrey Keynes. Oxford University Press, London, 1966. Reproduced by permission.—Bone, Robert. From *Down Home: A History of Afro-American Short Fiction from Its Beginnings to the End of the Harlem Renaissance.* Columbia University Press, 1975. Copyright © 1975 by Columbia University Press. Reproduced by permission.—Bontemps, Arna. From an introduction to *Cane* by Jean Toomer. Copyright © 1969 by Arna Bontemps. Reprinted by permission of Liveright Publishing Corporation.—Bosmajian, Hamida. From *Metaphors of Evil: Contemporary German Literature and the Shadow of Nazism.* University of Iowa Press, 1979. Reproduced by permission.—Burnham, James. From *The Machiavellians: Defenders of Freedom.* The John Day Company, 1943. Reproduced by permission.—Clausen, Christopher. From *The Moral Imagination: Essays on Literature and Ethics.* University of Iowa Press, 1986. Reproduced by permission.—Conacher, D. J. From *Euripidean Drama: Myth, Theme, and Structure.* University of Toronto Press, 1967. Reproduced by permission.—Cook, Michael. From *Muhammad.* Oxford University Press, Oxford, 1983. Reproduced by permission.—Cooke, John. From *The Novels of Nadine Gordimer: Private Lives/Public Landscapes.* Louisiana State University, 1985. Reproduced by permission.—Cooke, Michael G. From *Afro-American Literature in the Twentieth Century: The Achievement of Intimacy.* Yale University Press, 1984. Reproduced by permission.—Creel, H. G. From *Confucius: The Man and the Myth.* The John Day Company, 1949. Reproduced by permission.—Dahlie, Hallvard. From *Canadian Writers and Their Works, Vol. 7.* Edited by Robert Lecker, Jack David and Ellen Quigley. ECW Press, 1985. Reproduced by permission.—de Romilly, Jacqueline. From *A Short History of Greek Literature,* translated by Lillian Doherty. The University of Chicago Press, 1985. Reproduced by permission.—Eliot, T. S. From *Introduction of Selected Poems of Marianne Moore.* Edited by Marianne Moore. The Macmillan Publishing Company, 1935. Copyright 1935 by Marianne Moore; copyright renewed © 1963 by Marianne Moore and T.S. Eliot. Reproduced by permission.—Esposito, John L. From *Islam: The Straight Path: Expanded Edition.* Oxford University Press, 1991. Reproduced by permission.—Fine, Ellen S. From *Legacy of Night: The Literary Universe of Elie Wiesel.* State University of New York Press, 1982. Reproduced by permission.—Giddings, Paula. From *Black Women Writers (1950-1980): A Critical Evaluation.* Edited by Mari Evans. Copyright © 1983 by Mari Evans. Used by permission of Doubleday, a division of Bantam Doubleday Dell Publishing Group, Inc.—Giovanni, Nikki and Claudia Tate. From *Black Women Writers at Work.* Edited by Claudia Tate. Continuum, 1983. Reproduced by permission.—Gray, James. From *Edna St. Vincent Millay.* University of Minnesota Press, Minneapolis, 1967. Reproduced by permission.—Gray, Wallace. From *Homer to Joyce.* Macmillan Publishing Company, 1985. Reproduced by permission.—Hadas, Moses. From *A History of Greek Literature.* Columbia University Press, 1950. Reproduced by permission.—Hare, R. M. From *Plato.* Oxford University Press, 1982. Reproduced by permission.—Harris, William J. From *Black Women Writers (1950-1980): A Critical Evaluation.* Edited by Mari Evans. Copyright © 1983 by Mari Evans. Used by permission of Doubleday, a division of Bantam Doubleday Dell Publishing Group, Inc.—Heywood, Christopher. From *Nadine Gordimer.* Profile Books Ltd., 1983. Reproduced by permission of the author.—Hirsch, Edward L. From *Six Classic American Writers: An Introduction.* Edited by Sherman Paul. University of Minnesota Press, 1970. Reproduced by permission.—Howard, Donald R. From *The Idea of the Canterbury Tales.* University of California Press, 1976. Reproduced by permission.—Jackson, Blyden. From *The Waiting Years: Essays on American Negro Literature.* Louisiana State University Press, 1976. Reproduced by permission.—Jones, Anne Goodwyn. From *Tomorrow Is Another Day: The Woman Writer in the South,* 1859-1936. Louisiana State University Press, 1981. Reproduced by permission.—Josipovici, Gabriel. From *The Book of God: A Response to the Bible.* Yale University Press, 1988. Reproduced by permission.—Kearney, Colbert. From *Anglo-Irish and Irish Literature Aspects of Language and Culture, Vol. II.* Edited by Birgit Bramsback and Martin Croghan. Almqvist & Wiksell International, 1988. Reproduced by permission.—Knapp, Mona. From *Doris Lessing.* Frederick Ungar Publishing Co., 1984. Reproduced by permission.—Knight, G. Wilson. From *The Christian Renaissance.* Methuen & Co. Ltd, 1962. Reproduced by permission.—Knopp, Josephine and Arnost Lustig. From *Encountering the Holocaust: An Interdisciplinary Study.* Edited by Byron L. Sherwin and Susan G. Ament. Impact Press, 1979. Reproduced by permission of the authors.—Lear, Jonathon. From *Aristotle: The Desire to Understand.* Cambridge University Press, 1988. Reproduced by permission of the publisher and the author.—Lee, Don L. From *Dynamite Voices I: Black Poets of the 960's.* Broadside Press, 1971. Reproduced by permission.—Lincoln, Kenneth. From *Native American Renaissance.* University of California Press, 1983. Reproduced by permission of the publisher and the author.—Lloyd, G. E. R. From *Aristotle: The Growth and Structure of His Thought.* Cambridge at the University Press, 1968. Reproduced by permission of the publisher and the author.—Nietzsche, Friedrich. From *Basic Writings of Nietzsche.* Translated by Walter Kauffmann. The Modern Library, 1967. Copyright © 1967 by Random House, Inc. Reprinted by permission of Random House, Inc.—Paret, R. From *Arabic Literature to the End of the Umayyad Period.* Edited by A. F. L. Beeston and others. Cambridge University Press, 1983. Reproduced by permission.—Pitkin, Hanna Fenichel. From *Fortune Is a Woman: Gender and Politics in the Thought of Niccolo Machiavelli.* University of California Press, 1984. Reproduced by permission.—Quasimodo, Salvatore. From *The Poet and the Politician and Other Essays,* translated by Thomas G. Bergin and Sergio Pacifici. Southern Illinois University Press, 1964. Reproduced by permission.—Ralphs, Sheila. From *Dante's Journey to the Centre: Some Patterns in His Allegory.* Manchester University Press, 1972. Reproduced by permission.—Rehbein, Edna Aguirre. From *Critical Approaches to Isabel Allende's Novels.* Edited by Sonia Riquelme Rojas and Edna Aguirre Rehbein. Peter Lang, 1991. Reproduced by permission.—Robinson, Fred C. From an introduction to *Beowulf: A Verse Translation with Treasures of the Ancient North,* translated by Marijane Osborn. University of California Press, 1983. Reproduced by permission of the publisher and the author.—Russell, Bertrand. From *A History of Western Philosophy, and Its Connection with Political and Social Circumstances from the Earliest Times to the Present Day.* Simon & Schuster, 1945. Reprinted with the permission of Simon & Schuster and the Bertrand Russell Peace Foundation Ltd.—Schwartz, Benjamin I. From *The World of Thought in Ancient China.* Cambridge, Mass: The Belknap Press of Harvard University Press, 1985. Reproduced by permission.—Seyersted, Per. From *Kate Chopin: A Critical Biography.* Louisiana State University Press, 1969. Reproduced by permission.—Singleton, Mary Ann. From *The City and the Veld: The Fiction of Doris Lessing.* Bucknell University Press, 1977. Reproduced by permission.—Smith, Patricia Clark and Paula Gunn Allen. From *The Desert Is No Lady: Southwestern Landscapes in Women's Writing and Art.* Edited by Vera Norwood and Janice Monk. Yale University Press, 1987. Reproduced by permission.—Solomos, Alexis. From *The Living Aristophanes,* translated by Alexis Solomos and Marvin Felheim. The University of Michigan Press, 1974. Reproduced by permission.—Sorrentino, Gilbert. From *Something Said.* North Point Press, 1984. Copyright © 1984 Gilbert Sorrentino. Reprinted by permission of William Morris Agency, Inc. on behalf of the author.—Steiner, George. From *Language and Silence: Essays on Language, Literature, and the Inhuman.* Copyright © 1958, 1960, 1961, 1962, 1963, 1964, 1965, 1966, 1967 by George Steiner. Reprinted by permission of Georges Borchardt, Inc. for the author.—Taylor, Clyde. From *Modern Black Poets.* Edited by Donald B. Gibson. Prentice-Hall, 1973. Reproduced by permission.—Vaio, John. From *Hypatia: Essays in Classics, Comparative Literature, and Philosophy.* Edited by William M. Calder III, Ulrich K. Goldsmith and Phyllis B. Kenevan. Colorado Associated University Press, 1985. Reproduced by permission.—Van Doren, Carl. From *Benjamin Franklin.* The Viking Press, 1938. Copyright 1938 by Carl Van Doren. Renewed © 1966 by Margaret Van Doren Bevans, Anne Van Doren Ross and Barbara Van Doren Klaw. Used by permission of Viking Penguin, a division of Penguin Books USA Inc.—Vertreace, Martha M. From *American Women Writing Fiction: Memory, Identity, Family, Space.* Edited by Mickey Pearlman. The University Press of Kentucky, 1989. Reproduced by permission.—Vickers, Brian. From *Towards Greek Tragedy: Drama, Myth, Society.* Longman Group Limited, 1973. Reproduced by permission.—von Schelling, Friedrich Wilhelm Joseph. From *German Aesthetic and Literary Criticism: Kant, Fichte, Schelling, Schopenhauer, Hegel.* Edited by David Simpson, translated by Elizabeth Rubenstein and David Simpson. Cambridge University Press, 1984. Reproduced by permission of the publisher the translators.—Washington, Mary Helen. From *Sturdy Black Bridges: Visions of Black Women in Literature.* Edited by Roseann P. Bell, Bettye J. Parker and Beverly Guy-Sheftall. Anchor Press, 1979. Reproduced by permission of the author.—Watt, W. Montgomery. From *Islamic Revelation in the Modern World.* Edinburgh at the University Press, 1969. Reproduced by permission of the author.—Winnington-Ingram, R. P. From *Sophocles: An Interpretation.* Cambridge University Press, 1980. Reproduced by permission.—Yu-lan, Fung. From *A Short History of Chinese Philosophy.* Edited by Derk Bodde. Copyright 1948 by Macmillan Publishing Company; copyright renewed © 1976 by Chung Liao Feng and Derk Bodde. Reprinted with the permission of Simon & Schuster.

PHOTOGRAPHS AND ILLUSTRATIONS APPEARING IN *WLCS* WERE RECEIVED FROM THE FOLLOWING SOURCES:

Aeschylus, photograph of bust. AP/Wide World Photos. Reproduced by permission.—Alighieri, Dante, illustration.—Allende, Isabel, photograph. Archive Photos, Inc. Reproduced by permission.—Maya Angelou, photograph. AP/Wide World Photos. Reproduced by permission.—Aristophanes, engraving.—Aristotle, photograph. Corbis-Bettmann. Reproduced by permission.—Bambara, Toni Cade, photograph by Sandra L. Swans. Reproduced by permission.—Baraka, Amiri, Newark NJ, 1994, photograph by Christopher Felver. Archive Photos Inc. Reproduced by permission.—*Beowulf* manuscript, photograph.—Browning, Robert, photograph.—Chaucer, Geoffrey, photograph of a painting.—Chopin, Kate, photograph.—Confucius, photograph of a illustration. Corbis-Bettman. Reproduced by permission.—Cullen, Countee, leaning against tree, photograph by Carl van Vechten. The Beinecke Rare Book and Manuscript Library, Yale University Library. Reproduced by permission.—Euripides, photograph of bust. Archive Photo/Popperfoto. Reproduced by permission.—Franklin, Benjamin, photograph of painting. The Library of Congress.—Gawain, illustration. Pierpont Morgan Library, New York. Reproduced by permission.—Giovanni, Nikki, photograph by Nikki Giovanni. Reproduced by permission.—Gordimer, Nadine, photograph by Jerry Bauer. Reproduced by permission.—Heaney, Seamus, photograph by Jerry Bauer. Reproduced by permission.—Homer, bust. Archive Photos, Inc. Reproduced by permission.—Housman, A. E., photograph. Archive Photos, Inc. Reproduced by permission.—Hurston, Zora Neale, photograph by Carl Van Vechten. The Library of Congress.—King Arthur and the Knights of the Round Table, illustration. Archive Photos, Inc . Reproduced by permission.—King, Dr. Martin Luther, Jr., photograph. The Library of Congress.—Maxine Hong Kingston, photograph. Jerry Bauer. Reproduced by permission.—Lessing, Doris, photograph by Jerry Bauer. Reproduced by permission.—Longfellow, Henry Wadsworth, photograph. AP/Wide World Photos. Reproduced by permission.—Machiavelli, Niccolo, illustration. Archive Photos, Inc. Reproduced by permission.—Malcolm X (chin on hand), photograph. AP/Wide World Photos. Reproduced by permission.—Masters, Edgar Lee, photograph courtesy of Hilary Masters. Reproduced by permission.—Millay, Edna St. Vincent, photograph. AP/Wide World Photos. Reproduced by permission.—Millay, Edna St. Vincent, photograph by Carl Van Vechten. The Library of Congress.—Milosz, Czeslaw (in front of book cases), photograph by Jerry Bauer. Reproduced by permission.—Mohammed, drawing. The Bettmann Archive. Reproduced by permission.—Momaday, N. Scott, photograph by Jim Kalett. Reproduced by Permission.—Moore, Marianne, photograph by Jerry Bauer. Reproduced by permission.—Munro, Alice, photograph by Jerry Bauer. Reproduced by permission.—Naylor, Gloria, photograph. AP/Wide World Photos. Reproduced by permission.—O'Casey, Sean, lighting a pipe, photograph. Archive Photos, Inc. Reproduced by permission.—Plato, photograph of bronze bust. The Library of Congress.—Rushdie, Salman, photograph. AP/Wide World Photos. Reproduced by permission.—Saint Augustine, photograph of an illustration. The Library of Congress.—Silko, Leslie Marmon, photograph by Nancy Crampton. Reproduced by permission.—Sophocles, photograph of bust. The Bettman Archive. Reproduced by permission.—Three Dead Sea Scrolls displayed in glass, photograph. Archive Photos, Inc. Reproduced by permission.—Toomer, Jean and Margery Latimer, photograph. The Bettmann Archive/Newsphotos, Inc. Reproduced by permission.—Vergil, drawing. Archive Photos, Inc. Reproduced by permission.—Walker, Alice, photograph. AP/Wide World Photos. Reproduced by permission.—Wiesel, Elie, photograph. Archive Photos, Inc. Reproduced by permission.—Wilson, August. AP/Wide World Photos. Reproduced by permission.

WORLD LITERATURE CRITICISM

Supplement

INDEXES

WLC Cumulative Author Index

This index lists all author entries in *World Literature Criticism: 1500 to the Present* (**WLC**) and *World Literature Criticism Supplement* (**WLCS**). Authors are listed under the names by which they are best known, with suitable cross-references. Volume numbers are given for each author.

hebe, (Albert) Chinua(lumogu) 1930-
WLC: 1

schylus 525 B.C.-456 B.C.
WLCS: 1

ee, Edward (Franklin III) 1928-
WLC: 1

ott, Louisa May 1832-1888
WLC: 1

ghieri, Dante 1265-1321
WLCS: 1

ende, Isabel 1942-
WLCS: 1

dersen, Hans Christian 1805-1875
WLC: 1

derson, Sherwood 1876-1941
WLC: 1

gelou, Maya 1928-
WLCS: 1

stophanes 450 B.C.-385 B.C.
WLCS: 1

stotle 384 B.C.-322 B.C.
WLCS: 1

old, Matthew 1822-1888
WLC: 1

vood, Margaret (Eleanor) 1939-
WLC: 1

den, W(ystan) H(ugh) 1907-1973
WLC: 1

Augustine 354-430
WLCS: 1

sten, Jane 1775-1817
WLC: 1

Baldwin, James (Arthur) 1924-1987
WLC: 1

Balzac, Honore de 1799-1850
WLC: 1

Bambara, Toni Cade 1939-1995
WLCS: 1

Baraka, Amiri 1934-
WLCS: 1

Baudelaire, Charles 1821-1867
WLC: 1

Beauchamp, Kathleen Mansfield 1888-1923
See Mansfield, Katherine

Beauvoir, Simone (Lucie Ernestine Marie Bertrand) de 1908-1986
WLC: 1

Beckett, Samuel (Barclay) 1906-1989
WLC: 1

Behn, Aphra 1640?-1689
WLC: 1

Bellow, Saul 1915-
WLC: 1

Bierce, Ambrose (Gwinett) 1842-1914?
WLC: 1

Blair, Eric Arthur 1903-1950
See Orwell, George

Blake, William 1757-1827
WLC: 1

Boell, Heinrich (Theodor) 1917-1985
See Boll, Heinrich

Boll, Heinrich (Theodor) 1917-1985

WLC: 1

Borges, Jorge Luis 1899-1986
WLC: 1

Boswell, James 1740-1795
WLC: 1

Bradbury, Ray(mond Douglas) 1920-
WLC: 1

Brecht, (Eugen) Bertolt (Friedrich) 1898-1956
WLC: 1

Bronte, Charlotte 1816-1855
WLC: 1

Bronte (Jane) Emily 1818-1848
WLC: 1

Brooke, Rupert (Chawner) 1887-1915
WLC: 1

Brooks, Gwendolyn 1917-
WLC: 1

Browning, Elizabeth Barrett 1806-1861
WLC: 1

Browning, Robert 1812-1889
WLCS: 1

Bunyan, John 1628-1688
WLC: 1

Burke, Edmund 1729-1797
WLC: 1

Burns, Robert 1759-1796
WLC: 1

Burroughs, William S(eward) 1914-
WLC: 1

Butler, Samuel 1835-1902
WLC: 1

Byron, George Gordon (Noel), Lord 1788-1824
WLC: 1

Camus, Albert 1913-1960
WLC: 1

Capek, Karel 1890-1938
WLC: 1

Capote, Truman 1924-1984
WLC: 1

Carroll, Lewis 1832-1898
WLC: 1

Cather, Willa (Sibert) 1873-1947
WLC: 1

Cervantes (Saavedra), Miguel de 1547-1616
WLC: 2

Chaucer, Geoffrey 1340?-1400
WLCS: 1

Cheever, John 1912-1982
WLC: 2

Chekhov, Anton (Pavlovich) 1860-1904
WLC: 2

Chopin, Kate 1851-1904
WLCS: 1

Clemens, Samuel Langhorne 1835-1910
See Twain, Mark

Cocteau, Jean (Maurice Eugene Clement) 1889-1963
WLC: 2

Coleridge, Samuel Taylor 1772-1834
WLC: 2

Confucius 551 B.C.-479 B.C.
WLCS: 1

Congreve, William 1670-1729
WLC: 2

Conrad, Joseph 1857-1924
WLC: 2

Crane, (Harold) Hart 1899-1932
WLC: 2

Crane, Stephen 1871-1900
WLC: 2

Cullen, Countee 1903-1946
WLCS: 1

Cummings, E(dward) E(stlin) 1894-1962
WLC: 2

Davies, (William) Robertson 1913-
WLC: 2

Defoe, Daniel 1660?-1731
WLC: 2

De la Mare, Walter (John) 1873-1956
WLC: 2

Dickens, Charles 1812-1870
WLC: 2

Dickinson, Emily (Elizabeth) 1830-1886
WLC: 2

Dodgson, Charles Lutwidge
See Carroll, Lewis

Donne, John 1572-1631
WLC: 2

Doolittle, Hilda 1886-1961
See H(ilda) D(oolittle)

Dos Passos, John (Roderigo) 1896-1970
WLC: 2

Dostoyevsky, Fyodor 1821-1881
WLC: 2

Douglass, Frederick 1817?-1895
WLC: 2

Doyle, (Sir) Arthur Conan 1859-1930
WLC: 2

Dreiser, Theodore (Herman Albert) 1871-1945
WLC: 2

Dryden, John 1631-1700
WLC: 2

Du Bois, W(illiam) E(dward) B(urghardt) 1868-1963
WLC: 2

Dumas, Alexandre (Davy de la Pailleterie) (pere) 1802-1870
WLC: 2

Dunbar, Paul Laurence 1872-1906
WLC: 2

Eliot, George 1819-1880
WLC: 2

Eliot, T(homas) S(tearns) 1888-1965
WLC: 2

Ellison, Ralph (Waldo) 1914-
WLC: 2

Emerson, Ralph Waldo 1803-1882
WLC: 2

Euripides 485 B.C.-406 B.C.
WLCS: 1

Faulkner, William (Cuthbert) 1897-1962
WLC: 2

Fielding, Henry 1707-1754
WLC: 2

Fitzgerald, F(rancis) Scott (Key) 1896-1940
WLC: 2

Flaubert, Gustave 1821-1880
WLC: 2

Forster, E(dward) M(organ) 1879-1970
WLC: 2

Frank, Anne 1929-1945
WLC: 2

Franklin, Benjamin 1706-1790
WLCS: 1

Frost, Robert (Lee) 1874-1963
WLC: 2

Fuentes, Carlos 1928-
WLC: 2

Galsworthy, John 1867-1933
WLC: 2

Garcia Lorca, Federico 1898-1936
WLC: 2

Garcia Marquez, Gabriel (Jose) 1928-
WLC: 3

Gide, Andre (Paul Guillaume) 1869-1951
WLC: 3

Ginsberg, Allen 1926-1997
WLC: 3

Giovanni, Nikki 1943-
WLCS: 1

Goethe, Johann Wolfgang von 1749-1832
WLC: 3

Gogol, Nikolai (Vasilyevich) 1809-1852
WLC: 3

Golding, William (Gerald) 1911-1991
WLC: 3

Goldsmith, Oliver 1728?-1774
WLC: 3

Gordimer, Nadine 1923-
WLCS: 1

Gorky, Maxim 1868-1936
WLC: 3

Grass, Gunter (Wilhelm) 1927-
WLC: 3

Gray, Thomas 1716-1771
WLC: 3

Greene, Graham (Henry) 1904-1991
WLC: 3

Hardy, Thomas 1716-1928
WLC: 3

Harte, (Francis) Bret(t) 1836?-1902
WLC: 3

Hawthorne, Nathaniel 1804-1864
WLC: 3

H(ilda) D(oolittle) 1886-1961
WLC: 3

Heaney, Seamus 1939-
WCLS: 1

Heller, Joseph 1923-
WLC: 3

Hemingway, Ernest (Miller) 1899-1961
WLC: 3

Henry, O. 1862-1910
WLC: 3

Hesse, Hermann 1877-1962
WLC: 3

Hiraoka, Kimitake 1925-1970
See Mishima, Yukio

Homer c. 8th century B.C.
WLCS: 1

pkins, Gerard Manley 1844-1889
WLC: 3

usman, A. E. 1859-1936
WLCS: 1

ghes, (James) Langston 1902-1967
WLC: 3

go, Victor Marie 1802-1885
WLC: 3

rston, Zora Neale 1903-1960
WLCS: 1

xley, Aldous (Leonard) 1894-1963
WLC: 3

en, Henrik (Johan) 1828-1906
WLC: 3

esco, Eugene 1912-
WLC: 3

ing, Washington 1783-1859
WLC: 3

ckson, Shirley 1919-1965
WLC: 3

mes, Henry (Jr.) 1843-1916
WLC: 3

ffers, (John) Robinson 1887-1962
WLC: 3

hnson, Samuel 1709-1784
WLC: 3

nson, Ben(jamin) 1572?-1637
WLC: 3

ce, James (Augustine Aloysius) 1882-1941
WLC: 3

ka, Franz 1883-1924
WLC: 3

ats, John 1795-1821
WLC: 3

rouac, Jack 1922-1969
WLC: 3

rouac, Jean-Louis Lebris de 1922-1969
See Kerouac, Jack

sey, Ken (Elton) 1935-
WLC: 3

g, Martin Luther (Jr.) 1929-1968
WLCS: 1

gston, Maxine Hong 1940-
WLCS: 2

ling, (Joseph) Rudyard 1865-1936
WLC: 3

mb, Charles 1775-1834
WLC: 3

vrence, D(avid) H(erbert) 1885-1930
WLC: 3

, (Nelle) Harper 1926-
WLC: 4

sing, Doris 1919-
WLCS: 2

Lewis, C(live) S(taples) 1898-1963
WLC: 4

Lewis, (Harry) Sinclair 1885-1951
WLC: 4

Lindsay, (Nicholas) Vachel 1879-1931
WLC: 4

London, Jack 1876-1916
WLC: 4

London, John Griffith 1876-1916
See London, Jack

Longfellow, Henry Wadsworth 1807-1882
WLCS: 2

Lowell, Robert (Traill Spence, Jr.) 1917-1977
WLC: 4

Machiavelli, Niccolo 1469-1527
WLCS: 2

Malamud, Bernard 1914-1986
WLC: 4

Malcolm X 1925-1965
WLCS: 2

Malory, (Sir) Thomas 1410?-1471?
WLCS: 2

Mann, Thomas 1875-1955
WLC: 4

Mansfield, Katherine 1888-1923
WLC: 4

Marlowe, Christopher 1564-1593
WLC: 4

Marvell, Andrew 1621-1678
WLC: 4

Masters, Edgar Lee 1868-1950
WLCS: 2

Maugham, W(illiam) Somerset 1874-1965
WLC: 4

Maupassant, (Henri Rene Albert) Guy de 1850-1893
WLC: 4

McCullers, (Lula) Carson (Smith) 1917-1967
WLC: 4

McKay, Claude 1889-1948
WLC: 4

McKay, Festus Claudius 1889-1948
See McKay, Claude

Melville, Herman 1819-1891
WLC: 4

Millay, Edna St. Vincent 1892-1950
WLCS: 2

Miller, Arthur 1915-
WLC: 4

Miller, Henry (Valentine) 1891-1980
WLC: 4

Milosz, Czeslaw 1911-
WLCS: 2

Milton, John 1608-1674
WLC: 4

Mishima, Yukio 1925-1970
WLC: 4

Moliere 1922-1673
WLC: 4

Momaday, N. Scott 1934-
WLCS: 2

Montaigne, Michel (Eyquem) de 1533-1592
WLC: 4

Moore, Marianne 1887-1972
WLCS: 2

Morrison, Toni 1931-
WLC: 4

Muhammad 570?-632
WLCS: 2

Munro, Alice 1931-
WLCS: 2

Munro, H(ector) H(ugh) 1870-1916
WLC: 4

Nabokov, Vladimir (Vladimirovich) 1899-1977
WLC: 4

Naylor, Gloria 1950-
WLCS: 2

Neruda, Pablo 1904-1973
WLC: 4

Oates, Joyce Carol 1938-
WLC: 4

O'Casey, Sean 1880-1964
WLCS: 2

O'Connor, (Mary) Flannery 1925-1964
WLC: 4

O'Neill, Eugene (Gladstone) 1888-1953
WLC: 4

Orwell, George 1903-1950
WLC: 4

Osborne, John (James) 1929-
WLC: 4

Owen, Wilfred (Edward Salter) 1893-1918
WLC: 4

Pasternak, Boris 1890-1960
WLC: 4

Paton, Alan (Stewart) 1903-1988
WLC: 4

Paz, Octavio 1914-
WLC: 4

Pepys, Samuel 1633-1703
WLC: 4

Peshkov, Alexei Maximovich 1868-1936
See Gorky, Maxim

Pinter, Harold 1930-
WLC: 4

Pirandello, Luigi 1867-1936
WLC: 4

Plath, Sylvia 1932-1963
WLC: 4

Plato 428? B.C.-348? B.C.
WLCS: 2

Poe, Edgar Allan 1809-1849
WLC: 4

Pope, Alexander 1688-1744
WLC: 5

Porter, William Sydney 1862-1910
WLC: 5

Pound, Ezra (Loomis) 1885-1972
WLC: 5

Proust, Marcel 1871-1922
WLC: 5

Pushkin, Alexander (Sergeyevich) 1799-1837
WLC: 5

Pynchon, Thomas (Ruggles, Jr.) 1937-
WLC: 5

Rabelais, Francois 1494?-1553
WLC: 5

Rand, Ayn 1905-1982
WLC: 5

Richardson, Samuel 1689-1761
WLC: 5

Rimbaud, (Jean Nicolas) Arthur 1854-1891
WLC: 5

Rossetti, Christina Georgina 1830-1894
WLC: 5

Rossetti, Dante Gabriel 1828-1882
WLC: 5

Roth, Philip (Milton) 1933-
WLC: 5

Rousseau, Jean-Jacques 1712-1778
WLC: 5

Rushdie, Salman 1947-
WLCS: 2

Saki 1870-1916
WLC: 5

Salinger, J(erome) D(avid) 1919-
WLC: 5

Sand, George 1804-1876
WLC: 5

Sandburg, Carl (August) 1878-1967
WLC: 5

Saroyan, William 1908-1981
WLC: 5

Sartre, Jean-Paul (Charles Aymard) 1905-1980
WLC: 5

Scott, Sir Walter 1771-1832
WLC: 5

Service, Robert W(illiam) 1874?-1958
WLC: 5

Sexton, Anne (Harvey) 1928-1974
WLC: 5

Shakespeare, William 1564-1616
WLC: 5

Shaw, (George) Bernard 1856-1950
WLC: 5

Shelley, Mary Wollstonecraft Godwin 1797-1851
WLC: 5

Shelley, Percy Bysshe 1792-1822
WLC: 5

Sheridan, Richard Brinsley 1751-1816
WLC: 5

Silko, Leslie Marmon 1948-
WLCS: 2

Sinclair, Upton (Beall) 1878-1968
WLC: 5

Singer, Isaac Bashevis 1904-1991
WLC: 5

Solzhenitsyn, Aleksandr I(sayevich) 1918-
WLC: 5

Sophocles 496? B.C.-406? B.C.
WLCS: 2

Soyinka, Wole 1934-
WLC: 5

Spenser, Edmund 1552?-1599
WLC: 5

Stein, Gertrude 1874-1946
WLC: 5

Steinbeck, John (Ernst) 1902-1968
WLC: 5

Stendhal 1783-1842
WLC: 5

Sterne, Laurence 1713-1768
WLC: 5

Stevens, Wallace 1879-1955
WLC: 5

Stevenson, Robert Louis 1850-1894
WLC: 5

Stoker, Abraham 1847-1912
See Stoker, Bram

Stoker, Bram 1847-1912
WLC: 6

Stoppard, Tom 1937-
WLC: 6

Stowe, Harriet (Elizabeth) Beecher 1811-1896
WLC: 6

Strindberg, (Johan) August 1849-1912
WLC: 6

Swift, Jonathan 1667-1745
WLC: 6

Swinburne, Algernon Charles 1837-1909
WLC: 6

Tennyson, Alfred, Lord 1809-1892
WLC: 6

Thackeray, William Makepeace 1811-1863
WLC: 6

Thomas, Dylan (Marlais) 1914-1953
WLC: 6

Thoreau, Henry David 1817-1862
WLC: 6

Tolkien, J(ohn) R(onald) R(euel) 1892-1973
WLC: 6

Tolstoy, (Count) Leo (Lev Nikolaevich) 1828-1910
WLC: 6

Toomer, Jean 1894-1967
WLCS: 2

Trollope, Anthony 1815-1882
WLC: 6

Turgenev, Ivan 1818-1883
WLC: 6

Twain, Mark 1835-1910
WLC: 6

Undset, Sigrid 1882-1949
WLC: 6

Updike, John (Hoyer) 1932-
WLC: 6

Vergil 70 B.C.-19 B.C.
WLCS: 2

Voltaire 1694-1778
WLC: 6

Vonnegut, Kurt, Jr. 1922-
WLC: 6

Walker, Alice 1944-
WLCS: 2

Warren, Robert Penn 1905-1989
WLC: 6

Waugh, Evelyn (Arthur St. John) 1903-1966
WLC: 6

Webster, John 1580?-1634?
WLC: 6

Wells, H(erbert) G(eorge) 1866-1946
WLC: 6

Welty, Eudora (Alice) 1909-
WLC: 6

Wharton, Edith (Newbold Jones) 1862-1937
WLC: 6

Wheatley (Peters), Phillis 1753?-1784
WLC: 6

Whitman, Walt 1819-1892
WLC: 6

Wiesel, Elie 1928-
    WLCS: 2

Wilde, Oscar (Fingal O'Flahertie Wills)
    1854-1900
    WLC: 6

Wilder, Thornton (Niven) 1897-1975
    WLC: 6

Williams, Tennessee 1911-1983
    WLC: 6

Williams, William Carlos 1883-1963
    WLC: 6

Wilson, August 1945-
    WLCS: 2

Wolfe, Thomas (Clayton) 1900-1938
    WLC: 6

Woolfe, (Adeline) Virginia 1882-1941
    WLC: 6

Wordsworth, William 1770-1850
    WLC: 6

Wright, Richard (Nathaniel) 1908-1960
    WLC: 6

Yeats, William Butler 1865-1939
    WLC: 6

Zola, Emile 1840-1902
    WLC: 6

WLC Cumulative Nationality Index

This index lists all author entries in *World Literature Criticism: 1500 to the Present* (**WLC**) and *World Literature Criticism Supplement* (**WLCS**) by nationality. Authors are listed under the names by which they are best known. Volume numbers are given for each author.

ALGERIAN
Camus, Albert **WLC: 1**

AMERICAN
Albee, Edward **WLC: 1**
Alcott, Louisa May **WLC: 1**
Anderson, Sherwood **WLC: 1**
Angelou, Maya **WLCS: 1**
Auden, W. H. **WLC: 1**
Baldwin, James **WLC: 1**
Bambara, Toni Cade **WLCS: 1**
Baraka, Amiri **WLCS: 1**
Bellow, Saul **WLC: 1**
Bierce, Ambrose **WLC: 1**
Bradbury, Ray **WLC: 1**
Brooks, Gwendolyn **WLC: 1**
Burroughs, William S. **WLC: 1**
Capote, Truman **WLC: 1**
Cather, Willa **WLC: 1**
Cheever, John **WLC: 2**
Chopin, Kate **WLCS: 1**
Crane, Hart **WLC: 2**
Crane, Stephen **WLC: 2**
Cullen, Countee **WLCS: 1**
Cummings, E. E. **WLC: 2**
Dickinson, Emily **WLC: 2**
Dos Passos, John **WLC: 2**
Douglass, Frederick **WLC: 2**
Dreiser, Theodore **WLC: 2**
Du Bois, W. E. B. **WLC: 2**
Dunbar, Paul Laurence **WLC: 2**
Eliot, T. S. **WLC: 2**
Ellison, Ralph **WLC: 2**
Emerson, Ralph Waldo **WLC: 2**
Faulkner, William **WLC: 2**
Fitzgerald, F. Scott **WLC: 2**
Franklin, Benjamin **WLCS: 1**
Frost, Robert **WLC: 2**
Ginsberg, Allen **WLC: 3**
Giovanni, Nikki **WLCS: 1**
H. D. **WLC: 3**
Harte, Bret **WLC: 3**
Hawthorne, Nathaniel **WLC: 3**
Heller, Joseph **WLC: 3**
Hemingway, Ernest **WLC: 3**
Henry, O. **WLC: 3**
Hughes, Langston **WLC: 3**
Hurston, Zora Neale **WLCS: 1**
Irving, Washington **WLC: 3**
Jackson, Shirley **WLC: 3**
James, Henry **WLC: 3**
Jeffers, Robinson **WLC: 3**
Kerouac, Jack **WLC: 3**
Kesey, Ken **WLC: 3**
King, Martin Luther, Jr. **WLCS: 1**
Kingston, Maxine Hong **WLCS: 2**
Lee, Harper **WLC: 4**
Lewis, Sinclair **WLC: 4**
Lindsay, Vachel **WLC: 4**
London, Jack **WLC: 4**
Longfellow, Henry Wadsworth **WLCS: 2**
Lowell, Robert **WLC: 4**
Malamud, Bernard **WLC: 4**
Malcolm X **WLCS: 2**
Masters, Edgar Lee **WLCS: 2**
McCullers, Carson **WLC: 4**
McKay, Claude **WLC: 4**
Melville, Herman **WLC: 4**
Millay, Edna St. Vincent **WLCS: 2**
Miller, Arthur **WLC: 4**
Miller, Henry **WLC: 4**
Momaday, N. Scott **WLCS: 2**
Moore, Marianne **WLCS: 2**
Morrison, Toni **WLC: 4**
Nabokov, Vladimir **WLC: 4**
Naylor, Gloria **WLCS: 2**
Oates, Joyce Carol **WLC: 4**
O'Connor, Flannery **WLC: 4**
O'Neill, Eugene **WLC: 4**
Plath, Sylvia **WLC: 4**
Poe, Edgar Allan **WLC: 4**
Pound, Ezra **WLC: 4**
Pynchon, Thomas **WLC: 5**
Rand, Ayn **WLC: 5**
Roth, Philip **WLC: 5**
Salinger, J. D. **WLC: 5**
Sandburg, Carl **WLC: 5**
Saroyan, William **WLC: 5**
Sexton, Anne **WLC: 5**
Silko, Leslie Marmon **WLCS: 2**
Sinclair, Upton **WLC: 5**
Singer, Isaac Bashevis **WLC: 5**
Stein, Gertrude **WLC: 5**
Steinbeck, John **WLC: 5**
Stevens, Wallace **WLC: 5**
Stowe, Harriet Beecher **WLC: 6**
Thoreau, Henry David **WLC: 6**
Toomer, Jean **WLCS: 2**
Twain, Mark **WLC: 6**
Updike, John **WLC: 6**
Vonnegut, Kurt, Jr. **WLC: 6**
Walker, Alice **WLCS: 2**
Warren, Robert Penn **WLC: 6**
Welty, Eudora **WLC: 6**
Wharton, Edith **WLC: 6**
Wheatley, Phillis **WLC: 6**
Whitman, Walt **WLC: 6**
Wiesel, Elie **WLCS: 2**
Wilder, Thornton **WLC: 6**
Williams, Tennessee **WLC: 6**
Williams, William Carlos **WLC: 6**
Wilson, August **WLCS: 2**
Wolfe, Thomas **WLC: 6**
Wright, Richard **WLC: 6**

ARABIAN
Muhammad **WLCS: 2**

ARGENTINIAN
Borges, Jorge Luis **WLC: 1**

AUSTRIAN
Kafka, Franz **WLC: 3**

CANADIAN
Atwood, Margaret **WLC: 1**
Davies, Robertson **WLC: 2**
Munro, Alice **WLCS: 2**
Service, Robert W. **WLC: 5**

NATIONALITY INDEX

CHILEAN
Allende, Isabel **WLCS: 1**
Neruda, Pablo **WLC: 4**

CHINESE
Confucius **WLCS: 1**

COLOMBIAN
García Márquez, Gabriel **WLC: 3**

CZECHOSLOVAKIAN
Capek, Karel **WLC: 1**
Kafka, Franz **WLC: 3**
Stoppard, Tom **WLC: 6**

DANISH
Andersen, Hans Christian **WLC: 1**

DUTCH
Frank, Anne **WLC: 2**

ENGLISH
Arnold, Matthew **WLC: 1**
Auden, W. H. **WLC: 1**
Austen, Jane **WLC: 1**
Behn, Aphra **WLC: 1**
Blake, William **WLC: 1**
Boswell, James **WLC: 1**
Brontë, Charlotte **WLC: 1**
Brontë, Emily **WLC: 1**
Brooke, Rupert **WLC: 1**
Browning, Elizabeth Barrett **WLC: 1**
Browning, Robert **WLCS: 1**
Bunyan, John **WLC: 1**
Burke, Edmund **WLC: 1**
Butler, Samuel **WLC: 1**
Byron, Lord **WLC: 1**
Carroll, Lewis **WLC: 1**
Chaucer, Geoffrey **WLCS: 1**
Coleridge, Samuel Taylor **WLC: 2**
Congreve, William **WLC: 2**
Conrad, Joseph **WLC: 2**
De la Mare, Walter **WLC: 2**
Defoe, Daniel **WLC: 2**
Dickens, Charles **WLC: 2**
Donne, John **WLC: 2**
Doyle, Arthur Conan **WLC: 2**
Dryden, John **WLC: 2**
Eliot, George **WLC: 2**
Eliot, T. S. **WLC: 2**
Fielding, Henry **WLC: 2**
Forster, E. M. **WLC: 2**
Galsworthy, John **WLC: 2**
Golding, William **WLC: 3**
Goldsmith, Oliver **WLC: 3**
Gray, Thomas **WLC: 3**
Greene, Graham **WLC: 3**
Hardy, Thomas **WLC: 3**
Hopkins, Gerard Manley **WLC: 3**
Housman, A. E. **WLCS: 1**
Huxley, Aldous **WLC: 3**
Johnson, Samuel **WLC: 3**
Jonson, Ben **WLC: 3**
Keats, John **WLC: 3**
Kipling, Rudyard **WLC: 3**
Lamb, Charles **WLC: 3**
Lawrence, D. H. **WLC: 3**
Lessing, Doris **WLCS: 2**
Lewis, C. S. **WLC: 4**
Malory, Thomas **WLCS: 2**
Marlowe, Christopher **WLC: 4**
Marvell, Andrew **WLC: 4**
Maugham, W. Somerset **WLC: 4**
Milton, John **WLC: 4**
Orwell, George **WLC: 4**
Osborne, John **WLC: 4**
Owen, Wilfred **WLC: 4**
Pepys, Samuel **WLC: 4**
Pinter, Harold **WLC: 4**
Pope, Alexander **WLC: 5**
Richardson, Samuel **WLC: 5**
Rossetti, Christina **WLC: 5**
Rossetti, Dante Gabriel **WLC: 5**
Rushdie, Salman **WLCS: 2**
Saki **WLC: 5**
Scott, Sir Walter **WLC: 5**
Shakespeare, William **WLC: 5**
Shelley, Mary **WLC: 5**
Shelley, Percy Bysshe **WLC: 5**
Sheridan, Richard Brinsley **WLC: 5**
Spenser, Edmund **WLC: 5**
Sterne, Laurence **WLC: 5**
Stoppard, Tom **WLC: 6**
Swift, Jonathan **WLC: 6**
Swinburne, Algernon **WLC: 6**
Tennyson, Alfred, Lord **WLC: 6**
Thackeray, William Makepeace **WLC: 6**
Tolkien, J. R. R. **WLC: 6**
Trollope, Anthony **WLC: 6**
Waugh, Evelyn **WLC: 6**
Webster, John **WLC: 6**
Wells, H. G. **WLC: 6**
Wilde, Oscar **WLC: 6**
Woolf, Virginia **WLC: 6**
Wordsworth, William **WLC: 6**

FRENCH
Balzac, Honoré de **WLC: 1**
Baudelaire, Charles **WLC: 1**
Beauvoir, Simone de **WLC: 1**
Beckett, Samuel **WLC: 1**
Camus, Albert **WLC: 1**
Cocteau, Jean **WLC: 2**
Dumas, Alexandre **WLC: 2**
Flaubert, Gustave **WLC: 2**
Gide, André **WLC: 3**
Hugo, Victor **WLC: 3**
Ionesco, Eugène **WLC: 3**
Maupassant, Guy de **WLC: 4**
Molière **WLC: 4**
Montaigne, Michel de **WLC: 4**
Proust, Marcel **WLC: 5**
Rabelais, François **WLC: 5**
Rimbaud, Arthur **WLC: 5**
Rousseau, Jean-Jacques **WLC: 5**
Sand, George **WLC: 5**
Sartre, Jean-Paul **WLC: 5**
Stendhal **WLC: 5**
Voltaire **WLC: 6**
Zola, Emile **WLC: 6**

GERMAN
Böll, Heinrich **WLC: 1**
Brecht, Bertolt **WLC: 1**
Frank, Anne **WLC: 2**
Goethe, Johann Wolfgang von **WLC: 3**
Grass, Günter **WLC: 3**
Hesse, Hermann **WLC: 3**
Mann, Thomas **WLC: 4**

GREEK
Aeschylus **WLCS: 1**
Aristophanes **WLCS: 1**
Aristotle **WLCS: 1**
Euripides **WLCS: 1**
Homer **WLCS: 1**
Plato **WLCS: 2**
Sophocles **WLCS: 2**

IRISH
Beckett, Samuel **WLC: 1**
Burke, Edmund **WLC: 1**
Goldsmith, Oliver **WLC: 3**
Heaney, Seamus **WLCS: 1**
Joyce, James **WLC: 3**
Lewis, C. S. **WLC: 4**
O'Casey, Sean **WLCS: 2**
Shaw, Bernard **WLC: 5**
Sheridan, Richard Brinsley **WLC: 5**
Sterne, Laurence **WLC: 5**
Stoker, Bram **WLC: 6**
Swift, Jonathan **WLC: 6**
Wilde, Oscar **WLC: 6**
Yeats, William Butler **WLC: 6**

ITALIAN
Alighieri, Dante **WLCS: 1**
Machiavelli, Niccolò **WLCS: 2**
Pirandello, Luigi **WLC: 4**

JAMAICAN
McKay, Claude **WLC: 4**

JAPANESE
Mishima, Yukio **WLC: 4**

MEXICAN
Fuentes, Carlos **WLC: 2**
Paz, Octavio **WLC: 4**

NEW ZEALANDER
Mansfield, Katherine **WLC: 4**

NIGERIAN
Achebe, Chinua **WLC: 1**
Soyinka, Wole **WLC: 5**

NORWEGIAN
Ibsen, Henrik **WLC: 3**
Undset, Sigrid **WLC: 6**

POLISH
Conrad, Joseph **WLC: 2**
Milosz, Czeslaw **WLCS: 2**
Singer, Isaac Bashevis **WLC: 5**

ROMAN
St. Augustine **WLCS: 1**
Vergil **WLCS: 2**

RUMANIAN
Ionesco, Eugène **WLC: 3**

RUSSIAN
Chekhov, Anton **WLC: 2**
Dostoyevsky, Fyodor **WLC: 2**
Gogol, Nikolai **WLC: 3**
Gorky, Maxim **WLC: 3**
Nabokov, Vladimir **WLC: 4**
Pasternak, Boris **WLC: 4**
Pushkin, Alexander **WLC: 5**
Rand, Ayn **WLC: 5**
Solzhenitsyn, Aleksandr **WLC: 5**
Tolstoy, Leo **WLC: 6**
Turgenev, Ivan **WLC: 6**

SCOTTISH
Boswell, James **WLC: 1**
Burns, Robert **WLC: 1**
Scott, Sir Walter **WLC: 5**
Service, Robert W. **WLC: 5**
Stevenson, Robert Louis **WLC: 5**

SOUTH AFRICAN
Gordimer, Nadine **WLCS: 1**
Paton, Alan **WLC: 4**
Tolkien, J. R. R. **WLC: 6**

SPANISH
Cervantes, Miguel de **WLC: 2**
García Lorca, Federico **WLC: 2**

SWEDISH
Strindberg, August **WLC: 6**

SWISS
Hesse, Hermann **WLC: 3**
Rousseau, Jean-Jacques **WLC: 5**

WELSH
Thomas, Dylan **WLC: 6**

WLC Cumulative Title Index

This index lists all titles in *World Literature Criticism: 1500 to the Present* (**WLC**) and *World Literature Criticism Supplement* (**WLCS**). Volume and page numbers are given for each title.

"a-" (Cummings) **WLC 2**:842
À la recherche du temps perdu (*In Search of Lost Time; Remembrance of Things Past*) (Proust) **WLC 5**:2806, 2809, 2811, 2815, 2818
"A' the Airts" (Burns)
  See "Of A' the Airts"
"Aaron Hatfield" (Masters) **WLCS 2**:580
"L'abandonné" (Maupassant) **WLC 4**:2293
"The Abbey Grange" (Doyle) **WLC 2**:1013
Abdelazer; or, The Moor's Revenge (Behn) **WLC 1**:246
"Abencaján el Bojarí, muerto en su laberinto" ("Abenjacán the Bojarí, Dead in His Labyrinth") (Borges) **WLC 1**:335
"Abenjacán the Bojarí, Dead in His Labyrinth" (Borges)
  See "Abencaján el Bojarí, muerto en su laberinto"
"The Abode of Summer" (Welty) **WLC 6**:3891
The Abolition of Man (Lewis) **WLC 4**:2089-90
"About How Ivan Ivanovic Quarreled with Ivan Nikiforovic" (Gogol)
  See "The Tale of How Ivan Ivanovich Quarrelled with Ivan Nikiforovich"
"About the House" (Auden) **WLC 1**:137
Above the Barriers (Pasternak)
  See *Poverkh barierov*
"Abraham Lincoln Walks at Midnight" (Lindsay) **WLC 4**:2123-24
Absalom, Absalom! (Faulkner) **WLC 2**:1189, 1192-94, 1197-98
Absalom and Achitophel (Dryden) **WLC 2**:1051, 1054, 1056
The Absolute at Large (Capek)
  See *Továrna na absolutno*
"Absolution" (Fitzgerald) **WLC 2**:1232-33,

1235
The Accident (Wiesel) **WLCS 2**:847
"Accomplished Desires" (Oates) **WLC 4**:2528
An Account of a Battel between the Ancient and Modern Books in St. James's Library (Swift)
  See *A Tale of a Tub, Written for the Universal Improvement of Mankind, to Which is Added an Account of a Battel between the Ancient and Modern Books in St. James's Library*
An Account of Corsica (Boswell) **WLC 1**:350, 358
An Account of Corsica, The Journal of a Tour to that Island; and the Memoirs of Pascal Paoli (*Memoirs of Pascal Paoli; Tour of Corsica*) (Boswell) **WLC 1**:350, 360, 358
"Account of the Ensuing Poem" (Dryden) **WLC 2**:1057
The Account of the Life of Mr. Richard Savage (Johnson) **WLC 3**:1893
"An Account of Yesterday" (Tolstoy) **WLC 6**:3665
"Accountability" (Dunbar) **WLC 2**:1103
"Les accroupissements" (Rimbaud) **WLC 5**:295
"The Accuser" (Milosz) **WLCS 2**:610-11
The Acharnians (Aristophanes) **WLCS 1**:77-79
Het achterhuis (*Anne Frank: The Diary of a Young Girl; The Diary of a Young Girl*) (Frank) **WLC 2**:1277, 1279, 1282
Acia (Turgenev)
  See *Asya*
Acquainted with the Night (Boell)
  See *Und Sagte kein einziges Wort*
"Acquainted with the Night" (Frost) **WLC 2**:1293, 1299
Across Spoon River (Masters) **WLCS**

2:582-84
Across the Board on Tomorrow Morning (Saroyan) **WLC 5**:3080
Across the River and into the Trees (*The Things That I Know*) (Hemingway) **WLC 3**:1658
"Act of Union" (Heaney) **WLCS 1**:390
Ada (Nabokov) **WLC 4**:2497
Ada; or, Ardor: A Family Chronicle (Nabokov) **WLC 4**:2497
"Adagia" (Stevens) **WLC 5**:3437
Adam Bede (Eliot) **WLC 2**:1117, 1120, 1122-25
Adam stvoritel (*Adam the Creator*) (Capek) **WLC 1**:601, 605
Adam the Creator (Capek)
  See *Adam stvoritel*
Adam, Where Art Thou? (Boell)
  See *Wo warst du, Adam?*
"An Address Delivered Before the Senior Class in Divinity College, Cambridge" (Emerson)
  See "The Divinity School Address"
"Address of Beelzebub" (Burns) **WLC 1**:523-24
"Address to a Haggis" ("To a Haggis") (Burns) **WLC 1**:517
"Address to a Louse" (Burns)
  See "To a Louse, on Seeing One on a Lady's Bonnet at Church"
"Address to the De'il" ("To the De'il") (Burns) **WLC 1**:517, 523-26
Adjunta al Parnaso (Cervantes)
  See "Viage del Parnaso"
Adolescent (Dostoevsky)
  See *Podrostok*
Adonais: An Elegy on the Death of John Keats (Shelley) **WLC 5**:3224, 3233, 3236-38
Advent (Strindberg) **WLC 6**:3519
"Advent" (Grass) **WLC 3**:1506

Adventure (London) **WLC 4:**2139
"The Adventure of Lieutenant Jergounoff" (Turgenev)
  See "Istoriya leytenanta Ergunova"
"The Adventure of the Black Fisherman" (Irving) **WLC 3:**1820
The Adventure of the Black Lady (Behn) **WLC 1:**250
"The Adventure of the Copper Beeches" (Doyle) **WLC 2:**1015
"The Adventure of the Illustrious Client" (Doyle) **WLC 2:**1016
"The Adventure of the Retired Colourman" (Doyle) **WLC 2:**1013, 1016
"The Adventure of the Silver Blaze" (Doyle) **WLC 2:**1011
"The Adventure of the Speckled Band" (Doyle) **WLC 2:**1013, 1015
"The Adventure of the Sussex Vampire" (Doyle) **WLC 2:**1016
"The Adventure of the Three Gables" (Doyle) **WLC 2:**1013
"Adventure" (Anderson) **WLC 1:**85
Adventures du Baron de Gangan (Voltaire) **WLC 6:**3779
Adventures of a Young Man (Dos Passos) **WLC 2:**966
The Adventures of Augie March (Bellow) **WLC 1:**264-65, 268-69, 271-72, 274-75
The Adventures of Huckleberry Finn (Twain) **WLC 6:**3716, 3718, 3721, 3726-28
The Adventures of Sherlock Holmes (Doyle) **WLC 2:**1011, 1018, 1020
The Adventures of Tom Sawyer (Twain) **WLC 6:**3718
The Adventures of Wesley Jackson (Saroyan) **WLC 5:**3075
The Adventures of William Saroyan (Saroyan) **WLC 5:**3075
Adventures While Preaching the Gospel of Beauty (Lindsay) **WLC 4:**2117
"Advice to a Young Man" (Franklin) **WLCS 1:**322
"Advice to a Young Tradesman, Written by an Old One" (Franklin) **WLCS 1:**322
"Advice to Youth" (Cullen) **WLCS 1:**276
Aeneid (Vergil) **WLCS 2:**811-25
The Affected Ladies (Moliere)
  See *Les précieuses ridicules*
"An Affection for Cathedrals" (Golding) **WLC 3:**1456
Afloat (Maupassant)
  See *Sur l'eau*
"Africa Emergent" (Gordimer) **WLCS 1:**371
"After a Visit" (Dunbar) **WLC 2:**1100, 1103
"After Apple-Picking" (Frost) **WLC 2:**1290-91
"After Death" (Rossetti) **WLC 5:**2930, 2937
"After Holbein" (Wharton) **WLC 6:**3905
"After Magritte" (Stoppard) **WLC 6:**3483, 3494
After Many a Summer Dies the Swan (Huxley) **WLC 3:**1767-68
"After Mecca" (Brooks) **WLC 1:**456
"After the Death of John Brown" (Thoreau) **WLC 6:**3640
"After the Deluge" (Rimbaud)
  See "Après le déluge"

After the Fall (Miller) **WLC 4:**2370-72
"After the Funeral: In Memory of Anne Jones" ("In Memory of Ann Jones") (Thomas) **WLC 6:**3619
"After the Race" (Joyce) **WLC 3:**1936
"After the Storm" (Hemingway) **WLC 3:**1650
"After the Winter" (McKay) **WLC 4:**2337
"An Afternoon Miracle" (Henry) **WLC 3:**1675
"Afternoon of an Author" (Fitzgerald) **WLC 2:**1225, 1235
"An Afterthought" (Rossetti) **WLC 5:**2936
"An Afterward" (Heaney) **WLCS 1:**393, 396
"An Afterword to `Lolita'" (Nabokov) **WLC 4:**2498
Agamemnon (Aeschylus) **WLCS 1:**3, 10, 13-17
"The Age Demanded" (Pound) **WLC 5:**2792
The Age of Anxiety: A Baroque Eclogue (Auden) **WLC 1:**135-38
The Age of Innocence (Wharton) **WLC 6:**3904, 3908-10, 3912
Age of Shakespeare (Swinburne) **WLC 6:**3556
"Age" (de la Mare) **WLC 2:**890
"Agrippina in the Golden House of Nero" (Lowell) **WLC 4:**2167
Ah, Wilderness! (O'Neill) **WLC 4:**2561, 2563
"El ahogado más hermoso del mundo" ("The Handsomest Drowned Man in the World: A Tale for Children") (Garcia Marquez) **WLC 3:**1368-69
"Aigeltinger" (Williams) **WLC 6:**4020
L'aigle à deux têtes (*The Eagle Has Two Heads*) (Cocteau) **WLC 2:**729, 735
Airways (Pasternak) **WLC 4:**2627
Airways, Inc. (Dos Passos) **WLC 2:**960-61, 963
"Aisling" (Heaney) **WLCS 1:**390
Ajax (Sophocles) **WLCS 1:**779-80, 783, 785-87
Aké (Soyinka) **WLC 5:**3328-30, 3332
"Al Aaraaf" (Poe) **WLC 4:**2762
"Al-Mamon" (Gogol) **WLC 3:**1431
Al que quiere! (Williams) **WLC 6:**4020
"Alastor; or, The Spirit of Solitude" (Shelley) **WLC 5:**3233, 3236, 3238
"The Albanian Virgin" (Munro) **WLCS 2:**686-87
"Albert" (Tolstoy) **WLC 6:**3666
"Album of Dreams" (Milosz) **WLCS 2:**613
Alcestis (Euripides) **WLCS 1:**291, 293, 296
The Alchemist (Jonson) **WLC 3:**1908-13, 1915-19
"Alchemy of the Word" (Rimbaud)
  See "Alchimie du verbe"
"Alchimie du verbe" ("Alchemy of the Word") (Rimbaud) **WLC 5:**2921
"An Alcoholic Case" (Fitzgerald) **WLC 2:**1235
"El aleph" ("The Aleph") (Borges) **WLC 1:**342
"The Aleph" (Borges)
  See "El aleph"
"Alerted" (Heaney) **WLCS 1:**398
"Alësha Gorshók" (Tolstoy) **WLC 6:**3665
Alexander's Bridge (Cather) **WLC 1:**654-55, 658

"Alguien desordena estas rosas" ("Someone Has Disturbed the Roses") (Garcia Marquez) **WLC 3:**1363, 1365
The Alhambra (Irving) **WLC 3:**1820, 1822-23, 1825, 1828
Alice's Adventures in Wonderland (Carroll) **WLC 1:**637, 642, 644-9
"The Alien Corn" (Maugham) **WLC 4:**2282
"Alive in the Ice and Fire" (Brooks) **WLC 1:**457
All for Love; or, The World Well Lost (Dryden) **WLC 2:**1049, 1057-58
All God's Children Need Traveling Shoes (Angelou) **WLCS 1:**65-67
All God's Chillun Got Wings (O'Neill) **WLC 4:**2560, 2563
"All in the Streets" (Baraka) **WLCS 1:**146
All My Pretty Ones (Sexton) **WLC 5:**3137, 3139-42, 3144, 3149
"All My Pretty Ones" (Sexton) **WLC 5:**3137, 3141, 3139-42, 3144, 3149
All My Sons (Miller) **WLC 4:**2369-72
All Over (Albee) **WLC 1:**27, 30, 32
All Rivers Run to the Sea (Wiesel) **WLCS 2:**855-57
"All suddenly the Wind comes soft" (Brooke) **WLC 1:**434
All That Fall (Beckett) **WLC 1:**233
All That Rises Must Converge (O'Connor)
  See *Everything That Rises Must Converge*
All the King's Men (Warren) **WLC 6:**3805-07, 3809-10, 3812, 3814
All the Sad Young Men (Fitzgerald) **WLC 2:**1225
"All Worlds Have Halfsight, Seeing Either With" (Cummings) **WLC 2:**843
All's Well That Ends Well (Shakespeare) **WLC 5:**3159, 3174
All'uscita (*At the Exit; At the Gate*) (Pirandello) **WLC 4:**2719
"Allégorie" (Baudelaire) **WLC 1:**207
The Allegory of Love: A Study in Medieval Tradition (Lewis) **WLC 4:**2086, 2090
"L'Allegro" (Milton) **WLC 4:**2406-07, 2409
"Alley Rats" (Sandburg) **WLC 5:**3053
Almanac of the Dead (Silko) **WLCS 2:**770-71
Almanach du Bonhomme Richard (Franklin)
  See *Poor Richard. An Almanack*
The Almanach-Monger (Pushkin) **WLC 5:**2827
Almayer's Folly (Conrad) **WLC 2:**781
"The Almond Tree" (de la Mare) **WLC 2:**887
"The Aloe" (Mansfield) **WLC 4:**2216-17
Alone (Strindberg) **WLC 6:**3518
Aloneness (Brooks) **WLC 1:**462
Along Fields and Sea Shores (Flaubert) **WLC 2:**1245
"Along the Road" (Huxley) **WLC 3:**1765
"An Alpimalyan Dialogue" (Turgenev) **WLC 6:**3707
"An Alpine Idyll" (Hemingway) **WLC 3:**1651
Alps and Sanctuaries of Piedmont and the Canton Ticino (Butler) **WLC 1:**557, 560
"Altarwise by Owl-light" (Thomas) **WLC**

6:3617
lternating Current (Paz)
See *Corriente alterna*
Altogether: The Collected Stories of W. Somerset Maugham (Maugham)
See *East and West: The Collected Short Stories of W. Somerset Maugham*
L'altro figlio (*The Other Son*) (Pirandello) **WLC 4:**2726
Alturas de Macchu Picchu (*The Heights of Macchu Picchu*; *Macchu Picchu*) (Neruda) **WLC 4:**2504, 2506, 2508, 2514, 2518
"Always the Mob" (Sandburg) **WLC 5:**3051
"El amante liberal" ("The Generous Lover"; "The Liberal Lover") (Cervantes) **WLC 2:**679
Les amants magnifiques (*The Magnificent Lovers*) (Moliere) **WLC 4:**2436, 2445
"Amargura para tres sonámbulos" ("Bitter Sorrow for Three Sleepwalkers"; "Bitterness for Three Sleepwalkers") (Garcia Marquez) **WLC 3:**1363-65
"Amateur poet" (Service) **WLC 5:**3131
"Amazement" (Milosz) **WLCS 2:**609
Ambarvalia (Brooke) **WLC 1:**434
The Ambassadors (James) **WLC 3:**1859-60, 1866
Amédée; or, How to Get Rid of It (Ionesco)
See *Amédée; ou, Comment s'en débarrasser*
Amédée; ou, Comment s'en débarrasser (*Amédée; or, How to Get Rid of It*) (Ionesco) **WLC 3:**1798, 1800-01, 1803, 1809
Amelia (Fielding) **WLC 2:**1206-08, 1214-15
The Amen Corner (Baldwin) **WLC 1:**162, 170
Amendments of Mr. Collier's False and Imperfect Citations (Congreve) **WLC 2:**759
America (Kafka)
See *Amerika*
America: A Prophecy, 1793 (Blake) **WLC 1:**300
"America" (McKay) **WLC 4:**2331
The American (James) **WLC 3:**1857
American Blues (Williams) **WLC 6:**3989
The American Claimant (Twain) **WLC 6:**3719-20
"The American County Fair" (Anderson) **WLC 1:**78
The American Dream (Albee) **WLC 1:**20-1, 25, 28, 30-1
"American Humor" (Harte) **WLC 3:**1587
American Outpost: A Book of Reminiscences (Sinclair) **WLC 5:**3264
The American Scene (James) **WLC 3:**1866
American Scholar (*An Oration Delivered before the Phi Beta Kappa Society at Cambridge, August 31, 1837*) (Emerson) **WLC 2:**1172, 1174, 1177, 1180-83
An American Tragedy (Dreiser) **WLC 2:**1033
"The American's Tale" (Doyle) **WLC 2:**1017
Amerika (*America*) (Kafka) **WLC 3:**1942-43
Among Strangers (Gorky) **WLC 3:**1485
Amor de Don Perlimplín con Belisa en su jardín (*Don Perlimplín*; *The Love of Don Perlimplín for Belisa in His Garden*) (Garcia Lorca) **WLC 2:**1341-42, 1350, 1352
"Amor mundi" (Rossetti) **WLC 5:**2931
Amoretti (Spenser) **WLC 5:**3350-51
"The Amorous Jilt" (Behn) **WLC 1:**259
The Amorous Prince; or, The Curious Husband (Behn) **WLC 1:**245-46, 255-56
"Amos Barton" (Eliot)
See "The Sad Fortunes of the Rev. Amos Barton"
l' Amour Médecin (*Love Is the Best Doctor*) (Moliere) **WLC 4:**2436, 2444-45
"Amour" (Maupassant) **WLC 4:**2298, 2301
Amphitryon (Moliere) **WLC 4:**2436, 2445
"Anactoria" (Swinburne) **WLC 6:**3561-63
Analects (Confucius)
See *Lun Yü*
Analytical Studies (Balzac)
See *Etudes analytiques*
Analytics (Aristotle) **WLCS 1:**99
An Anatomie of the World (Donne)
See *The First Anniversarie. An Anatomie of the World. Wherein By Occasion of the untimely death of Mistris Elizabeth Drury, the frailtie and decay of this whole World is represented*
The Anatomy Lesson (Roth) **WLC 5:**2975-76
"Ancestral Houses" (Yeats) **WLC 6:**4112
"Anchar" ("The Upas Tree") (Pushkin) **WLC 5:**2832
The Ancient Child (Momaday) **WLCS 2:**632-33
"An Ancient Gesture" (Millay) **WLCS 2:**602
"The Ancient Marine" (Rossetti) **WLC 5:**2938
The Ancient Mariner (Coleridge)
See *The Rime of the Ancient Mariner: A Poet's Reverie*
Ancient Poems (Confucius)
See *Shih Ching*
& (And) (Cummings) **WLC 2:**838
"And Death Shall Have No Dominion" ("Death Shall Have No Dominion") (Thomas) **WLC 6:**3617-19
"And must I sing? what subject shall I chuse?" (Jonson) **WLC 3:**1921
And Never Said a Word (Boell)
See *Und Sagte kein einziges Wort*
"And One for My Dame" (Sexton) **WLC 5:**3146
And So Ad Infinitum (Capek)
See *Ze zivota hmyzu*
And Still I Rise (Angelou) **WLCS 1:**62
"And the Moon Be Still as Bright" (Bradbury) **WLC 1:**370
And the World Remained Silent (Wiesel) **WLCS 2:**854
And Where Were You, Adam? (Boell)
See *Wo warst du, Adam?*
"Andrei Kolosov" (Turgenev) **WLC 6:**3697, 3702, 3707
Androcles and the Lion (Shaw) **WLC 5:**3191
Andromeda (Euripides) **WLCS 1:**292
"The Andventure of the Devil's Foot" (Doyle) **WLC 2:**1012-13
"L'ane" (Maupassant) **WLC 4:**2293
Ange Pitou (Dumas) **WLC 2:**1092
"Angel Levine" (Malamud) **WLC 4:**2187, 2189-90
Angel of Light (Oates) **WLC 4:**2537
"The Angel of the Bridge" (Cheever) **WLC 2:**693-94, 696-97, 700
"Angelina" (Dunbar) **WLC 2:**1112
Angelo (Pushkin) **WLC 5:**2836
"Angels of the Love Affair" (Sexton) **WLC 5:**3146
Angle of Geese (Momaday) **WLCS 2:**628
"Angle of Geese" (Momaday) **WLCS 2:**630, 635
De Anima (Aristotle) **WLCS 1:**97
Animal Farm (Orwell) **WLC 4:**2575; **WLC 4:**2575-78, 2581-83, 2585
The Animals in That Country (Atwood) **WLC 1:**108, 111, 118
Ann Veronica (Wells) **WLC 6:**3870
Ann Vickers (Lewis) **WLC 4:**2103, 2108
Anna Christie (*Chris Christopherson*) (O'Neill) **WLC 4:**2559
Anna Karenina (Tolstoy) **WLC 6:**3664-70, 3674-75
"Anna on the Neck" (Chekhov) **WLC 2:**710
"Annabel Lee" (Poe) **WLC 4:**2757
Annales de l'empire (Voltaire) **WLC 6:**3770
Annals of Lu (Confucius)
See *Ch'un Ch'iu*
Anne Frank: The Diary of a Young Girl (Frank)
See *Het achterhuis*
"Anne Rutledge" (Masters) **WLCS 2:**585
"Anner Lizer's Stumblin' Block" (Dunbar) **WLC 2:**1106
"Annette Delarbre" (Irving) **WLC 3:**1820, 1828
"The Anniad" (Brooks) **WLC 1:**451-52, 455
Annie Allen (Brooks) **WLC 1:**450, 452, 454-55, 461
The Anniversaries (*The First and Second Anniversaries*) (Donne) **WLC 2:**940, 944-45
"Annus Mirabilis: The Year of Wonders, 1666" (Dryden) **WLC 2:**1047-48, 1056-58
"An Anonymous Story" ("A Story without a Title") (Chekhov) **WLC 2:**708-09
"Another Time" (Auden) **WLC 1:**133
Ansichten eines Clowns (*The Clown*) (Boell) **WLC 1:**316, 319, 324-26
"An Answer to Some Questions on How I Write" (Giovanni) **WLCS 1:**365
"An Answer to the Rebus" (Wheatley) **WLC 6:**3930
"Answers in Progress" (Baraka) **WLCS 1:**145
"Antaeus" (Heaney) **WLCS 1:**391
Anthem (Rand) **WLC 5:**2878, 2883-84
"Anthem for Doomed Youth" (Owen) **WLC 4:**2606-07, 2611
Anthills of the Savannah (Achebe) **WLC 1:**12-13
Antic Hay (Huxley) **WLC 3:**1762, 1767-

68, 1770
Antigone (Cocteau) **WLC 2:**735
Antigone (Sophocles) **WLCS 1:**776, 779-84, 786
The Antiquary (Scott) **WLC 5:**3105-08, 3110-12, 3114
"The Antique Ring" (Hawthorne) **WLC 3:**1605-06, 1608
Antony (Dumas) **WLC 2:**1088-90
Antony and Cleopatra (Shakespeare) **WLC 5:**3157
"anyone lived in a pretty how town" (Cummings) **WLC 2:**841
Ape and Essence (Huxley) **WLC 3:**1767
"Apologia pro poemate meo" (Owen) **WLC 4:**2609, 2614, 2618
"Apologie de Raimond Sebond" ("An Apology of Raymond Sebond") (Montaigne) **WLC 4:**2456, 2458
"Apology for Bad Dreams" (Jeffers) **WLC 3:**1884
"An Apology for Printers" (Franklin) **WLCS 1:**319
An Apology for the Life of Mrs. Shamela Andrews (*Shamela*) (Fielding) **WLC 2:**1210
"An Apology of Raymond Sebond" (Montaigne)
See "Apologie de Raimond Sebond"
"The Apostate" (London) **WLC 4:**2146
"Apostrophe to the Land" (Cullen) **WLCS 1:**283
"The Apostrophe to Vincentine" (Stevens) **WLC 5:**3429
"Apparent Failure" (Browning) **WLCS 1:**215
"The Appeal" (Bronte) **WLC 1:**430
"Appendix to the Anniad Leaves from a Loose-Leaf War Diary" (Brooks) **WLC 1:**451
The Apple Cart (Shaw) **WLC 5:**3191, 3193
"The Apple Tree" (Galsworthy) **WLC 2:**1331
"The Apple Tree" (Mansfield) **WLC 4:**2217
"The Apple Woman's Complaint" (McKay) **WLC 4:**2329-30
"Appleton House" (Marvell)
See "Upon Appleton House"
"The Applicant" (Plath) **WLC 4:**2743-44
"The Apprentice" (Bambara) **WLCS 1:**132-35
"Après le déluge" ("After the Deluge") (Rimbaud) **WLC 5:**2911, 2918-19
Arabesques (Gogol) **WLC 3:**1436
"Araby" (Joyce) **WLC 3:**1930-31
Archer-Maidens (Aeschylus) **WLCS 1:**6
"Archibald Higbie" (Masters) **WLCS 2:**577
El arco y la lira: El poema. la revelación poetica, poesia,e historia (*The Bow and the Lyre: The Poem, the Poetic Revelation, and History*) (Paz) **WLC 4:**2665, 2670, 2672-73
Areopagitica (Milton) **WLC 4:**2404-06
L'argent (Zola) **WLC 6:**4126
Argo (Aeschylus) **WLCS 1:**7
"The Argonauts of the Air" (Wells) **WLC 6:**3872
Aria de Capo (Millay) **WLCS 2:**590, 592
"Ariadna" (Chekhov)
See "Ariadne"
"Ariadne" ("Ariadna") (Chekhov) **WLC 2:**710
Ariel (Plath) **WLC 4:**2746, 2748
"Ariel" (Plath) **WLC 4:**2740, 2746, 2748
Arkhipelag GULag, 1918-1956: Op' bit khudozhestvennopo issledovaniia (*The Gulag Archipelago, 1918-1956: An Experiment in Literary Investigation*) (Solzhenitsyn) **WLC 5:**3302, 3305-06, 3308, 3310-12
Armance; ou, Quelques scènes d'un salon de Paris en 1827 (Stendhal) **WLC 5:**3396
"Armor's Undermining Modesty" (Moore) **WLCS 2:**651
"Arms and the Boy" (Owen) **WLC 4:**2613
Arms and the Man (Shaw) **WLC 5:**3193
Arrow of God (Achebe) **WLC 1:**5-7, 9-11
Arrowsmith (Lewis) **WLC 4:**2101, 2103, 2112-13
Ars Poetica: In the American Grain (Williams)
See *In the American Grain*
"Ars Poetica?" (Milosz) **WLCS 2:**604, 614
The Art of the Moving Picture (Lindsay) **WLC 4:**2124
"Art of Virtue" (Franklin) **WLCS 1:**322, 326, 329-30
The Art of War (Machiavelli) **WLCS 2:**533
The Artamonov Business (Gorky)
See *Delo Artmunovykh*
"Artemis, the Honest Well-Digger" (Cheever) **WLC 2:**698
"Arthur Gordon Pym" (Poe)
See *The Narrative of Arthur Gordon Pym*
Arthur Miller's Collected Plays (Miller) **WLC 4:**2369, 2373
Artifices (Borges)
See *Artificios*
Artificios (*Artifices*) (Borges) **WLC 1:**341
Artist Descending a Staircase (Stoppard) **WLC 6:**3487
"The Artist" (Heaney) **WLCS 1:**399
"An Artist's Story" ("The House with a Mezzanine"; "The House with an Attic"; "The House with the Maisonette") (Chekhov) **WLC 2:**710
"As Eagles Soar" (Toomer) **WLCS 2:**804
"As Freedom Is a Breakfast-Food" (Cummings) **WLC 2:**841
As I Lay Dying (Faulkner) **WLC 2:**1189, 1196-97
"As virtuous men pass mildly away" (Donne)
See "A Valediction: forbidding mourning"
As Well as Before, Better than Before (Pirandello)
See *Come prima, meglio di prima*
As You Desire Me (Pirandello)
See *Come tu mi vuoi*
As You Like It (Shakespeare) **WLC 5:**3159-62, 3174
"Ash-Cake Hannah and Her Ben" (Dunbar) **WLC 2:**1106
Ash-Wednesday (Eliot) **WLC 2:**1147
Ashenden; or, The British Agent (Maugham) **WLC 4:**2275
"The Ashplant" (Heaney) **WLCS 1:**400
Así que pasen cinco años (*If Five Years Pass*; *When Five Years Pass*) (Garcia Lorca) **WLC 2:**1341-42, 1349, 1352-53
"Asleep" (Owen) **WLC 4:**2616
Asolando (Browning) **WLCS 1:**214
"An Aspect of Love, Alive in the Fire and Ice" (Brooks) **WLC 1:**457
"Asphodel, That Greeny Flower" (Williams) **WLC 6:**4015-17
"Asphodel" (Welty) **WLC 6:**3881, 3884
The Assassins (Camus)
See *Les justes*
The Assassins: A Book of Hours (Oates) **WLC 4:**2531, 2535
"Assay of the Infinite Man" (Neruda)
See *Tentativa del hombre infinito*
Assembly of Women (Aristophanes) **WLCS 1:**82
The Assistant (Malamud) **WLC 4:**2175-76, 2178-81, 2184-86, 2190
L'assommoir (Zola) **WLC 6:**4118-27
Assorted Prose (Updike) **WLC 6:**3756
"The Assyrian" (Saroyan) **WLC 5:**3082
"Astrophel: A Pastoral Elegy" (Spenser) **WLC 5:**3349
Asya (*Acia*) (Turgenev) **WLC 6:**3701, 3703, 3707
"At a Calvary near the Ancre" (Owen) **WLC 4:**2611, 2615, 2617
"At a Month's End" (Swinburne) **WLC 6:**3565
"At Candle-Lightin' Time" (Dunbar) **WLC 2:**1112
"At Christmas-Time" (Chekhov) **WLC 2:**708, 710
At Fault (Chopin) **WLCS 1:**240, 246-47
At Heaven's Gate (Warren) **WLC 6:**3814
"At Melville's Tomb" (Crane) **WLC 2:**800
At My Heart's Core (Davies) **WLC 2:**852
"At Shaft 11" (Dunbar) **WLC 2:**1101, 1106, 1111
"At the 'Cadian Ball" (Chopin) **WLCS 1:**240
"At the Bay" (Mansfield) **WLC 4:**2215, 2219, 2221-23
"At the Caberet-Vert" (Rimbaud)
See "Au caberet-vert"
At the Exit (Pirandello)
See *All'uscita*
At the Gate (Pirandello)
See *All'uscita*
"At the Grave of Henry James" (Auden) **WLC 1:**136, 139
"At the Landing" (Welty) **WLC 6:**3882
"At the Rainbow's End" (London) **WLC 4:**2141
Atalanta in Calydon (Swinburne) **WLC 6:**3552, 3556, 3558-59, 3561, 3565
"Athenaise" (Chopin) **WLCS 1:**241-42, 248
"Atlantic City Waiter" (Cullen) **WLCS 1:**274, 276
"Atlantis" (Crane) **WLC 2:**801, 808
Atlas Shrugged (Rand) **WLC 5:**2877-78, 2880-82, 2884
Au bonheur des dammes (Zola) 4126-27
"Au caberet-vert" ("At the Caberet-Vert") (Rimbaud) **WLC 5:**2922
"Au lecteur" ("Hypocrite lecteur"; "To the Reader") (Baudelaire) **WLC 1:**201
"L'aube spirituelle" (Baudelaire) **WLC 1:**207

e Audience (Garcia Lorca)
See *El público*
"udley Court" (Tennyson) **WLC 6:**3583
udubon, A Vision (Warren) **WLC 6:**3814-15
er aufhaltsame aifstieg des Arturo ui (*The Resistible Rise of Arturo Ui*) (Brecht) **WLC 1:**391
"uguries of Innocence" (Blake) **WLC 1:**308
gust 1914 (Solzhenitsyn)
See *Avgust chetyrnadtsatogo*
"unt Helen" (Eliot) **WLC 2:**1146
nt Jo's Scrap-Bag (Alcott) **WLC 1:**50
"unt Mandy's Investment" (Dunbar) **WLC 2:**1106
"unt Tempy's Revenge" (Dunbar) **WLC 2:**1106
"unt Tempy's Triumph" (Dunbar) **WLC 2:**1106
ra (Fuentes) **WLC 2:**1310, 1317, 1322
ureng-Zebe (Dryden) **WLC 2:**1048
urora Leigh (Browning) **WLC 1:**467, 469-74, 478
"he Auroras of Autumn" (Stevens) **WLC 5:**3434-35
sgefragt (*Cross-Examined*) (Grass) **WLC 3:**1506
"n Author's Confession" (Gogol) **WLC 3:**1430-31
e Authoress of the 'Odyssey' (Butler) **WLC 1:**551
Autobiography (Trollope) 6;3688
e Autobiography of Alice B. Toklas (Stein) **WLC 5:**3361, 3367
tobiography of Benjamin Franklin (Franklin) **WLCS 1:**312, 315-18, 321-22, 324, 326-28, 331
e Autobiography of Leroi Jones (Baraka) **WLCS 1:**147, 149
e Autobiography of Malcolm X (Malcolm X) **WLCS 2:**538, 540-47, 549-50
e Autobiography of W. E. B. Du Bois (Du Bois) **WLC 2:**1065
e Autobiography of William Carlos Williams (Williams) **WLC 6:**4022
"utochthon" (Masters) **WLCS 2:**578
"utumn I" (Mansfield) **WLC 4:**2217
"utumn II" (Mansfield)
See "The Wind Blows"
e Autumn of the Patriarch (Garcia Marquez) **WLC 3:**1367-68, 1371
"utumn" (Pope) **WLC 5:**2782-83
"utumn" (Pushkin) **WLC 5:**2832
vare (*The Miser*) (Moliere) **WLC 4:**2436-39, 2445, 2447, 2449-50
e Avaricious Knight (Pushkin)
See *The Covetous Knight*
"ve atque Vale" (Swinburne) **WLC 6:**3566
venir est dans les oeufs (*The Future Is in Eggs*) (Ionesco) **WLC 3:**1800, 1802
enture indienne (Voltaire) **WLC 6:**3776
"verroes's Search" (Borges)
See "La busca de Averroes"
gust chetyrnadtsatogo (*August 1914*; *Krasnoe koleso: Povestvovanie v otmerennykh srokakh. Uzel I, Avgust chetyrnadsatogo*; *The Red Wheel, Knot I: August 1914*) (Solzhenitsyn) **WLC 5:**3302
e Awakening (Chopin) **WLCS 1:**242, 246-50

"Away from It All" (Heaney) **WLCS 1:**389
The Awful Rowing Toward God (Sexton) **WLC 5:**3142-43, 3146-47
The Awkward Age (James) **WLC 3:**1861, 1868-69
The Axe (Undset) **WLC 6:**3738
Ayala's Angel (Trollope) **WLC 6:**3681
"B—, A Song" ("Boswell: A Song") (Boswell) **WLC 1:**354
Baal (Brecht) **WLC 1:**385, 387-89
Der Baal tshuve (Singer)
See *Der Bal-tshuve*
Bababec (Voltaire) **WLC 6:**3775
Babbitt (Lewis) **WLC 4:**2100-01, 2103-12
"Babette" (Service) **WLC 5:**3131
"Baby Sketches" (Crane) **WLC 2:**818
"The Babylon Lottery" (Borges)
See "La lotería en Babilonia"
"Babylon Revisited" (Baraka) **WLCS 1:**145
"Babylon Revisted" (Fitzgerald) **2:**1234-35
The Bacchants (Euripides) **WLCS 1:**291, 293-94, 298-300
Bacchus (Cocteau) **WLC 2:**728-30, 738
"Bacchus" (Emerson) **WLC 2:**1172
Back to Methuselah (Shaw) **WLC 5:**3191-93, 3195-96, 3200
"The Backlash Blues" (Hughes) **WLC 3:**1724
A Backward Glance (Wharton) **WLC 6:**3908
"The Backwater" (Turgenev) **WLC 6:**3697, 3707
"Bad Dreams" (Browning) **WLCS 1:**208
"A Bad Night: A Lexical Exercise" (Auden) **WLC 1:**138
Badman (Bunyan)
See *The Life and Death of Mr. Badman*
Bailey's Cafe (Naylor) **WLCS 2:**703-04
The Bak-Chesarian fountain: A Tale of the Tauride (Pushkin)
See *Bakhchisaraiski Fontan*
The Bakhchisarai Fontan (Pushkin)
See *Bakhchisaraiski Fontan*
Bakhchisaraiski Fontan (*The Bak-Chesarian fountain: A Tale of the Tauride*; *The Bakhchisarai Fontan*) (Pushkin) **WLC 5:**2835
"Bal des pendus" (Rimbaud) **WLC 5:**2922
Der Bal-tshuve (*Der Baal tshuve*; *The Penitent*) (Singer) **WLC 5:**3295-96
"Le balcon" ("The Balcony") (Baudelaire) **WLC 1:**200
"The Balcony" (Baudelaire)
See "Le balcon"
The Bald Soprano (Ionesco)
See *La cantatrice chauve*
"Balder Dead" (Arnold) **WLC 1:**93-5
"The Ballad of Chocolate Mabbie" (Brooks) **WLC 1:**460
"A Ballad of Life" (Swinburne) **WLC 6:**3559
"The Ballad of One-Eyed Mike" (Service) **WLC 5:**3125
"Ballad of Pearl May Lee" (Brooks) **WLC 1:**460
"The Ballad of Reading Gaol" (Wilde) **WLC 6:**3952, 3956, 3966
"The Ballad of the Black Fox Skin"

(Service) **WLC 5:**3124
The Ballad of the Brown Girl (Cullen) **WLCS 1:**282
"The Ballad of the Brown Girl" (Cullen) **WLCS 1:**285
"The Ballad of the Harp-Weaver" (Millay)
See "The Harp-Weaver"
"The Ballad of the Long-Legged Bait" (Thomas) **WLC 6:**3612
"The Ballad of the Northern Lights" (Service) **WLC 5:**3124
The Ballad of the Sad Café (Albee) **WLC 1:**26
The Ballad of the Sad Cafe: The Novels and Stories of Carson McCullers (McCullers) **WLC 4:**2308-10, 2316, 2320
Ballads and Other Poems (Longfellow) **WLCS 2:**503
Ballads of Bohemian (Service) **WLC 5:**3130
Ballads of Cheeckako (Service) **WLC 5:**3121-22
"Balloons" (Plath) **WLC 4:**2740
"Balthazar's Marvelous Afternoon" (Garcia Marquez)
See "La prodigiosa tarde de Baltazar"
Banana Bottom (McKay) **WLC 4:**2336
"A Banjo Song" (Dunbar) **WLC 2:**1110
"The Banker's Daughter" (Lowell) **WLC 4:**2162, 2166
Los baños de Argel (Cervantes) **WLC 2:**682-83
"Un baptême" (Maupassant) **WLC 4:**2289, 2293, 2303
The Baptism (Baraka) **WLCS 1:**139, 152
"The Baptism of Fire" (Longfellow) **WLCS 2:**505
"Baptizing" (Munro) **WLCS 2:**682
Bar-Room Ballads (Service) **WLC 5:**3126, 3130
"Barbare" (Rimbaud) **WLC 5:**2918
La barcarola (Neruda) **WLC 4:**2516
Barchester Towers (Trollope) **WLC 6:**3681-82, 3688
"The Bard" (Gray) **WLC 3:**1520-21, 1524-27, 1530-31, 1533
Bare Life (Pirandello) **WLC 4:**2723
Bare Masques (Pirandello) **WLC 4:**2723
"Barker's Luck" (Harte) **WLC 3:**1589
"Barn Burning" (Faulkner) **WLC 2:**1196
Barnaby Rudge (Dickens) **WLC 2:**911
"The Barrier" (McKay) **WLC 4:**2331
Barry Lyndon (Thackeray)
See *The Memoirs of Barry Lyndon, Esq.*
Barsetshire Chronicle (Trollope) **WLC 6:**3681-82
Bartholomew Fair (Jonson) **WLC 3:**1909-13, 1915
"Baseball and Writing / Suggested by post-game broadcasts" (Moore) **WLCS 2:**647, 650
The Basement (Pinter) **WLC 4:**2704, 2706
"Basement" (Bambara) **WLCS 1:**130-31
"Basilica" (Bierce) **WLC 1:**291-92
Bassarae (Aeschylus) **WLCS 1:**6
"A Bat on the Road" (Heaney) **WLCS 1:**397
"The Bat" (Pirandello)
See "Il pipistrello"
Le bâtard de Mauléon (*The Half-Brothers;*

or, *The Head and the Hand*) (Dumas) **WLC 2:**1083
Le bateau ivre (*The Drunken Boat*) (Rimbaud) **WLC 5:**2098, 2910, 2914, 2921
Battle of Angels (Williams) **WLC 6:**3992, 3998, 4002-03
"Der bau" ("The Burrow") (Kafka) **WLC 3:**1951
Baudelaire (Sartre) **WLC 5:**3088
Bayou Folk (Chopin) **WLCS 1:**240
Be Angry at the Sun and Other Poems (Jeffers) **WLC 3:**1883
"The Bean Eaters" (Brooks) **WLC 1:**452, 455, 461
"The Bean-Field" (Thoreau) **WLC 1:**3631
"A Bear Hunt" (Faulkner) **WLC 2:**1196
"The Bear" (Faulkner) **WLC 2:**1194
"The Bear" (Momaday) **WLCS 2:**629-30, 634
Beat the Devil (Capote) **WLC 1:**618
The Beauties of Sterne (Sterne) **WLC 5:**3419
The Beautiful and Damned (Fitzgerald) **WLC 2:**1221-24
The Beautiful People (Saroyan) **WLC 5:**3072, 3081
Beauty and the Beast (Cocteau) See *La belle et la bête*
"Beauty" (Huxley) **WLC 3:**1764
Bech: A Book (Updike) **WLC 6:**3753
Becket (Tennyson) **WLC 6:**3574-75, 3578
Beckonings (Brooks) **WLC 1:**458, 461-63
"Bed Time" (Hughes) **WLC 3:**1723
The Bee (Goldsmith) **WLC 3:**1469
"The Bee Meeting" (Plath) **WLC 4:**2739
"Before a Crucifix" (Swinburne) **WLC 6:**3563
Before Adam (London) **WLC 4:**2139
"Before an Old Painting of the Crucifixion" (Momaday) **WLCS 2:**629
"Before the Mirror" (Swinburne) **WLC 6:**3559
A Beggar in Jerusalem (Wiesel) **WLCS 2:**849
The Beggar Maid (Munro) **WLCS 2:**683-84
The Beginning and the End and Other Poems (Jeffers) **WLC 3:**1880
"The Beginning is Zero" (Giovanni) **WLCS 1:**354
Beginning with My Streets (Milosz) **WLCS 2:**615, 619
"Behemoth" (Huxley) **WLC 3:**1763
"Behind a Mask: Or, A Woman's Power" (Alcott) **WLC 1:**49
Beim Bau der Chinesischen Mauer (*The Great Wall of China, and Other Pieces*; *The Great Wall of China: Stories and Reflections*) (Kafka) **WLC 3:**1945
Being and Nothingness: An Essay on Phenomenological Ontology (Sartre) See *L'être et le néant: Essai d'ontologie phénoménologique*
Being Here: Poetry, 1977-80 (Warren) **WLC 6:**3814
Bekenntnisse des Hochstaplers Felix Krull (*Confessions of Felix Krull, Confidence Man*) (Mann) **WLC 4:**2208
Bel-Ami (Maupassant) **WLC 4:**2291
Belfagor (Machiavelli)

See *A Fable: Belfagor, the Devil Who Took a Wife*
"Belief and Creativity" (Golding) **WLC 3:**1458
The Bell Jar (Plath) **WLC 4:**2735-36, 2746
"The Bell" (Andersen) **WLC 1:**59-60
"The Bella Lingua" (Cheever) **WLC 2:**691
"La belle dame sans merci" (Keats) **WLC 3:**1956
La belle et la bête (*Beauty and the Beast*) (Cocteau) **WLC 2:**723-25, 736
"La Belle Epoque" (Milosz) **WLCS 2:**617
"La Belle Zoraide" (Chopin) **WLCS 1:**239
Bellefleur (Oates) **WLC 4:**2536-37
Bells in Winter (Milosz) **WLCS 2:**607-08, 610, 614
"Bells in Winter" (Milosz) **WLCS 2:**610-11
"The Bells" (Poe) **WLC 4:**2757
Beloved (Morrison) **WLC 4:**2479-82
The Beloved Returns (Mann) See *Lotte in Weimar*
The Belton Estate (Trollope) **WLC 6:**3681
Beneath the Wheel (Hesse) See *Unterm Rad*
"Bénédiction" (Baudelaire) **WLC 1:**201, 205
"Benito Cereno" (Melville) **WLC 4:**2345
"The Benitous' Slave" (Chopin) **WLCS 1:**248
"Benjamin Pantier" (Masters) **WLCS 2:**584
Beowulf **WLCS 1:**156-74
Beppo: A Venetian Story (Byron) **WLC 1:**569, 572, 578
"Berenice" (Poe) **WLC 4:**2760
"Bermudas" (Marvell) **WLC 4:**2258-59
Bernarda Alba's Family (Garcia Lorca) See *La casa de Bernarda Alba*
"Bernice Bobs Her Hair" (Fitzgerald) **WLC 2:**1221, 1223
Il berretto a sonagli (*Cap and Bells*) (Pirandello) **WLC 4:**2719, 2721-22, 2726
The Bertrams (Trollope) **WLC 6:**3681, 3691
The Best Supernatural Tales of Arthur Conan Doyle (Doyle) **WLC 2:**1017
"The Bet" (Chekhov) **WLC 2:**708
"La bête à Maître Belhomme" (Maupassant) **WLC 4:**2293, 2301
Le bête humaine (Zola) **WLC 6:**4122, 4124, 4126-28
"Bethlehem" (Capek) See "Betlém"
"Betlém" ("Bethlehem") (Capek) **WLC 1:**605
Betrachtung (*Contemplation*; *Meditations*) (Kafka) **WLC 3:**1945-46
Betrachtungen eines Unpolitischen (*Meditations of a Non-Political Man*; *Reflections of a Non-Political Man*) (Mann) **WLC 2:**2207
Betrayal (Pinter) **WLC 4:**2704, 2706-07
"The Betrayer of Israel" (Singer) **WLC 5:**3290
Die Betrogene ("The Black Swan"; "The Deceived") (Mann) **WLC 4:**2204
"The Betrothal" (Millay) **WLCS 2:**590
"Betrothed" (Chekhov) **WLC 2:**710
A Better Class of Person (Osborne) **WLC**

4:2598-2600
"A Better Resurrection" (Rossetti) **WLC 5:**2938
Between the Acts (Woolf) **WLC 6:**4050-53, 4057-58
"Between the Porch and the Altar" (Lowell) **WLC 4:**2152
"Beverly Hills, Chicago" (Brooks) **WLC 1:**455
"Bewitched" (Wharton) **WLC 6:**3905
Beyond (Galsworthy) **WLC 2:**1335
Beyond Desire (Anderson) **WLC 1:**79
Beyond the Horizon (O'Neill) **WLC 4:**2558, 2569
"Beyond the Mexique Bay" (Huxley) **WLC 3:**1765
"Beyond the Wall" (Bierce) **WLC 1:**293
"Bezhin Meadow" (Turgenev) See "Byezhin Prairie"
Bible **WLCS 1:**175-96
"La biblioteca de Babel" ("The Library of Babel") (Borges) **WLC 1:**334, 339-40
Bid Me to Live (A Madrigal) (*A Madrigal*) (H. D.) **WLC 3:**1617-20, 1623
"Big Bessie Throws Her Son into the Street" (Brooks) **WLC 1:**456
"Big Black Good Man" (Wright) **WLC 6:**4088
"Big Boy Leaves Home" (Wright) **WLC 6:**4090
"Big Boy" (Wright) **WLC 6:**4090
"Big Mama's Funeral" (Garcia Marquez) See "Los funerales de la Mamá Grande"
The Big Sea: An Autobiography (Hughes) **WLC 3:**1736
Big Sur (Kerouac) **WLC 3:**1978, 1986-87
"Big Two-Hearted River" (Hemingway) **WLC 3:**1655
Billard um halbzehn (*Billiards at Half-past Nine*) (Boell) **WLC 1:**318-22, 324-25
Billiards at Half-past Nine (Boell) See *Billard um halbzehn*
Biographia Literaria; or, Biographical Sketches of My Literary Life and Opinions (Coleridge) **WLC 2:**745, 747, 750-51
"Birches" (Frost) **WLC 2:**1299
"Bird and Beast" (Rossetti) **WLC 5:**2936
The Bird's Nest (Jackson) **WLC 3:**1838-39, 1841-43, 1850
The Birds (Aristophanes) **WLCS 1:**77-79
"Birds of Prey" (McKay) **WLC 4:**2331
"The Birth in a Narrow Room" (Brooks) **WLC 1:**454
"Birth of Love" (Warren) **WLC 6:**3814
Birthday (Fuentes) **WLC 2:**1322
The Birthday Party (Pinter) **WLC 4:**2699-2701, 2704-05, 2707
"A Birthday Present" (Plath) **WLC 4:**2747
"A Birthday" (Mansfield) **WLC 4:**2216
"A Birthday" (Rossetti) **WLC 5:**2929
"The Birthmark" (Hawthorne) **WLC 3:**1600, 1606
"The Birthplace" (Heaney) **WLCS 1:**397
"The Bishop of Borglum" (Andersen) **WLC 1:**63
"The Bishop" (Chekhov) **WLC 2:**710
Bitter Oleander (Garcia Lorca) See *Bodas de sangre*
"Bitter Sorrow for Three Sleepwalkers" (Garcia Marquez) See "Amargura para tres sonámbulos"

Bitterness for Three Sleepwalkers" (Garcia Marquez)
See "Amargura para tres sonámbulos"
Blacamán el bueno vendedor de milagros" (Garcia Marquez)
See "Blacamán the Good, Vendor of Miracles"
Blacamán the Good, Vendor of Miracles" ("Blacamán el bueno vendedor de milagros") (Garcia Marquez) **WLC 3:**1367
Black Art (Baraka) **WLCS 1:**151
Black Art" (Baraka) **WLCS 1:**145
The Black Art" (Sexton) **WLC 5:**3142, 3144, 3149
Black Beetles in Amber (Bierce) **WLC 1:**291-92
Black Boy: A Record of Childhood and Youth (Wright) **WLC 6:**4087-89
Black Brown Yellow White" (Baraka) **WLCS 1:**147
The Black Cat" (Poe) **WLC 4:**2755, 2760-61
The Black Christ and Other Poems (Cullen) **WLCS 1:**282
The Black Christ" (Cullen) **WLCS 1:**280, 285
Black Dada Nihilismus" (Baraka) **WLCS 1:**145, 152
Black Feeling, Black Talk (Giovanni) **WLCS 1:**352, 355, 358-59, 361, 364-65
Black Fire (Baraka) **WLCS 1:**149
The Black Friar" (Chekhov)
See "The Black Monk"
The Black Glove (Strindberg) **WLC 6:**3519
Black Goblet" (Pasternak) **WLC 4:**2635
The Black Interpreters (Gordimer) **WLCS 1:**371
Black Is My Favorite Color" (Malamud) **WLC 4:**2189
Black Island Memorial (Neruda)
See Memorial de Isla Negra
Black Judgement (Giovanni) **WLCS 1:**352, 355, 359, 361
Black Magdalens" (Cullen) **WLCS 1:**277
Black Magic Poetry (Baraka) **WLCS 1:**145
Black Mass (Baraka) **WLCS 1:**145, 152
Black Mischief (Waugh) **WLC 6:**3821-22, 3824-26
The Black Monk" ("The Black Friar") (Chekhov) **WLC 2:**709, 711
Black Music (Baraka) **WLCS 1:**150
Black People" (Baraka) **WLCS 1:**145
Black Poems, Poseurs and Power" (Giovanni) **WLCS 1:**354
Black Reconstruction: An Essay toward a History of the Part Which Black Folk Played in the Attempt to Reconstruct Democracy in America, 1860-1880 (Du Bois) **WLC 2:**1066
Black Riders (Crane) **WLC 2:**815-17
The Black Sheep" (Boell)
See "Die schwarzen schafe"
Black Spring (Miller) **WLC 4:**2377, 2380, 2391-92
The Black Swan" (Mann)
See Die Betrogene
Black Tambourine" (Crane) **WLC 2:**799
Blackness (Jonson)
See Masque of Blacknesse

Blanco (Paz) **WLC 4:**2663, 2666, 2669-70, 2674-75
Blasts and Benedictions (O'Casey) **WLCS 2:**709
Bleak House (Dickens) **WLC 2:**903, 909, 911
Die Blechtrommel (The Tin Drum) (Grass) **WLC 3:**1501-13
"The Blessed Damozel" (Rossetti) **WLC 5:**2947-49, 2951, 2955-56
"A Blessed Deceit" (Dunbar) **WLC 2:**1107
"Blind Bartimeus" (Longfellow) **WLCS 2:**504
"Bliss" (Mansfield) **WLC 4:**2212, 2215, 2224
The Blithedale Romance (Hawthorne) **WLC 3:**1596
Bliznets v tuchakh (The Twin In the Clouds) (Pasternak) **WLC 4:**2627
"The Blizzard" (Pushkin) **WLC 5:**2836
The Blood of a Poet (Cocteau)
See Le sang d'un poète
The Blood of the Bambergs (Osborne) **WLC 4:**2597
"Blood of the Walsungs" (Mann)
See Wälsungenblut
Blood Wedding (Garcia Lorca)
See Bodas de sangre
"Blood" (Singer) **WLC 5:**3288
A Bloodsmoor Romance (Oates) **WLC 4:**2536
A Blot in the 'Scutcheon (Browning) **WLCS 1:**206
"The Blue Flag in a Bog" (Millay) **WLCS 2:**591, 595, 603
"The Blue Hotel" (Crane) **WLC 2:**818, 820, 826-27
"Blue Meridian" (Toomer) **WLCS 2:**796-97, 799, 804
"A Blue Woman with Sticking out Breasts Hanging" (Cummings) **WLC 2:**844
"Blueberries" (Frost) **WLC 2:**1299
"Blues for Men" (Hughes) **WLC 3:**1724
Blues for Mister Charlie (Baldwin) **WLC 1:**62
"The Blues I'm Playing" (Hughes) **WLC 3:**1733-34, 1736
Blues People (Baraka) **WLCS 1:**150
The Bluest Eye (Morrison) **WLC 4:**2471-73, 2477
"The Boarding House" (Joyce) **WLC 3:**1930
Bodalsia telenok s dubom (The Oak and the Calf) (Solzhenitsyn) **WLC 5:**3310-11
Bodas de sangre (Bitter Oleander, Blood Wedding; A Fatal Wedding) (Garcia Lorca) **WLC 2:**1342-43, 1350
Boece (Chaucer) **WLCS 1:**227
"The Bog King's Daughter" (Andersen)
See "The Marsh King's Daughter"
"Boles" ("Her Lover") (Gorky) **WLC 3:**1485
"Bona and Paul" (Toomer) **WLCS 2:**793, 795
A Bond Honoured (Osborne) **WLC 4:**2595, 2598
Bone-Collectors (Aeschylus) **WLCS 1:**8
"Bonnie Dundee" (Scott) **WLC 5:**3115
A Book about Myself (Dreiser) **WLC 2:**1035, 1037

A Book for Boys and Girls; or, Country Rhimes for Children (Bunyan) **WLC 1:**488
Book IV (Williams) **WLC 6:**4015
"Book-Lover" (Service) **WLC 5:**3130
Book of Changes (Confucius)
See Yi-king
Book of Dreams (Kerouac) **WLC 3:**1978, 1983-85
The Book of Folly (Sexton) **WLC 5:**3146
Book of Gypsy Ballads (Garcia Lorca)
See Primer romancero gitano
Book of Historical Documents (Confucius)
See Shu Ching
Book of History (Confucius)
See Shu Ching
Book of Odes (Confucius)
See Shih Ching
Book of Poetry (Confucius)
See Shih Ching
Book of Rites (Confucius)
See Li Chi
Book of Rituals (Confucius)
See Li Chi
The Book of Snobs (The Snobs of England) (Thackeray) **WLC 6:**3594, 3603, 3606
Book of Songs (Garcia Lorca)
See Canciones
"The Book of the Grotesque" (Anderson) **WLC 1:**78, 81, 84
The Book of the Lion (Chaucer) **WLCS 1:**229
Book of Vagaries (Neruda)
See Extravagario
A Book of Verses (Masters) **WLCS 2:**576
Book V (Williams) **WLC 6:**4015
"The Booker Washington Trilogy" (Lindsay) **WLC 4:**2120
"The Books in My Life" (Miller) **WLC 4:**2382
The Books of Pantagruel (Rabelais) **WLC 2:**868-69, 2872
Books of Rites and Ancient Ceremonies and of Institutions (Confucius)
See Li Chi
"Boomtown" (Wolfe) **WLC 6:**4040
The Bores (Moliere)
See Les fâcheux
Boris Godunov (Pushkin) **WLC 5:**2825-27, 2830, 2836
"The Boscombe Valley Mystery" (Doyle) **WLC 2:**1013
"The Boston Hymn" (Emerson) **WLC 2:**1171
Boston: A Documentary Novel of the Sacco-Vanzetti Case (Sinclair) **WLC 5:**3263, 3269
The Bostonians (James) **WLC 3:**1857, 1859, 1860-61
"Boswell: A Song" (Boswell)
See "B—, A Song"
Bothwell (Swinburne) **WLC 6:**3553
"Boule de suif" (Maupassant) **WLC 4:**2291, 2293, 2301-02
Bound East for Cardiff (O'Neill) **WLC 4:**2558
"Bound No'th Blues" (Hughes) **WLC 3:**1721
Le bourgeois gentilhomme (The Bourgeois Gentleman) (Moliere) **WLC 4:**2436-37, 2445

The Bourgeois Gentleman (Moliere)
See *Le bourgeois gentilhomme*
Bouvard et Pécuchet (Flaubert) **WLC 2:**1246
"The Bowl" (de la Mare) **WLC 2:**887
"The Bowl" (Fitzgerald) **WLC 2:**1231
"Bowls" (Moore) **WLCS 2:**651
Box (Albee) **WLC 1:**31
"The Boy and the Bayonet" (Dunbar) **WLC 2:**1107
"The Boy Died in My Alley" (Brooks) **WLC 1:**463
"Boy in Rome" (Cheever) **WLC 2:**696
A Boy's Will (Frost) **WLC 2:**1291, 1296-97, 1302
The Boys in the Band (Williams) **WLC 6:**4003
"Boys. Black." (Brooks) **WLC 1:**458
Bracebridge Hall (Irving) **WLC 3:**1822-23, 1828
Den braendende busk (Undset) **WLC 6:**3738, 3741-42
"Brahma" (Emerson) **WLC 2:**1171
Brand (Ibsen) **WLC 3:**1777, 1780, 1782, 1785-86, 1792
The Brass Butterfly (Golding) **WLC 3:**1446-47
"Brass Spittoons" (Hughes) **WLC 3:**1726
Bratya Razboiniki (*The Brigand Brothers*; *The Brothers Highwaymen*) (Pushkin) **WLC 5:**2835
Brave New World (Huxley) **WLC 3:**1758, 1760, 1762, 1767-71
Brave New World Revisited (Huxley) **WLC 3:**1758, 1767, 1769
"Bread and Freedom" (Camus) **WLC 1:**596
"Bread and Wine" (Cullen) **WLCS 1:**277
The Bread of Those Early Years (Boell)
See *Das Brot der frühen Jahre*
"Break, Break, Break" (Tennyson) **WLC 6:**3584
Breakfast at Tiffany's (Capote) **WLC 1:**618-19, 623, 628-30
Breakfast of Champions; or, Goodbye, Blue Monday! (Vonnegut) **WLC 6:**3792-93
"The Bride Comes to Yellow Sky" (Crane) **WLC 2:**818, 820, 824, 826
"The Bride of Abydos: A Turkish Tale" (Byron) **WLC 1:**569-70, 572
The Bride of Lammermoor (Scott) **WLC 5:**3108, 3112, 3114
"The Bride's Chamber" (Rossetti) **WLC 5:**2954
"The Bride's Prelude" (Rossetti) **WLC 5:**2953-55, 2958-59
Brideshead Revisited: The Sacred and Profane Memories of Captain Charles Ryder (Waugh) **WLC 6:**3823-24, 3826, 3828-31
The Bridge (Crane) **WLC 2:**797-99, 801, 805-06, 809
The Bridge of San Luis Rey (Wilder) **WLC 6:**3982-83, 3985
"The Bridge" (Baraka) **WLCS 1:**150
Brief an einen jungen Katholiken (Boell) **WLC 1:**325
"The Brief Cure of Aunt Fanny" (Dunbar) **WLC 2:**1107
Briefing for a Descent into Hell (Lessing) **WLCS 2:**493-96

The Brigadier and the Golf Widow (Cheever) **WLC 2:**692, 696, 700
"The Brigadier" (Turgenev)
See "Brigadir"
"Brigadir" ("The Brigadier") (Turgenev) **WLC 6:**3697, 3699
The Brigand Brothers (Pushkin)
See *Bratya Razboiniki*
"Bright and Morning Star" (Wright) **WLC 6:**4089
Brighton Rock (Greene) **WLC 2:**1537, 1539-40, 1542-43, 1545-47, 1549-52
"The Brigs of Ayr" (Burns) **WLC 1:**517
"Broken Field Running" (Bambara) **WLCS 1:**133-34, 136
"The Broken Heart" (Irving) **WLC 3:**1818, 1822
"The Broken Tower" (Crane) **WLC 2:**801, 805
"The Bronco That Would Not Be Broken" (Lindsay) **WLC 4:**2121
The Bronze Horseman (Pushkin)
See *Medny Vsadnik*
"A Bronzeville Mother Loiters in Mississippi. Meanwhile a Mississippi Mother Burns Bacon" (Brooks) **WLC 1:**451-53, 456
"Bronzeville Woman in a Red Hat" (Brooks) **WLC 1:**452
Das Brot der frühen Jahre (*The Bread of Those Early Years*) (Boell) **WLC 1:**317, 326
Brother to Dragons (Warren) **WLC 6:**3814
The Brothers Highwaymen (Pushkin)
See *Bratya Razboiniki*
The Brothers Karamazov (Dostoevsky) **WLC 2:**972-73, 975-76
"Brown Boy to Brown Girl" (Cullen) **WLCS 1:**274
"A Brown Girl Dead" (Cullen) **WLCS 1:**274, 283
"Brown of Calaveras" (Harte) **WLC 3:**1589
"Brown River, Smile" (Toomer) **WLCS 2:**796
"Brute Neighbours" (Thoreau) **WLC 6:**3631
"Bryan, Bryan, Bryan, Bryan" (Lindsay) **WLC 4:**2123-14
The Buccaneers (Wharton) **WLC 6:**3908-09, 3911-12
The Buck in the Snow (Millay) **WLCS 2:**591
"Buckthorne and His Friends" (Irving) **WLC 3:**1819, 1828
"The Buckwheat" (Andersen) **WLC 1:**63
"Bucolics" (Auden) **WLC 1:**137
Buddenbrooks (Mann) **WLC 4:**2192-2197, 2202, 2204, 2206, 2208
Las buenas consciencias (*The Good Conscience*) (Fuentes) **WLC 2:**1320
"Le buffet" (Rimbaud) **WLC 5:**2922
"The Building of the Ship" (Longfellow) **WLCS 2:**510
"Bull of Bandylaw" ("The Bull of Bendylaw") (Plath) **WLC 4:**2747
"The Bull of Bendylaw" (Plath)
See "Bull of Bandylaw"
Bullet Park (Cheever) **WLC 2:**699, 701-02
"The Bullfinches" (Hardy) **WLC 3:**1571

The Bulwark (Dreiser) **WLC 2:**1033, 1036-38
"Bums at Sunset" (Wolfe) **WLC 6:**4040
"Bunner Sisters" (Wharton) **WLC 6:**3904
"Burbank with a Baedeker: Bleistein with a Cigar" (Eliot) **WLC 2:**1147
"The Burden of Nineveh" (Rossetti) **WLC 5:**2951, 2956
Burger's Daughter (Gordimer) **WLCS 1:**375, 377
"The Buried Life" (Arnold) **WLC 1:**100, 102
Burmese Days (Orwell) **WLC 4:**2576-77, 2579, 2581
Burning Daylight (London) **WLC 4:**2139
"Burning the Christmas Greens" (Williams) **WLC 6:**4014
The Burning Wheel (Huxley) **WLC 3:**1761-62, 1764
"The Burning Wheel" (Huxley) **WLC 3:**1762
"The Burning" (Welty) **WLC 6:**3888
"Burnt Norton" (Eliot) **WLC 2:**1148
A Burnt-Out Case (Greene) **WLC 3:**1550, 1553-54
"The Burrow" (Kafka)
See "Der bau"
"The Bus to St. James's" (Cheever) **WLC 2:**696, 698
"La busca de Averroes" ("Averroes's Search") (Borges) **WLC 1:**333, 336
"but observe; although" (Cummings) **WLC 2:**840
"Buteo Regalis" (Momaday) **WLCS 2:**634
The Butterfly's Evil Spell (Garcia Lorca)
See *El maleficio de la mariposa*
By Avon River (H. D.) **WLC 3:**1616, 1618, 1624
"By Himself" (Pirandello)
See "Da sé"
"By Moonlight" (Mansfield) **WLC 4:**2219
"By Oneself" (Pirandello)
See "Da sé"
"By the North Sea" (Swinburne) **WLC 6:**3566-67
"By the Seaside" (Longfellow) **WLCS 2:**510
"Byezhin Prairie" ("Bezhin Meadow") (Turgenev) **WLC 6:**3702
Bygmester Solness (*The Master Builder*) (Ibsen) **WLC 3:**1779, 1781-82, 1784-86, 1790, 1792
Byvshii lyudi ("Ex-People") (Gorky) **WLC 3:**1485
The Cabala (Wilder) **WLC 6:**3981-83, 3985
"The Cabalist of East Broadway" (Singer) **WLC 5:**3291
Cabbages and Kings (Henry) **WLC 3:**1669, 1671
La cabeza de la hidra (*The Hydra Head*) (Fuentes) **WLC 2:**1311-12, 1314
Cabiri (Aeschylus) **WLCS 1:**7
"Caboose Thoughts" (Sandburg) **WLC 5:**3052
Cachiporra's Puppets (Garcia Lorca)
See *Los títeres de Cachiporra*
Cady's Life (Frank) **WLC 2:**1283
Les cahiers d'André Walter (Gide) **WLC 3:**1375, 1388
"Cahoots" (Dunbar) **WLC 2:**1107
Cain (Byron) **WLC 1:**568-70, 575

akes and Ale; or, The Skeleton in the Cupboard (Maugham) **WLC 4:**2270-71, 2275, 2281, 2284-85
aligula (Camus) **WLC 1:**589-91, 593
aligula (Dumas) **WLC 2:**1080-81
he Call of Blood (Cervantes)
See "La fuerza de la sangre"
he Call of the Wild (London) **WLC 4:**2136-37, 2139, 2145-46
"The Call of the Wild" (Service) **WLC 5:**3123
"La Calle Destruida" (Neruda) **WLC 4:**2509
"he Calling of Names" (Angelou) **WLCS 1:**63
ambio de piel (*A Change of Skin*) (Fuentes) **WLC 2:**1311-16
amino Real (*Ten Blocks on the Camino Real*) (Williams) **WLC 6:**3989, 3991-92, 3995-96
an Such Things Be? (Bierce) **WLC 1:**293
an You Forgive Her? (Trollope) **WLC 6:**3681
"A Canary for One" (Hemingway) **WLC 3:**1651
he Cancer Ward (Solzhenitsyn)
See *Rakovyi korpus*
"Canción tonta" ("Silly Song") (Garcia Lorca) **WLC 2:**1345
anciones (*Book of Songs*; *Songs*) (Garcia Lorca) **WLC 2:**1345, 1347-48, 1350
"Candelora" ("Candlemas") (Pirandello) **WLC 4:**2716
andide; or, Optimism (Voltaire)
See *Candide; ou, L'optimisme*
andide; ou, L'optimisme (*Candide; or, Optimism*) (Voltaire) **WLC 6:**3769, 3772-76, 3778, 3780, 3782
andle in the Wind (Solzhenitsyn)
See *Svecha na vetru*
"he Candle Indoors" (Hopkins) **WLC 3:**1715
andlemas" (Pirandello)
See "Candelora"
andour in English Fiction" (Hardy) **WLC 3:**1568
ane (Toomer) **WLCS 2:**791-93, 795-96, 799-802, 804
annery Row (Steinbeck) **WLC 5:**3387-88
"he Canonization" ("For Godsake hold your tongue, and let me love") (Donne) **WLC 2:**945
anopus in Argos: Archives (Lessing) **WLCS 2:**494, 496, 498
anta l'epistola" ("Chants the Epistle"; "He Sings the Epistle"; "He-Who-Intones-the-Epistle"; "Sing the Epistle") (Pirandello) **WLC 4:**2717
a cantatrice chauve (*The Bald Soprano*) (Ionesco) **WLC 3:**1798-1800, 1802-03, 1807-09, 1811
anterbury Settlement (Butler) **WLC 1:**555
e Canterbury Tales (Chaucer) **WLCS 1:**219, 223-30, 233-34
he Canterville Ghost: A Hylo-Idealistic Romance" (Wilde) **WLC 6:**3952
anto general de Chile (*General Song*) (Neruda) **WLC 4:**2511, 2514-16, 2518

"Canto I" (Pound) **WLC 5:**2793, 2801
"Canto II" (Pound) **WLC 5:**2794
"Canto III" (Pound) **WLC 5:**2794
"Canto IV" (Pound) **WLC 5:**2794
"Canto LII" (Pound) **WLC 5:**2795, 2802
"Canto LIX" (Pound) **WLC 5:**2793
"Canto LXXXI" (Pound) **WLC 5:**2791
"Canto V" (Pound) **WLC 5:**2794
"Canto VI" (Pound) **WLC 5:**2794
"Canto XC" (Pound) **WLC 5:**2796
"Canto XCVI" (Pound) **WLC 5:**2796
"Canto XIII" (Pound) **WLC 5:**2795
"Canto XL" (Pound) **WLC 5:**2793
"Canto XVI" (Pound) **WLC 5:**2795
"Canto XVII" (Pound) **WLC 5:**2795
"Canto XX" (Pound) **WLC 5:**2795-96
"Canto XXVII" (Pound) **WLC 5:**2793
"Canto XXXIX" (Pound) **WLC 5:**2795
"Canto XXXVI" (Pound) **WLC 5:**2795, 2801
"Canto" (Pound) **WLC 5:**2794
Cantos (Pound) **WLC 5:**2792, 2793, 2795, 2801-03
Cap and Bells (Pirandello)
See *Il berretto a sonagli*
Cape Cod (Thoreau) **WLC 6:**3635
"Cape Hatteras" (Crane) **WLC 2:**801
"The Capital of the World" (Hemingway) **WLC 3:**1651
Capitalism: The Unknown Ideal (Rand) **WLC 5:**2887
"Capri" (Milosz) **WLCS 2:**620
"Caprice" (Cullen) **WLCS 1:**276
"Captain Grose" (Burns)
See "On the Late Captain Grose's Peregrinations Thro' Scotland"
"The Captain of the Polestar" (Doyle) **WLC 2:**1017
Captain Singleton (Defoe)
See *The Life, Adventures, and Pyracies of the Famous Captain Singleton*
The Captain's Daughter; or, The Generosity of the Russian Usurper Pugatscheff (Pushkin) **WLC 5:**2829-30, 2836
The Captain's Verses (Neruda)
See *Versos del capitán*
Captains Courageous (Kipling) **WLC 3:**2012, 2021-22
The Captive in the Caucasus (Tolstoy) **WLC 6:**3667
The Captive Mind (Milosz) **WLCS 2:**607, 618-19
The Captive of the Caucasus (Pushkin)
See *Kavkazsky plennik*
The Captivity (Goldsmith) **WLC 3:**1476
"The Card-Dealer" (Rossetti) **WLC 5:**2950, 2952
"A Career" (Dunbar) **WLC 2:**1110
The Caretaker (Pinter) **WLC 4:**2700-02, 2704-05, 2711
"Carnegie Oklahoma, 1919" (Momaday) **WLCS 2:**635
Carnets (*Notebooks*) (Camus) **WLC 1:**594-99
Caroling Dusk (Cullen) **WLCS 1:**274, 278, 283
Carols of an Old Codger (Service) **WLC 5:**3130, 3132
"Carried Away" (Munro) **WLCS 2:**687-88
"Carrion Comfort" (Hopkins) **WLC 3:**1712
"A Carrion" (Baudelaire)
See "Une charogne"

"La cas de Madame Luneau" (Maupassant) **WLC 4:**2293
Un cas intéressant (Camus) **WLC 1:**590
La casa de Bernarda Alba (*Bernarda Alba's Family*; *The House of Bernarda Alba*) (Garcia Lorca) **WLC 2:**1350, 1352
La casa de los celos (Cervantes) **WLC 2:**683
La casa de los espíritus (Allende)
See *The House of the Spirits*
Casa Guidi Windows: A Poem (Browning) **WLC 1:**469, 472
The Case-Book of Sherlock Holmes (Doyle) **WLC 2:**1018
"The Case of 'Ca'line': A Kitchen Monologue" (Dunbar) **WLC 2:**1106
"The Cask of Amontillado" (Poe) **WLC 4:**2761
The Castle (Kafka)
See *Das Schloss*
Castle Richmond (Trollope) **WLC 6:**3681
"Casualty" (Heaney) **WLCS 1:**392-93
Cat and Mouse (Grass)
See *Katz und Maus*
Cat on a Hot Tin Roof (Williams) **WLC 6:**3989, 3992-93, 3995-96, 3998, 4002-03
Cat's Cradle (Vonnegut) **WLC 6:**3786, 3789, 3792-93
Catch-22 (Heller) **WLC 3:**1631-32, 1634-40, 1642-44
The Catcher in the Rye (Salinger) **WLC 5:**3015, 3019, 3022, 3024, 3028-29, 3032
Categories (Aristotle) **WLCS 1:**96-97
Cathay (Pound) **WLC 5:**2801, 2803
Catherine (Thackeray) **WLC 6:**3594-95
Cathleen ni Houlihan (Yeats) **WLC 6:**4108, 4110
Catiline (Jonson) **WLC 3:**1907, 1909-12
"Cato Braden" (Masters) **WLCS 2:**578
The Caucasian Captive (Pushkin)
See *Kavkazsky plennik*
The Caucasian Chalk Circle (Brecht)
See *Der kaukasische Kreidekreis*
"A Cauliflower in Her Hair" (Jackson) **WLC 3:**1837
"Cave Canem" (Millay) **WLCS 2:**603
The Cave Dwellers (Saroyan) **WLC 5:**3081
Les caves du Vatican (*Lafcadio's Adventures*; *The Vatican Swindle*) (Gide) **WLC 3:**1378, 1385
Cawdor, and Other Poems (Jeffers) **WLC 3:**1874-76
"Ce qu'on dit au poète à propos de fleurs" ("What One Says to the Poet on the Subject of Flowers") (Rimbaud) **WLC 5:**2917, 2921
"The Celebrated Jumping Frog of Calaveras County" (Twain) **WLC 6:**3718
The Celestial Omnibus (Forster) **WLC 2:**1260
"The Celestial Railroad" (Hawthorne) **WLC 3:**1595
Les célibataires (Balzac)
See *Le curé de Tours*
"El celoso extremeño" ("The Jealous Extremaduran"; "The Jealous Hidalgo") (Cervantes) **WLC 2:**680

The Cenci (Shelley) **WLC 5**:3234-35
The Centaur (Updike) **WLC 6**:3749-50, 3752-53, 3755-56, 3758, 3764
El cerco de Numancia (*La Numancia*) (Cervantes) **WLC 2**:681-83
Ceremony (Silko) **WLCS 2**:765, 767-70
"Ceremony after a Fire Raid" (Thomas) **WLC 6**:3612, 3614
Ch'un Ch'iu (Confucius) **WLCS 1**:255-56, 260
"Chac Mool" (Fuentes) **WLC 2**:1309
The Chairs (Ionesco)
  See *Les chaises*
Les chaises (*The Chairs*) (Ionesco) **WLC 3**:1800-01, 1803-04, 1808, 1809
"Châli" (Maupassant) **WLC 4**:2293
"La chambre double" ("The Double Chamber") (Baudelaire) **WLC 1**:204-05
"La chambre" ("The Room") (Sartre) **WLC 5**:3095
Chance (Conrad) **WLC 2**:782, 790
"The Chances" (Owen) **WLC 4**:2608, 2618
A Change of Skin (Fuentes)
  See *Cambio de piel*
"Changes" (Heaney) **WLCS 1**:389
"A Channel Passage" (Brooke) **WLC 1**:436, 440
"Chant d'automne" (Baudelaire) **WLC 1**:202
"Chant de guerre parisien" (Rimbaud) **WLC 5**:2923
Les chants de Crépuscule (Hugo) **WLC 3**:1749
"Chants the Epistle" (Pirandello)
  See "Canta l'epistola"
"The Character of Holland" (Marvell) **WLC 4**:2254
"A Character" (Tennyson) **WLC 6**:3584
"Characters of Dramatic Writers Contemporary with Shakespeare" (Lamb) **WLC 3**:2031
Characters of Men and Women (Pope) **WLC 5**:2774
"The Charge of the Light Brigade" (Tennyson) **WLC 6**:3584-88
"The Chariot" (Dickinson) **WLC 2**:918, 920
"Charlie" (Chopin) **WLCS 1**:246-47
"A Charm" (Dickinson) **WLC 2**:926
"Une charogne" ("A Carrion"; "A Rotting Corpse") (Baudelaire) **WLC 1**:202
The Charterhouse of Parma (Stendhal)
  See *La chartreuse de Parme*
La chartreuse de Parme (*The Charterhouse of Parma*) (Stendhal) **WLC 5**:3393, 3395-99, 3406
"The Chase" (Toomer) **WLCS 2**:804
Chastelard (Swinburne) **WLC 6**:3552, 3561
"Le châtiment de Tartuff" ("Tartuffe's Punishment") (Rimbaud) **WLC 5**:2916, 2922
Les Châtiments (Hugo) **WLC 3**:1748-49
Chayka (*The Seagull*) (Chekhov) **WLC 2**:713, 718
The Cheats of Scapin (Moliere)
  See *Les fourberies de Scapin*
"Chefs and Spoons" (Grass) **WLC 3**:1510
Chelkash (Gorky) **WLC 3**:1485

Les chemins de la liberté (*The Roads of Freedom*) (Sartre) **WLC 5**:3088, 3093
The Cherry Garden (Chekhov)
  See *Visnevyi sad*
The Cherry Orchard (Chekhov)
  See *Visnevyi sad*
"A cheval" (Maupassant) **WLC 4**:2297, 2300
Le chevalier d'Harmental (Dumas) **WLC 2**:1084
Le chevalier de Maison-Rouge (*Marie Antoinette; or, The Chevalier of the Red House: A Tale of the French Revolution*) (Dumas) **WLC 2**:1083, 1092
Les chevaliers (Cocteau) **WLC 2**:730
"La chevelure" (Baudelaire) **WLC 1**:208
"The Chicago Picasso" (Brooks) **WLC 1**:457
Chicago Poems (Sandburg) **WLC 5**:3051-52, 3054, 3063
"Chicago" (Sandburg) **WLC 5**:3054, 3061, 3063, 3066
Chickamauga (Bierce) **WLC 1**:281, 289
Chicot the Jester; or, The Lady of Monsareua (Dumas)
  See *La dame de Monsoreau*
"The Chief Characteristics of the Doctrine of Mahayana Buddhism" (King) **WLCS 1**:471
Chief Joseph of the Nez Perce (Warren) **WLC 6**:3812-13
"Le chien" (Maupassant) **WLC 4**:2293
"Child by Tiger" (Wolfe) **WLC 6**:4041
"The Child Who Favored Daughter" (Walker) **WLCS 2**:829
A Child's Garden of Verses (Stevenson) **WLC 5**:3446, 3453-56
Childe Harold's Pilgrimage: A Romaunt (Byron) **WLC 1**:568, 572, 574, 578
"Childe Roland to the Dark Tower Came" (Browning) **WLCS 1**:213
Childhood (Tolstoy)
  See *Detstvo*
Childhood (Tolstoy) **WLC 6**:3665-66
"Childhood and Poetry" (Neruda) **WLC 4**:2509, 2511
Childhood-Boyhood (Tolstoy) **WLC 6**:3665
"The Childhood of Ljuvers" (Pasternak)
  See "The Childhood of Luvers"
"The Childhood of Luvers" ("The Childhood of Ljuvers") (Pasternak) **WLC 4**:2627
The Children (Wharton) **WLC 6**:3908
Children of the Frost (London) **WLC 4**:2136, 2142-43
Children of the Game (Cocteau)
  See *Les enfants terribles*
Children of the Mire: Modern Poetry from Romanticism to the Avant-Garde (Paz)
  See *Los hijos del limo: Del romanticismo a la vanguardia*
"Children of Violence" (Lessing) **WLCS 2**:488, 493
"Children on the Post Road" (Kafka) **WLC 3**:1946
"Children on Their Birthdays" (Capote) **WLC 1**:619, 628
"The Children's Song" (Kipling) **WLC 3**:2017
Childwold (Oates) **WLC 4**:2531, 2535
"Chilterns" (Brooke) **WLC 1**:434

China Men (Kingston) **WLCS 2**:476-83
"Chinese Letters" (Goldsmith) **WLC 3**:1472-75
The Chinese Nightingale, and Other Poems (Lindsay) **WLC 4**:2120
Choephoroe (Aeschylus) **WLCS 1**:13
"A Choice of Profession" (Malamud) **WLC 4**:2190
"The Choice" (Rossetti) **WLC 5**:2955
"The Chorus Girl" (Chekhov) **WLC 2**:708
Chosen Country (Dos Passos) **WLC 2**:965
Les Chouans (Balzac) **WLC 1**:186
Chris Christopherson (O'Neill)
  See *Anna Christie*
"Christ in Alabama" (Hughes) **WLC 3**:1727
Christabel (Coleridge) **WLC 2**:744-45
Christian Behavior (Lewis) **WLC 4**:2081-82
The Christian Doctrine (Tolstoy) **WLC 6**:3664
"The Christian Pertinence of Eschatological Hope" (King) **WLCS 1**:471
"Le Christianisme" (Owen) **WLC 4**:2611
"Christmas Antiphones" (Swinburne) **WLC 6**:3563
"Christmas at Black Rock" (Lowell) **WLC 4**:2154
A Christmas Carol (Dickens) **WLC 2**:910
"Christmas Eve under Hooker's Statue" (Lowell) **WLC 4**:2152
"Christmas Eve" (Gogol)
  See "Noc pered rozdestvom"
"Christmas is a Sad Season for the Poor" (Cheever) **WLC 2**:698
"A Christmas Memory" (Capote) **WLC 1**:622, 626, 629-30
Christus: A Mystery (Longfellow) **WLCS 2**:513, 516
Chronicle of a Death Foretold (Garcia Marquez)
  See *Crónica de una muerte anunciada*
The Chronicles of Clovis (Saki) **WLC 5**:3011
Chroniques italiennes (Stendhal) **WLC 5**:3402
"The Chrysanthemums" (Steinbeck) **WLC 5**:3387-88
"The Church of Brou" (Arnold) **WLC 1**:93, 101
"The Church with an Overshot Wheel" (Henry) **WLC 3**:1667, 1675
"Churchyard" (Gray)
  See "Elegy Written in a Country Churchyard"
La chute (*The Fall*) (Camus) **WLC 1**:596
Cien años de soledad (*One Hundred Years of Solitude*) (Garcia Marquez) **WLC 3**:1357, 1360, 1363, 1367-71
Cien sonetos de amor (*One Hundred Love Sonnets*) (Neruda) **WLC 4**:2515, 2517
Le cinquième et dernier livre des faictz et dictz heroiques du noble Pantagruel (Rabelais) **WLC 5**:2872
Circe (Aeschylus) **WLCS 1**:8
"The Circle Game" (Atwood) **WLC 1**:108, 110-12, 118
"Circle of Prayer" (Munro) **WLCS 2**:684
"The Circular Ruins" (Borges)
  See "Las ruinas circulares"

ities of the Plain (Proust)
  See *Sodome et Gomorrhe*
The Citizen of the World (Goldsmith) **WLC 3:**1465, 1468-69, 1473-75, 1477
The City Heiress; or, Sir Timothy Treat-all (Behn) **WLC 1:**245, 248
"The City in the Sea" (Poe) **WLC 4:**2757
"A City Night-Peace" (Goldsmith) **WLC 3:**1474
The City of God (St. Augustine) **WLCS 1:**108
"CITYCity-city" (Kerouac) **WLC 3:**1986-87
"Civil Disobedience" ("The Rights and Duties of the Individual in Relation to the Government") (Thoreau) **WLC 6:**3630, 3635, 3636-40
"CIVIL RIGHTS POEM" (Baraka) **WLCS 1:**145
"Clancy in the Tower of Babel" (Cheever) **WLC 2:**698
"Clancy of the Mounted Police" (Service) **WLC 5:**3123
"Clara Milich" (Turgenev)
  See "Klara Milich"
"Clarence" (Harte) **WLC 3:**1583, 1584
Clarissa Harlowe (Richardson)
  See *Clarissa; or, The History of a Young Lady*
Clarissa; or, The History of a Young Lady (*Clarissa Harlowe*) (Richardson) **WLC 5:**2892, 2894, 2897-98, 2901-04
"Claude Gueux" (Hugo) **WLC 3:**1747
The Claverings (Trollope) **WLC 6:**3681
"Clay" (Joyce) **WLC 3:**1931
"A Clean, Well-Lighted Place" (Hemingway) **WLC 3:**1651, 1655, 1659
"The Cleric" (Heaney) **WLCS 1:**398
"Clerk's Prologue" (Chaucer) **WLCS 1:**231
"Clifford Ridell" (Masters) **WLCS 2:**580-83
Clizia (Machiavelli) **WLCS 2:**533
"The Cloak" (Gogol)
  See "The Overcoat"
Clock without Hands (McCullers) **WLC 4:**2310, 2312
"Clorinda and Damon" (Marvell) **WLC 4:**2253
"Clorindy; or, The Origin of the Cakewalk" (Dunbar) **WLC 2:**1111
"The Cloud" (Shelley) **WLC 5:**3225
Clouds (Aristophanes) **WLCS 1:**78-79
The Clouds (Williams) **WLC 6:**4015
"Clouds" (Brooke) **WLC 1:**439, 444
"The Clouds" (Williams) **WLC 6:**4020
The Clown (Boell)
  See *Ansichten eines Clowns*
"Clytie" (Welty) **WLC 6:**3880, 3882, 3888
Cobwebs from an Empty Skull (Bierce) **WLC 1:**292
Cock-a-doodle Dandy (O'Casey) **WLCS 2:**716
The Cocktail Party (Eliot) **WLC 2:**1149, 1151
"The Code" (Frost) **WLC 2:**1293, 1299
"The Coffee House of Surat" (Tolstoy) **WLC 6:**3664
"The Coffin-Maker" (Pushkin) **WLC 5:**2836
The Coiners (Gide)
  See *Les faux-monnayeurs*

"Cold Iron" (Kipling) **WLC 3:**2017
"Colin Clout" (Spenser)
  See *Colin Clouts Come Home Againe*
Colin Clouts Come Home Againe ("Colin Clout") (Spenser) **WLC 5:**3350
Collected Earlier Poems (Williams) **WLC 6:**4021, 4023
The Collected Essays, Journalism and Letters of George Orwell (Orwell) **WLC 4:**2575, 2587
Collected Later Poems (Williams) **WLC 6:**4020-21
Collected Letters (Dickinson) **WLC 2:**921, 924
Collected Plays (Shaw) **WLC 5:**3200
Collected Poems (Auden) **WLC 1:**134
Collected Poems (Cummings) **WLC 2:**841
Collected Poems (Dickinson) **WLC 2:**291
Collected Poems (Milosz) **WLCS 2:**616-18
Collected Poems (Moore) **WLCS 2:**642, 645
Collected Poems (Pasternak) **WLC 4:**2628
Collected Poems (Rossetti)
  See *The Poetical Works of Christina Georgina Rossetti*
Collected Poems (Sandburg) **WLC 5:**3066-67
Collected Poems, 1934-1952 (Thomas) **WLC 6:**3616
Collected Poems of H. D. (H. D.) **WLC 3:**1612-13, 1617-18, 1624
The Collected Poems of Octavio Paz, 1957-1987 (Paz) **WLC 4:**2674
Collected Stories (Malamud)
  See *The Stories of Bernard Malamud*
The Collected Stories of Isaac Bashevis Singer (Singer) **WLC 5:**3290-91
Collected Stories of William Faulkner (Faulkner) **WLC 2:**1196
Collected Verse (Service) **WLC 5:**3130
Collected Works (Rossetti)
  See *The Poetical Works of Christina Georgina Rossetti*
The Collected Works of Ambrose Bierce (Bierce) **WLC 1:**291
The Collection (Pinter) **WLC 4:**2704-06
Le collier de la reine (*The Queen's Necklace*) (Dumas) **WLC 2:**1083-84, 1092, 1094
"Le collier" (Maupassant) **WLC 4:**2293
"Colloquy in Black Rock" (Lowell) **WLC 4:**2154, 2161
"The Colloquy of Monos and Una" (Poe) **WLC 4:**2760
"Colloquy" (Jackson) **WLC 3:**1840
El colonel no tiene quien le escribe (*The Colonel Has No One to Write Him*; *No One Writes to the Colonel*) (Garcia Marquez) **WLC 3:**1366-68, 1370
The Colonel Has No One to Write Him (Garcia Marquez)
  See *El colonel no tiene quien le escribe*
Colonel Jack (Defoe)
  See *The History of the Most Remarkable Life and Extraordinary Adventures of the Truly Honourable Colonel Jacque, Vulgarly Called Colonel Jack*
"Colonel Starbottle's Client" (Harte) **WLC 3:**1579

"The Colonel's Awakening" (Dunbar) **WLC 2:**1101, 1106
Color (Cullen) **WLCS 1:**273-74, 276-77, 282
The Color Purple (Walker) **WLCS 2:**831-33, 835-36, 840
"Colored Blues Singer" (Cullen) **WLCS 1:**282
"The Colored Soldiers" (Dunbar) **WLC 2:**1103
Columbe's Birthday (Browning) **WLCS 1:**206
Columbus (Irving) **WLC 3:**1827
"Combat Cultural" (Moore) **WLCS 2:**650
Come Along with Me (Jackson) **WLC 3:**1936-39, 1851
"Come Down, O Maid" (Tennyson) **WLC 6:**3584
Come prima, meglio di prima (*As Well as Before, Better than Before*) (Pirandello) **WLC 4:**2719, 2721-22, 2728
Come tu mi vuoi (*As You Desire Me*) (Pirandello) **WLC 4:**2727
The Comedians (Greene) **WLC 3:**1553-54
Comedias (Cervantes)
  See *Ocho comedias y ocho entremeses nunca representados*
Comedias y entremeses (Cervantes)
  See *Ocho comedias y ocho entremeses nunca representados*
"Comédie de la soif" (Rimbaud) **WLC 5:**2917, 918
La Comédie Humaine: La Recherche de l'Absolu (Balzac) **WLC 1:**179, 182-83, 185-89, 193
"A Comedy in Rubber" (Henry) **WLC 3:**1671
The Comedy of Errors (Shakespeare) **WLC 5:**3161, 3174
"The Comforts of Home" (O'Connor) **WLC 4:**2547
"The Coming of Arthur" (Tennyson) **WLC 6:**3584
The Coming of William (Saki)
  See *When William Came: A Story of London under the Hohenzollerns*
Coming Up for Air (Orwell) **WLC 4:**2575-76, 2581, 2584
"Commander Lowell 1887-1950" (Lowell) **WLC 4:**2163
Comment c'est (*How It Is*) (Beckett) **WLC 1:**231, 233
Commentaire sur Corneille (Voltaire) **WLC 6:**3771
The Common Reader (*The Common Reader, First Series*; *The First Common Reader*) (Woolf) **WLC 6:**4048
The Common Reader, First Series (Woolf)
  See *The Common Reader*
Le compagnon du tour de France (*The Companion Tour of France*) (Sand) **WLC 5:**3048
The Companion Tour of France (Sand)
  See *Le compagnon du tour de France*
"Comparatives" (Momaday) **WLCS 2:**629
"The Complaint Ledger" (Chekhov) **WLC 2:**708
Complete Poems (Moore) **WLCS 2:**645-47
Complete Poems (Sandburg) **WLC 3:**61, 3063-64

The Complete Poems (Sexton) **WLC 5**:3144-45, 3147
The Complete Poems of Robert Service (Service) **WLC 5**:3130
The Complete Vindication (Johnson) **WLC 3**:1892
The Complete Works of Kate Chopin (Chopin) **WLCS 1**:249
Composition as Explanation (Stein) **WLC 5**:3357, 3367, 3369
"The Compost" (Whitman) **WLC 6**:3943
Le comte de Monte-Cristo (*The Count of Monte Cristo*) (Dumas) **WLC 2**:1084, 1087, 1089, 1090
La comtesse d'Escarbagnas (Moliere) **WLC 4**:2436, 2445
La Comtesse de Charney (Dumas) **WLC 2**:1092
Comus: A Maske (*Mask of Comus*) (Milton) **WLC 4**:2406, 2408-09
"Conclusion" (Hawthorne) **WLC 3**:1604-05
"Conclusion" (Thoreau) **WLC 6**:3633
"Concord Ode" (Emerson) **WLC 2**:1171
The Condemned of Altona (Sartre)
See *Les séquestrés d'Altona*
Condensed Novels (Harte) **WLC 3**:1585
The Conduct of Life (Emerson) **WLC 2**:1174, 1177
Confession (Gorky)
See *Ispoved*
"The Confession of Faith of a Savoyard Vicar" (Rousseau)
See "Profession du vicaire Savoyard"
"Confession" (Baudelaire) **WLC 1**:206
Les Confessions (Rousseau) **WLC 5**:2982-83, 2986
Confessions (St. Augustine) **WLCS 1**:112, 114
The Confessions of a Fool (Strindberg)
See *Le plaidoyer d'un fou*
Confessions of a Mask (Mishima)
See *Kamen no kokuhaku*
Confessions of Felix Krull, Confidence Man (Mann)
See *Bekenntnisse des Hochstaplers Felix Krull*
The Confidence-Man: His Masquerade (Melville) **WLC 4**:2356
"A Confidence" (Dunbar) **WLC 2**:1103
The Confidential Agent (Greene) **WLC 3**:1542, 1545-46
Configurations (Paz) **WLC 4**:2662
The Congo and Other Poems (Lindsay) **WLC 4**:2118
"Congo" (Lindsay) **WLC 4**:2120, 2124-25
Los conjurados (*The Conspirators*) (Borges) **WLC 1**:342
"The Conjuring Contest" (Dunbar) **WLC 2**:1106-07
A Connecticut Yankee in King Arthur's Court (Twain) **WLC 6**:3715, 3718, 3726-28
"The Conqueror Worm" (Poe) **WLC 4**:2754-55
"Conscious" (Owen) **WLC 4**:2608
The Conservationist (Gordimer) **WLCS 1**:371, 375
"Consider" (Rossetti) **WLC 5**:2931
"Consorting with Angels" (Sexton) **WLC 5**:3145
The Conspirators (Borges)
See *Los conjurados*
Constab Ballads (McKay) **WLC 4**:2327, 2329, 2335
"A Constable Calls" (Heaney) **WLCS 1**:397
"The Constant Tin Soldier" (Andersen)
See "The Steadfast Tin Soldier"
"The Constant Tin Solider" (Andersen) **WLC 1**:60
Consuelo (Sand) **WLC 5**:3043, 3044
A Contaminated Family (Tolstoy) **WLC 6**:3666
"Conte" (Rimbaud) **WLC 5**:2918
Contemplation (Kafka)
See *Betrachtung*
Les contemplations (Hugo) **WLC 3**:1746, 1749
"The Contemplative Soul" (Huxley) **WLC 3**:1764
Contemporaries of Shakespeare (Swinburne) **WLC 6**:3556
Contest for the Arms (Aeschylus) **WLCS 1**:8
"Contest of the Bards" (Ginsberg) **WLC 3**:1398, 1403
"Contrast" (Hemingway) **WLC 3**:1879
Du Contrat social (*Le Contrat Social*; *The Social Contract*) (Rousseau) **WLC 5**:2980, 2984, 2988, 2991, 2994
Le Contrat Social (Rousseau)
See *Du Contrat social*
"The Convent Threshold" (Rossetti) **WLC 5**:2942
Conversation at Midnight (Millay) **WLCS 2**:598
"The Conversation of Eiros and Charmion" ("Eiros and Charmion") (Poe) **WLC 4**:2761
"The Conversation of Prayer" (Thomas) **WLC 6**:3619
"A Conversation" (Turgenev) **WLC 6**:3707
"The Conversion of the Jews" (Roth) **WLC 5**:2963-64, 2970
"Cook Park and Ballylee, 1931" (Yeats) **WLC 6**:4111
"Cool Park, 1929" (Yeats) **WLC 6**:4111
"Cool Thoughts on the Present Situation of Our Public Affairs" (Franklin) **WLCS 1**:316
"The Cop and the Anthem" (Henry) **WLC 3**:1672
Copper Sun (Cullen) **WLCS 1**:282
"A Coquette Conquered" (Dunbar) **WLC 2**:1103
"Cor Cordium" (Swinburne) **WLC 6**:3563
"La corde" ("The Rope") (Baudelaire) **WLC 1**:209-10
Coriolanus (Shakespeare) **WLC 5**:3158, 3164
"The Corner Store" (Welty) **WLC 6**:3891
Cornhuskers (Sandburg) **WLC 5**:3051-53
"The Coronet" (Marvell) **WLC 4**:2258
"Correspondances" (Baudelaire) **WLC 1**:201
Correspondence (Gogol) **WLC 3**:1440
A Correspondence (Turgenev) **WLC 6**:3697, 3703
Corriente alterna (*Alternating Current*) (Paz) **WLC 4**:2670
The Corsair (Byron) **WLC 1**:572
Corydon (Gide) **WLC 3**:1375, 1379, 1386
Cosi-Sancta (Voltaire) **WLC 6**:3775
Cosiè (se vi pare) (*It Is So, If You Think So; se vi pare*) (Pirandello) **WLC 4**:2721, 2726-27
Cosmic Carols (Service) **WLC 5**:3130, 3132
"Cosmogony" (Borges) **WLC 1**:343
The Cosmological Eye (Miller) **WLC 4**:2391
Du côté de chez Swann (*Swann's Way*) (Proust) **WLC 5**:2806, 2815-18
Le côté des Guermantes (*The Guermantes Way; Guermantes' Way*) (Proust) **WLC 5**:2817-18
"Cottage by the Tracks" (Wolfe) **WLC 6**:4040
"The Cottar's Saturday Night" (Burns) **WLC 1**:518, 525-27
Cotton Candy on a Rainy Day (Giovanni) **WLCS 1**:355, 359, 361, 363-64
"Cotton Candy" (Giovanni) **WLCS 1**:363
"Cottonwood" (Silko) **WLCS 2**:763
"Could man be drunk for ever" (Housman) **WLCS 1**:434
"A Council of State" (Dunbar) **WLC 2**:1106, 1109
Count Nulin (Pushkin)
See *Graf Nulin*
The Count of Monte Cristo (Dumas)
See *Le comte de Monte-Cristo*
"Counter-Revolution of Property" (Du Bois) **WLC 2**:1066
The Counterfeiters (Gide)
See *Les faux-monnayeurs*
"Counterparts" (Joyce) **WLC 3**:1930
The Countess Cathleen (Yeats) **WLC 6**:4102
Counting the Ways: A Vaudeville (Albee) **WLC 1**:30-1
Country Doctor (Balzac)
See *Le Médecin de Campagne*
"The Country Doctor" (Kafka)
See "Ein landarzt"
The Country House (Galsworthy) **WLC 2**:1334
"The Country Husband" (Cheever) **WLC 2**:696
"The Country Inn" (Turgenev)
See "The Inn"
"The Country of the Blind" (Wells) **WLC 6**:3875
The Country Waif (Sand)
See *François le Champi*
"The Coup de Grâce" (Bierce) **WLC 1**:289
Couples (Updike) **WLC 6**:3749-51, 3755-58
"The Course of a Particular" (Stevens) **WLC 5**:3435
The Court of the King of Bantam (Behn) **WLC 1**:250
"The Courting of Dinah Shadd" (Kipling) **WLC 3**:2010-11
The Courtship of Miles Standish (Longfellow) **WLCS 2**:513
Le cousin Pons (Balzac) **WLC 1**:191-92
Cousin Henry (Trollope) **WLC 6**:3681
The Covetous Knight (*The Avaricious Knight*) (Pushkin) **WLC 5**:2826-27, 2836
"The Coy Mistress" (Marvell)

See "To His Coy Mistress"
Le crapaud (Hugo) **WLC 3:**1748
"Crapy Cornelia" (James) **WLC 3:**1865
"The crawlin' ferlie" (Burns) **WLC 1:**517
"The Creation of the World and Other Business" (Miller) **WLC 4:**2372
"Creation" (Bierce) **WLC 1:**291-92
"The Creative Impulse" (Maugham) **WLC 4:**2282
Creditors (Strindberg) **WLC 6:**3515, 3529
"The Cremation of Sam McGee" (Service) **WLC 5:**3124, 3129
Crepúsculario (*The Twilight Book*) (Neruda) **WLC 4:**2513
"Le crépuscule du soir" ("Evening Twilight"; "Paris at Nightfall") (Baudelaire) **WLC 1:**209
Crime and Punishment (Dostoevsky)
  See *Prestuplenie i nakazanie*
Crime Passionel (Sartre)
  See *Les mains sales*
"Crisis" (Auden) **WLC 1:**135
"The Critic as Artist" (Wilde) **WLC 6:**3954
The Critic; or, Tragedy Rehearsed (Sheridan) **WLC 5:**3244-45, 3247, 3256
"Critics and Connoisseurs" (Moore) **WLCS 2:**648-49
La critique de L'école des femmes (*The School for Wives Criticized*) (Moliere) **WLC 4:**2436, 2438, 2443
Critique de la raison dialectique, Volume I: Théorie des ensembles pratiques (*Critique of Dialectical Reason: Theory of Practical Ensembles*) (Sartre) **WLC 5:**3088, 3092-93, 3099, 3101
Critique of Dialectical Reason: Theory of Practical Ensembles (Sartre)
  See *Critique de la raison dialectique, Volume I: Théorie des ensembles pratiques*
Critique of Dogmatic Theology (Tolstoy) **WLC 6:**3664
Le crocheteur borgne (Voltaire) **WLC 6:**3780
Crome Yellow (Huxley) **WLC 3:**1760, 1762, 1765, 1767-70
Crónica de una muerte anunciada (*Chronicle of a Death Foretold*) (Garcia Marquez) **WLC 3:**1371
"Cross-Country Snow" (Hemingway) **WLC 3:**1651
Cross-Examined (Grass)
  See *Ausgefragt*
Cross Purpose (Camus)
  See *Le malentendu*
"Cross" (Hughes) **WLC 3:**1727
"Crossing the Bar" (Tennyson) **WLC 6:**3584
"Crowds" (Baudelaire)
  See "Les foules"
"Crowing-Hen Blues" (Hughes) **WLC 3:**1724
"The Croxley Master" (Doyle) **WLC 2:**1019
The Crucible (Miller) **WLC 4:**2364-65, 2369-73
The Crusade of the Excelsior (Harte) **WLC 3:**1589
Cry, the Beloved Country: A Story of Comfort in Desolation (Paton) **WLC 4:**2642-44, 2647-48, 2651-52, 2654
The Crying of Lot 49 (Pynchon) **WLC 5:**2840-44, 2848-49
"The Crystal Egg" (Wells) **WLC 6:**3874-75
The Cub at Newmarket. A Letter to the People of Scotland (Boswell) **WLC 1:**353, 355
"Cuba Libre" (Baraka) **WLCS 1:**151
"The Culprit" (Housman) **WLCS 1:**428
"The Cultivation of Christmas Trees" (Eliot) **WLC 2:**1148
"El culto, II" (Neruda) **WLC 4:**2515
Cumpleaños (Fuentes) **WLC 2:**1311
The Cup (Tennyson) **WLC 6:**3576
Cup of Gold: A Life of Henry Morgan, Buccaneer, with Occasional References to History (Steinbeck) **WLC 5:**3387
Le curé de Tours (*Les célibataires*; *The Curé of Tours*) (Balzac) **WLC 1:**182
Le curé de Village (*The Village Curate*) (Balzac) **WLC 1:**182, 189
The Curé of Tours (Balzac)
  See *Le curé de Tours*
"A Curious Man's Dream" (Baudelaire)
  See "Le rêve d'un curieux"
"Curse for Kings" (Lindsay) **WLC 4:**2123
"The Curse" (Millay) **WLCS 2:**590
"A Curtain of Green" (Welty) **WLC 6:**3880-81, 3883, 3892
The Custom of the Country (Wharton) **WLC 6:**3904, 3907-09, 3911
"Cut" (Plath) **WLC 4:**2738
Cyclops (Euripides) **WLCS 1:**291
"Le cygne" ("The Swan") (Baudelaire) **WLC 1:**202-03
Cymbeline (Shakespeare) **WLC 5:**3171, 3174
"Cymon and Iphigenia" (Dryden) **WLC 2:**1046
The Cynic's Word Book (Bierce)
  See *The Devil's Dictionary*
Cynthia's Revels (Jonson) **WLC 3:**1910
"Czar Nikita" (Pushkin)
  See "Tsar Nikita"
"D.C." (Millay) **WLCS 2:**590
"Da sé" ("By Himself"; "By Oneself") (Pirandello) **WLC 4:**2717
"Daddy" (Plath) **WLC 4:**2738, 2744-45
"The Daemon Lover" (Jackson) **WLC 3:**1851
Daggers and Javelins (Baraka) **WLCS 1:**154
Damaged Goods: The Great Play "Les avariés" by Brieux, Novelized with the Approval of the Author (Sinclair) **WLC 5:**3263
La dame de Monsoreau (*Chicot the Jester; or, The Lady of Monsareua*) (Dumas) **WLC 2:**1083
"The Damned Thing" (Bierce) **WLC 1:**289
"Der Dampfkessel-Effekt" ("The Steam Boiler Effect") (Grass) **WLC 3:**1507
Danaids (Aeschylus) **WLCS 1:**6
A Dance of Death (Albee) **WLC 1:**27
The Dance of Death (Strindberg)
  See *Dödsdansen första delen*
A Dance of the Forests (Soyinka) **WLC 5:**3322-25, 3327-28
Dance of the Happy Shades (Munro) **WLCS 2:**675-76, 678, 681, 683, 685, 688
"Dance of the Happy Shades" (Munro) **WLCS 2:**678, 681
"The Dance" (Crane) **WLC 2:**801
Dancing Girls, and Other Stories (Atwood) **WLC 1:**114-15, 118
Dandelion Wine (Bradbury) **WLC 1:**364, 366, 368, 377
"The Dandelion" (Lindsay) **WLC 4:**2123
"Dandy Jim's Conjure Scare" (Dunbar) **WLC 2:**1107
Dangling Man (Bellow) **WLC 1:**263-64, 268-69, 272-73, 275
Daniel Deronda (Eliot) **WLC 2:**1123-24, 1125-27
"Danny Deever" (Kipling) **WLC 2:**2016-17
Dante (Baraka) **WLCS 1:**139
"Dante and the Lobster" (Beckett) **WLC 1:**231
"Dante at Verona" (Rossetti) **WLC 5:**2955-56
Dar (*The Gift*) (Nabokov) **WLC 4:**2499, 2500
"The Daring Young Man on the Flying Trapeze" (Saroyan) **WLC 5:**3071, 3082
Dark Laughter (Anderson) **WLC 1:**75-6, 78-9
"The Darkling Thrush" (Hardy) **WLC 3:**1570
Darkness Visible (Golding) **WLC 3:**1458
"Darkness" (Byron) **WLC 1:**578
Darkwater: Voices from within the Veil (Du Bois) **WLC 2:**1062, 1064
"The Darling" (Chekhov) **WLC 2:**710
"Darwin among the Machines" (Butler) **WLC 1:**552
"Daughter of Albion" (Chekhov) **WLC 2:**706
A Daughter of the Snows (London) **WLC 4:**2136
Daughters of Phorcus (Aeschylus) **WLCS 1:**7
"The Daughters of the Late Colonel" (Mansfield) **WLC 4:**2215, 2224, 2226
"De Daumier-Smith's Blue Period" (Salinger) **WLC 5:**3022, 3027
"The Daunt Diana" (Wharton) **WLC 6:**3904
David Balfour: Being Memoirs of His Adventures at Home and Abroad (Stevenson)
  See *Kidnapped: Being Memoirs of the Adventures of David Balfour in the Year 1751*
David Copperfield (Dickens)
  See *The Personal History of David Copperfield*
Dawn (Wiesel) **WLCS 2:**847
Day by Day (Lowell) **WLC 4:**2168
"A Day in the Jungle" (Jackson) **WLC 3:**1836
"Day That I Have Loved" (Brooke) **WLC 1:**436
"The Day the Pig Fell into the Well" (Cheever) **WLC 2:**696
"Daybreak" (Hughes) **WLC 3:**1723
Days without End (O'Neill) **WLC 4:**2561
"Days" (Emerson) **WLC 2:**1171, 1174
"Dayspring Mishandled" (Kipling) **WLC 3:**2022
De l'amour (*On Love*) (Stendhal) **WLC 5:**3396

TITLE INDEX

"The Dead Beat" (Owen) **WLC 4**:2608
"Dead Every Enormous Piece"
 (Cummings) **WLC 2**:841
Dead Leaves (Garcia Marquez)
 See *La hojarasca*
The Dead Lecturer (Baraka) **WLCS 1**:146, 148, 151
"The Dead Man" (Borges)
 See "El muerto"
The Dead Priestess Speaks (H. D.) **WLC 3**:1624
Dead Souls (Gogol)
 See *Tchitchikoff's Journey; or Dead Souls*
The Dead Without Burial (Sartre)
 See *Morts sans sépulture*
"The Dead" (Brooke) **WLC 1**:438, 442-43
"The Dead" (Joyce) **WLC 3**:1931, 1936
Dealings with the Firm of Dombey and Son (*Dombey and Son*) (Dickens) **WLC 2**:907-10
"The Dean of the Faculty" (Burns) **WLC 1**:524
Dear Judas and Other Poems (Jeffers) **WLC 3**:1874-75, 1884
Death along the Wabash (Saroyan) **WLC 5**:3080-81
"The Death and Dying Words of Poor Mailie" ("Elegy on Poor Mailie"; "Mailie's Dying Words and Elegy"; "Poor Mailie's Elegy") (Burns) **WLC 1**:517
"Death and the Child" (Crane) **WLC 2**:814-15
Death and the King's Horseman (Soyinka) **WLC 5**:3330-31
Death Baby (Sexton) **WLC 5**:3146-47
Death Comes for the Archbishop (Cather) **WLC 1**:655-57, 660, 665
Death in Midsummer (Mishima) **WLC 4**:2422-24
"Death in Midsummer" (Mishima) **WLC 4**:2422-23
Death in the Afternoon (Hemingway) **WLC 3**:1650-51, 1659
"Death in the Dawn" (Soyinka) **WLC 5**:3323
"Death in the Woods" (Anderson) **WLC 1**:77-80, 84
Death in Venice (Mann)
 See *Der Tod in Venedig*
The Death Notebooks (Sexton) **WLC 5**:3146
"Death of a Favorite Cat" (Gray)
 See "Ode on the Death of a Favourite Cat, Drowned in a Tub of Gold Fishes"
Death of a Naturalist (Heaney) **WLCS 1**:392, 396-97, 400
Death of a Salesman (*The Inside of His Head*) (Miller) **WLC 4**:2362-64, 2366, 2368-72
"The Death of a Traveling Salesman" (Welty) **WLC 6**:3880, 3892
The Death of Artemio Cruz (Fuentes)
 See *La muerte de Artemio Cruz*
"The Death of Artists" (Baudelaire)
 See "The Death of Artists"
The Death of Bessie Smith (Albee) **WLC 1**:20-1
"The Death of Halpin Frayser" (Bierce) **WLC 1**:289, 293
"The Death of Justina" (Cheever) **WLC 2**:696, 700

"The Death of Lovers" (Baudelaire)
 See "La mort des amants"
The Death of Malcolm X (Baraka) **WLCS 1**:154
"The Death of Me" (Malamud) **WLC 4**:2183, 2186, 2190
"The Death of Methuselah" (Singer) **WLC 5**:3295
"The Death of Saint Narcissus" (Eliot) **WLC 2**:1144
"The Death of the Fathers" (Sexton) **WLC 5**:3138, 3146-47
"The Death of the Hired Man" (Frost) **WLC 2**:1293, 1299
"Death of the Lord Protector" (Marvell)
 See "Poem upon the Death of O. C."
The Death of the Moth, and Other Essays (Woolf) **WLC 6**:4047-49
"The Death of the Sheriff" (Lowell) **WLC 4**:2152
"Death of Tsotsi" (Paton) **WLC 4**:2650
"Death Shall Have No Dominion" (Thomas)
 See "And Death Shall Have No Dominion"
"Death the Proud Brother" (Wolfe) **WLC 6**:4040
The Death-Trap (Saki) **WLC 5**:3010
"Deaths and Entrances" (Thomas) **WLC 6**:3611-12, 3619
Deaths Duell; or, A Consolation to the Soule, against the dying Life, and living Death of the Body (Donne) **WLC 2**:941, 945-48
La débâcle (Zola) **WLC 6**:4118-20, 4126
"Debates in Magna Lilliputia" (Johnson) **WLC 3**:1893
"Debbie Go Home" (Paton) **WLC 4**:2656
"The Debt" (Wharton) **WLC 6**:3904
"The Decay of Lying" (Wilde) **WLC 6**:3954
"The Deceived" (Mann)
 See *Die Betrogene*
"A December Day in Dixie" (Chopin) **WLCS 1**:248
"December of My Springs" (Giovanni) **WLCS 1**:359
A Decent Birth, a Happy Funeral (Saroyan) **WLC 5**:3075-76
Decline and Fall (Waugh) **WLC 6**:3820-22, 3824-25, 3831
The Decoration of Houses (Wharton) **WLC 6**:3907
"Décoré" (Maupassant) **WLC 4**:2291
"Découverte" (Maupassant) **WLC 4**:2293
"Dedication for a Plot of Ground" (Williams) **WLC 6**:4023
Deep Song (Garcia Lorca)
 See *Poema del cante jondo*
"The Defeat of the City" (Henry) **WLC 3**:1670
The Defeat of Youth, and Other Poems (Huxley) **WLC 3**:1761, 1764
"The Defeat of Youth" (Huxley) **WLC 3**:1764
"The Defection of Mary Ann Gibbs" (Dunbar) **WLC 2**:1107
A Defence of Poetry (Shelley) **WLC 5**:3227
"A Defender of the Faith" (Dunbar) **WLC 2**:1107
"Defender of the Faith" (Roth) **WLC 5**:2963-64, 2971

The Defense (Nabokov) **WLC 4**:2497, 2500
"The Definition of Love" (Marvell) **WLC 4**:2258
The Deformed Transformed (Byron) **WLC 1**:568
"The Deil's Awa' wi' th' Exciseman" (Burns) **WLC 1**:524
"The Deliberation of Mr. Dunkin" (Dunbar) **WLC 2**:1106
A Delicate Balance (Albee) **WLC 1**:24-5, 27-30, 32
"The Delight Song of Tsoai-talee" (Momaday) **WLCS 2**:628, 635
Delo Artmunovykh (*The Artamonov Business*) (Gorky) **WLC 3**:1488, 1493
"Delphi" (Golding) **WLC 3**:1456
Delta Wedding (Welty) **WLC 6**:3885, 3888, 3892-93
Demian (Hesse) **WLC 3**:1692
Democratic Vistas (Whitman) **WLC 6**:3936
"The Demon of Perversity" (Poe)
 See "The Imp of the Perverse"
Departmental Ditties (Kipling) **WLC 3**:2013-14
"Departure;" (Millay) **WLCS 2**:590
"Departure" (Anderson) **WLC 1**:84
Le dépit amoureux (*Lovers' Spite*) (Moliere) **WLC 4**:2436, 2441
"Des Roma" (Lowell) **WLC 4**:2152
"A Descent into the Maelström" (Poe) **WLC 4**:2760, 2762
The Descent of Man (Wharton) **WLC 6**:3903
"The Descent of Odin, an Ode" (Gray) **WLC 3**:1530
"The Descent" (Williams) **WLC 6**:4023
"Description of a City Shower" ("Shower") (Swift) **WLC 6**:3535
"Description of the Morning" (Swift) **WLC 6**:3535, 3544-45
"Description without Place" (Stevens) **WLC 5**:3435
A Descriptive Catalogue (Blake) **WLC 1**:300
"The Desert Music" (Williams) **WLC 6**:4021
"The Deserted Plantation" (Dunbar) **WLC 2**:1099, 1103, 1110
Deserted Village (Goldsmith) **WLC 3**:1464, 1472, 1475-77
"Desire and the Black Masseur" (Williams) **WLC 6**:4003
Desire under the Elms (O'Neill) **WLC 4**:2560, 2563
Desolation Angels (Kerouac) **WLC 3**:1983, 1985, 1987
Despair (Nabokov) **WLC 4**:2500
Desperate Remedies (Hardy) **WLC 3**:1558, 1571
"Destiny" (Arnold) **WLC 1**:101
"The Destruction of Kreshev" (Singer) **WLC 5**:3291
"The Destruction of Personality" (Gorky) **WLC 3**:1493
"Detroit Conference of Unity and Art" (Giovanni) **WLCS 1**:362
Detstvo (*Childhood*) (Tolstoy) **WLC 6**:3665-66
Detstvo (*My Childhood*) (Gorky) **WLC**

3:1484-85, 1487-88
"Deutsches Requiem" (Borges) **WLC 1**:333, 336
Le deuxième sexe (*The Second Sex*) (Beauvoir) **WLC 1**:216, 218, 220-23
The Devil and the Good Lord (Sartre)
See *Le diable et le bon Dieu*
"The Devil and Tom Walker" (Irving) **WLC 3**:1820, 1826, 1828
Devil in Paradise (Miller) **WLC 4**:2382
The Devil is an Ass (Jonson) **WLC 3**:1910-12
"The Devil" (Tolstoy) **WLC 6**:3664-65
The Devil's Dictionary (*The Cynic's Word Book*) (Bierce) **WLC 1**:280, 284, 287
The Devil's Disciple (Shaw) **WLC 5**:3195
The Devil's Law-Case (Webster) **WLC 6**:3841, 3852
The Devils of Loudun (Huxley) **WLC 3**:1767, 1771
Devotions on Sundrie Occasions (Donne)
See *Devotions upon Emergent Occasions, and Severall steps in my sicknes*
Devotions upon Emergent Occasions, and Severall steps in my sicknes (*Devotions on Sundrie Occasions*) (Donne) **WLC 2**:941, 945-47
"Devyatsat pyaty god" ("The Year 1905") (Pasternak) **WLC 4**:2627, 2632
The Dharma Bums (Kerouac) **WLC 3**:1976-77, 1983
In di Velt hot Geshvign (Wiesel)
See *And the World Remained Silent*
Di Familie Moskat (*The Family Moskat*) (Singer) **WLC 5**:3292-95
Le diable et le bon Dieu (*The Devil and the Good Lord; Lucifer and the Lord*) (Sartre) **WLC 5**:3091-92
"Diálogo del espejo" ("Dialogue in a Mirror") (Garcia Marquez) **WLC 3**:1363
"The Dialogue between Franklin and the Gout" (Franklin) **WLCS 1**:314
Dialogue II (Pope) **WLC 5**:2782
"Dialogue in a Mirror" (Garcia Marquez)
See "Diálogo del espejo"
Dialogue Something Like Horace (Pope) **WLC 5**:2782
"Dialogues of the Dogs" (Burns)
See "The Twa Dogs"
"The Diamond as Big as the Ritz" (Fitzgerald) **WLC 2**:1223
"The Diamond Necklace" (Maupassant)
See "La parure"
Diary in North Wales (Johnson) **WLC 3**:1895
Diary of a Good Neighbor (Lessing) **WLCS 2**:497
"Diary of a Madman" ("A Madman's Diary"; "Notes of a Madman") (Gogol) **WLC 3**:1430-31, 1438
"The Diary of a Madman" (Tolstoy)
See *Zapiski sumasshedshego*
"Diary of a Naturalist" (Milosz) **WLCS 2**:610-11
"The Diary of a Superfluous Man" (Turgenev)
See "Dnevnik lishnego cheloveka"
The Diary of a Young Girl (Frank)
See *Het achterhuis*
The Diary of Samuel Marchbanks (Davies) **WLC 2**:848, 851

The Diary of Samuel Pepys (Pepys) **WLC 4**:2681-83, 2685-93
"Dick Boyle's Business Card" (Harte) **WLC 3**:1584
Dictionary (Johnson) **WLC 3**:1894, 1899-1901, 1903
Dictionnaire philosophique (*Portatif*) (Voltaire) **WLC 6**:3771-72, 3778
Dictyulci (Aeschylus) **WLCS 1**:13
Dido, Queen of Carthage (Marlowe) **WLC 4**:330, 336, 363, 369
La Difficulté d'être (Cocteau) **WLC 2**:737
"The Difficulty of Crossing a Field" (Bierce) **WLC 1**:287
"Digging" (Heaney) **WLCS 1**:391, 393
Dimitri Roudine (Turgenev)
See *Rudin*
Ding Dong Bell (de la Mare) **WLC 2**:888
"Dining-Room Tea" (Brooke) **WLC 1**:434, 438-39, 444
"Dirge for a Righteous Kitten" (Lindsay) **WLC 4**:2122
"Dirge" (Emerson) **WLC 2**:1171
Dirty Hands (Sartre)
See *Les mains sales*
Dirty Linen (Stoppard) **WLC 6**:3484, 3487, 3492-93
"Dis Aliter Visum" (Browning) **WLCS 1**:214
Los dís enmascarados (*The Masked Days*) (Fuentes) **WLC 2**:1309
"Disabled" (Owen) **WLC 4**:2612
"The Disappointment" (Behn) **WLC 1**:255
The Discarded Image: An Introduction to Medieval and Renaissance Literature (Lewis) **WLC 4**:2086
Discorsi di Nicolo Machiavelli (Machiavelli)
See *Discourses on Livy*
Discours sur l'Inégalité (Rousseau)
See *Discours sur l'origine et les fondements de l'inégalité parmi les hommes*
Discours sur l'origine et les fondements de l'inégalité parmi les hommes (*Discours sur l'Inégalité; Discourse on Inequality; Discourse on the Origins of Inequality; Second Discourse*) (Rousseau) **WLC 5**:2986
Discourse on Inequality (Rousseau)
See *Discours sur l'origine et les fondements de l'inégalité parmi les hommes*
Discourse on the Origins of Inequality (Rousseau)
See *Discours sur l'origine et les fondements de l'inégalité parmi les hommes*
Discourses on Livy (Machiavelli) **WLCS 2**:521-23, 526, 528, 533
"Discovered" (Dunbar) **WLC 2**:1103
Discoveries (Jonson)
See *Timber; or, Discoveries*
"The Discovery of the Future" (Wells) **WLC 6**:3861
"A Discovery of Thought" (Stevens) **WLC 5**:3436
"A Discreet Miracle" (Allende) **WLCS 1**:47
Disorder and Early Sorrow ("Early Sorrow") (Mann) **WLC 4**:2198
"The Displaced Person" (O'Connor) **WLC 4**:2542, 2554

"The Disquieted Muses" (Plath)
See "The Disquieting Muses"
"The Disquieting Muses" ("The Disquieted Muses") (Plath) **WLC 4**:2740
The Dissolution of Dominic Boot (Stoppard) **WLC 6**:3487
Distant Relations (Fuentes)
See *Una familia lejana*
"The Distracted Preacher" (Hardy) **WLC 3**:1567
District of Columbia (Dos Passos) **WLC 2**:966
Divan of the Tamarit (Garcia Lorca)
See *El Diván de Tamarit*
El Diván de Tamarit (*Divan of the Tamarit*) (Garcia Lorca) **WLC 2**:1347
La divina commedia (Alighieri)
See *Divine Comedy*
Divine Comedy (Alighieri) **WLCS 1**:21, 23, 25, 29-31, 33-35, 37
The Divine in Mode (Marvell)
See *Mr. Smirk; or, The Divine in Mode*
The Divine Tragedy (Longfellow) **WLCS 2**:513-14, 516
"The Diviner" (Heaney) **WLCS 1**:396
"The Divinity School Address" ("An Address Delivered Before the Senior Class in Divinity College, Cambridge") (Emerson) **WLC 2**:1180, 1182-83
"Dizzy-Headed Dick" (Dunbar) **WLC 2**:1106
"Dnevnik lishnego cheloveka" ("The Diary of a Superfluous Man"; "The Journal of a Superfluous Man") (Turgenev) **WLC 6**:3697, 3702
Do with Me What You Will (Oates) **WLC 4**:2525-2527, 2529-2530, 2535
"Docker" (Heaney) **WLCS 1**:397
Le docteur Pascal (Zola) **WLC 6**:4118, 4121, 4125-26, 4128
"The Doctor and the Doctor's Wife" (Hemingway) **WLC 3**:1651
Doctor Faustus (Marlowe) **WLC 4**:2237-39, 2241-44, 2246
Doctor Faustus: The Life of the German Composer Adrian Leverkühn as Told by a Friend (Mann)
See *Doktor Faustus: Das Leben des deutschen Tonsetzers Adrian Leverkühn, erzählt von einem Freunde*
The Doctor in spite of Himself (Moliere)
See *Le médecin malgré lui*
Doctor Jekyll and Mr. Hyde (Stevenson) **WLC 5**:3446-49, 3451, 3459
See *The Strange Case of Dr. Jekyll and Mr. Hyde*
Doctor Sax: Faust Part Three (Kerouac) **WLC 3**:1983, 1985
Doctor Thorne (Trollope) **WLC 6**:3680-81, 3691
Doctor Zhivago (Pasternak) **WLC 4**:2623, 2625-26, 2630-38
See *Dr. Zhivago*
"The Doctor's Duty" (Pirandello)
See "Il dovere del medico"
"The Doctor's Wife" (Updike) **WLC 6**:3751
Documents Relating to the Sentimental Agents in the Volyen Empire (Lessing) **WLCS 2**:497
Dödsdansen första delen (*The Dance of Death*) (Strindberg) **WLC 6**:3518,

3528
Dodsworth (Lewis) **WLC 4:**2103, 2112
The Dog It Was That Died (Stoppard) **WLC 6:**3487
Dog Years (Grass)
See *Hundejahre*
"The Dog" (Turgenev) **WLC 6:**3699, 3705, 3707
Dogg's Hamlet, Cahoot's Macbeth (Stoppard) **WLC 6:**3493
Doktor Faustus: Das Leben des deutschen Tonsetzers Adrian Leverkühn, erzählt von einem Freunde (*Doctor Faustus: The Life of the German Composer Adrian Leverkühn as Told by a Friend*) (Mann) **WLC 4:**2203-05, 2207-08
Doktor Murkes gesammeltes Schweigen, und andere Satiren (*Dr. Murke's Collected Silences; Murke's Collected Silences*) (Boell) **WLC 1:**328
A Doll's House (Ibsen)
See *Et dukkehjem*
"The Doll's House" (Mansfield) **WLC 4:**2215, 2219, 2223
"Dolph Heyliger" (Irving) **WLC 3:**1820, 1828
The Dolphin (Lowell) **WLC 4:**2168-70
Dom Garcie de Navarre; ou, Le prince jaloux (*Don Garcia of Navarre; Don Garcie de Navarre*) (Moliere) **WLC 4:**2436, 2438, 2440, 2442
"The Domain of Arnheim" (Poe) **WLC 4:**2757
Dombey and Son (Dickens)
See *Dealings with the Firm of Dombey and Son*
Domesday Book (Masters) **WLCS 2:**577, 580
Domik v Kolomne (*The Little House of Kolomna*) (Pushkin) **WLC 5:**2832
"Domination of Black" (Stevens) **WLC 5:**3434
Don Fernando (Maugham) **WLC 4:**2277, 2281
Don Garcia of Navarre (Moliere)
See *Dom Garcie de Navarre; ou, Le prince jaloux*
Don Garcie de Navarre (Moliere)
See *Dom Garcie de Navarre; ou, Le prince jaloux*
Don Juan (Byron) **WLC 1:**568-69, 572-80
Don Juan de Marana (Dumas) **WLC 2:**1081
Don Perlimplín (Garcia Lorca)
See *Amor de Don Perlimplín con Belisa en su jardín*
Don Quixote (Cervantes)
See *El ingenioso hidalgo Don Quixote de la Mancha*
Don Quixote in England (Fielding) **WLC 2:**1214
Don Sebastian, King of Portugal (Dryden) **WLC 2:**1058
Don't Go Away Mad (Saroyan) **WLC 5:**3075-76
"Don't Have a Baby Till You Read This" (Giovanni) **WLCS 1:**354
"Donald Caird" (Scott) **WLC 5:**3115
"Le donneur d'eau bénite" (Maupassant) **WLC 4:**2301
Doña Rosita la soltera (*Doña Rosita the Spinster; or, The Language of Flowers*) (Garcia Lorca) **WLC 2:**1342
Doña Rosita the Spinster; or, The Language of Flowers (Garcia Lorca)
See *Doña Rosita la soltera*
"Doom and She" (Hardy) **WLC 3:**1571
"The Door in the Wall" (Wells) **WLC 6:**3874, 3876
Door into the Dark (Heaney) **WLCS 1:**391
The Doors of Perception (Huxley) **WLC 3:**1766-67, 1769-71
"Dora Williams" (Masters) **WLCS 2:**584
"Las dos doncelas" ("The Two Maidens") (Cervantes) **WLC 2:**679
Dostoyevsky According to His Correspondence (Gide) **WLC 3:**1385
The Double (Dostoevsky) **WLC 2:**976
The Double Axe and Other Poems (Jeffers) **WLC 3:**1878, 1884
"The Double Chamber" (Baudelaire)
See "La chambre double"
The Double Dealer (Congreve) **WLC 2:**759, 762, 764, 767, 772-74
"A Double-Dyed Deceiver" (Henry) **WLC 3:**1675
"The Double Image" (Sexton) **WLC 5:**3137, 3139, 3141
"Dover Beach" (Arnold) **WLC 1:**92-3, 97-8, 100
"Il dovere del medico" ("The Doctor's Duty"; "The Physician's Duty") (Pirandello) **WLC 4:**2717
"The Doves Nest" (Mansfield) **WLC 4:**2215
Down and Out in Paris and London (Orwell) **WLC 4:**2581, 2586-87
"Down at the Cross" (Baldwin) **WLC 1:**168
"Down at the Dinghy" (Salinger) **WLC 5:**3019, 3024-26
"Down by the Riverside" (Wright) **WLC 6:**4086, 4089-90
"Down Pens" (Saki) **WLC 5:**3007
"Dr. Chevalier's Lie" (Chopin) **WLCS 1:**241
Dr. Murke's Collected Silences (Boell)
See *Doktor Murkes gesammeltes Schweigen, und andere Satiren*
"Dr. Woolacott" (Forster) **WLC 2:**1270
Dr. Wortle's School (Trollope) **WLC 6:**3681
Dr. Zhivago (*Doctor Zhivago*) (Pasternak) **WLC 4:**2623, 2625-26, 2630-38
Dracula (Stoker) **WLC 6:**3463-71, 3473-78
A Draft of Shadows (Paz)
See *Pasado en claro*
A Draft of XXX Cantos (Pound) **WLC 5:**2792
Drafts and Fragments (Pound) **WLC 5:**2801-03
"A Drama of Exile" (Browning) **WLC 1:**469
"Un drame au bord de la mer" ("A Seashore Drama") (Balzac)
"A Dream of Armageddon" (Wells) **WLC 6:**3874
"A Dream of Fair Women" (Tennyson) **WLC 6:**3575
"A Dream of Jealousy" (Heaney) **WLCS 1:**393
The Dream Play (Strindberg)
See *Ett drömspel*
"A Dream" (Burns) **WLC 1:**525
"The Dream" (Turgenev)
See "Son"
"The Dreams of Debs" (London) **WLC 4:**2146-47
"Dreams of Movie Stardom" (Frank) **WLC 2:**1283
Dreamtigers (Borges)
See *El hacedor*
"A Dreary Story" ("A Dull Story") (Chekhov) **WLC 2:**709
Die Dreigroschenoper (*The Threepenny Opera*) (Brecht) **WLC 1:**389-90
"Drenched in Light" (Hurston) **WLCS 1:**449-50
"A Dresden Lady in Dixie" (Chopin) **WLCS 1:**248
"Drifting Off" (Heaney) **WLCS 1:**398
"A Drink in the Passage" (Paton) **WLC 4:**2651
"Drink to Me Only with Thine Eyes" (Jonson)
See "Song to Celia"
"The Drinker" (Lowell) **WLC 4:**2159
Drums in the Night (Brecht) **WLC 1:**387, 390
See *Trommeln in der nacht*
"The Drums of the Fore and Aft" (Kipling) **WLC 3:**2010
The Drunken Boat (Rimbaud)
See *Le bateau ivre*
"The Drunken Fisherman" (Lowell) **WLC 4:**2152, 2159
"The Dry Salvages" (Eliot) **WLC 2:**1148
"The Dryad War" (Paz) **WLC 4:**2675
"The Dryad" (Andersen) **WLC 1:**61
Dubin's Lives (Malamud) **WLC 4:**2190
Dubliners (Joyce) **WLC 3:**1930-33, 1935-37
Dubrovsky (Pushkin) **WLC 5:**2829-30
The Duchess of Malfi (Webster) **WLC 6:**3838-39, 3843-44, 3846-52
The Duchess of Padua (Wilde) **WLC 6:**3955
"The Duckling" (Andersen)
See "The Ugly Duckling"
"The Duel" (Chekhov) **WLC 2:**709
"The Duelist" (Turgenev) **WLC 6:**3702
The Duenna; or, The Doubling Elopement (Sheridan) **WLC 5:**3243, 3253-56
A Duet, with an Occasional Chorus (Doyle) **WLC 2:**1020
"The Duke in His Domain" (Capote) **WLC 1:**629
The Duke's Children (Trollope) **WLC 6:**3682, 3688
"Dulce Et Decorum Est" (Owen) **WLC 4:**2608, 2613
"A Dull Story" (Chekhov)
See "A Dreary Story"
The Dumb Waiter (Pinter) **WLC 4:**2699-2701, 2704
"Duncan Gray" (Burns) **WLC 1:**517
Dunciad (Pope) **WLC 5:**2773, 2776, 2781
"Duns Scotus" (Lowell) **WLC 4:**2154
"During Fever" (Lowell) **WLC 4:**2164
"Dusk" (Saki) **WLC 5:**3007
Dust Tracks on a Road (Hurston) **WLCS 1:**447-48, 453

ust" (Brooke) **WLC 1:**434, 438
utch Courage" (Kipling) **WLC 3:**2010
he *Dutch Lover* (Behn) **WLC 1:**245-46
utchman (Baraka) **WLCS 1:**139-42, 144, 148, 152
vádtsat' shesti i odná (*Twenty-Six Men and a Girl*) (Gorky) **WLC 3:**1485, 1490
voryanskoe gnezdo (*The Nest of Gentlefolk; Nest of Noblemen; Nest of the Gentry; Noblemen's Home*) (Turgenev) **WLC 6:**3703-04, 3706, 3708, 3710
he *Dwarfs* (Pinter) **WLC 4:**2701
yadya Vanya (*Uncle Vanya*) (Chekhov) **WLC 2:**713, 717-18
ym (*Smoke*) (Turgenev) **WLC 6:**3704
he *Dynamics of a Particle* (Carroll) **WLC 1:**644
he *Dynamiter*" (Stevenson)
See *The New Arabian Nights*
he *Dynasts: A Drama of the Napoleonic Wars* (Hardy) **WLC 3:**1573
. P. Ode Pour L'Election de son Sepulchre" (Pound) **WLC 5:**2789
ach and All" (Emerson) **WLC 2:**1171
ach in His Role (Pirandello)
See *Il giuoco delle parti*
ach of Us His Own Part (Pirandello)
See *Il giuoco delle parti*
he *Eagle Has Two Heads* (Cocteau)
See *L'aigle à deux têtes*
he *Eagle That Is Forgotten*" (Lindsay) **WLC 4:**2118, 2121, 2124
arly Sorrow" (Mann)
See *Disorder and Early Sorrow*
arth Has Not Anything to Show More Fair" (Wordsworth) **WLC 6:**4073
he *Earth Men*" (Bradbury) **WLC 1:**370
arth's Holocaust" (Hawthorne) **WLC 3:**1595, 1606
ast and West: The Collected Short Stories of W. Somerset Maugham (*Altogether: The Collected Stories of W. Somerset Maugham*) (Maugham) **WLC 4:**2274
ast of Eden (Steinbeck) **WLC 5:**3379-84, 3387
ast Slope (Paz)
See *Ladera este*
ast, West (Rushdie) **WLCS 2:**753
he *East*" (Singer) **WLC 5:**3286
aster 1916" (Yeats) **WLC 6:**4108-10
he *Easter Egg*" (Saki) **WLC 5:**3001, 3007-08
aster Eve" (Chekhov) **WLC 2:**709
he *Easter Wedding*" (Dunbar) **WLC 2:**1107
astern Slope (Paz)
See *Ladera este*
aves-Dropping a Lodge of Free-Masons" (*A House of Gentlefolk*) (Harris) **WLC 6:**3701
cclesiastical Sketches (*Ecclesiastical Sonnets*) (Wordsworth) **WLC 6:**4073
cclesiastical Sonnets (Wordsworth)
See *Ecclesiastical Sketches*
choes of the Jazz Age" (Fitzgerald) **WLC 2:**1231
clatante victoire de Saarebrück" ("The Sinking Ship") (Rimbaud) **WLC 5:**2922
logues (Vergil) **WLCS 2:**809-11, 814
cole des femmes (*The School for Wives*) (Gide) **WLC 3:**1379, 1384
L'école des femmes (*The School for Wives*) (Moliere) **WLC 4:**2436-37, 2442, 2444, 2447
L'école des maris (*The School for Husbands*) (Moliere) **WLC 4:**2436-37, 2442, 2444, 2447
"Economics" (Thoreau) **WLC 6:**3633
"Economy" (Thoreau) **WLC 6:**3631
Ecossaise (Voltaire) **WLC 6:**3769
"The Ecstasy" (Donne)
See "The Exstasie"
"Eden Bower" (Rossetti) **WLC 5:**2948-49, 2953, 2956-57
"Edge" (Plath) **WLC 4:**2740, 2748
The Edible Woman (Atwood) **WLC 1:**109, 114
Edoni (Aeschylus) **WLCS 1:**6
L'éducation sentimentale: Histoire d'un jeune homme (*Sentimental Education: A Young Man's History*) (Flaubert) **WLC 2:**1241, 1246, 1252-55
"Edward Fane's Rose-Bud" (Hawthorne) **WLC 3:**1594
Edward II (Marlowe) **WLC 4:**2237-40
Edwin and Angelina (Goldsmith) **WLC 3:**1475
"Effects of Analogy" (Stevens) **WLC 5:**3438
"The Egg" (Anderson)
See "The Triumph of the Egg"
"The Egg" (Anderson)
See "The Triumph of the Egg"
Egmont (Goethe) **WLC 3:**1421
"Ego Dominus Tuus" (Yeats) **WLC 6:**4100
"Ego Tripping" (Giovanni) **WLCS 1:**364
Egor Bulychev and Others (Gorky) **WLC 3:**1488
"Egotism; or, The Bosom Serpent" (Hawthorne) **WLC 3:**1595, 1606
"Egypt from My Inside" (Golding) **WLC 3:**1455-56
"Egypt from My Outside" (Golding) **WLC 3:**1455
An Egyptian Journal (Golding) **WLC 3:**1455-56
The Egyptian Nights (Pushkin) **WLC 5:**2829
Eight Cousins (Alcott) **WLC 1:**41-3, 50
Eight Men (Wright) **WLC 6:**4091
"Eight O'Clock" (Housman) **WLCS 1:**428
Eight Plays (Cervantes)
See *Ocho comedias y ocho entremeses nunca representados*
Eight Plays and Eight Interludes: New and Never Performed (Cervantes)
See *Ocho comedias y ocho entremeses nunca representados*
18 Poems (Thomas) **WLC 6:**3612
"1887" (Housman) **WLCS 1:**433
Eimi (Cummings) **WLC 2:**840
"Ein Hungerkünstler" ("A Hunger-Artist") (Kafka) **WLC 3:**1950-51
"Ein landarzt" ("The Country Doctor") (Kafka) **WLC 3:**1950
Eirei no koe (Mishima) **WLC 4:**2420
"Eiros and Charmion" (Poe)
See "The Conversation of Eiros and Charmion"
Either of One or of No One (Pirandello)
See *O di uno o di nessuno*
Either Someone's or No-One's (Pirandello)
See *O di uno o di nessuno*
"Elaine" (Millay) **WLCS 2:**595
"Elaine" (Tennyson) **WLC 6:**3584
The Elder Statesman (Eliot) **WLC 2:**1148
Electra (Euripides) **WLCS 1:**293, 299-300
Electra (Sophocles) **WLCS 1:**783-84
"Electra on Azalea Path" (Plath) **WLC 4:**2740
"An Elegiac Poem on the Death of George Whitefield" ("On the Death of the Rev. Mr. George Whitefield") (Wheatley) **WLC 6:**3922
"Elegie IV: The Perfume" (Donne) **WLC 2:**943
"Elegie VIII: The Comparison" (Donne) **WLC 2:**935
"Elegie XIX: Going to Bed" (Donne) **WLC 2:**943
"Elegy for a friend killed in the civil war" (Paz) **WLC 4:**2659
"Elegy in a Rainbow" (Brooks) **WLC 1:**463
"Elegy on Poor Mailie" (Burns)
See "The Death and Dying Words of Poor Mailie"
"An Elegy on the Death of an Amiable Young Lady" (Boswell) **WLC 1:**353-54
"Elegy to the Memory of an Unfortunate Lady" (Pope) **WLC 5:**2778-79
"Elegy Written in a Country Churchyard" ("Churchyard") (Gray) **WLC 3:**1521-22, 1524, 1526, 1528-31, 1533
The Elemental Odes (Neruda)
See *Odas elementales*
Elementary Odes (Neruda)
See *Odas elementales*
"Elemetina" (Cheever) **WLC 2:**697-98
"Elévation" (Baudelaire) **WLC 1:**201
"Elevator Boy" (Hughes) **WLC 3:**1726
Eleven Years (Undset)
See *Elleve aar*
"The Elfin Mound" (Andersen) **WLC 1:**60
"Eli the Fanatic" (Roth) **WLC 5:**2970
"Elijah Browning" (Masters) **WLCS 2:**580
Elizabeth Bennet; or, Pride and Prejudice (Austen)
See *Pride and Prejudice*
"Elizabeth" (Jackson) **WLC 3:**1851
Elle et lui (*She and He*) (Sand) **WLC 5:**3044
Elleve aar (*Eleven Years*) (Undset) **WLC 6:**3742
Elmer Gantry (Lewis) **WLC 4:**2101, 2103, 2108, 2112-13
"Eloisa to Abelard" (Pope) **WLC 5:**2772, 2775, 2781
"Elza Ramsey" (Masters) **WLCS 2:**577
"The Embarkment for Cythera" (Cheever) **WLC 2:**691
"An Embarrassing Situation" (Chopin) **WLCS 1:**240
émile, ou de l'éducation (Rousseau) **WLC 5:**2983-86, 2988
"Emily Brosseau" (Masters) **WLCS 2:**578
"Emily Sparks" (Masters) **WLCS 2:**584
Emma (Austen) **WLC 1:**144-45, 148-49, 155-58
"Emmett Burns" (Masters) **WLCS 2:**578
Empedocles on Etna, and Other Poems (Arnold) **WLC 1:**101-02

"Empedocles" (Arnold) **WLC 1:**94, 101, 103
The Emperor Jones (O'Neill) **WLC 4:**2559
"The Emperor's New Clothes" (Andersen) **WLC 1:**55, 61, 64
"The Empire of the Ants" (Wells) **WLC 6:**3863, 3873
Empty Mirror (Ginsberg) **WLC 3:**1395-96
En attendant Godot (*Waiting for Godot*) (Beckett) **WLC 1:**228-29, 231-43
En bla bok (*Zones of the Spirit*) (Strindberg) **WLC 6:**3518
"En famille" (Maupassant) **WLC 4:**2293-94, 2297
En folkefiende (*An Enemy of the People*) (Ibsen) **WLC 3:**1777, 1780-81
"En su muerte" (Neruda) **WLC 4:**2515
The Enchanter (Nabokov)
See *Volshebnik*
The End of the Affair (Greene) **WLC 3:**1542, 1545, 1548, 1551, 1553
"The End of the Passage" (Kipling) **WLC 3:**2010-11, 2017
"The End of the Tether" (Conrad) **WLC 2:**781
"The End of the World" (Turgenev) **WLC 6:**3707
End to Torment: A Memoir of Ezra Pound (H. D.) **WLC 3:**1624
"The End" (Borges)
See "El fin"
"The End" (Owen) **WLC 4:**2611
Endeavors of Infinite Man (Neruda)
See *Tentativa del hombre infinito*
Endgame (Beckett)
See *Fin de partie*
Ends and Means (Huxley) **WLC 3:**1765-66
"The Enduring Chill" (O'Connor) **WLC 4:**2543
Endymion (Keats) **WLC 3:**1956, 1958, 1966-67
Enemies: A Love Story (Singer)
See *Sonim, di Geschichte fun a Liebe*
An Enemy of the People (Ibsen)
See *En folkefiende*
"Enfance" (Rimbaud) **WLC 5:**2918
Les enfants terribles (*Children of the Game*; *The Holy Terrors*) (Cocteau) **WLC 2:**725, 727, 729-30, 736-37
England Made Me (Greene) **WLC 3:**1542, 1545-46, 1552
The English People (Orwell) **WLC 4:**2575
English Traits (Emerson) **WLC 2:**1172
"The Englishman in Italy" (Browning) **WLCS 1:**211
"Enid" (Tennyson) **WLC 6:**3584
Enoch Arden (Tennyson) **WLC 6:**3579
The Enormous Radio, and Other Stories (Cheever) **WLC 2:**690, 695-96, 698
The Enormous Room (Cummings) **WLC 2:**834
"Enough" (Turgenev) **WLC 6:**3705
An Enquiry into the Present State of Polite Learning in Europe (Goldsmith) **WLC 3:**1465, 1472-73, 1475
Enrico IV (*Henry IV*; *The Living Mask*) (Pirandello) **WLC 4:**2721-22, 2727
Enter a Free Man (Stoppard) **WLC 6:**3481, 3494
The Entertainer (Osborne) **WLC 4:**2592, 2594-98, 2602
Entfernung von der Truppe (Boell) **WLC 1:**315, 317-18, 326
Entremeses (Cervantes)
See *Ocho comedias y ocho entremeses nunca representados*
La entretenida (Cervantes) **WLC 2:**683-84
"Entropy" (Pynchon) **WLC 5:**2842
L'Envers de L'Histoire contemporaine (Balzac) **WLC 1:**188
"L'Envoi" (Kipling) **WLC 3:**2013
"Envoi" (Pound) **WLC 5:**2791
"The Ephemera" (Franklin) **WLCS 1:**314
"The Epic" (Tennyson) **WLC 6:**3584
Epicene (Jonson)
See *Epicoene; or, the Silent Woman*
Epicoene; or, the Silent Woman (*Epicene*; *The Silent Woman*) (Jonson) **WLC 3:**1910, 1912, 1915-16, 1918-19
Epilogue to the Satires (Pope) **WLC 5:**2774, 2781, 2783-85
"Epilogue" (Masters) **WLCS 2:**579-80
"Epiphanies" (Joyce) **WLC 3:**1935
Epipsychidion (Shelley) **WLC 5:**3234, 3236-38
"An Epistle from Lycidas to Menalcas" (Boswell) **WLC 1:**353
"Epistle III" (Pope) **WLC 5:**2780-81
"Epistle IV" (Pope) **WLC 5:**2780
"Epistle to a Godson" (Auden) **WLC 1:**139
"Epistle to Dr. Arbuthnot" (Pope) **WLC 5:**2774, 2776-78, 2780, 2782-83
Epistles (St. Augustine) **WLCS 1:**108
"Epistles to Several Persons" ("Ethick Epistles") (Pope) **WLC 5:**2775, 2781
"The Epistles" (Burns) **WLC 1:**518
Epitaph for George Dillon (Osborne) **WLC 4:**2592, 2594
Epitaph for the Race of Man (Millay) **WLCS 2:**594
"Epitaph for the Race of Man" (Millay) **WLCS 2:**593, 599
"Epitaphs of the War" (Kipling) **WLC 3:**2017
"An Epithalamion, or mariage song on the Lady Elizabeth, and Count Palatine being married on St. Valentines day" (Donne) **WLC 2:**935
"Epithalamion" (Cummings) **WLC 2:**835
"Epithalamion" (Spenser) **WLC 5:**3350-51
"Epstein" (Roth) **WLC 5:**2964
"Ere Sleep Comes Down to Soothe the Weary Eyes" (Dunbar) **WLC 2:**1102, 1110-11
Erewhon Revisited Twenty Years Later (Butler) **WLC 1:**554, 558-60, 562
Erewhon; or, Over the Range (Butler) **WLC 1:**552, 555-63
Erma bifronte (*Two-faced Herma*) (Pirandello) **WLC 4:**2717, 2732
Ernest Pontifex; or, The Way of All Flesh (Butler)
See *The Way of All Flesh*
Eros at Breakfast, and Other Plays (Davies) **WLC 2:**852
"Escape" (Huxley) **WLC 3:**1761-62
The Escaped Cock (Lawrence)
See *The Man Who Died*
"La escritura del Dios" ("The God's Script") (Borges) **WLC 1:**342-43
"Eskimo" (Munro) **WLCS 2:**684
"Esmé" (Saki) **WLC 5:**3006
La espada encendida (Neruda) **WLC 4:**2515
España en el corazón: himno a las glorias del pueblo en la guerra (1936-1937) (*Spain at Heart*; *Spain in My Heart*; *Spain in the Heart*) (Neruda) **WLC 4:**2505, 2514
Essai sur les moeurs (Voltaire) **WLC 6:**3770, 3778
Essai sur les révolutions de la musique en France (Marmontel) **WLC 4:**2457-58, 2464-66
Essay of Dramatic Poesy (Dryden)
See *Of Dramatick Poesie: An Essay*
"An Essay on Criticism" (Pope) **WLC 5:**2769, 2771, 2774-76
An Essay on Man (Pope) **WLC 5:**2773, 2782
Essay on the Sublime and Beautiful (Burke)
See *A Philosophical Enquiry into the Origin of Our Ideas of the Sublime and Beautiful*
Essays (Emerson) **WLC 2:**1170, 1172
Essays in Criticism (Arnold) **WLC 1:**90
Essays of Elia (Lamb) **WLC 3:**2028, 2038
Essentials (Toomer) **WLCS 2:**796, 800
La estación violenta (*The Season of Violence*; *The Violent Season*) (Paz) **WLC 4:**2660
"Ester Lucero" (Allende) **WLCS 1:**47
"Esthétique du mal" (Stevens) **WLC 5:**3434
Et dukkehjem (*A Doll's House*; *Nora*) (Ibsen) **WLC 3:**1777, 1779-82, 1785, 1787, 1791-92, 1794
Etapper: Ny raekke (*Stages on the Road*) (Undset) **WLC 6:**3739
L'état de siège (*The State of Siege*) (Camus) **WLC 1:**589-91, 595
The Eternal Husband (Dostoevsky)
See *Vechny muzh*
The Eternal Return (Cocteau)
See *L'éternel retour*
L'Eternel retour (Cocteau) **WLC 2:**732
L'éternel retour (*The Eternal Return*) (Cocteau) **WLC 2:**732
Ethan Frome (Wharton) **WLC 6:**3898, 3902, 3904-05, 3909, 3912
"Ethick Epistles" (Pope)
See "Epistles to Several Persons"
Ethics (Aristotle) **WLCS 1:**100-01, 103
"Eton College Ode" (Gray)
See "Ode on a Distant Prospect of Eton College"
"Eton" (Gray)
See "Ode on a Distant Prospect of Eton College"
L'étourdi (Moliere) **WLC 4:**2436, 2441
L'étranger (*The Outsider*; *The Stranger*) (Camus) **WLC 1:**584, 586-88, 590-94
L'être et le néant: Essai d'ontologie phénoménologique (*Being and Nothingness: An Essay on Phenomenological Ontology*) (Sartre) **WLC 5:**3088, 3090, 3092, 3094, 3096-3100
Ett drömspel (*The Dream Play*) (Strindberg) **WLC 6:**3517-18, 3529

tudes analytiques (*Analytical Studies*) (Balzac) **WLC 1**:182
tudes philosophiques (*Oeuvres philosophiques*) (Balzac) **WLC 1**:182, 189, 193
"uclid" (Millay) **WLCS 2**:591
ugene Onegin (Pushkin)
See *Yevgeny Onegin*
umenides (Aeschylus) **WLCS 1**:6-7, 12-16
"uphrasie" (Chopin) **WLCS 1**:237-38
ureka: A Prose Poem (Poe) **WLC 4**:2757, 2759-60, 2763
urope: A Prophecy, 1794 (Blake) **WLC 1**:300
he Eustace Diamonds (Trollope) **6**;3690-92
"va está dentro de su gato" ("Eva Inside Her Cat") (Garcia Marquez) **WLC 3**:1362-63
"va Inside Her Cat" (Garcia Marquez)
See "Eva está dentro de su gato"
va Luna (Allende) **WLCS 1**:47
vangeline (Longfellow) **WLCS 2**:506, 509-11, 513
vangiles (Zola) **WLC 6**:4125
"he Eve of St. Agnes" (Keats) **WLC 3**:1956, 1964, 1966-67
"he Eve of St. John" (Scott) **WLC 5**:3114
"ve" (Rossetti) **WLC 5**:2936
"veline" (Joyce) **WLC 3**:1930
"vening Hawk" (Warren) **WLC 6**:3814
"vening on the Broads" (Swinburne) **WLC 6**:3566
"vening Twilight" (Baudelaire)
See "Le crépuscule du soir"
n Evening Walk in the Abbey-Church of Holyroodhouse" (Boswell) **WLC 1**:352
"vening" (Wheatley)
See "An Hymn to the Evening"
venings on a Farm near Dikanka (Gogol)
See *Vechera ná khutore bliz Dikanki*
"eventail" (Capek) **WLC 1**:600
"vents of That Easter" (Cheever) **WLC 2**:691
very Good Boy Deserves Favour: A Piece for Actors and Orchestra (Stoppard) **WLC 6**:3487, 3493
very Man in his Humour (Jonson) **WLC 3**:1909-10, 1912, 1914, 1917
verybody's Autobiography (Stein) **WLC 5**:3369
verything in the Garden (Albee) **WLC 1**:26
verything That Rises Must Converge (*All That Rises Must Converge*) (O'Connor) **WLC 4**:2546
vgeni Onegin (Pushkin)
See *Yevgeny Onegin*
he Evidence of Things Not Seen (Baldwin) **WLC 1**:175
"vil Allures, but Good Endures" (Tolstoy) **WLC 6**:3667
he Evil Hour (Garcia Marquez)
See *La mala hora*
he Evil" (Rimbaud)
See "Le mal"
volution, Old and New (Johnson) **WLC 1**:557
"x-People" (Gorky)
See *Byvshii lyudi*

"Excelsior" (Longfellow) **WLCS 2**:509
The Excursion, Being a Portion of "The Recluse" (*Prospectus to the Excursion*) (Wordsworth) **WLC 6**:4066-67, 4069-71
"The Execution of Troppmann" (Turgenev) **WLC 6**:3704
Exemplary Novels (Cervantes)
See *Novelas exemplares*
Exemplary Stories (Cervantes)
See *Novelas exemplares*
Exemplary Tales (Cervantes)
See *Novelas exemplares*
"The Exile's Return" (Lowell) **WLC 4**:2152
Exiles (Joyce) **WLC 3**:1935
Exit the King (Ionesco)
See *Le roi se meurt*
"The expense of spirit in a waste of shame" (Shakespeare)
See "Sonnet 129"
Expensive People (Oates) **WLC 4**:2526, 2528
"Experience and Fiction" (Jackson) **WLC 3**:1836
"Experience of the Theatre" (Ionesco) **WLC 3**:1808
"Experience" (Emerson) **WLC 2**:1176-77, 1180, 1183
Experiment in Autobiography (Wells) **WLC 3**:3872, 3876
An Experiment in Criticism (Lewis) **WLC 4**:2085
Experimental Death Unit #1 (Baraka) **WLCS 1**:152
L'expiation (Hugo) **WLC 3**:1748
"Explaining a Few Things" (Neruda)
See "Explico algunas cosas"
"Explico algunas cosas" ("Explaining a Few Things"; "I Explain a Few Things") (Neruda) **WLC 4**:2514
The Exploits of Brigadier Gerard (Doyle) **WLC 2**:1020
An Exposition of the Gospels (Tolstoy) **WLC 6**:3664
"An Expostulation with Inigo Jones" (Jonson) **WLC 3**:1921
"Exposure" (Heaney) **WLCS 1**:391-92, 396, 399
"Exposure" (Owen) **WLC 4**:2605, 2616
"The Exstasie" ("The Ecstasy") (Donne) **WLC 2**:945
The Exterminator (*Exterminator!*) (Burroughs) **WLC 1**:541-42, 545-46
Exterminator! (Burroughs)
See *The Exterminator*
"The Extinction of Man" (Wells) **WLC 6**:3863
"An Extravagance of Laughter" (Ellison) **WLC 2**:1165
Extravagario (*Book of Vagaries*) (Neruda) **WLC 4**:2515, 2517-18
The Eye (Nabokov) **WLC 4**:2497
An Eye for an Eye (Trollope) **WLC 6**:3681
Eyeless in Gaza (Huxley) **WLC 3**:1760-61, 1767-68, 1770
"Eyes and Tears" (Marvell) **WLC 4**:2252, 2258
"A Fable of Joan Miro" (Paz) **WLC 4**:2675
A Fable: Belfagor, the Devil Who Took a Wife (Machiavelli) **WLCS 2**:533
"Fable" (Golding) **WLC 3**:1458
Fables Ancient and Modern; Translated into Verse, from Homer, Ovid, Boccace, & Chaucer (Dryden) **WLC 2**:1046
"Face Lift" (Plath) **WLC 4**:2747-48
The Face of a Nation (Wolfe) **WLC 6**:4033
"The Face of the War" (Wolfe) **WLC 6**:4040
"A Face on Which Time Makes but Little Impression" (Hardy) **WLC 3**:1570
Les fâcheux (*The Bores*) (Moliere) **WLC 4**:2436, 2440, 2442
Facing the River (Milosz) **WLCS 2**:620-21
The Factory of the Absolute (Capek)
See *Továrna na absolutno*
"The Facts Concerning the Recent Carnival of Crime in Connecticut" (Twain) **WLC 6**:3721
"The Facts in the Case of M. Valdemar" (Poe) **WLC 4**:2753, 2760
Fadren (*The Father*) (Strindberg) **WLC 6**:3515, 3517, 3521-22, 3525, 3527-28
The Faerie Queene, Disposed into Twelve Bookes Fashioning XII Morall Vertues (Spenser) **WLC 5**:3337, 3339, 3341-48, 3351-52
Fahrenheit 451 (Bradbury) **WLC 1**:366-67, 373-75
The Fair Haven (Butler) **WLC 1**:554, 556-57, 559-60
The Fair Jilt; or, The History of Prince Tarquin and Miranda (Behn) **WLC 1**:250, 255, 258
"The Fair Singer" (Marvell) **WLC 4**:2258
The Fair Vow-Breaker (Behn)
See *The History of the Nun; or, The Fair Vow-Breaker*
The Fairy Tale of My Life (Andersen) **WLC 1**:67
"Fairy Tale of the Natchez Trace" (Welty) **WLC 6**:3891
Fairy-Tales (Capek) **WLC 1**:602
"The Faith Cure Man" (Dunbar) **WLC 2**:1106
The Faithful Wife (Undset)
See *Den trofaste hustru*
The Falcon (Tennyson) **WLC 6**:3575
Falconer (Cheever) **WLC 2**:700, 702
"Falk" (Conrad) **WLC 2**:781
The Fall (Camus)
See *La chute*
The Fall of America: Poems of These States 1965-1971 (Ginsberg) **WLC 3**:1393-95, 1398-99, 1402-03
The Fall of the House of Suzaku (Mishima)
See *Suzaku Ke no Metsudo*
"The Fall of the House of Usher" (Poe) **WLC 4**:2754, 2756, 2762
The Fallen Idol (Greene) **WLC 3**:1542, 1544
"Falsche Schönheit" ("Wrong Beauty") (Grass) **WLC 3**:1507
The False Alarm (Johnson) **WLC 3**:1895
"The False Collar" (Andersen) **WLC 1**:60
"The False Coupon" (Tolstoy) **WLC 6**:3665
False Dawn (Wharton) **WLC 6**:3911
False Notes (Pirandello)

See *Fuori di chiave*
Una familia lejana (*Distant Relations*) (Fuentes) **WLC 2:**1311-12
"Familiär" ("Family Matters") (Grass) **WLC 3:**1506
"A Family Feud" (Dunbar) **WLC 2:**1101, 1106
Family Happiness (Tolstoy)
See *Semeinoe schaste*
The Family Idiot: Gustave Flaubert, 1821-1857 (Sartre)
See *L'idiot de la famille: Gustave Flaubert de 1821 à 1857*
"The Family in Modern Drama" (Miller) **WLC 4:**2372
"Family Matters" (Grass)
See "Familiär" *The Family Moskat* (Singer)
See *Di Familie Moskat*
Family Pictures (Brooks) **WLC 1:**452, 457-58, 461-62
A Family Reunion (Albee) **WLC 1:**29
"The Family Reunion" (Eliot) **WLC 2:**1148
Family Voices (Pinter) **WLC 4:**2703
"The Fanatics" (Dunbar) **WLC 2:**1101, 1104, 1113
"Fancy's Show-Box" (Hawthorne) **WLC 3:**1594, 1607-08
Fantastic Fables (Bierce) **WLC 1:**281, 287
Le fantôme de Marseille (Cocteau) **WLC 2:**732
Far from the Madding Crowd (Hardy) **WLC 3:**1559, 1561
Farbenlehre (Goethe) **WLC 3:**1423
"A Farewell to America" (Wheatley) **WLC 6:**3923, 3929
A Farewell to Arms (Hemingway) **WLC 3:**1651, 1653, 1658-59, 1661-22
Farfetched Fables (Shaw) **WLC 5:**3200
"The Farmer's Wife" (Sexton) **WLC 5:**3140
Fatal Interview (Millay) **WLCS 2:**593, 599-600
A Fatal Wedding (Garcia Lorca)
See *Bodas de sangre*
"The Fate of the Jury" (Masters) **WLCS 2:**580
"Fate" (Emerson) **WLC 2:**1171
The Fateful Game of Love (Capek) **WLC 1:**600
"The Fates" (Owen) **WLC 4:**2618
The Father (Strindberg)
See *Fadren*
"Father Abraham's Speech" (Franklin) **WLCS 1:**314
"Father Alexey's Story" (Turgenev)
See "Rasskaz ottsa Aleksaya"
Father Sergius (Tolstoy)
See *Otetz Sergii*
"Father's Bedroom" (Lowell) **WLC 4:**2164-65
Fathers and Children (Turgenev)
See *Ottsy i deti*
Fathers and Sons (Turgenev)
See *Ottsy i deti*
"Fathers and Sons" (Hemingway) **WLC 3:**1650
Fattige skjaebner (*Poor Fortunes*) (Undset) **WLC 6:**3740
Faust (Goethe) **WLC 1:**1412-15, 1417-18, 1421-22
Faust (Turgenev) **WLC 6:**3697, 3701, 3703, 3707-08
"Faustus and Helen (II)" (Crane) **WLC 2:**802
La faute de l'Abbé Mouret (Zola) **WLC 6:**4118, 4127
Les faux-monnayeurs (*The Coiners; The Counterfeiters*) (Gide) **WLC 3:**1378-79, 1381-85
Fear and Misery of the Third Reich (Brecht)
See *Furcht und Elend des dritten Reiches*
"The Fear of Bo-talee" (Momaday) **WLCS 2:**628
"Fear" (Frank) 2;1283
"Fears and Scruples" (Browning) **WLCS 1:**208
The Feast during the Plague (Pushkin)
See *A Feast in Time of the Plague*
A Feast in Time of the Plague (*The Feast during the Plague*) (Pushkin) **WLC 5:**2826-27, 2836
"Feather" (Pirandello)
See "Piuma"
Fécondité (Zola) **WLC 6:**4118
The Feigned Courtesans; or, A Night's Intrigue (Behn) **WLC 1:**246-47
Felix Holt the Radical (Eliot) **WLC 2:**1123
"Le femme de Paul" (Maupassant) **WLC 4:**2293
La femme rompue (*The Woman Destroyed*) (Beauvoir) **WLC 1:**220
Les femmes savantes (*The Learned Ladies*) (Moliere) **WLC 4:**2436-37, 2439-40, 2445
Fences (Wilson) **WLCS 1:**862-66, 868-69, 874
"Les fenêtres" (Baudelaire) **WLC 1:**210
"Fergus and the Druid" (Yeats) **WLC 6:**4105
Ferishtah's Fancies (Browning) **WLCS 1:**208
"Fern Hill" (Thomas) **WLC 6:**3612
"Fern" (Toomer) **WLCS 2:**793
"The Fernery" (Crane) **WLC 2:**799
"Fêtes de la faim" (Rimbaud) **WLC 5:**2917-18
"Fever 103°" (Plath) **WLC 4:**2746-48
"A Few Crusted Characters" (Hardy) **WLC 3:**1566-67
A Few Figs from Thistles (Millay) **WLCS 2:**590, 592, 594, 600, 603
Ficciones, 1935-1944 (*Fictions*) (Borges) **WLC 1:**339, 341
"La ficelle" ("A Piece of String") (Maupassant) **WLC 4:**2293
Fictions (Borges)
See *Ficciones, 1935-1944*
"Fiddler Jones" (Masters) **WLCS 2:**577
"The Fiddler of the Reels" (Hardy) **WLC 3:**1566-67
Field Work (Heaney) **WLCS 1:**388, 390-94, 396-97
The Fiend's Delight (Bierce) **WLC 1:**286
"The Fiends" (Pushkin) **WLC 5:**2832
Fiesta (Hemingway)
See *The Sun Also Rises*
Fifth Business (Davies) **WLC 2:**848-50, 853-54, 857-60
The Fifth Child (Lessing) **WLCS 2:**499
The Fifth Column (Hemingway) **WLC 3:**1651-52
Fifth Decad of Cantos (Pound) **WLC 5:**2803
Fifty Poems (Cummings) **WLC 2:**841
"La figlia che piange" (Eliot) **WLC 2:**1146-47
"The Figure a Poem Makes" (Frost) **WLC 2:**1298, 1301
La fille aux yeux d'ors (Balzac) **WLC 1:**190
"Filmer" (Wells) **WLC 6:**3872-73, 3876
"La fin de la journée" (Baudelaire) **WLC 1:**205
Fin de mundo (Neruda) **WLC 4:**2515
Fin de partie (*Endgame*) (Beckett) **WLC 1:**230, 235
"El fin" ("The End") (Borges) **WLC 1:**342
"Final Soliloquy of the Interior Paramour" (Stevens) **WLC 5:**3439
The Financier (Dreiser) **WLC 2:**1025, 1027-30
"The Finding of Martha" (Dunbar) **WLC 2:**1107
"The Finding of Zach" (Dunbar) **WLC 2:**1102, 1106
Fine Clothes to the Jew (Hughes) **WLC 3:**1723, 1726
"The Finish of Patsy Barnes" (Dunbar) **WLC 2:**1106
Finnegans Wake (*Work in Progress*) (Joyce) **WLC 3:**1935
Fiorenza (Mann) **WLC 4:**2198
"The Fir-Tree" ("The Little Fir Tree") (Andersen) **WLC 1:**59, 64
Fire (Lessing) **WLCS 2:**492
"Fire and Cloud" (Wright) **WLC 6:**4089
"The Fire Balloons" (Bradbury) **WLC 1:**367
"The Firemen's Ball" (Lindsay) **WLC 4:**2119
The First and Second Anniversaries (Donne)
See *The Anniversaries*
"The First and the Last" (Galsworthy) **WLC 2:**1331
The First Anniversarie. An Anatomie of the World. Wherein By Occasion of the untimely death of Mistris Elizabeth Drury, the frailtie and decay of this whole World is represented (*An Anatomie of the World*) (Donne) **WLC 2:**940, 944
"The First Anniversary of the Government under O. C." ("The First Anniversary of the Government Under His Highness the Lord Protector") (Marvell) **WLC 4:**2254
"The First Anniversary of the Government Under His Highness the Lord Protector" (Marvell)
See "The First Anniversary of the Government under O. C."
The First Circle (Solzhenitsyn)
See *V kruge pervom*
"The First-Class Passenger" (Chekhov) **WLC 2:**708
The First Common Reader (Woolf)
See *The Common Reader*
First Encounter (Dos Passos)
See *One Man's Initiation--1917*
"First Epistle of the First Book of Horace"

(Pope)
See *Satires and Epistles of Horace, Imitated*
"A First Family of Tasajara" (Harte) **WLC 3:**1590
"The First Kingdom" (Heaney) **WLCS 1:**398
First Love (Turgenev)
See *Pervaya lyubov'*
"First Love" (Welty) **WLC 6:**3881-83
The First Men in the Moon (Wells) **WLC 6:**3856, 3859, 3862, 3864, 3867, 3869, 3871, 3873, 3876
First Person Singular (Maugham) **WLC 4:**2274
The First Rescue Party (Capek) **WLC 1:**606
"The First Seven Years" (Malamud) **WLC 4:**2189
"First Wedding Night" (Pirandello)
See "Prima notte"
"Fish Crier" (Sandburg) **WLC 5:**3066
"The Fish" (Brooke) **WLC 1:**434, 439, 444
"The Fish" (Moore) **WLCS 2:**642, 649
"A Fit of the Blues" (Gorky) **WLC 3:**1491
"Fits" (Munro) **WLCS 2:**683
"The Fitting" (Millay) **WLCS 2:**599
"The Five-Forty-Eight" (Cheever) **WLC 2:**696
"Five Men against the Theme, `My Name is Red Hot. Yo Name ain Doodley Squat'" ("My Name Is Red Hot. Yo Name Ain Doodley Squat") (Brooks) **WLC 1:**463
"The Five White Mice" (Crane) **WLC 2:**818, 825
The Fixer (Malamud) **WLC 4:**2173, 2178-80, 2184-86, 2190
Flags in the Dust (Faulkner)
See *Sartoris*
"Le flambeau vivant" (Baudelaire) **WLC 1:**207
"Flame-Heart" (McKay) **WLC 4:**2334, 2336-37
"Flanagan" (Crane) **WLC 2:**814-15
"Flanagan and His Short Filibustering Adventure" (Crane) **WLC 2:**826
Flappers and Philosophers (Fitzgerald) **WLC 2:**1224
"Flats Road" (Munro) **WLCS 2:**682
"Fletcher McGee" (Masters) **WLCS 2:**579, 582
Les fleurs du mal (*The Flowers of Evil*; *The Lesbians*; *Les Lesbiennes*; *Les Limbes*) (Baudelaire) **WLC 1:**197-98, 201, 203-09
The Flies (Sartre)
See *Les mouches*
"Flight" (Steinbeck) **WLC 5:**3385, 3387-88
Flood (Grass) **WLC 3:**1510
"Florentine Pilgrim" (Service) **WLC 5:**3132
"Flower and the Leaf" (Chaucer) **WLCS 1:**224
"The Flower of Mending" (Lindsay) **WLC 4:**2123
"The Flowering of the Rod" (H. D.) **WLC 3:**1613, 1615-16, 1618, 1624
"The Flowering of the Strange Orchid" (Wells) **WLC 6:**3863, 3874

The Flowers of Evil (Baudelaire)
See *Les fleurs du mal*
The Flying Doctor (Moliere)
See *Le médecin volant*
"The Flying Fish" (Lawrence) **WLC 3:**2045
"The Flying Trunk" (Andersen) **WLC 1:**60
Folks from Dixie (Dunbar) **WLC 2:**1101-02, 1104-06, 1108, 1111
Following the Equator (Twain) **WLC 6:**3414, 3716
Foma Gordeyev (Gorky) **WLC 3:**1490-93
The Food of the Gods, and How It Came to Earth (Wells) **WLC 6:**3867, 3869, 3876
"The Fool" (Service) **WLC 5:**3122
"Footnote to Howl" (Ginsberg) **WLC 3:**1404, 1406
"Footsteps of Angels" (Longfellow) **WLCS 2:**510
"For a Lady I Know" (Cullen) **WLCS 1:**276
"For a Poet" (Cullen) **WLCS 1:**277
"For a Virgin" (Cullen) **WLCS 1:**276
"For an Atheist" (Cullen) **WLCS 1:**276
"For Daughters of Magdalen" (Cullen) **WLCS 1:**277
"For Esmé—with Love and Squalor" (Salinger) **WLC 5:**3022-23, 3025-26
"For George Santayana" (Lowell) **WLC 4:**2162
"For Godsake hold your tongue, and let me love" (Donne)
See "The Canonization"
"For John, Who Begs Me Not to Enquire Further" (Sexton) **WLC 5:**3145
"For My Grandmother" (Cullen) **WLCS 1:**276
"For My Sister Molly Who in the Fifties" (Walker) **WLCS 2:**830
"For Paul Laurence Dunbar" (Cullen) **WLCS 1:**276
"For Sale" (Lowell) **WLC 4:**2164
"For Sandra" (Giovanni) **WLCS 1:** 352, 362
"For the Marriage of Faustus and Helen" (Crane) **WLC 2:**800-01, 806, 808
For the Time Being (Auden) **WLC 1:**130-31, 135-36
For the Union Dead (Lowell) **WLC 4:**2158-59, 2161, 2168
"For the Union Dead" (Lowell) **WLC 4:**2158-61, 2168, 2170
La force de l'âge (*The Prime of Life*) (Beauvoir) **WLC 1:**219-20, 224
"The Force of Blood" (Cervantes)
See "La fuerza de la sangre"
The Forced Marriage (Moliere)
See *Le mariage forcé*
The Forced Marriage; or, The Jealous Bridegroom (Behn) **WLC 1:**245-46
"Forced Retirement" (Giovanni) **WLCS 1:**359-60
"Ford Madox Ford" (Lowell) **WLC 4:**2162
"Foreign Lands" (Stevenson) **WLC 5:**3454
"Forerunners" (Emerson) **WLC 2:**1172
The Forest (Jonson) **WLC 3:**1920-21
The Foresters—Robin Hood and Maid Marian (Tennyson) **WLC 6:**3575-76
"The Forethought" (Du Bois) **WLC 2:**1067, 1072

"Le forgeron" (Rimbaud) **WLC 5:**2922, 2925
"La forma de la espada" ("The Shape of the Sword") (Borges) **WLC 1:**335
"A Forsaken Garden" (Swinburne) **WLC 6:**3563-64
"The Forsaken Merman" (Arnold) **WLC 1:**92, 101
"Forschungen eines hundes" ("Investigations of a Dog") (Kafka) **WLC 3:**1945
The Forsyte Saga (Galsworthy) **WLC 2:**1328-30, 1333
Fortaellingen om Viga-Ljot og Vigdis (*Gunnar's Daughter*) (Undset) **WLC 6:**3737, 3743
"Forth went the candid man" (Crane) **WLC 2:**817
"The Fortress" (Sexton) **WLC 5:**3142
The Fortunate Mistress (*Roxana*) (Defoe) **WLC 2:**871-72
La fortune de Rougon (Zola) **WLC 6:**4125-26
Fortune Heights (Dos Passos) **WLC 2:**964
Fortune, My Foe (Davies) **WLC 2:**852
The Fortunes and Misfortunes of the Famous Moll Flanders (*Moll Flanders*) (Defoe) **WLC 2:**867, 871-73, 876-81
The Forty-Five Guardsmen (Dumas)
See *Les quarante-cinq*
"Fosterling" (Heaney) **WLCS 1:**400
"Les foules" ("Crowds") (Baudelaire) **WLC 1:**210
"A Foundling" (Atwood) **WLC 1:**111
"The Fountain" (Wordsworth) **WLC 6:**4068
The Fountainhead (Rand) **WLC 5:**2878-79, 2883-84, 2886
Four Black Revolutionary Plays (Baraka) **WLCS 1:**149
"The Four Brothers" (Sandburg) **WLC 5:**3051
"Four Introductions" (Giovanni) **WLCS 1:**365
"The Four Lost Men" (Wolfe) **WLC 6:**4040
"Four Notions of Love and Marriage" (Momaday) **WLCS 2:**628
The Four Quartets (Eliot) **WLC 2:**1146, 1148, 1150
The Four Zoas: The Torments of Love and Jealousy in the Death and Judgement of Albion the Ancient Man (*Vala*; *Vala*) (Blake) **WLC 1:**301, 303, 306, 310
The Four-Gated City (Lessing) **WLCS 2:**489, 493-96
Les fourberies de Scapin (*The Cheats of Scapin*; *The Rogueries of Scapin*; *The Tricks of Scapin*) (Moliere) **WLC 4:**2436, 2438, 2440, 2445
"The Fourth Alarm" (Cheever) **WLC 2:**697
Fowre Hymnes (*Hymnes*) (Spenser) **WLC 5:**3352
The Fox; or, Volpone (Jonson)
See *Volpone; or, the Foxe*
"Fragment of an `Antigone'" (Arnold) **WLC 1:**100-01
"Fragment Thirty-Six" (H. D.) **WLC 3:**1612
"Fragment: Not One Corner" (Owen) **WLC 4:**2614

Fragments of a Journal (Ionesco) **WLC 3:**1804-O5, 1810
Framley Parsonage (Trollope) **WLC 6:**3681
François le Champi (*The Country Waif*) (Sand) **WLC 5:**3039, 3041, 3043, 3047-48
Frankenstein; or, The Modern Prometheus (Shelley) **WLC 5:**3204-08, 3210, 3213-19 18, 3219
"Frankfurt Lectures" (Boell) **WLC 1:**326
Franklin's Wit and Folly: The Bagatelles (Franklin) **WLCS 1:**314
"Franny" (Salinger) **WLC 5:**3019-20, 3022-23
Frederick and the Great Coalition (Mann) **WLC 4:**2208
"Frederick Douglass" (Dunbar) **WLC 2:**1103
Free Fall (Golding) **WLC 3:**1457
"Free" (Dreiser) **WLC 2:**1038
"Freedman" (Heaney) **WLCS 1:**388
Freedom under Parole (Paz)
See *Libertad bajo palabra*
"Freud and the Future" (Mann) **WLC 4:**2201
"Freud's Position in the History of Modern Thought" (Mann) **WLC 4:**2201
Friday's Footprint (Gordimer) **WLCS 1:**374
Friedrich und die grosse Koalition (Mann) **WLC 4:**2208
"A Friend of Kafka" (Singer) **WLC 5:**3293
Friend Of My Youth (Munro) **WLCS 2:**685
"Friends on the Road" (Neruda) **WLC 4:**2510
The Frivolous Prince (Cocteau) **WLC 2:**738
Frogs (Aristophanes) **WLCS 1:**80, 83-85, 87
Fröken Julie (*Miss Julie*) (Strindberg) **WLC 6:**3517, 3520, 3522-25, 3527-29
"From a Railway Carriage" (Stevenson) **WLC 5:**3454
From Death to Morning (Wolfe) **WLC 6:**4040-41
"From My Diary, July, 1914" (Owen) **WLC 4:**2608, 2618
"From the Pillar" (Huxley) **WLC 3:**1764
"From the Rising of the Sun" (Milosz) **WLCS 2:**616
"From the Rising Sun" (Milosz) **WLCS 2:**608
From under the Rubble (*Rubble*) (Solzhenitsyn) **WLC 5:**3312-13
Fru Hjelde (*Mrs. Hjelde*) (Undset) **WLC 6:**3740
Fru Marta Oulie (*Mrs. Marta Oulie*) (Undset) **WLC 6:**3735, 3739-40
Fruen fra havet (*The Lady from the Sea*) (Ibsen) **WLC 3:**1779, 1782, 1790, 1792
"Fruit of the Flower" (Cullen) **WLCS 1:**273
The Fruit of the Tree (Wharton) WLC 6:3907
"The Fruitful Sleeping of the Rev. Elisha Edwards" (Dunbar) **WLC 2:**1106
The Fruits of the Earth (Gide)
See *Les nourritures terrestres*
Il fu Mattia Pascal (*The Late Mattia Pascal*) (Pirandello) **WLC 4:**2718, 2722, 2724, 2726, 2731
"La fuerza de la sangre" ("The Call of Blood"; "The Force of Blood") (Cervantes) **WLC 2:**679
"Full Fathom Five" (Plath) **WLC 4:**2740
Full Powers (Neruda)
See *Plenos poderes*
"The Function of Criticism at the Present Time" (Arnold) **WLC 1:**96
"Funeral Rites" (Heaney) **WLCS 1:**391
"Funeral" (Arnold) **WLC 1:**93
"Los funerales de la Mamá Grande" ("Big Mama's Funeral") (Garcia Marquez) **WLC 3:**1366
Funk Lore (Baraka) **WLCS 1:**154
"Funk" (Service) **WLC 5:**3122
Fuori di chiave (*False Notes*) (Pirandello) **WLC 4:**2731
Furcht und Elend des dritten Reiches (*Fear and Misery of the Third Reich*) (Brecht) **WLC 1:**390
"The Furies" (Sexton) **WLC 5:**3144, 3146-47
"The Furnished Room" (Henry) **WLC 3:**1670, 1675
De Futilitate (Lewis) **WLC 4:**2089
"Futility" (Owen) **WLC 4:**2608, 2616-17
The Future Is in Eggs (Ionesco)
See *l'Avenir est dans les oeufs*
The Gadsbys (Kipling) **WLC 3:**2011
Gahagan (Thackeray) **WLC 6:**3595
"Galahad: King Arthur's Men Have Come Again" (Lindsay) **WLC 4:**2128
La Galatea (Cervantes) **WLC 2:**681
Galileo (Brecht)
See *Leben des Galilei*
El gallardo español (Cervantes) **WLC 2:**682
"The Gallery" (Marvell) **WLC 4:**2258
The Gambler (Dostoevsky) **WLC 2:**975
The Game (London) **WLC 4:**2138
"The Game of Chess" (Borges) **WLC 1:**335
"Gamlet i Don Kikhot" ("Hamlet and Don Quixote") (Turgenev) **WLC 6:**3707, 3709
The Garbage Man (Dos Passos)
See *The Moon Is a Gong*
"Garden Abstract" (Crane) **WLC 2:**799
A Garden of Earthly Delights (Oates) **WLC 4:**2523, 2531, 2535
"The Garden of Eden" (Andersen) **WLC 1:**66
"Garden of Paradise" (Andersen) **WLC 1:**60
"The Garden of the Forking Paths" (Borges)
See "El jardín de senderos que se bifurcan"
"Garden Paradise" (Andersen) **WLC 1:**60
The Garden Party, and Other Stories (Mansfield) **WLC 4:**2212
"The Garden Party" (Mansfield) **WLC 4:**2213, 2215, 2219, 2224-26
"Garden State" (Ginsberg) **WLC 3:**1404
"Garden" ("Heat") (H. D.) **WLC 3:**1623
"The Garden" (Marvell) **WLC 4:**2258-59, 2264-66
"The Gardener" (Kipling) **WLC 3:**2022
Gargantua (Rabelais) **WLC 5:**2860, 2869, 2872
The Gates of the Forest (Wiesel) **WLCS 2:**848
The Gates of Wrath: Rhymed Poems, 1948-1952 (Ginsberg) **WLC 3:**1393-95
Gather Together In My Name (Angelou) **WLCS 1:**58, 62, 64, 67-68
"Gathering of Shields" (Momaday) **WLCS 2:**635
The Gavriiliada (Pushkin)
See *Gavriiliada*
Gavriiliada (*The Gavriiliada*) (Pushkin) **WLC 5:**2833
"Gay Chaps at the Bar" (Brooks) **WLC 1:**451
"La géante" ("The Giantess") (Baudelaire) **WLC 1:**201
"Gehazi" (Kipling) **WLC 3:**2017
Gemini: An Extended Autobiographical Statement on My First Twenty-five Years of Being a Black Poet (Giovanni) **WLCS 1:**353, 355-56, 359
"Gemini--A Prolonged Autobiographical Statement on Why" (Giovanni) **WLCS 1:**354
"General Prologue" (Chaucer) **WLCS 1:**223-26, 228, 231
General Song (Neruda)
See *Canto general de Chile*
General William Booth Enters into Heaven, and Other Poems (Lindsay) **WLC 4:**2117
"General William Booth Enters into Heaven" (Lindsay) **WLC 4:**2119, 2125
De Generatione Animalium (Aristotle) **WLCS 1:**97, 101
"The Generous Lover" (Cervantes)
See "El amante liberal"
"The Genesis of Spoon River" (Masters) **WLCS 2:**582
"Genesis" (Swinburne) **WLC 6:**3563
Geneviéve (Gide) **WLC 3:**1384
Gengangere (*Ghosts*) (Ibsen) **WLC 3:**1777, 1780-81, 1785, 1788, 1791
The "Genius" (Dreiser) **WLC 2:**1024, 1026-27, 1029, 1032, 1036-38
The Genius and the Goddess (Huxley) **WLC 3:**1771
The Genteel Style in Writing (Lamb) **WLC 3:**2032
"Gentilesse" (Chaucer) **WLCS 1:**224
"The Gentle Boy" (Hawthorne) **WLC 3:**1600
The Gentle Grafter (Henry) **WLC 3:**1675
"The Gentleman from Cracow" (Singer) **WLC 5:**3291, 3293
"The Geometry of Love" (Cheever) **WLC 2:**697
George Dandin; or, The Baffled Husband (Moliere)
See *George Dandin; ou, Le mari confondu*
George Dandin; ou, Le mari confondu (*George Dandin; or, The Baffled Husband*) (Moliere) **WLC 4:**2436-38, 2445
George's Mother (Crane) **WLC 2:**814
Georges (Dumas) **WLC 2:**1089
Georgics (Vergil) **WLCS 2:**810-11, 813-14
Germinal (Zola) **WLC 6:**4118-19, 4122-23, 4125-30
"Gerontion" (Eliot) **WLC 2:**1147-48, 1150
"Gethsemane" (Kipling) **WLC 3:**2017

Getting Married (Strindberg) **WLC 6**:3535, 3536
"Getting There" (Plath) **WLC 4**:2747-48
The Ghost Sonata (Strindberg)
  See *Spöksonaten*
The Ghost Writer (Roth) **WLC 5**:2975
Ghosts (Ibsen)
  See *Gengangere*
"The Ghosts of the Buffaloes" (Lindsay) **WLC 4**:2121
"The Giantess" (Baudelaire)
  See "La géante"
Giaour (Byron) **WLC 1**:569-70, 572
Gideon Planish (Lewis) **WLC 4**:2108
The Gift (H. D.) **WLC 3**:1624
The Gift (Nabokov)
  See *Dar*
The Gift of Black Folk (Du Bois) **WLC 2**:1064
"The Gift of the Magi" (Henry) **WLC 3**:1675, 1677
"The Gift Outright" (Frost) **WLC 2**:1297
"Gift" (Milosz) **WLCS 2**:620
"The Gifts of Iban" (Steinbeck) **WLC 5**:3387
"Gifts of Rain" (Heaney) **WLCS 1**:389
The Gilded Age (Twain) **WLC 6**:3715, 3720-21
"The Gilded Six-Bits" (Hurston) **WLCS 1**:449-51
"Giles Corey of the Salem Farms" (Longfellow) **WLCS 2**:513-14, 516
"Gimpel Tam" ("Gimpel the Fool") (Singer) **WLC 6**:3290, 3292-93
"Gimpel the Fool" (Singer)
  See "Gimpel Tam"
The Gioconda Smile (Huxley) **WLC 3**:1771
Gipsies (Pushkin)
  See *Tsygany*
Gipsy Ballads (Lorca)
  See *Primer romancero gitano*
"The Girl of My Dreams" (Malamud) **WLC 4**:2190
"The Girl Who Trod on the Loaf" (Andersen) **WLC 1**:62
"Girl" (Henry) **WLC 3**:1677
"Giulia Lazzari" (Maugham) **WLC 4**:2277
I giuoco delle parti (*Each in His Role; Each of Us His Own Part*) (Pirandello) **WLC 4**:2719, 2729
"Giuseppe Caponsacchi" (Browning) **WLCS 1**:201
"Give All to Love" (Emerson) **WLC 2**:1171
"Give Your Heart to the Hawks" (Jeffers) **WLC 3**:1876
"Give" (Frank) **WLC 2**:1283
"Giving Birth" (Atwood) **WLC 1**:114, 118
"Giving Blood" (Updike) **WLC 6**:3760
Das Glasperlenspiel (*The Glass Bead Game; Magister Ludi*) (Hesse) **WLC 3**:1692-97, 1699
The Glass Bead Game (Hesse)
  See *Das Glasperlenspiel*
The Glass Menagerie (Williams) **WLC 6**:3989-93, 3995-97, 4000, 4004-06
"The Glass Scholar" (Cervantes)
  See "El licienciado vidriera"
Gleisdreieck (*Triangle Junction*) (Grass) **WLC 3**:1506
"Glenfinlas" (Scott) **WLC 5**:3114

"Glittering Pie" (Miller) **WLC 4**:2391
The Gnädiges Fräulein (*The Mutilated; Slapstick Tragedy*) (Williams) **WLC 6**:3996, 3998
"Go Down, Moses" (Faulkner) **WLC 2**:1192, 1194, 1197-98
"The Goblet of Life" (Longfellow) **WLCS 2**:504
"Goblin Market" (Rossetti) **WLC 5**:2929, 2932, 2941
God and the Bible: A Review of Objections to "Literature and Dogma" (Arnold) **WLC 1**:92
God Bless You, Mr. Rosewater; or, Pearls before Swine (Vonnegut) **WLC 6**:3786, 3797
"God Is Good—It Is a Beautiful Night" (Stevens) **WLC 5**:3431, 3439
The God of His Fathers (London) **WLC 4**:2135, 2141-42
"The God of His Fathers" (London) **WLC 4**:2135
"God Rest You Merry, Gentlemen" (Hemingway) **WLC 3**:1650
"God Send the Regicide" (Lindsay) **WLC 4**:2121
"God's Battle-Ground" (Service) **WLC 5**:3131
God's Grace (Malamud) **WLC 4**:2190
"God's Grandeur" (Hopkins) **WLC 3**:1713-14
"The God's Script" (Borges)
  See "La escritura del Dios"
"God's Skallywags" (Service) **WLC 5**:3131
"God's World" (Millay) **WLCS 2**:594
The Goddess and Other Women (Oates) **WLC 4**:2531
"Godliness" (Anderson) **WLC 1**:84-5
The Gods Arrive (Wharton) **WLC 6**:3908, 3911
Goethe's Works (Goethe) **WLC 3**:1412
Gogo no eiko (*The Sailor Who Fell from Grace with the Sea*) (Mishima) **WLC 4**:2426
"The Going Away of Liza" (Chopin) **WLCS 1**:240
Going Home (Lessing) **WLCS 2**:493
"Going Home" (Service) **WLC 5**:3122
Going to Meet the Man (Baldwin) **WLC 1**:174
Going to the Territory (Ellison) **WLC 2**:1165
"The Gold Bug" (Poe) **WLC 4**:2755, 2760-61
"The Gold of Tomas Vargas" (Allende) **WLCS 1**:46
The Golden Apples of the Sun (Bradbury) **WLC 1**:366
"The Golden Apples" (Welty) **WLC 6**:3885, 3889, 3893
The Golden Ass (Machiavelli) **WLCS 2**:533
The Golden Book of Springfield (Lindsay) **WLC 4**:2117, 2125, 2129, 2131
The Golden Bowl (James) **WLC 3**:1859, 1864, 1866
"The Golden Echo" (Hopkins) **WLC 3**:1704
"A Golden-Haired Girl in a Louisiana Town" (Lindsay) **WLC 4**:2127
The Golden Legend (Longfellow) **WLCS**

2:514, 516
The Golden Notebook (Lessing) **WLCS 2**:488, 492-96, 498
"The Golden Whales of California" (Lindsay) **WLC 4**:2122, 2124
"The Golem" (Borges) **WLC 1**:335
"Goliath of Gath. 1 Sam. Chap. XVII" (Wheatley) **WLC 6**:3918-19, 3928
"Gone" (Sandburg) **WLC 5**:3066
"Good-bye to the Mezzogiorno" (Auden) **WLC 1**:131
The Good Conscience (Fuentes)
  See *Las buenas consciencias*
"Good Country People" (O'Connor) **WLC 4**:2543
"Good Frend" (H. D.) **WLC 3**:1616
"Good Friday" (Donne)
  See "Goodfriday 1613: Riding Westward"
"Good Humor" (Andersen) **WLC 1**:60
"A Good Man Is Hard to Find" (O'Connor) **WLC 4**:2543, 2549-50
The Good Natur'd Man (Goldsmith) **WLC 3**:1477-78
The Good Terrorist (Lessing) **WLCS 2**:495, 497
The Good Woman of Setzuan (Brecht)
  See *Der gute Mensch von Sezuan*
Goodbye, Columbus (Roth) **WLC 5**:2962-63, 2965-66, 2969-71, 2974
"Goodbye, My Brother" (Cheever) **WLC 2**:695
"Goodfriday 1613: Riding Westward" ("Good Friday") (Donne) **WLC 2**:937, 948
Gorgias (Plato) **WLCS 2**:731
Gorilla, My Love (Bambara) **WLCS 1**:126
"Gorilla, My Love" (Bambara) **WLCS 1**:128
"The Gourd Dancer" (Momaday) **WLCS 2**:635
Grace Abounding to the Chief of Sinners (Bunyan) **WLC 1**:484, 488, 491-94
"Grace" (Joyce) **WLC 3**:1931
Graf Nulin (*Count Nulin*) (Pushkin) **WLC 5**:2832-33
The Grafting (Pirandello)
  See *L'innesto*
La gran sultana (Cervantes) **WLC 2**:682
Le grand écart (Cocteau) **WLC 2**:725-26, 734, 736
The Grand Design (Dos Passos) **WLC 2**:966
"The Grand Inquisitor" (Dostoevsky)
  See "The Legend of the Grand Inquisitor"
"Grand River Marshes" (Masters) **WLCS 2**:578
"Grandfather Arthur Winslow" (Lowell) **WLC 4**:2152
"Grandparents" (Lowell) **WLC 4**:2161-64
"Granite and Steel" (Moore) **WLCS 2**:650
"Grantchester" (Brooke) **WLC 1**:434, 435, 437
The Grapes and the Wind (Neruda)
  See *Las uvas y el viento*
The Grapes of Wrath (Steinbeck) **WLC 5**:3375, 3377-79, 3381, 3383, 3386-88
The Grass Harp (Capote) **WLC 1**:618-20, 622, 624, 628-30
The Grass Is Singing (Lessing) **WLCS 2**:488, 492, 494, 497
"The Grave of the Famous Poet" (Atwood) **WLC 1**:114-16

Gravity's Rainbow (Pynchon) **WLC 5:**2843-52
The Great American Novel (Williams) **WLC 6:**4015
"The Great American Novel" (Wharton) **WLC 6:**3908
"The Great Carbuncle" (Hawthorne) **WLC 3:**1594
The Great Days (Dos Passos) **WLC 2:**962, 965
The Great Divorce (Lewis) **WLC 4:**2086, 2091
Great Expectations (Dickens) **WLC 2:**897, 899, 901, 904, 906, 909, 912
"The Great Fillmore Street Buffalo Drive" (Momaday) **WLCS 2:**635
The Great Gatsby (Fitzgerald) **WLC 2:**1223-24, 1226, 1228-29, 1231-32
The Great God Brown (O'Neill) **WLC 4:**2560
Great Goodness of Life (Baraka) **WLCS 1:**152
The Great Highway (Strindberg)
 See *Stora landsvägen*
The Great Hoggarty Diamond (*The History of Samuel Titmarsh and the Great Hoggarty Diamond*) (Thackeray) **WLC 6:**3592, 3594-95
"The Great Interrogation" (London) **WLC 4:**2136, 2141
"The Great Keinplatz Experiment" (Doyle) **WLC 2:**1018
"The Great Lover" (Brooke) **WLC 1:**435-39, 444
"A Great Sorrow" (Andersen) **WLC 1:**58, 60
The Great Valley (Masters) **WLCS 2:**577
The Great Wall of China, and Other Pieces (Kafka)
 See *Beim Bau der Chinesischen Mauer*
The Great Wall of China: Stories and Reflections (Kafka)
 See *Beim Bau der Chinesischen Mauer*
"Greater Love" (Owen) **WLC 4:**2606, 2609, 2611, 2618
The Grecian History, from the Earliest State to the Death of Alexander the Great (Goldsmith) **WLC 3:**1467
"The Green Door" (Henry) **WLC 3:**1667
"Green Grow the Rashes O" (Burns) **WLC 1:**518
The Green Helmet (Yeats) **WLC 6:**4099
The Green Hills of Africa (Hemingway) **WLC 3:**1652, 1659
"Greenleaf" (O'Connor) **WLC 4:**2542
Grey Eminence (Huxley) **WLC 3:**1768
A Grief Observed (Lewis) **WLC 4:**2087
Grimus (Rushdie) **WLCS 2:**744
El gringo viejo (*The Old Gringo*) (Fuentes) **WLC 2:**1319-20, 1322-23
The Ground We Stand On (Dos Passos) **WLC 2:**955
Group Portrait with Lady (Boell)
 See *Gruppenbild mit Dame*
Gruppenbild mit Dame (*Group Portrait with Lady*) (Boell) **WLC 1:**327-28
The Guermantes Way (Proust)
 See *Le côté des Guermantes*
Guermantes' Way (Proust)
 See *Le côté des Guermantes*
"Guerre" (Rimbaud) **WLC 5:**2919
The Guest (Pushkin) **WLC 5:**2827

A Guest of Honour (Gordimer) **WLCS 1:**371, 375, 377, 380
"Guests from Gibbet Island" (Irving) **WLC 3:**1820
"Guests on a Winter Night" (Singer) **WLC 5:**3295
"Guid Mornin' to your Majesty" (Burns) **WLC 1:**517
"Guinevere" (Tennyson) **WLC 6:**3584
The Gulag Archipelago, 1918-1956: An Experiment in Literary Investigation (Solzhenitsyn)
 See *Arkhipelag GULag, 1918-1956: Op' bit khudozhestvennopo issledovaniia*
Gulliver's Travels (Swift) **WLC 6:**3535-43, 3546-47
A Gun for Sale (*This Gun for Hire*) (Greene) **WLC 3:**1542, 1545-46
Gunnar's Daughter (Undset)
 See *Fortaellingen om Viga-Ljot og Vigdis*
Der gute Mensch von Sezuan (*The Good Woman of Setzuan*) (Brecht) **WLC 1:**383, 389, 390-91
Guy Mannering (Scott) **WLC 5:**3108, 3110
Gymnadenia (*The Wild Orchid*) (Undset) **WLC 6:**3738, 3741-42
The Gypsies (Pushkin)
 See *Tsygany*
Gypsy Balladeer (Garcia Lorca)
 See *Primer romancero gitano*
Gypsy Ballads (Garcia Lorca)
 See *Primer romancero gitano*
"Ha'penny" (Paton) **WLC 4:**2650
"Habakuk Jephson's Statement" (Doyle) **WLC 2:**1017
"An Habitation Enforced" (Kipling) **WLC 3:**2014
"Habits" (Giovanni) **WLCS 1:**364
"Hablar y decir" (Paz) **WLC 4:**2673
El hacedor (*Dreamtigers*; *The Maker*) (Borges) **WLC 1:**338-39
"Hadjii murád" (Tolstoy)
 See "Khadzi murat"
"The Hag" (Turgenev) **WLC 6:**3707
"Hair Jewellery" (Atwood) **WLC 1:**114-16
"The Hairless Mexican" (Maugham) **WLC 4:**2281
The Hairy Ape (O'Neill) **WLC 4:**2559-60, 2563, 2569
"Haïta the Shepherd" (Bierce) **WLC 1:**288
"Halberdier of the Little Rheinschloss" (Henry) **WLC 3:**1675
The Half-Brothers; or, The Head and the Hand (Dumas)
 See *Le bâtard de Mauléon*
Hall of Healing (O'Casey) **WLCS 2:**717
"Hallowe'en" (Burns) **WLC 1:**518-19
"Hamatreya" (Emerson) **WLC 2:**1171
The Hamlet (Faulkner) **WLC 2:**1194, 1196-98
Hamlet (Shakespeare) **WLC 5:**3157-58, 3174
"Hamlet and Don Quixote" (Turgenev)
 See "Gamlet i Don Kikhot'"
"The Hand" (Service) **WLC 5:**3131
The Hand of Ethelberta (Hardy) **WLC 3:**1568
A Handful of Dust (Waugh) **WLC 6:**3821, 3824, 3826-27, 3830
The Handmaid's Tale (Atwood) **WLC 1:**120-22

"Hands" (Anderson) **WLC 1:**77-8, 81, 84-5
"The Handsomest Drowned Man in the World: A Tale for Children" (Garcia Marquez)
 See "El ahogado más hermoso del mundo"
Hangsaman (Jackson) **WLC 3:**1838-39, 1841-43, 1850
Hapgood (Stoppard) **WLC 5:**3493-95 **WLC 91:**171, 173, 174
"Happier Dead" (Baudelaire)
 See "Le mort joyeux"
"Happiness in Herat" (Paz) **WLC 4:**2674
"Happiness" (Chekhov) **WLC 2:**708-09
"Happiness" (Sandburg) **WLC 5:**3036
The Happy Age (Undset)
 See *Den lykkelige alder*
"Happy Birthday" (Bambara) **WLCS 1:**128
Happy Days (Beckett) **WLC 1:**233
"The Happy Family" (Andersen) **WLC 1:**63, 65
The Happy Journey to Trenton and Camden (Wilder) **WLC 6:**3971
"The Happy Prince" (Wilde) **WLC 6:**3952
"A Harbinger" (Chopin) **WLCS 1:**239
"Hard Candy" (Williams) **WLC 6:**4002-03
"Hard Luck" (Hughes) **WLC 3:**1723
Hard Times for These Times (Dickens) **WLC 2:**907-09, 911
"Hard Times" (McKay) **WLC 4:**2328
"The Hardy Tin Soldier" (Andersen)
 See "The Steadfast Tin Soldier"
"The Harlem Dancer" (McKay) **WLC 4:**2332-33
Harlem Shadows (McKay) **WLC 4:**2326, 2332-33, 2335
"Harlem Shadows" (McKay) **WLC 4:**2332
"The Harlot's House" (Wilde) **WLC 6:**3952, 3965
"Harmonie du soir" (Baudelaire) **WLC 1:**207
Harmonium (Stevens) **WLC 5:**3432, 3436
Harold (Tennyson) **WLC 6:**3573-75
Haroun and the Sea of Stories (Rushdie) **WLCS 2:**748, 753
"The Harp of Joy" (Mishima)
 See *Yorokobi no Koto*
"The Harp Song of the Dane Women" (Kipling) **WLC 3:**2017
The Harp-Weaver, and Other Poems (Millay) **WLCS 2:**599-601
"The Harp-Weaver" (Millay) **WLCS 2:**590, 603
Harper of Heaven (Service) **WLC 5:**3130
"Harriet Waage" (Undset) **WLC 6:**3740
"The Harvest Bow" (Heaney) **WLCS 1:**394
"Has Your Soul Sipped" (Owen) **WLC 4:**2608
The Haunch of Venison, a Poetical Epistle to Lord Clare (Goldsmith) **WLC 3:**1476
The Haunted (O'Neill) **WLC 4:**2561
The Haunted Marsh (Sand)
 See *La mare au diable*
"The Haunted Mind" (Hawthorne) **WLC 3:**1594
"The Haunted Oak" (Dunbar) **WLC 2:**1109, 1114

The Haunted Pool (Sand)
See *La mare au diable*
The Haunting of Hill House (Jackson) **WLC 3:**1838-39, 1843, 1850-51
Haus ohne Hüter (*Tomorrow and Yesterday; The Unguarded House*) (Boell) **WLC 1:**316, 319-24
Die Hauspostille (*A Manual of Piety*) (Brecht) **WLC 1:**386
"Hautot père et fils" (Maupassant) **WLC 4:**2300
"Have You Ever Made a Just Man?" (Crane) **WLC 2:**817
"Haworth Churchyard" (Arnold) **WLC 1:**104
"Hawthorne" (Lowell) **WLC 4:**2159
"The Hayswater Boat" (Arnold) **WLC 1:**102
"A Hazel Stick for Catherine Ann" (Heaney) **WLCS 1:**396
"He Also Serves" (Henry) **WLC 3:**1667
"He Appears" (Atwood) **WLC 1:**112
"He Is a Strange Biological Phenomenon" (Atwood) **WLC 1:**112
"He Is Last Seen" (Atwood) **WLC 1:**112
He Knew He was Right (Trollope) **6;**3688, 3693
"He Never Expected Much" (Hardy) **WLC 3:**1570
"He Sings the Epistle" (Pirandello)
See "Canta l'epistola"
"He-Who-Intones-the-Epistle" (Pirandello)
See "Canta l'epistola"
"The Headless Hawk" (Capote) **WLC 1:**618
The Heart Is a Lonely Hunter (McCullers) **WLC 4:**2307, 2309-16, 2319
The Heart of a Woman (Angelou) **WLCS 1:**58-62, 64, 67
"Heart of Autumn" (Warren) **WLC 6:**3814
Heart of Darkness (Conrad) **WLC 2:**780, 782-85, 787-88, 791-92
The Heart of Happy Hollow (Dunbar) **WLC 2:**1101-02, 1104-05, 1107
The Heart of Mid-Lothian (Scott) **WLC 5:**3108-09, 3112, 3115
"The Heart of Sourdough" (Service) **WLC 5:**3123
The Heart of the Matter (Greene) **WLC 3:**1537-43, 1545, 1547-48, 1550, 1552-54
The Heart of the West (Henry) **WLC 3:**1669, 1677
Heartbreak House (Shaw) **WLC 5:**3191-94
"Hearts and Crosses" (Henry) **WLC 3:**1675
"Heat" (H. D.)
See "Garden"
"Heathen Chinee" (Harte)
See "Plain Language from Truthful James"
"L'héautontimorouménos" (Baudelaire) **WLC 1:**202
Heaven and Earth (Byron) **WLC 1:**575
Heaven and Hell (Huxley) **WLC 3:**1766-67, 1769
"Heaven" (Brooke) **WLC 1:**435, 437, 439, 443-4
Heaven's My Destination (Wilder) **WLC 6:**3983-84
Hebrew Melodies (Byron) **WLC 1:**574

Hebrides Journal (Boswell)
See *Journal of a Tour to the Hebrides with Samuel Johnson, LL. D.*
Hecuba (Euripides) **WLCS 1:**291-92, 294-95, 300
Hedda Gabler (Ibsen) **WLC 3:**1779, 1781, 1784-85, 1791
Hedylus (H. D.) **WLC 3:**1623
The Heights of Macchu Picchu (Neruda)
See *Alturas de Macchu Picchu*
Die heilige Johanna der Schlachthöfe (*St. Joan of the Stockyards*) (Brecht) **WLC 1:**390-91
"Heine's Grave" (Arnold) **WLC 1:**104
"The Heir of the McHulishes" (Harte) **WLC 3:**1584
Helen (Euripides) **WLCS 1:**293, 296
Helen in Egypt (H. D.) **WLC 3:**1616-18, 1621-22, 1624
Helena (Waugh) **WLC 6:**3828, 3830
"Helena" (Capek) **WLC 1:**601
Heliodora, and Other Poems (H. D.) **WLC 3:**1612
"Hell Gate" (Housman) **WLCS 1:**429
Hellas (Shelley) **WLC 5:**3234
Hello Out There (Saroyan) **WLC 5:**3072, 3080
"Hendecasyllables" (Coleridge) **WLC 2:**744
Henderson the Rain King (Bellow) **WLC 1:**264-65, 269, 271, 275
"Henne Fire" (Singer) **WLC 5:**3290
Henri III et sa cour (Dumas) **WLC 2:**1090
La henriade (Voltaire) **WLC 6:**3769, 3772, 3779
Henry Esmond (Thackeray)
See *The History of Henry Esmond, Esq., a Colonel in the Service of Her Majesty Q. Anne*
Henry IV (Pirandello)
See *Enrico IV*
Henry IV Parts 1 and 2 (Shakespeare) **WLC 5:**3158-59, 3162, 3168-69, 3173, 3176-77
"Henry Tripp" (Masters) **WLCS 2:**579
Henry V (Shakespeare) **WLC 5:**3169, 3175
Her (H. D.)
See *HERmione*
"Her First Ball" (Mansfield) **WLC 4:**2219
"Her Kind" (Sexton) **WLC 5:**3141, 3144, 3149
"Her Lover" (Gorky)
See "Boles"
"Her Son" (Wharton) **WLC 6:**3905
"Her Sweet Jerome" (Walker) **WLCS 2:**837
Heracles (Euripides)
See *Heracles Mad*
Heracles Mad (Euripides) **WLCS 1:**291, 294, 296, 299-300
"Hercules and Antaeus" (Heaney) **WLCS 1:**391
Here and Beyond (Wharton) **WLC 6:**3904
"Here Comes the Maples" (Updike) **WLC 6:**3761
"Here's to the Mice" (Lindsay) **WLC 4:**2121
"The Heritage of Dedlow Marsh" (Harte) **WLC 3:**1590
"Heritage" (Cullen) **WLCS 1:**274-76, 281-

83, 285
"L'héritage" (Maupassant) **WLC 4:**2291, 2293-94, 2303
"Hermaphroditus" (Swinburne) **WLC 6:**3559, 3566
"Hermetic Definition" (H. D.) **WLC 3:**1618-19, 1624
HERmione (*Her*) (H. D.) **WLC 3:**1620, 1622, 1625
The Hermit and the Wild Woman (Wharton) **WLC 6:**3903
Hero and Leander (Marlowe) **WLC 4:**2239
"The Hero" (Moore) **WLCS 2:**651
The Heroic Slave (Douglass) **WLC 2:**1000, 1001
Herr Puntila and His Servant Matti (Brecht)
See *Herr Puntila und sein Knecht Matti*
Herr Puntila und sein Knecht Matti (*Herr Puntila and His Servant Matti; Puntila*) (Brecht) **WLC 1:**390, 392
"Hertha" (Swinburne) **WLC 6:**3563
Herzog (Bellow) **WLC 1:**265, 269, 271-74, 276
"The Hiding of Black Bill" (Henry) **WLC 3:**1671
High Time along the Wabash (Saroyan) **WLC 5:**3081
"The Higher Abdication" (Henry) **WLC 3:**1675
"Higher Laws" (Thoreau) **WLC 6:**3631
"The Higher Pragmatism" (Henry) **WLC 3:**1670
"Highland Mary" (Burns) **WLC 1:**518
"The Highland Reaper" (Wordsworth) **WLC 6:**4068
"The Highway" (Bradbury) **WLC 1:**367
Los hijos del limo: Del romanticismo a la vanguardia (*Children of the Mire: Modern Poetry from Romanticism to the Avant-Garde*) (Paz) **WLC 4:**2672
"The Hill and Grove at Bill-Borrow" (Marvell)
See "Upon the Hill and Grove at Billborow"
"The Hill" (Brooke) **WLC 1:**434, 437
"The Hill" (Masters) **WLCS 2:**579, 582
"Hills Like White Elephants" (Hemingway) **WLC 3:**1651
"Himno entre ruinas" ("Hymn among the Ruins") (Paz) **WLC 4:**2659, 2661
The Hind and the Panther (Dryden) **WLC 2:**1046, 1052, 1056, 1058
Hints from Horace (Byron) **WLC 1:**579
Hippolytus (Euripides) **WLCS 1:**291, 293, 296, 298-300, 302
Hippolytus Temporizes (H. D.) **WLC 3:**1624
"The Hippopotamus" (Eliot) **WLC 2:**1147
"Hiram Powers' Greek Slave" (Browning) **WLC 1:**468
"His Father's Son" (Wharton) **WLC 6:**3904
His Last Bow: Some Reminiscences of Sherlock Holmes (Doyle) **WLC 2:**1018
"His Last Bow: The War Service of Sherlock Holmes" (Doyle) **WLC 2:**1018
"L'histoire d'une fille de ferme" (Maupassant) **WLC 4:**2291, 2293
L'histoire de Jenni (Voltaire) **WLC**

TITLE INDEX

6:3776, 3780, 3782
Histoire de la grandeur et de la décadence de César Birotteau, parfumeur (*History of the Grandeur and Downfall of César Birotteau*) (Balzac) **WLC 1:**182
Histoire de ma vie (*My Life*; *The Story of My Life*) (Sand) **WLC 5:**3044, 3047
"A Historical Footnote to Consider Only When All Else Fails" (Giovanni) **WLCS 1:**359
History (Lowell) **WLC 4:**2168-69
History of a Foundling (Fielding)
See *The History of Tom Jones, a Foundling*
History of English Literature in the Sixteenth Century (Lewis) **WLC 4:**2090
The History of Henry Esmond, Esq., a Colonel in the Service of Her Majesty Q. Anne (*Henry Esmond*) (Thackeray) **WLC 6:**3592, 2597-98
The History of Jonathan Wild the Great (Fielding)
See *The Life of Mr. Jonathan Wild the Great*
The History of Joseph Andrews (*Joseph Andrews*) (Fielding) **WLC 2:**1204, 1206-08, 1210-11, 1214-17
"The History of Lieutenant Ergunov" (Turgenev)
See "Istoriya leytenanta Ergunova"
The History of Mr. Polly (Wells) **WLC 6:**3879
History of New York (*Knickerbocker's History*) (Irving) **WLC 3:**1822-24, 1827-28
A History of New York, from the Beginning of the World to the End of the Dutch Dynasty (Irving) **WLC 3:**1822-24, 1827-28
The History of Pendennis: His Fortunes and Misfortunes, His Friends and His Greatest Enemy (*Pendennis*) (Thackeray) **WLC 6:**3592, 3596-98, 3601-02
History of Peter I (Pushkin)
See *The History of Peter the Great*
The History of Peter the Great (*History of Peter I*) (Pushkin) **WLC 5:**2830
The History of Polish Literature (Milosz) **WLCS 2:**610
The History of Samuel Titmarsh and the Great Hoggarty Diamond (Thackeray)
See *The Great Hoggarty Diamond*
The History of Sir Charles Grandison (*Sir Charles Grandison*) (Richardson) **WLC 5:**2894-97, 2903
History of the Devil (Defoe) **WLC 2:**874
History of the Grandeur and Downfall of César Birotteau (Balzac)
See *Histoire de la grandeur et de la décadence de César Birotteau, parfumeur*
A History of the Life and Voyages of Christopher Columbus (Irving) **WLC 3:**1827
History of the Manor of Goryukhino (Pushkin) **WLC 5:**2828-29
The History of the Most Remarkable Life and Extraordinary Adventures of the Truly Honourable Colonel Jacque,

Vulgarly Called Colonel Jack (*Colonel Jack*) (Defoe) **WLC 2:**867, 871-72
The History of the Nun; or, The Fair Vow-Breaker (*The Fair Vow-Breaker*) (Behn) **WLC 1:**250
A History of the Plague (Defoe)
See *A Journal of the Plague Year*
The History of the Pugachev Rebellion (Pushkin) **WLC 5:**2830
The History of Tom Jones, a Foundling (*History of a Foundling*; *Tom Jones*) (Fielding) **WLC 2:**1206-10, 1212-13
"The Hitch-Hikers" (Welty) **WLC 6:**3880, 3882
"Hitherto Uncollected" (Moore) **WLCS 2:**651
The Hobbit; or, There and Back Again (Tolkien) **WLC 6:**3645-46, 3651, 3654, 3658
"Hod Putt" (Master) **WLCS 2:**579, 582
La hojarasca (*Dead Leaves*; *Leaf Storm*) (Garcia Marquez) **WLC 3:**1363, 1365-68, 1370
H j no umi (*The Sea of Fertility: A Cycle of Novels*) (Mishima) **WLC 4:**2427
The Hollow Men (Eliot) **WLC 2:**1147
"Holly" (Heaney) **WLCS 1:**399
The Holy City; or, The New Jerusalem (Bunyan) **WLC 1:**486, 488
"Holy Cross Day" (Browning) **WLCS 1:**211
"The Holy Fair" (Burns) **WLC 1:**517-19, 523-24, 528-29
"The Holy Grail" (Tennyson) **WLC 6:**3584
Holy Place (Fuentes)
See *Zona sagrada*
Holy Sonnets (Donne) **WLC 2:**940
"Holy Spring" (Thomas) **WLC 6:**3612, 3619
The Holy Terrors (Cocteau)
See *Les enfants terribles*
The Holy War (Bunyan) **WLC 1:**483-84, 486, 488
"Holy Willie's Prayer" (Burns) **WLC 1:**517, 518, 523
Homage to Catalonia (Orwell) **WLC 4:**2576, 2579, 2582-83, 2586-87
Homage to Clio (Auden) **WLC 1:**131
"Homage to Duke Ellington on His Birthday" (Ellison) **WLC 2:**1166
"Homage to Emerson, on Night Flight to New York" (Warren) **WLC 6:**3816
"Homage to Sextus Propertius" (Pound) **WLC 5:**2797-2801
Home (Baraka) **WLCS 1:**141, 148, 151-52
Home After Three Months Away (Lowell) **WLC 4:**2156, 2165
"The Home-Coming of 'Rastus Smith" (Dunbar) **WLC 2:**1107
"Home-Sickness...from the Town" (Huxley) **WLC 3:**1761-62
"Home-Thoughts" (McKay) **WLC 4:**2334, 2337
Home to Harlem (McKay) **WLC 4:**2324-27
Homecoming (O'Neill) **WLC 4:**2561
The Homecoming (Pinter) **WLC 5:**2697-99, 2703-04, 2706, 2709
"Homenaje y profanaciones" (Paz) **WLC 4:**2661, 2663
"Hometown Piece for Messers Alston and

Reese" (Moore) **WLCS 2:**648, 650
L'homme aux quarante écus (*The Man with Forty Ecus*) (Voltaire) **WLC 6:**3769, 3776, 3780
"L'homme juste" ("The Just Man") (Rimbaud) **WLC 5:**2920
L'homme qui rit (*The Man Who Laughs*) (Hugo) **WLC 3:**1742-43, 1745
L'homme révolté (*The Rebel*) (Camus) **WLC 1:**595
The Honorary Consul (Greene) **WLC 3:**1550
"Honoria" (Dryden)
See *Theodore and Honoria*
An Honoured Guest (Gordimer)
See *A Guest of Honour*
A Hoosier Holiday (Dreiser) **WLC 2:**1029, 1037
Hopes and Impediments: Selected Essays (Achebe) **WLC 1:**14
"Horae Canonicae" (Auden) **WLC 1:**137
"An Horatian Ode upon Cromwell's Return from Ireland" ("Ode") (Marvell) **WLC 4:**2253, 2259, 2261, 2263-64
The Horatians and the Curiatians (Brecht) **WLC 1:**390
"The Horatians" (Auden) **WLC 1:**137
Hordubal (Capek) **WLC 1:**603, 605-06
"Le horla" (Maupassant) **WLC 4:**2293
"L'horreur sympathique" (Baudelaire) **WLC 1:**205
"The Horse-Stealers" (Chekhov) **WLC 2:**709
"The Horse that Died of Shame" (Momaday) **WLCS 2:**628
"A Horse's Name" (Chekhov) **WLC 2:**708
"A Horseman in the Sky" (Bierce) **WLC 1:**288
Horses and Men (Anderson) **WLC 1:**79-80
"Horses—One Dash" ("One Dash--Horses") (Crane) **WLC 2:**818, 824
"Hospital Barge at Cérisy" (Owen) **WLC 4:**2618
Hospital Sketches (Alcott) **WLC 1:**49-50
The Hot Gates, and Other Occasional Pieces (Golding) **WLC 3:**1455-56, 1458
The Hotel in Amsterdam (Osborne) 4;2598
The Hothouse (Pinter) **WLC 4:**2704, 2707
"The Hottest Coon in Dixie" (Dunbar) **WLC 2:**1111
The Hound of the Baskervilles (Doyle) **WLC 2:**1013, 1018-19
"The Hounds of Fate" (Saki) **WLC 5:**3001, 3005, 3007, 3009
"The Hour and the Ghost" (Rossetti) **WLC 5:**2937
"An Hour" (Milosz) **WLCS 2:**608
House Made of Dawn (Momaday) **WLCS 2:**623, 625-27, 629, 631-32, 634
A House Not Meant to Stand (Williams) **WLC 6:**4006-07
The House of Bernarda Alba (Garcia Lorca)
See *La casa de Bernarda Alba*
The House of Fame (Chaucer) **WLCS 1:**231-33
"House of Flowers" (Capote) **WLC 1:**618
A House of Gentlefolk (Turgenev)

See "Eaves-Dropping a Lodge of Free-Masons"
The House of Life" (Rossetti) **WLC 5:**2951-55, 2958
The House of Mirth (Wharton) **WLC 6:**3907, 3909-12
The House of the Seven Gables (Hawthorne) **WLC 3:**1595, 1598, 1601, 1607-08
The House of the Spirits (Allende) **WLCS 1:**40-46, 53
The House with a Mezzanine" (Chekhov) See "An Artist's Story"
The House with an Attic" (Chekhov) See "An Artist's Story"
The House with the Maisonette" (Chekhov) See "An Artist's Story"
House" (Browning) **WLCS 1:**208
The Housebreaker of Shady Hill (Cheever) **WLC 2:**690, 696
The Householder" (Browning) **WLCS 1:**208
How a Little Girl Danced" (Lindsay) **WLC 4:**2123
How Bozo the Button Buster Busted All His Buttons when a Mouse Came" (Sandburg) **WLC 5:**3066
How Brother Parker Fell from Grace" (Dunbar) **WLC 2:**1107
How He Lied to Her Husband (Shaw) **WLC 5:**3193
How I Contemplated the World from the Detroit House of Correction and Began My Life Over Again" (Oates) **WLC 4:**2536
How I Went to the Mines" (Harte) **WLC 3:**1585
How It Is (Beckett) See *Comment c'est*
How It Strikes a Contemporary" (Woolf) **WLC 6:**4048
How Lucy Backslid" (Dunbar) **WLC 2:**1112
How oft when thou, my music, music play'st" (Shakespeare) See "Sonnet 128"
How Santa Claus Came to Simpson's Bar" (Harte) **WLC 3:**1589
How to Write a Poem About the Sky" (Silko) **WLCS 2:**761
How Yesterday Looked" (Sandburg) **WLC 5:**3053
Howards End (Forster) **WLC 2:**1258-59, 1261, 1265, 1269-70
Howdy, Honey, Howdy (Dunbar) **WLC 2:**1114
Howl, and Other Poems (Ginsberg) **WLC 3:**1399-1400, 1403
Howl" (Ginsberg) **WLC 3:**1396-98, 1404-07
Hudson River Bracketed (Wharton) **WLC 6:**3908, 3911
Hugh Selwyn Mauberley (Pound) **WLC 5:**2789-93, 2795, 2797, 2803
Huis clos (*No Exit*) (Sartre) **WLC 5:**3090-92, 3095-97, 3100
The Human Comedy (Saroyan) **WLC 5:**3075
The Human Drift (London) **WLC 4:**2140
The Human Factor (Greene) **WLC 3:**1550-51

"The Humble-Bee" (Emerson) **WLC 2:**1171
"A Humble Remonstrance" (Stevenson) **WLC 5:**3456
Humboldt's Gift (Bellow) **WLC 1:**265, 267, 271-72
The Humiliated and the Wronged (Dostoevsky) See *The Insulted and Injured*
"Humility" (Service) **WLC 5:**3131
"Hunchback Girl: She Thinks of Heaven" (Brooks) **WLC 1:**454
The Hunchback of Notre-Dame (Hugo) See *Notre-Dame de Paris*
Hundejahre (*Dog Years*) (Grass) **WLC 3:**1503, 1508-09, 1511
Hunger and Thirst (Ionesco) See *La soif et la faim*
"A Hunger-Artist" (Kafka) See "Ein Hungerkünstler"
The Hunted (O'Neill) **WLC 4:**2561
Hunter's Sketches (Turgenev) See *Zapiski okhotnika*
The Hunting of the Snark: An Agony in Eight Fits (Carroll) **WLC 1:**644
Huntsman, What Quarry? (Millay) **WLCS 2:**599-600, 602-03
"Hurry Up Please It's Time" (Sexton) **WLC 5:**3138
The Hydra Head (Fuentes) See *La cabeza de la hidra*
"Hygeia at the Solito" (Henry) **WLC 3:**1677
"Hyme" (Donne) See "Hymne to God my God, in my sicknesse"
Hymen (H. D.) **WLC 3:**1612, 1618, 1624
Hymenaei (Jonson) **WLC 3:**1920
"Hymme to God My God, in My Sicknesse" (Donne) See "Hymne to God my God, in my sicknesse"
"Hymn among the Ruins" (Paz) See "Himno entre ruinas"
"Hymn for Lanie Poo" (Baraka) **WLCS 1:**151
Hymn in Honor of the Plague (Pushkin) **WLC 5:**2827
"Hymn of Apollo" (Shelley) **WLC 5:**3232, 3234
"Hymn of Man" (Swinburne) **WLC 6:**3563
Hymn of the Pearl (Milosz) **WLCS 2:**617
"Hymn to Adversity" (Gray) See "Ode to Adversity"
"Hymn to Beauty" (Spenser) See "An Hymn in Honour of Beautie"
"An Hymn to Humanity" (Wheatley) **WLC 6:**3922-23, 3928, 3930
"Hymn to Ignorance" (Gray) **WLC 3:**1526, 1533
"Hymn to Intellectual Beauty" (Shelley) **WLC 5:**3233, 3238
"Hymn to Mercury" (Shelley) **WLC 5:**3236
"Hymn to Proserpine" (Swinburne) **WLC 6:**3562
"An Hymn to the Evening" ("Evening") (Wheatley) **WLC 6:**3918, 3924, 3927, 3930
"An Hymn to the Morning" ("Morning") (Wheatley) **WLC 6:**3918, 3927
"Hymn to the Night" (Longfellow) **WLCS 2:**509

"Hymn" (Milosz) **WLCS 2:**613
"An Hymne in Honour of Beautie" ("Hymn to Beauty"; "Hymne of Beauty") (Spenser) **WLC 5:**3339
"Hymne of Beauty" (Spenser) See "An Hymne in Honour of Beautie"
"An Hymne of Heavenly Beautie" (Spenser) **WLC 5:**3339
"Hymne to God my God, in my sicknesse" ("Hyme"; "Hymme to God My God, in My Sicknesse"; "Since I am comming") (Donne) **WLC 2:**942
"A Hymne to God the Father" ("Wilt thou forgive") (Donne) **WLC 2:**942
Hymnes (Spenser) See *Fowre Hymnes*
Hyperion (Keats) **WLC 3:**1956, 1958-59, 1967
Hyperion (Longfellow) **WLCS 2:**508-09, 511
The Hypochondriac (Moliere) See *Le malade imaginaire*
"Hypocrite lecteur" (Baudelaire) See "Au lecteur"
"Hysteria" (Eliot) **WLC 2:**1146
Hypsipyle (Aeschylus) **WLCS 1:**7
"i thank You God for most this amazing" (Cummings) **WLC 2:**842
"I Cannot Be Silent" (Tolstoy) **WLC 6:**3664
"I Didn't Get Over" (Fitzgerald) **WLC 2:**1235
"I do believe her though I know she lies" (Shakespeare) See "Sonnet 138"
"I don't love you" (Baraka) **WLCS 1:**151
"I Explain a Few Things" (Neruda) See "Explico algunas cosas"
"I Have a Dream" (King) **WLCS 1:**465-67, 469
"I Have a Thing to Tell You" (Wolfe) **WLC 6:**4041
"I Have Longed to Move Away" (Thomas) **WLC 6:**3617
"I Heard Immanuel Singing" (Lindsay) **WLC 4:**2119
I Know Why the Caged Bird Sings (Angelou) **WLCS 1:**56, 58-59, 62, 64-65, 67-68
"I Love Those Little Booths at Benvenuti's" (Brooks) **WLC 1:**452
"I May, I Might, I Must" (Moore) **WLCS 2:**648
"I Must Have You" (Oates) **WLC 4:**2530
"I See the Promised Land" (King) **WLCS 1:**467
"I Shall Never See You Again" (Masters) **WLCS 2:**578
I Sing the Body Electric! (Bradbury) **WLC 1:**371
"I Stood on Tiptoe" (Keats) **WLC 3:**1958
"I Think It Rains" (Soyinka) **WLC 5:**3319
"I Thought of Thee" (Wordsworth) **WLC 6:**4073
I vecchi e i giovani (*The Old and the Young*) (Pirandello) **WLC 4:**2718
"I Want to Sing" (Giovanni) **WLCS 1:**359
I Wanted to Write a Poem: The Autobiography of the Works of a Poet (Williams) **WLC 6:**4019
"I'm a Fool" (Anderson) **WLC 1:**79

"The Ice Maiden" (Andersen) **WLC 1**:66
"The Ice Palace" (Fitzgerald) **WLC 2**:1232
The Iceman Cometh (O'Neill) **WLC 4**:2561-63, 2565-66, 2569
Ida Elisabeth (Undset) **WLC 6**:3738, 3741-42
"Ida M'Toy" (Welty) **WLC 6**:3889
Idanre and Other Poems (Soyinka) **WLC 5**:3319, 3320
"An Ideal Craftsman" (de la Mare) **WLC 2**:892
An Ideal Husband (Wilde) **WLC 6**:3957, 3965
The Ides of March (Wilder) **WLC 6**:3976, 3984
L'idiot de la famille: Gustave Flaubert de 1821 à 1857 (*The Family Idiot: Gustave Flaubert, 1821-1857*) (Sartre) **WLC 5**:3093, 3099, 3101
"The Idiot Boy" (Wordsworth) **WLC 6**:4076
Idiots First (Malamud) **WLC 4**:2176, 2181, 2183, 2186
"An Idle Fellow" (Chopin) **WLCS 1**:242
Idler (Johnson) **WLC 3**:1894
"The Idyl of Red Gulch" (Harte) **WLC 3**:1580
"Une idylle" (Maupassant) **WLC 4**:2289
Idylls of the King (Tennyson) **WLC 6**:3575, 3579, 3584
"if i have made, my lady, intricate" (Cummings) **WLC 2**:840
If Beale Street Could Talk (Baldwin) **WLC 1**:175
"If Everything Happens That Can't Be Done" (Cummings) **WLC 2**:842
If Five Years Pass (Garcia Lorca)
See *Así que pasen cinco años*
"If My Head Hurt a Hair's Foot" (Thomas) **WLC 6**:3621
If the Old Could (Lessing) **WLCS 2**:497
"If We Must Die" (McKay) **WLC 4**:2326, 2330, 2336-37
"If You Should Go" (Cullen) **WLCS 1**:276
"If" (Kipling) **WLC 3**:2014
"If" (Pirandello)
See "Se ..."
Ignatius, His Conclave; or His Inthronisation in a Late Election in Hell: wherein many things are mingled by way of satyr (Donne) **WLC 2**:939
Ile (O'Neill) **WLC 4**:2558
The Iliad (Homer) **WLCS 1**:405-22
Les illuminations (*Illuminations*) (Rimbaud) **WLC 5**:2908, 2910-14, 2916, 2918-20
Illuminations (Rimbaud)
See *Les illuminations*
Illusions perdues (*Lost Illusions*) (Balzac) **WLC 1**:183, 190
"Illusions" (Emerson) **WLC 2**:1174
"The Illustrated Man" (Bradbury) **WLC 1**:366
"L'illustre estinto" ("The Illustrious Deceased") (Pirandello) **WLC 4**:2717
"The Illustrious Deceased" (Pirandello)
See "L'illustre estinto"
"The Illustrious Kitchen Maid" (Cervantes)
See "La ilustre fregona"
"The Illustrious Serving Wench" (Cervantes)
See "La ilustre fregona"
"La ilustre fregona" ("The Illustrious Kitchen Maid"; "The Illustrious Serving Wench") (Cervantes) **WLC 2**:679
Im dickicht der städte (*In the Jungle of Cities; In the Swamp*) (Brecht) **WLC 1**:389
"Im Ei" ("In the Egg") (Grass) **WLC 3**:1506
"The Image of the Lost Soul" (Saki) **WLC 5**:3007
"Images" (Munro) **WLCS 2**:675
The Imaginary Invalid (Moliere)
See *Le malade imaginaire*
Imitations (Lowell) **WLC 4**:2168
Imitations of Horace (Pope)
See *Satires and Epistles of Horace, Imitated*
"Imitations of Horace" (Swift) **WLC 6**:3535
The Immoralist (Gide)
See *L'immoraliste*
L'immoraliste (*The Immoralist*) (Gide) **WLC 3**:1377, 1381-84, 1388
"The Immortal" (Borges)
See "El inmortal"
"The Imp of the Perverse" ("The Demon of Perversity") (Poe) **WLC 4**:2760-61
"An Imperfect Conflagration" (Bierce) **WLC 1**:288
"Imperfect Sympathies" (Lamb) **WLC 3**:2032
The Importance of Being Earnest (Wilde) **WLC 6**:3955, 3957-59
The Imposter (Moliere)
See *Le tartuffe*
L'imposteur (Moliere)
See *Le tartuffe*
L'impromptu de l'alma; ou, Le cameleon du berger (*Improvisation; or, The Shepherd's Chameleon*) (Ionesco) **WLC 3**:1798-99, 1802
"Impromptu on Lord Holland's House" (Gray)
See "On Lord Holland's Seat near Margate, Kent"
Improvisation; or, The Shepherd's Chameleon (Ionesco)
See *L'impromptu de l'alma; ou, Le cameleon du berger*
"In a Far Country" (London) **WLC 4**:2141
In a German Pension (Mansfield) **WLC 3**:2216
"In a Gondola" (Browning) **WLCS 1**:204
In a Sanctuary (Pirandello) **WLC 4**:2726
"In a Station of the Metro" (Pound) **WLC 5**:2802
"In a Troubled Key" (Hughes) **WLC 3**:1721-22
"In and Out of Old Natchitoches" (Chopin) **WLCS 1**:249
"In Another Country" (Hemingway) **WLC 3**:1655
In Chancery (Galsworthy) **WLC 2**:1328
In Cold Blood: A True Account of a Multiple Murder and Its Consequences (Capote) **WLC 1**:625-30
"In Country Sleep" (Thomas) **WLC 6**:3614
"In der Strafkolonie" ("In the Penal Colony") (Kafka) **WLC 3**:1946-47, 1950
"In distrust of merits" (Moore) **WLCS 2**:643, 645
In Dubious Battle (Steinbeck) **WLC 5**:3381, 3385-88
In Evil Hour (Garcia Marquez)
See *La mala hora*
"In Harmony with Nature" (Arnold) **WLC 1**:100
"In Illo Tempore" (Heaney) **WLCS 1**:398
"In Lieu of the Lyre" (Moore) **WLCS 2**:650
In Love and Trouble (Walker) **WLCS 2**:836-37
In Memoriam (Tennyson) **WLC 6**:3579-81, 3583-84
"In Memory of Ann Jones" (Thomas)
See "After the Funeral: In Memory of Anne Jones"
"In Memory of Arthur Winslow" (Lowell) **WLC 4**:2162
"In Memory of Col. Charles Young" (Cullen) **WLCS 1**:277
"In Memory of Eva Gore-Booth and Con Markiewicz" (Yeats) **WLC 6**:4109
"In Memory of Major Robert Gregory" (Yeats) **WLC 6**:4111
"In Memory of Segun Awolowo" (Soyinka) **WLC 5**:3319
"In Memory of Sigmund Freud" (Auden) **WLC 1**:139
"In Memory of W. B. Yeats" (Auden) **WLC 1**:139-40
"In Montgomery" (Brooks) **WLC 1**:457
"In Ohnmacht gefallen" ("Powerless, with a Guitar") (Grass) **WLC 3**:1506
In Our Terribleness (Baraka) **WLCS 1**:145-46
In Our Time (Hemingway) **WLC 3**:1648-49, 1656-57, 1661
"In Praise of Johnny Appleseed" (Lindsay) **WLC 4**:2124
"In Praise of Limestone" (Auden) **WLC 1**:130-31, 137
In Reckless Ecstasy (Sandburg) **WLC 5**:3063
"In Search of a Majority" (Baldwin) **WLC 1**:169
In Search of Lost Time (Proust)
See *A la recherche du temps perdu*
In Search of Our Mothers' Gardens (Walker) **WLCS 2**:838
"In Shadow" (Crane) **WLC 2**:799
"In the Abyss" (Wells) **WLC 6**:3871, 3873
In the American Grain (*Ars Poetica: In the American Grain*) (Williams) **WLC 6**:4018, 4022-23
"In the Avu Observatory" (Wells) **WLC 6**:3863
In the Bar of a Tokyo Hotel (Williams) **WLC 6**:3996-98
"In the Beech" (Heaney) **WLCS 1**:398
"In the Carquinez Woods" (Harte) **WLC 3**:1582-83
In the Clearing (Frost) **WLC 2**:1297
"In the Days of Prismatic Color" (Moore) **WLCS 2**:649-50
In the Days of the Comet (Wells) **WLC 6**:3869, 3876
"In the Egg" (Grass)
See "Im Ei"
In the Frame of Don Cristóbal (Garcia Lorca)

See *Retablillo de Don Cristóbal*
In the Jungle of Cities (Brecht)
　See *Im dickicht der städte*
In the Mecca (Brooks) **WLC 1:**452, 456, 458, 461-62
"In the Mecca" (Brooks) **WLC 1:**456-57
In the Midst of Life (*Tales of Soldiers and Civilians*) (Bierce) **WLC 1:**281
"In the Morning" (Dunbar) **WLC 2:**1114
"In the old age black was not counted fair" (Shakespeare)
　See "Sonnet 127"
"In the Penal Colony" (Kafka)
　See "In der Strafkolonie"
In the Presence of the Sun (Momaday) **WLCS 2:**634-35
"In the Public Garden" (Moore) **WLCS 2:**650
"In the Ravine" ("In the River") (Chekhov) **WLC 2:**710-11
"In the Region of Ice" (Oates) **WLC 4:**2535
"In the River" (Chekhov)
　See "In the Ravine"
"In the Rukh" (Kipling) **WLC 3:**2019
"In the Same Boat" (Kipling) **WLC 3:**2017
In the Steppe (Gorky) **WLC 3:**1482
In the Swamp (Brecht)
　See *Im dickicht der städte*
"In the Time of Prince Charley" (London) **WLC 4:**2141
"In the Tules" (Harte) **WLC 3:**1589
"In the Valley of Cauteretz" (Tennyson) **WLC 6:**3584
"In the White Giant's Thigh" (Thomas) **WLC 6:**3614
"In the World, Not of It" (Lessing) **WLCS 2:**490
In the Zone (O'Neill) **WLC 4:**2558
"In Time of War" (Auden) **WLC 1:**132
"In Transit" (Auden) **WLC 1:**139
"In Utrumque Paratus" (Arnold) **WLC 1:**101
Inadmissible Evidence (Osborne) **WLC 4:**2594-99, 2601-02
"Inauguration Day: January 1953" (Lowell) **WLC 4:**2162, 2166
Incarnations: Poems, 1966-1968 (Warren) **WLC 6:**3814-15
Incident at Vichy (Miller) **WLC 4:**2371
"Incident" (Cullen) **WLCS 1:**275
"Include Me Out" (Service) **WLC 5:**3131
Incognita; or, Love and Duty Reconcil'd (Congreve) **WLC 2:**770-71
The Indian Emperour; or, The Conquest of Mexico by the Spaniards, Being the Sequel of the Indian Queen (Dryden) **WLC 2:**1058
Indian Journals, March 1962-May 1963 (Ginsberg) **WLC 3:**1393-94
"Indian Song: Survival" (Silko) **WLCS 2:**761
"The Indian to His Love" (Yeats) **WLC 6:**4105-06
"The Indian upon God" (Yeats) **WLC 6:**4106
Indiana (Sand) **WLC 5:**3035-38, 3042, 3045-46
The Infernal Machine (Cocteau)
　See *La machine infernale*
L'inferno (Alighieri) **WLCS 1:**21-22, 25, 30-31, 34-37

Inferno (Strindberg) **WLC 6:**3518, 3528
"Inferno, I, 32" (Borges) **WLC 1:**344
El ingenioso hidalgo Don Quixote de la Mancha (*Don Quixote*) (Cervantes) **WLC 2:**671-76, 678, 681-85
L'Ingénu (Voltaire) **WLC 6:**3776, 3780, 3782
"An Ingènue of the Sierra" (Harte) **WLC 3:**1584
"The Ingrate" (Dunbar) **WLC 2:**1106, 1107
"An Inhabitant of Carcosa" (Bierce) **WLC 1:**288
The Inheritors (Golding) **WLC 3:**1445-46, 1459
"The Inheritors" (Conrad) **WLC 2:**780
"The Inhumanist" (Jeffers) **WLC 3:**1879, 1884
"The Iniquity of the Fathers upon the Children" (Rossetti) **WLC 5:**2940
"Initial, Daemonic, and Celestial Love" (Emerson) **WLC 2:**1171
"Injudicious Gardening" (Moore) **WLCS 2:**651
Injury and Insult (Dostoevsky)
　See *The Insulted and Injured*
"The Injury" (Williams) **WLC 6:**4014
"El inmortal" ("The Immortal") (Borges) **WLC 1:**335
The Inn Album (Browning) **WLCS 1:**215
"The Inn" ("The Country Inn"; "The Wayside Inn") (Turgenev) **WLC 6:**3697, 3703
L'innesto (*The Grafting*) (Pirandello) **WLC 4:**2721
The Innocents Abroad; or, The New Pilgrim's Progress (Twain) **WLC 6:**3714-16, 3718
L'innommable (*The Unnameable*) (Beckett) **WLC 1:**231-33
The Insect Comedy (Capek)
　See *Ze zivota hmyzu*
Insect Life (Capek)
　See *Ze zivota hmyzu*
The Insect Play (Capek)
　See *Ze zivota hmyzu*
Insect Story (Capek)
　See *Ze zivota hmyzu*
Insects (Capek)
　See *Ze zivota hmyzu*
The Inside of His Head (Miller)
　See *Death of a Salesman*
"Insomniac" (Plath) **WLC 4:**2742
"Inspection" (Owen) **WLC 4:**2614
The Insulted and Injured (*The Humiliated and the Wronged*; *Injury and Insult*) (Dostoevsky) **WLC 2:**971-72
Intact Wind (Paz)
　See *Viento entero*
Intelligent Woman's Guide (Shaw) **WLC 5:**3192
Intentions (Wilde) **WLC 6:**3954-55
"The Interest of Great Britain in Regard to Her Colonies" (Franklin) **WLCS 1:**316
"The Interference of Patsy Ann" (Dunbar) **WLC 2:**1107
Interludes (Cervantes)
　See *Ocho comedias y ocho entremeses nunca representados*
"The Intervention of Peter" (Dunbar) **WLC 2:**1106
Intimacy, and Other Stories (Sartre)

See *Le mur*
Intimate Journal (Sand)
　See *Le secrétaire intime*
Intimate Journals (Baudelaire)
　See *Journaux intimes*
Intimate Relations (Cocteau)
　See *Les parents terribles*
"Intimations" (Wordsworth) **WLC 6:**4076
"Intrigue" (Crane) **WLC 2:**817
Introduction to Objectivist Epistemology (Rand) **WLC 5:**2887
"Introspection" (Giovanni) **WLCS 1:**360
Intruder in the Dust (Faulkner) **WLC 2:**1197-99
"Inventions" (Oates) **WLC 4:**2526
"Investigations of a Dog" (Kafka)
　See "Forschungen eines hundes"
Invisible Man (Ellison) **WLC 2:**1155-60, 1165-66
The Invisible Man (Wells) **WLC 6:**3856, 3859, 3862-63, 3867, 3869, 3871, 3876
"L'invitation au voyage" (Baudelaire) **WLC 1:**208
"The Invitation" (Shelley)
　See "To Jane: The Invitation"
L'invitée (*She Came to Stay*) (Beauvoir) **WLC 1:**219
"Invocation" (Bierce) **WLC 1:**291-92
Ion (Euripides) **WLCS 1:**291-93, 296
"Ionitch" (Chekhov)
　See "Ionych"
"Ionych" ("Ionitch") (Chekhov) **WLC 2:**710
Iphigenia (Aeschylus) **WLCS 1:**9
Iphigenia (Goethe) **WLC 3:**1416-17
Iphigenia among the Taurians (Euripides)
　See *Iphigenia in Tauris*
Iphigenia at Aulis (Euripides) **WLCS 1:**291, 296
Iphigenia in Tauris (Euripides) **WLCS 1:**291, 292, 294, 299
Irene (*Mahomet and Irene*) (Johnson) **WLC 3:**1893
"An Irish Airman Foresees His Death" (Yeats) **WLC 6:**4111
The Iron Heel (London) **WLC 4:**2138, 2147-49
"L'irrémédiable" (Baudelaire) **WLC 1:**202
"L'irréparable" (Baudelaire) **WLC 1:**202, 205
is 5 (Cummings) **WLC 2:**839
Is He Popenjoy? (Trollope) **WLC 6:**3681
"Is My Team Ploughing" (Housman) **WLCS 1:**434
"Is Theology Poetry?" (Lewis) **WLC 4:**2090
"Isabella" (Keats) **WLC 3:**1956
Isabelle (Gide) **WLC 3:**1379
"Isaiah Beethoven" (Masters) **WLCS 2:**579-80
Isarà (Soyinka) **WLC 5:**3332-33
Isla Negra: A Notebook (Neruda)
　See *Memorial de Isla Negra*
Island (Huxley) **WLC 3:**1762, 1769, 1771
The Island of Dr. Moreau (Wells) **WLC 6:**3859, 3862-64, 3867, 3869, 3871
"The Island of the Fay" (Poe) **WLC 4:**2760
The Island Pharisees (Galsworthy) **WLC 2:**1328
Isle Somante (Rabelais) **WLC 5:**2869
Ispoved (*Confession*) (Gorky) **WLC**

3:1486, 1491, 1493
"Israfel" (Poe) **WLC 4**:2759
Isthmiastai (Aeschylus) **WLCS 1**:13
"Istoriya leytenanta Ergunova" ("The Adventure of Lieutenant Jergounoff"; "The History of Lieutenant Ergunov"; "Lieutenant Yergunov's Story"; "The Story of Lieutenant Ergunov") (Turgenev) **WLC 6**:3699
It Can't Be Serious (Pirandello)
  See *Ma non è una cosa seria*
"It Is Everywhere" (Toomer) **WLCS 2**:804
It Is So, If You Think So (Pirandello)
  See *Così (se vi pare)*
It's a Battlefield (Greene) **WLC 3**:1545-47
"The Italian Banditti" (Irving) **WLC 3**:1828
Ivanhoe (Scott) **WLC 5**:3112, 3115
The Ivory Tower (James) **WLC 3**:1865
"Ivy Day in the Committee Room" (Joyce) **WLC 3**:1931
"J'accuse" (Zola) **WLC 6**:4119
J-E-L-L-O (Baraka) **WLCS 1**:152
Jack and Jill: A Village Story (Alcott) **WLC 1**:38, 41-2, 50
Jack; or, The Submission (Ionesco)
  See *Jacques; ou, La soumission*
Jacob Pasinkov (Turgenev)
  See *Yakov Pasynkov*
Jacob's Room (Woolf) **WLC 6**:4046, 4052-53, 4058
Jacques (Sand) **WLC 5**:3035, 3038, 3042
Jacques; ou, La soumission (*Jack; or, The Submission*) (Ionesco) **WLC 3**:1798-99, 1809
La jalousie de Barbouillé (*The Jealousy of Le Barbouillé*) (Moliere) **WLC 4**:2436, 2441, 2445
James Burnham and the Managerial Revolution (Orwell) **WLC 4**:2575
"Jan Van Hunks" (Rossetti) **WLC 5**:2959
Jane Eyre: An Autobiography (Bronte) **WLC 1**:399-410
"Janet's Repentance" (Eliot) **WLC 2**:1120
"El jardín de senderos que se bifurcan" ("The Garden of the Forking Paths") (Borges) **WLC 1**:340
"Je ne parle pas français" (Mansfield) **WLC 4**:2215-16
"The Jealous Extremaduran" (Cervantes)
  See "El celoso extremeño"
"The Jealous Hidalgo" (Cervantes)
  See "El celoso extremeño"
The Jealousy of Le Barbouillé (Moliere)
  See *La jalousie de Barbouillé*
"Jean Desprez" (Service) **WLC 5**:3122
Jeanne (Sand) **WLC 5**:3041
Jeannot et Colin (Voltaire) **WLC 6**:3772-73
Jennie Gerhardt (Dreiser) **WLC 2**:1025, 1027, 1031, 1035
Jenny (Undset) **WLC 6**:3735-37, 3740
"Jenny" (Rossetti) **WLC 5**:2948, 2950-51, 2956-57
"The Jerboa" (Moore) **WLCS 2**:641, 643
Jerry of the Islands (London) **WLC 4**:2140
Jerusalem: The Emanation of the Giant Albion (Blake) **WLC 1**:301
"Jesse and Meribeth" (Munro) **WLCS** 2:683
"Jesus Christ in Flanders" (Balzac)
  See "Jesus Christ in Flanders"
"The Jesus Papers" (Sexton) **WLC 5**:3146
"Jesus Suckles" (Sexton) **WLC 5**:3146
"Jésus-Christ en Flandre" (Balzac) **WLC 1**:189
"Jeunesse" (Rimbaud) **WLC 5**:2918
Jeux de massacre (*The Killing Game*) (Ionesco) **WLC 3**:1804
A Jew Today (Wiesel) **WLCS 2**:854-55
"The Jewbird" (Malamud) **WLC 4**:2190
The Jewel of Seven Stars (Stoker) **WLC 6**:3464
"The Jewels of the Cabots" (Cheever) **WLC 2**:697
"The Jews" (Turgenev) **WLC 6**:3697, 3702
A Jig for the Gypsy (Davies) **WLC 2**:852
Jim Dandy: Fat Man in a Famine (Saroyan) **WLC 5**:3072, 3075
"Jim's Probation" (Dunbar) **WLC 2**:1106
Jimmie Higgins (Sinclair) **WLC 5**:3263
"Jimsella" (Dunbar) **WLC 2**:1102, 1106, 1111, 1113
"Jinny" (Harte) **WLC 3**:1590
Jitney (Wilson) **WLCS 2**:863
Jo Turner's Come and Gone (Wilson) **WLCS 1**:862, 864-65, 869
Jo's Boys and How They Turned Out (Alcott) **WLC 1**:41, 43, 51
Joan and Peter: The Story of an Education (Wells) **WLC 6**:3859
The Job (Lewis) **WLC 4**:2108
John Barleycorn (London) **WLC 4**:2140
"John Bartine's Watch" (Bierce) **WLC 1**:289
"John Brown" (Lindsay) **WLC 4**:2120
"John Bull" (Irving) **WLC 3**:1827
John Caldigate (Trollope) **WLC 6**:3681
"John Endicott" (Longfellow) **WLCS 2**:513-14, 516
John Gabriel Borkman (Ibsen) **WLC 3**:1784, 1786-87
"John Inglefield's Thanksgiving" (Hawthorne) **WLC 3**:1605
"John Redding Goes to Sea" (Hurston) **WLCS 1**:449-50
John Thomas and Lady Jane (Lawrence) **WLC 3**:2053
John Woodvil (Lamb) **WLC 3**:2029
"Johnny Appleseed" (Lindsay) **WLC 4**:2122
"The Johnson Girls" (Bambara) **WLCS 1**:131
"The Jolly Beggars" (Burns) **WLC 1**:518-20, 528-29
"The Jolly Company" (Brooke) **WLC 1**:434
"The Jolly Corner" (James) **WLC 3**:1865
Jonah: Christmas 1917 (Huxley) **WLC 3**:1761, 1763-64
"Jonathan Edwards" (Lowell) **WLC 4**:2159
Jonathan Oldstyle (Irving) **WLC 3**:1827-28
Jonathan Wild (Fielding)
  See *The Life of Mr. Jonathan Wild the Great*
Joseph Andrews (Fielding)
  See *The History of Joseph Andrews*

Joseph der Ernährer (*Joseph the Provider*) (Mann) **WLC 4**:2205, 2207-08
Joseph the Provider (Mann)
  See *Joseph der Ernährer*
Le jour des rois (Hugo) **WLC 3**:1748
Le journal des faux-monnayeurs (*Journal of the Counterfeiters; Logbook of the Coiners*) (Gide) **WLC 3**:1378, 1383-84, 1387
Journal (Thoreau) **WLC 6**:3631, 3633-35
Journal du voyage de Michel de Montaigne en Italie par la Suisse et l'Allemagne en 1580 et 1581 (*Travel Journal*) (Montaigne) **WLC 4**:2467-68
"The Journal of a Superfluous Man" (Turgenev)
  See "Dnevnik lishnego cheloveka"
Journal of a Tour to the Hebrides with Samuel Johnson, LL. D. (*Hebrides Journal*) (Boswell) **WLC 1**:351, 356, 358-60
The Journal of Arthur Stirling (Sinclair) **WLC 5**:3261-62
Journal of the Counterfeiters (Gide)
  See *Le journal des faux-monnayeurs*
A Journal of the Plague Year (*A History of the Plague*) (Defoe) **WLC 2**:867, 870
The Journal to Eliza (Sterne) **WLC 5**:3418, 3421-22
The Journals of Ralph Waldo Emerson (Emerson) **WLC 2**:1170, 1172
The Journals of Susanna Moodie (Atwood) **WLC 1**:108, 110-12, 116, 118
Journals: Early Fifties, Early Sixties (Ginsberg) **WLC 3**:1398, 1405
Journaux intimes (*Intimate Journals*) (Baudelaire) **WLC 1**:199-201
Journey from this World to the Next (Fielding) **WLC 2**:1203-04
"Journey of the Magi" (Eliot) **WLC 2**:1147-48
Journey to a War (Auden) **WLC 1**:139
Journey to Love (Williams) **WLC 6**:4021
"Journey to Polessie" (Turgenev) **WLC 6**:3707-08
"Journey to the Dead" (Arnold) **WLC 1**:93
A Journey to the Western Islands of Scotland (Johnson) **WLC 3**:1895, 1902
Journeys between Wars (Dos Passos) **WLC 2**:955
"Jubal the Selfless" (Strindberg) **WLC 6**:3525
"Judas Iscariot" (Cullen) **WLCS 1**:277
Judas Maccabaeus (Longfellow) **WLCS 2**:514, 516
Jude the Obscure (Hardy) **WLC 3**:1561, 1565, 1567
"A Judgment of Paris" (Dunbar) **WLC 2**:1107
"The Judgment" (Kafka)
  See "Das Urteil"
"Jug of Silver" (Capote) **WLC 1**:619
Julia Bride (James) **WLC 3**:1865
"Julian and Maddalo" (Shelley) **WLC 5**:3228
Julie, ou La Nouvelle Héloïse (Rousseau)
  See *La Nouvelle Héloïse*
Julius Caesar (Shakespeare) **WLC**

5:3157, 3169
July's People (Gordimer) **WLCS 1:**372, 375, 377, 380
Jumpers (Stoppard) **WLC 6:**3481, 3483-84, 3487-90, 3492-95
"June Recital" (Welty) **WLC 6:**3893
The Jungle (Sinclair) **WLC 5:**3261-68, 3273-75, 3278-79
The Jungle Book (Kipling) **WLC 3:**2012, 2018-20
Juno and the Paycock (O'Casey) **WLCS 2:**707-09, 712-13, 717-20, 722
The Just Assassins (Camus)
See *Les justes*
"Just Before the War with the Eskimos" (Salinger) **WLC 5:**3026
Just Give Me a Cool Drink of Water 'fore I Diiie (Angelou) **WLCS 1:**62
"The Just Man" (Rimbaud)
See "L'homme juste"
"Just One More Time" (Cheever) **WLC 2:**696
Just So Stories (Kipling) **WLC 3:**2018
Les justes (*The Assassins*; *The Just Assassins*) (Camus) **WLC 1:**588-91, 595
"Justice Denied in Massachusetts" (Millay) **WLCS 2:**598-99
"Kabnis" (Toomer) **WLCS 2:**793, 800
"Kaddish" (Ginsberg) **WLC 3:**1398-99
"Kafka and His Precursors" (Borges) **WLC 1:**338
"The Kallyope Yell" (Lindsay) **WLC 4:**2125, 2130
Kamen no kokuhaku (*Confessions of a Mask*) (Mishima) **WLC 4:**2425-31
The Kanaka Surf (London) **WLC 4:**2140
Kantan (Mishima) **WLC 4:**2417
Karl Ludwig's Window (Saki) **WLC 5:**3010
"Kashtánka" (Chekhov) **WLC 2:**709
Kataku (Mishima) **WLC 4:**2417
Katherine Mansfield: Short Stories (Mansfield) **WLC 4:**2226
"Katherine's Dream" (Lowell) **WLC 4:**2154
Kathleen Listens In (O'Casey) **WLCS 2:**717, 722
Katz und Maus (*Cat and Mouse*) (Grass) **WLC 3:**1503, 1505, 1508-09, 1511
Der kaukasische Kreidekreis (*The Caucasian Chalk Circle*) (Brecht) **WLC 1:**383, 385, 391
"Kavanagh" (Longfellow) **WLCS 2:**508-09, 511-12
Kavkazsky plennik (*The Captive of the Caucasus*; *The Caucasian Captive*; *The Prisoner of the Caucasus*) (Pushkin) **WLC 5:**2835
Kean, on désordre et genie (Dumas) **WLC 2:**1091
"Keela, the Outcast Indian Maiden" (Welty) **WLC 6:**3882, 3892
"Keep Innocency" (de la Mare) **WLC 2:**887
Keep the Aspidistra Flying (Orwell) **WLC 4:**2576, 2579
"Keeping their world large" (Moore) **WLCS 2:**643
"Keesh, the Son of Keesh" (London) **WLC 4:**2142

The Kempton-Wace Letters (London) **WLC 4:**2137
A Key to Uncle Tom's Cabin: Presenting the Original Facts and Documents upon Which the Story Is Founded (Stowe) **WLC 6:**3504, 3509-10
"Key West: An Island Sheaf" (Crane) **WLC 2:**801
"The Key" (Welty) **WLC 6:**3882
"Khadzi murat" ("Hadjii murád") (Tolstoy) **WLC 6:**3665
"Khozyaika" ("The Landlady") (Dostoevsky) **WLC 2:**976
Khozyain i rabotnik (*Master and Man*) (Tolstoy) **WLC 6:**3663-65
Kidnapped (Stevenson)
See *Kidnapped: Being Memoirs of the Adventures of David Balfour in the Year 1751*
Kidnapped: Being Memoirs of the Adventures of David Balfour in the Year 1751 (*David Balfour: Being Memoirs of His Adventures at Home and Abroad*; *Kidnapped*) (Stevenson) **WLC 5:**3446-48, 3451
"Kiku on the Tenth" (Mishima) **WLC 4:**2427
"Killed at Resaca" (Bierce) **WLC 1:**289
The Killer (Ionesco)
See *Tueur sans gages*
"The Killers" (Hemingway) **WLC 3:**1661
The Killing Game (Ionesco)
See *Jeux de massacre*
Kim (Kipling) **WLC 3:**2012, 2014, 2018, 2022
"The Kind Ghosts" (Owen) **WLC 4:**2616, 2618
A Kind of Alaska (Pinter)
See *Other Places*
"Kinderlied" (Grass) **WLC 3:**1506
Kindly Ones (Aeschylus) **WLCS 1:**13
"Kindness" (Plath) **WLC 4:**2739
Kindui n gaku sh (Mishima) **WLC 4:**2425
King (Nabokov) **WLC 4:**2497
"King Arthur's Men Have Come Again" (Lindsay) **WLC 4:**2128
King Coal (Sinclair) **WLC 5:**3263, 3267-69
The King Dies (Ionesco)
See *Le roi se meurt*
"King Essarhadon" (Tolstoy) **WLC 6:**3664
King John (Shakespeare) **WLC 5:**3165-66
King Lear (Shakespeare) **WLC 5:**3157, 3171, 3173
"A King Lear of the Steppes" (Turgenev)
See "Stepnoy Korol 'Lir"
King Midas: A Romance (Sinclair)
See *Springtime and Harvest: A Romance*
"King Solomon and the Queen of Sheba" (Lindsay) **WLC 4:**2120
"The King's Dream" (Andersen) **WLC 1:**60
The King's Edict (Hugo)
See *Marion de Lorme*
The King's Henchman (Millay) **WLCS 2:**591-92
"The King's Tragedy" (Rossetti) **WLC 5:**2950, 2953, 2955, 2959
Kingdom of Earth: The Seven Descents of Myrtle (*The Seven Descents of Myrtle*)

(Williams) **WLC 6:**3995-97
"The Kingdom of Heaven Is within Us" (Tolstoy) **WLC 6:**3664
Kingsblood Royal (Lewis) **WLC 4:**2108
Kinkakuji (*The Temple of the Golden Pavillion*) (Mishima) **WLC 4:**2418, 2426-27, 2429-30
Kipps (Wells) **WLC 6:**3858, 3861, 3870
Kirjali (Pushkin) **WLC 5:**2829
"The Kirk's Alarm" (Burns) **WLC 1:**517, 524
"The Kiss" (Chopin) **WLCS 1:**240
Kit Brandon (Anderson) **WLC 1:**76
"A Kite for Michael and Christopher" (Heaney) **WLCS 1:**389
"Kitty" (Frank) **WLC 2:**1280
"Klara Milich" ("Clara Milich") (Turgenev) **WLC 6:**3699, 3705, 3707
"Kleckerburg" (Grass) **WLC 3:**1505
De kloge jomfruer (*The Wise Virgins*) (Undset) **WLC 6:**3736, 3740-41
Knave (Nabokov) **WLC 4:**2497
Knickerbocker (Irving) **WLC 3:**1817-18
Knickerbocker's History (Irving)
See *History of New York*
"Knight's Gambit" (Faulkner) **WLC 2:**1197
"Knight's Tale" (Chaucer) **WLCS 1:**226-27, 231
The Knightly Quest (Williams) **WLC 6:**4003
Knights (Aristophanes) **WLCS 1:**79-80
"Knock...Knock...Knock" (Turgenev)
See "Stuk...stuk...stuk"
Koholstomér (Tolstoy) **WLC 6:**3666
Kongi's Harvest (Soyinka) **WLC 5:**3325, 3327, 3328
Kongs emnerne (*The Pretenders*) (Ibsen) **WLC 3:**1790, 1792
Kora in Hell: Improvisations (Williams) **WLC 6:**4019, 4023
Koran (Muhammad) **WLCS 2:**657-72
Krakatit (Capek) **WLC 1:**602-03, 605, 609, 613
Krakonos's Garden (Capek) **WLC 1:**599-601
Krasnoe koleso: Povestvovanie v otmerennykh srokakh. Uzel I, Avgust chetyrnadsatogo (Solzhenitsyn)
See *Avgust chetyrnadtsatogo*
Kreitserova sonata (*The Kreutzer Sonata*) (Tolstoy) **WLC 6:**3664, 3675
The Kreutzer Sonata (Tolstoy)
See *Kreitserova sonata*
Kristin Lavransdatter (Undset) **WLC 6:**3732-38, 3743
"Kubla Khan" (Coleridge) **WLC 2:**743
Kunstmakher fun Lublin (*The Magician of Lublin*) (Singer) **WLC 5:**3286, 3293
"A la musique" (Rimbaud) **WLC 5:**2922
El laberinto de amor (Cervantes) **WLC 2:**683-84
El laberinto de la soledad (*The Labyrinth of Solitude*) (Paz) **WLC 4:**2667, 2669, 2672
"The Laboratory" (Browning) **WLCS 1:**209
"The Laboring Skeleton" (Baudelaire)
See "Le squelette laboureur"
The Labyrinth of Solitude (Paz)
See *El laberinto de la soledad*
"Lachrymae Christi" (Crane) **WLC 2:**800-

TITLE INDEX

"The Lacking Sense" (Hardy) **WLC** 3:1571
Ladera este (*East Slope; Eastern Slope*) (Paz) **WLC 4**:2672
Lady Anna (Trollope) **WLC 6**:3681
The Lady Aoi (Mishima) **WLC 4**:2417
Lady Chatterley's Lover (Lawrence) **WLC** 3:2052-55
"The Lady Cornelia" (Cervantes)
 See "La Señora Cornelia"
Lady Frederick (Maugham) **WLC 4**:2277
The Lady from Dubuque (Albee) **WLC** 1:30
The Lady from the Sea (Ibsen)
 See *Fruen fra havet*
"Lady Lazarus" (Plath) **WLC 4**:2738, 2744-48
"A Lady of Bayou St. John" (Chopin) **WLCS 1**:240
The Lady of Larkspur Lotion (Williams) **WLC 6**:3989
"The Lady of Shalott" (Tennyson) **WLC** 6:3583
The Lady of the Lake (Scott) **WLC** 5:3115, 3117
"The Lady of the Lake" (Malamud) **WLC** 4:2189
Lady Oracle (Atwood) **WLC 1**:109-11, 114-15
"A Lady Slipper" (Dunbar) **WLC 2**:1106
Lady Windermere's Fan (Wilde) **WLC** 6:3955
"The Lady with the Dog" ("Lady with the Little Dog") (Chekhov) **WLC 2**:710
"Lady with the Little Dog" (Chekhov)
 See "The Lady with the Dog"
"The Lady with the Pet Dog" (Oates) **WLC 4**:2535, 2536
Lafcadio's Adventures (Gide)
 See *Les caves du Vatican*
The Lair of the White Worm (Stoker) **WLC 6**:3464
Laius (Aeschylus) **WLCS 1**:8
"Lake Boats" (Masters) **WLCS 2**:578
"The Lame Shall Enter First" (O'Connor) **WLC 4**:2543
Lament for Ignacio Sánchez Mejías (Garcia Lorca)
 See *Llanto por Ignacio Sánchez Mejías*
Lament for the Death of a Bullfighter (Garcia Lorca)
 See *Llanto por Ignacio Sánchez Mejías*
"Lament" (Millay) **WLCS 2**:590
"Lament" (Plath) **WLC 4**:2740
Lamia (Keats) **WLC 3**:1964-67
"The Land Ironclads" (Wells) **WLC** 6:3867, 3872
"The Land of Counterpane" (Stevenson) **WLC 5**:3454
The Land of Heart's Desire (Yeats) **WLC** 6:4102
Land of Unlikeness (Lowell) **WLC** 4:2161, 2168
"The Land" (Kipling) **WLC 3**:2017
"The Landing" (Welty) **WLC 6**:3881
"The Landlady" (Dostoevsky)
 See "Khozyaika"
The Landleaguers (Trollope) **WLC** 6:3681
Landscape (Pinter) **WLC 5**:2705-06
"The Landscape" (Masters) **WLCS 2**:578

"The Lantern Out of Doors" (Hopkins) **WLC 3**:1714
"Laodamia" (Wordsworth) **WLC 6**:4068
Laon and Cythna (*The Revolt of Islam*) (Shelley) **WLC 5**:3227-28
"Laquelle est la vraie?" ("Which Is the True One?") (Baudelaire) **WLC 1**:210
Lara (Byron) **WLC 1**:570, 572
"The Lark" (Service) **WLC 5**:3122
"Larme" (Rimbaud) **WLC 5**:2918
"The Lass of Balloch myle" (Burns) **WLC** 1:518
The Last Battle (Lewis) **WLC 4**:2084, 2087
The Last Chronicle of Barset (Trollope) **WLC 6**:3680-81, 3688-90
"A Last Confession" (Rossetti) **WLC** 5:2947, 2950
"The Last Days of John Brown" (Thoreau) **WLC 6**:3640
"The Last Demon" (Singer) **WLC 5**:3290
"The Last Dream of the Old Oak" ("Old Oak Tree's Last Dream") (Andersen) **WLC 1**:64
"The Last Fiddling of Mordaunts Jim" (Dunbar) **WLC 2**:1107
"The Last Instructions to a Painter" (Marvell) **WLC 4**:2254
The Last Man (Shelley) **WLC 5**:3214
"Last May a braw Wooer" (Burns) **WLC** 1:517
"The Last Mohican" (Malamud) **WLC** 4:2175, 2181-83, 2186, 2189
"The Last of the Belles" (Fitzgerald) **WLC** 2:1233
Last Poems (Housman) **WLCS 1**:426-29, 435, 437
Last Poems (Yeats) **WLC 6**:4102
"The Last Special" (Doyle) **WLC 2**:1018
"The Last Supper" (Service) **WLC** 5:3131
The Last Tycoon (Fitzgerald) **WLC** 2:1223, 1226
"The Last Voyage of the Ghost Ship" (Garcia Marquez)
 See "El último viaje del buque fantasma"
The Late Bourgeois World (Gordimer) **WLCS 1**:370, 374-77
The Late Mattia Pascal (Pirandello)
 See *Il fu Mattia Pascal*
Later Collected Verse (Service) **WLC** 5:3132
"The Laughing Man" (Salinger) **WLC** 5:3023, 3026
The Laughing Matter (Saroyan) **WLC** 5:3075, 3083
Laughter in the Dark (Nabokov) **WLC** 4:2497
Laus Veneris, and Other Poems and Ballads (Swinburne)
 See *Poems and Ballads*
"Laus Veneris" (Swinburne) **WLC 6**:3557-58, 3563, 3566
"The Law of Life" (London) **WLC 4**:2142
"The Law of the Jungle" (Cheever) **WLC** 2:695
"The Law of the Yukon" (Service) **WLC** 5:3123
Laws (Plato) **WLCS 2**:730, 735, 737, 740
The Lay of the Last Minstrel (Scott) **WLC** 5:3115, 3116, 3117
Lazarus Laughed (O'Neill) **WLC 4**:2560

le misanthrope (Moliere) **WLC 4**:2436-40, 2445
"The Leaden-Eyed" (Lindsay) **WLC** 4:2131
"A Leaf From the Sky" (Andersen) **WLC** 1:59
Leaf Storm (Garcia Marquez)
 See *La hojarasca*
"The Leaf" (Warren) **WLC 6**:3814-15
"The League of Old Men" (London) **WLC** 4:2136
The League of Youth (Ibsen)
 See *De unges forbund*
"The Leap Frog" (Andersen) **WLC 1**:55, 60
"A Lear of the Steppes" (Turgenev)
 See "Stepnoy Korol 'Lir'"
The Learned Ladies (Moliere)
 See *Les femmes savantes*
"Leather Leggings" (Sandburg) **WLC** 5:3051
Leaven of Malice (Davies) **WLC 2**:848, 852, 854, 859
Leaves of Grass (Whitman) **WLC** 6:3936, 3938, 3940-48
Leben des Galilei (*Galileo; The Life of Galileo*) (Brecht) **WLC 1**:382, 391-92
La leçon (*The Lesson*) (Ionesco) **WLC** 3:1798, 1800, 1802-04, 1809
"Lecture on the Times" (Emerson) **WLC** 2:1174
Lectures in America (Stein) **WLC 5**:3362
Leda (Huxley) **WLC 3**:1761, 1764
"Leda and the Swan" (Yeats) **WLC** 6:4109-10
"Leda" (Huxley) **WLC 3**:1765
The Legend of Good Women (Chaucer) **WLCS 1**:226-27, 229, 231
A Legend of Montrose (Scott) **WLC** 5:3108, 3112
"The Legend of Saamstadt" (Harte) **WLC** 3:1581
"The Legend of Sleepy Hollow" (Irving) **WLC 3**:1820-21, 1825-28, 1832
The Legend of the Centuries (Hugo)
 See *La légende des siècles*
"The Legend of the Grand Inquisitor" ("The Grand Inquisitor") (Dostoevsky) **WLC 2**:975-78, 982, 985
The Legend of the Rhine (Thackeray) **WLC 6**:3592
"Legend" (Crane) **WLC 2**:799-800
La légende des siècles (*The Legend of the Centuries*) (Hugo) **WLC 3**:1746, 1748-49
Legends of Our Time (Wiesel) **WLCS** 2:854
Legends of the Conquest of Spain (Irving) **WLC 3**:1820
Lélia (Sand) **WLC 5**:3035-38, 3042, 3044-47
Lenin in Zurich (Solzhenitsyn) **WLC** 5:3310
"Lenox Avenue: Midnight" (Hughes) **WLC** 3:1728
"The Leper" (Swinburne) **WLC 6**:3557, 3559, 3563
Lesbia Brandon (Swinburne) **WLC** 6:3562
The Lesbians (Baudelaire)
 See *Les fleurs du mal*
Les Lesbiennes (Baudelaire)

See *Les fleurs du mal*
Leshy (*The Wood Demon*) (Chekhov) **WLC 2**:713-14
The Lesson (Ionesco)
See *La leçon*
"The Lesson" (Bambara) **WLCS 1**:128
"The Lesson" (Lowell) **WLC 4**:2159
"Let Us Be Content with Three Little Newborn Elephants" (Miller) **WLC 4**:2391
Letter from Birmingham Jail (King) **WLCS 1**:460-62, 464-65
A Letter from Mr. Burke, to a Member of the National Assembly: In Answer to Some Objections to His Book on French Affairs (*A Letter to a Member of the National Assembly*) (Burke) **WLC 1**:506
Letter from the Right Honourable Edmund Burke to a Noble Lord, on the Attacks Made upon Him and His Pension, in the House of Lords (Burke) **WLC 1**:505, 508
"Letter to a Bourgeois Friend Whom I Once Loved (and Maybe Still Do If Love Is Valid)" (Giovanni) **WLCS 1**:362
A Letter to a Member of the National Assembly (Burke)
See *A Letter from Mr. Burke, to a Member of the National Assembly: In Answer to Some Objections to His Book on French Affairs*
"Letter to Lord Byron" (Auden) **WLC 1**:139
"Letter Written on a Ferry Crossing Long Island Sound" (Sexton) **WLC 5**:3142
"Letter" (Hughes) **WLC 3**:1723
"The Letter" (Maugham) **WLC 4**:2275
"The Letter" (Owen) **WLC 4**:2608
"Letters" (Harte) **WLC 3**:1580-81
"Letters" (Lewis) **WLC 4**:2087
Letters from America (Brooke) **WLC 1**:442
Letters from England (Capek) **WLC 1**:602
Letters from Iceland (Auden) **WLC 1**:139
Letters from Italy (Capek) **WLC 1**:602
Letters from the Underworld (Dostoevsky)
See *Zapiski iz podpol'ya*
Letters of a Traveller (Sand)
See *Lettres d'un voyageur*
The Letters of J. R. R. Tolkien (Tolkien) **WLC 6**:3653
The Letters of Robert Louis Stevenson (Stevenson) **WLC 5**:3453
The Letters of T. S. Eliot: Volume One, 1898-1922 (Eliot) **WLC 2**:1149
Letters of Two Lovers (Rousseau)
See *La Nouvelle Héloïse*
Letters of Vachel Lindsay (Lindsay) **WLC 4**:2131
Letters on a Regicide Peace (Burke) **WLC 1**:502
Letters to Malcolm: Chiefly on Prayers (Lewis) **WLC 4**:2091
"Letters" (Emerson) **WLC 2**:1171
Letting Go (Roth) **WLC 5**:2964-67, 2972
Les lettres d'Annabel (Voltaire) **WLC 6**:3780
Lettres a Jean Marais (Cocteau) **WLC 2**:733
Lettres d'Amabed (Voltaire) **WLC 6**:3775-76

Lettres d'un voyageur (*Letters of a Traveller*) (Sand) **WLC 5**:3035, 3039
Li Chi (Confucius) **WLCS 1**:254, 258
Li ki (Confucius)
See *Li Chi*
"Li'l Gal" (Dunbar) **WLC 2**:1114
"The Liars" (Sandburg) **WLC 5**:3053
Libation Bearers (Aeschylus) **WLCS 1**:13, 15-16
"The Liberal Lover" (Cervantes)
See "El amante liberal"
Libertad bajo palabra (*Freedom under Parole*; *Liberty behind the Words*) (Paz) **WLC 4**:2659, 2672
"Liberty and Peace" (Wheatley) **WLC 6**:3917, 3922, 3926, 3929
Liberty behind the Words (Paz)
See *Libertad bajo palabra*
"The Library of Babel" (Borges)
See "La biblioteca de Babel"
Libro de poemas (*Poems*) (Garcia Lorca) **WLC 2**:1350
"Lichen" (Munro) (Munro) **WLCS 2**:684
"El licienciado vidriera" ("The Glass Scholar"; "Master Glass") (Cervantes) **WLC 2**:679-80
Lieutenant Schmidt (Pasternak) **WLC 4**:2627, 2632
"Lieutenant Yergunov's Story" (Turgenev)
See "Istoriya leytenanta Ergunova"
Life (Voltaire) **WLC 6**:3771
The Life, Adventures, and Pyracies of the Famous Captain Singleton (*Captain Singleton*) (Defoe) **WLC 2**:868, 870
Life among the Savages (Jackson) **WLC 3**:1838, 1849, 1851
The Life and Adventures of Martin Chuzzlewit (*Martin Chuzzlewit*) (Dickens) **WLC 2**:907
The Life and Adventures of Nicholas Nickleby (*Nicholas Nickleby*) (Dickens) **WLC 2**:898-99
The Life and Death of Mr. Badman (*Badman*) (Bunyan) **WLC 1**:482-83, 486
The Life and Death of the Mayor of Casterbridge: A Story of a Man of Character (Hardy)
See *The Mayor of Casterbridge: The Life and Death of a Man of Character*
Life and Habit (*Short Vindication*) (Butler) **WLC 1**:553, 560-61
The Life and Opinions of Tristram Shandy, Gentleman (*Tristram Shandy*) (Sterne) **WLC 5**:3413, 3415-16, 3418-20, 3422-25
The Life and Strange Surprising Adventures of Robinson Crusoe, of York, Mariner (Defoe) **WLC 2**:865-68, 871-72, 877, 881
Life and Times of Frederick Douglass, Written by Himself (Douglass) **WLC 2**:992-93, 998-99, 1002
"Life for a Life" (Paton) **WLC 4**:2656
"The Life I Led" (Giovanni) **WLCS 1**:359
Life of Duncan Campbell (Defoe) **WLC 2**:874
The Life of Edward II, King of England (Brecht) **WLC 1**:389
The Life of Galileo (Brecht)
See *Leben des Galilei*
The Life of George Washington (Irving) **WLC 3**:1823
The Life of Henri Brulard (Stendhal)
See *Vie de Henri Brulard*
Life of Johnson (Boswell)
See *The Life of Samuel Johnson, LL. D.*
The Life of Klim Samgin (Gorky) **WLC 3**:1493-95
"The Life of Lincoln West" (Brooks) **WLC 1**:457, 462
"Life of Ma Parker" (Mansfield) **WLC 4**:2224, 2227
The Life of Matvey Kozhemyakin (Gorky) **WLC 3**:1493
The Life of Mr. Jonathan Wild the Great (*The History of Jonathan Wild the Great*; *Jonathan Wild*) (Fielding) **WLC 2**:1203-06, 1208, 1210-12
The Life of Samuel Johnson, LL. D. (*Life of Johnson*) (Boswell) **WLC 1**:348, 350-52, 359
The Life of the Insects (Capek)
See *Ze zivota hmyzu*
Life on the Mississippi (Twain) **WLC 6**:3716, 3726
Life Studies (Lowell) **WLC 4**:2155-56, 2159-63, 2165-70
The Life to Come, and Other Stories (Forster) **WLC 2**:1270
"Life Without Principle" (Thoreau) **WLC 6**:3630
"Life's Tragedy" (Dunbar) **WLC 2**:1114
"Lifeguard" (Updike) **WLC 6**:3756
"Ligeia" (Poe) **WLC 4**:2754, 2760
Light in August (Faulkner) **WLC 2**:1189, 1194, 1197, 1199
"The Light o' the Moon" (Lindsay) **WLC 4**:2118
"The Light of Stars" (Longfellow) **WLCS 2**:509
The Light That Failed (Kipling) **WLC 3**:2012
Like a Bulwark (Moore) **WLCS 2**:649
"Like Decorations in a Nigger Cemetery" (Stevens) **WLC 5**:3434
"Lilacs" (Chopin) **WLCS 1**:240
"Lilith" (Rossetti) **WLC 5**:2950
Lille Eyolf (*Little Eyolf*) (Ibsen) **WLC 3**:1784, 1791-92
"Lily Daw and the Three Ladies" (Welty) **WLC 6**:3892
"The Lily's Quest" (Hawthorne) **WLC 3**:1594
Les Limbes (Baudelaire)
See *Les fleurs du mal*
Limbo (Huxley) **WLC 3**:1765
Linden Hills (Naylor) **WLCS 2**:693-94, 696, 698, 702-03
"Lines Above Tintern Abbey" (Wordsworth)
See "Lines Composed a Few Miles Above Tintern Abbey"
"Lines Composed a Few Miles Above Tintern Abbey" ("Lines Above Tintern Abbey"; "Tintern Abbey") (Wordsworth) **WLC 6**:4076
"Lines Written among the Euganean Hills" (Shelley) **WLC 5**:3225
"Lines Written in Dejection" (Yeats) **WLC 6**:4100
"Lines Written in Early Spring" (Wordsworth) **WLC 6**:4072
"Lines Written in Kensington Gardens"

TITLE INDEX

(Arnold) **WLC 1:**100
"Lines Written in the Bay of Lerici" (Shelley) **WLC 5:**3234
"Lines Written on Hearing the News of the Death of Napoleon" (Shelley) **WLC 5:**3234
"Lines...on...the Death of Napoleon" (Shelley) **WLC 5:**3234
The Lion and the Jewel (Soyinka) **WLC 5:**3323, 3325-26, 3328
The Lion and the Unicorn (Orwell) **WLC 4:**2575
The Lion, the Witch, and the Wardrobe (Lewis) **WLC 4:**2082-83, 2093-94
"The Lion's Mane" (Doyle) **WLC 2:**1010
Listening: A Chamber Play (Albee) **WLC 1:**30-3
"Les litanies de satan" ("The Litanies of Satan") (Baudelaire) **WLC 1:**203
"The Litanies of Satan" (Baudelaire)
See "Les litanies de satan"
"A Litany of Atlanta" (Du Bois) **WLC 2:**1062
"The Litany of the Dark People" (Cullen) **WLCS 1:**285
"The Litany of the Heroes" (Lindsay) **WLC 4:**2122
"The Literary Influence of Academies" (Arnold) **WLC 1:**96
Literature and Dogma: An Essay towards a Better Apprehension of the Bible (Arnold) **WLC 1:**92
Literature and Existentialism (Sartre)
See *Qu'est-ce que la littérature?*
Literature and Science (Huxley) **WLC 3:**1769
"Little Brown Baby" (Dunbar) **WLC 2:**1112
Little Dorrit (Dickens) **WLC 2:**903, 909, 911
Little Eyolf (Ibsen)
See *Lille Eyolf*
Little Fadette (Sand)
See *La petite Fadette*
"The Little Fir Tree" (Andersen)
See "The Fir-Tree"
"A Little Free-Mulatto" (Chopin) **WLCS 1:**248
"Little Gidding" (Eliot) **WLC 2:**1151
"The Little Girl" (Mansfield) **WLC 4:**2216
"Little Girl" (Sexton) **WLC 5:**3149
"The Little Hill" (Millay) **WLCS 2:**595, 603
The Little House of Kolomna (Pushkin)
See *Domik v Kolomne*
"Little Ida's Flowers" (Andersen) **WLC 1:**59
The Little Lady of the Big House (London) **WLC 4:**2140
"The Little Man in Black" (Irving) **WLC 3:**1820
"The Little Match Girl" ("The Little Match Seller") (Andersen) **WLC 1:**64-5
"The Little Match Seller" (Andersen)
See "The Little Match Girl"
Little Men: Life at Plumfield with Jo's Boys (Alcott) **WLC 1:**41, 43, 45, 50
"The Little Mermaid" ("The Little Sea-Maid") (Andersen) **WLC 1:**61, 64-6
"The Little Old Women" (Baudelaire)
See "Les petites vielles"
Little Poems in Prose (Baudelaire)
See *Petits poèmes en prose: Le spleen de Paris*
"The Little Sea-Maid" (Andersen) **WLC 1:**59-60
See "The Little Mermaid"
"The Little Shoemakers" (Singer) **WLC 5:**3288, 3290, 3293
Little Tragedies (Pushkin) **WLC 5:**2826, 2828
Little Women; or, Meg, Jo, Beth, and Amy (Alcott) **WLC 1:**37, 39-50
Live or Die (Sexton) **WLC 5:**3137, 3139, 3142-45, 3149
Lives of Girls and Women (Munro) **WLCS 2:**677-79, 681-83, 685, 687
Lives of the English Poets (Johnson)
See *Prefaces, biographical and critical, of the most eminent of the English Poets*
"Lives of the Poets" (Atwood) **WLC 1:**114, 116
The Living Corpse (Tolstoy) **WLC 6:**3665
The Living Mask (Pirandello)
See *Enrico IV*
"A Living Relic" (Turgenev) **WLC 6:**3699-3700
The Living Room (Greene) **WLC 3:**1541-42
Livingstone's Companions (Gordimer) **WLCS 1:**371
"Livvie" (Welty) **WLC 6:**3884
Liza of Lambeth (Maugham) **WLC 4:**2277, 2282
Llanto por Ignacio Sánchez Mejías (*Lament for Ignacio Sánchez Mejías*; *Lament for the Death of a Bullfighter*) (Garcia Lorca) **WLC 2:**1347-50
"The Loan" (Malamud) **WLC 4:**2189
Local Anaesthetic (Grass) 3;1508, 1512-13
Local Color (Capote) **WLC 1:**618
"Locksley Hall" (Tennyson) **WLC 6:**3584
"Lofty Malady" (Pasternak) **WLC 4:**2635
Logbook of the Coiners (Gide)
See *Le journal des faux-monnayeurs*
Lolita (Nabokov) **WLC 4:**2486, 2488-91, 2493, 2495-2501
"London" (Johnson) **WLC 3:**1892-93
"Lonesome" (Dunbar) **WLC 2:**1100
"Long Barren" (Rossetti) **WLC 5:**2931
"Long Black Song" (Wright) **WLC 6:**4090
The Long Christmas Dinner (Wilder) **WLC 6:**3971, 3985
Long Day's Journey into Night (O'Neill) **WLC 4:**2563, 2565-70
The Long Dream (Wright) **WLC 6:**4088, 4092
"The Long Night" (Bambara) **WLCS 1:**134-35
"The Long Shadow of Lincoln: A Litany" (Sandburg) **WLC 5:**3062
"A Long Story" (Gray) **WLC 3:**1526, 1530, 1532
The Long Valley (Steinbeck) **WLC 5:**3382
The Long Voyage Home (O'Neill) **WLC 4:**2558
A Long Way From Home (McKay) **WLC 4:**2335-36, 2338
"The Long Years" (Bradbury) **WLC 1:**370
The Longest Journey (Forster) **WLC 2:**1258-60, 1265-66, 1269
Look Back in Anger (Osborne) **WLC 4:**2592-94, 2596-2602
Look Homeward, Angel (Wolfe) **WLC 6:**4027-32, 4034, 4036-38
Look! We Have Come Through! (Lawrence) **WLC 3:**2049
Looking Back (Maugham)
See *Looking Backward*
"Looking Back" (Heaney) **WLCS 1:**396
Looking Backward (*Looking Back*) (Maugham) **WLC 4:**2283
"Looking in a Mirror" (Atwood) **WLC 1:**111
"The Loom" (Masters) **WLCS 2:**578
"Lord Arthur Savile's Crime: A Study of Duty" (Wilde) **WLC 6:**3952, 3965
"Lord Daer" (Burns)
See "Meeting with Lord Daer"
Lord Jim (Conrad) **WLC 2:**781, 790, 792
Lord Malquist and Mr. Moon (Stoppard) **WLC 6:**3486, 3489
"Lord Mountdrago" (Maugham) **WLC 4:**2281
The Lord of Fontenelle (Harte) **WLC 3:**1582
Lord of the Flies (Golding) **WLC 3:**1445-48, 1450-51, 1453-54, 1457-59
The Lord of the Isles (Scott) **WLC 5:**3116, 3117, 3118
The Lord of the Rings (Tolkien) **WLC 6:**3645, 3647-48, 3650-54, 3656-58
Lord Weary's Castle (Lowell) **WLC 4:**2152, 2155, 2158-62, 2168
Loser Takes All (Greene) **WLC 3:**1547
"Losing Battles" (Welty) 6;3885, 3888-90, 3893
"The Lost Boy" (Wolfe) **WLC 6:**4041
"The Lost Decade" (Fitzgerald) **WLC 2:**1226, 1235
Lost Face (London) **WLC 4:**2139
The Lost Girl (Lawrence) **WLC 3:**2052
The Lost Honor of Katharina Blum: How Violence Develops and Where It Can Lead (Boell)
See *Die verlorene Ehre der Katharina Blum: oder, Wie Gewalt entstehen und wohin sie führen kann*
Lost Illusions (Balzac)
See *Illusions perdues*
A Lost Lady (Cather) **WLC 1:**656
The Lost World (Doyle) **WLC 2:**1020
The Lost Zoo (Cullen) **WLCS 1:**280
"Lot No. 249" (Doyle) **WLC 2:**1018
"La lotería en Babilonia" ("The Babylon Lottery"; "The Lottery in Babylon"; "The Lottery of Babylon") (Borges) **WLC 1:**334
"The Lotos-Eaters" (Tennyson) **WLC 6:**3583, 3587
Lotte in Weimar (*The Beloved Returns*) (Mann) **WLC 4:**2204, 2207
"The Lottery in Babylon" (Borges)
See "La lotería en Babilonia"
"The Lottery of Babylon" (Borges)
See "La lotería en Babilonia"
"The Lottery" (Jackson) **WLC 3:**1835-37, 1840, 1844-45, 1848-49, 1851
Louis Lambert (Balzac) **WLC 1:**185
"Louis" (Saki) **WLC 5:**3005
"Louisa, Please Come Home" (Jackson) **WLC 3:**1851
Lourdes-Rome-Paris (Zola) **WLC 6:**4128
Love a Cheat (Pepys) **WLC 4:**2682

Love, Again (Lessing) **WLCS 2:**498-99
Love among the Artists (Shaw) **WLC 5:**3196
"Love among the Haystacks" (Lawrence) **WLC 3:**2048
Love and Its Derangements (Oates) **WLC 4:**2527
"The Love and the Hate" (Jeffers) **WLC 3:**1884
Love for Love (Congreve) **WLC 2:**759, 763-64, 767-68, 772-74
"Love in a Cottage Is Best" (Dunbar) **WLC 2:**1111
Love in Several Masques (Fielding) **WLC 2:**1213-14
Love Is the Best Doctor (Moliere)
See *l'Amour Médecin*
The Love of Don Perlimplín for Belisa in His Garden (Garcia Lorca)
See *Amor de Don Perlimplín con Belisa en su jardín*
The Love of Landry (Dunbar) **WLC 2:**1101, 1104, 1112-13
Love of Life, and Other Stories (London) **WLC 4:**2139
"The Love-Philtre of Ikey Schoenstein" (Henry) **WLC 3:**1675
Love Poems (Sexton) **WLC 5:**3138, 3143, 3145
"The Love Song of J. Alfred Prufrock" (Eliot) **WLC 2:**1140-41, 1146, 1150
"The Love Song of the Conquering Lovers" (Turgenev)
See "Pesn' torzhestruyushchey lyubvi"
"Love: Is a Human Condition" (Giovanni) **WLCS 1:**360
"Love" (Brooke) **WLC 1:**434
"Love's Apotheosis" (Dunbar) **WLC 2:**1111-12
Love's Labour's Lost (Shakespeare) **WLC 5:**3158-59, 3161-62, 3181
Love's Old Sweet Song (Saroyan) **WLC 5:**3072
"Love's Phases" (Dunbar) **WLC 2:**1112
Love's Pilgrimage (Sinclair) **WLC 5:**3263-64
The Loved One: An Anglo-American Tragedy (Waugh) **WLC 6:**3830-34
"Loveliest of Trees" (Housman) **WLCS 1:**433
"A Lovely Love" (Brooks) **WLC 1:**450, 455-56
The Lover (Pinter) **WLC 4:**2704
"Lovers of the Poor" (Brooks) **WLC 1:**452
The Lovers Watch (Behn)
See *La Montre; or, The Lover's Watch*
"The Lovers" (Andersen) **WLC 1:**60
"Lovers' Death" (Baudelaire)
See "La mort des amants"
Lovers' Spite (Moliere)
See *Le dépit amoureux*
"The Loving Shepherdess" (Jeffers) **WLC 3:**1875
"Low-Lands" (Pynchon) **WLC 5:**2854
The Lower Depths (Gorky)
See *Na dne*
"The Lowest Place" ("The Lowest Room") (Rossetti) **WLC 5:**2941
"The Lowest Room" (Rossetti)
See "The Lowest Place"
"Lucerne" (Tolstoy) **WLC 6:**3666
Lucien Leuwen (Stendhal) **WLC 5:**3399

Lucifer and the Lord (Sartre)
See *Le diable et le bon Dieu*
The Luck of Barry Lyndon (Thackeray)
See *The Memoirs of Barry Lyndon, Esq.*
"The Luck of Roaring Camp" (Harte) **WLC 3:**1578, 1582-83, 1587-90
Luck, or Cunning, as the Main Means of Organic Modifications? (Butler) **WLC 1:**557
The Lucky Chance; or, An Alderman's Bargain (Behn) **WLC 1:**248
The Lucky Mistake (Behn) **WLC 1:**250, 255
Lucrezia Floriani (Sand) **WLC 5:**3039
"Lucubratio Ebria" (Butler) **WLC 1:**553
Lucy Church, Amiably (Stein) **WLC 5:**3363
Lucy Gayheart (Cather) **WLC 1:**660-62
"Lucy Gray" (Wordsworth) **WLC 6:**4067
"Lui?" (Maupassant) **WLC 4:**2301
"The Lull" (Saki) **WLC 5:**3007
"Lullaby" (Silko) **WLCS 2:**758, 762
Lulu's Library (Alcott) **WLC 1:**51
"The Lumber Room" (Saki) **WLC 5:**3000
Luminous Depths (Capek) **WLC 1:**600-01
Lun Yü (Confucius) **WLCS 1:**254, 256-63, 266-67
"Luna Habitabilis" (Gray) **WLC 3:**1533
Luna silvestre (Paz) **WLC 4:**2664, 2671
"Lust" (Brooke) **WLC 1:**436
Lustra (Pound) **WLC 5:**2791, 2802-03
Luther (Osborne) **WLC 4:**2592, 2594-95, 2597
"Luxury, Idleness and Industry" (Franklin) **WLCS 1:**315
"Lycidas" (Milton) **WLC 4:**2407, 2409-11
Lycidus; or, The Lover in Fashion (Behn) **WLC 1:**248
Lycurgea (Aeschylus) **WLCS 1:**6
The Lying Days (Gordimer) **WLCS 1:**368, 374-75, 377
Den lykkelige alder (*The Happy Age*) (Undset) **WLC 6:**3735, 3739-40
"The Lynching of Jube Benson" (Dunbar) **WLC 2:**1102, 1107, 1109
"The Lynching" (McKay) **WLC 4:**2331
The Lyre of Orpheus (Davies) **WLC 2:**854-860
Lyrical Ballads (Coleridge) **WLC 2:**751
Lyrical Ballads, with a Few Other Poems (Wordsworth) **WLC 6:**4064, 4071, 4073-74, 4076
Lyrics of a Lowbrow (Service) **WLC 5:**3130
Lyrics of Love and Laughter (Dunbar) **WLC 2:**1103, 1109, 1113-14
Lyrics of Lowly Life (Dunbar) **WLC 2:**1102-03, 1110-11
Lyrics of Sunshine and Shadow (Dunbar) **WLC 2:**1103, 1114
Lyrics of the Hearthside (Dunbar) **WLC 2:**1103, 1111, 1113
Lysistrata (Aristophanes) **WLCS 1:**73, 77-78, 80, 82
"Ma bohème" ("My Bohemian Life") (Rimbaud) **WLC 5:**2922
"Ma femme" (Maupassant) **WLC 4:**2300
Ma non è una cosa seria (*It Can't Be Serious*) (Pirandello) **WLC 4:**2717
Ma Rainey's Black Bottom (Wilson) **WLCS 1:**860-67, 869

Macbeth (Shakespeare) **WLC 5:**3157, 3174
Macbett (Ionesco) **WLC 3:**1809-10
Macchu Picchu (Neruda)
See *Alturas de Macchu Picchu*
MacFlecknoe; or, A Satire upon the Trew-Blew-Protestant Poet, T. S. (Dryden) **WLC 2:**1051, 1054
La machine àécrire (Cocteau) **WLC 2:**729-32
La machine infernale (*The Infernal Machine*) (Cocteau) **WLC 2:**725, 729-30, 735
"A Mad Negro Soldier Confined at Munich" (Lowell) **WLC 4:**2162, 2166
Madame Bovary (Flaubert) **WLC 2:**1239-52, 1254
"Madame Celestin's Divorce" (Chopin) **WLCS 1:**240, 242
Madame de Sade (Mishima) **WLC 4:**2420
Madame de Treymes (Wharton) **WLC 6:**3907
Madame Dorthea (Undset) **WLC 6:**3743
Madeleine Férat (Zola) **WLC 6:**4123-24
"Mademoiselle Claude" (Miller) **WLC 4:**2391
"Mademoisselle Fifi" (Maupassant) **WLC 4:**2293
Madheart (Baraka) **WLCS 1:**152
A Madman's Defense (Strindberg)
See *Le plaidoyer d'un fou*
"A Madman's Diary" (Gogol)
See "Diary of a Madman"
"The Madness of King Goll" (Yeats) **WLC 6:**4104
A Madrigal (H. D.)
See *Bid Me to Live (A Madrigal)*
Maggie Cassidy (Kerouac) **WLC 3:**1983, 1985, 1987
"Maggie of the Green Bottles" (Bambara) **WLCS 1:**129
Maggie: A Girl of the Streets (Crane) **WLC 2:**814, 818, 820-21
The Magic Barrel (Malamud) **WLC 4:**2181, 2183, 2190
"The Magic Barrel" (Malamud) **WLC 4:**2174, 2176, 2189-90
The Magic Mountain (Mann)
See *Der Zauberberg*
The Magic Skin (Balzac) **WLC 1:**182
The Magician (Nabokov)
See *Volshebnik*
The Magician of Lublin (Singer)
See *Kunstmakher fun Lublin*
The Magician's Nephew (Lewis) **WLC 4:**2082-84, 2087
Magister Ludi (Hesse)
See *Das Glasperlenspiel*
The Magnetic Lady (Jonson) **WLC 3:**1911
The Magnificent Lovers (Moliere)
See *Les amants magnifiques*
"Magnolia Flower" (Hurston) **WLCS 1:**449
Mahagonny (Brecht) **WLC 1:**390
Mahomet (Irving) **WLC 3:**1827
Mahomet and Irene (Johnson)
See *Irene*
"The Maid of Saint Phillippe" (Chopin) **WLCS 1:**240
"Maidenhood" (Longfellow) **WLCS 2:**510

"Mailie's Dying Words and Elegy" (Burns)
See "The Death and Dying Words of Poor Mailie"
Main Street: The Story of Carol Kennicott (Lewis) **WLC 4**:2089, 2101-14
The Maine Woods (Thoreau) **WLC 6**:3635
Les mains sales (*Crime Passionel; Dirty Hands*) (Sartre) **WLC 5**:3091-92, 3095, 3101
"La maison Tellier" (Maupassant) **WLC 4**:2291, 2293-94, 2302-03
"Maithuna" (Paz) **WLC 4**:2666
Les maîtres sonneurs (Sand) **WLC 5**:3041, 3043
Major Barbara (Shaw) **WLC 5**:3191, 3195, 3197, 3199
Majors and Minors (Dunbar) **WLC 2**:1099. 1102, 1108, 1110-11
The Maker (Borges)
See *El hacedor*
The Making of Americans: Being a History of a Family's Progress (*The Making of Americans: The Hersland Family*) (Stein) **WLC 5**:3361, 3369
The Making of Americans: The Hersland Family (Stein)
See *The Making of Americans: Being a History of a Family's Progress*
"Making Strange" (Heaney) **WLCS 1**:389
"Making Strange" (Heaney) **WLCS 1**:397
The Makropoulos Affair (Capek)
See *Vec Makropulos*
The Makropoulos Secret (Capek)
See *Vec Makropulos*
Mal giocondo (Pirandello) **WLC 4**:2731
"Le mal" ("The Evil") (Rimbaud) **WLC 5**:2922
La mala hora (*The Evil Hour; In Evil Hour*) (Garcia Marquez) **WLC 3**:1367
Le malade imaginaire (*The Hypochondriac; The Imaginary Invalid*) (Moliere) **WLC 4**:2436-37, 2440, 2446
Malcolm (Albee) **WLC 1**:26
Malcolm X Speaks (Malcolm X) **WLCS 2**:550
Malcolm X: The Last Speeches (Malcolm X) **WLCS 2**:550, 552
El maleficio de la mariposa (*The Butterfly's Evil Spell; The Spell of the Butterfly; The Witchery of the Butterfly*) (Garcia Lorca) **WLC 2**:1339-40
Le malentendu (*Cross Purpose; The Misunderstanding*) (Camus) **WLC 1**:589-91
Malone Dies (Beckett)
See *Malone meurt*
Malone meurt (*Malone Dies*) (Beckett) **WLC 1**:232-33
"Malva" (Gorky) **WLC 3**:1482, 1485
Mama Day (Naylor) **WLCS 2**:696-98, 703
"Mammy Peggy's Pride" (Dunbar) **WLC 2**:1106
"A Man and Some Others" (Crane) **WLC 2**:825
Man and Superman (Shaw) **WLC 5**:3189, 3192, 3194, 3196, 3199-3200
"The Man and the Snake" (Bierce) **WLC 1**:287, 289
"Man and Wife" (Lowell) **WLC 4**:2156, 2165
Man, Beast, and Virtue (Pirandello)
See *L'uomo, la bestia, e la virtù*
"The Man from Athabaska" (Service) **WLC 5**:3122
"The Man from Mars" (Atwood) **WLC 1**:114-15
"Man of Law's Prologue" (Chaucer)
See "Man of Lawe's Tale"
"Man of Lawe's Tale" (Chaucer) **WLCS 1**:223, 227
The Man of Property (Galsworthy) **WLC 2**:1328, 1330, 1332
"The Man of the Crowd" (Poe) **WLC 4**:2760; **WLC 4**:2753
A Man of the People (Achebe) **WLC 1**:3, 5-6, 9, 12
"The Man of the Year Million" (Wells) **WLC 6**:3875
"A Man on the Beach" (Harte) **WLC 3**:1590
"The Man That Corrupted Hadleyburg" (Twain) **WLC 6**:3720
"The Man Who Became a Woman" (Anderson) **WLC 1**:78-9
"The Man Who Could Work Miracles" (Wells) **WLC 6**:3876
The Man Who Died (*The Escaped Cock*) (Lawrence) **WLC 3**:2045
The Man Who Laughs (Hugo)
See *L'homme qui rit*
"The Man Who Laughs" (Rimbaud) **WLC 5**:2920
"The Man Who Lived Underground" (Wright) **WLC 6**:4087, 4091
"The Man Who Would Be King" (Kipling) **WLC 3**:2011, 2013
The Man with Forty Ecus (Voltaire)
See *L'homme aux quarante écus*
"The Man with the Watches" (Doyle) **WLC 2**:1018
The Man Within (Greene) **WLC 3**:1542-43, 1546
"The Man without a Temperament" (Mansfield) **WLC 4**:2216
"The Man" (Bradbury) **WLC 1**:367
A Man's a Man (Brecht)
See *Mann ist Mann*
Manassas: A Novel of the War (Sinclair) **WLC 5**:3262-63, 3265, 3274
Les mandarins (*The Mandarins*) (Beauvoir) **WLC 1**:220, 223
The Mandarins (Beauvoir)
See *Les mandarins*
Mandela's Earth (Soyinka) **WLC 5**:3332
Mandragola (Machiavelli) **WLCS 2**:528, 531-36
Manfred (Byron) **WLC 1**:568, 575
Manhattan Transfer (Dos Passos) **WLC 2**:955-56, 960, 963-965
Mann ist Mann (*A Man's a Man*) (Brecht) **WLC 1**:386-87, 389-90
The Manor (Singer) **WLC 5**:3292-93
"The Manrique" (Longfellow) **WLCS 2**:504
Mansfield Park (Austen) **WLC 1**:149, 154-55
The Mansion (Faulkner) **WLC 2**:1197-98
The Manticore (Davies) **WLC 2**:848-50, 853-54
Mantrap (Lewis) **WLC 4**:2101
A Manual of Piety (Brecht)
See *Die Hauspostille*
"Manual System" (Sandburg) **WLC 5**:3053
Many Marriages (Anderson) **WLC 1**:75-6, 78
The Map of Love (Thomas) **WLC 6**:3612, 3618
"El mar del tiempo perdido" ("The Sea of Lost Time") (Garcia Marquez) **WLC 3**:1368
"The Maracot Deep" (Doyle) **WLC 2**:1020
The Marble Faun; or, The Romance of Monte Beni (*Transformation; or, The Romance of Monte Beni*) (Hawthorne) **WLC 3**:1596, 1600
Marcel Duchamp o el castillo de la castillo de la pureza (*Marcel Duchamp: Appearance Stripped Bare; Marcel Duchamp, or The Castle of Purity*) (Paz) **WLC 4**:2672
Marcel Duchamp, or The Castle of Purity (Paz)
See *Marcel Duchamp o el castillo de la castillo de la pureza*
Marcel Duchamp: Appearance Stripped Bare (Paz)
See *Marcel Duchamp o el castillo de la castillo de la pureza*
Marchbanks' Almanack (Davies)
See *Samuel Marchbanks' Almanack*
Marching Men (Anderson) **WLC 1**:75, 77-8
Marco Millions (O'Neill) **WLC 4**:2560, 2562
Mardi: And a Voyage Thither (Melville) **WLC 4**:2343
La mare au diable (*The Haunted Marsh; The Haunted Pool*) (Sand) **WLC 5**:3039-41, 3043, 3047
Margaret of Navarre; or, The Massacre of Saint Bartholome's Ev e (Dumas)
See *La reine Margot*
"Margaret" (Wordsworth) **WLC 6**:4071
Le mariage forcé (*The Forced Marriage*) (Moliere) **WLC 4**:2436, 2443
Marian Pineda (Garcia Lorca)
See *Mariana Pineda*
Mariana Pineda (*Marian Pineda*) (Garcia Lorca) **WLC 2**:1340-42, 1352
"Mariana" (Tennyson) **WLC 6**:3579-80, 3583
Marie Antoinette; or, The Chevalier of the Red House: A Tale o f the French Revolution (Dumas)
See *Le chevalier de Maison-Rouge*
"Marie Vaux of the Painted Lips" (Service) **WLC 5**:3131
Le mariés (Cocteau) **WLC 2**:730-31
Les mariés de la Tour Eiffel (*The Wedding on the Eiffel Tower*) (Cocteau) **WLC 2**:729-30
"Marina" (Eliot) **WLC 2**:1147-48
Mariner (Coleridge)
See *The Rime of the Ancient Mariner: A Poet's Reverie*
Marino Faliero: Doge of Venice (Byron) **WLC 1**:575
Mario and the Magician (Mann)
See *Mario und der Zauberer*
Mario und der Zauberer (*Mario and the Magician*) (Mann) **WLC 4**:2198-99
Marion de Lorme (*The King's Edict*) (Hugo) **WLC 3**:1746
Marion Fay (Trollope) **WLC 6**:3681

"Mariposa" (Millay) **WLCS 2:**594
"The Mark of the Beast" (Kipling) **WLC 3:**2013
"Markheim" (Stevenson) **WLC 5:**3451
Marmion (Scott) **WLC 5:**3115-17
Marmor Norfolciense (Johnson) **WLC 3:**1892
Le marquis de Villemer (*The Marquis of Villemer*) (Sand) **WLC 5:**3043
The Marquis of Villemer (Sand)
See *Le marquis de Villemer*
La marquise (Sand) **WLC 5:**3039
Marriage (Gogol)
See *Zhenit'ba; Sovershenno neveroyatnoye sobitye*
Marriage (Strindberg) **WLC 6:**3515-16
The Marriage of Heaven and Hell (Blake) **WLC 1:**306
The Marriage: An Utterly Incredible Occurence (Gogol)
See *Zhenit'ba; Sovershenno neveroyatnoye sobitye*
"Marriage" (Moore) **WLCS 2:**641, 646, 650
Marriages and Infidelities (Oates) **WLC 4:**2526, 2528, 2536
"Married" (Dreiser) **WLC 2:**1038
Marry Me: A Romance (Updike) **WLC 6:**3758
"The Marsh King's Daughter" ("The Bog King's Daughter") (Andersen) **WLC 1:**61-2
Marshlands (Gide)
See *Paludes*
Marsyas, or on the Margin of Literature (Capek) **WLC 1:**602
Martha Quest (Lessing) **WLCS 2:**492
The Martian Chronicles (Bradbury) **WLC 1:**364, 366, 368-72, 374-76
"The Martian" (Bradbury) **WLC 1:**370
Martin Chuzzlewit (Dickens)
See *The Life and Adventures of Martin Chuzzlewit*
Martin Eden (London) **WLC 4:**2138, 2147, 2149
"Maruja" (Harte) **WLC 3:**1583, 1590
The Marvellous Shoemaker's Wife (Garcia Lorca)
See *La zapatera prodigiosa*
Mary (Nabokov)
See *Mashen'ka*
"Mary and Gabriel" (Brooke) **WLC 1:**434
"The `Mary Gloster'" (Kipling) **WLC 3:**2016
"Mary Morison" (Burns)
See "Ye Are Na Mary Morison"
"Mary Postgate" (Kipling) **WLC 1:**65-6
"Mary Winslow" (Lowell) **WLC 4:**2161-62
"Mary" (Mansfield) **WLC 4:**2216
Marya: A Life (Oates) **WLC 4:**2535
Maschere nude (*Naked Masks*) (Pirandello) **WLC 4:**2718, 2732
Mashen'ka (*Mary*) (Nabokov) **WLC 4:**2497
Mask of Comus (Milton)
See *Comus: A Maske*
The Masked Days (Fuentes)
See *Los dís enmascarados*
The Masque of Anarchy (Shelley) **WLC 5:**3227, 3235
Masque of Blacknesse (*Blacknesse*) (Jonson) **WLC 3:**1914

The Masque of Pandora (Longfellow) **WLCS 2:**516
"The Masque of the Red Death" (Poe) **WLC 4:**2754-55, 2760
Die Massnahme (*The Measures Taken*) (Brecht) **WLC 1:**390
Master and Man (Tolstoy)
See *Khozyain i rabotnik*
The Master Builder (Ibsen)
See *Bygmester Solness*
"Master Glass" (Cervantes)
See "El licienciado vidriera"
"Master Hugues of Saxe-Gotha" (Browning) **WLCS 1:**210
"Master Misery" (Capote) **WLC 1:**620, 625, 629
The Master of Ballantrae: A Winter's Tale (Stevenson) **WLC 5:**3451-53, 3459
The Master of Hestviken (Undset) **WLC 6:**3734-35, 3738-39, 3743
"The Master of Mystery" (London) **WLC 4:**2143
Mäster Olof (Strindberg) **WLC 6:**3515
"The Masters" (Heaney) **WLCS 1:**398
"Masts at Dawn" (Warren) **WLC 6:**3815
Mat' (Gorky) **WLC 3:**1487, 1490-93, 1495
"The Match" (Marvell) **WLC 4:**2258
"A Match" (Swinburne) **WLC 6:**3559
The Matchmaker (Wilder) **WLC 6:**3976
"Material" (Munro) **WLCS 2:**676, 682
"Matinée d'ivresse" (Rimbaud) **WLC 5:**2920
"A Matter of Doctrine" (Dunbar) **WLC 2:**1107
"Matthew Arnold's New Poems" (Swinburne) **WLC 6:**3558
Maud, and Other Poems (Tennyson) **WLC 6:**3577, 3579, 3581-84, 3586, 3588
Maud Martha (Brooks) **WLC 1:**457
"Maude Clare" (Rossetti) **WLC 5:**2941
Mauprat (Sand) **WLC 5:**3039, 3042, 3048
Maurice (Forster) **WLC 2:**1267, 1269-70
Maximilian (Masters) **WLCS 2:**576
May-Day and Other Pieces (Emerson) **WLC 2:**1170
"May-Day" (Emerson) **WLC 2:**1171-72
"May Day" (Fitzgerald) **WLC 2:**1231-33, 1235
The Mayflower; or, Sketches of Scenes and Characters among the Descendants of the Puritans (Stowe) **WLC 6:**3506
The Mayor of Casterbridge (Hardy)
See *The Mayor of Casterbridge: The Life and Death of a Man of Character*
The Mayor of Casterbridge: The Life and Death of a Man of Character (*The Life and Death of the Mayor of Casterbridge: A Story of a Man of Character*; *The Mayor of Casterbridge*) (Hardy) **WLC 3:**1561-65, 1571
"The Mayor of Gary" (Sandburg) **WLC 5:**3053
"McAndrew's Hymn" (Kipling) **WLC 3:**2016
"McCluskey's Nell" (Service) **WLC 5:**3131
Measure for Measure (Shakespeare) **WLC 5:**3174, 3182

The Measures Taken (Brecht)
See *Die Massnahme*
The Medall. A Satire Against Sedition (Dryden) **WLC 2:**1051, 1056, 1058
Medea (Euripides) **WLCS 1:**291, 293, 299-301, 305, 307
The Medea and Some Poems (Cullen) **WLCS 1:**280, 282-83
"Medea" (Cullen) **WLCS 1:**280
Le médecin malgré lui (*The Doctor in spite of Himself*) (Moliere) **WLC 4:**2436, 2441, 2445
Le médecin volant (*The Flying Doctor*) (Moliere) **WLC 4:**2436, 2441
Le Médecin de Campagne (*Country Doctor*) (Balzac) **WLC 1:**181-82, 189
"A Medicine for Melancholy" (Bradbury) **WLC 1:**366
Meditations (Kafka)
See *Betrachtung*
"Meditations in Time of Civil War" (Yeats) **WLC 6:**4109-11
Meditations of a Non-Political Man (Mann)
See *Betrachtungen eines Unpolitischen*
"Medley" (Bambara) **WLCS 1:**125
Medny Vsadnik (*The Bronze Horseman*) (Pushkin) **WLC 5:**2824, 2832, 2835-36
"Meeting with Lord Daer" ("Lord Daer") (Burns) **WLC 1:**517
"Meiosis" (Auden) **WLC 1:**138
Meisters Wanderjahre (Goethe) **WLC 3:**1412, 1415
Melancholia (Sartre)
See *La nausée*
"Melanctha" (Stein) **WLC 5:**3360
"Melancthon" (Moore) **WLCS 2:**646
Mélicerte (Moliere) **WLC 4:**2436
The Member of the Wedding (McCullers) **WLC 4:**2309, 2311-14, 2316, 2318-19
Memnon (Aeschylus) **WLCS 1:**6
Memnon; ou, La sagesse humaine (Voltaire) **WLC 6:**3775, 3779
"Mémoire" (Rimbaud) **WLC 5:**2921
Memoires of a Physician (Dumas)
See *Mémoires d'un médecin: Joseph Balsamo*
Les mémoires d'un fou (Flaubert) **WLC 2:**1252
Mémoires d'un médecin: Joseph Balsamo (*Memoires of a Physician*) (Dumas) **WLC 2:**1092, 1094
Mémoires d'une jeune fille rangée (*Memoirs of a Dutiful Daughter*) (Beauvoir) **WLC 1:**224
Memoirs (Williams) **WLC 6:**3998, 4001-03
Memoirs from Underground (Dostoevsky)
See *Zapiski iz podpol'ya*
The Memoirs of a Billiard-Marker (Tolstoy) **WLC 6:**3666
Memoirs of a Cavalier (Defoe) **WLC 2:**870
Memoirs of a Dutiful Daughter (Beauvoir)
See *Mémoires d'une jeune fille rangée*
Memoirs of a Madman (Tolstoy)
See *Zapiski sumasshedshego*
Memoirs of a Midget (de la Mare) **WLC 2:**885-87, 892-94
The Memoirs of a Nihilist (Turgenev)
See *Ottsy i deti*
The Memoirs of a Protestant (Goldsmith) **WLC 3:**1472

The Memoirs of a Sportsman (Turgenev)
See *Zapiski okhotnika*
The Memoirs of a Survivor (Lessing) **WLCS 2:**489-90, 494
The Memoirs of Barry Lyndon, Esq. (*Barry Lyndon*; *The Luck of Barry Lyndon*) (Thackeray) **WLC 6:**3594-95
"Memoirs of M. de Voltaire" (Goldsmith) **WLC 3:**1472
Memoirs of Pascal Paoli (Boswell)
See *An Account of Corsica, The Journal of a Tour to that Island; and the Memoirs of Pascal Paoli*
The Memoirs of Sherlock Holmes (Doyle) **WLC 2:**1018
"Memoirs" (Franklin) **WLCS 1:**322, 324-31
Memorial to Isla Negra (Neruda)
See *Memorial de Isla Negra*
Memorial de Isla Negra (*Black Island Memorial*; *Isla Negra: A Notebook*; *Memorial to Isla Negra*; *Notes from Isla Negra*) (Neruda) **WLC 4:**2511, 2515, 2518-19
"Memorials of a Tour in Italy, 1837" (Wordsworth) **WLC 6:**4072
"Memories of West Street and Lepke" (Lowell) **WLC 4:**2165, 2167
"The Memory of Martha" (Dunbar) **WLC 2:**1107
A Memory of Two Mondays (Miller) **WLC 4:**2371
"A Memory Picture" (Arnold) **WLC 1:**100
"A Memory" (Welty) **WLC 6:**3880, 3883-84
Men at Arms (Waugh) **WLC 6:**3823, 3828
Men Like Gods (Wells) **WLC 6:**3862, 3869, 3871
Men without Women (Hemingway) **WLC 3:**1650-51
Men Without Shadows (Sartre)
See *Morts sans sépulture*
"Mending Wall" (Frost) **WLC 2:**1298
"Menelaus and Helen" (Brooke) **WLC 1:**436
"Menses" (Millay) **WLCS 2:**602
"Mental Cases" (Owen) **WLC 4:**2608, 2610, 2616, 2618
"A Mental Suggestion" (Chopin) **WLCS 1:**241
"Menuet" (Maupassant) **WLC 4:**2298
The Merchant of Venice (Shakespeare) **WLC 5:**3171, 3174
Mercy Street (Sexton) **WLC 5:**3146-47
Mere Christianity (Lewis) **WLC 4:**2083-84, 2090
"La mère sauvage" (Maupassant) **WLC 4:**2297
Meridian (Walker) **WLCS 2:**831
"Merlin and Vivien" (Tennyson) **WLC 6:**3584
"Merlin" (Emerson) **WLC 2:**1171
Mérope (Voltaire) **WLC 6:**3769, 3779
The Merry Men and Other Tales and Fables (Stevenson) **WLC 5:**3447, 3452
"Mes petites amoureuses" ("My Little Lovers") (Rimbaud) **WLC 5:**2923
"A Mess of Pottage" (Dunbar) **WLC 2:**1106, 1109
"The Messiah" (Pope) **WLC 5:**2771

"Messidor" (Swinburne) **WLC 6:**3563
The Metamorphosis (Kafka)
See *Die verwandlung*
"The Metaphysical Poets" (Eliot) **WLC 2:**1137
Metaphysics (Aristotle) **WLCS 1:**96-98
Meteor (Capek)
See *Provetron*
"Metro" (Pound) **WLC 5:**2794
The Metropolis (Sinclair) **WLC 5:**3263
"Metzengerstein" (Poe) 4;2753
Le meunier d'Angibault (*The Miller of Angibault*) (Sand) **WLC 5:**3041
Mexico City Blues (Kerouac) **WLC 3:**1983, 1985-86
Micah Clarke (Doyle) **WLC 2:**1019
Michael Angelo (Longfellow) **WLCS 2:**514, 516
Michael, Brother of Jerry (London) **WLC 4:**2140
Michael Robartes and the Dancer (Yeats) **WLC 6:**4110
"Michael" (Wordsworth) **WLC 6:**4068, 4071, 4076
Micromégas (Voltaire) **WLC 6:**3775, 3780-81
Mid-American Chants (Anderson) **WLC 1:**80
"Mid-Twentieth-Century Portrait" (Milosz) **WLCS 2:**620
Midcentury (Dos Passos) **WLC 2:**966
"The Middle Toe of the Right Foot" (Bierce) **WLC 1:**293
Middlemarch: A Study of Provincial Life (Eliot) **WLC 2:**1117, 1119, 1122-23, 1126-27, 1130-31
"Midnight Chippie's Lament" (Hughes) **WLC 3:**1723
Midnight's Children (Rushdie) **WLCS 2:**744-46, 748, 753
"Midpoint" (Updike) **WLC 6:**3755, 3757-58
"A Midsummer Holiday" (Swinburne) **WLC 6:**3566
A Midsummer Night's Dream (Shakespeare) **WLC 5:**3158-59, 3161-62, 3171, 3173
Mignons (Goethe) **WLC 3:**1413
"A Migration" (Heaney) **WLCS 1:**397
"El milagro secreto" ("The Secret Miracle") (Borges) **WLC 1:**341
"Miles City, Montana" (Munro) **WLCS 2:**683-84
De militia romana libri quinque (Lipsius) **WLC 2:**870
The Milk Train Doesn't Stop Here Anymore (Williams) **WLC 6:**3995-96, 3998
The Mill on the Floss (Eliot) 1117, 1119-20, 1123, 1127
The Miller of Angibault (Sand)
See *Le meunier d'Angibault*
"The Miller's Daughter" (Tennyson) **WLC 6:**3583
"Miller's Tale" (Chaucer) **WLCS 1:**230
"The Million-Year Picnic" (Bradbury) **WLC 1:**370
The Millionairess (Shaw) **WLC 5:**3193
The Mills of the Kavanaughs (Lowell) **WLC 4:**2161, 2168
"The Mills of the Kavanaughs" (Lowell) **WLC 4:**2161, 2168

Milton (Blake) **WLC 1:**310
Mind at the End of Its Tether (Wells) **WLC 6:**3859
Mind Breaths: Poems, 1972-1977 (Ginsberg) **WLC 3:**1403
"The Mind's Games" (Williams) **WLC 6:**4020
Mine the Harvest (Millay) **WLCS 2:**600, 602-03
"Miners" (Owen) **WLC 4:**2607, 2609, 2618
"The Minister's Black Veil" (Hawthorne) **WLC 3:**1597, 1601
The Ministry of Fear (Greene) **WLC 3:**1542, 1544-45
The Minstrelsy of the Scottish Border (Scott) **WLC 5:**3116, 3118
Miracles (Lewis) **WLC 4:**2082, 2090
Mirgorod (Gogol) **WLC 3:**1439
"Miriam" (Capote) **WLC 1:**618-19, 626
"The Mirror of the Enigmas" (Borges) **WLC 1:**344
The Mirror of the Sea (Conrad) **WLC 2:**782
"Mirrors" (Giovanni) **WLCS 1:**360
Misalliance (Shaw) **WLC 5:**3192
Miscellaneous Observations on the Tragedy of Macbeth (Johnson) **WLC 3:**1893
Miscellanies (Fielding) **WLC 2:**1203-04
"A Miscellany of Characters That Will Not Appear" (Cheever) **WLC 2:**691, 696
The Miser (Moliere)
See *L'avare*
Les misérables (*The Wretched*) (Hugo) **WLC 3:**1741, 1743, 1745-48
"Misery" (Chekhov) **WLC 2:**708
"A Misfortunate Girl" (Turgenev)
See "Neschastnaya"
"Miss Drake Proceeds to Supper" (Plath) **WLC 4:**2741
"Miss Harriet" (Maupassant) **WLC 4:**2293, 2300
Miss Julie (Strindberg)
See *Fröken Julie*
Miss Lucy in Town, A Sequel to the Virgin Unmasked (Fielding) **WLC 2:**1214
Miss Mackenzie (Trollope) **WLC 6:**3681
"Miss McEnders" (Chopin) **WLCS 1:**247
"The Mission of Mr. Scatters" (Dunbar) **WLC 2:**1107
"Mississippi Levee" (Hughes) **WLC 3:**1724
The Misunderstanding (Camus)
See *Le malentendu*
A Mixture of Frailties (Davies) **WLC 2:**848, 852-54, 857-59
Moby-Dick; or, The Whale (*The Whale*) (Melville) 2345, 2347, 2350-51
"A Model Millionaire: A Note of Admiration" (Wilde) **WLC 6:**3952
A Modern Comedy (Galsworthy) **WLC 2:**1329-30, 1333
"Modern Fiction" (Woolf) **WLC 6:**4048, 4054
The Modern Husband (Fielding) **WLC 2:**1213-14
A Modern Mephistopheles (Alcott) **WLC 1:**41
"A Modern Mephistopheles or The Fatal Love Chase" (Alcott) **WLC 1:**49
A Modern Utopia (Wells) **WLC 6:**3867,

3874
"Modest Enquiry into the Nature and Necessity of Paper Money" (Franklin) **WLCS 1:**315
Modest Proposal for Preventing the Children of the Poor People from Being a Burthen (Swift) **WLC 6:**3545-46
"Mogollon Morning" (Momaday) **WLCS 2:**635
Moi universitety (*My Universities*) (Gorky) **WLC 3:**1485-87
Moise and the World of Reason (Williams) **WLC 6:**4001
Moll Flanders (Defoe)
See *The Fortunes and Misfortunes of the Famous Moll Flanders*
Molloy (Beckett) **WLC 1:**231-33
Mon coeur mis à nu ("My Heart Laid Bare") (Baudelaire) **WLC 1:**200
"Mon oncle Jules" (Maupassant) **WLC 4:**2297
"Monadnoc" (Emerson) **WLC 2:**1172
Le monde comme il va (Voltaire) **WLC 6:**3779
"Money and How It Gets That Way" (Miller) **WLC 4:**2391
Money and Other Stories (Capek)
See *Trapné povídky*
"The Money Diggers" (Irving) **WLC 3:**1828
The Moneychangers (Sinclair) **WLC 5:**3263
The Monk and the Hangman's Daughter (Bierce) **WLC 1:**282, 287
"Monk's Tale" (Chaucer) **WLCS 1:**231
"Monna Innominata" (Rossetti) **WLC 5:**2941-42
Monologue (Pinter) **WLC 4:**2706-07
"Monologue of Segismund" (Borges) **WLC 1:**343
Monsieur de Pourceaugnac (Moliere) **WLC 4:**2436-37, 2445
"Monsieur les Deux Chapeaux" (Munro) **WLCS 2:**684
"Monsieur Parent" (Maupassant) **WLC 4:**2293-94
The Monster (Crane) **WLC 2:**818, 820
Les monstres sacrés (*Sacred Monsters*) (Cocteau) **WLC 2:**729
"Mont Blanc" (Shelley) **WLC 5:**3228, 3233, 3237-38
Montage of a Dream Deferred (Hughes) **WLC 3:**1727-28, 1731-32
A Month of Sundays (Updike) **WLC 6:**3756, 3758
La Montre; or, The Lover's Watch (*The Lovers Watch*) (Behn) **WLC 1:**248
"A Monument I Reared" (Pushkin) **WLC 5:**2835
Moods (Alcott) **WLC 1:**49, 51
The Moon and Sixpence (Maugham) **WLC 4:**2281
Moon for the Misbegotten (O'Neill) **WLC 4:**2563, 2566
"The Moon in the Orange Street Skating Rink" (Munro) **WLCS 2:**684
"The Moon in Your Hands" (H. D.) **WLC 3:**1616
The Moon Is a Gong (*The Garbage Man*) (Dos Passos) **WLC 2:**963
The Moon of the Caribbees (O'Neill) **WLC 4:**2558

The Moons of Jupiter (Munro) **WLCS 2:**683-84
The Moor of Peter the Great (Pushkin)
See *The Negro of Peter the Great*
The Moor's Last Sigh (Rushdie) **WLCS 2:**749, 752-55
"Moose Island" (H. D.) **WLC 3:**1624
"The Morals of Chess" (Franklin) **WLCS 1:**314
More Collected Verse (Service) **WLC 5:**3132
More Poems (Housman) **WLCS 1:**430-31, 437
More Pricks than Kicks (Beckett) **WLC 1:**231
"Morella" (Poe) **WLC 4:**2760
"Morning at the Window" (Eliot) **WLC 2:**1147-48
"Morning Scene" (Huxley) **WLC 3:**1764
"Morning" (Wheatley)
See "An Hymn to the Morning""Morning After" (Hughes) **WLC 3:**1724
"La mort des amants" ("The Death of Lovers"; "Lovers' Death") (Baudelaire) **WLC 1:**203
"La mort des artistes" (Baudelaire) **WLC 1:**205
"Le mort joyeux" ("Happier Dead") (Baudelaire) **WLC 1:**205
"The Mortal Immortal" (Shelley) **WLC 5:**3215
"Mortal Limit" (Warren) **WLC 6:**3816
Une morte très douce (*A Very Easy Death*) (Beauvoir) **WLC 1:**224
"Morte d'Arthur" ("The Passing of Arthur") (Tennyson) **WLC 6:**3583-84
Le Morte Darthur (Malory) **WLCS 2:**556-58, 563, 565-66, 569-70
"Mortmain" (Warren) **WLC 6:**3814
"Morts de quatre-vingt-douze et de quatre-vingt-treize" (Rimbaud) **WLC 5:**2922
Morts sans sépulture (*The Dead Without Burial*; *Men Without Shadows*; *The Victors*) (Sartre) **WLC 5:**3091-92, 3095
Moses, Man of the Mountain (Hurston) **WLCS 1:**453
"The Moss of His Skin" (Sexton) **WLC 5:**3140
"Mossbawn" (Heaney) **WLCS 1:**395
Mosses from an Old Manse (Hawthorne) **WLC 3:**1594, 1598-1600
Most Likely to Succeed (Dos Passos) **WLC 2:**962, 965
The Mother (Brecht)
See *Die Mutter*
Mother (Gorky) **WLC 3:**1487, 1490-93, 1495
Mother Courage and Her Children (Brecht)
See *Mutter Courage und ihre Kinder*
"Mother Hubberd's Tale" (Spenser)
See "Prosopopoia; or, Mother Hubberds Tale"
Mother Night (Vonnegut) **WLC 6:**3786, 3788-89, 3791-92, 3797
"Mother to Son" (Hughes) **WLC 3:**1725
"Mother" (Anderson) **WLC 1:**81
Mother's Garden (Walker)
See *In Search of Our Mothers' Gardens*
The Mother's Recompense (Wharton)

WLC 6:3908, 3911
Motley, and Other Poems (de la Mare) **WLC 2:**890
Les mots (*The Words*) (Sartre) **WLC 5:**3099
"Mouche" (Maupassant) **WLC 4:**2303
Les mouches (*The Flies*) (Sartre) **WLC 5:**3090, 3092, 3100
Mountain Interval (Frost) **WLC 2:**1292
"The Mountain" (Frost) **WLC 2:**1299
"Mountains" (Auden) **WLC 1:**131
"Mountjoy" (Irving) **WLC 3:**1821
"The Mourner's Bench" (Masters) **WLCS 2:**580
"The Mourners" (Malamud) **WLC 4:**2183, 2187
"Mournin' For Religion" (Masters) **WLCS 2:**580
Mourning Becomes Electra (O'Neill) **WLC 4:**2561, 2563, 2565-66
The Mourning Bride (Congreve) **WLC 2:**759, 763-64, 768, 770, 773-74
"Mourning" (Marvell) **WLC 4:**2252
"The Mouse" (Burns) **WLC 1:**517
A Moveable Feast (Hemingway) **WLC 3:**1659
A Moving Target (Golding) **WLC 3:**1455-56, 1458-59
"The Mower against gardens" (Marvell) **WLC 4:**2258
"Mowing" (Frost) **WLC 2:**1290-91
"Moxon's Master" (Bierce) **WLC 1:**288
Mozart and Salieri (Pushkin) **WLC 5:**2825-26, 2832, 2836
Mr. Bennett and Mrs. Brown (Woolf) **WLC 6:**4048-49
Mr. Britling Sees It Through (Wells) **WLC 6:**3858-59
"Mr. Cornelius Johnson, Office Seeker" (Dunbar) **WLC 2:**1106
"Mr. Costyve Duditch" (Toomer) **WLCS 2:**801
"Mr. Groby's Slippery Gift" (Dunbar) **WLC 2:**1107
"Mr. Harrington's Washing" (Maugham) **WLC 4:**2281
"Mr. Higginbotham's Catastrophe" (Hawthorne) **WLC 3:**1594
"Mr. Nixon" (Pound) **WLC 5:**2791
Mr. Polly (Wells) **WLC 6:**3858, 3861
Mr. Sammler's Planet (Bellow) **WLC 1:**265-67, 270-72, 276
Mr. Scarborough's Family (Trollope) **WLC 6:**3681
Mr. Smirk; or, The Divine in Mode (*The Divine in Mode*) (Marvell) **WLC 4:**2255
"Mrs. Battle's Opinions on Whist!" (Lamb) **WLC 3:**2027
"Mrs. Benjamin Pantier" (Masters) **WLCS 2:**584
Mrs. Dalloway (Woolf) **WLC 6:**4046-48, 4052-56, 4058
Mrs. Hjelde (Undset)
See *Fru Hjelde*
Mrs. Marta Oulie (Undset)
See *Fru Marta Oulie*
"Mrs. Mobry's Reason" (Chopin) **WLCS 1:**239
"Mrs. Small" (Brooks) **WLC 1:**451
"Mrs. Williams" (Masters) **WLCS 2:**584
"MS. Found in a Bottle" (Poe) **WLC 4:**2753, 2755-56, 2758, 2760-62

"Mt. Pisgah's Christmas Possum" (Dunbar) **WLC 2:**1106
Much Ado about Nothing (Shakespeare) **WLC 5:**3161, 3174
La muerte de Artemio Cruz (*The Death of Artemio Cruz*) (Fuentes) **WLC 2:**1310, 1319, 1321-22
"El muerto" ("The Dead Man") (Borges) **WLC 1:**335
"Mulatto" (Hughes) **WLC 3:**1727
Mules and Men (Hurston) **WLCS 1:**448
"Mumu" (Turgenev) **WLC 6:**3697, 3702-03
"The Municipal Gallery Revisited" (Yeats) **WLC 6:**4112
"A Municipal Report" (Henry) **WLC 3:**1669, 1674-75, 1677
Le mur (*Intimacy, and Other Stories; The Wall, and Other Stories*) (Sartre) **WLC 5:**3094
Murder in the Cathedral (Eliot) **WLC 2:**1148
"The Murders in the Rue Morgue" (Poe) **WLC 4:**2762
Murke's Collected Silences (Boell)
See *Doktor Murkes gesammeltes Schweigen, und andere Satiren*
Murphy (Beckett) **WLC 1:**233
"The Muse of the Coming Age" (Andersen) **WLC 1:**60
"Musée des Beaux Arts" (Auden) **WLC 1:**135
The Muses Are Heard: An Account of the Porgy and Bess Tour to Leningrad (Capote) **WLC 1:**618, 629
"The Musgrave Ritual" (Doyle) **WLC 2:**1009
"The Music Lesson" (Cheever) **WLC 2:**697
"Music Swims Back to Me" (Sexton) **WLC 5:**3140-41
"The Music Teacher" (Cheever) **WLC 2:**698
"Must the Novelist Crusade" (Welty) **WLC 6:**3890
"The Mutability of Literature" (Irving) **WLC 3:**1827
The Mutilated (Williams)
See *The Gnädiges Fräulein*
The Mutiny of the Elsinore (London) **WLC 4:**2140
Die Mutter (*The Mother*) (Brecht) **WLC 1:**390
Mutter Courage und ihre Kinder (*Mother Courage and Her Children*) (Brecht) **WLC 1:**384, 386-87, 391-92
"Muttsy" (Hurston) **WLCS 1:**449-50
"My Adventures As a Social Poet" (Hughes) **WLC 3:**1731-32
"My ain kind Dearie" (Burns) **WLC 1:**518
My ántonia (Cather) **WLC 1:**653-57, 659-60, 663-66
My Apprenticeship (Gorky) **WLC 3:**1487
"My Aunt" (Irving) **WLC 3:**1820
"My Bohemian Life" (Rimbaud)
See "Ma bohème"
My Bondage and My Freedom (Douglass) **WLC 2:**992-93, 996-1003
My Childhood (Gorky)
See *Detstvo*
"My Dream" (Rossetti) **WLC 5:**2937
"My Dungeon Shook" (Baldwin) **WLC 1:**169

"My Father Moved through Dooms of Feel" (Cummings)
See "My Father Moved through Dooms of Love"
"My Father Moved through Dooms of Love" ("My Father Moved through Dooms of Feel") (Cummings) **WLC 2:**841
"My Favorite Murder" (Bierce) **WLC 1:**281, 288
"My Fellow-Traveller" (Gorky) **WLC 3:**1485
"My First Article" (Frank) **WLC 2:**1279, 1283
"My First Book" (Golding) **WLC 3:**1459
My Friend Hitler (Mishima)
See *Wagatomo Hitler*
"My Friends" (Service) **WLC 5:**3123
"My Grandmother's Love Letters" (Crane) **WLC 2:**799-800
"My Heart Laid Bare" (Baudelaire)
See "Mon coeur mis à nu"
My Heart's in the Highlands (Saroyan) **WLC 5:**3072, 3076-77, 3079-80, 3084
My House (Giovanni) **WLCS 1:**359
"My House" (Giovanni) **WLCS 1:**363
"My Kinsman, Major Molineux" (Hawthorne) **WLC 3:**1605
"My Last Afternoon with Uncle Devereux Winslow" (Lowell) **WLC 4:**2163, 2167
"My Library" (Service) **WLC 5:**3130
My Life (Sand)
See *Histoire de ma vie*
My Life as a Man (Roth) **WLC 5:**2975
"My Life Had Stood—A Loaded Gun" (Dickinson) **WLC 2:**924
"My Life with R. H. Macy" (Jackson) **WLC 3:**1851
"My Life" (Chekhov) **WLC 2:**708, 710-11
"My Light With Yours" (Masters) **WLCS 2:**578
"My Little Lovers" (Rimbaud)
See "Mes petites amoureuses"
"My Lost City" (Fitzgerald) **WLC 2:**1235
"My Man Bovanne" (Bambara) **WLCS 1:**129
"My mistress' eyes are nothing like the sun" (Shakespeare)
See "Sonnet 130"
My Mortal Enemy (Cather) **WLC 1:**656
"My Name Is Red Hot. Yo Name Ain Doodley Squat" (Brooks)
See "Five Men against the Theme, `My Name is Red Hot. Yo Name ain Doodley Squat'"
"My Nanie O" (Burns) **WLC 1:**518
"My Own Heart Let Me More Have Pity On" (Hopkins) **WLC 1:**1715
"My Pal" (Service) **WLC 5:**3131
"My Partner and My Guide" (Wordsworth) **WLC 6:**4073
"My Poem" (Giovanni) **WLCS 1:**352
"My Side of the Matter" (Capote) **WLC 1:**619
My Sister, Life (Pasternak)
See *Sestra moia zhizn*
"My Sister's Sleep" (Rossetti) **WLC 5:**2950-51
My Soul's High Song (Cullen) **WLCS 1:**283
"My Star" (Browning) **WLCS 1:**208

"My Uncle John" (Irving) **WLC 3:**1820
My Uncle Toby (Sterne) **WLC 5:**3419
My Universities (Gorky)
See *Moi universitety*
My Universities (Gorky) **WLC 3:**1485-87
"Mycerinus" (Arnold) **WLC 1:**100
Myrmidons (Aeschylus) **WLCS 1:**8, 14
Mysians (Aeschylus) **WLCS 1:**9
"The Mysteries of the Joy Rio" (Williams) **WLC 6:**4003
Mysteries of Winterthurn (Oates) **WLC 4:**2536-37
"The Mysterious Chamber" (Twain) **WLC 6:**3720
The Mysterious Stranger (Twain) **WLC 6:**3718
"Mystic" (Plath) **WLC 4:**2740
"Myth of Mountain Sunrise" (Warren) **WLC 6:**3814
The Myth of Sisyphus (Camus)
See *Le mythe de Sisyphe*
Le mythe de Sisyphe (*The Myth of Sisyphus*) (Camus) **WLC 1:**584-86, 590-94
Na dne (*The Lower Depths*) (Gorky) **WLC 3:**1483-84, 1490
Na rannikh poezdakh (*On Early Trains*) (Pasternak) **WLC 4:**2628
"Nabo: The Black Man Who Made the Angels Wait" (Garcia Marquez) **WLC 3:**1363-65
Nakanune (*On the Eve*) (Turgenev) **WLC 6:**3703, 3708-10
Naked (Pirandello)
See *Vestire gli ignudi*
Naked Life (Pirandello)
See *La vita nuda*
Naked Lunch (Burroughs) **WLC 1:**534-38, 541-44
Naked Masks (Pirandello)
See *Maschere nude*
"Nam Bok the Unveracious" (London) **WLC 4:**2142
The Name and Nature of Poetry (Housman) **WLCS 1:**432, 434
"The Name-Day Party" ("The Party") (Chekhov) **WLC 2:**708-09
The Name of Action (Greene) **WLC 3:**1542, 1546
The Names (Momaday) **WLCS 2:**632
Nana (Zola) **WLC 6:**4118, 4124, 4126
"The Nana-Hex" (Sexton) **WLC 5:**3146
Nanine (Voltaire) **WLC 6:**3769
Nar vi døde vagner (*When We Dead Awaken*) (Ibsen) **WLC 3:**1777, 1781-82, 1784, 1786-87
Narcissus and Goldmund (Hesse)
See *Narziss und Goldmund*
"Narnia" (Lewis) **WLC 4:**2090
The Narrative of Arthur Gordon Pym ("Arthur Gordon Pym") (Poe) **WLC 4:**2753, 2755-57
Narrative of the Life of Frederick Douglass, an American Slave, Written by Himself (Douglass) **WLC 2:**989-994, 996-1003
The Narrow Corner (Maugham) **WLC 4:**2284-85
"Narthex" (H. D.) **WLC 3:**1624
Narziss und Goldmund (*Narcissus and Goldmund*) (Hesse) **WLC 3:**1693
Natalie Mann (Toomer) **WLCS 2:**801

"he National Pastime" (Cheever) **WLC 2**:696
"ationality in Drinks" (Browning) **WLCS 1**:208
tive Realm: A Search for Self-Definition (Milosz) **WLCS 2**:609, 614, 620-21
tive Son (Wright) **WLC 6**:4081-83, 4086, 4088, 4092-93
ativity Ode" (Milton)
  See "On the Morning of Christ's Nativity"
e Natural (Malamud) **WLC 4**:2173, 2176, 2178-81, 2184
ture (Emerson) **WLC 2**:1173-74, 1180, 1182
ature" (Longfellow) **WLCS 2**:507
ature" (Turgenev) **WLC 6**:3707
e Naulahka (Kipling) **WLC 3**:2012
usea (Sartre)
  See La nausée
nausée (Melancholia; Nausea) (Sartre) **WLC 5**:3088, 3091, 3098, 3100-01
ar the Ocean (Lowell) **WLC 4**:2168, 2170
ear White" (Cullen) **WLCS 1**:274
ecessary Angel" ("Shepherds' Hymn") (Stevens) **WLC 5**:3438
he Neckan" (Arnold) **WLC 1**:92-3
he Necklace" (Maupassant)
  See "La parure"
eeds Must" (Strindberg) **WLC 6**:3536
eg Creol" (Chopin) **WLCS 1**:248
egligible Tales" (Bierce) **WLC 1**:288
e Negro (Du Bois) **WLC 2**:1072
he Negro and the Constitution" (King) **WLCS 1**:471
he Negro Artist and the Racial Mountain" (Hughes) **WLC 3**:1729, 1731, 1733-34
he Negro Hero" (Brooks) **WLC 1**:453
Negro Love Song" (Dunbar) **WLC 2**:1111
e Negro of Peter the Great (The Moor of Peter the Great; The Nigger of Peter the Great) (Pushkin) **WLC 5**:2828
Negro Speaks of Rivers" (Hughes) **WLC 3**:1727
eighbour Rosicky" (Cather) **WLC 1**:657
else Hatton's Revenge" ("Nelse Hatton's Vengeance") (Dunbar) **WLC 2**:1106
else Hatton's Vengeance" (Dunbar)
  See "Nelse Hatton's Revenge"
mea (Aeschylus) **WLCS 1**:8
ené e Niní" (Pirandello) **WLC 4**:2717
ereids (Aeschylus) **WLCS 1**:8
eschastnaya" ("A Misfortunate Girl"; "The Unfortunate"; "An Unhappy Girl") (Turgenev) **WLC 6**:3699
e Nest of Gentlefolk (Turgenev)
  See Dvoryanskoe gnezdo
est of Noblemen (Turgenev)
  See Dvoryanskoe gnezdo
est of the Gentry (Turgenev)
  See Dvoryanskoe gnezdo
he Nest of the White Ant" (Mishima) **WLC 4**:2418
Net to Snare in the Moonlight" (Lindsay) **WLC 4**:2118
t-Draggers (Aeschylus) **WLCS 1**:7
t-Drawers (Aeschylus) **WLCS 1**:13
ever Again Would Birds' Song Be the Same" (Frost) **WLC 2**:1301, 1304

"Nevskij Avenue" (Gogol)
  See "Nevsky Prospect"
"Nevsky Prospect" ("Nevskij Avenue") (Gogol) **WLC 3**:1431, 1437
"The New Accelerator" (Wells) **WLC 6**:3874, 3876
New and Selected Poems: 1923-1985 (Warren) **WLC 6**:3814-16
The New Arabian Nights ("The Dynamiter") (Stevenson) **WLC 5**:3446-48
"The New Country House" (Chekhov)
  See "The New Villa"
New Eloise (Rousseau)
  See La Nouvelle Héloïse
New England Tragedies (Longfellow) **WLCS 2**:505, 513, 516
New-Found-Land (Stoppard) **WLC 6**:3493
New Hampshire (Frost) **WLC 2**:1297
The New Inn (Jonson) **WLC 3**:1911
A New Life (Malamud) **WLC 4**:2173, 2176, 2178-81, 2184-85
A New Lovesong for Stalingrad (Neruda)
  See Nuevo canto de amor a Stalingrado
The New Nationalism (Baraka) **WLCS 1**:153
"A New Psalm for the Chapel of Kilmarnock" (Burns) **WLC 1**:523
The New Spoon River (Masters) **WLCS 2**:577-78, 580-81
The New Tenant (Ionesco)
  See Le nouveau locataire
A New Testament (Anderson) **WLC 1**:80
"The New Villa" ("The New Country House") (Chekhov) **WLC 2**:710
A New Voyage Round the World (Defoe) **WLC 2**:870
"A New Year Greeting" (Auden) **WLC 1**:138
New Year Letter (Auden) **WLC 1**:135, 139
New Year's Day (Wharton) **WLC 6**:3911
New York Quartet (Wharton)
  See Old New York
The Newcomes: Memoirs of a Most Respectable Family (Thackeray) **WLC 6**:3587, 3601-05
"News of Paris—Fifteen Years Ago" (Fitzgerald) **WLC 2**:1235-36
"Newsreel: Man and Firing Squad" (Atwood) **WLC 1**:112
Nicholas Nickleby (Dickens)
  See The Life and Adventures of Nicholas Nickleby
Nicomachean Ethics (Aristotle) **WLCS 1**:103
"Nigger Book" (Rimbaud) **WLC 5**:2908
The Nigger of Peter the Great (Pushkin)
  See The Negro of Peter the Great
The Nigger of the "Narcissus" (Conrad) **WLC 2**:779, 782
"The night is freezing fast" (Housman) **WLCS 1**:435
Night (Pinter) **WLC 4**:2705-06
Night (Wiesel) **WLCS 2**:843, 845-48, 853-54, 856
Night and Day (Stoppard) **WLC 6**:3484, 3493, 3495
Night and Day (Woolf) **WLC 6**:4053-54, 4058
"The Night-Born" (London) **WLC 4**:2140

"The Night-Doings at `Deadman's'" (Bierce) **WLC 1**:293
"A Night in New Arabia" (Henry) **WLC 3**:1667
"Night Meeting" (Bradbury) **WLC 1**:370
"Night of Hell" (Rimbaud)
  See "Nuit de l'enfer"
"The Night of the Curlews" (Garcia Marquez)
  See "La noche de los alcaravanes"
The Night of the Iguana (Williams) **WLC 6**:3993, 3995-98
A Night Out (Pinter) **WLC 4**:2700-02, 2704
Night School (Pinter) **WLC 4**:2704
Night-Side (Oates) **WLC 4**:2536
"Night Sketches" (Hawthorne) **WLC 3**:1606, 1608
"The Nightingale" (Andersen) **WLC 1**:67
"Nightingale" (Keats)
  See "Ode to a Nightingale"
"A Nightmare" (Rossetti) **WLC 5**:2937
"Nikki-Rosa" (Giovanni) **WLCS 1**:359
"Nina Replies" (Rimbaud)
  See "Les reparties de Nina"
Nine Stories (Salinger) **WLC 5**:3018, 3020
Nineteen Eighty-Four (1984) (Orwell) **WLC 4**:2577-79, 2581-88
1914 and Other Poems (Brooke) **WLC 1**:435, 437, 441, 446
1919 (Dos Passos) **WLC 2**:965
95 Poems (Cummings) **WLC 2**:842-43
"91 Revere Street" (Lowell) **WLC 4**:2155, 2162, 2166
Ninety-Three (Hugo)
  See Quatre-vingt treize
Niobe (Aeschylus) **WLCS 1**:7, 14
No Abolition of Slavery (Boswell) **WLC 1**:355
"No Coward Soul Is Mine" (Bronte) **WLC 1**:430
"No Door" (Wolfe) **WLC 6**:4040
No Exit (Sartre)
  See Huis clos
"No Lilies for Lisette" (Service) **WLC 5**:3131
No Longer at Ease (Achebe) **WLC 1**:4-6, 12
No Man's Land (Pinter) **WLC 4**:2703, 2706-07, 2710
No Name in the Street (Baldwin) **WLC 1**:168-69
No One Writes to the Colonel (Garcia Marquez)
  See El colonel no tiene quien le escribe
No Parasan! (They Shall Not Pass): A Story of the Battle of Madrid (Sinclair) **WLC 5**:3270
No Thanks (Cummings) **WLC 2**:841
Nobel Lecture by Aleksandr Solzhenitsyn (Solzhenitsyn)
  See Nobelevskaia lektsii politerature 1970 goda
"The Nobel Rider and the Sound of Words" (Stevens) **WLC 5**:3438
Nobelevskaia lektsii politerature 1970 goda (Nobel Lecture by Aleksandr Solzhenitsyn) (Solzhenitsyn) **WLC 5**:3307-08
The Noble and Joyous Book Entytled Le Morte Darthur (Malory)

See *Le Morte Darthur*
"Noble Sisters" (Rossetti) **WLC 5**:2937
Noblemen's Home (Turgenev)
See *Dvoryanskoe gnezdo*
"Noc pered rozdestvom" ("Christmas Eve") (Gogol) **WLC 3**:1429
"La noche de los alcaravanes" ("The Night of the Curlews") (Garcia Marquez) **WLC 3**:1362-63
"A Nocturnal upon S. Lucies day, Being the shortest day" ("St. Lucies Day") (Donne) **WLC 2**:944
"Nocturno de San Ildefonso" ("San Ildefonso Nocturne") (Paz) **WLC 4**:2667, 2675
"Non dolet" (Swinburne) **WLC 6**:3536
None to Accompany Me (Gordimer) **WLCS 1**:382, 384
Nora (Ibsen)
See *Et dukkehjem*
North (Heaney) **WLCS 1**:390-92, 394, 396
"North Labrador" (Crane) **WLC 2**:799
North of Boston (Frost) **WLC 2**:1291, 1296-99
Northanger Abbey (Austen) **WLC 1**:149, 153, 155
"The Northern Farmer—New Style" (Tennyson) **WLC 6**:3572, 3584
"The Northern Farmer—Old Style" (Tennyson) **WLC 6**:3572, 3584
"The Norwood Builder" (Doyle) **WLC 2**:1013
"The Nose" (Gogol) **WLC 3**:1430-33
Nostromo (Conrad) **WLC 2**:780-82, 791
Not for Publication (Gordimer) **WLCS 1**:374
"Not for Publication" (Gordimer) **WLCS 1**:371
"Not Ideas about the Thing but the Thing Itself" (Stevens) **WLC 5**:3439
Note-Books of Samuel Butler (Butler) **WLC 1**:555-60
"Note on Blues" (Hughes) **WLC 3**:1721-22
"A Note on War Poetry" (Eliot) **WLC 2**:1146
Notebook (Lowell) **WLC 4**:2168
Notebooks (Camus)
See *Carnets*
Notes and Counter-notes (Ionesco)
See *Notes et contre-notes*
Notes et contre-notes (*Notes and Counter-notes*) (Ionesco) **WLC 3**:1805, 1808-09, 1811
"Notes for a Hypothetical Novel" (Baldwin) **WLC 1**:169
Notes from a Diary (Gorky) **WLC 3**:1485-86
Notes from Isla Negra (Neruda)
See *Memoríal de Isla Negra*
Notes from the Underground (Dostoevsky)
See *Zapiski iz podpol'ya*
Notes of a Hunter (Turgenev)
See *Zapiski okhotnika*
"Notes of a Madman" (Gogol)
See "Diary of a Madman"
"Notes of a Native Son" (Baldwin) **WLC 1**:163-64, 168, 174
"Notes on Nationalism" (Orwell) **WLC 4**:2582
"Notes on River Country" (Welty) **WLC** 6:3891
"Notes on the Petty Bourgeois Mentality" (Gorky) **WLC 3**:1493
"Notes on the Text of Shelley" (Swinburne) **WLC 6**:3565
Notes on Translating Shakespearean Tragedies (Pasternak) **WLC 4**:2629
Notes toward a Supreme Fiction (Stevens) **WLC 5**:3431, 3434-35, 3437-40
Notre-Dame de Paris (*The Hunchback of Notre-Dame*) (Hugo) **WLC 3**:1740-41, 1743-45, 1747, 1750, 1753-54
Les nourritures terrestres (*The Fruits of the Earth*) (Gide) **WLC 3**:1376-77, 1388-89
Le nouveau locataire (*The New Tenant*) (Ionesco) **WLC 3**:1800
La Nouvelle Héloïse (*Julie, ou La Nouvelle Héloïse*; *Letters of Two Lovers*; *New Eloise*) (Rousseau) **WLC 5**:2483-84
Nov' (*Virgin Soil*) (Turgenev) **WLC 6**:3704
Nova Express (Burroughs) **WLC 1**:535, 537-538, 545
"The Novel and the Nation in South Africa" (Gordimer) **WLCS 1**:375
Novelas exemplares (*Exemplary Novels*; *Exemplary Stories*; *Exemplary Tales*) (Cervantes) **WLC 2**:674, 679-80, 684
The Novels of Swinburne (Swinburne) **WLC 6**:358
Novembre: Fragments de style quelconque (Flaubert) **WLC 2**:1252
"Now hollow fires" (Housman) **WLCS 1**:431
"Now Sleeps the Crimson Petal" (Tennyson) **WLC 6**:3584
Nuevas odas elementales (Neruda) **WLC 4**:2516
Nuevo canto de amor a Stalingrado (*A New Lovesong for Stalingrad*) (Neruda) **WLC 4**:2514
"La nuit blanche" (Kipling) **WLC 3**:2017
La Nuit (Wiesel)
See *Night* (Wiesel)
"Nuit de l'enfer" ("Night of Hell") (Rimbaud) **WLC 5**:2919
"Nullo" (Toomer) **WLCS 2**:801-03
La Numancia (Cervantes)
See *El cerco de Numancia*
Number One (Dos Passos) **WLC 2**:966
Numquid et tu (Gide) **WLC 3**:1377
"Nuptial Sleep" (Rossetti) **WLC 5**:2947
Nurses of Dionysus (Aeschylus) **WLCS 1**:6
"The Nymph and the Faun" (Marvell)
See "The Nymph Complaining for the Death of Her Faun"
"The Nymph Complaining for the Death of Her Faun" ("The Nymph and the Faun") (Marvell) **WLC 4**:2252, 2256-57, 2259
"A Nymph's Passion" (Jonson) **WLC 3**:1922
"A Nympholept" (Swinburne) **WLC 6**:3566
"O City of Broken Dreams" (Cheever) **WLC 2**:698
O di uno o di nessuno (*Either of One or of No One*; *Either Someone's or No-One's*) (Pirandello) **WLC 4**:2728
"O malých pomerech" ("On a Small Scale") (Capek) **WLC 1**:605
O Pioneers! (Cather) **WLC 1**:654-55, 657, 659-60, 665
O Shepherd, Speak (Sinclair) **WLC 5**:3272
"O, Tempora! O Mores!" (Poe) **WLC 4**:2762
O vecech obecných cili ZOON POLITIKON (*On Political Things; or, Zoon Politicon*) (Capek) **WLC 1**:602, 605
"O Ye Tongues" (Sexton) **WLC 5**:3144, 3146-47
Oak and Ivy (Dunbar) **WLC 2**:1102, 1110-12
The Oak and the Calf (Solzhenitsyn)
See *Bodalsia telenok s dubom*
Oak Leaves and Lavender (O'Casey) **WLCS 2**:721
The Oath (Wiesel) **WLCS 2**:848-50
"The Obelisk" (Forster) **WLC 2**:1270
"Obituary for a Living Lady" (Brooks) **WLC 1**:461
"The Objectivist Ethics" (Rand) **WLC 5**:2887
"The Oblation" (Swinburne) **WLC 6**:3562
Obscure Destinies (Cather) **WLC 1**:657, 660
"Observations Concerning the Increase of Mankind and the Peopling of Countries" (Franklin) **WLCS 1**:315, 327
Observations, Good or Bad, Stupid or Clever, Serious or Jocular, on Squire Foote's Dramatic Entertainment entitled "The Minor," by a Genius (*Observations on "The Minor"*) (Boswell) **WLC 1**:353
Observations on "The Minor" (Boswell)
See *Observations, Good or Bad, Stupid or Clever, Serious or Jocular, on Squire Foote's Dramatic Entertainment entitled "The Minor," by a Genius*
Observations on a Late Publication Intituled "The Present State of the Nation" (Burke) **WLC 1**:506
"Observe how Myanoshita cracked in two. . . ." (Millay) **WLCS 2**:594
Obycejnýzivot (*An Ordinary Life*) (Capek) **WLC 1**:603, 605-06
Occasion for Loving (Gordimer) **WLCS 1**:372-74, 376-77
"An Occurrence at Owl Creek Bridge" (Bierce) **WLC 1**:281, 288, 290, 293
"Ocean's Love to Ireland" (Heaney) **WLCS 1**:390
Ocho comedias y ocho entremeses nunca representados (*Comedias*; *Comedias y entremeses*; *Eight Plays*; *Eight Plays and Eight Interludes: New and Never Performed*; *Entremeses*; *Interludes*) (Cervantes) **WLC 2**:681
"October, a Poem" (Boswell) **WLC 1**:352
"October and June" (Henry) **WLC 3**:1675
"October in the Railroad Earth" (Kerouac) **WLC 3**:1978
"October" (Dunbar) **WLC 2**:1110
"October" (Frost) **WLC 2**:1299
"An Octopus" (Moore) **WLCS 2**:641, 646-47, 651
"Oda a la claridad" (Neruda) **WLC 4**:2515
"Oda a la poesía" (Neruda) **WLC 4**:2515
"Oda a Salvador Dali" ("Ode to Salvador Dali") (Garcia Lorca) **WLC 2**:1345,

1349
"Oda al edificio" (Neruda) **WLC 4:**2508
"Oda al santísimo sacramento del altar: exposición y mundo" ("Ode to the Most Blessed Sacrament"; "Ode to the Most Holy Eucharist: Exposition and World"; "Ode to the Sacrament") (Garcia Lorca) **WLC 2:**1345, 1349
Odas elementales (*The Elemental Odes; Elementary Odes; Odes to Simple Things*) (Neruda) **WLC 4:**2508, 2511, 2515-17
Odd Man Out (Pinter)
See *Old Times*
"Ode by Dr. Samuel Johnson to Mrs. Thrale upon their supposed approaching Nuptials" (Boswell) **WLC 1:**352
"Ode for Music" (Gray) **WLC 3:**1532-33
"Ode for St. Cecilia's Day" (Pope) **WLC 5:**2771
"Ode on a Distant Prospect of Eton College" ("Eton"; "Eton College Ode") (Gray) **WLC 3:**1519, 1531-33
"Ode on a Drop of Dew" (Marvell) **WLC 4:**2252, 2258
"Ode on a Grecian Urn" (Keats) **WLC 3:**1957-58, 1962, 1964
"Ode on Indolence" (Keats) **WLC 3:**1964, 1966
"Ode on Melancholy" (Keats) **WLC 3:**1960-61, 1964, 1966
"Ode on Melancholy" (Owen) **WLC 4:**2614
"Ode on Spring" ("Ode on the Spring") (Gray) **WLC 3:**1519, 1526, 1528, 1530
"Ode on the Death of a Favourite Cat, Drowned in a Tub of Gold Fishes" ("Death of a Favorite Cat") (Gray) **WLC 3:**1519, 1526, 1529, 1531
"Ode on the Death of a Lamb" (Boswell) **WLC 1:**355
"Ode on the Pleasure Arising from Vicissitude" ("Ode on Vicissitude") (Gray) **WLC 3:**1526, 1530-31
"Ode on the Progress of Poesy" (Gray)
See "The Progress of Poesy"
"Ode on the Spring" (Gray)
See "Ode on Spring"
"Ode on Vicissitude" (Gray)
See "Ode on the Pleasure Arising from Vicissitude"
"Ode on Vicissitude" (Gray) **WLC 3:**1526, 1530-31
"Ode on Whistling" (Boswell) **WLC 1:**355
"Ode to a Nightingale" ("Nightingale") (Keats) **WLC 3:**1956, 1962, 1964-67
"Ode to Adversity" ("Hymn to Adversity") (Gray) **WLC 3:**1520, 1530
"Ode to Ambition" (Boswell) **WLC 1:**355
"Ode to an artichoke" (Neruda) **WLC 4:**2517
"Ode to Autumn" ("To Autumn") (Keats) **WLC 3:**1956-57, 1960-63
"Ode to Beauty" (Emerson) **WLC 2:**1172
"Ode to Duty" (Wordsworth) **WLC 6:**4071
"Ode to Ethiopia" (Dunbar) **WLC 2:**1103, 1110
"Ode to Fame" (Masters) **WLCS 2:**576
"Ode to Liberty" (Shelley) **WLC 5:**3233-34
"Ode to Mæcenas" ("To Mæcenas") (Wheatley) **WLC 6:**3922-23, 3928-29

"Ode to Memory" (Tennyson) **WLC 6:**3579
"Ode to Naples" (Shelley) **WLC 5:**3227
"Ode to Neptune" (Wheatley) **WLC 6:**3928
"Ode to Psyche" (Keats) **WLC 3:**1963, 1965-67
"Ode to Salvador Dali" (Garcia Lorca)
See "Oda a Salvador Dali"
"Ode to Silence" (Millay) **WLCS 2:**591, 595
"Ode to Terminus" (Auden) **WLC 1:**140
"Ode to the Elves" (Boswell) **WLC 1:**355
"Ode to the Medieval Poets" (Auden) **WLC 1:**137
"Ode to the Most Blessed Sacrament" (Garcia Lorca)
See "Oda al santísimo sacramento del altar: exposición y mundo"
"Ode to the Most Holy Eucharist: Exposition and World" (Garcia Lorca)
See "Oda al santísimo sacramento del altar: exposición y mundo"
"Ode to the Sacrament" (Garcia Lorca)
See "Oda al santísimo sacramento del altar: exposición y mundo"
"Ode to the Sky Lark" (Shelley) **WLC 5:**3225, 3233-34
"Ode to the West Wind" (Shelley) **WLC 5:**3233-34
Ode to Tragedy (Boswell) **WLC 1:**354
"Ode" (Marvell)
See "An Horatian Ode upon Cromwell's Return from Ireland"
"Ode" (Wordsworth) **WLC 6:**4068
Odes to Simple Things (Neruda)
See *Odas elementales*
Odin den' Ivana Denisovicha (*One Day in the Life of Ivan Denisovich*) (Solzhenitsyn) **WLC 5:**3300, 3311
The Odyssey (Homer) **WLCS 1:**413, 417, 420-21
"An Odyssey of the North" (London) **WLC 4:**2142-43
Oedipe (Gide) **WLC 3:**1375
Oedipus (Aeschylus) **WLCS 1:**8
Oedipus at Colonos (Sophocles) **WLCS 1:**776-77, 780, 782-84, 786
Oedipus Rex (Sophocles)
See *Oedipus Tyrannus*
Oedipus the King (Sophocles)
See *Oedipus Tyrannus*
Oedipus Tyrannus (Sophocles) **WLCS 1:**774-75, 778-80, 782-88
L'oeuvre (Zola) **WLC 6:**4126
Oeuvres philosophiques (Balzac)
See *études philosophiques*
"Of A' the Airts" ("A' the Airts") (Burns) **WLC 1:**518
"Of Alexander Crummell" (Du Bois) **WLC 2:**1070
Of Dramatick Poesie: An Essay (*Essay of Dramatic Poesy*) (Dryden) **WLC 2:**1043
Of Human Bondage (Maugham) **WLC 4:**2272, 2276, 2279, 2281, 2283
"Of Liberation" (Giovanni) **WLCS 1:**352
"Of Love: A Testimony" (Cheever) **WLC 2:**689, 695
Of Mice and Men (Steinbeck) **WLC 5:**3382-86, 3388
"Of Modern Poetry" (Stevens) **WLC**

5:3430
"Of the Coming of John" (Du Bois) **WLC 2:**1070, 1074-75
"Of the Faith of the Fathers" (Du Bois) **WLC 1:**1075
"Of the Passing of the First-Born" (Du Bois) **WLC 2:**1070, 1074
Of the Progres of the Soule (Donne)
See *The Second Anniversarie. Of the Progres of the Soule. Wherein, By Occasion Of the Religious death of Mistris Elizabeth Drury, the incommodities of the Soule in this life, and her exaltation in the next, are Contemplated*
"Of the Sorrow Songs" (Du Bois) **WLC 2:**1070
"Of the Wings of Atlanta" (Du Bois) **WLC 2:**1070
Of Time and the River (Wolfe) **WLC 6:**4029-30, 4032-33, 4035-38, 4040
"The Office" (Munro) **WLCS 2:**682
Officers and Gentlemen (Waugh) **WLC 6:**3823
"Often Rebuked, yet Always Back Returning" (Bronte) **WLC 1:**429, 431
"Oh death shall find me" (Brooke) **WLC 1:**438
"Oh, For a Little While Be Kind" (Cullen) **WLCS 1:**276
Oh Pray My Wings are Gonna Fit Me Well (Angelou) **WLCS 1:**62
"Oh see how thick the goldcup flowers" (Housman) **WLCS 1:**434
Oh What a Paradise It Seems (Cheever) **WLC 2:**700, 702
"Oil of Dog" (Bierce) **WLC 1:**281
Oil! (Sinclair) **WLC 5:**3263, 3267
Olalla (Stevenson) **WLC 5:**3452
"Old Abe's Conversion" (Dunbar) **WLC 2:**1107
"Old and New Art" (Rossetti) **WLC 5:**2955
"Old and New Year Ditty" (Rossetti) **WLC 5:**2938
The Old and the Young (Pirandello)
See *I vecchi e i giovani*
"The Old Apple Dealer" (Hawthorne) **WLC 3:**1606
The Old Bachelor (Congreve)
See *The Old Batchelour*
The Old Batchelour (*The Old Bachelor*) (Congreve) **WLC 2:**762, 764-65, 771-72, 775
The Old Beauty and Others (Cather) **WLC 1:**660, 662
"Old China" (Lamb) **WLC 3:**2032, 2034
The Old Curiosity Shop (Dickens) **WLC 2:**900, 910
"Old Doc Rivers" (Williams) **WLC 6:**4015
"Old Dwarf Heart" (Sexton) **WLC 5:**3142
"Old Fashion Farmers" (Gogol) **WLC 3:**1428, 1430
An Old-Fashioned Girl (Alcott) **WLC 1:**40, 42-3, 50
"Old Flame" (Lowell) **WLC 4:**2159
The Old Glory (Lowell) **WLC 4:**2168
The Old Gringo (Fuentes)
See *El gringo viejo*
"The Old Icons" (Heaney) **WLCS 1:**399
The Old Maid (Wharton) **WLC 6:**3911
The Old Man and the Sea (*The Sea in*

*Being) (Hemingway) **WLC 3:**1659
An Old Man Taught Wisdom; Or, The Virgin Unmasked (Fielding) **WLC 2:**1214
"Old Man" (Faulkner) **WLC 2:**1194
"The Old Man" (Singer) **WLC 5:**3286-88
"Old Marrieds" (Brooks) **WLC 1:**453, 460
Old Mortality (Scott) **WLC 5:**3108, 3111
"Old Mr. Marblehall" (Welty) **WLC 6:**3880, 3892
"Old Mrs. Harris" (Cather) **WLC 1:**657, 660-62
Old New York (New York Quartet) (Wharton) **WLC 6:**3911-12
"Old Oak Tree's Last Dream" (Andersen)
See "The Last Dream of the Old Oak"
"Old, Old, Old Andrew Jackson" (Lindsay) **WLC 4:**2124
"Old People's Home" (Auden) **WLC 1:**137
The Old Plantation Days (Dunbar) **WLC 2:**1101, 1104-06, 1111
Old Shellover (de la Mare) **WLC 2:**892
"An Old Time Christmas" (Dunbar) **WLC 2:**1106
" Old Timers" (Sandburg) **WLC 5:**3052
Old Times (Odd Man Out) (Pinter) 4;2705-06
"The Old Vicarage, Grantchester" (Brooke) **WLC 1:**439-40, 443
The Old Woman Izergil (Gorky) **WLC 3:**1485
"An Old World Thicket" (Rossetti) **WLC 5:**2942
Olinger Stories: A Selection (Updike) **WLC 6:**3753
Oliver Twist (Dickens) **WLC 2:**900, 902-03, 912
Omoo: A Narrative of Adventures in the South Seas (Melville) **WLC 4:**2343
"On a Book Entitled *Lolita*" (Nabokov) **WLC 4:**2499
"On a Political Prisoner" (Yeats) **WLC 6:**4109
"On a Small Scale" (Capek)
See "O malých pomerech"
On Active Service (Crane) **WLC 2:**814-15
On Baile's Strand (Yeats) **WLC 6:**4102
"On Becoming a Catholic" (McKay) **WLC 4:**2335
"On Being Asked What It's Like to Be Black" (Giovanni) **WLCS 1:**354
"On Being Brought from Africa to America" (Wheatley) **WLC 6:**3919, 3922, 3924, 3926, 3929-30
"On Desire. A Pindarick" (Behn) **WLC 1:**255
On Early Trains (Pasternak)
See *Na rannikh poezdakh*
"On Friendship" (Wheatley) **WLC 6:**3930
"On Greenhow Hill" (Kipling) **WLC 3:**2010, 2013
On Humor (Pirandello)
See *L'umorismo*
"On Justice and Generosity" (Goldsmith) **WLC 6:**3916, 3918, 3924
"On Lord Holland's Seat near Margate, Kent" ("Impromptu on Lord Holland's House") (Gray) **WLC 3:**1526, 1529
On Love (Stendhal)
See *De l'amour*

"On Major General Lee" (Wheatley)
See "Thoughts on His Excellency Major General Lee"
"On My Songs" (Owen) **WLC 4:**2613
On Political Things; or, Zoon Politicon (Capek)
See *O vecech obecných cili ZOON POLITIKON*
"On Recollection" ("Recollection") (Wheatley) **WLC 6:**3918, 3922, 3924, 3928
"On Social Plays" (Miller) **WLC 4:**2370
"On Stories" (Lewis) **WLC 4:**2088
"On the Artificial Comedy of the Last Century" (Lamb) **WLC 3:**2032, 2037
On the Boiler (Yeats) **WLC 6:**4103
"On the Circuit" (Auden) **WLC 1:**137
"On the Death of the Rev. Mr. George Whitefield" (Wheatley)
See "An Elegiac Poem on the Death of George Whitefield"
"On the Death of the Reverend Dr. Sewall" (Wheatley) **WLC 6:**3923
"On the distresses of the poor, exemplified in the life of a private centinel" (Goldsmith) **WLC 3:**1474
"On the Downs" (Swinburne) **WLC 6:**3563
On the Eve (Turgenev)
See *Nakanune*
"On the Hill and Grove at Billborow" (Marvell)
See "Upon the Hill and Grove at Billborow"
"On the Laboring Poor" (Franklin) **WLCS 1:**315
"On the Late Captain Grose's Peregrinations Thro' Scotland" ("Captain Grose") (Burns) **WLC 1:**517
"On the Makaloa Mat" (London) **WLC 4:**2140
"On the Morning of Christ's Nativity" ("Nativity Ode") (Milton) **WLC 4:**2406, 2408-09
"On the New Arts; or, The Risk in Artistic Production" (Strindberg) **WLC 6:**3529
"On the Rafts" (Gorky) **WLC 3:**1482, 1488, 1491
On the Razzle (Stoppard) **WLC 6:**3493
"On the River" (Dunbar) **WLC 2:**1110
On the Road (Kerouac) **WLC 3:**1973, 1975-78, 1980, 1986-88
"On the Road" (Heaney) **WLCS 1:**399
"On the Slave Trade" (Franklin) **WLCS 1:**315
On the Study of Celtic Literature (Arnold) **WLC 1:**96
On the Tragedies of Shakespeare (Lamb) **WLC 3:**2031, 2037
"On the Wide Heath" (Millay) **WLCS 2:**602
"On the Wing" (Rossetti) **WLC 5:**2930
"On the Works of Providence" (Wheatley)
See "Thoughts on the Works of Providence"
On These I Stand: An Anthology of the Best Poems of Countee Cullen (Cullen) **WLCS 1:**282-83
On this Island (Auden) **WLC 1:**129
"On Three Ways of Writing for Children" (Lewis) **WLC 4:**2085, 2087
"On Virtue" ("Virtue") (Wheatley) **WLC 6:**3918, 3928

"On Wenlock Edge the wood's in trouble" (Housman) **WLCS 1:**430
"Once I Passed through a Populous City" (Whitman) **WLC 6:**3940
"One Arm" (Williams) **WLC 6:**4002-03
1x1 (Cummings) **WLC 2:**842
"One Christmas at Shiloh" (Dunbar) **WLC 2:**1107
"One Dash--Horses" (Crane)
See "Horses—One Dash"
"One Day After Saturday" (Garcia Marquez) **WLC 3:**1367, 1369
One Day in the Life of Ivan Denisovich (Solzhenitsyn)
See *Odin den' Ivana Denisovicha*
One Flew over the Cuckoo's Nest (Kesey) **WLC 3:**1992, 1994-96, 1999-2002, 2004
One for the Road (Pinter)
See *Other Places*
One Generation After (Wiesel) **WLCS 2:**854
One Half of Robertson Davies: Provocative Pronouncements on a Wide Range of Topics (Davies) **WLC 2:**850
One Hundred Love Sonnets (Neruda)
See *Cien sonetos de amor*
100%: The Story of a Patriot (Sinclair) **WLC 5:**3263
One Hundred Years of Solitude (Garcia Marquez)
See *Cien años de soledad*
"One Kind of Officer" (Bierce) **WLC 1:**287-89
"One Man's Fortune" (Dunbar) **WLC 2:**1102, 1106, 1112
One Man's Initiation--1917 (First Encounter) (Dos Passos) **WLC 2:**955, 962
One, None, and a Hundred Thousand (Pirandello)
See *Uno, nessuno e centomila*
One of Ours (Cather) **WLC 1:**655
"One of the Missing" (Bierce) **WLC 1:**281, 287, 289
"One of These Days" (Garcia Marquez) **WLC 3:**1366-67
"One Officer, One Man" (Bierce) **WLC 1:**287
"One Ordinary Day, with Peanuts" (Jackson) **WLC 3:**1851
"One Slip-Slouch Twi" (Cummings) **WLC 2:**841
One Thousand Seven Hundred and Thirty Eight (Pope) **WLC 5:**2782
"One Trip Abroad" (Fitzgerald) **WLC 2:**1231, 1234
One Way to Heaven (Cullen) **WLCS 1:**282-83
One Writer's Beginnings (Welty) **WLC 6:**3892
"One's-Self I Sing" (Whitman)
See "Song of Myself"
"Oneiromancy" (Bierce) **WLC 1:**292
Onkel, Onkel (Grass) **WLC 3:**1510
The Only Jealousy of Emer (Yeats) **WLC 6:**4102-03
Only Ten Minutes to Buffalo (Grass) **WLC 3:**1510
"Onnagata" (Mishima) **WLC 4:**2423-24
"The Open Boat" (Crane) **WLC 2:**818, 820, 823-27

n Open Letter to My Sister, Miss Angela Davis" (Baldwin) **WLC 1**:173
e Open Sea (Masters) **WLCS 2**:577-78
en Secrets (Munro) **WLCS 2**:685-87
he Open Window" (Saki) **WLC 5**:3008
he Operation" (Sexton) **WLC 5**:3137
phélie" (Rimbaud) **WLC 5**:2921-22
ium (Cocteau) **WLC 2**:735
e Optimist's Daughter (Welty) **WLC 6**:3885-86, 3889-90, 3892-93
he Oracles" (Housman) **WLCS 1**:428
 Oration Delivered before the Phi Beta Kappa Society at Cambridge, August 31, 1837 (Emerson)
See American Scholar
e Orators (Auden) **WLC 1**:128, 133-35
rchard" (H. D.)
See "Priapus"
Orchids in the Moonlight (Fuentes)
See Orquídeas a la luz de la luna
he Ordeal at Mt. Hope" (Dunbar) **WLC 2**:1101, 1106
 Ordinary Evening in New Haven" (Stevens) **WLC 5**:3435-36
 Ordinary Life (Capek)
See Obycejnýzivot
he Ordination" (Burns) **WLC 1**:517, 524
read" (H. D.) **WLC 3**:1616, 1623
s oreilles du comte de Chesterfield (Voltaire) **WLC 6**:3776, 3780, 3782
reithyia (Aeschylus) **WLCS 1**:7
restea (Aeschylus) **WLCS 1**:5-6
resteia (Aeschylus) **WLCS 1**:11, 13-15, 17
restes (Euripides) **WLCS 1**:292, 294, 296, 299
he Organizer's Wife" (Bambara) **WLCS 1**:131, 133-34
rient Express (Greene)
See Stamboul Train
n Original Letter from a Gentleman of Scotland to the Earl of * * * in London" (Boswell) **WLC 1**:355
rlando (Woolf) **WLC 6**:4047, 4050, 4057
ley Farm (Trollope) **WLC 6**:3681
rnières" (Rimbaud) **WLC 5**:2918
roonoko; or, The Royal Slave (Behn) **WLC 1**:245, 249-52, 257-59
rphan Paul (Gorky)
See Paul the Unfortunate
rphée (Orpheus) (Cocteau) **WLC 2**:723-25, 727, 729-31, 736
rpheus (Cocteau)
See Orphée
rpheus Descending (Williams) **WLC 6**:3989, 3992-93, 3995-96, 3998
rquídeas a la luz de la luna (Orchids in the Moonlight) (Fuentes) **WLC 2**:1316-19
sorio (Coleridge)
See Remorse
tetz Sergii (Father Sergius) (Tolstoy) **WLC 6**:3665
thello (Shakespeare) **WLC 5**:3157, 3171
ther Inquisitions, 1937-1952 (Borges)
See Otras inquisiciónes, 1937-1952
ther People's Point of View (Pirandello)
See La ragione degli altri

Other Places (A Kind of Alaska; One for the Road; Victoria Station) (Pinter) **WLC 4**:2707-08
"The Other Rib of Death" (Garcia Marquez)
See "La otra costilla de la muerte"
"The Other Side of Death" (Garcia Marquez)
See "La otra costilla de la muerte"
The Other Son (Pirandello)
See L'altro figlio
"The Other Two" (Wharton) **WLC 6**:3903
Other Voices, Other Rooms (Capote) **WLC 1**:618, 620, 622, 627-30
"Others, I am not the first" (Housman) **WLCS 1**:434
"La otra costilla de la muerte" ("The Other Rib of Death"; "The Other Side of Death") (Garcia Marquez) **WLC 3**:1363
Otras inquisiciónes, 1937-1952 (Other Inquisitions, 1937-1952) (Borges) **WLC 1**:337-38
"The Ottawa Valley" (Munro) **WLCS 2**:677
"Otter" (Heaney) **WLCS 1**:388
Ottsy i deti (Fathers and Children; Fathers and Sons; The Memoirs of a Nihilist) (Turgenev) **WLC 6**:3702-04, 3706, 3709-10
"Our Bourgeois Literature" (Sinclair) **WLC 5**:3262
Our Man in Havana (Greene) **WLC 3**:1550
"Our Martyred Soldiers" (Dunbar) **WLC 2**:1110
"Our Mother Pocahontas" (Lindsay) **WLC 4**:2124
Our Mutual Friend (Dickens) **WLC 2**:903-04, 910-12
"Our Secret" (Allende) **WLCS 1**:47
Our Town (Wilder) **WLC 6**:3971-79, 3981, 3983-94
Out Cry (Williams)
See The Two-Character Play
"Out of the Cradle Endlessly Rocking" (Whitman) **WLC 6**:3847
Out of the Silent Planet (Lewis) **WLC 4**:2079, 2081, 2085, 2087, 2092-94
"Outcast" (McKay) **WLC 4**:2332
"The Outcasts of Poker Flat" (Harte) **WLC 3**:1576, 1581, 1583, 1589
"The Outing" (Baldwin) **WLC 1**:168
Outline of an Autobiography (Toomer) **WLCS 2**:793
The Outline of History (Wells) **WLC 6**:3859
Outre-Mer (Longfellow) **WLCS 2**:505, 508, 511
The Outsider (Camus)
See L'étranger
"The Oval Portrait" (Poe) **WLC 4**:2757, 2760
"Over Cities" (Milosz) **WLCS 2**:610-11
"Over-Soul" (Emerson) **WLC 2**:1174, 1183
"The Overcoat" ("The Cloak") (Gogol) **WLC 3**:1430-31, 1433-35
Overlaid (Davies) **WLC 2**:852
The Oxford Book of Light Verse (Auden) **WLC 1**:138
"The Oxford Volunteers" (Huxley) **WLC**

3:1763
"Oxford" (Auden) **WLC 1**:135
"Oysters" (Heaney) **WLCS 1**:392-93, 395
"Oysters" (Sexton) **WLC 5**:3149
"Pacchiarotto" (Browning) **WLCS 1**:211
"The Pace of Youth" (Crane) **WLC 2**:824
"Pagan Prayer" (Cullen) **WLCS 1**:274-76
Pagan Spain (Wright) **WLC 6**:4088
Une page d'amour (Zola) **WLC 6**:4118, 4126
"The Pahty" ("The Party") (Dunbar) **WLC 2**:1103, 1110-11
"A Painful Case" (Joyce) **WLC 3**:1931, 1935
Painful Stories (Capek)
See Trapné provídky
A Pair of Blue Eyes (Hardy) **WLC 3**:1568
"A Pair of Silk Stockings" (Chopin) **WLCS 1**:241
"The Palace of Art" (Tennyson) **WLC 6**:3578
Palamon and Arcite (Dryden) **WLC 2**:1046
Pale Fire (Nabokov) **WLC 4**:2497, 2500
Palimpsest (H. D.) **WLC 3**:1616, 1623
Paludes (Marshlands) (Gide) **WLC 3**:1376
Pamela; or, Virtue Rewarded (Richardson) **WLC 5**:2891-92, 2894, 2898-2903
Pansies (Lawrence) **WLC 3**:2045
The Panther and the Lash: Poems of Our Times (Hughes) **WLC 3**:1724, 1726
"Paper Pills" (Anderson) **WLC 1**:81
The Papers of Martin Luther King, Jr., Volume I: Called to Serve, January 1929-June 1951 (King) **WLCS 1**:470
"The Parable of the Old Man and the Young" (Owen) **WLC 4**:2615-16
Paracelsus (Browning) **WLCS 1**:213
Parade (Cocteau) **WLC 2**:730
Paradise Lost (Milton) **WLC 4**:2397-2402, 2406-09
Paradise Regained (Milton) **WLC 4**:2408
"Paradise" (Rossetti) **WLC 5**:2942
Il paradiso (Alighieri) **WLCS 1**:21-22, 35, 27-28, 30-31
"Paralytic" (Plath) **WLC 4**:2740
"Paraphrase" (Crane) **WLC 2**:800
"The Parenticide Club" (Bierce) **WLC 1**:288
Les parents terribles (Intimate Relations) (Cocteau) **WLC 2**:728-30, 732, 736
"The Parents: People Like Our Marriage, Maxie and Andrew" (Brooks) **WLC 1**:455
Paris (Zola) **WLC 6**:4121, 4125-26
"Paris at Nightfall" (Baudelaire)
See "Le crépuscule du soir"
Paris Spleen (Baudelaire)
See Petits poèmes en prose: Le spleen de Paris
"A Parisian Dream" (Baudelaire)
See "Rêve parisien"
The Parisian Prowler (Baudelaire)
See Petits poèmes en prose: Le spleen de Paris
"Parisina" (Byron) **WLC 1**:569
"Parker's Back" (O'Connor) **WLC 4**:2542
Parleyings with Certain People of Importance in their Day (Browning) **WLCS 1**:213
Parmenides (Plato) **WLCS 2**:729

TITLE INDEX

"Parson's Prologue" (Chaucer)
See "The Parson's Tale"
"The Parson's Tale" (Chaucer) **WLCS 1:**226, 228-29, 234
"Part of the Doctrine" (Baraka) **WLCS 1:**145
Parti-colored Stories (Chekhov) **WLC 2:**708
"Une partie de campagne" (Maupassant) **WLC 4:**2294
"The Party" (Chekhov)
See "The Name-Day Party"
"The Party" (Dunbar)
See "The Pahty"
"La parure" ("The Diamond Necklace"; "The Necklace") (Maupassant) **WLC 4:**2297-98, 2300
Pasado en claro (*A Draft of Shadows*) (Paz) **WLC 4:**2675
"Pascal's Sphere" ("The Sphere of Pascal") (Borges) **WLC 1:**338
"A Passage in the Life of Mr. John Oakhurst" (Harte) **WLC 3:**1576
A Passage to India (Forster) **WLC 2:**1258-59, 1261-63, 1265, 1267, 1269
"Passage" (Crane) **WLC 2:**800, 808-10
Le passé défini (Cocteau) **WLC 2:**733
"Passing Away, Saith the World, Passing Away" (Rossetti) **WLC 5:**2931
"The Passing of Arthur" (Owen) **WLC 4:**2618
"The Passing of Arthur" (Tennyson)
See "Morte d'Arthur"
"The Passing of Arthur" (Tennyson) **WLC 6:**3584
"The Passing Show" (Bierce) **WLC 1:**287
"The past is the present" (Moore) **WLCS 2:**644
The Pastoral Symphony (Gide)
See *La Symphonie pastorale*
La pastorale comique (Moliere) **WLC 4:**2436
"Pastorale" (Crane) **WLC 2:**799
Pastorals (Pope) **WLC 5:**2770-71, 2783-84
"Pastorals" (Pope) **WLC 5:**2770-71, 2783-84
"The Pasture" (Frost) **WLC 2:**1299
The Pastures of Heaven (Steinbeck) **WLC 5:**3382
"A Patch of Old Snow" (Frost) **WLC 2:**1303
The Patent (Pirandello)
See *La patente*
"Patent Leather" (Brooks) **WLC 1:**454
La patente (*The Patent*) (Pirandello) **WLC 4:**2726
Paterson (Williams) **WLC 6:**4010, 4015-16, 4018, 4021-23
Paterson I (Williams) **WLC 6:**4014, 4017
Paterson II (Williams) **WLC 6:**4022-23
Paterson III (Williams) **WLC 6:**4015
Paterson V (Williams) **WLC 6:**4015-17, 4022
"Paterson: Episode 17" (Williams) **WLC 6:**4014
"Paterson" (Ginsberg) **WLC 3:**1396
The Patrician (Galsworthy) **WLC 2:**1334
The Patriot (Johnson) **WLC 3:**1895
A Patriot For Me (Osborne) **WLC 4:**2595, 2598, 2602
"The Patriot" (Browning) **WLCS 1:**209

"La patronne" (Maupassant) **WLC 4:**2291
Paul the Unfortunate (*Orphan Paul*; *Paul the Wretched*) (Gorky) **WLC 3:**1490-91
Paul the Wretched (Gorky)
See *Paul the Unfortunate*
Paula (Allende) **WLCS 1:**52-53
"Les pauvres gens" (Hugo) **WLC 3:**1748
"The Pavilion on the Links" (Stevenson) **WLC 5:**3447
"Pay Day" (Hughes) **WLC 3:**1723
"The Payment" (Strindberg) **WLC 6:**3536
Peace (Aristophanes) **WLCS 1:**77, 79-80
"The Peace of Utrecht" (Munro) **WLCS 2:**681
"Peace" (Brooke) **WLC 1:**441-43
"Pear Tree" (H. D.) **WLC 3:**1616
"Pearl Button" (Mansfield) **WLC 4:**2223-24
"The Pearl of Good Fortune" (Andersen) **WLC 1:**60
"The Pearl" (Mishima) **WLC 4:**2423
"The Peasant Gentlewoman" (Pushkin) **WLC 5:**2828
"Peasants" (Chekhov) **WLC 2:**710
La peau de chagrin (*The Wild Ass' Skin*) (Balzac) **WLC 1:**185
Pedro de Urdemalas (Cervantes) **WLC 2:**683
Peer Gynt (Ibsen) **WLC 3:**1780-82, 1785-87, 1792
The Pelican (Strindberg) **WLC 6:**3519
"Pen, Pencil, and Poison" (Wilde) **WLC 6:**3954
Pendennis (Thackeray)
See *The History of Pendennis: His Fortunes and Misfortunes, His Friends and His Greatest Enemy*
Penelope (Aeschylus) **WLCS 1:**8
The Penitent (Singer)
See *Der Bal-tshuve*
"The Penitent" (Millay) **WLCS 2:**590
Pensaci, Giacomino! (*Think It Over, Giacomino!*; *Think of It, Giacomino!*) (Pirandello) **WLC 4:**2717, 2721, 2726
"Pensar, dudar" (Hugo) **WLC 3:**1749
"Il Penseroso" (Milton) **WLC 4:**2406-07, 2409
Pentheus (Aeschylus) **WLCS 1:**6
The People of the Abyss (London) **WLC 4:**2137
The People, Yes (Sandburg) **WLC 5:**3054, 3057-58, 3061, 3064-65, 3067
Per Amica Silentia Lunae (Yeats) **WLC 6:**4098
"Le père amable" (Maupassant) **WLC 4:**2293
Perelandra (Lewis) **WLC 4:**2081-82, 2085-87, 2092-93
The Perennial Philosophy (Huxley) **WLC 3:**1765-69
"A Perfect Day for Bananafish" (Salinger) **WLC 5:**3019-21, 3023-25
"The Peril in the Streets" (Cheever) **WLC 2:**695
Period of Adjustment: High Point over a Cavern (Williams) **WLC 6:**3995, 3997, 4002-03
Persae (Aeschylus) **WLCS 1:**10
"Persian Poetry" (Emerson) **WLC 2:**1170
Persians (Aeschylus) **WLCS 1:**12, 14-17
Persiles y Sigismunda (Cervantes)

See *Los trabajos de Persiles y Sigismunda*
The Personal Heresy (Lewis) **WLC 4:**2090
The Personal History of David Copperfield (*David Copperfield*) (Dickens) **WLC 2:**897, 906-7
Personal Recollections of Joan of Arc (Twain) **WLC 6:**3715, 3718
Persuasion (Austen) **WLC 1:**148-49, 155
Pervaya lyubov' (*First Love*) (Turgenev) **WLC 6:**3702-04, 3706-07
"Pesn' torzhestruyushchey lyubvi" ("The Love Song of the Conquering Lovers"; "The Song of the Triumphant Love") (Turgenev) **WLC 6:**3699, 3705
La peste (*The Plague*) (Camus) **WLC 1:**594
Peter Bell (Wordsworth) **WLC 6:**4076
"Peter" (Moore) **WLCS 2:**648
"Le petit fût" (Maupassant) **WLC 4:**2293
"Petit soldat" (Maupassant) **WLC 4:**2293
La petite Fadette (*Little Fadette*) (Sand) **WLC 5:**3039, 3041, 3043
"Les petites vielles" ("The Little Old Women") (Baudelaire) **WLC 1:**203
Petits poèmes en prose: Le spleen de Paris (*Little Poems in Prose*; *Paris Spleen*; *The Parisian Prowler*; *Poems in Prose from Charles Baudelaire*; *Prose Poems*; *Short Prose Poems*; *Le spleen de Paris*) (Baudelaire) **WLC 1:**205, 208, 210
"Petrificada petrificante" (Paz) **WLC 4:**2664
"The Petrified Man" (Welty) **WLC 6:**3880, 3892
Phaedrus (Plato) **WLCS 2:**735
The Phantom (de la Mare) **WLC 2:**890
"Phantoms" (Turgenev) **WLC 6:**3698, 3705, 3707
Pharos and Pharillon (Forster) **WLC 2:**1258
The Philadelphia Negro (Du Bois) **WLC 2:**1064, 1068, 1072
The Philanderer (Shaw) **WLC 5:**3196
Philebus (Aristotle) **WLCS 1:**92
Philebus (Plato) **WLCS 2:**730-34
Philip (Thackeray) **WLC 6:**3595, 3598
"Philoclea in the Forest" (Huxley) **WLC 3:**1761
Philoctéte (Gide) **WLC 3:**1377
Philoctetes (Aeschylus) **WLCS 1:**8
Philoctetes (Sophocles) **WLCS 1:**776, 780, 783, 785
A Philosophical Enquiry into the Origin of Our Ideas of the Sublime and Beautiful (*Essay on the Sublime and Beautiful*) (Burke) **WLC 1:**502
A Philosophical View of Reform (Shelley) **WLC 5:**3227
Phineas Finn (Trollope) **WLC 6:**3681
Phiness Redux (Trollope) 6;3683-85, 3692
Phoedo (Plato) **WLCS 2:**730-31
Phoenician Women (Euripides) **WLCS 1:**296
Phrygians (Aeschylus) **WLCS 1:**8, 14
"The Physician's Duty" (Pirandello)
See "Il dovere del medico"
Physiology and Calisthenics (Beecher) **WLC 1:**182

Il piacere dell'onestà (*The Pleasure of Honesty*; *Pleasure of Honor*) (Pirandello) **WLC 4:**2721, 2724, 2726
The Piano Lesson (Wilson) **WLCS 1:**861-62, 864, 868-71, 874
Pickwick Papers (Dickens)
 See *The Posthumous Papers of the Pickwick Club*
Picture-Book without Pictures (Andersen) **WLC 1:**58
The Picture of Dorian Gray (Wilde) **WLC 6:**3953, 3955, 3960-3961, 3963, 3965
Pictures of Fidelman: An Exhibition (Malamud) **WLC 4:**2174-75, 2178, 2180-81, 2184, 2190
"A Piece of News" (Welty) **WLC 6:**3882
"A Piece of String" (Maupassant)
 See "La ficelle"
"Pied Beauty" (Hopkins) **WLC 3:**1714
"The Pied Piper of Hamelin" (Browning) **WLCS 1:**211
Piedra de sol (*Sun Stone*; *Sunstone*) (Paz) **WLC 4:**2660-63, 2665, 2667, 2674-75
Las piedras de Chile (*The Stones of Chile*) (Neruda) **WLC 4:**2515
Pierre et Jean (Maupassant) **WLC 4:**2296
Pierre; or, The Ambiguities (Melville) **WLC 4:**2355-57
"Pierrot" (Maupassant) **WLC 4:**2296-97
Le piéton de l'air (*A Stroll in the Air*; *The Stroller in the Air*) (Ionesco) **WLC 3:**1803, 1807
Pigeon Feathers, and Other Stories (Updike) **WLC 6:**3756, 3759
"The Pigeons of St. Marks" (Service) **WLC 5:**3132
The Pilgrim's Progress from This World to That Which Is to Come (Bunyan) **WLC 1:**481-94
The Pilgrim's Regress (Lewis) **WLC 4:**2086, 2089
"Pilgrimage" (Stevens) **WLC 5:**3440
The Pillars of Society (Ibsen)
 See *Samfundets støtter*
Pillars of the Community (Ibsen)
 See *Samfundets støtter*
Pincher Martin (*The Two Deaths of Christopher Martin*) (Golding) **WLC 3:**1445-46, 1456
"Il pipistrello" ("The Bat") (Pirandello) **WLC 4:**2719
Pippa Passes (Browning) **WLCS 1:**208, 213
The Pisan Cantos (Pound) **WLC 5:**2793, 2795, 2801, 2803
"The Pit and the Pendulum" (Poe) **WLC 4:**2761
"The Pitchfork" (Heaney) **WLCS 1:**400
"Pity's Gift" (Lamb) **WLC 3:**2028
"Piuma" ("Feather") (Pirandello) **WLC 4:**2719
"Place in Fiction" (Welty) **WLC 6:**3891
"Place of Refuge" (Brecht) **WLC 1:**393
The Plague (Camus)
 See *La peste*
"The Plaid Dress" (Millay) **WLCS 2:**603-04
Le plaidoyer d'un fou (*The Confessions of a Fool*; *A Madman's Defense*) (Strindberg) **WLC 6:**3536

"Plain Language from Truthful James" ("Heathen Chinee") (Harte) **WLC 3:**1578
"Plain Truth" (Franklin) **WLCS 1:**315-16
"Plainview: 2" (Momaday) **WLCS 2:**628-29
Plaisirs de l'île enchantée (Moliere) **WLC 4:**2443
Plan of a Dictionary (Johnson) **WLC 3:**1893, 1899-1900
Planet News: 1961-1967 (Ginsberg) **WLC 3:**1401, 1403
"The Plattner Story" (Wells) **WLC 6:**3875
"The Play and I" (Mishima) **WLC 4:**2418
A Play of Giants (Soyinka) **WLC 5:**3331
Player Piano (*Utopia Fourteen*) (Vonnegut) **WLC 6:**3786, 3790-92
Playing with Fire (Strindberg) **WLC 6:**3527, 3529
Plays for England (Osborne) **WLC 4:**2594-95
"A Plea for Captain John Brown" (Thoreau) **WLC 6:**3640
The Pleasure of Honesty (Pirandello)
 See *Il piacere dell'onestà*
Pleasure of Honor (Pirandello)
 See *Il piacere dell'onestà*
The Plebeians Rehearse the Uprising: A German Tragedy (Grass) **WLC 3:**1508, 1512-13
Plenos poderes (*Full Powers*) (Neruda) **WLC 4:**2515
The Plough and the Stars (O'Casey) **WLCS 2:**712, 714, 716-18, 720, 722
Ploughman of the Moon: An Adventure into Memory (Service) **WLC 5:**3130
The Plumed Serpent (Lawrence) **WLC 3:**2045
Plutonian Ode: Poems, 1977-1980 (Ginsberg) **WLC 3:**1399, 1403-04
"Po' Boy Blues" (Hughes) **WLC 3:**1721
Podrostok (*Adolescent*; *A Raw Youth*) (Dostoevsky) **WLC 2:**979
"Poem (No Name No. 3)" (Giovanni) **WLCS 1:**352
"The Poem as a Field of Action" (Williams) **WLC 6:**4020
"Poem for Black Hearts" (Baraka) **WLCS 1:**145
"Poem for Half-White College Students" (Baraka) **WLCS 1:**145
"Poem in October" (Thomas) **WLC 6:**3612
"Poem IV" (Auden) **WLC 1:**127
"Poem IX" (Auden) **WLC 1:**127
Poem of the Cante Jondo (Garcia Lorca)
 See *Poema del cante jondo*
The Poem of the Deep Song (Garcia Lorca)
 See *Poema del cante jondo*
"Poem of These States" (Ginsberg) **WLC 3:**1402
"Poem on His Birthday" (Thomas) **WLC 6:**3620
"A Poem to Peanut" (Brooks) **WLC 1:**463
"Poem upon the Death of O. C." ("Death of the Lord Protector"; "A Poem Upon the Death of His Late Highness the Lord Protector"; "Upon the Death of the Lord Protector") (Marvell) **WLC 4:**2254
"A Poem Upon the Death of His Late Highness the Lord Protector" (Marvell)

 See "Poem upon the Death of O. C."
"Poem XXV" (Auden) **WLC 1:**127
Poema del cante jondo (*Deep Song*; *Poem of the Cante Jondo*; *The Poem of the Deep Song*) (Garcia Lorca) **WLC 2:**1344-45
Poemas (Paz) **WLC 4:**2673
Poems (Auden) **WLC 1:**127, 133, 138
Poems (Emerson) **WLC 2:**1170
Poems (Garcia Lorca)
 See *Libro de poemas*
Poems (Pasternak) **WLC 4:**2627
Poems (Rossetti) **WLC 5:**2931
Poems (Rossetti) **WLC 5:**2947
Poems (Wilde) **WLC 6:**3952
Poems—1832 (Tennyson) **WLC 6:**3578
Poems—1842 (Tennyson) **WLC 6:**3579
Poems 1906 (de la Mare) **WLC 2:**890
Poems, 1920 (Eliot) **WLC 2:**1147
Poems 1933-1938 (Auden) **WLC 1:**133, 135
Poems 1965-1975 (Heaney) **WLCS 1:**387
Poems and Ballads (*Laus Veneris, and Other Poems and Ballads*) (Swinburne) **WLC 6:**3552-53, 3563, 3565-66
Poems and Ballads, third series (Swinburne) **WLC 6:**3555, 3557, 3559, 3562
Poems before Congress (Browning) **WLC 1:**472
Poems, Chiefly Lyrical (Tennyson) **WLC 6:**3578-79
Poems in Prose (Turgenev) **WLC 6:**3705
Poems in Prose from Charles Baudelaire (Baudelaire)
 See *Petits poèmes en prose: Le spleen de Paris*
The Poems of Wilfred Owen (Owen) **WLC 4:**2605
Poesia politica (Neruda) **WLC 4:**2515
"Poesía de comunión y poesía de soledad" ("Poetry of Solitude and Poetry of Communion") (Paz) **WLC 4:**2672
Poesía en movimiento (Paz) **WLC 4:**2673
"La poesía" ("Poetry") (Paz) **WLC 4:**2659
Poèsies complètes (Rimbaud) **WLC 5:**2918-19
"The Poet and His Song" (Dunbar) **WLC 2:**1110
Poet in New York (Garcia Lorca)
 See *Poeta en Nueva York*
"The Poet" (Dunbar) **WLC 2:**1113
"The Poet" (Emerson) **WLC 2:**1170, 1183
"Poet's Reverie" (Coleridge) **WLC 2:**754
Poeta en Nueva York (*Poet in New York*) (Garcia Lorca) **WLC 2:**1345, 1349-51
The Poetaster (Jonson) **WLC 3:**1910
"Les poètes de sept ans" ("The Poets of Seven Years") (Rimbaud) **WLC 5:**2916-17, 2921
Poetic Equation (Giovanni) **WLCS 1:**360
Poetical Sketches (Blake) **WLC 1:**300
The Poetical Works of Christina Georgina Rossetti (*Collected Poems*; *Collected Works*) (Rossetti) **WLC 5:**2939
The Poetical Works of S. T. Coleridge (Coleridge) **WLC 2:**743
Poetics (Aristotle) **WLCS 1:**95, 99-101

"Poetry and Grammar" (Stein) **WLC 5:**3363-64
"Poetry and Imagination" (Emerson) **WLC 2:**1170
Poetry for the Advanced (Baraka) **WLCS 1:**147, 154
"Poetry of Solitude and Poetry of Communion" (Paz)
See "Poesía de comunión y poesía de soledad"
"Poetry" (Moore) **WLCS 2:**646
"Poetry" (Paz)
See "La poesía"
"The Poets of Seven Years" (Rimbaud)
See "Les poètes de sept ans"
"A Point at Issue" (Chopin) **WLCS 1:**238, 242
Point Counter Point (Huxley) **WLC 3:**1760, 1762, 1767-68, 1770-73
"A Point of Honor" (Conrad) **WLC 2:**781, 789
"Point Pinos and Point Lobos" (Jeffers) **WLC 3:**1884
Points of View (Maugham) **WLC 4:**2281
The Poison Belt (Doyle) **WLC 2:**1020
"The Poison of Subjectivism" (Lewis) **WLC 4:**2089-90
"Polarities" (Atwood) **WLC 1:**114, 118-19
"Polder" (Heaney) **WLCS 1:**388
Polikushka (Tolstoy) **WLC 6:**3666
Political Tracts (Johnson) **WLC 3:**1895
Politics (Aristotle) **WLCS 1:**101
"The Politics of Rich Painters" (Baraka) **WLCS 1:**151
Politicus (Plato) **WLCS 2:**739
Polydectes (Aeschylus) **WLCS 1:**7
"Pompilia" (Browning) **WLCS 1:**201
The Ponder Heart (Welty) **WLC 6:**3889, 3892
"The Ponds" (Thoreau) **WLC 6:**3631
"The Pool" (Maugham) **WLC 4:**2281
"The Poor Bird" (Andersen) **WLC 1:**57
Poor Fortunes (Undset)
See *Fattige skjaebner*
"A Poor Girl" (Chopin) **WLCS 1:**237
"Poor John" (Andersen) **WLC 1:**57
"Poor Little Black Fellow" (Hughes) **WLC 3:**1733
"Poor Mailie's Elegy" (Burns)
See "The Death and Dying Words of Poor Mailie"
"Poor Pierrot" (Masters) **WLCS 2:**578
"The Poor Poet" (Milosz) **WLCS 2:**614
Poor Richard Improved (Franklin) **WLCS 1:**321
Poor Richard. An Almanack (Franklin) **WLCS 1:**313, 317, 320, 322
"Poor Thumbling" ("Thumbling") (Andersen) **WLC 1:**57, 60
Poor White (Anderson) **WLC 1:**75-8
The Poorhouse Fair (Updike) **WLC 6:**3749, 3751-53, 3756
"The Pope" (Browning) **WLCS 1:**201
"Poppies in July" (Plath) **WLC 4:**2747
"Poppies in October" (Plath) **WLC 4:**2738
"Le port" (Baudelaire) **WLC 1:**210
Portatif (Voltaire)
See *Dictionnaire philosophique*
La porte étroite (*Strait Is the Gate*) (Gide) **WLC 3:**1377, 1382-85, 1387
Portnoy's Complaint (Roth) **WLC 5:**2968-69, 2972-75

"Portrait by a Neighbor" (Millay) **WLCS 2:**603
"Portrait of a Girl in Glass" (Williams) **WLC 6:**4006
The Portrait of a Lady (James) **WLC 3:**1859, 1861
"Portrait of a Lady" (Eliot) **WLC 2:**1146-47
"A Portrait of Bascom Hawke" (Wolfe) **WLC 6:**4041
The Portrait of Mr. W. H. (Wilde) **WLC 6:**3953-55
A Portrait of the Artist as a Young Man (Joyce) **WLC 3:**1925-29, 1932-34, 1937
"A Portrait" (Browning) **WLCS 1:**208
"The Portrait" (Gogol) **WLC 3:**1436-37, 1439
"The Portrait" (Rossetti) **WLC 5:**2949
Portraits-souvenir (Cocteau) **WLC 2:**735
Posdata (Paz) **WLC 4:**2667
Les possédés (*The Possessed*) (Camus) **WLC 1:**588-90
The Possessed (Camus)
See *Les possédés*
"Possessions" (Crane) **WLC 2:**800
"The Post Card" (Boell)
See "Die Postkarte"
"The Post" (Chekhov) **WLC 2:**708
"A Postcard form North Antrim" (Heaney) **WLCS 1:**392
The Posthumous Papers of the Pickwick Club (*Pickwick Papers*) (Dickens) **WLC 2:**900, 906
"Die Postkarte" ("The Post Card") (Boell) **WLC 1:**317
"Postscript, Found in the Handwriting of Mr. Knickerbocker" (Irving) **WLC 3:**1832
Pot-bouille (Zola) **WLC 6:**4126-27
"The Pot of Gold" (Cheever) **WLC 2:**695
"The Potatoes' Dance" (Lindsay) **WLC 4:**2120
Le Potomak (Cocteau) **WLC 2:**737
Poverkh barierov (*Above the Barriers*) (Pasternak) **WLC 4:**2627
The Power and the Glory (Greene) **WLC 3:**1539-40, 1542-43, 1545-47, 1550, 1552, 1554
Power Politics (Atwood) **WLC 1:**108-09, 111-12, 116, 118
"Powerhouse" (Welty) **WLC 6:**3880
"Powerless, with a Guitar" (Grass)
See "In Ohnmacht gefallen"
"Powhatan's Daughter" (Crane) **WLC 2:**806
"The Prague Orgy" (Roth) **WLC 5:**2975-76
"The Prairie Battlements" (Lindsay) **WLC 4:**2121
The Prairie Years (Sandburg) **WLC 5:**3055
"Prairie" (Sandburg) **WLC 5:**3051, 3053
"Praise for an Urn" (Crane) **WLC 2:**797, 800
"The Praise of Chimney-Sweepers" (Lamb) **WLC 3:**2028
"A Prayer for My Daughter" (Yeats) **WLC 6:**4100, 4110-11
"Prayer" (Service) **WLC 5:**3131
Prayers and Meditations (Johnson) **WLC 3:**1895, 1898

"Prayers of Steel" (Sandburg) **WLC 5:**3051
"Pre-Amphibian" (Atwood) **WLC 1:**111
Les précieuses ridicules (*The Affected Ladies*) (Moliere) **WLC 4:**2436, 2439, 2441
"Preface (English Dictionary)" (Johnson) **WLC 3:**1899-1900
"Preface on Bosses" (Shaw) **WLC 5:**3193
Preface to a Twenty Volume Suicide Note (Baraka) **WLCS 1:**146, 150
A Preface to Paradise Lost (Lewis) **WLC 4:**2090
"Preface to *Poems*" (Arnold) **WLC 1:**96, 102
Prefaces, biographical and critical, of the most eminent of the English Poets (*Lives of the English Poets*) (Johnson) **WLC 3:**1891, 1895-98, 1901, 1903
The Prelude (Wordsworth)
See *The Prelude; or, Growth of a Poets Mind: Autobiographical Poem*
The Prelude; or, Growth of a Poets Mind: Autobiographical Poem (*The Prelude*) (Wordsworth) **WLC 6:**4066, 4069, 4072-73
"Prelude" (Mansfield) **WLC 4:**2215-17, 2219, 2221-23
"Prelude" (Service) **WLC 5:**3126-27
"Preludes" (Eliot) **WLC 2:**1148
Le premier homme (Camus) **WLC 1:**588
"Première soirèe" (Rimbaud) **WLC 5:**2916, 2922
Preoccupations (Heaney) **WLCS 1:**391, 393, 398
"Present at a Hanging" (Bierce) **WLC 1:**287
Present Discontents (Burke)
See *Thoughts on the Cause of the Present Discontents*
Present Past, Past Present (Ionesco)
See *Présent passé, passé présent*
Présent passé, passé présent (*Present Past, Past Present*) (Ionesco) **WLC 3:**1809
Prestuplenie i nakazanie (*Crime and Punishment*) (Dostoevsky) **WLC 2:**971, 975
The Pretenders (Ibsen)
See *Kongs emnerne*
"Pretty Mouth and Green My Eyes" (Salinger) **WLC 5:**3018-19, 3023-24, 3036
"Priapus" ("Orchard") (H. D.) **WLC 3:**1616
The Price (Miller) **WLC 4:**2371-72
Pride and Prejudice (*Elizabeth Bennet; o, Pride and Prejudice*) (Austen) **WLC 1:**144, 146-50, 154-56
"The Pride of the Village" (Irving) **WLC 3:**1820, 1828
"The Priest of Shiga Temple and His Love" (Mishima) **WLC 4:**2422-24
Priestesses (Aeschylus) **WLCS 1:**6
"The Priestly Prerogative" (London) **WLC 4:**2141
"Prima notte" ("First Wedding Night") (Pirandello) **WLC 4:**2717
The Prime Minister (Trollope) **WLC 6:**3682, 3684
The Prime of Life (Beauvoir)

See *La force de l'âge*
Primer for Blacks (Brooks) **WLC 1:**458
Primer romancero gitano (*Book of Gypsy Ballads; Gipsy Ballads; Gypsy Balladeer; Gypsy Ballads; Romancero gitano*) (Garcia Lorca) **WLC 2:**1339-40, 1342, 1344-45, 1349-51, 1353
"A Primitive Like an Orb" (Stevens) **WLC 5:**3440
"Primitive Sources" (Atwood) **WLC 1:**111
The Prince (Machiavelli) **WLCS 2:**521-22, 525-34
The Prince and the Pauper (Twain) **WLC 6:**3715, 3721, 3726
The Prince of Abyssinia (*Rasselas*) (Johnson) **WLC 3:**1894, 1901, 1903
Prince Otto (Stevenson) **WLC 5:**3446
"The Prince's Progress" (Rossetti) **WLC 5:**2929, 2940, 2942
"The Princess and the Pea" ("The Princess on the Pea") (Andersen) **WLC 1:**60-1, 64
The Princess Casamassima (James) **WLC 3:**1857, 1860-61
"The Princess on the Pea" (Andersen)
See "The Princess and the Pea"
The Princess: A Medley (Tennyson) **WLC 6:**3579, 3581, 3584
"The Princess" (Chekhov) **WLC 2:**708
La princesse de Babylon (Voltaire) **WLC 6:**3776, 3780
De principiis (Gray)
See *De principiis cogitandi*
De principiis cogitandi (*De principiis*) (Gray) **WLC 3:**1533
"The Principles of Trade" (Franklin) **WLCS 1:**315
"Prioress's Tale" (Chaucer) **WLCS 1:**223, 225
"The Priory School" (Doyle) **WLC 2:**1011
The Prisoner of the Caucasus (Pushkin)
See *Kavkazsky plennik*
"The Privy Councilor" (Chekhov) **WLC 2:**708
"Problem No. 4" (Cheever) **WLC 2:**695
The Problem of Pain (Lewis) **WLC 4:**2090
"The Problem" (Emerson) **WLC 2:**1171
"Proc nejsem komunistou" (Capek) **WLC 1:**605
Procedures for Underground (Atwood) **WLC 1:**108, 111-12
"Procedures for Underground" (Atwood) **WLC 1:**111
"The Procession of Life" (Hawthorne) **WLC 3:**1595, 1606
"La prodigiosa tarde de Baltazar" ("Balthazar's Marvelous Afternoon") (Garcia Marquez) **WLC 3:**1366, 1368
"Profession du vicaire Savoyard" ("The Confession of Faith of a Savoyard Vicar"; "Profession of Faith") (Rousseau) **WLC 5:**2988
"Profession of Faith" (Rousseau)
See "Profession du vicaire Savoyard"
Professional Foul (Stoppard) **WLC 6:**3488, 3492-93
The Professor (Bronte) **WLC 1:**400-01, 406-07, 409
The Professor (Thackeray) **WLC 6:**3594
The Professor's House (Cather) **WLC 1:**656, 660, 662

Profitable Meditations Fitted to Man's Different Condition (Bunyan) **WLC 1:**486
De profundis (Wilde) **WLC 6:**3955-56, 3964, 3966
The Progress of Love (Munro) **WLCS 2:**683-85
"The Progress of Love" (Munro) **WLCS 2:**684
"The Progress of Poesy" ("Ode on the Progress of Poesy"; "The Progress of Poetry") (Gray) **WLC 3:**1320, 1523-28, 1530, 1532-33
"The Progress of Poetry" (Gray)
See "The Progress of Poesy"
The Progresse of the Soule (Donne) **WLC 2:**938
A Project for the Advancement of Religion (Swift) **WLC 6:**3548
Prologue in Heavan (Goethe) **WLC 3:**1419, 1422
"Prologue" (Sheridan) **WLC 5:**3245
"Promenade" (Maupassant) **WLC 4:**2294
Le Prométhée mal enchaîné (*Prometheus Illbound; Prometheus Misbound*) (Gide) **WLC 3:**1389
Prometheus (Aeschylus)
See *Prometheus Bound*
Prometheus Bound (Aeschylus) **WLCS 1:**5-6, 11-12, 14-16
Prometheus Bound (Lowell) **WLC 4:**2168
Prometheus Bound, and Miscellaneous Poems (Browning) **WLC 1:**468
Prometheus Illbound (Gide)
See *Le Prométhée mal enchaîné*
Prometheus Misbound (Gide)
See *Le Prométhée mal enchaîné*
Prometheus Unbound (Aeschylus) **WLCS 1:**6
Prometheus Unbound (Shelley) **WLC 5:**3226-28, 3230, 3233-34, 3236, 3238
The Promise of May (Tennyson) **WLC 6:**3576-78
"The Promisers" (Owen) **WLC 4:**2618
Promises: Poems, 1954-1956 (Warren) **WLC 6:**3814
"The Promoter" (Dunbar) **WLC 2:**1107
"Proof" (Milosz) **WLCS 2:**608
A Proper Marriage (Lessing) **WLCS 2:**493
Proper Studies: The Proper Study of Mankind Is Man (Huxley) **WLC 3:**1765-66
"Propertius" (Pound) **WLC 5:**2797
"The Prophet" (Pushkin)
See "Prorok"
"The Prophetic Pictures" (Hawthorne) **WLC 3:**1594, 1607-08
"Prorok" ("The Prophet") (Pushkin) **WLC 5:**2832
Les Proscrits (Balzac) **WLC 1:**189
Prose Poems (Baudelaire)
See *Petits poèmes en prose: Le spleen de Paris*
"Prosopopoia; or, Mother Hubberds Tale" ("Mother Hubberd's Tale") (Spenser) **WLC 5:**3352
"The Prospector" (Service) **WLC 5:**3123
Prospectus to the Excursion (Wordsworth)
See *The Excursion, Being a Portion of "The Recluse"*
"Le protecteur" (Maupassant) **WLC 4:**2300
"A Protégée of Jack Hamlin's" (Harte) **WLC 3:**1579, 1581
"Protestant Drums, Tyrone, 1966" (Heaney) **WLCS 1:**397
Prothalamion; or, A Spousall Verse (Spenser) **WLC 5:**3352
Proud Flesh (Warren) **WLC 6:**3812
"Proud Maisie" (Scott) **WLC 5:**3115
"Proust" (Beckett) **WLC 1:**240
Provetron (*Meteor*) (Capek) **WLC 1:**603, 605-06
Der Prozess (*The Trial*) (Kafka) **WLC 3:**1941, 1943, 1947-48
Prufrock and Other Observations (Eliot) **WLC 2:**1146, 1148, 1150
"A Psalm of Life" (Longfellow) **WLCS 2:**509
A Psalm of Montreal (Butler) **WLC 1:**560
Pseudo-Martyr: Wherein Out of Certaine Propositions and Gradations, This Conclusion is evicted. That Those Which Are of the Romane Religion in this Kingdome, may and ought to take the Oath of Allegiance (Donne) **WLC 2:**944
Psiché (Moliere) **WLC 4:**2436-37
"Psyche" (Andersen) **WLC 1:**65, 67
"Psychical Research" (Brooke) **WLC 1:**439
"Psycho-analysis and Literary Criticism" (Lewis) **WLC 4:**2090
Psychoanalysis and the Unconscious (Lawrence) **WLC 3:**2044
"Psychology" (Mansfield) **WLC 4:**2215-16
Psychostasia (Aeschylus) **WLCS 1:**14
The Public (Garcia Lorca)
See *El público*
"Public Garden" (Lowell) **WLC 4:**2152
El público (*The Audience; The Public*) (Garcia Lorca) **WLC 2:**1341
Pucelle (Voltaire) **WLC 6:**3769
"Puck of Pook's Hill" (Kipling) **WLC 3:**2014
"Puella Mea" (Cummings) **WLC 2:**835
Pullman Car Hiawatha (Wilder) **WLC 6:**3979, 3985
"Punin and Baburin" (Turgenev) **WLC 6:**3699
Puntila (Brecht)
See *Herr Puntila und sein Knecht Matti*
"Purdah" (Plath) **WLC 4:**2748
Il purgatorio (Alighieri) **WLCS 1:**21-22, 25-28
Purgatory (Alighieri)
See *Il purgatorio*
Purgatory (Yeats) **WLC 6:**4102-03
"The Purloined Letter" (Poe) **WLC 4:**2762
Purple Dust (O'Casey) **WLCS 2:**716-17, 722
"The Purple Hat" (Welty) **WLC 6:**3881, 3884
"The Purple Pileus" (Wells) **WLC 6:**3874
"A Pursuit Race" (Hemingway) **WLC 3:**1650
A Pushcart at the Curb (Dos Passos) **WLC 2:**963
Put Out More Flags (Waugh) **WLC 6:**3822
"Pyetushkov" (Turgenev) **WLC 6:**3697

The Pyramid (Golding) **WLC 3**:1457
Q.E.D. (Stein)
  See *Things As They Are*
Qu'est-ce que la littérature? (*Literature and Existentialism; What Is Literature?*) (Sartre) **WLC 5**:3088
"The Quadroon Girl" (Longfellow) **WLCS 2**:504
"The Quaker Graveyard at Nantucket (for Warren Winslow, Dead at Sea)" (Lowell) **WLC 4**:2153-54, 2160-61, 2170
"Quaker Hill" (Crane) **WLC 2**:797
Quando si è qualcuno (*When One Is Somebody; When Someone is Somebody*) (Pirandello) **WLC 4**:2727
Les quarante-cinq (*The Forty-Five Guardsmen*) (Dumas) **WLC 2**:1083
"The Quarrel of Two Ivans" (Gogol)
  See "The Tale of How Ivan Ivanovich Quarrelled with Ivan Nikiforovich"
Quart Livres (Rabelais) **WLC 5**:2859, 2861-62, 2869, 2871
Quatre-vingt treize (*Ninety-Three*) (Hugo) **WLC 3**:1740, 1743, 1746
Queen (Nabokov) **WLC 4**:2497
Queen Mab (Shelley) **WLC 5**:3227-28
The Queen Mary (Tennyson) **WLC 6**:3573-75
The Queen of Spades (Pushkin) **WLC 5**:2828-29, 2836
The Queen's Necklace (Dumas)
  See *Le collier de la reine*
The Queens of France (Wilder) **WLC 6**:3985
"A Queer Streak" (Munro) **WLCS 2**:683
The Quest of the Absolute (Balzac)
  See *La recherche de l'absolu*
Questa sera si recita a soggetto (*Tonight We Improvise*) (Pirandello) **WLC 4**:2727
Questioned (Grass) **WLC 3**:1510
Questions de méthode (*Search for a Method*) (Sartre) **WLC 5**:3093-94
The Quiet American (Greene) **WLC 3**:1545, 1553-54
"A Quiet Spot" (Turgenev) **WLC 6**:3703-04, 3706
"Quiet Work" (Arnold) **WLC 1**:100
Quint Livre (Rabelais) **WLC 5**:2862
Quitting (Albee) **WLC 1**:33
Quotations from Chairman Mao Tse-Tung (Albee) **WLC 1**:27
Qur'an (Muhammad)
  See *Koran*
R. U. R. (*Rossum's Universal Robots*) (Capek) **WLC 1**:601, 603-05, 607-08, 610
Rabbit Is Rich (Updike) **WLC 6**:3763-64
Rabbit Redux (Updike) **WLC 6**:3753, 3756, 3758, 3762-64
Rabbit, Run (Updike) **WLC 6**:3749, 3751-53, 3755, 3761
"The Race Question" (Dunbar) **WLC 2**:1107
Rachel Ray (Trollope) **WLC 6**:3681
"Rages de césars" (Rimbaud) **WLC 5**:2922
La ragione degli altri (*Other People's Point of View; The Reason of Others*) (Pirandello) **WLC 4**:2719-20, 2728
"Ragnarök" (Borges) **WLC 1**:338
"The Raid" (Tolstoy) **WLC 6**:3665

The Railroad Track Triangle (Grass) **WLC 3**:1510
The Rainbow (Lawrence) **WLC 3**:2043-44, 2050-52, 2056
"Rainy Mountain Cemetery" (Momaday) **WLCS 2**:629
Raio no Terrasu (*The Terrace of the Leper King*) (Mishima) **WLC 4**:2420, 2422
"Raise High the Roofbeam, Carpenters" (Salinger) **WLC 5**:3019-24
Raise Race Rays Raze (Baraka) **WLCS 1**:149, 153
Raising Demons (Jackson) **WLC 3**:1838, 1849, 1851
"The Rajah's Diamond" (Stevenson) **WLC 5**:3447
Rakovyi korpus (*The Cancer Ward*) (Solzhenitsyn) **WLC 5**:3300, 3304-06, 3311
"Ralph Ringwood" (Irving) **WLC 3**:1819
Rambler (Johnson) **WLC 3**:1894, 1899, 1901
Ransom of Hector (Aeschylus) **WLCS 1**:6, 8, 14
"Rape Fantasies" (Atwood) **WLC 1**:114, 116-17
The Rape of the Lock (Pope) **WLC 5**:2771-72, 2775, 2781
Rape upon Rape; Or, The Justice Caught in His Own Trap (Fielding) **WLC 2**:1213
"Rappaccini's Daughter" (Hawthorne) **WLC 3**:1600, 1605
"Rapunzel" (Sexton) **WLC 5**:3146
Rasselas (Johnson)
  See *The Prince of Abyssinia*
"Rasskaz ottsa Aleksaya" ("Father Alexey's Story"; "The Story of Father Alexis") (Turgenev) **WLC 6**:3705
"The Rathskeller and the Rose" (Henry) **WLC 3**:1671
The Raven, and Other Poems (Poe) **WLC 4**:2762
A Raw Youth (Dostoevsky)
  See *Podrostok*
"Raymond's Run" (Bambara) **WLCS 1**:129
Les rayons et les ombres (Hugo) **WLC 3**:1749
The Razor's Edge (Maugham) **WLC 4**:2279, 2281-82, 2284
Re:Creation (Giovanni) **WLCS 1**:355, 361, 364
"The Real Inspector Hound" (Stoppard) **WLC 6**:3483, 3489, 3492-94
The Real Life of Sebastian Knight (Nabokov) **WLC 4**:2497, 2500
"A Real Life" (Munro) **WLCS 2**:687
The Real Thing (Stoppard) **WLC 6**:3485, 3487-88, 3493-95
Real Utopias (Strindberg) **WLC 6**:3515
"Realism" (Milosz) **WLCS 2**:620-21
"The Reality of Dream" (Pirandello)
  See "La realtà del sogno"
Reality Sandwiches (Ginsberg) **WLC 3**:1400
"Really, Doesn't Crime Pay" (Walker) **WLCS 2**:837
"La realtà del sogno" ("The Reality of Dream") (Pirandello) **WLC 4**:2719
"Rearmament" (Jeffers) **WLC 3**:1883
The Reason of Others (Pirandello)

  See *La ragione degli altri*
The Rebel (Camus)
  See *L'homme révolté*
The Rebel Angels (Davies) **WLC 2**:854-57, 859
"Le rebelle" (Baudelaire) **WLC 1**:205
"Rebellion" (Lowell) **WLC 4**:2162
"Receipt for Diminishing a Great Empire" (Franklin) **WLCS 1**:314
"Recessional" (Masters) **WLCS 2**:578
La recherche de l'absolu (*The Quest of the Absolute*) (Balzac) **WLC 1**:179, 182-83, 185-89, 193
"Recitative" (Crane) **WLC 2**:800
The Recluse; or Views on Man, Nature, and on Human Life (Wordsworth) **WLC 6**:4069, 4072, 4076
"The Recollection" (Shelley)
  See "To Jane: The Recollection"
"Recollection" (Wheatley)
  See "On Recollection"
Recollections (Gorky) **WLC 3**:1485
Recollections of Andreev (Gorky) **WLC 3**:1486
Recollections of Tolstoy (Gorky) **WLC 3**:1486
"Records" (Giovanni) **WLCS 1**:358
"The Recovery" (Wharton) **WLC 6**:3902-03
"The Recruit" (Housman) **WLCS 1**:434
The Red and the Black (Stendhal)
  See *Le rouge et le noir*
The Red Badge of Courage: An Episode of the American Civil War (Crane) **WLC 2**:813-14, 816, 818, 820-23
Red Cross for Bronze (H. D.) **WLC 3**:1624
"The Red Mullet" (Warren) **WLC 6**:3815
The Red Pony (Steinbeck) **WLC 5**:3383, 3385
"The Red Retreat" (Service) **WLC 5**:3122
The Red Room (Strindberg)
  See *Röda Rummet*
Red Roses for Me (O'Casey) **WLCS 2**:716
"The Red Shoes" (Andersen) **WLC 1**:58, 60, 67
"Red Story" (Capek) **WLC 1**:600
"Red-Tail Hawk and Pyre of Youth" (Warren) **WLC 6**:3814
The Red Wheel, Knot I: August 1914 (Solzhenitsyn)
  See *Avgust chetyrnadtsatogo*
"The Red Wheelbarrow" (Williams) **WLC 6**:4020
Redgauntlet (Scott) **WLC 5**:3108-09, 3112
The Reef (Wharton) **WLC 6**:3907
"Reflection in a Forest" (Auden) **WLC 1**:131
Reflections in a Golden Eye (McCullers) **WLC 4**:2309, 2319-20
Reflections of a Non-Political Man (Mann)
  See *Betrachtungen eines Unpolitischen*
"Reflections on My Profession" (Giovanni) **WLCS 1**:365
Reflections on the French Revolution (Burke)
  See *Reflections on the Revolution in France and on the Proceedings in Certain Societies in London Relative to That Event*

Reflections on the Revolution in France and on the Proceedings in Certain Societies in London Relative to That Event (*Reflections on the French Revolution*) (Burke) **WLC 1:**504
"A Refusal to Mourn the Death, by Fire, of a Child in London" (Thomas) **WLC 6:**3612, 3619
Reginald (Saki) **WLC 5:**3011
Reginald in Russia, and Other Stories (Saki) **WLC 5:**3011
"The Region November" (Stevens) **WLC 5:**3435
La región más transparente (*Where the Air Is Clear*) (Fuentes) **WLC 2:**1309-11, 1314-15, 1319-21
"Regret" (Chopin) **WLCS 1:**241-42
The Rehearsall Transpros'd (Marvell) **WLC 4:**2255
La reine Margot (*Margaret of Navarre; or, The Massacre of Saint Bartholome's Eve*) (Dumas) **WLC 2:**1083, 1085
"A Reiver's Neck-Verse" (Swinburne) **WLC 6:**3555
The Reivers (Faulkner) **WLC 2:**1197
"The Rejuvenation of Major Rathborn" (London) **WLC 4:**2141
Religio Laici; or, A Layman's Faith (Dryden) **WLC 2:**1046, 1058
"The Relique" (Donne) **WLC 2:**938, 945
"The Remarkable Case of Davidson's Eyes" (Wells) **WLC 6:**3875
"Remarks Concerning the Savages of North America" (Franklin) **WLCS 1:**314
Rembrandt's Hat (Malamud) **WLC 4:**2175-76
"The Remedy: Geography" (Pirandello)
See "Rimedio: La geografia"
"Remember Me" (Rossetti) **WLC 5:**2937
"Remembering Malibu" (Heaney) **WLCS 1:**396
"Remembering Richard Wright" (Ellison) **WLC 2:**1166
Remembrance of Things Past (Proust)
See *A la recherche du temps perdu*
Remorse (*Osorio*) (Coleridge) **WLC 2:**745
"Le remplacant" (Maupassant) **WLC 4:**2291
Renascence, and Other Poems (Millay) **WLCS 2:**591
"Renascence" (Millay) **WLCS 2:**590, 592, 595
"Renegade" (Jackson) **WLC 3:**1849
"Les reparties de Nina" ("Nina Replies") (Rimbaud) **WLC 5:**2916
"Reply to Professor Haldane" (Lewis) **WLC 4:**2090
"A Reply to the Critics" (O'Casey) **WLCS 2:**718
Report from Part One (Brooks) **WLC 1:**453
"A Report to an Academy" (Kafka) **WLC 3:**1947, 1950
"Repose of Rivers" (Crane) **WLC 2:**800, 808-10
Representative Men: Seven Lectures (Emerson) **WLC 2:**1172
Republic (Plato) **WLCS 2:**726, 730-37, 739
Requiem for a Nun (Camus)

See *Requiem pour une nonne*
Requiem pour une nonne (*Requiem for a Nun*) (Camus) **WLC 1:**589-90
"Rescue with Yul Brenner" (Moore) **WLCS 2:**648, 651
Residence on Earth (Neruda)
See *Residencia en la tierra*
Residence on Earth and Other Poems (Neruda)
See *Residencia en la tierra*
Residencia en la tierra (*Residence on Earth; Residence on Earth and Other Poems; Residencia en la tierra, Vol. 1, 1925-31; Residencia en la tierra, Vol. 2, 1931-35; Residencia I; Residencia II; Residencia III*) (Neruda) **WLC 4:**2504-05, 2507, 2509-11, 2513-14, 2516-19
Residencia en la tierra, Vol. 1, 1925-31 (Neruda)
See *Residencia en la tierra*
Residencia en la tierra, Vol. 2, 1931-35 (Neruda)
See *Residencia en la tierra*
Residencia I (Neruda)
See *Residencia en la tierra*
Residencia II (Neruda)
See *Residencia en la tierra*
Residencia III (Neruda)
See *Residencia en la tierra*
"Resignation" (Arnold) **WLC 1:**100-02
The Resistible Rise of Arturo Ui (Brecht)
See *Der aufhaltsame aifstieg des Arturo ui*
"Resolution and Independence" (Wordsworth) **WLC 6:**4068, 4076
"Respectability" (Anderson) **WLC 1:**85
"A Respectable Woman" (Chopin) **WLCS 1:**240
"The Resplendent Quetzal" (Atwood) **WLC 1:**114, 116
Responsibilities, and Other Poems (Yeats) **WLC 6:**4099, 4108
Resurrection (Tolstoy)
See *Voskresenie*
Retablillo de Don Cristóbal (*In the Frame of Don Cristóbal*) (Garcia Lorca) **WLC 2:**1341
Retaliation (Goldsmith) **WLC 3:**1475
Le Retour de l'Enfant prodigue (Gide) **WLCS 3:**1377
"Retraction" (Chaucer) **WLCS 1:**226, 299
Retreat to Innocence (Lessing) **WLCS 2:**488
"Retro Me, Sathana!" (Rossetti) **WLC 5:**2955
"Retrospect" (Brooke) **WLC 1:**439
"Retrospect" (Huxley) **WLC 3:**1763
The Return (de la Mare) **WLC 2:**886-88
Return (Paz) **WLC 4:**2675
See *Vuelta*
The Return of Lanny Budd (Sinclair) **WLC 5:**3272
The Return of Sherlock Holmes (Doyle) **WLC 2:**1018
The Return of the Native (Hardy) **WLC 3:**1561, 1569-70
"The Return to Imray" (Kipling) **WLC 3:**2013
"The Return" (Conrad) **WLC 2:**780
"The Return" (Pound) **WLC 5:**2802
"Reuben Pantier" (Masters) **WLCS 2:**584
"Reunion" (Cheever) **WLC 2:**696

Le rêve (Zola) **WLC 6:**4118, 4127
"Le rêve d'un curieux" ("A Curious Man's Dream") (Baudelaire) **WLC 1:**205
"Rêve parisien" ("A Parisian Dream") (Baudelaire) 1.204-05
"Rêve pour l'hiver" (Rimbaud) **WLC 5:**2922
"Reveille" (Housman) **WLCS 1:**427
"Revelation" (O'Connor) **WLC 4:**2542-43
Rêveries du promeneur solitaire (Rousseau) **WLC 5:**2986
"Reversibilité" (Baudelaire) **WLC 1:**207
The Review (Lowell) **WLC 4:**2155
The Revolt of Islam (Shelley)
See *Laon and Cythna*
Révolte dans les Asturies (Camus) **WLC 1:**590
Revolution, and Other Essays (London) **WLC 4:**2138
"The Revolution in Low Life" (Goldsmith) **WLC 3:**1476
"Revolutionary Tale" (Giovanni) **WLCS 1:**354
"The Revolutionary Theatre" (Baraka) **WLCS 1:**142, 152
Rewards and Fairies (Kipling) **WLC 3:**2014
Rhetoric (Aristotle) **WLCS 1:**95, 99
Rhinoceros (Ionesco)
See *Rhinocéros*
Rhinocéros (*Rhinoceros*) (Ionesco) **WLC 3:**1798, 1800-02, 1809
"The Rhodora" (Emerson) **WLC 2:**1171
"Rhyme for My Tomb" (Service) **WLC 5:**3131
Rhymes For My Rags (Service) **WLC 5:**3130, 3132
Rhymes of a Rebel (Service) **WLC 5:**3130
Rhymes of a Red Cross Man (Service) **WLC 5:**3122
Rhymes of a Rolling Stone (Service) **WLC 5:**3121
Rhymes of a Roughneck (Service) **WLC 5:**3130-31
Rhymes to Be Traded for Bread (Lindsay) **WLC 4:**2117
"The Rich Boy" (Fitzgerald) **WLC 2:**1231, 1233
"Richard Cromwell" (Marvell) **WLC 4:**2254
Richard Darlington (Dumas) **WLC 2:**1087
Richard II (Shakespeare) **WLC 5:**3157-58, 3168, 3171, 3176
Richard III (Shakespeare) **WLC 5:**3158, 3164-65, 3167, 3171
The Riddle, and Other Stories (de la Mare) **WLC 2:**886-87
"Riddle in the Garden" (Warren) **WLC 6:**3815
"Riders to the Blood-Red Wrath" (Brooks) **WLC 1:**453
"The Right Eye of the Commander" (Harte) **WLC 3:**1589
"The Rights and Duties of the Individual in Relation to the Government" (Thoreau)
See "Civil Disobedience"
"Rigs o'Barley" (Burns) **WLC 1:**518
The Rime of the Ancient Mariner: A Poet's Reverie (*The Ancient Mariner, Mariner, The Rime of the Ancyent Marinere*)

(Coleridge) **WLC 2:**745, 750-54
The Rime of the Ancyent Marinere (Coleridge)
See *The Rime of the Ancient Mariner: A Poet's Reverie*
"Rimedio: La geografia" ("The Remedy: Geography") (Pirandello) **WLC 4:**2719
The Ring and the Book (Browning) **WLCS 1:**199, 203, 206, 208, 211, 213
"The Ring of Thoth" (Doyle) **WLC 2:**1018
Riot (Brooks) **WLC 1:**452, 457, 461-63
"Riot" (Brooks) **WLC 1:**457
"Rip Van Winkle" (Irving) **WLC 3:**1818, 1820-23, 1825-27
"Ripe Figs" (Chopin) **WLCS 1:**249-50
"The Rising of the Storm" (Dunbar) **WLC 2:**1102
"The Rites for Cousin Vit" (Brooks) **WLC 1:**455-56
The Rivals (Sheridan) **WLC 5:**3242-43, 3246-47, 3250, 3252-56
"The River" (O'Connor) **WLC 4:**2542, 2551
The Road (London) **WLC 4:**2148
The Road (Soyinka) **WLC 5:**3319, 3322-24, 3327-28
"The Road from Colonus" (Forster) **WLC 2:**1267-68
The Road through the Wall (Jackson) **WLC 3:**1838-41, 1850
The Road to Wigan Pier (Orwell) **WLC 4:**2579, 2582, 2585-88
Road to Within (Hesse)
See *Weg nach Innen*
The Roads of Freedom (Sartre)
See *Les chemins de la liberté*
"Roan Stallion" (Jeffers) **WLC 3:**1876, 1881-82
Rob Roy (Scott) **WLC 5:**3108, 3112
The Robber Bridegroom (Welty) **WLC 6:**3892
Robert (Gide) **WLC 3:**1379, 1384
The Rock (Stevens) **WLC 5:**3432
Rock-Drill (Pound) **WLC 5:**2795-96, 2801-02
Rock Wagram (Saroyan) **WLC 5:**3082-83
"The Rocket Man" (Bradbury) **WLC 1:**370, 377
"Rocket Summer" (Bradbury) **WLC 1:**370
Rocking Back and Forth (Grass) **WLC 3:**1510
Röda Rummet (*The Red Room*) (Strindberg) **WLC 6:**3516
Roderick Hudson (James) **WLC 3:**1857, 1861
Rodney Stone (Doyle) **WLC 2:**1019
"Roger Malvin's Burial" (Hawthorne) **WLC 3:**1605
The Rogueries of Scapin (Moliere)
See *Les fourberies de Scapin*
Le roi Candaule (Gide) **WLC 3:**1377, 1381
Le roi se meurt (*Exit the King; The King Dies*) (Ionesco) **WLC 3:**1804, 1808-09, 1811-12
"The Role of the Writer in a New Nation" (Achebe) **WLC 1:**9
"The Romance of a Busy Broker" (Henry) **WLC 3:**1675
Romancero gitano (Garcia Lorca)
See *Primer romancero gitano*
Rome (Zola) **WLC 6:**4118

"Rome" (Gogol) **WLC 3:**1431
Romeo and Juliet (Shakespeare) **WLC 5:**3158, 3164
Romola (Eliot) **WLC 2:**1123, 1127
Die Rondköpfe und die Spitzköpfe (*The Round Heads and the Pointed Heads; The Roundheads and the Peakheads*) (Brecht) **WLC 1:**391
The Room (Pinter) **WLC 4:**2699, 2701, 2704
A Room with a View (Forster) **WLC 2:**1258-59, 1264, 1269
"The Room" (Sartre)
See "La chambre"
"Roosevelt" (Lindsay) **WLC 4:**2124
Rootabaga Stories (Sandburg) **WLC 5:**3065-66
"The Rope" (Baudelaire)
See "La corde"
Rosa; or, The Black Tulip (Dumas)
See *La tulipe noire*
"Rosabelle" (Scott) **WLC 5:**3115
Rosalind and Helen (Shelley) **WLC 5:**3225
Rosamond Gray (Lamb) **WLC 3:**2030
"The Rose Bush" (Giovanni) **WLCS 1:**359
Rose et Blanche (Sand) **WLC 5:**3045
Rose in Bloom (Alcott) **WLC 1:**39, 43, 50
"Rose Mary" (Rossetti) **WLC 5:**2950, 2958-59
"A Rose of Glenbogie" (Harte) **WLC 3:**1584
"A Rose Plant in Jericho" (Rossetti) **WLC 5:**2931
The Rose Tattoo (Williams) **WLC 6:**3992, 3995-96, 4000
"The Rose Tree" (Yeats) **WLC 6:**4109
Rosencrantz and Guildenstern Are Dead (Stoppard) **WLC 6:**3482-90, 3493-94
"Le rosier de Madame Husson" (Maupassant) **WLC 4:**2300
Roslavlev (Pushkin) **WLC 5:**2829
Rosmersholm (Ibsen) **WLC 3:**1777, 1785, 1788-89, 1791-92
Rossum's Universal Robots (Capek)
See *R. U. R.*
The Rosy Crucifixion (Miller) **WLC 4:**2385, 2391
"A Rotting Corpse" (Baudelaire)
See "Une charogne"
Le rouge et le noir (*The Red and the Black; Scarlet and Black*) (Stendhal) **WLC 5:**3396-99, 3406
Rough Crossing (Stoppard) **WLC 5:**3493
"Rough Magic" (Golding) **WLC 3:**1459
Roughing It (Twain) **WLC 6:**3715-16
"La rouille" (Maupassant) **WLC 4:**2291
"The Round Dozen" (Maugham) **WLC 4:**2275
The Round Heads and the Pointed Heads (Brecht)
See *Die Rondköpfe und die Spitzköpfe*
"A Round of Visits" (James) **WLC 3:**1865
"Round Tower at Jhansi" (Rossetti) **WLC 5:**2937
Roundabout Papers (Thackeray) **WLC 6:**3598-99
"The Roundel" (Swinburne) **WLC 6:**3559
The Roundheads and the Peakheads (Brecht)
See *Die Rondköpfe und die Spitzköpfe*

The Roundheads; or the Good Old Cause (Behn) **WLC 1:**245
The Rover; or, The Banished Cavalier (Behn) **WLC 1:**245-46, 248
"The Rowing Endeth" (Sexton) **WLC 5:**3147
"Rowing" (Sexton) **WLC 5:**3147
Roxana (Defoe)
See *The Fortunate Mistress*
Rubble (Solzhenitsyn)
See *From under the Rubble*
Rudin (*Dimitri Roudine*) (Turgenev) **WLC 6:**3703-04, 3708
El rufián dichoso (Cervantes) **WLC 2:**682-83
"Las ruinas circulares" ("The Circular Ruins") (Borges) **WLC 1:**335, 340
"Rule by Machines" (Capek) **WLC 1:**612
Rumour at Nightfall (Greene) **WLC 1:**1542, 1546
"Runes on Weland's Sword" (Kipling) **WLC 3:**2017
"Rupture" (Pasternak) **WLC 4:**2629
Rusalka (*The Water Nymph*) (Pushkin) **WLC 5:**2827
Ruslan and Lyudmila (Pushkin)
See *Ruslan i Lyudmila*
Ruslan i Lyudmila (*Ruslan and Lyudmila*) (Pushkin) **WLC 5:**2832-33
"Russell Kincaid" (Masters) **WLCS 2:**580
"The Russian Language" (Turgenev) **WLC 6:**3705
A Russian Pelham (Pushkin) **WLC 5:**2829
"Ruth" (Oates) **WLC 4:**2531
S Is for Space (Bradbury) **WLC 1:**371
S. S. Glencairn (O'Neill) **WLC 4:**2558
"Saadi" (Emerson) **WLC 2:**1171
Sabotage (Baraka) **WLCS 1:**151
"Sacrament" (Cullen) **WLCS 1:**277
"Sacred Chant for the Return of Black Spirit and Power" (Baraka) **WLCS 1:**145
Sacred Cows and Other Edibles (Giovanni) **WLCS 1:**364
The Sacred Factory (Toomer) **WLCS 2:**801
The Sacred Fount (James) **WLC 3:**1869
"The Sacred Marriage" (Oates) **WLC 4:**2528
Sacred Monsters (Cocteau)
See *Les monstres sacrés*
The Sacred Wood: Essays on Poetry and Criticism (Eliot) **WLC 2:**1151
The Sacred Zone (Fuentes)
See *Zona sagrada*
"The Sad Fortunes of the Rev. Amos Barton" ("Amos Barton") (Eliot) **WLC 2:**1119, 1125-26
The Sad Shepherd (Jonson) **WLC 3:**1909-11
"Sadie and Maude" (Brooks) **WLC 1:**461
Safe Conduct (Pasternak) **WLC 4:**2627-29; 2632
"Safety" (Brooke) **WLC 1:**437, 443-44
"Sagesse" (H. D.) **WLC 3:**1616, 1624
"Sailing Home from Rapallo" (Lowell) **WLC 4:**2164
"Sailing to Byzantium" (Yeats) **WLC 6:**4105-06, 4112
The Sailor Who Fell from Grace with the Sea (Mishima)

See *Gogo no eiko*
"The Sailor's Mother" (Wordsworth) **WLC 6:**4067
"A Saint about to Fall" (Thomas) **WLC 6:**3622
"The Saint and the Goblin" (Saki) **WLC 5:**3007
Saint-Antoine (Flaubert) **WLC 2:**1241
"Saint Francis and Lady Clare" (Masters) **WLCS 2:**578
Saint Joan (Shaw) **WLC 5:**3192, 3194-95
La Saisiaz (Browning) **WLCS 1:**214-15
Une saison en enfer (*A Season in Hell*) (Rimbaud) **WLC 5:**2908, 2910, 2912, 2917-19, 2921, 2925
"Sakyamuni Coming Out from the Mountain" (Ginsberg) **WLC 3:**1396
The Salamander (Paz)
See *Salamandra*
Salamandra (*The Salamander*) (Paz) **WLC 4:**2661, 2663
Salammbô (Flaubert) **WLC 2:**1241, 1252
Salmagundi (Irving) **WLC 3:**1816-18, 1820, 1823, 1827
Salomé (Wilde) **WLC 6:**3955
The Salt Eaters (Bambara) **WLCS 1:**124, 126
The Salterton Trilogy (Davies) **WLC 2:**852
Sam Ego's House (Saroyan) **WLC 5:**3075
Samfundets støtter (*The Pillars of Society; Pillars of the Community*) (Ibsen) **WLC 3:**1780-81, 1785
Samson Agonistes (Milton) **WLC 4:**2407, 2409
Samuel Marchbanks' Almanack (*Marchbanks' Almanack*) (Davies) **WLC 2:**848, 851
"San Ildefonso Nocturne" (Paz)
See "Nocturno de San Ildefonso"
"Sanatorium" (Maugham) **WLC 4:**2281
Sanctuary (Faulkner) **WLC 2:**1189, 1193, 1195-99
The Sandbox (Albee) **WLC 1:**20, 30-1
"The Sandpit" (Heaney) **WLCS 1:**396
"Sandstone Keepsake" (Heaney) **WLCS 1:**389
Le sang d'un poète (*The Blood of a Poet*) (Cocteau) **WLC 2:**723-25
"Sanity of True Genius" (Lamb) **WLC 3:**2036
"The Santa Fé Trail" (Lindsay) **WLC 4:**2119
Sapphira and the Slave Girl (Cather) **WLC 1:**660, 663
"Sarah Dewitt" (Masters) **WLCS 2:**578
Sartoris (*Flags in the Dust*) (Faulkner) **WLC 2:**1190, 1195, 1197-98
Satan in Goray (Singer)
See *Shoten an Goray*
The Satanic Verses (Rushdie) **WLCS 2:**743-46, 748-49, 751, 753
Satin-Legs Smith (Brooks)
See "The Sundays of Satin-Legs Smith"
Satires (Donne) **WLC 2:**933
Satires and Epistles of Horace, Imitated ("First Epistle of the First Book of Horace"; *Imitations of Horace*) (Pope) **WLC 5:**2775
Satires of Dr. Donne Versified (Pope) **WLC 5:**2779

Satori in Paris (Kerouac) **WLC 3:**1978
"Saturday's Child" (Cullen) **WLCS 1:**273-75
"Saturn" (Grass) **WLC 3:**1506
"Le satyre" (Hugo) **WLC 3:**1749
Satyres (Donne) **WLC 2:**933
Saül (Gide) **WLC 3:**1388
"Saul" (Browning) **WLCS 1:**214
Savage Holiday (Wright) **WLC 6:**4088, 4091
"The Scapegoat" (Dunbar) **WLC 2:**1107
Scarlet and Black (Stendhal)
See *Le rouge et le noir*
The Scarlet Letter (Hawthorne) **WLC 3:**1595, 1597-99, 1601-05, 1607
The Scarlet Plague (London) **WLC 4:**2140
Scarmentado (Voltaire) **WLC 6:**3779-80
Scenes from Russian Life (Turgenev)
See *Zapiski okhotnika*
Scenes of Clerical Life (Eliot) **WLC 2:**1117, 1119, 1123
Scenes of Military Life (Balzac) **1:**182
Scenes of Parisian Life (Balzac)
See *Scènes de la vie Parisienne*
"Scenes of Passion and Desire" (Oates) **WLC 4:**2530
Scenes of Political Life (Balzac)
See *Scènes de la vie politique*
Scenes of Private Life (Balzac)
See *Scènes de la vie privée*
Scenes of Provincial Life (Balzac)
See *Scènes de la vie de province*
Scènes de la vie de province (*Scenes of Provincial Life*) (Balzac) **WLC 1:**182
Scènes de la vie militaire (Balzac) **WLC 1:**182
Scènes de la vie Parisienne (*Scenes of Parisian Life*) (Balzac) **WLC 1:**182
Scènes de la vie politique (*Scenes of Political Life*) (Balzac) **WLC 1:**182
Scènes de la vie privée (*Scenes of Private Life*) (Balzac) **WLC 1:**182
"The Schartz-Metterklume Method" (Saki) **WLC 5:**3008
Das Schloss (*The Castle*) (Kafka) **WLC 3:**1943, 1948
"The Scholar-Gipsy" (Arnold) **WLC 1:**91-2, 103
The School for Husbands (Moliere)
See *L'école des maris*
The School for Scandal (Sheridan) **WLC 5:**3243, 3245-46, 3248, 3250-51, 3253, 3256
"The School for Tenors" (Grass)
See "Die Schule der Tenöre"
The School for Wives (Gide)
See *L'école des femmes*
The School for Wives (Moliere)
See *L'école des femmes*
The School for Wives Criticized (Moliere)
See *La critique de L'école des femmes*
"Die Schule der Tenöre" ("The School for Tenors") (Grass) **WLC 3:**1506
"Schwallinger's Philanthropy" (Dunbar) **WLC 2:**1107
"Die schwarzen schafe" ("The Black Sheep") (Boell) **WLC 1:**326
"La Science du Bonhomme Richard" (Franklin) **WLCS 1:**314
"Science, Liberty and Peace" (Huxley)

WLC 3:1766-67
Scoop (Waugh) **WLC 6:**3821
"Scots Wha Hae wi' Wallace Bled" (Burns) **WLC 1:**518
The Screwtape Letters (Lewis) **WLC 4:**2081, 2084, 2086, 2091
Scum (Singer) **WLC 5:**3293-95
se vi pare (Pirandello)
See *Cosíè (se vi pare)*
"Se ..." ("If") (Pirandello) **WLC 4:**2719
"The Sea and the Mirror: A Commentary on Shakespeare's *Tempest*" (Auden) **WLC 1:**135-36
The Sea Birds Are Still Alive (Bambara) **WLCS 1:**132, 134-36
"The Sea Birds Are Still Alive" (Bambara) **WLCS 1:**134-35
"The Sea-Elephant" (Williams) **WLC 6:**4014
Sea Garden (H. D.) **WLC 3:**1623-24
The Sea in Being (Hemingway)
See *The Old Man and the Sea*
The Sea Lady (Wells) **WLC 6:**3874, 3876
Sea of Cortez: A Leisurely Journal of Travel and Research (Steinbeck) **WLC 5:**3388
The Sea of Fertility: A Cycle of Novels (Mishima)
See *H j no umi*
"The Sea of Lost Time" (Garcia Marquez)
See "El mar del tiempo perdido"
"The Sea Raiders" (Wells) **WLC 6:**3863-64, 3876
"Sea-Shore" (Emerson) **WLC 2:**1171
"Sea Unicorns and Land Unicorns" (Moore) **WLCS 2:**641
The Sea Wolf (London) **WLC 4:**2137, 2143, 2147-48
"The Sea's Green Sameness" (Updike) **WLC 6:**3751
The Seagull (Chekhov)
See *Chayka*
Search for a Method (Sartre)
See *Questions de méthode*
Search for a Method (Sartre) **WLC 5:**3093-94
"A Seashore Drama" (Balzac)
See "Un drame au bord de la mer"
The Seaside and the Fireside (Longfellow) **WLCS 2:**510, 513
"The Seaside Houses" (Cheever) **WLC 2:**696-97
"Seaside" (Brooke) **WLC 1:**438
A Season in Hell (Rimbaud)
See *Une saison en enfer*
"The Season of Divorce" (Cheever) **WLC 2:**695
The Season of Violence (Paz)
See *La estación violenta*
The Second Anniversarie. Of the Progres of the Soule. Wherein, By Occasion Of the Religious death of Mistris Elizabeth Drury, the incommodities of the Soule in this life, and her exaltation in the next, are Contemplated (*Of the Progres of the Soule*) (Donne) **WLC 2:**944
Second April (Millay) **WLCS 2:**592, 603
The Second Birth (Pasternak) **WLC 4:**2627
"The Second Choice" (Dreiser) **WLC 2:**1038
"The Second Coming" (Yeats) **WLC**

6:4108, 4110
The Second Common Reader (Woolf) **WLC 6:**4048, 4050
Second Discourse (Rousseau)
  See *Discours sur l'origine et les fondements de l'inégalité parmi les hommes*
The Second Jungle Book (Kipling) **WLC 3:**2019-20
"Second Nun's Tale" (Chaucer) **WLCS 1:**227, 233
"The Second Sermon on the Warpland" (Brooks) **WLC 1:**453
The Second Sex (Beauvoir)
  See *Le deuxième sexe*
The Secret Agent (Conrad) **WLC 2:**780, 782, 790-92
Secret Love; or, The Maiden Queen (Dryden) **WLC 2:**1048
"The Secret Miracle" (Borges)
  See "El milagro secreto"
"The Secret of Macarger's Gulch" (Bierce) **WLC 1:**288
"The Secret of the Sea" (Longfellow) **WLCS 2:**510
"The Secret Rose" (Yeats) **WLC 6:**4102
"The Secret Sharer" (Conrad) **WLC 2:**790
Le secrétaire intime (*Intimate Journal*) (Sand) **WLC 5:**3039
"The Secular Masque" (Dryden) **WLC 2:**1051
"Seduction" (Giovanni) **WLCS 1:**363-64
"See where Capella with her golden kids" (Millay) **WLCS 2:**594
"The Seed of Faith" (Wharton) **WLC 6:**3905
Seeds for a Hymn (Paz)
  See *Semillas para un himno*
Seeing Things (Heaney) **WLCS 1:**399
Sei personaggi in cerca d'autore (*Six Characters in Search of an Author*) (Pirandello) **WLC 4:**2719-23, 2725, 2728-32
Seize the Day (Bellow) **WLC 1:**263-65, 268-69, 271-74
Sejanus (Jonson) **WLC 3:**1907, 1909-10
Selected Letters (Forster) **WLC 2:**1270
Selected Plays and Prose of Amiri Baraka/Leroi Jones (Baraka) **WLCS 1:**146, 152
Selected Poems (Brooks) **WLC 1:**455-56
Selected Poems (McKay) **WLC 4:**2336
Selected Poems (Milosz) **WLCS 2:**607-08, 610, 612
Selected Poems (Pound) **WLC 5:**2792
Selected Poems, 1923-1975 (Warren) **WLC 6:**3816
Selected Poems 1965-1975 (Atwood) **WLC 1:**111-12
The Selected Poems of Nikki Giovanni (Giovanni) **WLCS 1:**365
Selected Poems: New and Old, 1923-1966 (Warren) **WLC 6:**3814
Selected Poetry of Amiri Baraka/Leroi Jones (Baraka) **WLCS 1:**146
Selected Stories (Gordimer) **WLCS 1:**370, 375
"Self Criticism" (Cullen) **WLCS 1:**282
"Self-Deception" (Arnold) **WLC 1:**100
"Self-Dependence" (Arnold) **WLC 1:**100
"Self-Reliance" (Emerson) **WLC 2:**1176-77, 1179-80, 1183
"The Selfish Giant" (Wilde) **WLC 6:**3952
"The Semblables" (Williams) **WLC 6:**4014
Semeinoe schaste (*Family Happiness*) (Tolstoy) **WLC 6:**3666
Semele (Aeschylus) **WLCS 1:**6
Semillas para un himno (*Seeds for a Hymn*) (Paz) **WLC 4:**2660
"The Send-Off" (Owen) **WLC 4:**2608
"Sending" (Arnold) **WLC 1:**93
Senilia (Turgenev)
  See *Stikhotvoreniya v proze*
"Sensation" (Rimbaud) **WLC 5:**2922
Sense and Sensibility (Austen) **WLC 1:**149, 155
A Sense of Detachment (Osborne) **WLC 4:**2597-98, 2600-01
The Sensitive Plant (Shelley) **WLC 5:**3228, 3235-36
Sentimental Education: A Young Man's History (Flaubert)
  See *L'éducation sentimentale: Histoire d'un jeune homme*
A Sentimental Journey through France and Italy (Sterne) **WLC 5:**3412, 3414, 3418, 3421-23
"A Sentimental Soul" (Chopin) **WLCS 1:**240
"Sentimental Summer" (Huxley) **WLC 3:**1761-62
"The Sentry" (Owen) **WLC 4:**2611
Señora Carrar's Rifles (Brecht) **WLC 1:**390
"La Señora Cornelia" ("The Lady Cornelia") (Cervantes) **WLC 2:**679
The Separate Notebooks (Milosz) **WLCS 2:**617
"Separating" (Updike) **WLC 6:**3760
"Les sept vieillards" ("The Seven Old Men") (Baudelaire) **WLC 1:**203
"September 1913" (Yeats) **WLC 6:**4108-10
"September on Jessore Road" (Ginsberg) **WLC 3:**1398
"September Song" (Heaney) **WLCS 1:**394
Septimius Felton, or the Elixir of Life (Hawthorne) **WLC 3:**1600-01
Les séquestrés d'Altona (*The Condemned of Altona*) (Sartre) **WLC 5:**3091-92, 3095
"The Seraphim" (Browning) **WLC 1:**468
Sermons (Johnson) **WLC 3:**1895
The Sermons of Mr. Yorick (Sterne) **WLC 5:**3424-25
"The Service" (Thoreau) **WLC 6:**3628-31
Sestra moia zhizn (*My Sister, Life*) (Pasternak) **WLC 4:**2627
"The Settle Bed" (Heaney) **WLCS 1:**400
"The Settlers" (Bradbury) **WLC 1:**370
"Sevastopol in August, 1855" (Tolstoy) **WLC 6:**3666
"Sevastopol in December 1854" (Tolstoy) **WLC 6:**3665
"Sevastopol in May, 1855" (Tolstoy) **WLC 6:**3666
Seven against Thebes (Aeschylus) **WLCS 1:**8, 10, 12, 14-15
"The Seven Bridges" (Mishima) **WLC 4:**2423
The Seven Descents of Myrtle (Williams)
  See *Kingdom of Earth: The Seven Descents of Myrtle*
Seven Guitars (Wilson) **WLCS 1:**872, 874
"The Seven Old Men" (Baudelaire)
  See "Les sept vieillards"
"The Seven Vagabonds" (Hawthorne) **WLC 3:**1594
Seventh Letter (Plato) **WLCS 2:**735
"Seventy Thousand Assyrians" (Saroyan) **WLC 5:**3082
73 Poems (Cummings) **WLC 2:**843
Sganarelle, ou le cocu imaginaire (*Sganarelle; or, The Cuckold in His Own Imagination*) (Moliere) **WLC 4:**2436, 2442
Sganarelle; or, The Cuckold in His Own Imagination (Moliere)
  See *Sganarelle, ou le cocu imaginaire*
"Shadow, a Parable" (Poe) **WLC 4:**2754, 2761
Shadow and Act (Ellison) **WLC 2:**1165
"The Shadow Line" (Conrad) **WLC 2:**781
The Shadow of a Gunman (O'Casey) **WLCS 2:**707, 709, 712-14, 717, 720, 722
"The Shadow" (Andersen) **WLC 1:**60
Shadows on the Rock (Cather) **WLC 1:**655-57, 660, 665
"Shakespeare in Harlem" (Hughes) **WLC 3:**1721-22, 1724
"Shakespeare, the Poet" (Emerson) **WLC 2:**1170
"Shakespeare" (Arnold) **WLC 1:**100
Shakespeare's Boy Actors (Davies) **WLC 2:**848
Shakespeare's Tragedies (Lamb) **WLC 3:**2032
Shame (Rushdie) **WLCS 2:**744-46, 748, 753
"A Shameful Affair" (Chopin) **WLCS 1:**239-40
Shamela (Fielding)
  See *An Apology for the Life of Mrs. Shamela Andrews*
"The Shape of the Sword" (Borges)
  See "La forma de la espada"
The Shape of Things to Come (Wells) **WLC 6:**3869, 3871
"The Shape of Things" (Capote) **WLC 1:**619
Shapes of Clay (Bierce) **WLC 1:**291-92
She and He (Sand)
  See *Elle et lui*
She Came to Stay (Beauvoir)
  See *L'invitée*
She Stoops to Conquer (Goldsmith) **WLC 3:**1464, 1470, 1477-78
"Sheltered Garden" (H. D.) **WLC 3:**1612
The Shepheardes Calender: Conteyning Twelve Æglogues Proportionable to the Twelve Monethes (Spenser) **WLC 5:**3349-50
"The Shepherd's Brow, Fronting Forked Lightning" (Hopkins) **WLC 3:**1715
"The Shepherdess and the Chimney Sweep" (Andersen) **WLC 1:**59, 64-5
"Shepherds' Hymn" (Crashaw)
  See "Necessary Angel"
"The Sheridans" (Mansfield) **WLC 4:**2219
Sherwood Anderson's Memoirs (Ander-

son) **WLC 1:**74-5, 77, 83
"The Shield of Achilles" (Auden) **WLC 1:**137
Shih (Confucius)
See *Shih Ching*
Shih Ching (Confucius) **WLCS 1:**254, 256-57
See *Ancient Poems*
Shih king (Confucius)
See *Shih Ching*
Shikasta (Lessing) **WLCS 2:**489-91
"Shine, Perishing Republic" (Jeffers) **WLC 3:**1882
"Shingles for the Lord" (Faulkner) **WLC 2:**1196
"Shining Houses" (Munro) **WLCS 2:**680
"Shipman's Tale" (Chaucer) **WLCS 1:**227
Shirley (Bronte) **WLC 1:**399-402, 404, 407
Shiro ari no su (Mishima) **WLC 4:**2418
The Shoemaker's Prodigious Wife (Garcia Lorca)
See *La zapatera prodigiosa*
"The Shooting of Dan McGrew" (Service) **WLC 5:**3123, 3128
"Shop" (Browning) **WLCS 1:**2-9
"Short Friday" (Singer) **WLC 5:**3287, 3290-91
"The Short Happy Life of Francis Macomber" (Hemingway) **WLC 3:**1651-52
Short Prose Poems (Baudelaire)
See *Petits poèmes en prose: Le spleen de Paris*
"A Short Recess" (Milosz) **WLCS 2:**610-11
"The Short Story" (Welty) **WLC 6:**3891
Short Vindication (Vanbrugh)
See *Life and Habit*
"The Shot" (Pushkin)
See "Vystrel"
Shoten an Goray (*Satan in Goray*) (Singer) **WLC 5:**3286, 3292-93
"Should, Should Not" (Milosz) **WLCS 2:**615
"The Shovel Man" (Sandburg) **WLC 5:**3066
"The Show" (Owen) **WLC 4:**2608, 2617-18
"Shower" (Swift)
See "Description of a City Shower"
A Shropshire Lad (Housman) **WLCS 1:**426-27, 429-31, 433-36
"The Shroud of Color" (Cullen) **WLCS 1:**273-74, 276, 285-86
Shu (Confucius)
See *Shu Ching*
Shu Ching (Confucius) **WLCS 1:**254-56
Shu King (Confucius)
See *Shu Ching*
"Shut a Final Door" (Capote) **WLC 1:**618
Si le grain ne meurt (Gide) **WLC 3:**1379
"Siblings" (Gordimer) **WLCS 1:**380
"Sibrandus Schafnaburgensis" (Browning) **WLCS 1:**208
"A Sibyl" (Atwood) **WLC 1:**111
Sibylline Leaves (Coleridge) **WLC 2:**746
"Sicilian Limes" (Pirandello) **WLC 4:**2726
The Sicilian; or, Love the Painter (Moliere)
See *Le sicilien; ou, L'amour peintre*
Le sicilien; ou, L'amour peintre (*The Sicilian; or, Love the Painter*) (Moliere)

WLC 4:2436-37, 2445
"The Sick King in Bokhara" (Arnold) **WLC 1:**101
Siddhartha (Hesse) **WLC 3:**1686-88
Siècle de Louis XIV (Voltaire) **WLC 6:**3770
Siècle de Louis XV (Voltaire) **WLC 6:**3770-71
The Siege of Corinth (Byron) **WLC 1:**569
"Siena" (Swinburne) **WLC 6:**3563
"Siesta in Xbalba and Return to the States" (Ginsberg) **WLC 3:**1400, 1402
"Sigismunda and Guiscardo" (Dryden) **WLC 2:**1046
The Sign of Four (Doyle) **WLC 2:**1011
"The Sign" (Masters) **WLCS 2:**578
Signora Morli One and Two (Pirandello) **WLC 4:**2727
"Signs of the Times" (Dunbar) **WLC 2:**1103
"Silas Jackson" (Dunbar) **WLC 2:**1106
Silas Marner, the Weaver of Raveloe (Eliot) **WLC 2:**1119-20, 1123
Silence (Pinter) **WLC 4:**2704-06
"Silence, a Fable" (Poe) **WLC 4:**2754
"Silence" (Masters) **WLCS 2:**578
"Silent Samuel" (Dunbar) **WLC 2:**1107
"The Silent Towns" (Bradbury) **WLC 1:**370
The Silent Woman (Jonson) **WLC 3:**1908, 1910, 1912-13
See *Epicoene; or, the Silent Woman*
"Silly Song" (Garcia Lorca)
See "Canción tonta"
The Silmarillion (Tolkien) **WLC 6:**3645, 3654-58
The Silver Chair (Lewis) **WLC 4:**2083
Silver Pitchers (Alcott) **WLC 1:**50
The Silver Spoon (Galsworthy) **WLC 2:**1328
The Silver Tassie (O'Casey) **WLCS 2:**709, 716, 721-23
"Simile" (Momaday) **WLCS 2:**628
Simon (Sand) **WLC 5:**3039
"Simon Legree" (Lindsay) **WLC 4:**2120-21, 2127
"Simon the Cyrenian Speaks" (Cullen) **WLCS 1:**277
Simonsen (Undset) **WLC 6:**3740
"A Simple Enquiry" (Hemingway) **WLC 3:**1650
"Simple Maria" (Allende) **WLCS 1:**46
The Simpleton of the Unexpected Isles (Shaw) **WLC 5:**3193
"since feeling is first" (Cummings) **WLC 2:**840
"Since I am comming" (Donne)
See "Hymne to God my God, in my sicknesse"
"Sincerity and Art" (Huxley) **WLC 3:**1762
Sing (Bradbury) **WLC 1:**372
"The Sing-Song of Old Man Kangaroo" (Kipling) **WLC 3:**2018-19
"Sing the Epistle" (Pirandello)
See "Canta l'epistola"
"The Singers" (Turgenev) **WLC 6:**3702, 3706
Singin' and Swingin' and Gettin' Merry Like Christmas (Angelou) **WLCS 1:**58, 62, 67
"The Singing Lesson" (Mansfield) **WLC 4:**2215

"The Singing School" (Heaney) **WLCS 1:**391
"The Sinking Ship" (Rimbaud)
See "L'eclatante victoire de Saarebrück"
"Sins of the Third Age" (Gordimer) **WLCS 1:**379
Sir Charles Grandison (Richardson)
See *The History of Sir Charles Grandison*
"Sir Galahad" (Masters) **WLCS 2:**578
Sir Gawain and the Green Knight **WLCS 1:**333-49
Sir Harry Hotspur (Trollope) **WLC 6:**3681
"Sir Humphrey Gilbert" (Longfellow) **WLCS 2:**510
Sir Nigel (Doyle) **WLC 2:**1015, 1019-20
Sir Patient Fancy (Behn) **WLC 1:**246-48
The Sirens of Titan (Vonnegut) **WLC 6:**3786, 3790-92, 3797
"The Siskin Who Lied and the Truth-Loving Woodpecker" (Gorky) **WLC 3:**1485
Sister Carrie (Dreiser) **WLC 2:**1025, 1031-32, 1034, 1036-38
"Sister Helen" (Rossetti) **WLC 5:**2949-50, 2953, 2955-57
"Sister Maude" (Rossetti) **WLC 5:**2937
"The Sisters" (Joyce) **WLC 3:**1930
Sisyphus (Aeschylus) **WLCS 1:**6
"Six-Bit Blues" (Hughes) **WLC 3:**1723
Six Characters in Search of an Author (Pirandello)
See *Sei personaggi in cerca d'autore*
Six Feet of Country (Gordimer) **WLCS 1:**374
"Six O'Clock in Princes Street" (Owen) **WLC 4:**2618
The Six of Calais (Shaw) **WLC 5:**3193
"Skazka o Tsare Sultane" ("The Tale of the Tsar Sultan"; "Tsar Sultan") (Pushkin) **WLC 5:**2832
"The Skeleton in Armor" (Longfellow) **WLCS 2:**503-04, 510
The Sketch Book (Irving)
See *The Sketch Book of Geoffrey Crayon, Gent.*
The Sketch Book of Geoffrey Crayon, Gent. (*The Sketch Book*) (Irving) **WLC 3:**1816-20, 1822, 1825-28
"Sketch" (Sandburg) **WLC 5:**3063
Sketches from a Hunter's Album (Turgenev)
See *Zapiski okhotnika*
The Skin of Our Teeth (Wilder) **WLC 6:**3977-79, 3981, 3984
"Skunk Hour" (Lowell) **WLC 4:**2156-58, 2165, 2167
"The Skunk" (Heaney) **WLCS 1:**397
Slapstick Tragedy (Williams)
See *The Gnädiges Fräulein*
"The Slaughterer" (Singer) **WLC 5:**3293
Slaughterhouse-Five; or, The Children's Crusade: A Duty-Dance with Death (Vonnegut) **WLC 6:**3786, 3789-90, 3792-3801
The Slave (Baraka) **WLCS 1:**139, 141-43, 148, 152
"Slave on the Block" (Hughes) **WLC 3:**1733
Slave Ship (Baraka) **WLCS 1:**152
"Sleep and Poetry" (Keats) **WLC 3:**1958-59

"Sleep at Sea" (Rossetti) **WLC 5**:2938
"The Sleep Worker" (Hardy) **WLC 3**:1571
"Sleepy" (Chekhov) **WLC 2**:708-09
A Slight Ache (Pinter) **WLC 4**:2701, 2704
"Slip-Shoe Lovey" (Masters) **WLCS 2**:577
"Slipfoot and How He Nearly Always Never Gets What He Goes After" (Sandburg) **WLC 5**:3066
"Sludge" (Browning) **WLCS 1**:211
Small Craft Warnings (Williams) **WLC 6**:3996, 3998, 4002-03
The Small House at Allington (Trollope) **WLC 6**:3681, 3689
"The Small Personal Voice" (Lessing) **WLCS 2**:487
"The Small Rain" (Pynchon) **WLC 5**:2854
"Small Tactics" (Atwood) **WLC 1**:112
"A Small Variation" (Paz) **WLC 4**:2675
"Smile, Smile, Smile" (Owen) **WLC 4**:2611, 2616
Smoke (Turgenev)
  See *Dym*
Smoke and Steel (Sandburg) **WLC 5**:3052-53
"Smoke and Steel" (Sandburg) **WLC 5**:3053
"Smoke" (Thoreau) **WLC 6**:3627
The Snobs of England (Thackeray)
  See *The Book of Snobs*
Snopes (Faulkner) **WLC 2**:1198-99
"The Snow Fairy" (McKay) **WLC 4**:2334, 2337
"Snow-Flakes" (Hawthorne)
  See "Snowflakes"
"The Snow Man" (Stevens) **WLC 5**:3434, 3437
"The Snow Queen" (Andersen) **WLC 1**:59-61, 63-4, 67
"The Snow Storm" (Emerson) **WLC 2**:1171
"Snowflakes" ("Snow-Flakes") (Hawthorne) **WLC 3**:1594
"The Snows of Kilimanjaro" (Hemingway) **WLC 3**:1651-52, 1655, 1657
"The Snowstorm" (Pushkin) **WLC 5**:2828
The Social Contract (Rousseau)
  See *Du Contrat social*
Sodom and Gomorrah (Proust)
  See *Sodome et Gomorrhe*
Sodome et Gomorrhe (*Cities of the Plain*; *Sodom and Gomorrah*) (Proust) **WLC 5**:2818-20
"Les soeurs Rondoli" (Maupassant) **WLC 4**:2289, 2291, 2293, 2303
The Soft Machine (Burroughs) **WLC 1**:535-37, 542, 544-45
The Soft Voice of the Serpent (Gordimer) **WLCS 1**:374
"Soft Wood" (Lowell) **WLC 4**:2159
"Sohrab and Rustum" (Arnold) **WLC 1**:93-95, 103
La soif et la faim (*Hunger and Thirst*) (Ionesco) **WLC 3**:1804-06, 1809
"Un soir" (Maupassant) **WLC 4**:2300
"The Soldier" (Brooke) **WLC 1**:440, 443-44
"Soldier's Dream" (Owen) **WLC 4**:2614
"Soldiers Three" (Kipling) **WLC 3**:2020-22
"Soleil et chair" ("Sunlight and Flesh") (Rimbaud) **WLC 5**:2920, 2922, 2924-25

"Soles occidere et redire poussunt" (Huxley) **WLC 3**:1765
"The Solitary Reaper" (Wordsworth) **WLC 6**:4073
"Some Foreign Letters" (Sexton) **WLC 5**:3137-38, 3146
Some Monday for Sure (Gordimer) **WLCS 1**:370
"Some Monday for Sure" (Gordimer) **WLCS 1**:370, 372
"Some Notes on Recent American Fiction" (Bellow) **WLC 1**:265
"Some Novelists I Have Known" (Maugham) **WLC 4**:2278
Some People, Places, and Things That Will Not Appear in My Next Novel (Cheever) **WLC 2**:690, 696
"Someone Has Disturbed the Roses" (Garcia Marquez)
  See "Alguien desordena estas rosas"
Something Cloudy, Something Clear (Williams) **WLC 6**:4007
Something Happened (Heller) **WLC 3**:1640
Something I've Been Meaning to Tell You (Munro) **WLCS 2**:676, 678, 683, 685
"Something I've Been Meaning to Tell You" (Munro) **WLCS 2**:676
Something of Myself (Kipling) **WLC 3**:2018
Something Out There (Gordimer) **WLCS 1**:372, 379
"Something Out There" (Gordimer) **WLCS 1**:375-77
"Something to Be Said for Silence" (Giovanni) **WLCS 1**:359
Something Wicked This Way Comes (Bradbury) **WLC 1**:364, 366
Sometimes a Great Notion (Kesey) **WLC 3**:1994, 1996, 2000-01
A Son at the Front (Wharton) **WLC 6**:3908
Son excellence (Zola) **WLC 6**:4125
The Son of a Servant (Strindberg)
  See *Tränstekvinnans son*
The Son of the Wolf: Tales of the Far North (London) **WLC 4**:2141-42
"The Son of the Wolf" (London) **WLC 4**:2141
"Son" ("The Dream") (Turgenev) **WLC 6**:3699
"A Song for Simeon" (Eliot) **WLC 2**:1147
"Song of a Man Who Has Come Through" (Lawrence) **WLC 3**:2045
Song of Hiawatha (Longfellow) **WLCS 2**:512, 514
"Song of Myself" ("One's-Self I Sing") (Whitman) **WLC 6**:3936, 3938, 3940-41, 3945
Song of Solomon (Morrison) **WLC 4**:2474, 2476-79
"The Song of the Bower" (Rossetti) **WLC 5**:2948
The Song of the Lark (Cather) **WLC 1**:654-55, 665
The Song of the Mad Prince (de la Mare) **WLC 2**:892
"The Song of the Mouth-Organ" (Service) **WLC 5**:3122
"The Song of the Triumphant Love" (Turgenev)

  See "Pesn' torzhestruyushchey lyubvi"
"A Song of Winter Weather" (Service) **WLC 5**:3122
"Song of Women" (Masters) **WLCS 2**:578
"A Song on the End of the World" (Milosz) **WLCS 2**:610
"Song to Celia" ("Drink to Me Only with Thine Eyes") (Jonson) **WLC 3**:1920
"Song" (Heaney) **WLCS 1**:391
"Song" (Tennyson) **WLC 6**:3579-80, 3583
Songs (Garcia Lorca)
  See *Canciones*
Songs and Sonets (Donne) **WLC 2**:940, 943
Songs and Sonnets, Second Series (Masters) **WLCS 2**:575-76
Songs before Sunrise (Swinburne) **WLC 6**:3562-63
Songs for My Supper (Service) **WLC 5**:3130, 3132
Songs of a Sun-Lover (Service) **WLC 5**:3130-31
Songs of Childhood (de la Mare) **WLC 2**:890
Songs of Innocence and of Experience: Shewing the Two Contrary States of the Human Soul (Blake) **WLC 1**:300-01, 309
Songs of Jamaica (McKay) **WLC 4**:2327-28, 2330, 2335
"Songs of the Transformed" (Atwood) **WLC 1**:112
Songs of the Western Slavs (Pushkin) **WLC 5**:2836
Songs of Two Nations (Swinburne) **WLC 6**:3562
Sonim, di Geschichte fun a Liebe (*Enemies: A Love Story*) (Singer) **WLC 5**:3293
"Sonnet 116" (Shakespeare) **WLC 5**:3179
"Sonnet 120" (Shakespeare) **WLC 5**:3179
"Sonnet 127" ("In the old age black was not counted fair") (Shakespeare) **WLC 5**:3180
"Sonnet 128" ("How oft when thou, my music, music play'st") (Shakespeare) **WLC 5**:3178, 3180, 3183
"Sonnet 129" ("The expense of spirit in a waste of shame") (Shakespeare) **WLC 5**:3178, 3180-83
"Sonnet 130" ("My mistress' eyes are nothing like the sun") (Shakespeare) **WLC 5**:3178, 3180-81
"Sonnet 131" (Shakespeare) **WLC 5**:3181
"Sonnet 132" (Shakespeare) **WLC 5**:3181
"Sonnet 133" (Shakespeare) **WLC 5**:3179
"Sonnet 134" (Shakespeare) **WLC 5**:3179
"Sonnet 135" (Shakespeare) **WLC 5**:3181
"Sonnet 136" (Shakespeare) **WLC 5**:3181
"Sonnet 137" (Shakespeare) **WLC 5**:3178, 3180-81
"Sonnet 138" ("I do believe her though I know she lies"; "When my love swears

that she is made of truth")
(Shakespeare) **WLC 5:**3178, 3181
"Sonnet 139" (Shakespeare) **WLC 5:**3181
"Sonnet 141" (Shakespeare) **WLC 5:**3181
"Sonnet 142" (Shakespeare) **WLC 5:**3181-83
"Sonnet 143" (Shakespeare) **WLC 5:**3181
"Sonnet 144" (Shakespeare) **WLC 5:**3178-79, 3181-82
"Sonnet 145" ("Those lips that Love's own hand did make") (Shakespeare) **WLC 5:**3178, 3181-83
"Sonnet 146" (Shakespeare) **WLC 5:**3178, 3181-83; **WLC 5:**3178, 3181
"Sonnet 147" (Shakespeare) **WLC 5:**3178
"Sonnet 149" (Shakespeare) **WLC 5:**3182
"Sonnet 150" (Shakespeare) **WLC 5:**3178, 3180
"Sonnet 151" (Shakespeare) **WLC 5:**3182
"Sonnet 152" (Shakespeare) **WLC 5:**3182
"Sonnet 35" (Shakespeare) **WLC 5:**3181
"Sonnet 40" (Shakespeare) 5;3179
"Sonnet 41" (Shakespeare) **WLC 5:**3179
"Sonnet 42" (Shakespeare) **WLC 5:**3179
"Sonnet: To a Child" (Owen) **WLC 4:**2618
"Sonnets from an Ungrafted Tree" (Millay) **WLCS 2:**600, 602
Sonnets from the Portuguese (Browning) **WLC 1:**468-69, 474-78
Sons and Lovers (Lawrence) **WLC 3:**2043-44, 2050-52, 2056
Sophist (Plato) **WLCS 2:**729, 732
"Sophistication" (Anderson) **WLC 1:**82, 84
Sophistici Elenchi (Aristotle) **WLCS 1:**99
Sor Juana Inés de la Cruz, o, Las trampas de la fe (*Sor Juana; Or, The Traps of Faith*) (Paz) **WLC 4:**2672
Sor Juana; Or, The Traps of Faith (Paz)
See *Sor Juana Inés de la Cruz, o, Las trampas de la fe*
"The Sorrows of Gin" (Cheever) **WLC 2:**696
"Sort of Preface" (Bambara) **WLCS 1:**126
The Soul of a Bishop: A Novel (With Just a Little Love in It) about Conscience and Religion and the Real Troubles of Life (Wells) **WLC 6:**3859
"The Soul of the City" (Lindsay) **WLC 4:**2119
Soul-Conductors (Aeschylus) **WLCS 1:**7
The Souls of Black Folk (Du Bois) **WLC 2:**1062, 1064, 1067-68, 1070-72, 1074-75
The Sound and the Fury (Faulkner) **WLC 2:**1189-90, 1194, 1197-99
The Sound Waves (Mishima) **WLC 4:**2426
"Sounds Out of Sorrow" (Masters) **WLCS 2:**578
"Soup on a Sausage Peg" (Andersen) **WLC 1:**61
"South of the Slot" (London) **WLC 4:**2146-47

"Southeast Corner" (Brooks) **WLC 1:**454
"Souther Pacific" (Sandburg) **WLC 5:**3052
Souvenirs de la cour d'Assises (Gide) **WLC 3:**1378
Souvenirs dégotisme (Stendhal) **WLC 5:**3405-07
"Spaceships Have Landed" (Munro) **WLCS 2:**686, 688
Spain at Heart (Neruda)
See *España en el corazón: himno a las glorias del pueblo en la guerra (1936-1937)*
Spain in My Heart (Neruda)
See *España en el corazón: himno a las glorias del pueblo en la guerra (1936-1937)*
Spain in the Heart (Neruda)
See *España en el corazón: himno a las glorias del pueblo en la guerra (1936-1937)*
The Spanish Friar (Dryden) **WLC 2:**1048
"The Spanish Needle" (McKay) **WLC 4:**2334, 2336-37
Spanish Student (Longfellow) **WLCS 2:**516
The Spark (Wharton) **WLC 6:**3911
"A speech according to Horace" (Jonson) **WLC 3:**1921
"Speakin o' Christmas" (Dunbar) **WLC 2:**1100
Specimens of English Dramatic Poets Who Lived About the Time of Shakespeare (Lamb) **WLC 3:**2028, 2035-36, 2038-39
"The Spectre Bridegroom" (Irving) **WLC 3:**1820, 1827
"The Speech of Mistress Polly Baker" (Franklin) **WLCS 1:**314
Speech on the Acts of Uniformity (Burke) **WLC 1:**511
Spektorsky (Pasternak) **WLC 4:**2627
The Spell of the Butterfly (Garcia Lorca)
See *El maleficio de la mariposa*
Spell of the Yukon and Other Verses (Service) **WLC 5:**3121-23
"The Spellin' Bee" (Dunbar) **WLC 2:**1100, 1103
"Spelt from Sibyl's Leaves" (Hopkins) **WLC 3:**1712
"Spenser's Ireland" (Moore) **WLCS 2:**649
"The Sphere of Pascal" (Borges)
See "Pascal's Sphere"
"The Sphinx without a Secret: An Etching" (Wilde) **WLC 6:**3952, 3956
"The Sphinx" (Emerson) **WLC 2:**1172
"The Sphinx" (Poe) **WLC 4:**2762
"The Spinoza of Market Street" (Singer) **WLC 5:**3293
The Spire (Golding) **WLC 3:**1456
"The Spire Cranes" (Thomas) **WLC 6:**3622
Spiridion (Sand) **WLC 5:**3035
Spirit-Raisers (Aeschylus) **WLCS 1:**7
"Spiritual View of Lena Horne" (Giovanni) **WLCS 1:**354
Le spleen de Paris (Baudelaire)
See *Petits poèmes en prose: Le spleen de Paris*
Splinten av troldspeilet (*The Splinter of the Magic Mirror; The Splinter of the Troll Mirror*) (Undset) **WLC 6:**3736,

3740-41
The Splinter of the Magic Mirror (Undset)
See *Splinten av troldspeilet*
The Splinter of the Troll Mirror (Undset)
See *Splinten av troldspeilet*
The Spoils of Poynton (James) **WLC 3:**1866
Spöksonaten (*The Ghost Sonata; The Spook Sonata*) (Strindberg) **WLC 6:**3519
"Sponono" (Paton) **WLC 4:**2650
The Spook Sonata (Strindberg)
See *Spöksonaten*
Spoon River Anthology (Masters) **WLCS 2:**575-77, 579-83, 585-86
"Spooniad" (Masters) **WLCS 2:**579-80
The Sport of the Gods (Dunbar) **WLC 2:**1102, 1104-06, 1109, 1113
A Sportsman's Sketches (Turgenev)
See *Zapiski okhotnika*
"Spring, 1938" (Brecht) **WLC 1:**394
Spring and All (Williams) **WLC 6:**4014-16
Spring and Autumn (Confucius)
See *Ch'un Ch'iu*
Spring and Autumn Annals (Confucius)
See *Ch'un Ch'iu*
"Spring and Fall" (Hopkins) **WLC 3:**1712, 1714, 1716
Spring Freshets (Turgenev)
See *Veshnie vody*
Spring in New Hampshire (McKay) **WLC 4:**2332, 2334, 2336-37
"Spring in the Igloo" (Atwood) **WLC 1:**111
"Spring Offensive" (Owen) **WLC 4:**2608, 2611, 2616-18
"Spring Reminiscence" (Cullen) **WLCS 1:**277
"The Spring Running" (Kipling) **WLC 3:**2019
Spring-Torrents (Turgenev)
See *Veshnie vody*
"Spring" (Pope) **WLC 5:**2782
Springtime (Undset)
See *Vaaren*
Springtime and Harvest: A Romance (*King Midas: A Romance*) (Sinclair) **WLC 5:**3261
"Spunk" (Hurston) **WLCS 1:**449-50
Squaring the Circle (Stoppard) **WLC 6:**3487-88
"Squaring the Circle" (Henry) **WLC 3:**1670-71
"Le squelette laboureur" ("The Laboring Skeleton") (Baudelaire) **WLC 1:**205
"Sredni Vashtar" (Saki) **WLC 5:**3000, 3002-03, 3008, 3011
"St. Brandan" (Arnold) **WLC 1:**92-3
St. Ives: Being the Adventures of a French Prisoner in England (Stevenson) **WLC 5:**3454
St. Joan of the Stockyards (Brecht)
See *Die heilige Johanna der Schlachthöfe*
"St. Kentigern" (Harte) **WLC 3:**1581
"St. Lucies Day" (Donne)
See "A Nocturnal upon S. Lucies day, Being the shortest day"
St. Patrick's Day; or, The Scheming Lieutenant (Sheridan) **WLC 5:**3242-43, 3252-56
"St. Simeon Stylites" (Tennyson) **WLC**

6:3583
"The Staff and Scrip" (Rossetti) **WLC** 5:2948-49, 2953, 2955-56, 2958
"Stage Illusion" (Lamb) **WLC** 3:2037-38
Stages on the Road (Undset)
See *Etapper: Ny raekke*
"Staley Fleming's Hallucination" (Bierce) **WLC 1**:293
Stalky and Co. (Kipling) **WLC 3**:2021-22
Stamboul Train (*Orient Express*) (Greene) **WLC 1**:1542, 1545-46, 1552
Stand Still like the Hummingbird (Miller) **WLC 4**:2391
"The Stanton Coachman" (Dunbar) **WLC 2**:1107
"Stanzas from the Grande Chartreuse" (Arnold) **WLC 1**:104
"Stanzas in Memory of Edward Quillinan" (Arnold) **WLC 1**:102, 104
"Stanzas in Memory of the Author of `Obermann'" (Arnold) **WLC 1**:102, 104
"Stanzas Written at Night in Radio City" (Ginsberg) **WLC 3**:1393
"Stanzas" (Bronte) **WLC 1**:429
The Staple of News (Jonson) **WLC 3**:1911
The Star Rover (London) **WLC 4**:2146
The Star Turns Red (O'Casey) **WLCS 2**:716, 721
"The Star" (Masters) **WLCS 2**:578
"The Star" (Wells) **WLC 6**:3863-64, 3873, 3876
"Stark Major" (Crane) **WLC 2**:799
The Stark Munro Letters (Doyle) **WLC 2**:1020
"The Starry Night" (Sexton) **WLC 5**:3144
"Starry Night" (Sexton) **WLC 5**:3144
Starved Rock (Masters) **WLCS 2**:577
The State of Innocence, and Fall of Man (Dryden) **WLC 2**:1055
The State of Siege (Camus)
See *L'état de siège*
State of the Nation (Dos Passos) **WLC 2**:955
Statesman (Plato) **WLCS 2**:737
Station Island (Heaney) **WLCS 1**:389, 393-94, 396, 398
"Station Island" (Heaney) **WLCS 1**:389, 391-92, 394, 397
"The Stationmaster" (Pushkin) **WLC 5**:2828
The Statue Guest (Pushkin)
See *The Stone Guest*
"The Steadfast Tin Soldier" ("The Constant Tin Soldier"; "The Hardy Tin Soldier") (Andersen) **WLC 1**:64-5
"The Steam Boiler Effect" (Grass)
See "Der Dampfkessel-Effekt"
"Steam Song" (Brooks) **WLC 1**:463
"The Steeple-Jack" (Moore) **WLCS 2**:648
"Stella" (Nin) **WLC 1**:60
"Stepnoy Korol 'Lir'" ("A King Lear of the Steppes"; "A Lear of the Steppes"; "A Village Lear") (Turgenev) **WLC 6**:3697, 3699-3701, 3704
"The Steppe" (Chekhov) **WLC 2**:708-09
Steppenwolf (Hesse)
See *Der Steppenwolf*
Der Steppenwolf (*Steppenwolf*) (Hesse) **WLC 3**:1689, 1691, 1693, 1696
Stikhotvoreniya v proze (*Senilia*) (Turgenev) **WLC 6**:3705

"A Still Moment" (Welty) **WLC 6**:3882-83
"Stings" (Plath) **WLC 4**:2747
The Stoic (Dreiser) **WLC 2**:1033
"A Stoic" (Galsworthy) **WLC 2**:1331-32
"The Stoker" (Kafka) **WLC 3**:1950
The Stolen Bacillus and Other Incidents (Wells) **WLC 6**:3872
"The Stolen Bacillus" (Wells) **WLC 6**:3871, 3873
"The Stolen Body" (Wells) **WLC 6**:3874
A Stone, A Leaf, A Door (Wolfe) **WLC 6**:4033
The Stone Guest (*The Statue Guest*) (Pushkin) **WLC 5**:2825-27, 2836
The Stones of Chile (Neruda)
See *Las piedras de Chile*
"The Stones" (Plath) **WLC 4**:2746, 2748
"Stopped Dead" (Plath) **WLC 4**:2748
"Stopping by Woods on a Snowy Evening" (Frost) **WLC 2**:1288, 1290, 1293, 1299
Stora landsvägen (*The Great Highway*) (Strindberg) **WLC 6**:3518, 3529
Stories (Pasternak) **WLC 4**:2627
Stories from One Pocket (Capek)
See *Tales from Two Pockets*
Stories from the Other Pocket (Capek)
See *Tales from Two Pockets*
The Stories of Bernard Malamud (*Collected Stories*) (Malamud) **WLC 4**:2188
The Stories of Eva Luna (Allende) **WLCS 1**:46-47
The Stories of F. Scott Fitzgerald (Fitzgerald) **WLC 2**:1225
The Stories of John Cheever (Cheever) **WLC 2**:697
Stories of Three Decades (Mann) **WLC 4**:2198
"The Storm Cone" (Kipling) **WLC 3**:2017
"Storm Ending" (Toomer) **WLCS 2**:801-03
"The Storm" (Chopin) **WLCS 1**:246-48
"A Story from the Dunes" (Andersen) **WLC 1**:63, 65
The Story of a Horse (Tolstoy) **WLC 6**:3666
"The Story of a Mother" (Andersen) **WLC 1**:59-60, 64-5
The Story of a Novel (Wolfe) **WLC 6**:4032, 4039
"The Story of a Well-Made Shield" (Momaday) **WLCS 2**:628
"The Story of an Hour" (Chopin) **WLCS 1**:240, 242
"The Story of Father Alexis" (Turgenev)
See "Rasskaz ottsa Aleksaya""The Story of Lieutenant Ergunov" (Turgenev)
See "Istoriya leytenanta Ergunova"
The Story of My Life (Andersen) **WLC 1**:60
The Story of My Life (Sand)
See *Histoire de ma vie*
"The Story of St. Vespaluus" (Saki) **WLC 5**:3007
"A Story of the Days to Come" (Wells) **WLC 6**:3862, 3864, 3866, 3873-74, 3876
"The Story of the Late Mr. Elvesham" (Wells) **WLC 6**:3875
"A Story of the Stone Age" (Wells) **WLC 6**:3873-74
A Story Teller's Story (Anderson) **WLC 1**:75-6
"A Story without a Title" (Chekhov)
See "An Anonymous Story"
Storyteller (Silko) **WLCS 2**:760, 763, 769-70
"Storyteller" (Silko) **WLCS 2**:762
"Storytelling" (Silko) **WLCS 2**:764
"The Stout Gentleman" (Irving) **WLC 3**:1826, 1828
Strait Is the Gate (Gide)
See *La porte étroite*
"The Strand at Lough Beg" (Heaney) **WLCS 1**:392, 398
The Strange Case of Dr. Jekyll and Mr. Hyde (*Doctor Jekyll and Mr. Hyde*) (Stevenson) **WLC 5**:3446-49, 3451, 3459
"Strange Fits of Passion" (Wordsworth) **WLC 6**:4075
Strange Interlude (O'Neill) **WLC 4**:2561, 2564
"Strange Meeting" (Owen) **WLC 4**:2605, 2608, 2610, 2612-19
"The Strange Ride of Morrowbie Jukes" (Kipling) **WLC 3**:2013
"Strange Stories by a Nervous Gentleman" (Irving) **WLC 3**:1828
"A Strange Story" (Turgenev)
See "Strannaya istoriya"
The Stranger (Camus)
See *L'étranger*
"The Stranger" (Mansfield) **WLC 4**:2214
"Strannaya istoriya" ("A Strange Story") (Turgenev) **WLC 6**:3699
"Stratton Water" (Rossetti) **WLC 5**:2949
"Stray Children" (Oates) **WLC 4**:2536
The Strayed Reveller, and Other Poems (Arnold) **WLC 1**:100-01
"The Stream's Secret" (Rossetti) **WLC 5**:2947
"Streams" (Auden) **WLC 1**:139
A Street in Bronzeville (Brooks) **WLC 1**:450, 452-54, 459-61
A Streetcar Named Desire (Williams) **WLC 6**:3989, 3992-93, 3995-97, 4001, 4004-06
Streets of Night (Dos Passos) **WLC 2**:955, 963
The Strength of Gideon and Other Stories (Dunbar) **WLC 2**:1101-02, 1104-06, 1109, 1111-13
A Stroll in the Air (Ionesco)
See *Le piéton de l'air*
The Stroller in the Air (Ionesco)
See *Le piéton de l'air*
The Strong Breed (Soyinka) **WLC 5**:3327
"Strong Men, Riding Horses" (Brooks) **WLC 1**:451
"Struggle of Wings" (Williams) **WLC 6**:4020
"The Student of Salamanca" (Irving) **WLC 3**:1828
A Study in Scarlet (Doyle) **WLC 2**:1008, 1011-13, 1018
"The Study of Poetry" (Arnold) **WLC 1**:96
"Stuk...stuk...stuk" ("Knock...Knock...Knock"; "Toc...toc...toc") (Turgenev) **WLC 6**:3699, 3705
"Style" (Moore) **WLCS 2**:650-51
A Subject of Scandal and Concern (Osborne) **WLC 4**:2594

The Subterraneans (Kerouac) **WLC 3:**1976, 1978, 1980, 1983, 1986-87
"A Sudden Trip Home in the Spring" (Walker) **WLCS 2:**831
Suddenly Last Summer (Williams) **WLC 6:**3991-92, 3995-97, 4002-03
The Suicide Club (Stevenson) **WLC 5:**3448
"Suicide" (Hughes) **WLC 3:**1723
Sula (Morrison) **WLC 4:**2473, 2476-77
The Sullivan County Sketches of Stephen Crane (Crane) **WLC 2:**818
Summer (Gorky) **WLC 3:**1491
Summer (Wharton) **WLC 6:**3905
Summer and Smoke (Williams) **WLC 6:**3993, 3995-96, 3999
The Summer before the Dark (Lessing) **WLCS 2:**494, 499
"The Summer Farmer" (Cheever) **WLC 2:**695, 698
"A Summer Night" (Arnold) **WLC 1:**100, 102
"The Summer Night" (Bradbury) **WLC 1:**370
"Summer Theatre" (Cheever) **WLC 2:**695
"A Summer Wish" (Rossetti) **WLC 5:**2942
"Summer" (Pope) **WLC 5:**2782-83
The Summing Up (Maugham) **WLC 4:**2277, 2281, 2283
The Sun Also Rises (*Fiesta*) (Hemingway) **WLC 3:**1650-57
"The Sun and the Rain" (Wolfe) **WLC 6:**4040
Sun Stone (Paz)
    See *Piedra de sol*
Sunday after the War (Miller) **WLC 4:**2391
"Sunday at Home" (Hawthorne) **WLC 3:**1606
"Sunday Morning Apples" (Crane) **WLC 2:**799
"Sunday Morning" (Stevens) **WLC 5:**3431, 3434
"Sunday" (Hughes) **WLC 3:**1723
"The Sundays of Satin-Legs Smith" (*Satin-Legs Smith*) (Brooks) **WLC 1:**450, 452, 454
The Sundial (Jackson) **WLC 3:**1838, 1843, 1850
"The Sunlanders" (London) **WLC 4:**2142
"sunlight was over" (Cummings) **WLC 2:**840
"Sunlight and Flesh" (Rimbaud)
    See "Soleil et chair"
"Sunshine" (Lindsay) **WLC 4:**2121
Sunstone (Paz)
    See *Piedra de sol*
"Super Flumina Babylonis" (Swinburne) **WLC 6:**3563
"The Superintendent" (Cheever) **WLC 2:**695, 698
"A Supper by Proxy" (Dunbar) **WLC 2:**1107
"Supper Time" (Hughes) **WLC 3:**1722
The Suppliant Maidens (Aeschylus)
    See *Suppliants*
Suppliants (Aeschylus) **WLCS 1:**6, 9, 11, 12, 14-16
The Suppression of the African Slave-Trade to the United States of America, 1638-1870 (Du Bois) **WLC 2:**1064, 1068
Sur l'eau (*Afloat*) (Maupassant) **WLC 4:**2297
"Sur la destruction des monuments en France" (Hugo) **WLC 3:**1754
Surfacing (Atwood) **WLC 1:**108-10, 114-15
"Surgery" (Chekhov) **WLC 2:**708
"Surprised by Joy" (Wordsworth) **WLC 6:**4073
"Sursum Corda" (Emerson) **WLC 2:**1171
Survival: A Thematic Guide to Canadian Literature (Atwood) **WLC 1:**120
"Susy" (Harte) **WLC 3:**1583-84
Suzaku Ke no Metsudo (*The Fall of the House of Suzaku*) (Mishima) **WLC 4:**2420
Svecha na vetru (*Candle in the Wind*) (Solzhenitsyn) **WLC 5:**3302
"Swaddling Clothes" (Mishima) **WLC 4:**2423-24
The Swamp Dwellers (Soyinka) **WLC 5:**3324
Swan Song (Galsworthy) **WLC 2:**1327, 1329-31
"The Swan" (Baudelaire)
    See "Le cygne"
"The Swan's Nest" (Andersen) **WLC 1:**57
Swann's Way (Proust)
    See *Du côté de chez Swann*
Swanwhite (Strindberg) **WLC 6:**3517
"Sweat" (Hurston) **WLCS 1:**449-50
Sweeney Astray (Heaney) **WLCS 1:**389-90, 394, 396-97
Sweeney in the Trees (Saroyan) **WLC 5:**3072
"Sweeney Redivivus" (Heaney) **WLCS 1:**389, 398
"Sweeney's Returns" (Heaney) **WLCS 1:**399
Sweet Bird of Youth (Williams) **WLC 6:**3989, 3992-96, 3998, 4003
"Sweet Town" (Bambara) **WLCS 1:**127
"The Sweethearts" (Andersen) **WLC 1:**65
"The Swiftest Runners" (Andersen) **WLC 1:**55
"The Swimmer" (Cheever) **WLC 2:**697
"The Swineherd" (Andersen) **WLC 1:**60, 64
"Switzerland" (Arnold) **WLC 1:**100
Sylvia (Sinclair) **WLC 5:**3263
Sylvia's Marriage (Sinclair) **WLC 5:**3263
Sylvie and Bruno (Carroll) **WLC 1:**644-5
"Sympathy" (Thoreau) **WLC 6:**3626
La Symphonie pastorale (*The Pastoral Symphony*) (Gide) **WLC 3:**1379, 1381-85, 1387
"A Symphony in Yellow" (Wilde) **WLC 6:**3952
Symposium (Plato) **WLCS 2:**731
The System of Dante's Hell (Baraka) **WLCS 1:**139, 148, 152
"The System" (Capek) **WLC 1:**600
"T.T. Jackson sings" (Baraka) **WLCS 1:**145
"Ta" (Cummings) **WLC 2:**838
Table Talk (Pushkin) **WLC 5:**2830
The Table Talk of Samuel Marchbanks (Davies) **WLC 2:**848, 851
"Tableau" (Cullen) **WLCS 1:**274
A Tale (Pasternak) **WLC 4:**2635
Tale of a Tub (Jonson) **WLC 3:**1911

A Tale of a Tub, Written for the Universal Improvement of Mankind, to Which is Added an Account of a Battel between the Ancient and Modern Books in St. James's Library (*An Account of a Battel between the Ancient and Modern Books in St. James's Library*) (Swift) **WLC 6:**3535-36, 3541, 3545-46
"The Tale of How Ivan Ivanovich Quarrelled with Ivan Nikiforovich" ("About How Ivan Ivanovic Quarreled with Ivan Nikiforovic"; "The Quarrel of Two Ivans"; "The Tale of Two Ivans"; "The Two Ivans") (Gogol) **WLC 3:**1430, 1439
"Tale of the Tiger Tree" (Lindsay) **WLC 4:**2121
"The Tale of the Tsar Sultan" (Pushkin)
    See "Skazka o Tsare Sultane"
"The Tale of Two Ivans" (Gogol)
    See "The Tale of How Ivan Ivanovich Quarrelled with Ivan Nikiforovich"
Tales (Baraka) **WLCS 1:**145, 149, 152
Tales by Belkin (Pushkin)
    See *The Tales of Ivan Belkin*
Tales from a Troubled Land (Paton) **WLC 4:**2647-48, 2650, 2656
Tales from One Pocket (Capek)
    See *Tales from Two Pockets*
Tales from the House Behind (Frank) **WLC 2:**1282
Tales from the Other Pocket (Capek)
    See *Tales from Two Pockets*
Tales from Two Pockets (*Stories from One Pocket*; *Stories from the Other Pocket*; *Tales from One Pocket*; *Tales from the Other Pocket*) (Capek) **WLC 1:**603, 611
Tales of a Traveller (Irving) **WLC 3:**1820, 1825, 1827-28
Tales of a Wayside Inn (Longfellow) **WLCS 2:**506, 513-14
The Tales of Ivan Belkin (*Tales by Belkin*) (Pushkin) **WLC 5:**2828-30
Tales of Men and Ghosts (Wharton) **WLC 6:**3903-04
Tales of My Landlord (Scott) **WLC 5:**3112
Tales of Soldiers and Civilians (Bierce)
    See *In the Midst of Life*
Tales of the Jazz Age (Fitzgerald) **WLC 2:**1224
"A Talisman" (Moore) **WLCS 2:**640
"Tam Glen" (Burns) **WLC 1:**517
"Tam o' Shanter" (Burns) **WLC 1:**517-18, 521, 523-24, 529
Tamar and Other Poems (Jeffers) **WLC 3:**1878, 1881, 1884
Tamarlane, and Other Poems, By a Bostonian (Poe) **WLC 4:**2762
Tamburlaine (Marlowe) **WLC 4:**2237-39, 2244-47
The Taming of the Shrew (Shakespeare) **WLC 5:**3158, 3161
Tancréde (Voltaire) **WLC 6:**3779
Tanglewood Tales for Girls and Boys: Being a Second Wonder-Book (Hawthorne) **WLC 3:**1596
Taps at Reveille (Fitzgerald) **WLC 2:**1225
Tar Baby (Morrison) **WLC 4:**2479-80
Tar: A Midwest Childhood (Anderson) **WLC 1:**76
"Taras bulba" (Gogol) **WLC 3:**1430-31,

TITLE INDEX

143-49
Target Study (Baraka) **WLCS 1**:151
Le tartuffe (*The Imposter; L'imposteur; Tartuffe*) (Moliere) **WLC 4**:2435-36, 2438-40, 2443-44
Tartuffe (Moliere)
See *Le tartuffe*
"Tartuffe's Punishment" (Rimbaud)
See "Le châtiment de Tartuff"
Tasks and Masks: Themes and Styles of African Literature (Nkosi) **WLC 3**:1516-17, 1521
Le taureau blanc (Voltaire) **WLC 6**:3776
Taxation no Tyranny (Johnson) **WLC 3**:1895
"The Taxpayer" (Bradbury) **WLC 1**:370
Tchitchikoff's Journey; or Dead Souls (*Dead Souls*) (Gogol) **WLC 3**:1431, 1441
"Le Te Deum du Ier Janvier" (Hugo) **WLC 3**:1748
Tea Party (Pinter) **WLC 4**:2704
"The Teacher of Literature" (Chekhov) **WLC 2**:709-10
"Tears, Idle Tears" (Tennyson) **WLC 6**:3584
"Teddy" (Salinger) **WLC 5**:3022, 3027
Teeth (Stoppard) **WLC 6**:3488
"Teibele and Her Demon" (Singer) **WLC 5**:3293
"Telemachus, Friend" (Henry) **WLC 3**:1674
"Telephone Conversation" (Soyinka) **WLC 5**:3322
"Telephone Poles" (Updike) **WLC 6**:3751
Tell Me, Tell Me (Moore) **WLCS 2**:650
"Tell Me Yes or No" (Munro) **WLCS 2**:676, 678
"The Tell-Tale Heart" (Poe) **WLC 4**:2760-61
"Tema del traidor y del héroe" ("The Theme of the Traitor and the Hero") (Borges) **WLC 1**:336
The Tempest (Shakespeare) **WLC 5**:3171
Tempest-Tost (Davies) **WLC 2**:848, 852, 854
The Temple Beau (Fielding) **WLC 2**:1213-14
"The Temple of Fame" (Pope) **WLC 3**:270, 316
The Temple of the Golden Pavillion (Mishima)
See *Kinkakuji*
"A Temple of the Holy Ghost" (*Woman of the River*) (O'Connor) **WLC 4**:2544
Le temps retrouvé (*Time Regained*) (Proust) **WLC 5**:2817
The Temptation of Jack Orkney (Lessing) **WLCS 2**:498
The Temptation of St. Anthony (Flaubert)
See *La tentation de Saint Antoine*
"Temptation" (Dunbar) **WLC 2**:1112
Temy i var'iatsii (Pasternak)
See *Temy i variatsi*
Temy i variatsi (*Temy i var'iatsii; Themes and Variations*) (Pasternak) **WLC 4**:2627, 2638
Ten Blocks on the Camino Real (Williams)
See *Camino Real*
The Tenants (Malamud) **WLC 4**:2178, 2180-81, 2184, 2190

Tender Buttons: Objects, Food, Rooms (Stein) **WLC 5**:3359, 3361, 3365, 3367-70
Tender Is the Night (Fitzgerald) **WLC 2**:1225-28, 1231, 1234
"A Tender Man" (Bambara) **WLCS 1**:125
"Tennessee's Partner" (Harte) **WLC 3**:1576, 1589
La tentation de Saint Antoine (*The Temptation of St. Anthony*) (Flaubert) **WLC 2**:1249
Tentativa del hombre infinito ("Assay of the Infinite Man"; *Endeavors of Infinite Man*; *Venture of the Infinite Man*) (Neruda) **WLC 4**:2513
La tentative amoureuse (Gide) **WLC 3**:1384
"Tenth-Day Chrysanthemums" (Mishima)
See *Toka no Kiku*
"Teoría y juego del duende" ("The Theory and Art of the `Duende'"; "Theory and Game of the Goblin"; "The Theory and Play of the *Duende*"; "Theory and practice of the Goblin") (Garcia Lorca) **WLC 2**:1344
Tercer libro de odas (Neruda) **WLC 4**:2516
"La tercera resignación" ("The Third Resignation") (Garcia Marquez) **WLC 3**:1362-63
Tercera residencia, 1935-1945 (*The Third Residence; Third Residence*) (Neruda) **WLC 4**:2510
"Terminal Day at Beverly Farms" (Lowell) **WLC 4**:2163
"Terminus" (Emerson) **WLC 2**:1171
"The Terms in Which I Think of Reality" (Ginsberg) **WLC 3**:1396
Terra nostra (Fuentes) **WLC 2**:1311-12, 1314
"The Terrace at Berne" (Arnold) **WLC 1**:100
The Terrace of the Leper King (Mishima)
See *Raio no Terrasu*
La terre (Zola) **WLC 6**:4121-23, 4126-27
"A Terre" (Owen) **WLC 4**:2606, 2614
Tess of the D'Urbervilles: A Pure Woman Faithfully Presented (Hardy) **WLC 3**:1565-66, 1570-71
The Testament (Wiesel) **WLCS 2**:854
"Testanaento de otoño" (Neruda) **WLC 4**:2515
Teverino (Sand) **WLC 5**:3039
Thank You, Fog: Last Poems (Auden) **WLC 1**:138
Thankful Blossom (Harte) **WLC 3**:1582
"Thanks for the Ride" (Munro) **WLCS 2**:657, 679, 688
"Thanksgiving for a Habitat" (Auden) **WLC 1**:137
The Thanksgiving Visitor (Capote) **WLC 1**:630
"THANKSGIVING (1956)" (Cummings) **WLC 2**:842
"That Enough Is as Good as a Feast" (Lamb) **WLC 3**:2033
That Hideous Strength: A Modern Fairy Tale for Grown-Ups (Lewis) **WLC 4**:2084-85, 2087-88, 2091-93
"That Nature Is a Heraclitean Fire and of the Comfort of the Resurrection" (Hopkins) **WLC 3**:1713-16

"the season 'tis, my lovely lambs" (Cummings) **WLC 2**:840
"the skinny voice" (Cummings) **WLC 2**:844
The Bow and the Lyre: The Poem, the Poetic Revelation, and History (Paz)
See *El arco y la lira: El poema. la revelación poetica, poesia,e historia*
"The-Child-Who-Was-Tired" (Mansfield) **WLC 4**:2219
"Theater" (Toomer) **WLCS 2**:793-94
Théâtre de Poche (Cocteau) **WLC 2**:731
Theft (London) **WLC 4**:2138
Their Eyes Were Watching God (Hurston) **WLCS 1**:441-44, 446-48, 451-53
"Thekla's Answer" (Arnold) **WLC 1**:101
"Thelassius" (Swinburne) **WLC 6**:3560, 3565
"The Theme of the Traitor and the Hero" (Borges)
See "Tema del traidor y del héroe"
Themes and Variations (Huxley) **WLC 3**:1767-68
Themes and Variations (Pasternak)
See *Temy i variatsi*
Then and Now (Maugham) **WLC 4**:2272-2274, 2280
Theodore and Honoria ("Honoria") (Dryden) **WLC 2**:1046
"Theodore the Poet" (Masters) **WLCS 2**:582
Theoetetus (Plato) **WLCS 2**:731
"The Theologians" (Borges) **WLC 1**:342
"The Theory and Art of the `Duende'" (Garcia Lorca)
See "Teoría y juego del duende"
"Theory and Game of the Goblin" (Garcia Lorca)
See "Teoría y juego del duende"
"The Theory and Play of the *Duende*" (Garcia Lorca)
See "Teoría y juego del duende"
"Theory and practice of the Goblin" (Garcia Lorca)
See "Teoría y juego del duende"
"There Are No Thieves in This Town" (Garcia Marquez) **WLC 3**:1368-69
"There Is Mist on the Mountain" (Scott) **WLC 5**:3115
"There Was a Saviour" (Thomas) **WLC 6**:3619
"There Will Come Soft Rains" (Bradbury) **WLC 1**:370
"There's Wisdom in Women" (Brooke) **WLC 1**:434
Thérèse Raquin (Zola) **WLC 6**:4122-24, 4126, 4128
"Thermos Bottles" ("Thermos Flasks") (Mishima) **WLC 4**:2423
"Thermos Flasks" (Mishima)
See "Thermos Bottles"
"These Walls Are Cold" (Capote) **WLC 1**:619
"These" (Williams) **WLC 6**:4014, 4023
"Thesis and Counter-Thesis" (Milosz) **WLCS 2**:620
Things As They Are (*Q.E.D.*) (Stein) **WLC 5**:3361, 3370
Things Fall Apart (Achebe) **WLC 1**:3-10, 12
The Things That I Know (Hemingway)
See *Across the River and into the Trees*

Think It Over, Giacomino! (Pirandello)
See *Pensaci, Giacomino!*
Think of It, Giacomino! (Pirandello)
See *Pensaci, Giacomino!*
"The Third Expedition" (Bradbury) **WLC 1:**370
"The Third Ingredient" (Henry) **WLC 3:**1675, 1677
The Third Life (Walker) **WLCS 2:**836
The Third Man (Greene) **WLC 3:**1542, 1544, 1547, 1553
Third Residence (Neruda)
See *Tercera residencia, 1935-1945*
The Third Residence (Neruda)
See *Tercera residencia, 1935-1945*
"The Third Resignation" (Garcia Marquez)
See "La tercera resignación"
The Third Violet (Crane) **WLC 2:**814-15
Thirst and Other One-Act Plays (O'Neill) **WLC 4:**2558
"This Bread I Break" (Thomas) **WLC 6:**3617
This Gun for Hire (Greene)
See *A Gun for Sale*
"This Is a Photograph of Me" (Atwood) **WLC 1:**111
"This Is the Track" (Owen) **WLC 4:**2618
This Side of Paradise (Fitzgerald) **WLC 2:**1221-24
"This Side of Truth" (Thomas) **WLC 6:**3619
This Was the Old Chief's Country (Lessing) **WLCS 2:**492
"The Thistle, The Nettle" (Milosz) **WLCS 2:**618
Thomas l'imposteur (*Thomas the Imposter*) (Cocteau) **WLC 2:**726-27, 733, 736
Thomas the Imposter (Cocteau)
See *Thomas l'imposteur*
"Thomas Trevelyn" (Masters) **WLCS 2:**579
"A Thorn Forever in the Breast" (Cullen) **WLCS 1:**284
"The Thorny Path of Honor" (Andersen) **WLC 1:**57
Those Barren Leaves (Huxley) **WLC 3:**1762, 1767-68
"Those lips that Love's own hand did make" (Shakespeare)
See "Sonnet 145"
"Those Times" (Sexton) **WLC 5:**3146
Those Who Ride the Night Winds (Giovanni) **WLCS 1:**360
Thoughts and Details on Scarcity Originally Presented to the Right Hon. William Pitt in the Month of November, 1795 (Burke) **WLC 1:**506, 509
"Thoughts on His Excellency Major General Lee" ("On Major General Lee") (Wheatley) **WLC 6:**3917, 3919
Thoughts on Religion (Swift) **WLC 6:**3547
"Thoughts on the African Novel" (Achebe) **WLC 1:**15
Thoughts on the Cause of the Present Discontents (*Present Discontents*) (Burke) **WLC 1:**506
Thoughts on the late Transactions respecting the Falkland Islands (Johnson) **WLC 3:**1895
"Thoughts on the Shape of the Human Body" (Brooke) **WLC 1:**439
"Thoughts on the Works of Providence" ("On the Works of Providence") (Wheatley) **WLC 6:**3921, 3926, 3928, 3930
Thoughts on Various Subjects (Swift) **WLC 6:**3535
"A Thousand Deaths" (London) **WLC 4:**2141
Thracian Women (Aeschylus) **WLCS 1:**8
"Thrawn Janet" (Stevenson) **WLC 5:**3447
The Three Clerks (Trollope) **WLC 6:**3681, 3691
Three Deaths (Tolstoy)
See *Tri smerti*
"Three Encounters" (Turgenev) **WLC 6:**3708
"The Three Enemies" (Rossetti) **WLC 5:**2931
Three Essays in Homage to John Dryden (Eliot) **WLC 2:**1137
"Three Hours between Planes" (Fitzgerald) **WLC 2:**1235
Three Lives (Stein) **WLC 5:**3360-61, 3363, 3367-70
"Three Meetings" (Turgenev) **WLC 6:**3702
"The Three Million Yen" (Mishima) **WLC 4:**2423
Three Musketeers (Dumas)
See *Les trois mousquetaires*
The Three Musketeers; or, The Feats and Fortunes of a Gascon Adventurer (Dumas)
See *Les trois mousquetaires*
"Three Nuns" (Rossetti) **WLC 5:**2942
The Three of Them (Gorky) **WLC 3:**1490, 1492
Three Plays (Wilder) **WLC 6:**3981, 3983
"Three Portraits" (Turgenev) **WLC 6:**3697, 3702
The Three Sisters: A Drama in Four Acts (Chekhov) 708, 710, 713, 715-18, 720
Three Soldiers (Dos Passos) **WLC 2:**955, 963
"The Three Strangers" (Hardy) **WLC 3:**1566
"Three Talks on Civilisation" (Milosz) **WLCS 2:**620
"Three Vagabonds of Trinidad" (Harte) **WLC 3:**1583, 1589
"The Three Voices" (Service) **WLC 5:**3123
"Three Years" (Chekhov) **WLC 2:**709
"Three" (Capek) **WLC 1:**601
"The Threefold Destiny" (Hawthorne) **WLC 3:**1605
The Threepenny Opera (Brecht)
See *Die Dreigroschenoper*
Threnodia Augustalis (Goldsmith) **WLC 3:**1476
"Threnody" (Emerson) **WLC 2:**1171-72, 1178
Thrones, 96-109 de los cantares (Pound) **WLC 5:**2801-02
"Through Death to Love" (Rossetti) **WLC 5:**2951
"Through the Dutch Waterways" (Golding) **WLC 3:**1456
Through the Looking-Glass and What Alice Found There (Carroll) **WLC 1:**637, 642-3, 647-9
"Throughout Our Lands" (Milosz) **WLCS 2:**613-14
"Thumbelina" (Andersen) **WLC 1:**65
"Thumbling" (Andersen)
See "Poor Thumbling"
"Thursday" (Millay) **WLCS 2:**590
"Thurso's Landing" (Jeffers) **WLC 3:**1874-75
"Thyrsis" (Arnold) **WLC 1:**104
"Ti Frere" (Chopin) **WLCS 1:**241
"Tiare Tahiti" (Brooke) **WLC 1:**439, 443-44
The Ticket That Exploded (Burroughs) **WLC 1:**535-37, 542
Tiempo mexicano (Fuentes) **WLC 2:**1312-13
Le tiers livre des faictz et dictz heroiques du noble Pantagruel (Rabelais) **WLC 5:**2859-60, 2862-63, 2869
Tiers Livre (Rabelais) **WLC 5:**2859-60, 2862-63, 2869
Till Damaskus (*To Damaskus*; *Toward Damscus*) (Strindberg) **WLC 6:**3517-19, 3525, 3529
Till We Have Faces: A Myth Retold (Lewis) **WLC 4:**2087, 2090, 2093-94
Timaeus (Plato) **WLCS 2:**726, 735
Timber; or, Discoveries (*Discoveries*) (Jonson) **WLC 3:**1916, 1919-20
The Time Machine (Wells) **WLC 6:**3859, 3861-62, 3864-66, 3868-70, 3872, 3874
Time Must Have a Stop (Huxley) **WLC 3:**1767-69
"The Time of Death" (Munro) **WLCS 2:**681
The Time of Your Life (Saroyan) **WLC 5:**3070-73, 3076-80
Time Present (Osborne) **WLC 4:**2596, 2598, 2600-01
Time Regained (Proust)
See *Le temps retrouvé*
Timoeus (Plato) **WLCS 2:**731, 733
Timus (Plato) **WLCS 2:**733
The Tin Drum (Grass)
See *Die Blechtrommel*
"The Tinder-Box" (Andersen) **WLC 1:**57, 64-5, 67
"Tintern Abbey" (Wordsworth)
See "Lines Composed a Few Miles Above Tintern Abbey"
Tiny Alice (Albee) **WLC 1:**23-5, 27, 30-1
"Tiresias" (Swinburne) **WLC 6:**3563
The Titan (Dreiser) **WLC 2:**1025-30
Los títeres de Cachiporra (*Cachiporra's Puppets*) (Garcia Lorca) **WLC 2:**1341
"Tithonus" (Tennyson) **WLC 6:**3583
"Titmouse" (Emerson) **WLC 2:**1171
"Tjodolf" (Undset) **WLC 6:**3741
"To a Brown Boy" (Cullen) **WLCS 1:**274
"To a Brown Girl" (Cullen) **WLCS 1:**274
"To a Child" (Longfellow) **WLCS 2:**510
"To a Contemporary Bunk-Shooter" (Sandburg) **WLC 5:**3054
"To a Friend" (Arnold) **WLC 1:**100
"To a Gipsy Child by the Sea-shore" (Arnold) **WLC 1:**101
To a God Unknown (Steinbeck) **WLC 5:**3387
"To a Haggis" (Burns)
See "Address to a Haggis"
"To a Lady and Her Children, On the

Death of Her Son and Their Brother" (Wheatley) **WLC 6:**3929
"To a Little Girl, One Year Old in a Ruined Fortress" (Warren) **WLC 6:**3814
"To a Louse, on Seeing One on a Lady's Bonnet at Church" ("Address to a Louse") (Burns) **WLC 1:**523
"To a Magnate" (Pushkin) **WLC 5:**2832
"To a Man" (Angelou) **WLCS 1:**64-65
"To a Republican Friend" (Arnold) **WLC 1:**100
"To a Solitary Disciple" (Williams) **WLC 6:**4012
"To a Strategist" (Moore) **WLCS 2:**651
"To a Wealthy Man" (Yeats) **WLC 6:**4108
"To a Winter Squirrel" (Brooks) **WLC 1:**457
"To an Athlete Dying Young" (Housman) **WLCS 1:**433, 437
"To Autumn" (Keats)
See "Ode to Autumn"
"To Be in Love" (Brooks) **WLC 1:**456-57
To Bedlam and Part Way Back (Sexton) **WLC 5:**3136-37, 3139-41, 3144-45
"To Certain Critics" (Cullen) **WLCS 1:**284
To Clothe the Naked (Pirandello)
See *Vestire gli ignudi*
To Damascus (Strindberg)
See *Till Damaskus*
"To Delmore Schwartz" (Lowell) **WLC 4:**2162, 2167
To Disembark (Brooks) **WLC 1:**458
"To Dog" (Bierce) **WLC 1:**292
"To Don at Salaam" (Brooks) **WLC 1:**458
"To E. FitzGerald" (Tennyson) **WLC 6:**3584
"To Fausta" (Arnold) **WLC 1:**101
To Find Oneself (Pirandello)
See *Trovarsi*
To Have and Have Not (Hemingway) **WLC 3:**1658
"To Helen" (Poe) **WLC 4:**2759
"To Hell with Dying...." (Walker) **WLCS 2:**837
"To his Mistris Going to Bed" (Donne) **WLC 2:**945
"To His Coy Mistress" ("The Coy Mistress") (Marvell) **WLC 4:**2253, 2255-56, 2258-59, 2264-66
"To His Excellency General George Washington" (Wheatley) **WLC 6:**3917, 3922, 3926
"To His Honor the Lieutenant Governor on the Death of His Lady" (Wheatley) **WLC 6:**3922
"To His Watch" (Hopkins) **WLC 3:**1708
"To Imagination" (Bronte) **WLC 1:**429
"To J. W." (Emerson) **WLC 2:**1171
"To Jane: The Invitation" ("The Invitation") (Shelley) **WLC 5:**3234
"To Jane: The Recollection" ("The Recollection") (Shelley) **WLC 5:**3234
"To John Keats, Poet: At Springtime" (Cullen) **WLCS 1:**277
"To Keorapetse Kgositsile (Willie)" ("Willie") (Brooks) **WLC 1:**458
To Kill a Mockingbird (Lee) **WLC 4:**2062-63, 2065-68, 2070-74
"To Kill Time" (Gorky) **WLC 3:**1485
To Let (Galsworthy) **WLC 2:**1328
"To Marguerite--Continued" (Arnold) **WLC 1:**100

"To Mæcenas" (Wheatley)
See "Ode to Mæcenas"
"To Mr R. W. `If as mine is'" (Donne) **WLC 2:**934
"To Negro Writers" (Hughes) **WLC 3:**1731
"To Night" (Shelley) **WLC 5:**3234
"To One Who Said Me Nay" (Cullen) **WLC 1:**276
"To Raja Rao" (Milosz) **WLCS 2:**612
"To Robinson Jeffers" (Milosz) **WLCS 2:**613, 620
"To S. M., A Young African Painter, on Seeing His Works" (Wheatley) **WLC 6:**3929
"To Sir Edward Herbert, at Julyers. `Man is a lumpe'" (Donne) **WLC 2:**945
"To Speak of Woe That Is in Marriage" (Lowell) **WLC 4:**2165-66
"To the Countesse of Bedford. `Madame, reason is'" (Donne) **WLC 2:**934
"To the Countesse of Bedford. `This twilight of'" (Donne) **WLC 2:**934
"To the De'il" (Burns)
See "Address to the De'il"
"To the Diaspora" (Brooks) **WLC 1:**459
"To the Duke of Wellington" (Arnold) **WLC 1:**100
"To the Foot from Its Child" (Neruda) **WLC 4:**2517
To the Lighthouse (Woolf) **WLC 6:**4046-47, 4052-53, 4056-58
"To the Memory of My Beloved, the Author, Mr. William Shakespeare, and What He Hath Left Us" (Jonson) **WLC 3:**1921
"To the New South" (Dunbar) **WLC 2:**1109, 1113-14
"To the Not Impossible He" (Millay) **WLCS 2:**590
"To the One of Fictive Music" (Stevens) **WLC 5:**3429, 3438
"To the Reader" (Baudelaire)
See "Au lecteur"
"To the Rev. Mr. Pitkin on the Death of His Lady" (Wheatley) **WLC 6:**3918
"To the Right Honorable William, Earl of Dartmouth, His Majesty's Principal Secretary of State for North America" (Wheatley) **WLC 6:**3817, 3921-22, 3926
"To the same" (Jonson) **WLC 3:**1920
"To the South" (Dunbar) **WLC 2:**1114
"To the United States Senate" (Lindsay) **WLC 4:**2118
"To the University of Cambridge, in New England" (Wheatley) **WLC 6:**3917, 3919, 3921-22, 3925
"To the White Fiends" (McKay) **WLC 4:**2331, 2338
"To Victor Hugo of My Crow Pluto" (Moore) **WLCS 2:**650
"To Waken an Old Lady" (Williams) **WLC 6:**4014
"To What Serves Mortal Beauty" (Hopkins) **WLC 3:**1713
"To You Who Read My Book" (Cullen) **WLCS 1:**274, 277
"Tobermory" (Saki) **WLC 5:**3008-09
"Toc...toc...toc" (Turgenev)
See "Stuk...stuk...stuk"
Der Tod in Venedig (*Death in Venice*) (Mann) **WLC 4:**2198-2200, 2202, 2204
Todos los gatos son pardos (Fuentes) **WLC 2:**1312
"Toe'Osh: A Laguna Coyote Story" (Silko) **WLCS 2:**761
The Toilers of the Sea (Hugo)
See *Les travailleurs de la mer*
The Toilet (Baraka) **WLCS 1:**139-40, 142, 152-53
Toka no Kiku ("Tenth-Day Chrysanthemums") (Mishima) **WLC 4:**2418
Tom Jones (Fielding)
See *The History of Tom Jones, a Foundling*
"Tommy's Burglar" (Henry) **WLC 3:**1667
Tomorrow and Yesterday (Boell)
See *Haus ohne Hüter*
Tonight We Improvise (Pirandello)
See *Questa sera si recita a soggetto*
Tonio Kröger (Mann) 4;2198, 2207
Tono-Bungay (Wells) **WLC 6:**3858, 3860-61, 3870
Too Dear (Tolstoy) **WLC 6:**3664
Too Far to Go: The Maples Stories (*Your Lover Just Called: Stories of Joan and Richard Maple*) (Updike) **WLC 6:**3760
Too Late the Phalarope (Paton) **WLC 4:**2643-44, 2647, 2649-51
Too True to Be Good (Shaw) **WLC 5:**3193, 3201
"The Toome Road" (Heaney) **WLCS 1:**392
"The Tooth" (Jackson) **WLC 3:**1851
"The Top and the Ball" (Andersen) **WLC 1:**64
Topics (Aristotle) **WLCS 1:**99
Topoemas (Paz) **WLC 4:**2674
"Torch Song" (Cheever) **WLC 2:**695, 698
The Torrents of Spring (Turgenev)
See *Veshnie vody*
The Torrents of Spring: A Romantic Novel in Honor of the Passing of a Great Race (Hemingway) **WLC 3:**1661
Tortilla Flat (Steinbeck) **WLC 5:**3384-85, 3387-88
"Tosca" (Allende) **WLCS 1:**46
"Totem" (Plath) **WLC 4:**2747
"A Touch of Realism" (Saki) **WLC 5:**3007
A Touch of the Poet (O'Neill) **WLC 4:**2566
La tour de Nesle (*The Tower of Nesle*) (Dumas) **WLC 2:**1091
Tour of Corsica (Boswell)
See *An Account of Corsica, The Journal of a Tour to that Island; and the Memoirs of Pascal Paoli*
"A Tour of the Forest" (Turgenev) **WLC 6:**3698, 3705
A Tour on the Prairies (Irving) **WLC 3:**1822, 1825
"The Tour" (Plath) **WLC 4:**2743-44
"Tourist" (Service) **WLC 5:**3132
Továrna na absolutno (*The Absolute at Large; The Factory of the Absolute*) (Capek) **WLC 1:**601, 603-05, 609-10, 613
Toward Damscus (Strindberg)
See *Till Damaskus*
Toward the Gulf (Masters) **WLCS 2:**577
The Tower (Yeats) **WLC 6:**4100
The Tower Beyond Tragedy (Jeffers) **WLC 3:**1875-76

The Tower of Nesle (Dumas)
See *La tour de Nesle*
The Town (Faulkner) **WLC 2:**1197-98
The Town and the City (Kerouac) **WLC 3:**1976, 1984-85
The Town Beyond the Wall (Wiesel) **WLCS 2:**848, 850, 856
The Town Fop; or, Sir Timothy Tawdrey (Behn) **WLC 1:**246
Los trabajos de Persiles y Sigismunda (*Persiles y Sigismunda*) (Cervantes) **WLC 2:**681-2
Trachiniae (Sophocles) **WLCS 1:**780, 783, 785-86
"La tragedia di un personaggio" ("The Tragedy of a Character") (Pirandello) **WLC 4:**2720
"The Tragedy at Three Corners" (Dunbar)
See "The Tragedy at Three Forks"
"The Tragedy at Three Forks" ("The Tragedy at Three Corners") (Dunbar) **WLC 2:**1102, 1106-07, 1109
"The Tragedy of a Character" (Pirandello)
See "La tragedia di un personaggio"
Tragedy of an Elderly Gentleman (Shaw) **WLC 5:**3192
The Tragedy of Pudd'nhead Wilson (Twain) **WLC 6:**3719-21
"The Tragic" (Emerson) **WLC 2:**1175, 1177
The Trail of Ninety-Eight: A Northland Romance (Service) **WLC 5:**3131
"The Train and the City" (Wolfe) **WLC 6:**4040
"The Train Was on Time" (Boell)
See "Der Zug war pünktlich"
"The Train Whistled" (Pirandello)
See "Il treno ha fischiato"
Training (Atwood) **WLC 1:**114, 117-18
Trainor the Druggist" (Masters) **WLCS 2:**584
"Le traité du Narcisse" (Gide) **WLC 3:**1376
Traité de métaphysique (Voltaire) **WLC 6:**3771
"The Traitor" (Maugham) **WLC 4:**2277
A Tramp Abroad (Twain) **WLC 6:**3716, 3718
Transformation; or, The Romance of Monte Beni (Hawthorne)
See *The Marble Faun; or, The Romance of Monte Beni*
"Transformation" (Hawthorne) **WLC 3:**1598
Transformations (Sexton) **WLC 5:**3138, 3143, 3145
Transport to Summer (Stevens) **WLC 5:**3439
"Transposition" (Lewis) **WLC 4:**2091-92
Tränstekvinnans son (*The Son of a Servant*) (Strindberg) **WLC 6:**3517
"The Trap" (Lindsay) **WLC 4:**2118
"The Trap" (Pirandello)
See "La trappola"
Trapné provídky (*Money and Other Stories; Painful Stories*) (Capek) **WLC 1:**601
"La trappola" ("The Trap") (Pirandello) **WLC 4:**2716
El trato de Argel (*Los tratos de Argel*) (Cervantes) **WLC 2:**681-83
Los tratos de Argel (Cervantes)

See *El trato de Argel*
Travail (Zola) **WLC 6:**4126
Les travailleurs de la mer (*The Toilers of the Sea*) (Hugo) **WLC 3:**1742-43, 1745, 1748-49
Travel Journal (Montaigne)
See *Journal du voyage de Michel de Montaigne en Italie par la Suisse et l'Allemagne en 1580 et 1581*
"A Travel Piece" (Atwood) **WLC 1:**114, 117
Traveller (Goldsmith) **WLC 3:**1464, 1466-67, 1472, 1475-76
"The Travelling Companion" (Andersen) **WLC 1:**63-65
Travels with My Aunt (Greene) **WLC 3:**1550
Travesties (Stoppard) **WLC 6:**3481, 3483-84, 3489, 3493-95
Treasure Island (Stevenson) **WLC 5:**3446, 3448, 3451, 3454, 3456-59
A Treatise on the Astrolabe (Chaucer) **WLCS 1:**227
Treatises (St. Augustine) **WLCS 1:**108
A Tree of Night, and Other Stories (Capote) **WLC 1:**619
"A Tree of Night" (Capote) **WLC 1:**618, 620, 630
"The Tree" (Pound) **WLC 5:**2802
"Il treno ha fischiato" ("The Train Whistled") (Pirandello) **WLC 4:**2719
The Trespasser (Lawrence) **WLC 3:**2043-44
Tri smerti (*Three Deaths*) (Tolstoy) **WLC 6:**3666
"A Triad" (Rossetti) **WLC 5:**2930
The Trial (Kafka)
See *Der Prozess*
"The Trial Sermon on Bull-Skin" (Dunbar) **WLC 2:**1106
The Trials of Brother Jero (Soyinka) **WLC 5:**3324, 3326
Triangle Junction (Grass)
See *Gleisdreieck*
"Tribuneaux rustiques" (Maupassant) **WLC 4:**2293
Tribute to Freud (H. D.) **WLC 3:**1616, 1619, 1624-25
Tribute to the Angels (H. D.) **WLC 3:**1613, 1615-16, 1618, 1624
The Tricks of Scapin (Moliere)
See *Les fourberies de Scapin*
"Tricolour" (Service) **WLC 5:**3122
Trilogy (*War Trilogy*) (H. D.) **WLC 3:**1621, 1624-25
De trinitate (St. Augustine)
See *The Trinity*
The Trinity (St. Augustine) **WLCS 1:**119
"Trinity Peace" (Sandburg) **WLC 5:**3053
A Trip to Scarborough (Sheridan) **WLC 5:**3255-56
Tripmaster Monkey (Kingston) **WLCS 2:**481-83
"Triptych" (Heaney) **WLCS 1:**392
Tristan (Mann) **WLC 4:**2198
Tristessa (Kerouac) **WLC 3:**1978, 1987
"Tristram and Iseult" (Arnold) **WLC 1:**93, 95, 100
Tristram of Lyonesse (Swinburne) **WLC 6:**3557, 3559-60, 3564, 3566
Tristram Shandy (Sterne)
See *The Life and Opinions of Tristram Shandy, Gentleman*
The Triumph of Life (Shelley) **WLC 5:**3224, 3229, 3231-34, 3236-38
The Triumph of the Egg: A Book of Impressions from American Life in Tales and Poems (Anderson) **WLC 1:**78
"The Triumph of the Egg" ("The Egg"; "The Egg") (Anderson) **WLC 1:**78
"The Triumph of Time" (Swinburne) **WLC 6:**3557, 3563-64
Den trofaste hustru (*The Faithful Wife*) (Undset) **WLC 6:**3738, 3741-42
Troilus and Cressida (Shakespeare) **WLC 5:**3171
Troilus and Criseyde (Chaucer) **WLCS 1:**226-27, 229-33
Les trois mousquetaires (*Three Musketeers; The Three Musketeers; or, The Feats and Fortunes of a Gascon Adventurer*) (Dumas) **WLC 2:**1083-91
Trojan Women (Euripides) **WLCS 1:**291, 293, 299-300
Trommeln in der nacht (*Drums in the Night*) (Brecht) **WLC 1:**387, 390
Tropic of Cancer (Miller) **WLC 4:**2377, 2379-80, 2382-83, 2386-92
Tropic of Capricorn (Miller) **WLC 4:**2377, 2380-82, 2387, 2391-92
"The Tropics in New York" (McKay) **WLC 4:**2334, 2337
"The Trouble about Sophiny" (Dunbar) **WLC 2:**1106
"The Trousers" (Dunbar) **WLC 2:**1107
Trovarsi (*To Find Oneself*) (Pirandello) **WLC 4:**2727
"Troy Town" (Rossetti) **WLC 5:**2948, 2953, 2956
"The Truce of the Bear" (Kipling) **WLC 3:**2017
"Truck-Garden-Market Day" (Millay) **WLCS 2:**602
"The True Import of Present Dialogue, Black vs. Negro" (Giovanni) **WLCS 1:**352, 359, 362
"The Trustfulness of Polly" (Dunbar) **WLC 2:**1106, 1113
"The Truth About Pyecraft" (Wells) **WLC 6:**3874
"The Truth of Fiction" (Achebe) **WLC 1:**15
"The Truth of Masks" (Wilde) **WLC 6:**3954
"The Truth the Dead Know" (Sexton) **WLC 5:**3141
"Truth" (McKay) **WLC 4:**2334
"Tsar Nikita" ("Czar Nikita") (Pushkin) **WLC 5:**2832-33
"Tsar Sultan" (Pushkin)
See "Skazka o Tsare Sultane"
Tsygany (*Gipsies*; *The Gypsies*) (Pushkin) **WLC 5:**2825, 2832, 2835
"Tubal-Cain Forges A Star" (Garcia Marquez)
See "Tubal-Caín forja una estrella"
"Tubal-Caín forja una estrella" ("Tubal-Cain Forges A Star") (Garcia Marquez) **WLC 3:**1363
"The Tuesday Afternoon Siesta" (Garcia Marquez)
See "Tuesday Siesta"
"Tuesday Siesta" ("The Tuesday Afternoon

Siesta") (Garcia Marquez) **WLC 3:**1366-68
Tueur sans gages (*The Killer; The Unrewarded Killer*) (Ionesco) **WLC 3:**1798-99, 1801-02, 1804, 1809, 1811-12
La tulipe noire (*Rosa; or, The Black Tulip*) (Dumas) **WLC 2:**1084
Tulips and Chimneys (Cummings) **WLC 2:**832, 837-38, 842-43
"Tulips" (Plath) **WLC 4:**2742-44, 2746-47
"The Tunnel" (Crane) **WLC 2:**797
The Turn of the Screw (James) **WLC 3:**1863, 1865
"The Turtles of Tasman" (London) **WLC 4:**2140
Tutto per bene (Pirandello) **WLC 4:**2722
"The Twa Dogs" ("Dialogues of the Dogs") (Burns) **WLC 1:**517, 519, 525-26, 528-29
"The Twa Herds" (Burns) **WLC 1:**524
Twelfth Night (Shakespeare) **WLC 5:**3158-59, 3161-62, 3174
"The Twelve Mortal Men" (McCullers) **WLC 4:**2320
Twenty Bath-Tub Ballads (Service) **WLC 5:**3130
Twenty-Five Poems (Thomas) **WLC 6:**3612
Twenty Love Poems and a Despairing Song (Neruda)
See *Veinte poemas de amor y una canción desesperada*
Twenty Love Poems and a Desperate Song (Neruda)
See *Veinte poemas de amor y una canción desesperada*
Twenty Love Poems and a Song of Despair (Neruda)
See *Veinte poemas de amor y una canción desesperada*
Twenty Love Poems and One Song of Despair (Neruda)
See *Veinte poemas de amor y una canción desesperada*
Twenty Poems (Neruda)
See *Veinte poemas de amor y una canción desesperada*
Twenty-Six Men and a Girl (Gorky)
See *Dvádtsat' shesti i odná*
Twenty Years After; or, The Further Feats and Fortunes of a Gascon Adventurer (Dumas)
See *Vingt ans après*
Twice-Told Tales (Hawthorne) **WLC 3:**1594-95, 1599-1600, 1607
"Twicknam Garden" (Donne) **WLC 2:**935
The Twilight Book (Neruda)
See *Crepúsculario*
Twilight in Italy (Lawrence) **WLC 3:**2044
"Twilight Reverie" (Hughes) **WLC 3:**1722
Twilight Sleep (Wharton) **WLC 6:**3904, 3908
The Twin In the Clouds (Pasternak)
See *Bliznets v tuchakh*
"Two-an'-Six" (McKay) **WLC 4:**2328
"The Two April Mornings" (Wordsworth) **WLC 6:**4074-75
Two Books (Pasternak) **WLC 4:**2627
The Two-Character Play (*Out Cry*) (Williams) **WLC 6:**3996, 3998
"The Two Children" (Bronte) **WLC 1:**426

The Two Deaths of Christopher Martin (Golding)
See *Pincher Martin*
Two-faced Herma (Pirandello)
See *Erma bifronte*
"Two Fathers" (Capek) **WLC 1:**601
Two Friends (Turgenev) **WLC 6:**3703
"Two Friends" (Cather) **WLC 1:**657
"Two Gallants" (Joyce) **WLC 3:**1930
The Two Gentlemen of Verona (Shakespeare) **WLC 5:**3161
Two-Headed Poems (Atwood) **WLC 1:**118
Two Hussars (Tolstoy) **WLC 6:**3666-67
"Two in the Campagna" (Browning) **WLCS 1:**214
"The Two Ivans" (Gogol)
See "The Tale of How Ivan Ivanovich Quarrelled with Ivan Nikiforovich"
"The Two Maidens" (Cervantes)
See "Las dos doncelas"
"Two Morning Monologues" (Bellow) **WLC 1:**263
The Two Noble Kinsmen (Shakespeare) **WLC 5:**3182
"Two Old Men" (Tolstoy) **WLC 6:**3664
Two on a Tower (Hardy) **WLC 3:**1568
"Two or Three Ideas" (Stevens) **WLC 5:**3439
Two Plays (O'Casey) **WLCS 2:**708
"Two Portraits" (Chopin) **WLCS 1:**241
"The Two Races of Men" (Lamb) **WLC 3:**2032-33
"Two Rivers" (Emerson) **WLC 2:**1170
"The Two Spirits: An Allegory" (Shelley) **WLC 5:**3234
Two Trains Running (Wilson) **WLCS 1:**870-71
"The Two Voices" (Tennyson) **WLC 6:**3580-81
"Two Who Crossed a Line (He Crosses)" (Cullen) **WLCS 1:**277
"Two Words" (Allende) **WLCS 1:**47
"The Two" (Naylor) **WLCS 2:**692
"The Tyneside Widow" (Swinburne) **WLC 6:**3555
Typee: A Peep at Polynesian Life (Melville) **WLC 4:**2343, 2355
Typhoon (Conrad) **WLC 2:**781-82, 784
"Typhoon" (London) **WLC 4:**2141
"Typhus" (Chekhov) **WLC 2:**708
Tyrannick Love; or, The Royal Martyr (Dryden) **WLC 2:**1057
U.S.A. (Dos Passos) **WLC 2:**952-56, 962, 964-67
"Über die Brücke" (Boell) **WLC 1:**316
"The Ugly Duckling" ("The Duckling") (Andersen) **WLC 1:**55, 58, 63-4
"Ugly Honkies, or The Election Game and How to Win It" (Giovanni) **WLCS 1:**353
"An Ulster Twilight" (Heaney) **WLCS 1:**397
"El último viaje del buque fantasma" ("The Last Voyage of the Ghost Ship") (Garcia Marquez) **WLC 3:**1367
Ulysses (Joyce) **WLC 3:**1925-36
"Ulysses" (Tennyson) **WLC 6:**3580, 3583
L'umorismo (*On Humor*) (Pirandello) **WLC 4:**2716, 2731
The Unbearable Bassington (Saki) **WLC 5:**2999, 3002-05, 3008-11
The Uncalled (Dunbar) **WLC 2:**1101,
1104, 1111-13
Uncle Bernac (Doyle) **WLC 2:**1019-20
"Uncle Jim and Uncle Billy" (Harte) **WLC 3:**1589
"Uncle Simon's Sunday Out" (Dunbar) **WLC 2:**1106
Uncle Tom's Cabin; or, Life among the Lowly (Stowe) **WLC 6:**3498-99, 3501-10
Uncle Tom's Children (Wright) **WLC 6:**4089, 4091
"Uncle Tony's Goat" (Silko) **WLCS 2:**761
Uncle Vanya (Chekhov)
See *Dyadya Vanya*
"Uncle Wiggily in Connecticut" (Salinger) **WLC 5:**3019, 3021-22, 3025
Unconditional Surrender (Waugh) **WLC 6:**3823
Unconscious Memory (Butler) **WLC 1:**557
Und Sagte kein einziges Wort (*Acquainted with the Night; And Never Said a Word*) (Boell) **WLC 1:**319-21, 323-24
"The Undefeated" (Hemingway) **WLC 3:**1650
"The Under-Dogs" (Service) **WLC 5:**3131
"Under Glass" (Atwood) **WLC 1:**114, 118-19
Under Milk Wood (Thomas) **WLC 6:**3614
Under Plain Cover (Osborne) **WLC 4:**2598
"Under Sirius" (Auden) **WLC 1:**137
Under the Greenwood Tree (Hardy) **WLC 3:**1558, 1565-66
"Under the Knife" (Wells) **WLC 6:**3875
Under the Lilacs (Alcott) **WLC 1:**38, 41, 50
"Under the Rose" (Rossetti) **WLC 5:**2940-41
Under the Wheel (Hesse)
See *Unterm Rad*
"Under the Willow-Tree" (Andersen) **WLC 1:**58
Under Western Eyes (Conrad) **WLC 2:**780-82, 785, 791
The Under-wood (Jonson) **WLC 3:**1921
"The Underground" (Heaney) **WLCS 1:**396
"The Undertaker" (Pushkin) **WLC 5:**2828
"Undine" (Heaney) **WLCS 1:**388
The Undying Fire (Wells) **WLC 6:**3859
"The Unexpected" (Chopin) **WLCS 1:**241
"Unexpressed" (Dunbar) **WLC 2:**1111
"An Unfinished Story" (Henry) **WLC 3:**1674, 1677
The Unfortunate Happy Lady (Behn) **WLC 1:**250-51, 255
"Unfortunate" (Brooke) **WLC 1:**434
"The Unfortunate" (Turgenev)
See "Neschastnaya"
De unges forbund (*The League of Youth*) (Ibsen) **WLC 3:**1780
The Unguarded House (Boell)
See *Haus ohne Hüter*
"An Unhappy Girl" (Turgenev)
See "Neschastnaya"
Unholy Loves (Oates) **WLC 4:**2535
"A Unison" (Williams) **WLC 6:**4014
The Universal Gallant; or, The Different Husbands (Fielding) **WLC 2:**1213-14
"The Universe of Death" (Miller) **WLC 4:**2379

Unknown Girl in the Maternity Ward" (Sexton) **WLC 5:**3140
Unmailed, Unwritten Letters" (Oates) **WLC 4:**2528, 2535
The Unnameable (Beckett)
See *L'innommable*
Uno, nessuno e centomila (*One, None, and a Hundred Thousand*) (Pirandello) **WLC 4:**2718
Unreal Estates" (Lewis) **WLC 4:**2086
The Unrest Cure" (Saki) **WLC 5:**3008
The Unrewarded Killer (Ionesco)
See *Tueur sans gages*
The Unseen" (Singer) **WLC 5:**3291
An Unsocial Socialist (Shaw) **WLC 5:**3196
Unterm Rad (*Beneath the Wheel*; *Under the Wheel*) (Hesse) **WLC 3:**1693
The Untold Lie" (Anderson) **WLC 1:**83-4
An Unusual Young Man" (Brooke) **WLC 1:**440
The Unvanquished (Faulkner) **WLC 2:**1198
The Unveiling" (Milosz) **WLCS 2:**610-11
L'uomo, la bestia, e la virtù (*Man, Beast, and Virtue*) (Pirandello) **WLC 4:**2717
Up at the Villa (Maugham) **WLC 4:**2279, 2280
Up Hill" (Rossetti) **WLC 5:**2931
The Upas Tree" (Pushkin)
See "Anchar"
Upon Appleton House" ("Appleton House") (Marvell) **WLC 4:**2253, 2255, 2257-59
Upon Returning to the Country Road" (Lindsay) **WLC 4:**2118
Upon the Death of the Lord Protector" (Marvell)
See "Poem upon the Death of O. C."
Upon the Hill and Grove at Billborow" ("The Hill and Grove at Bill-Borrow"; "On the Hill and Grove at Billborow") (Marvell) **WLC 4:**2252, 2258
Uprooted" (Chekhov) **WLC 2:**708
Urfaust (Goethe) **WLC 3:**1421
Urien's Voyage (Gide)
See *Le voyage d'Urien*
Das Urteil ("The Judgment") (Kafka) **WLC 3:**1950
Us" (Sexton) **WLC 5:**3149
Useful Knowledge (Stein) **WLC 5:**3360
Utopia Fourteen (Vonnegut)
See *Player Piano*
Las uvas y el viento (*The Grapes and the Wind*) (Neruda) **WLC 4:**2515-16
V chiom moya vera" ("What I Believe") (Tolstoy) **WLC 3:**3664
V kruge pervom (*The First Circle*) (Solzhenitsyn) **WLC 5:**3300-01, 3304-06, 3311
V." (Pynchon) **WLC 5:**2840-42, 2844, 2847, 2854
Vaaren (*Springtime*) (Undset) **WLC 6:**3736, 3740-41
Vacillation" (Yeats) **WLC 6:**4101
The Vagrant Mood (Maugham) **WLC 4:**2281
Vala (Blake)
See *The Four Zoas: The Torments of Love and Jealousy in the Death and Judgement of Albion the Ancient Man*
Vala (Blake)

See *The Four Zoas: The Torments of Love and Jealousy in the Death and Judgement of Albion the Ancient Man*
"A Valediction: forbidding mourning" ("As virtuous men pass mildly away") (Donne) **WLC 2:**935, 947
"A Valediction: of weeping" (Donne) **WLC 2:**934
Valentine (Sand) **WLC 5:**3038, 3044-46
Válka s mloky (*War with the Newts*) (Capek) **WLC 1:**603-05, 607-09, 611, 613
The Valley of Decision (Wharton) **WLC 6:**3907
The Valley of Fear (Doyle) **WLC 2:**1011, 1018
The Valley of the Moon (London) **WLC 4:**2140
"The Valley of the Spiders" (Wells) **WLC 6:**3863
Vanity Fair: A Novel without a Hero (Thackeray) **WLC 6:**3592, 3595-96, 3598-99, 3601-04
Vanity of Duluoz: An Adventurous Education, 1935-1946 (Kerouac) **WLC 3:**1978, 1980, 1984
"The Vanity of Human Wishes" (Johnson) **WLC 3:**1893, 1898
"Vánka" (Chekhov) **WLC 2:**708
"Vanvild Kava" (Singer) **WLC 5:**3291
The Vast Earth (Pasternak) **WLC 4:**2628
"Vastness" (Tennyson) **WLC 6:**3584
The Vatican Swindle (Gide)
See *Les caves du Vatican*
Vec Makropulos (*The Makropoulos Affair*; *The Makropoulos Secret*) (Capek) **WLC 1:**601, 603-04, 609
Vechera ná khutore bliz Dikanki (*Evenings on a Farm near Dikanka*) (Gogol) **WLC 3:**1431, 1439
Vechny muzh (*The Eternal Husband*) (Dostoevsky) **WLC 2:**975
The Vegetable (Fitzgerald) **WLC 2:**1223
Veinte poemas de amor y una canción desesperada (*Twenty Love Poems and a Despairing Song*; *Twenty Love Poems and a Desperate Song*; *Twenty Love Poems and a Song of Despair*; *Twenty Love Poems and One Song of Despair*; *Twenty Poems*) (Neruda) **WLC 4:**2504, 2507, 2510, 2513, 2516
"Une vendetta" (Maupassant) **WLC 4:**2297
Venetian Epigrams (Goethe) **WLC 3:**1412
Le ventre de Paris (Zola) **WLC 6:**4118, 4125
Venture of the Infinite Man (Neruda)
See *Tentativa del hombre infinito*
"Vénus anadyomène" (Rimbaud) **WLC 5:**2916
"Venus's Looking-Glass" (Rossetti) **WLC 5:**2930
Vera; or, The Nihilists (Wilde) **WLC 6:**3955
"The Verdict" (Kafka) **WLC 3:**1946
El verdugo (Balzac) **WLC 1:**190
Vérité (Zola) **WLC 6:**4118-19
Die verlorene Ehre der Katharina Blum: oder, Wie Gewalt entstehen und wohin sie führen kann (*The Lost Honor of Katharina Blum: How Violence Develops and Where It Can Lead*) (Boell) **WLC 1:**328
"Vers nouveaux et chansons" (Rimbaud) **WLC 5:**2925
"A Verseman's Apology" (Service) **WLC 5:**3130
"Verses on the Death of Dr. Swift" (Swift) **WLC 6:**3535, 3544
Verses to the Memory of an Unfortunate Lady (Pope) **WLC 5:**2771
Los versos del capitán (Neruda)
See *Versos del capitán*
Versos del capitán (*The Captain's Verses*; *Los versos del capitán*) (Neruda) **WLC 4:**2517
"Vertige" (Rimbaud) **WLC 5:**2912
Die verwandlung (*The Metamorphosis*) (Kafka) **WLC 3:**1945-51
A Very Easy Death (Beauvoir)
See *Une morte très douce*
Veshnie vody (*Spring Freshets*; *Spring-Torrents*; *The Torrents of Spring*) (Turgenev) **WLC 6:**3697, 3699, 3704, 3707
Vestire gli ignudi (*Naked*; *To Clothe the Naked*) (Pirandello) **WLC 4:**2719, 2721-22
"Viage del Parnaso" (*Adjunta al Parnaso*; "Voyage to Parnassus") (Cervantes) **WLC 2:**674
The Vicar of Wakefield (Goldsmith) **WLC 3:**1466-72, 1475
Le Vicomte de Bragelonne (Dumas) **WLC 2:**1083
The Victim (Bellow) **WLC 1:**263-64, 268-69, 271-72, 275
Victimes du devoir (*Victims of Duty*) (Ionesco) **WLC 3:**1801-02, 1808-09
Victims of Duty (Ionesco)
See *Victimes du devoir*
Victoria Station (Pinter)
See *Other Places*
The Victors (Sartre)
See *Morts sans sépulture*
Victory (Conrad) **WLC 2:**780, 782, 790
Vie de Henri Brulard (*The Life of Henri Brulard*) (Stendhal) **WLC 5:**3401, 3405-07
Viento entero (*Intact Wind*) (Paz) **WLC 4:**2661
Vieux carré (Williams) **WLC 6:**4002
A View from the Bridge (Miller) **WLC 4:**2365-66, 2369-72
A View of the Edinburgh Theatre during the Summer Season, 1759 (Boswell) **WLC 1:**352
"A View of the Woods" (O'Connor) **WLC 4:**2550
Vildanden (*The Wild Duck*) (Ibsen) **WLC 3:**1777, 1781-82, 1792
Vile Bodies (Waugh) **WLC 6:**3821, 3824-26
"The Village Blacksmith" (Longfellow) **WLCS 2:**503, 509
The Village Curate (Balzac)
See *Le curé de Village*
"A Village Lear" (Turgenev)
See "Stepnoy Korol 'Lir"
"The Village That Voted the Earth Was Flat" (Saki) **WLC 5:**3003
"Villes" (Rimbaud) **WLC 5:**2918
Villette (Bronte) **WLC 1:**399-401, 404,

TITLE INDEX

406-10
A Vindication of Natural Society (Burke) **WLC 1:**506
See *A Vindication of Natural Society; or, A View of the Miseries and Evils Arising to Mankind from Every Species of Artificial Society*
A Vindication of Natural Society; or, A View of the Miseries and Evils Arising to Mankind from Every Species of Artificial Society (*A Vindication of Natural Society*) (Burke) **WLC 1:**506
"Viney's Free Papers" (Dunbar) **WLC 2:**1106
Vingt ans après (*Twenty Years After; or, The Further Feats and Fortunes of a Gascon Adventurer*) (Dumas) **WLC 2:**1083
"Vint" (Chekhov) **WLC 2:**708
The Violent Bear It Away (O'Connor) **WLC 3:**2542-44, 2548-53
The Violent Season (Paz)
See *La estación violenta*
Virgin Soil (Turgenev)
See *Nov'*
The Virginians: A Tale of the Last Century (Thackeray) **WLC 6:**3602-03
Virginibus Puerisque (Stevenson) **WLC 5:**3446-47
The Virtue of Selfishness: A New Concept of Egoism (Rand) **WLC 5:**2887
"Virtue" (Wheatley)
See "On Virtue"
La vision de Dante (Hugo) **WLC 3:**1748
"Vision And Prayer" (Thomas) **WLC 6:**3612, 3614, 3169
Vision de Babouc (Voltaire) **WLC 6:**3781
The Vision of Judgment (Byron) **WLC 1:**569, 575, 578
Vision of Spangler's Paul (Wolfe) **WLC 6:**4041
"A Vision of Spring in Winter" (Swinburne) **WLC 6:**3563, 3566
"A Vision of the World" (Cheever) **WLC 2:**691, 693-94, 701
"The Vision" (Burns) **WLC 1:**517
Visions of Cody (Kerouac) **WLC 3:**1979, 1982-85, 1987
Visions of Gerard (Kerouac) **WLC 3:**1985
"A Visit to Avoyelles" (Chopin) **WLCS 1:**240
"A Visit to the Asylum" (Millay) **WLCS 2:**595
"Visit" (Cocteau) **WLC 2:**734
Visnevyi sad (*The Cherry Garden; The Cherry Orchard*) (Chekhov) **WLC 2:**710, 713-15, 717-20
La vita nuda (*Naked Life*) (Pirandello) **WLC 4:**2718
La vita nuova (Alighieri) **WLCS 1:**30-31
"La viuda de Montiel" (Garcia Marquez) **WLC 3:**1367
ViVa (*VV*) (Cummings) **WLC 2:**840-41
"Vivien" (Tennyson) **WLC 6:**3584
"Viy" (Gogol) **WLC 3:**1430-31, 1439
"A Vocation and a Voice" (Chopin) **WLCS 1:**241
Voice from the Attic (Davies)
See *A Voice in the Attic*
A Voice in the Attic (*Voice from the Attic*) (Davies) **WLC 2:**848, 850, 858
"The Voice of Rock" (Ginsberg) **WLC 3:**1393
"The Voice" (Arnold) **WLC 1:**101
"The Voice" (Brooke) **WLC 1:**438
"Voices of Poor People" (Milosz) **WLCS 2:**620
The Voices of the Heroic Dead (Mishima) **WLC 4:**2427
Voices of the Night (Longfellow) **WLCS 2:**503, 509
Voina i mir (*War and Peace*) (Tolstoy) **WLC 6:**3661, 3663-70, 3672-75
Volpone; or, the Foxe (*The Fox; or, Volpone*) (Jonson) **WLC 3:**1906, 1908, 1910, 1912, 1912-16, 1920-21
Volshebnik (*The Enchanter, The Magician*) (Nabokov) **WLC 4:**2499
"Voluntaries" (Emerson) **WLC 2:**1171
Die Vorzüge der Windhühner (Grass) **WLC 3:**1504-06
Voskresenie (*Resurrection*) (Tolstoy) **WLC 6:**3665-66, 3670, 3674-75
"A Vow" (Ginsberg) **WLC 3:**1403
"Le voyage à Cythère" ("Voyage to Cythera") (Baudelaire) **WLC 1:**203
Le voyage d'Urien (*Urien's Voyage*) (Gide) **WLC 3:**1376
The Voyage Out (Woolf) **WLC 6:**4045, 4053, 4058
A Voyage to Arzrum (Pushkin) **WLC 5:**2830
"Voyage to Cythera" (Baudelaire)
See "Le voyage à Cythère"
"Voyage to Parnassus" (Cervantes)
See "Viage del Parnaso"
"Voyage VI" (Crane) **WLC 2:**804
"Le voyage" (Baudelaire) **WLC 1:**203, 205
"Voyages I: Poster" (Crane) **WLC 2:**802, 804
"Voyages II" (Crane) **WLC 2:**802-03
"Voyages III" (Crane) **WLC 2:**803-04
"Voyages VI" (Crane) **WLC 2:**803-04
"Voyages" (Crane) **WLC 2:**801-04, 806, 808
"Voyelles" (Rimbaud) **WLC 5:**2917
"Les Voyelles" (Rimbaud) **WLC 5:**2917
Vuelta (*Return*) (Paz) **WLC 4:**2675
VV (Cummings)
See *ViVa*
"Vystrel" ("The Shot") (Pushkin) **WLC 5:**2828, 2836
"W. S. Landor" (Moore) **WLCS 2:**650
Wagatomo Hitler (*My Friend Hitler*) (Mishima) **WLC 4:**2420
"The Wage Slave" (Service) **WLC 5:**3125
"A Waif of the Plains" (Harte) **WLC 3:**1583-84
Waiting for Godot (Beckett)
See *En attendant Godot*
"The Waiting Supper" (Hardy) **WLC 3:**1567
"Wakefield" (Hawthorne) **WLC 3:**1606, 1608
"Waking in the Blue" (Lowell) **WLC 4:**2156, 2165
"Waldemar Daa and His Daughters" (Andersen)
See "The Wind Tells of Valdemar Daae and His Daughters"
Walden; or, Life in the Woods (Thoreau) **WLC 6:**3628-29, 3631-35, 3638-40
"Wales Visitation" (Ginsberg) **WLC 3:**1401-03
"Walimai" (Allende) **WLCS 1:**47
A Walk on the Water (Stoppard) **WLC 6:**3481
"Walker Brothers Cowboy" (Munro) **WLCS 2:**683
"The Walking Man of Rodin" (Sandburg) **WLC 5:**3062
"Walking on Water" (Munro) **WLCS 2:**676
The Wall, and Other Stories (Sartre)
See *Le mur*
"The Wall" (Brooks) **WLC 1:**457, 463
The Walls Do Not Fall (H. D.) **WLC 3:**1613, 1615-18, 1624
"The Walls of Jericho" (Dunbar) **WLC 2:**1107
Wälsungenblut ("Blood of the Walsungs") (Mann) **WLC 4:**2198, 2204
"The Wanderer from the Fold" (Bronte) **WLC 1:**428
The Wandering Beauty (Behn) **WLC 1:**250, 257
"The Wanderings of Oisin" (Yeats) **WLC 6:**4099-4100
"Wanting to Die" (Sexton) **WLC 5:**3143-44
The Wapshot Chronicle (Cheever) **WLC 2:**690, 699-700
The Wapshot Scandal (Cheever) **WLC 2:**690, 699-702
War and Peace (Tolstoy)
See *Voina i mir*
War Bulletins (Lindsay) **WLC 4:**2124
"The War in the Bathroom" (Atwood) **WLC 1:**114-15
War Is Kind (Crane) **WLC 2:**815-17
The War of the Air (Wells) **WLC 6:**3859, 3871
The War of the Classes (London) **WLC 4:**2138
The War of the Worlds (Wells) **WLC 6:**3856-57, 3859, 3862, 3864, 3866-67, 3869, 3871, 3873, 3876
War Trilogy (H. D.)
See *Trilogy*
War with the Newts (Capek)
See *Válka s mloky*
The War Years (Sandburg) **WLC 5:**3055-56
"Ward No. Six" (Chekhov) **WLC 2:**709
"A Ward of the Golden Gate" (Harte) **WLC 3:**1590
The Warden (Trollope) **WLC 6:**3681-82, 3688
Wasps (Aristophanes) **WLCS 1:**78, 80, 83
"Wassermann Test" (Pasternak) **WLC 4:**2634
The Waste Land (Eliot) **WLC 2:**1137, 1142-45, 1147, 1149-51
"The Waste Land" (Paton) **WLC 4:**2650
Watch It Come Down (Osborne) **WLC 4:**2600-01
"The Watchers" (Bradbury) **WLC 1:**370
The Water Nymph (Pushkin)
See *Rusalka*
"Water" (Lowell) **WLC 4:**2160
The Watsons (Austen) **WLC 1:**154
Watt (Beckett) **WLC 1:**233
Waverley (Scott) **WLC 5:**3108-3112, 3115
Waverley Novels (Scott) **WLC 5:**3105-08,

3106, 3107, 3108, 3116, 3118
The Waves (Woolf) **WLC 6:**4051-53, 4057-58
"The way that Lovers use is this" (Brooke) **WLC 1:**434
"The Way of a Woman" (Dunbar) **WLC 2:**1107
The Way of All Flesh (*Ernest Pontifex; or, The Way of All Flesh*) (Butler) **WLC 1:**555-60
The Way of the World (Congreve) **WLC 2:**761, 763-65, 768-69, 772, 774-75
The Way Some People Live (Cheever) **WLC 2:**689-90, 695-96
"The Way through the Woods" (Kipling) **WLC 3:**2017
"The Way to Hump a Cow Is Not" (Cummings) **WLC 2:**841
"A Way to Love God" (Warren) **WLC 6:**3815-16
The Way to Rainy Mountain (Momaday) **WLCS 2:**625, 627-28, 632
The Way to Wealth (Franklin) **WLCS 1:**321
"The Way to Wealth" (Franklin) **WLCS 1:**314, 317
The Way We Live Now (Trollope) **WLC 6:**3682
"The Wayfarers" (Brooke) **WLC 1:**436
The Ways of White Folks (Hughes) **WLC 3:**1733, 1736
Wayside Crosses (Capek) **WLC 1:**600-01, 603
"The Wayside Inn" (Turgenev)
 See "The Inn"
The Wayward and the Seeking (Toomer) **WLCS 2:**800-01
The Wayward Bus (Steinbeck) **WLC 5:**3387-88
We Have Always Lived in the Castle (Jackson) **WLC 3:**1835, 1837-39, 1844, 1850-51
"We Real Cool" (Brooks) **WLC 1:**450, 452
We the Living (Rand) **WLC 5:**2877, 2879-80
"We Wear the Mask" (Dunbar) **WLC 2:**1110
The Weary Blues (Hughes) **WLC 3:**1725-26, 1731-32
"The Weary Blues" (Hughes) **WLC 3:**1724, 1726
"The Weary Wedding" (Swinburne) **WLC 6:**3555
The Web and the Rock (Wolfe) **WLC 6:**4030, 4033, 4035, 4038
"The Web of Earth" (Wolfe) **WLC 6:**4040
"Webster Ford" (Masters) **WLCS 2:**581-82, 585-86
The Wedding Day (Fielding) **WLC 2:**1213
The Wedding on the Eiffel Tower (Cocteau)
 See *Les mariés de la Tour Eiffel*
"Wedding Preparations" (Kafka) **WLC 3:**1951
A Week (Thoreau) **WLC 6:**3630
A Week on the Concord and Merrimack Rivers (Thoreau) **WLC 6:**3631-32, 3634-35, 3638
Weg nach Innen (*Road to Within*) (Hesse) **WLC 3:**1687
Weighing of Souls (Aeschylus) **WLCS 1:**6, 8, 14

Weight and Weightlessness (Branley) **WLC 3:**1790, 1792
Weir of Hermiston (Stevenson) **WLC 5:**3452-53
"The Wereman" (Atwood) **WLC 1:**111
Werner (Byron) **WLC 1:**575
Werther (Goethe) **WLC 3:**1411-12, 1416
West of Suez (Osborne) **WLC 4:**2598, 2600-01
West-Östlicher Divan (Goethe) **WLC 3:**1412
"Westering" (Heaney) **WLCS 1:**397
"Westminster Abbey" (Irving) **WLC 3:**1826-27
"A Wet Night" (Beckett) **WLC 1:**231
The Wet Parade (Sinclair) **WLC 5:**3263
"Whacking Off" (Roth) **WLC 5:**2967-68
The Whale (Melville)
 See *Moby-Dick; or, The Whale*
"What Father Does" (Andersen) **WLC 1:**64
"What for Us, My Heart, Are Pools of Blood" (Rimbaud) **WLC 5:**2921
"What I Believe" (Tolstoy)
 See "V chiom moya vera""What I Lived For" (Thoreau) 6;3630
"What is Capitalism" (Rand) **WLC 5:**2887
What Is Literature? (Sartre)
 See *Qu'est-ce que la littérature?*
What Is Man? (Twain) **WLC 6:**3718
"What Is the Connection between Men and Women" (Oates) **WLC 4:**2527
What Maisie Knew (James) **WLC 3:**1865-67, 1869
"What One Says to the Poet on the Subject of Flowers" (Rimbaud)
 See "Ce qu'on dit au poète à propos de fleurs"
What to Do (Tolstoy) **WLC 6:**3664
What Was the Relationship of the Lone Ranger to the Means of Production? (Baraka) **WLCS 1:**153
What's Bred in the Bone (Davies) **WLC 2:**854-57, 859-60
The Wheel of Love, and Other Stories (Oates) **WLC 4:**2528, 2536
"when god decided to invent" (Cummings) **WLC 2:**841
"When a lovely woman stoops to folly" (Goldsmith) **WLC 3:**1475
"When All Is Done" (Dunbar) **WLC 2:**1112
"When de Co'n Pone's Hot" (Dunbar) **WLC 2:**1103, 1110
"When Death Came April Twelve 1945" (Sandburg) **WLC 5:**3061
When Five Years Pass (Garcia Lorca)
 See *Así que pasen cinco años*
"When Gassy Thompson Struck It Rich" (Lindsay) **WLC 4:**2120
"When I Buy Pictures" (Moore) **WLCS 2:**651
"When I Die" (Giovanni) **WLCS 1:**359
"When It Happens" (Atwood) **WLC 1:**114, 118-19
"When Lilacs Last in the Dooryard Bloom'd" (Whitman) **WLC 6:**3943
"When Lilacs Last in the Dooryard Bloomed" (Whitman) **WLC 6:**3943
"When Malindy Sings" (Dunbar) **WLC 2:**1103

"When my love swears that she is made of truth" (Shakespeare)
 See "Sonnet 138"
When One Is Somebody (Pirandello)
 See *Quando si è qualcuno*
When She Was Good (Roth) **WLC 5:**2966-67, 2972
When Someone is Somebody (Pirandello)
 See *Quando si è qualcuno*
"When summer's end is nighing" (Housman) **WLCS 1:**429
"When the Lamp Is Shattered" (Shelley) **WLC 5:**3234
When the Sleeper Wakes (Wells) **WLC 6:**3862, 3864, 3866, 3869, 3874, 3876
When We Dead Awaken (Ibsen)
 See *Nar vi døde vagner*
When William Came: A Story of London under the Hohenzollerns (*The Coming of William*) (Saki) **WLC 5:**3005, 3008-09
"When You've Forgotten Sunday" (Brooks) **WLC 1:**463
Where Angels Fear to Tread (Forster) **WLC 2:**1258-60, 1264, 1269
"Where Are You Going, Where Have You Been?" (Oates) **WLC 4:**2528, 2532, 2533-2535
Where Do We Go From Here: Chaos or Community (King) **WLCS 1:**458
"Where I Live in This Honorable House of the Laurel Tree" (Sexton) **WLC 5:**3140
"Where is David, the Next King of Israel?" (Lindsay) **WLC 4:**2118
"Where is the Voice Coming From" (Welty) **WLC 6:**3887
"Where Is the Real Non-Resistant?" (Lindsay) **WLC 4:**2121
Where the Air Is Clear (Fuentes)
 See *La región más transparente*
"Where the Rainbow Ends" (Lowell) **WLC 4:**2153
"Where the Slow Fig's Purple Sloth" (Warren) **WLC 6:**3815
"Which Is the True One?" (Baudelaire)
 See "Laquelle est la vraie?"
"Which Side Am I Supposed to Be On?" (Auden) **WLC 1:**134
Whirligigs (Henry) **WLC 3:**1677
"The Whistle" (Welty) **WLC 6:**3882
"Whistling Sam" (Dunbar) **WLC 2:**1112
White Buildings (Crane) **WLC 2:**799-800, 808-09
"White Christmas" (Service) **WLC 5:**3131
"The White City" (McKay) **WLC 4:**2330
The White Company (Doyle) **WLC 2:**1016, 1019-20
The White Devil (Webster) **WLC 6:**3838-44, 3846, 3848-52
The White Doe of Rylstone; or, The Fate of the Nortons (Wordsworth) **WLC 6:**4073
"White Dump" (Munro) **WLCS 2:**683-84
White Fang (London) **WLC 4:**2139, 2145
"The White House" (McKay) **WLC 4:**2338
White-Jacket; or, The World in a Man-of-War (Melville) **WLC 4:**2355, 2357
The White Monkey (Galsworthy) **WLC 2:**1328
The White Peacock (Lawrence) **WLC 3:**2043
The White Plague (Capek) **WLC 1:**605,

609
"The White Ship" (Rossetti) **WLC 5:**2949, 2959
"Who Dat Say Chicken in a Crowd" (Dunbar) **WLC 2:**1111
Who Do You Think You Are? (Munro) **WLCS 2:**677, 679-80, 682, 685
"Who Made Paul Bunyan" (Sandburg) **WLC 5:**3060
"Who Stand for the Gods" (Dunbar) **WLC 2:**1106
"Who Was My Quiet Friend" (Harte) **WLC 3:**1590
Who's Afraid of Virginia Woolf? (Albee) **WLC 1:**21-30
Why Do People Intoxicate Themselves? (Tolstoy) **WLC 6:**3664
"Why I Live at the P. O." (Welty) **WLC 6:**3880, 3882-83, 3892
"Why I Voted the Socialist Ticket" (Lindsay) **WLC 4:**2123
"Why I Write" (Orwell) **WLC 4:**2580, 2582, 2587
"Why Is Your Writing So Violent?" (Oates) **WLC 4:**2535
"Why the Negro Won't Buy Communism" (Hurston) **WLCS 1:**453
"Wichita Vortex Sutra" (Ginsberg) **WLC 3:**1396, 1401, 1404
The Wicked Cooks (Grass) **WLC 3:**1510
Wide Is the Gate (Sinclair) **WLC 5:**3271
"The Wide Net" (Welty) **WLC 6:**3880-2, 3884, 3892
"The Widow and Her Son" (Irving) **WLC 3:**1819, 1827
"Widow La Rue" (Masters) **WLCS 2:**578
"The Widow's Lament in Springtime" (Williams) **WLC 6:**4014
"The Widow's Ordeal" (Irving) **WLC 3:**1820
Widowers' Houses (Shaw) **WLC 5:**3196, 3200
"The Wife of a King" (London) **WLC 4:**2141, 2143
"The Wife" (Irving) **WLC 3:**1819, 1822, 1827-28
"wild (at our first) beasts uttered human words" (Cummings) **WLC 2:**843
The Wild Ass' Skin (Balzac)
See *La peau de chagrin*
The Wild Boys: A Book of the Dead (Burroughs) **WLC 1:**542, 545
The Wild Duck (Ibsen)
See *Vildanden*
The Wild Gallant (Dryden) **WLC 2:**1048
The Wild Orchid (Undset)
See *Gymnadenia*
The Wild Palms (Faulkner) **WLC 2:**1188-89, 1195
The Wild Swans at Coole (Yeats) **WLC 6:**4099-4100
"The Wild Swans" (Andersen) **WLC 1:**61, 65
"Wilderness" (Sandburg) **WLC 5:**3052
Wilhelm Meister (Goethe) **WLC 3:**1412-13, 1415
"William Marion Reedy" (Masters) **WLCS 2:**578
"William Wilson" (Poe) **WLC 4:**2760
"Willie" (Brooks)
See "To Keorapetse Kgositsile (Willie)"
"The Willing Mistress" (Behn) **WLC 1:**255

"Wilt thou forgive" (Donne)
See "A Hymne to God the Father"
"Wiltshire" (Golding) **WLC 3:**1456
The Wind among the Reeds (Yeats) **WLC 6:**4099
"The Wind Blows" ("Autumn II") (Mansfield) **WLC 4:**2217
"The Wind Tells of Valdemar Daae and His Daughters" ("Waldemar Daa and His Daughters"; "The Wind Tells the Story of Valdemar Daa and his Daughters"; "The Wind's Tale") (Andersen) **WLC 1:**64
"The Wind Tells the Story of Valdemar Daa and his Daughters" (Andersen)
See "The Wind Tells of Valdemar Daae and His Daughters"
"The Wind's Tale" (Andersen)
See "The Wind Tells of Valdemar Daae and His Daughters"
Windfalls (O'Casey) **WLCS 2:**720
"The Windhover" (Hopkins) **WLC 3:**1716
The Winding Stair (Yeats) **WLC 6:**4100
"Winds" (Auden) **WLC 1:**138
"Windsor-Forest" (Pope) **WLC 5:**2771, 2775, 2782
Windy McPherson's Son (Anderson) **WLC 1:**77-8
Wine from These Grapes (Millay) **WLCS 2:**602
"The Wine Menagerie" (Crane) **WLC 2:**800-01
Winesburg, Ohio (Anderson) **WLC 1:**73, 75-8, 80-6
Winged Chariot (de la Mare) **WLC 2:**892
The Wings of the Dove (James) **WLC 3:**1863-66
Winner Take Nothing (Hemingway) **WLC 3:**1650-51
"Winter Dreams" (Fitzgerald) **WLC 2:**1232
"Winter Evening" (Pushkin)
See "Zimniy Vecher"
"Winter in Dunbarton" (Lowell) **WLC 4:**2162-63
Winter Love (H. D.) **WLC 3:**1624
The Winter of Our Discontent (Steinbeck) **WLC 5:**3388
"Winter on Earth" (Toomer) **WLCS 2:**801
"Winter Sleepers" (Atwood) **WLC 1:**111
"Winter Song" (Owen) **WLC 4:**2618
Winter Trees (Plath) **WLC 4:**2743-44
"Winter: My Secret" (Rossetti) **WLC 5:**2941
"Winter" (Giovanni) **WLCS 1:**363
"Winter" (Pope) **WLC 5:**2782-83
The Winter's Tale (Shakespeare) **WLC 5:**3171, 3174, 3177
"A Winter's Tale" (Thomas) **WLC 6:**3612
Wintering Out (Heaney) **WLCS 1:**397
"The Wisdom of Silence" (Dunbar) **WLC 2:**1107, 1109
The Wisdom of the Heart (Miller) **WLC 4:**2391
Wise Blood (O'Connor) **WLC 4:**2542, 2546, 2548, 2550-53
"The Wise Men" (Crane) **WLC 2:**815
"The Wise Old Dwarf" (Frank) **WLC 2:**1280, 1283
The Wise Virgins (Undset)
See *De kloge jomfruer*
"Wiser Than a God" (Chopin) **WLCS 1:**237, 239, 242
"A Wish" (Arnold) **WLC 1:**100
"The Witch-Mother" (Swinburne) **WLC 6:**3555
"The Witch of Atlas" (Shelley) **WLC 5:**3224, 3234, 3236
"The Witch of Coös" (Frost) **WLC 2:**1294
"A Witch Trial at Mount Holly" (Franklin) **WLCS 1:**319
The Witchcraft of Salem Village (Jackson) **WLC 3:**1839
The Witchery of the Butterfly (Garcia Lorca)
See *El maleficio de la mariposa*
"With a Guitar, to Jane" (Shelley) **WLC 5:**3234
"With Mercy for the Greedy" (Sexton) **WLC 5:**3142
"With rue my heart is laden" (Housman) **WLCS 1:**431
"The Withered Arm" (Hardy) **WLC 3:**1566-67
"Withered Skin of Berries" (Toomer) **WLCS 2:**801
Within the Gates (O'Casey) **WLCS 2:**716-17, 721
"Without Benefit of Clergy" (Kipling) **WLC 3:**2013
"The Witnesses" (Longfellow) **WLCS 2:**504
Wo warst du, Adam? (*Adam, Where Art Thou?*; *And Where Were You, Adam?*) (Boell) **WLC 1:**315, 319-20, 323, 326
"Wolfert Webber" (Irving) **WLC 3:**1820, 1828
"Wolfert's Roost" (Irving) **WLC 3:**1820
"The Wolves of Cernogratz" (Saki) **WLC 5:**3007, 3009
"The Woman at the Store" (Mansfield) **WLC 4:**2216
The Woman Destroyed (Beauvoir)
See *La femme rompue*
"The Woman in his Life" (Kipling) **WLC 3:**2017
The Woman of Andros (Wilder) **WLC 6:**3982-85
A Woman of No Importance (Wilde) **WLC 6:**3955, 3965
Woman of the River (Alegria)
See "A Temple of the Holy Ghost"
The Woman Warrior (Kingston) **WLCS 2:**475-78, 482-83
"The Woman Who Was a Tree" (Huxley) **WLC 3:**1762
"A Woman without a Country" (Cheever) **WLC 2:**692, 696
"The Woman" (Giovanni) **WLCS 1:**359-60
The Women and the Men (Giovanni) **WLCS 1:**355-56, 359, 361
The Women at Point Sur (Jeffers)
See *The Women of Point Sur*
Women in Love (Lawrence) **WLC 3:**2044, 2050-52, 2056
Women of Aetna (Aeschylus) **WLCS 1:**7
The Women of Brewster Place (Naylor) **WLCS 2:**691, 693-95, 700-03
The Women of Point Sur (*The Women at Point Sur*) (Jeffers) **WLC 3:**1874-75, 1884
Women of Salamis (Aeschylus) **WLCS 1:**8

he Women of Trachis (Sophocles)
See *Trachiniae*
Wonder-Book for Girls and Boys (Hawthorne) **WLC 3:**1596
onderland (Oates) **WLC 4:**2526, 2527, 2531, 2535
he Wood Demon (Chekhov)
See *Leshy*
he Woodfelling" (Tolstoy) **WLC 6:**3666
he Woodlanders (Hardy) **WLC 3:**1561, 1571-72
oodnotes" (Emerson) **WLC 2:**1172
he Woodpile" (Frost) **WLC 2:**1299
, Word for Me...Also" (Giovanni) **WLCS 1:**360
ord from the Right Wing" (Baraka) **WLCS 1:**145
e Words (Sartre)
See *Les mots*
ords for Hart Crane" (Lowell) **WLC 4:**2162, 2167
ords into Fiction" (Welty) **WLC 6:**3891
ords" (Plath) **WLC 4:**2748
ork, Death, and Sickness" (Tolstoy) **WLC 6:**3664
ork Gangs" (Sandburg) **WLC 5:**3053
ork in Progress (Joyce)
See *Finnegans Wake*
ork: A Story of Experience (Alcott) **WLC 1:**50
e Works of Anne Frank (Frank) **WLC 2:**1279
e Works of Sir Thomas Malory (Malory) **WLCS 2:**559, 565-66, 569-70
he World and the Door" (Henry) **WLC 3:**1677
he World and the Quietist" (Arnold) **WLC 1:**100-01
orld Enough and Time (Warren) **WLC 6:**3814
he World Is Too Much with Us" (Wordsworth) **WLC 6:**4073
he World of Apples" (Cheever) **WLC 2:**697
e World of Paul Slickey (Osborne) **WLC 4:**2592, 2594, 2600
World of Strangers (Gordimer) **WLCS 1:**374-75, 377
orld of Wonders (Davies) **WLC 2:**848-850, 853-54
e World Set Free (Wells) **WLC 6:**3867, 3869, 3871
he World-Soul" (Emerson) **WLC 2:**1172, 1178
e World We Live In: The Insect Comedy (Capek)
See *Ze zivota hmyzu*
he World" (Rossetti) **WLC 5:**2930
he World's Desire" (Masters) **WLCS 2:**578
orlds" (Masters) **WLCS 2:**578
Worn Path" (Welty) **WLC 6:**3880
he Wreck of the Deutschland" (Hopkins) **WLC 3:**1712-13, 1715-16
he Wreck of the Hesperus" (Longfellow) **WLCS 2:**503-04, 510
reckage" (Momaday) **WLCS 2:**635
e Wretched (Hugo)
See *Les misérables*
rite it Right (Bierce) **WLC 1:**287
Writer's Notebook (Maugham) **WLC 4:**2280, 2283-84

The Writing of Fiction (Wharton) **WLC 6:**3908
"Written in Emerson's Essays" (Arnold) **WLC 1:**100
"Wrong Beauty" (Grass)
See "Falsche Schönheit"
Wuthering Heights (Bronte) **WLC 1:**416-21, 423-24, 426-29, 431
Xaipe: Seventy-One Poems (Cummings) **WLC 2:**842
Xantriae (Aeschylus) **WLCS 1:**6-7
Xingu, and Other Stories (Wharton) **WLC 6:**3908
XLI Poems (Cummings) **WLC 2:**838
"The Yachts" (Williams) **WLC 6:**4014
Yakov Pasynkov (*Jacob Pasinkov*) (Turgenev) **WLC 6:**3697, 3703
"Ye Are Na Mary Morison" ("Mary Morison") (Burns) **WLC 1:**518
"The Year 1905" (Pasternak)
See "Devyatsat pyaty god"
The Years (Woolf) **WLC 6:**4052-53
"The Yellow Peril" (London) **WLC 4:**2138
"Yellow Woman" (Silko) **WLCS 2:**759, 761, 763-64
The Yellowplush Papers (Thackeray) **WLC 6:**3594-95
"Yentl the Yeshiva Boy" (Singer) **WLC 5:**3293
Yerma (Garcia Lorca) **WLC 2:**1342-43, 1350
"Yet Do I Marvel" (Cullen) **WLCS 1:**275
"Yeux Glauques" (Pound) **WLC 5:**2791
Yevgeny Onegin (*Eugene Onegin*; *Evgeni Onegin*) (Pushkin) **WLC 5:**2822-25, 2828, 2832-33
"YgUDuh" (Cummings) **WLC 2:**842
Yi-king (Confucius) **WLCS 1:**254, 256
"Ylla" (Bradbury) **WLC 1:**370
Yorokobi no Koto ("The Harp of Joy") (Mishima) **WLC 4:**2419
You Are Happy (Atwood) **WLC 1:**109-10, 112, 116, 118
You Can't Go Home Again (Wolfe) **WLC 6:**4029-30, 4033, 4038
"You Can't Tell a Man by the Song He Sings" (Roth) **WLC 5:**2964
"You cannot hurt / Muhammad Ali, and stay / alive" (Baraka) **WLCS 1:**145
You, Emperors, and Others: Poems, 1957-1960 (Warren) **WLC 6:**3814
You Never Can Tell (Shaw) **WLC 5:**3193
"Young Goodman Brown" (Hawthorne) **WLC 3:**1597, 1605
The Young King; or, The Mistake (Behn) **WLC 1:**246
"The Young Men Run" (Brooks) **WLC 1:**463
"Young" (Sexton) **WLC 5:**3142, 3149
The Younger Brother; or, The Amorous Jilt (Behn) **WLC 1:**259; **WLC 30:**
Your Lover Just Called: Stories of Joan and Richard Maple (Updike)
See *Too Far to Go: The Maples Stories*
Youth (Tolstoy)
See *Yunost*
"Youth and Calm" (Arnold) **WLC 1:**103
"The Youth of Man" (Arnold) **WLC 1:**100
"The Youth of Nature" (Arnold) **WLC 1:**100, 102
"Youth" (Conrad) **WLC 2:**780-82, 790
Yüeh (Confucius) **WLCS 1:**256

"Y koku" (Mishima) **WLC 4:**2418, 2423-24, 2427, 2430
Yunost (*Youth*) (Tolstoy) **WLC 6:**3665
Zadig (Voltaire) **WLC 6:**3769, 3775, 3779-81
Zaïre (Voltaire) **WLC 6:**3769, 3772, 3779
La zapatera prodigiosa (*The Marvellous Shoemaker's Wife*; *The Shoemaker's Prodigious Wife*) (Garcia Lorca) **WLC 2:**1341
Zapiski iz podpol'ya (*Letters from the Underworld*; *Memoirs from Underground*; *Notes from the Underground*) (Dostoevsky) **WLC 2:**975
Zapiski okhotnika (*Hunter's Sketches*; *The Memoirs of a Sportsman*; *Notes of a Hunter*; *Scenes from Russian Life*; *Sketches from a Hunter's Album*; *A Sportsman's Sketches*) (Turgenev) **WLC 6:**3700, 3702-05
Zapiski sumasshedshego ("The Diary of a Madman"; *Memoirs of a Madman*) (Tolstoy) **WLC 11:**463-64, 478
Zapolya: A Christmas Tale (Coleridge) **WLC 2:**745
Der Zauberberg (*The Magic Mountain*) (Mann) **WLC 4:**2196, 2199-2200, 2204-06, 2208
Ze zivota hmyzu (*And So Ad Infinitum*; *The Insect Comedy*; *Insect Life*; *The Insect Play*; *Insect Story*; *Insects*; *The Life of the Insects*; *The World We Live In: The Insect Comedy*) (Capek) **WLC 1:**601, 603-04
Zhenit'ba; Sovershenno neveroyatnoye sobitye (*Marriage*; *The Marriage: An Utterly Incredible Occurence*) (Gogol) **WLC 3:**1440
"Zimniy Vecher" ("Winter Evening") (Pushkin) **WLC 5:**2832
Zona sagrada (*Holy Place*; *The Sacred Zone*) (Fuentes) **WLC 2:**1311, 1316-17
Zones of the Spirit (Strindberg)
See *En bla bok*
"Zoo Celeste" (Huxley) **WLC 3:**1763
"Zoo Keeper's Wife" (Plath) **WLC 4:**2741
The Zoo Story (Albee) **WLC 1:**19, 21, 23, 25-6, 28-9, 32
"Zooey" (Salinger) **WLC 5:**3020, 3022-23
Zora Neale Hurston: Folklore, Memoirs, and Other Writings (Hurston) **WLCS 1:**451
Zora Neale Hurston: Novels and Stories (Hurston) **WLCS 1:**451
Zuckerman Bound: A Trilogy and an Epilogue (Roth) **WLC 5:**2975-76
Zuckerman Unbound (Roth) **WLC 5:**2975
"Der Zug war pünktlich" ("The Train Was on Time") (Boell) **WLC 1:**315, 318, 320
Die Zweite Revolution (Goebbels)
See *Die Zweite Revolution*

ISBN 0-7876-1913-2